AMERICA IN THE TWENTIES AND THIRTIES

Also by Sean Dennis Cashman

Prohibition: The Lie of the Land (THE FREE PRESS)

America in the Gilded Age (NEW YORK UNIVERSITY PRESS)

America in the Age of the Titans: The Progressive Era and World War I
(NEW YORK UNIVERSITY PRESS)

America, Roosevelt, and World War II (NEW YORK UNIVERSITY PRESS)

AMERICA IN THE TWENTIES AND THIRTIES

The Olympian Age of Franklin Delano Roosevelt

SEAN DENNIS CASHMAN

NEW YORK UNIVERSITY PRESS

NEW YORK & LONDON

Library of Congress Cataloging-in-Publication Data
Cashman, Sean Dennis.
America in the twenties and thirties.
Bibliography: p.
Includes index.
1. United States—Civilization—1918–1945.
2. Roosevelt, Franklin D. (Franklin Delano), 1882–1945.
I. Title.
E169.1.C297   1988   973.91   88-5278
ISBN 0-8147-1412-9 (alk. paper)
ISBN 0-8147-1413-7 (pbk.)

New York University Press books are Smyth-sewn and
printed on permanent and durable acid-free paper.

Book design by Ken Venezio

For Colin Morris

CONTENTS

ILLUSTRATIONS

PREFACE AND
ACKNOWLEDGMENTS

THIS BOOK is intended as an interdisciplinary history of the
United States in the period 1920–1941, ending with the Japanese attack on Pearl Harbor. It charts the course of domestic
politics and foreign policies, and tells something of the stories of
industrial and economic, social and cultural history. These were
crucial years for the United States, in which profound developments occurred in politics, transportation and communication,
culture, and world affairs. The achievements of the New Deal of
1933–1939 and the lost generation of artists were set against the
dramatic backdrop of the Great Depression, the advent of World
War II, and revolutions of Left and Right in Europe and Asia.

The book is a work of synthesis, based partly on primary
sources, partly on recent scholarship. It is a companion volume to
America in the Age of the Titans, covering the Progressive Era and
World War I in the period 1901–20. The book aims at a clear
presentation of essential facts and a synthesis of academic interpretations, and places some emphasis on the personalities of the
principal actors.

I began this book in August 1984 at the invitation of Colin Jones, who, throughout its composition, offered constructive advice about structure and detail. My initial research was facilitated by two travel grants provided by the University of Manchester, England. The support and encouragement of my former colleagues in the Department of American Studies there, notably Professor Peter Marshall, were most appreciated. The book was completed in 1987 at New York University when I was visiting professor in history, having been invited to teach there by Professors Carl Prince and David Reimers.

The book was written concurrently with *America in the Age of the Titans* but took longer to complete. Toward the end of final revisions in summer 1987 I was invited by Dr. Peter Diamandopoulos, president of Adelphi University, Garden City, Long Island, to apply for the post of dean of arts and sciences there. The interesting sequences of interviews at Adelphi and the appointment capped what had been a most stimulating year and the loyal faculty and administrators at Adelphi gave me warm support in the various stages of production.

To some people, three years would seem a long, to others, a short, time to write a book such as this. In fact, this period brought to fruition years of studying and teaching the period, beginning with my D.Phil. thesis at Oxford and continuing at the University of Manchester, England, in a series of interdisciplinary courses with my esteemed colleague, Godfrey Kearns. Thus, this is a book I had started to write in my mind several times before being given the opportunity to do so for publication. While wanting to give appropriate weight to political history, both Colin Jones and I also wanted to emphasize major developments in social and cultural history, including inventions, transportation, and the arts. Even so, the history is not complete. It does not treat such important subjects as philosophy, education, and sports, and only touches upon music. To ensure thorough presentation of black history, I have reviewed the period 1865–1920 as well as the 1920s and 1930s.

Without the assistance and participation of several friends and colleagues, my task would have been far harder. Iain Halliday undertook preliminary work, locating material, synthesizing previous scholarship, and writing drafts on various subjects, including Los Angeles as a metropolis, and the arts. The extent and variety of his work were much appreciated. Daniel Couzens both found material and prepared draft sections on the subjects of radio and music. Chris Hasson provided an account of workers and labor organizations. Chris Harries read widely in the field of black history, made a judicious choice of texts for me to study, and provided an outline of black history. In every case, my friends' help prepared the ground for what had to be done. Dr. Daniel Cornford, formerly of the Universities of California at Santa Barbara and San Francisco, and of Manchester, and an expert on labor history, read the chapter on labor. He had vigorous arguments to make about what extra scholarship was required. I also owe much to the encouragement of my mother, Margaret Cashman, and my good friend, Kenneth McArthur throughout the period writing this book.

The illustrations were found in the Museum of Modern Art, the Whitney Museum of American Art, and, principally, in the Prints and Photographs Division of the Library of Congress. Ms. Mary Ison, head of the reference section, and Ms. Maja Felaco were most helpful in advising on the selection of illustrations. Mrs. Eileen Grimes of Manchester typed most of the manuscript and typing was completed by Mrs. Lee Plaut of Adelphi University. At Manchester Ms. Caroline Sutton typed most of the voluminous correspondence. The index was devised by Robert Madison.

INTRODUCTION

COMPOSER AND lyricist Kurt Weill once observed that, for every generation, there was a special part of the world about which fantasies were conceived—for Shakespeare and his circle it was Italy; for Mozart and his contemporaries it was Turkey. For twentieth-century artists it was the United States, and during a precise period at that—1920–1941—now remembered as great years in the development of American society.

Politically, the period came to be dominated by one man, Franklin Delano Roosevelt, elected president for an unprecedented four terms and who served for over twelve years in office (1933–1945). As surely as Zeus had led a new race of Olympian gods who superseded the defunct titans of Greek mythology, in America FDR led his cabinet colleagues and political allies alike in a program of wide-ranging federal reforms, using progressive ideas to reorder government in the wake of half a century of industrial and economic expansion achieved by the titans of American industry and politics. Yet in the early 1920s Roosevelt's career, having begun so promisingly as assistant secretary to the navy (1913–1920), went into eclipse following a profound personal tragedy.

In the early 1920s downtown Chicago was dominated by a medley of skyscrapers, turning the city center into a series of vertical, manmade canyons. The Chicago Tribune Tower (left) of Raymond Hood and John Mead Howells (1925) was a Gothic creation crowned by a circle of buttresses, while the tower of the white Wrigley Building (right) by Graham, Anderson, Probst, and White (1921) was inspired by the Giralda (the Moorish tower) in Seville, Spain. (Library of Congress).

Paradoxically, what was a disastrous presidential campaign by Democratic nominee James B. Cox, governor of Ohio, in 1920 was, on balance at least, a *succès d'estime* for Roosevelt, his vice-presidential running mate. For FDR had made himself nationally widely known and personally liked. Nevertheless, when Warren Harding and Calvin Coolidge were elected president and vice-president, Roosevelt was out of public life for the first time in ten years. The Republican landslide seemed a rejection of the progressive spirit as much as a rejection of Wilsonian liberalism at home and abroad. Roosevelt retreated into the legal profession. Yet he continued to manage a variety of social, political, and charitable activities, many of which generated public appearances and guaranteed press copy. He set his sights on winning nomination and election as senator for New York in 1922. He supported the way the Republicans resolved the fiasco of the Senate's rejection of the Treaty of Versailles and League of Nations by making, first, a separate peace with Germany and, second, by organizing the Washington Naval Conference of 1921–1922.

Roosevelt and his family—his wife, Eleanor, and their four sons and one daughter, Anna—spent their summer vacation of 1921 off Campobello, New Brunswick. On Wednesday, August 10, 1921, they alighted from their yacht, the *Vireo,* to help put out a forest fire on one of the islands. "Late in the afternoon we brought it under control," he remembered. "Our eyes were bleary with smoke; we were begrimed, smarting with spark burns, exhausted." Then, to relieve tension, they raced across the island at Campobello and ended the day by taking a swim in the frigid sea off the Bay of Fundy. "I didn't feel the usual reaction, the glow I'd expected. When I reached the house the mail was in, with several newspapers I hadn't seen. I sat reading for a while, too tired even to dress. I'd never felt quite that way before." He went to bed before supper was over. The next day brought the crisis to a head. "When I swung out of bed my left leg lagged but I managed to move about and to shave. I tried to persuade myself that the trouble with my leg was muscular, that it would disappear as I used it. But presently it refused to work, and then the other." He had a temperature of 102°.

On Friday morning, August 12, he could not stand and by the evening could not even move his legs. A specialist diagnosed paralysis caused by a blood clot and prescribed massage, a remedy performed resolutely by Eleanor Roosevelt and confidant Louis Howe. His uncle, Franklin A. Delano, consulted various specialists who suspected poliomyelitis and this was confirmed by Boston specialist Dr. Robert W. Lovett on August 25. Although his political career was already formidable, Roosevelt was still only thirty-nine. Thus he was cut down, literally, in his prime. Franklin and Eleanor wanted to stay in public life and they were indomitable. Louis Howe kept the terrible news of Roosevelt's illness out of the newspapers until August 27, by which time it was truly possible to declare he was recovering. Thus Howe deliberately created and nurtured the impression that there was nothing fundamentally wrong—essential if FDR were to resume his political career. In an instant the social butterfly in Roosevelt was extinguished and with it the opportunities for political advance by display. In its place was a cocoon, an invalid confined to bed or wheelchair and sometimes encased in plaster.

The worst was not really over. In January 1922 his knee muscles began to tighten, drawing his legs up behind him. His physician, Dr. Draper's, remedy was to put both legs in plaster casts and use wedges driven farther each day, to stretch the tendons back. In February steel braces were fitted from hips to feet and, by maneuvering himself from his hips and moving, FDR could give an impression that he was walking, albeit clumsily, although he had no balance at all and no power in his legs. Through arduous exercise, he built up his upper body and transformed his shape from slim to stocky.

Eleanor Roosevelt told historian and biographer Frank Freidel in an interview in 1952 that Franklin's polio strengthened his already formidable self-control. Because he had to choose a particular course of treatment and stick to it for one or two years, he recognized the advantage of deciding upon a political policy and abiding by it. Many politicians, having made a decision over which they have no further control, remain worried lest it is not the right one. However, FDR developed a capacity to free his mind from worry about things he could not change. Thus in the Great Depression and World War II alike he was free to concentrate on what he could usefully do.

The man who could not walk found limitless fortitude, stamina, and political skill. It was he who, as president, would drive the nation forward in the Great Depression and World War II, while, at the same time, being able to identify with, and be identified with, the forgotten man at the base of the economic pyramid.

1

DRIVING AMBITION
The Continuing Revolutions
in Transportation

IN 1922 photographer Paul Strand began to take photographs of working parts of his motion picture camera and, fascinated, went on to photograph such other machines as drills and lathes, commenting on the beauty of their forms and workmanship and proclaiming them as one part of a new Trinity: "God the Machine, Materialistic Empiricism the Son, and Science the Holy Ghost." For the United States the period 1920–1941 could not be described in classical terms as an age of such precious metals as gold, silver, or bronze. However, it was one in which much of American civilization owed its forms to the industrial metals steel and aluminum, and to the mineral oil. It was, indeed, an age of *machinery: m*otor cars, *a*irplanes, *c*ameras, *h*ydroelectric power, *i*nternal combustion engines, *n*ewspaper printing presses, *e*lectrical engines, *r*adio, and *y*arns of artificial fibers.

In their *Art and the Machine* (1936) critics Sheldon and Martha Cheyney claimed how the "age of machine-implemented culture

Plymouth automobile assembly line. By mass production, standardization, and interchangeable parts, Ford and other auto manufacturers brought motor cars within reach of their workers' pockets, not only increasing the revolution in transportation but also preempting any claim of socialism that American capitalism divorced workers from the results of their labor. (Library of Congress).

had begun." In "The Americanization of Art" for a machine-age exhibition catalog of 1927, constructionist Louis Lozowick stressed how "The history of America is a history of stubborn and ceaseless effort to harness the forces of nature . . . of gigantic engineering feats and colossal mechanical construction." Here was an inspiration for art, the raw material of industrial function, structure, and standardization that could be discerned in the "rigid geometry of the American city: in the verticals of its smoke stacks, in the parallels of its car tracks, the squareness of its streets, the cubes of its factories, the arcs of its bridges, the cylinders of its gas tanks." Such mathematical order, indeed, organization, invited the "plastic structure" of art to capture the "flowing rhythm of modern America" in an idiomatic American art.

Despite the dramatic economic profile of each decade—superficial prosperity in the 1920s, the agonies of the Great Depression in the 1930s, followed by the miracle of recovery and growth in 1940s—many Americans understood that this was a period with its different industrial and social strands drawn together by science and technology, with ever-faster communication and an ever more diverse range of consumer products. As historian Richard Guy Wilson explains in the 1986 catalog for the exhibition, *The Machine Age in America 1918–1941,* "The machine age meant actual machines such as giant turbines and new machine materials such as Bakelite, Formica, chrome, aluminum, and stainless steel. The machine age meant new processes—mass production, 'Fordism'—factories, great corporations, and new ways of hiring. . . . The machine age encompassed the vast new skyscraper city, with its transportation systems compacted one on top of the other, and the new horizon city composed of filling stations, drive-ins, and superhighways."

The ever-increasing number of new inventions had led to the creation of a new vocabulary to describe them. In 1888 a group of academics undertook to make a dictionary in ten volumes of all the words in English. The project was to last forty years. As they labored, the world moved ahead of them. Thus, in 1893, while they were still on letter A, appendicitis came into common use but too late for inclusion. When they got past letter C the cinema came into being and the lexicographers decided to include it among the Ks as kinema. Over 400 words beginning with C were also too late for inclusion. By the time the project was complete in April 1928 about one new word had entered the language for every old one. A supplementary volume was already necessary. Whereas in the nineteenth century there were only two colors of stocking—black and white—now there were forty-three. The 1929 edition of *Webster's International Dictionary* found over 3,000 words had come into being in the period 1909–27. Of the 299 words beginning with letter A, 221 (two-thirds) were in the fields of science, medicine, and invention, and 82 of those were in aviation; 7 were in machinery. Only 1 was in art—atonality.

The heroes of America's advanced, increasingly technological society were Henry Ford and Charles A. Lindbergh, Jr. In 1920 one car in two throughout the world was a Ford Tin Lizzie. Pioneer car manufacturer Henry Ford had transformed the society into which he was born through an astute combination of advanced technology and paternalist management. A more authentic folk hero than Ford was Charles Lindbergh, whose solo $33\frac{1}{2}$-hour transatlantic flight from New York to Paris in May 1927 also combined new technical expertise with the traditional pioneer spirit. On his return New York brought down a storm of ticker tape to celebrate an achievement in which all Americans could take pride.

The Transportation Revolution of the 1920s and 1930s

Whatever the contribution to society of such men as Lindbergh, it was the automobile that shaped the new machine society and its culture most decisively. It was not only an agent of mobility but also a potent symbol of a new order. The scale of the continuing revolution in transportation achieved by cars between the world wars is suggested by the following statistics. In 1920 1,905,500 passenger cars were produced; in 1930, 2,787,400. In 1920 there were, altogether, 7.5 million cars on America's roads; in 1930 26.5 million—or one car for every five Americans. In 1940 3,717,300 cars were sold in the United States. The rise in the number of miles traveled was equally dramatic—from 1921 with 55,027 miles per vehicle to 1930 with 206,320 miles per vehicle and then 1940 with 302,188 miles per vehicle. In the 1920s private intercity motor car traffic soon exceeded rail traffic and by 1930 it was six times greater. Very soon cars were not only a convenience but also a necessity for mind as well as body. When Sinclair Lewis came to satirize the small-town world of a middle-aged real estate man in *Babbitt* (1922), he observed, "To George F. Babbitt, as to most prosperous citizens of Zenith, his motor-car was poetry and tragedy, love and heroism. The office was his pirate ship but the car his perilous excursion ashore." By the 1920s the automobile was automatically linked in most minds to the glamorous world of the happiness of pursuit created by advertising and to upward social mobility.

André Siegfried in *America Comes of Age* (1927) asserted how "it is quite common to find a working-class family in which the father has his own car, and the grown-up sons have one apiece as well." The wife of an unemployed worker in *Middletown* told the Lynds, "I'll never cut on gas! I'd go without a meal before I'd cut down on using the car." In fact, less than half of blue-collar families owned automobiles. In his article, "Affluence for Whom?" for *Labor History* of Winter 1983, Keith Stricker concludes that there were probably 16.77 million cars for 36.10 million consumer units (families and individuals) and thus about 46 percent of the units had cars. An automobile was not a sign of affluence when a used car could be bought for $60 outright or for a deposit of $5 and delayed purchase by monthly instalments of $5. Of course, Americans were more likely to have cars than Europeans and the urban family probably had about a fifty-fifty chance of owning a car. Many automobiles belonged to companies; some families had more than one car; and many single people had cars. Some cars were scrapped during the year; some cars belonged to farms.

By the mid-1920s the automobile industry was dominant in the American economy and had made tributaries of such other American industries as petroleum (using 90 percent of petroleum products), rubber (using 80 percent), steel (20 percent), glass (75 percent), and machine tools (25 percent). Socially, the automobile increased opportunities for leisure and recreation, bridging town and country, affording escape and seclusion from small town morality, and generally shaping the view of an ever more mobile population to an urban perspective.

The Big Three: Ford, GM, and Chrysler

Just after World War I Henry Ford dominated automobile manufacture, both nationally and internationally, although on the domestic scene he would face increasingly serious competition from General Motors. In fact, the 1920s saw the full emergence of two

New lamps for old. Shopworn Democratic standard-bearer William Jennings Bryan and Henry Ford, the mechanical genius whose name was synonymous with the new age of machines, in a publicity photo to promote Ford's peace ship in 1915. Ironically, Ford came to detest many new values of the society he himself had done more to transform than any other individual and set about recreating a tribute to a bygone rural Arcadia in his Dearborn museum, while fundamentalist Bryan, who was usually taken as a symbol of bygone agrarian protest, became in the 1920s a front man for a Florida real estate company dedicated to creating an idyllic leisure retreat for the affluent. (Library of Congress).

other giant auto companies, General Motors (GM) and the Chrysler Corporation, to take their place at the side of Ford as the Big Three companies among automobile manufacturers.

Among other leading producers General Motors, founded in 1908 by William Durant, was originally intended to become a combine of other companies. As initially formed, it included the companies of Buick, Cadillac, Oldsmobile, and Oakland, and several lesser firms. By a series of rapid financial combinations, acquisitions, and mergers, Durant created a network of suppliers,

assembly plants, and distributors. However, following an unex-
pected decline in sales, in 1910 Durant was forced out of General
Motors. He then acquired Chevrolet and, supported by Pierre Du
Pont and John Julius Raskob and the wealth of the Du Pont
family, he recaptured control of General Motors in 1915. (The
Du Ponts were an American family of French descent with a
fortune originally based in textiles, chemicals, and explosives.
Their concerns were incorporated in 1902 by Henry Algernon Du
Pont. His three cousins, Thomas Colman, Alfred Irénée, and
Pierre Samuel Du Pont, served as directors.)

By the end of World War I William C. Durant was planning
construction of plants and facilities on such a vast scale that he
required extra funds not only from the Du Ponts but also their
British associates, the Nobels, and the House of Morgan. Indeed,
it was only the outsize contribution of this powerful trio that
saved General Motors from bankruptcy in the postwar recession.
However, when William Durant tried to maintain the price of
General Motors above its current market rate, he was forced to
retire for the second, and last, time.

Henry Ford dealt with a postwar recession by cutting prices,
insisting on rigorous economies throughout his company, and
obliging suppliers and dealers to help him out; the suppliers by
selling parts more cheaply, the dealers by accepting additional
stocks that they could not sell immediately. Moreover, Ford attempted vertical integration, control of all processes from start to
finish, acquiring raw materials and transportation to achieve an
even flow from source to production to distribution. His aim was
a giant and incessant conveyor belt for the universal car. Ford's
new plant on River Rouge became a prime example of modern,
integrated production, in which Ford produced nearly all parts
for the Model T and even made his own glass and steel. Although
it was a superb achievement as technology and industrial integration, the Rouge plant was less successful as a business venture
since it was inflexible and run on high fixed costs. The complex
had been created to make a product that was already fifteen years
old. Even minor changes could only be introduced at great expense. Ford's difficulties arose not only out of his failure to recognize changing customer demands and their implications for

marketing, but also the swift success with which General Motors managers exploited the new situation.

Pierre Du Pont replaced Durant as president of General Motors and began to reorganize the corporation's administration and finances, and to revise its policies in production and marketing. Pierre Du Pont took his cue from Alfred P. Sloan, Jr., president of one of the firms acquired by Durant in 1916, and allowed such operating divisions as car, truck, parts, and accessories to retain their own autonomy. Thus the division managers continued to control their own production, marketing, purchasing, and engineering—as they had under Durant. However, what was new in the Du Pont-Sloan system was a new general office, comprising general executives and advisory staff specialists, to assure planning, coordination, and overall control.

First, Du Pont and Sloan (who then succeeded Du Pont as president in 1923) defined the roles of various executives in the general office and senior division managers in order to clarify authority and communications. Second, they arranged for the continuous collection and circulation of statistics to disclose the performances of the operating divisions and, indeed, the entire corporation. In time, much of this information and the decisions it inspired came to depend on market forecasts about production, costs, prices, and employment. It served as a yardstick for measuring performance.

General Motors led the way in improved mechanics and design. When automobile pioneer Charles K. Kettering became general manager of General Motors' research laboratories (1925–1947), he directed research on improving diesel engines and the development of a nontoxic and noninflammable refrigerant. He also devised and conducted research into higher octane gasoline, adding tetraethyl lead. Cars became more comfortable; until the 1920s most new automobiles were open cars but by 1929 the great majority were closed models. In order to entice consumers, General Motors' marketing included the development of an extensive range of models, an annual model, massive advertising, schemes to allow customers to trade in their old car in part payment for a new one, and regular and systematic analyses of the market. However, by using some of the same parts and supplies for their different models, General Motors hoped to retain one major advantage over the Ford system—economy of scale. Thus, between them, Pierre Du Pont and Alfred Sloan, by their rational innovations, boosted General Motors' share of total sales from 12.7 percent of the market in 1921 to 43.9 percent in 1931 and 47.5 percent in 1940. General Motors created a new, decentralized form of management at the precise time that Henry Ford was ridiculing systematic management while drawing the threads of control of his own company more tightly into his own autocratic hands.

The Chrysler Corporation was formed out of the failing Maxwell Motor Company in 1925 by Walter P. Chrysler who introduced his own design of car, featuring a high compression engine. He also acquired the Dodge Brothers Manufacturing Company in 1928 and produced the Plymouth, a successful model that allowed Chrysler to compete with Ford and General Motors, thereby becoming one of the Big Three car manufacturers. In 1929 Chevrolet introduced the six-cylinder engine and set a pattern for future development wherein auto manufacturers concentrated on engineering improvements, suspension, engines, and overall design.

Thus the American automobile market was to be dominated by the Big Three producers. Independent manufacturers could only survive if they produced automobiles for a narrow, specialized market, such as motor cars for the affluent. However, in general they either declined, went out of business, or were absorbed by the Big Three.

Early automobiles were designed in the fashion of horse-drawn carriages and, as late as the 1920s, they continued the basic feature of clearly separated parts in their overall design. However, in the course of the 1920s manufacturers were made forcibly aware of the significance of body styling, especially after the introduction of closed cars, which increased their share of the market from 10 percent in 1919 to 85 percent in 1927. The most significant designer was Harley Earl of General Motors. Coming from a background of custom-body building in Los Angeles and, having specialized in creating unique designs for individual Hollywood film stars, Earl knew how to create the widest range in styles from the same essential design and to provide even greater sophistication by subtle changes in body, attachments, and color within different price ranges. By 1928 designer Norman Bel Geddes refined the conventional angular design of cars into a rounder, more harmonious form in a design that was never put into production by manufacturer Graham Page but which influenced others' work.

Walter P. Chrysler had his top engineers, Fred Zeder, Owen Skelton, George McCain, and Barl Breer, and outside designers William Earnshaw and H. V. Hendersson, produce a streamlined automobile, the *Airflow*, for 1934 and in successive years. It had a torpedo-like body, bullet-shaped headlamps, slanted windshields, and curved window covers. The overall shape was a parabolic curve, like the then fashionable teardrop. However, such striking changes in the front of the vehicle were less significant than Chrysler's visible alterations to the body, with the engine placed farther forward and lower between the two front wheels—rather than in its usual position behind the front axle—and a lower frame seating passengers between front and rear axle, and all in a steel body welded to a steel frame. The interiors used chrome tubing for the seats and marbled rubber for the floor. Here was one of the most beautiful of all designs of the machine age, complete with a long, low-slung look decorated with a triad of horizontal speed lines to accentuate the car's purpose.

Cars conveyed more than their passengers. They could carry packages containing alcohol and did so in the period of national prohibition of alcohol. They certainly carried change—the conventions of the countryside were challenged by those of the city. They provided means and opportunity for sexual freedom impossible in a static society. In the Lynds' study *Middletown* one judge referred to the car as "a house of prostitution on wheels." Because they were used so much by bootleggers and gangsters, automobiles were never dissociated from criminal activities in the public mind. "Don't shoot, I'm not a bootlegger," was the caption popular among car owners in Michigan, and prohibited there by the attorney general in 1929. Whereas at the beginning of the 1920s automobiles represented an alternative to alcohol, at its end they symbolized booze and beer running and everything that was

Charles Sheeler, *River Rouge Plant,* (1932), 20″ × 24⅛″. (Photo by Geoffrey Clements; Collection of Whitney Museum of American Art, New York). In 1927 the Ford Motor Company commissioned precisionist artist Charles Sheeler to take a series of photographs of its River Rouge Plant, the first factory capable of manufacturing a complete automobile on one site. The definitive collection of thirty-two photographs and thirteen paintings, drawings, and prints were a celebration of the modern factory and its products in which all is sleek and immaculate.

subversive of national prohibition of alcohol. In addition, they provided an unfortunate comparison with liquor: how a potentially lethal invention could be controlled and made comparatively safe.

In *Responsible Drinking* (1930) Robert Brinkley compared the ill effects of alcohol with those of the automobile. He concluded that morals had withstood centuries of drinking but had broken down after two decades of driving. Driving was intoxicating. Cars had facilitated crime. Driving was habit-forming. Millions of people would hardly be able to use their legs again. However, the temperance movement had concentrated on the prohibition of alcohol. It had remained unconcerned by the social upheaval caused by the car. Of course, cars were part and parcel of contemporary social and economic life. They were controlled by careful drivers and compulsory insurance policies, by legislation and licenses. Could not liquor be regulated in the same way? The penalties of the automobile included urban congestion, road accidents, and gasoline pollution.

The motor vehicle facilitated the growth of suburbia, but, it must also be noted, the specific needs of the motor vehicle itself began to change the look of urban America. As traffic jams began to occur increasingly in the 1920s, citizen protest prompted the organization of local safety councils and encouraged cities to enact ordinances limiting speeds and parking and to erect traffic lights to control movement. In 1922 New York introduced the first manually operated traffic lights that were soon developed into an automatic system by Philadelphia and Cleveland. In Boston the parking charge was first invented, but not until 1932 did the parking meter make its debut in Oklahoma City. The first shopping center with adjoining parking lot opened in Kansas City in 1924 and in 1929 the first ramp garage was in use in Detroit. These are all important, but by now overly familiar elements in the makeup of the contemporary urban scene in America.

Detroit, in common with other cities engaged in production, had, and still has, a special relationship with the automobile. The motor capital grew by 126 percent during the decade 1910-1920, a ratio second only to that of Akron, the tire capital, at 173 percent. Los Angeles and Houston, both centers of oil production, experienced such phenomenal rates of growth in the 1920s and beyond when the automobile was exploited to its fullest potential.

The motor vehicle revolution led to ever-wider use of trucks for goods and buses for passengers as well as of private motor cars. Trucks carried mail, farm produce and livestock, and manufactured goods. In 1899 the Post Office began to experiment with delivery of mail by truck in some cities. In 1904 only 700 trucks were sold but most auto manufacturers added a truck line to their regular production and by 1918 over half a million were in use. In particular, trucking expanded in the 1930s. There were 4.5 million registered trucks in 1940, a seventh of all vehicles. Unemployed truck drivers bought trucks on credit to establish a tiny one-man business, carrying furniture, animals, and farm produce. Truck operators were not regulated until 1935.

Americans soon became aware of the convenience and cleanliness of buses, especially for intracity journeys. The first buses were simply elongated passenger cars with a stronger chassis and extra seats. The prototype of modern buses was designed and created by Frank and William Fageol, a bus close to the ground with a low step at the entrance and a lower center of gravity. A subsequent model placed the engine under the floor so that the entire inner space of the body was available for passengers. Hundreds of small bus companies competed for passengers and by 1930 there were enough good roads for intercity bus services to become firmly established. In that year about a fifth of all intercity commercial travel was by bus.

Buses had considerable advantages over railroads for shorter journeys because they could vary routes and were cheaper than trains requiring tracks and stations. America's (eventual) 3 million miles of roads and highways gave car, bus, and truck a flexibility that railroads simply could not provide. The smaller size and seating capacity of buses also allowed greater variety of service. Needless to say, both trucks and buses were dependent on improved roads and more of them. During the 1930s the number of registered buses rose by 80 percent. In 1930 buses were providing about 25 percent more passenger miles than intercity railroads. In 1940 they supplied about 40 percent more. During the 1930s bus fares were about 10 percent cheaper than railroad fares, a factor in the sharp reduction in rail fares during the depression.

Changing Strategies of the Big Three Auto Manufacturers

However, whatever public demand for automobiles in the 1920s and 1930s, it was greatly exceeded by the potential supply. Manufacturers could make far more cars and trucks than they could sell. By the mid-1920s most Americans who could afford a motor car had bought one and the market for automobiles was a replacement market. Thus the automobile industry moved from initial growth to a competitive stage between the different manufacturers. The market was saturated and thus marketing, rather than sheet production, became the prime concern of manufacturers. As Alfred Dupont Chandler, Jr., explains in *Giant Enterprise* (1964), "Marketing now became a greater challenge than production. The underlying marketing problem was no longer to sell an individual his first car but to get the man who already owned one to buy a new car. And management became a greater challenge than finance. Effective coordination, appraisal, and planning were essential if costs were to be kept down and the market was not to be oversold." While General Motors forged ahead with its new methods of management and marketing, Henry Ford stubbornly persisted in his shopworn strategy. Thus his share of the market fell steadily from 55.7 percent in 1921 to 24.9 percent in 1931, and then to 18.9 percent in 1940.

We might say the cause of Ford's tragedy was his success. Having shaped American society for the 1920s in a most decisive fashion, he failed to move with the times. He failed to appreciate the dynamic character of the mass market for cars that he himself had done so much to create. He refused to let Edsel, his only son and the national president of the company, exercise any real control over his creation. His tyranny damaged Edsel's health and, at times, came close to destroying the firm. In his "Sketch for a Portrait of Henry Ford," poet William Carlos Williams refers to Ford, somewhat laconically, as "a tin bucket," full of "heavy sludge," and "steel grit." The bucket with the dent swings round at ever-faster speed and its handle soon "gives way and the bucket is propelled through space. . . ."

The Ford family drama was a topsy-turvy version of *King Lear* in which the father conspired against his son and drove him to an early grave. The outwardly loyal Harry Bennett modeled his professional character on the type of man played by James Cagney in the movies. He was a fixer who got things done, such as taking care of the mother of Henry's illegitimate son and hiring strong-arm gorillas to beat up union leader Walter Reuther. "If Mr. Ford told me to blacken out the sun tomorrow," remarked Bennett, "I might have trouble fixing it. But you'd see a hundred thousand sons-of-bitches coming through the Rouge gates in the morning all wearing dark glasses." Bennett created an illegal private police force, the "outside squads," closer to fascist black shirts than anything else. Ford repeatedly humiliated Edsel, always backing Bennett in disputes. Thus Edsel, forced to endure endless frustration, developed "Ford Stomach," the illness and anxiety experienced by men on the shop floor and caused by relentless adherence to timetables on the assembly line. Edsel died of an ulcer and cancer at the age of forty-nine.

Henry Ford kept the Model T in production for too long. In his *Ford* (1986), Robert Lacey sums up Ford's propensity for managerial autocracy as "Absolute control plus divided attention equals a recipe for disaster." Ford belatedly learnt that the new mass society he had helped shape would not just select goods on the basis of cost. It expected efficiency and choice of style. The new society of mass consumption was also a new society of mass communications in which radio, movies, and advertising stirred aspirant needs and desires in people all the way from New York to San Francisco. Because of his limited design, Ford was excluded from the world of upward social mobility and he simply did not realize how deep was the need for individual fulfillment. The common man did not want to stay common. Ford's loyalty to the Model T was not simply a matter of personal pride. He did not want to foreclose a line that had long been popular and, more importantly, he did not really want to have to close down his workshops while they were being reequipped and thereby lose markets to his competitors in the interim before he did introduce a new car.

However, the Ford company was part of a capitalist system in which the weakest competitor went to the wall. No matter how false were the new values that led the public to move from the cheap Model T, because it was cheap, simple, black, and ugly, to other models, no matter how far Ford wanted to rely on internal company strength, he was eventually forced to respond to the public crisis of confidence in his car. When profits declined dramatically, he decided to extinguish the Model T in 1927, close his plants, and reequip them for an improved model, the Model A. Ford's strategy was essentially a retreat. Yet, having done all this, in 1929, the first full year of the Model A, Ford took only 31.3 percent of the market while General Motors retained 32.3 percent. Moreover, their profits were rising. In 1928 General Motors reported a profit of $296.25 million—one of the largest ever by an American corporation to that time. During the period 1927–1937, including eight years of the Great Depression, General Motors took an average profit of $173.2 million, while Ford took an average annual loss of $1.4 million. The depression hit Ford at an especially awkward time when he was constructing a large new plant, River Rouge, and needed to buy back shareholders' stock to raise the capital. He survived the depression but his period of near monopoly control had passed.

Ford clung to a forlorn belief that his company was more efficient than was General Motors. Ironically, he believed his company recognized ability in younger men more quickly than they did in General Motors—ironically, because many of his executives left him for General Motors in the 1930s. The best of the renegades included William S. Knudsen in production and Norval Hawkins in sales. In the Ford company authority became concentrated among a few unscrupulous and hardheaded favorites. However, Ford's old-fashioned views on the way to administer a modern business were less damaging than his refusal, or inability, to recognize his competitor's superior innovations in marketing.

The General Motors' executive committee and international sales committee tried to increase their share of the market by steadily improving the performance and regularly changing the design of their cars. Charles Kettering and his research staff concentrated on improving such things as axles, transmissions, and crankshafts in order to make their cars easier and more comfortable to drive. Harley Earl and his styling section made the cars' design and colors most attractive. General Motors cultivated good relations with local dealers and showed acute understanding of the dealers' changing needs in the depression, raising the dealers' margin of profit on new cars to 24 percent, encouraging them to

The United States prepared for the postwar boom in automobile sales and their promise of suburban life with such compelling symbols as this 1945–1946 model of the Nash Ambassador Six. (Library of Congress).

apply modern accounting procedures, and, above all, trying to prevent them from becoming overstocked.

Chrysler adopted General Motors' strategy. By concentrating on the inexpensive Plymouth, Walter P. Chrysler had 25.4 percent of the market in 1937, compared with Ford's 21.4 percent, and in 1940, 23.7 percent, compared with Ford's 18.9 percent. Despite the introduction of the Ford V-8 in 1934, Ford's sales continued to fall and the company lost an average of $1.4 million per year in the period 1931–1941. By the mid-1940s the Ford company might have gone bankrupt but for the wartime spending of the government of Franklin Roosevelt that he despised. Apart from some production triumphs in World War II, Ford's later career was marred by bitter conflicts with management and labor alike. The Henry Ford of $5 a day could not understand that workers really did want to belong to organized labor unions and were ready to strike in pursuit of union recognition. Ford was a ghost of his former self. The man who created the future now gave himself up to recreating the past. He turned to such social pursuits as folk dancing, new editions of the McGuffey *Readers,* and collecting artifacts for his special museum, a sentimental reconstruction of the rural past he had fled before the turn of the century.

However, in general, the Great Depression further aided the domination of the Big Three companies by eliminating the remaining major independents. Moreover, General Motors' new decentralized industry set a model not only for the other auto manufacturers Ford and Chrysler but also for other areas of American industry. Just as the great industrial concerns of the late nineteenth century had used the railroads as their model for organization at a time when railroads were at the heart of the American economy, so in the mid-twentieth century other industries and manufacturing enterprises adapted the structure of auto manufacturers when automobile production was central to the entire system of industry and manufacturing. Alfred Dupont Chandler concluded in *Giant Enterprise* (1964), "By 1925 General Motors' innovations in management had produced a new decentralized type of organization for the large industrial enterprise. It became a model for much of American industry because it supplied a viable alternative to the centralized, functionally departmentalized structure (that is, a department for each major function—production, sales, purchasing, research, and so forth) that had been developed in the second part of the nineteenth century, first by the railroads and then by the early large integrated industrial enterprises. It provided as well a more effective administrative form than did the loosely controlled holding company in which only financial ties connected the several operating subsidiaries with each other and with the general office."

At the turn of the century the United States had an extensive railroad network, not truly flexible because its tracks were fixed but yet responsive enough to contemporary needs for passengers and freight. However, by comparison, its intercity road network was truly primitive, a shambles of unsafe dirt tracks. Such road construction schemes as were conceived during the early twentieth century were essential for intracity traffic and even here the emphasis was on boulevards to make cities beautiful, such as the McMillan Plan for Washington, D.C., (1907–1912) or the Chicago Plan (1906–1909).

Richard Guy Wilson recalls how traffic problems were widely discussed in newspapers and magazines throughout the 1920s and 1930s. They included such conjuror's tricks as diminishing several traffic lanes to only two to enter tunnels approaching major cities, traffic jams stretching for miles along two-lane highways; erratic uncontrolled drivers whose cars careened from side to side; bridges across navigable rivers that got stuck when they were being opened or closed; railroad grade crossings not always run with model efficiency and thus with occasional, terrifying crashes. Moreover, motor vehicles were multiplying in size and numbers beyond the capacity of new roads. In August 1936 R. B. Toms, chief of design at the Bureau of Public Roads, was reported by *Future* as saying that at least a quarter and perhaps a half of modern roads built over the previous twenty years were "unfit" for use. Automobile roadside culture of gas stations and garages and ugly billboards disfigured the landscape. People obsessed with the advantages of the automobile required their representatives in Congress and the State assemblies to have highways and superhighways constructed so that they could travel with maximum ease and minimum inconvenience.

The preferred solution was a specially designed environment — superhighways to cater for automobiles, buses, and trucks traveling resolutely at a maximum speed consistent with safety and with minimum interruption. These highways were entities separate from homes, businesses, pedestrians and cross traffic. As critics Lewis Mumford and Benton McKay observed in their seminal article, "Townless Highways for the Motorist: Proposal for the Automobile Age" in *Harper's* of August 1931: "The Townless Highway would be, like the railroad, an institution in itself, a system."

The highway accommodated two or more lanes of traffic in both directions but without a central strip to separate left and right. However, in the course of the 1920s builders introduced a three-lane highway in which the central lane was to be used for turning and passing in both directions. Alternative titles were motorway, freeway, parkway, turnpike, expressway, and, even, limited way.

The freeway was distinguished by multiple traffic lanes and a central median strip. It moved across the natural landscape of the countryside and the man-made cityscape, such as the Pulaski Skyway over Jersey City or the Outer Drive around Chicago, both constructed in the 1930s.

The parkway's most distinctive features were its limited access and being placed in a carefully designed landscape. The leading parkway designer of the period was Gilmore D. Clarke. However, the first automotive parkway was the Bronx River Parkway, authorized by the New York State Assembly in 1907, and constructed in the period 1919–1923 from the North Bronx to White Plains in Westchester County. It set the pattern for future parkways, with an initial road of four lanes, two in each direction, occasionally separating to enfold hillocks and copses but generally following the undulating meander of the Bronx River. Wherever it was not possible to demolish signs or intrusive buildings, trees were planted to mask them. Encouraged by the success of the Bronx River Parkway, the Westchester County Park Commission began to construct various other parkways, partly to convert the recreational areas of Westchester County and partly to provide more convenient access to New York City. Thus, in the period 1923–1933 the commission had eighty-eight miles of parkways and ten miles of freeways constructed. The leading designer, Gilmore D. Clarke, went on to a successful career as the designer of the Taconic State, the Long Island, New York City, and George Washington Memorial parkways.

By 1936 the Bureau of Public Roads had spent almost $2 billion altogether on the construction and improvement of 324,000 miles of federal highways. The idea of highways and freeways penetrating yet accommodating the natural landscape of rivers, hills, and valleys, and of piercing cities and towns, and the ways they were achieved were major accomplishments of the 1920s and 1930s. Swiss architectural historian Siegfried Giedion was enraptured by

America's numerous highways and observed in his *Space, Time and Architecture* (1941) how "Full realization is given to the driver and freedom to the machine. Riding up and down the long sweeping grades produces an exhilarating dual feeling, one of being connected with the soil and yet of hovering just above it, a feeling which is nothing else so much as sliding swiftly on skis through untouched snow down the sides of high mountains."

It was World War II, with its special needs of transporting workers, war materiel, and supplies of food and manufactured goods across great stretches of country, that provided a major impetus to the extension and renewal of the American highway system. Perhaps the most notable highway project was the Alaskan Highway (Alcan). Construction began on March 12, 1942, and was completed by December 1 that year. Alcan extended 1,523 miles from Davison Creek, British Columbia, through Canada and the Yukon Territory to Fairbanks, Alaska. Conceived as a military supply route, it cost $138 million to build and was opened to tourists in summer 1948.

Service Stations

The most widely known form of architecture inspired by the automobile was the gas, or service station. Different oil companies established different sorts of structures to promote their own special images. The Texas Star and Mobil flying horse were recognized nationwide atop clean, efficiently run buildings. Holabird and Roth designed prototype stations for Texaco's distributors with flat, overhanging roofs atop distinctive glass boxes. Gulf also achieved prototype stations with a large display room but with curved glass, horizontal strips and fins, and a setback towered entrance. The prototype building for Standard Oil by Alfred Clauss and George Daub of Philadelphia, with distinctive porcelain panels in red, white, and blue, was sufficiently festive to appeal to organizers Philip Johnson and Henry-Russell Hitchcock who included it in the Museum of Modern Art International Style exhibit of February and March 1932.

The most successful and widely known standardized service stations were prototypes designed for Texaco in 1936 by Walter

Dorwin Teague as part of Texaco's assertive marketing campaign. Along with the prototype stations, with large display windows, a canopy with fins, and crowned by the giant Texaco Star, came a new advertising campaign promoting the premier gasoline "for those who want the best," and clean rest rooms checked by an inspection team. By 1940 500 Texaco stations had been built based on Teague's original design.

Aviation

For a time flying and airplane development stumbled after World War I but then, toward the end of the 1920s, they gathered momentum once again, thanks to new research, both public and private. In 1926 the Guggenheim Foundation established a special fund that provided grants of $3 million altogether, partly to promote aeronautical knowledge, partly to help extend the boundaries of aeronautical science, partly to encourage commercial and civil aviation and assist the development of planes and equipment, and partly to encourage wider use of airplanes. By the time the fund was liquidated in 1930, it had achieved many of its objectives.

By the mid-1920s it was clear that a market for new aircraft was emerging. Thus government administrators realized that there was a need for a firm governmental hand, exercising some control and coordination, both to ensure safety and to avoid the sort of unbridled chaos that had marked the years of railroad construction. Accordingly, the administration of President Calvin Coolidge (1923–1929) created a board to plan a national aviation policy. In turn, their recommendations were incorporated into the Air Commerce Act of 1926, the Navy Five-Year Aircraft Program of 1926, and the Army Five-Year Program.

American passenger airlines grew out of the Post Office service. Firstly, it was the airmail service that laid out an extensive route system. Then, in 1925, distribution of airmail was contracted out to private companies who were encouraged to carry passengers in order to part-subsidize the operation. Finally, legislation was enacted to connect a number of major cities through the transcontinental mail routes. The first regular passenger service, based on the mail system, opened on April 4, 1927, between Boston and New York.

Lindbergh's Solo Flight Across the Atlantic

Two epochal flights demonstrated the potential of planes as a means of mass, rapid transportation: Louis Blériot's record flight across the English Channel of July 25, 1909; and Charles A. Lindbergh, Jr.'s, solo flight across the Atlantic Ocean on May 20–21, 1927. (In 1919 two English pilots, Alcock and Brown, first flew across the Atlantic from Newfoundland to Ireland.)

Charles A. Lindbergh, Jr., son of a Minnesota congressman but born in Detroit in 1902, was of Swedish extraction. He grew up in Detroit and Washington, and attended the University of Wisconsin as well as flying schools in Lincoln, Nebraska, and the army in Texas. In 1926 he served as an airmail pilot on the run from St. Louis to Chicago. His nonstop transatlantic flight, promoted by a press competition, turned Lindbergh into a folk hero whose receptions in various European and American cities were turned into victory tours. As Anne Michaelis explained in a poem, "Lindbergh,"

> Alone, yet never lonely,
> Serene, beyond mischance,
> The world was his, his only,
> When Lindbergh flew to France.

A crucial factor to explain Lindbergh's amazing popularity was due to the timing of his solo flight. The uncomfortable barnstorming warplanes, hastily converted for peacetime use, were getting older and some were being taken out of service. Lindbergh demonstrated the amazing potential of flight as a rival to conventional modes of travel. He revitalized public interest in aviation at a time when aircraft research and development had become somewhat stagnant. His timing was in tune with the rising expectations of the few people who chose to travel by air. They wanted newer, more comfortable planes, and the airlines had to respond to their passengers because they were competing with such longer established modes of travel as railroads, ships,

Charles A. Lindbergh, Jr., the attractive, gangling pioneer aviator whose solo transatlantic flight of May 1927 not only demonstrated the enduring American traditions of rugged determination and technical skills in new fields but also revived flagging public interest in aviation. (Library of Congress).

and automobiles, all of which were more comfortable and accessible.

People ascribed Lindbergh's heroism to his personality and praised his Swedish self-containment, his mechanical precision, and even his commercial ambition. His personality was taken as a representation of the restraints associated with aviation. Man's ability to fly depended on a balanced combination of disciplines that were the exact opposite of carefree. Lindbergh liked to give an impression of casualness, prompting the *Times* of London to call him "the flying fool." In fact, his numerous achievements depended on meticulous preparation and care.

He was soon regarded as an expert in the comparatively new field of aviation and became a technical adviser for Transcontinental Air Transport and Pan Am and personally pioneered some of their routes. He received the Medal of Honor.

Other epochal flights suggested expanding horizons of achievement in the air. C. C. Champion set an early record for altitude by flying 37,995 feet above Washington (1927); Bert Hinkler flew solo from London to Australia (1928); and Commander Bird flew over the South Pole (1929). In the 1930s daring aviators attempted flights around the world. Lindbergh flew to Shanghai, China; Amelia Earhart made two attempts at crossing the world in 1937; Howard Hughes tried to do so in 1938. Other feats included intercontinental races, such as the MacRobertson International Race from England to Australia in 1934. Although it was won by a British plane, American planes came second and third and thus the race introduced the DC-3 and Boeing 247D to a wider public, prompting European airlines to buy these American models. The Schneider Cup revived racing in closed courses, notably the USA National Air Races in Cleveland.

Castles in the Air — The Big Four and Pan Am

Civil aviation developed out of a central American need. In a country as large as the United States with as scattered a population and large cities, people were quick to appreciate the speed and convenience of air travel, compared with more traditional forms. Increasing passenger expectations coincided with the advent of new, improved planes. Moreover, the mail service had already established a network of routes and flight paths, with lighted beacons providing necessary signals to guide airplanes. Once again, people saw air travel as a way of rising above the restrictions of national territory and of opening up new relationships across the world. British investigative journalist Anthony Sampson comments in *Empires of the Sky* (1984) "But the pilots and entrepreneurs soon discovered that they could not fly without their governments' support, and that even within their own country they could not make their airlines pay without subsidies or the mail contracts which governments awarded. In every country the soaring ambition of the aviators and their financiers came up against the controls and military designs of their governments."

By 1930 the United States had four major airlines, all launched on the model of shipping lines: Bill Boeing and engine makers Pratt and Whitney had formed the United Aircraft and Transportation Corporation, later United Air Lines; the Aviation Corporation, founded by railroad magnate W. A. Harriman in 1929, eventually developed into American Airlines; and entrepreneur C. M. Keys, chairman of the Curtiss airplane company, was a pivotal figure in the creation of North American Airlines, predecessor of Eastern Airlines, and TAT, later TWA. By 1930 these four airlines—United, Eastern, TWA, and American—had all established transcontinental routes, their prime catchment area for the next half century. Altogether, 73 million passenger miles were flown in 1930, the first year of air hostesses, part attendant, part waitress, and part nurse, to serve passengers. In 1938 the Big Four were joined by Continental Airlines, founded in Denver by Robert Six.

The airlines also had their tycoons—Cyrus Smith (American), Bill Patterson (United), Eddie Rickenbacker (Eastern), and Jack Frye (TWA)—each obsessed with the challenge of creating networks and opening up the continent. The airline pioneers competed furiously with one another but retained a spirit of friendly rivalry like barroom gamblers. After all, they were bound together by their mutual obsession and the novel experience of flight that had captured public imagination in less than a generation. Their competition for landing rights and the need to find

A new age of transportation dawned with the advent of ever larger airplanes. The Florida Flyer arrives at Newark airport, New Jersey, in 1934. (Library of Congress).

refueling stages led to the further development of Fort Worth, St. Louis, and Kansas City. Aviation was largely untouched by the depression. Dozens of companies, large and small, with hundreds of planes flew ever more passengers and carried increasing loads of mail in the 1930s. Between 1930 and 1940 air passenger traffic multiplied twelve times to just over a billion passenger miles in 1940, while airfreight traffic more than tripled in volume. In 1934, for the first time, over a million airline tickets were sold in a single year.

Many of the minute airports that served as refueling stages were truly isolated places—quite different from frontier railroad stations of the previous century. F. Scott Fitzgerald described the type in his last, unfinished novel, *The Last Tycoon*.

I suppose there has been nothing like airports since the days of the stage-stops—nothing quite as lonely, as sombre-silent. The old red-brick depots were built right into the towns they marked—people didn't get off at those isolated stations unless they lived there. But airports lead you way back in history like oases, like the stops on the great trade routes. The sight of air travellers strolling in ones or twos into midnight airports will draw a small crowd any night up to them. The young people look at the planes, the older ones look at the passengers with a watchful incredulity.

During the 1920s commercial airplanes carried between twelve and fifteen passengers, sometimes more. However, in the 1930s overall airplane design greatly improved the associated technology of engines, propellers, movable wing surfaces (or flaps), and retractable undercarriages, and this allowed for larger planes, carrying between thirty and forty passengers, the first economically viable transport aircraft.

The depression and World War II provided a turning point for commercial aviation. This was most obvious in the early 1930s when airlines began to benefit from earlier research, both governmental and private, and an ever growing corps of young, and optimistic aeronautical scientists and engineers, committed to the development of commercial airplanes. By 1932 aircraft design was far superior to that of the planes of World War I. In a word, it was streamlined. New airplanes were internally braced, low-strung monoplanes, built entirely of metal. They had such improved features as air-cooled engines, controllable pitch propellers, retractable undercarriages, and insulated and sound-proofed compartments for pilots and passengers. Although later developments included such features as jet engines, more powerful propeller engines, and much larger capacity, the all-metal monoplane of the very early 1930s has provided the essential prototype for all later civil aircraft design.

In 1932 Donald Douglas sold TWA several DC-2 planes. They carried fourteen passengers at 170 mph. From 1936 his new all-metal DC-3, powered by two 900 horsepower Wright cyclone motors, became the most popular model on all major airlines and was known as "the Model T of aircraft." It carried twenty-one passengers and revolutionized air travel on account of its safety and reliability. The DC-3 combined maximum economy, safety, and speed and carried twenty-one passengers. It was the first passenger plane to make a profit without benefit of an airmail route subsidy. The DC-3 flew a route from New York to Los Angeles, a journey lasting twenty-four hours, including eighteen hours in the air, with three or four stops for refueling.

Canada was one of the few developed countries without a scheduled national air service and until the late 1930s American airlines carried Canadians across their country. The Canadian government founded Trans-Canada Airlines but the new air networks crossed the frontier with the United States along the forty-ninth parallel and began to erode Canada's separate economy irreversibly.

Modern aircraft design in the United States was stimulated by the arrival of German immigrants Max Munk and Theodore von Karman, the creation of the Daniel Guggenheim Fund for the Promotion of Aeronautics in 1926, and research by the National Advisory Committee for Aeronautics (NACA).

In the late twenties and thirties the appearance of airplanes was much enhanced by a number of technological improvements such as the powerful and elegant radical engineering of Pratt and Whitney, and Curtis-Wright. Cantilevered wings, better braced and attached to the fuselage than the old flat wings attached by external wires and struts, allowed designers to achieve more streamlined designs overall. Thus John K. Northrop's Vega of 1927 for Lockheed and his Sirius of 1929 set new standards of design, while providing superior machines as to range and speed for pioneers Lindbergh, Amelia Earhart, and Wiley Post. In 1931 Russian immigrant Igor Sikorsky designed and built the first Clippers for Pan Am. Following closely, Glen Martin's flying boats, such as the M-130W China Clipper of 1934, demonstrated a new integral aircraft design, notably in the way the wings rose naturally from the body.

Industrial designers contributed to improved interiors. For the never realized Air Liner Number 4 Norman Bel Geddes and Otto Koller provided the plane's interior design with all the accoutrements of a luxury ocean liner. In Martin's China Clippers, as modified by Worthen Paxxon and Frances Waite Geddes, there was a lounge with sofas that converted into sleeping berths at night. As further modified by Henry Dreyfuss and Howard Ketcham, the Pan Am Clippers gained an exotic reputation as the airline extended its operations into Latin America and the Orient.

The most significant developments in aviation design were the almost simultaneous achievement of the 247 by Boeing and the DC-1 by Douglas. The Boeing 247 flew its maiden flight on February 8, 1933; the Douglas DC-1 first flew on July 1, 1933. The Boeing was an all-metal monoplane with two short-cowled radial engines and retractable landing gear that could carry ten passengers from coast to coast in twenty hours, including seven stops for refueling en route. The DC-1, designed by Donald Douglas to replace the discredited Fokker trimotor planes, was also superior to the Boeing 247. It drew on innovations by Jack Northrop to provide an all-metal, multicullar wing mounted beneath the fuselage. By the time of its third revision, the DC-3 of 1935–1936, it could accommodate twenty-eight passengers. The streamlined fuselage was constructed of special lightweight aluminum, riveted to the frame and polished to perfection. Its flowing appearance and sterling performance alike captured public imagination as it reduced the transcontinental journey to fifteen hours, thereby stimulating passenger sales and relieving airlines from dependence on federal mail contracts. In time, companies right across the world adopted DC-2 and DC-3 airplanes that became standard everywhere.

In the early 1930s there were only about 200,000 passengers traveling by air in the United States and Europe each year. Fatalities were high with one passenger killed in an accident for every 8 million passenger miles traveled. By the end of the 1930s, when several million passengers were traveling each year, there was one fatality for every 100 million passenger miles traveled.

Transatlantic flight was most significant, heralding a new era of travel to follow in the years after World War II. Between 1932 and 1937 transatlantic flights were by airships, such as the *Graf Zeppelin* and the *Hindenburg,* flying between Frankfurt, Germany, and Lakehurst, New Jersey. The day of the airship was brief, brought to an abrupt end by the crash and explosion of the *Hindenburg* at Lakehurst in 1937.

The first of the forty-seater Handley Page airliners ready for delivery to Britain's Imperial Airways—the first aircraft designed for passenger comfort, providing a drawing room with eighteen seats (here), a cocktail bar, a saloon with twenty seats, a chart room, and a wireless cabin. (Photo by Underwood and Underwood; Library of Congress).

The flying boat was then the staple carrier for intercontinental flights until 1938 when it was replaced by the Boeing 314 clipper widely adopted in 1939, the year transatlantic flights began. The major intercontinental carrier was Pan American World Airways, founded in 1928 and originally operating a route from Florida to Cuba. By 1938 and 1939, under its dynamic president Juan Trippe, it was running passenger services on routes to South America, across the Pacific to Manila in the Philippines, and to England. Pan Am introduced a new Martin M-130 four engine on its Pacific routes in 1935. That year Imperial and Pan Am began a series of pioneer transatlantic flights. In August 1939 they started a regular transatlantic service with inflight refueling by flying boats. The service was interrupted by World War II and, at first, Pam Am clippers could only land in Ireland. Nevertheless, the North Atlantic Return Ferry introduced a year-round service, eventually run by BOAC. Commercial aviation was disrupted by the war and military attention shifted to the use of airplanes. Nevertheless, the destructive experience of war stimulated substantial developments in airplane design and construction and these benefited civil as well as military aviation. The state of military transport aviation shaped commercial aviation in the immediate postwar years, providing the world with flying boats for civil transportation.

As with every new form of manufacturing and commerce introduced since the American Civil War, air transportation posed special problems for government regulation. At first the Department of Commerce assigned routes, awarded pilot certificates and licenses, and determined standards of safety through its Aeronautics branch. However, the system was rocked by scandal and airmail contracts were canceled in 1934 after the discovery of a number of illegal arrangements. In 1934 Senator Hugo Black of Alabama led sensational hearings to investigate how former postmaster general Walter Brown had awarded airmail contracts. Jim Farley, the new postmaster general, accused Brown of conspiracy and collusion. Indeed, airline chiefs were brought to testify about their relations with the man who had helped create their airlines. Although they were opening up a continent all over again and encouraging mankind to review its horizons, airline companies had an early reputation as buccaneers. To the public it seemed here was a new race of robber barons.

President Franklin D. Roosevelt (1933–1945) distrusted the Big Four and Pan Am but, when he tried to find an alternative to commercial airlines, he failed. He canceled all domestic airmail contracts and called in the army to fly the mail, but army pilots could not handle the quantity or the routes and ten of them were killed. FDR had to reinstate the airline contracts. First, the government introduced a temporary airmail law to return mail delivery to the private sector. The bill provided for the appointment of a Federal Aviation Commission (FAC) to study the general situation and make recommendations for the future organization of aviation. Its views were implemented in the Civil Aeronautic Act of 1938, creating a Civil Aeronautics Authority (CAA), within the Department of Commerce. In 1940 the CAA became the licensing and regulating body for civil aviators and a Civil Aeronautics Board (CAB) was created under the secretary of commerce to control the economic organization of airlines and determine standards of safety. The new board continued a system of so-called controlled competition by which airlines sought routes from government to be approved by the president. In practice, the Big Four, who were not well established, were awarded "grandfather rights," that is, permanent certificates on domestic routes, while Pan Am continued to enjoy its foreign monopoly.

However, FDR did achieve a critical change when he separated manufacturing companies, such as Boeing and United, from owning or controlling airlines. This fundamental shift in policy encouraged the airlines to pick and choose between manufacturers, thereby stimulating competition and increasing the pace of advances in technology. On the West Coast such aircraft companies as Boeing, Douglas, and Lockheed competed for airline custom until just before, and during World War II, when orders for military planes became even more lucrative.

World Fairs

It was not only the art, industry, and gadgets of the machine age that were on the agenda for transformation but also the general environment. This was a special feature of two world's fairs, the Century of Progress Fair, Chicago, in 1933–1934, and the World of Tomorrow Fair, New York, 1939–1940, both of which boasted pavilions devoted to new worlds. In Chicago visitors could see a General Motors assembly line devised by Albert Kahn, while in New York they could view *Democracity* by Henry Dreyfuss and thereby enter a future made by machines. *Democracity* was a model city within the Persisphere, a round building of 200 feet in diameter wherein people passed through the Trylon, 700 feet tall, and finally descended a ramp, the Helicline to the ground.

The way science and technology were enriching American civilization was a theme dear to the National Research Council (NRC), funded by big business and supported by university scholars. The NRC was instrumental in the Century of Progress and World of Tomorrow expositions in Chicago and New York. In particular, the Chicago exposition was regarded as a showcase for "the transformation of life through the ministrations of sciences." An official slogan was "Science Finds—Industry Applies—Man Conforms." The buildings provided visitors with a progress from primitive machine shops of the 1830s to the mass production lines of Ford and General Motors of the 1930s, while the structures themselves were designed to exploit metallic sheafs, electric cascades, and suspended roots. The New York World's Fair offered visitors a similarly idealistic vision of tomorrow's world. As its president, Grover Whalen, commented, "a glimpse of the community of the future—a future conditioned by science." Albert Einstein, the preeminent physicist whose name was synonymous with scientific advance, acted as front man to an Advisory Committee on Sciences. His most popular contribution was the movie, *The City,* directed by Ralph Steiner and Willard Van Dyke and with a score by Aaron Copland, as a celebration of greenbelt towns. Pavilions dedicated to business were designed to look like laboratories of the future.

The most significant was *Futurama* designed by Norman Bel Geddes as part of the General Motors Pavilion. Visitors entered through a gigantic curved wall painted like an automobile in a silver metalic finish and thence proceeded to a large, darkened auditorium which they crossed aboard a rubber-tired train on a route to simulate an air trip across the United States of 1960. They saw miniature automobiles, orchards, and fields encased by glass, and a modern metropolis composed of skyscrapers. The final destination was a full-size version of a street intersection they had just passed over in model form and now containing the latest products from General Motors. The message was clear. Technology and machines were not the essential problem for America in the Great Depression but, rather, the solution.

FDR opens the New York World's Fair of 1939, the last great demonstration of the peaceful potential of the new machine age before its destructive forces were unleashed by World War II. (Photo by courtesy of Charles Ober).

2

THE 1920s
An American Dream That
Became a Nightmare

THE ROARING TWENTIES, a gangster film released in 1939, shows
how the world of entertainment has romanticized the history
of the 1920s and made icons of the gangster, the tycoon, the
movie star, and the flapper. Legend has it that America was
suddenly different at the end of World War I, with the controversy over the League of Nations, the Great Red Scare, the commercial use of radio, the scoring of jazz, the imposition of national
prohibition, the introduction of woman suffrage, the campaign
for normalcy, and immigration restriction. The historical boundaries of the decade were clearly defined by these events and, at its
close, by the Wall Street Crash of 1929.

Because our view of the 1920s has been colored by its various
portrayals on screen, by the boom in advertising, and the chaos
and license associated with prohibition, it has been tempting for
historians to take the Age of Ballyhoo at its word and describe it
as a period of newfound prosperity, with high earnings for work-

An emancipated flapper, a nymphet with bobbed hair, outsize necklace, short shift, and unfurled stockings, teaches an old dog how to dance the Charleston in John Held's cover design for *Life* of February 18, 1926. Held was one of the most admired cartoonists of the Jazz Age, noted for his deft satires of its high jinks, especially in illustrations to stories by F. Scott Fitzgerald. (Library of Congress).

ers and low rates of unemployment. Moreover, the stark contrast with widespread destitution in the Great Depression has lent point to the metaphor of prosperity rolling merrily down Main Street until 1929. It seemed there was a genuine shift in consumer spending to such durables as automobiles and domestic appliances. Thus Jim Potter in *The American Economy between the World Wars* (1974) speaks for many historians when he argues how "the bread and butter problems of survival of earlier decades were now replaced for a majority by the pursuit of happiness in the form of the traditional minority pursuits of wine, women and song."

Aggregate statistics on production, income, and consumption are, indeed, impressive. The real Gross National Product (GNP) rose by 39 percent between 1919 and 1929, and real per capita GNP by 20 percent in the same period, while personal disposable income rose by 30 percent. Appliances flooded the market, and general personal consumption increased. According to Harold G. Vatter in "Has There Been a Twentieth-Century Consumer Durables Revolution?" in the *Journal of Economic History* for March 1967, whereas between 1909 and 1918 the annual sale of durables to consumers was, on average $4.29 billion, between 1919 and 1929 it was, on average $7.06 billion, an increase of 65 percent.

The revolution in consumption was most apparent in the home. The percentage of households with inside flush lavatories rose from 20 to 51 percent between 1920 and 1930. The number of homes with radios rose from zero to 40 percent over the same decade. There were equally significant increases, but on a smaller scale, in the percentage of homes with vacuum cleaners, rising from 9 to 30 percent; of washing machines from 8 to 24 percent; and of mechanical refrigerators from 1 to 8 percent. (These are the conclusion of Stanley Lebergott in *The American Economy: Income, Wealth, and Want* [1976].) The proliferation of relatively cheap electrical and mechanical devices for cooking and cleaning eased the physical chores of housekeeping. Moreover, more houses relied on canned and frozen foods to provide their basic diet.

As a result of technological changes, the capacity of electric generating stations rose from 22 million horsepower to 43 million between 1922 and 1930. These changes included a better design of machinery that reduced the cost of generating power, improvements in the means of transmission of power over long distances, and interconnection between separate stations to make the distribution of power more even between localities. Thus, whereas in 1920 35 percent of the population lived in homes lit by electricity, by 1924 over 50 percent did so, and by 1930 68 percent. Moreover, whereas in 1910 there was one telephone for every 14½ people, in 1920 there was one for every 8½ people.

It is scarcely surprising that such developments should have produced a new generation of salesmen and advertising executives to carry various products to middle America. The successful salesman, like the sports star, was meant to exude magnetism and vitality. Sinclair Lewis's fictional real estate salesman, George F. Babbitt, referred to the ideal salesman as "the real He-man, the fellow with Zip and Bang," the fellows who have "hair on their chests and smiles in their eyes and adding machines in their offices."

The new emphasis on material things is clearly illustrated by changing understanding of the verb "to sell." Dictionaries up to the 1930s confined its meaning to transfer goods for a price. Yet what this exchange suggested had expanded. Sell had invaded the worlds of the mind and the spirit. To convert someone to a new belief you would "sell him the idea," to impress him favorably you would "sell yourself to him." Thus a missionary would "sell religion to unbelievers." A statesmen who would have "gone to the people" on the issue of secession in the 1860s, or "educated the people" on gold and silver in the 1890s, would, in the 1910s, "sell the League of Nations to the country." If he was successful, he would have made a good deal, congratulate himself that he had "put it over."

The traditional view of widespread prosperity in the 1920s based on consumption has been offset by exhaustive studies, such as the Brookings Institution's *America's Capacity to Consume* (1934) that emphasized the poverty of most Americans in the 1920s. Irving Bernstein in *The Lean Years: A History of the American Worker, 1920–1933* (1966) concluded that the 1920s were golden "only for a privileged segment of the population" and, among others, Robert Ozanne in *Wages in Practice and Theory* (1968) has shown how wage increases in the 1920s were relatively small. On the whole, labor historians have admitted that the distribution of income became more unequal and that certain industries (and, indeed, regions) failed in a period of general affluence. The sick industries included farming, coal mining, textiles, railroads, shipping and shipbuilding, and shoe and leather production. Geographically, the Northeast, Mid Atlantic, and Pacific states were the most prosperous regions. Least prosperous were the agricultural states of the South and the Northwest. Moreover, the distribution of wealth throughout society was most uneven and this provided the prime source of social tension. The top 1 percent of the population earned almost 15 percent of all earned incomes. In 1926 207 people paid taxes on incomes of $1 million or more—the highest number then recorded. Corporate net profits rose in the decade by 76 percent. The Brookings Institution report showed how unequal was consumption. It found that in 1929 the highest 24 percent of all spending units made 50 percent of all purchases; the highest 20 percent made 50 percent of all expenditure on housing; and the top 20 percent made 36 percent of all purchases of food and 50 percent of all expenditure on such items as health, education, and recreation.

The United States was facing profound economic problems beside those of postwar conversion. However, their nature was imperfectly understood by government and people. Although the war had apparently strengthened American industry, its economic structure was now seriously warped. For one thing, the war had expanded and speeded up industrial capacity, firstly to supply Europe and, later, to supply the United States. In 1920 exports had reached $8.25 billion, an increase of 4 percent over 1919 and of 333 percent over 1913. The cost of imports was about $5.75 billion, an increase of 35 percent over 1919 and almost 300 percent over 1913. However, America's capacity to produce was far beyond its capacity to consume during peacetime or to export abroad once other nations had resumed their normal production. As the economic crisis hit various industries in the period 1919–1921, many firms in business and farms went bankrupt but manufacturers survived by curtailing production and laying off men. Perhaps 4.75 million men altogether were out of work in 1919. The upshot of industrial confusion was labor strife and strikes. The

first in the long series of strikes and lockouts was a strike of dock
workers in New York from January 9, 1919, followed by strikes
of dress- and waistmakers, shipworkers, engineers, and firemen,
culminating in the Great Steel Strike, beginning on September 22,
1919.

To make matters worse, there were also "strikes" by consumers, protesting the high cost of living. In 1918 the index of retail
food prices was 168.3; in 1920, it was 203.4. The government
reacted to the buyers' strike by fixing maximum prices for bread,
milk, and coal. In Washington Congress forbade increases in rents
and state and city governments followed suit. Manufacturers
gradually reduced their prices and in 1922 the retail price index
fell to 141.6 as America entered a recession.

The Narrow Gate: Immigration Restriction

A prime source of social tension was ethnic rivalry. Forty years
of continuous immigration on a massive scale had made the United
States the most heterogeneous nation ever. In 1920 the population
was 105,710,620 people in the continental United States and
12,279,997 in its overseas possessions. Of this population, 58.5
percent were children of white native parents; 7.0 percent of
mixed native and foreign parentage; 15.5 percent of foreign parents; 10.5 percent were black Americans; and 13.75 percent were
first-generation immigrants. Following the Great Red Scare of
1917–1921 and the rout of Woodrow Wilson's foreign policy over
the League of Nations, the country became suspicious, even hostile, to all things foreign, including immigration. The war had
revealed how close were the sympathies of millions of American
citizens to their countries of origin. Their double loyalty led to
charges of "hyphenated Americanism." In his forlorn defense of
the Treaty of Versailles, Wilson maintained "Hyphens are the
knives that are being stuck into this document."

Racism was now corroborated more than ever before by pseudo-
scientific analyses. Thus in *The Passing of the Great Race* (1916)
Madison Grant maintained that it was race that determined the
quality of civilization and that only Aryans had built great cultures. "The man of the old stock," opined Grant, "is being crowded

by these foreigners, just as he is today being literally driven off the streets of New York City by the swarms of Polish Jews. These immigrants adopt the language of the native American, they wear his clothes, they steal his name and they are beginning to take his women, but they seldom adopt his religion or understand his ideals. . . . " Lothrop Stoddard in *The Rising Tide of Color* (1920) and Professor Edwin East of Harvard warned how the white races were being overwhelmed by more fertile colored races. Perhaps the most influential diatribes of all were articles by Kenneth Roberts for the *Saturday Evening Post* in which he urged a revision of immigration laws to permit fewer Polish Jews, whom he described as "human parasites," to enter the United States.

By February 1921 Ellis Island, the immigrant reception center, was jammed by the number of immigrants seeking entry and the immigration authorities diverted ships to Boston to loosen the bottle neck. Congress was panic-stricken and precipitately passed an emergency measure to restrict immigration. It passed the House in a few hours without the vote being recorded and was adopted by the Senate shortly afterward by 78 votes to 1. This first immigration act, the Emergency Quota Act, signed by President Warren Harding on May 19, 1921, was intended as an interim measure.

It decreed that no more than 357,000 immigrants could be admitted to the United States in one year. This figure was about a third of the annual totals in the years before World War I. Moreover, the fixed number was broken down into a series of national quotas. Each quota represented 3 percent of the immigrants from any particular country in the United States in 1910. Thus the new, restricted immigration was to be based on a mix of old and new immigrant groups. The act was intended to last for one year only but it was subsequently extended until 1924. In those three years Congress discovered that the assigned quotas were at variance with the proposed ceiling and that far more immigrants than it intended were entering the United States. In 1924 the total number was more than 700,000. Furthermore, the act failed to discriminate against immigrants from southern and eastern Europe as much as its advocates wanted.

The definitive act of 1924, the National Origins Act, cut the maximum figure to 164,000 by pushing the base year for the quota proportions to 1890 and cutting the annual quota for each nationality to 2 percent. The year 1890 was chosen as being six years before the new immigration exceeded the old. During congressional debates congressmen reviled and ridiculed the new immigrants of the great cities, especially New York, to whom they imputed every contemporary evil. "On the one side," claimed Congressman Jasper Napoleon Tincher of Kansas, a farmer and stock raiser, "is beer, bolshevism, unassimilating settlements and perhaps many flags—on the other side is constitutional government; one flag, stars and stripes. . . . "

The 1924 act stated that after 1927 the annual quota for each nationality was not to be computed from the number of foreign-born in the United States at any given time but from "the number of inhabitants of 1920 whose origin by birth *or ancestry*" could be attributed to a specific national area. The secretaries of state, commerce, and labor had the invidious task of fixing national origins. However they found "national origins" so difficult to define that they postponed this part of the law until 1929.

The act of 1924 had other special features. Quotas established in 1921 applied only to Europe, the Near East, Africa, and Australia and New Zealand. There were no restrictions for countries in the western hemisphere. However, arrangements for certain Asian countries, notably Japan, ensured the virtual exclusion of Japanese immigrants. While each restricted nation was allowed a minimum of 100 immigrants per year, Japan was pointedly insulted by the declaration, "No alien ineligible to citizenship shall be admitted to the United States." Secretary of State Charles Evans Hughes (1921–1925) tried to persuade Congress that this provision was a wanton insult to a supersensitive nation with whom the United States was seeking naval limitations at Washington. However, Congress, itself sensitive to anti-Japanese opinion on the Pacific coast, would not be deterred. Moreover, the Supreme Court decided in the case of *Ozawa* v. *The United States* (1923) that people of Japanese birth were ineligible for naturalization. The intention and effect of the law was crystal clear. By its callous disregard of human rights, Congress was providing Japanese militants with an additional reason for hating the United States.

In short, the effect of the act of 1924 was to hold immigration from 1925 to 1930 to an annual average of 300,000. In the 1930s the combined effect of the act and the Great Depression held immigration down to an annual average of about 50,000. People in other countries complained when families were kept apart by the new measures, with wives denied permission to join their husbands in America. An interesting side effect of the new laws and different from those intended by their sponsors was increased immigration to the United States by people of Hispanic and Indian origin from Mexico and Puerto Rico and of French origin from Canada.

In addition to reactionary xenophobes, the laws were welcomed by progressives, liberals, and many ordinary folk who felt that many of the problems of American society could be solved, only if the composition of society remained static. Moreover, organized labor, led by the AFL, favored such restriction. So prevalent was the feeling and the traditional thinking behind it, that while the quotas and ceiling were relaxed in succeeding decades, the principles behind them were not overturned until the Immigration Act of 1965.

The law finally took effect in 1929, establishing a total limit of 153,714, excluding the Western Hemisphere and Asia. Britain was allowed an annual quota of 65,361 immigrants, whereas Italy was allowed only 5,803, Poland, 6,524, and Russia, 2,784 immigrants. In response to demands, under President Herbert Hoover's administration the State Department instructed American consuls to refuse to issue visas to prospective immigrants who did not have $50 in cash, the amount deemed essential to be self-supporting. Ironically, the new immigrants, accused of trying to subvert American values and institutions, had not been able to exercise sufficient political influence to get the act defeated in Congress.

Another source of social tension was the widening division between town and country. For the first time the number of people living in towns—communities of 2,500 or more—exceeded those

"SHE HAD SO MANY CHILDREN, SHE DIDN'T KNOW WHAT TO DO!"

"She Had So Many Children, She Didn't Know What To Do." A cartoon of the federal government overwhelmed by the social problems of
the 1920s, ranging from prohibition and gangsterism to sexual permissiveness and its critics, fundamentalism, and racism. The resulting social conflicts took such forms as intolerant extremism and antisocial self-
indulgence. (Library of Congress).

living in the countryside (51.4 percent in towns, compared with 48.6 percent in the countryside). Sixty-eight cities contained 100,000 or more inhabitants, and each of these major cities was the center of a larger population. By 1930 there were ninety-six such cities and their total population accounted for 44.6 percent of the whole nation. This reflected the ever increasing shift from agriculture to industry since for every forty-six people now working in agriculture there were fifty-four engaged in manufacturing and mechanical industries. Moreover, the gross value of manufacturing was almost three times that of agriculture.

American cities offered their inhabitants a variety of experience, whether for work, recreation, or social life, that was beyond the capacity of the countryside and small towns. Country dwellers dreaded the encroaching political power of the growing cities with their jazz and bootlegging, racketeering and municipal corruption, and their diverse mix of ethnic groups.

Los Angeles as Metropolis

In the period from 1920 it was Los Angeles rather than New York or Chicago that provided the essential model and spatial plan of the typical twentieth-century American city. This was the new metropolis dominated by the automobile. In 1920 Los Angeles was the tenth largest city in the nation with a population of some 577,000 people, about the same size as Pittsburgh. On the eve of World War II that figure had increased to 2,785,000 with the real explosion coming during the war and afterward so that, by 1970, the population was 9,475,000 and the metropolitan area was the third largest manufacturing center in the United States after Chicago and New York.

In the same way that geography determined Washington's and Chicago's growth and success as cities, so it did with Los Angeles. Waves of migration to California and the Southwest ensured the city's expansion, while new resources and industries fueled its economic growth. For Chicago, it had been railroads, prairie farms, the forests of Michigan and Wisconsin, and iron ore from Lake Superior that had made of the city a center for transportation, food processing, lumber, steel, and machinery. A warm and sunny climate, the presence of oil, and airlines were turning Los Angeles into a capital of petroleum refining, of national distribution of fruit and vegetables, of motion picture production, and the focal point of the aircraft, aerospace, and war research industries. During the 1920s and 1930s a combination of factors led to the city's expansion: irrigated agriculture, oil discoveries, the motion picture boom, and waves of midwestern and Texan immigrants seeking work, fortune and, possibly, fame. Oil revenues contributed to the cost of the construction of an ocean port at Long Beach, and rail connections to the East and the Southwest were laid. These improvements in transportation made Los Angeles a preferred site for warehouses and the branch plants of national corporations. In the 1920s both Ford and Goodyear built Pacific plants in the city and were followed by many other firms.

However, one element of manufacturing remained underdeveloped in Los Angeles until the 1940s. The city's factories were very isolated, being some 2,000 miles from the western edge of the midwestern manufacturing belt at St. Louis, Missouri. Thus metalworking and general machinery did not feature as part of the city's industrial potential until the great and unusual demand for aircraft during World War II resulted in the birth of an aerospace industry and all its concomitant manufacturing capabilities.

A special feature of Los Angeles is that, in being quintessentially a city of the twentieth century, it has a very special land use and transportation structure in comparison with older cities such as Chicago and New York. It has a low density of settlement, the majority of its inhabitants move about with ease, and it is not dominated by a single downtown area. Los Angeles is an amorphous metropolis. Although, like other cities, it does have slum tenements and apartment buildings, it is characterized by the single-family dwelling unit. There are three main reasons for this predominance of the single house, and none of them can be traced back to the schemes of town planners: the culturally-induced predilection of certain Americans for detached homes; the need and the business opportunity involved in supplying water and transportation for burgeoning land development; and, perhaps, most important of all, the freedom and sheer pleasure bestowed by the automobile.

In the early years of the twentieth century some three out of four newcomers to Los Angeles were white, native-born Americans from eastern cities and midwestern farms and towns. Both white city dwellers and farmers alike brought with them the tradition of the detached single-family home. Fulfilling this demand meant the creation of suburbia and the provision of water and public transport. Speculators were not slow to provide these services and they built a complex of interurban streetcars that had some lines stretching from twenty to thirty-five miles out from the city center. The widespread use of the automobile in the 1920s encouraged the trend toward diffusion and, in fact, increased the extent of suburbia to massive proportions. The automobile allowed developers to build housing beyond walking distance from the interurban streetcars. Eventually and inevitably, the interurban lines began to lose money from competition with automobiles and then, when traffic jams in downtown Los Angeles became intolerable, the municipality called for the construction of the city's famed rapid-transit system to alleviate traffic, revitalize the street railways, and save the downtown area from congestion. It is interesting to note that the citizens of Los Angeles, unlike the citizens of many other cities in the 1920s, voted against proposals for a subway system. In their view, their city was new and open plan and bore no relation to the cramped conditions of other, older, cities that could not do without underground transportation.

Whatever their virtues as places for residence and recreation, it was the vices of the cities, real or imaginary, that exercised country folk in the 1920s. As English radio producer Daniel Snowman explains, during the 1920s America was in the midst of a whole series of transitions, "No longer rural, but not yet dominated by either industry or the white-collar professions; no longer overwhelmingly Anglo-Saxon or Protestant but not yet resigned to becoming a genuinely pluralistic society." One result was continuous conflict between the new urban civilization and traditional rural values. At stake was social, political, and religious tolerance. The darker side of the decade surfaced with alarming frequency as if to demonstrate that society could not accommodate all its conflicts. As Daniel Snowman says, "These manifestations took two major forms: intolerant extremism and anti-social self-indulgence." The accompanying table shows how the political and social phenomena of the decade may be distributed into these categories.

Intolerance	Indulgence
National Prohibition	
Senate rejection of the League of Nations	Ohio gang in Washington
	Veterans' Bureau Scandals
Great Red Scare and Palmer Raids	Teapot Dome Scandal
Sacco–Vanzetti Case	Florida land boom
Revival of the Ku Klux Klan	Mellon tax proposals
Immigration restriction	Gangsterism and racketeering
Fordney-McCumber Tariff System of foreign debt repayments	Sexual license
	Great Bull Market
Case of *Adkins* v. *Children's Hospital*	
Scopes Trial	
1928 presidential election	

Sacco and Vanzetti

The case of Italian immigrants and anarchists Nicola Sacco and Bartolomeo Vanzetti reflects this. The central crime in the case was the theft of a $16,000 payroll of the Slater and Morrill shoe factories in the industrial town of South Braintree, twelve miles south of Boston, on April 15, 1920. During the robbery, the paymaster Frederick A. Parmenter, and his guard, Alessandro Berardelli, were shot and killed by two thieves who made their getaway in a stolen car with other bandits. Twenty days later cobbler Nicola Sacco and fish peddler Bartolomeo Vanzetti were arrested although they both had alibis.

The evidence that convicted Sacco and Vanzetti before the Norfolk County Superior Court at Dedham on July 14, 1921, concerned identification, ballistics, and consciousness of guilt. The district attorney, Frederick A. Katzmann, was a skilled counsel who ruthlessly exploited the defendants' poor command of English to goad and slight them, making it seem to the jury that their imperfectly expressed explanations were deliberate malice against the United States. Katzmann also appealed to the biased jury's basest emotions and he was abetted by the incompetent and malicious judge, Webster Thayer. Popular anecdotes have him referring to the accused as "dagoes" and "anarchist bastards."

The case quickly became a sensation at home and abroad. What roused Americans of all classes was not so much whether Sacco and Vanzetti were guilty but whether they should live or die, and what determined people's attitudes was, primarily, their own social perspective. The general public, what we might today call Middle America, demanded death.

The American friends of Sacco and Vanzetti organized themselves to save their heroes. The Sacco-Vanzetti Defense Committee was led by a succession of ordinary working-class men, notably Aldino Felicani and Gardner Jackson, ready to risk social ostracism on behalf of the class war. Over the years it distributed over 200,000 pieces of printed material, including an irregular *Official Bulletin,* published between December 1925 and September 1930. Its aim was to exploit every reasonable line of action to reverse the conviction and use it until a better came along.

Over the period 1921–1925 Judge Webster Thayer staunchly resisted various requests for a new trial that were advanced on various grounds of which the most persuasive was the inconclusive nature of the ballistic evidence. At one point a convicted murderer, Celestino F. Medeiros (or Madeiros), confessed to the South Braintree robbery and murder by way of a note to Sacco on November 18, 1925. So shocked were the staff of the Boston *Herald,* previously hostile to the defense, when Thayer denied a new trial after the Medeiros confession, that the newspaper reversed its attitude. Its chief editorial writer, F. Lauriston Bullard, wrote his famous leader "We Submit" that won him a Pulitzer prize. In particular, Bullard found Thayer's innuendos distressing. Medeiros's confession ought to be tested in court for "the criterion here is not what a judge may think about it but what a jury might think about it."

Like later members of ethnic minorities in prison, Sacco and Vanzetti were educated and radicalized by their experiences, becoming proficient in English and, in Vanzetti's case, skilled in social analysis. When their line of defense was exhausted, they were brought again before Judge Thayer on April 9, 1927, and made moving pleas asserting their innocence and the prejudice of the judge before being condemned to death. Vanzetti told Judge Thayer

I would not wish to a dog or to a snake, to the most low or misfortunate creature of the earth—I would not wish to any of them what I have had to suffer for things that I am not guilty of. But my conviction is that I have suffered for things that I am guilty of. I am suffering because I am a radical and indeed I am a radical; I have suffered because I was an Italian, and indeed I am an Italian; I have suffered more for my family and for my beloved than for myself; but I am so convinced to be right that if you could execute me two times, and if I could be reborn two other times, I would live again to do what I have done already.

Sacco and Vanzetti were electrocuted shortly after midnight on August 22, 1927. Medeiros died with them. Their funeral procession in Boston on August 28 became a riot between family mourners, 50,000 spectators, and police in which women marchers and innocent onlookers were attacked and beaten without provocation. There were also demonstrations elsewhere, notably in Chicago and Seattle, attended by IWW members. However, mass public grief did not atone for the shame felt by artists, radicals, and intellectuals. Novelist John Dos Passos declared that, from the moment of their execution, America was two nations and Sacco and Vanzetti had been victims in the struggle for supremacy. As graphic designer Ben Shahn observed later, the case was a searing experience for American artists—like "living through another crucifixion"—and a most formative one.

The tensions between Left and Right, young and old, town and country that had been exacerbated by the Sacco-Vanzetti case extended to other matters—serious, frivolous, and bizarre.

The New Woman and the Cult of Youth

Among the supposedly new features of society after World War I were the new woman, symbolized by the flapper, and the ascendancy of youth. Indeed, a milestone of political history was reached when the Senate voted for woman suffrage by fifty-six votes to twenty-five on June 14, 1919, and the Nineteenth Amendment was submitted to the states. Tennessee was the thirty-sixth state to pass the amendment on August 18, 1920, and it was declared duly ratified by Secretary of State Bainbridge Colby (1920–1921) on August 26. It was estimated that the Woman's Suffrage amendment would add 9.5 million women voters to the existing electorate of 17.5 million men. In the event, women stayed away from the polls in 1920 and 1924 and, when they did vote, they were no better informed than men.

Moreover, as historian Carl Degler has remarked, "Suffrage, once achieved, had almost no observable effect upon the position of women." Thus the majority of American women were still treated as an underprivileged minority, less equal as individuals and as citizens. A logical extension of NAWSA's (the National American Woman Suffrage Association's) suffrage program would have been a new campaign for another constitutional amendment to remove all legal discrimination as regards such matters as jury service, property rights, child custody, and protection for working women. This was the route that Alice Paul, the dominant voice in the National Women's party, chose to follow, calling for a constitutional amendment providing that "equality of rights under the law shall not be denied or abridged by the United States or by a State on account of sex." This is sometimes called the ERA (Equal Rights Amendment).

However, the majority of former suffragists considered the ERA a betrayal of all they had fought for because it would nullify existing special protective laws for women. "The cry Equality, Equality, where Nature has created inequality," declared Florence Kelley of the National Consumers' League, "is as stupid and as deadly as the cry Peace, Peace, where there is no Peace." To give up protective legislation for working women who had so little protection would be to subject them even more to men. The proposed amendment would open a Pandora's box of divisive litigation and no one would be able to predict the consequences. Thus, when the Supreme Court declared, in the case of *Adkins* v. *Children's Hospital,* decided by a vote of five to three on April 9, 1923, that a minimum wage law for women in Massachusetts was unconstitutional because it infringed the rights of management, it divided the two arms of the women's movement. The National Women's party regarded it as a victory for equal rights, while most women's, labor, and liberal associations denounced it as a regressive decision, breaching the precedent of *Muller* v. *Oregon* (1908).

A singular demonstration of the emergence of the new woman in society was the cult of the flapper. The term "flapper" was first used in England and introduced by H. L. Mencken to the United States in 1915. A girl who flapped had not yet attained full maturity and her flapper dresses were intended to transform juvenile, angular figures into an aesthetic ideal. Her hairstyle was a Ponjola bob, as first worn in the United States by dancer Irene Castle during the war. Her dresses were short, tight, and somewhat plain with a low waist; her stockings were silk or rayon and flesh colored and could be rolled below the knee or taken off in hot weather. According to John C. Fügel in *The Psychology of Clothes* (1930), the whole effect carried the eye from body to limbs to emphasize the long lines of arms and legs. The so-called boyish figure and face were still ultrafeminine in the excessive use of makeup and provocative display of leg.

Moreover, flapper styles were not restricted to adolescent girls. Even the Sears Roebuck catalog deliberately aimed at women in Middle America, drew on the fashions of New York society and *Vogue* magazine, offering modish designs at moderate prices. Thus F. Scott Fitzgerald noted how the flapper was passé by 1923 when other age groups began to copy her style. Such simple clothes as the flappers wore could be produced for almost any figure, saving time and money on fitting and alterations, and were manufactured in great quantities. As Elizabeth Sage observes in *A Study of Costume* (1926),

With the entrance of women into the business world the demand came for comfortable dress which did not hamper the wearer in any way, and would hold its own no matter in what situation its owner found herself. It must have lasting qualities as well, for the business woman like the business man must not be bothered with constant repairs. It must be easy to put on. The designers set to work and the one-piece slip on gown was the result.

Mass production not only led to uniformity and simplicity but also to greater variety by way of textures, styles, and colors and to more types of clothes for different occasions—professional, formal, and casual. Thus it dawned on the rag trade that women grew up to wear certain dress sizes, seven of which would fit half of the women in the whole country.

Critics of the flapper were more disturbed by her aggressive modernity than her sexuality and they were more perplexed by the fact that she represented only the most overt changes in the presentation and, indeed, life-styles of many American women. Samuel Byrne, editor of the *Observer* of Pittsburgh, was one who tackled this theme in June 1922.

There has been a change for the worse during the past year in feminine dress, dancing, manners, and general moral standards. The causes are the lack of an adequate sense of responsibility in the parents or guardians of girls, a decline in personal religion, a failure to realize the serious ethical consequences of immodesty in girls' dress, a dulling of moral susceptibilities, an inability to grasp the significance of the higher things in human life, and, last, but not least, the absence of sufficient courage and determination to resist the dictates of what is known as Fashion when these are opposed to decency.

The gist of such articles was that modesty and morality were somehow indivisible from traditional female presentation. Once one was relaxed, all was lost in the other. Contemporary dress and modern behavior were attacked together by middle-aged, middle-class women who clung to certain nineteenth-century values of their class in which marriage was seen as the price men paid for sex and sex the price women paid for marriage. The new woman who showed off her body and enjoyed sex before marriage was threatening traditional American values.

Society was paying greater attention to the young than ever before, partly out of respect for the thousands of youths lost in the war. Another influence in this respect was current psychological thinking that individuals must be nurtured while they are young, before their habits are set. A third factor was the growing significance of machines, primarily the automobile, that could be handled most dexterously by young people. A fourth factor in the new emphasis on youth was that social changes gave youth economic independence and, following close behind, moral and intellectual independence. Whatever his age, any youth who had taken part in the war emerged as a mature man, licensed to behave as the superior of those who had not taken part.

Moreover, the proportion of high school graduates among all seventeen-year-olds increased from 16.3 percent in 1920 to 27.5 percent in 1929. A minority of middle-class folk could keep their children in education for longer, not only sending them to college for an undergraduate course but also, sometimes, supporting them through a postgraduate program. Thus children finished school at age seventeen, graduated, perhaps, as late as twenty-three, and completed a Ph.D. by the time they were thirty. Thus the number of students in higher education rose by about 50,000 each year. In 1926 one out of every eight young Americans between the ages of eighteen and twenty-one was in college. This was four or five times the number achieved by other developed countries. Perhaps standards for undergraduate programs became more lax as curriculae widened. The reverse was true of graduate schools that made high demands in the fields of medicine, law, and engineering, and, in the case of Ph.D. programs, most rigorous ones. Universities cultivated research students and their teachers began to concentrate more on research and scholarship, throwing undergraduates more on their own initiative.

Thus youth received unprecedented opportunities for advancement and fulfillment and began to display greater defiance of traditional values. The natural arrogance of youth and the new opportunities for its display afforded by society reversed traditional patterns of behavior. Youth, rather than maturity, provided the model for others. This was certainly the case on the dance floor, in the beauty parlor, and the sports field. When it came to clothes, manners, and fashions, mature folk strove to act like their children and sometimes their grandchildren. Indeed, to an unusual extent, American culture in the 1920s was prefigurative, with adults learning from the younger generation of adolescent girls, creative writers and artists, intelligentsia, and students.

In this climate it is not surprising that sexual fulfillment and orgasm were no longer taboo subjects. Lesser writers, taking advantage of the trail of sexual discovery blazed by such varied and distinguished authors as Sherwood Anderson, John Dos Passos, and Theodore Dreiser, made a great deal of money out of books about sex. Warner Fabian in *Flaming Youth* and *Unforbidden Fruit* titillated his readers with what journalist Mark Sullivan calls an "apotheosis of pruriency." James Branch Cabell achieved special notoriety when his *Jurgen* was suppressed after its publication in 1920. The heroine of Victor Marguerite's *The Bachelor Girl* was a hostess in Paris who treated her guests to the ultimate in hospitality. To appeal to the smart set, sex had either to take place in exotic locations, filled with eastern promise, or amidst opulent but neurotic cafe society, as portrayed by Ben Hecht, Carl Van Vechten, and Maxwell Bodenheim. Poet Edna St. Vincent Millay expressed the Greenwich Village cult of bohemian freedom in a much quoted stanza.

> My candle burns at both ends;
> It will not last the night;
> But ah, my foes, and oh, my friends,
> It gives a lovely light.

The Roaring Twenties

There was a revolution in the world of communications as the expanding mass media of newspapers and magazines, radio, and cinema began to shape popular culture toward an increasingly urban point of view. Thus the presentation of fashions, sports, entertainment, and a minimum of political reporting were becoming increasingly standardized, giving society a similar view of itself all the way from New York to San Francisco and from Chicago to New Orleans. The cults associated with movie stars and sports heroes gave America certain well-focused images of itself, its fashions, and its customs.

In 1919 the first tabloid newspaper, the New York *Daily News,* was published. It set a pattern and encouraged a vogue for a new form of journalism copied, in New York, by Bernard Macfadden's *Evening Graphic* and William Randolph Hearst's *Daily Mirror,* and, in Chicago, by the *Daily Illustrated Times.* The *Daily*

News eventually had the largest circulation of any American paper. It carried more photographs and cartoons than news and
comment, and more advertisements than either. Indeed, its copy
was devoted more to gossip than to news and more to entertainment than information, what one critic called "more sex than
sense."

All the tabloids came to specialize in crime stories, divorce
reports, national disasters, sports, strip cartoons, and personal
columns offering readers advice on sex and marriage. All these
subjects provided plenty of opportunity for titillation. What was
missing was serious news on politics, economics, and social issues, and critical reviews of the arts. The tabloids encouraged a
new form of the literature of exposure, sometimes called "key-
hole journalism," providing intimate detail (or conjecture) of the
secret lives of people in show business, sports, and high society.
The new reporters became masters of innuendo and their doyen
was Walter Winchell. Originally from the Lower East Side, Winchell had finished school at sixth grade, pretended he had only
once read a book, and dismissed intellectuals by describing a
philosopher as "somebody who knows all the platitudes and copies
things that are clever out of books."

As well as celebrating heroes like Ford and Lindbergh, papers
sensationalized sordid dramas. The Hearst chain was the most
adept in exploiting sex and crime to the utmost. The murderess
Ruth Snyder achieved posthumous notoriety by being photographed during her execution. The *Daily News* regaled its apparently gourmet readers about how she was going "to cook, *and
sizzle,* AND FRY!" in the electric chair.

In 1922 ten magazines each claimed a paid circulation of over
2.5 million and another twelve claimed a circulation of over 1
million. The majority were pulp magazines, printed on cheap
wood-pulp paper, and devoted mainly to lowbrow detective,
western, or movie fiction. Some specialized in true confessions of
fits of wrongdoing followed by bouts of repentance. Compared
with the magazines of the early Progressive Era, magazines of the
1920s carried far fewer serious articles and devoted more space to
sports, fashion, and leisure activities. Whereas in the 1900s bio-

graphical articles were about politicans and businessmen, in the 1920s and 1930s they were about sportsmen, movie stars, and radio personalities.

Most notable of the new magazines was *Time* magazine, founded in 1923 with Henry Luce as its first editor. From the start, it tried to make politics a popular subject without trivializing the issues and personalities, except when they called for it. In the 1930s it experimented with a missionary style of film newsreel, *The March of Time,* intended not only to inform the public about major political issues but also to shape their opinions.

Entertainment played a significant part in social life. It reduced tensions and helped maintain equilibrium between the divisions in society. The trivial games crazes of the 1920s—Mah Jongg in 1922, crossword puzzles in 1924, golf every year—all had their part to play. More important still were spectator sports, especially team sports as devices to maintain social equilibrium. The player expended his emotional energy in physical competition; the spectator sublimated his in adulation of a favorite star. In football Harold E. ("Red") Grange of Illinois enjoyed a meteoric but ephemeral career. According to the *New York Times* of October 19, 1924, 67,000 people watched him and the University of Illinois team beat Michigan in the Illinois Memorial Stadium. Of all the games, baseball was the most celebrated. Of all the sports' starts, the most idolized was George Herman ("Babe") Ruth, first of the Boston Sox and, after 1920, of the New York Yankees. In 1920 a man died of excitement when he saw Babe Ruth hit a ball into the bleachers. In the season of 1921 Ruth hit fifty-nine home runs and he maintained his superiority over other players throughout the decade.

The financial incentive for stars, promoters, and managers, as well as newspaper reporters and radio commentators, was unprecedented. The public's capacity for vicarious satisfaction reached a peak in attendance at the two boxing matches between Jack Dempsey and Gene Tunney in Philadelphia in 1926 and Chicago in 1927, both of which Tunney won on points. For the first match, 120,000 people paid almost $2 million; for the second, 145,000 paid $2.5 million. The Chicago amphitheater, Soldiers' Field, was so enormous that two-thirds of the audience on the

Dempsey and Firpo by George Bellows (1924), 5″ × 63¼″. (Geoffrey Clements Photography; Collection of Whitney Museum of American Art, New York). Boxing contests allowed spectators to sublimate ethnic loyalties in enthusiasm for the skill and prowess of a new generation of champions. Assigned to cover the September 3, 1923, fight between Jack Dempsey and Luis Firpo of Argentina for the *New York Evening Journal,* Bellows chose the episode in the first round when Firpo knocked Dempsey through the ropes into Bellows's own lap. Dempsey climbed back into the ring and, in the second round, knocked Firpo out. For the painting Bellows modestly moved himself to the extreme left.

periphery did not know who had won; almost 50 million people listening to commentator Graham McNamee on radio did and eleven of them died of excitement during the bout. As a recent analyst, Elliot J. Gorn, observes, "Spectacles like the Dempsey-Tunney fights were (now) part of a larger fantasy world of popular idols, status symbols and leisure time pleasures which offered

Americans vicarious release from an oppressively rationalized society."

Gorn shows how Dempsey and Tunney both represented different but central social values and their two prize fights helped exorcize social tensions and contradictions. James Joseph ("Gene") Tunney was the son of an Irish-American working-class family in Greenwich Village who served in the marines during the war from which he emerged as light-heavyweight champion of the AEF, hence the "fighting marine." He was tall, blond, and handsome and his poise, physical grace, and strength were a tribute to his professional commitment to clean living and arduous training. Despite sixty fights, he was unscarred and this was because he was a defensive fighter who parried blows rather than dealt them out until in time he wore down stronger opponents. When Henry Ford attributed his own commercial success to managerial intelligence, mixing speed, power, and accuracy with economy, system, and community, he was using exactly the vocabulary sports commentators used to describe Tunney's fighting style. Like Ford and Lindbergh, Tunney owed his tremendous success to his fusion of Puritan restraint, heroic individualism, and technical skill. Thus the fighting marine was a mixture of manager and hero, embodying the spirit that had tamed a wilderness and conquered its inhabitants.

In comparison, William Harrison ("Jack") Dempsey excited both tremendous adulation and vicious hate. He was the ninth of thirteen children of a luckless Colorado miner, a young tough who drifted through the violent copper mining camps of Utah and Colorado, part laborer and part hobo, dividing his youth between the pits and the ring. His vicious fighting style when he won the championship against Jess Willard in 1919 earned him the title of the "Manassa Mauler." Furthermore, he was associated with an unsavory collection of hangers on, including gamblers and gangsters, and, for a time, it seemed he was more interested in living off his reputation than in defending his title. Thus, established and upwardly mobile Americans could not adopt him as a mascot of American virtues as they could Gene Tunney. Nevertheless, he appealed to working-class men across the country who saw him as an unreclaimed outlaw. Dempsey was a long representative of what Elliot J. Gorn calls the "deep subterranean well of discontent" and he and his cronies "projected a fantasy of unreconstructed virility and independence" against the threat of depersonalization in modern society.

Like radio, movies, and other forms of mass culture, sports helped persuade a nation divided by race, class, and ethnicity that it had a common identity. For white- and blue-collar workers alike, bored with their work, but with more money to spend on entertainment than ever before, sports not only represented escape from routine but also celebrated physical skill, courage, and endurance.

The Roaring Twenties is also celebrated for its high jinks, absurd activities, such as marathon dances, in which people engaged as a means of frenetic escape or to attain momentary publicity. The idea of marathon dances began in Britain and became popular in New York after Alma Cummings established a new world record of twenty-seven hours in New York on March 31, 1923. On April 19 a new record of ninety hours was set at Cleveland. Physical collapse was common enough and, occasionally, dancers died from overexertion.

America Dry: The Tragicomedy of Prohibition

During the twenties national prohibition was the most avidly discussed subject in American society. It was a subject of far more interest than foreign affairs or party politics and indissoluble from fashion, entertainment, and crime. What, when, why, and how people drank were questions affording limitless speculation. Drys believed that drinking among poor people was reduced; that there was a decline in absenteeism from, and inefficiency at, work; that people spent more money on food, clothing, and shelter; and that everyone shared more evenly in the general prosperity of society. Wets charged that drinking became more fashionable than ever; that prohibition and its excesses led to a decline in social behavior; that an immoderate law could not be enforced; that it led to greater corruption in city government and an increase in gangsterism and racketerering. To this day historians argue about how successful was the reform.

Not only was the task of keeping America dry impossible for the federal government, especially after 1923, but also the Anti-Saloon League did not have the sort of structure and techniques to cope with the new situation. According to K. Austin Kerr in *Organized for Prohibition* (1985), the League was organized to achieve prohibition legislation, but not organized for prohibition observance. All it had was a facade of power that it used insidiously in politics in the early 1920s. It was divided into two factions. One, led by its charismatic but megalomaniac counsel Wayne Wheeler wanted ever stricter enforcement laws and control of appointments to law enforcement agencies. The other faction, led by Ernest Cherrington, wanted to leave enforcement to government and concentrate on educating the public through its giant press at the American Issue Company in Westerville, Ohio.

Enforcement of the Eighteenth Amendment, which took effect on January 16, 1920, was provided by the National Prohibition Enforcement Act of October 27, 1919, devised by Wayne Wheeler of the Anti-Saloon League but named after Andrew Volstead of Minnesota who presented it in the House. An "intoxicating liquor" was defined as one with a two-hundredth part of alcohol or 0.5 percent. It did not, of course, define the amount of alcohol that it would take to make someone drunk. Yet the definition of an intoxicating beverage as 0.5 percent of alcohol surprised some people who had previously supported prohibition. They had assumed that, as was the case in many dry states, only distilled spirits would be banned. Thus it was the Volstead Act, rather than the Eighteenth Amendment, that proscribed beer and wine as well as distilled spirits. However, farmers were still allowed their sweet cider.

Some wets did agree with drys that the amount of liquor people drank decreased substantially. In the period 1911 to 1914 the average annual amount was 1.69 gallons per head. In the period of wartime restrictions, 1918 to 1919, the amount decreased to 0.97. At the outset of national prohibition in 1921 to 1922, there was a further decrease to 0.73 gallons. Only in the later years, from 1927 to 1930, did the amount rise again to 1.14 gallons. These are the figures of Clark Warburton, writing in the early 1930s for volume twelve of the *Encyclopedia of Social Sciences*.

Although these statistics were moderate, drys considered them too generous about the amount of alcohol consumed. The most enduring legend associated with prohibition—the one that has captured public imagination—is that of the abuse of law. To begin with, the illicit supply of beer, wine, and spirits was a mere trickle. Later, from 1923 onward, it became a torrent. The principal ways of obtaining alcohol were by smuggling, by bootlegging, by homebrewing and moonshining, and by misappropriating wine intended for medicine or church services.

In early 1920 a new phrase was coined to describe the smuggling of liquor—"rum running." Smuggling provided the surest way of getting liquor of high quality into the United States. The total frontier was 18,700 miles, made up of approximately 12,000 miles of coast, 3,700 miles of land borders, and 3,000 miles of lake and river front. Alcohol was smuggled into the United States from Canada, Mexico, and the West Indies, and from ships outside the three miles of territorial waters around the coast, the so-called "Rum Row." Smuggling did not long remain a matter of individuals against the state; it became big business. In New York Arnold Rothstein saw how to smelt gold from the amber hue of whiskey. Rothstein was parodied by F. Scott Fitzgerald as Meyer Wolfsheim, an unctuous bootlegger in *The Great Gatsby*. He was supposed to have bribed eight players of the Chicago White Sox baseball team $100,000 to play badly and lose the first games in the 1919 World Series. The story broke, to the embarrassment of the White Sox and subsequent losses for Rothstein and his partners. According to legend, he tried to organize a national syndicate of crime based on sectional cooperation between different gangs. Rothstein created a central buying office to procure alcohol for wholesale and retail from Canada, the West Indies, and even England and Scotland. By 1927 the syndicate, known variously as the Big Seven and the Seven Group, enjoyed a monopoly of liquor traffic on the North Atlantic coast from Boston to Baltimore. It was to be the prototype of national syndicates based on any illicit trade. According to Rothstein's principles, the success of the syndicate depended on cooperation between the different ethnic groups—Italian, Irish, Jewish—rather than internecine competition.

A novel situation now existed for brewers who still wanted to make and sell real beer. Brewers who had the capital, the product, and the expertise began to cooperate with gangsters who provided them with distribution and protection. More than anything else it was the invention of the beer truck that led to the inception of nationwide criminal syndicates in the prohibition years. Unlike wine and spirits, beer was a bulky commodity. It could not be manufactured or transported in secret and it was only profitable when sold in large quantities. Therefore, beer peddlers required considerable resources: a fleet of trucks; weapons, ammunition, and hit men to ward off competitors; funds to bribe police and authorities to ignore the obvious evidence of brewing and distribution *en masse*. Only large and brutal gangs would supply what was required.

In Chicago the brewer Joseph Stenson and his three brothers collaborated with the gangsters Terry Druggan, Frankie Lake, and Johnny Torrio in the operation of five breweries. From 1925 Torrio's successor, Al ("Scarface") Capone, became the most flamboyant, the most widely publicized, and most notorious gangster of the era for his brutal control of gangland territories in Chicago. In Detroit the Purple Gang was a loose coalition of two different Jewish groups, the Oakland Sugar House Gang of Harry Altman, Harry Keywell, and others and the original Purple Gang of Harry Fleisher, Henry Shore, and others. It was similar in other cities. In Boston Charles Solomon, in Philadelphia Max Hoff, in Denver Joseph Roma, and in Cleveland the Mayfield Road Mob peddled beer and carved out gangland territories for its distribution. Moreover, since gangsters provided a front as directors of the brewery they also took the fall—legal liability when something went wrong.

Speakeasies were illegal bars during national prohibition. The term was first used to describe an unlicensed saloon in 1889 and, according to H. L. Mencken, originated in Ireland as "speak softly shop." Whereas before prohibition traditional saloons were often situated at the corner of the block, speakeasies were located in a basement, a back room, or an upstairs apartment. Speakeasies were accredited with three social revolutions. They introduced women, other than prostitutes, to bars. They led to uneasy alliances between the proprietors and gangsters who protected them from police harassment. In general, they sold raw liquor at high prices and were common scenes of fights, raids, and unlicensed behavior. Furthermore, they led to the establishment of night-clubs that survived the repeal of national prohibition in 1933.

Clients of speakeasies and nightclubs delighted in a new mixed drink. The cocktail was a concoction of wine or spirits mixed with fruit juice or soda. Three hundred varieties of cocktail had existed before national prohibition, including the mint julep and the scotch highball. The mix now masked the foul taste of recon-verted industrial alcohol. Thus, cocktails first punished the palate with a bizarre taste before the alcohol went on to pollute the stomach.

The significance of prohibition for Chicago lies partly in the flamboyance of Al Capone, partly in the excesses of his crimes, and partly in the nature of the Chicago underworld. Prohibition was being imposed in the United States at a time when the Italians, a comparatively new immigrant group, were making their bid for full acculturation in the city and for some political control of their environment. That new environment was largely determined by syndicated crime, hitherto the preserve of Jewish and Irish groups who fought back against the mixed South Side Gang of Capone with its Italians, Jews, and Poles.

The notorious climax of Chicago's gang warfare was the St. Valentine's Day Massacre of February 14, 1929, when seven members of the North Side Gang were mown down by machine-gun fire in a warehouse at 2122 North Clark Street. Like other assassinations of the period, the murders served a double func-tion, satisfying the requirements of a blood feud and preparing for some sort of consolidation of crime to which these gangsters would be an impediment. Capone, it seemed, ruled with impu-nity but without remorse. He certainly was not afraid of official retribution. Between 1927 and 1930 there were at least 227 gang-land killings in Chicago. However, in that time, only two gang-sters were tried and convicted of murder.

Nevertheless, the wars did not last forever; self-preservation was as keen an instinct as vendetta. Then there was a truce of sorts. Probably the first national summit of organized crime in

The most popular among all prohibition agents were Izzy (Einstein) and Moe (Smith) whose dexterity in disguise earned them an unequaled record of entrapping unsuspecting bootleggers and speakeasy operators. Apparently, going to work was never a drag in costumes as dazzling and disingenuous as these. (Library of Congress).

the United States took place at the Hotel Statler, Cleveland, on December 5, 1928, when twenty-seven gang leaders from Chicago, St. Louis, Buffalo, New York City, Gary, Newark, and Tampa met to discuss the national distribution of whiskey and future criminal syndicates of Sicilians and Sicilian-Americans. A second conference, at the President Hotel, Atlantic City, New Jersey, from May 13 to May 16, 1929, was open not only to Sicilian and Italian but also Jewish and Irish gangsters. The Sicilian monopoly had been broken. The conclave was representative of crime throughout the nation. It is possible that the conference established territories in a loose federation of criminal syndicates across the nation. By the power of might the local boss who proved himself most efficient became head of his territory: gangs were to unite and forbear feuds. Mafia historian Fred Cook believes that a multimillion dollar fund was established from a pool of resources to be used for bribery of politicians and public officers on a massive scale. It was also decided that L'Unione Siciliana, a fraternal organization of Sicilian immigrants that had been penetrated by criminal elements as a nucleus for an American mafia, would be reorganized from head to foot.

Prohibition was supposed to be enforced by a federal agency, called the Prohibition Unit until March 3, 1927, and, thereafter, known as the Prohibition Bureau. The Unit had none of the prerequisites for making a success of its job: good salaries to make graft superfluous; continuity of personnel; cooperation from government and the general public. Throughout the twenties the annual appropriation from Congress was modest—an average of $8.8 million. Of course, deprived of its excise taxes during prohibition, the federal government had less revenue to spend on enforcement of liquor laws. The total number of agents in the Prohibition Unit varied between 1,500 and 2,300 men and the entire staff was never more than 4,500. The rate of pay was between $1,200 and $2,000 a year in 1920 and about $2,300 a year in 1930. In the first eleven years of the service 17,972 appointments were made but there were 11,982 resignations and 1,608 dismissals for various corrupt practices.

It was, perhaps, the failure of courts to maintain prohibition that most discredited the new law. First offenses usually carried fines of not more than $1,000 or six months' imprisonment; later offenses usually carried fines of between $200 and $2,000 and imprisonment of between one month and five years. The Jones Act of 1929, which made violations a felony, provided maximum penalties of a $10,000 fine, or five years' imprisonment, or both, for the first offense. However, the national average of fines remained $130 and the average prison sentence was 140 days. In some parts of the country prosecutors and judges were so hostile to prohibition that true enforcement was not possible. Sometimes juries refused to convict bootleggers. The number of prohibition cases was much more than the judicial system could accommodate. In 1920 federal courts tried 5,095 prohibition cases out of a total of 34,230 criminal cases altogether. During the twenties the number of prohibition cases went up fifteenfold. In 1929 federal courts tried 75,298 prohibition cases alone.

It had been in rural areas that the prohibition movement had first tested its strength. Once rural isolation was ended by the invasion of press, automobiles, and movies, rural prejudice could not long survive. City papers, now regularly critical of prohibition, were becoming the press of all the states. Between 1925 and 1930 rural subscriptions to city papers doubled. As prohibition historian Andrew Sinclair suggests, "The automobile became so much the representative of the new way of life that its use in nullifying national prohibition was inevitable." Cars and beer trucks carried the precious commodity of alcohol. Whereas at the beginning of the decade automobiles represented an alternative to alcohol, at its end they symbolized booze and beer running and everything that was subversive of prohibition.

From the ranks of doctors, lawyers, businessmen, and labor a new association emerged against national prohibition. This was the Association Against the Prohibition Amendment (AAPA) founded by Captain William H. Stayton on November 12, 1918, and formally incorporated on December 31, 1920. Stayton was an elderly man who had served in the navy, practiced at the bar, and was working in Washington for the Navy League, a lobby for increased naval defenses. His political experiences had left him profoundly disillusioned with the federal government on account of what he considered its inappropriate interference in the lives of individuals.

The size of AAPA membership fluctuated but by 1926 it may have stood at 726,000. Stayton cultivated affluent businessmen who could easily afford to cover the considerable expenses of a political lobby. Among early members were Stuyvesant Fish, president of the Illinois Central Railroad, and Charles H. Sabin, president of Guaranty Trust Company of New York, a Morgan bank. Most important among later recruits were General Motors executives John Julius Raskob and the three Du Pont brothers of Wilmington, Delaware, (Pierre, Irénée, and Lammot). In their paternalistic outlook, prohibition reform was a mission, a question of social responsibility.

Alcoholism and alcohol abuse were serious problems for American society. While national prohibition may have dried up the United States more than the legend propagated by gangster movies from 1930 onward would have us believe, it was not working at all properly by the end of the decade and was yielding new problems of gangsterism and racketeering. The tragedy was not simply that prohibition failed but that, because of the way it failed, politicians abandoned serious attempts to discuss federal control of stimulants, drugs, hallucinogens, and alcohol lest they appear foolish. A new legend developed that outright bans on cigarettes, spirits, and marijuana were bound to backfire on those who had introduced them. Hence the underlying problems of addiction and their putative solutions remained untreated. While politicians prevaricated, America remained amused and aghast at the failure of the countryside to put the clock back with the reform that became a folly.

The tragicomedy of prohibition was a setback for such Protestant churches as the Baptists, Methodists, and Presbyterians, all of whom had supported the dry crusade. In any case, Protestantism was having great difficulties as people spent more and more leisure time in various secular pursuits. In 1927 the *Christian Century* reported how the evangelical churches had lost over half a million members in twelve months. The exceptions were fringe movements that attracted a wide variety of fanatics. In the East

Dr. Frank Buchman, originally a Lutheran minister from North Dakota, enticed the wealthy to religious house parties where his initiates, including graduates from Ivy League colleges, attended group confessions. Buchmanism, sometimes known as the Oxford Movement or Moral Rearmament, invited members to seek "God guidance," after a personal "washing out" of sins, by a daily period of spiritual silence.

The Revival of the Ku Klux Klan

The reaction to modernism was strongest in the South. In popular legend the South was a place forgotten by time and marooned in ignorance. Columnist H. L. Mencken's contempt and loathing for the South know no bounds. The South was "the bunghole of the United States, a cesspool of Baptists, a miasma of Methodism, snake-charmers, phoney real-estate operators, and syphilitic evangelists."

A more informed but equally hostile attack against the South was launched by William Henry Skaggs, formerly of Alabama but later of New York. In *The Southern Oligarchy* of 1924 he produced a vitriolic catalog of its numerous evils: political corruption, illiteracy, peonage, racism, lynching, and various abuses by landlords. Less bitter but equally perceptive was the interpretation provided by Columbia professor Frank Tannenbaum in a slim collection of essays, also of 1924, *Darker Phases of the South*. In order to preserve its much vaunted racial purity, the South had segregated its Anglo-Saxons so effectively that it had buried them in mill villages. The white plague of the South was cotton. The exploitation of cotton accounted for soil erosion, the poor state of race relations, and for poverty, ignorance, and peonage.

One potent expression of primitive fear was the revival of the Ku Klux Klan. The second Klan, the "Invisible Empire, Knights of the Ku Klux Klan, Inc.," lasted from 1915 to 1944. It was as secret, violent, and subversive as the Reconstruction Klan and was ultrapatriotic, nativistic, and moralistic. Its revival was the work of William J. ("Colonel") Simmons of Alabama, a former Methodist circuit preacher who specialized in organizing fraternities. He chose Stone Mountain, Georgia, sixteen miles from Atlanta, as the venue for a special Klan launching ceremony on October 26, 1915. He told Congress later that it was there at midnight, "bathed in the sacred glow of the fiery cross, the invisible empire was called from its slumber of half a century to take up a new task." This was a week before the Atlanta run of D. W. Griffith's film, *The Birth of a Nation*.

The revived Klan's catchment area was not simply the South but, more particularly, the Southwest (especially Texas), the Midwest (especially Indiana, Ohio, and Oklahoma), and Far West (especially Oregon and California). The elaborate rituals and secret signs of the Invisible Empire appealed to a rural populace, bombarded with propaganda against the Germans in the war, but cheated of its prey at the end. In 1920 there were no more than 50,000 members but the Klan provided an outlet for nativist hysteria.

Whereas the impressive-looking Simmons was an ineffectual dreamer, two of his disciples, Edward Young Clarke and Mrs. Elizabeth ("Bessie") Tyler, were born organizers. They were canny enough to appreciate the commercial opportunities of a secret organization collecting high initiation fees. By July 1921 Clarke had sent 214 organizers, or Kleagles, across the country to recruit initiates. Estimates vary but it was said that Clarke had converted at least 90,000 people to the hooded order within fifteen months. In 1923 total Klan income was $3 million. Business also boomed for southern manufacturers involved with the Klan. The Gate City Manufacturing Company of Atlanta, Georgia, was designated sole manufacturer of Klan regalia. Each white robe, worn with a pointed cap to resemble a ghost of the Confederate dead, cost $6.50.

From being a somewhat simple-minded fraternal organization in its early days the Klan became openly racist from 1920 onward. It started to represent itself as a defender of white against black, Gentile against Jew, and Protestant against Catholic. Bessie Tyler told New York newspapermen that to be for the white race meant to be against all others. Clarke proposed sterilizing black Americans. Simmons declared that never in the history of the world had a "mongrel civilization" survived: his goal was "one-hundred-per-cent Americanism." Opposition to Catholicism was not based primarily on differences in theology but, rather, ethnicity. As we know, in the main Catholics were new immigrants. Their religion was taken as a symbol of the cultural differences between the new immigration and the old. Simmons warned the Junior Order of United American Mechanics in Atlanta on April 30, 1922, that, far from being a melting pot, America was "a garbage can! . . . When the hordes of aliens walk to the ballot box and their votes outnumber yours, then that alien horde has got you by the throat."

The Klan also appealed to those new inhabitants of towns and cities who had assumed an urban hide but who retained their rural outlook. John M. Mecklin explained the attraction of the Klan for the small-town hick adrift in the big city,

He is tossed about in the hurly-burly of our industrial and so-called democratic society. Under the stress and strain of social competition he is made to realize his essential mediocrity. Yet according to traditional democratic doctrine he is born free and equal to his fellow who is outdistancing him in the race. Here is a large and powerful organization offering to solace his sense of defeat by dubbing him a knight of the Invisible Empire . . . the chosen conservator of American ideals, the keeper of the morals of the community.

Thus the Klan afforded recreation and fraternity to its inmates. In the small towns its rituals relieved the boredom of everyday routine and the mass initiation of new members was a popular entertainment in southern communities.

However, Klan leaders could no more redress the grievances of their members than they could undo the Industrial Revolution or American immigration. Instead, they indulged in bribery, intimidation, and torture by flogging, branding, and acid burning, and even in mutilation and murder. Discontented former Klansmen exposed the Klan and its atrocities to the New York press that syndicated their tales across the country. The New York *World* ran a series of well-documented, alarmist, and sensational articles from September 6 to 26, 1921, laying bare the Klan's history and aims. The intention was, in part, to depress Klan membership. In fact, the articles had the opposite effect: they gave it wide publicity and encouraged membership in the North and East.

The Klan continued on its foul path of murder and mayhem

and established a pattern of man's inhumanity to man in every state that it defiled by its presence. A historian of the Klan, David Chalmers, rates the number of victims of assault in the 1920s at well over a thousand in Oklahoma and Texas, at over a hundred in each of Alabama, Georgia, and Florida, and at scores in the other Klan states. The victims were usually errant whites.

The most notorious and gross of Klan atrocities were the Mer Rouge murders in Louisiana. In Morehouse Parish, Louisiana, two men who criticized the Klan, planter's son Watt Daniels and garage mechanic Tom Richards, were kidnapped and murdered on August 24, 1922. They were killed by being run over by a large road-grading tractor that crushed and splintered their bodies. Then they were dismembered and their mutilated corpses were deposited in Lake Lafourche, whence the pieces rose in December. An open hearing lasted from January 5 to 25, 1923, during which the state called over fifty witnesses, including Klansmen. However, it could not prove who had murdered the young men.

The Klan was not only a simple-minded fraternity engaged in cruel terrorist outrages but it was also a force to be reckoned with in politics. In 1922 and 1923 the Klan helped elect governors in Oregon and Georgia, congressmen in several states, and local officials throughout the country. In 1924 it helped elect governors in Maine, Ohio, Colorado, and Louisiana. It elected senators for Texas in 1922 and for Oklahoma in 1924. Warren Harding belonged to the Klan and disgraced the White House by being inducted there.

From 1921 to 1923 the internal feuds of the Klan were well publicized in a series of court cases, most notoriously the attempt by Dallas dentist Hiram Wesley Evans to oust Colonel Simmons. It was proved in court that Simmons alone held the copyright to the Klan's name, charter, constitution, and regalia. A later, but apocryphal, story has Hiram Evans giving Simmons some heartfelt advice about Klan costume. "Why don't you throw in the towel?" he asked. Simmons replied, "Because I need it to wrap round my head."

However, the eventual usurpation of Hiram Evans was not the end of the Klan's troubles. In Indiana David C. ("Steve") Stephenson, the kingmaker who had engineered Evans's coup, built up the Klan as a mass organization that could form the basis of a political machine. Unfortunately, his self-indulgence got the better of his political acumen. First, he saved the office of state superintendent of public instruction that his opponents had wanted to abolish. Then, he expected the incumbent, plump spinster Madge Oberholtzer, to repay him with sex. He had her hustled aboard a train bound for Chicago and forced himself on her. The next day she took bichloride of mercury tablets, a poison that caused her agony. Stephenson had to let Madge return home to her parents where she subsequently died. Her father charged him with second degree murder and, after a sensational trial, Stephenson was found guilty and sentenced to life imprisonment in the penitentiary in Michigan City. What happened to the Klan after 1924 was less disintegration than decomposition. The *Washington Post* of July 6, 1929, estimated that there were only 82,000 Klansmen left. On November 3, 1930, it said the number had dwindled further to 35,000. This was partly on account of public disgust at Klan atrocities and feuds but more because the initial causes—postwar xenophobia and inner city frustration-had been dissipated and the onset of the depression had engulfed all other social problems. The Klan had no answer for this calamity.

The Scopes Trial

The conflict between old and new, countryside and town, extended to religion and reached another climax with the Scopes trial of 1925, centered on the conflict between modernism and Darwin's theory of evolution on the one hand and religious fundamentalism, the literal interpretation of the Bible, on the other.

The Scopes trial represented, in the words of George I. Schwartz and Philip W. Bishops, "the last significant attempt to discredit Darwin's theory by those who sincerely believed that the Biblical story of the creation of man was a complete explanation of the origin of species." For that very reason it roused intense feelings among fundamentalists and evolutionists. Thus the Scopes trial was, to Carlyle Marney, "a seizure, a paroxysm, a grand colic in the bowel of the American folk-religion." Walter Lippmann ex-

The Scopes trial of 1925 in which John Scopes was convicted of teaching evolution in contradiction to the state laws of Tennessee that required all teaching about Creation to conform literally to the myths of Genesis. Scopes was defended by Clarence Darrow, standing in front of the table, whose eloquent arguments educated America about the merits of Darwin's theory of natural selection. John Scopes is seated immediately behind Darrow. (Library of Congress).

plained the social significance of the case, "The campaign in certain localities to forbid the teaching of 'Darwinism' is an attempt to stem the tide of the metropolitan spirit, to erect a spiritual tariff against an alien rationalism which threatens to dissolve the mores of the village civilization."

While man's scientific knowledge was increasing, his understanding of himself and his place in the universe failed to keep pace. As to southerners, it is tempting to say that their understanding was actually shrinking. Indeed, the South was overwhelmed by what seemed the inconceivable nature of new scientifiic discoveries and the complexities and contradictions of the new urban and industrial civilization. Education in the South was largely controlled by the church with each major denomination providing at least one university or college in every state. The curriculums were out of date, emphasizing only religion and the classics. There was not a single top-quality university in the entire South. The disciplines of science and engineering were somewhat neglected and libraries were inadequate. Proponents of fundamentalism celebrated common ignorance. Hal Kimberly, a Georgia assemblyman, thought that all that was worth knowing was contained in only three books. "Read the Bible. It teaches you how to act. Read the hymn book. It contains the finest poetry ever written. Read the almanac. It shows you how to figure out what the weather will be. There isn't another book that is necessary for anyone to read, and therefore I am opposed to all libraries."

The state of Tennessee had contributed to the debate between fundamentalism and Darwinism in 1925 by passing the Butler law against the teaching of evolution in public schools. Quite simply, the law proscribed the teaching of "any theory that denies the story of the Divine Creation of man as taught in the Bible, and to teach instead that man has descended from a lower order of animals." Few state politicians cared about it one way or the other.

It was not the law's proponents but its enemies who decided to bring a test case to court and try and get it repealed. In Dayton, Tennessee, George W. Rappelyea, a manager of iron and coal mines, persuaded John Scopes, a young biology teacher, to provide the American Civil Liberties Union (ACLU) with a test case. All he had to do was to teach evolution and get arrested. In New York Roger Baldwin announced, "We shall take the Scopes case to the United States Supreme Court if necessary to establish that a teacher may tell the truth without being thrown in jail." The ACLU launched a defense appeal fund that eventually raised $11 million.

Both sides wanted to attract maximum publicity by getting celebrities to take part. William Jennings Bryan, now a front man for Florida Realtors, announced on May 13 that he had accepted an invitation by the World's Christian Fundamentals Association (WCFA) to prosecute the case. "We cannot afford to have a system of education that destroys the religious faith of our children," he declared. "There are about 5,000 scientists, and probably half of them are atheists, in the United States. Are we going to allow them to run our schools? We are not." According to John Scopes himself, Bryan's entry into the case threw a monkey wrench into the gears of the ACLU. They had to field a defense counsel of equal weight. This was to be Clarence Darrow, "attorney for the damned." Darrow had never prosecuted anyone; he was a tireless advocate of free speech, nonviolent resistance, and the rights of the individual against the collective power of the state.

Public interest in the Scopes trial was so great that it received wider press coverage than had any previous trial. Moreover, the trial set a precedent by being the first trial ever broadcast. Judge Raulston boasted, "My gavel will be heard around the world." A heatwave struck Dayton on the very first day of the sessions, July 10, making the tiny overcrowded courtroom almost unendurably hot and serving to heighten tension.

The state's position was that if Scopes had taught that man was descended from animals he implicitly denied the story of Creation as told in Genesis. The case for the defense rested on three grounds: that the Butler Act was unconstitutional because it violated freedom of religion by making the Bible the test of truth; that it was unreasonable, given modern knowledge of evolution; and that it was indefinite because people interpreted the Bible differently. In the course of his argument Darrow tried to show that the Bible, taken literally, was a maze of contradictions. But if it was interpreted with insight and intelligence the story of Creation in Genesis was quite compatible with the theory of evolution. The implications of his argument were that truth is inimical to any closed order because it threatens basic assumptions. Judge Raulston allowed defense attorney Arthur Garfield Hays to read transcripts from seven distinguished scientists that explained the prehistory of the world. They gave special emphasis to the relationship between homo sapiens and other animals and their evidence was supported by scientific data. The defense also drew on testimony

from four theologians who discussed interpretations of the Bible
and the relationship of religion to science. Although the judge
prevented the defense from presenting such statements in their
entirety to the jury, he could not stop the syndicated press carrying them verbatim across the country. Thus was America taught
about evolution and biblical scholarship.

It was because all other avenues had been closed to him that
Darrow eventually decided to call Bryan for cross examination.
How was it estimated that Noah's flood happened in 4004 B.C.?

"I never made a calculation," said Bryan.

"A calculation from what?"

"I could not say."

"From the generations of man?" asked Darrow.

"I would not want to say that."

"What do you think?"

"I do not think about things I don't think about."

"Do you think about things you do think about?"

"Well, sometimes."

The crux came with a simple question that devastated Bryan.

"Do you think the earth was made in six days?"

"Not six days of twenty-four hours."

The crowd gasped. When he realized his error, Bryan jumped
to his feet, purple with rage, and exclaimed, "I am simply trying
to protect the word of God against the greatest atheist or agnostic
in the United States." At last, Bryan had compromised Genesis
with evolution, had made himself ridiculous, and destroyed the
prosecution's case.

The next day Darrow made the most of the situation by inviting the judge to instruct the jury to find John Scopes guilty. He
wanted the case to go to the State Supreme Court. Accordingly,
the jury found Scopes guilty on July 21. Nothing could hide the
fact that Bryan was crushed and broken. However, though he
was an ardent prohibitionist, Bryan was a glutton for food. His
eating was as hearty as ever and on July 26, 1925, he died of
apoplexy in his sleep. Thus Bryan had, appropriately enough,
gone with the wind.

The Tennessee Supreme Court heard the appeal at Nashville
and finally announced its decision on January 14, 1927. It upheld

the Butler Act but it reversed the original judgment of a technical (but uncontested) issue of the fine of $100. The victory of fundamentalism led to its defeat. Everywhere there was an argument about evolution became a prime market for books on the subject. Universal Pictures recognized this and in 1931 produced a 42-minute movie about evolution, *The Mystery of Life,* in which Darrow appeared to appreciative audiences and good reviews.

3

THE INCOMPLETE POLITICS OF THE REPUBLICAN ASCENDANCY

THE PROBLEMS associated with economic dislocation, labor strife, and radical agitation in 1919 and 1920 were clear indications that many of the mechanisms regulating society were not working. On May 14, 1920, Senator Warren Gamaliel Harding of Ohio explained his understanding of America's needs. "America's present need is not heroics, but healing; not nostrums, but normalcy; not revolution, but restoration; not agitation, but adjustment; not surgery, but serenity; not the dramatic, but the dispassionate; not experiment, but equipoise; not submergence in internationality, but sustainment in triumphant nationality. . . ."

"Normalcy" could mean all sorts of things, except what Harding intended. The American norm was not relaxed stability but social mobility, economic development, political agitation, and cultural experiment. Such restlessness was in part the result of the fact that American society lacked a homogeneous social structure. Nevertheless, Harding inadvertently expressed a social truth, that a society perplexed by deep problems is not likely to try and cure them, least the remedy prove more painful than the disease and prejudice the comfortable lot of its more privileged members.

As the decade advanced it became clear that America's undoubted social problems would be ignored by both main parties. Novelty of fashion, entertainment, and invention were prized while radical dissent and fundamental criticism were derided or suppressed. When Fitzgerald observed "it was characteristic of the Jazz Age that it had no interest in politics at all," he was not only referring explicitly to the low popular vote in the presidential elections of 1920 and 1924, when less than half the electorate (respectively 49.3 percent and 49.1 percent) went to the polls, but also implicitly to public unwillingness to address politics to social ills.

The Available Man

Harding was the tool of an ambitious corporation lawyer, Harry Daugherty. When Daugherty first met Harding in 1900 at a small-town hotel in Richwood, Ohio, he was struck by Harding's perfect physical proportions, his natural grace, and his resonant voice. Thus he was supposed to have said, "Gee, what a president he'd make." What Daugherty meant was that Harding would make a good-looking candidate and that, once in office, he would fulfill a popular conception of a president. He had been editor of the Marion *Star,* then lieutenant governor of Ohio, before becoming a senator. Superficially, he had all the necessary experience of high office to make him a suitable candidate. Moreover, he was genial. After the high-minded autocratic style of Woodrow Wilson, congressmen yearned for an amenable, amiable president who was one of themselves.

The Republican National Convention of 1920 met in Chicago but it was in the dark recesses of the original smoke-filled room in the Blackstone Hotel that the key decision was made to nominate Harding. The men from the smoke-filled room of the Blackstone Hotel had already agreed that, to balance their conservative candidate, the best man for vice-president would be Senator Irvine Lenroot of Wisconsin. However, no sooner had Lenroot

This mawkish photograph of President Calvin Coolidge (center) surrounded by members of his cabinet, including Secretary of State Charles Evans Hughes (seated second from left) and Secretary of the Treasury Andrew Mellon (seated third from right), beneath a memorial photograph of the late Warren Harding, was taken in 1923 to emphasize Republican solidarity and an orderly succession. However, it is difficult to tell who are living and who are dead among such glum waxworks. (Library of Congress).

been proposed to the delegates in Chicago than Wallace McCamant, delegate from Oregon, climbed on his chair, and put forward the name of Governor Calvin Coolidge of Massachusetts, popular hero of the Boston police strike. Immediately the stenographer at the convention recorded "an outburst of applause of short duration but of great report." Coolidge's nomination by 674½ votes out of 984 was recorded "with tumultuous applause and cheers"—the only spontaneous event in the entire convention.

Meeting at San Francisco, the Democrats nominated Governor James M. Cox of Ohio, a small city editor and publisher and former congressman. As governor, he had championed progressive legislation, especially in the field of workmen's compensation acts, and thus brought to an end the spate of lawsuits instigated by injured employees against their employers. His running mate was Assistant Secretary of the Navy Franklin D. Roosevelt.

Like McKinley in 1896, Harding chose to conduct the campaign from the comfort and convenience of his own front porch in Marion, Ohio. The centerpiece of Cox's campaign was a twenty-nine-day whistle-stop tour of eighteen states west of the Mississippi from which he garnered not one electoral vote. He could not believe the country's indifference to the League of Nations. As Franklin K. Lane, once secretary of the interior under Wilson, remarked, "Cox will be defeated not by those who dislike him but by those who dislike Wilson."

In the election Harding took 16,143,407 popular votes (60.4 percent) to Cox's 9,130,328 (34.2 percent). The Socialist, Eugene V. Debs, took 919,799 votes (3.4 percent). Thus Harding carried 37 states, and 404 votes in the electoral college to Cox's 11 states and 127 votes. The election returns were broadcast for the first time by the pioneer radio station KDKA in Pittsburgh. The result was taken as an overwhelming repudiation of Wilsonian liberalism at home and abroad. The United States was now committed to twelve years of Republican ascendancy.

As president, Harding (1921–1923) proved an amiable simpleton manipulated by sinister forces. It was said that, whereas George Washington could not tell a lie, Warren Harding could not tell a liar. Thus he took into office with him his old small-town friends, the Ohio gang, principally Harry Daugherty who became attorney general. From the Senate he took with him John W. Weeks as secretary of war, Harry S. New as postmaster general, and most sinister of all, Senator Albert B. Fall of New Mexico. After Republican elders dissuaded him from appointing the devious and unsuitable Fall as secretary of state, he moved him to the interior, an appointment that the Senate, for once, and to its subsequent shame, confirmed without the formality of referring it to a committee. Also out of misplaced sentiment, Harding appointed Edwin N. Denby as secretary of the navy. A former congressman, he had enlisted as a private in the Marine Corps in 1914 (although he was already forty-seven) and subsequently had risen to the rank of major. Harding made the unscrupulous Colonel Charles R. Forbes, whom he had met casually while on vacation in Honolulu, head of the Veterans Bureau. In fact, Forbes was a self-seeking opportunist who had won round Mrs. Harding. To a man, they shrank from the irksomeness of their jobs.

Half way through his cabinet selection, Harding got the urge to raise its stature and appointed Charles Evans Hughes secretary of state, Herbert Hoover secretary of commerce, Henry C. Wallace secretary of agriculture, and Andrew W. Mellon secretary of the treasury. Mellon, who owed his fortune to aluminum steel, was obliged to resign directorships in sixty corporations before his appointment was confirmed. It was to be said of Mellon that three presidents served under him.

Harding could move from particular acts of kindness to generous acts of political skill. In order to settle the continuing steel dispute, Harding invited forty-one steel magnates to the White House in 1922 when he persuaded them that twelve hours was too long and arduous a period for a regular working shift. Thus on August 2, 1923, Judge E. H. Gary, head of U. S. Steel, announced the abolition of the twelve-hour day and on August 13 the plant at Gary, Indiana, was put on an eight-hour day, setting a precedent followed by the entire industry.

Harding repeatedly announced his commitment to economy in government. The Budget and Accountancy Act of June 20, 1921, provided for the establishment of the Budget Bureau in the Treasury, with powers to revise, reduce, or increase the estimates of the various departments. Its intention was to put each on a business basis by making it accountable to one section. In addition, the act tried to compel Congress to keep its appropriations within limits set by budget offices. Harding appointed Chicago banker Charles Gates Dawes to the new post of budget director.

Dawes was one of the most striking political personalities of the age. He first made his mark on public opinion when he gave evidence to Congress as to whether the Democrats had indulged in war profiteering. (During the war he had been head of the supply procurement division in France). "Damn it all," he told the committee, "the business of an army is to win the war not to quibble around with a lot of cheap buying. Hell and Maria, we weren't trying to keep a set of books, we were trying to win the war." Throughout his subsequent career he remained "Hell and Maria" Dawes to the public. He was also the only vice-president and ambassador (to Britain) who wrote popular songs, such as "It's All in the Game."

Business wanted the Republicans to lower taxes, raise tariffs, and provide government subsidies without imposing restrictions on business practice, except for the curbing of labor. They achieved much of what they wanted. Secretary of the Treasury Mellon accordingly urged Congress to repeal the wartime excess profits tax outright and reduce the maximum surtax on incomes above $66,000 from 65 percent to 40 percent. To compensate the Treasury for the losses, he proposed a wider distribution of indirect tax on the less wealthy by doubling the stamp tax on documents, imposing a tax of 2 cents on postcards and bank checks, and introducing a federal license tax on cars. Accordingly, in the Revenue Act of November 23, 1921, Congress removed the excess profits tax and revised the maximum surtax to 50 percent. The specious justification for the relief of the rich was that burdensome taxes on wealth inhibited creative investment. If government continued to cream off the cat's share of profits, then business would not take the risks necessary for industrial and commercial expansion.

To propitiate the less affluent, the tax threshold for heads of families with $5,000 or less was raised from $2,000 to $2,500, and the exemption for each dependent was raised from $200 to $400. Nuisance taxes were abolished. The tax on the net profits of corporations was set at 12.5 percent, instead of 10 percent. In general, government policies were deflationary and served to curb business expansion. The federal government collected about $4 billion in annual revenue and spent just over $3 billion. It used the surplus to liquidate the national debt, that fell from about $24 billion in 1920 to about $16 billion ten years later. Prosperity returned. Unemployment, having reached a peak of 5.73 million in 1921, began to decline and settled at about 2.5 million. Those in work found that their purchasing power, if not their actual wage, was rising.

The greatest ally of business at the courts of Harding and his successor, Calvin Coolidge, was Secretary of Commerce Herbert Hoover, a constructive critic of business practices. He deployed the bureaus of standards and of foreign and domestic commerce to research ways of eliminating waste and gave wide publicity to their findings. In 1928 Hoover's Committee on Economic Trends reported how per capita production had improved by 35 percent in the 1920s. Herbert Hoover actively encouraged the formation of trade associations along the lines of the oldest, the United States Brewers Association, founded in 1862, and the National Association of Manufacturers of 1895. These associations funded central agencies that collated and distributed information on such matters as prices, production, credit, insurance, and relations between employers and employees for the benefit of their member corporations and individual stockholders. In addition, they funded lobbies to advance or retard legislation, according to the special interests of their interest group. Under Hoover's benevolent eyes they grew in number and influence.

Conservative business interests wanted to restrain government from using its right to regulate business according to formidable powers vested in the ICC (Interstate Commerce Commission) by the Hepburn Act of 1906, the Federal Reserve Board of 1913, the Federal Trade Commission of 1914, and the Federal Power Commission of 1920. For whatever reason, business was usually successful.

Let us look at just one industry, the generation of electric power, and the way its particular commission, the Federal Power Commission, operated. The production of electric power was greatly expanded during the 1920s and its distribution became available to ever more people. This was achieved by means of technological improvements and interconnections between different companies. However, these changes were initially most expensive and only the strongest companies could afford them. The route to strength was amalgamation. In 1926 there were over 1,000 mergers in public utilities. Many involved municipal plants that were sold out to private companies. Public utility magnates wanted to eliminate public ownership. By 1930 ten "groups of systems" controlled three-quarters of the nation's electric power. They sold to industry at lower prices than those charged to domestic consumers, lest industry should invest in its own plants. However, the price charged to domestic consumers also fell and the rate of domestic consumption went up.

It was the duty of the Federal Power Commission to supervise the manufacture and distribution of electric power. The act of 1920 gave the commission power to grant licenses for the construction of new plants, regulate rates of currents across state borders, require uniform systems of accounting from the companies, and decide on the issue of new securities. Because the commission initially comprised the secretaries of war, agriculture, and the interior, it assumed the political complexion of the new administration.

Senator George W. Norris of Nebraska, exasperated by the way Harding and Coolidge, by conservative appointments, had helped destroy the new federal system of regulatory commissions, wrote a scathing attack on Republican policies that both *Collier's Weekly* and the *Forum* refused to print. It finally appeared in the *Nation* of September 16, 1925. Norris's chief conclusion was that Republican policies had "set the country back more than twenty-five years." With heavy sarcasm he noted, "It is an indirect but positive repeal of Congressional enactments, which no administration, however powerful, would dare to bring about by any direct means. It is the nullification of federal law by a process of boring from within. If trusts, combinations, and big business are to run the government, why not permit them to do it directly rather than through this expensive machinery which was originally honestly established for the protection of the people of the country against monopoly and control?" In the light of such comments, historian John D. Hicks concludes how "In a sense, the slanting of government during the 1920s to support whatever stand the dominant business interests wanted was far more scandalous than the merely political depravity for which the Harding regime was noted."

Both industry and agriculture demanded a protective tariff against cheap foreign produce and persuaded Congress to pass the Fordney-McCumber tariff of September 21, 1922. However, it passed Congress on party lines only after acrimonious debate in which the Senate proposed some 2,082 amendments to the original House bill. The underlying and overwhelming sentiment was that the American producer must have the advantage in the American market. It was especially aimed at such products of Germany and Japan as silk and rayon, china, cutlery, and toys.

In one respect, the Fordney-McCumber tariff was an improvement on its predecessors since it provided for a more efficient administration of tariff regulations, based on a systematic classification of products. Moreover, on the advice of the commission, the president could raise or lower duties by up to 50 percent on specific items in order to achieve parity between American and foreign costs. However, of thirty-seven changes under Harding and Coolidge, thirty-two were upwards. The five decreases were picayune; on millfeeds, bobwhite quail, paintbrush handles, cresylic acid, and phenol. Whatever the incidental benefits to certain industrialists, the new tariff harmed American agriculture and industry in the long run.

The Sheppard-Towner Act of 1921 provided for maternal and infant health care under the charge of the Children's Bureau in the Department of Labor. It was intended to provide a basis for future development, a basis necessary for the kind of welfare state most Western European countries have instituted. However, yielding to pressure from the American Medical Association, Congress refused to renew the act in 1929. Critic and historian Linda Gordon remarks of their decision how "the demise" of the act "marked America's turn away from a permanent governmental responsibility for the health and welfare of its citizens."

The most famous acts of the Harding administration were the notorious misuses of federal resources and public monies. At the Veterans Bureau Forbes proved an energetic organizer who diverted the massive congressional appropriation of $36 million for medical care of injured veterans and the construction of hospitals to fradulent contractors and to himself. Hearing of the extent of Forbes's misdeeds, Harding and Daugherty arranged that he should first go abroad and then resign. The Senate started an investigation. However, while Forbes was away, his legal assistant, Charles F. Cramer, shot himself dead in his bathroom.

It became an open secret that the surest way of advancing sinister interests was to bend the ear of the unscrupulous attorney general and the easiest way to do that was through Daugherty's protégé, Jess Smith. One of their ruses to make money was to sell bootleg liquor impounded by the prohibition authorities and held in a house at 1625 K Street whence it was sold illegally and at great profit. William J. Burns ran the Department of Justice for Daugherty as a private protection racket. In particular, his agent Gaston B. Means, was supposed to have taken $7 million altogether from bootleggers who bought pardons for their convictions. The money was left in a goldfish bowl before being turned over to the Department of Justice. Unfortunately, the gullible and greedy Smith did not have the sort of cast-iron constitution required of those involved in political intrigue and shady deals while they are continuously in the public gaze. Smith could not stand the strain and he, too, committed suicide by shooting himself.

Harding was deeply worried by mounting evidence of misconduct by the Ohio gang. Quite simply, he was out of his depth as president and knew it. "My God, this is a hell of a place for a man like me to be," he said. He threw himself with ever greater abandon into his hobbies of golf during the day and poker at night.

Harding's health was certainly not up to the arduous tour to the West and Alaska that he undertook in late June 1923. Speaking at cities en route exhausted him and he died in San Francisco on August 2. Some of his doctors concluded that he had suffered a heart attack and was developing bronchial phneumonia. There was nothing odd in a man of Harding's age and soft constitution dying from apoplexy. For years he had overindulged himself in food, drink, and finally worry. Yet he was greatly mourned and the long train journey of the casket of the dead president from San Francisco to Washington, the lying in state at the Capitol,

and the final journey to Marion, Ohio, provided a splendid opportunity for public display of hysteria and grief.

Vice-President Calvin Coolidge was staying at his family's
farmhouse in Plymouth, Vermont, when he was awakened at
2:00 A.M. on August 3, with the news of Harding's death. His
father, who was a public notary, then administered the oath of
office to his son in the sitting room. "What was your first thought
when you heard that Harding had died?" portrait painter Charles
Hopkins asked of Coolidge later. "I thought I could swing it."

The contrast between the two presidents could hardly have
been more marked. Where Harding was the available man, Coolidge (1923–1929) was a puritan in Babylon. Harding was large
and handsome while Coolidge was shriveled and insignificant.
Where Harding had been genial and well liked, Coolidge was
aloof and austere. Someone said that he spoke so little that each
time he did open his mouth, a moth flew out. However, his
reputation for silence is belied by numerous anecdotes that suggest a mordant wit. Of a Baptist preacher who ate very little
before a revival meeting because, he said, abstinence improved
his preaching, Coolidge remarked after the sermon, "Might as
well have et." To the society woman who said to him at dinner,
"I made a bet that I could get more than two words out of you,"
he said curtly, "You lose." "What is your hobby?" "Holding
office."

Teapot Dome Scandal

In April 1922 an obscure citizen of Wyoming complained to
Senator John B. Kendrick that certain oil lands, usually known as
Teapot Dome on account of the unusual shape of one hill, and
intended to supply the navy, were being secretly and wrongfully
leased by Secretary of the Interior Albert B. Fall to a private
corporation, Mammoth Oil Company, owned principally by one
Harry F. Sinclair. Under pressure from the Senate, the Department of the Interior admitted that not only had Teapot Dome
been leased to the Sinclair Company but that it was also about to
lease the Elk Hills reserve in California to the Pan-American
Petroleum and Transportation Company of which the head was

"NONSENSE! IF IT GETS TOO DEEP, YOU CAN EASILY PULL ME OUT!"

"Nonsense, if it gets too deep, you can easily pull me out!" cries the very fat lady of excessive government spending to the emaciated taxpayer as she drags him from the shallows of deficit to the larger waves of debt in this 1920s cartoon by Herbert Johnson. (Library of Congress).

Edward L. Doheny. The explanation was that the oil was being drained from these reserves by wells on adjoining lands and that, within a few years, government reserves would be exhausted.

However, Senator Robert La Follette of Wisconsin was not satisfied and persuaded the Committee on Public Lands to instigate a formal investigation through a special committee chaired by Senator Thomas J. Walsh of Montana. Walsh was an Irish-American Catholic of penetrating mind, restrained manner, and inexhaustible energy who labored assiduously over the oil scandals for the next eighteen months. At the public hearings beginning on October 25, 1923, the weight of technical evidence was that leasing of oil reserves to anticipate drainage at the edges was quite unjustified. The oil supply was intended for the navy and it had been most irregular of Secretary of the Navy Edwin Denby to allow Secretary of the Interior Fall to issue leases to commercial companies. Although Coolidge was willing to stand by the hapless secretary of the navy, Denby could not endure the situation, and resigned.

At first, Walsh had next to no evidence against his suspects (Fall, Denby, Doheny, and Sinclair), but the process of inquisition began to arouse attention from various people who wanted to settle old scores with Fall. From their accounts it transpired Fall had moved from penury to opulence within two years and now had considerable ranch lands in New Mexico. It became evident that Doheny had "loaned" Fall $100,000 to improve his ranch. Thus Fall stood condemned: he was an experienced politician who, while he held public office, had received $100,000 from a man to whom, it his official capacity, he was about to grant a valuable lease. Moreover, he had lied about the money.

Because of Daugherty's involvement with the oil scandal, the Senate preferred to have charges against Fall and Doheny brought by a special counsel independent of the Department of Justice. For this task Coolidge chose Owen J. Roberts, a Republican lawyer from Philadelphia, and Atlee W. Pomerone, a former Democratic senator from Ohio.

The various trials of Fall, Sinclair, and Doheny on several charges of conspiracy and fraud resulted in the surprising acquittal of Doheny and Fall for fraud (December 16, 1926), and of Fall and Sinclair (April 21, 1928). However, Fall was convicted for having accepted a bribe (October 25, 1929), sentenced to a year's imprisonment, and fined $100.000. Thus was Fall the first cabinet officer of the United States to go to jail. Paradoxically, Doheny was acquitted in March 1930 on a charge of bribing Fall. Harry F. Sinclair, who refused to give the Walsh committee straight answers, was cited for contempt by the Senate, and tried and convicted in the criminal courts. He was sentenced to pay a fine of $1,000 and spend three months in jail. Later, when he was charged with Fall of having conspired to defraud the government, it was discovered that he employed detectives to shadow the jury and he was sentenced to another six months in jail.

Public confidence in public officers was visibly shaken. Accordingly, to remedy the damage, Coolidge and the new attorney general, Harlan Fiske Stone, attempted to improve the watchdog of public activities, the Bureau of Investigations, originally founded as an investigative branch of the Department of Justice in July 1908. In 1924 Stone had it reorganized under a new director, J. Edgar Hoover, who remained its head until his death in 1972. The title Federal Bureau of Investigations (FBI) was adopted in July 1935. It was the bureau's task to investigate crimes and undertake domestic intelligence activities and in 1930 it began to collate and publicize reports on crime from various police forces, subsequently published as *Uniform Crime Reports*.

Hoover had already worked in the Justice Department for seven years, notably as a special agent in the Enemy Aliens Bureau. His special gifts had been most apparent during the Great Red Scare of 1917–1921, particularly in 1919 when he became special assistant to the attorney general, A. Mitchell Palmer. While Palmer was a zealot of exaggerated ambitions whose enthusiasm was rewarded with legendary authorship of the Palmer Raids, it was Hoover who masterminded the kangaroo courts and deportations of radicals and subversives, real or imagined.

In his biography *Secrecy and Power* (1987), Richard Gid Powers notes that, since it was anti-Communist fervor that brought Hoover to power, it was anti-Communism that defined his political career. His central principle was continuous opposition to all who threatened the authority of lawful government especially "communists, subversives, and pseudo-liberals." In the 1930s he established a counterintelligence program or Cointelpro against the Communist party, penetrating and exposing its cadres. He investigated and harried suspects to the point of breaking the law. In his own manifesto against Communists, *Masters of Deceit* (1958), Hoover relished a stereotype of evil radicals based on popular images from science fiction, comic books, and detective novels. Hoover's values were those of his childhood and youth in Washington at the turn of the century—provincial white morality.

In private Hoover admitted mistakes. His public image was of unswerving certainty of purpose. According to an apocryphal story, once he announced the death of an agent in a shootout who was, in fact, only wounded, other FBI agents drew straws to select which of them should visit the hospital to turn Hoover's announcement into reality. He liked his typist to leave wide margins so that he could add personal comments to memos. Once he wrote at the side of a narrow margin, "Watch the borders," thereby prompting agents to put bureau offices near Canada and Mexico on full alert.

He was deeply jealous of individual agents who scored personal successes. Thus when Melvin Purvis received due credit for the entrapment and summary execution of outlaws John Dillinger and Pretty Boy Floyd, Hoover despatched inspectors to Purvis's office in Chicago who wrote adverse reports about him. Thus pressured, Purvis resigned in 1935. He found himself unable to get a job elsewhere, whether in movies or among the Senate staff. Purvis never realised who his real enemy was and remained obsessively loyal to Hoover. In 1960, he shot himself. As a final insult, Hoover decided not to sent a letter of condolence to the bereaved family of his unknowing victim.

The Progressive Revival and the Election of 1924

The test of the reformed federal government came with the presidential election of 1924. On the first ballot at the Republican National Convention, Coolidge won the nomination in Cleveland in June by courting Republican regulars, thus earning Borah's public support. "Give him a chance to make good. I think he is an able man." Behind the scenes Coolidge wooed business, with whom he was popular, and succeeded in giving them even greater control of the party. The Republican campaign slogan was "Keep Cool and Keep Coolidge," emphasizing Cal's imperturbable serenity. Asked by a reporter if he had a statement to make about the campaign, he answered, "No." Asked, "Can you tell us something about the world situation?" he answered, "No." "Anything about prohibition?" "No—Now remember, don't quote me."

However, the Democrats' principal problem was the association of many leading politicians with the revived Ku Klux Klan. The Klan had two principal objectives at the Democratic National Convention of 1924. It wanted to help William Gibbs McAdoo win the presidential nomination and it was determined to prevent the party from condemning it by name. This first objectives would involve trouncing McAdoo's rivals, wet Governor Alfred E. Smith of New York and dry Senator Oscar N. Underwood of Alabama, both of whom were declared opponents of the Klan. In pursuit of its goals, the Klan had participated in the Democratic state conventions in Arkansas, Oklahoma, Texas, and elsewhere. As a result, perhaps 80 percent of delegates from Arkansas and Texas were at least sympathetic to the Klan if not actual knights. Indeed, the New York *World* estimated that about 300 delegates to the national convention were Klansmen.

The convention met on June 24, 1924, in the sweltering auditorium of Madison Square Garden, New York. When he rose on the second day to nominate Oscar Underwood for president, Alabama delegate Forney Johnson first called on the convention to take a stand against secret un-American organizations such as the Ku Klux Klan. This attack brought the issue into the open. It sharply divided delegates in northern states from those in the South. As the controversy became ever more heated, it transpired that a majority of delegates did not intend to condemn the Klan.

For the Democrats the decision was a disaster. It embittered the convention and prevented the nomination of either of their leading candidates. John W. Davis, a Wall Street lawyer from West Virginia, was a compromise candidate nominated after 103 ballots cast over seventeen riotous days. The total number of votes cast at the convention would be 1,098. The convention, broadcast by radio, divided Democrats across the country on a scale unknown since the Civil War and unsurpassed until 1968. "How true was Grant's exclamation," observed Hiram Johnson to his family, "that the Democratic party could be relied upon at the right time to do the wrong thing!"

The Republicans' indifference to reform and the Democrats' incapacity led to the rise of alternative groups pledged to reform. The most widely known leader of the reform movement was Senator Robert M. La Follette of Wisconsin, briefly unpopular for his opposition to American intervention in the war, but now, through his speeches, reaching a wider audience than just the state readers of his own *La Follette's Magazine*. Almost his equal in influence was Senator George W. Norris of Nebraska, tireless champion of public rights against the interests of monopolies, especially the utility empires. Other progressives included Senators Edwin F. Ladd and Lynn J. Frazier of North Dakota, Burton K. Wheeler of Montana, Magnus Johnson and Henrik Shipstead of Minnesota, and Smith W. Brookhart of Iowa. Outside the Senate they included Congressman Fiorello La Guardia of New York (later mayor), John R. Commons of the University of Wisconsin, Felix Frankfurter of the Harvard Law School, and journalists William Allen White of the Emporia *Gazette* and Chester H. Rowell of the San Francisco *Chronicle*. They were all disaffected with the Republican party.

Accordingly, these progressives now organized themselves into three different political groups: the American Labor party of 1919, based on trade unions; the Committee of Forty-eight, composed of old Bull-Moose progressives—those who had supported Theodore Roosevelt for president in 1912—and led by J.A.H. Hopkins, a New Jersey insurance broker, who finally formed a Farmer-Labor party in 1920; and the Conference for Progressive Political Action (CPPA), based on railroad brotherhoods and formed in Chicago in February 1922. Their projected reforms included the abolition of the electoral college and the use of direct primaries for all elective officers, including the presidency, the rapid convening of new Congresses, and the exclusion of special privilege interests from government.

Encouraged by the problems of both main parties, the CPPA held a national convention in Cleveland in July 1924 that was attended by 600 delegates from labor unions, farmers' organizations, and the Socialist party. At the insistence of Robert La Follette, they decided not to form a third party and thus jeopardize the seats of many sympathetic progressives in Congress who held seats as nominal Democrats or Republicans. Instead, they would concentrate on the presidential contest, nominating La Follette with Democratic Senator Burton K. Wheeler of Montana as his running mate.

The progressive plank declared that "the great issue" was "the control of government and industry by private monopoly," that had "crushed competition" and "stifled private initiative and independent enterprise" in pursuit of "extortionate profits." However, progressives were reluctant to accept the socialist remedy of government ownership of industry. Thus, their platform reiterated the nineteenth-century remedies of the Populists against great monopolies. However, they did advocate the right of organized labor to collective bargaining, urged the abolition of the use of injunctions in labor disputes, favored a constitutional amendment to restrict the use of judicial veto (by which federal courts could declare laws void), proposed ten-year terms for federal judges, and suggested a revision of the Treaty of Versailles.

In the election Coolidge took 15,718,211 popular votes, exceeding the combined total of Davis's 8,385, 283 and La Follette's 4,831,289. Thus Coolidge had 54.0 percent of the popular vote while Davis had 28.8 percent and La Follette 16.6 percent. La Follette carried only his home state, Wisconsin, while Coolidge had thirty-five states, giving him 382 votes in the electoral college, and Davis, with twelve states, had 136 votes. The Coolidge landslide also gave the Republicans control of Congress. In the House there were now 247 Republicans to 183 Democrats and 2 Farmer-Laborites and 2 Socialists; in the Senate there were 56 Republicans to 39 Democrats and 1 Farmer-Laborite.

On the surface, it seemed that La Follette had been beaten badly. Yet his campaign had made a considerable impact on politics. He scared bosses in both parties by coming second in eleven states (California, Idaho, Iowa, Minnesota, Montana, Nevada, North Dakota, South Dakota, Oregon, Washington, and Wyoming). In thirteen others he took enough votes so that Coolidge carried them by pluralities rather than outright majorities. Those dissatisfied with the Republicans were as likely to vote for La Follette, who was liberal, as for Davis, who was not. Thus, leading Democrats concluded that if the Democrats were ever to win again, they would have to field liberal candidates with liberal programs.

Despite the setback, La Follette tried to stir the CPPA for the midterm congressional elections of 1926. However, the AFL would not continue to work with a third party and, without its considerable support, the CPPA dissolved. However, before this happened La Follette died of a heart attack on June 18, 1925, and was succeeded in the Senate by his son, Robert M. La Follette, Jr., who took his seat as a Republican.

A Puritan in Babylon

Supported by comfortable Republican majorities, Secretary of the Treasury Andrew Mellon could now get his preferred tax proposals enacted. The Revenue Act of 1926 repealed gift taxes outright and reduced minimum surtaxes and estate taxes from 40 to 20 percent, raising only corporation tax from 12 to 12½ percent. In 1928 this was again reduced to 12 percent. These various revisions were a boon to the truly rich. A man with an income of $1 million now paid less than $200,000 in income tax, compared with $600,000 before the alteration. According to Harvey O'Connor in *Mellon's Millions* (1933) the annual amount released by the new tax schedules to the Mellons for extra investment was about $350 million.

In the late 1920s all seemed well with the economy on the surface. American capitalism enjoyed a boom: between 1925 and 1929 the number of factories had increased from 183,877 to 206,663 and the value of their production for the domestic market rose from $34 billion to $37.78 billion. The Federal Reserve index of industrial production had risen from 67 in 1921 to 100 in 1925, and then 126 in June 1929. However, there were cracks in the economic plates just below the surface. Economic growth in the early twenties was most notable in construction and the automobile industry. From 1925 onward both were in decline. New residential construction earned $5 billion in 1925 but only $3 billion in 1929. Automobile production continued to grow in these years but at a much slower rate and this in turn reduced the production of steel, rubber, glass, and its other tributary industries. By 1929 it was clear that all of these were dangerously overextended. Since there was no new industry to supersede the auto industry as the pivot of the industrial economy, it was inevitable that a serious recession would ensue.

In agriculture the crisis was chronic. From 1921 onward American farmers paid the inevitable price for capacity production during the war. Once the war was over, Europe had less need of American grain. In consequence, the steady supply of bumper harvests in the United States amounted to gross overproduction. The impending disaster for American agriculture in the 1930s is best suggested by the fall in the value of farm products from $21.4 billion in 1919 to $11.8 billion in 1929. Other statistics confirm the depressing trend. Farm tenancy increased from 38.1 percent of farms in 1920 to 42.4 percent in 1930. The percentage of farms mortgaged also rose from 37.2 percent in 1920 to 42 percent in 1930.

In Congress farmers were supported by an active pressure group that was predominantly Republican in character and usually known as the farm bloc. It was the guiding force behind farm legislation of the decade designed to ease agricultural problems. The Packers and Stockyards Act of 1921 gave the Department of Agriculture considerable powers over the meat-packing industry and broke the big meatpackers' monopoly over the stockyards. The Grain Futures Act eliminated much of the fraud and grain speculation in the grain exchanges. The Capper-Volstead Act of 1922 released farm cooperatives from the antitrust laws. Most active in the farm bloc was Senator George W. Norris who proposed a revolutionary scheme whereby government warehouses would store the surplus, public corporations would buy it, and government agencies would sell and transport it abroad. Instead, Congress passed the Agriculture Credits Act of 1923, aimed principally at livestock farming and which allowed the farmer to borrow money, using his crop as collateral, postponing its sale, and storing it for periods lasting from six months to three years until prices were more favorable.

Two midwestern industrialists also succeeded in getting Congress to act. George N. Peek and General Hugh S. Johnson had first worked together in the War Industries Board and in the twenties led the Moline Plow Company of Moline, Illinois, which, like other farm servicing industries, was under great financial pressure. Peek and Johnson realized that the essential problem was that farmers had to buy their equipment in a domestic market in which industry was protected by high tariffs but that they had to sell their produce in a world market that was not so protected. What agriculture needed, surely, was for some form of parity or equality between its purchasing power and that of industry, a "fair exchange value." This could be achieved if agriculture could regulate its supply of produce to meet the domestic demand. This would involve dumping the surplus abroad at current world prices, and maintaining high prices for produce sold at home by a tariff. The losses sustained by the government on produce sold cheaply abroad would be compensated by special equalization fees to be paid by the farmers.

The Peek-Johnson scheme was first proposed in Congress in 1924 by Senator Charles L. McNary of Oregon (a wheat state) and Congressman Gilbert N. Haugen of Iowa (a corn state). Despite support from business as well as farm organizations, and by Secretary of Agriculture Henry C. Wallace, it was defeated in the House on June 3, 1924, by eastern Republicans acting on instructions from Coolidge. However, the farm bloc then proposed a measure with wider coverage of such crops as cotton, tobacco, and rice. In this way they enticed support from southern Democrats and their second bill was passed by Congress in 1927. It listed only six basic commodities (cotton, wheat, corn, rice, hogs, and tobacco) and proposed a Federal Farm Board of twelve members, one for each Federal Land Bank District, to administer the scheme. The Board could raise domestic prices to the level of the official tariff on each item. The equalization fee was not to be assessed on the farmers but on the processing, transportation, and sale of crops. Coolidge vetoed the bill in 1927 and again in 1928 when it was passed a second time by Congress. On neither occasion could the farm bloc find the necessary two-thirds majority to override the veto. Nevertheless, the parity scheme and other plans for agriculture united farmers and farm organizations as had no previous movement.

Lean years for farmers were also hard for the industries that served the farm. One indication is that rural banks failed in this period and so, too, did other banks. In the prosperous year of 1928 as many as 549 banks failed: in 1929, 640 did so. Here were sure signs of an economy deep in trouble.

The Bitter Harvest of 1928

The most exciting and divisive political event of the 1920s was the presidential election of 1928 when the wet, Democratic, and

Catholic governor of New York, Al Smith, stood against the dry, Republican, and Quaker secretary of commerce, Herbert Hoover. At the outset it looked as if the 1928 election would be fought on the economic problems of agriculture. However, in the end the campaign was the climax of the conflict between rural America with its allegiance to proven values and urban America with its masses committed to social and political experiments. It also represented the climax of fifty years' debate about prohibition in which nativist pride, religious prejudice, legal pedantry, and political bigotry were the determining factors.

Al Smith was the son of poor Irish Catholics and had started work in Fulton Street Fish Market, New York, when he was twelve. As a loyal Tammany man who was also a progressive reformer, he rose in the Democratic party and served four terms as governor of New York between 1919 and 1929. His prestige was taken as an illustration of "Americanism," the philosophy that merit determined success in a pluralistic society. Smith was now preeminent in the Democratic party. From 1926 onward there was open public debate about the suitability of a Catholic for the presidency and discussion as to whether Smith would break the "unwritten law" that no Catholic could ever become president. There was a general misapprehension that a Catholic president would put the duties of church before state, involve America in entangling alliances, and subvert democracy. In 1926 Catholics accounted for 15.97 percent of the total population. (When Kennedy ran for the presidency in 1960 they accounted for 23.2 percent.) However, of the remaining 84.03 percent in 1926, only 27.36 percent belonged to Protestant churches and only 3.50 percent attended Jewish synagogues: 53.17 percent had no religious affiliation. The statistics, however, belied the incipient religious intolerance of the age.

Ironically, Smith, a city slicker if ever there was one, was to be promoted as champion of the downtrodden farmers and, not surprisingly, repudiated by them on account of his religion, his background, and his opposition to prohibition. Smith compounded his problems by taking advice from a "golfing cabinet" of nouveaux riches industrialists, including General Motors executive John J. Raskob, whom he made his campaign manager.

Unsuccessful Democratic presidential candidate Al Smith puts his case on the radio in 1928. Radio was a medium that cruelly exposed his regional limitations of voice and political style, thereby underlying his Tammany origins, his association with the new immigrants, and his opposition to prohibition, all of which were as objectionable to hide-bound rural America as was his Catholicism. (Library of Congress).

Smith hoped to convince the public that the Democrats did have the support of big business. However, Raskob alienated the party on account of his own well-publicized Catholicism, and, as a leading member of the Association Against the Prohibition Amendment (AAPA), his wetness. Nevertheless, Raskob spent at least $5.3 million on Smith's campaign, a record to that time.

After his nomination as Republican candidate, Herbert Hoover promised a federal commission to investigate prohibition, which he referred to as "a great social and economic experiment, noble in motive and far-reaching in purpose." His words were reduced by others to "noble experiment"—offensive to both wets and drys. But his proposal undermined Smith's appeal to all wets who could now vote for Hoover on the assumption that he would first investigate and then change the law.

Smith's main strategy was a whistle-stop tour of the country but he was harassed in the South, West, and Midwest by the Ku Klux Klan. In 1928 it was still a vibrant force and, against Smith, it received covert support from various Protestant churches led by Methodist Bishop James A. Cannon, Jr., of the Anti-Saloon League. Cannon diverted Democratic monies to a campaign against the party nominee (and also into his own pocket). He undertook extensive campaign tours deliberately inciting religious hatred.

The vivacious Smith could not be persuaded to stand still before a radio microphone and the effect of his voice, with its pronounced East Side accent, moving in and out of earshot, was grotesque and his words unintelligible to many in the South and West. By comparison, Hoover, who was known as a dull speaker, disciplined himself to talk directly into the microphone, have his shyness mistaken for modesty, and give a general impression of midwestern sobriety.

There was a heavy turnout at the polls with 67.5 percent of voters casting their ballots. Smith won the largest popular vote given to any Democrat to that time, 15,016,169 (40.7 percent). Hoover took 21,391,993 (58.2 percent). He had 444 votes in the electoral college to Smith's 87. Six southern states went Republican (Florida, Kentucky, North Carolina, Tennessee, Texas, Virginia). But industrial Massachusetts and Rhode Island went Democrat for the first time since the Civil War. Although Smith lost Pennsylvania, Illinois, and Wisconsin, he narrowed the Republican lead there.

Never again would the Democrats count on the Solid South but, instead, search out new catchment areas. Thus the electoral significance of the South would diminish. Smith, moreover, inaugurated a trend that was to make the Democrats the future majority party of the nation. In the twelve most populous cities the Democrats had a majority of 38,000 whereas the Republican majorities there had been 1,638,000 in 1920 and 1,252,000 in 1924. The Republican hold on these cities was broken by Smith who, thus, cleared the path for Franklin D. Roosevelt's victory in 1932. More women voted than before and Catholic women gave their votes to Smith. As for Congress, the Republicans took 267 seats in the House, against 163 for the Democrats and 1 for the Farmer-

Laborites, and now had 56 seats in the Senate against 39 for the Democrats and 1 for the Farmer-Laborites. In the gubernatorial contests the Republicans won 30 and the Democrats 18.

Smith's consolation prize was the result of another of Raskob's pet schemes. Raskob wanted New York to have its own equivalent of the Eiffel Tower. On August 29, 1929, Al Smith, now president of the Empire State, Inc., announced that the organization would build the world's tallest skyscraper. It would be 1,200 feet high, with 102 stories of offices for 25,000 people. It would stand on Fifth Avenue at Thirty-Fourth Street and the Waldorf-Astoria Hotel would be demolished to make room for it. The Empire State Building was to be a physical representation of the inevitable triumph of modernism.

On the eve of his retirement from the presidency, Calvin Coolidge's old neighbors in Vermont gave him a farewell present of a handmade rake. At the presentation ceremony the orator described the sterling qualities of the hickory wood from which it was made. "Hickory, like the president, is sturdy, strong, resilient, unbroken." Coolidge turned the rake over and remarked quite simply, "Ash." For the last time, Coolidge had exercised his special talent for unwitting irony in his choice of the right word. The decade of invention, intolerance, and indulgence was about to come to an end.

4

SNOW IN HARVEST
The Onset of the Great
Depression

WE MIGHT characterize the 1920s as an American dream that became a nightmare. Despite the publicity about progress and prosperity, it seemed that, in economic terms, society was digging its own grave, its citizens the victims of an inadequate economic mechanism. American prosperity in the 1920s stood on brittle glass. However, in 1929 the mirror cracked when the economy was shattered by the Wall Street Crash. The crisis for the old order had been brewing for many years and the climax lasted three months—September, October, and November of 1929. The consequences continued for a decade afterward as the Great Depression spread its shadow over the land.

Heedless of the basic flaws in the American economic system, those with money to invest did so eagerly and greedily in the 1920s. For, as historian William E. Leuchtenburg explains, "The prosperity of the 1920s produced the contagious feeling that everyone was meant to get rich." Thus well before the Wall Street

Crash of 1929 there was the Florida Land Boom of the mid-twenties, an episode that had all the hallmarks of a classic speculation bubble.

No single individual was responsible for the Wall Street Crash. No single individual was the architect of the babel of speculation that preceded it. Thousands of people contributed freely to the debacle. In the early twenties stock prices were low; in the mid-twenties they began to rise. The main index for these years is provided by the *New York Times* industrial averages, an aggregate of twenty-five leading industrial stocks. Between May 1924 and December 1925 the *Times* averages rose from 106 to 181. By December 1927 the *Times* averages were 245, a gain of sixty-nine points in the year.

The rise was partly a response to a British decision about the exchange rate that had widespresd repercussions. In 1925 Winston Churchill, chancellor of the exchequer, returned Britain formally to the gold standard, making the pound sterling the equivalent of £1 = $4.86. He did so for mistaken reasons of prestige and failed to recognize the subtle but disastrous effects of overvaluation. The American response was decisive. In August 1927 the Federal Reserve System lowered the rediscount rate from 4 percent to 3.5 percent. It did this partly to discourage the flow of gold from Europe to the United States, partly to encourage the flow of European imports and thus help certain European countries stabilize their currencies, and partly to stimulate American business. Unfortunately, the Federal Reserve overstimulated the stock market.

The great bull market began in earnest on Saturday, March 3, 1928. For instance, General Motors rose from 140 to 144 that day and in the next week crossed the psychologically significant figure of 150. There was a specific explanation. Since Henry Ford had discontinued the Model T in 1927 and reequipped his plants for the Model A, production of Ford cars would obviously be somewhat impeded. Thus General Motors would gain customers at Ford's expense. One indication that trading was at astonishing, unprecedented levels was the fact that day after day the stock ticker, unable to cope with the demand, was late: on June 12 it was almost two hours late in recording prices on the floor.

Fifth Avenue at 42nd Street, New York, 1933, dominated by the Empire State Building (1931), the most famous skyscraper in the world, designed by Shreve, Lamb, and Harmon with most skillful massing to make optimum use of the city's zoning laws and with a facade of limestone, granite, aluminum, and nickel capped by a crown of setbacks and a rounded tower. It both dominates the landscape and merges into it. Close by is the New York Public Library (1897–1911) by Carrere and Hastings, a modest, neoclassical building. (Photo by Irving Underhill; Library of Congress).

The ecstasy of speculation sent American investors in the 1920s into a wonderland where all had won and all must have prizes. The great Wall Street stockbroking firms opened an increasing number of branch offices across the country. Where there had been about 500 branch offices in 1919, in October 1928 there were 1,192. Business was not confined to the New York Stock Exchange, that accounted for only about 61 percent of transactions; the stock markets of Boston, Chicago, and San Francisco were also most active.

Few bankers urged caution. One who did so was Paul M. Warburg of the International Acceptance Bank who was reported by the *Commercial and Financial Chronicle* of March 9, 1929, as calling for a stronger Federal Reserve policy and predicted that, if the exuberant bonanza of unrestricted speculation was not stopped, then there would eventually be a disastrous collapse. A minority of journalists never lost touch with reality. Poor's *Weekly Business and Investment Letter* referred to the "great common-stock delusion." Both the *Commercial and Financial Chronicle* and the *New York Times* warned that a day of reckoning would come.

Of course, very few people were actually buying and selling stocks and shares. In 1929, when the total population of the United States was 121,767,000, the member firms of twenty-nine exchanges had no more than 1,548,707 clients altogether. And of these, 1,371,920 were clients of member firms of the New York Stock Exchange. Those involved in the precarious and potentially damaging marginal trading were only slightly more than 50,000. Thus, as J. K. Galbraith emphasizes, "The striking thing about the stock market speculation of 1929 was not the massiveness of the participation. Rather it was the way it became central to the culture." It was as if by foolhardy, spendthrift actions, a whole society was digging its own economic grave, a victim of its own inadequate economic mechanism. Such foolhardiness was to bring snow in harvest.

The economy had already entered a depression ahead of the stock market. Industrial production peaked in June 1929, when the Federal Reserve index stood at 126. Thereafter, it began to decline. By October, the Federal Reserve index of industrial production was 117. Thus economist Thomas Wilson later maintained that the ensuing fall in the stock market was reflecting a change that had already occurred in industry, rather than the other way round.

A few shareowners, suspicious of market fluctuations, quietly sold stock at advantageous prices. In time everyone began selling as much as possible. Real panic set in on the morning of "Black Thursday," October 24, 1929, when 12,894,650 shares changed hands in a vicious spiral of deflation. In the mad scramble to sell people were ready to part with shares for next to nothing. Among visitors to the New York Stock Exchange that day was Winston Churchill who might have rued his decision to return Britain to the gold standard four years earlier. To the *New York Herald Tribune* of October 25, 1929, Wall Street on Black Thursday was like a carnival with huge crowds in a holiday mood surging around the narrow streets of the financial centers and with hotels nearby overflowing with brokers' men. The atmosphere was most tense with enraged brokers vandalizing stock tickers and (largely unsubstantiated) rumors of others having jumped from windows. But it was prices that were falling through the floor.

At noon organized support rallied at 23 Wall Street, the offices of J. P. Morgan and Company. Led by Thomas W. Lamont, the senior partner of the House of Morgan, a pool of six bankers was formed to save the situation. Nevertheless, "Black Tuesday," October 29, 1929, was the bitter climax of everything that had gone wrong before. The amount of trading and the fall in prices was greater than ever. Altogether, 16,410,030 sales took place and the *Times* averages fell 43 points, wiping out all the gains of the previous twelve months. The worst losses were sustained by overvalued investment trusts. Goldman, Sachs Trading Corporation fell from 60 to 35; Blue Ridge fell from 10 to 3. The collapse of the stock market was greeted with blunt vulgarity by the weekly stage paper, *Variety*. Its headline of October 30, 1929, was "WALL STREET LAYS AN EGG."

The period of great bankruptcies began. The first major casualty of the crash outside New York was the Foshay enterprises of Minneapolis, a floundering utilities company, supposedly worth $20 million but already deeply in debt. The Wall Street Crash had eliminated potential investors who might have rallied to it. Now their savings had been wiped out. The market continued to fall inevitably until Wednesday, November 13, 1929. The *Times* averages then stood at 224, compared with 542 in early September. Altogether stocks and shares had lost $40 billion in the autumn of 1929.

The crisis continued along its remorseless and inevitable path of economic disintegration. Despite temporary gains in early 1930, the stock market continued to fall until July 8, 1932, when the *Times* averages were 58, as compared with 224 at their low ebb on November 13, 1929.

Causes and Consequences of the Wall Street Crash

The Wall Street Crash exposed the underlying instability of the American economic system—the overexpansion of industry and the farm surpluses, the unequal distribution of wealth, and the weak banking structure. In *The Great Crash—1929* (1954) J. K. Galbraith emphasizes five principal weaknesses of an unsound economy. The first was the bad distribution of income. The top 5 percent of the population took a third of all personal income. This inequality meant that the survival of the economy depended on a very high level of investment by the wealthy few, or a high level of luxury spending, or both. Since there was a limit to the amount of food, housing, and clothing the rich could consume they must either spend their money on luxuries or investment. However, both luxury and investment spending were subject to a variety of changing circumstances. They could not remain steady.

A second unsound feature was the bad corporate structure. The most damaging weakness was the great, and comparatively recent, infrastructure of holding companies and investment trusts. Holding companies controlled a majority of shares in production companies, especially in the fields of railroads, public utilities, and entertainment. Even in economic crises holding companies insisted on their dividends, whatever the essential economic needs of the operating (that is the productive) companies from which they derived their great wealth. Thus the operating companies had to give priority to paying dividends rather than being able to invest in new plants or improved machinery that might have led to higher production. The system kept the operating companies weak and fueled deflation.

A third feature was the inherently weak banking structure of the United States with an excessive number of independent banks. In the first six months of 1929 as many as 346 banks with average deposits of $115 million failed. This was a tyranny of the weak. When one bank failed, others froze their assets, thus inviting investors to ask for their money back. In turn, such public pressure led to the collapse of ever more banks. Thus isolated instances of bank mismanagement led to a chain reaction in which neighboring banks collapsed like a row of dominoes. When a depression hit employment and people withdrew their savings, bank failures proliferated.

A fourth feature was the imbalance of trade. As we have observed, the United States became a creditor nation in the course of World War I. However, afterward the surplus of exports over imports, which had once paid for European loans, continued. High tariffs restricted imports and this factor impeded the ability of other countries to repay their loans. During the twenties they tried to meet their payments in gold while at the same time the United States was increasing its loans to foreign countries. Congress impeded further repayment of foreign loans by trade when it passed the Hawley-Smoot tariff, signed by Hoover on June 17, 1930, that raised tariff levels quite decisively. The upshot was a sharp reduction in trade and general default on repayment.

The fifth feature was the poor state of economic intelligence. The people running the economic machinery simply did not fully understand the system they were operating. Official dependence on outdated clichés—such as maintaining the gold standard, balancing the budget, and opposing inflation—all posed insuperable barriers to an early solution to the crisis. Moreover, it was harmful to the economy as a whole for the people in charge to equate the national interest with the special interests of the businesses they served.

Nevertheless, the greater fell with the lesser. Charles E. Mitchell of the House of Morgan, Ivan Kreuger, the Swedish Match

King, and officials of the Union Industrial Bank of Flint, Michigan, were among financiers found out for various forms of sharp practice.

Another crook who was made a scapegoat was Samuel Insull of Chicago. Insull was an English immigrant whom Thomas Edison had employed successively as secretary, assistant, and then general manager. At the turn of the century he was head of Edison's offices in Chicago and in 1908 formed the Commonwealth Edison Company, a $30 million corporation consolidating the Edison companies around Chicago, of which he became president. Insull's speciality was combining small power companies into ever larger units with improved facilities for generating electric power and then distributing it. He was a director of eighty-five companies, chairman of sixty-five boards, and president of another eleven. He owed his fabulous wealth to a conglomerate of 150 utility companies, serving 3.25 million people, and employing 50,000. It was valued at $3 billion. Unfortunately, he had a sinister side, his mania for creating pyramids of holding companies that were no better than a chaotic financial jumble. He refused to take account of the fact that a fall in profits of the operating companies, fundamental to the whole system, would reduce the unstable tiers to rubble. In early 1932 his empire collapsed, partly because it was overextended and overcapitalized and partly on account of fraud. The value of its stock fell to 4 percent of its 1931 level and two of Insull's investment trusts were declared bankrupt. In July 1932, having been indicted by a Cook County grand jury for outrageous debts of $60 million, Insull fled to Europe. He moved from Paris to Rome and, finally, to Athens because Greece had no extradition treaty with the United States. When an extradition treaty was signed in November 1932, he escaped to Turkey disguised as a women. He was eventually returned to the United States and stood trial. However, he was found not guilty as a result of a major loophole in the law: holding companies were not subject to regulation.

The causes of the Wall Street Crash were complex. The results were plain for all to see. The tawdry affluence of the twenties went out like a light.

The Years of the Locust

After the seven fat years of prosperity of 1922–1929, America entered a devastating and extended economic depression that lasted longer than seven lean years. The worst period was the notorious "Years of the Locust" of 1929–1932. Industry foundered. Instead of expanding, railroads and utilities contracted. Their new capital issues of bonds and stocks fell from $10 billion in 1929 to $1 billion in 1932. In 1932 the physical production of industry was 54 percent of what it had been in 1929. The automobile industry was working at a fifth of its previous capacity in 1929. By 1932 steel production was only operating at 12 percent of capacity and railroad freight was half of what it had been in 1929. The Gross National Product fell from $103.1 billion in 1929 to $58 billion in 1932, that is, a fall per captia from $847 in 1929 to $465 in 1932.

The story in agriculture was much the same. Capital investment in agriculture fell gradually from $79 billion in 1919 to $58 billion in 1929 and then precipitately to $38 billion in 1932. Realized gross income from farming fell from $13.9 million in 1929 to $6.4 million in 1932. The decline was most severe in basic export crops such as wheat, cotton, and tobacco.

At first industries tried to conserve their failing resources and faltering organization by such devices as cutting the working week or reducing wages. U.S. Steel became the first major corporation to reduce wages on September 22, 1931, when it announced a cut of 10 percent. It was followed by General Motors, Bethlehem Steel, and other corporations.

As sales continued to fall and the depression showed no signs of improving, business and industry cut costs further by discharging some of their work force. Those who were out of work could not afford to buy goods. This led to a vicious spiral of deflation. Sales fell yet again, leading to ever more layoffs and the further contraction of purchasing power. It was a vicious circle affecting farmers and industrial workers alike. Neither could afford to buy the products of the other. The problem was double-headed: chronic overproduction and perennial underconsumption, both at the same time.

The most profound consequence was unemployment on a massive, unprecedented scale. As historian William E. Leuchtenburg observes, the statistics of unemployment read like casualty figures in the great battles of the world war. In the three years following the crash an average of 100,000 workers were being discharged every week. According to the Bureau of Labor Statistics of the U.S. Department of Labor, published on June 29, 1945, there were 1.49 million unemployed in 1929 and this number increased gradually over the months to 11.9 million in 1932. This represented a percentage rise from 3.1 percent of the civilian labor force in 1929 to 24.0 percent in 1932. Other sources, such as the National Industrial Conference Board, the AFL, and the Labor Research Association (LRA), disputed these figures. The LRA said that the true number was 16.78 million.

Such unemployment was not shared evenly across the regions or between social and ethnic groups. By 1932 a million were unemployed in New York and so were 660,000 others in Chicago. In Cleveland 50 percent of the labor force was idle, in Akron 60 percent, and in Toledo 80 percent. In an article, "Negroes Out of Work," of April 22, 1931, the *Nation* showed that black unemployment was four to six times as high as white, particularly in industrial towns. In the depression blacks were displaced by whites in the lowly occupations of waiters, hotel workers, and elevator operators. In the specially created jobs in public works there was also positive discrimination against blacks.

The Protestant work ethic died hard. Millions who lost their jobs blamed themselves for their misfortune. A generation raised on the belief that hard work inevitably led to success could not come to terms with collective failure. Poverty was shameful and, to the middle class, something that had to be concealed from their friends and neighbors. Your neighbor opposite may have looked like an executive but, perhaps, when he left home each morning, he subsequently changed his suit to go begging, work in construction, or sell shoelaces or apples on street corners. Perhaps he spent his days looking for work.

Mass unemployment had grave consequences for marriage and

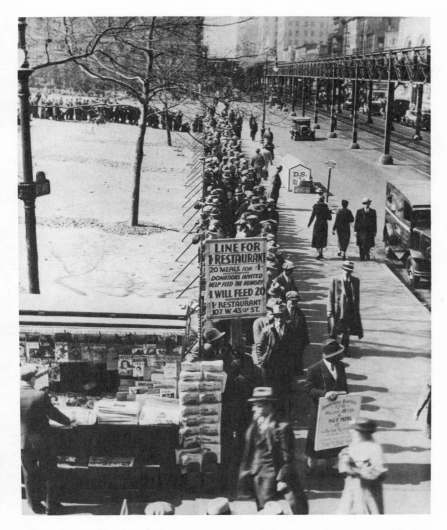

A breadline of haunted, hungry men waits for a meal in a soup kitchen
supported by private charity alongside Bryant Park, 42nd Street, close
to the New York Public Library in this classic depression photograph
of February 1932. (Library of Congress).

birth rates and for immigration. With no prospect of employment young people either postponed marriage or, if they were already married, postponed having children. In 1929 there were 1.23 million marriages, in 1932, 982,000. In 1929 the birth rate was 21.2 per 1,000 population; in 1932 it was 19.5 per 1,000. In 1932 emigration exceeded immigration: 35,576 immigrants arrived and 103,000 emigrants left.

However, the most obvious consequence of mass unemployment was that those who could afford neither rent nor mortgage payments were put out of house and home. Masses of unemployed and destitute folks set up squalid camps on the edges of cities. These grotesque suburbs were a mixture of tents made from old sacking and shacks built with corrugated iron and even cardboard. They were called Hoovervilles. Their inhabitants depended on charity to stay alive. If that was not forthcoming, they combed the streets looking for garbage in the gutter and trash in the cans to find something to eat. Author Thomas Wolfe described such scenes in New York as "homeless men who prowled in the vicinity of restaurants, lifting the lids of garbage cans and searching around inside for morsels of rotten food."

Soup kitchens were provided by missions, churches, and hospitals, by the Salvation Army and, in Chicago, by Al Capone. The fare was meager, the portions diminutive. Thomas Minehan, a graduate student at the University of Minnesota, studied breadlines at close quarters. Everywhere he saw the prominent ribs, concave abdomens, and emaciated limbs that were the hallmarks of malnutrition.

The extent of the problem of human misery and want is indicated by a survey of *Fortune* magazine, in September 1932. *Fortune* estimated that 34 million men, women, and children, that is 28 percent of the total population, were without any income at all. (This estimate did not include America's 11 million farm dwellers, who represented 25 percent of the population trying to live off the land.) Private charity accounted for only 6 percent of the funds altogether spent on the poor in 1932. Public welfare was unequal to the other 94 percent. Municipal income came from taxes on real estate, all grossly overappraised. When local taxes fell 20 or 30 percent behind payment, cities cut their costs by reducing such services as maintaining roads and clearing snow.

It was extremely hard for people to get on a relief roll. Before an applicant could be considered, he had to sell all his possessions, including his home, cancel all his insurance policies and become literally destitute. The social stigma attached to relief discouraged all but the most needy. Ten states deprived the recipients of relief of their constitutional right to vote. Some churches barred families who received welfare from attending services. *Fortune* also disclosed in September 1932 that only 25 percent of duly qualified families were getting some form of relief. Unmarried people and couples without children were often excluded.

Schools, their children and teachers, suffered most on account of the improvidence or incapacity of local government to meet the depression. At the outset teachers' pay was cut to finance welfare. As the school population grew, classes became ever more overcrowded, textbooks dirtier and more dog-eared. At last schoolteachers were even denied their pay. In 1932 a million children were not being educated because of lack of funds. In Dayton, Ohio, schools were open but three days a week. In Arkansas more than 300 schools were shut for ten months of the year.

Before 1932 no state had a program for unemployment insurance. In 1929 only eleven states provided old age pensions. The total sum paid was $220,000. In 1931 there were 3.8 million one-parent families headed by a woman and only 19,280 of these families received any form of state aid. The average monthly award varied from $4.33 in Arkansas to $69.31 in Massachusetts. The Massachusetts award was the highest in any of the states but, even so, the yearly total was only $832, well below the sum of $2,000 that economists considered sufficient to supply an average family with basic necessities.

New York State was the first to accept state responsibility for relief on a massive scale. Here the influence of Governor Franklin D. Roosevelt was decisive. During the winter of 1930–1931 he had the State Department of Social Welfare and the State Charities Aid Association undertake a joint study of unemployment and relief. Their report insisted that the greater part of relief must come from public, and not private, funds. The Assembly, dominated by the Republicans, was reluctant and Roosevelt used a well-planned radio campaign to focus public opinion on the need for state aid. Thus he put pressure on the Assembly. It established a Temporary Emergency Relief Administration (TERA) to help city and county governments solve the problem of relief. The first administrator was a New York social worker, Harry Hopkins.

Men, women, and children who could find no sustenance at home simply took to the roads—more particularly the railroads where they became nonpaying, unwanted, stowaway passengers. By 1932 there were between one and two million roaming the states on freight cars. The transients or vagrants were a mix of hoboes, dispossessed farmers and sharecroppers, unemployed school leavers, and unemployable middle-class executives. Newton D. Baker told the *New York Times* of May 4, 1932, how

Every group in society is represented in their ranks from the college graduate to the child who has never seen the inside of the schoolhouse. Expectant mothers, sick babies, young childless couples, grim-faced middle-aged dislodged from lifetime jobs—on they go, an index of insecurity in a country used to the unexpected. We think of nomads of the Desert—now we have nomads of the Depression.

Novelist Thomas Wolfe contrasted the wretched plight of the dispossessed at night in New York with the shimmering skyscrapers of commerce nearby. To him these were towering symbols of indifference and man's inhumanity to man. Above and beyond the public toilets frequented by vagrants were

the giant hackles of Manhattan shining coldly in the cruel brightness of the winter night. The Woolworth Building was not fifty yards away, and a little farther down were the silver spires and needles of Wall Street, great fortresses of stone and steel that housed enormous banks. The blind injustice of this . . . seemed the most brutal part of the whole experience, for there . . . in the cold moonlight, only a few blocks away from this abyss of human wretchedness and misery, blazed the pinnacles of power where a large section of the entire world's wealth was locked in mighty vaults.

His point was that an economic system that tolerated exploitation to the extent of widespread unemployment and pitiful destitution could surely not survive indefinitely. People expected federal intervention, that is, specifically, presidential action, to raise the Great Depression.

Herbert Hoover brought a variety of talents and experience, both political and commercial, to the presidency in 1929 but, when he left office in March 1933, he was condemned as inefficient and inhumane. An apocryphal story has Hoover walking along the street with Andrew Mellon whom he asked for a nickel to make a phone call to a friend. "Here's a dime," replied the secretary of the treasury. "Call up both of them."

Hoover's cardinal sin was that he failed to raise the Great Depression. It is a popular, but erroneous, misconception that he did nothing about it. Critic Robert S. McElvaine observes, "He was a man of principle but his inflexibility proved his undoing in the face of economic collapse." He believed that his ideas about politics and economics were unassailable because they had been forged in, and tempered by, long experience. He recognized that enterprises such as public utilities entailed common interests and carried public responsibility. Accordingly, they must be regulated by government acting on behalf of its citizens. Nevertheless, government had no right to interfere with a free market economy. The American system had achieved the highest standard of living in the world precisely because the power of the federal government was limited. The economy allowed equality of opportunity and encouraged individual initiative. In his *1933: Characters in Crisis,* Herbert Feis, then an economic adviser in the State Department, recalls "Hoover was not an insensitive nor inhumane man; quite the contrary. But he could not grasp or would not face the grim realities which called for deviations from principles and practices that he deemed essential to American greatness and freedom."

However, Hoover was sensitive to growing areas of discontent against his own party. One such was in the very seedbed of Republicanism, the farm belt of the Midwest and Great Plains, from which the party had garnered seven presidents. Farmers already caught in the grip of agricultural recession resented the domination of their party by eastern interests. Since the farm belt would always play a pivotal role in the outcome of elections, Hoover recognised that he must improve the farmers' lot. He had first called the Seventy-First Congress into a special session before the crash in April 1929 to consider the pressing problems of agriculture.

Hoover would not countenance legislation on the lines of the McNary-Haugen proposals. Therefore, the Agricultural Marketing Act of June 1929 was intended to provide the farmers with a form of self-help. The act established a Federal Farm Board with funds of $500 million that it was to use to create farmers' marketing cooperatives and so-called "stabilization corporations." The stabilization corporations were assigned the task of storing and then disposing of surplus in order to help stabilize farm prices. What the farm boards could not do was restrict production, and excessive production in 1931 and 1932 resulted in huge surpluses and, thus, prices fell through the floor.

Moreover, the board clearly had no power to control the worldwide agricultural depression. As the European depression deepened, Europe reduced its imports of American produce even further while trying to sell its own surplus grain on the world market. The consequences of excessive surplus at home and abroad were devastating. The price of wheat fell from an average of $1.04 a bushel in 1929 to 67 cents in 1930 and then to between 30 cents and 39 cents in 1932. These prices were well below the cost of production. A system of voluntary cooperatives could not handle problems on this scale. The Farm Board appealed to Congress to restrict acreage and production.

Hoover's attempts to bring relief by raising the tariff on farm produce were also futile. Apart from sugar and butter, fruit and wool, very few imports were in competition with American agriculture. Tariff legislation had traditionally become a subject for barter between different interest groups in Congress. The Hawley-Smoot Act, which became law on June 17, 1930, was a classic instance of this. The average rates on all duties rose to new heights. The Fordney-McCumber tariff of 1922 had set the previous record with average duties of 33 percent. But it was surpassed by the Hawley-Smoot tariff in which the average duty was

40 percent. While affording some relief to diary and meat products, the new tariff was of no general use to agriculture. In turn, Britain and Germany abandoned free trade and set up economic barriers of their own. Other nations soon followed suit. International trade, already impeded by the depression, was thus further reduced.

Hoover met the problem of unemployment partly by calling on local government and private welfare agencies to provide extra employment and partly by extending the amount of public works undertaken by the federal government. He secured additional appropriations from Congress for public works from $250 million in 1929 to $410 million in 1930 and, thereafter, by stages to $726 million in 1932. However, individual welfare schemes were undernourished and quite inadequate for the needs of the time. There was more to welfare work than just forming committees. The Federal Home Loan Bank Act of July 1932 was intended to save mortgages by easing credit. It established a series of Federal Home Loan Banks to ease the problems of loan associations, insurance companies, and other organizations involved in mortgages. However, since the maximum loan was only to 50 percent of the value of the property, the measure was largely ineffective.

The most significant recovery measure of the early depression was the Reconstruction Finance Corporation (RFC). The RFC was based on the War Finance Corporation of the war and chartered by Congress on January 22, 1932, to lend funds of $500 million to banks and railroads, construction companies and various lending associations, especially those in danger of bankruptcy. This was the agency that funded projects such as the Golden Gate Bridge in San Francisco and the Mississippi River Bridge in New Orleans. But its support of certain banks made it an easy target for criticism. The first president of the RFC was noted banker Charles Gates Dawes, author of the Dawes plan on reparations and former vice-president under Coolidge. Shortly after Dawes retired from the RFC and returned to the Central Republic Bank of Chicago, the RFC awarded his bank a loan of $90 million, a sum almost as great as its supposed deposits.

However, the mood of the dispossessed changed dramatically in 1931 and 1932. Hitherto, the depression had astonished a generation who accepted the legend of the richest nation in the world without understanding how the dream could turn sour. The government faced truculent, disruptive action by farmers and war veterans.

It was the countryside that stirred itself first. The first signs of unrest came in isolated incidents of violence born of incredible frustration at the turn of events. Such was the Cow War, in which Iowa dairy farmers resisted the state's compulsory TB tests on cattle. Farmers armed with clubs and staves turned on state deputies appointed to oversee the tests and were only quelled by the intervention of the state militia equipped with tear gas.

Various farm groups organized themselves as the Farmers' Holiday Association. It eventually fell under the charismatic leadership of Milo Reno who had first proposed a farm strike in 1927. This would have involved farmers refusing to market their produce in order to make the towns and cities aware of their problems and bring about a rise in prices. They turned their slogan into a jingle:

> Let's call a "Farmers' Holiday"
> A Holiday let's hold
> We'll eat our wheat and ham and eggs
> And let them eat their gold.

The use of the term "Holiday" in place of "strike" was intended as a sardonic parody of the way banks closed their doors on bank holidays to customers they could not serve.

Farmers who could not meet their mortgage payments lost their farms in foreclosures. The dramatic increase in the number of farms being sold in the early depression is suggested in statistics released by the U.S. Department of Agriculture Bureau of Agricultural Economics. In 1929 58.0 farms in every 1,000 changed hands and of these 19.5 were forced sales; in 1932 76.6 farms in every 1,000 changed hands and 41.7 of these sales were forced. Thus did years of work count for nothing and a generation of farmers was dispossessed. Their grievances at such injustice took more serious and constructive forms. In early 1933 as many as seventy auctions of farm property took place in which the friends and neighbors of the dispossessed thwarted the auctioneers by

As president, Herbert Hoover (1929–1933) failed to fulfill his reputation as "the Great Engineer" who had fed Europe and America in World War I and sustained business as secretary of commerce in the 1920s. (Photo by Harris and Ewing of 1928; Library of Congress).

bidding a few cents for the items on sale and then returning them to their original owner. Such auctions were called "penny auctions" or "Sears Roebuck Sales." One farm in Haskins, Ohio, with a mortgage debt of $800 was acquired for $1.90. When such tactics did not work and an outsider took the farm he might be intimidated by an empty noose placed on a tree or with threats. After a spate of penny auctions, John A. Simpson, president of the National Farmers Union, warned the Senate Committee on Agriculture in January 1933, "The biggest and finest crop of revolutions you ever saw is sprouting all over the country right now." Edward A. O'Neal III, president of the American Farm Federation, said, "Unless something is done for the American farmer we'll have revolution in the countryside in less than twelve months." Because of mounting pressure Governors Charles Bryan of Nebraska and Floyd Olson of Minnesota signed state bills declaring a moratorium on farm mortgages.

War veterans provided a greater show of discontent. In 1924 Congress had voted a pension or bonus to war veterans. This was in the form of adjusted compensation certificates redeemable in 1945. In the early years of the depression veterans called for immediate payment when the money could be put to more effective use for personal relief, financial investment, or material support for their families. In Portland, Oregon, they elected Walter W. Waters, a former sergeant and cannery superintendent, to organize a march to the Capitol to dramatize their plight. This was the Bonus Expeditionary Force (BEF) that attracted thousands of veterans and transients as it moved across the country in the spring and summer of 1932. Other groups from different regions also began streaming into Washington, many with their wives and children. By mid-June there were between 15,000 and 20,000 bonus marchers in the city. They took up residence in various Hoovervilles. Their main camp was in southeast Washington on the other side of the Anacostia River across the Eleventh Street Bridge.

Roused by the bonus marchers' desperate plight, the House, on June 15, by a vote of 226 to 175, passed an enabling bill proposed by Congressman Wright Patman of Texas. It would have allowed immediate payment of the bonus. The estimated cost was $2.4

A detachment of 700 men from the Far West among the bonus army encampment on the east side of the Capitol in Washington, D.C., vowing they will remain there until Congress enacts a special bonus law to provide veterans with their pensions immediately. (Photo by Underwood and Underwood of July 13, 1932; Library of Congress).

billion. However, the bill was rejected by the Senate on June 17. Some veterans agreed to leave, using loans for travel home provided by the government and to be deducted from the payment in 1945. Others refused to budge. Their truculent mood disturbed both President Hoover and the commissioners of the District of Columbia whose anxiety increased when Congress adjourned.

On the night of June 17 some bonus marchers had begun to occupy a group of derelict red brick buildings on Pennsylvania Avenue. The occupation had the tacit support of the District police superintendent, Pelham D. Glassford, a retired brigadier who sympathized with the veterans and had food and blankets distributed to them. The squatters along Pennsylvania Avenue within three blocks of the Capitol itself were a humiliating eyesore to the Hoover administration because their presence exposed the inadequacy of the federal government. The authorities feared that the uninvited guests were harbingers of a revolution. For the first time since 1918 the White House gates were chained, barricades were erected around the executive mansion, and traffic was not allowed within a block. Secretary of War Patrick Hurley was determined to use any incident as a pretext for dislodging the marchers. One such occurred on July 28, 1932.

The evacuation of a small building on the corner of 3rd Street and Pennsylvania Avenue deteriorated into a full-scale riot. This was sufficient excuse for Hurley to summon federal troops under General Douglas MacArthur who, despite counsel of moderation from his aide, Major Dwight D. Eisenhower, proceeded to disperse the bonus marchers with infantry, cavalry, and tanks. The veterans were driven back across the Eleventh Street Bridge into the main camp at Anacostia Flats. The tents, shacks, and packing crates of the camp in which the bonus marchers were sheltered were all set on fire. The entire camp was razed to the ground. Two babies died of tear gas. A soldier deliberately ran a bayonet through the leg of a seven-year-old boy, Eugene King, who was trying to rescue his pet rabbit. As night fell women and children were ferried to Salvation Army hostels. Men with battered heads and eyes streaming from tear gas were carried off to the hospital by ambulance. The routed marchers were officially barred from Maryland and Virginia although police escorted a few stragglers through Maryland to Pennsylvania whence they were herded in turn by state police to Ohio. And so from state to state the weary band was dispersed. By the fall they were indistinguishable from the rest of America's huge transient population.

It was clear that by his actions, a mixture of arrogance, insensitivity, and cowardice, compounded by MacArthur's excesses, that Hoover had committed a gross political blunder that was to cost him dear. It was as if he were stage-managing his own defeat in the election of 1932.

The Rise of Franklin Delano Roosevelt

The Republican National Convention assembled in Chicago on June 14, 1932, and renominated Hoover dutifully but without any enthusiasm. The platform repeated the time-honored commitment to the gold standard, protection of the tariff, and traditional government economies whilst supporting the farmers' cooperative efforts to control agricultural production. On the issue of prohibition it was neither wet nor dry but moist, favoring resubmission of the Eighteenth Amendment to the states.

Hoover and the Republican party were most uneasy about what lay ahead. By 1932 the impact of the Great Depression was causing an irreversible shift in the political loyalty of millions. This was especially apparent among farmers, blacks, and the middle class. Thus, after decades of status as a party of honorable opposition, the Democrats were about to emerge as the natural party of government. In part, this was because the persuasive lobby of wets committed to the repeal of prohibition helped transform it after the resounding defeat of 1928. Opposition to national prohibition played a decisive part in the election of 1932 and its aftermath.

The role played by Democratic national chairman and General Motors executive John Julius Raskob in remodeling the party was pivotal. It had been Raskob's ambition to transform the Democratic party into "an organization which parallels, as nearly as conditions will permit, a first rate business enterprise operating all the time; spending money effectively and meeting the real issues at hand." Raskob recognized that the recipe for sustained electoral success was continuous work. Accordingly, in 1929 he put Jouett Shouse of Kansas, a former congressman, and Charles Michelson, former Washington correspondent for the New York *World,* in charge of publicity. Within two years he had created a permanent, professional national organization, the first of its kind and a model for the future.

The leading contender for the Democratic presidential nomination in 1932 was Governor Franklin D. Roosevelt of New York.

FDR's background, upbringing, and early political career barely suggest that he could become the greatest president of the United States in the twentieth century. He was born on January 30, 1882, in Hyde Park, New York, the only son of an elderly father and youthful mother. They were a wealthy Hudson River family of Anglo-Dutch extraction. Thus FDR received a privileged education. He entered Harvard in 1900 and finished his undergraduate courses in three years. In 1904 he went to Columbia University Law School and in 1905 married a fifth cousin, Anna Eleanor Roosevelt, who was given away by her uncle, President Theodore Roosevelt. In time the couple had four sons and a daughter. After passing the New York State bar examinations, FDR entered a Wall Street law firm as a junior clerk, but his political ambitions were already set on the presidency. In 1910 he was elected state senator for the Democrats and at Albany he led an insurgent group against Tammany Hall.

In 1913 President Woodrow Wilson brought him into his administration as assistant secretary of the navy—like Theodore Roosevelt before him—and he made himself popular with admirals, cultivated labor and business, but found himself in open disagreement with his superior, Secretary of the Navy Josephus Daniels, and Woodrow Wilson himself, over such matters as naval expenditures and rearmament. However, he was reconciled with Tammany Hall when he worked for Al Smith in 1918 during Smith's campaign for governor of New York. Thus in 1920 FDR was nominated for the vice-presidency as a candidate acceptable to Wilsonian, independent, and Tammany Democrats alike. He even gained by the rout of the Democrats that year because he had the advantage of national exposure without carrying any responsibility for the defeat.

At this point greater tragedy struck him when in 1921 he contracted poliomyelitis. It was incorrectly diagnosed and treated at first and it left him permanently paralyzed from the waist down. Against the wishes of his always indulgent and interfering mother but supported by his energetic wife and his closest confidant, political reporter Louis M. Howe, he concentrated first on gaining physical strength and then resumed his political career. Urged by Smith and supported by Raskob, he became Democratic candidate for governor of New York in 1928 when Al Smith ran for the presidency, winning by 25,000 votes whereas Smith, himself, lost the state.

As governor, Roosevelt treated the traditional problems of industrial monopolies and the new ones of the depression. He achieved cheaper electric power, both through the promotion of public power and more effective regulation of private utility companies. He met the two problems of unemployment and conservation by putting unemployed young men to work on land reclamation and tree-planting throughout the state. In short, no governor worked harder to ease the depression.

In a speech of April 7, 1932, Roosevelt declared that the country faced a more grave emergency than in 1917. He compared the Hoover administration to Napoleon at Waterloo who had staked too much on his overextended cavalry and forgotten his infantry. Thus the administration had forgotten "the infantry of our economic army." "These unhappy times call for the building of plans that rest upon the forgotten, the unrecognized but the indispensable units of economic power, . . . that put their faith once more in the forgotten man at the bottom of the economic pyramid." Precisely because of his illness, the wealthy Roosevelt could identify with the forgotten man and, by virtue of the way he had fought his illness to resume a political career, he became a symbol of the will to triumph over terrible adversity.

However, to political pundits, Roosevelt seemed to offer little beyond his illustrious name. He was much criticized by conservatives and radicals alike. Underlying all the censure, sometimes implicit and sometimes spoken, was the notion that here was simply another Hoover. This was a theme common to the Scripps-Howard chain of newspapers and to the *Nation*. Walter Lippmann opined of Roosevelt in the *New York Herald Tribune* of January 8, 1932, "He is a pleasant man who, without any important qualifications for the office, would very much like to be President."

Roosevelt entered the Democratic National Convention, which met in Chicago on June 27, 1932, with a large majority of delegates pledged to support him. However, his majority fell substantially short of the two-thirds necessary at that time to secure a presidential nomination. Roosevelt's nomination on the fourth ballot came as a result of the intercession of Joseph P. Kennedy of Boston with William Randolph Hearst. The newspaper magnate effectively controlled the California delegation, nominally led by William Gibbs McAdoo. Hearst was in his mansion at San Simeon, California. Kennedy called him by phone. Unless Hearst released the California votes, Roosevelt's nomination would be blocked. It would be the deadlock of 1924 all over again. Either Al Smith or Newton D. Baker would claim the prize. Hearst detested Smith for impeding his own political ambitions after the war. He distrusted Baker because he was a champion of the League of Nations and Hearst was an inveterate isolationist. On July 1, William Gibbs McAdoo, anticipating the withdrawal of Mississippi from Roosevelt's side, announced that California "did not come here to deadlock this convention, or to engage in another desolating contest like that of 1924." He then gave all forty-four votes of California to Roosevelt. Thus was he revenged on Al Smith for having been denied the nomination in 1924. Illinois, Indiana, and Maryland came round to Roosevelt. At the end of the fourth ballot he had 945 votes.

Only Smith from his hotel remained obdurate and refused to allow his delegates to release their votes to make the nomination unanimous. Not only was he resentful of Roosevelt's success as governor but also embittered by the way Roosevelt struck bargains with his former allies in order to secure the nomination. As H. L. Mencken observed, Smith looked on Roosevelt as a cuckoo who had seized his nest.

Until 1932 it was the custom for nominees to deliver their acceptance speeches weeks later from their homes. This was what Hoover did in Washington on August 11. However, Roosevelt broke all precedents. He arranged to fly to Chicago immediately

General Douglas MacArthur, army chief of staff, personally supervised the breaking up of the bonus camps, razing them to the ground, and finally dispersing the exhausted veterans and their families—a maneuver that contributed to the further decline of Hoover in public esteem. (Photo by Underwood and Underwood of July 29, 1932; Library of Congress).

to address the convention that had nominated him. The decision
to fly was itself a novelty when commercial flights were infrequent. Roosevelt proved he was good copy across the nation as
well as in his state. In his address of July 2 he declared: "I pledge
you, I pledge myself, to a new deal for the American people. Let
us all here constitute ourselves prophets of a new order of competence and of courage. This is more than a political campaign; it
is a call to arms. Give me your help, not to win votes alone, but
to win in this crusade to restore America to its own people." The
next day a cartoon by Rollin Kirby was reproduced in papers
across the country. It showed a farmer looking at an airplane in
the sky. The plane bore the inscription "New Deal." The phrase,
coined by Judge Samuel Rosenman of New York, was a hybrid
of Theodore Roosevelt's "Square Deal" and Woodrow Wilson's
"New Freedom." To boost public morale Roosevelt's campaign
song, now played everywhere, was the optimistic "Happy Days
Are Here Again."

The Democratic platform of 1932 not only favored repeal of
the Eighteenth Amendment but also proposed loans to the states
for unemployment relief, approved the principle of old age insurance to be achieved by state laws, and advocated control of surplus crops whilst paying lip service to the orthodox wisdom of a
balanced budget and a hard currency.

Roosevelt replaced John J. Raskob as chairman of the Democratic National Committee with Jim Farley, secretary of the New
York Democratic Committee. Farley was an Irish Catholic who
had never belonged to Tammany Hall. Unlike Raskob, he had
the common touch. He neither drank nor smoked. Yet he was a
wet and enough of a celebrity in his own right as a salesman of
construction materials to advertise Lucky Strike cigarettes for the
American Tobacco Company. Raskob's appointee as publicity
agent, Charles Michelson, released a barrage of publicity for FDR
and against Hoover. Roosevelt's academic advisers, the Brain
Trust, led by Professors Raymond Moley, Rexford G. Tugwell,
and Adolf A. Berle, Jr., of Columbia University, and General
Hugh S. Johnson, provided well-researched data and effective
briefs for Roosevelt to draw on.

Roosevelt's strategy was to concentrate on the West. New

York he knew he could hold and the South was not likely to treat him the way it had Al Smith in 1928. In order to entice the farm vote, he toured the West and Midwest extensively, securing support from maverick Republicans and old Progressives, such as George W. Norris, Henry C. Wallace, Basil Manly, and Judson King. Radio was even more important in the campaign than it had been in 1928. Hoover's sententiousness was no match for Roosevelt's uncanny ability to project exuberance, compassion, and humor. Indeed, his personality transcended the campaign.

In the election of November 8, 1932, Roosevelt received 22,809,638 votes, 57.4 percent of the total, against Hoover's 15,758,901, 39.7 percent. In the electoral college he had 472 votes to Hoover's 59. He carried all but six states, a larger victory than any Democrat before him. Norman Thomas, the Socialist candidate, received only 881,951 votes and William Z. Foster, the Communist candidate, took only 102,785. Both failed to exploit and gain from widespread unrest and discontent. In Congress the Democrats had 310 seats in the House and the Republicans had 117. In the Senate the Democrats had 60 seats, the Republicans 35.

Both observers and participants alike thought prohibition had been decisive in the outcome of the election. The *New York Times* of November 10, 1932, calculated that the forthcoming Seventy-third Congress would have 342 wet congressmen and 61 wet senators. Eleven states had held referenda on prohibition during the elections. In nine states the electorate voted to repeal state laws on prohibition. In Connecticut and Wyoming sizable majorities petitioned Congress for repeal of national prohibition. As the historian of repeal, David Kyvig, observes, the juxtaposition of three things: the election of 1932; the repeal movement; and the Great Depression produced an electoral result that seemed absolutely clear. People wanted a change of government; the repeal of prohibition; and new economic policies.

Hunger and Thirst

National prohibition was being made a scapegoat for the Great Depression. Arguments against prohibition were neither more nor less true than before the Wall Street Crash but its repeal was effectively urged by those who thought here was a panacea for the country's economic ills. Hence, hunger was a better advocate than thirst. It was far more eloquent against prohibition than any speech or sentence. As historian John D. Hicks explains, "It was the psychology of depression that made people change their minds. In prosperous times voters could tolerate the inefficiency of prohibition, make jokes about it, let it ride. But with the advent of depression its every fault was magnified, and the best jokes turned stale. The people were in a mood for change. Zealots who had promised the millennium as a result of prohibition, and had delivered bootleggers and racketeers instead, were in a class with politicians who had promised prosperity and delivered adversity. It was about time to wipe the slate clean and start over."

The AAPA decided to provide the public with more substantial evidence of the failure of prohibition than it had received hitherto. It created departments of research and information under John G. Gebhart, a New York social worker. His task was to collate information and publicize the ills of prohibition. Between April 1928 and January 1931 his department distributed over a million copies of thirteen pamphlets.

The AAPA's series of well-researched pamphlets brought public recognition of the need for a full-scale and reliable government enquiry into prohibition. In office, Herbert Hoover expanded his original plan for a national investigation into prohibition. Under the chairmanship of George W. Wickersham, who had served under Taft as attorney general, the eleven commissioners met for nineteen months from May 28, 1929. The commission elicited advice from experts, both academic and professional, on such subjects as crime and courts, police and prisons, and juvenile delinquency. The vast majority of people writing to, and appearing before, the commission told members in no uncertain terms that prohibition was not working and that it should be repealed.

The Wickersham Commission issued its final report on January 7, 1931. Although as many as seven members of the commission were openly critical of prohibition, all but one signed a final summary endorsing it. The contradiction between the individual reports declaring for reform and the shared summary declaring for further trial that had been forced on the commission by Hoover

caused an uproar in the press. For example, Franklin P. Adams
ridiculed the commission in a famous satirical verse for the *New
York World* in February 1931:

> Prohibition is an awful flop.
>   We like it.
> It can't stop what it's meant to stop.
>   We like it.
> It's left a trail of graft and slime,
> It don't prohibit worth a dime,
> It's filled our land with vice and crime.
>   Nevertheless, we're for it.

Hitherto, it had been generally assumed by both sides that
women supported the Eighteenth Amendment. In fact, women
were just as sensitive to the scandal of prohibition as men and
became equally militant in their opposition to it. Their opposition
in a new lobby, the Women's Organization for National Prohibition
Reform (WONPR), was decisive in the movement for repeal.
The WONPR was the creation of Pauline Morton Sabin, wife of
Charles H. Sabin, president of Guaranty Trust, a Morgan bank.
He was also treasurer of the AAPA. Not only did she persuade
New York socialites Mrs. Coffin Van Rensselaer, Mrs. Caspar
Whitney, and others, to join her, but she also enlisted upper-class
women in the regions, all with time on their hands and a flair for
publicity. Joining the WONPR became the fashionable thing to
do. A "Sabin woman" could be received anywhere. On May 28,
1929, twenty-four such socialites from eleven states met at Chicago's fashionable Drake Hotel to launch the WONPR. Chicago
was chosen rather than New York because its widely publicized
crime problem was indissoluble from prohibition.

At the WONPR's first national convention, held in Cleveland
in 1930, the Sabin women declared for outright repeal of prohibition. Pauline Sabin attached great importance to a huge membership. She understood that protest movements could succeed only
if they continued to grow. As chairman, she worked assiduously
from a small office in New York, writing articles, enrolling members, and making speeches. In April 1931 the WONPR claimed
300,000 members altogether and in 1932 it claimed 600,000 members in forty-one state branches.

Once the election was over and leading politicians had accepted the result as a clear indication that the public wanted repeal, events moved quickly. Repeal was necessarily the first step to raise the depression. Thus, where Congress would act ahead of Roosevelt's inauguration, and act decisively, was in the matter of prohibition. Republican Senator John J. Blaine of Wisconsin drafted a new constitutional amendment to be ratified by state legislatures. It proposed three things: an end to national prohibition; that the federal government retain the right to protect dry states against the importation of liquor; and that Congress should have concurrent power with the states to forbid the return of the saloon. On February 16, 1933, Senator Joseph T. Robinson, Democratic majority leader, led a group of senators who revised the Blaine measure to provide for ratification by specially elected state conventions, and removed the provision to prevent the return of the saloon. Thus they gave the Twenty-First Amendment its definitive form. The new amendment repealed the Eighteenth Amendment while prohibiting the importation of intoxicating liquor into states that forbade it. Moreover, the amendment was to be subject to ratification by state conventions within seven years. In this final form the resolution was approved by the Senate by 63 votes to 23 on February 16, 1933. On February 20, 1933, it was passed by the House by a vote of 289 votes to 121.

On April 10, 1933, the first state convention to vote for repeal was held in Michigan at Lansing. Of the one hundred delegates elected to consider ratification of the Twenty-First Amendment on April 3 only one was a dry. As convention followed convention it became clear that even such traditionally dry states as Alabama, Arkansas, and Tennessee now favored repeal. It was rare for the wet majority to fall below 60 percent. Of the total popular vote, 15 million, or 72.9 percent, favored repeal.

The federal government precipitated repeal by anticipating it. One of Roosevelt's first acts, after taking office on March 4, 1933, was to request a special session of Congress on March 13 to revise the Volstead Act, pending repeal of prohibition, to allow beer of 3.2 percent alcohol. Among his arguments was the need for additional federal revenue that could be raised by a tax on beer. Thus beer became legal under new federal dispensation on April 7, 1933. It was freely consumed on that day in Washington and in nineteen states. It was so scarce in New York that the stock joke was that people longed for prohibition so that they could get a drink. A week later an Associated Press release claimed that the federal government had already taken $4 million in license fees and taxes on barrels of beer. A Federal Alcohol Control Administration was established by FDR under the National Recovery Administration on December 4, 1933.

Best Cellars

Unfortunately, the repeal of prohibition was not the end of the story for criminal syndicates.

Deep public outrage at the scope of criminal activities was, nevertheless, somewhat appeased by the entrapment and conviction in 1931 of the most outrageous criminal, Al Capone. He was caught not for his most notorious crimes but, on the orders of Hoover and Mellon, for income tax evasion, thereby bypassing his known suborning of Chicago's officers and police. He was found guilty and sentenced to a total of eleven years' imprisonment, fined $50,000, and charged $30,000 in costs—a record for tax avoidance to that time. Capone was imprisoned first in the Atlanta Penitentiary and later in the newly opened prison at Alcatraz where he eventually slid into madness, a victim of neurosyphilis. As actress and screenwriter Mae West observed, "There are no withholding taxes on the wages of sin."

However, the elimination of Capone was a comparatively minor achievement given the scale of underworld activities as a whole. The Wall Street Crash was as crucial an event to the underworld as to the rest of society. During the depression gangsters' clients, shorn of their former affluence, could no longer afford their special services. Because of recession the gangs were once more in competition with one another. Rivalries that had become submerged in the revelry of the twenties once more burst into the open. Especially notorious was the feud between Giuseppe ("Joe the Boss") Masseria and Salvatore Maranzano in New York.

The settlement of their so-called Castellammarese War of 1930–1931 was synonymous with the institution of a Mafia on a national scale.

The pivotal players in New York were Salvatore Lucania and Meyer Lansky. Lucania belonged to the new generation of Italians and Sicilans who formed alliances based on common interests with men from different ethnic groups. His right hand man was Francesco Castiglia, or Frank Costello, of Calabria and his closest ally was Meyer Lansky, a Jew. An exceptional mathematician, Lansky began his career in organized crime as an automobile mechanic who provided gangs with fleets of souped-up trucks and cars before he entered the bootlegging industry. Lansky and Lucania were protégés of Arnold Rothstein and members of the Big Seven group from its inception. When Rothstein was killed in 1928 over a gambling debt, they became his heirs and continued to run a syndicate based on a mix of ethnic groups—Italians, Jews, and Poles. Ranged against them were Sicilian gangs, such as those of Masseria and Maranzano, that prided themselves on their elite ethnic composition.

Lansky and Lucania (Lucky Luciano as he was now called after returning from a one-way ride) stirred up trouble between Masseria and Maranzano, allowing Maranzano a temporary victory. Some historians date the founding of the American Mafia to Maranzano's decisions implemented at a secret meeting of unknown date. He instituted criminal governace by a chain of command from a supreme boss of all bosses, to family bosses, and underbosses. In order to anticipate wasteful feuds families would be apportioned regional areas. Mafia historian Gaia Servadio lists the cities that were to become the new centers of syndicate crime: Boston, Buffalo, Chicago, Cleveland, Detroit, Kansas City, Los Angeles, Newark, New Orleans, Philadelphia, Pittsburgh, San Francisco, Miami, and Las Vegas. Havana in Cuba would remain open to all. New York City would be divided among five families: the old Masseria gang now led by Frank Costello and Salvatore Luciano with Vito Genovese; the old Reina gang led by Tom Gagliano with Thomas Lucchese; the Maranzano gang divided into two families, one led by Joseph Profaci and the other by Joe Bonanno;

and in Brooklyn a coalition of Philip and Vincent Mangano with Albert Anastasia.

However, the war was not yet over. On September 11, 1931, four men pretending to be income tax inspectors entered Maranzano's Park Avenue office and killed him in a most brutal fashion. Maranzano's death was a sensation in the popular press that carried lurid accounts of scores of murders of "Mustache Petes," old style bosses, across the country on September 10, 1931. However, all that Lansky and Luciano needed to do was to cut off the head of the big fish in order to bring the lesser fry into line. Lansky was twenty-nine and Luciano was thirty-four when they stood at the threshold of supreme criminal power. They succeeded in part because they did not seek the title *capo di tutti capo*.

Under Luciano the syndicate, or Mafia, exploded its traditional boundaries of recruitment. Between 1931 and 1934 it began to take in so-called full Italians, that is Italians and Italian-Americans whose parents were both Italian. Lucky realized that the Wall Street Crash that had brought incipient tensions in the underworld to a head would, in the long run, also provide it with greater stability. It gave gangsters a golden opportunity to compensate themselves against future losses in the inevitable demise of prohibition. They could now enter legitimate business with honest citizens who had lost their assets. They alone could provide funds for needy businessmen. For instance, in 1931 Frank Costello formed an association with the Mills Novelty Company of Chicago, the largest manufacturers of slot machines. With a partner, Dandy Phil Kastel of New Orleans, he established a whole series of companies such as the Tru-Mint, the Village Candy, and the Monroe Candy companies. Their machines were placed in bars, candy and cigar stores, and stationery shops across the country.

With the aid of another of Rothstein's men, Frank Erickson, they developed a network of illegal off(race)track betting among small shopkeepers and their customers in the ghettos. Shopkeepers were paid $150 a week for handling the bets—the sum had been finely calculated by syndicate accountants from an average of gains, losses, and expenses. These bookkeeping businesses were safe from the police who were bribed to turn a blind eye to them. For those days when horses were not running they developed the numbers racket, a means of allowing punters the opportunity to bet a few cents on the random selection of a three digit figure, anything from 000 to 999. The numbers racket was first tried in Harlem in 1925 among poor blacks whom their white predators thought too immature to see how slim were the chances of winning. A craze developed and spread. Thousands of people were required to run the system across the country and all shared in the profits on a percentage basis.

The Chicago conclave of 1931 was not the end of the matter. Over the next three years subsequent meetings were held in Cleveland, Chicago, and New York. Representatives from syndicates in New York, Chicago, Cleveland, Minneapolis, Boston, Philadelphia, Miami, New Orleans, and New Jersey sometimes met in the new Waldorf Astoria Hotel, New York City. It was one of the homes of Lucky, now a businessman, Charles Ross. On the advice of Aaron Shapiro, a Fifth Avenue lawyer, this criminal syndicate took the National Recovery Administration of June 16, 1933, as its model with a commission governing the operation and development of the principal syndicates. It seemed happy days were here to stay.

Of course, it is never truly so. For almost sixty years the Crash of 1929 held a special place in economic history and folklore and had almost assumed the enjoyable status of myth. It did seem that the controls and safeguards introduced in the 1930s by the federal government served to control the vagaries of the stock market and forestall another such crash. However, in 1987 the dramatic fall of share prices on "Black Monday," October 19, quite eclipsed the single-day record of "Black Tuesday," October 29, 1929, and spread ominous chills across world markets about the continuous perils of prosperity.

5

HAPPY DAYS ARE HERE AGAIN
Franklin D. Roosevelt and
the Early New Deal

Roosevelt and the Bank Crisis

I N EARLY 1933 the depression continued along its relentless path.
Industrial production foundered, unemployment mounted, farm
mortgage foreclosures became more common than ever, banks
failed, and state authorities could not meet their relief obligations.
One obstacle in the way of positive executive action was the
rather long period of four months between the presidential election on November 8 and inauguration on March 4. This had long
been a quadrennial problem for American politics. Accordingly,
to remedy matters, the Twentieth Amendment had already been
proposed by Senator George W. Norris of Nebraska and passed
by Congress on March 3, 1932. It eliminated the so-called "lame
duck" session of an old Congress by requiring the new Congress
to meet on January 3 following the election. It also brought
forward the date of the presidential inauguration from March 4 to
January 20. However, the Twentieth Amendment was not rati-

fied until February 1933 and thus would not take effect until 1935 and 1937.

In the meantime, there was a stultifying loss of confidence between election and inauguration. Herbert Hoover tried to arrange for a smooth transition by attempting a dialogue with Roosevelt. He tried to extract assurances from FDR that he would comply with his ideas on tariffs and taxes, currency and the budget, if only for the sake of public confidence. But Roosevelt was a past master at parrying suggestions that implied commitment to any previous policy.

A series of bank failures, most notably in February 1933, made the collapse of Hoover's intended dialogue most unfortunate. As we have observed, the weak American banking system was a prime cause of the Great Depression. Bank failures were something of a chronic feature of American economic life during the early thirties. There had been 1,345 in 1930, 2,298 in 1931, and 1,456 in 1932. By 1932 and 1933 the American banking system was in a state of acute crisis.

The crisis deepened in October 1932 when the governor of Nevada anticipated the failure of an important banking chain by closing the state banks in a bank holiday. Then at midnight on February 14, 1933, Governor William A. Comstock of Michigan issued a proclamation closing all 550 banks in the state for eight days. The crisis had been precipitated by a run on the Union Guardian Trust Company of Detroit. The Michigan bank holiday led to panic across various states and a whole series of bank holidays. In a speakeasy in New York a man in his cups asked the bartender how many states had declared bank holidays. "Thirty-eight," was the answer. "Ah!" said the customer. "That ratifies the depression!"

One important side effect of these closures was the flow of gold reserves from the Federal Reserve System and banks in New York City both to support the deposits of banks across the country and at the demand of panic-stricken foreign investors. Thus, in just over two months, from January to early March 1933, the nation's gold reserves fell from over $1.3 billion to $400 million. By early 1933 America's 18,569 banks had only about $6 billion altogether in cash to meet $41 billion in deposits. In the two days before the

Franklin Delano Roosevelt, the greatest president of the twentieth century, achieved the highest office in the United States despite his crippling condition of poliomyelitis. Identifying himself with the forgotten man at the base of the economic pyramid, he led the New Deal, a comprehensive program of legislation designed to raise the Great Depression and remedy basic inequalities in the structure of American society, before directing America's military and domestic strategies in World War II to bring the United States to a summit of global power. This publicity still for the presidential election of 1932 was said to be FDR's favorite photograph. (Library of Congress).

inauguration clients withdrew $500 million from banks across the country. Increasingly, the bank crisis made people of all classes recognize the imperative need for decisive executive action, even modified dictatorship. Walter Lippmann declared in his "Today and Tomorrow" column for the *Tribune* of February 17, 1933, that, "The danger we have to fear is not that Congress will give Franklin D. Roosevelt too much power, but that it will deny him the powers he needs."

Roosevelt stage-managed his own inauguration on March 4, 1933, with impeccable flair that captured the imagination of the entire country. Hence, Miguel Covarrubias painted the regal scene for *Vanity Fair* in the classical manner of David's *Coronation of Napoleon,* a brooding monument of ensemble. Instead of simply saying, "I do," after Chief Justice Charles Evans Hughes had read out the oath of office, Roosevelt repeated the full text. He then embarked on a stirring inaugural speech. "Let me first assert my firm belief that the only thing we have to fear is fear itself— nameless, unreasoning, unjustified terror which paralyzes needed efforts to convert retreat into advance." These ringing words resounded across the nation. No phrase had been borrowed. As the radio broadcast continued, listeners far and near were stopped in their tracks. "I shall ask the Congress for the one remaining instrument to meet the crisis—broad Executive power to wage a war against the emergency, as great as the power that would be given me if we were in fact invaded by a foreign foe." Hoover looked askance.

Roosevelt's portentous text was delivered with such impeccable diction that the audience far and wide all but tasted his words. In his narrative history, *Since Yesterday* (1939), Frederick Lewis Allen summed up the impression made by FDR on the vast radio audience thus:

You can turn off the radio now. You have heard what you wanted to hear. This man sounds no longer cautious, evasive. For he has seen that a tortured and bewildered people want to throw overboard the old and welcome something new; that they are sick of waiting, they want some-body who will *fight* this Depression for them and with them; they want leadership, the thrill of bold decision. And not only in his words but in the challenge of the very accents of his voice he has promised them what they want.

The bank crisis and FDR's determination to meet it demonstrate just how decisive would be his new start. On Sunday, March 5, Roosevelt summoned Congress into extraordinary session on Thursday, March 9, to consider the bank crisis. Taking advantage of legislation from the war that gave the president wide executive authority in case of a bank emergency, he then declared a four-day national bank holiday on Monday, March 6. He thus prevented further panic withdrawals and gold hoarding, whilst allowing time for Treasury officials to devise emergency draft legislation. During the bank holiday people improvised a temporary extra currency, a mix of barter and credit, stamps and streetcar tokens, Mexican pesos, and Canadian dollars.

The Bureau of Engraving and Printing acquired 375 extra workers and they worked round the clock printing bale after bale of money and using the outdated dies plates of 1929 since there was no time to have new ones engraved. Nevertheless, the various measures that were about to be taken to rescue the banks had already been discussed by Hoover's cabinet and advisers. However, because Hoover was irresolute and reluctant to close the banks by presidential proclamation, he failed to act on his colleagues' advice. However, FDR would act where Hoover would not and, to ensure the strategy was a success. he retained Hoover's men at the Treasury, notably Arthur Ballantine, undersecretary, and Floyd Awalt, acting comptroller of the currency.

On March 9 a special session of Congress approved the Emergency Banking Relief Act. In the House the debate lasted only forty minutes. The act provided aid for hard-pressed but solvent banks. The RFC could buy the preferred stock of banks, giving them additional operating funds from the Federal Reserve Banks. On April 19, 1933, Roosevelt forbade the hoarding and exporting of gold. He decided to do this to preempt the revival in Congress of the discredited idea of coining silver to achieve inflation. Banks examined and approved by government assessors could reopen immediately. Those that required further examination—about a quarter—could pay out only part of their deposits. After a few days banks that had previously accounted for 90 percent of all deposits were allowed to reopen.

On March 12 Roosevelt gave his first radio address, or fireside chat, as president. His aim was to make the emergency action intelligible to all and his gentle but invigorating words also encouraged reinvestment. By April over $1 billion in currency had been returned to bank deposits. The crisis was over. In the words of Frederick Lewis Allen, "The New Deal had made a brilliant beginning."

The name of Franklin Delano Roosevelt was to become synonymous with twelve years of assertive leadership, and a major extension of executive powr. This was even implied by the way Roosevelt was known simply by his initials, FDR, with their suggestion of an enclosed word FEDERAL. FDR was the only president to be elected four times and his second election in 1936 set a record for overwhelming victory. Roosevelt's enigmatic personality was the most teasing of any twentieth-century American leader, part patriarch, part child. To his allies he appeared exuberant, charming, and generous. His inviting manner often gave his visitors the impression he agreed with their recommendations and there is little doubt that, like all other leaders, but in his own special way, he used ambiguity as a political tool to rouse support or silence criticism. To his enemies he seemed a duplicitous and vindictive megalomaniac. Despite his patrician education, his experiences in practical politics and his courageous fight to overcome the crippling limitations of his paralysis combined to make him compassionate toward those with physical, social, and psychological disabilities.

He was not an intellectual. Indeed, he was not widely read. He did not have a particularly original mind nor was he capable of sustained analysis. However, he was creative in the imaginative use he could make of the superior talents of others and in the constructive use he could make of apparently conflicting ideas. "A second class intellect—but a first class temperament" was Oliver Wendell Holmes's comment on FDR. His intuitive, flexible approach allowed him to combine both new and old ideas, to retain what worked and to discard what did not. Before making his decisions he sought divers opinions and weighed the myriad questions of public interest and political consequence. His reorganization of the executive was an outstanding administrative achievement. Indeed, contemporary Washington was largely his creation. Thus, as his director of the budget observed, he was "a real artist in government."

Roosevelt transformed the presidency not only beyond its abject position in the years of the Republican ascendancy but also beyond the last formidable resurrection of the office achieved by Theodore Roosevelt and Woodrow Wilson in the progressive period. He dispatched messages to Congress along with draft legislation, and put pressure on committee chairmen and other key figures in Congress through letters and meetings. Thus, by the end of the thirties, Congress expected presidential initiatives. It looked for guidance from the administration from whom it expected a regular program of proposed legislation.

Furthermore, FDR dominated the front pages of newspapers as had no other president before and as none has done since. By his unsurpassed number of 998 press conferences, by getting his aides to answer all letters, which totaled between 5,000 and 8,000 each working day and, most of all, by his 28 radio broadcasts, called "fireside chats" by CBS manager Harry C. Butcher, FDR made himself the most accessible president since Theodore Roosevelt. Roosevelt's fireside chats were, in themselves, models of directness and simplicity, and imbued with his warmth and courage. Indeed, all his speeches and his performance of them showed grace and finish. Roosevelt was in his element with the press, sharpening his political talents and developing his special techniques in conversation, a mix of humor, seriousness, sincerity—and evasion.

Roosevelt's career before and during his presidency was much advanced by the distinctive support of his wife, Eleanor. Theirs was an astonishing political collaboration. She had had the advantage of being Theodore Roosevelt's niece but the disadvantages of being orphaned by the time she was nine and of growing up tall and awkward with protruding teeth. Yet her amazing energy, initiative, and social conscience stirred her to work for social improvement, and, in so doing, find fulfillment. Where FDR was crippled, she was mobile and she moved across the country and reported what she found back to him. But if theirs was a professionally harmonious business relationship, his longest romantic relationship was with Eleanor's part-time social secretary, Lucy Mercer Rutherford, with whom he had started an affair as early as 1913.

Being first lady was, at first, a liberating experience for Eleanor Roosevelt as she delivered lectures, visited slums, and talked to the people. Her column, *My Day,* was syndicated in 135 newspapers and she also wrote a question-and-answer column for the *Woman's House Companion.* In addition, she broadcast on radio twice a week, being sponsored by such products as Sweetheart toilet soap and Simmons mattresses, and she gave her fee to the American Friends Service Committee. But in time she found her role frustrating. Whereas she was committed to various radical and cooperative projects, she could not carry FDR with her. To her critics, her good works were ill-judged and improper interferences. Nevertheless, she enhanced the status of professional women by conferring awards on those whose research had led to social improvement like Alice Hamilton, Harvard expert on industrial toxicology. Throughout her life her constant companion was inner loneliness—the price she paid for professional fulfillment.

The New Dealers and Their Policies

Any examination of the various policies of the New Deal suggests that it was experimental, inconsistent, and diverse. One reason for this is the varied characters and qualities of the New Dealers. Roosevelt's cabinet appointments were a mix of the conventional and the progressive. Secretary of State Cordell Hull, formerly senator from Tennessee, was a typical southern conservative, except on the tariff, which he wanted to reduce, and on international affairs, on which he was, perhaps, more of an expert than anyone else of his generation. Already sixty-one in 1933, he served until 1944—longer than any other secretary of state. In time FDR proved himself closer to the undersecretary, Sumner Welles, than he did to Cordell Hull.

Migrant Mother by Dorothea Lange is one of the classic icons of the Great Depression. Dorothea Lange (1895–1965) of New York began to work as a professional photographer in San Francisco after the theft of her money forced her to abandon a planned trip around the world. Along with thousands of others, this portrait of a modern madonna was taken to publicize Farm Security Administration programs to relieve rural poverty. The young mother of thirty-two was living in a tent with her family in a camp for migrant farm workers in Nipomo, California, in February 1936. They had just sold the car tires to buy food. (Library of Congress).

The most distinctive appointments were those of Harold L. Ickes, Frances Perkins, and Henry A. Wallace. Harold L. Ickes of Chicago, who became secretary of the interior, was a progressive Republican turned Democrat. His lawyer's training gave him instant understanding of corruption in office and his progressive zeal led him to weed it out. He had a fiery temper and liked to be known as "the old curmudgeon." However, he proved a most cautious administrator. Behind his back FDR called him "Donald Duck." Frances Perkins, the first woman in any cabinet, had been a social worker who had served with Smith and FDR at Albany, and now became secretary of labor. Her colleagues disliked her assertiveness and sharp tongue. Yet in Congress Perkins made firm and valuable allies of Senator Robert F. Wagner of New York and Congressman David J. Lewis of Maryland. However, the staid leaders of the AFL disliked her simply because she was a woman. Henry A. Wallace, secretary of agriculture, was the son of Henry C. Wallace, secretary of agriculture under Harding and Coolidge. The son had deserted the Republicans for Al Smith in 1928 and for FDR in 1932. Once in office, he moved decisively into the great problems of agriculture. His solutions were pragmatic and ingenious.

Another innovation was the extensive use of a brains trust, or brain trust, a group of academic advisers somewhat like those used by Theodore Roosevelt and Woodrow Wilson. But FDR broadened the basis of selection, expanded its role, and gave wider publicity to his brains trust to the point of institutionalizing it. From Columbia University Roosevelt used Professors Raymond Moley, Adolf A. Berle, Jr., and Rexford G. Tugwell. These various academics were not just confined to the sidelines as advisers without power. Thus, Raymond Moley was assistant secretary of state in 1933, and Rexford G. Tugwell was assistant secretary of agriculture in 1933 and undersecretary in 1934–1937. Thus were intellectuals transformed into practical experts.

Roosevelt also employed General Hugh ("Ironpants") Johnson, originally of the Army and the Moline Plow Company, who helped write speeches and draft agricultural and business legislation before becoming head of the National Recovery Administration. Lawyers Thomas A. Corcoran and Benjamin

Cohen of Harvard drafted legislation that was "lawyer-proof," including the Securities Exchange Act of 1934. They were eventually superseded as presidential assistants by social worker Harry L. Hopkins who came from New York to head the Federal Emergency Relief Administration in 1933 and then served as administrator of the Works Progress Administration (1935–1938), secretary of commerce (1938–1940), and administrator of Lend-Lease in 1941. It was said of Hopkins that he had the purity of Saint Francis of Assisi combined with the shrewdness of a race-course tout.

Because of the expanded role it allotted to the federal government and the unprecedented volume of legislation, the New Deal encouraged the growth of the legal profession. More lawyers were needed to frame laws, to work as government administrators, and to advise and act for firms and private citizens. Thus, as Jerold S. Auerbach suggests, the New Deal "enabled a new professional elite to ascend to power," a privileged class drawn from those social and ethnic backgrounds that had hitherto excluded them from the white, Anglo-Saxon Protestant legal establishment. Thus "Between 1933 and 1941 professional power in the public arena shifted from a corporate elite, served by Wall Street lawyers, to a legal elite, dominated by New Deal lawyers."

Among the bright young lawyers who came to the capital to work for the New Deal were Dean Acheson, who became, for a brief time, undersecretary of the Treasury; J. W. Fulbright, who worked in the Department of Justice; Hubert Humphrey, who worked as a relief administrator; and Henry Fowler, who worked in the TVA (Tennessee Valley Authority). The Department of Agriculture attracted a formidable array of such talents, including Thurman Arnold, Abe Fortas, Adlai Stevenson, Lee Pressman, and Alger Hiss. Being lawyers, they were obsessed with process. Their obsession with mechanism was a prime factor behind the New Deal's opportunism, its predilection for compromise, and its readiness to accept the existing balance of power between competing interest groups.

The New Dealers were genuinely reform minded and confident they could improve society by reshaping it. To this end they combined the experience of national planning in World War I; the urban social reforms of Progressives at the turn of the century; the Populists' aims for agriculture and finance of the 1890s. Ralph F. de Bedts distinguishes four principal schools of thought among the New Dealers. Conservatives, such as Jesse Jones and Lewis Douglas, adhered to traditional laissez-faire economics, accepting only a limited amount of government interference to reflate the economy by way of public works, and maintaining the gold standard at all costs. Their arguments were opposed by the inflationists, successors to the Populists, who wanted monetary inflation and who were willing to use silver as legal tender and alter the gold content of the dollar. Not surprisingly, this school of thought was centered in silver states and represented by Senators Burton K. Wheeler of Montana and Key Pittman of Nevada. A third school of Progressives favored trust-busting as a means of breaking up the overwhelming influence of giant corporations for the sake of the economic health of the whole nation. These Wilsonians included Louis D. Brandeis of the Supreme Court and Felix Frankfurter of the Harvard Law School.

The most influential New Dealers we could term economic planners. They advocated central, planned intervention by the federal government in the economy, based on the academic reasoning of economic progressives like Herbert Croly and Thorstein Veblen. However, even this fourth group was divided between conservatives, who wanted to see a partnership between business and government with business in the lead, and reformers, who wanted the federal government to regulate business on lines subsequently suggested by English economist John Maynard Keynes. According to this school, not only was a balanced budget unnecessary but it might also stand in the way of recovery. By trying to balance the books orthodox accountants were further constricting demand and helping to intensify the depression they were trying to raise. The way out of the depression was in debt, carefully calculated government spending on public works to create employment in bad times and, thereafter, nicely calculated government taxation in good times. Thus the government would act as a stimulating or retarding factor according to circumstances. Among the economic planners, the conservatives were led by Raymond Moley and Hugh Johnson and the reformers by Adolf A. Berle, Jr., and Rexford G. Tugwell.

One of Roosevelt's prime political skills was his ability to synthesize different ideas. Roosevelt tried to secure the utmost from his team by treating the individuals within it as rivals who were thus obliged to compete with one another and become ever more productive. Thus FDR found the optimum solution to any problem by creating a trial by combat between different theories. Not only did the New Deal attempt to raise the depression with programs for relief and public works but Roosevelt was also concerned about malfunctioning in the American political and economic system as a whole. He was motivated to correct inequalities that the system seemed to perpetuate.

The emphases of the New Deal changed considerably in the period 1933–1938. Thus, for convenience, historians distinguish between the "first" New Deal of 1933–1935, which was primarily devoted to recovery and relief, and the "second" New Deal of 1935–1938, which was aimed at a wide reform of the economic system, by long-term measures to pass on the benefits of modern technology to farmers and consumers whilst providing safeguards against any future depressions. However, there were elements of the "first" New Deal in the "second," and vice versa. But the major emphasis in both is evident. Some historians, such as Barry D. Karl, also distinguish a "third" New Deal in the legislation of 1937 and 1938 that was intended to introduce national planning but foundered in the stormy sea of adversary politics.

The First Hundred Days and the Early New Deal

Because the Democrats had said next to nothing in the election about the need for national economic planning, the impact of the first hundred days was overwhelming. Part of Roosevelt's extraordinary political success in getting his legislation through Congress lay in the new situation. After the twelve years of Republican ascendancy, the new Congress was overwhelmingly Democratic and its freshmen were eager to respond to bold initiatives.

Contemporary revelations by an investigating subcommittee of the Senate Finance Committee had made the public aware of how great was the need for reforms in banking, securities, and the stock market. Under the skillful chairmanship of Democratic Senator Duncan U. Fletcher of Florida and the penetrating and tenacious counsel, Ferdinand Pecora, it exposed exactly how bankers had appropriated funds for their own use and also evaded income tax. The Pecora committee constituted what Frederick Lewis Allen calls "a sort of protracted coroner's inquest upon American finance." Its procession of unwilling witnesses disclosed "a sorry story of public irresponsibility and private greed" that was "spread upon the front pages of the newspapers." Perhaps the most notorious case was that of Charles E. Mitchell.

Great public outrage and the New Dealers' response to these revelations led to the Glass-Steagall Banking Act of June 1933. It separated commercial banks from their investment affiliates so that they could not use either their depositors' funds or the resources of the Federal Reserve for speculation. It also gave the Federal Reserve more control over its tributary, or member, banks. Moreover, it established the Federal Deposit Insurance Corporation (FDIC), which insured clients' deposits up to $2,500 initially, and, later in 1935, up to $5,000, $10,000 in 1950, and subsequently, $15,000. This particular proposal was deeply resented by the American Banking Association, who claimed it was governmental interference. Here the New Deal's support from western and southern banking interests was decisive in getting the act passed.

The Truth-in-Securities Act of 1933 and the Securities Exchange Act of 1934 were inspired by further discourses of the Pecora committee that J. P. Morgan, Jr., had a select list of friends to whom the House of Morgan offered stocks below the market price. They included conservative Democrats Bernard Baruch, John Julius Raskob, and William Gibbs McAdoo, and Republicans Calvin Coolidge and Owen J. Roberts. The drama of the investigations was given wit and point when, during the course of J. P. Morgan's testimony, a circus promoter managed to put a midget on Morgan's knee. Here was capitalism, both large and small, for all America to see. Another discovery was that "pools" had operated to bring about rapid rises in particular stocks, usually by spreading false reports of their value or by intense buying and selling activities. In such ways, a pool created a public appetite for the stock of Radio Corporation of America (RCA), through the agency of the brokers M. J. Meehan and Co. It succeeded in increasing the value of RCA stock from 79 to 109 in seven days, after which the participants sold out to capitalize on their good fortune. Such discoveries led the public to seek protection for investors as well as depositors. Such was the background to two important pieces of stock market legislation.

The Truth-in-Securities Act of 1933 required brokers to furnish complete information to prospective investors as to the true value of securities. Moreover, it held the underwriter and corporate officer responsible for the truthfulness of the stock's registration and the arrangements under which it was sold. The Securities Exchange Act of 1934 established the Securities Exchange Commission (SEC) as a nonpartisan agency to oversee and regulate the activities of all stock exchanges and to prevent fraud and manipulation. Outraged by threat of government surveillance, leaders of the New York Stock Exchange, which accounted for more than 90 percent of national securities trading, threatened to move the exchange to Canada if the bill were passed. But the overwhelming evidence of past malpractice convinced public and Congress alike that the measure was essential. The subsequent trial and imprisonment of Richard Whitney, president of the New York Stock Exchange, for embezzlement in 1938 confirmed public opinion of this. Those who opposed the legislation at first were later convinced that it afforded banking and securities much-needed government protection. On the advice of Raymond Moley, FDR appointed speculator Joseph Kennedy to head the SEC. Moley reasoned that, precisely because Kennedy was a speculator, he knew all the loopholes in the law, and would, therefore, be best equipped to plug them. Perhaps this was why his appointment roused the implacable, but impotent, fury of Wall Street. Kennedy's fortune was so large that he could afford to act against the interest of a speculator clan of which he was a member.

Roosevelt understood that the core of the economic crisis in 1933 was the very low level of prices. The clear remedy was to reverse the process, first by restoring confidence in the banks (which had been recently achieved), and second, by increasing the amount of currency in circulation.

On March 6, 1933, Roosevelt prohibited the redemption of currency in gold coin. On April 5 he issued an executive order whereby gold (coin, certificates, and bullion) had to be delivered to the Federal Reserve in exchange for an equivalent amount in currency or coin. Two weeks later the Treasury announced that it would no longer grant licenses for the export of gold. These several measures had the effect of taking the United States off the gold standard at home while still retaining gold to support its currency and allowing government payments abroad in gold. Lewis Douglas, director of the budget, was aghast at the very idea of taking the dollar off the gold standard. Roosevelt's action, he said, would mean "the end of Western civilization." However, on April 23, 1933, Will Rogers reminded his readers just how irrelevant was all the talk of undermining civilization by abandoning hard money. "The best way to tell when each of us went off the gold is to figure back how many years it was since we had any." Indeed, more informed conservatives than Lewis Douglas, led by such bankers as Charles Gates Dawes, Russell Leffingwell, and J. P. Morgan, Jr., approved FDR's policy of devaluation wholeheartedly.

Roosevelt's policy still left open the possibility that creditors could require debtors to repay loans in gold, instead of currency, and thus they would gain an advantage. Therefore, in June 1933 Congress passed a joint resolution that voided clauses in loan contracts requiring payment in gold. The joint resolution was upheld by the Supreme Court in 1935. The overriding intention behind these various measures was to bring down the value of the dollar on foreign exchanges while raising prices at home. By May 1933 the international value of the dollar had fallen to $0.85 in gold, meaning that other countries could buy 15 percent more American goods than before. At home wholesale prices also showed a slight increase. This success placed FDR in a quandary during the London Economic Conference attended by Secretary of State Cordell Hull in June and July. Delegates from other countries wanted a general stabilization of currencies, including the dollar,

The New Deal goes to war. Fontana Dam, completed in 1944, was built to generate electricity for the U.S. defense effort during World War II. Built on the Little Tennessee River in western North Carolina, Fontana is the highest dam east of the Rocky Mountains. Its three turbine-generator units can produce 238,500 kilowatts of electricity. (Tennessee Valley Authority).

but Roosevelt could not agree to that when the falling value of the dollar was revitalizing the American economy. Thus, for the sake of immediate economic benefits at home, FDR refused American support for any multilateral monetary policy, thereby causing considerable embarrassment to Cordell Hull in London, torpedoing the whole conference, and incurring hostility from Western Europe.

However, the policy of allowing the dollar simply to float in the exchange market produced neither the right level of exchange abroad nor economic recovery at home. Hence, on the advice of the brain trust, FDR decided to bid up the price of gold. The secretary of the treasury, William H. Woodin, was ill at this time and the undersecretary, Dean Acheson, was utterly opposed to the idea. Thus he was obliged to resign and was succeeded by Henry Morgenthau, Jr. On October 22, 1933, FDR announced that the RFC would buy gold on government account above world market price (initially at $31.36 an ounce). The price of gold was fixed by FDR and his advisers each morning. Once Roosevelt increased the price by 21 cents an ounce simply because he liked the number 21. As the price for gold rose, so the value of the dollar declined. In January 1934 the ratio stood at $34.45 = 1 ounce of gold (in comparison with March 1933 when it had stood at $20.67 = 1 ounce of gold). In effect, the dollar had been devalued by 40 percent. This was what Al Smith called a "baloney dollar."

FDR now decided to stabilize things. In the Gold Reserve Act of January 30, 1934, Congress set the price of gold at $35 an ounce. However, the silver lobby was sufficiently influential to oblige FDR and Congress to accept a Silver Purchase Act of June 1934, requiring the Treasury to buy silver both at home and abroad until a quarter of all United States monetary stocks was in silver or until the market price of silver had reached $1.29 an ounce. This quite unnecessary piece of legislation was no more than a bribe to a powerful special interest group. It seemed every cloud had a silver lining.

For its chief strike against the depression the government proposed a special agency, the National Recovery Administration (NRA). The National Industrial Recovery Act was passed by Congress on June 16, 1933 (the last of the first hundred days). It tried to achieve planning and cooperation between the three sectors of business, labor, and government. Industry received government support in its aims to reduce cutthroat competition and unfair practices and, in return, made certain concessions to labor that were thought to be in the national interest and would promote recovery. Title I of the act declared a state of national emergency and suspended some antitrust laws. It established the National Recovery Administration (NRA), required government and industry to draw up codes of practice as to business competition, and hours and wages. Public hearings would be held before the NRA to determine that the interests of business, labor, and government (as the guardian of consumer and general interests) were being observed in individual industries. After approval by the president, individual codes of practice, agreed at the hearings, would become legally binding and, thereafter, action under the code would be exempt from the antitrust laws. Section 7a declared that employees could join unions, appoint officers, and were entitled to collective bargaining. Thus the act accepted the existence of giant corporations and, to protect the public from abuse, relied solely on cooperation between business and government.

Title II authorized the president to create an emergency Public Works Administration (PWA) with $3.3 billion for "pump priming" expenditures on such public works as highways, dams, schools, and federal buildings. The PWA was put in charge of Secretary of the Interior Harold L. Ickes. General Hugh S. Johnson was given control of the NRA.

Johnson was a troubleshooter of diverse experience and considerable initiative. At the very outset he predicted for the *New York Times* of June 17, 1933, just how chequered would be the career of the NRA in an extraordinary mix of metaphors, "It will be red fire at first and dead cats afterwards. This is just like mounting the guillotine on the infinitesimal gamble that the ax won't work." Within three weeks Johnson had persuaded the heads of the textile industry to agree to the first set of NRA codes. Finally, 557 basic codes were approved, encompassing every sort of business from bottle caps to brassieres and burlesque theaters. To expedite proceedings, Johnson devised a blanket code, known as the President's Reemployment Agreement, that allowed small businesses to subscribe to the main tenets of the NRA on hours and conditions of work and wages without the inconvenience of lengthy hearings. In this way he hoped to increase employment and purchasing power quickly. Those who conformed were entitled to display an emblem, the Blue Eagle, underneath which was inscribed the motto, "We Do Our Part." To achieve maximum publicity Johnson also organized rallies and parades with songs and dances.

However, the NRA aroused widespread dissatisfaction. Consumers said the NRA had led to a steep rise in prices ahead of wages. Labor said Section 7a was inadequate for its needs and that, anyway, it could be circumvented by unscrupulous employers. Small businesses said the codes were drafted by big business in its own interests. Moreover, they did not have the resources to comply with the sort of far-reaching regulations devised for large firms. In particular, they could not always afford the minimum wages prescribed by the codes. Although it held the trump cards, big business was increasingly alarmed at the prospect of increased government regulation and the gains of organized labor. It regarded the NRA as the thin end of a most unwelcome wedge.

Unexpectedly, opposition to the NRA grew in other quarters. On March 7, 1934, Congress established the National Recovery Review Board under criminal lawyer Clarence Darrow to study monopolistic tendencies in the codes. Its report emphasized that the NRA encouraged the monopoly tactics of big business. Public respect for the NRA was damaged further when a dry cleaner was sent to jail in New Jersey for pressing trousers for less than the regular code price. Furthermore, FDR realized that Johnson, whom he admired, was something of a liability for his outspoken comments in the face of so much criticism. When the press discovered his liking for alcohol and love for his secretary, he justified her high salary by saying "she was more than a stenographer" and when they reported that he complained, "Boys you're hitting below the belt." FDR replaced him with Donald Richberg, and then relaxed some of the codes.

The final blow came on May 27, 1935, when the Supreme Court, in the case of *Schechter Poultry Corporation* v. *The United States,* invalidated the NRA. The *Schechter* case concerned an appeal by operators of a slaughterhouse against conviction for having broken the code of fair competition agreed by the live poultry industry in New York City. The Court unanimously declared that the NRA was unconstitutional on two grounds. First, Congress had delegated its powers to the executive in violation of the constitutional principles of separation of power. Second, it had wrongly laid down federal regulation of intrastate commerce as well as of interstate activities. FDR was outraged and told his press conference of May 31, 1935, "We have been relegated to the horse-and-buggy definition of interstate commerce." This bitter climax to mounting public censure of the NRA masked the fact that the NRA had to face almost insurmountable obstacles.

Years later Moley and Tugwell thought the *Schechter* decision against the NRA was a turning point for the New Deal. FDR was deeply disillusioned and abandoned his early idealism. Instead of another umbrella reform, Roosevelt decided to extract the NRA's good features, such as collective bargaining, maximum hours, and minimum wages, and enact them separately.

Agricultural recovery was just as complex a problem as industrial recovery. Moreover, its solution was even more urgent since the ills of agriculture had led to violence in some parts of the Midwest. There were two principal problems: the increasing number of mortgage foreclosures on farms; and the fact that farm purchasing power, in terms of the industrial goods farmers had to buy, was at its lowest level ever. Thus FDR proposed another series of emergency measures. On March 27, 1933, he centralized those agencies dealing with agricultural credit in the Farm Credit Administration. In April 1933 Congress passed the Emergency Farm Mortgage Act to fund emergency loans for farmers in immediate danger of losing their farms and, subsequently, short-term loans for livestock farmers. The Frazier-Lemke Farm Bankruptcy Act of June 1934 enabled farmers to recover farms previously lost when mortgages had been foreclosed and it allowed them to do so on terms prescribed by a federal court with interest set at only 1 percent.

As to long-term measures, there was the same variety of opinions about agriculture as there had been on industrial recovery. FDR and Secretary of Agriculture Henry A. Wallace conferred with farm leaders to consolidate various ideas in the Agriculture Adjustment Act of May 12, 1933. The new supervising agency was the Agricultural Adjustment Administration (AAA) that declared the following were staple crops: wheat, corn, cotton, tobacco, rice, milk, hogs—and, later, added livestock and sugar. Individual farmers made an agreement by which, in exchange for acres taken out of cultivation, they were given benefit payments. The money to finance the program came from a tax levied on processors of staple foods who passed on the tax to consumers by way of higher prices. George N. Peek became head of the AAA and, through his agents, he persuaded cotton farmers to plow under 10 million acres, a quarter of the crop, in return for benefit payments. The AAA also bought 6 million piglets that were slaughtered and processed to feed the unemployed. Thus was plenty destroyed in the midst of want. Public outcry on behalf of the slaughtered piglets vented itself in abuse of AAA officials. Few, including the farmers, understood the underlying principles behind government policy. Cotton farmers plowed under a quarter of the crop in exchange for benefits but overfertilized the remaining land so that the 1933 crop actually surpassed the 1932 crop of 13 million bales by 45,000 bales. In response to this counterproductive activity, Congress passed the Bankhead Cotton Control Act of 1934 that set production quotas for cotton and placed a prohibitive tax on all cotton sold in excess of the quota. The Kerr-Smith Tobacco Act of June 1934 introduced the same sort of restrictions on tobacco farmers.

To solve the problems of farm tenancy, the Resettlement Administration, established in April 1935 under Rexford G. Tugwell, tried to move farmers from poor land to new cooperative communities but without much success. In the Bankhead-Jones Farm Tenant Act of July 1937 Congress tried to raise farm tenants and sharecroppers to the status of owners. It established the Farm Security Administration that allowed tenants to borrow money at 3 percent interest to purchase land. Over a three-year period it made available small rehabilitation loans of an average of $350 each to 750,000 tenant farmers.

The achievements of the AAA were considerable. In 1933 10.4 million acres were taken out of production; in 1934, 35.7 million acres; and in 1935 30.3 million acres. Partly because of these policies of crop limitation and partly because of serious droughts, farm prices rose. A bushel of wheat fetched, on average, only 33 cents in 1933, but, thereafter, the price rose gradually to 88 cents in 1938. In sum, total farm income rose from $4.5 billion in 1932 to $6.9 billion in 1935. Thus farmers were a third better off financially by 1935 than they had been in 1932.

Above all, the AAA was also a creation of considerable political significance since it allowed FDR and the New Dealers to put into practice their central conception of balance between the various sections of the economic community and to persuade urban congressmen that a revitalized economy could not be built upon a declining agriculture.

Dam the Flowing Tide

The reform that became synonymous with the New Deal in the early days was the Tennessee Valley Authority. It combined agricultural and industrial blows at the depression. The valleys of southern Alleghenies were a poverty-stricken area, their soils washed away by a fatal combination of exploitive hillside farming, heavy rainfalls, and frequent flooding. Conservationists wanted a coordinated strategy to preserve the region from itself. In 1908 Theodore Roosevelt sent Congress a report of the Inland Waterways Commission that proposed a coordinated approach to the problems. By the National Defense Act of 1916, Woodrow Wilson intended the building of an Alabama nitrate plant at Muscle Shoals to avoid dependence on foreign sources of energy, especially in wartime. However, the plants were not finished until the end of the war. Sensing their future industrial potential, in 1921 Henry Ford offered the secretary of war an annual rental of $1.5 million for the facilities to produce electric power and to manufacture nitrates for use as fertilizers. However, the plants had cost $80 million to build and, thus, progressive Senator George W. Norris of Nebraska, chairman of the Senate Agriculture Committee, successfully opposed this fraudulent offer on the grounds that it was a gross act of exploitation of community resources. Norris's own bill to make the Muscle Shoals project the center of a vast water and regional power project was vetoed by Coolidge in 1928 and then by Hoover in 1929. In contrast, FDR supported the idea.

On April 10, 1933, having conferred with Norris, FDR asked Congress to create the Tennessee Valley Authority (TVA), which was achieved in an act passed on May 18, 1933. Under the terms of the act, the TVA was to complete and extend the Muscle Shoals project, creating a new 650-mile inland waterway to connect the South with the Great Lakes, the Ohio River, and the

Missouri and Mississippi river systems. The TVA was to construct new dams and improve existing ones, to control floods, to generate cheap hydroelectric power, to manufacture fertilizers, to check erosion, and to provide reforestation. It had the right to fix the resale rates of power it generated—"the yardstick"—by which the rates of competing private utility companies could also be elevated. In general, under a board of three directors, it was to promote the economic and social welfare of people in seven states, extending for an area of 80,000 square miles with a population of 2 million.

The waterway allowed the importation of sorely needed automobiles, iron, cement, and gas to the region via barges. The TVA invented new fertilizers, showed farmers how to conserve moisture in the soil, and how to use contour plowing and cover crops. Thus, farm income in Tennessee improved by 200 percent in the period 1929–49, compared with a national average improvement of 170 percent during the same time. The TVA encouraged wider and greater use of electricity and the penetration of industry into the region to benefit from cheap hydroelectric power. By the early 1940s the TVA's average annual consumption of electricity was 1,180 kilowatt-hours per person at the rate of 2 cents per hour, compared with a national average of 850 kilowatt-hours per person, at the rate of 4 cents an hour.

The TVA statute of incorporation put the manufacture and distribution of electricity into a secondary role as a byproduct. This was partly because the New Dealers expected the private power companies to complain of unfair competition to the Supreme Court. Thus they forced the Court to find that the actual wording of the act would not allow it to decide against the TVA. In the cases of *Ashwander* v. *TVA* of February 1936 and *Tennessee Electric Power Company* v. *TVA* of January 1939 the Court upheld the constitutionality of the TVA and its right to sell electricity. The leader of the concerted attack by nineteen private companies against the TVA was Wendell L. Willkie, president of Commonwealth and Southern, who then sold the entire facilities of the Tennessee Electric Power Company to the TVA for $78.6 million, a rather high price.

The concept of the yardstick provoked greater controversy. It

was impossible to distinguish between the cost of actually producing electricity from such necessary safety precautions as dam
maintenance and flood control. In later years, the TVA provided
power for the entire aluminum industry and also for the development of the atomic bomb. It led to the creation of new areas of
recreation for tourists. Most significant, it advanced the opportunities for an entire region, an impressive, if overdue, experiment
in social renewal.

The great dams of the 1930s were as formidable a contribution
to the world of American machines as were the suspension bridges.
Not only did such creations as the Hoover, Grand Coulee, and
Tennessee Valley Authority dams provide irrigation, prevent
flooding, generate electricity, and allow more land to be farmed
but they also, in turn, transformed the living conditions of millions, while ushering in a new era of hydroelectric power. The
creation of such huge multifunctional dams captured the imagination of all classes and generations who lived through the Great
Depression and who recognized in this one striking feature of the
New Deal a benevolent achievement of governmental planning.
They also recognized that here was a potent symbol of man's
ability to control the environment and harness the forces of nature
for the improvement of society.

Although the United States had enjoyed the benefits of such
dams as the Arrowrock, Idaho, (1912–1916) and the Deadwood,
Idaho, (1929–1930), it was in the 1930s that the country entered a
formative period of dam building, commencing with the Hoover
Dam, Boulder City, Nevada (1930–1936). This dam, situated
over the Colorado River in the hostile, torrid desert, thirty miles
from Las Vegas, gave rise to Boulder City, a dormitory and
service town for its numerous engineers, 5,000 construction
workers, and their families. At the time of completion, at over
726 feet and with 3.40 million cubic yards of concrete, it was the
highest and largest dam in the world with the largest reservoir,
Lake Mead, with 28,53 million acre feet of water. It also had the
largest power capacity. Continuous construction by day and night
was undertaken in daunting circumstances, with summer temperatures on and under the site of between 120° and 140° and winter
temperatures below 20° with such hazards as blustery winds.

There was also the mighty Colorado River that threatened to engulf the entire project, and workers imperiled by natural and machine-made hazards as they swung along canyon walls to strip away rock. The excitement and drama of construction were captured by photographer Ben Glaha for the Bureau of Reclamation.

Before actual construction, it was necessary to divert the Colorado River through man-made tunnels, erecting temporary cofferdams to block the river, and finally, excavating the site. These were monumental feats of engineering and only afterward could dam and power plant be constructed. There were other, major, technical problems. If the concrete used for retaining was simply poured down, it would have taken about a hundred years to cool and harden and it would then have shrunk so much as to crack the entire edifice. The solution was to pour individual slabs of concrete and hasten their cooling by circulating refrigerated water through them by means of tubes, thereby cooling each section in seventy-two hours.

As to the appearance of the dam, the engineers used consultant architect Gordon B. Kaufmann of Los Angeles to provide a facade that would arise naturally from the landscape and yet dominate it by means of setbacks, surmounted by winged bronze monuments designed by Oskar J. W. Hansen, and a powerhouse designed in an orthodox streamlined fashion.

The Hoover Dam set the pattern for the eight dams of the Tennessee Valley Authority constructed in the period 1933–1941 that also included such construction villages as Norris, Tennessee, named after the progressive senator for Nebraska who had championed the scheme. The Norris Freeway was a two-lane, limited-access road linking dam and town to Knoxville. Not only did civil engineer Arthur E. Morgan want the best possible technical engineering for construction but he also wanted the best possible social engineering for the construction workers and their families and not just some hastily erected shanty town that would become a desolate ghost town as soon as the immediate project was completed. Architectural historian Richard Guy Wilson observes in *The Machine Age in America* (1986) how "TVA architecture— the dams, powerhouses, locks, visitors centers, and mounted buildings—exhibits a common aesthetic, the attempt to monumentalize and emphasize machine iconography. Simple forms, great sheer surfaces where possible, the particularization of details, and the machines themselves—whether Gantry Cranes at Kentucky Dam, 1938–41, or the turbines at the Pickwick Landing Dam, 1934–1938—make the dams more than functional engineering; they became works of great art."

Relief

A central aim of the New Deal in its early days was to provide relief on a scale never previously attempted. What had most deterred the Hoover administration from a vast program of federal relief was the cost involved. The federal government simply did not have sufficient revenue. And it was clear that, while the orthodox wisdom of a balanced budget remained government policy, nothing could be done.

Unlike his predecessor, FDR was willing to depart from the conventional wisdom to relieve widespread distress. The first significant relief measure was aimed at young people between the ages of eighteen and twenty-five, a proportion of the unemployed that was quite disproportionate to the actual numbers of the group. The Civilian Conservation Corps Reforestation Relief Act of March 31, 1933, created the very first New Deal agency, and the one that most bore the imprint of FDR and his earlier reforestation projects in New York State. The Civilian Conservation Corps (CCC), managed jointly by the departments of Labor and the Interior, organized projects of reforestation, soil conservation, building firebreaks and forest lookout towers, and constructing recreational facilities in national parks. FDR was singularly impressed by the organizational skills of General Douglas MacArthur and Colonel George C. Marshall. Between 1933 and 1942 more than 2 million young men served in the agency, usually for periods of about nine months. Their pay was $30 per month, plus board and lodging, and $25 was sent to the youths' families in order to spread relief and purchasing power.

To provide relief for the urban unemployed the Federal Emergency Relief Act of May 12, 1933, established the Federal

Emergency Relief Administration (FERA) under Harry L. Hopkins. It divided its appropriation of $500 million evenly between the states, providing $1 for every $3 spent by the local authorities, with the remaining half going outright to the poorest states for direct relief.

The Public Works Administration of July 1933, established under Title II of the National Industrial Recovery Act (NIRA) and placed under the supervision of Secretary of the Interior Ickes, was intended to revitalize industry by creating public works to stimulate the need for capital goods. However, Ickes proved so cautious in dispensing the allocation of $3.3 billion that the PWA did very little to stimulate recovery or provide relief. FDR, somewhat disturbed by this and acting on the advice of Harry Hopkins, took $400 million of PWA money and created a new, temporary agency, the Civil Works Administration (CWA) in November 1933 and asked Hopkins to run it. It was this that led directly to the rise of Hopkins within the New Deal and his eventual ascendancy over all of FDR's other advisers. The CWA put more than 4 million people to work in the winter of 1933–1934 in various makeshift projects, but it drew opposition from both Republicans and Democrats and FDR closed it in early 1934. FERA was then given extra funds and thus increased its family allowance payments to $35 per month by July 1935. However, the PWA became a major achievement, creating schools, bridges, dams, sewers, post offices, and court houses.

To prevent foreclosure of domestic mortgages, Congress, by the Home Owners Refinancing Act of May 13, 1933, created the Home Owners Loan Corporation. It rescued urban home mortgages by refinancing the loans at lower rates of interest over longer periods of time. In June 1934 Congress established the Federal Housing Administration (FHA), a system of federal mortgage insurance, permitted to insure up to 80 percent, and later, 90 percent of newly constructed homes costing $6,000 or less at low rates of interest payable over long periods. Thus, it also tried to revive the stagnant construction industry. Moreover, it made home ownership possible for many who would otherwise never have had the opportunity to buy their own house.

Such extensive spending on relief increased the federal debt from $19.5 billion in early 1933 to $22.5 billion in late 1933. Once various state, municipal, and other resources had been depleted and the federal government assumed greater burdens, it rose to $28.7 billion in 1935 and then, in 1937, to $36.4 billion. Thereafter, its rise was the direct result of military expenditures. Later, when the debt reached astronomical heights, there was much less criticism of deficit financing than in the early days, when its levels were modest. Thus objections were not really about the actual size of the debt so much as the way the money was spent.

As business gradually revived in 1933, there was talk of a Roosevelt market. The Federal Reserve Board's adjusted index figure for industrial production rose from 59 in March 1933 to 100 in July 1933 (compared with the 1929 high of 125). However, there followed a setback. In August the index fell from 100 to 91 and by November it had receded further to 72. Not until December 1933 did it recover its position at 101. This fall was damaging psychologically. People had expected much of the New Deal and the NRA in particular, and their disappointment was keen. For this and other reasons, FDR and his cabinet were well aware that their emergency legislation had still not brought recovery and that more fundamental reforms were necessary. Thus did FDR's own progressivism become more sharply defined and more readily implemented.

The humanitarianism of the New Deal deeply touched the electorate, which rewarded the administration in the midterm congressional elections with an unprecedented Democratic majority. The Republicans lost twenty-six out of thirty-five contested seats in the Senate and the Democratic majority in the House was increased to 318 against 99 Republicans and 11 others, who normally voted with the Democrats. In the state elections only seven states survived the Democratic landslide. The midterm elections proved conclusively that the political balance had shifted from the Republicans to the Democrats. Congress would now have a far more liberal complexion than ever before and the new congressmen were increasingly impatient of compromise legislation. Moreover, the problems of the depression would actually get more complex and demand more radical solutions than anything yet attempted.

The Dust Bowl

The coming of the New Deal may have brought happy days to Washington but elsewhere it was still hard times. In certain regions the depression had actually deepened. Perhaps the greatest terrors were reserved for the inhabitants of the Dust Bowl, the states of North and South Dakota, Montana, western Kansas, eastern Colorado, Oklahoma, and northern Texas. Here, an inhospitable climate and harsh geography were transformed by human mismanagement into a graveyard for the American dream of agrarian opportunity.

Once the Great American Desert was settled with improved methods of farming, it was exploited by overplowing with John Deere plows that cut below the topsoil and by overgrazing. During World War I tractors for large-scale machine farming were used to expand crop production in order to supply America and Europe with more grain, principally wheat. What remained of the steppe grass and sod covering that protected the Great Plains was ruthlessly plowed away. This was a triumph of factory methods over the farm and the process continued its relentless, exploitive way during the twenties. At first, years of exceptional, heavy rain hid the true significance of human mismanagement. However, in dry years, the topsoil simply blew away. As the tragedy unfolded, the government began to count the cost. The National Resources Board estimated in 1934 that 35 million acres of previously arable land had been destroyed, that the soil of another 125 million acres had been exhausted or removed, and that another 100 million acres of land were threatened. By this time the Dust Bowl comprised 756 counties in 19 states.

The extent of the tragedy drew a wealth of commentary. In an article, "Saga of Drought," for *Commonwealth* of September 14, 1934, Charles Morrow Wilson recorded a common enough scene in a series of staccato statements, each with the precision of a telegram message.

Southwest is parched. Temperature above 100 in shade for forty-three successive days. Missouri Pacific Railway hauling tankcars of water for

Farmer and Sons Walking in the Face of a Dust Storm, 1936, by Arthur Rothstein. Rothstein was the first photographer to join the Farm Security Administration project. In this photograph he had father and older son pose carefully, leaning against the wind as they walked in front of a shed, partly submerged by dust, and had the smaller son hold back, covering his face with his hands. Thus Rothstein dramatized their poverty at the mercy of the elements. (Library of Congress).

use of livestock. First time in history. Sam Nance, farmer near Ardmore, Oklahoma, shoots 143 head of cattle to save them from starving. Cotton crop one-half normal. Apples, peaches, small fruits 30 percent normal. Livestock congesting packing centers. Beef selling on foot as low as $.01 a pound. Pasturage exhausted. States too broke to grant drought aid. United States adjudges 81 counties for primary emergency relief; 119 for secondary. Arkansas river four feet below normal record. Town and city reservoirs failing. Churches praying for rain in many parts of Arkansas, Oklahoma and Texas.

Chronic agricultural problems were then worsened by a series of great windstorms of which the first began in South Dakota on

November 11, 1933, and spread its pall as far south as Texas. This was the great black blizzard. In her article, "Dust," for the *New Republic* of May 1, 1935, commentator Avis D. Carlson described what it was like to be caught in a dust storm.

The impact is like a shovelful of fine sand flung against the face. People caught in their own yards grope for the doorstep. Cars come to a standstill, for no light in the world can penetrate that swirling murk.

Dust masks are snatched from pockets and cupboards. But masks do not protect the mouth. Grit cracks between the teeth, the dust taste lies bitter on the tongue, grime is harsh between the lips. . . .

In time the fury subsides. If the wind has spent itself, the dust will fall silently for hours. If the wind has settled into a good steady blow, the air will be thick for days. During those days as much of living as possible will be moved to the basement, while pounds and pounds of dust sift into the house. It is something, however, to have the house stop rocking and mumbling.

Then, after years of praying for rain, settlers and townsfolk had their requests answered with a terrible vengeance. When the rains came they did not stop. The *New York Times* of January 23, 1937, reported how floods had made 150,000 homeless in twelve states. Conditions were worst in Indiana, Kentucky, Ohio, and Tennessee. Refugees sheltered from snow and sleet in box cars, public buildings, churches, and tents. *Time* magazine of February 8, 1937, recorded how the Ohio River "looked like a shoreless yellow sea studded here and there with tree tops and half submerged buildings. To people crouching on house roofs, it was an immeasurable amount of ugly yellow water surging higher and higher hours without end. . . ." Finally, perhaps half a million people were made homeless. In all, floods and windstorms claimed 3,678 lives in the mid-thirties.

In national terms drought and flood achieved what the federal limitation on crops could not. They eliminated surplus. For the hapless individuals involved, it was utterly disastrous. Thousands upon thousands of farms failed. When their owners could not meet their mortgage payments, the banks foreclosed them. The U.S. Department of Agriculture Bureau of Agricultural Economics estimated that in 1933 93.6 farms in every 1,000 changed hands and 54.1 of these sales were forced or somehow related to defaults. This was the greatest number of farm transfers in the 1930s, but every year the number was in the low 70s or high 60s per 1,000 farms, until 1939 when it fell to 63.8 sales per 1,000 farms.

Most farmers who lost their farms did so because they got into a bottomless pit of debt to banks, insurance companies, or private investors. Some were held by the government for nonpayment of taxes. In 1934 the National Resources Board estimated that almost 30 percent of the value of farm land in the West and Midwest was owned by government agencies or private creditors. In the Great Depression as many as 42 percent of farmers were tenants, compared with only 25 percent in 1880. Moreover, in 1935 less than two-thirds of tenant farmers had lived on their land for more than a year. Tenancy had various disadvantages. Tenants were much less likely to settle than owners and they did not share owners' special concern for land and equipment. The whole agricultural system encouraged restless mobility down the socioeconomic scale.

By its policies, the New Deal's agricultural agency, the AAA, encouraged the process. A farm owner who was being subsidized for growing less could afford to evict his tenants or sharecroppers, live off the federal check, buy tractors and other labor-saving implements, and then hire labor by the day instead of throughout the year. The displacement of agricultural workers was most noticeable in cotton production. In 1930–1937 sales of farm tractors in ten cotton states rose by 90 percent. Whereas the actual number of farms increased in the rest of the country, in the southern and southwestern states it actually declined. Paul S. Taylor, who studied two cotton producing counties in Texas, observed on the sharp decline in the number of farms, "commonly, the landlord who purchases a tractor throws two 160-acre farms operated by tenants into an operating unit and lets both tenants go. Sometimes the rate of displacement is greater, rising to 8, 10, and even 15 families of tenants."

One consequence common to both industrial and agricultural depressions was that millions of people were uprooted. The thirties was a decade of great migrations. Some states lost population —Vermont, the Dakotas, Kansas, Nebraska, and Oklahoma. The largest migrations were from the South and the Appalachians to the industrial centers of Ohio, Illinois, Indiana, and Michigan. However, it was states with warm climates that were most likely to be attractive to migrants—Arizona, California, and Florida. Indeed, the general movement to the Pacific was, eventually, to make California the most populous state.

One sort of migration was more famous than another of the others. In 1934 and 1935 Okies, dispossessed farmers, not only from Oklahoma but also Arkansas, Texas, and elsewhere, began to cross into California, looking for work as fruit pickers. They traveled in old jalopies along U.S. Highway 30 through the Idaho hills and along Highway 66 across New Mexico and Arizona.

The most famous record of the Okies' migration was provided by John Steinbeck in his best-selling novel, *The Grapes of Wrath* (1939). Steinbeck recorded the early movement of the migrant families who, ironically, could only ensure the survival of their individual members by splitting up. He followed the declining fortunes of a fictitious family, the Joads, whose miseries are caused by the intransigence of banks, the indifference of government, and their own incapacity to adjust to a changing world.

However, the mass migration was not welcome to residents of California who dreaded the sudden influx of destitute Okies and the social dislocation it would cause. A billboard on the Nevada-California border of 1935 proclaimed "Okies Go Home: No Relief Available in California." Once they were actually in California the Okies found themselves in desperate competition for work with such other itinerant families as evicted sharecroppers from Alabama, tenant farmers from Arkansas, and perennial vagabonds. In no time at all the California labor market for fruit pickers and other menial agricultural work became glutted. Thus, in the words of Frederick Lewis Allen, "to the vast majority of the refugees the promised land proved to be a place of new and cruel tragedy."

6

STORMY WEATHER
The Later New Deal

Thunder from Right and Left

ONCE BIG business discerned the beginnings of recovery, it began to vent unreasonable diatribes on "that man in the White House" and his progressive measures. Whereas to his admirers, FDR was leading the country through a period of momentous reforms, to his critics, he was fomenting class rivalry, undermining the American system of free enterprise, and trying to undermine the Constitution. Marquis W. Childs analyzed the hatred FDR aroused in an article, "They Hate Roosevelt," for *Harper's* of May 1936. He described this hatred as a passion and an irrational fury that permeates "the whole upper stratum of American society." Among the lackeys of the plutocracy it became something of a status symbol to revile Roosevelt in the most scurrilous terms. There were bitter jokes such as the one about the eminent psychiatrist summoned prematurely to Heaven to treat God "because He has delusions of grandeur—He thinks He is Franklin D. Roosevelt."

It was said of Roosevelt by his enemies that he was a traitor to his class. What they meant was that, since Roosevelt came from an upper-class Hudson River family, it should have been his intention to protect the old plutocracy. However, instead of rewarding industrial entrepreneurs and landowners for their contribution to American society, the New Deal made relief to the indigent poor a priority. This, according to the orthodox wisdom, was tantamount to encouraging idleness among the workshy, as well as going against the Protestant work ethic and the American myth of rags to riches.

More significantly, the dominant plutocracy objected to the fact that relief payments, programs of public works, and an expanded bureaucracy to administer them could only be paid for by increased taxation on themselves. This came most decisively in the Revenue Act of 1936 that imposed higher taxes on gifts and estates, on corporate incomes and high personal incomes. What they most resented, therefore, was not the theory but paying for the relief. In addition, the plutocracy resented legislation that curbed their own financial activities, in such measures as the Glass-Steagall Banking Act and the Truth-in-Securities Act, both in 1933, and the Securities Exchange Act of 1934.

Of course, far from being a traitor to his class, Roosevelt was its savior. Government supervision of banking and the stock market not only ensured prevention of the worst abuses of the 1920s but also provided an implicit government seal of approval of the way finances, both high and low, checking and speculative, were conducted. Moreover, those despised later measures of social reform, such as the Social Security and Wagner acts of 1935, and the more equable distribution of wealth achieved by other acts, undercut the appeal of revolutionary movements that sought to overturn the entire capitalistic system. Thus FDR and the New Dealers reformed the system in order to preserve it. The essence of the New Deal was a conservative treatment of radical problems.

However, at the time the plutocracy could not see the wood for the trees. In August 1934 business leaders, including former ardent supporters of FDR in 1932 in the former AAPA, constituted themselves the American Liberty League, determined to

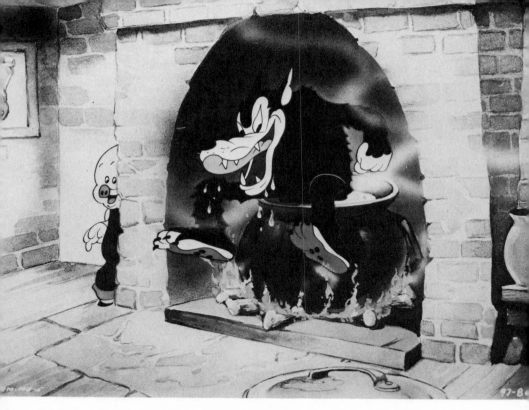

"Who's Afraid of the Big, Bad Wolf?" The wise little pig who built his house of bricks, unlike the foolish pigs who built theirs of straw or hay, has the pleasure of seeing the big, bad wolf descend the chimney only to get a roasting in the stewpot over the hearth. The situation and song in Walt Disney's classic cartoon movie were taken as symbols of the United States' cheerful determination to defy and beat the ravenous wolves of the Great Depression at home and cataclysmic wars in Europe and Asia overseas. (Walt Disney Productions; RKO Pictures; Museum of Modern Art Film Stills Archive).

encompass his destruction. It was bipartisan but led by John Julius Raskob, and R. R. M. Carpenter, brother-in-law to the Du Ponts and vice-president of the Du Pont Corporation. The new league could count on other big guns of business and their considerable financial resources. It adopted the same membership and had the same influence as had its predecessor, the AAPA, attracting such capitalists as newspaper magnate William Randolph Hearst, the three Du Pont brothers, Sewell L. Avery of Montgomery Ward, and Colby M. Chester, president of General Foods. They orchestrated press campaigns criticizing FDR's dictatorial methods, the invasion of individual freedoms by the New Deal, and the allegedly communistic legislation in support of labor unions. R. R. M. Carpenter was supposed to have told Raskob with much indignation, "five Negroes on my place refused to work this spring, saying that they had an easy job with the government," and, "a cook on my houseboat quit because the government was paying him $1 an hour as a painter."

There was also thunder from the Left. In California novelist Upton Sinclair had published a campaign document, *I, Governor of California and How I Ended Poverty,* in 1933, which sold about a million copies and encouraged the growth of an insurgency movement, EPIC (End Poverty in California). Its program was a mix of state socialism and rural cooperatives, in which unemployed people were to be allowed to produce work on cooperative farms or factories leased by the state. They would be paid in scrip that could be used only to buy food or goods produced by the cooperatives. Upton Sinclair won the support of novelist Theodore Dreiser, poet Archibald MacLeish, and lawyer Clarence Darrow. He roused Democrats in the state party and took the nomination for governor from party favorite George Creel in the primary election of August 1934 with a far greater majority than the incumbent governor, Frank Merriam, achieved in the Republican party.

Sinclair's campaign provoked concerted opposition from conservatives of both parties and the federal government allied together in an attempt to defeat him. It drew on the resources of Hollywood, which produced fake newsreels showing jobless hordes swarming across the state lines to become expensive wards of California. As a result of their nicely timed and well-orchestrated campaign, Merriam trounced Sinclair by 260,000 votes in the election and another 303,000 votes went to a third-party candidate.

More troublesome to FDR was Dr. Francis E. Townsend, a retired medical doctor, originally from Illinois but now living in Long Beach, California, where he had worked as assistant county health officer until forced to retire in 1933 at the age of sixty-six with less than $200 in savings and no other means of earning his living. He proposed old age pensions for people retired at sixty who would receive $200 per month, provided they took on no extra work and spent the entire sum within the month in the United States. The Townsend plan was to be financed (initially) by a 2 percent tax on all business transactions. This was later amended to direct income tax on corporations and individuals. The Townsend scheme appealed to millions across the country whose plight and feelings of hopelessness were similar to his own. Moreover, Townsend claimed that the retirement of people over sixty would create vast job opportunities for the young unemployed and that the introduction of monthly pensions would further stimulate the economy by creating a demand for goods and services that would, in turn, generate more jobs.

Townsend took on a partner, Robert E. Clements, an energetic Texas realtor of thirty-nine, and together they incorporated Old Age Revolving Pensions, Ltd., on January 1, 1934, dispatching literature to all and sundry. Having launched Townsend Clubs across the country and built up a membership of 1.5 million, they started publishing a newspaper, the *Townsend National Weekly,* and began lobbying Congress with a series of mass petitions. As a result of their campaign, Congressman John S. McGroarty of California, who owed his election to the support of local Townsend Clubs, introduced a pension bill into the House in early 1935. It was opposed by the administration as expensive and impractical.

By far the most aggressive and noisome criticisms of the New Deal came from Senator Huey Long of Louisiana and Father Charles Coughlin of Michigan. Drawing on the residue of the old Populist movement in the South and Midwest, they both launched effective crusades against the encroaching power of the federal government. Alan Brinkley, a recent historian of the Long and Coughlin movements, observes in his *Voices of Protest* (1982) how the two leaders used their eloquence to evoke and express a dissident ideology. They affirmed values and institutions threatened by modern developments and offered their followers promise of a fairer society in which traditional values and institutions would be protected. They ascribed current social and economic problems to a selective list of scapegoats, principally the unseen interests of Wall Street, and they promised to prevent any further expansion of government.

Senator Huey P. Long, the self-styled "Kingfish" of Louisiana, was an amazing phenomenon even among southern demagogues. He combined genuine compassion for the dispossessed with ruthless political ambition. Born in 1893 into an extremely poor area of Louisiana, Winn Parish, where his father rose from obscurity to owning the town bank, Huey Long first went to work as a door-to-door salesman. After studying at the Tulane University Law School for only eight months, he learned enough to pass a bar examination and began to practice law. In 1918, at the age of twenty-five, he was elected to the State Railroad Commission, the only political office for which he was then eligible. Thereafter, he steadily advanced his political career to become governor in 1928.

Huey Long was tall but graceless, with tousled brown hair and pudgy jowls, but, although he moved like an oaf, he had an impish, pert face and his whole personality was unruly and mischievous, suggesting his inner impatience and driving ambition. Indeed, his whole persona appealed to the rural population but was most threatening to the atrophied society of Baton Rouge and its oligarchy of planters, merchants, and industrialists.

Within three years of taking office he had abolished state poll taxes, declared a moratorium on debts, and excused the poor from property taxes. In 1928 Louisiana had only 300 miles of paved highways and 3 bridges. By 1933 it had 3,754 miles of paved highways, 40 bridges, and almost 4,000 miles of gravel farm roads. Moreover, as well as organizing a campaign to eliminate adult illiteracy, Long transformed Louisiana State University from a provincial college into a major institution. The new public buildings he commissioned, including the state capitol, governor's mansion, and New Orleans airport, not only satisfied Long's personal vanity and outsize ego but also provided extra work and boosted public morale.

According to state law, Long could not run for governor again in 1932 and thus he ran, instead, for the U.S. Senate in 1930, won, but delayed taking his seat until 1932 when he could install a stooge, Oscar K. Allen, as governor in his place. However, he continued to participate in front of, as well as behind, the scenes of state politics by taking charge of debates in the assembly and ordering the representatives to pass his proposed measures. On one day in November 1934 the state senate passed forty-four bills in only two hours, that is, one every three minutes. In this way and by selective use of bribery, torture, and intimidation, Long made himself dictator in his state.

Although he was an adept self-publicist, sometimes his boorishness was counterproductive. A trivial incident in August 1933 caused Long excessive embarrassment. It arose out of the flamboyant behaviorism he had now adopted. When he got drunk at a party at the Sands Point Casino, Long Island, New York, he tried to relieve himself in the men's room through the legs of a man already using a urinal. History does not say whether he was every inch a king—only that he was rewarded with a black and bloody eye for his cheek. "Kingfish to Crawfish" was the comment of the *New Republic*. A journalist in New Orleans inquired if it were true that Long had accepted an engagement to appear in a freak show at Coney Island for $1,000 per night.

Huey Long's own plan for national recovery was "Share Our Wealth," which he announced on the radio on February 23, 1934. It called for a wide redistribution of wealth among the lower economic groups. This was to be achieved by liquidating all personal fortunes above $3 million and providing every family with $4,000 or $5,000 to buy a house, an automobile, and a radio. The program also prescribed old age pensions, a bonus for veterans, minimum wages, and a free college education at government expense for young people of tested intelligence. To promote his point of view Huey Long issued pamphlets, made effective speeches, and promoted a song extolling the virtues of his scheme. The "Share Our Wealth" scheme was crude and, in its present form, impracticable, but it expressed a self-evident truth about just how unfair was the uneven distribution of wealth. Thus it was also a modestly successful political movement from which Long could advance his presidential ambitions.

FDR was exasperated by Long's attempt to appropriate control of the New Deal and his colossal rudeness. At a White House meeting Long kept his hat on, only removing it to tap the crip-

The effervescent Huey Long, first governor and, later, senator of Louisiana, where he reigned as the self-styled Kingfish, was a dangerous foil for FDR, partly because his "Share Our Wealth" campaign threatened to undermine the appeal of New Deal economic policies, partly because he could divide the Democratic party in the South. (Library of Congress).

pled president on the knees to emphasize his points. FDR took his revenge by distributing federal patronage to Long's political enemies in Louisiana.

Another thorn in FDR's side was Father Charles E. Coughlin, the radio priest. He was of Irish-American descent, Canadian birth, and had first come to the United States in the 1920s to Royal Oak, Michigan, near Detroit. He soon borrowed $79,000 from the archdiocese of Detroit to build a brown-shingled church of St. Therese, the Little Flower of Jesus, seating 600 people. In July 1926 the new church was threatened by a huge burning cross planted on the front lawn by the local Ku Klux Klan, who, it will be recalled, were opposed to Catholics and immigrants.

Despite this act of intimidation and because Coughlin's various efforts at fund-raising were still producing the revenue necessary to run the church, he persuaded Leo Fitzpatrick, manager of the local radio station, WJR, to let him broadcast his appeals on the air. From his first broadcast on October 17, 1926, he was an immediate success. Wallace Stegner recalls in *The Aspirin Age,* Isabel Leighton's 1949 collection of impressionistic synopses of the age, how Coughlin had "a voice of such mellow richness, such manly, heart-warming confidential intimacy, such emotional and ingratiating charm, that anyone turning past it on the radio dial almost automatically returned to hear it again." His voice was a vessel that could be filled or drained at will. It was "without doubt one of the great speaking voices of the twentieth century." The strength of his personality was such that by 1930 he was able to mount regular Sunday evening broadcasts, "The Golden Hour of the Little Flower," for seventeen CBS stations.

His early radio addresses were essentially religious, interpretations of the Bible. From 1930 onward they became almost exclusively political in content. The reason was not hard to find. After the Wall Street Crash, Detroit, which was almost entirely dependent on the automobile industry, had the highest unemployment rate of any large American city. The most common criticisms leveled at Coughlin were that he was an upstart priest interfering in politics. The CBS network was most sensitive to these charges and, fearful of offending the federal government, in April 1931 they refused to renew his contract. Not daunted, Coughlin went back to WJR in Detroit and arranged individual contracts with eleven private stations in the East and Midwest. By the end of 1934 more than thirty stations were broadcasting his addresses. By 1934 Coughlin was so popular that he was receiving more mail than FDR—sometimes over a million letters a week, requiring 150 clerks to process them.

The Charity Crucifixion Tower, his new granite and marble church, stood seven stories high and was decorated with a huge, bas-relief figure of Christ, illuminated by spotlights at night. At the side of the tower were a gasoline station, "Shrine Super-Service," and a Little Flower hot dog stand. Thus it was fair game for journalistic ridicule. *Time* magazine declared on April 10,

1933, that the "Charity Crucifixion Tower reminds many Detroiters of a silo" and called the architect "Silo Charlie."

Like Huey Long, Coughlin was an early supporter of FDR whom he used to call "Boss." Unlike Long, he had no personal political ambitions but he was disturbed by the failure of the early New Deal to move quickly to the Left. Coughlin's prescriptions for raising the depression were two: reform the currency and reorder the financial institutions. Silver donations had made Coughlin the greatest owner of silver, which he described as "the Gentile metal." He advocated the coinage of silver in a new dollar containing 75 percent gold and 25 percent silver, in order to increase the amount of money in circulation and thus increase purchasing power and stimulate the economy. In late 1934 and early 1935 Coughlin moved further to the Left, calling for the abolition of the privately controlled Federal Reserve System and the creation of a national bank to be controlled by popularly elected representatives. To achieve these reforms Coughlin organized the National Union for Social Justice in 1935. It was said the prospective constituency was 8.5 million people

The dissident ideology propounded by Coughlin and Long drew from a traditional idea that individuals should be able to control their own destiny and not have it controlled by some faceless bureaucracy serving the financial interests of unseen corporations. It was concentrated wealth that had come close to destroying the community in the great bull market and the Wall Street Crash. The community could be revitalized by a new economic order with decentralized government, limited ownership of property, and controlled capitalism. Yet, ironically, it was the radio, itself a means of greater centralization, that made it possible for Coughlin and Long to propound their arguments for decentralization.

Since neither Long nor Coughlin could achieve a working relationship with the New Deal, they turned to their newly created organizations with extra broadcasts, recruiting drives, and public speaking engagements wherever the authorities would permit them an audience. The Long organization spread from the South along the states bordering the Atlantic coast as far north as Connecticut and had footholds in Pennsylvania, Missouri, Wisconsin, and

Indiana. However, it was naturally stronger in the West than the Midwest, with California the most receptive state outside the South. The National Union for Social Justice spread from the Midwest to New England and the northeastern seaboard generally.

Coughlin and Long were formidable enough separately. Together, they could organize a huge constituency and they were being drawn together by their supporters, so closely did public opinion associate one with the other. Furthermore, various organizations, such as the Farmer-Labor Party and the Farmers' Holiday Association, and the Townsend Clubs, were united in what they saw as the common aim of the Long and Coughlin movements—"SHARE OUR WEALTH."

The electoral threat of Huey Long and the Share Our Wealth movement to FDR disappeared on September 9, 1935, when Long was fatally wounded inside the Louisiana State Capitol. Long's assassin, Dr. Carl Austin Weiss, who was immediately gunned down by Long's bodyguards, was the son-in-law of Judge Benjamin Pavy, a political enemy to the Kingfish. With Long gone, his movement split into two bitter factions and soon fell apart.

There was yet more thunder on the Left. Governor Floyd B. Olson of Minnesota was the dynamic leader of a Farmer-Labor party, whose platform proposed fundamental economic reforms, including state appropriation of idle factories to put the unemployed to work, state ownership of public utilities, a moratorium on farm mortgage foreclosures, exemption of low-income families from property taxes, and a government bank. However, while his administration accomplished environmental legislation and some regulation of public utilities, it proved less radical than his election promises. In 1936 he died of cancer at the early age of forty-five.

In Wisconsin Robert La Follette's sons, the unassuming Robert, Jr. ("Young Bob") and the extrovert Philip, dissatisfied with the pace of the New Deal, founded a new Progressive party in May 1934 and were elected as senator and governor, respectively, that year, while seven Progressive candidates were elected to the House of Representatives. They were supported by the League for Independent Political Action, an insurgent movement of eastern intellectuals that included John Dewey, Lewis Mumford, and Archibald MacLeish. This group favored a third party to unite leading midwestern movements, including its own creation of 1933, the Farmer-Labor Political Federation (FLPF).

Disenchantment with the old machines was also seen in New York City in 1933 where Republican Fiorello H. La Guardia was elected mayor after the Democratic machine of Tammany Hall was shown, in a sensational investigation, to have corrupted municipal politics. In office, La Guardia instituted a series of welfare programs on the lines of the New Deal. He was supported by the American Labor party that helped his reelection in 1937 and contributed to FDR's own electoral victory of 1936.

These various activities, commonly known as "Thunder on the Left," were, collectively, a significant factor in pushing the New Deal itself farther to the Left. FDR drew off their fire by kindling it for his own blazing reforms. Social security drew much of its momentum from Dr. Townsend's plan and the Revenue Act and the Holding Company Act were largely inspired by FDR's determination to refute Huey Long's charge that he was the creature of the utility corporations. Of yet more fundamental and ironic significance was the fact that FDR turned criticism of the New Deal from the Left to generate even wider public support for his policies. Historian Robert H. Walker puts it this way: "Franklin D. Roosevelt made visible use of the popular fear of violent revolution in gaining acceptance for a politico-economic program which many Americans might otherwise have regarded as itself unacceptably radical." Indeed, when Congress met for its second session on January 4, 1935, FDR asked for a "second New Deal" of sweeping reforms: security against illness, old age, and unemployment; slum clearance; and a program of works for the unemployed.

The New Deal at Flood Tide

Perhaps the most significant legislative achievement of early 1935 was the expansion of federal relief. By early 1935 perhaps as many as 5.5 million people were in receipt of relief; if their dependents were also included, then the total was 20.5 million, 17 percent of the total population. If those who were only in work because they were working for government relief projects are included, then it is clear the government was supporting over 20 percent of its citizens.

These statistics were not welcome to the New Dealers. Both FDR and Hopkins shared the traditional American view that relief by itself undermined character. Therefore, FDR and Hopkins wanted the 3.5 million people who were out of work but able-bodied and skilled to be given work through federal monies rather than a dole. Accordingly, the Emergency Relief Employment Act was designed to meet this special requirement. It passed the House by 317 votes to 70 and the Senate by 67 votes to 13 to be signed by FDR on April 8, 1935.

The Emergency Relief Appropriation Act established new agencies, notably the Works Progress Administration (WPA), for its purposes. (The following account is, like that for other legislation in this chapter, closely based on Ralph de Bedts's interpretation in *Recent American History.*) The Works Progress Administration, which changed its name in 1939 to Works Projects Administration, was awarded an appropriation of $5 billion, the largest in American history. It led to open conflict between Ickes and Hopkins. Ickes wanted to concentrate on recovery rather than relief and gave support to large public works projects to aid industry through expenditure on capital goods. This would ensure recovery in the long run. Hopkins, however, wanted to put as many people as possible into truly productive jobs and thus rely on their spending their wages to help business revive. He was supposed to have said, "People don't eat in the long run," and his approach to problems won him control of the WPA. Wages were somewhat above the dole but lower than wages in private industry. This led to opposition from liberals who wanted to raise wages and the compromise was to give the president "discretionary control" to raise wages. In 1936 the average wage was $52.4 per month. The average number of people employed by the WPA at any one time was 2 million—although by 1941 altogether 8 million, or 20 percent of the workforce, had at some time or other worked for the WPA. The WPA could not enter all fields.

It could not compete with private business and, because of costs, it could not engage in home construction.

Nevertheless, it built 12,000 playgrounds, 1,000 airport landing fields, 8,000 school buildings and hospitals, and, by instruction, publishing, and libraries, waged a campaign against adult illiteracy. It was, argues William Manchester, the WPA that transformed America's cities, creating the potential for additional transport, access, and other facilities. In New York it cut the Lincoln Tunnel linking Manhattan and New Jersey and built the Triborough Bridge linking Manhattan and Long Island. In Washington it created the mall and the Federal Trade Commission. In Dallas it laid Dealey Plaza; in California it built the Camarillo Mental Hospital; in Kentucky, the Fort Knox gold depository. Moreover, during this period federal appropriations for the armed services were minuscule in comparison with the need. Thus the contribution of the WPA to the maintenance of army posts and naval stations ensured their physical survival. Furthermore, the WPA provided the nucleus for, first, the wartime and, second, the postwar industrial expansion of business.

The WPA was under continuous attack from various quarters, including militant unionists (both within and without the WPA). Conservatives returned to traditional criticisms that federal relief undermined the Protestant work ethic, that many WPA projects were of dubious value in themselves and were being used for party political advantage. This last criticism was met by Congress that passed the Hatch Act in August 1939 forbidding federal employees (except officials at higher levels of policy making) from taking part in politics. The WPA aimed to create work for young people in its subsidary, the National Youth Administration (NYA), administered by Aubrey Williams, which gave priority to those who had graduated from high school and tried to persuade as many as possible to remain in education and stay out of the labor market. By 1941 it had employed about 1.5 million young people, favoring college students whom it paid between $10 and $20 per month.

Despite the expansion of federal relief in the early part of the year, it seemed to many of his supporters that FDR was becoming indecisive in 1935 until May when the U.S. Chamber of

Commerce announced it would not cooperate any longer with the New Deal and when the Supreme Court declared the NRA unconstitutional in the case of *Schechter Poultry Corporation v. The United States* on May 27, 1935. FDR reacted vigorously to both setbacks, denouncing both capitalists and the court in vehement tones and presenting to Congress in June 1935 five important new pieces of legislation. All were sweeping reform measures urged by liberals and progressives alike. These measures were the heart of the Second Hundred Days.

The first of these, the Wagner–Connery National Labor Relations Act, had originally been introduced by Senator Robert Wagner of New York. It was aimed at the many company unions set up to undermine labor's attempts to organize independently. FDR and Frances Perkins originally opposed the bill and they gave it their enthusiastic support only after it had passed the Senate by 63 votes to 12 on May 16, 1935, and after the Supreme Court had invalidated the NRA in the *Schechter* case eleven days later. FDR was not, at first, committed to the bill, yet his later support ensured that it passed the House by a large majority before he signed the Wagner Act on July 5, 1935. Workers were guaranteed the right to collective bargaining through unions of their own choice and the union chosen by the majority became the bargaining voice for all. The bill, moreover, established a three-member National Labor Relations Board (NLRB), headed by Professor J. Warren Madden of Pittsburgh, to supervise its enforcement, if necessary, by holding elections. Thus did the company union become illegal. Employers were forbidden to resort to "unfair practices," such as discrimination against union members or refusal to accept collective bargaining with union representatives.

The NLRB's wide powers aroused considerable controversy. Employers could maintain they had fired workers for inefficiency, whereas those workers would insist that their discharge was really owing to their union activities. The AFL and its craft unions claimed that the board was too partial to the Committee for Industrial Organization (CIO) and its industrial unions. Fifty-eight lawyers associated with the American Liberty League confidently predicted that the act would be adjudged unconstitutional and advised employers not to comply with it but, instead, to seek injunctions against it from sympathetic courts. However, in 1937 the Supreme Court upheld the new law in a series of decisions of which the most celebrated was *NLRB* v. *Jones and Laughlin Steel Corporation,* declaring that workers had a fundamental right to organize through unions. In 1938 the court went further by ending the legal abuse of injunctions to prevent strikes.

The Wagner Act was one of the most important acts in the history of American labor, aiding the rise of "big labor" as part of New Deal strategy to balance the component parts of society. It was said that it averted 869 threatened strikes in its first five years. Thus did the New Deal's policy to labor accomplish what Milton Derber of the Institute of Labor and Industrial Relations regards as "a fundamental restructuring of the industrial relations system." Whereas the immediate effects supported labor and made possible the unionization of those industries engaged in mass production, the result in the long term was to give to the federal government the pivotal role of arbitrator between labor and management, an arbitrator who decided upon and enforced the rules. By widening the scope of its social responsibility in providing minimum standards of pay at work and social security payments for unemployment and illness, the federal government encouraged the active participation of organized labor in the theater of national politics, especially within the Democratic party.

The second of FDR's five proposals became the Social Security Act. Only a few states provided old age pensions, and all were inadequate. Only Wisconsin had laws governing unemployment compensation. Thus the Social Security Act, in large measure stimulated by thunder from the Left, was a departure from all previous practice. However, knowledge of Townsend's more excessive demands prompted congressmen, who might otherwise have been reluctant, to find FDR's more modest proposals palatable by comparison. The bill moved easily through Congress, passing the House by 372 votes to 33 and the Senate by 76 votes to 6, and became law on August 15, 1935.

The Social Security Act provided an unemployment insurance plan and old age and survivors' pensions. Unemployment insurance was to be administered by the states and not the federal government. A federal unemployment tax was imposed on all

Mexican migrant fieldworker, on edge of frozen peafield, Imperial Valley, California, in March 1937 by Dorothea Lange. Both Dorothea Lange's first husband, painter Maynard Dixon, and her second, economist Paul S. Taylor, encouraged her work and, with Taylor, she recorded the plight of migrant farm workers for the Farm Security Administration. Herself a childhood victim of poliomyelitis, she, too, identified with the forgotten man. (Library of Congress).

employees. In order to encourage the states to keep their side of the bargain and pass enabling legislation, Congress provided that employers would be allowed a credit of up to 90 percent of the tax for contributions made to state unemployment compensation funds. In the end, all the states had passed the requisite legislation within two years. The act covered 27 million people but excluded many in agriculture, domestic service, and those working for small employers. In 1938 maximum payments were $18 per week, but much less in the South, and the national average was less than

$11. Payments extended for sixteen weeks only. The old age pension portion of the act created a federal annuity system to be financed by equal contributions from employer and employee, beginning at 1 percent of wages and increasing gradually. Payments were to begin in 1940. Fewer than 50 million people were covered by the original act and those reaching age 65 were to receive a pension in proportion to their contributions. Retired workers would receive a minimum of $10 and a maximum of $85 per month. Both sums were later raised. Frances Perkins said in her account of the Roosevelt years that FDR took greater satisfaction in the Social Security Act of 1935 than in anything else he achieved on the domestic front. The Social Security Act was a major landmark of social reform that made social security a basic function of the government.

Roosevelt's third proposal was the Banking Act of August 23, 1935, which was intended to give the federal government control of such matters in banking as reserve requirements and rediscount rates. Marriner S. Eccles of Utah, governor of the Federal Reserve Board, believed Wall Street exercised too much power in national finance and determined to revise the Federal Reserve Act of 1913, despite well-orchestrated opposition from the banking community led by Senator Carter Glass of Virginia, who resented any revision to the 1913 act that he himself had partly drafted. The result was a compromise between the Glass and Eccles points of view.

In future each Federal Reserve Bank elected its own head but he had to be approved by the board of governors of the Federal Reserve System (FRS). Thus was the Federal Reserve System made subject to more centralized control, moving the capital of banking from New York to Washington. Decisions on reserve requirements and discount rates were given to the board of governors. Moreover, the Open Market Committee of the FRS, which controlled open market operations in government securities, was put under a policy-making committee over which the central board had majority control, instead of being subordinated to the member banks and in a purely advisory capacity. All large state banks seeking the benefit of the new federal deposit insurance (achieved earlier in 1933) were now required to join the FRS and accept its jurisdiction. Thus, despite compromise, the act set a precedent in removing control of the nation's finances from private banking and placing it with the federal government.

The fourth measure, the Public Utility Holding Company Act of August 1935, was passed despite unprecedented lobbying against it by the giant public utility companies. However, not only Congress and FDR but also public opinion were convinced of the need to reform a whole set of abuses. Stocks issued were often overvalued or fradulent; sometimes public utility companies bribed legislators to advance or block legislation in their interest; the rates paid to holding company investors were usually excessive in order to support the top-heavy structure of the system. All of this was widely known. Therefore, Roosevelt and his allies wanted the dissolution of utilities holding companies in order to protect consumers against excessive rates and prevent unhealthy concentrations of economic power. The act was proposed by Congressman Sam Rayburn of Texas and Senator Burton K. Wheeler of Montana.

The act ordered the liquidation of holding companies more than two times removed from their operating companies (instead of all holding companies more than once removed from the operating companies, which the administration wanted). All utilities combines had to register with the Securities Exchange Commission (SEC), and this body could decide which holding companies could survive, that is, whether or not they were one or two times beyond the operating companies. If it thought any holding companies were not in the public interest it could order their elimination. In addition, the SEC was given control over all financial transactions and stock issuance of the utilities companies, which had to register with it. Some companies refused to register but the Supreme Court upheld the act and the great utilities companies were broken up within three years. The most significant achievement of the act was to stop the issue of fradulent utilities stocks.

An additional agency created at this time was the Rural Electrification Administration (REA) of May 1935, established to build generating plants and power lines in rural areas since only 10 percent of American farm families had electricity. Under the

Rural Electrification Act of 1936, farmers were encouraged to take advantage of REA loans at low rates of interest and form their own cooperatives in order to build their own plants. This encouraged private power companies to build power lines into remote rural areas, previously considered unprofitable. Thus, by 1941 40 percent of farms received electricity and, by 1950, 90 percent.

The Revenue Act of 1935 or Wealth Tax Act was greeted with more abuse than any of the Seventy-Fourth Congress's other laws. Newspaper magnate William Randolph Hearst called it "Soak the Successful" Act. FDR, undeterred, wanted to encourage a wider distribution of wealth and, also, reduce the need for deficit financing. Hitherto, tax on the wealthy was minimal. A man with an income of $16,000 paid only $1,000 in tax. In his message to Congress of June 19, 1935, recommending a revision of the tax system, FDR said, "Social unrest and a deepening sense of unfairness are dangers to our national life we must minimize by rigorous methods. People know that vast personal incomes come not only through the effort or ability or luck of those who receive them, but also because of the opportunity for advantage which Government itself contributes. Therefore the duty rests upon the Government itself to restrict such incomes by high taxes."

The new act set higher taxes on gifts and estates, raised corporate income taxes, and imposed an excess profits tax on profits above 15 percent. Moreover, it placed surtaxes on personal taxable income above $50,000, according to a graduated scale from 31 percent at the starting figure of $50,000 to a maximum of 75 percent on net incomes over $5 million. In addition, the act taxed undistributed corporation profits. The new tax law did not achieve the ambitious changes desired by its advocates and feared by its enemies. However, it did make the system of taxation far more equitable, although the monopoly of wealth by the top 1 percent remained substantially intact.

Congress also enacted ad hoc legislation in reaction to the scuttling of the NRA by the Supreme Court. Thus, the Guffey-Snyder Act of 1935 created a National Bituminous Coal Commission to supervise production quotas and prices, hours and wages. Because it guaranteed collective bargaining and attempted to set uniform wages and hours it, too, was set aside by the Supreme Court. Congress, therefore, replaced it with the Guffey-Vinson Act of 1937 that reproduced all the original terms of 1935, except for this last one concerning uniform hours and wages. Congress also passed the Connally Act of 1935 on the shipment of oil; the Alcohol Control Act of 1935, which reintroduced the NRA liquor code and placed its supervision under the Treasury; the Robinson-Patman Act of 1936 against favoritism through differential pricing; and the Miller-Tydings Act of 1937, allowing establishment of fair-trade minimum retail prices by manufacturers.

Most substantive was the Motor Carrier Act of 1935 that brought all interstate passenger bus and trucking lines under ICC control. The act also produced a model code based on the railroad code. This prohibited rate discrimination, provided maximum hours for labor, and allowed the ICC to review stock issues and proposals for mergers. A supplementary Transportation Act of 1940 made domestic water carriers and truck companies subject to the same requirements. In 1936 Congress passed the Patman bonus bill, giving war veterans immediate payment of their "bonus" instead of in 1945, something FDR had previously opposed but on which he had now changed his mind.

Once the Supreme Court had declared the AAA unconstitutional in January 1936, Congress devised an alternative, the Soil Conservation and Domestic Allotment Act of 1936, to continue arrangements by which the federal government paid subsidies to farmers who curtailed production. The Merchant Marine Act of 1936 created a maritime commission (headed by Joseph P. Kennedy) to plan trade routes, labor policies, and shipbuilding programs. Moreover, in order to discourage the practice of employing foreigners in order to depress wages, it required that three-quarters of ships' crews were American. The commission was also to build up an auxiliary merchant fleet in case of war.

The Election of 1936

Both sides agreed that the election of 1936 would be a battle of momentous significance. Democrats believed victory was theirs and were most concerned that it should be large enough to carry on the momentum of the most recent New Deal legislation. The Republicans were apprehensive. They welcomed any Democratic defectors and, to stave off a rout, counted on the undoubted fact that millions of people were still unemployed. It was Republican strategy to field a candidate who would alienate neither conservatives nor progressives. Thus Governor Alfred M. Landon of Kansas became the sole contender. He was a progressive from the Midwest who was not associated in any way with the discredited administration of Herbert Hoover. He was duly nominated in Cleveland on June 11, 1936. To journalist Walter Lippmann, Landon was "a dull and uninspired fellow, an ignorant man." Landon was called the Kansas Coolidge by Henry Ford, an epithet that drew an effective riposte from FDR who remarked that the Kansas sunflower was yellow, had a black heart, and always died before November.

After his inevitable renomination on June 12, 1936, FDR compared his critics to "a nice old gentleman" rescued from drowning by a friend in 1933 but who subsequently complained that, though his life had been saved, his fine silk hat had been lost in the misadventure. He returned to his effective distinction between politics and government that he had first made in 1932. FDR admitted "Governments can err, Presidents do make mistakes, but the immortal Dante tells us that divine justice weighs the sins of the cold-blooded and the sins of the warm-hearted in different scales." For, "Better the occasional faults of a Government that lives in a spirit of charity than the constant omission of a Government frozen in the ice of its own indifference." Moreover, "Government in a modern civilization has certain inescapable obligations to its citizens, among which are protection of the family and the home, the establishment of a democracy of opportunity, and aid to those overtaken by disaster. . . . There is a mysterious cycle in human events. To some generations much is given. Of others much is expected. This generation of Americans has a rendezvous with destiny."

The Democrats had to contend with more than their Republican rivals. After the assassination of Huey Long in 1935, Father Coughlin had to carry the double constituency by himself and, finding it difficult to channel the emotional momentum he had helped generate, preferred to draw on a new political ally, Congressman William ("Liberty Bill") Lemke of North Dakota, in a newly formed Union party, to which Gerald L. K. Smith and Dr. Townsend also committed themselves. Lemke became their presidential candidate. He was a shrill speaker who sported outsize clothes, a gray cloth cap, and a glass eye. From the outset relations between these allies were most tense and the ill-fated alliance fell victim to petty jealousies. At the climactic national convention of the Townsend Clubs, held in Cleveland in mid-July 1936, Coughlin, removing his coat and collar, decided to exceed Gerald Smith in his vicious abuse of FDR, to the great embarrassment of the pitifully small delegation of 5,000. His vituperation knew no bounds. "The great betrayer and liar, Franklin D. Roosevelt, who promised to drive the money changers from the temple, has succeeded (only) in driving the farmers from their homesteads and the citizens from their homes in the cities. . . . I ask you to purge the man who claims to be a Democrat from the Democratic Party, and I mean Franklin Double-Crossing Roosevelt." The greater were Coughlin's attacks on FDR, the larger was the desertion of his followers. His constituency declined to a lunatic fringe of Irish-Catholic fanatics.

Political pundits, with the evidence of public opinion polls adverse to FDR, thought that Landon had a fair chance of winning. It was certainly possible to argue that the election of Roosevelt in 1932 was a freak of circumstance and that the New Deal had failed to raise the depression. According to the Bureau of Labor Statistics (BLS), unemployment was 8.59 million whereas the Labor Research Association (LRA) claimed it was 12.61 million. Moreover, prominent Democrats were withdrawing their support from the New Deal. Taking its cue from press censure, the Literary Digest predicted that Landon would take 32 states with 370 electoral votes and that Roosevelt would take only 16 states and 161 electoral votes. However, Dr. George Gallup used different methods for his newly formed American Institute of Public Opinion and predicted a Roosevelt landslide of 477 electoral votes against 42 for Landon.

Not content with relying on the record of the New Deal, FDR went on the attack with a whistle-stop tour. The tenor of FDR's remarks are suggested by his final campaign speech of October 31, in Madison Square Garden, when he said:

For twelve years this nation was afflicted with hear-nothing, see-nothing, do-nothing government. The nation looked to the government but the government looked away. Nine mocking years with the golden calf and three long years of the scourge! Nine crazy years at the ticker and three long years in the breadlines! Nine mad years of mirage and three long years of despair! Powerful influences strive today to restore that kind of government, with its doctrine that that government is best which is most indifferent. . . .

Never before in our history have these forces been so united against one candidate as they stand today. They are unanimous in their hatred for me—and I welcome their hatred.

He concluded with open defiance of the plutocracy, in a ringing remark thrown out with ecstatic arrogance.

I should like to have it said of my first administration that in it the forces of selfishness and of lust for power met their match. I should like to have it said of my second administration that in it these forces met their master.

In the event, FDR won every state except Maine and Vermont, just as his campaign manager, Jim Farley, had predicted. He took 27,752,869 votes to Landon's 16,674,665. Thus was Roosevelt the first Democrat in eighty years to be elected president by a popular majority, taking 60.8 percent of the total to Landon's 36.5 percent. In the electoral college he had 523 votes to Landon's 8. The Union party took only 882,479 votes, the Socialists, 187,720 votes, and the Communists, 80,159 votes. Roosevelt's victory thus set standards for all future elections and his popular vote was not exceeded until Lyndon Johnson's 61.1 percent in 1964.

The credibility of the *Literary Digest* evaporated overnight. It had used outdated methods in its poll, taking the opinions of telephone subscribers, both present and former, who had yet to recover from the depression and were still blaming government for their misfortune. The sales of the *Literary Digest* declined and it soon sold out to *Time* magazine.

The overwhelming Democratic victory created a preponderance of Democrats in the House of almost three to one. In the

Senate 75 out of 96 members were now Democrats; only 16 were Republicans. In the state elections Democrats took 26 of 33 contested elections, including Kansas, Landon's own state.

For a brief time Roosevelt was carried away by his sweeping electoral victory and in his arrogance he momentarily lost his remarkable capacity for knowing what was politically feasible and what was not. Thus the great mandate of 1936 led to unexpected pitfalls for FDR in 1937.

The Storm over the Supreme Court

At his second inauguration, instead of expounding on the New Deal's achievements, Roosevelt struck a new militant note: "In this nation I see tens of millions of its citizens—a substantial part of its whole population—who at this very moment are denied the greater part of what the very lowest standards of today call the necessities of life. . . . I see one third of a nation ill-housed, ill-clad, ill-nourished." Indeed, according to a report by the National Resources Planning Board, *Security, Work, and Relief Policies* (1942), in 1936 18.3 million families, 60 million people altogether, received less than $1,000 per year. Excluding those who received relief, the average family income was $1,348 and this had to support a father, mother, and one or two children in a rented house or apartment. As William Manchester remarks, "The inconvenience and economies of the Depression had been institutionalized." Roosevelt's second inaugural speech became one of the most quoted and has been frequently referred to by analysts to suggest increasing New Deal commitment to end poverty. But, ironically, the problems of "one third of a nation" were to receive considerably less attention in Roosevelt's second term than in his first.

In his first address to the new Congress Roosevelt tried to expose the causes of much of the failure of existing institutions to accommodate themselves to the new requirements of government. In particular, he commented on the Supreme Court's reluctance to accept the New Deal. During the depression the Court had consistently voted—usually by a majority of five to four—against state laws seeking new economic remedies for the depression. In 1935 and 1936 the Court brought much New Deal legislation to an abrupt stop on the grounds that Congress was delegating its power to the president. The extent of the problem is simply illustrated. In the previous 140 years the Supreme Court had nullified only sixty laws. In 1935 and 1936 it invalidated eleven. Moreover, FDR, at the end of his first term, became the first president ever to serve a full four-year term without being able to make a single Court appointment.

In 1933 the Supreme Court had been an extremely conservative body although the other senior branches of government clearly wanted a change. Four of the justices were archconservative: James McReynolds, Willis Van Devanter, Pierce Butler, and George Sutherland. Of these, McReynolds, in his mid-seventies, was considered one of Woodrow Wilson's mistaken appointments, while Van Devanter, at seventy-six, was so infirm that he could not even complete his share of the clerical work of the Court, writing out its decisions, which, therefore, had to be undertaken by his colleagues. All of the conservative justices held that private property was sacrosanct and that an economic policy of laissez faire was the only right course in the depression.

The liberal justices were Benjamin Cardozo, Harlan Fiske Stone, and Louis D. Brandeis. Both Cardozo and Brandeis were Jewish and all were committed to civil rights. Brandeis, the oldest justice, brought to judicial problems a new emphasis upon facts, statistics, and a pragmatic approach to social problems. His decisions and those of Cardozo and Stone implied that government and laws must change with the times. The remaining two justices are sometimes called "the swing men." They were Owen Roberts, who had prosecuted the Teapot Dome Scandal in the 1920s, and Chief Justice Charles Evans Hughes, former governor of New York and former secretary of state. Hughes tried to keep the peace between all the factions. While lacking the compassion of the liberals, Hughes was a rare mix of statesman and jurist whose austere, Jove-like presence commanded respect and awe. In the end he moved his politics from right to left.

The first adverse decision came in January 1935 in *Panama Refining Co.* v. *Ryan*. This was a case about Section 9c of the National Industrial Recovery Act that allowed the president, under certain circumstances, to prohibit the transportation of oil across state lines. By a vote of 8 to 1 the Court declared Section 9c unconstitutional because it was incomplete: it established neither guidelines for, nor restrictions upon, presidential authority. The Court was also hostile to any modest redistribution of wealth. In the case of *Railroad Retirement Board* v. *Alton Railroad,* also in 1935, by a vote of 5 to 4, the Court declared unconstitutional a railway retirement act on the grounds that the Constitution did not provide for the compulsory institution of railway pensions, which were a misuse of the property of the employers.

The most notorious adverse decisions were those of Black Monday—May 27, 1935. The Court found the Frazier-Lemke Farm Mortgage Act unconstitutional, ruled that the removal of Federal Trade Commissioner William E. Humphrey was a matter for Congress and not the president, and, as we know, in *Schechter* v. *The United States,* found the NIRA unconstitutional because it interfered with interstate commerce. It should be emphasized that the adverse decision in the *Schechter* case was unanimous. The liberals sided with the conservatives. Sensing the significance of this decision, the *Daily Express* of London opined: "America Stunned: Roosevelt's two years' work killed in twenty minutes." In January 1936 the Court went further and ruled 6 to 3 against the AAA in *United States* v. *Butler et al.* By 5 to 4 it ruled against the Municipal Bankruptcy Act (requested by cities across the country). By 5 to 4 it found in *Carter* v. *Carter Coal Company* against the Guffey-Snyder Coal Conservation Act, an act specifically written after the NIRA decision in the *Schechter* case of the previous year. Al Smith jubilantly told a Liberty League dinner how the Supreme Court was "throwing out the alphabet three letters at a time."

Supreme Court rejection of the New Deal had reached epidemic proportions. Thus, as British political scientist John Lees declares, "The conjunction of a grave political and economic emergency, an assertive and popular President, and a strong-willed judiciary, provided in 1933 the ingredients for a constitutional conflict of major dimensions." Roosevelt and his supporters feared that the nonelected justices were preventing the duly elected branches of government from doing their job. The Court and its supporters feared that the will of the majority was being used by the president to make himself a dictator.

The president and his team had long considered how best to remedy matters. FDR favored the plan of Attorney General Homer S. Cummings, the court-packing bill S. 1392, announced on February 5, 1937. Its premise was that Court personnel in general were deficient, particularly because too many judges were too old for the job. Therefore, FDR proposed that if a federal judge who had served ten years waited more than six months beyond the age of 70 to retire, then the president could appoint an additional justice—up to six on the Supreme Court and forty-four to lower federal courts. In his message FDR deliberately avoided any reference to the judges' widely publicized conservatism.

As far as increasing the actual number of justices to the Supreme Court was concerned, FDR had ample precedent since the number had been revised from six to ten and, finally, nine in the nineteenth century—and always for reasons of party politics. Moreover, his plan was based on one offered to Woodrow Wilson by his attorney general, James C. McReynolds, now the archconservative architect of court decisions against the New Deal. However, by disguising what was a blatant political stratagem as a means of restoring efficiency to the courts and using old age as a criterion, FDR had miscalculated. The oldest member of the Court, Louis D. Brandeis, at seventy-nine was the most liberal. Everyone knew it was not the age of other justices that was in question but their political opinions. Many distinguished congressmen over seventy also felt themselves threatened. It was frankly disingenuous to incubate such a profound change in secret, to tie reform of the Supreme Court to reform of the judiciary, to avoid admission of the differences between the Court and the New Deal, and to do all this so soon after an election in which the proposal had not even been mentioned.

Not only did the American Liberty League, the National Association of Manufacturers, the U.S. Chamber of Commerce, and the DAR campaign against the scheme, as expected, but also a host of local community associations, whose opposition was more disinterested. In his column of June 6, 1937, Walter Lippmann accused FDR of "proposing to create the necessary precedent, to

Cartoonist Clifford Berryman was as imaginative in exploring the comic possibilities of FDR as he had been with Theodore Roosevelt. This cartoon of March 9, 1937, shows how the Democratic donkey and the dove of peace scatter in dismay upon hearing Franklin Roosevelt's plan to pack the Supreme Court, a plan as offensive to FDR's allies as to his opponents. (Library of Congress).

establish the political framework for, and to destroy the safeguards against, a dictator." Previously loyal liberals, such as Senator Burton K. Wheeler of Montana, now joined with the opposition.

Nevertheless, the impasse between FDR and the Court was resolved and a serious crisis passed. First, Charles Evans Hughes wrote a letter to Wheeler in the Senate Judiciary Committee, which had been agreed by Willis Van Devanter (one of the conservatives) and Louis D. Brandeis (one of the liberals), showing that the Court was abreast of its work, and that an increase of judges would make for greater, not less, inefficiency. As Hughes explained, "There would be more judges to hear, more judges to confer, more judges to be convinced and decide. The present number of Justices is thought to be large enough so far as the prompt, adequate and efficient conduct of the work of the Court is concerned."

Second, the Court began to return decisions favorable to the New Deal. On March 29, 1937, in *West Coast Hotel Company* v. *Parrish,* by a majority of 5 to 4, it upheld a minimum wage law enacted by Washington State that was almost exactly the same as the one passed by New York State that it had nullified the year before. Public opinion preferred to believe the remark of a wit that "a switch in time saves nine." Apparently, Owen J. Roberts changed his mind realising that, unless the Court moved with the times, its influence would decline.

Third, in five decisions in April 1937 the Court allowed Congress control of interstate commerce, most notably in *NLRB* v. *Jones and Laughlin Steel Corporation.* In May in two decisions it upheld the Social Security Act by majorities of 5 to 4. Fourth, in May 1937, the physically senile Justice Van Devanter retired at long last, thus allowing FDR the opportunity to appoint a more liberal successor. As a result of these various events the more urgent reasons for reforming the Court evaporated.

FDR's worst tactical error in the whole episode was to insist on passage of the original court-packing bill even after the political need for it had disappeared. Thus he aroused deep antagonism in Congress. When the bill was eventually passed in August 1937 as the Judicial Reform Act, it was in emasculated form with no mention of the Supreme Court. However, FDR described the Court fight as "a lost battle which won a war." Between 1937 and 1940 FDR appointed liberals Hugo Black, Stanley Reed, Felix Frankfurter, William O. Douglas, and Frank Murphy to various vacancies on the Supreme Court. There was now a "Roosevelt Court," the most liberal since the mid-nineteenth century, committed to civil liberties, minority rights, and progressive legislation in general.

Ironically, the battle over the Supreme Court allowed many who had abandoned the New Deal earlier to move back into the mainstream of liberalism, claiming that they, rather than FDR, were the true heirs of progressivism. It was a small bloc of southern conservatives in Congress, led by Senator Carter Glass of Virginia, that first began to oppose the New Deal more forcibly. These men had begun to move away from the New Deal as early as 1935, but the storm over the Supreme Court gave them the excuse they needed to fight FDR openly.

The antagonisms aroused by the Court battle were fueled by the dissatisfaction of conservatives with the gains of labor, increased welfare and relief, and began to take on something of the character of the feud between town and country that had disfigured the 1920s. The conservatives were essentially from a background of rural politics themselves and from states in which rural politics were predominant. They opposed proposals for low-cost public housing, federal regulation of hours and wages, and legislation to achieve civil rights. What they feared was the advent of an interdependent, possibly collectivized, urban society. They saw increasing centralization in government without understanding the changes in growth of population and demands that underpinned it.

Roosevelt also suffered defections from the high ranks of the New Dealers such as Raymond Moley, General Hugh Johnson, and George Peek, all of whom distrusted the increased supremacy of government over labor, agriculture, and industry that they had, themselves, done so much to bring about. Among the former progressives who lost sympathy with the New Deal were Oswald Garrison Villard, Walter Lippmann, and Dorothy Thompson, all of whom were trenchant critics in journals and newspapers. They simply would not accept that increased centralization of government came out of ever greater public demands for governmental services or the need to regulate economic forces, partly to raise the standard of living for the most disadvantaged. They could not reconcile themselves to a system of national social security that was based on a degree of coercion by law. To these critics the New Deal was imposing a Servile State—the phrase borrowed from G. K. Chesterton. They made mistaken analogies between FDR and European dictators, and failed to appreciate that the totalitarian governments of Europe had come to power not because democratic governments had assumed too much power but, rather, because they had not done enough to support their principles.

The New Deal at Ebb Tide

Because of the furor over the court-packing scheme, FDR was unable to accomplish anything substantive of his ambitious program for the "one-third-of-a-nation" address. Nevertheless, in 1937 Congress acted on behalf of the destitute migrants of the Dust Bowl, the Okies.

The Bankhead-Jones Farm Tenant Act of July 1937 was a product of a government report, showing that family-owned farms were becoming something of the past as mortgages were foreclosed when crops failed. As we know, some families slid into tenancy and sharecropping, and the Okies and Arkies (migrants from Arkansas) took to the roads. The act created a Farm Security Administration (FSA) and incorporated it within the Resettlement Administration (RA) to help tenants and sharecroppers acquire farms from a special loan fund to provide for the purchase, refinancing, and rehabilitation of farms at low rates of interest. Thus, the FSA was to counteract the unfortunate side effects of the first AAA that contributed to dispossession when marginal lands were withdrawn from production in return for subsidies. The FSA also established thirty camps to provide temporary housing for thousands of destitute migratory families. In addition, it created medical and dental centers and funded cooperative aid for the purchase of heavy machinery by small farmers. Within ten years 40,000 families had bought their own farms through FSA loans and 900,000 families had borrowed a total of $800 million to rehabilitate their farms or, even, relocate them on more arable land.

One of the most impressive government documents of the depression years is not a book of statistics of the experience but the remarkable portfolio of photos taken by artists and photographers of the Farm Security Administration. Jack Delano, Carl Mydans, Walker Evans, Arthur Rothstein, John Vachon, and others, captured the plight and determination of impoverished America. Two of the group, Dorothea Lange and Ben Shahn, were especially gifted in encapsulating the desperate experience of migrants from the Dust Bowl and showing listlessness, despair, and helplessness in children, courage and stamina in their parents. Such prolific and talented artists provided the nation with graphic proof that the soil was exhausted, that the system had broken down, and that it was the urgent duty of the body politic to put things right.

The Wagner-Steagall National Housing Act of September 1, 1937, was designed to meet the problems of slum clearance and public housing. It established the United States Housing Authority (USHA) to act through public housing bureaus in large cities, loaning them sufficient money (up to 100 percent) at low rates of interest to build new homes. It was to be financed by issues of bonds. By 1941 160,000 units had been built for slum dwellers at an average rent of $12 or $15 per month.

The New Agriculture Adjustment Act of February 1938 was based on the so-called "ever normal granary" plan, storing surplus in fat years for distribution in lean years. It established how quotas in five basic staple crops—cotton, tobacco, wheat, corn, and rice—could be imposed by a two-thirds majority of farmers in a referendum. Those who adhered to the quota received subsidies based on prices of the favorable period of 1909–1914. In case of overproduction, the Commodity Credit Corporation could make storage loans up to 75 percent of parity price (later 85 percent). Thus, if the market price fell below that amount, then the farmer could store his crop in return for a loan at that level of 75 (or 85) percent. When the market price rose, then the farmer could repay the loan and sell the surplus. Because of the fierce droughts of previous years, crop insurance was made available to farmers. The premiums could be paid for either in wheat or its cash equivalent. A second new feature was the Food Stamp Plan under which farm surpluses were distributed through the Federal Surplus Commodities Corporation to persons on relief who received 50 cents of such produce free for every $1 they spent on other groceries. These relief payments, especially among the urban poor, helped reduce farm surplus, and increased the business of retail stores.

The last major law of the New Deal was the Fair Labor Standards Act of June 25, 1938, a most controversial measure that was only passed by Congress meeting in special session after numerous concessions by FDR and the New Dealers. It fixed minimum wages and maximum hours for all industries engaged in interstate commerce: it established a minimum wage of 25 cents per hour, with provisions for a gradual increase to 40 cents an hour; and it set maximum hours at forty-four hours per week, with a goal of forty hours within three years. Moreover, overtime work was to be paid at the rate of time-and-a-half. The act also set laws on child labor. It forbade interstate shipment of goods made either in whole or in part by children under sixteen. Further, children under eighteen could engage only in nonhazardous occupations. To supervise the new law a Wage and Hour Division was created in the Department of Labor with power to impose heavy fines for breach of regulations. As a result of the act, about 650,000 workers received wage rises and over 2 million had their hours of work reduced. Because of the need to secure the votes of grudging conservative congressmen, FDR accepted exemptions of benefit to their particular economic interests. Thus seamen, fishermen, domestics, and farm laborers were exempt from the provisions of the act. However, the bill outlawed child labor; it abolished the worst abuses of sweatshops; and it brought some protection to the three-quarters of working people not in organized labor.

The Food, Drug, and Cosmetics Act of 1938 expanded the Pure Food Act of 1906, giving the Department of Agriculture additional powers to control fraud by the manufacturers of foods and drugs. In particular, it required labels on bottles listing their contents. Nevertheless, Congress had not turned FDR's recommendations in his second inaugural address into positive legislative achievements and there followed an even more effective break on the New Deal than congressional intransigence.

Without question, the economy had shown signs of recovery from the worst of the depression in the period 1933–1936. The national income rose from little more than $42 billion in 1933 to $57 billion in 1935. Accordingly, the government began to plan for a balanced budget by 1939, gradually reducing its deficit. However, in August 1937 business fell back and there was a wave of selling on the stock market. In nine months in 1937–1938 the Federal Reserve Board's adjusted index of industrial production lost two-thirds of the gains it had made during the painful ascent of the New Deal years. It fell from 117 in August 1937 to 76 in May 1938. This was a faster collapse than in the devastating period 1929–1932. Farm prices fell by nearly 20 percent and, in the autumn, unemployment increased by more than 2 million. Harry Hopkins, Harold Ickes, and others argued for the continued injection of government funds into the economy, spending even to the point of deficit financing. Roosevelt reluctantly agreed. He was won round by stories of starvation in the South and extreme and widespread poverty in northern cities and, thus, asked Congress for a $3 billion program of relief and public works expenditures. By December 1938 this, and continuing New Deal programs, had halted the decline.

Believing that private business had failed to play its part in recovery, FDR also wanted increased surveillance of business monopolies. Therefore, Congress set up the Temporary National Economic Committee (1938–1941) under Senator Joseph O'Mahoney of Wyoming. It produced the most thorough study ever of American monopolies. But in 1941 its findings were overshadowed by foreign affairs.

The traditional regional division in the Democratic party, which the battle over the Supreme Court had widened, was confirmed by the failure of the Wagner-Van Nuys bill that would have made lynching a federal crime and allowed the families of lynch victims to sue the county in which the crime was committed. It was defeated by a southern filibuster. FDR, and his advisers, especially Hopkins and Ickes, were furious at the way southern Democrats used FDR's popularity to get themselves elected and, once in office, deserted the New Deal. Thus they tried to institute a purge of disloyal congressmen, such as Senators Millard F. Tydings of Maryland, "Cotton Ed" Smith of South Carolina, and Walter F. George of Georgia, in the midterm elections of 1938. FDR wanted

With her penetrating gaze fixed on the horizon, an indomitable grandmother among the Okies looks ahead to the future. (Photo by Dorothea Lange; Library of Congress).

to oust these southern conservatives and to transform the Democratic party from a loose coalition of local and sectional interests,
in which its congressmen conveniently blurred the issues when it
suited them, into a tightly knit and cohesive bloc of definite,
liberal views.

It is a political truism that for some men to live by principle
others must live by compromise and when Roosevelt sought to
overlook this and defy political reality, he was fighting a losing
game. Not only was the strategy mistaken but also the tactics.
Roosevelt tried and failed to have popular and influential Democrats dropped from the party ticket for the midterm elections of
1938. Thus Senators George, Smith, and Tydings survived FDR's
attacks. Only Congressman John O'Connor of New York, albeit

chairman of the powerful House Rules Committee, succumbed to Roosevelt's withdrawal of support and was defeated. He was nominated by the Republicans as their candidate but lost the election.

Moreover, in the midterm elections of 1938, the Republicans almost doubled their seats in the House from 88 to 169 against 261 Democrats—still a workable majority. In the Senate the results left sixty-nine Democrats against twenty-three Republicans. Nevertheless, the swing of public approval away from the New Deal could not be ignored. Thus in January 1939 no new reform measures were proposed. The political impulses that had allowed, even needed, the New Deal in the early 1930s were almost extinct. The New Dealers sought no more fundamental laws and the brief overwhelming ascendancy of the Democratic party was somewhat tarnished in many minds by the mistaken court packing scheme and by the comparative electoral setback of 1938. People were exhausted by adversary politics and both organized labor and business now preferred to follow a more moderate course in the interests of reducing class tension. Thus FDR's annual message on January 4, 1939, acknowledged the New Deal had come to an end.

However, the New Deal ended as it had begun with a demonstration that the greatest power of the federal government devolved from presidential initiative. FDR realized that if he, or any less energetic successor, were to survive the political strain of the presidency, then it would be necessary to institutionalize its administrative staff and reform the various agencies to make them more effective. However, his attempt to secure congressional approval for a reorganization bill had fallen foul of the soured atmosphere of 1938. The bill narrowly passed the Senate in March to be defeated by 204 votes to 196 in the House on April 8, 1938. Roosevelt's critics charged him with an attempt at Hitlerian despotism, a criticism fueled by Father Coughlin's unwanted return to political broadcasts in 1938, but many were really motivated by jealousy and malice.

FDR was neither defeated nor deterred and by Executive Order 8248 of September 8, 1939, he established the Executive Office of the President, staffed with six administrative assistants. Subsequently, the Council of Economic Advisers, the National Security Council, and the Central Intelligence Agency were moved into the Executive Office. In *The American Presidency* (1956) Clinton Rossiter concludes that this decision "converts the Presidency into an instrument of twentieth-century government; it gives the incumbent a sporting chance to stand the strain and fulfill his constitutional mandate as a one-man branch of our three-part government; it deflates even the most forceful arguments . . . for a plural executive; it assures us that the Presidency will survive the advent of the positive state. Executive Order 8248 may yet be judged to have saved the Presidency from paralysis and the Constitution from radical amendment."

The major legacy of the New Deal was that the operation of the national economy was made the responsibility of government in the interests of all its citizens and not just those of a particular class. Thus the federal government became an institution shared by all the people. For the first time they experienced its presence as it taxed hundred of thousands directly and distributed pensions and relief to millions. No longer was it a neutral arbiter between different branches or levels of government but, in the words of Felix Frankfurter, the "powerful promoter of society's welfare."

The state was personified by FDR whom millions regarded as a protector. In his *Being an American* (1948), Justice William O. Douglas remarked: "He was in a very special sense the people's President, because he made them feel that with him in the White House they shared the Presidency. The sense of sharing the Presidency gave even the most humble citizen a lively sense of belonging." Or, in the words of William E. Leuchtenburg in *Franklin D. Roosevelt and the New Deal* (1963), "Roosevelt's importance lay not in his talents as a campaigner or a manipulator. It lay rather in his ability to arouse the country and, more specifically, the men who served under him, by his breezy encouragement of experimentation, by his hopefulness, and—a word that would have embarrassed some of his lieutenants—by his idealism."

Historian Dexter Perkins has acutely observed, "The President . . . took his place at the head of the procession only when it was quite clear where the procession was going." The procession was, of course, the New Deal and public support for it, and, in one sense, FDR cannot be given credit for originality. The individual reforms of the New Deal were all variations upon earlier proposals, as Perkins also makes clear. The legislation of the New Deal grew out of the recent past.

While the New Deal achieved a more equitable society it left much undone. It left largely untouched the problems of tenant farmers, sharecroppers, migrant workers in agriculture and, among ethnic groups, blacks, Puerto Ricans, and Mexican-Americans. New Deal efforts in slum clearance were scarcely proportionate to the magnitude of the problem. Although FDR had called attention to one-third of a nation "ill-nourished, ill-clad, ill-housed" in 1937, only thirty years later Michael Harrington showed in *The Other America* that the proportion was almost as great.

It was especially frustrating for the most egalitarian New Dealers that their program bypassed black Americans, made only symbolic concessions to the status of women, and did little to improve the general standard of education. The New Deal was essentially devoted to economic and material recovery and thus civil rights between the sexes and the races were largely ignored. New Deal discrimination against blacks took various forms, such as banning them from construction work on the TVA, interpreting crop restriction policies of the AAA in such a way as to allow their eviction from farms, and pandering to the racist sentiments of federal administrators in the South. Even the Federal Housing Administration practiced discrimination. All of this was partly because FDR knew he dare not antagonize southern congressmen utterly and completely. But it was also because the New Deal was, as we have observed in its reform program, acting as an honest broker between different sections of the community and the greatest benefits were to be awarded to the best organized or politically influential groups.

The American political and economic system was strengthened by the New Deal but the depression and widespread unemployment remained. According to the minimal statistics of the U.S. Department of Labor, Bureau of Labor Statistics, unemployment rose from 1.49 million (3.1 percent of the labor force) in 1929 to 12.63 million (25.2 percent) in 1933. Thereafter, the level fell gradually until it was 7.27 million (13.8 percent) in 1937, only to rise to 8.84 million (16.5 percent) in 1939. As has been emphasized, these statistics were regarded as serious underestimates by the AFL, CIO, and LRA. Even the BLS admitted that wholesale prices remained well below their index number of 100 in 1926. Thus in 1929 prices were at 95.3 of the high level, falling successively to 65.9 in 1933, and rising gradually to 86.3 in 1937, and then declining to 77.1 in 1939. The Federal Reserve Board charted the physical volume of industrial production in these years according to an average of 100 for the years 1935–1939. In 1929 the index was 110. It was at its lowest in 1932 at 58. Thereafter, it rose to 113 in 1937, falling back to 88 in 1938, before rising to 108 in 1939. We can attribute some poverty to factors other than the unprecedented economic crisis, but they made the Great Depression more severe. One such factor was the increasing number of old people in the population. The number of people over sixty-five rose from 4.9 million in 1920 to 9 million in 1940, an increase from 4.6 percent to 6.9 percent. Another factor was the bitter climax of the long-term exploitation of the soil in certain areas that culminated in the Dust Bowl.

Given the unprecedented crisis it was surprising that the New Deal achieved as much as it did, rather than it left so many problems unsolved. In less than six years more significant changes were wrought by government than ever previously. Much of what the New Deal attempted but did not complete was halted by the war, by its own moderation and loss of momentum, and by the growth of opposition resulting from FDR's adversary politics of 1936 and 1937. Moreover, the New Deal fostered and encouraged widespread discussion about the values of society, the proper role and relationships of its various economic components —industry, business, agriculture, labor, and government—and just how mutually responsible and caring these groups in society should be to one another. In short, the New Deal educated the American people that industrial and social life must be a shared experience.

7

A HOUSE DIVIDED
Workers, Labor, and
Ethnic Groups

Welfare Capitalism of the 1920s

THE GREAT Red Scare of 1917–1921 and the extinction of the postwar wave of strikes crippled the union movement for the next dozen years. During the course of the 1920s, the proportion of the nonagricultural labor force organized in unions declined from 18.6 percent to only 12 percent. The AFL scurried back into its shell of conservatism as the nation's factories and mills roared forward at an ever quickening pace. Employers, anxious to prevent another 1919, set about nurturing a sense of loyalty among their employees, and applied modern technology to the world of the worker.

Nevertheless, employers had come to the conclusion that they could get more out of their workers by cultivating their loyalty and dependence, rather than relying forever on the threat of wage cuts and unemployment. Housing, pension schemes, stock sharing, recreational services, health care, and educational benefits were offered to some workers who agreed not to join unions and avoided strike action. A 1919 Bureau of Labor Statistics special report on industrial welfare indicated a broad movement by management to stimulate corporate loyalty among employees. Of 431 establishments surveyed, 375 had begun some type of medical program and 265 reported having hospital facilities, 75 had pension plans, 80 had established disability benefit plans, and 152 had constructed recreation facilities for their workers. The selective nature of welfare capitalism was a point not lost on the president of International Harvester, Harold McCormick, who wrote in a letter to employees, "As you know, our Pension Plan is a purely voluntary expression of the company's desire to stand by the men who have stood by it." At least 6 million workers came to be covered by welfare programs in the 1920s, and a survey of 1926 found that half of the 1,500 largest American companies were operating comprehensive schemes.

It should be emphasized that, even at its peak, welfare capitalism covered only a minority of the work force, and often the schemes were somewhat piecemeal. The influence of welfare capitalism was felt strongest in company towns, where stringent rules already restricted workers' lives in and outside the plant. For example, strikers and their families in steel mill towns found that they were evicted from company-owned housing and denied access to the social clubs, libraries, and health clinics built by the corporation. The illusion of corporate paternalism was also developed in the form of "employee representation plans" and "works councils." Drawing on the arbitration guidelines established by the War Labor Board, companies offered workers the right to a formal grievance procedure within strictly defined limits. Between 1919 and 1924, some 490 firms established representation plans that served not only to redress petty complaints, but also to deflect and absorb more militant demands. "Given a channel for expression of legitimate grievances," writes economist Richard Edwards in *Contested Terrain* (1979), " 'loyal' workmen would not be driven into the ranks of the unions." Thus, company unions came to feature strongly in corporate publicity as a shining example of America's industrial democracy.

However, it was the change in the structure of the workplace

The calm and sobriety of prewar small town America is captured in this 1941 photograph of the business section of Taft, California, behind which loom the oil derricks of prosperity. (Wittemann Collection, Library of Congress).

that proved crucial in undermining the power of workers on the shopfloor. Companies set up personnel departments to remove decisions over hiring and firing from the foreman and commissioned scientific management studies to increase efficiency. Moreover, the administration of day-to-day factory life was put into the hands of a new army of professional managers.

Throughout the nineteenth and early twentieth centuries, attempts had been made to reduce the need for highly skilled labor by mechanizing the production process. For example, the Ford assembly line achieved enormous increases in productivity by transferring the decision as to the pace of work away from the worker, and into the hands of the manager who controlled the production line. "The delivery of work instead of leaving it to the workmen's initiative to find it" was how Henry Ford described it. With the new product in high demand, the Ford Motor Company's plants were able to produce 31,200 automobiles in 1925 with virtually the same machinery that had produced 25,000 cars in 1920.

Because of his scientific advances and his highly successful factory management, Henry Ford's schemes of employment were accepted by society at large. His $5 a day minimum wage for workers and his insistence on a high standard of social behavior from them were generally assumed to beneficial. However, minister and theologian Reinhold Niebuhr, who had a parish in Detroit, knew differently. He became a contributing editor of *Christian Century* in 1923 and, gleaning evidence from his parishioners, began a series of articles criticizing Ford. He showed that Ford's average annual wage was low and exposed other malpractices of the system. Ford's employees were broken by their work despite the $5 wage and the five-day week. Niebuhr knew that they were often dismissed in summary fashion in middle age, unfit for work elsewhere and emotionally dejected. Niebuhr found himself increasingly concentrating on welfare work for Ford's employees. After General Motors began to outsell him, in 1927 Ford discontinued production of the model T, closed his factories, modernized them, and then reopened them for his production of the new model A. In the interim period some 60,000 workers were unemployed. When the factories reopened, the former workers were engaged as new employees, starting again at $5 a day. Thus the new Ford car cost Ford's men at least $50 million in lost wages, not to mention the families broken up in the period of unemployment.

Reinhold Niebuhr believed certain factors in the capitalist system made this sort of injustice possible. One was the development of the city—a society without moral standards held together by a mechanical, productive process—and another was the selfishness inherent in human nature: "We are all responsible. We all want the things which the factory produces and none of us is sensitive enough to care how much in human values the efficiency of the modern factory costs." Thus Niebuhr concluded that the natural energy of man was harnessed to the inhuman drives of society. Men worked for a society that actually deprived them of the emotional benefits they thought came from it. Niebuhr did not merely criticize Ford and other industrialists but accused society as a whole for its indifference to human suffering. In *Does Civilization Need Religion?* (1927), he declared that the threat of depersonalization of the individual was inherent in modern industrial society and should be met by social reconstruction.

Problems of Labor

Even in the 1920s unemployment was much higher than was generally supposed and a continuous worry for most workers. However, estimates vary greatly. According to the *Historical Statistics of the United States* (1975), unemployment was 11.7 percent of the civilian labor force in 1921 and then fell to an average of 3.3 percent in the period 1923–1929, with the figure of 1.8 percent for 1926 being a modern peacetime record for the United States. Robert M. Cohen in "Labor Force and Unemployment in the 1920s and 1930s" for the *Review of Economics and Statistics* (1973) gives an average unemployment rate of 5.1 percent for 1923–1929. However, Paul H. Douglas, surveying only transportation, mining, building, and construction in *Real Wages in the United States, 1890–1926* (1930), provides an average of 12.95 percent in 1921–1926 and even the very best years of 1923, 1925, and 1926 average 8.1 percent.

The discrepancy is partly explained by the fact that those in work included many who wanted to work full-time but had only part-time employment. Without the sort of welfare support provided later, part-time work was hardship and made it more difficult to save for periods of total unemployment. As Caroline Manning noted in *The Immigrant Woman and Her Job* (1930), "due to the amount of part-time work during the past year or two, they have found it impossible to accumulate a financial reserve to fall back on when out of a job." In Muncie, Indiana, in 1924 43 percent of one sample of working-class families for the Lynds' *Middletown* (1929) lost at least a month of work and 24.2 percent lost three or more months of work. Thus, in the first nine months of 1929, average unemployment of these working-class families was 17.5 percent. A survey in Philadelphia by J. Frederick Dewhurst and Ernest A. Tupper, *Social and Economic Character of Unemploy-*

ment in Philadelphia (April 1929), showed 10.4 percent out of work because there was no work to be found (7.8 percent) or because of sickness, old age, and similar causes (2.6 percent). The analysts discussed 18.9 percent unemployed in industrial neighborhoods.

If many working-class families were poor in employment, unemployment plunged them into deep poverty. The wife of an unemployed roofer told Clinch Caulkins in *Some Folk's Won't Walk* (1930), "When my husband's working steady, I can just manage, but when he's out, things go back. First I stop on the damp wash, then on the food, and then the rent goes behind." Some families would rather almost starve than accept charity and one lived on nothing but bread and tea for six weeks. A father waited on a streetcorner at lunchtime "for fear if he came home he would be tempted to eat what they have been able to put on the table for the children." Those who suffered malnutrition were prone to such illnesses as pneumonia. Some people had nervous breakdowns or committed suicide by gassing themselves.

Despite the decline in European immigration, there was a glut of industrial workers after 1923. As the decade progressed, workers had a harder time finding jobs. The move of ever more people from countryside to city more than compensated for the abrupt end of immigration. It was an employers' market. Productivity increased and the increase was possible with the same number, or fewer, workers. Thus there were about the same numbers of industrial workers in 1928 and 1929 (respectively 8.1 million and 8.6 million) as there had been in 1919 and 1920 (8.6 million). Increased mechanization and reorganization of work displaced workers who might endure several months of unemployment before finding work again, as Isador Lubin shows in *The Absorption of the Unemployed by American Industry* (1929).

The mountains of paperwork generated by the modern corporation created a need for clerical workers, a need filled by women secretaries. The so-called feminization of the clerical labor force drew nearly 2.25 million women to work in offices by the end of the decade. Between 1910 and 1930, the proportion of women who worked in domestic service fell from a third of all women wage earners to a quarter. However, even with as many as 4 million women wage earners in the work force in 1930, the doors of organized labor remained difficult for them to prise open. Already largely excluded from the male-dominated internationals, a proposal by the Women's Trade Union League to organize separate federal locals for women was also rejected by the AFL. As a result, only 250,000 women belonged to unions at the end of the decade and half of them were in the garment industry. Moreover, the progressive principle of protecting women and children workers was rejected by the courts. In the case of *Adkins* v. *Children's Hospital,* decided by 5 votes to 3 on April 9, 1923, the Supreme Court invalidated an act of Congress setting a minimum wage for women and children in the District of Columbia. The majority found that the law was a price-fixing measure in violation of freedom of contract protected by the Fifth Amendment.

In the bituminous coal industry, the boom of the war years was followed by a crisis of overproduction, with domestic markets becoming glutted. Too many mines producing too much coal was the context in which miners struck in 1919 and 1922. The new president of the United Mine Workers (UMW), John L. Lewis, was forced to accept a settlement that preserved existing wage rates but gave no protection for jobs. Between 1920 and 1927, the number of miners working in the industry fell from over 700,000 to approximately 575,000. The UMW's losses in membership were even more spectacular, from a high of half a million bituminous coal members in 1921–1922, to, perhaps, 80,000 by mid-1928.

The problems of the coal industry had reached chronic proportions years before shareholders saw their surplus wealth crash on Wall Street in 1929. The continuous surplus of labor meant that a typical miner was working between 142 and 220 days a year, and often bringing home less than $2 a day, instead of the expected $7.50 union minimum. Miners and their families lived on diets of beans (euphemistically nicknamed "miners' strawberries"), gravy, and bread. Respiratory and intestinal diseases were widespread in mining communities. For those who complained too loudly about their impoverished existence, company officials were swift with the reminder that "there's a barefoot, hungry man outside waiting for your job."

Powerless to rescue the economy of coal, the UMW's president, John L. Lewis, concentrated on securing his grip on the union's internal organization. The son of Welsh immigrants who had settled in Iowa in the 1870s, John L. Lewis rose to become the most important and perplexing labor leader of the twentieth century. He assumed control of the miners' union in 1919, when a debilitated Frank Hayes was obliged to retire. Lewis was a big burly man with a luxurious lion's mane of hair, eyebrows like furry caterpillars, and a foghorn voice. His rhetoric mixed metaphors from the Bible, Homer, and Shakespeare, combining the commonplace and the grotesque to inspired effect. Of his own genius for self-publicity he once remarked, "He who tooteth not his own horn, the same shall not be tooted."

According to his biographers, Melvyn Dubofsky and Warren Van Tine, Lewis was a "man driven by ambition and perhaps eager to compensate for his lowly social origins by achieving parity with America's economic and political elite." Through a combination of subtle scheming, deceitful maneuvering, and ruthless opportunism, he accumulated power within the UMW as a model union autocrat. From this lofty position, Lewis also prospered as a bank president, investor, country-clubber, and dinner guest to leading businessmen and politicians. Yet, conversely, while he assimilated the values of business, John Lewis also maintained a deep commitment to the coal industry and to the organization of its workers. Forever the pragmatist, Lewis shifted his allegiances and demands as the contemporary political climate permitted. Thus, in the 1920s he remained passive while the membership of his union and the wages of miners plummeted. However, as the tide of events turned in 1932, the UMW leader became an advocate of militancy, demanding, first, governmental action to revive the economy, and, then, trade union action to mobilize the nation's industrial workers. Later, Lewis would stand alone among union leaders in resisting the government's efforts to manipulate the organized labor movement during World War II. Liberals regarded him as a politician of conscience and vision while to his conservative critics, he was proletarian evil incarnate.

John Lewis's career demonstrated how the political economy of

The gregarious and vociferous miners' leader, John Llewellyn Lewis
(left), a man of luxurious hair who led the movement for the unionization of unskilled and semiskilled industrial workers, eventually breaking with the AFL to form the Congress of Industrial Organizations.
(Photo by Underwood and Underwood; Library of Congress).

the period was more conducive to trade union autocracy than it was to working class militancy. Hard hit by open shop drives, and the depression that crippled some weaker industries, such as coal and textiles, union leaders often found that the only way to preserve their organizations at all was to centralize power and stamp out internal dissent. Gangsterism was also able to use union leadership struggles to creep into the labor movement. Meanwhile, conservative business unionists, such as William ("Big Bill") Hutcheson of the Carpenters, dominated the AFL's executive council, and held sway over the mild-mannered William Green who succeeded Samuel Gompers as president in 1924. Of Green, John L. Lewis later remarked, "Alas poor Green: I knew him well. He wishes to join in fluttering procrastination, the while intoning, 'O tempora, O mores!' "

AFL leaders stubbornly refused to pay attention to members' demands—let alone the 85 to 90 percent of unorganized workers —since the full power of American capitalism had a firm stranglehold around the neck of the labor movement. In an era that was marked by its low strike rate and falling union rolls, corporate paternalism could switch rapidly to overt repression if workers stepped too far out of line. Of 1,845 injunctions issued by federal courts to ban strike action in the period 1800 to 1930, almost half were issued in the 1920s. Indeed, the legal right of workers to bargain with their employers through labor unions remained in doubt right through to the 1930s.

In spite of the barrage of judicial and management attacks, the acquiescence of the rank and file was never absolute. On the shop floor, informal groups of workers continued to restrict output and undermine management's attempts to restructure the workplace. Elsewhere, workers made increasingly militant demands through works councils that occasionally took on a life of their own. Moreover, the scattering of radicals who had managed to escape the full force of the Great Red Scare also began to regroup and organize at grass roots level.

Throughout the 1920s, the Communist party, first founded in 1919 as the Workers' party, followed a strategy of boring from within the AFL unions. Led by the roving industrial organizer, William Z. Foster, the Communists attempted to capture the national movement for a Farmer-Labor party in 1922–1924, but their efforts were undermined by sectarianism and factionalism. They were more successful in trade union work, leading strikes in the textile and fur industries. However, communism was usually associated in the public mind with foreign ideologies and terrorist outrages and this was a liability in an age of increased nativism, making the task of converting English-speaking workers in the skilled trades difficult and often dangerous.

By 1928, when the newly emerged Soviet leader Josef Stalin called for a more revolutionary dual union line from the Communist party, many radicals had virtually abandoned hope of changing the AFL from the inside. However, Foster remained committed to trade union organizing and was displaced as party leader. Ironically, these disputes over strategy occurred just as a rank-and-file revolt was beginning within the UMW. John Brophy's "Save the Union" movement in 1927–1928 challenged Lewis's dominion, but Brophy was defeated in a characteristic display of diplomacy and brute force by the union president.

Theodore Draper's portrait of American communism in the 1920s in *The Roots of American Communism* is the work of an accomplished miniaturist. He rarely leaves the tiny smoke-filled rooms of New York and Moscow, disclosing the claustrophobic and obsessive world of the marginal communist movement of the 1920s ridden by intrigue and faction. Draper argues how three key events of the early 1920s transformed the Communist party's emulation of the Bolsheviks. The first was Lenin's pamphlet on "Left-Wing Infantilism" in which he criticized Western communists for failing to base themselves on mainstream labor organizations. Lenin's sensible argument moved Communists across the world to "a point of no return" in which, "For the first time, every Communist in the world was called on to change his mind in accordance with a change of line."

The second "fateful step" came when the Communist International, or Comintern, in Moscow was asked to choose and arbitrate between John Reed and Louis Fraina as representatives of two rival CPs in the United States. Thus, for the first (but not the last) time, American Communists, despite their bitter internal squabbles, wanted Moscow to arbitrate between them. "Even if there had been a greater willingness in Moscow to pursue a hands off policy, the Americans themselves would not have permitted it."

This led to the third fateful step. The Comintern imposed unity on the underground American CP and wanted it to work above ground. Ironically, "The first change of line was every other change of line in embryo. A rhythmic rotation from Communist sectarianism to Americanized opportunism was set in motion at the outset and has been going on ever since." Thus by 1922 American communism "was transformed from a new expression of American radicalism to the American appendage of a Russian revolutionary power."

In future, committed American radicals were to be blown about in gales of contrary doctrine.

Labor in the Great Depression

During the Great Depression of the 1930s many workers became deeply disillusioned and embittered by the apparent inability of government to ameliorate their suffering and the indifference of businessmen and industrialists to the harsh fate of the working class. Here it seemed was the crisis of capitalism that could lead to improvement by revolution.

Employers, struggling to regain their balance in the upheavals of the early 1930s, withdrew housing and health benefits, and slashed the size of their work forces. However, in discharging workers and turning whole families into scavenging transients, companies also lost the loyalty and confidence that welfare capitalism had been nurturing so carefully in the 1920s. Although some company welfare schemes continued to operate right the way through the depression, many workers became disenchanted and embittered by the apparent indifference or inability of industrialists and politicians to ameliorate their suffering. David Brody goes so far as to argue that "had not the Depression shattered the prevailing assumptions of welfare capitalism, the open shop might well have remained a permanent feature of American industrialism."

As coal miners were among the first major body of workers to experience the instability and arbitrariness of the American economy, it is not surprising that it was in the coal industry that labor unrest began to reemerge in the early 1930s, after a decade of relative calm. While the UMW was preoccupied with internal struggles over the leadership, miners in Kentucky, Ohio, western Pennsylvania, and West Virginia instigated a series of strikes, which, by 1933, accounted for 58 percent of all time lost to American industry.

Paralleling the insurgency in the mines, Communists, Socialists, and a new generation of radical activists, were helping to mobilize the mass of the urban unemployed whose needs had swamped the resources of private charities. Unemployed councils organized marches and rallies that often ended in violent confrontations with police. In March 1930 a demonstration by 35,000 people in New York's Union Square was dispersed when, according to the *New York Times*, "Hundreds of policemen and detectives, swinging night sticks, blackjacks and bare fists, rushed into the crowd, hitting out at all with whom they came into contact, chasing many across the street and into adjacent thoroughfares and rushing hundreds off their feet." In 1931 three people died during an anti-eviction struggle in Chicago, and a crowd of 60,000 people of mixed races marched on City Hall in protest over the incident.

The revival of the labor movement depended not just on the impact of the depression and the increase in local militancy, but also on the changed political context represented by the New Deal. Trade union experiences in the 1920s had shown how impossible was the task of unionization, if the government actively supported corporate repression of labor. The first piece of pro-labor legislation implemented by the administration of Franklin D. Roosevelt, as it desperately tried to stabilize the economy, was Section 7a of the National Industrial Recovery Act of 1933. This gave employees the right to bargain collectively through representatives of their own choice and without interference from employers. However, as the NIRA codes were to be hammered out within individual industries, and in the absence of adequate enforcement machinery, companies either ignored the act or reactivated "employee representation plans" and company unions. By

1935, nearly 2.5 million workers were covered by such plans, as compared with the 4.1 million members of trade unions. Although Section 7a lacked any concrete strength, it had a significant symbolic effect. It seemed as if the federal government, for the first time, was not only acknowledging but also legitimizing the right of workers to organize. However, the NIRA was declared unconstitutional by the Supreme Court in the *Schechter* case of May 27, 1935.

Senator Robert Wagner of New York and Congressman William Connery of Massachusetts then introduced a new bill, creating a National Labor Relations Board (NLRB), that established the right of workers to bargain collectively with management through various representatives chosen in elections supervised by the federal government. It also defined unfair labor practices. Congress passed it precipitately and it received Roosevelt's assent on July 5, 1935. Again, employers responded bitterly through repressive and obstructive actions, and successfully delayed the act in the courts for a further two years. However, American workers preceived the Wagner Act as a statement of support from president and federal government in line with their popular image of the New Deal. The Supreme Court finally upheld the Wagner Act in the case of *NLRB* v. *Jones and Laughlin Steel Company* on April 12, 1937, by 5 votes to 4.

Congress also helped labor by passing the Norris-La Guardia Anti-Injunction Act of 1932 that limited the use of court injunctions in industrial disputes; and in the Senate, the La Follette committee, as we have observed, was beginning to document scores of corporate violations of civil rights.

In 1938 Congress established a minimum wage of 25 cents an hour to rise to 40 cents within three years. However, to secure necessary support from southern Democrats, the sponsors agreed to exclude domestic workers and farm laborers and to allow regional wage differences. Sometimes such well-intentioned legislation had unfortunate results. For instance, in 1938 there were 8,000 Mexican-Americans working as pecan shellers in San Antonio, Texas. According to Selden Menefee and Orin C. Cassmore in *The Pecan Shellers of San Antonio* (1940), they were employed on a seasonal basis and earned 5 to 6 cents an hour, making a median wage of $2.73 in a working week of fifty-one hours. Their employers could not afford to pay them the minimum wage of 25 cents per hour without mechanizing their plants. Thus many closed down. When the plants were mechanized and reopened they employed, altogether, 3,000 shellers only, having fired another 5,000, the victims of technological change.

Again and again, it was the grass roots activity of militant cadres of workers that proved crucial in stirring individual workers into demanding their rights. Indeed, industrial workers began putting politicians and employers under mounting pressure to raise the depression. The number of workers involved in strikes rose from 324,210 in 1932 to 1.16 million in 1933. In 1934 working-class militancy reached a level not seen in the United States since 1919, as violent industrial conflicts paralyzed three major cities.

Striking electrical workers and members of the Unemployed League joined forces in Toledo, Ohio, to imprison 1,500 strikebreakers inside the city's Auto-Lite plant. A seven-hour battle between National Guardsmen and pickets followed, in which two strikers died and fifteen were wounded. In San Francisco, a strike by longshoremen extended to other workers and paralyzed the whole city when police shot dead two unarmed strikers on a picket line. Some 130,000 of the city's workers walked out in a display of solidarity that concerned the editors of the *Los Angeles Times* to the point of declaring "There is but one thing to be done —put down the revolt with any force necessary." The conservative leadership of the AFL was equally dismayed by the militancy of union members. William Green disowned the strike on July 18, 1934, and, three days later, the General Strike Committee voted for a return to work. Meanwhile, in Minneapolis on July 20, police fired into a crowd of striking teamsters, killing two and wounding more than fifty. Governor Floyd Olson of Minnesota placed the city under martial law, but, faced by the continued determination of the strikers and massive public outcry, was eventually forced to withdraw the troops. A national textile strike of the same year saw over 370,000 workers from Maine to Alabama stop work. In total, at least forty workers were killed in the industrial conflicts of 1934, and troops were called out in sixteen states.

Much of the trouble in the 1930s was caused by the companies' strong-arm strategies and provocative tactics. The La Follette Civil Liberties Committee learned in December 1934 that over 2,500 firms employed strikebreaking companies, of which the largest were Pearl Bergoff Service and the Pinkerton National Detective Agency. Both maintained a standing army, equipped with machine guns, tear gas, and clubs. They also hired spies to penetrate the work force and entrap radical agitators. Harassment of workers even extended to making them work at gunpoint. The Pittsburgh Coal Company kept machine guns aimed on employees in its coal pits. Chairman Richard B. Mellon explained to a congressional committee, "You cannot run the mines without them." Such operations were big business. The Pinkerton Agency earned about $2 million between 1933 and 1936, much of it from Detroit, center of the automobile industry.

Frances Fox Piven and Richard A. Cloward argue in *Poor People's Movements* (1977) that the most extraordinary feature of the increase in labor militancy was the spontaneity of many strikes, and the relatively small role of existing trade unions in promoting and directing local protest. Although many workers' battles were fought to win union recognition, if any union structure already existed, it usually remained on the sidelines. John L. Lewis and the UMW could claim little responsibility for the coal strikes during the period 1930–1933. Likewise, labor historian Jeremy Brecher notes in *Strike* (1979) that the flying squadrons of pickets that helped spread the 1934 textile strike across the country were "at first tolerated and perhaps encouraged by union officials, but as the squadrons led to confrontations, union officials tried to bring them to a halt." The relative militancy of particular groups of workers in particular industries often seemed to depend on small cadres of class-conscious radicals, ready to instigate confrontations. Communists, Trotskyists, and Musteites (followers of radical A. J. Muste) had been at the heart of the mobilization of strikers in Toledo, San Francisco, and Minneapolis in 1934. John L. Lewis observed on various tragedies of the period, "Labor, like Israel, has many sorrows. Its women keep their fallen and lament for the future of the race." From the point of view of labor, the most bitter cup was that most of the victims had died in vain. While local unions won recognition in the cities of Minneapolis, San Francisco, and Toledo, employers remained adamantly opposed to organized labor in the big industries — automobiles, steel, rubber, and textiles.

In the early thirties, according to the highest estimates, AFL membership rose from 2.96 million in 1930 to 3.04 million in 1934 and then 3.51 million in 1936. In that year there were, altogether, 4.1 million members of all trade unions. Provoked by the hardship of the depression, and spurred on by the actions of radicals and the rhetoric of New Dealers, militancy from the rank and file sent shock waves through the organized trade union movement. The AFL had consistently resisted attempts to extend its influence beyond craft-based organization because its leadership either disdained immigrant and nonwhite unskilled labor, or regarded the task of organizing in the mass-production industries as virtually impossible.

However, by the 1930s, the divisive influence of ethnic fragmentation was not as significant as it had once been. For example, in the steel industry, the proportion of European-born workers had declined from 50 percent in 1910 to 30 percent in 1930. These workers were also no longer confined to the least skilled and lowest paid work. More confident of their place in American society than their parents had been, the sons and daughters of immigrants were frequently in the vanguard of many of the period's industrial conflicts.

The AFL was hopelessly conservative. Its insistence on adhering to the craft form of unionism in the face of a total crisis for industry, labor, and the country was quite absurd and deeply angered new leaders like Lewis. Moreover, the AFL was ultra-conservative on central political issues — being opposed to the whole notion of unemployment insurance. Indeed, many AFL leaders were Republicans — as was Lewis himself until the 1930s.

John L. Lewis now insisted that the AFL mount an intensive drive to bring millions of factory workers into union ranks. Lewis called for a new form of industrial union, whereby workers in such mass-production industries as construction and steel would have one union big enough to bargain with the giant corporations. At the convention in Atlantic City in October 1935 he led a formidable group of insurgents, including Sidney Hillman of the Amalgamated Clothing Workers, David Dubinsky of the International Ladies' Garment Workers, Thomas McMahon of the Textile Workers, and Charles Howard of the Typographers' Union. The confrontation between old and new schools of thought led to a fight on the platform between Lewis and "Big Bill" Hutcheson of the Carpenters in which Lewis punched Hutcheson, after Hutcheson had insulted a speaker from the rubber workers. He was carried out with blood streaming from his face. Lewis remarked later, "They fought me hip and thigh and right merrily did I return their blows." "With this historic punch," writes James Green, "Lewis signified the formal beginning of the industrial-union rebellion within the House of Labor and made himself the leading rebel."

Lewis and his allies soon met to form the Committee for Industrial Organization (CIO), ostensibly to work within the AFL to aid it in unionizing the basic industries. The AFL executive council ordered the CIO to disband and, when they refused, first suspended the ten renegade unions in August 1935 and, finally, in March 1937 expelled them. In splitting from the conservative main body of the AFL to form the CIO, Lewis and his followers had created a militant industrial union organization around which local militants could gather.

New militancy was characterized by a new tactic, the sit-down strike. On January 29, 1936, rubber workers in Akron, Ohio, laid down their tools and occupied the Firestone plant. Workers at the nearby Goodrich and Goodyear companies rapidly followed the example of the Firestone strikers by implementing labor's new-found weapon of the sit-down strike. Through plant occupations, workers used the techniques of nonviolent resistance to bring shame on their bosses and forced management to the negotiating table. As far as management was concerned, the sit-down strike was an outrage against private property, an underhand act of trespass in which Communists carpeted the shop floors with human bodies because they knew the company would not risk the

Edward Hopper, *New York Movie* (1939), oil on canvas, 32⅛″ × 40⅛″. (Collection, The Museum of Modern Art, New York). Edward Hopper captured the essential solitariness of people absorbed in their own thoughts, whether in crowded or desolate places in realistic works by arresting off-center composition, abrupt chiaroscuro of light and shade, and, sometimes, deliberate distortions of size. Here the ephemeral pleasures of well-heeled life on screen elude the contemplative usherette.

adverse publicity following the bloodshed of forcible removal or damage to its own plants and material. In Akron, the old AFL local was reorganized as the United Rubber Workers and affiliated with the new CIO.

Toward the end of 1936 the United Auto Workers sought a conference on collective bargaining with William S. Knudsen, executive vice-president of General Motors (GM). When he refused, men on the shop floors in Cleveland's Fisher Body Plant

No. 1 took spontaneous action on December 28 by sitting down and ignoring the moving assembly line belt. Their protest spread to Fisher Body Plant No. 2 in Flint, Michigan, and thence to Pontiac, Atlanta, Kansas City, and Detroit. Soon 484,711 men from sixty plants in fourteen states were involved. GM obtained an injunction ordering evacuation of the plants but it had no moral force once the press disclosed that the judge who issued the order was a major stockholder in General Motors.

On the eve of the General Motors sit-down strike, only a small proportion of workers were fully paid-up members of the United Auto Workers. However, once the strike began, many previously apathetic workers displayed very high levels of militancy and class consciousness. During the first eight months of 1937, the membership of the UAW increased from 88,000 to 400,000. At Flint, a psychologist declared that the strike created "a veritable revolution of personality" among the workers. One of the strikers, Bob Stinson, recalled that

Morale was very high at the time. It started out kinda ugly because the guys were afraid they [had] put their foot in it and all they was gonna do is lose their jobs. But as time went on, they begin to realize they could win this darn thing, 'cause we had a lot of outside people comin' in showin' their sympathy.

Whole communities rallied to the support of those on strike. Women workers and strikers' wives coordinated many of the demonstrations outside the plants, and organized a system of strike relief and food convoys. "I found a common understanding and unselfishness I'd never known in my life," said one woman. "I'm living for the first time with a definite goal. . . . Just being a woman isn't enough anymore. I want to be a human being with the right to think for myself."

The silence of Roosevelt, Secretary of Labor Frances Perkins, and other sympathetic New Dealers put extra pressure on Governor Frank Murphy of Michigan. A second court injunction obtained by GM lawyers threatened the sit-down strikers with prison sentences and a fine of $15 million if they did not give up by February 3, 1937. GM then chose its Chevrolet plant in Flint as the testing ground and Murphy called out the National Guard to surround the plant. John L. Lewis did not like the strike because it was a diversion from his campaign for union recognition in the steel industry. Yet he did not want to lose the car workers. Thus Lewis told Murphy he supported the strike and that he would order the men to disregard any order to evacuate the plant. "I shall walk up to the largest window in the plant, open it, divest myself of my outer raiment, remove my shirt and bare my bosom. Then, when you order your troops to fire, mine will be the first breast that those bullets will strike. And as my body falls from the window to the ground, you will listen to the voice of your grandfather as he whispers in your ear, 'Frank, are you sure you are doing the right thing?' " This was a telling touch. Murphy's grandfather had been hanged after an Irish uprising.

Murphy knew he could not abandon the strikers to the unmerciful GM company and, instead, insisted that food was delivered to them. Thus the UAW triumphed because of the tacit support of president, governor, and the conversion of Lewis, all of which broke the morale of General Motors. Through its strategy of a concerted attack on General Motors to immobilize its plants and only token demonstrations at Chrysler, Ford, Nash, and Packard, the UAW had divided and ruled. Instead of siding with GM, the other auto manufacturers simply took advantage of its embarrassment and exploited the market for their own automobiles. Thus by February 7 GM directors were forced to cut the dividend in half. After a crisis of forty-four days, William Knudsen agreed to the conference. All the other auto manufacturers recognized the UAW, except Ford, who held out until 1941, and they also signed agreements on grievance committees, seniority, a forty-hour week, and payment of time-and-a-half for overtime.

A prime target of the CIO in its drive to create and organize industrial unions was the steel industry. In June 1936 Phil Murray formed the Steel Workers Organizing Committee (SWOC), the first significant attempt at a steel union since the Homestead Strike of 1892. Not only did it entice thousands of workers out of company unions into its ranks but it also, with tacit government support, threatened and instituted costly strikes to force the steel companies to recognize it. The large steel companies, known as Big Steel and led by United States Steel, the corporation based on the original Carnegie companies, accepted SWOC. Myron Charles Taylor, chairman of the board of directors and chief executive, met Lewis by chance in the Mayflower Hotel, Washington, on January 9, 1937, and then and there arranged a series of private meetings with him to thrash out differences between Big Steel management and SWOC. The Carnegie-Illinois Steel Company signed a contract on March 2, 1937, and the other United States Steel subsidiaries followed with contracts granting union recognition, the forty-hour week, a 10 percent increase in wages, and overtime pay at the rate of time-and-a-half.

Because Big Steel had decided on a strategy of accommodation with the new union in the interests of harmony, it was widely expected that the remaining smaller companies, known collectively as Little Steel, would follow suit. However, three of them opposed SWOC. Republic Steel, Bethlehem Steel, and Youngstown Sheet and Tube resisted a new strike of 70,000 men in twenty-seven plants for union recognition in May 1937. They summoned their strikebreaking armies and threw them at striking workers.

On Memorial Day several thousand strikers and their families had assembled in prairie land east of Republic Steel's South Chicago plant. The mayor of Chicago had given his permission for a peaceful parade with marchers falling in behind banners with such notices as "Republic Steel violates Labor Dispute Act" and "Win With the CIO." Ahead of the marchers was a line of 500 Chicago police, all heavily armed. A police captain called out, "You dirty sons of bitches, this is as far as you go." Without any further warning, some of the police began attacking strikers' wives, pummeling their breasts with nightsticks. The strike leaders called out, "We got our legal rights to protect." "You got no rights" came the retort. Some workers threw a few empty soda pop bottles at the police and this was sufficient provocation to start a massacre, beginning with tear gas grenades and followed by gunfire. The police in South Chicago killed ten people and wounded ninety others outside the Republic Steel plant. The casualties were shot in the back as they fled in terror. Such conflicts became part of working class folklore—and art. In *An American Tragedy* (1937) Philip Evergood (1901–1973) dramatized workers and their families in a vicious clash with police against a background of a closed factory.

Subsequently, the Senate Civil Rights Subcommittee led by Robert La Follette, Jr., of Wisconsin began an investigation into the violation of the workers' civil rights and the shooting incidents. Their investigations disclosed that the Little Steel companies maintained illegal private armies and had extensive stores of munitions, including machine guns and tear gas. The adverse publicity was such that Little Steel was eventually compelled to recognize SWOC. Thus by 1941 over 600,000 workers had achieved union recognition in the very industry most bitterly opposed to labor organization.

In the course of 1937 a total of 4.7 million workers were involved in 4,740 strikes. For the first time in American history, all of the nation's key industries—steel, coal, auto, rubber, electricity—were affected by major industrial disputes. As historian William Manchester explains, labor violence was part of an American tradition. It was by violence that the United States had gained independence, conquered the West, and freed the slaves. Moreover, it was violence that "had raised working men up from the industrial cellar. Labor might forget that and turn conservative, but for liberals to deny other oppressed groups the right to revolt would prove impossible. Thus were the seeds of later anguish planted in innocence, even in idealism."

By the end of 1937 the new CIO unions claimed some 4 million members in 32 international unions and 600 independent locals. Genuine efforts were made to overcome differences in gender, nationality, and race. The number of women in unions tripled in the 1930s to stand at 800,000 in 1940. As to the activity of black and immigrant workers in this period, historian James Green says, "The CIO unions did not dissolve ethnic and racial group consciousness or end cultural antagonism, but they did give a highly divided workforce a basis for cooperation on issues of common concern."

In the lean years of the late 1930s, it was the AFL, revitalized by the challenge of its new rival, the CIO, that achieved the greatest increases in membership. Craft unions such as the Machinists, Teamsters, Electrical Workers, and Meat Cutters, began to organize vigorously on an industrial union basis, and proved more resilient against the recession and counteroffensive by employers. From October 1938 the CIO was known as the Congress of Industrial Organizations. In 1937, the first year of the two major unions, there were, according to official statistics, 3.18 million members of the AFL and 1.99 million members of the CIO. By 1940 there were 4.34 million members of the AFL and 2.15 million members of the CIO. That year there were 7.28 million trade union members of all unions.

The often confusing relationship between union leaders and the rank and file must always be set against the extremely vulnerable position of unions in America's major industries. It was the strike movement at grassroots level that was the prime force behind the creation of the CIO. Moreover, during several of the decade's major industrial struggles, CIO leaders were prepared to suppress or disown rank-and-file militancy (the sit-down strike, for example, was never officially endorsed), in return for union recognition from management. However, the opportunism and sporadic conservatism exhibited by Lewis and other union leaders often stemmed from a reluctance to encourage premature actions from workers that might lead a fledgling union into positions it could not effectively support. Nothing weakens a union so much as a lost strike. That is not to say that Lewis did not concern himself with monopolizing power as the archetypal union "boss"; and he often, in his own words, "put a lid on the strikers." However, as the Memorial Day Massacre had so violently demonstrated, working-class radicalism had limits even during the turmoil of depression America.

Radical Visions and American Dreams

Although Communists, Socialists, and other radicals had played a crucial role in the revival of the labor movement, their influence beyond grass roots organizations was negligible.

The Socialist party ceased to be an effective political force in the 1930s. The very fact of the depression makes even this surprising. However, it is not an exaggeration to say that New Deal legislation preempted many of the Socialists' proposals. Norman

Thomas, Socialist leader after the death of Debs in 1926, maintained for many years that the Socialist collapse was due to popular support for, and interest in, the New Deal. In his article, "Not So 'Turbulent Years' " (1979), Melvyn Dubofsky concludes that "By frightening the ruling class into conceding reforms and appealing to workers to vote as a solid bloc, Roosevelt simultaneously intensified class consciousness and stripped it of its radical potential." The Socialists might have gained by the great interest in social welfare but the party disintegrated and by the time of Pearl Harbor had become a diminutive sect. In the early days of the New Deal the Socialist party continued to rise to 23,600 members in May 1934, of whom 5,000 members were new in that year. However, this increased numerical support was lacking in financial substance. Ironically, as numbers went higher, financial support was a small fraction of that given in 1928 when membership was low. In 1932 only $26,000 in funds were raised from all sources whereas in 1928 the total of funds was $110,000. The Socialist party could have continued to profit in the 1930s but did not. The Socialists fell out among themselves and the opposing groups of militant youngsters and more conservative old guard became increasingly factious. Many of the younger Socialists, such as Paul Douglas, went to work in New Deal agencies while others, like David Dubinsky, rose to positions of leadership in organized labor and supported New Deal policies. They wanted to see their ideas of reform realized from positions of power.

There were other reasons for the decline of the Socialist party in the 1930s. One of Norman Thomas's biographers, Bernard K. Johnpoll in *Pacifist's Progress* (1970), mentions how new reform movements drew support from within the existing two-party system, primarily those of Fiorello La Guardia in New York and Upton Sinclair in California. Moreover, the Spanish Civil War diverted and divided radicals. There were, also, Trojan Horse activities of Trotskyites and other communist sects that were penetrating the Socialist party. Norman Thomas's own pacifism and isolationism alienated certain ethnic groups with European loyalties and, at the same time, antagonized radicals committed to reform in the United States. Thus the Socialist party was divided over domestic and foreign policies and its isolationist campaigns from 1938 onward resulted in a decline to only 1,141 members by January 1942. By then the Socialist party was nothing more than a minuscule sect.

The Communist party of America, while hardly larger than the Socialist party, with an estimated membership only 25,000 or 30,000, exercised much greater influence during the 1930s. American intellectuals, oblivious to the political brutalities of Stalin's dictatorship in the USSR, compared its supposed economic successes with the fumbling inability of the United States, the world's richest country, to treat mass poverty and unemployment. Some were active in the Communist party; others promoted socialist ideals in their writings.

In their *The American Communist Party, A Critical History: 1919– 1957* (1957), Irving Howe and Lewis Coser believe that the key to understanding the CP from the 1930s was to see how it had been transformed in the 1920s into a totalitarian organization. Moreover, they tried to explain Stalinism in Russia with its cult of personality, show trials, and mass purges as one part of a general crisis for modern mass society.

Communism and its cruel caricature, Stalinism, derived not from a psychological malaise unique to or predominant among its adherents but from a general breakdown of society. . . . In a time of permanent crisis Stalinism seemed to provide a faith, to cry forth a challenge and make possible an ideal. . . . The tragedy of Stalinism arose when the quest for justice among its followers became indistinguishable from their loyalty to a profoundly unjust system of totalitarian domination.

The Communist party managed to broaden its appeal after 1935 through the Popular Front Against Fascism. However, by obediently, if reluctantly, following Moscow's alternating and ambiguous shifts in policy, communism in the United States was never able to hold sway in more than a few CIO locals and intellectual groups. This did not prevent many employers, union leaders, and right-wing politicians from claiming that the CIO was dominated by reds. John L. Lewis did allow Communists to recruit for the CIO, reckoning that they had the toughness and dedication to take on difficult tasks. One such, Len De Caux, became editor of

Many ethnic and religious communities retained their distinctive customs and appearances until, and beyond, World War II. A Mennonite couple at a public sale in Lititz, Pennsylvania, in November 1942, photographed by Marjory Collins for the Office of War Information. (Library of Congress).

CIO News, and another, Lee Pressman, served Lewis as chief counsel. By 1939 the United Electrical Union, the International Longshoremen and Warehouse Union, the Mine, Mill, and Smelter Union, the Fur Workers' Union, and the United Cannery Workers' Union were infiltrated by Communists, who had also penetrated certain sections of the Transport Workers' Union and Furniture Workers' Union. However, from 1939 onward Communist influence began to decline.

The antipathy of American political culture to left-wing radicalism encouraged the House Un-American Activities Committee —the body more commonly associated with the intolerance of the postwar McCarthy era—to begin its investigations and hearings as early as 1938.

During this period President Franklin Roosevelt's attitude toward labor was ambivalent and he certainly was not a pro-union politician. When the CIO revived an earlier slogan "The President Wants You To Organize" in 1936, FDR's administration considered (but declined) taking legal action against the unions. "The point was," as David Brody correctly asserts, "that workers believed it was true; they thought the president did want them to organize. Its underlying labor sympathy was the New Deal's special contribution to making the conditions for organizing America's industrial workers."

Another important contribution of the New Deal was, of course, the reshaping of national electoral politics. In alienating many sections of the business community, the Democratic party under FDR came to rely on the support of a coalition of working-class and labor groups. For example, in the 1936 election campaign, the Non-Partisan League was formed by AFL and CIO activists to mobilize working-class support for FDR. On the one hand, his reliance on union support pushed Roosevelt into adopting policies more sympathetic to labor. On the other, labor's fortunes, and the interests of its leaders, became increasingly tied to the success of the Democratic party. However, John L. Lewis resisted organized labor's growing dependence on the government. When the flow of pro-labor measures began to dry up after 1937, and the administration started to adopt an interventionist strategy toward the war in Europe, Lewis split first with the president, and, then, from the CIO. Lewis was concerned about increased collaboration between labor and government and, in retrospect, we can see that his fears were justified. However, instead of going on to form a labor party, which might have been the logical step to take, Lewis endorsed the Republicans in the 1940 election and stepped down from his position as CIO chief in favor of Phil

Murray of SWOC. The labor movement once again failed to translate its newfound numerical strength into an effective independent political organization.

The persistent difficulty of linking shop-floor militancy with electoral politics had been clearly evident during the CIO's local election campaigns in 1937. For example, in Akron, birthplace of the sit-down strike and possibly the most unionized city in the country, the CIO candidate for mayor was defeated by the Republicans because the working-class vote was split on issues of union strategy, growing public dissatisfaction with the New Deal, and claims that a radical city government would drive away business.

Thus, as America prepared for World War II, the labor movement was making divergent signals. In the twelve years to 1941, the number of workers organized in unions had almost tripled to stand at 8.41 million, or 27 percent of all industrial workers. For the first time in history, unions had made significant inroads into the mass production sector of the economy, and new legislation guaranteed the rights of workers to organize freely. However, in the wake of the upheavals and dramatic victories of the 1933–1937 period, unions struggled to maintain their newly won gains. Workers on the shop floor were asked to tone down their demands and stifle their militancy, as union leaders sought to build stable bridges between labor, management, and government. In the years to come, this strained relationship emerged as the key factor behind labor's ever shifting fortunes.

The Working Class on the Eve of the War

The United States was still largely a nation of small towns and rural communities in 1940. Of the 131,699,275 citizens listed in the census as living in the continental United States and the 118,933 living in overseas territories and dependencies, 74.4 million (56.5 percent) were designated as urban dwellers. However, as we know, urban meant only a community of 2,500 or more inhabitants. If we consider urban a community of far greater numbers, then a different picture emerges. Less than 50 percent of all Americans lived in cities with over 10,000 inhabitants; less than 40 percent lived in cities with over 25,000 inhabitants; and only 30 percent lived in cities with over 100,000. Thus in 1940 70 million people (55 percent) lived in places with fewer than 10,000 inhabitants. In other words, small towns were a dominant fact of American life.

Historian Richard Polenberg declares in *One Nation Divisible* (1980) that "American society on the eve of World War II was sharply divided along class, racial, and ethnic lines." He demonstrates the truth of his assertion about class and ethnicity in a penetrating analysis. His conclusion is also that of many sociologists who followed the Lynds' pioneering study, *Middletown,* with quasi-anthropological and scientific studies of such towns as Newburyport, Massachusetts, Indianola, Mississippi, and Morris, Illinois. "The social system of Yankee City (Newburyport) was dominated by a class order," said W. Lloyd Warner and Paul S. Lunt in *The Social Life of a Modern Community* (1941). The criteria for membership of the upper, middle, and lower classes and their various subsections differed little from place to place. Between 60 and 70 percent of people belonged to the lower-middle and upper-lower categories; about 15 percent belonged to the upper-middle classes; the remaining 15 to 25 percent were in the lower-lower class. Richard Polenberg sums up his interpretation of the class system in the declaration: "Class membership determined virtually every aspect of an individual's life: the subjects one studied in high school, the church one attended, the person one married, the clubs one joined, the magazines one read, the doctor one visited, the way one was treated by the law, and even the choice of an undertaker. Movement across class lines, if not impossible, was markedly infrequent."

Class was also, of course, largely determined by income. In 1939 factory workers earned, on average, about $1,250 a year. However, a highly skilled, experienced tool inspector in an automobile plant might earn as much as $1,600. An advertisement quoted a man who planned to retire on $150 a month, enjoying "life-long security and freedom to do as I please." Thus a salary of $2,500 would make one well-to-do. But only 4.2 percent of working people earned that much in 1939. Among the most highly paid group—urban men in full-time employment—only

11.8 percent earned as much as $2,500. Thus when public opinion polls asked people what they would consider a completely satisfactory income, over half of those who replied gave a sum less than $2,500. Annual earnings of more than $5,000 were way beyond what most people could imagine.

At the base of the economic pyramid were the underemployed, the seasonally employed, and the unemployed. The severe recession of 1938 probably led to an increase in unemployment from 7.5 million to over 11 million. Even in 1940, after the federal government had yet again expanded its programs of relief and national defense, unemployment was still about 9 million people. Furthermore, almost a quarter of the people in work worked less than nine months every year. Partial employment and unemployment account for some most revealing statistics. In 1939, if we exclude that 2.5 million people working on public relief, 58.5 percent of men and 78.3 percent of women were working for, or looking for work that paid, less than $1,000.

It was also people's social class that determined the quality of their medical care. The National Health Survey, a canvass of 740,000 families by the U.S. Public Health Service, published in *Public Health Reports* during 1940, disclosed that families with low incomes were sick longer and more often than better-off families but called doctors less often. In 1936 American families spent an average of $59 a year on medical care but poor families spent less than half that and wealthy families spent twice as much. Serious illness made people poorer. One in 250 heads of families earning $2,000 was permanently disabled but 1 in 20 heads of families on relief was physically unable to work. Moreover, dismal living conditions in themselves made people unhealthy. For example, a study in Cincinnati discovered that the high death rate from intestinal illnesses was centered in congested areas where houses lacked adequate sanitation.

The failure of the Wagner national health bill in 1939 and 1940 illustrated the failing fortunes of the New Deal. Not only had the Republicans made a strong showing in the midterm elections of 1938 and were determined to resist further social reforms but also vested interests lobbied congressmen to work against such legislation. The Wagner bill would have authorized federal aid for maternity and child care, public health services, and hospital construction. Furthermore, it proposed federal supervision of state efforts to implement compulsory insurance. Although the bill was intended to assist the indigent, those most in need of care but least able to afford it, the bill met with a hostile reception in Congress and FDR's indifference. The AMA opposed the bill because it thought the program threatened the relationship between doctor and patient and officials in the Public Health Service did not like the controversy the bill was causing. In the end, Roosevelt endorsed a limited proposal to build (but not maintain) "forty little hospitals" in poor, usually rural, areas at a cost of $50 million. The Senate approved the measure in 1940; the House never considered it.

Education was another gauge of social position. Just as quite small differences in income had a significant impact on standards of living, so minor differences in schooling had considerable repercussions on careers and prospects. In 1940 of the 74.8 million Americans who were twenty-five or older, only 2 in 5 had gone beyond eighth grade; only 1 in 4 had graduated from high school; only 1 in 10 had gone to college and only 1 in 20 had graduated from college. Nevertheless, a college education and degree were becoming recognized as the visa and passport to a career in the white-collar professions. Thus about 875,000 students were enrolled full-time in colleges in 1939. Half the graduates in the Wesleyan class of 1939 expected to make a career in business, medicine, law, or education. Yet the cost of college tuition, accommodation, and board ranged from $453 per annum at state colleges to $979 at private universities and was way beyond most people's pockets.

In 1940 11,419,000 residents, 8.5 percent of the population, had been born abroad. They included 1,624,000 people from Italy; 1,323,000 from Russia, Lithuania, and Rumania; 1,238,000 from Germany; 993,000 from Poland; 845,000 from Denmark, Norway, and Sweden; 678,000 from Ireland; and 163,000 from Greece. There were also 23 million second-generation white immigrants, born in the United States, one or both of whose parents were immigrants, and this accounted for 17.5 percent of the popula-

Not a finale to a Busby Berkeley musical but routine work for women, finishing transparent bomber noses for reconnaissance and fighter planes in the Douglas Aircraft plant in Long Beach, California, in 1942. (Library of Congress).

tion. Thus over one in four Americans was a first- or second-generation immigrant.

Immigrants and their children still accounted for the majority of the population in twenty large industrial cities, comprising two-thirds of the people in Cleveland, Ohio; three-quarters of the population in New York; and three-fifths of the people in Newark, New Jersey. There were large numbers of Finns in Montana, Norwegians in North Dakota, Germans in Wisconsin, and Czechs in Iowa. Immigrants, primarily French Canadians, constituted 40 percent of the population of Burlington, Vermont.

The census of 1940 discovered 377,000 residents who had been born in Mexico and were entitled to be in the United States. The true number, including illegal immigrants, was much larger. In political terms, these illegal immigrants were invisible. Because they were aliens, they could not work on public works projects and worked, whenever possible, in California in lettuce fields, in Texas in cotton fields, and in Michigan in beet fields. They tended to move about so much that they never comprised a significant political bloc. The rate of infant mortality among Mexican-Americans was twice the national average, while the death rate from tuberculosis was three or four times as great.

Mutual aid societies still had their halls, the centers of social life in ethnic communities, often with libraries or newspaper reading rooms, games rooms, and bars. There were also twenty-five fraternal associations for different ethnic groups, comprising almost 3 million members in 32,000 branches.

According to the census of 1940, English was not the mother tongue of almost 22 million people. There were not only foreign language newspapers and magazines but also foreign language bookstores, movie houses, and theaters. About 200 radio stations broadcast foreign language programs, providing, in the largest cities, almost a continuous series of programs in German, Polish, Yiddish, and other languages. They appealed primarily to older immigrants who could return to an aural world of once-familiar music, stories, and jokes. In North End, Boston, 85 percent of Italian immigrants listened regularly to such broadcasts—more than listened to programs in English.

Foreign languages were still widely used and helped foster ethnic identities. In 1940 237 foreign language periodicals were being published in New York; 96 in Chicago; 38 in Pittsburgh; 25 in Los Angeles; and 22 in Detroit. Richard Polenberg estimates that over 1,000 newspapers and periodicals with an aggregate circulation of almost 7 million were printed wholly or partly in a foreign language.

It would be easy to exaggerate the association of particular ethnic groups with certain occupations. Not all Jews worked in the rag trade but Maurice J. Karpf in *Jewish Community Organization in the United States* (1938) discovered that 10.7 percent of Jewish people in the New York telephone book worked in the needle trades, compared with 1.7 percent of those named Smith. Three-quarters of shoe repair and shoeshine shops in New York were owned by Italian Americans.

While older immigrant areas were disintegrating in major cities, certain ethnic groups were still associated with particular sections. Thus in New York City, the Italian community dominated the South Bronx; the Jews, Brownsville; the Germans, Yorkville; the Irish, Manhattanville. Even in small cities, such as Manchester, New Hampshire, there were ethnic quarters, notably Little Canada, Irish Acre, German town, and Norwegian village.

Indians and the New Deal

Anthropologists were beginning to appreciate the cohesive values of cultural heritage, rather than seeing different cultural values as somehow subversive of some idealized American way. Hence American Indians were becoming admired precisely for those characteristics that had, only a few years earlier, led to their being scorned as hopelessly primitive and, hence, inferior. These were their lack of individualism and sense of a progressive historical destiny and their emphasis on intuition and religious belief. Not surprisingly, Indians anxious to improve the quality of their life grew sick and tired of primitive characterizations of themselves as noble savages. When salon dilettante Mable Dodge Luhan tried to prevent the introduction of modern sanitation in the Taos Pueblo, one progressive Indian offered to exchange his primitive home for hers with all its modern conveniences.

Although the new anthropology was limited, it had its distinct political uses and was employed constructively by former New York social worker John Collier. In his autobiography, *From Every Zenith* (1963), John Collier expressed the impact Indian communities were having upon reformers:

The discovery that came to me, there, in that tiny group of a few hundred Indians, was of personality-forming institutions, even now unweakened, which had survived repeated and immense historical shocks, and which were going right on in the production of states of mind, attitudes of mind, earth-loyalties and human loyalties, amid a context of beauty which suffused all the life of the group. . . . It might be that only the Indians, among the peoples of this hemisphere at least, were still the possessors and users of the fundamental secret of human life—the secret of building great personality through the instrumentality of social institutions. And it might be, as well, that the Indian life would not survive.

In the 1920s John Collier challenged federal policy toward certain Indian communities, notably the Bursum bill that proposed to dispossess Pueblo Indians of certain land and water rights. Collier had developed a profound commitment to Indian culture that he saw as preferable to conventional American commercial values. He interpreted what he saw in the light of *Mutual Aid* by Kropotkin, an instance of how to endure by cooperative communal values rather than become engulfed by economic competition in the name of individual will.

In 1934 Collier became commissioner of Indian affairs in Roosevelt's administration, the very same year that Columbia University anthropologist Ruth Benedict's influential work, *Patterns of Culture,* was published. In her book, Ruth Benedict clearly preferred Pueblo culture with its emphasis on communal values to the somewhat possessive Northwest coast fishing cultures. Collier generalized from Benedict's hypotheses and from what he knew of the Pueblo Indians with their cohesive society. He then applied his generalizations to such different groups as the Plains Indians whose culture emphasized individual expression and who had adjusted to a system of individually owned farmland. Collier believed that previous federal policies had been misconceived. Whatever the motives, they had damaged Indian culture. Thus Collier wanted to remedy things.

Collier's wide-ranging proposals were enacted in a modified form in the Wheeler-Howard or Indian Reorganization Act of 1934. It applied to all states except Oklahoma and was, in time, accepted by 192 of 263 tribes who voted on it. The act had three principal aims: to bring an abrupt end to the discredited policy of allotment and continued white appropriation of Indian land; to establish a system of tribal government, providing Indians with some self-determination, "certain rights of home rule"; and to enhance the economic welfare of Indian reservations by creating a revolving credit fund and adding to Indian territory. In his pamphlet, *Modern Indians* (1982), David Murray concludes, "These were undoubtedly helpful and well-intentioned proposals, which in the end helped to ease the poverty and demoralization of many Indians, preserving their land-holdings and setting in motion the complex process of achieving a degree of self-determination." At the same time, the Wheeler-Howard Act proposed that the Bureau of Indian Affairs (BIA) should exercise a far more active role than hitherto according to the expertise of social scientists. The contradiction between the aim of granting the Indians greater autonomy while, at the same time, strengthening the hand of the BIA proved too much for Collier's new colonial policy.

Collier made enemies left and right. He knew that some of the Navahos' chronic economic problems were caused by continuous overgrazing by their sheep. In accordance with New Deal policy elsewhere, Collier's solution was to reduce the flock by slaughter. Whatever the merits of slaughter in terms of cost-effectiveness, to the Navaho it appeared a wanton act against their future security. The decision disclosed the gulf between the impersonal expertise of the administration and the cultural values of the Indians the administration was supposed to be preserving. Collier was essentially autocratic, insisting that the BIA was offering advice and that that advice must be heeded since the experts who gave it were bound to know best. In addition, Collier proved indifferent and, sometimes, downright hostile to Indian resistance to big corporations ready and anxious to extract precious minerals from their lands. Since he preferred land held by tribes to land held by individuals, Indians who wanted to adopt American economic values accused him of trying to send them "back to the blanket." Moreover, he was committed to reversing previous school policies. Instead of instilling white values in boarding schools, he wanted a return to traditional Indian values, a policy that some argued would produce young adults underequipped to cope with earning a living in contemporary America.

The sort of Indian government Collier wanted to establish was the form he considered most representative—an accountable democracy based on a constitution and elections by universal adult suffrage in which the winner was the candidate with the highest plurality. Many Indians considered this a white form of government not suited to Indian needs. Some would have no part in it. Consequently, it was those Indians who played the system and cooperated with federal policies who tended to get elected. They were also those who most conformed to white life-styles and were, often, of mixed race with less Indian blood than white. These "Indians" were sometimes called "progressives" and considered not truly representative. Thus traditional Indians still considered themselves ignored and dispossessed. Once again, the federal government's attempt to reform its Indian policy had resulted in a compromise that favored Indians who preferred assimilation. As Steve Talbot remarks in an article, "The Meaning of Wounded Knee, 1973," for Gerritt Huizer and Bruce Mannheim in *The Politics of Anthropology* (1979), "In essence the [Wheeler-Howard] Act marked a shift from the government's policy of direct rule of reservations as internal colonies to one of indirect rule, a shift from outright colonialism to a system of neocolonialism."

From the beginning of 1942 Collier's program was being steadily deprived of money. Moreover, it fell victim to the slowly mounting political opposition to the New Deal and, in terms of the Indian problem, this took the form of yet another swing in federal policy. The conventional wisdom now believed that Indian communities should be awarded funds in order to facilitate the Indians' prompt acculturation as integrated American citizens. At the same time as this shift was occurring, many Indians were becoming more active politically. In 1944 they founded the National Congress of American Indians (NCAI), an organization that mixed national and tribal aspirations. Many of its leaders were tribal leaders also and after World War II the NCAI was sustained by the interest of former Indian servicemen (25,000 in all) who, like black Americans, had been radicalized by their wartime experiences. The NCAI, urged onward by younger, educated Indians, was to focus its efforts on legal cases and occupations to secure an extension or return of Indian lands from the whites.

8

WHAT DID I DO TO BE SO BLACK AND BLUE? Black America

DISCRIMINATION AND harsh treatment of its black citizens was to become the most persistent social evil of America in the twentieth century. In an age when a central theme of art has been the oppression of the individual by the state, the plight of blacks was to be taken as a potent metaphor for imprisonment, whether social, physical, or psychological. Indeed, the black experience was a prime example of man's inhumanity to man. As novelist Richard Wright once observed in a much quoted remark, "The Negro is America's metaphor." Moreover, the black experience makes a stark comment on a central paradox of American history —how a nation composed of such diverse ethnic groups and beliefs could endure and survive. Thus novelist James Baldwin (1924–1987) declared, "The story of the Negro in America is the story of America, or, more precisely, it is the story of Americans."

Out of the total American population of 105,710,620 in 1920,

W. E. B. DuBois, noted black polemicist, photographed by C. M. Battey in 1918. After taking three degrees at Harvard, he became a professor of history at Atlanta University and began to devote himself to race relations and other black problems on which he adopted a militant position. He helped launch the Niagara movement for racial equality in 1905 and in 1910 he became director of publicity and research for the NAACP, a post he held for twenty-four years, during which he organized the Pan-African Congress (1919) before returning to Atlanta University as head of the department of sociology (1933–1944). (Library of Congress).

10,951,000 were blacks—about 10.5 percent of the whole. Eighty-five percent of them lived in the South—the eleven states of the old Confederacy and five others, Oklahoma and Kentucky to the west and Delaware, Maryland, West Virginia, and the District of Columbia to the north. Of the total population of 33,126,000 of this "Census South," 8,912,000 were blacks. Thus, whereas the ratio of blacks to whites across the country as a whole was, approximately, one in ten, in the South it was one in four. In two states, Mississippi and South Carolina, blacks predominated.

The abolition of slavery and the destruction of the rebel Confederacy in the Civil War (1861–1865) had led to the granting of equal social and political rights to blacks in the period of Reconstruction (1865–1877). The Thirteenth Amendment (1865) proscribed slavery. The first section of the Fourteenth Amendment (1866) defined American citizens as all those born or naturalized in the United States and enjoined states from abridging their rights to life, liberty, property, and process of law. The second section threatened to reduce proportionately the representation in Congress of any state denying the suffrage to adult males. Congress determined to protect black suffrage in the South by the Fifteenth Amendment (1869–1870) by which the right to vote was not to be denied "on account of race, color, or previous condition of servitude." Yet forty years later these rights had been assailed or eroded by white racists. The abject position of blacks was such that historian Rayford Logan in *The Betrayal of the Negro* (1954; 1969) described the turn of the century as "the nadir" of Afro-American history, notwithstanding the existence of slavery up to 1865.

The Nadir of Race Relations

The regular intimacy of contact under slavery was being superseded by a caste system with next to no sustained contact and resulted in an inexorable gulf between black and white. Although blacks were the largest of America's ethnic minorities, they were segregated in schooling, housing, and places of public accommodation, such as parks, theaters, hospitals, schools, libraries, courts, and even cemeteries. The variety and fluidity of access of the late nineteenth century were abandoned as state after state adopted rigid segregation in a series of so-called "Jim Crow" laws. ("Jim Crow" was the title of a minstrel song of 1830 that presented blacks as childlike and inferior.)

In *The Strange Career of Jim Crow* (1955; 1974) historian C. Vann Woodward argues that cast-iron segregation was a product of the late nineteenth and early twentieth centuries, and that the avalanche of Jim Crow laws began when poor white farmers came to power. Moreover, a new generation of black citizens had grown up who had never known slavery. Previously, aristocratic southerners had shown a paternalistic attitude to blacks, protecting them from some overt racist attacks by poor whites. They knew they did not need segregation laws to confirm their own privileged social position. Nevertheless, none of the states passed a single comprehensive segregation law. Instead, they proceeded piecemeal over a period of thirty to fifty years. Thus South Carolina segregated the races in successive stages, beginning with trains (1898) and moving to streetcars (1905), train depots and restaurants (1906), textile plants (1915 and 1916), circuses (1917), pool halls (1924), and beaches and recreation centers (1934). Georgia began with railroads and prisons (1891), and moved to sleeping cars (1899), and, finally, pool halls (1925), but refused to segregate places of public accommodation until 1954.

The South reacted against the natural tide of black resentment to its new restrictive policies with more repression. Mississippi was the first state effectively to disfranchise black citizens by a constitutional convention in 1890. It was followed by South Carolina in 1895, Louisiana in 1898, North Carolina (by an amendment) in 1900, Alabama in 1901, Virginia in 1901 and 1902, Georgia (by amendment) in 1908, and the new state of Oklahoma in 1910. Four more states achieved the same ends without revising their constitutions: Tennessee, Florida, Arkansas, and Texas.

Edgar Gardner Murphy, a humanitarian journalist, reported in *The Basis of Ascendancy* (1909) how extremists had moved "from an undiscriminating attack upon the Negro's ballot to a like attack upon his schools, his labor, his life—from the contention that no Negro shall vote to the contention that no Negro shall learn, that no Negro shall labor, and (by implication) that no Negro shall live." The result was an "all-absorbing autocracy of race," an "absolute identification of the stronger race with the very being of the state." Deploring the sorry state of affairs, Governor N. B. Broward of Florida told the state legislature in 1907 that "relations between the races are becoming strained and acute." In 1903 black analyst Charles W. Chestnutt said that "the rights of the Negroes are at a lower ebb than at any time during the thirty-five years of their freedom, and the race prejudice more intense and uncompromising."

As far as black history is concerned, we can interpret the period 1900–1941 as a journey over a giant suspension bridge across a turbulent river, the dark waters of racism. On near and far sides, the bridge is suspended between the poles of two very different Supreme Court decisions. The first is the notorious "separate but equal" ruling in *Plessy* v. *Ferguson* of 1896, symbol of the heinous institutional racism of the period 1890–1910; and the second is the ruling that separate is unequal of *Brown* v. *Board of Education* of 1954, the most momentous post–World War II court decision yet and a mighty symbol of the victories of the great civil rights movement of 1950–1970. The outlying buttresses of the bridge are provided by four of the most enduring civil rights or separatist groups that were formed in the period: the National Association for the Advancement of Colored People (NAACP) (1910), the Urban League (1911), the Nation of Islam (1931), and, in the 1940's, the Committee, later the Congress, for Racial Equality (CORE) (1943). The apex of the suspension bridge is provided by the great flowering of black cultural talent of the 1920s, known variously as the "Black" or "Negro" or "Harlem Renaissance." During these years four charismatic black leaders guided their followers across the bridge, albeit to different destinations: Booker T. Washington, W. E. B. DuBois, Marcus Garvey, and Asa Philip Randolph.

Moreover, certain of the phenomena that account for the way civil rights moved to the center of the political stage in the 1950s and then shifted emphasis to black power in the course of the 1960s were already present early in the century. These include: the Great Migration of blacks from countryside to city and from

South to North, making black problems known to the North and transforming blacks into a potentially potent political force to be courted by both parties and radical groups; increasing black literacy and awareness of the discrepancy between the ideals of the American Constitution and the blatant practice of racism, most notably in World War II; the development of nonviolent tactics to protest discrimination, initially by religious groups; various Supreme and lesser court hearings that provided forums for such eloquent black attorneys as Moorfield Storey, Walter F. White, and Thurgood Marshall to press for rulings on racial equality that exposed discrimination, established the legal principle of equality before the law, and legitimized the civil rights movement. Furthermore, the later tension between civil rights and black power was anticipated in the 1920s by the controversy between W. E. B. DuBois and A. Philip Randolph on one side and Marcus Garvey and his short-lived United Negro Improvement Association (UNIA) organization (1914) on the other.

Before 1900 black protest existed only in local groups, apart from a series of black conventions summoned to endorse presidential candidates. Nevertheless, state and local conventions debated the new laws on public accommodation and disfranchisement. Their protests were handicapped by black poverty, illiteracy, and fragmentation. Leaders found it almost impossible to develop black consciousness and unity on a scale to combat the considerable white forces arrayed against them, notably the adverse political climate, the indifference of the Supreme Court, and white intimidation and violence. Their political voice was silenced. There was no black congressman for twenty-seven years, between 1901, when George H. White of North Carolina left Congress, and 1928, when Oscar De Priest was elected for Chicago.

Booker T. Washington and W. E. B. DuBois

Since blacks were being displaced from their traditional trades and confined to menial jobs in the towns, those who did succeed in entering the worlds of business and the professions were obliged by white society to adopt its attitudes in order to retain their hard won position. Their undeclared leader was Booker T. Washington, head of Tuskegee Industrial Institute, Alabama. Washington was invited to speak at the opening of the Cotton States and International Exposition in Atlanta on September 18, 1895, by businessmen who recognized his remarkable powers of expression. His address was one of the most effective political speeches of the Gilded Age, a model fusion of substance and style.

In what was later called the Atlanta Compromise he abandoned the postwar ideal of racial equality in favor of increased economic opportunity for blacks. "The wisest among my race understand that the agitation of questions of social equality is the extremest folly and that progress in the enjoyment of all the privileges that will come to us must be the result of severe and constant struggle rather than of artificial forcing." He preached patience, proposed submission, and emphasized material progress. Those blacks who rejected the Atlanta Compromise, such as rising activist W. E. B. DuBois, considered it a capitulation to blatant racism. But Washington was telling white society exactly what it wanted to hear, that blacks accepted the Protestant work ethic. His most widely reported remark was a subtle metaphor about racial harmony: "In all things social we can be as separate as the fingers, yet one as the hand in all things essential to mutual progress."

Washington's emphasis on racial pride, economic progress, and industrial education encouraged white politicians and businessmen, such as steel tycoon Andrew Carnegie, to subsidize the black institutions he recommended. Through his close connections with business he was able to raise the funds necessary to create the National Negro Business League in 1900. Moreover, he used money not to advance black acquiescence but to fight segregation. Others sought a more open insistence on racial pride. In 1890 T. Thomas Fortune, a black journalist of New York, persuaded forty black protection leagues in cities across the country to join in a national body, the Afro-American League. Historian C. Vann Woodward assesses Washington's work thus: "Washington's life mission was to find a pragmatic compromise that would resolve the antagonisms, suspicions, and aspirations of 'all three classes directly concerned—the Southern white man, the Northern white man, and the Negro.' It proved, he admitted, 'a difficult and at times a puzzling task.' But he moved with consummate diplomacy, trading renunciation for concession and playing sentiment against interest."

The publication of *The Souls of Black Folk* by W. E. B. DuBois in 1903 solidified black protest around a new spokesman. William Edward Burghardt DuBois was born in Great Barrington, Massachusetts, in 1868, graduated from Fisk and Harvard, and attended the University of Berlin. After returning to America in 1894, he taught at Wilberforce University, Ohio, and Pennsylvania University, before becoming professor of sociology at Atlanta. Widely known for being a natty dresser, DuBois was also a creative writer who produced two novels, *The Quest of the Silver Fleece* (1900) and *The Dark Princess* (1928), and two volumes of essays and poems, *Dark Water* (1920) and *The Gift of Black Folk* (1924). One of DuBois's early supporters, James Weldon Johnson, said of *The Souls of Black Folk* that "it had a greater effect upon and within the Negro race than any single book published in the country since *Uncle Tom's Cabin.*" One of the essays was a withering attack on what DuBois considered Washington's acceptance of the heinous doctrine of black inferiority. DuBois insisted on an end to accommodation. "By every civilized and peaceful method we must strive for the rights which the world accords to men."

Deeply angered by Washington's counterrevolutionary tactics and intensely hostile to the strategy of accommodation, DuBois invited likeminded activists to a national conference at Fort Erie in July 1905 that established the Niagara movement. This was an elite cadre of about 400 college-educated professional people. The Niagara movement committed itself to continuing vocal protest against "the abridgment of political and civil rights and against inequality of educational opportunity." DuBois and others published the *Moon* and, later, the *Horizon* as unofficial journals of the movement. Nevertheless, the Niagara movement failed to establish itself as a distinctive national voice.

At a meeting in New York on May 31 and June 1, 1909, black and white radicals proposed a new national organization to protect the rights of blacks and a similar conference held in 1910 established the National Association for the Advancement of Colored People (NAACP) with its declared goal of "equal rights and opportunities for all." Under its first president, Moorfield Storey, the NAACP formed several hundred branches. Under the editorship of W.E.B. DuBois, the NAACP journal, the *Crisis*, reached a circulation of 100,000. DuBois's own column, "As the Crow Flies," attacked white racism. Together with the *Chicago Defender*, the *Pittsburgh Courier*, and the *Baltimore Afro American*, the *Crisis* made an ever-increasing spectrum of literate blacks aware of their national responsibilities and what the nation owed them.

The NAACP's distinctive strategy was litigation to challenge racist laws. For example, in 1917 the NAACP challenged a statute of Louisville, Kentucky, requiring "the use of separate blocks for residence, places of abode, and places of assembly by white and colored people respectively." Moorfield Storey took the case to the Supreme Court at a time when it was, in the terms of analyst Richard Kluger, peopled by men of Paleolithic perspective, notably Justices Willis van Devanter and James Clark McReynolds. Nevertheless, in the case of *Buchanan* v. *Warley* the Court unanimously, and surprisingly, decided on November 5, 1917, that "All citizens of the United States shall have the same right in every state and territory, as is enjoyed by white citizens thereof, to inherit, purchase, lease, sell, hold and convey real and personal property." However, the *Buchanan* decision resulted in a spate of private restrictive covenants under which residents agreed to sell or rent their property to individuals of one race only. The Court subsequently upheld this pernicious practice in *Corrigan* v. *Buckley* in 1926, maintaining that civil rights were not protected against discrimination by individuals.

The second-oldest surviving black organization, the Urban League, was founded in New York in 1911. It was primarily a social welfare organization assisting black migrants in finding work and accommodation and trying to relieve the worst excesses of black urban poverty. It, too, had a journal, *Opportunity*, founded in 1923, and, in the 1930s, the extreme circumstances of the depression allowed the organization the occasion for special pleas against economic as well as political oppression of black citizens. Of these first concerted attempts at black association, Harvard Sitkoff concludes in *A New Deal for Blacks* (1978), "The civil

For over thirty years, Paul Robeson proved himself among the most versatile of American artists, whether as college athlete, singer of spirituals, or a noble actor in plays by Shakespeare and Eugene O'Neill. In the film of O'Neill's *The Emperor Jones* he moved from cocky self-assurance to doubt and terror. However, throughout his successful career, Paul Robeson never lost touch with the dilemma of black Americans and he adopted increasingly radical political stands, culminating in his appeal for "Black Power" during the Little Rock crisis of 1957. (Musuem of Modern Art Film Stills Archive).

rights organizations of the early twentieth century lacked adequate finances, political leverage, the support of most blacks, influential white allies, and access to the major institutions shaping public opinion and policy."

Race discrimination, important in itself, had more momentous consequences because of the contemporary exodus of blacks from South to North. For the 1910s and 1920s were also the years of the Great Migration. The immediate reason for the exodus was the industrial requirements of World War I. Whites were being drawn increasingly into the armed services and newly created war industries. However, the war prevented European immigrants from coming to America and taking their place as laborers. Thus in 1915 agents for northern employers began recruiting black labor from the South. However, at least four times as many blacks went North on word of mouth than did so at the prompting of labor agents. The exodus was mainly spontaneous and largely unorganized; whatever the personal motives for individual moves, the collective motive was bad treatment in the South. The Great Migration was facilitated by railroad transportation and continued after the war was over. In sum, the South lost 323,000 black citizens in the 1910s and 615,000 in the 1920s—about 8.2 percent of its black population.

Carter G. Woodson recognized the significance of the phenomenon and founded the Association for the Study of Negro Life and History in September 1915 to review the momentous sociological changes in a regular publication, the *Journal of Negro History,* of which he was editor. In 1915 the association published Woodson's *A Century of Negro Migration* that described the exodus as "giving the Negro his best chance in the economic world out of which he must emerge a real man with power to secure his rights as an American citizen."

At home black leaders felt ambivalent toward American intervention. W. E. B. DuBois moved from opposing the war effort to support in June 1918 on the assumption that an Allied victory would yield blacks the right to vote, work, and live without continuous harassment. Other activists disagreed. The included Asa Philip Randolph and Chandler Owens, editors of the *Messenger,* a journal they had founded in 1915 as part of a strategy to recruit black hotel workers into a labor union.

A. Philip Randolph, born in Crescent City, Florida, would emerge as one of the most significant black leaders of the twentieth century. The son of James Randolph, an African Methodist Episcopal Church preacher, A. Philip moved to New York and joined the Socialist party in 1911. He was fired from successive jobs as an elevator operator, maintenance man, and waiter for having tried to start unions with his fellow workers. Roi Ottley describes him in *Black Odyssey* as "unique among Negro leaders in that he was neither preacher, educator, nor rabble rousing politician, but a labor organizer. Tall, dark, and brooding, Randolph impressed Negroes as being all soul." Along with fellow socialist Chandler Owens, Randolph condemned the war in the *Messenger* and traversed the country making speeches in opposition to it. He declared in the *Messenger,* "Lynching, Jim Crow, segregation, and discrimination in the armed forces and out, disfranchisement of millions of black souls in the South—all these things make your cry of making the world safe for democracy a sham, a mockery, a rape of decency, and a travesty of common justice." After an antiwar meeting in Cleveland in 1918 Randolph was arrested and jailed for a few days. In the antiradical hysteria following the war, the *Messenger* was banned from federal mails.

In the North black migrants were condemned by circumstances to a life in squalid tenement ghettos. They faced resentment and hostility from white workers who feared for their livelihood. In 1917 there were race riots in towns and on army bases. In July 1917 a savage race riot in East St. Louis killed between 40 and 200 blacks and drove almost 6,000 from their homes. The first year of peace, 1919, was the most violent in black history since Reconstruction: there were twenty-five race riots across the country.

With the death of prominent black spokesman Booker T. Washington in 1915 the initiative in the black political movement passed to the NAACP. Within ten years W. E. B. DuBois, editor of the NAACP journal, the *Crisis,* had made himself the leading black spokesman of the age. The NAACP's base was in the North but its principal officers were natives of the South—William Pickens, Robert W. Bagnall, Walter White, and James Weldon Johnson. Johnson had graduated from Atlanta University and was a distinguished novelist and poet who had served the State Department in Nicaragua and Venezuela. As secretary he expanded the NAACP's activities. In 1919 the association had 88,448 members distributed among 300 branches, of which 155 were in the South. This rapid increase in size since 1913 (when there had been only fourteen branches) laid the NAACP open to racist criticism that it had fueled postwar riots. This was ironic. The NAACP was an elite organization committed to legal protest against injustice. Nevertheless, it was determined that black citizens should be made aware of their civil rights.

DuBois was also the father of the Pan African movement with its belief in special cultural and political links between American blacks and Africa. Thus the NAACP supported the Pan African Congress in Paris in 1919 and lobbied statesmen at the peace conference for self-determination for African colonies. It was DuBois who recognized the connection between the struggles by African blacks for national independence from Europe and by American blacks for civil rights in the United States.

Southern senators, such as Walter F. George, John Sharp Williams, and James F. Byrnes, were utterly complacent in their faith that white supremacy was inviolable. On the surface, it seemed that statistical evidence was on their side. In the South only 21.1 percent of blacks worked outside of agriculture. Only 7 percent of blacks in towns had professional, managerial, or clerical occupations. Furthermore, blacks were still being systematically disenfranchised. In the South the real contest was not in the election itself but for the Democratic nomination. Thus the Democratic party prevented its black members from voting in primaries. It did this by state laws in eight states and by county or city laws in three others.

Texas was one of the states that decided to use the device of excluding blacks from Democratic primaries. However, Dr. A. L. Nixon, a black citizen of El Paso, supported by the NAACP, challenged the racist law in the case of *Nixon* v. *Herndon,* in which he was represented by Moorfield Storey, then aged eighty-two. The case reached the Supreme Court that ruled on March 7, 1927, that the Texas law violated the Fourteenth Amendment. The Texas state legislature decided to undermine the ruling by investing the state executive committees of the political parties with authority to decide who could, and who could not, vote. Thus the Democratic party committee restricted voting in primaries to "all white Democrats who are qualified under the constitution and laws of Texas." Dr. Nixon continued to press his, and the NAACP's, case and was now represented by attorney Nathan Margold, author of a report recommending the NAACP to oblige states to make black educational facilities equal to white. In the case of *Nixon* v. *Condon* the Supreme Court decided by 5 votes to 4 on May 2, 1932, that the power of executive committees to exclude blacks from primaries was a form of state power and, therefore, unconstitutional.

Within weeks the devious Texas Democrats had convened a state convention that declared that all white citizens could vote in primaries but blacks could not. When black Texan William Grovey tried to get a ballot for the Democratic primary election of July 1934, he was refused. Supported by black lawyers Carter Wesley and J. Alston Atkins, he fought the test case of *Grovey* v. *Townsend* to the Supreme Court, which, on April 1, 1935, unanimously ruled that the Texas Democratic party was within its rights because it was a private organization and not subject to the Fourteenth Amendment.

Sometimes blacks were allowed to vote in municipal elections, especially in Texas and Virginia. They played a decisive part in local elections in Louisville in 1920, Nashville in 1921, and Savannah in 1923. In Atlanta in 1921 and NAACP mobilized black voters to ensure the passage of a $4 million school bond of which $1 million was pledged to black schools. Some urban bosses elicited black support and repaid it in kind. In San Antonio, Texas, Charles Bellinger had a regular supply of black votes. Thus he controlled city elections in San Antonio from 1918 until 1935. In return, he provided blacks with schools and parks, a library and an auditorium, as well as paved streets and sewers.

Strange Fruit

Not content with holding blacks in social chains, vicious whites sometimes sought their lives. Many blacks were victims of lynch law, especially in the South where the trees of small towns bore strange fruit about once in every generation. The common charge was that the black victims of white lynch mobs had tried to rape white women. According to black surveys, there were over a thousand lynchings between 1900 and 1915. Moreover, as historian Harvard Sitkoff observes, "Petty brutality, lynchings, and pogroms against the Negro sections of towns occurred so frequently in the first decade of the twentieth century that they appeared commonplace, hardly newsworthy." American intervention in the war and its vicious propaganda to smash the Hun released a new tide of savagery. Between 1918 and 1927, according to NAACP officer Walter F. White in his *Rope and Faggot* (1929), 456 people were victims of lynch mobs. Of this number 416 were black, 11 were women and 3 of them were pregnant. Forty-two of the victims were burned alive, 16 were cremated after death, and 8 were either beaten to death or dismembered and cut to pieces.

Racist Winfield H. Collins defended this vile practice in a scurrilous book of 1918, *The Truth About Lynching:* "The white man in lynching a Negro does it as an indirect act of self-defense against the Negro criminal as a race." The practice of lynching was necessary "in order to hold in check the Negro in the South." Senator James F. Byrnes agreed. He told Congress that lynching was the surest way of defending white women from rape. Perversely turning the burden of guilt to the victims of lynching, he declared that "rape is responsible directly and indirectly for most of the lynching in America."

For some communities the act of lynching became what historian George Brown Tindall has called in *The Emergence of the New South* (1967) "a twentieth century auto-da-fé." It was an event for white men, women, and children to attend in order to relieve the boredom of small town life. They wanted entertainment and prolonging the torture of a hapless victim and taking bizarre photographs of the cruel scene gave them sadistic pleasure. A contributory factor in the epidemic of lynching was the depressed provincialism of isolated southern communities. According to historian James H. Chadbourn in *Lynching and the Law* (1933), a county given to lynching was "characterized in general by social and economic decadence." Its family incomes were well below average and 75 percent of its inhabitants were likely to belong to Southern Methodist and Baptist churches. Moreover, W. E. Wimpy of Georgia believed in an article for *Manufacturers' Record* of December 25, 1919, that the horrible practice could persist because the United States was divided into hundreds of minuscule sovereign governments. "These tiny kingdoms can kill their subjects like hogs if they want to, and under State rights they know there is no law on earth to prosecute them but their own law; no judge ever prosecutes himself."

The epidemic of lynchings allowed black leaders the opportunity to lance the boil of white hypocrisy and evasion. The NAACP assumed that if it publicized the outrages, mass public indignation would demand reform. Thus it organized public meetings, lobbied public officials, and stimulated press investigation. Walter F. White of Atlanta, appropriately enough, could pass for white. Thus he gained access to public officials in the South who held records of lynchings. Those officials who discovered he was black were more antagonized by his methods than they were by his disclosures.

The NAACP published its research findings as *Thirty Years of Lynching, 1889–1918*. The report was published to coincide with a national conference on the subject held in New York in May 1919. The review challenged popular stereotypes about lynching. In particular, it showed that fewer than one in six victims of lynching had even been accused of rape by their assailants. The conference called for a federal law against lynching.

In 1921 the NAACP established an office in Washington. Its aim was to lobby Congress in support of Congressman L. C. Dyer of St. Louis who had introduced an antilynching bill in 1919. The Dyer bill proposed to eliminate lynching by making counties in which the offence occurred responsible. If they failed to protect citizens or prisoners from mob rule and a lynching took place, then the county would be fined. The Dyer bill passed the House by 230 votes to 119 in 1922. However, it was defeated in the Senate because of a southern filibuster.

Although the Dyer bill failed in Congress, the publicity it earned helped reduce the extent of the evil. The South grew ashamed of lynching. Southern papers asserted that southern courts

Throughout the 1920s and 1930s the NAACP maintained a campaign against the notorious racist abuse of lynching, publishing terrifying photographs of hapless victims trapped by the merciless sadism of the most bigoted southern towns, ready to corrupt little children by scenes of torture and murder. (Library of Congress).

could handle the problem and punish aggressors without needing a federal law to show them how. According to the *Negro Year Book* (1932), whereas the total number of lynchings was eighty-three in 1919 it fell to sixteen in 1924. It rose to thirty in 1926 and then declined further to eleven in 1928. The NAACP did not work alone. In 1929 reporter Louis I. Jaffe of the Norfolk *Virginian Pilot* won an editorial prize for his campaign against lynching.

Another association working for improved race relations was the Commission on Interracial Cooperation (CIC). It was founded on April 9, 1919, by a group of whites and blacks in Atlanta, disturbed by the events of 1919. They gave priority to the special social needs of black soldiers and their families in the process of demobilization. The commission secured a grant from the National War Work Council and organized conferences to advise white and black social workers. The strategy was to persuade one white and one black social worker to act as liaison officers in each southern community. Their aim was to reduce social tensions. In 1920 there were 500 interracial committees and by 1923 there were about 800. The CIC was well aware of the extent of the problem as it uncovered "vast areas of interracial injustice and neglect that could not be cleared up in a few months or a few years."

After the first two years the CIC began to receive funds regularly from various Protestant churches and public foundations, and it instituted a campaign to redress black grievances. By this time Will W. Alexander, a former Methodist minister and YMCA worker from Nashville, had emerged as leader of the commission. His strategy was to get whites and blacks to cooperate with one another by sharing a common task of welfare. The CIC was supported by the NAACP, the black press, and the Methodist church and governors in seven states. It persuaded Governor Hugh M. Dorsey of Georgia to publish an account on April 22, 1921, of 135 atrocities against blacks in the previous two years. However, the CIC, fearing loss of funds from its white sponsors, failed to take a stand on the issue of desegregation.

Another social evil in the South was peonage, a sinister variant of contract labor. Peonage was illegal but it was common in labor camps throughout the South. Peons were immigrants enticed by fraudulent advertisements placed in labor agencies in the larger cities. They worked in the cotton belt from Texas to the Carolinas, the turpentine areas of Florida, Georgia, and Alabama, and on railroads, sawmills, and mines elsewhere. Unlike slaves, they had no value as investment. They were kept at subsistence level and only for as long as they could work. In 1921 John Williams killed eleven black workers at his farm near Covington, Georgia, rather than admit he was making them work out fines he had paid the county. Governor Hugh Dorsey disclosed over twenty cases of peonage in Georgia that year.

The New York *World* began a campaign against peonage. On November 24, 1929, the *World* published findings of Orlando Kay Armstrong, a former dean of journalism at the University of Florida. Armstrong exposed the abuse of forced labor in Florida. A state law of 1919 deemed that anyone who promised his labor in advance but failed to give it was guilty of a misdemeanour. The law could be used by unscrupulous bosses to misrepresent labor contracts and thus force men to work as peons against their will.

The New York *World* also revealed that the leasing of convict labor still persisted. It told the lurid story of Martin Tabert of North Dakota who was caught train hopping in Tallahassee and sent to a lumber camp where he was whipped to death. The camp doctor had tried to cover the traces of the malevolent whip master by saying the victim had died of malaria. The *World*'s exposure of the Tabert case prompted various investigations by Florida papers and an official investigation by the state legislature. As a result, convict leasing was eventually abolished.

However, fictional accounts of the penal system based on real life experience proved the most penetrating indictments of its excessive brutality. In 1932 two novels, *Georgia Nigger* by John L. Spivak and *I am a Fugitive from a (Georgia) Chain Gang* by Robert Elliot Burns, spoke more eloquently than official reports and aroused mass indignation.

The Garvey Movement

During the course of the 1920s feelings of alienation, outright rage, and, above all, despair among blacks encouraged extremism and division. One logical expression of this was emigration to

Africa, or repatriation, for blacks, as first proposed by sea captain Paul Cuffee in the 1810s and political separatist Touissaint L'Ouverture in the 1820s.

It was now Marcus Garvey who provided blacks with an avenue of escape from the Americas. Born in Jamaica in 1887, Marcus Moziah Garvey emigrated to London and worked there for several years as a printer. After his return to Jamaica, he led an unsuccessful printers' strike and lost his job. However, he was inspired by Booker T. Washington's autobiography, *Up From Slavery* (1901), to organize the Universal Negro Improvement and Conservation Association (later known as the UNIA), in August 1914. The aims of the new organization were to establish a universal cofraternity of blacks, civilize tribes in Africa, encourage race pride, and develop a "conscientious Christianity." Having been encouraged by Washington to visit Tuskegee, he arrived after Washington's death. Undeterred, he established the UNIA in Harlem, firstly among other West Indian immigrants. The organization reached its peak of membership in 1921 with between, perhaps, 1 million and 4 million supporters.

Garvey was a commanding and charismatic speaker who promoted the slogan "Africa for Africans at home and abroad" (a variant on a phrase first coined by Martin R. Delany in 1860), and exhorted his followers with "Up you mighty race, you can accomplish what you will." The UNIA established the Black Star Steamship Line to carry migrants across the Atlantic. It also petitioned the League of Nations to transfer the former German colonies in Africa, South West Africa and German East Africa, held as mandates by South Africa and Britain, respectively, to Garvey's control. In 1922 Garvey designated himself president of a new African republic. He organized a militia and created dukes of the Nile among his lieutenants. The panoply of grand titles and imperial uniforms soon seemed foolish. However, the UNIA was the first truly mass movement of black Americans, a predecessor of later black organizations, especially those advocating black power and black pride.

However, because Garvey criticized the lighter skinned integrationists and middle-class blacks of the NAACP for being ashamed of their ancestry, he himself drew withering attacks from such as

A. Philip Randolph, Chandler Owens, and W. E. B. DuBois. Randolph and Owens abused Garvey for concentrating on the issue of race and ignoring what they considered more important, the issue of class. The mutual attacks and recrimination were venomous in the extreme. DuBois described Garvey as "A little fat black man, ugly but with intelligent eyes and a big head." Garvey retorted, calling DuBois a racial monstrosity on account of his mixed African, French, and Dutch ancestry. He was "a lazy dependent mulatto." DuBois published his most virulent attack on Garvey in an editorial "A Lunatic or a Traitor" in the *Crisis* of May 1924, saying Garvey had convicted himself by his own "swaggering monkey shines." "Marcus Garvey is, without doubt, the most dangerous enemy of the Negro race in America and in the world. He is either a lunatic or a traitor."

In *Race First* (1976) Tony Martin comments,

What was most fascinating about the Garvey-DuBois struggle was that it was in a most real sense a continuation of the Washington-DuBois debate. The ideological questions raised were largely the same. Furthermore, Garvey was very self-consciously a disciple of Washington. Along with his admiration for Washington, Garvey had early imbibed a dislike for DuBois. He therefore saw himself as the heir to Washington's fight against DuBois and never missed an opportunity to compare the two, to the detriment of DuBois.

Garvey realized that Washington had accommodated himself to white racism but preferred to believe that, had he lived longer, Washington would have shifted emphasis from gradualism to black nationalism. He shared Washington's opposition to social equality, which he interpreted as free and unhindered social intercourse between the races. Moreover, unlike DuBois, Washington had preached and practiced self-reliance and formed a power base, independent of white influence.

Hostility between integrationists and separatists was so great as to split the UNIA convention in Harlem in 1922. James W. H. Eason, a Philadelphia minister and prominent member of the UNIA, quarreled violently with Garvey on the platform. He withdrew from the UNIA and set up a rival organization, the Universal Negro Alliance, pledged to concentrate on the problems of blacks in the United States. He was also due to testify against Garvey over various irregularities in the Black Star finances but was shot at a speaking engagement in New Orleans in January 1923. Two Jamaicans were indicted for attempted murder, Garvey's chief of police, William Shakespeare, and a patrolman, F. W. Dyer. However, Eason died before he could identify them and they were released. Outraged by this bizarre murder, the Committee of Eight, a group of black leaders, sent a letter to Attorney General Harry M. Daugherty, protesting about the length of time it was taking to bring Garvey to trial for irregularities in the funding of the Black Star Steamship Line. He was arrested on a charge of using the federal mails to defraud the public, convicted in 1923, and after his appeal failed, imprisoned in Atlanta in 1925. In December 1927 he was deported to Jamaica and died in obscurity in London in 1940.

The Garvey movement represented a new black consciousness in which millions of black citizens could sublimate their despair and disillusionment in the promise of a better and more fulfilled future. Most significantly, Garvey also convinced blacks that it was white racism and not black failings or inadequacy that was responsible for their poverty and sense of powerlessness. James Weldon Johnson of the NAACP commented how Garvey collected more money "than any other Negro organization had ever dreamed of." In a most prophetic statement, the *Amsterdam News* of November 30, 1927, declared how "Marcus Garvey made black people proud of their race. In a world where black is despised he taught them that black is beautiful."

The Harlem Renaissance

During the 1920s black consciousness in the North was being nourished by the Harlem Renaissance. Hitherto, even substantive achievements in literature, such as *The Litany of Atlanta* that DuBois wrote to commemorate the Atlanta Riot of 1906, were sporadic, hardly part of a movement. In contrast, the 1920s produced a wealth of black artistic and literary talent that paralleled similar achievements by whites. Both expressed the conflict of values in society between old and new, countryside and town, following

World War I and artists' alienation from small town bourgeois society.

Black arts now received extensive patronage from wealthy whites. The Great Migration that had swelled the black community of Harlem had also made it prosperous. Since New York was the artistic capital of the United States, it was in the interests of producers, publishers, and agents there to promote good art from those ethnic groups who could make a distinctive contribution. While Norman Mailer's perceptive and prophetic remarks of 1957 on "hipsters" and "the white negro" were still far into the future, the seeds of black influence on white fashions, customs, and articulation were already being sown. As writer Langston Hughes commented, "It was the period when the Negro was in vogue." In his *From Slavery to Freedom* (1947; 1967) historian John Hope Franklin explains how the black writers of the Harlem Renaissance expressed the social and economic grievances of blacks.

Despite his intense feelings of hate and hurt, [the black writer] possessed sufficient restraint and objectivity to use his materials artistically, but no less effectively. He was sufficiently in touch with the main currents of American literary development to adapt the accepted forms of his own materials, and therefore gain a wider acceptance. These two factors, the keener realization of injustice and the improvement of the capacity for expression, produced a crop of Negro writers who constituted the "Harlem Renaissance."

The pivotal figure was NAACP leader James Weldon Johnson, who both took part in and recorded the history of the Harlem Renaissance. Johnson produced his *Fifty Years and Other Poems* (1917), following it with a collection of others' work, *The Book of Negro Poetry* (1922), two books of Negro spirituals (1925 and 1926), a book of black sermons in verse, *God's Trombones* (1927), and an indictment of discrimination against black Gold Star mothers, entitled *Saint Peter Relates an Incident of the Resurrection Day* (1930). Johnson's considerable achievement was capped by the reissue of his 1912 *Autobiography of an Ex-colored Man* (1927) and two works that told the story of the Harlem Renaissance, *Black Manhattan* (1930) and *Along This Way* (1933).

Alain Locke of Philadelphia, who took a Ph.D. at Harvard and was the first black Rhodes scholar, published *The New Negro: An Interpretation* (1925), a collection of articles, essays, stories, and poems, first published in the *Survey Graphic*. His preface expressed boundless optimism about the future of black Americans, believing "The vital inner grip of prejudice has been broken" and "In the very process of being transported, the Negro is becoming transformed." "We are witnessing the resurrection of a people. . . ," a "rise from social disillusionment to race pride."

The first writer to capture a wide readership was Claude McKay, who immigrated from the West Indies in 1912 when he was twenty-one. After attending Tuskegee and the University of Kansas, McKay settled in Harlem and published poems in such magazines as the *Seven Arts,* the *Liberator,* and the *Messenger.* However, it was his *Harlem Shadows* (1922) that placed him in the fore of American poets with the plangent defiance of poems like "The Lynching," "If We Must Die," and "To The White Fiends." Therefore, he turned increasingly to prose, producing a novel of black life in New York, *Home to Harlem* (1928), an autobiography, *A Long Way From Home,* and a panoramic study of everyday black life in New York, *Harlem: Negro Metropolis.* The most cosmopolitan and prolific writer, Langston Hughes, was also the most wide-ranging and rebellious in terms of content and form. Thus he earned the nickname "Shakespeare in Harlem." He could move from the passionate defensive pride of race in *The Negro Speaks of Rivers* or mix noble expression in low-life settings in *Brass Spittoons.* His achievements in *Weary Blues* (1926) and *Fine Clothes to the Jew* (1927) were crowned by a novel, *Not Without Laughter* (1930), and *The Ways of White Folks* (1934), and his autobiography, *The Big Sea* (1940).

Other leading writers included Jean Toomer, Countee Culleen, Jennie Redmond Fauset, and Nella Larsen. NAACP antilynching campaigner Walter White was also an accomplished novelist who wrote *Fire in the Flint* (1924), a fast-moving tragedy of southern blacks, and *Flight* (1926), about a woman light enough to pass as white. In 1929 he wrote *Rope and Faggot: A Biography of Judge Lynch,* an acute summary of his research into the problem.

From 1910 onward black actors began to disappear from plays presented downtown and there soon developed a black theater in

Harlem in which black actors appeared before black audiences in both black and white roles. In April 1917 a group sponsored by Emily Hapgood appeared in three one-act plays by Ridgley Torrence at the Garden Theater, Madison Square Garden, that were widely reviewed by the white press. However, press concentration on America's formal entry into World War I immediately afterward obscured the achievement. In 1919 the black actor Charles Gilpin played Rev. William Custis in *Abraham Lincoln* by John Drinkwater and his performance reminded critics of the wealth of black acting talent.

Now white artists, writers, musicians, and dramatists began to draw on the black experience to explore the themes of rootlessness, restlessness, and alienation. One such was playwright Eugene O'Neill who was, like T. S. Eliot, greatly influenced by European expressionism and used modern psychology to analyse biblical and classical myths. In 1920 O'Neill's *The Emperor Jones* was produced in New York with Charles Gilpin as the deposed and ostracized dictator of a West Indies island who declines through persecution to a state of paranoia, all to the accompaniment of accelerating drums and within sets that symbolize his fears. Gilpin found the strain of having to use the term "nigger" again and again every night intense and he began to amend the text onstage and to drink heavily off it. Eventually, he was replaced by Paul Robeson. In *All God's Chillun Got Wings* (1924) O'Neill examined a marriage between a black husband and white wife. The scene at the close when the white actress must kiss the hand of the black actor caused a storm of protest when the play was published and led to threats against O'Neill.

In 1927 *Porgy,* a folk play by Dorothy and DuBose Heyward about the black community in Charleston, was presented by the Theater Guild with Rose McClendon and Frank Wilson. The greatest commercial success of the black legitimate theater was *The Green Pastures* (1930) by Marc Connelly. It retold the story of the Old Testament as if the playwright were Uncle Tom, and in which Richard B. Harrison played de Lawd.

Black performing artists had scored especial success as dancers, comedians, and singers in a variety of musical shows ever since Bert Williams and George Walker had brought their vaudeville

Richard Wright, author of *Native Son,* a moving novel of black consciousness that contains effective satire of whites, whether racist, liberal, or radical, and that set a new standard for black literature, providing a model followed by such diverse writers as Ralph Ellison and Alex Haley. (Carl Van Vechten Collection; Library of Congress).

act to New York in 1896. Black American music, whether jazz, blues, spirituals, or soul, has been among the most influential of all twentieth-century art forms across the world. These forms also shaped black music and its performers onstage in theaters. The writer-producer team of F. E. Miller, Aubrey Lyle, Eubie Blake, and Noble Sissle mounted the black revue *Shuffle Along* (1920), considered the most brilliant by any company to that time, and with a string of popular songs, including "I'm Just Wild About Harry" and "Love Will Find a Way." It established a vogue for black revues, such as Irving Miller's '*Liza,* Miller and Lyle's *Runnin' Wild,* and Blake and Sissle's *Chocolate Dandies,* which introduced Josephine Baker, (all 1923), and *Dixie to Broadway* (1924), which starred Florence Mills, "the little black mosquito," who also appeared in *Blackbirds* (1926).

Among white artists who painted black subjects were Mexican born Miguel Covarrubias and Winold Reiss who illustrated Alain Locke's *The New Negro.* Black artist Henry Ossawa Tanner enjoyed a reputation at the turn of the century that remained unsurpassed by his successors—Laura Wheeler Waring, who painted scenes from the lives of affluent blacks, and Edward A. Harleston, who concentrated on artisans.

With the coming of the depression, the initial flame that had fueled the Renaissance in Harlem began to flicker and the New York wits carried their torches to different parts of the country or Europe. Some new talents began to emerge and kept the spirit of the Renaissance alive until it should come into its second flowering at the end of the decade. Among these transitional writers was the anthropologist Zora Neal Hurston, a student of Franz Boas at Columbia, who collected a mass of folklore in the United States and from the Caribbean on which she would base scholarly articles and novels between 1931 and 1943.

The Great Depression

The Great Depression of the 1930s was a greater catastrophe for the black community than for the white. For those blacks who had a job, the average income during the depression in the South was only $634 in cities and $566 in the countryside. Black sociologist Kelly Miller described the black American in 1932 as "the surplus man, the last to be hired and the first to be fired." By 1933 50 percent of urban blacks could not find jobs of any kind and most rural blacks could not sell their crops at a price that would repay their costs. In the cities unemployed whites contested for menial work they would once have thought beneath them and thus "negro jobs" disappeared as domestic service and garbage collection suddenly became white occupations. Black communities across the country were threatened by privation, malnutrition, and even starvation. Not only did southern states provide the lowest levels of unempolyment benefit and relief but white officials also openly discriminated against blacks in administering them. Thus in Mississippi, where over half the population was black, less than 9 percent of Afro-Americans received any relief in 1932, compared with 14 percent of whites.

The Great Migration slowed down. Blacks were just as keen to move from South to North as previously, not because they thought they could find work more easily but because they heard relief was administered more equitably in northern cities and that schools there were better than in the South. However, the costs of transportation were beyond most blacks. Thus only 347,000 came North in the course of the 1930s.

At first, the depression had a crippling effect on civil rights organizations, reducing financial contributions from industry and charitable foundations. At one point the *Crisis,* starved of funds and subscriptions, was almost forced to close down. Faced with the possibility of extinction, the NAACP, the Urban League, the CIC, and other black groups agreed to pool their resources and share the cost of lobbying operations. They formed a Joint Committee on National Recovery to supervise and coordinate various programs. In the process the Urban League was transformed from an organization responsible for a broad range of social services into a protest and lobbying group. However, the NAACP expanded its activities to include cooperation with the CIO, lobbying Congress, and a small number of court cases, led by Charles Houston, dean of Harvard Law School, William H. Hastie, and Thurgood Marshall. Rather than challenge Jim Crow outright,

Houston began a painstaking assault on inequality in public accommodation.

The Great Depression also exacerbated racial tensions. The
number of lynchings provides a barometer of race relations, rising
from seven in 1921 to twenty-one in 1930 and twenty-eight in
1933. However, the NAACP campaign against lynching attracted
widespread support although southern Senators repeatedly secured the defeat of antilynching bills. Lynching united the opposition of both black and white liberals, thereby swelling support
for civil rights. The notorious murder of Claude Neal in Florida
on October 23, 1934, was widely publicized in the NAACP
pamphlet by Howard Kester, recounting how the mob vivisected
its victim and hung his mutilated limbs from a tree outside a court
house.

A bill proposed by Senators Edward Costigan of Colorado and
Robert Wagner of New York called for the fining or jailing of
state or local officials found delinquent, either in protecting black
or white citizens from lynch mobs or in arresting and prosecuting
violators of the law. Furthermore, it provided for a fine of $10,000
to be levied against the county in which the lynching took place.
It was supported by governors of twelve states, including David
Sholtz of Florida where Claude Neal had been murdered. Nevertheless, the Costigan bill was rejected in April 1935 after a filibuster of southern senators that lasted six days. However, many
southern newspapers had now changed their minds and now
favored legislation. Congressman Joseph A. Gavagan of New
York proposed a new bill that passed the House in April 1937 by
277 votes to 120 after a terrible incident at Duck Hill, Mississippi,
where a mob killed two blacks with a blowtorch. However, it
was abandoned in the Senate on February 21, 1938, after a filibuster led by Senators Tom Connally of Texas and Theodore Bilbo
of Mississippi.

The NAACP campaign had, as usual, been conducted by Walter
White, who had become its executive secretary in 1930. White
won nationwide recognition for his efforts, including the title of
Man of the Year by *Time* magazine in January 1939. Perhaps
because of all the adverse publicity, the number of lynchings
gradually began to fall—from eighteen in 1935 to two in 1939.

Black Muslims

A number of black nationalist movements emerged during the 1930s, including the National Movement for the Establishment of a Forty-Ninth State, founded in Chicago in 1934 by Oscar Brown, Sr., and Bindley C. Cyrus. The most famous of such organizations was the Nation of Islam, popularly called the Black Muslims, and founded in Detroit circa 1931 by Wallace D. Fard (or Farrod Mohammed or Wali Forrod), a peddler of silks and raincoats of obscure origins, possibly black, possibly part Arab. The Black Muslims represented the most extreme reaction of black Americans to white racism.

Basing their beliefs on the Muslim religion and a version of the Koran, Black Muslims taught that all whites were devils, perverse creations of an evil scientist, Yakub, and that only blacks were the true children of Allah. Absurd? Well, as we have observed elsewhere, both the Jewish Torah and Christian Bible allow the book of Genesis not one but two different stories of the creation of the world and neither is consistent with subsequent scientific interpretations. Religions are conceived by men of faith rather than men of science and they enshrine myths, imaginative stories that help us understand the mysteries of human existence. The myth of the evil Yakub expresses a profound truth, the systematic exploitation of blacks by white society, notably in human slavery and, also, the ways society finds to justify and institutionalize white racism. Moreover, in the 1930s the myth became terrible prophecy. Thus in Germany the Nazis set out to perfect a master race of Aryans, to exterminate the Jews, and also dabbled in terrible sexual and scientific experiments on their victims in concentration camps. In the United States, scientists chose to study the degeneration of black sufferers of venereal disease by allowing them to survive but deteriorate without remedial treatment in the "Bad Blood" experiment at Tuskegee, chronicled by James Jones. The subjects were simply told they suffered from bad blood. Here in the 1930s were two instances of white science fulfilling the worst of contemporary black fears.

By 1933 the Black Muslims had established a temple, created a ritual, founded a University of Islam, and formed the Fruit of Islam, a bodyguard. The sect drew followers from other similar organizations, notably the Moorish Science Temple in Newark, New Jersey. This sect had been first founded in 1913 by Timothy Drew of North Carolina who subsequently opened temples in New York, Chicago, Detroit, and other major cities that were attended by an aggregate congregation of between 20,000 and 30,000.

By 1933 Fard had established a hierarchy in the Nation of Islam, notably his minister, Robert Poole of Georgia, known as Elijah Muhammad. When Fard disappeared mysteriously in 1934, Elijah Muhammad assumed control moving headquarters from Detroit to Chicago. During the 1930s membership stabilized around 10,000 but was damaged by the onset of war. Elijah Muhammad and some others were convicted of draft evasion and he was imprisoned from 1942 to 1946. During the war membership fell to below 1,000 with four temples in Detroit, Chicago, Milwaukee, and Washington, D.C. An obscure religious sect for almost thirty years, the Nation of Islam gained wide publicity in the late 1950s with the rise of its most charismatic leader, Malcolm X.

The cult of separatism had repercussions in the NAACP. In 1934 DuBois broke with the NAACP over his ideas for developing a separate state for blacks, a "Nation within a Nation." He averred that "if the economic and cultural salvation of the American Negro calls for an increase in segregation and prejudice, then that must come." DuBois was to return to the NAACP in 1944 and leave it once again four years later over another policy dispute. In the meantime, he had become a consultant to the United Nations and was more involved in the activities of the Communist party. These led to his indictment for subversion and subsequent acquittal and his unsuccessful campaign for election to the Senate on the American Labor ticket in 1950. Eventually convinced that Afro-Americans could not achieve justice in the United States, he emigrated to Africa and in 1962 he became a citizen of Ghana where he died in 1963 whilst engaged as director of a government-sponsored *Encyclopedia Africana.*

The Scottsboro Boys

Some blacks were attracted to communism because of its emphasis on economic and racial equality and its strategy of working-
class solidarity. Radical interest in racial matters was furthered by
white Communists, including James S. Allen, Herbert Aptheker,
and Philip S. Foner who wrote about black culture and argued
that racial prejudice must be erased. No single person represented
the fusion of black protest and radicalism better than celebrated
actor and singer Paul Robeson. He made no secret of his Communist sympathies, visited Russia in the 1930s, and praised the
Soviet system for its apparent equality.

While it is true that blacks were potentially a fertile field for
communism and perhaps 2,500 blacks belonged to the Communist
party in the mid-1930s, black radicalism was essentially indigenous to the United States, uninterested in theory, especially foreign ideologies, and suspicious of Communist motives at home
and abroad. The verdict of many was "It's enough to be black
without being red, as well."

The Scottsboro incident of 1931 provided the Communists
with the opportunity to rally black support. Here was something
that had the hallmarks of a black variation of the *Sacco-Vanzetti*
case of the 1920s.

The Scottsboro boys were nine black youths falsely accused of
multiple rape on a freight train near Scottsboro, Alabama, on
March 25, 1931, by two foul-mouthed white harlots, Victoria
Price and Ruby Bates, who needed to explain their presence
among the youths. The black youths, all aged between thirteen
and twenty, were Charlie Weems, Ozie Powell, Clarence Norris,
Olen Montgomery, Willie Roberson, Haywood Patterson, Eugene
Williams, and Andrew and Leroy Wright. Viewed dispassion-
ately, the allegations were none too likely. Willie Roberson was
suffering from syphilis and gonorrhea and Olen Montgomery
was blind in one eye. However, the sensational case touched an
exposed nerve of race relations, sexual intercourse between black
men and white women. The metaphor of imprisonment of white

over black was here made physical, the unjust incarceration of innocent men.

At the first trial of Clarence Norris and Charlie Weems on March 30, 1931, two doctors gave medical evidence that the girls were not injured in any way consistent with rape. Nevertheless, in the hysterical atmosphere of Alabama in the 1930s all white juries doubtless felt they had no option but to convict blacks accused of raping white women and the only possible penalty was death. The sentence of electrocution was cheered by the crowd. At trials held later that week the other defendants were found guilty and also sentenced to death.

The publicity generated by the case, the speed of the trial, and the savage nature of the sentences, reached all parts of the country and led the Communist party to convene protests in Cleveland and New York. The International Labor Defense (ILD), a committee with close ties to the Communists, hired George W. Chamlee, a famous southern lawyer, to defend the youths. The way the Communists appropriated the case antagonized the NAACP and divided potential sources of support for the defense. Nevertheless such organizations as the American Civil Liberties Union (ACLU) and the Southern Commission on Interracial Cooperation (SCIC) sustained the defendants and helped save their lives through a long series of appeals before the state supreme court and the U.S. Supreme Court.

On March 24, 1932, the case reached the Alabama Supreme Court that sustained all the convictions but commuted the death penalty for Leroy Wright to imprisonment on account of his extreme youth. However, on November 7, 1932, the Supreme Court ruled in *Powell* v. *Alabama* that there must be a retrial on the basis that the prejudice of the all-white juries had denied the defendants due process of law as guaranteed by the Fourteenth Amendment.

At the first retrial (of Haywood Patterson), held at Decatur, Alabama, fifty miles west of Scottsboro, on March 27, 1933, ILD defense attorney Samuel Leibowitz failed to get any blacks elected to the jury but he had persuaded star witness Ruby Bates to appear for the defense and repudiate her earlier allegations of rape. The jury was obdurate and impervious to the new weight of evidence, again finding Haywood Patterson guilty and recommending the death penalty. The other defendants were also found guilty at their second trials and the Alabama Supreme Court set the date for their execution as August 31, 1934. Once again, the defense appealed to the Supreme Court. On April 1, 1935, in *Norris* v. *Alabama* the court duly and unanimously ruled that the exclusion of blacks from juries and grand juries was contrary to the Fourteenth Amendment.

The defense now drew its conflicting forces together and the ILD, NAACP, ACLU, and the League for Industrial Democracy created a special Scottsboro Defense Committee on December 19, 1935. However, for its part, the prosecution began to fall apart, ready to compromise with prison sentences for all but Norris. President Franklin D. Roosevelt tried to persuade Governor "Bibb" Graves of Alabama to parole the Scottsboro boys but Graves was under intense local pressure to resist him.

At this point the case was complicated by an incident on January 25, 1936, in which Ozie Powell, baited by the police, attacked a deputy, Edgar Blalock, in a car, slashing his throat, and was himself shot and seriously wounded in the head. He survived but with permanent brain damage. The prosecution now decided to concentrate on his crime of assault and overlooked the original allegation of rape. He was sentenced to twenty years' imprisonment.

By July 1937 the prosecution was ready to compromise, insisting on death for Clarence Norris, prison for four others (Charlie Weems, Ozie Powell, Andy Wright, and Haywood Patterson) and withdrawing the case against the remaining four (Olen Montgomery, Roy Wright, Willie Roberson, and Eugene Williams). Thus four defendants were released on evidence that had convicted four others. The *Times-Dispatch* of July 27, 1937, suggested that the dropping of charges against four "serves as a virtual clincher to the argument that all nine of the Negroes are innocent." The governor then commuted Norris's sentence to life imprisonment. State authorities began to release all the remaining defendants under various terms of parole between 1943 and 1950.

Another case that provided the Communists with an opportunity to entice blacks was that of Angelo Herndon, arrested for leading a demonstration in Atlanta in 1932, and charged on the basis of an old slave law with incitement to insurrection. He was sentenced to eighteen years' hard labor on a chain gang. The Supreme Court overturned the verdict in 1937 after a well-orchestrated campaign for Herndon's release.

By the mid-thirties organized labor was shifting its position with regard to blacks. In the early decade the AFL had refused to discuss discrimination. There were few black unions, apart from A. Philip Randolph's Brotherhood of Sleeping Car Porters (BSCP), founded on August 5, 1925. However, the upheaval in organized labor caused by the new demands of industrial workers, leading to the creation of the CIO and its subsequent secession from the AFL, and the determination of certain Communist organizers to inject the race issue into union affairs helped promote the black case. The communist National Textile Workers emphasized the need for racial equality, in contrast to the all-white exclusiveness of the United Textile Workers. Similarly, the Sharecropper Union in Alabama, the United Citrus Workers in Florida, and the Southern Tenant Farmers Union all practiced open membership. White institutions in general were showing themselves increasingly receptive to open discussion of race relations. Thus the Carnegie foundation sponsored Swedish sociologist Gunnar Myrdal to undertake the research and writing of his mammoth study of race, *An American Dilemma* (1937).

This subtle change in radical climate among better educated people began to have a marked effect on the attitudes of the political parties. In particular, blacks were becoming disaffected wth the Republicans. In 1932 Robert Vann, publisher of the *Courier,* the black newspaper with the largest circulation, wrote "My friends, go turn Lincoln's picture to the wall. That debt has been paid in full." Both the NAACP and the Urban League urged independent voting. Nevertheless, most blacks still voted for Hoover in 1932. Not until 1934 would they desert the Republicans in significant numbers.

New Deal or Cold Deck

The impact of the New Deal on the black community as a whole was, at best, indirect. The first major code of the National Recovery

Administration (NRA) for cotton textiles provided neither fewer hours nor higher pay for unskilled work, jobs that blacks normally occupied, and this differential treatment set a precedent for other textile codes. NRA codes in other industries, like steel and tobacco, specifically allowed lower wages for blacks than for whites. Where there was no legal discrimination, employers could still hire whites rather than blacks. In general, the shortcomings of the NRA toward blacks led to some calling it "Negroes Ruined Again."

Moreover, the administration of relief in the New Deal programs was decentralized and this allowed local and party officials to exercise their prejudices against black recipients. Of over 10,000 WPA supervisors in the South, only eleven were black. Not surprisingly, public assistance for blacks in the South was meager and difficult to obtain. White planters and landlords took advantage of the total or partial illiteracy of blacks and their economic dependence on them to prevent their AAA reduction checks from reaching them. When AAA procedure was changed to allow direct payments to tenants, certain landlords decided to dispense with tenants, whom they evicted, and collect the crop reduction bonuses themselves. Such dishonesty fueled discontent among both black and white sharecroppers who united in the biracial Southern Tenant Farmers Union. Later, the FSA encouraged black farmers to buy their own land.

However, by the time of the 1936 election a series of factors combined to aid the cause of civil rights. In 1934 Arthur Mitchell of Chicago became the first black Democratic congressman, having defeated the Republican Oscar De Priest. By 1936 the northern black vote was sizable enough to merit serious consideration by both major parties. The Republicans tried to present their presidential candidate, Alf Landon, as a defender of black rights in the party of Lincoln. Indeed, he had openly favored a law against lynching and a Republican pamphlet tried to take the credit for saving the Scottsboro boys from the electric chair.

However, the most striking changes occurred in the Democratic party: for the first time black delegates—thirty in all—attended the Democratic convention. Roosevelt chose a black minister to open the convention and had Arthur Mitchell deliver the first address, much to the disgust of southern representatives. Historian William Manchester comments ruefully, "In that year the black vote was still to be had for a prayer." Yet *Time* magazine accurately reported how, for the first time, the Democrats were making a serious bid for the black vote. Indeed, no other voting section shifted its allegiance so markedly: a Gallup poll disclosed that 76 percent of northern blacks voted for FDR. The Roosevelt coalition of farmers, workers, labor, intellectuals, and blacks was decisive in his landslide victory of 60.8 percent of the popular vote. Various black leaders interpreted this as the start of a new phase of black influence in politics. Earl Brown, a black political analyst, considered the black vote was now a key sector of the northern electorate. If the Democrats were to maintain, or the Republicans were to recapture, the black vote, they would have to offer blacks more in the industrial states.

Although southerners occupied half the chairs of congressional committees in every Congress throughout the New Deal, several leading administrators began to show an unprecedented concern for black rights. One of the most notable was Secretary of the Interior Harold Ickes who was also a former head of a Chicago chapter of the NAACP. However, it was Eleanor Roosevelt who was the most conspicuous New Dealer to demonstrate this new humanitarianism by her visits to Harlem, to black schools and projects, and her readiness to speak at black functions. She made the president accessible to black leaders, notably Walter White of the NAACP and Mary McLeod Bethune, president of the National Council of Negro Women, who were allowed interviews with FDR from 1936 onward—something that would have been unthinkable even three years earlier.

Roosevelt's personality and the extraordinary way he had overcome his poliomyelitis were likely to make him an attractive candidate to black voters. The warmth of his voice, the charisma of his style, and his uncanny ability to identify himself with human exploitation encouraged blacks, somewhat ironically, to think here was their stoutest champion since Lincoln.

Unlike previous presidents who had simply sought unofficial black advice, Roosevelt employed more blacks in office. Thus Mrs. Mary McLeod Bethune became director of the Division of

Negro Affairs in the NYA; William H. Hastie, dean of Howard University Law School, became first, assistant solicitor in the Department of the Interior, and, later, the first ever black federal judge; Robert C. Weaver also worked in the Interior and, later, in the Federal Housing Authority; Eugene K. Jones of the Urban League served as adviser on Negro Affairs in the Department of Commerce; Edgar Brown had a similar post in the CCC; and veteran social worker Lawrence A. Oxley was in charge of the Department of Labor's Division of Negro Labor. These and other such appointments were sufficiently numerous to earn the collective title of "Black Cabinet."

Furthermore, the expansion of the executive during the New Deal opened additional career opportunities for black, as for white, Americans. Whereas in 1932 the Civil Service employed fewer than 50,000 blacks, by 1941 it employed three times as many. The NYA under the liberal Aubrey Williams of Mississippi pursued a policy of appointing black state and local supervisors in those areas with a sizable black population. The NYA provided young blacks with funds to attend school from grammar schools to graduate schools.

These things stimulated greater political consciousness in black communities, especially in the South. Although only 5 percent of adult blacks voted in the South in 1940, others were forming a number of new voting organizations to try and persuade blacks to register to vote. For example, the Negro Voters League was formed in Raleigh, North Carolina, in 1931 and Committees on Negro Affairs were established in Charlotte, Durham, Greensboro, and Winston-Salem that together held a pro–Roosevelt rally in 1936.

Thus the political consciousness of blacks was being developed and they turned increasingly to the Democratic party. Toward the end of the 1930s Democratic candidates received as much as 85 percent of the vote in such black areas as Harlem in New York and the South Side of Chicago.

This phenomenon was to prove a decisive factor in Roosevelt's three campaigns for reelection. Of 15 major black wards in 9 cities, Roosevelt had carried only 4 in 1932. In 1936 he carried 9 and in 1940 all 15 wards elected him by large majorities. The

After a boxing exhibition at an air base in England, heavyweight champion Sgt. Joe Louis gets into the cockpit of a P-51 bomber and is advised about flying by pilot Col. George Peck. While the armed forces remained totally segregated during World War II, the irony of black servicemen separated from whites in a war widely publicized as a war against racism was not lost on a more militant generation of black activists. (Library of Congress).

marginal Democratic victory of 1944 was supplied by black votes in several states. For instance, in Michigan, which the Republicans had carried in 1940, the Democratic plurality of only 22,500 votes in the state as a whole was more than accounted for by the black Democratic vote in Detroit alone. In New Jersey black voters in 5 major cities provided Roosevelt with a plurality of almost 29,000 in a state that went Democratic by only 26,500.

However, the notorious poll tax, white primaries, and the maze of regulations about registration still thwarted black voting campaigns. In 1939 eight states used a poll tax of between $1 and $25 to disfranchise blacks (Alabama, Arkansas, Georgia, Mississippi, South Carolina, Tennessee, Texas, and Virginia). Moreover, four of these states (Alabama, Georgia, Mississippi, and Virginia) also enforced an annual liability (or fine) on every voter who failed to pay. All but South Carolina enforced payment for primary voting as well. Liberals joined forces with civil rights leaders to try and get such practices outlawed. Democratic Congressman Lee E. Geyer of California introduced a bill against poll taxes that passed the House in October 1941 but was blocked by southern senators in the upper house. The House voted various forms of anti-poll tax legislation in 1943, 1945, 1947, and 1949, only to see them all buried in Senate committees or blocked by filibusters.

There were advances for blacks in litigation. A series of con-structive decisions by the Supreme Court during the 1930s paved the way for the major civil rights decisions of the postwar period. As the Supreme Court moved to the left, it changed the criteria for its decisions on civil rights showing decreased interest in the rights of property and an increased interest in the rights of the individual. This shift, too, stemmed from the upheaval of the New Deal. The Supreme Court greatly expanded the powers of the national government, reduced the principle of state's rights and, by implication, began to undermine the validity of political and social discrimination preserved by state governments.

In June 1935 Lloyd Lionel Gaines, a graduate of Lincoln University, the state-supported black college of Missouri, applied for a place at the law school of the University of Missouri, which was, then, all white. Although he was duly qualified, the univer-sity refused him admission and advised him either to apply to Lincoln (which had no law school) or to apply out of state. Gaines took legal action and the test case of *Missouri ex rel. Gaines* v. *Canada* was decided by the Supreme Court on December 12, 1938. By 7 votes to 2 the Court ruled against the state. In the words of Chief Justice Charles Evans Hughes, "A state denies equal protection of the laws to a black student when it refuses him admission to its all white law school, even though it volun-teers to pay his tuition at any law school in an adjacent state. By providing a law school for whites but not for blacks the state has created a privilege which one race can enjoy but the other cannot." Equally significant was the Supreme Court's repudiation of southern subterfuges to deny blacks the vote. In the case of *Love* v. *Wilson,* on May 22, 1939, the Court finally ruled against the Oklahoma law replacing the grandfather clause the Court had nullified in *Guinn* v. *United States* (1915). It declared the replacement law as "a violation of the Fifteenth Amendment ban on racial discrimination in voting."

During the years of the Scottsboro trials a series of other cases provided unequivocal evidence that the absence of blacks from state juries was prima facie evidence of the denial of due process of law to blacks. For example, in *Brown* v. *Mississippi* the Court ruled on February 17, 1936, that use of torture to extract confessions from defendants was clear denial of due process of law.

When Harlan Stone succeeded the somewhat conservative Charles Evans Hughes as chief justice in 1941, NAACP attorney Thurgood Marshall became more optimistic about the outcome of civil rights cases. Stone's accession marked an even more decisive liberal shift in the court. It was also true that other recently appointed justices, Hugo Black (appointed 1937), Stanley Reed (1938), Frank Murphy (1940), and Robert Jackson (1941), had all served the New Deal and appreciated the significance of the black vote for the Democratic party.

On May 26, 1941, in *United States* v. *Classic* (a case arising out of corruption in white primaries in Louisiana and brought by white voters), the Court, by 5 votes to 3, awarded Congress the power to regulate primary elections, thereby reversing earlier decisions. This ruling gave NAACP attorneys William Hastie and Thurgood Marshall the confidence to use the *Classic* opinion as a basis for contesting all-white primaries in *Smith* v. *Allwright.* Marshall declared, "We must not be delayed by people who say, 'The time is not ripe,' nor should we proceed with caution for fear of destroying the status quo. People who deny us our civil rights should be brought to justice now." The Court decided on the *Smith* case on April 3, 1944, and ruled by 8 votes to 1 that actions by a political party to prevent blacks from voting in primaries were subject to the Fourteenth and Fifteenth Amendments. Whereas the impact of the Court's decisions on southern practices was negligible, its influence on the criteria for postwar decisions was vital.

Black Stars

Once again, the worlds of sports and entertainment attested to the continuing strength and vibrancy of black stars. Adolf Hitler's claims about Nordic supremacy were challenged by the great black American sprinter Jesse Owens of Ohio. At the 1936 Olympics in Berlin, German track officials deliberately handicapped Jesse Owens who, nevertheless, scored signal victories. Hitler made his disgust obvious by refusing to make the awards of gold medals himself and several other American athletes protested against the insult by refusing to accept their medals from Hitler. Two years later, heavyweight boxing champion Joe Louis, "the brown bomber," hammered home the point by pounding German boxer Max Schmelling (who had previously defeated him) to defeat at Madison Square Garden. By the time America went to war in 1941, Joe Louis had successfully defended his heavyweight title nine times. He was well aware of his social responsibilities. "I want to fight honest," he said, "so that the next colored boy can get the same break I got. If I act the fool, I'll let them down."

White society prized black singers and musicians for their range of emotional expression but denied them full recognition as citizens. When Benny Goodman, "King of Swing," employed black artist Teddy Wilson in his band, various hotel managers refused to allow Wilson to play with the band on dance floors. Duke Ellington and his band were allowed to perform at Loew's State Theater on Broadway but not at the Paramount or Strand. Singer Billie Holiday had to enter hotels by the back door. In Detroit a theater manager thought she looked too light and she was told to put on darker make-up. She remarked of a southern tour with Artie Shaw's band, "It got to the point where I hardly ever ate, slept, or went to the bathroom without having a major NAACP type production."

On one celebrated occasion white racism misfired and aided black pride. In 1939 black classical contralto Marian Anderson planned to give a concert at Constitution Hall on Easter Day. "A voice like yours," said conductor Arturo Toscanini to her, "comes but once in a century." Nevertheless, Marian Anderson encountered serious resistance. Her proposed auditorium was managed by the Daughters of the American Revolution (DAR). Journalist Mary Johnson, sensing a story, provoked the DAR president, Mrs. Henry M. Robert, Jr., into announcing that neither Marian Anderson nor any other black artist would ever be heard in Constitution Hall. Liberals were scandalized.

However, at the suggestion of Walter White, Harold Ickes gave permission to give the concert on the steps of the Lincoln Memorial, a far more prestigious and symbolic site. Eleanor Roosevelt resigned from the DAR and she and Ickes made sure that the front rows of the audience would comprise cabinet members, senators, congressmen, and Supreme Court justices. The widespread publicity ensured an audience of 75,000 who were engrossed by the contralto's power, range, and expression in a variety of songs from "America" to "Nobody Knows The Trouble I've Seen." Among the ensuing crush of people around Marian Anderson was a young black girl in her Easter best whose hands were already toughened by manual work. Walter White noticed her expression that seemed to say, "If Marian Anderson can do it, then I can, too."

Whereas the Great Depression and World War II inhibited certain cultural activities, they saw no lessening of black artistic achievement. The new poets included Melvin B. Tolson of Wiley College, who published a collection *Rendezvous with America* (1944), which included his most famous piece "Dark Symphony"; and Robert Hayden of the University of Michigan, whose first volume was *Heart-Shape in the Dust* (1940). Commentator Arna Bontemps produced *God Sends Sunday* (1931), and two historical novels, *Black Thunder* (1936) and *Drums at Dusk* (1939), before collaborating with Jack Conroy on *They Seek a City* (1945), an enthralling account of the urbanization of black Americans. George W. Lee described Memphis life in *Beale Street* (1934) and then brought out *River George* (1936), while Waters Turpin concentrated on the upper South of Maryland in *These Low Grounds*

(1937) and *O Canaan* (1939). Sculptor Augusta Savage was widely praised for her head of DuBois and her sculpture *Lift Every Voice and Sing,* exhibited at the New York World's Fair of 1939.

Chester Himes described racial tension and friction in a wartime industrial community, *If He Hollers, Let Him Go* (1945), which vividly evokes the confusions felt by blacks recently moved to industrial towns and their bitterness. In *Let Me Breathe Thunder* (1939) and *Blood on the Forge* William Attaway showed he could treat white as well as black characters and themes.

The most celebrated new talent of the second period was Richard Wright, who rapidly produced a collection of short stories, *Uncle Tom's Children* (1938), a folk history, *Twelve Million Black Voices* (1941), and his account of his Mississippi childhood, *Black Boy* (1945), as well as his most celebrated novel, *Native Son* (1940).

Native Son is about the social, psychological, and physical incarceration of the marginal man. Bigger Thomas, an unemployed black youth, is taken on as chauffeur by a supposedly liberal family, the Daltons, who are, in fact, the exploitive landlords of his slum home. He is compromised by their daughter, Mary, whose superficial gestures of friendship and equality confuse and terrify him so much that he smothers her by accident, and, frightened out of his wits, disposes of the body in a furnace. In the course of his getaway he brutally murders his black girlfriend, Bessie.

The story is told with a series of effective dramatic metaphors, beginning with the cornered rat Bigger kills in his home, continuing with Bigger's attempted escape across Chicago, where, like Eliza across the ice floes in *Uncle Tom's Cabin,* his very blackness is emphasised by the falling snow that renders the entire city a prison of whiteness, until it is Bigger himself who is trapped like a cornered rat. The language, images, and elaborate, surreal court scenes in which the political utterances of conservatives, liberals, and Communists are shown as stereotypes of sophistry—all are effectively treated to the literary equivalent of the dramatic and stark Soviet cinema posters of the period such as Grigory Rychkov's *The Tractor Drivers* (1939).

The genius of Wright's work is not only in the way he exposes the superficiality of white understanding but also, like William

Faulkner with the racially ambiguous Joe Christmas, how he makes articulate the hidden, confused emotions of his inarticulate hero by playing white rhetoric against black restraint and sullenness. The very title, *Native Son,* makes its own ironic comments, suggesting natives of Africa, children of the United States, who have an indigenous right to equal citizenship in the country of their ancestors and of their birth.

Black America on the Eve of World War II

In 1940 there were 12,866,000 black Americans, most of whom worked at unskilled and menial jobs with low pay. Only one in twenty black males worked in a white-collar profession (compared with one in three white males). Of every ten black women who worked, six worked as maids (compared with one in ten white women). Although twice as many blacks as whites worked on farms, a much smaller proportion farmed their own land.

Four times as many blacks as whites lived in houses with more than two people per room and only half as many blacks lived in houses with two rooms per person. The black mortality rate was almost twice that of whites. Thus in Washington, D.C., for example, the infant mortality rate among whites was 37 per 1,000 whereas for blacks it was 71 per 1,000. If they survived infancy, black citizens could expect to live, on average, twelve years less than whites. Of black citizens over twenty-five, one in ten had not completed a single year of school; only one in a hundred had graduated from college. Racism was still widespread and institutionalized. Thirty states proscribed marriage between blacks and whites. In the South not only did blacks have to use separate waiting rooms at bus and railroad stations, separate railroad cars, separate seating sections in movie theaters, separate churches and schools, separate restaurants and drinking fountains, but they also had to endure all manner of white refusals to allow them even a modicum of social respect. It was difficult, and most rare, for blacks to serve as police officers or become practicing lawyers. In the Deep South blacks were almost never employed as policemen. In 1940 the states of Mississippi, South Carolina, Louisiana, Georgia, and Alabama (states in which blacks made up over a third of the population) had not one black policeman between them. Nor did Arkansas and Virginia (where blacks accounted for a third of the population). There were only 4 black lawyers in Alabama, compared with 1,600 whites, and 6 in Mississippi, compared with 1,200 whites. Judges and court officials were invariably white. Blacks seldom served on juries. In consequence, blacks received odd, ill-balanced forms of justice. Thus courts tended to be lenient to blacks accused of committing crimes against other blacks but especially harsh to blacks accused of crimes against whites.

World War II and the Civil Rights Movement

World War II clarified attitudes toward race as government propaganda fashioned political ideology in an attempt to cover the contradictions of fighting a war against racism abroad while maintaining segregation at home. Thus the shortcomings of the American democratic system were tested to the limit. It was now all too easy for liberals and radicals alike to equate poll taxes and grandfather clauses, lynching, and the segregation of blacks in the United States with Hitler's persecution of Jews in the Third Reich. The *Crisis* published a photograph of a defense industry factory with a "whites only" notice outside and commented bitterly about aircraft made by whites, flown by whites, but paid for by blacks. "It sounds pretty foolish to be *against* park benches marked 'Jude' in Berlin, but to be *for* park benches marked 'Colored' in Tallahassee, Florida."

The New Deal and Roosevelt's foreign policy rhetoric had roused black expectations of change but left them unsatisfied. With consummate, newfound political skills, black leaders were quick to exploit the situation. In January 1941, at a meeting that included Walter White, Mary McLeod Bethune, and Lester Grange (of the Urban League), A. Philip Randolph announced plans for a mass march on Washington to protest against discrimination in defense industries. Some commentators were skeptical of success. The Chicago *Defender* commented on February 8, 1941, "To get 10,000 Negroes assembled in one spot, under one banner, with justice, democracy, and work as their slogan would be the miracle of the century." However, Randolph was firmly convinced of black solidarity and believed he knew how to channel black indignation into constructive political action while preventing the Communists from exploiting the occasion. Indeed, Randolph's appeal transcended his immediate aims and touched a sensitive nerve in the black community at large. Across the country blacks formed committees to coordinate support and began organizing transportation to Washington. Thus encouraged, Randolph chose July 1 for the event.

Randolph's command and activities produced feelings of consternation bordering upon panic in Roosevelt's administration. It sought national unity and FDR did not want his plans for the war to be jeopardized by ethnic divisions at home. On June 18, 1941, Roosevelt met with Randolph and White and tried to separate bluff and realism in their tactics. "Walter, how many people will really march?" "No less than 100,000," replied White. Thus cornered, on June 25 Roosevelt issued Executive Order 8802, requiring that all employees, unions, and government agencies "concerned with vocational and training programs" must "provide for the full and equitable participation of all workers in defense industries without discrimination because of race, creed, color, or national origin." The march was called off. To enforce the order, FDR created a Fair Employment Practices Committee (FEPC).

The FEPC had no punitive powers and was even loath to penalize white violators. However, because it held hearings in public, many employers preferred to change their policies rather than risk unfavorable publicity. Nevertheless, the black press was jubilant and greeted Executive Order 8802 as a second emancipation proclamation. Unfortunately, the FEPC was scuttled by racists at the end of the war.

9

SOUNDS IMPOSSIBLE
The Golden Age of Radio

Radio in the 1920s

AFTER THE years of experiment and innovation in 1900–1920, radio broadcasting for the general public was born in the early 1920s and almost immediately expanded, first as a novelty, and then as a major recreation of the decade. The radio boom that started in 1921 should not be seen as an inevitable part of a cultural and technological tide. Indeed, it is often more significant how such tides have failed to roll on schedule. Despite the flood, the emergence of public broadcasting was not entirely relentless. The critical steps toward the birth of American broadcasting were taken between 1918 and 1922. Despite some calls in Congress for governmental control of radio, all private communication stations were returned to their original owners on March 1, 1920, while amateur enthusiasts had been allowed back on the air in the fall of 1919. The elite of radio's major interests believed radio would be used primarily for transoceanic and marine communiction and secondarily for long-distance telephone communications. Some wanted to mold the situation by an informal association between manufacturers and the federal government. Nevertheless, companies manufacturing radio parts believed that they must find a new market for their postwar surpluses. Almost immediately, the existing state of affairs in radio was challenged.

In March 1919, when Guglielmo Marconi was negotiating to buy the rights to the Alexanderson alternator from General Electric, the Marconi Company seemed to be the only possible customer and only possible winner of exclusive rights to this new, most powerful transmitter. However, such a monopoly control over American communication was deplored by the federal government, and particularly by the navy. Under Secretary of the Navy Franklin D. Roosevelt and other members of government gave encouragement to the General Electric representative, Owen D. Young, and the company's directors to revise the deal. General Electric would buy a controlling interest in American Marconi, anticipating and quieting any congressional objections about British Marconi having too great an influence. British Marconi agreed. As a manufacturer, General Electric was loath to run the American Marconi stations and, therefore, created the Radio Corporation of America (RCA). Eighty percent of its stock had to be American, with a government representative on the board of directors. The formation of RCA assured the United States of a new powerful position in world communication and satisfied the determination of Woodrow Wilson's administration to challenge and supersede Britain in this new field.

On July 1, 1920, General Electric, RCA, and AT & T ended a bitter dispute over patent rights by signing a broad patent pooling agreement. AT & T had purchased most of the rights to use the central device of the crystal radio set before the war. The deal with British Marconi meant that General Electric and RCA possessed the old American Marconi rights to the other two crucial parts of radio, the Alexanderson alternator and the vacuum tube. (The early history of radio discoveries and inventions was told in *America in the Age of the Titans,* chapter eight.) Consequently, production and use of the vacuum tube could begin in earnest. The patents pool was completed when the electrical manufacturer, Westinghouse, decided to join the other companies. So, by 1921, around 2,000 patents had been pooled. From the point of view of the giants, the infant radio industry was being nicely divided up. RCA would sell radio receivers that had been produced by General Electric and incorporated the latest in radio technology, the Armstrong patent for a supersensitive receiver, possessed by Westinghouse. AT & T could use radio telephone equipment for its business and produce transmitters. Thus in 1920 no one expected that the prime use of radio would be public broadcasting. When this was what happened, it soon shattered the comfort of the radio oligarchy.

On November 2, 1920, what would become the oldest and longest running station, KDKA, began broadcasting from Pittsburgh, announcing the Harding–Cox presidential election returns. As would be the case with the other pioneer stations, KDKA had begun as a successful amateur operation, 8XK, run by Dr. Frank Conrad, a Westinghouse engineer. It was when a Pittsburgh department store advertised radio sets to listen to 8XK that H. P. Davies, vice president of Westinghouse, decided to set up a radio station to promote sales of the company's receivers. Notably, this was before Westinghouse joined the patent pool and, so, was inclined to consider such an independent, innovatory tactic within its strategy. The first transmissions came, initially, from a rough shack and, then, a tent on top of a Westinghouse factory.

After KDKA came on the air, radio broadcasting seemed to grow but slowly in its first years. By January 1922 only thirty broadcasting stations had been licensed and by the end of the year only 100,000 radio sets had been purchased. In actual fact, there was a great deal of activity. Most radio sets were homemade and amateur licensed stations broadcast concerts, weather reports, lectures, and recorded music. By May 1922 the Board of Navigation in the Department of Commerce listed 218 such stations. The following spring, there were 556.

The breakthrough year for radio was 1922. Public interest across the world spurred inventors, engineers, and executives to create nationwide services. France began regular broadcasts from the Eiffel Tower, Paris; the first Soviet station began broadcasts from Moscow; Nederlandsche Radio Industrie began operations in Holland; and in England the BBC began life as the British Broadcasting Company. International agreement on copyright, wavelengths, and program exchanges were decided at a series of international conferences, beginning in Washington in 1927.

In the United States, even though amateurs seemed to lead the field in initiating public broadcasting, the full emergence of broadcasting was not a matter of independent, individual enterprise. The creation of KDKA showed the critical importance of corporate involvement. From September 1921, Westinghouse opened up a succession of stations. The other major companies were slow to enter broadcasting, mainly because they still thought the mainstay of their business lay in international communications. It was not until December 1922 that RCA created WDY in Roselle Park, New Jersey. General Electric had opened WGY in Schenectady (New York), KOA in Denver (Colorado), and KGO in Oakland (California). The domination of the patent pool members in broadcasting was evident when, in February 1923, of the 376 stations that the U.S. Department of Commerce listed, 222 were owned by General Electric, RCA, Westinghouse, or AT & T. Newspapers like the *Detroit News* (station WWJ) owned 69; educational institutions, 72 and department stores, 29. These early stations were largely publicity ventures, although churches and universities did use their stations for preaching, extension courses, and study programs. Broadcasters divided themselves into three groups—those selling radio sets, those seeking goodwill, and those seeking free advertising.

Since they were sidelines to other enterprises, the first radio stations were primitive and run on shoestring budgets. Many broadcasts were transmitted from hotel rooms because the main hotel was the tallest building in most cities. A studio simply consisted of a piano and a microphone or two. There was no volume control and mixing so that a broadcast of lusty opera singers with powerful voices large enough to fill a giant theater, could jeopardize the future of a station by blowing out expensive vacuum tubes. The early transmitters were often handmade and low-powered. A typical transmitter could take 100 watts. The mortality rate of pioneering stations was high. In 1922, 94 stations closed down while, over the spring and early summer months of 1923, another 150 stations folded.

Although many stations did cease broadcasting once some public interest in their novelty value faded, on the whole people were becoming addicted to radio. Ever more people exchanged their homemade crystal sets for readymade receivers. In 1923 between $30 and $45 million worth of radio sets were sold. In 1924 sales climbed to $100 million. Between 1922 and 1925 the industry produced and sold 4.1 million sets.

The success of broadcasting caused tension within the patent pool. AT & T challenged the casual way that early stations were subsidized by the companies. After setting up its own station, WEAF, in New York in the summer of 1922, AT & T declared that the pooling agreement had been contravened for it alone had the right to manufacture and sell transmitters for broadcasting. Moreover, AT & T held that it possessed exclusive right to sell time for advertising and to interconnect stations by telephone wire for network broadcasting. Thus the Telephone Groups of AT & T and Western Electric were ranged against the Radio Groups of RCA, General Electric, and Westinghouse. Most stations capitulated. Radio Group stations tried to create networks along the inferior telegraph wires of Western Union. The Radio Group fought back, successfully demanding that all manufacturers of radio sets had to acquire licenses from RCA in order to make any receiver part. Consequently, the bubble burst for the 748 radio manufacturers who had appeared between 1923 and 1926. In 1927 only 72 remained. In 1925 AT & T threatened to break the vital patents' pool. This tactic of confrontation led to a settlement of the dispute in 1926. AT & T received a monopoly of wire interconnections between stations while selling off WEAF to RCA and agreeing not to reenter broadcasting for eight years.

However, the attention of radio listeners was on the content of programs rather than the organization of radio broadcasting. The programming of early radio involved much experimentation but tended toward the broadcasting of variety shows consisting of music and comedy acts. A brief and distinct feature of early American radio was the extremely formal style of presentation of the various programs. Presenters were known only by their initials. Although they could not be seen by the public, they wore tuxedos and spoke from studios decorated like hotel dance floors with potted palm trees.

The airwaves of early radio were mainly given over to music. In the 1925 schedules of the major stations in New York, Kansas City, and Chicago, over 70 percent of airtime was devoted to performed music, of which 25 percent was dance music. Music was performed live. In 1922, Secretary of Commerce Herbert Hoover prohibited the broadcasting of phonograph records. He thought that, by broadcasting music from disks, stations would be cheating the public by giving them nothing more than they could enjoy without radio. Early wireless dance bands, many of which played live from hotal ballrooms, included the Vincent Copes Group and Coon Sanders Nighthawks. Many early radio stars were plucked out of the dying vaudeville theater circuit. Ukulele player and singer Wendell Woods Haze rose to become the first major radio personality and his marriage was even broadcast over the air in 1924. Such individual stars competed with the song and patter teams like the Happiness Boys and Tastee Loafers with whom stations filled their variety spots. By the late 1920s Broadway stars like Al Jolson and Eddie Cantor were making radio broadcasts. The staple diet of vaudeville songs was varied by stations like WLS of Chicago that broadcast country and western music. The highbrow audience was catered for by classical music played by symphony orchestras, thereby cultivating the respectable image of many stations.

Although early radio programming consisted mainly of light entertainment, stations produced programs featuring talks, discussions, and providing information. Following the precedent of KDKA, radio stations devoted themselves to large-scale election coverage, beginning with the 1924 election. The notorious Democratic National Convention in New York with all its unbridled chaos and apparently endless votes was widely heard and this partly accounted for the Democrats' temporary eclipse. Yet regular news bulletins were rare in the 1920s. Sometimes news items were used as fillers while stations owned by newspapers would mention a story only briefly in order to rouse interest and stimulate newspaper sales. Early stations specialized in covering sudden news events, for which radio was ideally suited, and caught the immediacy of the event. Since stations were also used to to monitor the maritime distress channel, shipwrecks provided special news items. Midwestern, landlocked stations provided weather reports for farmers and carried early storm warnings, though the Chicago station, WGN, distinguished itself with the $1,000 per day coverage of the Scopes trial in Dayton, Tennessee, somewhat in the manner of its election coverage. Although telephone and radio brought people more closely together, they also made separation more palatable through the aural illusion of intimacy. In radio alone audience participation was more possible then, for example, for an audience at a vaudeville theater. Interest was expressed in choice, firstly between turning on or off, later by selecting one program rather than another.

Many of the familiar types of programs were initiated in the first years. The U.S. Army began religious programs when it broadcast a church service in Washington, D.C., in August 1919. However, it was KDKA that made church services a regular feature in its schedule in 1921. In its broadcasts, radio technicians at the service were disguised, rather implausibly, as choirboys. Surprisingly, radio stations rarely broadcast sports programs. Boxing was among the first sports to be covered, with ringside reports from KDKA in 1921. The Dempsey-Tunney fights were especially successful as commercial ventures heard by 50 million listeners and causing mass hysteria. The World Series of baseball games was broadcast from 1923. There was little drama on the radio in the 1920s, although there were some experiments with the radio adaptation of successful Broadway shows.

The diversity of early radio programming lay in what might now seem unusual, the broadcasting of lectures on the widest possible variety of subjects. It is interesting that those stations owned by radio manufacturers broadcast lectures on the technical aspects of the new medium, lectures primarily aimed at radio enthusiasts whom such stations considered the nucelus of the new audience. Despite its popularity, listening to the radio was not yet an entirely passive affair because home audiences always required someone with technical expertise to adjust the various crystals, batteries, and tubes in the receivers. Radio hams vied with one another as to who could get the clearest reception and who could reach the most distant station, this was known as " 'DX'ing."

Starlet Clara Horton listens to a Hollywood concert on a radio set decorated with photos of stars Colleen Moore and Corinne Griffith. A publicity photograph of June 1, 1925, by Underwood and Underwood. (Library of Congress).

Local stations encouraged hams to indulge in this and helped by closing down at night.

The preeminence of the radio specialist came to an end with the refinement of the radio receiver. In the autumn of 1920 factory-made crystal radio sets like the Westinghouse "Aeriola Jr." became available. For a brief time there was a proliferation of small firms making their own sets or assembling those of Westinghouse and General Electric. By 1923 advertising in radio, as elsewhere, following the visible hand of marketing, was stressing brand name reliability, an indication of how much the public now realized that expensive radio sets were far preferable to cheap sets that gave very inferior reception. The competition for customers was beginning to decimate the numbers of small manufacturers, even though sales had risen from about 500,000 sets in 1923 to 2 million in 1925 and prices had doubled from the earlier average of $50.

Radio sets were intended to be simple to use and more attractive to look at, and to form the centerpiece of a family living room. By 1926 families could dispense with their numerous, heavy, and ugly batteries and plug their new sets directly into the mains. Volume, tuning, and the on-off switch were all controled from one knob. The early sets had used a bread board as a base for the mechanism, but in 1926 sets tended to be fitted inside mahogany cases. One result of the continuing national craze for radio was that by 1926 1 radio set had been sold for every 6 households. (In 1921 this ratio had stood at 1 in every 500.)

Ironically, as audiences grew, radio broadcasting in America was heading for a crisis. There were too many stations saturating the airwaves, and, consequently, reception was deteriorating. Given the very slender band allocated for broadcasting, a large city could only possess around 7 stations but there were, for example, as many as 20 in Los Angeles and 40 in Chicago. Some cities attempted a fair division of wavelengths and sharing of broadcasting time. The answer of those stations owned by major companies was to increase their power, thus fortifying their signal against interference. In 1924, David Sarnoff of RCA revealed plans for a number of superpower 50,000 watt stations. This solution brought only temporary respite for the other stations soon increased their wattage and the interference began again. As Edwin E. Slosson remarked in his article, "Voices in the Air," for the *New York Independent* of April 1922, "Broadcasting has turned the nation into a town meeting. But there is no chairman and no parliamentary law. This will bring about anarchy in the ether."

Radio seemed to be jeopardizing its recent successes. The situation begged for strict federal regulation. Yet, to a certain extent, the application of what little regulation existed had aggravated the problem. The Radio Act of 1912 was inadequte, having been ratified before broadcasting was even seriously contemplated. The act simply empowered the secretary of commerce to pass all applications for station licenses, regardless of available frequencies. The only criteria for ownership was American citizenship. Moreover, government officials repeatedly failed to foresee the overloading of the airwaves and, consequently, failed to execute forceful, realistic measures. Prior to the boom, one wavelength of 360 metres was allocated for broadcasting experiments. In December 1921 another wavelength of 485 metres was added. By the spring of 1922, the growing number of stations necessitated another wavelength, 400 metres. The outcome was the cramming of stations in each of the three wavelengths.

The mounting number of complaints about interference spurred on Secretary of Commerce Herbert Hoover to convene a conference on the subject of regulatory radio legislation. In February 1922 the conference recommended that government should allocate specific frequencies and other terms by which stations should operate. However, there was still no legislation by March 1923 and the interference had grown. A second conference made all the same recommendations as the first and further proposed a creation of three classes of stations—those requiring high power, medium power, or low power—and a five way regional division of radio. Herbert Hoover then introduced a new system of frequency assignments. Stations were alloted a specific wavelength within either an A or B band. Even so, there was still no legislation to supersede the 1912 Radio Act and Hoover had to call two more conferences in October 1924 and November 1925. Congress proved to be indifferent to the immediate need for legislation and passage of radio bills was slow.

Yet, after four years of discussion, the problem of interference remained unchanged. One senior government official involved with radio recalled the chaotic state of radio in 1925 as "interference between broadcasters on the same wave length became so bad at many points on the dial that the listener might suppose (how), instead of a receiving set, he had a peanut roaster with assorted whistles." Nevertheless, an Illinois Federal District Court, supported by the opinion of the attorney general, decided that the secretary of commerce possessed no legal powers to prevent the Zenith and other radio stations from jumping from their alloted wavelengths. This was a nonsense causing endless confusion, and the resulting uproar finally brought about legislation. The Radio Act of 1927 established the Federal Radio Commission to oversee the entire business of radio. As we shall observe, such regulation proved effective in the New Deal administration of President Franklin D. Roosevelt.

Advertising and the Networks—NBC and CBS

As radio stations became more than simply sideline operations, broadcasters became increasingly concerned about how to fund their programs. Among the stations this crucial issue competed with the concern for excessive interference and was discussed at the four inconclusive radio conferences. Radio executives did not immediately consider selling time for advertising to pay for programs. David Sarnoff, commercial manager of RCA, suggested a 2 percent tax on receiver sales. This was tried out only locally. One New York station envisaged an "invisible theater of the air" from which it tried to collect $20,000 in box office receipts. The plan failed. The AT & T station, WEAF, was the first to broadcast advertisements when a salesman extolled the virtues of living in Jackson Heights, in one of New York's earliest condominiums, for fifteen minutes on August 28, 1922. Tidewater Oil and American Express were among the first clients. The adoption of radio advertising did not become widespread immediately. Many stations were initially cautious about the concept, not least because of AT & T's policy of demanding royalties for the use of radio telephony for wire.

AT & T played a large role in initiating the modernization of American broadcasting when, in January 1923, the company inaugurated network broadcasting, connecting WNAC of Boston with WEAF of New York for the transmission of a saxophone solo. In March 1925 the inauguration ceremony of President Calvin Coolidge was relayed to twenty-four stations of which twenty were centered on WEAF.

Therefore, prior to 1926 the two prime characteristics of American broadcasting, toll advertising and network affiliation, had appeared. The settlement of the dispute between the Radio and Telephone Groups in 1926 rationalized radio and, subsequently, the widespread adoption of advertising and development of national radio networks began in earnest. Over the next seven years, radio broadcasting became a sophisticated industry, resembling the later arrangement of American broadcasting and finally shedding its amateur, experimental roots.

American radio would thus follow a very different path from radio in Britain, where the BBC followed the strict precepts about content, hours, sponsorship (by prepaid public license fees), and autocratic management laid down by the architect of British broadcasting, John Reith. So, the essential commercial nature of American broadcasting was formed and imposed within a decade. Moreover, it soon turned the listener into a consumer of radio rather than a customer.

As part of the 1926 settlement, RCA purchased the AT & T station, WEAF, that now became the nucleus of its new corporation, the National Broadcasting Company (NBC). On November 18, 1926, NBC began its network programming with a variety extravaganza transmitted from New York, Chicago, and Kansas City. Subsequently, NBC took over the RCA station, WJZ of New York, as the basis for a second network. The WEAF and WJZ networks became known as, respectively the Red and Blue networks. By 1928 NBC began regular coast-to-coast network programs and in 1933 was at the peak of its power. The company owned ten stations outright while another twenty-eight were affiliated to its Red network and another twenty-four to the Blue. A further thirty-six stations were nominally part of the NBC networks, having arranged to take network programming occasionally. These stations constituted fifteen percent of all stations in America. The domination of NBC was especially evident in those major cities where there were two NBC affiliates. The high status of NBC was made clear when, toward the end of 1933, it moved out of its Fifth Avenue offices and studios and into its new headquarters in the Rockefeller Center, deliberately entitled Radio City.

In 1927 the business manager of the Philadelphia Orchestra, Arthur Johnson, attempted to challenge the newly formed company, NBC, by setting up a rival network, United Independent Broadcasting, Inc. However, this venture seemed to offer only a paper threat to NBC, for AT & T refused to provide the new network with the vital telephone connections between stations because UIB lacked the necessary liquid capital. Yet, this "paper network" was the origin of the Columbia Broadcasting System (CBS), the future rival of NBC. Immediate financial disaster was averted when a merger was arranged with the ailing Victor Talking Machine Company. From their pooled resources, the network found enough cash to commence operations. The newly named Columbia Phonograph Broadcasting System went on the air in September 1927. The beginnings of CBS were marred by mishaps. The first night broadcast from the Metropolitan Opera, New York, was ruined by static electricity from an electric storm. In the first month, the network lost over $100,000, enough for the phonograph company to pull out of the merger. Thereafter, the survival of the infant network depended upon winning the support of several wealthy individuals. The owner of an affiliate station, Dr. Lear Levy, arranged for a millionaire sportsman, Jerome H. Louchheim, to buy control of UIB and provide it with enough money to keep the network running. However, at this time CBS was losing out to NBC in selling advertising time. Louchheim decided to drop what appeared to be an irreversibly bad investment.

In September 1928 the new owner of the network proved to be the savior of the company. UIB-CBS had run a successful series of advertisements for the Congress Cigar Company whose vice-president, William S. Paley, was so impressed that he and his family's firm bought a controlling interest in the network. Paley refashioned the company, consolidating the twin separate networks into one, buying a new flagship station, WABC of New York, and renegotiating the contract with the affiliates so that the company would pay a station $50 per hour, rather than a weekly $500 for ten hours, regardless of the actual time used. The company was rapidly revived so that, in 1933, the network encompassed ninety-one stations. Paley had first envisaged a career of selling cigars, but he remained chief executive of CBS until late 1977 and, so, a consistently influential figure in American broadcasting.

The development of the two national networks was a major

factor in the growth of advertising on radio. At last advertisers were impressed by how coast-to-coast coverage radio could penetrate nearly 70 percent of American homes. Radio advertisements allowed the sponsors to thrust themselves into people's homes directly. Harry P. Davis of Westinghouse declared that "broadcast advertising is modernity's medium of business expression. It made industry articulate. American businessmen, because of radio, are provided with a latch key to nearly every home in the United States."

Moreover, certain radio art forms were conceived and broadcast at this time, thereby establishing prototypes for situation comedies, dramas, and documentaries. The situation comedy, or sitcom, was one in which standard characters got themselves both into and out of several humorous situations in each episode. The first and most famous of these radio comedy dramas evolved from the minstrel double act of Freeman F. Gosden and Charles J. Correll, performed in blackface. Gosden and Correll were vaudevillians, who had performed their act at a local radio station in exchange for free meals from the hotel owner of the station, and were eventually hired by the *Chicago Tribune* station, WGN (World's Greatest Newspaper), to do over 600 performances of their *Sam 'n' Henry* act. The show was so successful that the pair were bought up by WGN's rival, WMAQ. Since WGN refused to allow the use of the original name the act was renamed *Amos 'n' Andy* and their adventures revolved around the Freshair Taxicab Company and the fraternal lodge of the Mystic Knights of the Sea. It was not until after the whole show was sold to the NBC-Blue network in the summer of 1929 that *Amos 'n' Andy* became a national phenomenon. It has been said that everybody listened to the evening shows and that cinema managers would delay the screening of films so that audiences could listen to *Amos 'n' Andy*.

The immense popularity of *Amos 'n' Andy* and other programs must have acted as a catalyst in convincing advertisers of the viability of radio advertising. Between 1928 and 1932 radio advertising rose from 2 percent of all expenditure on advertising to 11 percent, representing a growth from $20 million to $75 million. Originally, radio advertisements had been run during the day but by 1932 were broadcast throughout the day, particularly in the newly identified evening prime time. As a further indicator of its growth, radio advertising became a business in itself, supporting a range of managerial and publicity staff working for sponsors and networks. Local stations employed representatives to sell their time in major cities and thereby developed the national and regional business of quite small stations. For their part, large advertising agencies developed very close relationships with the major networks. At first, the agencies merely purchased time for their clients, but soon they began to create an attractive package of advertisements and programs. The networks welcomed this development because the production of national programs was proving to be expensive and complicated. So in 1931 and 1932 agencies controlled program selection and production. Moreover, advertising became more technically proficient and sophisticated, so that in the early 1930s advertisements no longer needed to be performed live but were prerecorded and mailed to many stations, allowing simultaneous nationwide sales campaigns.

At the Department of Commerce Herbert Hoover breathed a sigh of relief. He was sensitive to the controversies about audience changes and the clutter of radio advertising and pleased that the large companies upon whom he relied heavily for advice were taking the initiative and finding a solution. He also allowed the indiscriminate sale of wavelengths. As a result, radio became increasingly a matter of private property and the original concept of temporary licenses was abandoned. The outcome clearly belied Hoover's early statement that he would "establish public right over the ether roads." Thus some critics see the government selling out radio to private interests while concealing the truth about private ownership.

In 1931 36 percent of airtime was commercially sponsored. Paradoxically, the depression pushed networks and stations alike into devoting more airtime to advertising and made them increasingly dependent on its revenues. There was a period of considerable investment in expensive equipment to improve stations between 1927 and 1930. To make their signals clear and strong, the average wattage of stations was increasing so that, while in 1927 28 percent of stations managed to operate on 100 watts, only

3 percent did so in 1933. Moreover, the newly formed Federal Radio Commission demanded and successfully enforced higher standards of transmission, further increasing the expenditures of broadcasters. Understandably, then, broadcasters sought advertising revenue. The coincidence of the economic crisis and a need to fund such technical improvements and support ever more hours of programs meant that it became imperative to sell even more airtime for advertising. The central importance of advertising was apparent when networks and sponsors became interested in audience research, recognizing its value in organizing advertising. In 1929, Archibald M. Crossley formed the Cooperative Analysis of Broadcasting that served both networks.

Radio in the 1930s

During the depression the position of the two major networks was consolidated while many individual and small stations suffered or closed down. The income of the networks rose in the first years of the depression. The income of NBC climbed from $798,200 in 1929 to $2.16 million in 1930 and, then, to $2.66 million in 1931. In that year the income of CBS surpassed that of NBC, standing at $2.67 million, whereas, the previous year, the network had made only $985,400. However, income dramatically declined in the next year when the Great Depression deepened and businesses cut back their advertising budgets.

Small, local stations suffered more than the great networks. As local economies retrenched, interest in the new advertising medium was cut short. Yet, it should be emphasized that the majority of bankrupt stations had closed before the depression. The reorganization of the airwaves by the Federal Radio Commission and the trend toward more power and better equipment forced the small, often amateur, stations off the air. However, in general, radio survived and almost flourished during the first years of the depression. After their initial purchase of a radio set, people regarded listening to the wireless as free entertainment. At this time, the broadcasting industry met with a varied mix of success and failure rather than outright disaster or triumph. In 1931 333 stations reported profits while 180 were in deficit. In the early

1930s listening to the radio ceased to be a novelty or complex hobby and became an everyday, common habit. The audience was still growing, with half of urban families owning receivers and a growing number of rural listeners, for whom radio was the first affordable and available direct communication. The depression made the retailing of radio sets more of a buyer's market, with companies steadily lowering their prices so as to sell off their large stocks of unsold receivers. The average price of a radio set fell from $90 in 1930 to $47 in 1932.

This growing audience for radio enjoyed a developing range of programming, either paid for by business sponsors or wholly sustained by the stations or networks. At first, network programming was minimal, counting for only about three and a half hours of broadcasting every day in 1927. As advertising revenues increased and affiliate stations demanded ever more shows, network programs increased in number and spread from the original evening hours to fill up the daytime slots by 1933. This rush of programming proved a curtain raiser for the golden age of radio later in the decade. Many of the famous shows and many of the famous careers in broadcasting began during this period.

Music and variety remained the core of radio programming. The typical music program was of an orchestra or professional singer playing popular or light classical music. Such shows were usually sponsored, for example, by companies such as Michelin. Singers who became radio stars included Joseph M. White who performed as the "Silver Masked Tenor" and always wore his mask when he sang. Vocalist Bing Crosby began crooning on radio in 1931. More major firms preferred to sponsor and be associated with prestigious classical orchestras. Large variety shows were a staple of network programming that became noted for its more lavish production values. The first of these, the Fleischmann Yeast program, starring the singer Rudy Vallee, started in October 1929. Ed Sullivan, whose later television show would be particularly famous and successful, began hosting a variety show with more conversation than usual in 1931. As the depression devastated Broadway and many theaters closed, many stage stars and certainly many vaudeville players came into the new field of radio. Comedians George Burns and Gracie Allen formed a popular husband and wife comedy act in 1932. That same year, blackface singer Al Jolson, wit Jack Benny, and anarchic comedians the Marx Brothers made network shows. Even more than the networks, local stations found they could choose from a large pool of unemployed theatrical talent and offer payment of little more than food and shelter.

Radio drama began to grow into distinct and familiar forms. In 1929 the success of the serial, *The Rise of the Goldbergs,* a drama about the everyday life of a Jewish-American family, established the idea of a continuing cast in a different situation each week. Along with *Vic and Sadie* and *One Man's Family,* such serials aimed at women at home were the first soap operas, so-called because various soap powder companies sponsored them. Among the most popular and longest running were *Helen Trent* and *Ma Perkins.* Soap operas quickly developed a special formula for captivating and retaining a special consumer audience. In contrast with movies that were primarily concentrated on the male audience, radio soaps concentrated on women of all ages and, indeed, on people of both sexes who might feel themselves marooned in a home and required surrogate fictional families to engage their inner fantasies. The dominant character in a soap was usually a mother who had to help her family and friends resolve their problems and, indeed, the whole thrust of soaps remained matrifocal in the golden age of radio and the television era that followed. Later, soap operas devoted their story lines to the sexual needs of their heroines, while television situation comedies parodied this genre by ridiculing the periodic attempts of housewives Lucille Ball and Joan Davis to enter the professional worlds.

Radio of the 1930s began to thrill the listener and create more truly radio drama when *The Shadow* was first broadcast. Imaginative use of sound gave the show its eerie quality. The Shadow, a crimefighter called Lamont Cranston, was supposed to be able to "cloud men's minds" so that they could not see him and this effect was created by having Cranston speaking through a filter that made his voice sound distant and distorted. The program was also notable because Cranston was played for a time by Orson Welles, one of the supreme innovators of wireless. In *March of Time,* first broadcast in 1931, radio was used to disguise the fact that the reports of current events were, in fact, dramatized with actors who were excellent mimics. The White House complained so strongly about the verisimilitude of the soundalike for FDR that he was dropped. It is interesting to note that radio programs were beginning to use specific catchphrases. The Shadow would give a chilling laugh and say, "Crime does not pay . . . the Shadow knows!" Westbrook Van Voorhis of the *March of Time* would declare, "Time . . . marches on."

In the fall of 1930, the NBC-Blue network began to broadcast a fifteen-minute news program five times a week. Prior to this, news programs had been weekly, but this development at NBC-Blue started a trend toward regular news bulletins of hard journalism. The major radio news story of the late 1920s had been the solo transatlantic flight of Charles A. Lindbergh, Jr. In the early 1930s the prime news story was of the Lindbergh baby kidnapping in 1932. The success of the news bulletins about the case, which the networks and stations inserted into their evening schedule, and the huge interest in any coverage of the presidential election campaign suggested to many broadcasters that news could win large audiences. Yet the initial development of radio news immediately brought radio broadcasting into conflict with the newspapers. With radio cutting into their advertising revenue, newspapers became hostile toward radio, firstly, preventing the wire services, Associated Press, United Press, and International News Service, from supplying the fledgling newscasts and, secondly, beginning late in 1933, by ending all free listings of programs and demanding payment. Radio gave way to this pressure. For its news imformation, it was totally dependent on the wire services and the networks had to sign the Biltmore agreement (named after the New York hotel where it was drafted) which restricted radio to only two five-minute news broadcasts every day at 9:30 A.M. and 9 P.M. that could comment on, and interpret, only the news provided by a special news service, the Press–Radio Bureau. However, within a year, because so few stations subscribed to the Press–Radio Bureau and two of the wire services resumed their supply to radio, the agreement was abandoned. This paved the way for the fuller development of radio journalism later in the decade.

Radio news was overshadowed by renewed and expanded coverage of current affairs and shows outside conventional light entertainment, such as talk shows. The networks filled their daytime schedules with such programs. Walter Winchell hosted a popular gossip show on NBC-Blue in 1932. The U.S. Department of Agriculture cooperated in the running of *National Farm and Home Hour*. The most distinctive shows were the religious talk and comment programs, for example the Protestant *National Vespers* and *The Catholic Hour*. The broadcasts of Father Coughlin from the Shrine of the Little Flower in Royal Oak near Detroit for CBS were most controversial. Coughlin indulged in demagoguery on political and economic issues. He was one of the first and most effective radio speakers, with a magnificent sonorous voice, like a vessel that could be drained or changed at will with such varied and potent emotions as tenderness, anger, and pride.

In the late 1920s and early 1930s radio broadcasting entered a period of decisive development and consolidation thanks to greater organization throughout the industry. Alongside the influence of the networks, broadcasting was being influenced by more effective government regulation. The Federal Radio Commission started operating in March 1927. It had control over all interstate and foreign radio communications that came from the United States. Although prohibited from censoring broadcasts, the FRC could dictate the general operation of radio stations, their frequencies, power, and equipment. The FRC was given the necessary licensing powers to eradicate interference, but, at first, for only a year. Indeed, the FRC was really considered by Herbert Hoover and other officials as a part-time organization mainly to augment self-regulatory practices of the industry and adjudicate in disputes. So little consideration had been given to its everyday finances that the new agency had to beg office space for its meager staff from the Departments of Commerce and the Navy. On the other hand, the FRC was being put on probation. Congress was loath to give any new federal authority carte blanche freedom. Throughout its six-year history, the FRC depended upon Congress to renew its powers for yet another year.

In its first year the FRC began to tackle the congestion of the airwaves by widening the broadcasting band to between 550 kHz and 1500 kHz. After questioning stations about their operations, the FRC granted new, temporary licenses, specifying power, time limits, and frequencies. Some stations were closed down. Following renewal of its licensing authority in March 1928, the FRC found that Congress had complicated its task. The 1927 Radio Act had suggested that the FRC should keep radio coverage of the nation relatively equal between regions, but the new Davis amendment required the FRC to achieve such equality. This would mean challenging the obvious concentration of stations in the area of greatest population, the East Coast. Later that summer, the FRC closed down 109 stations that had caused serious disruption. Portable stations that functioned by moving around to find the best conditions for transmission were banned.

Subsequently, the FRC devised a new classification scheme whereby there would be eight "cleared" stations in each of the five regional zones that could transmit at the high power of 25,000 and, later, 50,000 watts so as to give the best reception for distant rural areas. Moreover, only one of these stations could be allowed to transmit at a time during the night, ensuring even better, long-distance reception. The other two classes were for thirty-five stations of no more than 1,000 watts and twenty-one low-power local stations in each zone. Finally, in 1929, the FRC was given licensing authority for an unspecified time. By 1930, interference was dramatically reduced. Thus, in the early 1930s, the FRC spent more time tackling the equalization issue, setting up a system of quotas. However, the imbalance of station numbers remained irreversible.

More significantly, the FRC became increasingly involved in legal and programming issues. In a number of legal cases that were concerned with broadcasting and heard in the federal courts, the FRC had its right to regulate, refuse to grant licenses, prevent transfer to station ownership, and act with discretionary powers, upheld. A good example of one of these precedent-setting cases would be the first, concerning a medical advice show on a Kansas station. In a popular "medicine question box" program, the station owner, Dr. John R. Brinkley, had peddled a quack remedy for sexual rejuvenation that consisted of goat glands. Brinkley's

During the 1920s radio served to extend people's horizons, sharpen their perceptions, and, like the automobile, carry the values of urban civilization to rural America. At first the machines had awkward ear pieces for each listener and many tangling wires. Here John Joseph Pershing and a group listen to a set. (Library of Congress).

license was not reissued and this decision was supported by a court in 1931.

In 1934 the FRC was replaced by the Federal Communications Commission. One of Roosevelt's first decisions in 1933 had been to appoint a committee to examine the role of government in regulating radio. This concluded that the FRC should become a permanent agency, concerned with the private, public, and governmental use of radio and of interstate telephone and telegraph communications. The Communications Act of 1934 created this agency. The establishment of the FCC represented the fruition of the FRC's aims. It also suggested future greater tension between the government and the broadcasting industry because, in the congressional hearings, the National Association of Broadcasters was extremely hostile to the idea of effective federal regulation.

The latter years of the 1930s represented a golden age for radio. Radio became increasingly accepted as an essential part of American life and, before competition from television materialized, it was the supreme form of home entertainment, offering a wide range of programs. Indeed, the success of radio struck severe blows at the record industry and even shook the dominance of the film industry. Those who had invested in radio in the 1920s now found their decision repaid by large profits.

The growth of the radio audience advanced at a rapid pace. Between 1935 and 1941 the number of houses that listened to the radio climbed from around 7 million to 28.5 million. By the end of the decade half the homes in America contained at least two radios and one could hear a radio playing, on average, for about five hours every day. It was evident that radio had made its way into American life by 1941 when 7.5 million American cars were fitted with radio. Moreover, the prices of radio sets continued to fall during this period, and inexpensive but reliable table radio sets became very popular. The trend in radio set manufacture was for a sharpening of competition between companies and, consequently, more aggressive salesmanship and price-cutting, rather than major technical developments. The result was that radio circuitry and parts became increasingly standardized and the factory process more streamlined. Even so, the considerable development of radio broadcasting before the war still left about 20 million rural Americans with only a partial radio service or no radio service at all.

After 1935, as the national economy began to improve moderately, radio broadcasting went through a period of renewed expansion. By 1941 there were 200 new radio stations. As an entire industry radio broadcasting employed 27,000 people in 1941, almost double the work force in 1935. Although many towns got their first radio station, coverage of the nation remained fundamentally imbalanced with, in 1936, 43 percent of all stations in areas with populations of 100,000 or more. With the repeal of the

Davis amendment in 1936, the licensing of urban stations dramatically increased. This period of growth threatened to lead to new waves of interference, and the government adopted a number of countermeasures. Some stations were restricted to transmitting only during allotted daytime periods. Others had to reduce the broadcasting power at night. The main method of limiting interference, which became common before World War II, was the installation of a directional antenna that concentrated transmission in one direction rather than another. By 1941 over 200 stations used this technique.

In 1939, to guarantee good reception over a large area, the Federal Communications Commission expanded the number of clear channel stations, creating a secondary class of 50,000 watt stations. Many attacked the clear channel stations for skimming off the cream of advertising revenue. However, rural politicians pointed out that high-powered stations provided remote, rural communities with their only radio service. This debate reached a climax in the late 1930s after WLW, a superpower 500,000 watt station, began broadcasting from Cincinnati in 1934. Its signal reached the whole of the Midwest and a sizable part of the South and East, thus offering a serious alternative to the dominance of the networks. Calling itself the "Nation's Station," WLW soon attracted a wealth of national and regional advertising. Yet, the domination of WLW was cut short by a Senate resolution in 1938 stating that 50,000 watts was enough power for an AM station to broadcast with. This decision set an upper limit that still applies. In 1939, then, WLW's license to broadcast at 500,000 watts was rescinded.

During the late 1930s the networks increased their domination of broadcasting in America. Some statistics seem to suggest otherwise though, for in 1939 the networks apparently only owned 4 percent of all stations. Yet, the majority of stations were small, local operations while the networks owned 25 percent of all clear channel, high-power stations and, through affiliation, controlled fifty of the remaining fifty-two clear channel stations.

With the addition of Mutual in 1934, the actual number of national networks grew to four in the 1930s: NBC-Red, NBC-

Blue, CBS, and Mutual. There were also twenty regional networks, of which six covered more than one state, for example, the Yankee Network of New England.

The newest national network, Mutual, was a cooperative venture between three 50,000 watt stations, WGN (Chicago), WOR (Newark and New York), WLW (Cincinnati), and WXYZ (Detroit). It was the affiliation of the New England Colonial Network and the Dan Lee Network on the West Coast in 1936 that transformed Mutual into a national network. CBS and NBC were never seriously threatened by the existence of Mutual, which was reduced to providing fillers for such stations.

Indeed, over this period CBS and NBC tightened their control over their affiliates, for example, binding stations to a five-year contract that the networks could end after the first year. Furthermore, once affiliated to a network, a station could not take programs from another network, unless their main supplier agreed. The networks had the option to appropriate broadcasting time at short notice and CBS could seize a whole day for its programs. Finally, stations could not refuse to air commercially sponsored network programs. Significantly, even the largest stations gave way to the demands of the networks because the major networks of NBC and CBS provided the most, and some of the best and cheapest, programs available.

Therefore, by 1940 radio broadcasting in America became centrally organized from the New York headquarters of the two major national networks. The relationship between radio and advertising reinforced the centralization of program planning and production. Radio advertising had continued to grow and agencies created not just the advertisements but also the programs, and combined them into "packages." Again, in this climate of economic depression, the valuable savings to be made from handing over such tasks to an advertising agency were attractive.

From the mid-thirties radio broadcasting had adopted a definite pattern in its dependence on advertising revenue that would continue into the television era. About 60 percent of the revenue from selling airtime went to the networks and their few stations. The remaining 40 percent was distributed among the other 700 stations. The networks and the agencies had identified the most profitable time slots for advertising: in the late morning and early afternoon for a large housewife audience and an evening prime time between about 7:00 P.M. and 11:00 P.M. Advertisers and networks were able to assess the habits and composition of the listening audience, thanks to the parallel development of audience research organizations. The original Cooperative Analysist of Broadcasting was joined by Clark-Hooper in 1934. These companies soon offered both ratings for individual programs and a breakdown of audiences into specific income groups and their geographic location. The final result of the development of advertising on radio and the networks was that, by 1941, two-thirds of all programs carried advertisements. In 1930 fewer than a third had done so. Moreover, from the new audience research data, advertising agencies, networks, and stations learnt and applied the important concept of audience flow, whereby a single program could increase the audience for the programs broadcast immediately before and after it. Therefore, broadcasters scheduled blocks of similar programs to build up the audiences for that time of day. Overall, then, broadcasting became a more sophisticated and, perhaps, then, a more stable business.

The oligarchy in broadcasting was not left undisturbed in the late 1930s and early 1940s. In March 1938 the FCC announced that it would be investigating whether the networks operated monopoly control over broadcasting. After hearing the testimonies of ninety-four witnesses and other evidence, a *Report on Chain Broadcasting* was issued on June 12, 1940. The proposed new regulations directly challenged the practices of the networks that had been developed over the previous ten years. Both the station and network would be contracted together for one year. An affiliate could use programs from other networks. The right of networks to demand options on large sections of station time would cease. An affiliate possessed the right to reject any network program. NBC would no longer be allowed to run two networks. Finally, the ownership of two stations within one market would be prohibited.

Both NBC and CBS fought the implementation of the rules in the federal courts in 1941. Mutual supported the new regulations, believing they would create greater competition. However, the

FCC repeatedly postponed the imposition of the new regulations, leaving the issue of network monopoly unresolved as the nation entered the war. Also, on the eve of World War II, the FCC began to investigate the desirability of newspapers to own nearly 30 percent of all stations.

Over the same time a dispute arose between the American Society of Composers, Authors and Publishers (ASCAP) and the broadcasters over the rates payable for use of music on the radio. ASCAP had increased its rates by 70 percent in 1937 and the broadcasters responded by creating their own licensing organization, Broadcast Music, Inc. From 1940, broadcasters tried to proceed without ASCAP music, for example, changing all of their program theme music. The dispute ended in 1941 with ASCAP agreeing to lower its rates.

A Golden Age

The period 1935–1941 is sometimes known as the golden age of radio, principally because of the programming. By this time radio stations were broadcasting for longer periods, many for eighteen hours or more a day. Thus there was a need for not just more but a greater diversity of programs. A survey in 1938 revealed that 53 percent of radio programs were music, 11 percent were talk shows, 9 percent drama, 9 percent news bulletins, 5 percent religious programs, 2 percent coverage of special events and, finally 2 percent miscellaneous subjects.

Music continued to dominate the schedules of all radio stations, but increasingly less music was performed live. From 1929 radio stations had begun to use electrical transcriptions, $33\frac{1}{3}$ rpm disks that played for about 15 minutes on each side and produced a better quality of sound than the 78 rpm records. Since these transcriptions were successful and offered listeners entertainment they could not buy for themselves, the FRC permitted this form of mechanical broadcasting. In 1938, 21 percent of programming was from electrical transcriptions and, in the following year, 573 stations were supplied with electrical transcriptions. Given the savings in wages for a singer, orchestra musicians, and technicians that were made, small local stations that were not part of a network depended upon such transcriptions to make up a good deal of their daily schedules.

The music of radio in the 1930s was predominantly big band music from the bands of Benny Goodman, Ozzie Nelson, Tommy Dorsey, Russ Morgan, and Sammy Kaye. This was the popular music of the decade, regularly playing on one of radio's top rated programs, *Your Hit Parade,* that began in 1935. Interestingly, nearly all of these famous bands had entered broadcasting and built up a following at local stations and, indeed, it seems generally the networks would acquire such existing bands rather than cultivate newcomers with original ideas and talent. Chicago radio stations were often the source of new programs.

Amateur talent shows were popular with audiences and broadcasters who used such shows as cheap filler material between their main programs. *Major Bowes and His Original Amateur Hour* was the leader of the pack, having started in 1934, discovered vocalist Frank Sinatra, and then moved to the NBC-Red network in 1935. The show regularly topped the ratings and was the ancestor of television's *The Gong Show,* so called because Major Bowes would strike his gong as a signal to eject inept performers. As in previous years, a growing number of network and station programs were variety shows with both comedy and music. Among the ex-vaudevillians to break into radio broadcasting successfully at this time was comic actor Bob Hope whose show began on CBS in 1935.

It was, perhaps, in the presentation of drama and news that radio in the late 1930s most excelled. The networks produced a steady stream of serious drama. In the main these were anthology series, consisting of adaptations from the theater, cinema, or literature, and some specially commissioned work. *Lux Radio Theater* presented hourlong radio verions of recently popular films. *Columbia Workshop,* starting in 1936 on CBS, was noted for its experimental drama.

Another CBS program, the *Mercury Theater on the Air,* which started in 1938, created a major sensation with one of radio's most famous events. Orson Welles led the Mercury Theater Company of Actors and on Sunday, October 30, 1938, broadcast his and Howard Koch's version of English novelist H. G. Wells's classic science fiction novel, *War of the Worlds*. This broadcast caused a mass panic in the eastern United States, and had thousands believing that Martians had actually invaded the Earth. The reasons for this were obvious and subtle. Wells and Koch changed the location and time of the first landing of the Martians in Wells's book from England at the turn of the century to New Jersey in the late 1930s. More significantly, the play took the form of a conventional radio broadcast that was repeatedly interrupted by news flashes of the invasion that became increasingly serious and, finally, terrifying. The earlier reports of a gas cloud sighted on Mars were rapidly followed by the landing of the Mars spacecraft, reports of casualties, the death of the radio reporter on the spot, and the evacuation of New York. Besides its verisimilitude, the program made an impact because of the curious patterns of program selection by radio audiences on Sunday nights. A majority of listeners preferred to miss the first minutes of the evening radio play on CBS so they could hear all of a popular ventriloquist show on NBC. They would turn over to CBS. Consequently, on that night many listeners missed the opening explanation of the program and believed here was a terrible news broadcast.

There were two other external factors that encouraged the spread of terror. First, from September 19 onward, the worst hurricane ever devastated the Atlantic seaboard, claiming houses, mansions, the land itself, and 700 lives. Second, Britain and France had reached the nadir of their notorious appeasement of German dictator Adolf Hitler and acquiesced in the dismemberment of Czechoslovakia in the Munich crisis, also in September 1938. Here was victory of an evil empire abroad and physical devastation at home that had profound psychological consequences for many Americans.

Although the work of Orson Welles and other radio dramatists is justly praised, it should be remembered the bulk of programming consisted of soap operas, situation comedies, and thrillers. By 1940 all of the networks broadcast about 75 hours per week of soap operas, the majority of which were commercially sponsored. These programs came in daily 15 minute episodes that were broadcast during the day and each began with a signature tune, a recapitulaton, or recap, of "what happened last time" and, then, plunged straight into the action. This genre was diversifying. For example, there were *Back Stage Wife* (the trials and tribulations of being the wife of a Broadway star), *Road of Life* (life in a hospital), and *Our Gal Sunday* (whose dilemma was encapsulated by the station blurb as, "Can this girl from a mining town in the West find happiness as the wife of a wealthy and titled Englishman?").

Adventure series became more sophisticated. *Gangbusters,* which started in 1935, was characterized by its opening cacophony of sirens, machine-gun fire, and marching feet. *Mr. Keen, Tracer of Lost Persons* and *Mr. District Attorney* were other popular mystery shows. Children were offered their own adventure serials, often about cowboys like Tom Mix or pilot heroes such as *Captain Midnight* and *Hop Harrigan.* In 1938, the already popular *Lone Ranger* was joined by the crime crusader, *The Green Hornet,* whom station WXYZ claimed was the masked cowboy's grand nephew. In his eradication of "public enemies that even the G-Men cannot catch," *The Green Hornet* was a show that epitomized the New Deal ethos of a moral and economic rearmament in the war against both depression and an imagined crime wave.

Half-hour situation comedies were also a developing staple of thirties radio. *Lil' Abner* began in 1939 and competed with, among other popular programs, Fanny Brice's portrayal of *Baby Snooks* who terrorized the lives of her father and baby brother, Robespierre.

Radio drama of all types proved to be incredibly popular in the late 1930s, with many shows heard by large and loyal audiences. It seemed that radio drama caught the imagination of Americans, not just because of its creative use of sound that was refreshingly different from the movies or theater, but because its drama depended upon the listeners' participation in visualizing settings and action fully. Indeed, programs in which listeners could actively participate were guaranteed to attract large audiences in the thirties. A very erudite show, *The University of Chicago Roundtable,* on NBC, in which faculty members and guests discussed current topics, was far more popular than conventional entertainment shows according to the ratings and participants received sizable mail from listeners requesting transcripts of the debates. *America's Town Meeting* on NBC took this format a step further by inviting members of a studio audience to express their opinions in a radio debate. Not surprisingly, then, quiz shows grew in popularity from about two hours of all programs a week in 1935 to 10 hours a week in 1941. One of the most popular shows was *Kay Kyser's Kollege of Musical Knowledge* and those other shows in which the audience tested its or an expert's general knowledge, for example *Dr. I.Q.* and *Information, Please!* In 1941 one of the most famous quiz shows, and one that involved almost an orgy of public participation, was *Truth or Consequences,* in which the failure of contestants to answer stupid questions led to the same contestants having to embarrass themselves by performing stupid stunts.

We might be inclined to interpret this willingness of Americans to participate in their radio listening as reflecting the belief, generally cultivated in the media, that Americans and their massive democratic institutions were, at long last, working together to vanquish unemployment and poverty. Since radio was free, and carried the propaganda of the New Deal, perhaps it was truly a populist media of the 1930s. Whatever the case, the diverse programs of the thirties bequeathed a crucial legacy, for they provided the original models for the standard programs of future television broadcasting, most obviously the situation comedy, quiz shows, soap operas, and anthology story series.

When considering the development of news programs before World War II, we might return to the broadcasting of *War of the Worlds* in 1938. The panic that the false newscasts caused indicated just how much Americans had begun to believe in what radio told them. Researchers have discovered that, as CBS told them the Earth had been invaded, listeners did not telephone their friends or other sources of news. Indeed, by 1940, for a majority of people, radio news had supplanted newspapers as the prime source of information. The growth of news on radio can be traced back to the collapse of the Biltmore agreement in 1935 when most of the major wire services broke the embargo on supplying radio. Most radio stations began news programs consisting mainly of local stories but also supplied with national news by a wire service. As their service expanded, the national networks broadcast more international news and, partly because this was such a good audience-puller, they also broadcast more major crime stories than did the newspapers.

Radio was unrivaled in providing fast and colorful reports direct from the scene of major and sudden events, especially natural or man-made disasters. An outstanding example of this was the explosion of the *Hindenburg* passenger airship as it docked at Lakehurst, New Jersey, in May 1937. Herb Morrison of the Chicago WLS station happened to be at Lakehurst and was able to make a disk recording of his and other eye witnesses' surprise and horror at watching the sudden inferno. Undoubtedly, broadcasters discovered that live, on the spot, reporting of such disasters attracted audiences by offering a vacarious thrill of being present at such tragedies. The coverage of the trial of Bruno Hauptmann for the murder of the Lindbergh baby in 1935 also enthralled listeners. It also led to new limits being imposed on radio journalism in the interests of justice and good taste. The courtroom bristled with microphones and Gabriel Heatter of Mutual acted as a host for the final, grisly, and live coast-to-coast radio presentation of the electrocution of the hapless Hauptmann. Consequently, the American Bar Association severely restricted radio coverage in courtrooms in the future.

Besides the overturning of the Biltmore agreement, the other factor behind the expansion of radio news in the late 1930s was how world events, especially the rise of Nazi Germany in Europe, became increasingly newsworthy. Paul White, news director of CBS, was instrumental in pioneering newscasts from foreign correspondents. In 1936, he arranged both the coverage of the abdication crisis in England, when King Edward VIII renounced the throne to marry American divorcée Wallis Simpson, and the outbreak of the Spanish Civil War with the rebellion of General Franco. In Spain H. V. Kaltenborn sent reports from a haystack sitting between the firing guns of both armies. So, at quite an early stage, it was understood that radio news was best when it was dramatically related. With the Anschluss or annexation of Austria, in 1938, White inaugurated a familiar device of radio journalism, having reporters based in several countries discuss current events as seen from their different vantage points. In the Munich crisis of 1938 when Hitler forced the partition of Czechoslovakia, NBC scooped the first glance at the terms of the Munich agreement only minutes after it was signed.

Even before America finally joined the Allies in fighting, World War II boosted news broadcasting. The figures for the number of hours in a year given over to news disclose how, whereas in 1937 news totalled 800 hours on all networks, in 1939 this had risen to 1,250 hours. In 1941 the number of hours of network news had nearly tripled to 3,450 hours.

During the 1930s radio also established itself as an integral part of the political process. The principal and most successful pioneer of political broadcasting was Franklin D. Roosevelt whose series of "Fireside Chats" had a tremendous effect on the American public. Altogether, there were only twenty-eight such chats and they were conducted as an informal conversation between the president and the citizen listening in his home. Moreover, these broadcasts were always made at prime listening time. Since the Republicans could not field a public speaker of Roosevelt's ability and presence, during the 1930s the GOP tended to experiment more with its party political broadcasts. In the 1936 campaign, besides using frequent radio commercials, the Republican party had Senator Arthur Vandenberg record a supposed debate with the president in which the answers of FDR to Vandenberg's questions were, in fact, excerpts from past speeches by Roosevelt. This tactic was banned by CBS on the grounds that it was misleading. To put their case to the public, the Republicans eventually produced an allegorical play detailing their electoral promises.

By 1940 the pivotal role of radio in politics was recognized when surveys suggested that most voters considered radio to be their first source of political news. Thus, in the battle for ratings and votes that Roosevelt's performance won in 1940, perhaps it was significant that Republican candidate Wendell Wilkie had seriously strained his voice early in the campaign. Moreover, on the night before the election, the Democrats marshaled together stars of stage, screen, and radio to lead a radio entertainment extravaganza and final party political broadcast.

FM

Technical advances continued, and transmission and reception were refined. Yet, even during the 1930s, the sound quality of radio was tinny and frequently disturbed by static electricity. However, there were significant new developments to correct this problem.

FM, or Frequency Modulation, radio was the answer, ensuring reception free of static electricity by canceling out the effect of atmospheric amplitude modulation by including similar modulation in the radio signal. Yet, most engineers felt that the best and easier solution to static was to muffle the static by increasing the transmitter power and force it down a narrower channel. FM became a practicable concept, thanks to the work carried out by Edwin Armstrong, who had been active in radio engineering before World War I. In the late 1930s, he reasoned that, for FM to succeed, it required a broader channel of 200 kHz, many times wider than the typical AM channel of 10 kHz (kilohertz). This band width produced excellent sound, free from interference made by electrical storms and other radio stations. In 1933, after the system was patented, Armstrong persuaded his friend, David Sarnoff of RCA, to finance experiments with FM. However, in 1935 FM transmission from the RCA aerials on top of the Empire State Building ceased; Armstrong left RCA and took the FM system with him because RCA would not support the necessary huge development costs, thereby making its massive investment in AM (amplitude modulation) obsolete. Such economic self-interest and skepticism of the major radio businesses would delay the commercial growth of FM in the 1930s. Eventually, after a year spent supporting his FM experiments with his personal fortune, Armstrong convinced John Shepherd, who owned the Yankee Network in New England, to set up an FM station. In fact, the first FM station was Armstrong's own experimental WZXMN in Alpine, licensed in 1938. Yankee began FM broadcasting from one station in 1939 and was followed by General Electric. FM receivers were manufactured and a fair number sold.

By 1940, FM radio was almost fully developed and ready for commercial operation. It offered the possibility of drastic changes in broadcasting, not least because the quality of the FM signal allowed a program to be relayed by radio transmission at an equal and even better quality than the usual, expensive AT&T connections to a network. In 1946, FM broadcasters went before the

FCC to lobby for commercial FM broadcasting. Significantly, the case for commercial FM broadcasting would only gradually edge forward, not just because of resistance from AM broadcasters but also because of resistance from the advocates of commercial television. Commercial FM radio began in 1941, using one of the available experimental television channels.

10

SEEING IS DECEIVING
Hollywood and the Movies

IN 1927 there were 17,000 movie theaters across the United States and in many towns the movie theater was the most impressive new building. In general movie theaters made the most of modern architecture as advertisement, emphasizing that, within their portals, was a fantasy world offering patrons escape from reality with such enticing attachments as crystalline towers and illuminated marquees. Movie production, exhibition, and attendance formed a continuous self-fulfilling cycle in which huge audiences required numerous, capacious theaters and enormous production from the great studios. It was this emphasis on quantity, rather than creative quality, that necessitated a production system based on studios working to industrial capacity. Hollywood studios were giant factories using the same organizational strategy to separate production into a series of parts in which each component unit would have its designated function. Thus writers of stories, screenplays, and subtitles worked in a specific section, while such activities as set construction, costume making, and technical services each had their alloted space also.

British character actor Boris Karloff lent the gangling monster of *Frankenstein* (1931) a touching pathos in the most famous screen version of Mary Shelley's early nineteenth-century novella that, as written by Garrett Font and Francis Edwards Faragoh and directed by James Whale, also borrowed material from Wegener's *The Golem*. The result was later described by the *New York Times* as "probably the most famous of all horror films and one of the best." (Museum of Modern Art Film Stills Archive).

When the great Hollywood studios converted to sound production, it was by expanding their facilities, adding such additional departments as sound mixing and dubbing, and music recording. The consequences were even more extensive as writing screenplays became more specialized and required division of labor into three areas: providing general treatments of original and adapted stories; breaking the scenario into a visual sequence, shot by shot; and writing the actual dialogue. Thus a film began as an idea or concept, based on original or adapted material, and moved through the studio system, department by logical department, from writing to design, production, and editing, with the same sort of momentum and ease as a Ford Model T car on the assembly line. Very few directors had the prestige to exercise a decisive influence on the shape of a script before production and on the finished version during cutting. Actual shooting lasted between fifteen and thirty days, depending on the complexity of production. It was the need to govern production according to a system that determined the finished artistic form of all films.

Each studio had a particular style of film. MGM mounted glossy musicals, melodramas, and comedies about high society, Warner Brothers specialized in thrillers, and Columbia was given to experiments in exposing political and social problems. Successful films thrived on proven formulas—star personalities, studio images, and manufactured dreams. All of this did not mean that Hollywood was efficient economically. The potential for economic disintegration was present in Hollywood before World War II. Perhaps this was what dramatist George Bernard Shaw recognized when he refused to sell Samuel Goldwyn the rights to film his plays: "The trouble, Mr. Goldwyn, is that you are only interested in art and I am only interested in money." Philip French, the historian of *The Movie Moguls* (1969), concluded that "Few of the studios were run in a way that approximated to any standard notion of business efficiency; their administration and accountancy were quite unlike those of large corporations." Beneath the surface of order and regulation producers, directors, and stars were confused by the Hollywood system and their own place in it. As English novelist J. B. Priestley said about Hollywood before World War II: "Its trade, which is in dreams at so many dollars per thousand feet, is managed by businessmen pretending to be artists and by artists pretending to be businessmen. In this queer atmosphere, nobody stays as he was; the artist begins to lose his art, and the businessman becomes temperamental and overbalanced."

The Director as Industrial Coordinator

The day of improvisation in filmmaking passed with pioneer director D. W. Griffith. As Hollywood studios became more like other production factories, the product became ever more standardized. From being the principal auteur, the director became simply an executive responsible for drawing together the different contributions of screenplay writer, producer, actors, and technicians and overseeing a product from the middle to the finish. Individual films were considered but one unit in the studio's annual production of many.

Even leading directors were assigned all sorts of different material and expected to move easily from thriller to comedy to musical with the same impersonal determination as the studio. In the period 1930–1933 versatile director Mervyn Le Roy directed twenty-three films, including the very different crime thriller *Little Caesar,* the brutal social realism of *I Am a Fugitive From a Chain Gang,* and the backstage histrionics of *Gold Diggers of 1933.* In short, filmmaking had become another system of industrial production, like many others.

On the whole, Hollywood films of the 1920s were custom-made according to very tired formulas and this applied to the entire range of activities involved in making films and not only acting and directing. Whatever special gifts various technicians and designers may have possessed, they were restricted by the studios' insistence on conformity and repetition because conformity and repetition ensured mass production as regular as that of any other factory. Experiment was considered costly, time-consuming, and dangerous because no one could predict the commercial outcome. Yet successful innovative films had always been copied by competing directors.

Hollywood's dependence on huge financial investment in the 1920s made such copying essential. Thus films conformed to a particular genre that would be made according to precedent. A few gifted directors, such as Erich von Stroheim and Ernst Lubitsch, could prise open the formula and introduce their own insights, developing character and situation by their own imaginative use of shots, crosscutting, and so forth.

The director most clearly influenced by the shift from artistic innovation to industrial production was Thomas Ince, who became the first film producer of any significance. Ince was most concerned to sustain audience interest by keeping the story moving. He cut as freely and felicitously as Griffith but only to this end. Ince also championed shooting film outdoors in the West, to capture the drama and excitement of cowboys and Indians pitted against one another on horses in motion and dwarfed by the towering canyons and endless deserts in the background. Unlike Griffith, Ince welcomed his elevation from director to producer and enjoyed supervising several films at once, ordering shooting according to a preplanned and detailed script. Thus Ince's directors were expected to make a finished product from a blueprint that specified dialogue, shooting, and production schedule exactly. Each was planned to ensure that the entire process of filming was cost-effective by assembling cast, crew, and equipment for the shortest time.

Ironically, Ince's career, like Griffith's, faded in the studio era he had helped introduce. Mogul Harry Aitken took Ince, Sennett, and Griffith from Mutual into a new company, the Triangle Film Corporation. Much was expected of the new company but it failed in 1919 when Sennett and Griffith failed to produce films that continued to attract audiences. Ince himself died mysteriously in 1924. It was rumored that he was pushed over a cliff after showing too great an interest in Marion Davies, mistress and protégée of William Randolph Hearst.

Another transitional artist was Douglas Fairbanks, swash-buckling hero of romantic comedies devised by Anita Loos and directed by her husband John Emerson. These comedies, made in the period 1915–1920, satirized the new film genres and American mores. They capitalized on Fairbanks's inability to underplay and turned his overacting into displays of athletic exhilaration, swinging from balconies and ceilings and across ravines. The films contrasted the dull routine of conventional life with wild, extrovert fantasy.

Censorship

From the very start movie makers found themselves attacked by prurient moralists for attempting to debase standards, supposedly encouraging laziness and sexual license. In the early 1920s the gulf between old-fashioned morality and cinematic permissiveness yawned wide. Films reflected growing urban values and became more suggestive and, indeed, realistic. Some implied that those who disobeyed the ten commandments still managed to live happily ever after.

Certain self-appointed guardians of public morality, lacking official justification for judgment, passed their own private censure on to their constituents. They included the Federal Motion Picture Council in America and the Women's Christian Temperance Union (WCTU). Their charges of undue license were based in part on covert anti-Semitism, implying that Jewish moguls were corrupting Christian morals.

Moral license on screen was accompanied by extramarital license off it. A series of widely publicized scandals involving Hollywood stars damaged the reputation of the entire industry because Hollywood had placed such emphasis on creating the star system. In September 1922 the mysterious death of call girl Virginia Rappe whilst at a party given by comedian Fatty Arbuckle in the St. Francis Hotel, San Francisco, led to Arbuckle's trial for involuntary manslaughter. He was acquitted at a second trial but not until revelations and, worse, innuendos that his great weight had ruptured Rappe's gall bladder, causing her death, ended Arbuckle's career before the camera. He worked in *Hollywood,* a bitter satire by James Cruze, and, thereafter, only worked behind the cameras directing films and using a new name. In 1923 English romantic actor Wallace Reid died prematurely and was pronounced a confirmed morphine addict. Hollywood had turned him into a habitual drug user by giving him morphine to help him continue acting whilst recovering from injuries sustained while filming. When director William Desmond Tanner (or Taylor) also died prematurely, rumors of his particular brew of sex and drugs tarnished the images of actresses Mabel Normand and Mary Miles Minter. It later transpired he was shot dead by Minter's mother.

Such scandals roused the indignation of Congress and it seemed Hollywood might even be threatened by federal censorship. It was this threat, above all, that prompted the movie moguls to create their own censor. They chose big-eared, buck-toothed Will Hays, former campaign manager to Warren Harding and current postmaster general. He was everything the wailing wall of Hollywood moguls was not—Gentile, Protestant, and Wasp. He became president of the Motion Picture Producers and Distributors of America (MPPDA), commonly known as the Hays Office. However, Hays was not content to provide a front of Christian decency in the lounge so that Hollywood could enjoy Babylonian license in the bedroom. The Arbuckle scandal and others convinced the tycoons that Hollywood would require a code of public morality for its films and a code of private morality for its stars. In practice this meant the imposition of small town morality. It was to be the same sort of imposition of intolerance on indulgence as prohibition. At a Hollywood ball they might "need nothing at all," but Hays would make them say goodbye to all that.

The Hays office code, correctly the Production Code, was drawn up by Martin Quigley, a Chicago publisher, and the Reverend Daniel A. Lord, S.J., of St. Louis University, in 1929. It was submitted to the West Coast Association of Producers of 1924 who, with the MPPDA, approved it in 1930. In 1934 the Code was made compulsory when a Catholic and former journalist, Joseph I. Breen, took charge of its administration. A fine of $25,000 was imposed on any member company of the MPPDA that released a film without Breen's seal of approval. The purpose of the Code was explained in a preamble: "No picture shall be produced which will lower the moral standards of those who see it. Hence the sympathy of the audience shall never be thrown to the side of crime, wrong-doing, evil or sin."

From such an opening the Code attempted to enforce morality by legislating what could and what could not be shown. However, not all of its provisions were ridiculous nor was its assumption that an audience "is most receptive of the actions and ideals presented by their most popular stars."

The Hays Code was not imposing an artificial convention by insisting that "the sanctity of marriage and the home shall be upheld." Yet most of the Code was given to prurient speculation on sex outside marriage: "Impure love must not be presented as *attractive* and *beautiful* . . . . It must not be presented in such a way as to *arouse passion* or morbid curiosity on the part of the audience." All in all, the Code imposed a world picture on films that was quite inconsistent with adult experience. Yet it remained in effect for thirty-six years from 1930. Joseph Breen was its leading administrator and in 1953 he received an Academy Award for his "conscientious, open-minded and dignified management." Hollywood's observance of the Code was at best superficial and at worst hypocritical, a practice that turned vice into versa. The studios set out to titillate their public and they succeeded. Biblical subjects in particular lent themselves to explicit sexual display, for which director Cecil B. De Mille was especially notorious. His new religious look in décolleté gowns was always lo! and behold!

The Hays and Breen offices had not restricted themselves to morality. They were also in the business of political censorship. In 1937 Samuel Goldwyn submitted a screenplay by dramatist Lillian Hellman for *Dead End,* a gangster thriller, to Joseph Breen. Breen replied: "We would like to recommend . . . that you be less emphatic . . . in showing the contrast between conditions of the poor in tenements and those of the rich in apartment houses." Breen was less concerned with the rights of the poor than their smell. He did not want any emphasis on "the presence of filth or smelly garbage cans, or garbage floating in the river, into which the boys jump for a swim." His motives in suppressing these aspects of the script were, of course, pure. He was concerned with the social welfare of the working class: "This recommendation is made under the general heading of good and welfare because our reaction is that such scenes are likely to give offense." To whom they would give offense was not specified.

For all their impersonal emphasis on industrial efficiency in the interests of commerce, the great studios in their heyday responded to certain deep psychic needs in the American public. Almost all feature films in the studio years played on people's need to believe that human determination could triumph over adversity, such as the Great Depression. There was a concomitant corollary, that such benevolent human values as love, justice, and sincerity must inevitably succeed over selfishness, hypocrisy, and callousness, whether the story was domestic or political.

Hollywood in the 1920s

It was Erich von Stroheim and Cecil B. De Mille who were the natural successors of Griffith and Ince as innovator and showman in the 1920s. Gerald Mast perceptively satirizes the differences between them when he says, "Von Stroheim gave the public what he wanted, De Mille gave it what he thought it wanted. Von Stroheim was a ruthless realist committed to his art and his vision, De Mille was willing to throw any hokum into a film that was faddish or striking. Von Stroheim's films, despite their excesses and occasionally overstated moralizing, were controlled by the director's taste and intelligence; De Mille's films had everything but taste and intelligence."

Whereas both directors decided to capitalize on public obsession with infidelity among the idle rich, there is a world of difference between *Male and Female* by De Mille and *Blind Husbands* by von Stroheim, both of 1919. *Male and Female* is an extravagant, superficial, and meretricious examination of class attitudes toward sex, too much of which revolves around the cold miniature actress Gloria Swanson taking a bath. Ever conscious of the need to make a sensation, Gloria Swanson insisted that Cecil B. De Mille allow her to enter a lion's cage in *Male and Female*. At a preview of the completed film she overheard one member of the audience observe, "I wonder which one is stuffed."

However, von Stroheim's triangular melodrama, *Blind Husbands,* pares away excess incidents and trivia in order to expose the intensity of a neglected wife's desire for a German officer who courts her in front of her blind husband. Von Stroheim used detail expressively to evoke passion but his felicitous camera shots allowed him a range of subtle expressions. Like Griffith, von Stroheim was an expert at cutting and in creating authentic sets and costumes. However, von Stroheim's obsession with authenticity was costly in terms of money and time and he fell foul of Irving Thalberg who disliked his extravagance, his apparent inefficiency, and his disregard of studio bosses. Although von Stroheim's films were commercially successful and, in effect, subsidizing other productions, Thalberg dismissed him. Von Stroheim moved to Metro Pictures, another ailing studio he helped rescue before being sacked for a second time by Irving Thalberg.

At Metro von Stroheim worked first on a film version of the novel, *McTeague,* by Frank Norris and planned a thorough and literal interpretation with close attention to animal imagery and shot on location in San Francisco and Death Valley. The first version extended to forty-two reels, over three times as long as *Birth of a Nation.* When von Stroheim had cut it by more than half, to twenty reels, he refused to cut any further. Thalberg, now at Metro, fired him a second time. Thalberg then had resident studio scenarist June Mathis reduce the film further to ten reels, and ordered the destruction of all the excised sections. Despite the butchery, some of von Stroheim's personal vision survives. One of von Stroheim's most bitter climaxes comes when he shows how thirst for gold takes precedence over the natural human need for life-giving water in a desert with a man chained to his gold although his starving and parched body can only become food for vultures.

Von Stroheim was easy to hate and easier to fire, being extravagant and dictatorial. When he left Metro for Zukor he ran into all his old problems. Joseph Kennedy intended *Queen Kelly* as a celebration of his mistress Gloria Swanson but in von Stroheim's hands the film became ever more elaborate and sinister. Exasperated, Swanson had Kennedy finally pull the plug on Stroheim's career as a director by having the film abandoned in the midst of shooting just as sound was being introduced in the studios. Stroheim directed only one other film although he continued to act in various roles but always as a Prussian martinet, notably in Jean Renoir's *Grand Illusion* (1937) and Billy Wilder's *Sunset Boulevard* (1950). In this last film he played a dispossessed character whose tragic career in films echoed his own. He was the obsessed chauffeur of a faded and self-deluding star whom he had previously served as director and husband. Ironically, it was Gloria Swanson who played this part, inadequately but true to form.

Other significant directors of the 1920s included Henry King who made *Tol'able David;* James Cruze, who made *The Covered Wagon* (1923); Rex Ingram, who made *The Four Horsemen of the*

Apocalypse; Josef von Sternberg, *Salvation Hunters* and *Underworld;* John Ford, *The Iron Horse;* and King Vidor, *The Big Parade.* Among these other leading directors James Cruze was a master of satire, Rex Ingram was a specialist in composition, Josef von Sternberg excelled in the evocation of atmosphere, and John Ford began a very long career in westerns.

Documentary filmmaker Robert Flaherty made a naturalistic film of the everyday life of Eskimos in Hudson's Bay, *Nanook of the North* (1922). Flaherty was one of the few directors to enjoy true artistic freedom because he could film alone and on modest means. Nanook himself was quite uninhibited and lacking in any self-consciousness before the camera. Thus he lived his life for Flaherty whose artistic control of his means was such that concept and execution were one. Flaherty captured the beauty of immaculate frozen plains and also the rigors of the Eskimos' lives, their continuous struggle for food and shelter, complaisant and unaware that human life could be lived any other way.

Classic Comedies

The most enduring classics among silent films of the 1920s were the comedies. Among the newcomers were Stan Laurel and Oliver Hardy who were brought together by producer Hal Roach as a perfect comic fit of fat and thin. Their films were based on a visual anarchic convention akin to the musical convention of a slow-burning crescendo in a Rossini overture. Laurel and Hardy comedies were tight. If a Christmas tree catches in the doorway of a house, then tree, house, and parked cars nearby must all be destroyed as disaster follows calamity. In their acting Laurel and Hardy unfolded the spiteful child in the adult, reveling in the tyranny of the weak as tearful Stan undermines pompous Ollie's incompetent attempts to ride out hazardous situations.

When director Hal Roach chose Harold Lloyd as a leading man he wanted someone to combine the pathos of Chaplin with the zest of Fairbanks and the charm and zaniness of both. However, Lloyd's episodic comedies did not draw humor from character, simply from a series of potentially dangerous situations. In *High and Dizzy* (1921) he plays a newly qualified doctor who falls in

Chaplin's ascendancy as the preeminent comic genius of the silent screen was confirmed by such masterpieces as *The Gold Rush* (1925). In a celebrated sequence, desperately hungry, he cooked and ate an outsize boot, consuming it, sole and all, like a cordon bleu shellfish, and once again proving in his resourceful use of objects that versatility was the soul of wit. (Museum of Modern Art Film Stills Archive).

love with a somnambulist. The subsequent plot allowed Lloyd his trademark of a comedy of thrills when he has to protect the somnambulist walking on a perilous window ledge many stories above ground. When she moves back inside the building and locks the window behind her, it is he who is trapped and now performs a dazzling gymnastic routine of trips and stumbles that keep the audience on the edge of their seats in an original mix of perplexity and amusement. Lloyd's comedies were magic as pure sensation.

Buster Keaton came closest to equaling Chaplin's evocation of the tension between isolated individual and mechanized society and his exploration of the surface and undercurrent human relationships. Keaton specialized in a deadpan expression of a man resolutely determined to attain his goals, despite such monstrous obstacles as steamboat, hurricanes, locomotives, and whole tribes of savages. In *Daydreams* he eludes the police by hiding in the paddle wheel of a ferryboat that moves, forcing him to stay upright by walking without stopping, a metaphor for the sort of treadmill man must endure through life but cannot control.

Buster Keaton's masterpiece, *The General*, is cohesive from first to last, a comic epic about a railroad and the triumph of one man over others as well as such natural enemies as fire and water. The hero is clearly unequal to the task and the comedy is sustained by the disparity between human prowess and the natural forces he is pitted against. Keaton plays Johnny Gray, a confederate hero in the Civil War, who simply wants to run a train that the Union army wants to appropriate and use to wipe out his fellow Confederates. He is always saved by chance. A cannon aimed at him goes off only when the train has turned a corner, thus hitting the enemy straight in the flank instead. The film explains acts of heroism as absurd accidents—much the same point as was being made by the lost generation of war novelists.

Chaplin's *The Gold Rush* (1925) was an episodic film unified by Chaplin's continuous quest for physical wealth through gold and emotional security through love in a hostile, frozen world. The divertissements have become cinema classics. In an icy Alaskan cabin Charlie Chaplin cooks his shoe, carves it like best beef, salts it to taste, and chews it like a cordon bleu meal, twirling shoelaces like spaghetti, and sucking nails like chicken bones. In a dance hall he turns a spare rope into a belt unaware that a dog is tethered to the other end. The dog has to follow him around the dance floor, interrupting the other dancers, but when it darts after a stray cat, it is Charlie who has to run for his life. The consistent theme of the film is the way gold makes man inhuman, turning even conventional romantic leads, like the handsome lover, into callous cynics. When roommate Big Jim McKay becomes ravenous, he sees Charlie as a chicken to catch and eat. Though the sequence is hilarious, it is also disturbing because of its implied cannibalism. When their cabin teeters on the edge of a crumbling cliff the two friends turn enemies, with each trying to get out by scrambling over the other. Chaplin's choice of shots and his editing, while fully expressive, were unobtrusive, allowing mime to unfold story, situation, and humor as a continuous thread.

Sound

The talkies did not suddenly burst on the silver screen with the premiere of *The Jazz Singer* on October 5, 1927. The introduction of pictures with words was the result of three decades of experiment. The early film inventors had experimented with sound films, beginning with William Dickson in 1889. Leon Gaumont showed various films with synchronized sound in Paris after the turn of the century and German filmmaker Oscar Messter produced *The Green Forest* (1910) with synchronized sound.

The main problems were those of true synchronization between sound and picture, particularly when projected film was mechanically separate from recorded disk. However, German pioneers found a way of recording sound directly on film by using the principle of an oscilloscope, converting sound into beams of light recorded on the edge of the film strip next to the image. In the United States Lee de Forest perfected a similar process and also solved the second problem—amplification. A film had to be loud enough to reach (literally) thousands of people in the audience in huge theaters whose acoustics would carry according to capacity. De Forest had invented the audion tube in 1906—a vacuum tube that magnified sounds and relayed them through a speaker.

By 1923 de Forest was producing short films with synchronized sound. Moreover, in 1925 the Bell Telephone Company, through its research team at Western Electric, had produced a rival process of sound on disks, a system known as the Vitaphone. However, the Bell Company failed to persuade any Hollywood studio to use the Vitaphone. Producers were chary of an expensive and unproven innovation whose potential success would cause havoc in their, by now, more settled and more profitable business. The mere process of recording adequate sound alone would slow down film production. Furthermore, sound reproduction would be an extra economic imposition upon exhibitors who would have to acquire additional, expensive equipment and adapt their motion picture palaces accordingly.

Eventually, Bell and Western Electric offered the Vitaphone to Warners, an ailing company on the verge of bankruptcy. At first, Warners experimented with programs of short, sound films in 1926 and 1927 featuring Will Hays and various musicians. However, a rival, William Fox, began to make much the same sort of novelty programs, and, also, a newsreel with synchronized commentary. Fox was using his own separate system, Movietone. It had the sound recorded direct onto the filmstrip, something made possible by Theodore Case, who had pirated Lee de Forest's system. Thus Warners decided they had to bite the bullet and make a feature film with sound— *The Jazz Singer* with Al Jolson.

The artistic significance of *The Jazz Singer* was that it was the first film to use synchronized sound as the principal means of telling a dramatic story. In fact, the majority of the film was made as a silent with music added and synchronized. Only two sequences used synchronized speech, one building to a climax when Al Jolson sings *Mammy* to a theater audience. Whereas the silent sequences retained the fluidity of the better silent camera work, the sound sequences lacked movement and were dramatically inert, with the actors huddled close so that their voices could be captured by the microphones. Despite the visual plasticity of the silent sections and the static nature of the sound sequences, it was those very same sound sequences that provided the actors with greater opportunity to give voice and flesh to their characters.

Commercially, *The Jazz Singer* was an outstanding success whose very dimensions obliged the otherwise reluctant movie moguls to convert to sound if they wanted to retain their shaken hold of public taste. People wanted to hear as well as see films and Hollywood, desperate to please, converted wholesale to the new process.

However, talking pictures experienced various technical, artistic, and commercial problems. The camera, so fluent in silent films, was once again rooted to the spot so that the actors could be adequately recorded by the stationary microphone. Once again, filmmaking became an inferior means of recording theater performances. Now directors had to learn how to capture voice as well as face and master the requisite technical skills. Sound recording caught all noise and film cameras were notoriously audible with their incessant whirring. Thus, for a time, cameras were placed in a glass booth where they moved even less than before.

The introduction of sound led to reconsideration of the system developed over thirty years and a questioning of basic movie assumptions. Once again, filmmakers tried to find a parallel with the stage. They employed playwrights, stage actors, and theater directors and there was a brief period of misapplied stage principles. However, films could show any image while words were spoken. The synchronization of image and sound also allowed for disjunction of picture and sound in which a different image from an actor's face might be more effective than a literal presentation of a conversation. Moreover, movies could employ a greater range of sound effects than any play or opera—not only speech and natural sound effects, songs and musical accompaniment, but also distortion and subjective thoughts—all with perfect timing.

The whole process of conversion by studios and theaters was so expensive that they required massive injections of capital from banks. Thus did the movies become adjuncts to the great commercial banks who, incidentally and ironically, controlled the two major sound processes by Western Electric and RCA because these companies were themselves subdivisions of the Morgan and Rockefeller families. Thus the banks had created a sort of motion pictures version of the Dawes Plan for German reparations—one in which the studios had to borrow money from the banks to acquire equipment whose development the banks had themselves financed in the first place.

Sometimes the most illustrious artists of the silent era proved encumbrances in the age of sound. Foreign accents were inadmissible except in character parts. Native English speakers whose voices suggested rather different characters from their appearance —such as a handsome leading man with a high-pitched voice— might have been better off as mute artists (like Harpo Marx). The most famous of such casualties was John Gilbert, one of Greta Garbo's leading men, whose voice, as reproduced, seemed too fast and high. Different explanations have been given to account

for his failure in sound, ranging from vocal inadequacy to technical sabotage on the orders of Louis B. Mayer.

Studios required very different material with effective dialogue.
Not only did they import stage actors from Broadway but also
established playwrights and novelists to provide scripts for them.
Yet certain directors, notably the Russian Sergei Einstein, were
convinced that film could absorb sound and Einstein made much
of the symphonic possibilities of a film scene by engaging composer Sergei Prokofiev to enhance visual images with appropriate
music.

Eventually came the invention of the camera blimp, a mask to
cover its whirring sound while allowing it to film more freely.
Director Rouben Mamoulian introduced the use of two microphones to record a scene, allowing for a final composite mix of
their recording after balancing and regulating the volumes. The
introduction of the boom, an instrument that allowed the microphone to move in earshot but out of sight just above the actor's
head, allowed actors to move while speaking.

It was essential to transform sound into a positive asset to the
entire artistic range of filmmaking. Innovative director Ernst Lubitsch exploited some of the possibilities of sound to support
vision in his *The Love Parade* (1929) by having Maurice Chevalier
make witty asides and a series of deliberate mistimed sound effects
to jolt bride, groom, and congregation during a marriage ceremony. In *Trouble in Paradise* Lubitsch exploited sound as a means
of innuendo by concentrating camera and microphone outside a
room where a crucial scene of seduction is taking place. It was
Lubitsch who first conceived the mix of rhythmic song and
speeding train for *Monte Carlo* (1930) with both music and train
getting faster as the song nears its climax.

The most imaginative use of sound and pictures was found by
Walt Disney in his early animated cartoons. Walt Disney had
moved to Hollywood from Kansas, where he had had a successful
career as a commercial artist, in 1923. He and his animator, Ub
Iwerks, soon mastered the technique of animated cartoons, but
his adept use of sound made him preeminent in Hollywood.

Because he was not filming real people, Disney bypassed the
restrictions of sound recording. Cartoon sound could always be

added later and the fact that cartoons are fantastic, anyway, released sound (as well as vision) from immutable laws of realistic reproduction. The animals in a Disney cartoon could acquire human characteristics, and, indeed, act like people in the old films of Mack Sennett or Georges Méliès. Disney realised that sound and vision could be complementary in his *Steamboat Willie* (1928). When a goat devours a guitar and sheet music for the song *Turkey in the Straw* like so much grass, Mickey Mouse twists its tail, causing notes to stream from the goat's mouth as the soundtrack plays them aloud. Mickey Mouse then accompanies the tune with whatever tool he can turn into instruments of percussion—pots, pails, and washboard, along with squeaks and quacks from cat, pig, and duck—and finally, Mickey plays a cow's teeth like a xylophone.

Disney recognized similarities in superficially dissimilar sounds and pictures. The opening sequence of *The Skeleton Dance* (1929), the first of Walt Disney's *Silly Symphonies,* combines the eerie atmosphere of goblins at night, supported by owls hooting, bats flying, and wind whistling through percussion and a tense high note on a violin. Once the scene is set and the right atmosphere created, skeletons emerge from opened tombs and their jangling dances are underscored by appropriate rhythmic percussion.

Hollywood in the 1930s

The onset of the Great Depression hardly touched film prosperity. People needed entertainment and many could find the small change that was the price of admission to movie houses. However, the movies were hit by a temporary recession in 1933. The studios responded by rigorous economics and by eliciting some government assistance.

The studios now found it necessary to offer audiences two films for the price of one and double features became standard fare, as did novelty games such as Bingo and Screeno played for domestic prizes between screenings. Hollywood survived recessions in 1933 and 1938 and, thereafter, sailed through World War II on a flood of prosperity to its most profitable year ever in 1946.

While the studio system was successful in turning out films like

an industrial factory turns out machines, it was much less successful in producing art of lasting value. Gerald Mast estimates that,
of 7,500 feature films made in the heyday of the studio years of
1930–1945, perhaps only about 200 films made any lasting
impression and survive as vital examples of the century's most
potent performing art.

There were numerous parallels between the Elizabethan and
Jacobean theater of 1576 to 1642, the primo ottocento of Italian
opera of 1800–1851, and the great studio years of Hollywood.
Each produced an art form—play, opera, feature film—that appealed to a wide audience. Each was performed by a repertory of
artists supported by a company of writers, managers, costumiers,
and designers. Each drew on artists who could adapt their technique and stage type to similar roles—whether prima donna,
romantic tenor, tragic hero, comedian, or villain. Shakespeare
had Richard Burbage and Will Kemp, Verdi had Gaetano Fras-
chini and Felice Varesi, and MGM had Clark Gable and Greta
Garbo. Each form was steeped in its own conventions and clichés
that a major creative genius could transform by his personal art.
Moreover, much of the original material on which plays, operas,
and films were based came from popular literature of the time.
The Elizabethans enjoyed romances and histories by Holinshed
and Plutarch; the Italians wanted the British romantics such as
Byron and Scott and stories set in Tudor England; and film
audiences wanted such literary masterpieces as *La Dame aux Ca-
mélias* and *Les Misérables* turned into films. It was a case of one art
form helping perpetuate the myths and icons of another by lending them a new depth and perspective.

The studio system was responsible for choice of material and
the style in which the finished film was made. Studio bosses
assumed that a formula that was proven would work well again.
This estimation of public taste and reliance on an established form
accounts for the series of film cycles beginning with gangster
movies in the early 1930s.

In 1932 gangster movies were the most popular of all film
genres. Their vogue was greater than that of romances and musicals and far greater than that of westerns. As Dorothy Manners in
Motion Picture Classic of June 1931 observed, "Gangsters . . . gun-

men . . . gamblers . . . hoodlums . . . heist guys . . . hold-ups
. . . 'baby-faced killers' . . . bandits . . . bullets . . . murders . . .
morgues . . . molls. Hollywood is going at the pace that 'kills' at
the box office! Of all the theme picture epidemics none has equaled
the intense rush of gangsters to the box office." It was Paramount
that first developed the genre and other studios—MGM, Fox, De
Mille Pictures, Columbia, and Universal—followed its example.
One studio, Warner Brothers, made the genre its specialty.

Gangster thrillers held a double fascination for the public. They
combined the realism of a social documentary with the emotional
power of a dream. They played on fears that American society
during prohibition and the economy during the depression were
unstable and foundering. Gilbert Seldes in *The Years of the Locust
—America 1929–1932* (1932) said the gangster film was particularly effective at representing aspirations and desires in the depression: "Rude manners, brutality, and action—contempt of authority, the theme of the bowl of cherries and the raspberry; and the
desire for work." Gangster protagonists projected an image of
energy and self-assurance that lent encouragement to the public.

Gangsters in early films were city cousins of western outlaws
like Billy the Kid and Jesse James who had supposedly robbed the
rich to help the poor. They were presented as good-natured hoodlums conspiring to overthrow corrupt officers. Outlaws stole
from banks and railroad companies rather than people, who were
the prey of politicians and public officials. Whereas the western
outlaw roamed the countryside—a horizontal world—and the
eastern gangster hustled in the cities—a vertical world—both
inhabited canyons. The outlaw lived in the natural environment
of mountains, cliffs, crevices; the gangster dwelt in the man-made
environment of skyscrapers, office blocks, and bonded warehouses. Vertical planes suggested impossible odds, a corrupt civilization curbing freedom, and complemented the protagonist's
rise and fall. Bootlegging in the movies made gangsters popular
in the cinema and in real life. Films such as *The Bootlegger's
Daughter* (1922), *Contraband* (1925), *Poison* (1924), *Four Walls* (1928),
and *Broadway* (1929) supplied audiences with the cheap thrill of
seeing services rendered and the satisfaction of knowing that though

Little Caesar (Edward G. Robinson) arrives at the Big Boy's place, an art deco mansion replete with Flemish tapestries, rococo furniture, crystal chandelier, and inlaid marble floor. Hollywood adopted a double standard in such gangster movies as *Little Caesar* (1930), ensuring that, while the screenplay emphasized that crime does not pay, it provided viewers with vicarious pleasure as they gaped at criminal opulence. (Museum of Modern Art Film Stills Archive).

the law was being flouted rough justice would be meted out to the criminals.

Underworld (1927), written by Ben Hecht for Paramount, was erroneously hailed as the first gangster film, because it was certainly the most successful example of the genre to that time critically and commercially. The director, Josef von Sternberg, skillfully evoked the atmosphere of a city at night. The gangsters' world was dark, with flashes of light from car headlights, matches, mirrors, and chandeliers. Gangster thrillers remained lugubrious, their very darkness implying a relationship between environment and crime.

Little Caesar (1930) and *Public Enemy* (1931) offered a summation of what had been achieved in the genre hitherto. However, their plots lack coordination between the different elements, and the characterization is crude. The huge public success of the films owed much to the atmosphere of the time they were released. Al Capone was at the height of his notoriety. Some knowledge of his career is essential for understanding the twists and turns of the plots. Contemporary audiences were familiar with the allusions and expected to interpret the inconsistencies of the stories accordingly. *Little Caesar* (1930), directed by Mervyn LeRoy from a novel by W. R. Burnett, is not about a big shot but a small time crook, Caesar Enrico Bandello (Edward G. Robinson), who begins by robbing a gas station and then goes East with his partner, Joe (Douglas Fairbanks, Jr.). *Public Enemy*, directed by William A. Wellman and based on a story *Beer and Blood* by John Bright, begins with a series of episodes to show how a boy brought up in the slums turns to crime as a means of escape. Tom Powers (James Cagney) and Matt Doyle (Edward Woods) graduate from petty crimes to warehouse robberies. On the run for killing a police officer, they become, first, truck drivers for a bootlegger (Robert Emmet O'Connor) and, then, partners with Nails Nathan (Leslie Fenton) in an operation to divert liquor from a bonded warehouse. When they become involved in gang war over disputed territory, Matt is killed. Tom attempts to wreak revenge on the rivals but is badly wounded outside their headquarters. His rivals manage to kidnap him from the hospital where he is recovering and then they deposit his corpse on the doorstep of his mothers' house.

According to John Spivak in *America Faces the Barricades* (1935), such characters as Rico in *Little Caesar,* Tom Powers in *Public Enemy,* and others were made to die as scapegoats for the depression. A capitalist system that could not bring about its recovery for over a decade required an excuse for its own shortcomings. Nevertheless, despite censorship codes and moral tags, gangster movies consistently projected their protagonists as energetic and egalitarian heroes. As Eugene Rosow finds in *Born to Lose* (1978),

"When the national mood was characterized by apathy, defeat, disorientation, and insecurity, movie gangsters were active; they knew what they wanted and they knew how to get it; they were self-reliant and unafraid in pursuit of their goals; and they projected a quality of forthrightness that stood in contrast to the hypocrisies of the Hoover regime and the media's coverage of the Depression."

The tradition of the American gangster film was founded on a paradox. The genre celebrates freedom of the individual in a nostalgic evocation of the underworld although the contemporary inception of a national criminal syndicate destroyed that freedom. The irony is that the myth was perpetrated by movie moguls who, within another American tradition, business monopoly, contributed to the growth of large corporations. Therefore, it is not surprising that, although gangster films have offered the public escape of a sort, they have never carried a universal message of freedom triumphing over tyranny with any conviction. An economic system that has enormous problems is not likely to seek their resolution by political means lest the process of solving them prove injurious to interested parties. Nor is it likely to encourage others to seek such a solution. Instead, studios offered audiences subtle propaganda in the guise of escapism. While real citizens were hard up in the depression, film characters were well-heeled. The elegance of studio sets and costumes, the inevitable poetic justice of plot answered a genuine need. They encouraged audiences to try and attain in their lives the affluence they saw on screen. If that failed, people could still share in the luxury of their favorite stars—but at a distance and only once or twice a week. When the Breen code insisted on a higher tone, Hollywood recast its mobsters as policemen and simply moved them across the street to the right side of the law. Thus conscience made heroes of James Cagney and Edward G. Robinson.

Another early genre was the journalist movies in which a tough-talking newspaper man covered the daring escapades of gangsters and police in such films as *Big News, The Front Page,* and *The Power of the Press.* The pivotal author was former pressman Ben Hecht of Chicago whose assertive dialogue conveyed the tough world of prisons, dives, and precincts as few others have done.

Hollywood had a commercially profitable but curious and uneasy relationship with the great American novelists of the period. It used Ernest Hemingway's stories, notably *A Farewell to Arms* (1932). It also used *To Have and Have Not* (1944), with the title, Humphrey Bogart and Lauren Bacall, but not much of the plot and, in two later versions, different titles. It was said Hemingway wrote *For Whom the Bell Tolls* specifically with Hollywood in mind and the film (1943) adjusted this account of an incident in the Spanish Civil War to fit the disparate talents of American Gary Cooper, Swedish Ingrid Bergman, and Greek Katina Paxinou. Hollywood also, and at different times, encouraged F. Scott Fitzgerald, William Faulkner, and John Dos Passos to work on genres quite unsuited to their considerable talents. Faulkner, master of southern surfaces, paradoxes, and psychological intensity, collaborated on the original version of Hemingway's *To Have and Have Not* (1944), Chandler's *The Big Sleep* (1946), and a ludicrous historical hokum *Land of the Pharoahs* as a vehicle for British regular Jack Hawkins and continuously aspirant star Joan Collins (1955). Not surprisingly, Faulkner's idea of working at home, rather than in the Hollywood studio office, was to return to his house in Mississippi. Sometimes, the choice of author was more apposite but, once again, studio insistence on industrial production and maintaining a roster of star names resulted in interesting combinations of original and screenplay writers. While Raymond Chandler was allowed to work on his own *The Big Sleep* and *The Lady in the Lake* (both 1946) and other Marlowe stories, he was also employed as a collaborator for James M. Cain's *Double Indemnity* (1944). Ben Hecht (1894–1964), who wrote authentic-sounding dialogue for press and hoodlums, was allowed to write his own screen version of his play *The Front Page* (1931), but moved through such different material as the trifling *Goldwyn Follies* (1938) and the screen version of Emily Brontë's passionate romance, *Wuthering Heights* (1939).

Sound made it possible to make musical films in which complex dance sequences were performed to complex music and rhythm. So potent was the appeal of music in films that most early talkies included song or song and dance routines often set in a nightclub, as in *The Lights of New York* and *The Blue Angel*.

However, very soon musicals became a fully fledged genre in their own right, whether based on Broadway shows or traditional musical comedies with such artists as Maurice Chevalier, Jeanette MacDonald, and Jack Buchanan. This form was succeeded by the backstage genre in which struggling artists triumphed against considerable odds. They included among their leading players such characters as the ingenue chorine suddenly promoted to leading lady who then becomes a star overnight, and a millionaire composer who is hiding his true identity (and wealth) so that he can rise by his creative genius alone. Director and choreographer Busby Berkeley devised a series of elephantine dance sequences with kaleidoscopic and acrobatic formations by countless dancers. Later musical films were dominated by the more intimate solo dancing of Fred Astaire whose preferred form was bourgeois comedies, supported by various comic artists, such as Edward Everett Horton, in well-routined performances and, usually, by his best dancing partner, the somewhat churlish actress, Ginger Rogers. America's leading theater composers—George and Ira Gershwin, Cole Porter, Richard Rodgers, and Jerome Kern—all provided special songs or complete scores for Hollywood's musical films of the 1930s. Other musicals were traditional operettas in Ruritanian costumes with casts led by Jeanette MacDonald and Deanna Durbin.

There were film series based on popular characters such as Chinese detective Charlie Chan and ingenuous youngster Andy Hardy, the role that established Mickey Rooney. Other films drew on a studio's ensemble of leading actors in complementary plots united by place *(Grand Hotel)* or time *(Dinner at Eight)* but without any true stylistic ensemble of playing together.

Film Comedy in the 1930s

Comedy remained a distinctive form and many of Hollywood's best films of the 1930s were comedies.

Chaplin retained his highly individual style because his pictures were so popular and commercially successful that he needed to make only superficial gestures to Hollywood's demands for talking pictures. Moreover, his visual style, based on straightforward, rather than inventive, camera work, which emphasized the subject rather than the way it was shot, was in accord with the typical talking picture and its conventions of even lighting, stationary camera, and straightforward exposition. In *Modern Times* (1936) Charlie is an industrial everyman at the mercy of the automated assembly line and cast adrift as security guard in the consumer paradise of an outsize department store. In *The Great Dictator* (1940), a comedy of mistaken identity and destiny, Chaplin played a forlorn Jewish barber who survives World War I and finds his country, Bacteria, overrun by the dictator Hynkel, and governed by a party ruling under the sign of the double cross. Chaplin daringly capitalized on the coincidental, if superficial, similarity between the appearance of his favorite tramp and the despot Adolf Hitler to play both roles with short-back-and-sides haircut and toothbrush mustache.

Director Ernst Lubitsch also graduated successfully from silent to sound films. His earlier hallmark had been expressive use of visual detail and now he used sound effects to the same ends. His most successful films relied on witty dialogue that exploited studio convention, notably *Design for Living* (1933), and *Ninotchka* (1939). In *Trouble in Paradise* (1932), a triangle about a master thief (Herbert Marshall) caught between his victim (Kay Francis) and his accomplice (Miriam Hopkins), Lubitsch cleverly exposed the difference between the glistening surface of cafe society and the mire of his characters' inner lives. Herbert Marshall and Kay Francis fall in love as they compulsively steal one another's personal items—watches, wallets, and jewelry. Lubitsch drew sparkling dialogue from Simon Raphaelson.

Frank Capra's comedies of manners were set in a United States of Main Streets and country roads with dialogue provided by Robert Riskin. Many were moralities in which a resilient innocent triumphed over social manipulators by winning over a girl who embodied false values. In *It Happened One Night* (1934) reporter Clark Gable encounters society girl Claudette Colbert as she pursues a worthless match. Together they discover the pleasures and penalties of long-distance travel. The tone of Capra's deliberately populist material was lightened by deft underplaying and characterization. In *Mr. Deeds Comes to Town* (1936) rural nouveau riche

Gary Cooper discovers that he must use his fortune to help the poor, rather than spend it selfishly on snob reporter Jean Arthur. In *Mr. Smith Goes to Washington* (1939) the problem is political, rather than financial, manipulation. In *You Can't Take It With You* (1938) an eccentric family are set against a world of elegance and sophistication.

The Marx Brothers represented the quintessence of American comic films—exaggerated physical types directed to draw the maximum effect from their personalities and spiced by acidulous verbal wit. The Marx Brothers' first film was a version of their successful stage show, *Cocoanuts* (1929). They set out to look and act outrageously—Groucho with heavy mustache, Chico with bulbous eyes, Harpo with frizzy hair and inane smiles. Their films used a conventional romantic story as excuse for gross behaviorism by the brothers. *Duck Soup* (1933), *A Night at the Opera* (1936), and *At the Circus* (1939) relied on audience amusement at a stage tradition being ridiculed by well-routined anarchy performed with split second timing. In *Go West* (1940) the trio stripped an entire train of its wood in order to fuel the locomotive.

Actress and screenwriter Mae West's dramatic persona was a parody of the predatory blonde, first as a mature woman who could still attract young men, later as a caricature of woman as part siren, part landscape, and part gorgon. In *Night After Night* (1932) her immortal answer to the remark of the hatcheck girl who admires her jewelry, "Goodness, what beautiful diamonds," was, "Goodness had nothing to do with it, dearie." Her throwaway remark, accompanied by a shrug and wiggle, defined her persona beyond a brief film career. Her success was certainly resented by the nominal star, George Raft, who recalled that Mae West "stole everything but the cameras." Mae West subsequently disclosed that she and George Raft had made love in a broom cupboard: "It was love on the run with half the buttons undone." It was astonishing, given her languid delivery, that she became a legend for a series of celebrated and salacious wisecracks, each delivered from the side of the mouth. Of her own plot for *I'm No Angel* (1933) she said, "It's all about a girl who lost her reputation but never missed it." Of her character, Tira, she remarked, "She's the kind of girl who climbed the ladder of success wrong by wrong." The butt of her satire was the golddigger, the predatory vamp whose hard character was delineated elsewhere by Joan Blondell and Jean Harlow. However, her stories conformed to prevailing values, pitting the shady lady against hypocritical forces of law and order and allowing her to elude punishment because her impulses were sympathetic. She was much restricted by the Breen office. In *Belle of the Nineties* (1934), when she sang "My Old Flame," she had to make clear why the fire was a smoulder- ing ember by suggestive use of eyes and voice. The tepid lyrics by themselves do not even imply there was a flicker in the first place. Having dismissed a rival with a shove she ordered her maid (in a parody of "Give me a break"), "Beulah, peel me a grape."

Mae West's onetime partner in *My Little Chickadee* (1940), W. C. Fields, was a bibulous comedian with a sardonic wit to match his comic shape and gravelly voice. He had also moved from vaudeville to silent films. It was clear from this earlier period in silent comedies that Fields owed his success primarily to adept use of his ridiculous appearance of outsize tummy, luminous nose, and ludicrous historical costumes. Thus the funniness of Fields was essentially funny at its best in certain purely visual sequences, such as his awkward attempts at croquet in *Poppy* (1936) and his confusion with bent pool cues in *Six of a Kind* (1934). W. C. Fields cultivated a vulgar character of external gentility that barely concealed his boorish interior and inability to love. Yet his targets struck a responsive chord in film audiences who wanted to see mincing children and the sacred institution of marriage ridiculed by at least one comic master.

These films were based on dialogue, much of it effective screen dialogue convincingly caught by microphones. It was, indeed, dialogue, that dominated the way the films were made. Thus images were less important than speech. The dominance of speech over symbol determined that films would be shot in a straightfor- ward manner that precluded imaginative or daring camera shots by way of odd angles, exaggerated close-ups, and special moving effects. Even lighting remained uniformly bright so as not to divert any attention from the artists' words to the atmosphere. Nevertheless, film lighting was more than purely functional and used to enhance the stars' appearances, highlighting their best features. Thus, in the 1930s, films followed the line established by Thomas Ince, concentrating on telling an interesting story clearly and concisely. Psychology and character motivation were shown by ritual—not by probing beneath the surface.

Of new developments increasing use of color was the most important. In the early cinema directors had used color tints for specific sequences. Some of the films of George Méliès were tinted by hand, frame by frame. Because sixteen pictures were projected every second, a film lasting only ten minutes would require 10,000 frames each painted separately. Some of the films of D. W. Griffith and Abel Gance were printed with color casts —blue for night scenes, red for passionate scenes, and yellow and green for others. Each of these directors was looking for a visual complement to the atmospheric music that accompanied the film in the cinema. Of course, the effect was not the same as color photography. In 1908 Charles Urban developed a color photographic process, Kinemacolor. It was opposed by the film trust and never used in the movies. However, the Technicolor Corporation, founded in 1917, was supported by the film industry. Technicolor perfected its process in 1933, using three strips of emulsion sensitive to blue, to red, and to yellow.

Yet Hollywood postponed its conversion to color. Black and white film was more responsive to different lights and afforded more subtlety of shade. It was easier to use and quicker to process. Besides, the financial priority was to complete the conversion to sound. Thus Hollywood reserved color for special effects, such as a Disney cartoon like *Snow White and the Seven Dwarfs* (1937) or a spectacle, such as Victor Fleming's *Gone with the Wind* (1939). Later, in World War II, color films were an occasional luxury. Priority was given to black and white films because they were easier and less costly to produce.

Walt Disney was best able to profit from color as could few others. While studios were wrestling with the vexed problems of needing color to make pictures more realistic, while needing to tone down the garish hues of color stock, Disney exploited vivid colors that could lend additional force, variety, and poignancy to

In his first full-length animated cartoon, *Snow White and the Seven Dwarfs* (1937), Walt Disney mixed elements from American and European art. The wicked queen was a glacial American society woman who transforms herself into a comical old hag from Central Europe; Snow White was a younger, prettier version of American adventuress Wallis Simpson, while her dwarfs looked European but sounded like Californian miners in the Gold Rush. (Walt Disney Productions; Museum of Modern Art Film Stills Archive).

his animated features. Moreover, subject, music, and color could all be reconciled as each shifted. Disney was free to manipulate color as the directors of feature films were not and he used color for his animals, Mickey Mouse and Donald Duck, and, as mentioned, in his first full-length film, *Snow White and the Seven Dwarfs* (1937).

Most fascinating was the mix of American and European styles of art. This is most clearly seen in the two personae of the wicked queen. At first, she is a cold glacial figure, clearly defined by the sort of ruthless American career woman often played by Joan Crawford—elegant, predatory, and modern. Later, when the queen takes a potion to transform herself into an old crone who will give Snow White the near-fatal apple, the artists' inspiration is clearly any old witch of European provenance who might find herself in Hansel and Gretel—gnarled, hunchbacked, and wart-encrusted. Snow White herself was like an improved version of Wallis Simpson, the American divorcée for whom King Edward VIII of Britain abdicated his throne. The dwarfs were European in a traditional visual sense but their vocal characterization and their immortal mining song, "Heigh ho!" were clearly all-American.

Disney's most grandiose feature film was *Fantasia* (1941), a sequence of cartoon shorts inspired by classical music played by the Philadelphia Orchestra conducted by Leopold Stokowski. Running for well over four hours, *Fantasia* set new standards for movies in color and sound and its imaginative concept has never been surpassed. While some of the choice and use of material was predictable—Beethoven's Pastoral Symphony set in a classical world of saccharine gods and centaurs, gamboling in an Arcadian landscape, and the insertion of Mickey Mouse as the Sorcerer's Apprentice—much was not. Disney and Stokowski turned a Bach prelude into a kaleidoscopic tone poem of rich orchestral sonorities and abstract designs; Stravinsky's then controversial ballet, *The Rite of Spring,* was turned into a history of evolution; the ballet, the *Dance of the Hours,* from Ponchielli's opera, *La Gioconda,* was turned into a parody of opera and ballet with outsize hippos performing dainty ballet steps in minuscule tutus until pursued for dear life by predatory alligators. Even the *Sorcerer's*

Apprentice allowed for a terrifying cascade of automated broom-sticks carrying so much water from the well that they threaten Mickey Mouse with drowning—a frightening symbol of mass production. Most successful was program music that deliberately calls for a picture—the *Nutcracker Suite* from Tchaikovsky's ballet and Mussorgsky's *Night on a Bare Mountain*—because here the material lent itself most easily to the sort of pictures at which Disney excelled—faeries, demons, and goblins cavorting amidst autumn leaves, mist, and fireworks. Most telling of all was the Chinese dance performed by waddling mushrooms. Yet here, too, the limitations of Disney's art were also disclosed, confining him to the same formula of faeries, goblins, and demons forever. However, Disney soon returned to conventional human repro-duction and emphasis on American regional values in his other feature films. *Bambi* (1942), about the growing pains of a deer, was free from the inhibitions of human characters and succeeded perfectly.

Face Value

The stars of the 1930s shone as brightly as those of the 1920s. There were even more of them and their screen personae were tailored and manicured to conform to enduring archetypes. Clark Gable was generally considered the decade's most handsome and desirable leading man, with large and widely spaced eyes, razor sharp moustache, and roguish charm, whether the parts called for a rough diamond or a sly wit. Swedish immigrant Greta Garbo was assigned a range of parts drawn from history and literary classics, notably Camille, Queen Christina of Sweden, and Anna Karenina. Her forte was to convey deep emotions by adroit use of a husky voice still bearing traces of a Scandinavian accent, a natural commanding presence, and deep commitment. Com-menting on her ability to capture psychological undercurrents, English critic Kenneth Tynan once remarked that what men saw in other women drunk, they saw in Garbo sober. English immi-grant and former Korda player Charles Laughton was used in a series of exaggerated, histrionic, not to say grotesque, parts, rang-ing from Captain Bligh in *Mutiny on the Bounty* to Quasimodo in

The Hunchback of Notre Dame. Exaggerated mannerisms were also a hallmark of Bette Davis, a miniature actress who tackled melodramas with the relish of an octopus caressing a shellfish. If the part did not call for period dress with flounces and frills, she provided them in her acting.

The most debonair leading man was Welsh immigrant and former acrobat Cary Grant, whose career in sophisticated roles requiring throwaway delivery of lines and a touch of menace beneath the offhand manner extended well over thirty years. The glacially arresting Joan Crawford was the archetypal career woman of ruthless determination willing to use or suppress her feminine charms as she continuously rose from rags to riches. Her character was best defined in the role of predatory tigress in *The Women.* Humphrey Bogart alternated roles on wrong and right sides of the law in much the same manner as James Cagney and Edward G. Robinson but with a keener wit, expressing bitter resentment of upper-crust indolence. In *Casablanca* he reminded former girlfriend Ingrid Bergman of their last meeting: "The Germans wore grey; you wore blue."

Hollywood performed truly special services to enhance the appearance of its leading players. Style and quality of makeup accentuated good features, stylish costumes redeemed awkward physical shapes, and becoming hairstyles, whether by hair curling, wigs, or toupees, capped what was intended to be a lustrous appearance. The homely appearance of Irving Thalberg's wife, Norma Shearer, was transformed by all means available. In the process of beautifying its players, Hollywood transformed an entire society's ideas of what was beautiful in the face. Close-ups were the essential means of capturing emotion and perfectly symmetrical or arresting features were essential for leading artists. Since sound films were based on dialogue, mouth and teeth were far more important on film than in life. Teeth had to be even, emphasized and, sometimes, brought forward cosmetically. Concentration on the mouth and lips in film generally not only accentuated these features in the players but in their audiences' expectations of what was desirable.

Hollywood makeup might be heavy but it could not be successful—unlike stage makeup—if it were crude. Thus the Hollywood studios' concentration on subtlety of eyeliners, eyelashes, accentuated cheekbones, and tight jaws was of considerable significance for the cosmetic industry as a whole, precisely because Hollywood raised people's expectations about their own appearance. Put crudely, this might mean that girls living on modest incomes might want to look like their favorite actresses. More profoundly, people appreciated the benefits of subtle makeup for themselves so that they could present themselves to best advantage. This was a revolution of sorts. Some of these changes, such as large and prominent teeth and slightly hollow cheeks, would have been thought unattractive and almost ugly in certain earlier societies. Initially, they did not amount to universal ideals of beauty but they were so persuasively and emphatically presented in film after film that they established basic criteria for beauty in a whole society.

With the advent of synthetic fabrics and mass-produced tailoring, the whole concept of fashion and style in dress had already changed profoundly. The lines of clothes became longer and more svelte. Moreover, slimness rather than curvature was promoted in advertising photographs. Because drawings and photographs are essentially two-dimensional, what was important was not so much that clothes looked well on the human figure in the round but on line drawings and photographs in print. Thus it was less important for a costume to look well on a person than for it to look elegant in print. Horizontal and vertical lines were far more important than depth. Not only the drawings but also the models who first displayed the clothes had to look well in photos and needed to be as slim and elongated, and, by implication, as two-dimensional as possible in order to show the two-dimensional designs off to greatest effect. Hollywood carried this cult further. People captured on film and, later, television, tended to look slightly heavier than in real life. Hence, it was most important for leading and romantic players to be slightly underweight if they were to look their best on film and have flesh impact—unless, of course, there was a deliberate point to their being fat (like Ollie Hardy and W. C. Fields) or with an odd shape that could be used in character parts (like Charles Laughton or Boris Karloff).

The emphasis on a certain artificial idea of what was handsome or beautiful enhanced the reputation of its players and ensured its image of physical perfection but often limited the dramatic quality of its principal product, the films. This can be seen in the partnership of German immigrants Josef von Sternberg and Marlene Dietrich. Josef von Sternberg directed several films with Marlene Dietrich rich in exotic atmospheres and in shimmering chiaroscuro of light and shade that make them seem significant in comparison to the anodyne lighting of other films. However, they are essentially empty, suffering from the same vapid plots and characterization as most other Hollywood films.

His second sound film, *The Blue Angel* (1930), was the most celebrated and probably the best Sternberg-Dietrich collaboration. It is a modern version of the Greek legend of Circe, a temptress who bewitches men who should know better and thus turns them into swine. It is also a tragedy of the downfall of the authoritarian but sterile schoolteacher, Professor Unrat, played by Emil Jannings, who is her principal victim. He follows her recklessly into a disastrous marriage and an ignominious end as night club cleaner and buffoon. His classroom is a cage but when he flies the coop, Lola-Lola uses him and casts him away like the cuckold she has made of him. Both Unrat's callous pupils and his indifferent night club coworkers fail to appreciate his human qualities. The students, in particular, are shown as incipient Nazis.

Von Sternberg's films after *The Blue Angel* became ever more elaborate and sumptuous, reaching an apogee in *The Scarlet Empress* (1934) with Dietrich as Catherine the Great and Harpo Marx as her discarded husband, Peter III. However, despite such powerful evocations of period atmosphere as the marriage ceremony between the timid ingenue princess from Germany and the half-crazed tsarevitch, von Sternberg's film rarely peers beneath the surface. This was a perennial problem in the whole series of baroque Sternberg-Dietrich collaborations, such as *Morocco* (1930), *Shanghai Express* (1932), and *The Devil Is a Woman* (1934). Too much was surrendered in the attempt to transform Marlene Dietrich into a timeless beauty of dazzlingly luminous appearance. Nothing she did dramatically had real thrust or emphasis. Her face was plasticized by cosmetic artists and lighting men and remained inexpressive rather than enigmatic or mysterious.

Directors in the 1930s

Despite the emphasis on glamor and surface, certain directors did emerge with strong personal visions during the 1930s.

John Ford had the same sentimental values as D. W. Griffith and he celebrated ordinary people and their homegrown institutions in films that were accessible as well as posing major symbols. In telling his stories Ford emphasized canyons, plains, and skies. However he minimised symbol and metaphor in order to propel exciting stories forward. The first film in which he revealed his strength was *The Informer,* about a traitor to the IRA during "the troubles" who pays physically and psychologically for his error. Not only did Ford have the considerable advantage of a strong screenplay by Dudley Nichols but also telling photography by Joseph Angst. Ford maximized the photography in a series of dissolves and blurred focuses to convey the tortured mental state of his antihero. Ford chose as his symbol of relentless pursuit by the betrayed revolutionaries a blind man, akin to Blind Pew in *Treasure Island,* whose black form, tapping its way along with a cane, follows Gypo, the traitor, wherever he goes. Blind justice as an avenging angel was an obvious enough symbol but it succeeded far more than von Sternberg's ornate symbols as a representation of internal and external guilt because it could also be taken literally.

Ford's most famous film, *Stagecoach* (1939), was successful enough to revive the fading fortunes of the western. This was somewhat ironic because the film was essentially a conventional interior drama of conversation and surfaces, capped by a crude chase between cowboys and Indians for the finale. The stagecoach was intended as a symbol of settled society on the move, a machine built to win the untamed west, although a railroad train would have been a more appropriate symbol. Its occupants were intended as a microcosm of society, with such archetypes as an outlaw and shady dance hall girl with hearts of gold, a young matron in need of being awoken to others' values, a drunken doctor who reforms, and a hypocritical banker who has stolen from his own bank but inveighs continuously against the errors

Twenty-six year old newcomer Orson Welles (upper left) dominated *Citizen Kane* (1941), his first film. Widely praised for skillful and evocative use of montage, dissolve, and sound, the film was a complex screen biography of a press tycoon, clearly based on William Randolph Hearst, and a lugubrious indictment of American pursuit of wealth and power at the expense of personal integrity. (RKO; Museum of Modern Art Film Stills Archive).

of his companions. The banker character might have been written and defined by Griffith, as might the prim busybodies who hound doctor and dance hall girl out of town at the start of the movie. Ford's special talents for emphasizing the interior strengths of little people were seen at their best in his film versions of John Steinbeck's novel, *The Grapes of Wrath* (1940). This protest work about the injustices that befall the dispossessed Oakies drew especially strong performances from Henry Fonda and Jane Darwell.

Howard Hawks made more active, and more violent films with an even stronger emphasis on plot than Ford. In this respect he was somewhat like Thomas Ince and also in his concentration on the difference between outer and inner strength. A routine Hawks film would focus on a strong man who discovers his vulnerability under pressure but survives, and a more fragile man who has surprising reserves of resilience to make him join his tougher companion, as happened in *The Criminal Code* (1931). Hawks's legacy was a series of dramatic thrillers in praise of macho men—*Scarface* (1932), *To Have and Have Not* (1944), and *The Big Sleep* (1948). All were shot with conventional studio paraphenalia, except for the westerns that convey the excitement of taming a wilderness.

British immigrant Alfred Hitchcock managed the transition from English to American filmmaking after 1939. His entire career was a tribute to the close relationship between American and British filmmaking after the introduction of sound. Hitchcock's films were apolitical and inevitably took place in the well-heeled world of cafe society, where smooth men wooed outwardly cool women. Gerald Mast suggests that Hitchcock's films took the form of mysteries with psychology or psychological dramas with mystery. The plots usually mixed drama and suspense with macabre comedy and revolved around international conspiracies or disturbed antiheroes. Hitchcock's films had murders committed in such public places as theaters, parks, and trains and they often culminated in improbable chases in famous locations that were dramatic enough in themselves. Hitchcock's special hallmarks were intense suspense, bathos, and irony, supported by deft cutting and sure command of detail, as in *The 39 Steps* (1935), *Rebecca* (1940), *Suspicion* (1941), and *Saboteur* (1942). In *The 39 Steps* a Scottish landlady discovers the film's first corpse and begins to scream while Hitchcock cuts to the whistle of a train moving toward Scotland, thereby superseding, while exaggerating, the natural scream.

Unlike other significant directors with several films that were artistically successful, Orson Welles's reputation rests primarily on three films: *Citizen Kane* (1941), *The Magnificent Ambersons* (1942), and *Chimes at Midnight* (1966), a screen adaptation of Shakespeare's history plays with Falstaff. Welles had been sought by RKO of Hollywood because of his successes in the theater with the Mercury Theater group. He chose for his first, and most famous project, *Citizen Kane,* a fictional biography suggested by the career of William Randolph Hearst. Welles was only twenty-six yet he acted in, directed, wrote, edited, and designed a film that was controversial on three levels—as a debunking biography; for its stylistic innovations and complexity; and as a sociological exposure of the hollowness of power politics. Welles devised and cunningly played with the most innovative camera work, managing to shoot close-up and distant scenes together and keep each in focus, with many scenes lit from behind, and with parodies of such newsreels as *The March of Time* to comment ironically on the passing of a celebrated man. The use of shadows and depth in *Citizen Kane* was partly the result of the use of new incandescent studio lighting (in contrast with the old carbon-arc lamps) and the use of high-speed panchromatic film that permitted a deeper field of vision. Welles's proven experience in radio was also much in evidence with a whole variety of sound effects.

The plot is a maze, leading to discovery of the significance of Charles Foster Kane, the great newspaper man's, last word, "Rosebud." It begins with the exterior of the mansion and moves step by step closer to the heart of the fallen man. Like a classical drama in five acts, the story begins with an exposition (the superficial newsreel). It is followed by a second act of development (the banker's version of Charles Foster Kane's youth). The third act is incident and crisis (the associate's account of Kane's business ventures and unfulfilled first marriage). The fourth act is the unraveling (the best-friend-turned-enemy's account of Kane's abandonment of principles and his failure to win political office, followed by his living entombment in a fantastic castle, Xanadu). The final act of catastrophe (the breaking up of Xanadu by workmen after Kane's death) ends with the destruction of his property, including the burning of a childhood sleigh, the "Rosebud." "Rosebud" represents all the life that has been drained away from the old tyrant, coming from innocence rather than maturity. As Robert Frost observed, "Rosebud" was the road not taken.

Welles's central probing question was why Charles Foster Kane's career began with such promise and ended in ignominy. Film historian Gerald Mast believes that the implied answer is a con-

Two stars who could not see into the future. *Dark Victory* (1940), directed by Edmund Goulding, had pouting socialite Bette Davis going resolutely blind to the sound of music and set a trend toward unhappy endings. Any irony in the title could not possibly have been foreseen by the star and her supporting player, young Ronald Reagan. (Museum of Modern Art Film Stills Archive).

demnation of certain American values—that love is a casualty in the relentless pursuit of wealth and power. Moreover, the film suggests that wealth and power are no compensation for a life without love. Kane believes in bulk buying, whether the commodity is newspapers, furnishings, or political votes. The public resists his hollow demonstrations of love and he fails to win high office. As an impresario he can train his second wife to become an opera singer but he cannot breathe talent into her poor voice and her career fails. Thus he confines the two of them in a loveless marriage amid a fantastic mausoleum of dead objects.

The parallels between the real tycoon William Randolph Hearst and Welles's creation, Charles Foster Kane; between Hearst's mistress and protégée and Kane's second wife; and between Hearst's

Californian mansion, San Simeon, and Kane's outlandish castle, Xanadu, in Florida, were not lost on any informed person. Not only did the Hollywood moguls find the satire upon Hearst too close for comfort as well as too explosive politically, but they were also disturbed by the film's failure at the box office. It was not what people wanted to see—a sombre melodrama that required audience concentration and openly criticized American goals, instead of a conventional, glossy story.

Whatever the film's merits as sociological comment, the whole is not equal to the sum of its parts. The nub of the story, the significance of "Rosebud," is dramatically uninteresting, not to say abstruse. Moreover, the characters are not fully developed because they are secondary to directorial inventiveness, including the breaking up of the screenplay into five separate synopses. *Citizen Kane* provided other directors with insights as to what could be achieved by montages, complex composition, and shots to the ceiling, but it reminded them not to neglect an audience's needs. While having no doubts about Welles's versatility, RKO was concerned about his failure to draw the crowds and thus began to restrict his control of his own work.

Welles's second film, *The Magnificent Ambersons* (1942), also explored the harmful effect that an egomaniac can wreak on family and friends and, once again, Welles employed some striking compositions in shadow and depth and effective montage sequences to show time passing and fortunes changing. Despite stylish acting, a conventional and somewhat implausible ending in which the callow young scion (Tim Holt) is transformed, and formulaic editing imposed on the film by the studio, the finished film was also a commercial failure. Welles now found Hollywood's gates closed to him, although he could prise them open briefly from time to time.

By the late 1930s it was clear to most informed members of the film community that Hollywood could not survive in the same form much longer. The very success of the great studio system was to be the cause of its downfall. The elephantine system could be hugely successful for a short time until initially undiscriminating audiences became satiated with a diet of similar products. Once this had happened, the studios were too immured in their

Thank Your Lucky Stars (1943) was typical of Hollywood's buoyant musical films during World War II in which all-star tuneful extravaganzas ended in a resounding finale. Here tinsel stars and planets glisten amid dry ice and a curtain call line up of Alexis Smith (center back) and (at front) Dennis Morgan, Joan Leslie, Eddie Cantor, and Dinah Shore. (Museum of Modern Art Film Stills Archive).

own industrial system to be able to respond quickly and decisively enough to the postwar challenges of television, the drift to the suburbs, and, with it, the increasing range of leisure pursuits on offer. In the meantime, the problem was postponed by the boom years of World War II in which the advent of television was itself postponed and audiences at home and abroad were so eager for entertainment that nearly all films, whether good, bad, or indifferent, did well at the box office.

Meanwhile, in 1938 the Department of Justice instituted an antitrust investigation into such restrictive practices in the film industry as block-booking, price-fixing, and pooling agreements between the theaters. Most notorious of all Hollywood's supposed abuses was the convention of a company producing and distributing its movies and also owning the cinemas where they were shown. This would reach a climax in 1948 when all the major companies agreed to give up the so-called restrictive practices. This allowed the "Little Three" studios (Universal, Columbia, and United Artists) to retire from the case because they owned few theaters. By 1952 all of the "Big Five" (Loew's, MGM, Paramount, Warner Brothers, and Twentieth Century Fox) had agreed to separate production and distribution from exhibition.

11

REQUIEM, BUT NO PEACE
The Lost Generation
and the Arts

"**Y**OU ARE all a lost generation," is the first of the two epigraphs to Ernest Hemingway's novel, *Fiesta,* or *The Sun Also Rises* (1926). The remark is accredited to Gertrude Stein and this pithy observation has remained as the unofficial title for the dominant literary generation of the 1920s, although Hemingway subsequently regretted using the phrase and Gertrude Stein denied ever having uttered it.

The writers of the lost generation were, strictly speaking, expatriates such as Hemingway himself, F. Scott Fitzgerald, Sherwood Anderson, and John Dos Passos, who all spent at least months, if not years, in Paris, but membership can be extended to include those writers who stayed at home and resisted the opportunity for exile with a comfortable bohemian life-style that Paris offered Americans owing to the strength of the dollar. However, in many ways, even those who stayed at home, such as Sinclair Lewis, Ring Lardner, and Eugene O'Neill, were in exile, internal exile. Writers were alienated by the culture of commerce that permeated the superficial, tawdry affluence of America in the 1920s.

The epithet "lost generation" has survived because it evokes the themes of alienation, disillusionment, and cynicism with tradition, religion, and even literature itself that dominated the literature of the 1920s. Yet in many ways these negative attitudes also helped consolidate the beginnings of modernism in America's written culture. The second epigraph to *The Sun Also Rises,* taken from Ecclesiastes, provides the novel with its title and is a poignant expression of Ernest Hemingway's outward pessimism and nihilism: "One generation passeth away, and another generation cometh; but the earth abideth for ever. . . . The sun also riseth, and the sun goeth down, and hasteth to the place where he arose."

Why was the lost generation so cynical, especially toward authority? They knew from their experience in World War I that governments were hardly likely to describe the harsh realities of modern warfare in concrete terms. Instead, official language described the war in terms of a chivalrous crusade, repeating such catchwords as "honor," "sacrifice," "country," such phrases as a "war to end all wars" and a "war to make the world safe for democracy," implying that the hosts of righteousness were doing battle for God against Evil. It was one thing to take up arms to save Anglo-Saxon civilization; it was quite another to endure the boredom and terror of trench warfare. World War I was, as Ernest Hemingway wrote, "the most colossal, murderous, mismanaged butchery that has ever taken place on earth. Any writer who said otherwise lied. So the writers either wrote propaganda, shut up, or fought."

The reality of the war could not be conveyed to those who had not taken part. A gap yawned between those (mainly young) men who had fought and their civilian elders who had not, the first true generation gap of the twentieth century. To the young who endured the war, the crimes of their elders must have seemed endless. Not only had they first blundered into war, but they had also lost a generation of young men and then lost the peace. All that remained intact was the machine—the machine of government as well as the divisions and the weapons of industrialized warfare. According to poet Ezra Pound, in one of the most quoted comments on the war, young men had died "For an old bitch gone in the teeth, / For a botched civilization."

One result was the sheer hatred by some artists and writers of all traditional forms of authority. Another was a search for a clean slate. In Europe these impulses led to the Dada movement that ridiculed bourgeois worship of great monuments of culture past and dead artists as divine creators. Thus the French artist Marcel Duchamp, an intermittent resident in the United States, painted a mustache and goatee beard on the Mona Lisa in *L.H.O.O.Q.* (1919), a title with letters chosen to make, in French, a lewd title meaning "She's got a hot ass."

Despite their criticisms of the way the war was waged, some of the novelists admitted to a sensual enjoyment of it. It was an initiation as Malcolm Cowley explained in *Exile's Return:* "The war created in young men a thirst for abstract danger, not suffered for a cause but courted for itself; if later they believed in the cause, it was partly in recognition of the danger it conferred on them." But this sentimental view and accumulative sense of nostalgia that pervades the war novels, "the wish to capture some remembered thing," had no practical value. The ambulance drivers, the young men betrayed by the war, were, truly, "a lost generation." "It was lost because its training had prepared it for another world than existed after the war and the war prepared it for nothing." Yet this generation had a unity and therefore a strength: "They were, in the first place, a generation and probably the first real one in the history of American letters. They came to maturity during a period of violent change, when the influence of time seemed temporarily more important than that of class or locality. Everywhere after the war people were fumbling for a word to express their feeling that youth had a different outlook."

The Impotent Hero

The Sun Also Rises by Ernest Hemingway (1898–1961) is one of the definitive documents of the lost generation and portrays a group of expatriates in Europe in all their futile dissipation and jaded cynicism. The central character of this novel, and its first-person narrator, is far from being a conventional hero. Indeed, Jake Barnes is the archetypal protagonist of the literature and the history of the twenties, the impotent hero. An injury sustained during World War I has emasculated him and condemns him to an unrequited and emotionally destructive love for nyphomaniac Lady Brett Ashley. She tells him at the end of the novel, "We could have had such a damned good time together." Jake responds with characteristic and emblematic cynicism, "Yes. Isn't it pretty to think so?" Men, we gather, pay for life by experience, or chance, or even money. It takes a relatively untarnished young man, the bullfighter, Pedro Romero, to get the better of violence by virtue of his profession. Brett renounces the young bullfighter, having contented herself by teasing Robert Cohn, the Jewish writer, as well as Mike Campbell (her fiancé), and Jake. For Jake himself there is no solace, either physical or mental, in his rejection. He had entered the war as a test of his manhood and it had destroyed his manhood. The novel owes some of its inspiration to T. S. Eliot's poem, *The Waste Land* (1922), which set the pattern and established the mood for the subject of disintegration in twentieth-century literature. Like Eliot's poem, Hemingway's novel reworks the legend of the Holy Grail. In Hemingway's version, Jake Barnes is both questing knight and fisher king with an incurable wound. The mythical cup and lance are life-size.

Jake Barnes must fight for balance. His fascination with bullfights represented a final attempt to get some meaning out of life —a life that has been displaced by the war and turned into a continuous hangover. The bullfight is, both for Jake Barnes and Ernest Hemingway, a palliative to their bewilderment. The matador creates and manipulates his danger; at least in the bullring, chance, the gods, and even governments have no say. "Purity of line" and "grace under pressure" are the responsibility of the individual in this environment. Malcolm Cowley says *Fiesta* captured the mood of a generation: "Young men tried to get as imperturbably drunk as the hero, young women of good families took a succession of lovers in the same heartbroken fashion as the heroine, [and] they all talked like Hemingway characters."

However, Hemingway presented himself as anything but an impotent hero and today his popular reputation as a writer depends to a large extent on the masculine mystique that surrounds his memory. In his youth he developed that passion for active outdoor pursuits, such as hunting and fishing, that was to mark his life and fiction deeply. After working briefly as a journalist in Kansas, eighteen-year-old Hemingway joined a volunteer ambulance unit in France before America entered World War I and then later transferred to the Italian infantry. In 1918 near the Austrian frontier he was severely wounded, an experience after which he "ceased to be hard-boiled," as he expressed it, and, having discovered his own vulnerability, set out to exorcise his own fear of death by confronting it himself or closely observing others in the process of confronting it. Hence, his obsession with violence and terror in boxing, bullfighting, safari, deep-sea fishing, war, and in his writing. Hemingway was a deeply competitive writer in the same way that he lived life as a competition against fear and the emotional void of the modern world. Hemingway's nihilism and his insistence on man's right to choose between stoicism or suicide—this last being the choice Hemingway himself, like his father before him, made in 1961—makes him a truly modern writer and links him to the many moderns who have pondered the human predicament and how to express it. Only illness and numerous physical accidents impeded (but did not end) his astonishing efficiency. It was as if the physical punishment he put his body through was some sort of boxing match with an invisible opponent.

Hemingway's style inspired an entire generation of writers with its directness and apparent simplicity. His first book, *In Our Time* (1925), was a collection of straightforward, attractive, and sometimes brutal short stories written from the expatriate viewpoint and intended to express Hemingway's vision of his home through the largely autobiographical figure of young Nick Adams. His next book *The Torrents of Spring* (1926), was an excursion into the realm of parody and is considered a comic masterpiece. In it Hemingway parodies Sherwood Anderson's novel *Dark Laughter* (1925) with its commonplace portrayal of blacks as the sensual and mystical children of nature who are ingenuously in possession of the secret of life. Hemingway also parodies himself in *The Torrents of Spring,* for the book eventually becomes a satire on the cult of masculinity in American society and American literature. *Fiesta* (or *The Sun Also Rises*) was published in the same year and thus Hemingway was established as a significant and promising young novelist. In 1929 *A Farewell to Arms*—a romantic tragedy of love and war based on the author's own experience during World War I—went a long way toward fulfilling his early promise by virtue of his, by now, characteristic close attention to structure.

Hemingway devised his writing strategies quite early in his career. When he wrote a short story, he would withhold mention of a central fact or problem. When he wrote a novel, he would place it clearly in geography and time. In either form, he devised sentences that carried an emotional impact not by claiming it outright but by giving the reader a crystal-clear understanding of the experience that caused the emotion. Although the last thing we think of Hemingway as being is Victorian, this was exactly the way Queen Victoria herself recorded her experiences in her numerous letters and journals—intense emotion expressed by precise representational facts. The most noted weapon in Hemingway's stylistic armory was his rigorous ability to compress meaning and emotion, giving his work tremendous authority and thrust. His clarity expressed his genius and, at first, made him widely appreciated as the most significant writer in English. In the 1920s his works were fresh, the stories moved quickly, and every page of clear prose seemed to pass a judgment on any excesses in all previous writing. The author's voice was ever present and always hostile to pretense. Thus Hemingway's words always disclosed his dislike of rhetoric and cant.

A Farewell to Arms is also the title of a poem to Queen Elizabeth I by George Peele. Its subject is the ephemeral, fading nature of young and physical pleasure in comparison with more lasting, sterling virtues:

> Beauty, strength, youth, are flowers but fading seen;
> Duty, faith, love, are roots, and ever green.

Hemingway turns this point to ironic and dramatic effect in his novel.

A Farewell to Arms opens with a heavily ironic passage that shows how individual death is absorbed into a bland and uncaring statistical estimate: "At the start of the winter came the permanent rain and with the rain came the cholera. But it was checked and in the end only seven thousand died of it in the army." Although this story of a romance between American medical officer Frederic Henry and English nurse Catherine Barkley, set against the dramatic background of the Italian front in World War I, is generally regarded as a typical antiwar novel, Hemingway's treatment of his characters and their response to the situation are complex and ambivalent. This is not some conventional story of a modern Romeo and Juliet torn apart by authority in World War I. While clearly indicting the entire conduct of the war and its slogans, Hemingway presents Frederic Henry as neither romantic nor idealist but, rather, as a callow youth who starts an affair with Catherine because this will be a more pleasant way of enjoying sex than going down to the officers' brothel. Catherine, having denied sex to her English fiancé who has been killed, is full of the pleasures of the body for Frederic Henry. Their attitude is entirely childish. At one point, when he is in hospital recovering from his injury, they worry that a lack of supply of wounded men in the war to the hospital will mean Catherine must be redeployed and their nocturnal trysts will come to an end. Sometimes he is irritated by her need to be told he loves her, for he does not care for the emotional complications of a lasting relationship that he, at first, finds difficult to sustain.

The only suitable reaction to the absurd chaos of war, as demonstrated in the chapters describing the retreat from Caporetto, is a personal retreat into oneself, making "a separate peace." The rhetoric of war is consciously rejected:

I was always embarrassed by the words sacred, glorious, and sacrifice and the expression in vain. We had heard them, sometimes standing in the rain . . . and I had seen nothing sacred, and the things that were glorious had no glory and the sacrifices were like the stockyards at Chicago if nothing was done with the meat except to bury it. There were many words that you could not stand to hear and finally only the names of places had dignity. . . . Abstract words such as glory, honor, courage, or hallow were obscene beside the concrete names of villages, the numbers of roads, the names of rivers, the numbers of regiments and the dates.

The result is not just an attitude to war but an attitude to life that Frederic Henry sums up in his description of ants falling off a log into a camp fire.

Eventually, hero and heroine feel impelled by their emotions to desert their posts. Yet it does conflict with Frederic Henry's sense of duty. And he suffers a judgment when both Catherine and his newborn son die, for presuming that he still has a world of his own imagination to retreat to. It is not only military arms but also the arms of the woman he loves that Frederic Henry must bid farewell to. The meek may only inherit the earth if the earth is left to them. One cannot exist peaceably in a world of violence. Some critics suggest Hemingway's characters can only fulfill themselves by sublimating their emotional energies in some act that ends in their death. Otherwise, they are faced with an alternative, emasculation. At the close of the book, during a shower of rain, Henry's feelings are more passionately expressed when he feels sentence has been passed on him for running away:

Poor little kid, I wished the hell I'd been choked like that. No I didn't. Still there would not be all this dying to go through. Now Catherine would die. . . . You never had time to learn. They threw you in and told you the rules and the first time they caught you off base they killed you.

In the army the simplest decisions are made for one, and in war, the greatest also. Hemingway moves from society to self in his concentration on the lonely, troubled hero. He is revolted by the phoney values of the world. He seems aware of the essential tragedy of man's existence. All he can do, like Frederic Henry when he walks from the hospital in the rain, is meet it with dignity and stoical endurance.

If we were to select one author as archetype of the lost generation in terms of both literary output and personal history, then F. Scott Fitzgerald would come closest. His first book, *This Side of Paradise,* appeared appropriately in 1920 at the beginning of the decade that has become irrevocably linked with his name and it

Novelist and short story writer F. Scott Fitzgerald, a key player among the lost generation, is highly regarded for the stylistic grace, emotional impact, and penetrating, psychological characterizations in his best works. In the 1930s, when the public mood shifted, it was no longer ready for the perceptions of a writer becoming increasingly alcoholic and tormented by the mental problems of a deranged wife. By the time Carl Van Vechten took this photograph on June 4, 1937, the glamor had worn thin. (Library of Congress).

immediately established his reputation as an acutely poignant and cynical commentator on the vagaries of his time. Critics and readers alike expected great things that were fulfilled neither by the publication of two selections of short stories, *Flappers and Philosophers* (1920) and *Tales of the Jazz Age* (1922), nor by the weak play, *The Vegetable* (1923), and his second novel, *The Beautiful and Damned* (1922). However, 1925 saw the publication of *The Great Gatsby*, a literary masterpiece and a powerful evocation of all that was rotten in the American dream in general and the dream decade of the 1920s in particular. The hero, Jay Gatsby, is a true romantic hero of his time who tragically expends vast amounts of time, energy, emotion, and money in his useless courtship of Daisy Buchanan, unfulfilled wife of the insensitive and adulterous Tom Buchanan. Yet no matter how tragic Gatsby is, his heroism is tainted by the fact that his money—the vital piece of charm he was lacking five years previously when Daisy first spurned him—has been acquired through illegal means, probably bootlegging.

Fitzgerald's heroes are measured less by their attempt to do things well than to do them stylishly. His heroes do not love a woman; they love youth and their inability to accept aging is accompanied by realization of their own romantic inadequacy. His composition of characters was plastic, a synthesis of half a dozen people. Thus, like the reader, he never saw Jay Gatsby clear himself, as he explains in a letter to John Peale Bishop of August 1925, because "he started as one man I knew and then changed into myself."

Jay Gatsby dominates the novel. The mystery of his past is carefully turned into suspense by effective use of gossip at parties. His adolescent romanticism is humorously obvious at the tea party and it is this innocent naivety that renders him vulnerable and eventually leads to his murder. The novel contains a whole series of aligned images—water, sport, couples, riches, class, family, and self-image—that reinforce the undercurrents of doubt and uncertainty. Thus sportswoman and snob Jordan Baker is fashioned in the image of a golf champion, a fact that makes her first attractive, then less so to the narrator, Nick Carraway, who eventually recognizes her sportsmanship as a jaunty but contemptuous charade played especially for a gullible public. Her cheating in a golf tournament is on a par, so to speak, with Tom Buchanan's cheating with Myrtle Wilson and then over the murder of Gatsby. They are both careless people who use their wealth and position to screen themselves from inconvenient reality. Gatsby needs wealth to court Daisy and will do anything to acquire it through Meyer Wolfsheim, the underworld gangster who supposedly fixed the World Series in 1919, prompting Nick to remark, "It never occurred to me that one man could start to play with the faith of fifty million people—with the single-mindedness of a burglar blowing a safe." The explicit link between sport and criminality underlines the irony of a nation childishly investing so much faith in a sporting fix. Fitzgerald can be a violent writer, notably in his account of Tom Buchanan's sportsman's physique as "a body capable of enormous leverage—a cruel body," and with a punch hard enough to break his mistress's nose in a single swipe at a party.

Nick Carraway is passionately attracted to Gatsby's glamor while being deeply aware of the tawdriness that underlies the tinsel. Nick attends Gatsby's parties and feels at ease with the elitist Buchanans. He shows both his general ignorance and inside knowledge about Gatsby but does not discover the whole truth about the millionaire's past as James Gatz until near the close of the novel. The novel emphasizes the power and glamor of money and the way it distorts people's emotions. Carraway makes much of his honesty but at the outset encapsulates the central theme of the novel by stating how his great uncle avoided danger by paying for a substitute to fight in his place in the American Civil War, then built up a profitable hardware business, and used the money to buy a cloak of respectability. It is Gatsby's tragedy that he enters the game too late and is proved maladroit.

It was, perhaps, inevitable that Fitzgerald should never attain such formal artistic perfection again in his career. Inevitable, partly because of the difficulty in repeating such a feat and partly because his personal life degenerated progressively into confusion and tragedy with his wife, Zelda, suffering from severe mental illness, his own declining financial resources, and a lack of confidence in his ability as a writer. Although Fitzgerald did what Gatsby had failed to do, earned enough money to win back the girl he loved but who wanted affluence, malign events turned the fairy story into a horror tale since Zelda slid into madness. She probably conspired against Fitzgerald and he proved himself unable to confront his problems. Thus his two collections of short stories, *All the Sad Young Men* (1926), *Taps at Reveille* (1935), and his novel, *Tender Is the Night* (1934), paled in comparison with *Gatsby* and were received without anything like the same enthusiasm.

Fitzgerald felt at a very low ebb in 1933 when his obsession with style condemned him to a literary treadmill of technical variations on a few themes. "We authors must repeat ourselves," he wrote in the *Saturday Evening Post* of March 4, 1933. "We have two or three great and moving experiences in our lives . . . then we learn our trade, well or less well, and we tell our two or three stories—each time in a new disguise—maybe ten times, maybe a hundred, as long as people will listen."

Tender Is the Night was planned as an epic novel with many diverse targets and, perhaps, its subjects could not be managed easily, certainly not neatly. One of the central themes is the demoralization of a promising American psychiatrist, Dick Diver, tempted and bought by the affluent family of a girl, Nicole, emotionally disturbed after being forced into incest with her father. He marries her and they prove sexually incompatible. Nicole, like a parasite, absorbs her husband's failing energies until she is completely cured and his true professional life is over. His youth spent, his charm evaporated, he has to eke out a broken life as an alcoholic doctor in small-town America. In a sense, the story is about Nicole's cure. In the case of Dick Diver, Fitzgerald's transformation of his character from one based on others to one based on himself was only half-completed. Since he had always emphasized primary personal emotion and had not concerned himself overmuch with narrative and conventional literary techniques, his work went wrong when he could not summon up the requisite personal emotion at will.

English critic Donald Monk explains how the strands of the plot snarl and tangle in both the first version, with its glittering beginning as seen by film starlet Rosemary Hoyt, heroine of *Daddy's Girl,* who provides "Rosemary's Angle" on the Divers at play on the Riviera, and the second, which is a straightforward chronological narrative. Fitzgerald, with his easy stylistic grace, found it difficult to distinguish between erotic love and familial love. However, attracted to the formidable women characters, Nicole and her sister, Baby Warren, and Rosemary and her mother, he found himself brooding on the corrosion of willpower, instead of analyzing it. It is the uncertain definition of a point of view that undermines the novel and the filaments of style are scattered in too many directions. *Tender Is the Night* is awash with images breaking surface but lacking direction. The themes of Nicole's cure and Dick's deterioration are supported by a series of trans-sexual mammary images, notably Nicole's dependence on him as "her dry suckling on his lean chest."

The moment of crisis never arrives. The plot of *Tender Is the Night* is predicated on a continuous postponement of a moment of dramatic truth until the need for it has passed. This is undoubt-edly true to certain situations in real life but it leaves the reader dissatisfied. The final page contains what is perhaps the most understated and, therefore, brutal and dramatically effective, dis-missal of any fictional hero in modern literature. *Tender Is the Night* does contain significant images of cars, notably the sharp persuasive image of a mountain-climbing car that is used to ex-press Dick Diver's own predicament.

Mountain-climbing cars are built on a slant similar to the angle of a hat brim of a man who doesn't want to be recognised. As water gushed from the chamber under the car, Dick was impressed with the ingenuity of the whole idea—a complementary car was now taking on mountain water at the top and would pull the lightened car up by gravity, as soon as the breaks were released.

Dick's preoccupation with this unexceptional car is the natural response of an ambitious, ingenious man who wants to rise to the top without effort. The pulled-down hat brim reinforces Dick's future speculation as to how far relations can be stretched between doctor and patient. What is most telling is the explanation of mechanical balance and symbiosis, transference of mass and en-ergy, that reverses Dick's dream of an easy climb and, ironically, implies how his strength will be poured into Nicole.

Fitzgerald died in Hollywood, alcoholic and exhausted from hackwork at the age of forty-four.

Unlike Fitzgerald, John Dos Passos (1896–1970), illegitimate son of a Portuguese immigrant lawyer and a southern woman, worked in Hollywood for just one year of his full and varied career. In 1934, in the midst of economic depression, Dos Passos found the big money in the Hollywood dream factory. The fact that he lasted only one year there was not surprising. Dos Passos's importance lies more in his uniquely personal contribution to the development of American literature than in his membership of any literary school. He spent the obligatory time in Europe, first as a member of the French, then the American, medical corps during World War I, and then, briefly, as a literary expatriate in Paris where he met writers such as Gertrude Stein, Hemingway, Fitzgerald, and Sherwood Anderson. Here the similarity ends. Although Dos Passos shared the lost generation's disillusionment with the postwar world, he was neither nihilistic nor disaffected and preferred to expend his energies in both writing books that closely expressed the problems of American society, and in supporting various political causes that he deemed crucial to the well-being of the nation's democracy.

His first book was *One Man's Initiation—1917* (1920), a clumsy but emotionally powerful war novel about an ambulance driver. This was followed by *Three Soldiers* (1921) that successfully explored the dislocating effects of war on three different character types. The inhuman qualities of the war are emphasised by images of metal. The attempt of the army in *Three Soldiers* to fashion tin soldiers out of young men of flesh and blood is indicated by the consistent use of words and phrases of metallic connotation in the sequence of chapter titles. Five of the total six have this connotation: "Making the Mold," "The Metal Cools," "Machines," "Rust," and "Under the Wheels." The men's debasement and initiation is also suggested by sexual experiences. The shock of first intercourse is tantamount to initiation into the war, and this is used in two ways. First, it provides a social comment on changing patterns of behavior by indicating the lapse of romantic ignorance before marriage. Second, the degradation of men before whores and the hypocritical military arrangements in procuring women but punishing men who contract disease, provide easy targets for criticism of the running of the war. However, it was the novel *Manhattan Transfer* (1925) that marked the emergence of both Dos Passos's mature style and his mature outlook on the world. It is a collective portrait of the vast and varied, but, to Dos Passos, diseased life of New York City, made up of scores of fictional episodes. Dos Passos used impressionism, expressionism, montage, simultaneity, reportage—all the new literary techniques that appeared for the most part in the twentieth century and can be conveniently labeled as literary modernism. His diverse style unfolding like a kaleidoscope facilitated his attempt to fill the role of novelist, in his opinion, "a sort of second-class historian of the age he lives in."

Time has shown that Dos Passos was in fact underrating his own talents as a novelist and historian. Since the trilogy of novels, *The Forty-Second Parallel* (1930), *1919* (1932), and *The Big Money* (1936), were collected under the title *U.S.A.* in 1938, he has proved that fiction can effectively and admirably fill the role of history, and has directly inspired in thematic and stylistic terms many leading contemporary novelists, including Norman Mailer and E. L. Doctorow, and the historian William Manchester. *U.S.A.* is an unparalleled epic—or rather, anti-epic, since this book is a criticism, not an exaltation, of American society—and covers the nation's history from the turn of the century to the end of the 1920s. It achieves this through devices such as "Newsreel" (reconstructions or news reporting), the "Camera Eye" (impressionistic visions analogous to the cinematographic viewpoint), and slanted biographies of leading historical figures such as Carnegie, Edison, Debs, and Frank Lloyd Wright, who represent the entire range of the political spectrum. The fictional and factual stories end in what Marcus Cunliffe has called "the defeat of the individual on every front." As the reader learns of the different fates of the characters he is meant to understand that most of them are destroyed within themselves by their experience in war. Man's heroism is measured not by his achievements but by the difficulties he overcomes. Thus Dos Passos shows his radicals, Mary French and Ben Compton, with whom he sympathizes, suffering more from their own limitations than the injustices of society. In fact, the three novels gain from their understated sense of irony —the ironies of fate by which acquaintanceships begin and end, and the ironies of history that bring bad deeds from good men, and reduce the well-meaning attempts of the wise to the ineffectual efforts of the incompetent.

Dos Passos was close to the Communist party during the 1920s and most of the 1930s although he never actually joined, and by 1939, with the publication of the novel, *Adventures of a Young Man* whose protagonist is betrayed by the Communists, he had moved firmly to the center of the political arena. His early political radicalism was the most obvious feature that distinguished him from the lost generation and it was a radicalism rooted in pure American soil: a concern for, and ultimate faith in, democratic values; an acute appreciation of the theories of the social scientist Thorstein Veblen; an open admiration for the heroes of the early American Left, Emma Goldman, Max Eastman, and the IWW. He looked on World War I as a giant conspiracy against humanity. To him, the war was part of a capitalist attack on the values and ideals of Jeffersonian democracy, a conspiracy that continued into the 1920s with the Great Red Scare, the persecution of labor and labor leaders, and the shooting of strikers. The plight of the Italian immigrant anarchists, Nicola Sacco and Bartolomeo Vanzetti, exemplified this attack. Dos Passos wrote a pamphlet, "Facing the Chair," on behalf of these two unfortunates. Immediately after their execution, Dos Passos went to work on *The Forty-Second Parallel,* the first of the *U.S.A.* trilogy.

Sherwood Anderson (1876–1941), too, was barely a member of the lost generation although, like Dos Passos, he shared some themes in common with Hemingway and Fitzgerald. Anderson's best-known work is *Winesburg, Ohio* (1919), a series of interrelated tales about the thwarted lives of small-town people, trapped in ignorance and intolerance, yet groping for life. In most of the tales there appears the figure of George Willard, a young newspaper reporter and, like Hemingway's Nick Adams, a surrogate for the author himself. Willard eventually rejects the town of Winesburg and sets off in search of the qualities and values of personal freedom, sexual vitality, lyric insight, and blood brotherhood that are in very short supply amongst the narrow-minded

REQUIEM, BUT NO PEACE • 399

and suffocatingly conservative inhabitants of the small town. At the age of fifty-one Anderson returned to Winesburg, Virginia, having bought two weekly country newspapers and between 1927 and 1931 he wrote personal essays in the form of editorials, character sketches, and mood pieces. Anderson had his greatest successes in the short story rather than the novel and this was where his real talent lay. He once assessed himself as, "The minor author of a minor masterpiece." While this is essentially true, it fails to express the powerful influence that he had on other writers as Hemingway and Faulkner. Indeed, William Faulkner once called him, "The father of my generation of American writers and the tradition of American writing which our successors will carry on."

Jewish-American novels captured the essence of the immigrant experience because of their continuous unfolding of stories about an individual at odds with the world around him. For the heroes, and, one suspects, the authors, life is difficult, anyway, and the pressures of an urban, fragmented society upon individuals make it doubly so. Yet the novels are essentially optimistic, rather than pessimistic, since a central theme is that while life may be harsh, it is man's duty to try and understand his role in it and show understanding and compassion for the difficulties of his fellow men.

Ludwig Lewisohn, a German Jew, arrived in the United States in 1890 when he was seven. He came from a tradition of German Jews who had developed Reform Judaism. Lewisohn was dismayed to find how American society practiced subtle but hard forms of discrimination against even modern Jews. He described his disappointment in *Up Stream* (1922) and to maximum effect in his best work, *The Island Within* (1928). Lewisohn became convinced that the only way Jews could become well-adjusted was as individuals and for this they must revive their sense of a Jewish people.

The Island Within examines the psychological impact of anti-Jewish feeling on first- and second-generation American Jews. The novel moves from its opening in Europe to the United States. The hero, Arthur Levy, is initially confident that he is a true American, but gradually he becomes aware of differences between himself and other Americans because of their attitude toward him. The novel is set mainly in the very late nineteenth and early twentieth centuries, a period when Wasp society was resisting the rise of successive groups of Jews in American society. Lewisohn had great difficulty in obtaining a teaching post at university because he was Jewish. Much of *The Island Within* is based on Lewisohn's own experiences and his increasing awareness of Jewish consciousness. In the novel Arthur's Jewishness becomes the central factor in his life as he tries to reach out for the American ideal of equality for all. Eventually, he turns to the idea that Jews must preserve their sense of peoplehood, if they are to remain whole and not become self-hating through forlorn attempts at gaining access to gentile society.

Other second-generation Jewish immigrants were hit by discrimination and expressed the problems they experienced as marginal men while exploring the larger, social issues raised by prejudice. Some second-generation American Jews, especially in New York and Chicago, turned to a new orthodoxy to help them resolve such problems, the Communist party. Their contribution was significant and out of all proportion to their numerical membership, whether as organizers, activists, ideologues, or orators. In his pamphlet, "The Immigrant Experience in American Literature" (1982), Edward A. Abrahamson explains, "Whereas the writers of . . . the expatriate tradition had represented an educated, literate elite, able to travel abroad and experience an older, fuller, more confident culture, the writers who portrayed the immigrant experience marked a 'proletarianizing' influence which in some ways reflected more accurately what was happening in the United States itself."

Henry Roth was born in Galicia in 1906 and came to the United States as a small child with his mother to meet his father, the experience he draws on at the beginning of his novel, *Call It Sleep* (1934). He enjoyed some security in the Jewish section of the Lower East Side but lost it when the family subsequently moved to Harlem and he encountered anti-Semitism from Irish-Americans. In the Prologue Henry Roth describes the arrival of David Shearl and his mother, Genya, in New York, where they are met by his father, Albert. David is still wearing old-fashioned European clothes and his father, who cannot tolerate the idea of being thought a greenhorn, throws David's blue straw hat into the bay, a symbolic rejection of Europe. The entire scene of their arrival is presented as grim and despondent, rather than optimistic. Even the Statue of Liberty is perceived as something frightening. Liberty was evidently not a Jewish mother. The family live first in the Brownsville section of Brooklyn, later on the Lower East Side. Roth deliberately shifted the emphasis of his description of the Lower East Side to a harsher, cruder environment than the one he remembered. "In reality, I took the violent environment of Harlem—where we lived from 1914 to 1928—and projected it back onto the East Side."

To the boy, David, both his home and the streets outside are dangerous places—the streets because of the roaming gangs of gentile youths, his home because his father has become paranoid, uncertain whether David really is his son, and given to unpredictable bouts of irritation and bad temper. Roth shows tensions between various cultures, Irish and Jewish and Italian, and between two generations of American Jews. The father, Albert's, problems are largely caused by the need to come to terms with new urban society but compounded by his own awkward temperament.

The Impact of Freud

Eugene O'Neill (1888–1953) was the founding father of the modern American theater. O'Neill was the son of the actors James O'Neill (noted for his rendition of the Count of Monte Cristo) and Ellen Quinlan. Eugene O'Neill's early career was very checkered and included periods of acting, office work, gold prospecting, reporting, and, most significantly for his drama, a spell as a seaman. In 1912 he entered a sanitorium and, while recovering there from tuberculosis, he read the great dramatists of the world and began to write himself. In 1916 his first performed play, *Bound East for Cardiff,* was given its premiere at the Provincetown Players' new Playwrights' Theater in New York and thus dates the beginning of serious drama in the United States.

Eugene O'Neill with his wife, Carlotta. O'Neill's plays, with their obsessive characters and highly charged language, owed much to Sigmund Freud. The photograph is among hundreds of people in the worlds of literature, entertainment, and the arts between the 1930s and the 1960s by maverick writer and photographer Carl Van Vechten. (Library of Congress).

O'Neill was fascinated by the vagaries of human motivation and by mankind's self-destructive qualities, and he employed these themes with a pessimistic determinism that qualifies him for associate membership of the lost generation. He is also distinguished from the lost generation by virtue of his intellectual heritage that links him more with such heavyweight literary figures as James Joyce, T. S. Eliot, and August Strindberg, rather than Fitzgerald and Hemingway who never carried intellectual pretensions. The influence of Nietzsche in particular was to prove particularly relevant to O'Neill's work since—when combined with his natural American tendency toward individualistic concerns—it led him into exploration of the nature of self-reliance and heroic individualism in the face of social alienation, geographic isolation, and fervent competition.

There was another influence O'Neill never openly acknowledged. From the start the ideas of Viennese psychiatrist Sigmund Freud were received enthusiastically in America, but this enthusiasm hid the fact that these same ideas were also misperceived and abused by the vast majority of people. In books such as *The Interpretation of Dreams* (1900) and *The Psychopathology of Everyday Life* (1901) Freud explained the importance of the subconscious as a motivating factor in human behavior and provided certain guidelines for interpreting human motivation through analysis of our behavior and our dreams—the only element of our subconscious that we come into direct and knowing contact with. These new analytical techniques were, on the one hand, to prove indispensable to serious artists in their investigations into the mysteries of life and living and, on the other hand, proved extremely diverting and titillating to those who saw Freudian psychology as a means of escape from the inhibiting legacies of previous decades: sexual repression, patriotism, fundamentalist religion, and political idealism. Freud's ideas, apparently, licensed some people to throw these legacies out of the window. This was, of course, a complete distortion of the purposes to which Freud developed his theory. Freud was not an advocate of permissive behavior, but a dour, conservative, and deeply moralistic rationalist who disliked America. It was too brash and vulgar in comparison with the claustrophobic atmosphere and stuffy refinement of his native Vienna. A visit to America in 1909 to lecture at Clark University in Worcester, Massachusetts, did nothing to change his opinion.

Many popular writers produced a synthesis of his work that did nothing to endear America to Sigmund Freud. For example, André Tridon was prolific in his output of books that were a distillation of the more titillating ideas of Freud, Alfred Adler, and Carl Jung. Tridon took their ideas and stirred them enthusiastically as they boiled away in the pot. He was also capable of throwing in his own deeply considered psychological analysis of human behavior as seasoning to this psychological potpourri. Did you know, for example, that rice and old shoes at a wedding are obvious symbols of the semen and the female genitals? As cultural historian Robert Crunden summarizes Freud: "In his analyses of his patients' dreams and neuroses, he discovered what seemed to be an inherent conflict between the demands of human instinct, and the demands of society as a whole. The individual said, 'I want,' and society, from its broader experience, said, 'You can't.' " This was an argument tailor-made for those who hated the ideas of the previous decades and had seen them result in World War I.

Freud's ideas, long known to readers of classic drama—Shakespeare, Sophocles, Euripides, et al.—but now presented in a pseudo-scientific format had a profound impact on artists such as Eugene O'Neill. There are other numerous instances. In a letter to Ernest Hemingway of June 1934 F. Scott Fitzgerald found that "the purpose of a work of fiction is to appeal to the lingering after-effects in the reader's mind as differing from, say, the purpose of oratory or philosophy which respectively leave people in a fighting or a thoughtful mood." Fitzgerald agreed with one romantic tradition that insisted on the primacy of emotional intensity. "Almost everything I write in novels goes, for better or worse, into the subconscious of the reader." He told his daughter, Scottie, in a letter of 1936, "If you have anything to say, anything you feel nobody has ever said before, you have got to feel it so desperately that you will find some way to say it that nobody has ever found before, so that the thing you have got to say and the way of saying it blend as one matter—as indissolubly as if they were conceived together." Max Eastman, editor of *The Masses,* regarded Freud, correctly, not as a scientist "but an artist—a demonological poet—who insisted on peopling an underworld with masked demons who move about in the unlocal dark, controlling our thoughts and the action of our bodies." This was Freud's important contribution to art; he stimulated the artistic intellect and gave new depth to the possibilities for representation and analysis of human motivation.

In his play *The Emperor Jones* (1921), Eugene O'Neill expresses the psychology of his leading character through an experimental drama. This is a tale of a black Pullman porter who has managed to become dictator of a declining West Indian state. Jones suffers from "little formless fears" that are, in fact, in his subconscious, but that appear to him to be physical presences in the jungle that surrounds him. *All God's Chillun Got Wings* (1923) is a treatment of the problems of miscegenation and a diagnosis of how shock can provoke a regression to the mental state of childhood. It was expressed dramatically with the aid of a sophisticated stage set that contracted in size progressively throughout the play. *Desire Under the Elms* (1925) presented a variation on the theme of the Oedipus complex that O'Neill claimed was familiar to him from the original Greek source, rather than as distilled and refined through the mind of Sigmund Freud. *The Great God Brown* (1926) is a bitter examination of the personality masks that people use in their relationships with one another. *Marco Millions* (1928) was a satire on American commercialism transposed to Marco Polo's Venice. *Mourning Becomes Electra* (1931) had a rare psychological intensity, a play indebted to both Aeschylus and Freud, with Greek tragedy transposed to the life of the Mannon family of New England during the era of the American Civil War. O'Neill is undoubtedly America's greatest playwright and this is in no small part due to his understanding and exploitation of psychological factors.

Psychoanalysis became overwhelmingly popular and this affected not only sexual morality but the entire range of human consciousness. By advocating an alternative to society and economics as explanations for human behavior, the emphasis is thrown on the self apart from society. That "self" may be the subliminal-self or the id but it is still the self. Frederick Hoffmann writes that the literature of the 1920s shows ". . . many examples of the mind turning in upon itself, examining, explaining and excusing itself in psychological terms. Interest in self took the place and argued the futility of a sense of social responsibility." This preoccupation with oneself, separate from community and society, explains why politics and economics did not much interest the writers of the 1920s. Apparently, the way to keep psychologically healthy was to indulge one's libido and encourage one's flapper friends to do the same! Newspaper reporters offered instant psychological explanations for murder and divorce cases while columnists asked, "What are little boys made of? Oedipus Rex and

Infantile Sex." Margaret Mead's (1901–1979) book, *Coming of Age in Samoa* (1927), exploited this insatiable curiosity about sex under the guise of analytic anthropology. It quickly became the most surprising best-seller of the decade. However, by omitting Freud's biological determinism and arguing that a free society bred peace and harmony and well-adjusted adults, she offered a utopian adolescent vision that was enthusiastically embraced by the young.

From the start, Margaret Mead's *Coming of Age* was much criticized by more rigorous anthropologists for its lack of factual accuracy and poor discipline. *Coming of Age* may, or may not, be an academic fraud but it is a powerful fiction. Not only did Mead titillate her readers with old-fashioned romances about dusky natives having trysts under the palms but she wrote in most effective novelette style, inviting readers to compare their own repressed adolescence in provincial America with fulfilled sex on a fantasy island. Some of the subjects—rape, promiscuity, homosexuality—were, then, almost forbidden, but dangerous and thus exciting. Her master stroke was to focus on the adolescent girl in an age when society at home had made an icon of the adolescent girl as flapper. *Coming of Age* drew deep from American folklore and Mead hit a jackpot of sales. There are numerous signs in the book itself that her interpretation is at odds with the facts even she presents. The Samoan archipelago was not unspoilt. Already missionaries had imposed their will on certain sections; the economy was bound up with the United States and Europe; and Samoan natives who wanted greater education and social freedom were treated as social deviants. Now we are more likely to emphasize the text's significance as a bisexual's plea for greater toleration.

A more direct and equally popular representation of the nymphet as part siren, part ingenue, and part landscape was provided by Anita Loos (1894–1981) in *Gentlemen Prefer Blondes* (1925), Here the professional not-so-dumb blonde, Lorelei Lee, gives the reader her disingenuous protestations about her predatory intentions toward wealthy men in the form of a diary recording her single-minded devotion to orchids, champagne, and diamonds.

"Kissing your hand may make you feel good but a diamond bracelet lasts forever."

Journalists and Realists

Psychological treatment was not a prerequisite for literary success in America. Ring Lardner (1885–1933) established his name as a sports writer before the great success of his short stories brought him fame as a sardonic humorist and satirist. The best of his many collections of short stories are *How to Write Short Stories (with Samples)* (1924) and *The Love Nest and Other Stories* (1926). In these and later collections the stupidity and dullness of his protagonists, usually ordinary, working people, are analyzed with his usual pessimistic wit. In 1927 Lardner even turned his incisive wit on himself with the publication of his autobiography, *The Story of a Wonder Boy*. His use of the American vernacular brought him praise and gratitude from the most influential literary pundit of the time, H. L. Mencken (1880–1956).

Mencken himself, like Lardner, was hardly an intellectual. His formal education ended at high school and from then onward he immersed himself in the world of newspaper, magazine, and literary journalism. He attained his influence through his lively and daring editorships and criticisms that were often vehicles for his scathing wit. Mencken arrived at a fortuitous time in American history. The 1920s were peculiarly responsive to his iconoclasm that arose out of his feeling that American culture had become stultified by its rigid adherence to a particularly "Puritan" form of Christian morality and a foolishly persistent belief in egalitarianism.

The 1920s afforded Mencken plenty of opportunity to develop and express his iconoclasm through his editorship of the magazines *Smart Set* (1914–1923) and *American Mercury* (1924–1933). Moreover, Mencken was himself a prolific writer and, despite, or perhaps because of, his reliance on impressionism as a critical method, did his job with such gusto and panache that his name and his ideas spread far. However, the depression of the 1930s was certainly not a subject suited to Mencken's style. Indeed,

Mencken at first refused to believe in the depression's existence and dismissed it as "newspaper talk." He could not handle it and lost his readers.

Sinclair Lewis (1885–1951) was a writer who dealt with themes that were never far from mind whenever H. L. Mencken put his caustic pen to paper. Indeed, Lewis's most noted fictional character, George F. Babbitt, might be described as the prototype of Mencken's apocryphal human species, *Boobus Americanus*. Mencken and his followers applied this pejorative term dismissively to virtually everyone except themselves, but George Babbitt belonged to a race of Americans that require and deserve specific consideration.

Lewis himself was a journalist rather than a literary artist, and his fiction expresses this. However, he was the first American to be awarded the Nobel Prize for literature, an event that marked the apogee of his career in 1930. In his fiction Lewis used the tenets of realism as they had been worked out in the nineteenth century, even though in his Nobel acceptance speech he attacked the realist tradition as instigated by W. D. Howells. Nevertheless, he praised younger writers such as Ernest Hemingway and the ambitious and innovative Thomas Wolfe (1900–1938) whose *Look Homeward Angel* was published in 1928 and took literature into uncharted territory whither Lewis, with his conventional approach, was ill equipped to follow. However, this criticism cannot detract from the fact that, with *Babbitt* (1922), about a small-time, small-town real estate agent living in Zenith, Lewis created a classic American novel and a classic American character whose name has entered the English language.

The economic boom of the 1920s inevitably produced legions of Babbitts, middle-class aspirants who fulfilled their role as "boosters" in American society. Babbitt believes he is master of his own destiny; yet he is actually following the herd. Lewis's affectionate parody of popular slogans of optimism, health, and progress was uncannily prophetic of the fads of the decade and of consumerism and conformism long afterward. Lewis cannot be strictly classified as a member of the lost generation since his own reaction to the vulgar materialism and cultural impoverishment of the 1920s was ambivalent. For example, in *Babbitt* the force of his satire on the city of Zenith and its population of boosters is diminished by his recognition of the rebellious, individualistic impulses of George Babbitt, but what constitutes a loss for satire is a gain for the cause of psychological realism. Babbitt is saved from being utterly ridiculous by his friendship with Paul Riesling who encourages him to question the whole tribal structure. For a while, Babbitt becomes a rebel, violating social, political, and sexual taboos. However, Lewis does not permit any uplifting or revolutionary conclusion. Babbitt recognizes the heroism of strikers who openly display their "alien, red notions" but, nevertheless, he returns to his standardized, middle-class life. Sinclair Lewis creates a convincingly complex picture of the group pressure on an individual; yet Lewis manages to maintain, at the same time, a concentration on the idea of that individual's sense of being apart from society.

Sinclair Lewis drew entirely from everyday life, preparing his novels by recording names appropriate for particular characters from telephone directories, sketching precise maps of imagined towns, devising suitable backgrounds for his characters and defining their pets, garden plants, and favorite anecdotes—all in loose-leaf notebooks and usually before he began writing his novels.

At the end of a decade of prolific writing, including not only *Main Street* and *Babbitt* but also *Arrowsmith, Mantrap,* and *Elmer Gantry, The Man Who Knew Coolidge,* and *Dodsworth,* he was awarded the Nobel Prize for literature, an honor he had coveted and, indeed, lobbied for. When he received the award from King Gustav V of Sweden in December 1930 he turned his acceptance speech into a tirade on the poverty of American culture, prompting Calvin Coolidge to answer the storm of indignation at home with the dismissive remark, "No necessity exists for becoming excited." Lewis thought his career was over but his later, uneven, novels, *Ann Vickers, Work of Art,* and *It Can't Happen Here* were commercial successes and he became noted for playful wit, especially wordplay and wicked impersonation of John L. Lewis, FDR, Father Coughlin, and Huey Long. Fascinated by the theater, he collaborated with Lloyd Lewis on *Jayhawker* which played for only three weeks on Broadway in 1934, and he also adapted *It Can't Happen Here,* which opened to WPA productions in eighteen cities in 1936. Yet he had little understanding of the technical demands of the theater and sought advice on elementary matters from inexperienced actors in summer stock.

He met his second wife, journalist Dorothy Thompson, in Berlin where she was a newspaper correspondent for the *New York Evening Post* and the *Philadelphia Public Ledger*. Immediately, he sensed that this energetic, compassionate woman might help sustain him and proposed to her that very night and went on proposing until she accepted him a month later. Both were restless nomads and never settled on the farm they planned as a sort of country idyll. As Dorothy Thompson's career waxed, Lewis's waned and he hit the bottle more resolutely, rounding on his wife as some sort of malevolent Big Nurse. He complained he had to share a bed with world affairs and threatened to divorce her, naming Adolf Hitler as corespondent. When he was on the wagon, he would gnash his teeth at soirées dominated by her wit and insight as she held court to adoring young professionals. When someone said Dorothy Thompson should run for president in 1936, he retorted, "Fine. Then I can write 'My Day.'" When he argued with her, her response was to ridicule his arguments in a column, "Grouse for Breakfast."

The year that witnessed the publication of *Babbitt*, 1922, is a crucial one in the history of literature and intellectual activity including publications of T. S. Eliot's *Waste Land,* Joyce's *Ulysses,* and Walter Lippmann's *Public Opinion*. Moreover, in Italy the fascist dictator, Mussolini, came to power. In a preface to a collection of her essays published in 1936 Willa Cather (1873–1947) declared, "The world broke in two in 1922 or thereabouts, and the persons recalled in these sketches slide back into yesterdays seven thousand years." Cather was a novelist slow and meticulous in her prose style and her use of myth and symbol. Her early writing was much under the influence of Henry James, but with the publication of *Alexander's Bridge* in 1912 she began to find her own voice and was able to leave her job on the staff of the muckraking magazine, *McClure's,* and devote herself full time to fiction. Her most noted novels are *My Antonia* (1918), set amongst the immigrant farmers of Nebraska where she grew up, and *One of Ours* (1922) that won her the Pulitzer Prize. It tells the story of a young man's escape from an oppressive life on his family's mid-western farm to a vitalizing but, ultimately, fatal experience on the French battlefields of World War I. It was precisely the experience and the aftereffects of war that led Cather to make her apocalyptic statement about the year 1922. The writers of the lost generation would have agreed with her since their world was continually breaking in two, and, inevitably, like the unfortunate children they were, they were always left with the smaller piece.

American Poets

The poet T. S. Eliot would also have agreed with Willa Cather. In 1922 he published his seminal vision of a world materially and spiritually devastated by the experience of the war to end all wars. (He wrote *The Waste Land* while recovering from a devastating mental illness in 1915.) *The Waste Land* was recognized by Ezra Pound and other poets as a masterpiece of the modern movement when it was published. It was Pound who cut the first fifty-four lines from an opening line "First we had a couple of feelers down at Tom's place," with its obscure, suspicious double entendres, to the striking

> April is the cruellest month, breeding
> Lilacs out of the dead land, mixing
> Memory and desire, stirring
> Dull roots with spring rain,

with its echoes of Chaucer. It immediately established Eliot as the leading American poet of the day. No other poem in the English language provokes such extremes of feeling in critics and readers alike. Some see it as a poignant poetical rendition of what Eliot took to be the spiritual and moral plight of postwar Europe, while others see it as an obscure poem, pretentious in its classical allusions, and gratuitously pessimistic in tone. Eliot himself once— perhaps jocularly—dismissed *The Waste Land* as "just a piece of rhythmic grumbling." The poem certainly at first reads as a random series of symbolic images, but it is subtly and tenuously controlled throughout by a continuing narrative and an albeit inconstant narrator, Tiresias.

Eliot was born and raised in St. Louis, Missouri, but came from a Unitarian family whose roots were in New England. He graduated from Harvard in 1910 where he had been taught by the philosopher George Santayana, the linguist Irving Babbitt, and the literary historian Barrett Wendell. He first read Dante at Harvard, the poet who, in his own opinion, exerted the greatest permanent influence on his work. By 1911, at the age of twenty-three, he had completed *The Love Song of J. Alfred Prufrock,* a precocious poem with its vivid and sensuous images, its flexible tone, and its expressive rhythms.

In part, *Prufrock* is an investigation of Hell, defined as the pretentiousness of the women visitors to the gallery, the triviality of a life measured in coffee spoons, the uncertainty of toast and tea, and the fragmentary experiences of incoherent people. It is a "fog" and "yellow fog" that blots everything out and ensures one stays at home. Eliot's most assertive early poems are all set in the adolescent keys of unresolved self-doubt, self-absorbed hypersensitivity, and defensive, cold posturing. As critic M. L. Rosenthal has observed, *The Love Song of J. Alfred Prufrock* "positively sweats panic at the challenge of adult sexuality and of living up to one's ideal of what it is to be manly in any sort of heroic model."

In fact, various disclosures about Eliot's disastrous first marriage to Vivien Haigh-Wood that, perhaps, pushed him close to madness have recently threatened to overshadow Eliot's artistic achievement. Between his two happy periods—childhood and his second marriage to Valerie Eliot—Eliot drew from his personal anxieties and deep anguish and wrote his greatest poetry. *Rhapsody on a Windy Night* offers a squalid context of murky streets late at night, horror of sex with a prostitute who "hesitates towards you in the light of the door / Which opens on her like a grin," the moon depicted as a crackbrained old whore, and, at the close, a fear of waking into ordinary life. Such early works and those of other poets carry deep resonances because their adolescent terror is seen as a psychological complement to the gathering storm of World War I that was to shatter old forms of western civilization.

Irregular verse patterns, the procession of distorted, skeletal images with phallic symbols rendered sterile, add up to the shock of puberty, realization of death, and a vision of the macabre side of life.

After obtaining his B.A. and M.A., and embarking on his doctoral studies, T. S. Eliot settled in London in 1915 where, at first, he only just managed to scrape a precarious living by teaching, reviewing, and working for Lloyd's Bank. In 1927 he was confirmed in the Church of England and became a British citizen. Throughout his working life Eliot showed that human life was made up of an endless series of dying moments. The subject of T. S. Eliot's Ph.D. thesis, interrupted by the war, was English philosopher F. H. Bradley (1840–1924) and one of Bradley's prime concerns was the relationship between any given subject and the outside world that he regarded as one, existentially. To Eliot and Bradley our psychological perception of things was related to our geographical sense and this sense of identity varied according to our particular place at any given time. In the *Four Quartets* (1943) Eliot emphasized that culture was defined by place, by the way people were bound up in their environment and this included time. It seems that the culture of civilizations past has been turned into a chaotic jumble by the war. Accumulated knowledge cannot help us interpret the present nor see into the future. Nevertheless, we have to trust the universe because it is that, rather than our different cultures and languages, that binds us together. At its best, Eliot's poetry had an ability to make his readers feel the interaction of different experiences and realize that they, too, were in sum, a total of various complex internal and external factors. However, his plays, heavily imbued with Jacobean and Greek references but dramatically implausible, managed the astonishing feat of being both gross and coy at the same time.

Ezra Pound (1885–1972) was also an expatriate. He left America in 1908 for Europe and did not return until 1946 under tragic circumstances. If T. S. Eliot was the "invisible poet," then Ezra Pound was the "elusive poet," a scholar who remained suspicious of the tradition of English literature. Pound's M.A. was in Romanist literature. Throughout his career he did many translations of others' work and also worked such translations into his own poetry, such as the *Seafarer* (1912) that mimics the movement of an Anglo-Saxon line. After a period in Paris, Pound moved to Rapallo, Italy, where he remained until the end of World War II and where he composed the *Cantos*. In 1945 he was arrested for treason by U.S. army officers on the grounds of his previous public support of fascism. He was imprisoned in a cage in the open air and at his trial in 1946 found unfit to plead for reasons of insanity. He was confined in Elizabeth's Hospital for the Criminally Insane, Washington, D.C., until 1956 when pressure from other poets, such as Robert Frost, persuaded the authorities to release him. In the meantime, he had won the Bollinger Prize in 1949 for *Cantos* written in prison. Eliot saw Pound as a truly catalytic figure and called him "the animator of artistic activity in any milieu in which he found himself." In preference to the iambic pentameter, already discarded by Walt Whitman (1819–1892), Pound started to hammer out his own hard surface in a so-called imagist phase of 1912–1914. His work as a translator convinced him that, in translation, language was concerned with transmitting information and experience as clearly as possible and thus became neutral. He believed that, although the Americans had inherited the English language, they had not inherited the tradition and experience that that language was originally intended to convey. Thus he wanted to alter language (as in a translation), in order to carry the sense of breadth of American experience, stretching existing language to that end.

Pound had several obsessions of which only the poetical brought good, while the political and the racial brought only harm and tragedy. He was instrumental in the formation of the liberating theory of imagism that grew out of his obsession with the Japanese *haiku* or pictographic poetry. Imagism was the ultimate in economy and entailed using no superfluous word—no adjective, article, adverb, verb, or conjugation—that did not reveal something crucial to the reader. The most singular example of Pound's imagism is the poem "In a Station of the Metro," taken from the collection *Lustra* of 1915, and here reproduced in its minimal entirety:

> The apparition of these faces in the crowd;
> Petals on a wet, black bough.

Pound's explanation was that, "In a poem of this sort one is trying to record the precise instant when a thing outward and objective transforms itself, or darts into a thing inward and subjective."

As European editor between 1912 and 1919 of the "little" magazine, *Poetry,* owned by Harriet Monroe of Chicago, Pound was responsible for the publication of important works by such new authors as T. S. Eliot and Robert Frost. As English editor of the *Little Review* from 1917 to 1919, he placed James Joyce's *Ulysses* with one of its first publishers. Thus Pound was truly a catalyst in encouraging new literary talent and in helping to ensure the success of the little magazine movement that continues throughout the century as the major testing ground for avant-garde writers.

Pound the poet is remembered today for two works. First and foremost, by virtue of their sheer scale, are *The Cantos* (1925–1968) that, at almost a thousand pages, constitute Pound's attempt at creating a twentieth-century equivalent of Walt Whitman's masterpiece, *Leaves of Grass* (1855–1892). *The Cantos* are inconsistent in quality and too ambitious a project to have ever wholly succeeded. However, they do constitute a stunning compendium of poetical technique.

The finest section, "The Pisan Cantos," were written during his period of incarceration. (We must recall that in 1945, when he gave himself up to the American authorities in Italy, he was taken to the United States Army Disciplinary Training Center near Pisa and placed in a small cage made of airstrip landing mats above which an arc light burned throughout the night.) The first draft of "The Pisan Cantos" was written in this cage with a pencil stub in a children's notebook given him by a Jewish chaplain. He had no books except for Confucius and a poetry anthology he found in the lavatory. After he suffered his nervous breakdown, he was moved to a tent and allowed to use a typewriter. Yet he supplied the numerous and diverse details of history and literature from memory. He could do this because his quite incredible memory was aural rather than visual. He became impatient with his inability to type as fast as he could think and in his fury he hit blindly at the keys, causing them to jump all over the page and make erratic spacings, curious indentions, and odd dashes and capital letters that became punctuation. He usually kept two machines so that when one broke and had to be repaired he still had a spare. Pound's models for the *Cantos* were the epic poems of Homer and Dante that he transformed by echoes of Browning, Rosetti, and Whitman, and his experiments with collages of thirteen different languages, including Chinese. In fact, ten cantos (LII–LXI) are of early Chinese history, explaining how China prospered when a good emperor followed Confucian principles. Pound is also remembered for the poem, *Hugh Selwyn Mauberly* (1920) which, like *The Waste Land,* is a landmark in modern poetry. Pound and Eliot did what no poets had done before. They sacrificed their own authorial voice for the sake of their subject matter and left personae in the form of Mauberly and Tiresias, respectively, to face the aridity, the unreality, and the superficiality of postwar urban society.

Eliot and Pound's morbid vision of inner reality, their sense of human destiny moving down an irreversible death march, confirmed the deep pessimism about the human condition to the generation that attained maturity in the 1930s and 1940s and faced the horrors of World War II. As W. H. Auden later remarked, Eliot transmitted "the unmentionable odor of death" of our century. He also expressed a sense of a world out of kilter and out of control. Eliot "showed us a decisive image of ourselves in the mirror of a terrified age being quick-marched nowhere though still capable of making wonderful jokes about it all."

Hart Crane (1892–1932) is more important for what he set out to do rather than for what he actually achieved. Crane was a tragic figure, driven by compulsive and self-destructive alcoholic and sexual urges that culminated in a spectacular suicide. In 1932 he leaped into the sea on returning from Vera Cruz where he had hoped to write an epic poem on Montezuma and the Spanish conquest of Mexico. It is too easy to take a facile view of Crane and see him either as an amoral dissipate or as the romantically lonely scapegoat of an intolerant and brutal civilization. *The Bridge* (1930) is his longest and most important poem, modeled on *The Waste Land* in its form and intended as a kind of optimistic riposte to Eliot's negative view of the modern metropolis. *The Bridge,* like *The Waste Land* and *Ulysses,* follows a protagonist through the modern city. Crane's protagonist wakes in the morning, crosses over Brooklyn Bridge, wanders about the city, and then returns in the evening by the subway under the Hudson River. Crane tried to create an American mythology in this poem out of scraps of literature, history, and tradition with such figures as Columbus, Rip Van Winkle, the Wright Brothers, Walt Whitman, Edgar Allen Poe, Emily Dickinson, and Isadora Duncan. In the section entitled "Powhattan's Daughter" Pochahontas represents the American earth itself and its Red Indian heritage. However, it is the Brooklyn Bridge that is the unifying symbol of the poem, connecting the two halves of the city and, through the railroad that it carries, uniting the city with the country and the present to the past. This celebration of a great feat of engineering makes Crane an American representative of Futurism, an artistic movement expounded by the Italian Filippo Marinetti in 1909 when he called on art to exalt machines and imitate their motion.

Four poets who achieved their greatest successes and recognition after 1945 were active and influential during the first five decades of the twentieth century: Robert Frost (1874–1963), William Carlos Williams (1883–1963), Wallace Stevens (1879–1955), and E. E. Cummings (1894–1962).

Frost was a deeply ambiguous poet who hungered for success and created a larger-than-life popular image and an equally large supply of popular poetry that ensured him wide recognition yet hid his real nature. He is, perhaps, America's best-known poet, but his modernist awareness of the predicament of modern man goes largely unremarked by the many people who read his poetry. He made much of his crusty rural exterior and there was nothing abstruse about his work that was generally taken as a spontaneous, organic response to the wonders of nature. Nevertheless, as critic Richard Francis explains, his poems disclose a second, deeper meaning. When he urges a farmer not to mend a drystone wall separating his land from his neighbor's because territorial claims are not necessary in the natural world, he is really urging the paradox that territorial imperative is a perfectly natural response (in humans and in animals) to the environment. Similarly, taken superficially, his *Stopping by Woods on a Snowy Evening* is a traditional summation of the conflict between civilization and nature built up by an accumulation of images and a simple rhyme scheme. However, it is the horse, who wants to get back to the stable as quickly as possible, and escape possible dangers, whose response to descending night is far more natural than that of the self-indulgent man who wants to linger as long as possible to survey the scene. It is the horse that knows he and his master are better back in their social compact, that it is unnatural and dangerous to stay out late in the woods that afford him no gratification.

Birches is a poem about complex human needs, including sex, that children must learn by experience, in this case the boyish pleasure of finding the right balance by riding the branches of a birch tree as if to subdue them. Frost's simple titles are drawn from the natural world and imply love of the simple life of a golden age and the romantic tradition of Wordsworth. The *Ovenbird* does not simply die as do other birds but by enriching the life of a family it becomes part of the cycle of life.

Frost did not see nature as a sanctuary from the world of industry but he did believe that poetry, when successful, drew on deep roots of human consciousness and provided its readers with the means of resisting those forces in the world that erode human confidence and stability. As individuals we may be overwhelmed by events but we live again in poetry to celebrate the processes of self-expression. Thus, in part, poetry is about the human need to write poetry. In fact, Frost took his readers into the realms of irony and paradox.

William Carlos Williams was a doctor as well as a poet who found himself in a particularly advantageous position for writing of the American spirit since he saw it in sickness and in health tramping through his office in New Jersey for almost fifty years. Initially, his reputation existed only among other writers such as Ezra Pound and Hart Crane. Not until the publishing house New Directions started publishing his work in the late 1930s did he begin to attract a wider audience. Most of his first dozen books were printed privately or were subsidized. Williams always wrote in a mode based on the rhythms of the speaking voice, replete with idiomatic language, colloquialisms, and an intense interest in locale as both setting and subject. Indeed, his concentration on detail from everyday life and speech distances him from the elitist intellectualism of expatriates such as Eliot and Pound. This rejection of abstraction is succinctly expressed in his dictum, "No ideas but in things," that is, in turn, demonstrated in his poems whether they deal with, say, a red firetruck, or, "The Red Wheelbarrow." The four books of the poem *Paterson* (1946–1958) constitute his most celebrated and technically successful work with its epic exploration of the life of a man in the small city of the title.

Wallace Stevens was a man of deep contradictions. He was a most sensuous yet intellectual poet who spent most of his life working as an executive of the Hartford Life and Accident Insurance Company in Connecticut. He placed a very high value on poetry in particular and art in general, yet would only ever write in his spare time. Thematically, Stevens was at odds with most other American writers of the twentieth century who were deeply critical of their age. Instead of seeing dislocation and chaos in the destruction of old ways of life and living, he saw an opportunity for recreation that would be based on anarchic individualism, on an arrogant sense of self. Poetry would be a replacement for mankind's shattered faith in religion and God, but this poetry would be a highly personal process of subjective analysis of meaning. We are all poets, was Stevens's suggestion. The pity is that only very few of us have the gift of poetic expression. Stevens was optimistic in the way that he viewed his art as an antidote to meaninglessness: "Poetry is the Supreme Fiction," and the supreme fiction can cope with any chaos. His poetry and his poetic vision with its mystical overtones progressed from his first published collection of poetry, *Harmonium* (1923), through other collections, such as *The Man with the Blue Guitar* (1937) and *Notes Toward a Supreme Fiction* (1942).

E. E. Cummings should have belonged to the lost generation by virtue of the fact that he engaged in many of their prescribed pursuits—ambulance driving during World War I, expatriate living in Paris between 1921 and 1923, and pioneering experimentation with literary modernism. Yet, philosophically and stylistically, Cummings was a long way from the lost generation. He grew up in Cambridge, close to Harvard, where he later studied with distinction, and his Unitarian background provided him with a transcendental view of the world that permeates his poetry and contrasts starkly with the pessimism of the lost generation. During World War I Cummings was imprisoned in a French concentration camp because his companion, William Slater Brown, had written discontented letters to a German professor at Columbia University. Cummings was freed within three months, but only after his father had written to President Woodrow Wilson. As a direct result of this experience, he wrote *The Enormous Room* (1922), a prison journal that is full of comic invention, reportorial insight, and, even by virtue of its unconventional use of syntax, asserts a theme of humorous yet serious antiauthoritarianism.

Tulips and Chimneys was a large manuscript containing 152 of Cummings's poems that no publisher would accept. Only with the help of his ex-classmate John Dos Passos was he able in 1923 to publish a shortened version of the book containing sixty poems. In 1937 the original manuscript was issued in its entirety under its original title and it now stands as one of the classics of modernist literature. His poems caught the spirit of the jazz age through their great variety of tone, voice, and technique. Cummings was fascinated by the asyntactic language of Gertrude Stein (1874–1946) and the dismantled shapes of modernist painting. The new art made spontaneous perception the basis of expression and creation, just as in jazz music the soloist often departs from what is written. Cummings dismantled all the components of poetry and reassembled them: punctuation became a series of arbitrary signals sometimes used even as words. The function of nouns, pronouns, adverbs, and adjectives was often interchanged. Typography itself became a tool in the process of expressing what was essentially a lyric gift. His experiments are the direct literary equivalent of what happened in modern painting at this time. In fact, Cummings himself was also an accomplished and considered painter.

One playwright who benefitted from Gertrude Stein's ideas on language and form was Thornton Wilder (b. 1897), whose most famous play, *Our Town* (1936), is an American pastoral following a small regional community through a cycle of birth, marriage, and death and performed without scenery. This foolproof masterpiece is a gift for all amateur and professional companies, provided the players can assume their roles with sincerity and conviction. *The Skin of Our Teeth* (1942) is also somewhat experimental, following a representative family, the Antrobuses, through such cataclysmic events as Noah's Flood and Civil War and pitting traditional stereotypes, including prodigal son and obdurate father, and homely wife and lubricious mistress, against one another with satirical effect. Both these plays won Pulitzer Prizes and *The Skin of Our Teeth* became a preferred soubrette vehicle for Vivien Leigh.

Wilder was born in Wisconsin and grew up partly in Shanghai, where his father was consul general, before studying at Yale, the American Academy in Rome, and Princeton, and then teaching at Chicago University (1930–36). His first novel, *The Cabala* (1927), was inspired by his sojourn in Rome. In 1927 *The Bridge of San Luis Rey* established him as a leading novelist whose philosophic works of fate and chance owed much to the observations about civilization by Henry James and Marcel Proust before him. Wilder's imitative novels and plays carry deep philosophical undertones but his unerring consideration to keep readers and audiences continuously entertained prevent him from ever jolting them too greatly. If life is cyclical, then he argues, events will take their own course. Of his later pieces, the most enduring has proved to be *The Matchmaker* (1954), suggested by a Viennese tale but set in and around New York at the turn of the century and which provided the basis for the 1960s musical *Hello, Dolly!*

The cartoons and prose of James Thurber (1894–1961) for the *New Yorker,* in the days when it was edited by Harold Ross, were noted for a unique blend of precision, incisive wit, and provocative fantasy. Thurber's world was one of little men dominated by outsize wives (once presented as a woman becoming a house in a return-to-the-womb cartoon), as it might have been perceived by omniscient dogs. His work appeals to those readers whose sense of refinement and control is challenged by their own growing sense of anarchy and absurdity. His themes included the triumph of moral innocence in a society being transformed by the mass media, the cult of psychoanalysis, and sexual revolution. Among his sadly amusing short stories, the most famous, *The Secret Life of Walter Mitty,* carries an enduring myth—how a man over-powered by the demands of contemporary society makes up for his inadequacies by leading a combative, inner life in a series of imaginary, glamorous careers as crack pilot, leading medical consultant, and ace detective. In creating this secret world, later turned into a Hollywood vehicle for Danny Kaye (1947), Thurber appeals to all our interior dialogues between wish fulfillment and the dullness, apathy, and inertia of our daily routines. He drew upon life remembered from his eccentric family of Columbus, Ohio, and from his early careers as an aide in the American Embassy in Paris (1918–20) and as a journalist.

His keen-eyed vision of the world depended on acute observation from limited means. In his own words, during his boyhood, "He fell down a great deal . . . because of a trick he had of walking into himself. His goldrimmed glasses forever needed straightening which gave him the appearance of a person who hears somebody calling but can't make out where the sound is coming from. Because of his badly focused lenses, he saw, not two of everything, but one and a half. Thus a four-wheeled wagon would not have eight wheels for him, but six." Thurber's disability of very poor sight worsened progressively over the years to the point of blindness just before his death.

Thurber's wit and wisdom yielded more anecdotes and telling remarks than Mae West. An irate telephone caller who has dialed the wrong digits, cuts the answering party with, "Well, if I Called the Wrong Number, Why Did You Answer the Phone?" A patient man tells his date in an apartment lobby in a curious reversal of conventional sex roles, "You Wait Here and I'll Bring the Etchings Down." An outspoken guest exclaims to a scandalized couple whose son has just come into the room, "Why I Never Dreamed Your Union Had Been Blessed With Issue!" Many Thurber cartoons showed fantasy turned into reality as with the cross wife who rejoins to her husband, who has woken her up in bed, "All Right, Have It Your Way—You Heard a Seal Bark." And, of course, the seal is above the headboard. An artistic original, Thurber created an entire genre and became its master.

Music

Modernism was expressed even more clearly in music, especially in songs, than in poetry. Since music is one of the performing arts, successful music has to conform to a basic law of creative life: change and develop or stultify and die. The development of American music was astonishing. Jazz, with its broken cadences and strong rhythmic beat, constituted a radical departure from musical norms and was America's unique contribution to world modernism. The 1920s are often known as the jazz age, not because this was when jazz first appeared, but because this was the era in which jazz was first scored and made accessible to an audience beyond its roots in the culture of black Americans. Ironically enough, the most successful exponent of scored jazz music during the 1920s and beyond was a rotund band leader by the appropriate name of Paul Whiteman. It was Whiteman who in 1924 commissioned George Gershwin to write the first ever formal composition based on the elements of jazz. Whiteman's "semiclassical" orchestra gave *Rhapsody in Blue* a sensational premiere with Gershwin himself at the piano on February 12, 1924, at the Aeolian Hall, New York City.

During the twentieth century American popular music became a highly commercialized art form, a commodity mass-produced by a multinational music entertainment industry. The beginnings of this development can be traced back to changes that occurred in the first half of the century when, in addition, the substance of popular music was significantly affected by a stream of new music styles.

The foundation of the art and business of American popular music had been laid down in the last fifteen years of the nineteenth century when music publishing had become increasingly dominated by a number of companies based in New York and specifically located on 28th Street between Fifth Avenue and Broadway. This was Tin Pan Alley where companies like Thomas B. Harms, Inc., Willis Woodward, and Isidore Witmark typified a profitable business of writing and publishing popular songs on the basis of

A wartime audience of sailors on leave and their girlfriends enjoys swing music at O'Reilly's at Third Avenue and 54th Street, New York, on a Saturday night in February 1943. (Photograph for the Office of War Information by Marjory Collins; Library of Congress).

extensive market research. Songwriters were salaried employees rather than freelance artists while the market research was carried out by song pluggers, musicians who played drafts of new songs to selected audiences. In its harnessing of art to industry and commerce, the organization of Tin Pan Alley in 1900 was a forerunner for the studio system of Hollywood in later decades.

The music business in 1900 was one of selling sheet music to a piano-playing public. Publishers used the nationwide circuit of vaudeville venues to publicize their latest songs. Thus the importance of a close relationship between the music-makers and music-disseminators was established at an early stage. Undoubtedly, the later relationship between the recording industry and radio and television originated from this earlier business interdependency.

The musical talent and market research of Tin Pan Alley and vaudeville produced a succession of songs that were best-sellers and became firmly fixed in the emerging popular culture of the century: for example, "Give My Regards to Broadway" (George Cohan, 1904), "Shine on Harvest Moon" (Nora Bayers and Jack Norworth, 1908), "By the Light of the Silvery Moon" (Gus Edwards, 1909, and "When Irish Eyes are Smiling" (Ernest R. Ball, 1912). Songs from Tin Pan Alley developed a certain homogeneity. The general tone was sentimental and lyrics frequently referred to the city as a lively, colorful place or dealt with warm memories of a country childhood. Through market research these songs were responding to a common mood of the time, reflecting the fact that growing numbers of Americans were living and working in major cities. People were aware that they were cutting themselves off from a rural heritage and in the climate of progressivism were concerned about the standard of city life. Significantly, "popular music" would deviate from this diet of urban celebration and rural nostalgia only when America entered World War I and patriotic songs became popular. The way that the typical Tin Pan Alley song consisted of simple melodies, verses, and an emphasis on the repetition of the chorus helped to define the basic composition of the popular song in this century.

Even as Tin Pan Alley ruled, the first of a series of infusions of music from the black community was transforming the sound of all popular music. Between 1920 and 1941 the main influence was from jazz, but in the early 1900s it was ragtime and its success set the pattern for the introduction of jazz. Ragtime was a rigorous, vivid marriage of harmony and rhythm. It had emerged from the parlors of brothels because these were the only places where black pianists could play. The black classically trained composer, Scott Joplin, was its leading exponent, having written what was probably the first popular ragtime tune, "Maple Leaf Rag," in 1899. Joplin competed with other ragtime players like Jelly Roll Morton and Eubie Blake. The music of Scott Joplin was not, at first, written down and, indeed, musical notation could only give an approximate idea of his unconventional rhythms with their off-beat accents and varied timings.

Ragtime became popular because the simplicity of its tunes

meant that the large number of living-room pianists could play this form of music. Indeed, sheet music sales of ragtime made the first large profits for the music business in this century. "Maple Leaf Rag" sold over 1 million copies.

The best ragtime pieces involved a complex and energetic syncopation whereby beats in the music switch from being strong to weak and vice versa. Yet the majority of ragtime music was "junk rag," simply the playing of a string of catchy, jingling tunes at a breakneck speed. This reflected how, increasingly, rag became associated with player pianos. Its repetitive tunes were easy to punch out on the piano rolls. Moreover, junk rag was usually written by white men while the original black ragtime composers, like Joplin, often aspired to develop rag into a significant black art form.

Significantly, ragtime declined as the player piano was superseded by a superior means of mechanical recording and playback of music. Public enthusiasm for the gramophone broadened the appeal of popular music and transformed the place of music in society. In 1900 there were 100 companies in America manufacturing pianos, but the significant statistic of 1920 was that 100 million records were pressed in that year. (Thomas Edison had invented the phonograph in the 1870s and perfected it in 1888.) By 1920 the old cylinder system was replaced by the grooved disc and record players were being mass produced by Columbia and the Victor Talking Machine Company. When recorded on a disc, popular music became a true consumer item and industrial product. The ability to read music and play the piano were no longer prerequisites for a night of home entertainment. In the twenties the enjoyment of music became a more passive pleasure and the demand for records boomed. The scale of the popularity of gramophone records was such that serious composers like Aaron Copland not only commented upon it but also felt that their music should respond to this unleashing of popular culture. Furthermore, toward the end of the 1920s radio broadcasting and talkies provided additional forces for the popularization of music.

Therefore, jazz was drawn into the mainstream of American popular music at an opportune time. As befitted the free improvisation and rhythms associated with jazz, the popular music business in the 1920s became expansive, both artistically and commercially. The recording industry was relatively new and thus amenable to change. The demand for gramophone records required an expanded supply of popular music and one that was ever more diverse. Jazz music would eclipse the brief fashion for ragtime and have a greater influence on defining the style of popular music.

A new generation of popular music composers came to the fore in the twenties. Their music was distinguished by its use of jazz. The very public success of Irving Berlin, George Gershwin, and Cole Porter also indicated how the composers began to escape the anonymity associated with the successful Tin Pan Alley composers of the early 1900s. The popular composers of the 1920s displayed a common virtuosity in understanding jazz and synthesizing its qualities into the traditional form of the American popular song that they had learned from Tin Pan Alley. The work of these composers would set the scene for the 1930s and 1940s when they would further their reputations by working in Hollywood or continue to write for Broadway.

In 1893 the Balines, a family of Russian Jews, landed and made their home in New York. Their son, Irving, was then five years old. By his teens he was well known as a street singer and worked as a singing waiter for Pelham's cafe in Chinatown. In 1907 he published his first song, "Marie from Sunny Italy." It was through a printer's error on the title page of that song that he came to be known as Irving Berlin. Thus began the career of perhaps America's most successful popular composer. Although he lacked a formal music education and was unable to read music, Berlin eventually published 1,500 songs.

Soon after the publication of his first songs, Berlin made his stage debut and, subsequently, pursued a career of sometimes performing, but mainly writing for the musical variety theater of the day. In 1911, he contributed music and lyrics for *Alexander's Ragtime Band,* a show that was an international success. The 1914 revue, *Watch Your Step,* represented his first complete musical score and lyrics. As Broadway theaters began to boom, Berlin's own standing grew, for example, with his writing for the Ziegfeld Follies. By 1921 Berlin's position in popular entertainment was such that he felt he could build and run his own theater, the Music Box, upon which he staged his own revues. Consistently good box office returns proved Berlin correct. At the Music Box Berlin was not only making money, but also developing the stage musical into an increasingly sophisticated and versatile genre. For example, in 1925, Berlin collaborated with the Marx Brothers to write the first integrated musical comedy, *The Cocoanuts.*

Berlin was coming to prominence at a propitious time in the entertainment business. By the late twenties Hollywood studios were converting from silent to sound film production. The Broadway musical was immediately recognized as ideal subject matter for the new talkies. With their often lavish staging and chorus lines, Broadway musicals seemed almost to proclaim hosannas for the arrival of sound on screen. It was also less time-consuming to synchronize music and song in moving pictures than it was to synchronize speech. In addition, as Hollywood beckoned toward Broadway, the lights of Broadway were dimmed by the onset of the depression. Box office sales slumped and theaters and companies began to close.

Berlin was one of the many examples of Broadway talent attracted to Hollywood in the late twenties and early thirties. He would be one of the principal innovators of the film musical. In 1935 he wrote the score for *Top Hat,* a film that starred Fred Astaire and Ginger Rogers. Thereafter, Berlin wrote a succession of musical film hits, such as *The Gay Divorcée* (1937), *Holiday Inn* (1940), and *Annie Get Your Gun* (show 1945; film 1950), many based on his original theater shows. In the process he not only made his own fortune, but also helped to establish and further the careers of Bing Crosby, Fred Astaire, and Ethel Merman. His stage shows and films included songs that became popular classics, most notably "White Christmas" from *Holiday Inn* and "There's No Business like Show Business!" from *Annie Get Your Gun.*

The career of Irving Berlin is a case study in how popular music has developed in this century. After success on Broadway, Berlin's career truly took off once he became involved in the new mass mediums for music—motion pictures, radio broadcasting, and the phonograph industry. Indeed, Berlin is probably the greatest seller of gramophone records: his song "White Christmas" has sold 25 million copies of its original version and 100 million of other versions. Like later figures in popular music as diverse as Elvis Presley, the Beatles, and Bob Dylan, Berlin's success can also be attributed to his readiness and ability to adapt and synthesize the style and nuances of other musical influences. Berlin folded some of the distinctive characteristics of ragtime and jazz into his sentimental, money-spinning hit songs. Thus, Berlin's status in popular culture can be explained by a meshing of his own talent for artistic innovation (rather than invention) and the technical, commercial innovations (rather than inventions) occurring in America in the mid-twentieth century.

The music and lyrics of Cole Porter are characterized by a cool, urbane wit. This properly reflects the background and life-style of a composer whose grandfather had been a millionaire speculator. He was born in 1892 in Peru, Indiana, and studied at Yale (where he wrote football songs), Harvard Law School, and the Harvard Graduate School of Arts and Science. After serving in the American army in 1917–1918, Cole Porter led the life of a playboy, first in Europe and later in America. From an early age Cole Porter had been interested in music and by his teens was composing songs.

The success of the show *50 Million Frenchmen* in 1929 established him as a leading Broadway writer. The thirties were his most productive period. He wrote a string of stage successes, including *The Gay Divorcée* (1932), *Anything Goes* (1934), *Dubarry Was a Lady* (1939), and *Panama Hattie* (1940). Over the same time, Porter also wrote music for the movies. Of the songs he wrote for Hollywood between 1934 and 1940, many have become popular classics, for example "I Get a Kick out of You" (1934), "Begin the Beguine" (1936), and "I've Got You under My Skin" (1936). As significant as his melodies were his witty lyrics, especially in "Solomon," "My Heart Belongs to Daddy," "Miss Otis Regrets," and "Let's Do It."

George Gershwin spent his childhood in poverty on Manhattan's Lower East Side. However, there were, apparently, opportunities for the young George to listen to both jazz and concerts of classical music. George became interested in music and learnt

Versatile composer George Gershwin delighted audiences with music
that mixed syncopated rhythms and lyrical melodies as he moved across
the different forms of songs, piano concertos, orchestral tone poems,
and opera. He combined the diverse strains of Afro-American, Latin-
American, jazz, and popular music with the elegance of European operettas in a dazzling career cut short by his premature death at the age
of thirty-eight. (Carl Van Vechten; Library of Congress).

piano from the age of twelve. Despite numerous music teachers, Gershwin never really mastered reading music, though he did become proficient in composing and orchestration. His teachers also introduced him to the work of a wide variety of composers. Indeed, his significance as a figure in popular music was his blending of classical music with the nuances and styles of popular music and jazz. Indeed, Gershwin sought out the latest, most idiosyncratic of contemporary American composers, such as Henry Lowell and Joseph Schillinger, and proceeded to learn their music philosophy.

Gershwin came to the attention of the public not with the publication of his first song "When You Want 'Em, You Can't Get 'Em," but the song "Swanee" that Al Jolson sang in *Sinbad* in 1918. The song was a best-seller on gramophone records and music sheets. With his reputation fully established, Gershwin wrote his first entire score, *La, La Lucille*. That Gershwin was committed to experimentation was evident when he pushed aside the composition of songs for other people's musicals and revues to concentrate on a short modern opera that he wrote in 1922, first called *Blue Monday* and, later, *135th Street*. Such an imaginative step caught the attention of Paul Whiteman, then probably the most famous bandleader, who commissioned Gershwin to write a symphony in a jazz style. This was *Rhapsody in Blue*, and usually considered Gershwin's first masterpiece.

In 1924 George persuaded his younger brother, Ira, to collaborate as a lyricist for future projects. *Lady Be Good* (1924) was their first big success, followed by *American in Paris* (1925), *Tip Toes* (1925), *Oh Kay* (1926), *Funny Face* (1927), *Strike Up the Band* (1927), and *Girl Crazy* (1930). George also wrote four film scores, including music for some Astaire musicals.

George Gershwin saw himself as more than the writer of light musical escapism and, with Ira, created, first, the political musical satire *Of Thee I Sing* in the early 1930s, and, in 1935, his other masterpiece, *Porgy and Bess*. For this opera Gershwin spent a summer on a South Carolinian island so as to research a black peasant community. *Porgy and Bess* was incorrectly termed a folk opera when, in fact, what the Gershwins did was take a traditional operatic format and mold it to suit the black characters and settings of DuBoise Heyward's brutal drama, bringing together the diverse musical styles of popular Tin Pan Alley music, jazz, and operatic arias. Despite mixed critical reaction and an, initially, cool public reception, the opera produced a number of popular songs: "Summertime," one of the most immortal of all twentieth-century melodies, "I Got Plenty o' Nuttin'," and "It Ain't Necessarily So," and the duet, "Bess, You Is My Woman Now." Tragically, George Gershwin died in 1937 of a brain tumor; Ira continued to write lyrics in partnership with, among others, Moss Hart, Jerome Kern, and Kurt Weill. George Gershwin wrote popular songs characterized by sweet melodies and repetitive refrains. His talent was limited, for often his long pieces include abrupt pauses. Yet all of his music was distinguished by its healthy cross-fertilization of musical influences, including elements of Jewish folk and synagogue music, and dynamic, jazz rhythms.

Richard Rodgers was born on Long Island in 1902. He studied at Columbia University where he wrote the music and lyrics for amateur musical productions. When he met Lorenz Hart in 1918, Rodgers found a collaborator who agreed with his complaint that too many songs relied on banal lyrics. With this in mind, the two men began their musical partnership.

Their first major success was a revue, *The Garrick Gaieties*. By the late twenties, Rodgers and Hart concentrated on musical dramas that dispensed with the song and dance format. *Chee-Chee* and *Present Arms,* written in 1928, were examples of this trend. After an unsuccessful time in Hollywood in the early part of the decade, they returned to Broadway, writing successes like *Babes in Arms,* a backstage musical about the aspirations of adolescent talents. This production demonstrated how much Rodgers and Hart had become two of the most versatile practitioners of the Broadway musical. The score was incredibly varied, with songs ranging from the lyrical "My Funny Valentine," through the sophisticated "The Lady is a Tramp," to the highly rhythmic "Johnny One Note."

On Your Toes satirized the conventions of backstage musicals and added an amusing sketch of Russian emigré ballet dancers, of whom there were many in the West in the 1920s and early 1930s, who affect an intensity of emotion they cannot sustain. The musical also burlesques such ballets as the Diaghilev–Bakst *Scheherazade* and its climax is a ballet that fuses jazz and American and Russian dance choreography, "Slaughter on Tenth Avenue." In 1940, the cynically realistic musical *Pal Joey* represented the final outcome of Rodgers and Hart's disgust with banal lyrics and story lines in Broadway musicals. It was not, in the first instance, a commercial success. Three years later Lorenz Hart was dead. Rodgers's partnership with Hart had produced works that advanced the art form of the American stage musical.

On joining forces with the lyricist Oscar Hammerstein II, Rodgers refined the art form even further, winning serious critical applause. *Oklahoma* (1943) was a yet more complete integration of song, dance, and drama. The conventions of the song and dance routine had gone, the chorus line replaced by ballets of square dance routines. Spurred on by Hammerstein, Rodgers discovered that he could successfully break from the cast-iron convention of a song having a recurring verse and chorus. Indeed, this early work of Rodgers and Hammerstein first suggested how the Broadway musical could mature into a dramatic whole and, finally, release itself from its crude revue antecedents. It began with an offstage serenade, "Oh, What a Beautiful Morning!" while Aunt Eller silently churned milk and, then, it moved through routines, setting cowboys and farmers, first, at odds and, then, as friends, through conventional love songs such as "Surrey with the Fringe on Top," and the love duet, "People Will Say We're in Love," to a rousing populist celebration, "Oklahoma!" Though more saccharine than the Rodgers–Hart shows, Rodgers and Hammerstein musicals always had a dark side, represented in *Oklahoma!* by the sinister, brooding Jed. In *Carousel* the principal character is an antihero, a wastrel, bully, and unsuccessful thief. In *South Pacific,* set on a Pacific island during the navy's campaign against Japan in World War II, the target was racial prejudice.

Although his most famous compositions use folk tunes to celebrate the American West, Aaron Copland came from a quite different background. He was born in 1900 into a Russian Jewish family living in Brooklyn, New York. Later he described his early life as drab and hard. Yet, after learning the piano from an elder sister, Copland strove to complete a full musical education through correspondence courses and one day become a composer. In 1921, he went to study music in France. When he returned to New York in 1924, his music was highly experimental. That same year the New York Symphony Orchestra performed his *Symphony for Organ and Orchestra* at Carnegie Hall. For the next ten years Copland continued to experiment, using jazz rhythms for his *Piano Concerto* of 1926 and later assuming a lean, spare musical style for works like *Piano Variations* (1930) and *Statements for Orchestra* (1933–1935), a work that showed the influence of Russian expatriate composer Igor Stravinsky.

Copland then made a critical decision. He has referred to the dissatisfaction that he felt at the time about the considerable distance that had developed between modern "classical" composers and the general public. Therefore, in the mid-1930s, Copland deliberately chose to enter the mainstream of popular taste and write modern pieces that would be accessible to the large audiences of radio, film, and gramophone recordings. Copland has said, "It made no sense to ignore them [radio, film, and gramophone records] and to continue writing as if they did not exist. I felt that it was worth the effort to see if I couldn't say what I had to say in the simplest possible terms."

Copland began to write a series of ballets about subjects that were particularly familiar to ordinary Americans. *Billy the Kid* (1938), *Rodeo* (1942), and *Appalachian Spring* (1944) for choreographer Martha Graham drew on American folk tunes and stories. In 1939, Copland wrote one of his first film scores for the screen version of John Steinbeck's *Of Mice and Men* (1939). As America was drawn into World War II, Copland responded by composing music pieces that examined the issue of warfare by very American references, for example his *Lincoln Portrait* of 1942. This was the most productive period of the composer's life and one in which he achieved international fame. The music itself was usually relaxed and expansive. One might see Copland's avoidance of artistic elitism as reflecting the preeminence of populism in American society and politics, the ideals of the New Deal policies, and the myths surrounding FDR's personality. Copland was active in the organization of concerts that were aimed at the ordinary, nonconcertgoing people.

Ultimately, Copland wrote music tailored for an increasingly industrial and urban society. He exploited the latest methods of mass communication and incorporated a folksy jauntiness into his symphonies and ballets that perhaps satisfied a nostalgia for a simpler rural past that was thought to have disappeared recently. It was significant that his work was associated with the writings of novelist John Steinbeck and that the best of his music involves patterns of interweaving threads of precise, almost metallic, sounds and the freewheeling tunes of folk song and dance.

The creative achievements of popular composers who wrote for Broadway and Hollywood would have been much less had they not been able to fashion art from their subconscious, their cultural heritage, and their consciousness of the rich American tradition of performing and interpreting. In turn, the singers and musicians who performed the works of such composers as Gershwin, Porter, and Rodgers gave their music a color, vitality, and distinction that was special to the age.

European composers were fascinated by America's ascendancy in the machine age, but such works as Arthur Honegger's *Pacific 231* and Edgard Varèse's *Amériques* were rarely performed in the United States. Nevertheless, American composers did celebrate the machine age. Expatriate George Antheil wrote his *Ballet mécanique* in Paris. Frederick Shepard Converse wrote his *Flivver Ten Million* to honor the ten millionth Model T car and it was performed by the Boston Symphony Orchestra under conductor Serge Koussevitsky in 1927. The score had parts for a factory whistle, a Ford horn, and both wind and anvil machines. Jazz music also featured mechanical elements. John Alden Carpenter's jazz ballet, *Skyscrapers,* drew upon the frenzied sounds of the ever-restless modern city. In the ballet *Vanities* (1928) by Earl Carroll, one crucial sequence was a visit to a Ford plant choreographed by Busby Berkeley, whose later dance numbers in Hollywood musicals combined motorized stages and machinelike ensembles.

Musicians

In the 1920s the black blues singer and songwriter Bessie Smith was popularly acclaimed as the "Empress of the Blues." She had been born in 1898 in Chattanooga, Tennessee. Her early life was spent in the customary poverty of the black community of the South. Ma Rainey, who was, then, the most renowned blues singer, came across the young Bessie Smith and encouraged her to follow a professional singing career. When Clarence Williams, a black pianist and representative of Columbia Records, discovered Bessie Smith in 1923, she had already spent several years singing in Atlanta, Birmingham, and Memphis.

Bessie Smith was not the first singer to record blues music, since Mamie Smith had done so back in 1920. Yet, she did become the most successful blues recording artist of the time, making disks of 150 songs, often with the accompaniment of jazzmen like Louis Armstrong, Fletcher Henderson, and Benny Goodman. Her first recording session produced "Downhearted Blues" and her last, in 1933, "Down in the Dumps." Her recording success reflected how gramophone records were increasingly becoming consumer items in the 1920s. The earlier recordings of blues had been made for archival reasons, while Bessie Smith's records were best-sellers. Her first record, "Downhearted Blues," sold 780,000 copies in its first six months.

Bessie Smith also made innumerable live performances across the nation. Onstage she was a singer whose success was very much of the period of the national prohibition of alcohol. In New York she was a well-known figure at "Bufet Flats," high-class speakeasies where sexual encounters were also on the menu. A bold and confident artist who would frequently refuse to use a microphone in her live performances, Bessie Smith expressed both the hopes and frustrations of black Americans. She was associated with the so-called Harlem Renaissance that was at its peak in the 1920s. In 1929, Bessie starred in an all-black musical, *Pansy,* and film, *St. Louis Blues.*

However, by the early thirties, Bessie Smith's career was declining. The fashion for blues was over, record sales were greatly reduced on account of the depression, and she was now having to compete with a new generation of black women singers led by Ella Fitzgerald and Billie Holiday. It was while touring Mississippi in 1937 that Bessie Smith died of injuries caused by a car accident. Since she was refused immediate medical care from a

The vibrant singer Bessie Smith, "Empress of the Blues," whose soul-searching powers of communication melted musical hearts but not well enough to prevent her bleeding to death after a road accident when an ambulance refused to take her to a nearby hospital for whites only. (Photographed by Carl Van Vechten in 1936; Library of Congress).

nearby white hospital, it can be justly said that the Empress of the Blues was killed by Jim Crow—southern de jure segregation. Bessie Smith was both a success and casualty of the American recording industry's first attempt to exploit black music. By 1920 large numbers of blacks had migrated to the major cities, creating a market for what the record companies called euphemistically and inaccurately "race" records. Consequently, black musicians were signed up to make recordings and there was even a black-owned music label, Black Swan. When the economy collapsed in 1929, the purchase of records was one of the first luxuries to be cut. Suddenly, the remaining market for "race" records was killed off as the ailing record companies discarded their black recording artists.

In the twenties and thirties bandleaders and musicians Paul Whiteman and Benny Goodman were the leading popularizers of jazz music. Ironically, the success of such white men playing jazz paved the way for the general acceptance of black bandleaders and musicians such as Louis Armstrong playing the same music.

Paul Whiteman was born in Denver, Colorado, in 1890. His own instrument was the viola and, for a while, he led his band playing the violin. In the twenties his band became known as the premier dance band for the new, energetic styles of the Shimmy and Charleston. Benny Goodman had been born in Chicago in 1909. He learnt the clarinet at Hull House, the settlement house founded by Jane Addams. By the 1920s Goodman was a proficient enough musician to go out to Los Angeles to play with the Ben Pollack jazz band. His recording career began in 1926.

Whiteman promoted jazz as popular music by his employment of a succession of talented jazz soloists, most notably Bix Beiderbecke, Jack Teagarden, Eddie Lang, and Bunny Berigan. Moreover, it was Whiteman who encouraged George Gershwin to write *Rhapsody in Blue,* a work that Whiteman's orchestra was the first to perform in 1924. By 1930 much of the music that he and his orchestra played was strongly influenced by jazz. Thus in the early 1930s white bands were beginning to play jazz. Musicians had noted the success of the jazz-influenced music of Berlin, Gershwin, and Whiteman. Probably the first of the major white big bands was the Casa Loma Orchestra that became popular in

1930. As future big bands would do, the Casa Loma Orchestra performed a mix of slow and fast dance numbers. Moreover, their music was very much a youth phenomenon as the band was most popular on college campuses.

It was the orchestra that Goodman formed in New York in 1934 that spearheaded a new fashion for swing music and won him the title of "King of Swing." Swing is a form of popular jazz music with a pulsating, often fast, beat. The performance that Benny Goodman and his orchestra gave at the Palomar Ballroom, Los Angeles, has traditionally been seen as the birth of the swing era. The way that the orchestra had four saxophones playing parallel four-note chords epitomized the swing sound. It has been suggested that the term "swing" was coined by a BBC announcer sometime in the mid-1930s. Even as his orchestra encouraged the vogue for big band music, Goodman set up trio and later, quartet, ensembles that improvised in the traditional style and prefigured the future trend of modern, more idiosyncratic, jazz. In the 1940s, Goodman discontinued his orchestra and began to hire black musicians and eventually formed some of the first racially mixed popular jazz bands in America.

Unlike many of his contemporary musicians, Glenn Miller was not from New York or Chicago but was a midwesterner, born in 1904 in Iowa. After studying at the University of Colorado at Boulder, Glenn Miller, a talented trombonist, joined Ben Pollack's jazz band. By 1930 he was considered a seasoned professional musician, who did a great deal of freelance, session work. For a while Miller helped to organize bands for other people, working for the Dorsey brothers in 1934 and Ray Noble in 1935. Yet, eventually, Miller became eager to form his own orchestra and did so in 1938. At a time when radio broadcasting had become fully organized into two major networks and music programs dominated the airwaves, Miller rapidly won nationwide and, later, worldwide fame as a big band leader. In the 1930s Benny Goodman had broadened his appeal by film appearances. Similarly, Glenn Miller's reputation and record sales were boosted somewhat by his films, *Sun Valley Serenade* (1941) and *Orchestra Wives* (1942).

The appeal of Miller's big band music lay in the way that sweet,

simple melodies and rhythms were played with disciplined orchestration. His band had an instantly recognizable saxophone
sound. His music was not exactly jazz, since the usually improvised rhythms were tightly regulated. The success of Glenn Miller
emphasized how much "sweet" swing dominated popular music
by the late thirties. some of the biggest sellers of the decade were
the Artie Shaw band playing Cole Porter's "Begin the Beguine"
and Miller's own "In the Mood" and "A String of Pearls." Another emerging trend was the popularity of singers such as Frank
Sinatra, Doris Day, Jo Stafford, and Perry Como who were
employed to sing ballads in front of the band. It can be argued
that Glenn Miller and the vogue for big bands represented the end
result of a process whereby black music had been appropriated by
whites and so made palatable for a larger, wealthier audience.

It was rather fitting that Americans became enamored with the
big band sound and spectacle as the country moved toward entry
into World War II. Miller's band and others were noted for their
smart uniforms and an almost military marshaling of musicians
to produce music. Glenn Miller joined the U.S. Air Force, eventually becoming a major and leader of the Air Force Big Band in
Europe. Besides his musical talent, Glenn Miller is also remarkable for the posthumous intensity of his reputation. He disappeared on a flight between England and France in 1944. The
considerable interest in Glenn Miller has been fueled not just by
the mysterious circumstances of his death but also by the ability
of gramophone recordings and films to provide a means of cultural immortality. Thus, Glen Miller and his music seem to epitomize the considerable degree to which American popular music
had developed by 1945 largely as a function of the growth of mass
communications and entertainment.

In 1933 John Lomax, a collector of folk songs, discovered an
exceptional blues singer serving a sentence for murder in the
Louisiana State Penitentiary. Huddie ("Leadbelly") Ledbetter was
a black singer and guitarist who knew 500 blues songs by heart.
After recording him for the Library of Congress, Lomax succeeded in having Ledbetter paroled. Ledbetter was regarded as
one of the last great blues musicians, the principal custodian of its
tradition. He had been born in Mooringsport, Louisiana, in 1885,

learnt the twelve-string guitar at an early age, and had subsequently been the accompanist for a blues singer, Blind Lemon Jefferson. In the late 1930s and 1940s Ledbetter made many recordings, for example, "Honey I'm All Out and Down" and "Becky Deere, She Was a Gambling Gal." "Good Morning Blues" of 1940 was his most admired song. He died in 1949.

By 1945 the development of popular music as a major business was almost complete. The role of television in broadcasting popular music would be discovered after World War II. Jazz had been fully integrated into the mainstream of popular music and smooth, swing music prevailed. Yet, during the forties, there were signs pointing to the future appearance and impact of rock 'n' roll. The increase in industrial production for the war effort had accelerated the drawing in of large numbers of poor southern whites and blacks to work and live in the major cities of the USA. These groups brought not only unskilled labor into the cities but also their music. Rhythm and blues, a new style of blues singing with a faster, jazz beat, was increasingly enjoyed by urban blacks. It was also beginning to influence current popular music and was described as "novelty" music by whites who were amused by the furious speed of some songs. Ledbetter's "Goodnight Irene" was an example of novelty music. Significantly, such black music was enjoyed alongside the enthusiasm of poor southern whites for their "hillbilly," or country, music. This music involved both male and female singers with a backing of guitars, harmoniums, violins, and mandolins. Much of its particular style was derived from a tradition of church music. It was winning wider interest with its exposure on the radio and the success of performers like Gene Autry and Hank Williams, whose music bridged the hillbilly style and conventional popular music. Rock 'n' roll would be a blending of these emerging black and white music styles. Although it did not truly happen before 1945, it would require a white, country musician to cross over and play rhythm and blues for rock 'n' roll to begin to become marketable popular music.

In 1945 American popular music was on the verge of entering a new international phase. By virtue of its freedom from the devastation of war wrought in Europe and Asia, America was in a position to dominate the world not only politically and economically but also culturally. Gramophone recordings, radio, and movies had already cultivated a prewar interest in American popular music abroad. However, the stationing and advance of American troops in Europe had introduced a greater number of European countries to even more American music and, so, created a demand for more. Moreover, the European recording industry was shattered by the war and a low priority in the many programs for reconstruction, while the American music industry was intact.

Literature in the 1930s

Some leading writers of the 1930s shared the social concern that motivated many painters and there is a similar conflict between realism and grotesque perception. Nathanael West (c. 1902–1940), for example, wrote four short novels in his brief literary career that add up to one of the most telling criticisms of the United States ever produced. In West's view, the American dream was in fact a grotesque nightmare and his first novel, *The Dream Life of Balso Snell* (1931), is an examination of the subconscious mind that would have been impossible without Freud's innovative psychological theories. This novel is not typical of West's works in the sense that it is concerned with the disintegration of the isolated self, outside the social context, and constitutes a twisted and contemptuous expression of an individual's alienation. *Miss Lonelyhearts* (1933) provides us with an anonymous protagonist who cannot afford any such displays of private despair. He is the author and adviser for a newspaper agony column who is gradually overcome by the weight of genuine untreatable suffering, revealed in the letters he receives from his readers. His confused and often frantic attempts both to evade and to confront the enormity of pain and suffering end in failure and perturbing bathos when he is killed by one of his own readers as he runs toward him, arms outstretched, full of love. West's handling of his author's clients is deliberately poignant and grotesque, with an effective selection of animal imagery to undermine any sympathy the reader may have for their plight. *A Cool Million* is a more overtly social and political denunciation of America, with an innocent protagonist who is literally dismantled by American society in an uninhibited parody of the Horatio Alger myth of the Gilded Age in which the children's storyteller Horatio Alger propounded a myth of poor boys rising from rags to riches by dint of hard work and thrift. Lemuel Pitkin in *A Cool Million,* however, loses his teeth, an eye, a leg, and his scalp in the laissez-faire world and is then exploited by both communist and fascist organizations. *The Day of the Locust* (1939) is West's second masterpiece, and probably the best Hollywood novel in American literature. West himself worked in Hollywood on screenplays for the last five years of his life before he died tragically in a car crash in 1940, and this, his last novel, is peopled with bizarre and grotesque characters of the movie world. The book is replete throughout with suppressed violence and hatred that boil over in the last pages in an account of a mob riot at a film premiere.

Another author who was published during the thirties and specialized in reporting human grotesquery was William Faulkner (1897–1962). However, Faulkner, perhaps because of his southern heritage, focused on the family as an individual unit rather than society as a whole. Neither was Faulkner's work critical of humanity in the sense that, although he used a naturalistic style to emphasize such unattractive human qualities as brutality and violence, his work does balance this harsh view with an affirmation of positive human qualities and values that he listed in 1950 when he accepted the Nobel Prize for literature: "courage and honor and hope and pride and compassion and pity and sacrifice." This list might appear to indicate the work of a conservative and idealistic writer but Faulkner was, in fact, progressive and experimental in his style and use of form. In books such as *The Sound and the Fury* (1929), *As I Lay Dying* (1930), and *Absalom, Absalom!* (1936), he employed Joycean stream of consciousness, scrambled chronology, mythic and biblical parallels, and the manipulation within one book of seemingly disparate narrative lines.

In *The Sound and the Fury* Faulkner elaborates on typical southern stereotypes, such as a promiscuous girl, an idiot child, an unbalanced student, a sharp-witted cad—all scions of a dissolute southern family—and their harried, genteel hypochondriac mother and dependable black retainer, and plays most daringly with the material. The story is told by four characters, at first and most

grippingly by Benjy, the idiot son, who cannot distinguish idealized childhood past and more deprived adulthood present. Thus
eight family characters across two generations share only four
names. Here is an archetype of a stagnant family, a tale told by
Macbeth's idiot, full of sound and fury but signifying nothing,
living in the agrarian South, a place forgotten by time, its people
marooned by ignorance. The most imaginative creation of *Light
in August* (1932) is the central character, Joe Christmas, an orphan
unsure whether he is black or white and reared by foster parents
whose punishments he can cope with but whose occasional kindness he cannot. Years later, as a man living on the shady side of
the law, he makes love to, and then, in a bizarre scene, kills, a
white woman of some pronounced masculine traits. Here is the
sort of gross murder perpetrated by numerous petty criminals in
many different regions, who can only express themselves in inarticulate violence. However, in this instance, Faulkner unfolds the
background, situation, and motive without any artistic distortion
to dialogue or situation. The same novel carries forward the story
of the life-giving, unmarried, and pregnant girl, Lena Grove, a
Grecian urn who will give birth and be light in August. She is
poor white trash but blessed with an outward-looking attitude to
life that invites, and receives, all manner of help just when she
requires it.

Faulkner's stark stories hint at long-hidden family secrets that
have cast dark shadows over his characters. His world is violent,
lurid even, but the somber scene is illuminated by biting shafts of
humor and varied by the color and diversity of his characters.
This is, perhaps, most apparent in his most monumental single
novel, *Absalom, Absalom!* Thomas Sutpen tries to create a planta-
tion and found a dynasty but his design founders on his own
racial prejudice and his family's inability to love. The major crisis
is the fratricide by one son of another (hence the allusion to King
David's son, Absalom), rejected because he is part-colored. The
dream of a dynasty is finally laid to ashes by the Civil War and,
eventually, the line peters out in ignominy.

Carson McCullers (1917–1967) drew from her life in a small
Georgia town and distilled the experiences in a series of unroman-
tic romances set amid drab homes and burning summer heat.

Whatever the physical or psychological aspects of her characters, her central theme is love, fulfilled, forlorn, or thwarted. In *The Heart is a Lonely Hunter* (1940), the central character is a deaf mute, John Singer, whose compassionate nature encourages four other lonely people to try and communicate with him. *Reflections in a Golden Eye* (1941) portrays uncomfortable, ill-matched liaisons in a southern army camp. *Member of the Wedding* (1946) explores the emotional adjustment of an adolescent girl coming to terms with herself and her world. Besides Faulkner's epic novels, these were all miniatures in minor keys but keys that opened up wider doors and visions. Film versions of variable quality awaited a later, postwar, generation of artists and changed susceptibilities among cinema audiences.

The Civil War remained the most dramatic episode in American history and one for which there was an insatiable appetite among readers. Margaret Mitchell, the wife of an Atlanta advertising executive, provided exactly what they required in her mammoth novel, *Gone with the Wind* (1936), a novel it took her nine years to write. When Macmillan editor H. L. Latham met Margaret Mitchell in the lobby of his hotel in Atlanta in 1935 she was "a tiny woman sitting on a divan, and beside her the biggest manuscript I have ever seen, towering in two stacks almost up to her shoulders."

The story of how southern belle Scarlett O'Hara survives the Civil War and Reconstruction, how she rises above the barriers of poverty, caste, and sex amid the collapse of a civilization "gone with the wind," rises and prospers materially at a high emotional cost in a harsher, more demanding environment of the New South, was enthralling. It encapsulated a familiar American theme that riches can prove empty. Scarlett finally understands that her third husband, Rhett Butler, is her soul mate, once she has lost him. She remains indomitable.

Gone with the Wind sold 178,000 copies within its first three weeks of publication on June 30, 1936. This was, and remains, a unique accomplishment for an unknown author. It remained on best-seller lists for twenty-one consecutive months and by April 1938, when sales began to drop off, it had already sold 2 million copies. Fifty years later it had sold 25 million copies in twenty-seven langauges and thirty-seven countries and there were 185 official editions in print. Within a month of publication, movie rights had been sold to David Selznick for $50,000, a considerable sum in the 1930s. While the role of Rhett Butler was clearly attuned to the roguish charm of Clark Gable, search and competition for the coveted role of spitfire heroine Scarlett O'Hara was attended with the sort of publicity normally reserved for a presidential election. It was eventually resolved by the casting of little-known English actress Vivien Leigh. Numerous troubles followed, including a change of director when Gable and Leslie Howard (who played Ashley) found George Cukor too interested in the women's roles of Scarlett and Melanie (Olivia de Haviland) and he was replaced by Victor Fleming. The premiere at Loew's Grand in Atlanta on December 16, 1939, was a national event and the film set a special record, earning nine Hollywood Oscar awards, and for many years it was, at 231 minutes, the longest American film.

Rhett and Scarlett are not stock characters but engaging scoundrels of real depth and emotional intensity. Margaret Mitchell was dismissed as a hack writer but her account of the siege and arson of Atlanta and Scarlett's escape back to Tara along with Melanie and Prissy are most imaginatively handled and as a background to Scarlett's developing independence and her deepening, complex relationship with Rhett Butler. The story lives and is told in such a way as to retain, indeed, capture the reader's interest and imagination. The novel drew deep on American folklore, the myth of the Old South, and the sense of loss the continuing myth implies. The characters like Scarlett and Rhett who survive suffer the most tragic losses—both their loved ones and an imagined peace of mind. Critic Tom Wolfe explains Gone with the Wind's continuing hold on the public: " . . . the idea of loss is also at the heart of the novel. A world irrevocably vanished, whether real or not, and Scarlett's personal losses—the ideal of Ashley, the reality of Rhett—evoke the losses in our own lives, those we comprehend as well as those we only sense."

Among the most popular form of American fiction was the so-called hard-boiled crime thriller, especially the works of Ray-

mond Chandler (1888–1959), James M. Cain (1892–1977), and
Dashiell Hammett (1894–1961). Their scintillating dialogue, spoken by deftly defined and truly urban characters, called for dramatization on screen and, indeed, this was recognized by the movie
moguls who snapped up their properties for transformation by
Hollywood.

Although Raymond Chandler was born into a Quaker family
in Chicago, he went with his mother to England at the tender age
of eight and was educated at Dulwich College, a traditional,
private boarding school. After further education in France and
Germany, he went to live in California in 1912, served in the
army during World War I, and then worked for various oil companies. He did not begin writing until he was forty-four and
between 1933 and 1939 published over twenty stories, usually for
the *Black Mask,* a leading magazine of hard-boiled detective fiction. He moved his leading detective Philip Marlowe, the solitary, questing knight, through the neon landscape of Los Angeles
in a series of darkly humorous cases, beginning with *The Big
Sleep* (1939), *Farewell, My Lovely* (1940), *The High Window* (1942),
and *The Lady in the Lake* (1943). In every case the killer was a
leading lady, a modern Morgan Le Fay, who had, briefly, deceived the honorable Marlowe. Chandler wanted as charismatic,
debonair, and tall a leading man as Cary Grant for Marlowe when
Hollywood began to make screen versions of his works that were
not especially faithful to the plots of the originals but which did
capture their biting wit and the tense surfaces of characters under
pressure with much to conceal. Instead, Hollywood fielded a
series of actors adept at wisecracking to play the somewhat enigmatic Marlowe, notably Dick Powell and, later, James Garner,
and, most definitively, the small Humphrey Bogart in *The Big
Sleep* (1946).

Chandler's dialogue and recollections by Philip Marlowe are
famous for their provocative wit. "She approached me with enough
sex appeal to stampede a business men's lunch and tilted her head
to finger a stray, but not very stray, tendril of softly glowing
hair." Moose Malloy "was a big man but not more than six feet
five inches tall and not wider than a beer truck. . . . Even on
Central Avenue, not the quietest dressed street in the world, he

looked about as inconspicuous as a tarantula on a slice of angel food." The isolated Marlowe has his fair share of sexual encounters as with the predatory and aptly named Mrs. Grayle of *Farewell, My Lovely*. "She fell softly across my lap and I bent down over her face and began to browse on it. She worked her eyelashes and made butterfly kisses on my cheeks. When I got to her mouth it was half open and burning and her tongue was a darting snake between her teeth." Yet, when it comes to sex, Chandler's hero, carrying the last name of Christopher Marlowe, a notorious Elizabethan playwright who led a double life as a government spy, promises more than he delivers. Like Dashiel Hammett's Sam Spade, Marlowe must remain a self-contained loner, untarnished by the tawdry world he moves through, and preserving his integrity from all forms of corruption.

In fact, Chandler's most persistant theme is the raw disorder of the great metropoles, especially Los Angeles with its garish neon signs and tawdry glitter amid downtown nightclubs, as well as the dark pavements of innumerable mean streets, shining with traces of midnight rain. His sympathetic and villainous characters alike are victims of the greed of the prevailing commercial order as well as their most lascivious (but implied) desires. The underside of the search for sexual or financial gratification is the unfulfilled barrenness of many California lives. Marlowe assesses some victims in *Farewell, My Lovely*.

I leafed through the bunch of shiny photographs of men and women in professional poses. The men had sharp foxy faces and racetrack clothes or eccentric clown-like makeup. Hoofers and comics from the filling station circuit. Not many of them would ever get west of Main Street. You would find them in tank town vaudeville acts, cleaned up, or down in the cheap burlesque houses, as dirty as the law allowed and once in a while just enough dirtier for a raid and a noisy police court trial, and then back in their shows again, grinning sadistically filthy and as rank as the smell of stale sweat. The women had good legs and displayed their inside curves more than Will Hays would have liked. But their faces were as thread-bare as a book-keeper's office cat. Blondes, brunettes, large cow-like eyes with a peasant dullness in them. Small sharp eyes with urchin greed in them.

James M. Cain, born in Annapolis, moved in his forties from work as a journalist and screenplay writer to become a novelist of lurid melodramas, beginning wtih *The Postman Always Rings Twice* (1934) and *Double Indemnity* (1936). His works abounded in sensation in realistic settings, featuring such infernal triangles as dissatisfied wife, discarded husband, and enraptured lover in both *The Postman* and *Double Indemnity;* a hetero-and homosexual triangle of Mexican-Indian prostitute, opera singer, and ambitious conductor in *Serenade* (1937); and an incestuous liaison in *The Butterfly* (1946). *The Postman Always Rings Twice* was, initially, banned in Boston and French writer Albert Camus later acknowledged its influence on his own writing. "No one has ever stopped in the middle of one of Jim Cain's books," claimed the *Saturday Evening Post* and it was almost true. The pace and brevity, the visceral excitement of illicit love, and calculated twists in the plot, contrive to sustain reader interest, in breathless narratives. His genre was violence in low-life settings—the same as the verismo opera composers whose works he had earlier studied as a singing student.

More credible, because less macabre and rooted in the social phenomenon of ever-increasing suburbanization was *Mildred Pierce* (1941), about the tortuous relationships between unfulfilled divorcée and restauranteuse Mildred, her little minx of a daughter whose singing career she sponsors, and various shiftless men. The women's roles were, apparently, tailormade for Joan Crawford and Ann Blyth in the film version, allowing la Crawford an artificial but credible display of maternal love on screen. Her public persona of gracious mother was utterly destroyed after her death in 1977 by the corrosive revelations of her adopted children. They told how, behind the scenes, she was a careless parent, almost psychopathic in her oscillations between hollow protestations of love and outbursts of sadistic cruelty.

After serving as a sergeant in World War I, which shattered his health, Dashiel Hammett worked as a private detective for a Pinkerton Agency in San Francisco, a career that provided him with material for his series of detective crime thrillers. In *Red Harvest* (1929), he first showed his ability to catch the cool tone of an American urban hero, a talent further developed in *The Dain Curse* (1929), and reaching fuller expression with the creation of wisecracking detective Sam Spade, first in *The Maltese Falcon* (1930). This effective crime thriller was filmed three times by Warners, of which the best account was the 1941 version with Humphrey Bogart as Sam Spade and a rogues' gallery led by Mary Astor, Sidney Greenstreet, and Peter Lorre, all at their most ghoulish.

Hammett modeled his most famous heroine, Nora, wife of Nick Charles, for *The Thin Man* (1932) on his longtime companion, playwright Lillian Hellman (1905–1985). New Orleans-born Hellman scored a *succès de scandale* with her murky play *The Children's Hour* (1934) with its undertones of sexual perversion in a girls' boarding school—a scandal that tarnishes the two principal teachers and tests their emotional resilience with tragic consequences. Her most commercially successful play, *The Little Foxes* (1939), showed an aristocratic Alabama family fall prey to the machinations of a malign trio of two unscrupulous brothers and their rapacious sister. While the melodrama requires a strong cast able to project various southern stereotypes and play well together as an ensemble, the part of Regina is a gift for any actress who can assume a series of feline characteristics and, alternately, cajole, wheedle, and dominate the other characters, sending out chills of biting frost. Tallulah Bankhead, who created the part with idiosyncratic drawl, hauteur, and mannerisms, was much copied by early interpreters of the role, notably Bette Davis in the film version (1941). Lillian Hellman's plays were notable for psychological insight, well-modulated violence, and the liberal attitudes of her most sympathetic characters. In her various memoirs, she later idealized herself as heroine, both in the 1930s as a Jew helping her friend, "Julia," save European Jewish refugees from the Nazis and in the 1950s for refusing to testify fully before the House Un-American Activities Committee and betray friends from the past whom she knew had previously supported various radical organizations or causes. Hammett fared less well and was imprisoned for being a former fellow traveler with the Communists. Subsequently, critic Mary McCarthy and Hellman's biographer doubted her veracity about crucial episodes. Far from being ennobling experiences, they believed that her escapades were largely products of her imagination.

Hammett also idealized Hellman as Nora Charles, the witty and sporting wife of urbane detective Nick Charles, in *The Thin Man* (1932). Although the thin man was the murderer's first victim, the name got attached to the detective, especially as played by William Powell in the first film (1934) and its five sequels (1937–1946). Nora was played by the witty Myrna Loy and her domestic scenes with William Powell were considered the first realistic portrayal on screen of an affectionate marriage of sophisticated people, like a modern Millamant and Mirabel from Congreve's *The Way of the World*.

Hollywood also turned the thirties' major regional novel into a plangent and commercially successful film. John Steinbeck (1902–1968) created his most celebrated novel, *The Grapes of Wrath,* in 1938. It is, indeed, a 1930s novel in terms of both subject matter and date of publication for it deals with the story of the "Okies," driven out of the dustbowl by a cruel combination of depression, drought, and inefficient use of the land. Steinbeck's book is an epic that uses alternate chapters and "interchapters" to follow the Joad family in particular and American society in general through the experience of dispossession and deracination. This technique of using a microcosmic and macrocosmic point of view proved both immediately effective in contributing to the novel's success and, eventually, influential in inspiring writers of another generation to use it once again. Like Faulkner, Steinbeck concentrates on the family and its significance although his message is perhaps more didactic. His main spokesperson is Ma Joad, "Use'ta be the fambly was fust. It aint't so now. It's anybody." While Steinbeck is clearly on the side of the dispossessed Okies, he is also critical of their ignorant methods of farming that had helped precipitate their tragedy and then Ma Joad's obsessive insistence on the family staying together, although it is only by the individuals going their separate ways that any of them has a chance of progress beyond mere survival. However, in this book Steinbeck's vision is just as modernist as, say, William Faulkner's, because, despite his use of realism to promote the cause of cooperation amongst human beings, the conclusion of *The Grapes of Wrath* remains ambiguous with young Rosasharn in a stable offering her milk that was intended for her stillborn child to a dying old man. The modernist point of view was essentially pessimistic in its sophistication and Steinbeck in this book was certainly not offering any optimism, beyond Rosasharn's later understanding that she must become more outward-looking and giving. At first we are shown the relationship between the family unit and "the people." The people is an older agrarian concept, from time immemorial linked to the land, while the family is a collection of individuals. However, the people, or prisoners, who tamed nature are now an anachronism in the world of modern farming. The concept of the people must be replaced by a new concept of "the group," itself an instrument of technology, just as the Joads need a truck to survive.

The success of Clifford Odets's (1906–63) play, *Waiting for Lefty* (1935), showed just how popular was the new social ethic of the 1930s. The play examines the personal dramas of a mixed group of taxi drivers debating whether to strike or not and ends with their united cry to strike. This shows Odets's recognition of the failure of a system in which self-interest supposedly produces prosperity for society as a whole. It seems that, for Odets, the creative individual of the 1920s is being replaced by the reforming group of the 1930s, a recognition that men had to work together for the common good in both public and private life and that the federal government had to intervene when individual initiative failed.

In 1937 Ernest Hemingway produced a novel with a measure of social awareness, *To Have and Have Not,* his only novel with an American setting, whose very title proclaims his awareness of injustice and inequality. The central theme of early Hemingway, man working out his salvation alone, is far less sure now. Harry Morgan says at one point, "I've got no boat, no cash, I got no education. . . . All I've got is my cojones to peddle," and yet his much-quoted, dying words are "One man alone ain't got no bloody f—ing chance." Morgan is without any orthodox social awareness. When Cuban revolutionary Emilio rants about the tyranny of imperalistic capitalism, Morgan shouts: "The hell with their revolutions. All I got to do is make a living for my family and I can't do that. Then he tells me about his revolution. The hell with his revolution." As critic Alfred Kazin notes: "The hero . . . is not, like most of Hemingway's heroes, an elaborately, self-conscious man against society; he is rather a mass-man, a man like any other, whose life has a beginning, a middle, and a significant end. Harry Morgan's voice is his excessive self-reliance, the pride in his own tough loneliness."

Ernest Hemingway developed his ideas on war and peace and social commitment in his novel about the Spanish Civil War, *For Whom the Bell Tolls* (1940), also the vehicle for a successful film. *For Whom the Bell Tolls* extends some of Hemingway's own philosophy, not least in the common involvement and responsibility of men indicated by the title. Yet the importance of the historical crisis of the war is minimized. The chief interest lies in the continuous presentation of sensory experience recorded as time passes, rather than in political commitment—something Hemingway had little interest in. The story tells of the successful attempt, at a fatal cost, of a group of loyalist guerrilla fighters to blow up a bridge in the Spanish Civil War of 1936–39. The Spanish conflict was extremely suitable for Hemingway's highly sophisticated style, and for his general purposes. It was contemporary; both sides felt themselves committed to an ideal; and the fighting was extremely bitter. Although the fighting was confined within Spain, the debate on the ethics of the war was universal; it became a true crusade for its intellectuals. The principal character of the novel, Robert Jordan, is an American university teacher for whom the attempt is also a working out of a personal destiny, the proving to himself that his life has significance. At the close of the novel, when he has been abandoned by his friends, he awaits immobile and wounded to be killed by the falangist guards. While waiting, he sifts true and false values to find a permanent meaning to life:

The anger and emptiness and the hate that had come with the let down after the bridge, when he had looked up from where he had lain, and crouching, seen Anselmo dead, were still all through him. In him, too, was despair from the sorrow that soldiers turn to hatred in order that they may continue to be soldiers. . . .

And then, not suddenly, as a physical release could have been (if the woman would have put her arms around him, say) but slowly and from his head he began to accept it and let the hate go out.

12

ARTISTIC LICENSE

IN HIS painting, *Watch,* of 1925, artist Gerard Murphy enlarged the inside of a pocket watch, unfolding its labyrinthine mechanism and, thereby, showing how much everyday life in industrial society depends on precise regulation. The irony is that a small mechanical timepiece not only dictates the workings of larger human beings but also that the complex intricate system of any industrial society is mastered by the machines invented to serve it. Such a paradox was much appreciated by America's artists, sculptors, and architects working between the world wars.

In "The New Condition of Literacy Phenomena" for the art magazine, *Broom,* of April 1922, critic Jean Epstein claimed that, in certain circumstances, machines became extensions of the self. Thus, "spatial speed, mental speed, multiplication of intellectual images, and the deformations of these images" were the essential conditions of modernity. He projected a world in which technology dominated all human activity. In the 1920s and 1930s the worlds of American painting and sculpture were riven by the sort of conflicts between town and country that had characterized American social and political history in the 1920s. The new machines continued to make as formative an impact on art as upon everything else; realistic and regional art continued an often hostile dialogue with abstract art.

Whether their medium was painting, photography, or sculpture, American artists emphasized machines in their works. First, Alfred Stieglitz (1864–1946) documented such new artifacts as skycrapers, bridges, dynamos, and automobiles. Later, in the 1920s painters and sculptors explored geometric images that disclosed something of the speed and power of machines. By the 1930s the spread of machines into the countryside was so pervasive that artists began to consider interconnections between different areas of technology. While Walker Evans and Charles Demuth pondered the impact of the machine in the country, Charles Sheeler documented it as a total system. In his extensive mural for the Mining Industries Building of the West Virginia University at Morgantown (1940–1942) Robert Lepper (b. 1906) showed how coal and gas were first extracted and then transformed into energy before being distributed to industrial and domestic consumers. Thus his panorama of organic, mechanical, and biological forms related two instances of machine-age products in one locality to the scene nationwide. Sculptor John Storrs (1885–1956) etched the soaring form of skycrapers in a series of geometric, constructionist works that used such varied materials as polychromed stone, mirror glass, and metal strips and gave an impression of monumental forms most economically.

The Brooklyn Bridge assumed mythic significance in the art of John Marin (1870–1953), Louis Guglielmi (1906–56), and, most notably, Joseph Stella (1877–1946) who, through a series of remarkable paintings, showed the American public and critics that the bridge was a most potent symbol of their deepest aspirations. The most comprehensive of such works was his quintych of five panels, *The Voice of the City of New York Interpreted* (1920–1922), in which the outer panels of the Port of New York and the Brooklyn Bridge are succeeded by two inner panels of the "Great White Way of Broadway" and culminate in a central panel of Manhattan skyscrapers. Since automobiles represented speed, futurists chose to capture the movement of cars by using the elided, fragmented forms of cubism.

What was true of easel art was true of photography. In her

Charles Demuth, *I Saw the Figure 5 in Gold* (1925), 36″ × 29¾″. (The Metropolitan Museum of Art, The Alfred Stieglitz Collection, 1949). Demuth's "poster" painting, dedicated to his friend, poet William Carlos Williams, mixes words, arbitrary circles, a street lamp, and various distorted buildings in a mode that owes much to European cubists but yet remains essentially American.

Brooklyn Bridge, Water and Dock Streets, Brooklyn (1936) photographer Berenice Abbott (b. 1898) placed the bridge upper left between a disused warehouse in the foreground and the Manhattan skyline in the background, thereby implying the significance of technology in the transformation of New York. By the upward angle of *Manhattan Bridge: Looking Up* (1936), Abbott transformed its support into a monumental pylon, once again emphasizing technology as it was reforming society.

Yet artists continued to show an ambivalence to the machine, admiring its geometry and benevolent potential but recognizing its irrational and potentially destructive results. Because their art forms were many, and their images subtle, they could make ambiguous statements about the machine age, disclosing both myth and reality, good and evil inherent in modern technology. William Gropper (1897–1977) drew a series of pointed cartoons against the capitalist order. For the *Liberator* of 1922 he had a tailor entrapped in a sewing machine of utmost efficiency endure a caption "Work like hell and be happy." In *Hitchhiker* (1935) he had a forlorn angel of peace vainly trying to flag down a procession of Nazi tanks with an olive branch. Yet when he worked for the Department of Labor, Gropper chose to emphasize the heroism and prowess of American construction workers, building the Hoover Dam in *Construction of the Dam* (1937). Here men were fully in charge of their machines.

Overwhelmed by the array of motors and propellers on display at the *Salon d' Aviation,* Paris, in 1911, Marcel Duchamp observed to fellow artist Constantin Brancusi, "Painting is finished. Who can do anything better than this propeller? Can you?" In 1922 innovative photographer Alfred Stieglitz (1864–1946) had his colleagues attend a symposium on the subject "Can a photograph have the significance of art?" The discussion was published in *Manuscripts* for December 1922. Marcel Duchamp answered the question directly. "You know exactly what I think of photography. I would like to see it make people despise painting until something else will make photography unbearable." But photographers were not necessarily consistent for they shifted their emphasis. At the turn of the century reform-minded photographer Lewis W. Hine had followed in the honorable tradition of progressive journalist Jacob Riis in stark photographs documenting the drudgery of men, women, and children in inhospitable mills and factories across America. In his later years Hine celebrated the prowess of workers, notably those engaged in such fearless endeavors as the epic construction of the Empire State Building, most notably in his *Icarus* of 1931. In contrast, Margaret Bourke White concentrated on more formal studies. Her photographs of a textile mill at Amoskeag, New Hampshire, in 1932 emphasized just how efficient was American industry without hinting at the cost in human terms, implicitly approving the way things were being run, although she did protest against social conditions to the American Artists' Congress in 1935.

Not only did the machine widen the range of subject matter for all forms of art, providing them with new themes and powerful images, but it also introduced new materials and techniques. Twenty years after the public began to refer to a coterie of New York artists as the "Ash Can School," on account of their playful, quixotic treatment of urban scenes, Charles Burchfield (1893–1967) turned epithet into metaphor in his watercolor of a trash heap and weeds in a culvert entitled *Still Life—Scrap Iron* (1929). The junk of a machine age scattered over the countryside was a central image in a period when the town was overtaking the countryside.

Immigrant artists Marcel Duchamp (1887–1967) and Francis Picabia (1879–1953) were iconoclasts who were thrown into nihilism by their outrage at the carnage of World War I. Picabia's machine drawings for the Alfred Stieglitz review *291* emphasized the hard edges of machines and challenged the conventional academic wisdom as to what constituted a standard acceptable subject for a drawing or painting. In order to challenge the resolution and conviction of the Independents, the American artists who affected to adore his work, Duchamp, under the alias of "R. Mutt," a plumber, submitted a porcelain urinal entitled *Fountain,* for their exhibition of 1920. The Independents Committee was scandalized and rejected the exhibit: Duchamp resigned and proclaimed that it was the artist's selection of an object for display that turned it into an objet d'art. This, and this only, was the correct criterion for art. Because *Fountain* was, in fact, a machine for passing urine, it was obscene to a genteel art committee. The significances of the incident, sometimes known as the "Richard Mutt Case," was not the object itself but the happening, the way the urinal as sculpture tested public taste to the extreme. As Dickran Tashjian explains in *The Machine Age in America* (1986), "Duchamp had subverted deeply entrenched cultural norms for art by introducing an artifact from an industrial network into an art network involving studios, galleries, and exhibitions." In *Kora is Hell* (1920) poet William Carlos Williams claimed that Duchamp's *Fountain* was "a representative piece of American sculpture." To a credulous public, eager for titillation, Duchamp was now the "Buddha of the bathroom." Duchamp claimed how "The only works of art America has given are her plumbing and her bridges," thereby underscoring the irony of a situation already rich in irony whereby commonplace machine objects might be taken as serious works of art. The debate about what constitutes art continued to the end of the twentieth century and its comic possibilities were mercilessly exploited by Dada artists. In 1918 Morton Schamberg (1881–1918) joined a miter box and plumbing trap and entitled his sculpture-by-collage *God,* thus provocatively exposing the status awarded to sanitation in American society. It was in this context that realistic and regional art continued a hostile dialogue with abstract art.

Painting in the 1920s and 1930s

Stuart Davis (1894–1964) was a painter whose work was in many ways analogous to the poetry of E. E. Cummings. His mature style did not develop fully until he returned from study in Europe in 1929, but his inspiration came directly from the urban landscape of the twenties:

American wood and iron work of the past; Civil War and skyscraper architecture; the brilliant colors on gasoline stations; chainstore fronts, and taxicabs . . . electric signs; the landscape and boats of Gloucester, Mass.; 5 and 10 cent store kitchen utensils; movies and radio; Earl Hines hot piano and Negro jazz music in general.

Davis worked with all of these influences—often abstracting them in a stylized manner—to create colorful paintings that captured the commercial vigor of the decade. He was an individualist who avoided joining movements and was also one of the most articulate spokesmen for abstract painting while always describing himself as a realist painter. This may appear to be a contradiction in terms, but Davis often forcefully explained that his realism was not founded on naturalistic representation but consisted, again like an improvising jazz musician, of interpreting existing subject matter through an abstract style. Davis acknowledged the influence of jazz music on his paintings and the debt is quite evident in many of his works with their strong colors and sense of vigorous movement.

Another aspect of Davis's art worth noting is the fact that, together with the American school of painters known as the Precisionists, he was a precursor of the Pop artists. Some of Davis's work, such as his 1924 rendering of a packet of Odol disinfectant, brings to mind the icon of 1960s' pop art—Andy Warhol's representations of Campbell's soup cans. In the 1920s American painters first began to incorporate into their work the letters, words, and numerals that were becoming an integral part of the urban landscape. The social fabric was increasingly held together by a commercial culture that relied on signs, particularly advertisements, to get its message across. The Pop artists were to exploit this subject matter more fully in the 1950s and 1960s, but in the 1920s the Precisionists anticipated Pop artists with their highly stylized renderings of the urban and industrial scene. They took the commonplace and turned it into the monumental, as with Charles Demuth's (1883–1935) urgent, but splintered, representation of a fire truck moving in the city at night in *I Saw the Figure 5 in Gold,* inspired by a poem by his friend, William Carlos Williams, *The Great Figure.*

Together with Demuth, Charles Sheeler (1883–1965) was a leader of the Precisionists and between 1927 and 1930 he created a series of paintings based on the burgeoning automobile plants of Michigan. Sheeler was also a photographer and he developed a painting style that moved away from his early concern for French modernism and centered on a simple, almost photographic, realism. However, like Demuth, he was fascinated by the stark geometry of the new industrial plants and often his choice of subject matter in itself lent his paintings a quality of abstraction. *Classic Landscape* (1931), based on photographs of the Ford River Rouge Plant, for example, is, at first glance, a realistic representation of the Ford factory, but a closer look reveals that the factory is quite simply too clean to be a real one. The painting is even "too realistic" to be a photograph—it is without the atmospheric distortions of the camera that inevitably adorn photographs of industrial scenes taken at such long range. Sheeler's *Church Street El* of 1920 shows how realism can verge on abstraction. The buildings have been simplified to their geometric shapes. Sheeler's paintings bring to mind two other names that are sometimes used to describe the Precisionists—the Immaculates and the Cubist-Realists. It is strangely paradoxical that a painting can become too realistic by too much concentration on detail to seem real. The phenomenon has been exploited not only by the Precisionists, but in the 1970s and 1980s by the American Super-Realists, in particular Richard Estes.

The Precisionists never formed a movement in the strict sense of the word; they did not issue a manifesto, nor did they meet regularly. But they undoubtedly formed a movement in their shared concern for America's new industrial landscape. Demuth and Sheeler were two leading figures, but others included Preston Dickinson (1891–1930), Niles Spencer (1893–1952), Ralston Crawford (1906–78), and Georgia O'Keeffe (1887–1986).

However, O'Keeffe differed from these other artists by virtue of her application of precisionist principles to both industrial and organic forms. Her work is uniquely and unmistakably marked by the stamp of her forceful individualism, yet at the same time it is an absorbed synthesis of most of the progressive tendencies in American painting up to World War II. By the mid-twenties she was painting her famous studies of enlarged flowers, which, for all their rhythmic line movements, are essentially abstract compositions, reminiscent of Arthur Dove's free-form abstractions drawn from nature, Charles Demuth's crisp surfaces, and Charles Sheeler's sterile forms. Many critics have chosen to interpret her work in terms of stereotypical femininity, using such adjectives as "elegant," "pretty," and "typically feminine," in appreciations of her work. But a more significant explanation of her art is to be

Georgia O'Keeffe, *Lake George Window* (1920), oil on canvas, 40″ × 30″. (Collection, The Museum of Modern Art, New York. Acquired through the Richard D. Brixey Bequest). Here Georgia O'Keeffe has isolated a shuttered window door from its surroundings and, by eliminating details that might disturb her immaculate presentation of form, has heightened the overall visual impact.

found in a consideration of where she came from and the various influences she assimilated.

She was born near Sun Prairie, Wisconsin, in 1887 and spent her childhood in Virginia before moving to Texas. She retained a deep affinity with the enormous landscape of America's Midwest and West. Before meeting her future husband, Alfred Stieglitz, she had studied at Teachers' College, New York, with Arthur Dove (1880–1946), a teacher who based his instruction on an unorthodox source—the principles of design that he had discerned in Oriental art. He emphasized flat patterns and harmonious compositions that were to attract the interest of Stieglitz and his coterie when they were first shown O'Keeffe's work. O'Keeffe was influenced by other American painters who were drawing on European modernism for inspiration and technique but the most significant fact about O'Keeffe's painting is that she herself never actually studied in Europe. Not only did she create a synthesis of all the progressive tendencies in American painting but she also managed this without crossing the Atlantic to see at first hand the innovations of the European modernists. Her debt is to fellow Americans, not to Europeans. Gerald Murphy's (1888–1964) *Razor* of 1924 was noted at the time as being distinctively American in its choice and treatment of subject. The dash of colors and the stylized representation of three very American objects (safety razor, matchbox, and fountain pen) bring this painting even closer to Pop art than the work of the Precisionists.

Edward Hopper (1882–1967) was another painter who has been celebrated as a particularly American artist. Hopper, a realist who was not concerned with modernist styles, remarked, "To me, form, color and design are merely a means to an end, the tools I work with, and they do not interest me greatly for their own sake." Between 1906 and 1910 he made three journeys to Europe and spent most of his time in Paris. His strongest stylistic influence during these early years came from the French Impressionists and for a while he painted in a frankly Impressionist manner. However, American critics disliked these early works because they were too close to the art of Europe. After returning to America, Hopper abandoned his bright colors and adopted a more somber palette that was more in keeping with the subject matter he drew from his native country. Ironically, critics later charged Hopper with provincial nationalism in his painting.

Hopper's art has certainly come to epitomize the genre of American scene painting, but it is far from parochial or merely nationalistic. His early training in painting was at the New York School of Art and, although he studied under the traditionalist William Merritt Chase, it was Robert Henri, who joined the school in 1903, who was the greater influence. Henri passed on to Hopper the main drive of the Ash Can School—the desire to paint the life and sights around him. For Hopper this meant the city and the country. He painted both with a peculiarly individual vision.

Unlike the Ash Can School and early modernists, such as John Marin, when Hopper looked at the life around him in the American city he perceived not vitality but loneliness and melancholy. In contrast to the Precisionists, his canvases were often peopled, but rarely is there any sense of communication or interaction between characters. His *New York Movie* of 1939 illustrates Hopper's masterly handling of light. The lonely, isolated usherette separated from the auditorium can be seen as a symbol of humanity lost in its individual thoughts. The painting explores the tension between physical reality and our perception of our place in the scheme of things. Hopper himself was, by nature, a reserved and distanced character. His physical appearance had much to do with this. By the age of twelve he was an ungainly six feet tall and was ridiculed by his peers. His understandable embarrassment and resentment caused him to turn his back on his contemporaries and led him into solitude, a state of being that became a major theme in his painting.

Hopper is just as much a painter of the 1920s as, say, the lively and colorful figure of Stuart Davis. Edward Hopper once said of critical examinations of his work, "the loneliness thing is overdone," but loneliness is definitely to be found even in those of his paintings that expressed his passion for architecture and are not peopled. Many of Hopper's paintings provide us with scenes that are endowed with the same poignant symbolism as F. Scott Fitzgerald's "valley of ashes" in *The Great Gatsby*. In the midst of apparent prosperity there will always exist places "where ashes grow like wheat into ridges and hills and grotesque gardens, where ashes take the form of houses and chimneys and rising smoke and, finally, with a transcendent effort, of ash-grey men, who move dimly and already crumbling through the powdery air." You will search in vain for such a scene in the work of Edward Hopper but you will find the same chilly meaning in the first painting of his that you look at.

However, Hopper did not consciously set out to create an art that analytically criticized American society. That task was taken up mainly in the 1930s by the Social Realist painters. Foremost among them was Ben Shahn (1898–1969) who, like John Dos Passos, was particularly inspired by the *Sacco and Vanzetti* case of the late 1920s. Shahn was actually in Europe when the execution took place on August 23, 1927, but, on returning to America in 1929, he began work on a series of paintings depicting the trial and its aftermath. Shahn was born in Lithuania but grew up in an immigrant quarter of New York City where hatred of injustice and distrust of authority were common. At the age of sixteen he was apprenticed to a lithographer from whom he acquired an eye for telling detail. However, his painting relies less on realistic detail than on the devices he absorbed from the work of early German Expressionists. Amongst these devices are the use of oversized hands and heads that forcefully project the characters in his paintings, lending them a poignance and a significance that served his ends as a Social Realist. Shahn once said of the *Sacco and Vanzetti* case: "Ever since I could remember I'd wished that I'd been lucky enough to be alive at a great time—when something big was going on, like the Crucifixion. And suddenly I realized I was. Here I was living through another Crucifixion. Here was something to paint!" Between 1935 and 1938 Shahn took almost 6,000 photographs for the New Deal's Farm Security Administration, documenting the effects of depression on the rural poor. He later used many of these photographs as starting points for paintings.

Engineering Art

Critic Jane Heap, coeditor of the *Little Review,* wanted artists to affiliate themselves with one another and with scientists, engineers, and other constructive professional men of the age. Her hope for works based on a spirit of technological cooperation culminated in the Machine Age Exposition held in Steinway Hall, New York, in spring 1927, considered an ideal, plain setting for the various machines, paintings, and drawings on show. They were all displayed together, rather than with art and technology confined to separate rooms as was historically the case at great expositions. This reflected Jane Heap's conviction that engineers had much to learn from artists, not least basic ideas of artistic sensibility in terms of machine design. As she explained in her contemporaneous article, "Machine-Age Exposition," for the *Little Review* supplement of May 1927, which served as catalogue for the exhibition, she had decided on an exhibition of machines and art and architecture in juxtaposition. The cover was an elegant abstract design by Fernand Léger (1881–1955) and artists and architects represented included John Storrs, Charles Demuth, Louis Lozowick, Hugh Ferriss, Walter Gropius, and Raymond Hood.

The exposition stimulated discussion about Soviet society that was meant to fulfill the true union of arts and technology desired by Jane Heap. However, the exhibition attracted far less attention than the Exposition of Art in Trade, sponsored by Macy's in the first week of May, and which was more attractive because it promised those who attended a consumers' paradise.

It also prompted discussion about Constructivism. Initially a Soviet-inspired art movement, it represented a committed effort by artists to cooperate with industry, that is to use the new resources of industry, notably raw metals, and fashion from them a universal art that would be appreciated by aesthetes and proletariat alike. Among Jane Heap's constructivist heroes was Russian-American painter Louis Lozowick who drew and painted machines as forms of geometric ornament until he discovered how easily other commercial artists could transfer and develop his ornaments into advertising logos, feeding consumer, that is to say, capitalist desires. Dickran Tashjian observes in *The Machine Age in America* how, "Tacitly acknowledging the hegemony of American capitalism, Lozowick suggested that the American revolutionary artist should picture the machine environment 'more as a prognostication than as a fact,' a projection of 'rationalization and economy which must prove allies of the working class in the building of socialism.' " Lozowick shifted emphasis from abstract art to realistic depiction of urban life. In his *High Voltage—cos cob* (1930), he positioned a worker in front of the electric wires he had erected, thereby placing the actual mechanic rather than the engineer or designer in front.

Although Constructivism was a significant political movement in art for a handful of American artists in the 1920s, its political emphasis was successively weakened in the 1930s as there were ever more European styles and movements to stimulate American artists. However, abstract art was increasingly popular among emerging new artists although it was disliked by many radicals and most of the middle class, the potential customers. In fact, abstraction became a central issue for other young artists who lacked opportunities to show their abstract paintings. Rejected by the established art world, in 1936 they formed an association of American Abstract Artists to promote their work. It included Stuart Davis, who was president, Ilya Bolotowsky, Charles Shaw, and Paul Kelpe. In their *Yearbook of 1938* Rosalind Bergelsdorf defended abstract art in general terms, claiming how "the machine guided us to a logical combination of simplicity and functionalism" and that "so-called abstract painting is the expression of art of this age," the age of the machine. The most committed to making works of art from raw materials was Ibram Lassaw (b. 1913) who used sheet metal and steel to fashion biomorphic forms.

One exceptional sculptor made machines work for him and thus transcended the boundaries of his art. Alexander Calder (1898–1976), born into a family of sculptors, moved decisively away from his father's allegorical figures that used equestrian statues, most inappropriately, to symbolize such new forms of energy as electricity, into new, moving forms of sculpture, suggesting a motorized *Universe* (1934). In *Praying Mantis* (1936), Calder drew from his wide range of experiences and used biomorphic shapes, kinetic art, surrealism, and constructivism in his various works. Yet Calder, an American artist whose early career in Paris was significant more for its lack of distinctive achievement than anything else, eventually astounded Europe with his wire toys and metal circus figures. Eventually, he produced the

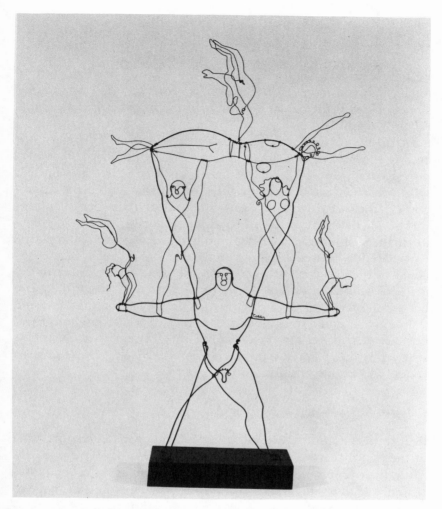

Alexander Calder, *The Brass Family* (1929), brass wire sculpture, 64″ ×
41″ × 8½″. (Collection of Whitney Museum of American Art, New
York; gift of the artist). The son and grandson of sculptors, Alexander
Calder (1898–1976) became himself America's most famous sculptor,
noted for his invention of the mobile, a hanging sculpture in motion.
He began his professional career as a freelance newspaper artist and
sketched both the Ringling Brothers' and the Barnum and Bailey Circuses that remained a continuous source of artistic inspiration for him,
as did the city of Paris. *The Brass Family,* in which an outsize athlete
balances six other acrobats, demonstrates Calder's irrepressible humor
as well as his skill in ink drawings. Indeed, Calder's wire sculptures
seem to transform drawn lines into space.

mobile, a hanging sculpture that moved of its own accord and no longer showed its origins in the machine. Thus, as Dickran Tashjian observes, in Calder's hands, "technology became the natural once again."

Ironically, in the 1930s it was three sculptors who were not among the American abstract artists—Charles Biederman, Theodore Roszak, and José de Rivera—who became most identified with constructivist art, itself a form of abstraction. Charles Biederman (1906–   ) used metal and glass as reliefs on paintings that recalled works by Piet Mondrian. Theodore Roszak (1907–81) made sculptures out of steel and bronze, aluminum and plastic that were like futurist architecture. In time, convinced that artists could not work with industry, Roszak abandoned Constructivism. José de Rivera (1904–85) a former machinist who had also been the owner of a tool shop, provided fascinating, graceful shapes that seemed to open and close the space surrounding them. His *Form Synthesis* (1938) of morel metal seemed to anticipate spaceships; his painted aluminum *Red and Black: Double Element* (1938) was both rectilinear and volumetric.

Art in the Great Depression

Realism in painting came to the fore during the depression. One of the major reasons for this shift away from abstraction toward naturalistic representation was the intervention of the federal government with its unparalleled program of wide-scale patronage of the arts. The New Deal encouraged a sense of nationalism radically different from earlier outbursts of xenophobic protectionism. American society was, to a certain extent, united in common misery. The New Deal was a symbol of some hope for the decade. The repercussions of government intervention for American painting were immense. Critical opinion is, as usual, divided over the value of the Federal Art Project and its associated programs and some commentators have emphasized the conservative aspects of its nature, particularly its lack of concern with abstract painting. However, it is undeniable that it sustained many important progressive painters, both realists and modernists, at a time when they may otherwise have been forced to abandon art.

The man who initiated government patronage of the arts in the 1930s was himself a progressive artist and was particularly concerned with mural painting. George Biddle was a member of an influential Philadelphia family and had attended Groton School and Harvard University with Franklin D. Roosevelt. He spurned the career in law that his family expected of him and sailed for France in 1911 where he began his career as a painter. His work always displayed a sensitive social conscience and, in common with the Social Realist painters, he strongly believed that art had not functioned as a positive influence on society for centuries, that it had been, "so to speak, a prostitute, well paid, sleeping in expensive beds, but divorced . . . from our program of life."

On May 9, 1933, Biddle wrote to Roosevelt suggesting that young American painters would support his New Deal and were eager to express the ideals of a social revolution in mural form on the walls of America's public buildings. The inspiration for Biddle's belief came from the experiment sponsored by the Mexican president, Alvaro Obregon, in the 1920s. Public buildings in Mexico City were covered with murals expressing the ideals of the Mexican revolution and the artists had received a small wage from the government for their work. The Mexican muralists created what some critics have considered to be the greatest national school of mural painting since the Italian Renaissance. Their leaders were Diego Rivera, José Clemente Orozco, and David Alfaro Siqueiros. In the late 1920s and early 1930s Orozco and Rivera worked in America and stimulated interest in the mural form. Their presence was particularly beneficial for America's best-known muralist, Thomas Hart Benton. Diego Rivera (1886–1957), the prolific Mexican muralist whose principal subjects were industrial production and political revolution, was one of the very few social artists outside Russia and Germany to devote his career to social art. The range of his art and the extraordinary prestige it enjoys in Mexico were the result of special historical circumstances. The people of Mexico (like those of Russia) were of a partially industrialized generation. Few could read and write. However, they were used to looking at popular devotional art as a prime source of moral instruction.

FDR was enthusiastic about Biddle's proposals and he enlisted the support of Secretary of Labor Frances Perkins, Secretary of the Interior Harold L. Ickes, Assistant Secretary of Agriculture Rexford G. Tugwell, and Eleanor Roosevelt. Yet, despite these impressive governmental supporters, the proposals ran into conservative opposition from an existing artistic agency within the government. The National Commission of Fine Arts had been created by Congress in 1910 and was strongly biased in favor of classical art. Charles Moore had been chairman of the commission since 1915 and he instructed that a long letter be sent to Roosevelt, criticizing Biddle's proposals on the grounds that they were subversive of traditional art. However, in the crisis years of the New Deal the government was open to influence along unorthodox channels and Biddle, along with an artistic ally from the Treasury Department, Edward Bruce, was able to get the project funded through the recently formed relief organization led by Harry Hopkins, the Civil Works Administration (CWA).

The formula that George Biddle and Edward Bruce devised for the administration of the new project was basically that of a central committee in Washington, D.C., with decentralized regional advisory committees each with a regional chairman selected by the central committee. Biddle himself was more concerned with painting than with administration and Bruce eventually became the project's guiding light. As a result, the emphasis on mural painting was expanded to include sculptors and easel painters as well. The Public Works of Art Project (PWAP) was operational by December 1933 when eighty-six artists throughout the sixteen geographic divisions received their first pay checks. Forbes Watson, a former art critic, was appointed technical director for the entire project and became its chief philosopher and spokesman.

However, the PWAP only lasted as long as Harry Hopkin's ill-fated CWA. In using the $400 million allocated to him from Harold Ickes's Public Works Administration (PWA), Hopkins had adopted a policy of administering relief across the board without means tests or other forms of qualified distribution. By early spring of 1934 these unorthodox methods had aroused such strong conservative opposition that Roosevelt was obliged to close down the CWA. This was by no means the end of government patronage of the arts. A major exhibition of PWAP art held at the Corcoran Gallery of Art in Washington, D.C., between April 24 and May 20, 1934, proved to be a success. Five hundred items were chosen as exhibits out of thousands submitted by the regional committees. The organizers were optimistic. The weekend before the opening Forbes Watson proclaimed that the exhibition would be, "the greatest art event in this country since the Armory Show."

While its success did not quite match that of the Armory Show of 1913, the Corcoran exhibition was sufficiently well received to ensure continued government involvement in patronage throughout the decade. Indeed, during the 1930s several government agencies would find themselves competing to employ the best artists available. Edward Bruce continued his involvement in government patronage through the Treasury Relief Art Project (TRAP), created in July, 1935. TRAP was funded with a grant from the recently established Works Progress Administration (WPA) controlled by Harry Hopkins. However, the WPA instituted its own Federal Art Project (FAP) that received fourteen times more money than Bruce's Treasury project and gave aid to ten times the number of artists. The FAP retained the structure of the PWAP and had many important artists on its payroll at one time or another, including some who became leading modern painters in the movement known as Abstract Expressionism: Arshile Gorky (1904–1948), Philip Guston (1930–1980), and Jackson Pollock (1912–1956), for example. Gorky was a painter of Armenian origin who deliberately went through a range of styles—Cubist, Surrealist, and Fauvist—before arriving at his mature style in the 1940s. His painting, *The Artist and His Mother* of 1926–1929, is not typical of that mature style in that it is somewhat naturalistic, but this painting portends something of the sadness and tragedy that overtook Gorky's life in his last years. Between 1946 and 1948 he suffered a major fire at his studio, cancer, marital breakup, and a major car crash in which he broke his neck and damaged his painting arm. In July of 1948 Gorky took his own life.

However, the FAP, despite its sponsorship of modernists such as Gorky, was, on the whole, more committed to realist painting because of its avowed purpose to create a popular art that gave expression to the aspirations and achievements of the American people. The director of the FAP was Holger Cahill whose specific concern was folk art. In fact, the FAP did much to propagate serious painting outside the urban centers, chiefly New York, and was particularly responsible for the rise of the school of painters known as the Regionalists. The Regionalists were undoubtedly disaffected with modernist painting and their ideals concurred with those of the PWAP officials in Westport, Connecticut, who forbade their artists to experiment with "cubism, futurism, and all forms of modernism."

Private sponsors also encouraged American understanding of, and self-expression through, art and wanted people to appreciate modern works. In 1929 the Museum of Modern Art was founded in New York by Lillie P. Bliss, Mrs. Cornelius Sullivan, and Abby Aldrich Rockefeller, as a permanent museum for the best modern works of art produced since the 1880s and to encourage and develop public appreciation of all the visual arts, including film. In 1930 Gertrude Vanderbilt Whitney, sculptor and art collector, founded the Whitney Museum of American Art, firstly in her Greenwich Village studio. She believed that living American artists deserved recognition and encouragement and donated over 600 American works in her possession. During the 1930s the Museum of Modern Art staged two crucial shows that influenced all serious young painters: *Cubism and Abstract Art* (1936) and *Fantastic Art, Dada, Surrealism* (1936–1937). Also, in 1939 the Valentine Gallery exhibited *Guernica* (1937), Picasso's protest at the German bombing and devastation of the defenseless Basque capital on April 27, 1937, in the Spanish Civil War. These exhibitions served to introduce a new generation of American artists to the Cubist revolution of Picasso and Braque.

The Regionalist school of painters, led by John Steuart Curry, Grant Wood, and Thomas Hart Benton, impressed on all their pupils that modernism was useless, unwanted, and decadent, that its techniques were irrelevant to the United States, and that what the American people really wanted was representational art of such American scenes as pasture, field, and harvest. Benton was the most vociferous advocate of this point of view. This was not

Thomas Hart Benton, *People of Chilmark* (Figure Composition) (1921), oil on canvas, 65⅝″ × 77⅝″. (Hirshhorn Museum and Sculpture Garden, Smithsonian Institution, Washington, D.C.). Preeminent regional artist Thomas Hart Benton of Neosho, Missouri, was son and grandnephew to congressmen and, throughout his youth, his family were discussing the factors that had shaped the Midwest. After an early period of experimentation, he rejected cubism and other modern European styles in favor of the more monumental mural art of the Italian Renaissance, and the easel paintings of El Greco. He wanted to forge an American art that would draw on the history, folklore, and daily life of the United States for subject matter but unfold the themes in stylized compositions dominated by thrusting curved lines.

surprising when we consider that he had begun his career as a modernist, a close friend of Stanton MacDonald Wright, who now turned on his modernist associates with great venom.

Yet much of the criticism of regionalist artists that stressed the conservative aspects of their art is exaggerated and fails to take account of their progressive qualities. Grant Wood (1892–1942) was one of America's foremost regionalist painters and spent most of his life in his native Iowa. He made two journeys to Europe where he was first influenced by Impressionism and later by the meticulous creations of medieval Flemish painters. When he returned to Iowa in the mid-1920s, he concentrated on painting the American scene. However, it was in the 1930s that his art reached its fullest expression and significance, and during this time he supervised most of the government art projects that operated in Iowa. He worked as technical chief on a cooperative mural at the University of Iowa. From the very first day in their workshop (an old swimming pool), Wood found the team of twenty-two painters divided into equal numbers of modernists and realists. Initially, the atmosphere was strained but gave way to a community of feeling that made the completion of the mural project their top priority. At one stage when the PWAP regional quotas were decreased, the twenty-two artists redistributed the incoming pay checks rather than have any artist laid off.

America's leading regionalist was Thomas Hart Benton (1889–1975), much influenced by the work of the Mexican muralists. However, his art evolved independently of them during the 1920s and, like Grant Wood's, reached its fullest expression in the 1930s. During World War I he volunteered for duty and was assigned as an architectural draftsman to the Norfolk Naval Base, Virginia. While studying in a Norfolk lodging house, he came across a nineteenth-century, four-volume history of the United States written by J. A. Spencer and illustrated with engravings. In his professional and technical autobiography, *An American in Art* (1969), he explained the significance of these illustrations for the evolution of his painting of the 1920s and 1930s: "Why could not such subject pictures dealing with the meanings of American history possess aesthetically interesting properties, deliverable along with their meanings? History painting, religious or secular, had occupied a large place in the annals of art. Why not look into it again, I asked, and try to fill the contextual void of my own painting, give it some kind of meaning?" The particular enterprise Benton had in mind was a mural project to be called *History of America*. By 1926 he had completed his first two "chapters" of the American history and had successfully exhibited them at the Architectural League in New York. However, by 1929, when he was invited to create a mural for the New School of Social Research in New York, his concern for history was replaced with a desire to document the contemporary scene. The immediate reason for this change in emphasis was the topical work of José Clemente Orozco who was also creating murals for the New School at the same time as Benton.

Benton himself did little work under government patronage, primarily because he was enjoying success in the private field. Nevertheless, he is closely linked to the art of the 1930s that sought to capture and document American life in all its aspects. The charges of political and artistic conservatism that have been leveled at these Regionalists are largely unfounded. For example, while using traditional artistic techniques, Wood was a New Deal Democrat in his politics, while Benton was a latter-day Populist whose realistic art is hardly conservative in its colorful yet lugubrious depictions of the American scene.

However, the Regionalists were not the only painters to concern themselves with aspects of American life in the 1930s. Jacob Lawrence (b. 1917) grew up in Harlem during the depression and, being black, was naturally aware of the cultural heritage and the hardships of black Americans during the decade. His career began in a settlement house art class that was supported by the FAP and his very first paintings dealt with historical figures who had played important roles in the liberation of slaves: for example, the Haitian Toussaint L'Ouverture and the southerners Frederick Douglass and Harriet Tubman. Between 1940 and 1941 he drew directly on his experience of the depression and created the series of sixty paintings entitled *The Migration of the Negro*. These paintings provide a telling description of the plight of dispossessed blacks in the 1930s. Lawrence has pointed out that this migration was an integral part of his life: "My parents were part of this migration

—on their way North when I was born in Atlantic City in 1917."
His use of stark compositions, bright poster colors, and angular,
often contorted, human figures, serve to increase the already
considerable emotional impact of his subject matter.

Two other leading Social Realists were Philip Evergood (1901–
1975) and Jack Levine (b. 1915). Evergood enrolled in the PWAP
in 1933 and created his most militant social protest paintings
during the next few years. Levine's social protests are often tempered by his ability for comic satire that has made him one of the
most durable of all the American painters of this century. Social
Realism in painting was essentially an optimistic, socially committed art form and, when Jack Levine spoke of his own painting,
he could easily have been talking for his colleagues: "I took my
place in the late thirties as part of the general uprising of social
consciousness in art and literature. It was part of the feeling that
things were the right way; we were all making a point . . . we
had a feeling of confidence about our ability to do something
about the world." Indeed, such confidence was strengthened by
the arrival in America of a kindred European spirit. The Social
Realists were deeply indebted to German Expressionists for their
manner. In 1933 the leading Expressionist George Grosz (1893–
1959) fled from Hitler's Germany and sought asylum in New
York. In 1938 he became an American citizen. Grosz's bitter
satires were an inspiration for many Social Realists. Other European artists also found at least temporary refuge from fascism in
America—Yves Tanguy, Pavel Tchelitchew, Max Ernst, and Salvador Dali—and the weight of their influence became apparent
after World War II.

World War II itself was to prove most influential in changing
the course of the development of American painting in the twentieth century. The shock of another war after the experience of
the war to end all wars proved too much for the American artist
and the American art world. Thomas Hart Benton wrote regret-
fully of the fact that, although he had successfully created a meaningful art in the 1930s, during World War II he saw "most of the
meanings, which it took so many years to formulate, disappearing with the dissolution of the world that generated them." Socially concerned artists such as Benton were to be replaced as

leaders after the war by the angst-ridden and essentially introspective Abstract Expressionists such as Pollock and Gorky.

Abstract Expressionism

It would be all too tempting and logical enough to conclude that the next major development in art—Abstract Expressionism—was a direct descendant from Cubism, with the shattering of conventional human and other traditional forms and their redesigning. Once one form had been broken, then its shattering or splintering must follow, just as World War II shattered societies almost everywhere but the United States. The years of World War II were not years of artistic sterility. This was the period when Abstract Expressionism was being developed by a handful of artists working in or near New York: Jackson Pollock (1912–1956), Arshile Gorky (1904–1948), Willem de Kooning (b. 1904), and Mark Rothko (1903–1970). Abstract Expressionism was to emerge as the dominant style of the postwar world.

In his *How New York Stole the Idea of Modern Art* (1985) Serge Guilbaut shows how New York intellectuals and artists moved in the late 1930s from popular front interest in the artist's relationship with the masses to a profound sense of alienation and concern for a special audience. Instead of wanting to change society, they became obsessed by the fate of creativity in modern society. In his 1939 essay for *Partisan Review* Clement Greenberg presented the crisis not in terms of society or social justice but in terms of the threat that the mass production of contemporary culture presented to artistic quality. Thus to continue producing painting or writing of high quality in the face of depression and war was, in itself, a radical act. American writers and painters were not immune from those devastating political experiences that had deeply disillusioned the American Left: Stalin's purges and show trials of 1936–1938; the Nazi-Soviet Pact of 1939; the Holocaust of 1941–1945; and the use of the atomic bomb in 1945. Such events forced them to reconsider their position and painters moved to an art form that was apolitical. They began to explore the possibilities of nonrepresentational art. In 1937 Meyer Schapiro had emphasized the humanity of abstract art in an article, "The Nature of

Abstract Art," for the *Marxist Quarterly,* and that abstract art was connected with social experience.

In *Hide-and-Seek* (1940–1942) Pavel Tchelitchev (1898–1957) showed the influence of surrealism in which the central tree surrounded by children's faces can be seen as representing the changing seasons of the year, while the color and composition suggest the internal biological workings of the human body. *The Red Stairway* (1944) shows Ben Shahn's experience in the Office of War Information where he dealt with photographs of bombing in Europe. Here a gleaming red stairway is in marked contrast to its devastated, bombed setting but it leads nowhere for its crippled passenger. The one sign of optimism is a laborer rising from the ground and facing forward, carrying on his back a basket loaded with stones with which to begin rebuilding. Shahn commented on the endless stream of photographs documenting "bombed-out places, so many of which I knew well and cherished. There were the churches destroyed, the villages, the monasteries. . . . I painted Italy as I lamented it, or feared that it might become." Instead of realism, he chose "A symbolism which I might once have considered cryptic" because it "now became the only means by which I could formulate the sense of emptiness and waste that the war gave me, and the sense of the littleness of people trying to live on through the enormity of war."

Faced with the only partly told horrors of the 1940s, art critic and historian Thomas Bender observes how

some painters, Mark Rothko in particular, found possibilities in the universality of primitive and archaic myths. They were able to believe that in speaking to the universal in man they had in fact expanded rather than contracted their connection with the public, even while narrowing their actual audience. By the end of the 40's, these artists thought their work represented not only their private anxiety but the anxiety of the age. They believed its illegibility was the only possible response to media and Government efforts to discuss the bomb in "normal" language and languages.

Of all these gifted, explosive talents, the most widely publicized was Jackson Pollock who studied at the Art Students League under prominent Regionalist Thomas Hart Benton. Benton conveyed his strong sense of vocation and the stature of art to his shy pupil. "You've the stuff, old kid—all you have to do is to keep it up," he is supposed to have told Pollock. From the very beginning, whether his work was regionalist or abstract, Pollock's work showed assured conception, dynamic rhythm and clear touch, and marked contrasts of dark and light. His expressionism was nourished by the work of the Mexican muralists, notably in the nightmarish *Woman* (1930–1933), which many critics see as a private family allegory, with its members surrounding an outsize mother like satellites in a dark sky. His pastoral work, like *Going West* (1934–1938), was nostalgic and melancholy. Yet there were always signs in his loose forms that he would move to abstraction. The New Deal rescued him from penury when he was employed in the FAP of the WPA, joining its painters in 1936 and staying until it was closed down in early 1943. It was his task to paint works for public buildings. He joined an experimental workshop of Alfaro Siquerios in Union Square, New York, where he was stimulated by Siquerios's own experimentation with new materials—spray guns and airbrushes, synthetic paint and lacquers. Pollock also discovered Picasso and his vocabulary of distended, reassembled, and primitive forms.

Since adolescence, Pollock had had a disturbing record of alcoholism and he underwent psychoanalysis with a number of psychiatrists in the period 1937–1943. During this time he made a series of "psychoanalytic drawings" and paintings with awkward limbs and eyes cleverly jumbled. Not only did they serve as therapy but they also served to exercise Pollock's need for the interconversion of form, the transmutation of figures into abstract form, and back again, notably in *White Horizontal* (c. 1938–1941) and *Composition with Masked Forms* (1941). These are fierce, disturbed works, akin to the last terrifying images of Goya or Van Gogh.

Pollock had been working to a breakthrough into major painting, heralded by his participation in a show organized by John Graham at McMillen, Inc., in January 1942, where relatively unknown American artists, such as Willem de Kooning and Lee Krasner, joined more famous ones, such as Stuart Davis and Walt Kuhn, and European notables such as Picasso and Braque. His work was now almost entirely abstract and on a very large scale, incorporating Cubist and Surrealist techniques in three paintings of 1942: *The Moon-Woman, Male and Female,* and *Stenographic Figure.* Elizabeth Frank writes of *Male and Female* that

it is possible to see male and female attributes in each of the figures. Passage yields to passage in an enriched virtuoso vocabulary of spatters, dips, swirls, scumbles, gestures, arabesques, filled-in shapes, and inscribed numbers, hieroglyphics of a painter by calligraphy that, for all its energy, never crowds or squeezes the picture.

As his companion and future wife, Lee Krasner, remembered, he would always continue painting if a recognizable image surfaced because "I choose to veil the imagery." In his *Guardians of the Secret* (1943), he combined a horizontal dog and two vertical figures, a bull and a woman, as "guardians" of his own psyche. He carried the bull imagery into *Pasiphaë* (1943), where the moon goddess of Crete consummates her love for a bull sent to her husband, King Minos.

Pollock moved to ever-larger and more abstract paintings and began pouring and dripping paint onto his canvases now stretched out on the floor, since some were far too large to be supported by an easel. In his *Composition with Pouring II* of 1943 for Peggy Guggenheim, a painting measuring 7' 11¾" by 19' 9½", he used thin vertical lines winding across the canvas in a mix of painting and drawing. In *Night Ceremony* each individual drawn shape exists quite independently in its own space. Sometimes, he returned to clear images as in his Equine series of 1944 that show his fascination with Picasso's horses in his bullfighting paintings. Pollock's *Totem Lesson 1* (1944) and *Totem Lesson 2* (1945) for his second one-man show at Art of This Century in November 1945 achieved complete solutions to the problems of mixing Abstract Expressionism figuration, and a mix of drawings as shapes and as "allover" lines. Clement Greenberg claimed that the show established Pollock "as the strongest painter of his generation." He believed the works were deeply pessimistic. "The only optimism in his smoky turbulent painting comes from his own manifest faith in the efficacy, for him personally, of art." Moreover, "he is not afraid to look ugly—all profoundly original art looks ugly at

Arshile Gorky, *The Artist and His Mother* (1926–1929), oil, 60″ × 50″.
(Collection of Whitney Museum of American Art, New York; gift of
Julien Levy for Maro and Natasha Gorky in memory of their father).
Armenian artist Arshile Gorky, whose original name was Vosdanig
Manoog Adoian, immigrated to the United States in 1920, and in the
1930s became friendly with abstract artists Stuart Davis and Willem de
Kooning. He set himself the task of translating European modernism
into American modes by retracing the European artistic revolution from
impressionism to cubism and surrealism, generation by generation, in
his own works. In this transitional painting he acknowledges the influence of Picasso, adopting the sort of composition of Picasso's early works.

first." Much the same criticism had been made of cubist art just after the turn of the century.

Abstract Expressionism was the new distinctive American art that allowed New York to supersede Paris as the international center of art, just when American politicians encouraged a high art that would give the United States a new cultural authority, commensurate with its economic, political, and military aims in the postwar world. Clement Greenberg challenged the shopworn idea of the supremacy of Paris and insisted that New York had replaced it. "The conclusion forces itself," he declared, "that the main premises of western art have at last migrated to the United States, along with the center of gravity of industrial power and political power."

American Architecture

Although skyscrapers were first created in the 1870s and 1880s and took definitive form under the expert innovations of Louis Sullivan in the 1890s and 1900s, it was in the 1910s and 1920s that they came to be widely regarded as the most substantive contribution of the United States to modern architecture, representing American determination to excel and turning America's major cities into vertical, man-made canyons.

While modernism in architecture was defined in various sophisticated ways, essential components were the use of modern materials and modern techniques to create a contemporary interior environment and an unqualified modern facade. Thus modernist architects used not only steel, brick, and glass but also aluminum, concrete, and formica in their buildings, many of which in size and spaciousness extolled the power of corporate America. In domestic architecture the aim was to provide homes with the maximum of efficient, cost-effective modern conveniences. Once again, it is the imaginative organizers of the exhibition, *The Machine Age in America,* and the authors of its accompanying catalogue, who help us understand the way modern architecture was an inevitable product of machine age ideas, technology, and images.

At the American Institute of Architects' Convention of 1930

modernist George Howe defined modernism in architecture as essentially technique, functionalism, the use of "modern construction and modern materials to the full, for architectural expression as well as for practical ends." At the time Howe (1886–1955) and his partner William Lescaze (1896–1969) were designing the Philadelphia Savings Fund Society Building, Philadelphia (1928–1932), that drew upon and, indeed, maximized the use of such raw materials and technologies as glass, steel, and electricity in an age where the car also demanded a new sort of building, the garage, to shelter it.

While much concerned with appearances, some architects concentrated on using the machine and its processes to determine the architectural form of their buildings. Here the main influence was all sorts of industrial buildings but, most notably, factories. By the 1910s such industrial architects as Albert Kahn of Detroit had helped create a distinctive American idiom. In 1917 he was commissioned by Henry Ford to create steel frame structures in which some walls were made up of light metal or brick and glass. In his Ohio Steel Foundry Roll and Heavy Machine Shop, Lima, Ohio (1938), Albert Kahn further refined industrial design, emphasizing certain features, such as the sawtooth clerestory and butterfly roofs, while treating the different sections as units within a continuous surface with great luminous spaces in the inside and tall glass walls atop a pediment of light-colored brick on the exterior.

The main schools of architectural style in the 1920s and 1930s were the International and Neoclassical styles, competing idioms that were, nevertheless, simplified in comparison with all previous idioms and much influenced by the starkness of abstract art. While the new buildings were far more mechanically complex on the inside than any previously, they were yet far simpler on the outside.

In their *The International Style* (1932) Philip Johnson and Henry-Russell Hitchcock explained the three principles of the new architecture; architecture as volume rather than mass; regular, rather than axial symmetry as the unit factor in determining design; and the absence of arbitrary, surface ornament. To Johnson and Hitchcock, the International Style did not depend upon function or materials. Walls might look wafer thin yet be composed of thick brick. Nevertheless, the International Style had developed from technology and function. According to Richard Guy Wilson in *The Machine Age in America* (1986), "severity, flat Spartan surfaces, revealed structure, and mechanics as objects became its identifying features; the man-made object in the landscape and white interior its trademarks." Such was the Aluminaire House, Syosset, New York (1931), by A. Lawrence Kochner (1888–1969) and Albert Frey (b. 1903). Made of a light steel and aluminum frame covered by insulated board, tarpaper, and aluminum sheets, it was erected in ten days in 1931.

Architect and architectural artist Hugh Ferriss recognized the energy of massed twisting shapes and his illustrations for his *Metropolis of Tomorrow* are a celebration of towering man-made cliffs lightened by a chiaroscuro of setbacks, dramatic crevices punctuating the grainy texture of the buildings. While Ferris denied that contemporary cities were devoid of humanity and humanizing influences, his sketches are somewhat impersonal with men at the mercy of seemingly obdurate skyscrapers. Modern American cities were, to many, enormous, complex machines— multifaceted and capable of hosting all sorts of activities—yet impervious to many of man's inner needs.

Another crucial architect was Bertram Grosvenor Goodhue (1869–1924), one of the most significant modernists for his building designs that echoed the machine-as-parts approach to automobile design. Thus his most famous building, the Nebraska State Capitol (1920–1931), while retaining such traditional features as tower, dome, and decoration, overall achieved a, then, unique form, a setback tower in which ornament served geometry rather than gratifying it.

A crucial factor influencing skyscraper design was the New York zoning law of 1916, widely copied elsewhere, that limited the height of a building at immediate street level, in order to provide the street with as much light as possible, thereby inspiring architects to introduce setbacks, partly to create ever-higher towers within the letter of the law, partly to achieve greater plasticity of form. A notable example is the New York Telephone Company or Barclay-Vesey Building (1922–1926) by architect Ralph Walker (1889–1973) of the firm of McKenzie, Voorhees, and Gmelin. The site was in the shape of a parallelogram, thus inducing Walker to introduce, through successive designs, a twist between the base of the building and the gothic, art nouveau tower, supported by the raised surrounding setbacks.

The most inventive architect of New York skyscrapers was Raymond Hood (1881–1934) who, between 1922 and his death in 1934, produced a series of dazzling towers. The American Radiator (1924) had a sheath of black brick outside its steel-framed setbacks with a golden gothic tower; the Daily News (1929–1931) played with assertive vertical strips; the McGraw-Hill (1930–1931) alternated dark green horizontal slabs with light green vertical panels and windows.

The Chrysler Building (1930) was conceived primarily as an advertisement. William Van Allen transformed the original design of site developer William Reynolds, eliminating the proposed glass dome, increasing the height to 1,050 feet and seventy-seven stories, and crowning it with a Krupp "KA2" crest of stainless steel with triangular windows lit at night to enhance the effect.

For many, the crowning glory of this period of intense competition between corporations as to which could build the highest skyscraper, and an enduring architectural achievement in its own right, was the Empire State Building, New York (1931), by Shreve, Lamb, and Harmon. Its five-story base gave way to what Paul Goldberger calls "an immensely skillful piece of massing" of 102 stories surmounted by a rounded tower, 1,250 feet above street level. Moreover, its facade mixed granite and limestone of the Stone Age with nickel and aluminum of the machine age.

Radio's most distinctive advertisement was the RCA tower, center of the Rockefeller Center, New York (1932–1940). Widely hailed as a milestone in urban civilization, the Rockefeller Center made its greatest impact through its massive scale and soaring skyscrapers. For the first time a series of skyscrapers were designed as an integral group. In its patterns of building and space, planes and light, the Rockefeller Center was a truly historical achievement. Most of all, it succeeded as glorious advertisement for big business during the depression, a time when few would glorify business in the printed word.

In the course of the 1930s American architects began to achieve a balanced, satisfying synthesis of the various diverse strands of modern architecture—the International Style, setback skyscrapers, and streamlined buildings. The results represented what critic Talbot Hamlin called "a contemporary American Style" in his article of that title for *Pencil Points* of February 1938. These were clean, sparse, neoclassical buildings with conventional proportions and incorporating classical motifs where appropriate. They included the Folger Shakespeare Library, Washington, D.C. (1929–1932) by Paul Cret (1876–1945). This is a white marble building with fluted piers alternating with high narrow windows whose spandrels carry neoclassical sculptured reliefs. Another stripped classical building was the National Airport in Washington, D.C. (1940), built by the PWA and with Howard L. Cheney as consultant architect, a semicircular building with concave entrance and convex glass wall looking upon the landing strip and with immense cylindrical columns.

Chicago became a center for machine housing with such projects as the Battledeck House (1929–1930) by Henry Dubin (1892–1963), so-called because wood was eliminated and because the system of roof and floor of welded steel plate and beams was somewhat like the construction of a ship. George Fred Keck was another architect committed to machine housing, perhaps on account of his background in architectural engineering at the University of Illinois.

For the Century of Progress Exposition he devised a duodecagon House of Tomorrow that could set off an optimum number of new gadgets and materials: General Electric provided appliances, H. W. Howell, the tubular metal furniture, U.S. Gypsum the floors, and Holland Furnace, the air conditioning. Apart from the concrete foundations and floors carried by core steel columns, the house was prefabricated and took only two months to erect. Underlying the design was Keck's assumption that modern life was dependent upon the machine and that the interiors must be adjustable through a sequence of movable, insulation board walls in order to accommodate successive changes in life-style. In the second year of the exposition Keck constructed a second, more refined house, largely prefabricated, the Crystal House, for which all exterior walls were of glass and the only room to be fully enclosed was the kitchen. Other architects who experimented with machine-produced houses included Howard Fisher and Norman Bel Geddes.

In contrast with the more conservative Northeast and Midwest, architects in southern California, such as Richard Neutra and Rudolph Schindler, found their affluent clients welcomed experimental building, partly because they liked to consider themselves part of the avant-garde, partly because of the economic boom and fantasy of Hollywood, partly because the milder climate of California favored more experiments in building. Richard Neutra acknowledged how a new style was being forged by the manufacturers of building materials and specialties, and his work used the technology of construction in a fashion far ahead of any European architect. The Beard House, Altadena, California (1934–1935), was built for William and Melba Beard, respectively a university teacher of engineering and the son of historians Charles and Mary Beard, and his wife, an aviator. The house used hollow steel channels for the walls, open-web steel trusses for the roof, and steel web beams as the base for the concrete floor. The exterior was painted silver gray while the interior had aluminum steel columns, a gray linoleum floor, brown masonite walls, and tubular steel furniture. More dramatic was Neutra's house for film director Josef von Sternberg in the San Fernando Valley (1934–1935) protected by long blank metal walls and a superfluous moat.

Rudolph Schindler (1887–1953) was less successful commercially and artistically than Neutra, partly because he was far less gifted as a publicist, partly because he synthesized a far greater range of influences and, therefore, lacked Neutra's single-minded development. In his Dr. Philip Lovell Beach House, Newport Beach, California (1925–1926), Schindler exploited modern technology; yet the overall effect was deliberately indeterminate, challenging conventional ideas of enclosure. Dissatisfied with Schindler's eclectic style, architect, curator, and critic Philip Johnson refused to allow his work to be exhibited in the MOMA International Style Show. Thus, rejected, Schindler tried to develop new sorts of projects using cheaper materials than steel.

Los Angeles architect Gregory Ain (b. 1908) worked at different times for both Schindler and Neutra and was influenced by

New York Hospital Cornell University Medical College Association Buildings, York Avenue from 68th to 70th Streets, New York, designed by architects Coolidge, Shepley, Bullfinch and Abbott and completed in 1933, is an example of architectural fusion between classical, medieval, and modern styles. (Photo by Irving Underhill, 1932; Library of Congress).

both of them. He wanted to build inexpensive modern housing using, as Schindler planned, cheap modern technology, but with broad, plain surfaces, as Neutra would have wished. Typical of Ain's work was his small, inexpensive Becker House on a hillside in the Silver Lake district of Los Angeles (1938). Made of a wood frame with plywood and stucco, it cost only $3,000 to build. Everything was run on economical lines because of the efficient layout, and Ain's use of open space was broad and subtle. Ain's Dunsimuir Flats, Los Angeles (1937), was another instance of a fully integrated structure using four different building elements to reduce costs, yet, by creating a series of cubes allowing light to enter all major rooms on three sides in each and every room.

Whatever the most ambitious plans of the most progressive architects, mass-produced housing was very expensive in terms of factory tooling and transportation. Moreover, even if a huge volume of production could be achieved in the interest of cutting the cost of individual units, this would not eliminate much of the expense of housing that revolved around costs on site: acquiring land, laying foundations, providing utilities, and meeting local building codes. Yet standardization could be applied to such traditional forms as wooden houses. After World War II mass-produced housing became a practicable proposition and suburbs and towns often built by the Levitt company to specific standards sprung up across the United States.

In February and March 1932 the Museum of Modern Art (MOMA), New York, mounted the International Exhibition of Modern Architecture, which was subsequently shown in another thirty cities and accompanied by a substantial catalog and book. It had three sections: one showed the extent of the International Style; another showed its influence on housing; and the third showed work by nine leaders of the style, including the Americans Richard Neutra, Irving and Monroe Bowman, Raymond Hood, George Howe, and William Lescaze. Maverick architect Frank Lloyd Wright (1869–1959) was also included, although his work was of a very different and romantic order, because his preeminence was widely recognized. The exhibition was jointly planned by Henry-Russell Hitchcock, Philip Johnson, and MOMA's director, Alfred H. Barr, Jr. The emphasis was on a lighter, more volumetric form of building than the rigid setback skyscrapers of the 1920s and one shorn of excessive decoration.

Yet, for all his differences, Frank Lloyd Wright's work was likened to that of architects influenced by the new machines. Critic Richard Guy Wilson comments how the Kaufmann Residence, later known as Fallingwater, in Bear Run, Pennsylvania (1936), the most notable of Wright's organic building designs, is a

machine in the wilderness with its broad, machine-produced, reinforced-concrete decks. Yet *Fallingwater* is tied to the site, part of the waterfall. Rocks push up through the living-room floor, and substantial stone piers carry the machine-like decks. . . . Wright's arguments for, and use of, materials in their nearly natural state—wood with the grain, stone in the rough, and the application of "natural" colors or finishes to the concrete, copper and brick—became a hallmark of organic design. . . .

Wright's fascination with organic shapes also led to his most famous office design of the period, the Johnson Wax Building, Racine, Wisconsin (1938), notable for its twenty-two "Dendiform Shafts," or mushroom, tapering columns, pinned on brass shoes at the bottom and growing outward at the ceiling of gleaming pyrex tubing. They served to divide the office space and enhance it by forming a contrast to the light streaming from the skylight.

Frank Lloyd Wright's professional life was conducted by continuous financial brinkmanship and marred by bouts of ill health, bronchitis, and pneumonia, that drove him to the desert camp at Taliesin West, Arizona. When his clients proved fractious or cowardly, he remonstrated with them. He berated client Alice Birdsall, for whom he had designed the Hollyhock House in California, in 1920, in a rigorous letter of several pages, accusing her of being wayward and headstrong, for going on overseas voyages when she could not cope with building problems.

You had flung my work to clerks who were naturally envious or suspicious. . . . My soul is sore and my mind stiff with this insult. . . . But if . . . in spite of what I have seen to be a disinclination on your part to stand the discipline of steady sustained endeavor . . . if you can break through the obstructions to any understanding with me you have yourself set up and fostered, then I will stand up to my duty to myself and to my work and to you. . . . Whatever its birth pangs [Hollyhock] will take its place as your contribution and mine to the vexed life of our time. What future it will have?—who can say?

Critic Ada Louise Huxtable comments how extraordinary it was that, despite considerable struggles, Wright still managed to produce a body of work, both completed and left at the planning stage, that changed the course of world architecture. Yet his personal vision was swiftly synthesized by avant-garde architects abroad. Indeed, there was much cross-fertilization even between

Wright and immigrant German architect Ludwig Mies van der Rohe who came to America in 1938: "There are some remarkable parallels in the planes and masses of their brick-walled houses. Modernism was fed by many streams, meeting and mingling in a shared vision that the doctrinaire modernist historian has never allowed." Wright's designs were carefully worked out over long periods. Fallingwater had its origins in his Gale House (1910); the Price Tower (1953) of Bartlesville, Oklahoma, had its origins in the 1929 projects of St. Marks-in-the Bouwerie. As Ada Louise Huxtable maintains,

[Wright's] architecture is not about image first and structure after, or a look embellished by some intellectual trimming, as in today's trivializing trends. It is based on the ability to visualize and understand a building simultaneously in every relationship, to see and feel the way its inner and outer forms and spaces are modeled by material, structure and light, and to invest this knowledge with spirit and style.

13

NEW HORIZONS, CLOSED FRONTIERS
America in World Affairs After 1920

THE UNITED States had three overlapping and contesting forms of foreign policy in the 1920s and early 1930s: the rhetoric of isolation with its unfortunate diplomatic impressions of neglect and lassitude upon Britain, France, Germany, and Japan; the sporadically active diplomacy by which the United States tried to resolve international disputes amicably; and commercial penetration of the rest of the world, notably in the matter of oil diplomacy and aviation rivalry, pursued by new multinational companies. The first led to misunderstandings at home and abroad; the second to temporary easing of international tensions; and the third helped lay the foundations for America's rise to globalism in the 1940s.

The shadow of Woodrow Wilson continued to loom over American foreign policy in the 1920s. Statesmen, determined to avoid the sort of controversy surrounding Wilson's handling of foreign affairs, reacted against his policies of intervention and his moralistic rhetoric. The shift in American foreign policy from outright intervention to apparent isolation was accepted, even welcomed, by the public, weary of the war and the political bitterness of 1919 and 1920. Isolationism did not mean withdrawing from economic involvement or political contact with other nations. It meant, rather, a return to the old American insistence on freedom of action, an outright rejection of collective security.

However, the story of America's foreign policy in the 1920s is not quite as isolationist as the myth. Isolationism was more a matter of instinct than of reason. It is certainly true that America enacted a series of measures—the immigration laws of 1921 and 1924 and the high tariffs of 1922 and 1930—that were isolationist. It is also true that America's absence from the League of Nations was a diplomatic handicap for American statesmen. America's commitments in Latin America and its financial loans to the Western powers involved it in negotiations with other nations that could not be conducted formally through the League. Yet we can set against the narrow self-interest of certain policies the altruism of others—such as the proposed reduction of the navy by the agreement of the Washington Conference, President Herbert Hoover's moratorium on war debts, and even the Kellogg Pact.

The economic reasons for American involvement were overwhelming. The United States had emerged stronger than ever from the war. Not only did it still have its superb natural resources and advanced industrial technology but it had also benefited materially from the catastrophe of war. Increased demand for products at home and abroad had stimulated invention and production. Furthermore, the wartime disruption of world trade had enabled American businesses to develop new markets abroad. The financial capital of the world had moved from London to New York. Among the powers, only the United States could expect continued economic progress. In 1920 the United States was producing about 40 percent of the world's coal—far more than twice as much as Britain, its nearest rival; an even greater proportion of the world's pig iron; and almost 70 percent of all crude petroleum. Its wealth in such raw materials as lumber and agricultural crops was prodigious. Despite its deficiency in a few crucial metals (manganese, chromite, and tungsten), rubber, and the crops of coffee, tea, and sugar, it was more nearly self-sufficient than any other country.

Throughout the 1920s the United States consolidated its position as the world's preeminent commercial power. According to the Department of Commerce *Commerce Yearbook of 1930,* it accounted for almost 16 percent of the world's exports, and 12 percent of imports. Its industrial track record was greater still. By the end of the 1920s the value of American industrial production was 46 percent of the world total. As to national income, according to *The United States in the World Economy* (1943), the total for the United States in 1929 was the same as the sum total for twenty-three other leading industrial nations, including Britain, France, Germany, Canada, and Japan.

In finance, the war had reversed the prewar position. In 1914 the United States was a debtor nation with net obligations of $3.7 billion. In 1919 it was a creditor nation owed $12.5 billion by other countries. Of this, $10 billion was in war debts. However, analysis of the figures suggests that in the private sector what was owed to American companies had almost doubled, while what they owed had been almost cut in half. By 1929 additional foreign loans and direct investment had increased private net assets to over $8 billion.

Thus, despite the official rhetoric of its foreign policy, the United States was to play a decisive role in international economic affairs. Through gifts and loans it supported the rehabilitation of Europe, in particular providing France, Germany, and Italy with huge advances to stabilize their currencies. In addition, the United States funded construction in Austria, Poland, and Yugoslavia. American money was also used to fund the digging of oil wells in the Middle East, planting rubber trees in Malaya and the Dutch East Indies and sugar cane in Cuba, and developing public utilities in Tokyo and Shanghai. Furthermore, giant corporations, such as Standard Oil, Ford, General Motors, International Harvester, Singer, and IBM, established various manufacturing companies in China, Europe, and the Caribbean.

The penetration of the rest of the world by American interests was seen most clearly in American pursuit of oil and ascendancy in aviation. In the fields of oil and aviation diplomacy the Americans were hotly pursued by their European former diplomatic allies and current commercial competitors.

International Oil Politics

The seven major oil companies (Exxon, Socal—also known as Chevron—Mobil, Gulf, Texaco, Shell, and BP), sometimes known as the seven sisters, dominated the world of oil from the 1920s onward. They became the first multinational corporations. English investigative journalist Anthony Sampson comments that

Each of them soon developed into an "integrated oil company" controlling not only its own production, but also transportation, distribution and marketing. With their own fleets of tankers, they could soon operate across the world in every sector of the industry, from the "upstream" business of drilling and producing at the oilfields, to the "downstream" activity of distributing and selling at the pumps or the factories. And each company strove, with varying success, to be self-sufficient at both ends, so that their oil could flow into their tankers through their refineries to their filling-stations. It was this world-wide integration, together with their size, which was the common characteristic of these seven.

On the surface, the oil companies were engaged in fierce competition to sell their product, especially as gasoline for motor cars.

Moreover, in the 1920s, the United States was by far the greatest consumer of oil, especially with the dramatic rise in the number of automobiles and the transformation of an entire society based on a superfluity of cheap oil. In the 1920s oilmen and government officials contemplated a world shortage with resources much depleted by the war and the ever-increasing number of automobiles. The director of the United States Geological Survey disclosed how the American oil situation "can best be described as precarious." Disturbed by their realization, American and European oil companies and governments began a scramble for oil, as bitterly contested as the earlier imperialist scramble for colonies. Britain and France tried to turn the Middle East into an Anglo-French oil field from which they planned to exclude the

United States. However, the United States retorted that it was clearly impossible for America to continue to provide the world with oil from its own diminishing supply. Moreover, it had played a decisive part in winning World War I and was thus entitled to a share in world reserves. Consequently, under Harding, the State Department began to support the American oil companies' pursuit of fresh fields. It was, of course, the casual support given the oil companies by the Ohio Gang that led to the Teapot Dome Scandal. Anthony Sampson characterizes the contests: "Ostensibly the [various oil] companies were the boxers in the big fights, and the governments were the seconds, providing encouragement or reproof. This meant that when the fight was most critical, the governments were out of the ring."

On the surface, and to critics of federal policy, it looked as if the State Department were letting the oil companies improvise its own diplomacy. Behind the scenes many diplomats and the secretariat in the State Department deeply distrusted the companies but they were reluctant to create any formal organization to conduct an oleaginous foreign policy. Thus they chose to use the oil companies, as discreetly as possible, to work out foreign policy for them. Government officers wanted to encourage the oil companies' search for fresh fields and began to apply such doctrines as the Open Door to oil, meaning that, in future, the former war allies should not discriminate against one another in the matter of oil supplies.

For their part, Britain and France used their "mandates" of Arab territory acquired from the defunct Ottoman Empire to search for new oil fields. In 1919 at San Remo they revived a prewar oil agreement of 1914 in which Armenian entrepreneur Calouste Gulbenkian had created an oil syndicate, the Turkish Petroleum Company (TPC). It was originally owned by BP, Shell, the Deutsche Bank, and Gulbenkian. The revision gave the Germans' quarter-share to France. When the (initially secret) agreement was discovered, the American ambassador in London protested that Britain was trying to corner the world's share of oil. Britain could argue that, since the United States had never declared war on Turkey, any peace treaty or other agreement with Turkey was beyond its scope. This was technically correct

Modern Brunnhilde. Vivacious aviatrix Amelia Earhart was in the early generation of pioneer pilots who demonstrated the potential of flight. In June 1937 she attempted the first round-the-world flight near the Equator but, after taking off from New Guinea for Howland Island in the Pacific, she and her navigator vanished. A large naval search failed to trace them and, later, rumors abounded that she had not been lost at sea but had been taken in Saipan by the Japanese and been killed. (Library of Congress).

but, perhaps, not the fundamental reason. For its part, America claimed, yet again, that its decisive part in helping Britain and France to win the war merited some compensation. British foreign secretary Lord Curzon said that oil within the British Empire and in Persia amounted to no more than 4.5 percent of world production, while the United States, together with Mexico, accounted for about 82 percent. Nevertheless, after prolonged pressure, Britain was ready to compromise with the United States. In August 1922 Britain offered the United States, first, 12 percent of the TPC and, then, 20 percent, which was accepted. This allowed (initially seven) American oil companies, led by Exxon and Mobil, into the new mandate, later state, of Iraq.

After the small state of Mosul was placed in Iraq under the British mandate, the new government in Iraq signed an agreement, the company was to remain British with a British chairman and would pay Iraq a royalty of 4 gold shillings (about $1 at that time) per ton. The original San Remo concession of 20 percent to Iraq was excluded from the new agreement. This prompted two Iraqi ministers to resign in protest and it remained a continuous source of bitterness with the Iraquis. Gulbenkian not only retained his original 5 percent but also the original clause by which the participants agreed not to seek concessions in the territory of the defunct Ottoman Empire, from Turkey in the north through Jordan, Syria, and Saudi Arabia in the southeast. This was in flat contradiction of the principle of the Open Door but, as the American companies were eager to settle the matter, all partners agreed to the terms in July 1928 at Ostend, Belgium. The TPC was thereafter called the Iraq Petroleum Company (IPC). In fact, none of the participants was exactly sure what had comprised the old Ottoman Empire, which had, after all, been in decline for a hundred years before its final collapse. Calouste Gulbenkian defined what he meant by drawing a line on a map round the territory with a red pencil. The so-called Red Line agreement included all the richest oil-producing areas of the Middle East except Iran and Kuwait. Thus, (initially) five American companies, including Exxon and Mobil, had penetrated the Middle East taking 23.7 percent of the company and the Open Door slammed shut behind them. Drilling began in April 1927 and six months later prospectors struck one of the richest oil fields in the world.

The Iraq Petroleum Company provided the prototype for other joint ventures in the Middle East. Because it included two American and two British companies, it made actual control of production comparatively easy and limited competition. However, it stoked resentment in those advanced countries without their own supply of oil.

In the early 1920s there were only three major contenders in the contest for world oil—the American Exxon, and the European Shell and BP. They now began to draw closer together, lest price-cutting wars should ruin one and all, increasingly convinced by Sir Henri Deterding of Shell's arguments about the dangers of internecine competition. Thus, in 1928, prompted by Walter Teagle of Exxon, the Big Three started a series of secret conferences with the aim of restraining one another from ruinous competition. In August 1928 Sir Henri Deterding rented Achnacarry Castle in the Scottish Highlands where he met with Sir John Cadman (since 1927 chairman of BP) and Walter Teagle (of Exxon). Ostensibly, they were there for trout and grouse. However, as representatives from other oil companies and various oil experts began to augment this select gathering, the British press grew curious about the outcome. The *Sunday Express* of London found the castle "an impenetrable fortress which harbors one of the most interesting groups of silent personalities in the world," whereas "the Scottish lochs themselves are no more communicative than the oil companies." According to Anthony Sampson, the party agreed to divide the world of oil into an international cartel. Their pool association, later known as the Achnacarry agreement, or "As Is," was never implemented in full but its echoes reverberated across the oil world until the 1950s.

In place of "excessive competition" that had led to "tremendous overproduction," it proposed collaboration based on seven principles. In the first, the parties agreed to abide by their present volume of business and to limit any future increases in production in proportion to their existing levels. (Thus, as a mechanism to reduce the possibility of excessive competition, the first principle was obliquely following something like the principle of the 5:5:3 naval agreement in Washington in 1922.) Moreover, according to the third principle "only such facilities [are] to be added as are necessary to supply the public with its increased requirements of petroleum products in the most efficient manner." Underlying the cartel was Deterding's favorite Dutch proverb—*Eendracht maakt macht*—cooperation provides power. Each party knew it could not achieve a global monopoly. Only by cooperation could the companies prosper. Whatever the economic rationale for an international cartel, it was politically insupportable on democratic grounds. Thus it was to be kept secret until 1952. The Achnacarry agreement was a plutocrats' plot to fix prices and generally divide the trade in oil. The basis for the oil cartel was the maintenance of American prices and thus it was especially attuned to the immediate needs of Exxon and Walter Teagle. Anthony Sampson asserts how

The arbiter of the world price of oil was the "Gulf Plus System." To protect American oil, the oil from anywhere else was fixed at the price in the Gulf of Mexico, whence most United States oil was shipped overseas, *plus* the standard freight charges for shipping the oil from the Gulf to its market. While the United States was the only major producing country the system had some justification; but, as American oil was becoming more expensive and threatened by much cheaper oil from Iran or Venezuela, it was a blatant device to keep up prices.

The Achnacarry, or As Is, agreement did not fix rules. It was a statement of intent, agreed first by Exxon, Shell, and BP, and then by fifteen American companies, including the four remaining sisters—Gulf, Socal (or Chevron), Texaco, and Mobil. It did not fix oil absolutely throughout the world because it could not discipline the USSR, but it allowed the largest Western companies to supervise the quota system and create two export associations.

Paradoxically, the Red Line agreement was to lead to an outsider taking the richest prize of all. Ironically, Socal achieved its footholds in two Middle Eastern countries precisely because of its lack of previous involvement. These were, first, Bahrain, and, second, Saudi Arabia, which had the most spectacular oil reserves.

In 1930 the profligate King Ibn Saud was in desperate need of money and his British adviser, Harry St. John Philby, who had left the Colonial Service and converted to Islam, advised him to exploit Saudi Arabia's mineral resources. They had an American geologist Karl Twitchell survey the land but, although he was excited by what he discovered, he failed to rouse Texaco, Exxon, and Gulf. However, Socal, not bound by the Red Line agreement, approached Twitchell, made him an adviser and also promised to pay Philby if he could secure a concession. This he achieved despite the temporary intervention by BP who made a much lower bid. Socal offered the king an immediate loan of £30,000, to be followed by a second loan of £20,000 in eighteen months, and an annual rent of £5,000—all in gold. King and company reached agreement in August 1933 and Philby received an annual salary of £1,000 from Socal. These Arabian oil fields were ready for production in May 1939, an event celebrated by a royal progress to the new oil town and two days of touring and feasting. The king initiated production by turning the valve on the pipeline. He was delighted and soon increased the size of the concession to 444,000 square miles.

The establishment of Socal, a completely American company, not only changed the face of Saudi Arabia irrevocably but also changed the balance of power in the Middle East. At the time of the agreement in 1933 there were no more than fifty Westerners in Jedda, the Saudi capital on the coast, and no American diplomat there at all. Not until 1939 when Bert Fisher, minister to Egypt, was accredited to Saudi Arabia as well, was there an American diplomatic presence. Anthony Sampson remarks that,

On the one hand was a desert kingdom ruled by an absolute monarch with medieval autocracy, with about five million people, many of them nomads. On the other hand were American technologists, as Philby [Saud's adviser] described them, "descending from the skies on their flying carpets with strange devices for probing the bowels of the earth in search of the liquid muck for which the world clamours to keep its insatiable machines alive."

Each new discovery of oil in the Middle East served to weaken still further the authority of the national government in whose territory it was found, as each discovery added to the world glut. In Iran BP retained its monopoly despite the acumen of a formidable ruler, Reza Shah, and it secured a new agreement in 1933 that extended the concession until 1993. In Iraq the IPC consortium made huge profits without giving the government its due return. Between 1934 and 1939 Exxon made a profit of around 52 cents per barrel, double what it paid the Iraqi government. It was said that for an initial investment of $14 million Exxon's share in IPC was worth $130 million by 1937.

American economic penetration of other countries had a profound sociological and cultural impact on them. It was not simply that American cars, bicycles, sewing machines, typewriters, and household goods appeared in ever-greater volume around the world but also that their presence transformed the nature of both European and Asian industries. Competing native companies were obliged to adopt American techniques of mass production and assembly lines. The transformation was most marked in Japan but even the relatively backward industrial system of the U.S.S.R. began to consider new technology called "Fordismus." This led to criticism on both sides of the Atlantic of what Charles Beard, writing for *Harper's* in March 1929 about "The American Invasion of Europe," called "prose against poetry; dollars against sacrifice; calculation against artistic abandon." The debate still continues today. The most significant development, as Beard explained, was that the export of American industrial products, cultural ideas, and customs was remodeling modern societies throughout the world. When American bankers loaned money to foreign countries and their firms, they often retained rights of supervision. This practice was even more pronounced among American corporations investing in foreign factories, assembly plants, or distributing companies.

Of all the American cultural influences, the most insidious and overwhelming was the cinema in which Hollywood dominated the countries of Europe as much as it did the United States. For millions around the world, Hollywood was American civilization. After that, American music and lyrics, especially those in ragtime or jazz, were all-pervasive, whether sung on radio, in theaters, or on disks.

At the same, and for the first, time Europe was being invaded by American tourists *en masse,* at the rate of about 500,000 each year in the 1920s. This was far more than the expatriate writers of the lost generation of Hemingway, Dos Passos, Eliot, Cummings *et al.* who had led the way. Whether on business or pleasure American travelers in Europe, and Asia, began to insist on American cultural standards in a way that was to transform foreign cultures slowly but inexorably. "Can Paris be retaken by the Parisians?" asked the New York *Herald Tribune* of January 24, 1926. "The French claim they cannot walk on the Boulevard St. Germain and hear a word of their native tongue. They claim that the high prices following in the wake of the American visitor are driving them from the best restaurants in Paris. They mourn the days of yesterday and scorn the Americanized Latin Quarter of today."

In view of all these factors, the United States could no more return to its supposed isolation in 1921 than it could have ignored World War I in 1914. Moreover, the coils of commerce set in motion in Cuba and China at the turn of the century were to wind up foreign policy in a way few could have predicted. As the historian of American expansion, Foster Rhea Dulles, concludes, "The United States controlled so much of the world's material wealth and industrial production, so great a proportion of international trade, and such a large share of world capital resources that American policy could not fail to have decisive consequences in every part of the globe."

Despite all these things and increasing press comment on them, the American people in general and their leaders in particular had very little understanding of the changing world that the United States was doing so much to shape. The United States never developed a coordinated economic strategy. If the story of international affairs in the period 1920–1932 is somewhat confused, then the United States's own confusion is partly responsible. These uneasy years and the greater disturbances they led to in the 1930s have led some to call them the years of the lost peace.

Washington Naval Conference

Despite his lack of diplomatic experience, Charles Evans Hughes was an imaginative and persuasive secretary of state (1921–1925). His dignified manner and Jove-like appearance lent style and prestige to any event he attended. However, any controversial proposal in favor of international cooperation from Hughes would have aroused suspicion among certain formidable members of Congress. Wilson's implacable foe, Henry Cabot Lodge of Massachusetts, remained chairman of the Senate Foreign Relations Committee until his death in November 1924 when he was succeeded by William E. Borah of Idaho, whose intransigent isolationism was supported by that of another leading member of the committee, Hiram Johnson of California. Nevertheless, after a Senate resolution that declared the war was over and that the United States reserved rights mentioned in the Treaty of Versailles, Hughes negotiated treaties with Germany, Austria, and Hungary, that were ratified in October 1921.

Having rejected Wilsonian remedies, President Warren Harding was conscious that the Republicans needed to do something "just as good as the League." This was to be the Washington Naval Conference. Peace sentiment in the United States, nurtured by Wilson and frustrated by the turn of events in 1919 and 1920, bridled at the thought of another arms and naval race between the great powers. Even Senator Borah thought that the incipient naval rivalry between America and Japan would end the way of all such rivalries. On December 14, 1920, he tabled a resolution in Congress calling for a reduction in armaments that was in July 1921 opposed by only four members in the House. Moreover, he suggested to Charles E. Hughes that the United States, Britain, and Japan should abstain from further shipbuilding. Hughes had the prestige and personal skill to avoid the sort of partisan antagonism between president and Senate that had so disfigured Wilson's last two years. Furthermore, he was anxious to repair declining American relations with Japan. He feared that Japan, resentful of the Immigration Quota Act of 1921 and antagonized by American economic rivalry in the Far East, might invoke the

The Republicans' attempt "to do something as good as the League" was the Washington Naval Conference of 1921–1922 whose principal achievement was the Five Power Naval Treaty concluded in the Diplomatic Room of the State Department on February 6, 1922, and signed by (from left to right at the table) Augusto Rosso of Italy, H. G. Chilton of Britain, Secretary of State Charles Evans Hughes, André de la Boulaye of France, and Masanao Hanihara of Japan. (Photo by National Photo Company; Library of Congress).

Anglo-Japanese Alliance of 1902 to claim British support against the United States. Britain agreed to a naval conference in Washington because it had no intention of losing American friendship over Japan.

To ensure maximum public support, the Harding administration prepared the ground well in advance. In the first place, the conference would be held in Washington; in the second, the president would not take part himself and the American delegation would consist of Secretary of State Charles Evans Hughes, elder statesman Elihu Root, and, from the Senate Foreign Relations Committee, Henry Cabot Lodge for the Republicans and Oscar W. Underwood for the Democrats. The implication was clear. Had Wilson showed such discretion, the outcome at Paris would have been very different. Moreover, the very fact of the conference, officially the "Conference on the Limitation of Armament," but more widely known as the "Peace Conference," implied that the United States was about to mend its bridges with the other powers.

Ironically, the various tensions between the powers added immeasurably to the success of the conference. On the day before the first session, November 12, 1921, the unknown soldier was buried at Arlington, an ideal ceremonial prelude to the meeting. In his opening address Hughes boldly took the initiative and asked representatives of Britain, Japan, France, Italy, Belgium, the Netherlands, Portugal, and China to sink 1,878,093 tons of capital ships—half the vessels afloat and in dry dock. The total tonnage for battleships and cruisers finally agreed by the powers was:

United States	525,850	to be distributed among 18 ships
Britain	558,950	to be distributed among 20 ships
Japan	301,320	to be distributed among 10 ships
France	221,170	to be distributed among 10 ships
Italy	182,800	to be distributed among 10 ships.

The agreement was simplistically expressed in the ratio 5 : 5 : 3. In addition, the powers accepted Hughes's proposal that no new ships should be built for ten years, and a limit of 35,000 tons to be imposed on new battleships. The conference also provided for restriction of aircraft carriers, normally of no more than 27,000 tons each, whereby Britain and the United States were each allowed 135,000 tons altogether, with Japan allowed 81,000 tons, and Italy and France, 60,000 tons apiece. Britain proposed the outright abolition of submarines but the other powers would not agree. Nevertheless, public opinion demanded some limitation as to submarine tonnage and usage, embodied in a separate five power treaty that lapsed when France refused to ratify it.

The main Five Power Treaty was supposed to last until 1936,

but from December 31, 1934, any country could give two years' notice of withdrawing from it. Japan's determination to secure a bigger ratio was submerged by an agreement with America that neither nation would expand its Pacific naval bases. Hughes knew that Congress would not have approved funds for building up American defenses in Guam and the Philippines. Moreover, he hoped that, if Japan were free from fear of attack, her statesmen would pursue a moderate foreign policy. To this end, and to allay mutual suspicions between the United States, Britain, and Japan, a Four Power Treaty, also signed with France, superseded the 1902 Anglo-Japanese Alliance. The four powers pledged themselves to "respect their rights in relation to their insular possessions in the region of the Pacific Ocean." In addition, a Nine Power Treaty acknowledged the Open Door to China. All nations attending the conference agreed to respect China's sovereignty and integrity. Japan agreed to restore the Shandong Peninsula (taken from Germany) to China and to start withdrawing troops from eastern Siberia. Initially, the powers made half-hearted efforts to abide by their agreements. However, they avoided proper discussion of provisions for enforcement of the naval limitations. Throughout the twenties the U.S. Navy was to be maintained at maximum strength and modernized. Only its overage vessels and those still under construction were scrapped according to the terms of the Washington Conference.

As if recognizing that a successful foreign policy could only be conducted by an expanded and informed civil service, successive presidents and secretaries of state had the State Department reorganized in the course of the 1920s. The diplomatic and consular services were merged and the civil service expanded to administer them, providing increased professional opportunities for career diplomats. Even so, the expansion was probably smaller than the need. According to Graham H. Stuart in *The Department of State* (1949), the State Department's annual budget was about $2 million in the 1920s and its personnel based at home numbered about 600.

Once the Washington Conference was over, public opinion began to lose interest in foreign affairs. Furthermore, isolationist sentiment was nourished by the activities of revisionist historians and pacifists. Revisionist histories of the origins of the war were to have a profound impact on a whole generation and its attitude to foreign affairs. They made particular the grievances expressed in metaphorical terms by the lost generation of war novelists. Both historians and novelists agreed that propaganda had debased language and that in the war the state had become a servile mechanism to malign forces. Revisionism began as an investigation into the causes of World War I and developed into a justification of American isolationism. The most immediate reason for the sudden appearance of revisionist histories about the war was the opening of the archives of the fallen imperial powers of Russia, Germany, and Austria that disclosed the prewar and wartime negotiations of both the Central and Entente powers, and revealed the great disparity between the fraudulent wartime propaganda of the nation states and the ugly reality of backstairs diplomacy.

The first major piece of American revisionist writing was provided by Sidney Bradshaw Fay of Smith College in three articles for the *American Historical Review* in 1920 and 1921, in which he refused to accept government propaganda about the origins of the war. Using Austrian and Russian documents, he derided the war-guilt clause of the Treaty of Versailles. Germany, he argued, had not wanted war and in 1914 had tried to persuade Austria against a declaration of war against Serbia. But Fay did not absolve Germany from blame completely for "in a wider sense, also, Germany is responsible, because one may say that militarism was one of the great causes of the war. . . . And for the growth of militarism in Europe, no country was so much responsible as Germany." Later he repeated his conclusions in *The Origins of the World War* (1928).

The supposed duplicity of Woodrow Wilson in achieving American intervention was a cardinal feature of the argument of *Shall It Be Again?* by J. K. Turner that appeared in 1922. Turner concluded that America had never been in danger of invasion, that Britain was more guilty of violations against American neutrality than Germany and that, in the war of rival imperialism, Wilson was willing to serve the special interests of American businessmen. "The great myth of the world war was Wilson idealism. Our noble President was simply a one hundred per cent American politician. The secret of Wilson is hypocrisy." Moreover, while presidents served Wall Street interests there would always be a danger of getting involved in wars. The real villain was the businessman who wanted to make a fast buck even if it involved plunging America into war. This particular criticism was to bear very bitter fruit in the 1930s. Other leading revisionists were Frederick Bausman, Harry Elmer Barnes, C. Hartley Grattan, Charles A. Beard, and, later, Walter Millis.

A more astute use of prewar and wartime history than these attempts to rewrite the past was made by progressive journalist Walter Lippmann in his influential *Public Opinion* (1922). He summed up the confusion of public and politicians resulting from their bitter experience of international diplomacy and the bombardment of pro-and anti-Wilson propaganda. *Public Opinion* was a pioneer analysis of the way people receive, and are influenced by, news, and the book's general analysis has not been surpassed. The central argument is that democracy is not based on an intelligent, informed, or rational public opinion. People, Lippmann argued, do not react to reality but to their personal view of reality determined by the pictures in their minds that he called "stereotypes." Individuals have their own view of the world—a "pseudo-environment . . . a representation of the environment"—that determines their ideas and opinions. Clemenceau, for example, had gone to the Peace Conference of 1919 determined to wreak vengeance on the Germans because of a stereotyped view of Germany dating back to the Franco-Prussian War.

The impact of the revisionists' moral tracts against Wilson's diplomacy was widespread. Theologian Reinhold Niebuhr, then a young minister working in Detroit, expressed the keen disillusionment of a generation when he set down his own reactions to the revisionist histories in his diary in 1923.

Gradually the whole horrible truth about the war is being revealed. Every new book destroys some further illusion. How can we ever again believe anything when we compare the solemn pretensions of statesmen with the cynically conceived secret treaties. Here was simply a tremendous contest for power between two great alliances of states in which the caprice of statesmen combined with basic economic conflicts to dictate the peculiar form of the alliance. Next time the cards will be shuffled in a different way and the "fellowship in arms" will consist of different fellows.

Many people who shared Niebuhr's great moral outrage had already begun to work for peace in various pacifist societies, both new and old. The term "pacifist," to describe someone who advocates the abolition of war and who will not take part in war, was not coined until 1909. In the following year former steel tycoon Andrew Carnegie gave $10 million in bonds for an organization to "hasten the abolition of international war." This was to be the Carnegie Endowment for International Peace that was led by Nicholas Murray Butler after the war. Hitherto, secular peace societies in America had been principally of this type—organizations committed to educating public and politicians about the horrors of war. But the movement was divided on the issue of American intervention in 1917. Only ardent socialists, social gospel clergymen, and feminists had maintained their opposition, founding such new pacifist societies as the American Union against Militarism. During the twenties the most active were two lobbying societies based in Washington. They were the National Council for the Prevention of War (NCPW) founded in 1921, led by its executive secretary, Frederick Libby, and the Women's International League for Peace and Freedom (WILPF), originally founded by social worker Jane Addams in 1915 but subsequently led by its executive secretary, Dorothy Detzer. In the NCPW Libby managed to bring together pacifists in farming and labor movements and published a monthly magazine, *Peace Action,* that had a circulation of 20,000.

Although revisionist historians and pacifists alike rejected Wilson's diplomacy, they were not isolationists. They wanted greater international cooperation between the nations of the world. American organizations to promote the idea of international cooperation were established on the premise that if people knew more they would understand more. The Foreign Policy Association, founded in 1921, made systematic attempts to inform people about international events. The contemporaneous Council on

Foreign Relations published a quarterly, *Foreign Affairs,* firstly under Archibald Cary Coolidge and later under Hamilton Fish Armstrong. By 1926 there were more than a thousand groups, whether international or isolationist, publishing news on foreign affairs.

Among America's foreign policy makers there remained a residual interest in genuine international cooperation, such as by American membership in the World Court. A World Court in which international law could be enforced and perfected had been discussed by a committee of jurists appointed by the League Council in 1920. It included Elihu Root, the New York corporation lawyer who had served Theodore Roosevelt as both secretary of state and secretary of war. Their recommendations were accepted by the League Assembly that devised a system for electing judges in 1921. Because this Court of International Justice at The Hague was affiliated with the League, it was anathema to some of the American public and to many congressmen. However, on January 26, 1927, the Senate voted 76 to 17 for United States' membership with five reservations. The Senate further stipulated that the reservations had to be accepted individually by all of the court's forty-eight member states. This stance would be interpreted as a way of saying no simply by making the price of membership too high. Of the American reservations one proved quite unacceptable to the other nations—that the United States remain free of any Court decisions given without American assent —although countries on the League Council actually had this privilege. President Calvin Coolidge refused to renegotiate this point and the possibility of American adherence died for the time being.

Economic Affairs

World economic affairs in the twenties were governed by three interrelated problems: reparations demanded of Germany by the victorious European powers; repayments of debts contracted by the Allies from the United States; and the development of American business and its desire for protection from overseas competition.

During the war the United States became a creditor nation. Wartime and postwar loans to friend and foe lent at 5 percent interest had stimulated the American economy and the total debt of $12.5 billion by the early twenties was too large a part of the economy to be overlooked by the government. Three presidents —Wilson, Harding, and Calvin Coolidge—took the attitude that the debts had to be paid in full without reference to other debts and reparations owed to America's debtors. Coolidge's supposed remark, "They hired the money, didn't they?" was much quoted and approved. However, Wilson admitted something that Harding and Coolidge were unwilling to—that only by trade with the United States could Europeans repay their loans.

Nevertheless, by the Fordney–McCumber Act of 1922 Congress raised the average level of duties on imports to a record height. However, the act did allow the president to raise or lower duties by as much as 50 percent but both Harding and Coolidge exercised this prerogative only thirty-seven times and thirty-two of these were upwards. Only on bobwhite quails, mill feed, cresylic acid, phenol, and paint brush handles were the duties lowered. It was on basic commodities of butter, cheese, and pig iron that duties were raised. The Fordney–McCumber tariff was the outcome of a compromise between different bargaining interests in Congress. The *Wall Street Journal* did not mince words in its condemnation calling it "One of the most selfish, short-sighted and extravagant laws of the kind ever enacted." Debts could not be paid without money or surplus products and the act gave Europeans no opportunity of earning dollars to repay their loans. In retaliation, they introduced protective tariffs of their own. Thus the resulting tariff war damaged the United States's foreign trade, persuaded some industrialists to establish plants abroad, and provoked several bankers and manufacturers to doubt the value of protection. Between 1922 and 1929 industrial production within America rose by 50 percent but exports rose only by 38 percent. Because imports rose at a slower rate than exports the United States accumulated a surplus of $11 billion in exports by 1929 and this was to be a contributory cause of the depression.

Administrations might be willing to adopt a flexible approach to the collection of debts, according to the varying abilities of debtor nations to repay loans, but Congress was obdurate. On February 9, 1922, it stipulated that the maximum deadline for repayment would be June 15, 1947, and that the minimum rate of interest would be 4.25 percent. Repayment was to be administered by a World War Foreign Debt Commission. Britain and France took offense at the Debt Funding Act that laid down these provisions. Not only did they consider that they had from the outset borne the highest losses of a common war—human fatality and economic disruption—but they also claimed a close relationship between their own debts and the reparations owed to them by Germany. Nevertheless, in January 1923 Britain and the United States agreed to repayment of Britain's debt of $4.6 billion over a period of 62 years at an average interest of 3.3 percent. The agreement set a precedent and the United States then went on to make similar agreements with fifteen other countries by 1927. France and Italy secured easier terms than Britain. So Britain set about collecting its debt and this entailed finding a way of exacting tribute Germany.

In 1919 John Maynard Keynes, a former British Treasury official, had argued against reparations in his book, *The Economic Consequences of the Peace*. Keynes had been the chief representative of the British Treasury at the Paris Peace Conference. But he had resigned on June 5, 1919, in disgust at the harsh terms of the Treaty of Versailles. He immediately set to work on his great book, paying for the printing himself and negotiating distribution with various publishers such as, in the United States, the new firm of Harcourt, Brace, and Howe. Although, in response to constructive criticism from family and friends, he toned down his personal attacks on politicians, deleting references to Wilson as a fly to Lloyd George's spider, the tenor of his attack was unmistakable. The book became an international best-seller. By April 1920 almost 70,000 copies had been sold in the United States. Readers were roused by Keynes's scornful and passionate denunciation of the failings of Wilson, Clemenceau, and Lloyd George. The heart of the book was a lucid analysis of the problems of reparations. The essential argument was that Europe could only regain its old affluence by restoring Germany to its former economic strength. It was underlined by Keynes's descriptions of a civilization at the point of collapse.

Though their peoples might be stirred, nations did not heed Keynes's arguments. Various countries continued to insist on excessive payments of $33 billion reparations from Germany. The Weimar Republic could not possibly meet these demands but, nevertheless, they were approved by the League on May 5, 1921. Two installments were paid in 1921 but none in 1922. On January 11, 1923, under instructions from French prime minister Raymond Poincaré, French troops occupied the Ruhr to punish Germany for default. German finances, already foundering, were now in chaos and the deutsche mark became worthless. The French army of occupation was withdrawn and Hughes suggested the formation of a European payment commission. In November it was established under the chairmanship of Chicago banker Charles Gates Dawes. Solutions were proposed—and accepted—for the reorganization of German finances.

The Dawes Plan, intended as an interim arrangement, aimed to make Germany solvent and to transfer any surplus of reserves over to the Allies. To stabilize the German currency, Dawes proposed an international loan of $200 million in gold, the reorganization of the Reichsbank under Allied supervision, and a new coinage, the reichsmark, set at 23.8 cents. As to reparations, he proposed payments on a sliding scale, beginning at $250 million and rising over five years to $625 million, with arrangements supervised by a new agent general (S. Parker Gilbert of the House of Morgan) who had to ensure payments were made regularly from a mix of funds, including the international loan, mortgages on principal industries and railroads, and taxes. The new scheme went into operation from September 1, 1924.

In time a new committee headed by New York industrialist Owen D. Young produced final and definitive arrangements, agreed by seventeen nations at The Hague on January 20, 1930. Germany's total liability was now set at $9 billion, with interest at 5.5 percent to be paid over fifty-nine years. Yearly payments were no more than $153 million—much less than the Dawes Plan had proposed. However, they were about the same as the total amount the Allies had agreed to pay the United States in war debts each year.

Germany could only meet its heavy reparations payments by borrowing. Investors, confident of German recovery, supported Germany by buying German securities regularly. The sums loaned by the United States up to July 1, 1931, were not less than $2.6 billion, the sum the United States collected from its Allies in war debts. The connection between German reparations, American loans, and Allied war debts became crystal clear. The United States loaned money to Germany with which it paid reparations to the Allies and they, in turn, repaid some of their debts to the United States. As historian William E. Leuchtenburg has observed in a much quoted sentence, "It would have made equal sense for the United States to take the money out of one Treasury building and put it into another." Far from being Uncle Shylock, the American people were underwriting the entire system of the debts and reparations.

The Young Plan also achieved the final evacuation of the Rhineland in which foreign troops left Coblenz on December 14, 1929, and Mainz on June 30, 1930.

Russo-American relations, embittered by aid given to the White Russian campaign of Admiral Alexander V. Kolchak in Siberia against the Bolsheviks in 1919 and early 1920, were also impeded by United States' insistence on full repayment by communist Russia of czarist debts. Throughout the twenties the United States refused to recognize the Soviet Union. However, Senator Borah argued for recognition after the Communists incorporated the Ukraine, Belorussia, and the Transcaucasian Federation with Russia into the Union of Soviet Socialist Republics (U.S.S.R.) in December 1922, and agreed on a first constitution in January 1924. The proposal was most astonishing coming as it did from Borah, because he was an inveterate isolationist. He was an effective public speaker—usually opposing whatever proposal was being mooted. According to an apocryphal story, Coolidge once met Borah riding through Rock Creek Park and after they had parted he commented, "Must bother the senator to be going in the same direction as the horse!" Borah's arguments for recognition of Russia were pragmatic. Only advantages could follow trade expansion. It had, hitherto, been standard American policy to recognize existing regimes whatever their moral origins. Against this Secretary Hughes argued that little economic gain could be gleaned from closer relations, that investment in a communist country was hazardous if not impossible, and there was no shred of evidence to suggest that countries recognizing the Bolsheviks had fared better economically than those that did not. Moreover, the Bolsheviks had annulled the czars' debts and refused to offer compensation for the confiscation of American property in Russia. This point of view was reaffirmed by Hughes's successors, Frank B. Kellogg (1925–1929) and Henry L. Stimson (1929–1933).

Collective Security, Disarmament, and the League

Between 1921 and 1924 the European powers tried to turn the prescriptions of the Covenant of the League of Nations into a practical program for collective security. The Draft Treaty of Mutual Assistance of 1923 provided the Council of the League, after an outbreak of hostilities, with authority to designate aggressor and victim. Furthermore, it obligated member states to give military support to the victim and take economic sanctions against the aggressor. As a concession and to entice the United States, the treaty said that nations were not obliged to assist the League outside the continent of the initial hostilities. However, Charles Evans Hughes said that since the United States was not a member of the League it could not assent to the proposals. The Geneva Protocol of October 2, 1924, went further than the Draft Treaty with specific proposals for enforcing collective security by sanctions. This, too, was rejected by the United States and, also, by the governments of Britain and the Dominions.

Europe could not be whole until Germany was readmitted to the concert of nations. Gustav Stresemann, chancellor of the Weimar Republic for 100 days in 1923 and, thereafter, foreign minister until his death six years later, attempted to overcome the suspicions of other European powers about the ambitions of Germany. Countering opposition within Germany and hesitation without, Stresemann's strategy was to tie German admission to the League and its Council to a review of territory in Europe. He achieved this in a series of treaties agreed on October 16, 1925, and known later as the Locarno Pact. On September 18, 1926, Germany was admitted to the League and became a permanent member of the Council that now had its numbers raised from ten to fourteen.

British and American delegations to the Peace Conference of 1919 had assured the French that they would together guarantee France's territorial integrity against any future German aggression. But when the United States Senate refused to ratify the Treaty of Versailles the chance of an Anglo–American guarantee also lapsed. In 1927 James T. Shotwell, a professor of Columbia University and associate director of the Carnegie Endowment for International Peace, visited Paris. He persuaded the French foreign minister, Aristide Briand, that he had a practical alternative. This was the Outlawry of War. Rejecting collective security because it was based on force, the American Committee for the Outlawry of War, founded in 1921 by Chicago businessman Salmon O. Levinson, conceived of a new international law prohibiting the use of force between nations.

The Outlawry of War had absolutely no appeal for Presidents Harding and Coolidge nor for Secretaries Hughes and Kellogg. The analogy with the tragicomedy of prohibition was obvious: the scourges of alcoholism and war to be abolished by inadequate legislation. However, Briand did not intend the Outlawry of War to be an empty scabbard. He now proposed a bilateral treaty between France and America. What he really wanted, of course, was the original American guarantee. Neither Coolidge nor Kellogg was deceived. They could not enter into an "entangling alliance" with France. Neither could they ignore the well-organized support for the scheme in America among pacifist societies —especially in the year of Lindbergh's solo flight across the Atlantic to Paris. By comparison with Hughes, Kellogg was an ineffective secretary of state. Perpetually harassed, he was called "Nervous Nellie" by sneering colleagues. Coolidge, on the other hand, was ill-informed about foreign affairs but unwilling to admit it. Yet together president and secretary saw how to outmaneuver Briand with a counterproposal. Senator Borah sug-

gested making the scheme multilateral. Once other leading powers had agreed, the French had to accept the international ban on
war that they, themselves, had first proposed. Foster Rhea Dulles
observes, "Rarely if ever have moral and ethical factors been
played up in such sharp contradiction of reality. The outlawry of
war was accepted as the final realization of a historic dream even
as the nation refused any sacrifice that might have given that
dream substance." On August 27, 1928, the Kellogg-Briand Treaty
or Pact of Paris was signed initially by representatives of fifteen
nations. The Senate ratified it in jocular, dismissive vein on January 15, 1929, with only a single dissenting vote.

It received a better complement than it deserved in attempts at
disarmament. Perhaps the spirit of the pact was responsible for
transferring the hesitancy of a naval conference in Geneva in 1927
to more positive declarations in London in 1930. The London
Conference from January 21 to April 22, 1930, was attended by
the new secretary of state, Henry L. Stimson, and the secretary of
the navy, Charles E. Adams. The upshot was a reduction in
tonnages leaving the United States with 464,300, Britain with
474,500, and Japan with 272,000. A new provision, Article XXII,
forbade submarines to attack without warning or without caring
for passengers and crew. The London Treaty was ratified by the
Senate by 58 votes to 9. Afterwards it became a matter of pride
for the different nations to boast about their flagrant violations,
especially with regard to submarines.

There were some signs that the Kellogg Pact was leading to
better relations between the powers. In 1929, Britain, France,
Italy, and Belgium agreed with Germany in a conference at The
Hague to evacuate the Rhineland by the summer of 1930—five
years before they were due to do so—and to conclude decisions
about reparations. But their calculations were another casualty of
the breakdown of the economic order that year.

Air Power

Air power was as significant a new factor in world affairs as oil
power and American foreign policy in the 1920s and 1930s had to
take account of the fact, especially as the great airlines were

drawing their governments into their own empires of the sky. The story has been engagingly told by Anthony Sampson in his *Empires of the Sky* (1984). Leading Republican Wendell Wilkie observed in 1943 how "The modern airplane creates a new geographical dimension. A navigable ocean of air blankets the whole surface of the globe. There are no distant places any longer; the world is small and the world is one. The American people must grasp these new realities if they are to play their essential part in . . . building a world of peace and freedom."

European governments recognized how aviation could be used to tie colonies and other settlements overseas more closely to the homeland. In particular, France wanted to lead the new world of air travel and deploy planes to bind together its empires in Africa and the Far East through its airlines Air Union, (1923), Air Orient (1930), and The Line (1919), and thence a merger of all three as Air France (1933).

By 1934 air travel in Europe was sufficiently popular for Bradshaw's of London to start publication of a monthly *International Air Guide*. Yet, although flights cost only a quarter as much again as a first-class sea voyage and took only half the time, they were too hazardous, unreliable, and fatiguing for most travelers. Long journeys were a bizarre mixture of frivolous luxuries and wearisome discomfort. Thus travelers in the East might be served caviar or lobster and allowed to walk about and admire the view through portholes of flying boats but they were also expected to rise at 4:30 A.M. so that the plane could have an early takeoff.

Different nationalities showed their different characteristics in the air as on the ground. Americans were the most adventurous and informal travelers, accounting for up to 75 percent of passengers on flights from London to Paris. The French showed little interest in comfort for its own sake while the British ascended with all the antiquated snobbery of the officers' mess. Nevertheless, in 1919 a Briton, George Holt Thomas, persuaded six airlines to meet at The Hague to form the International Air Traffic Association (IATA) "with a view to co-operate to mutual advantage in preparing and organising international aerial traffic." By 1929, IATA had twenty-three members and its headquarters at The Hague attempted to standardize timetables and safety systems.

While IATA stoutly maintained it was not a cartel, it followed the pattern of European trade associations that tried to curtail competition.

In 1928 the United States ratified the Havana Air Convention that established the first rules for air traffic in the Americas. Like the convention in Paris in 1919, the Havana convention repudiated the idea of complete freedom of the air and established the principle of air sovereignty. This principle, jealously guarded, limited airplanes far more than ships on the high seas. Nations became concerned that airplanes flying above their territory, whence they could spy, drop bombs, or invade, were more dangerous than ships that were supposed to be able to call at any port they wanted to.

Pan Am and World Affairs

In October 1927 a new airline, Pan American Airways, led by its young executive Juan Trippe, established the first permanent service from the United States to a foreign country. It carried mail from Key West, Florida, to Havana, 100 miles away. It used Fokker F7 trimotor planes and the journey lasted an hour.

Trippe expanded in Latin America. Soon Pan Am joined forces with the Grace trading empire to establish the Panagra airline that flew down the west coast from Ecuador to Peru and Chile and thence across the Andes to Argentina on the east coast. Moreover, he obliged Peter Paul von Bauer to sell his airline SCADTA (Sociedad Colombo Alemana de Transportes Aeros) to him. Trippe's airline was much criticized in Latin America, where it was considered an adjunct to Wall Street and the State Department. By 1929, when he was thirty, Trippe's board included chairman Sonny Whitney, banker Robert Lehman, and diplomat David Bruce, son-in-law to Secretary of the Treasury Andrew Mellon. However, within the United States Pan Am's national profile was above suspicion. It had no domestic land routes to speak of, did not have to compete for passengers, and this, coupled with its overseas monopoly, gave it a dignified image.

During Senate investigations into airline-mail frauds in 1934

Postmaster General Jim Farley disclosed how Juan Trippe had received special favors and how he had concealed Pan Am profits by juggling with accounts in different regions—an early instance of a multinational corporation outfoxing government. Nevertheless, Farley understood that the Pan Am network was essential for American commerce. For his part, Trippe knew how to raise an unwelcome specter—the challenge of foreign airlines to American hegemony of the western hemisphere should Congress decide against Pan Am. Moreover, because Pan Am had not been involved in the way domestic routes were alloted among the airlines, it came through the exposures relatively unscathed.

Juan Trippe also set out to conquer the Pacific, twice the width of the Atlantic but interspersed with numerous islands, large and small, that could provide aircraft with refueling stages. However, the first lap was from the West Coast to Hawaii, a journey of 2,000 miles and longer than the shortest route then established across the Atlantic. By 1935 Pan Am was using Martin flying boats to cover this journey before flying on to China. In 1933 Trippe acquired a half share in the China National Aviation Corporation that flew planes from Shanghai to Canton. The Pacific route was already studded with American naval bases on Honolulu, Midway, Guam, and Manila. However, between Midway and Guam there was only the barren Wake Island, acquired during the War of 1898 but neglected afterward. Trippe petitioned the federal government for a five-year lease of Wake Island. The State Department, already disturbed by Japanese ambitions in the Pacific, was pleased to have an opportunity to extend American naval influence there under the guise of a commercial airline. Accordingly, FDR agreed to place Wake, and other islands, under naval administration that allowed Pan Am access to Wake.

Trippe quickly established airfields and radio stations on various remote islands and thus secured the lucrative airmail contract for the entire route from San Francisco to Canton in October 1935. The first plane, the *China Clipper*, arrived at Manila after sixty hours' flying over seven days and received massive publicity, including issue of a special postage stamp to celebrate the most spectacular of official air routes. In the 1930s American businessmen and diplomats thought the Pacific crossing was a major strategy for the United States to extend American interests in the Far East and to check Japanese expansion.

Trippe encountered British opposition when he wanted to land Pan Am planes in Hong Kong to complete the last lap of the route from Manila to China. However, when he threatened to use the Portuguese island of Macao as an alternative gateway to China, the British colony, fearful of losing trade, agreed to let Pan Am land on the island. Thus Trippe realized his aim of linking Pan Am with his China airline across the Pacific. His empire of the skies was already superseding the empire of the seas and encouraging American interests to encroach on European possessions in the Far East.

Trippe then moved toward Australia which had established a regular service across Asia to Britain by 1934. The obvious staging post en route to Australia and New Zealand was Fiji, a British colony. Trippe was again challenged by a British airline, Imperial Airways, planning a rival route from Vancouver. However, Imperial needed to land on Hawaii and hoped to bargain British landing rights on Hawaii for American landing rights on Fiji. The Americans would not concede Hawaii and Trippe found an alternative for Fiji in the South Pacific in Samoa, the American archipelago that included a magnificent natural harbor of Pago Pago. Moreover, Trippe secured landing rights in New Zealand, simply by threatening (as he had with Hong Kong) to exclude it from his network. Thus Trippe used the ruthless strategy of the early railroad entrepreneurs, demanding rights from whole territories rather than states or single towns.

Nevertheless, there were huge distances between islands in the South Pacific, sometimes called the empty hemisphere, and it proved a most treacherous region. Amelia Earhart disappeared without trace north of New Guinea in July 1937. Then in January 1938, Ed Musick, chief pilot to Pan Am, was killed when his plane, the *Samoa Clipper,* exploded in midair north of Pago Pago. For a time the Pan Am service to New Zealand was suspended but a regular service was resumed by July 1940. In the South Pacific, airlines made neighbors of islands far away from one another. Thus the South Pacific missed out the intervening age of railroad and steamships and yet now moved decisively into the global community.

The North Atlantic was potentially the most lucrative route for cargoes and passengers but in practical terms the most hostile in the 1930s. Its fierce headwinds, lack of any staging post between Canada and Ireland, except the frost-bound Greenland and Iceland to the north or the Azores to the south, made it a far more inhospitable region than the Pacific. Thus Lindbergh's historic solo transatlantic flight of 1927 was followed by prolonged anticlimax: one man might fly the Atlantic but no airplane could then carry mail and passengers for 2,000 miles without a stop. Furthermore, in one sense, air transport was in competition with the easy communication of the telephone, which was far more convenient for most businessmen to use.

Moreover, the North Atlantic proved a diplomatic minefield. Juan Trippe found the Europeans far more intractable about landing rights nearer home than they had been in the Far East. This time Britain and Imperial Airways had a bargaining point, Bermuda, a British island colony 800 miles southwest of New York, the crucial, and only, staging post on the southerly route via the Azores. The upshot was an agreement between Juan Trippe and Pan Am and Sir Eric Geddes of Imperial in 1930 wherein they formed a joint development corporation. As part of its strategy for closing the Atlantic, Britain sought agreement with Canada and Ireland, or Eire, newly independent, in Ottawa in November 1935 by which the three nations would form a joint Atlantic Company, of which Britain would hold 51 percent and Ireland and Canada half each of the remaining 49 percent. Meanwhile, America and Britain agreed to provide one another with reciprocal landing rights. Pan Am's arrangements with various European airlines, including the Dutch KLM company, created in 1924, broke both letter and spirit of the antitrust laws but the government allowed tactful wording in the contracts to conceal what was, in effect, restraint of trade.

Pan Am and Imperial chose Botwood in Newfoundland as their western terminus and Shannon, in Ireland, as their eastern terminus. After a year studying winds and clouds both companies undertook their first survey flights in July 1937. The new Pan Am flying boat, Clipper III, left Botwood in the evening and arrived at Foynes twelve and a half hours later. Yet neither airline had planes that could carry passengers on such a long flight. According to the agreement, Pan Am could not commence regular flights until Imperial was also ready and Imperial was behind Pan Am in research and development. In fact, the Germans were ahead of the Americans and the British. In 1938 Lufthansa flew a fourteen-engine Fokker-Wulf landplane from Berlin to New York in less than twenty-five hours.

Once the British became more engrossed in, first, the threat, and, then, the fact of war, and rapidly expanded the Royal Air Force, Pan Am steadily advanced its transatlantic passenger flights. In May 1939 Pan Am flew the first of the big Boeings, the Yankee Clipper, with twenty-two passengers aboard, from the Marine Terminal, New York (now next to La Guardia Airport), to Lisbon and Marseilles, via the Azores. Anthony Sampson concludes how

The airlines had completed their circumnavigation of the globe and a tireless passenger could now fly round it, with a bit of luck, in ten days —a bewildering change of perspective over the three decades since Blériot had first crossed the English Channel. It was a staggering technical achievement. But the political rhetoric of air transport about bringing peace and understanding was already sounding hollow after warplanes had revealed their destructiveness in Spain and Manchuria. . . . Behind their apparently infinite mobility, the airlines were becoming still more bound by the imperatives of sovereignty and national ambition.

In the 1930s European nations began to sense that aircraft would play a decisive role with lethal potential by dropping bombs in any future war. At a League of Nations disarmament conference in 1932, France, supported by Spain and Belgium, argued for an international air force and civil air service that alone would have the right to own and fly larger planes. Sweden advocated a modified system by which the international organization would simply run airports and supervise national airlines. However, Russia and Germany were opposed to either proposal and other leading countries, such as the United States, Britain, Canada, and Japan, were either skeptical or uninterested. After, first, Germany and, then, other countries began to rearm, French aviation economist Henri Bouche submitted a report to the League of Nations in 1935 that asked, "How could the governments of a mistrustful Europe allow the indefinite development of a powerful means of transport when aircraft sent on peaceful missions over national territories, and to the very heart of those territories, may also carry out their missions?"

In September 1939 Britain, France, and Germany were at war. Pan Am's flights to Europe stopped at Foynes in Ireland or Lisbon in Portugal, since Ireland and Portugal remained neutral. The skies above the Atlantic Ocean were reserved for Pan Am with its Boeing planes. Their supremacy could survive the war.

Latin America and the Good Neighbor Policy

Throughout the twenties American statesmen tried to revise Woodrow Wilson's diplomacy toward Latin America. As we know, in order to discourage revolutions in Latin America and to prevent political adventurers gaining power by assassination, Woodrow Wilson had applied his own special criteria of recognition to new regimes, that of constitutional legitimacy. But his policy had antagonized Latins and created more problems than it solved. In addition, Latins believed that the true motive underlying American interest was economic penetration of their countries, the so-called dollar diplomacy. The United States had superseded Britain as the principal source of capital for development in Latin America. American companies established branches in Latin America, American investors bought Latin-American bonds, and American corporations looked increasingly to Latin America for materials and markets. In certain respects, the two economies of the northern and southern hemispheres were complementary. The United States exported manufactured goods, notably machinery and motor cars, and imported such commodities as rubber, tin, copper, and nitrates, and sugar, bananas, and coffee. However, in other respects, there was a clash of interests. For example, both the United States and Argentina wanted to export their agricultural surplus and were thus in competition for markets. Moreover, the Latin states could not become self-suffi-

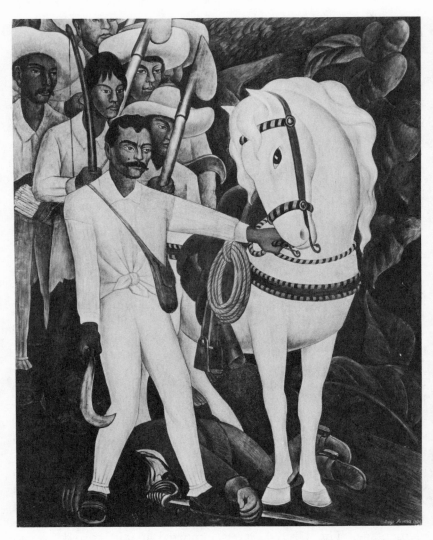

Diego Rivera, *Agrarian Leader Zapata* (1931), fresco 7′9″ × 6′2″. (Collection, The Museum of Modern Art, New York. Abby Aldrich Rockefeller Fund). The Mexican muralist Diego Rivera exercised a potent influence not only upon his people, who responded to political teaching through paintings and symbols, but also American regional artists such as Thomas Hart Benton and John Steuart Curry who wanted to celebrate pasture and harvest in graphic art that had an immediate impact.

cient economically while they grew ever more dependent on the United States for industrial goods. In addition, they felt more akin in cultural terms to Latin states in Europe than they did to the colossus of the north.

Successive Republican administrations now attempted to repair poor relations by introducing a Good Neighbor policy in Latin America. One sign of this shift was their promotion of more Pan-American conferences. The United States was host to a special conference on Central America in Washington from December 4, 1922, to February 7, 1923. In general, the United States worked for the peaceful settlement of disputes in Latin America and at promoting cooperative efforts in the fields of economics, transportation, and health.

The priority of American foreign policy in the western hemisphere was to maintain security in the Caribbean and in the isthmus between North and South America. The isthmus states were unstable politically and, to protect the Panama Canal, the United States despatched marines whenever and wherever it thought trouble was brewing. However, in the twenties presidents and secretaries of state cared more than ever before about cultivating the good will of these tiny but crucial allies. On April 20, 1921, Harding persuaded the Senate to approve the Treaty of Bogotá of April 6, 1914, by which Colombia was reconciled to the United States over the loss of Panama in 1903. There was method underlying this act of magnanimity. The United States was allowed to expand American operations in the oil fields of Colombia and soon recovered the initial outlay of its grant. Harding and Hughes also persuaded Panama to settle a boundary dispute with Costa Rica in favor of Costa Rica.

Harding also tried to propitiate Mexico and President Álvaro Obregón agreed to modify Mexican restrictions on American business but refused to offer compensation for all American losses in Mexico since 1920 or to agree to guarantee the rights of American nationals in Mexico. Nevertheless, Harding wanted to recognize the new Mexican government and the Bucareli agreements of August 15, 1923, brought to a formal end the hostility engendered by Wilson's policies. In 1924 Coolidge raised the arms embargo on Mexico and allowed American financiers to extend credit to the Mexican government for the purchase of a "few muskets and a few rounds of ammunition."

However, a new Mexican president, Plutarco Elías Calles, was less inclined to friendly relations with the United States than had been Álvaro Obregón. In 1925 the Mexican Congress passed an alien lands law that allowed foreigners to buy land in Mexico on condition that, in this matter, they renounced all rights to protection from foreign governments. It also passed a petroleum law that declared oil deposits were the inalienable and imprescriptible property of Mexico and provided strict laws about concessions to foreigners. Oil companies were ordered to apply for renewal of their rights under the law by January 1, 1927, or else, forfeit them. President Calles estimated that 380 companies, holding 26.83 million acres, assented to the new law while 22 companies, with 1.66 million acres, refused. These included such American interests as Doheny, Sinclair, Standard, and Gulf. Through their press allies they had newspapers circulate accounts that Mexico was adopting revolutionary socialist policies and fomenting communism throughout the western hemisphere. American politicians were not taken in. Borah declared in a speech of May 9, 1927, "The truth is that effort is being made to get this country into a shameless, cowardly little war with Mexico. . . . They talk communism and bolshevism, but what they mean is war."

As a pledge of noninterference, the United States began to withdraw its marines from Latin America and the Caribbean. However, the withdrawal of U.S. Marines from Nicaragua on August 1, 1925, was followed by a most violent civil war beginning on October 25. Coolidge ordered marines to return first in May and, then, in August 1926. He justified his action to Congress on January 10, 1927, on the basis of protecting both the Panama Canal and American investments. But he also sent Henry L. Stimson, a former secretary of war, to Nicaragua to try and persuade the two sides to come to terms. This Stimson achieved in the Peace of Tipitata on May 11, 1927, whereby both sides agreed to a coalition government under Adolfo Díaz until the United States could arrange elections. The election of 1928 was won by a former rebel, José M. Moncada. From February 1931

Stimson, now secretary of state, began to withdraw troops in successive stages.

The civil war in Nicaragua soured Mexican-American relations anew because the two countries supported opposite sides. The new deterioration in relations between the United States and its neighbor prompted what was, perhaps, Coolidge's most inspired decision in foreign policy. In 1927 he appointed Dwight W. Morrow as ambassador to Mexico to succeed the unpopular James R. Sheffield. Morrow had been in Coolidge's class at Amherst College and had an engaging personality. Morrow cleverly defused the situation. To redeem America's image, he had Lindbergh fly to Mexico City where he was received tumultuously. Then Morrow achieved a compromise over subsurface oil rights by persuading the Mexican Supreme Court to declare the most objectionable clauses of the new law unconstitutional. He also induced the Mexican government and the Catholic church, who were at odds over the proposed nationalization of church property, to accept a new accord by which the church withdrew an interdict on certain services in exchange for a government undertaking that it would not attempt the destruction of the church. The tensions between the United States and Mexico that had seemed so important in the early 1920s had dissolved ten years later.

Underlying these various American policies to individual countries was the realization by successive presidents and secretaries that they had to convince Latin America as a whole that the United States neither coveted additional territory nor wanted to interfere in others' internal affairs. Unlike the United States, sixteen Latin-American countries had joined the League of Nations by March 1921. Only Argentina, Ecuador, Mexico, and the Dominican Republic remained outside it. In these circumstances, it is not surprising that the United States eventually recognized the advantages of using the League to mediate in Latin-American disputes. In 1932 and 1933 the State Department twice accepted arbitration by the League, firstly, in the so-called Chaco War between Paraguay and Bolivia about a track of jungle and, secondly, in the war between Peru and Colombia over the village of Leticia. These quarrels made it clear that, no matter how constructive were United States strategies in pursuit of Good Neighbor policies, the machinery to keep the peace in Latin America was unreliable. The conventions on arbitration and conciliation were imperfect vehicles for joint consultation. Nevertheless, the United States could not collaborate effectively with the League while it remained an occasional guest rather than a permanent member.

Hoover and Stimson

When Herbert Hoover became president in March 1929 he was the most widely traveled man to take the office to that time. As secretary of commerce under Harding and Coolidge (1921–1929), Hoover had worked assiduously to secure American investment abroad and diplomatic compromise at home. Between his election and inauguration as president he toured Latin America, the only part of the world he had not previously visited. It seemed here at last was a president better informed on world affairs. Unfortunately, Hoover's crippling limitations of personality that weakened his ability to handle the depression also adversely affected his foreign policy. Moreover, the combination of the cautious new president and his alert, impulsive, and hyperactive secretary of state, Henry L. Stimson, was not harmonious. Stimson was a successful New York lawyer who had previously served as secretary of war under Taft. He admitted he knew little about European affairs but he was willing to act, and to act decisively in crisis.

The system of debts and reparations payments broke down in the wake of the Wall Street Crash. In March 1931 French bankers called in short-term German and Austrian notes. Unable to meet the demands upon it, the Kreditanstalt in Vienna collapsed and this set off a chain reaction. The Weimar Republic defaulted on reparations payments and President Paul von Hindenburg appealed to Hoover. In June 1931 Hoover proposed a one-year moratorium on the payment of international debts and reparations payments. At Lausanne in June 1932 Britain, France, Italy, Japan, and Belgium agreed to reduce the residue of German reparations to $750 million. Cuba alone paid off its American debt in full, $15 million by 1920. Finland, which had contracted a post-war loan of $9 million, was the only country to continue payments after 1935 and to discharge its loan.

Invasion of Manchuria

The Japanese invasion of Manchuria on September 18, 1931, was subsequently recognized as the turning point between peace and war. It symbolized the collapse of attempts to ensure peace, either by arbitration or collective security. It was a climax to Russo-Japanese antagonism since the 1890s. Furthermore, it inaugurated a period of Japanese politics called the *kurai tanima* or dark valley. Like the United States, Japan had emerged from World War I with increased economic and industrial capacity. Japan became a creditor nation and its financial and industrial combines, the *zaibatsu,* did well out of the protracted European struggle. However, Japan could only maintain production by finding additional reserves of raw materials abroad.

Industry, legitimately developed by the Japanese in Manchuria according to treaty, attracted increasing numbers of Chinese settlers north of the Great Wall. Subject to the despotic control of a brigand chief, Zhang Zuolin, Manchuria was not an integral part of China. But after years of confusion following the revolution of 1911 China now seemed ready for reunification. Jiang Jieshi, who was the leader of the conservative wing of the Guomindang or National People's party, established a capital on June 8, 1928, in Beijing. On July 25, 1928, the United States recognized his government. One of Jiang's aims was the recovery of Chinese control of territories leased to foreigners. This policy produced dynamic opposition from the Japanese army determined to resist it. The eventual pretext for the Japanese army's invasion of Manchuria was a minor explosion on the South Manchurian Railway stationed by Japanese soldiers. Their reprisal was an attack on the city of Shenyang and by October 1931 they had begun to bomb cities in southern Manchuria. At this time China was being devastated by floods. Although the Japanese prime minister, Wakatsuki Reijiro, and the foreign minister, Shidehara Kijuro, were indignant at the army's invasion, to save face in public they upheld their country's honor. Thus their envoy to the League, Yoshizawa, enlarged on the vital importance of Manchuria to Japan and the numerous, supposed broken agreements of the Chinese, while world disapproval of the invasion solidified native patriotism among the Japanese people.

The Japanese invasion was an act of flagrant aggression. How did the powers react? The League authorized a Commission of Inquiry headed by Lord Lytton to travel to Manchuria and review the situation. America was represented by General Frank McCoy. Hoover cynically judged European expressions of horror about the invasion as hypocritical. The only distinction between Japan's morals and those of the European imperial powers "was one of timing. The old empires had held the titles longer and thus were more sacrosanct." Nevertheless, he thought that the Japanese had played a dirty game by their "act of rank aggression." "The whole transaction is immoral. The offense against the comity of nations and the affront to the United States is outrageous." For Hoover there were two courses of action, either some form of collective economic sanctions against Japan or diplomatic pressure. He preferred diplomatic pressure because he thought sanctions would lead inevitably to war. His critics said he feared Congress would object to economic boycotts on the grounds that George Washington had never advocated boycotts.

Hoover recalled that William Jennings Bryan had, as Wilson's first secretary of state, used nonrecognition as a diplomatic device in 1915 when Japan made the notorious Twenty-One Demands of China. On November 9, 1931, Hoover suggested to Stimson that he did the same. Prompted by Hoover and urged on by Walter Lippmann, Stimson despatched a note declaring "The United States government . . . cannot admit the legality of any situation de facto" to both China and Japan on January 7, 1932. Acquisition by aggression had no legal validity.

International opposition to Japan did not coalesce. China was left alone to offer what resistance it could. After the first note, Japanese rear admiral Kuichi Shiozawa started a second war within the Great Wall, 200 miles south of Shenyang at Shanghai, on January 28, 1932. Stimson's desire to emphasize nonrecognition then took a different form, an open letter to Senator Borah of

February 23, 1932, in which his view was restated to warn Japan, to encourage China, and to rouse the League. When the Lytton report was published, it exonerated China and condemned Japan. On February 24, 1933, the League accepted the report and refused to recognize Manchuria. On March 27 Japan withdrew from the League. Fighting now extended to south of the Great Wall and, to avert more losses, Jiang Jieshi agreed to a truce on May 31, 1933. In the meantime, the last party cabinet of the thirties in Japan had been brought down after the assassination of the current prime minister, Inukai Tsuyoshi, on May 15, 1932, by a secret association of fanatics, "the League of Blood."

Collective security had fallen apart. The slide to another world war began. The Japanese sought living room. In their search they would enter a room none thought possible, the mushroom of 1945.

14

"WHO IS THIS HITLER, AND WHAT DOES HE WANT?"
Isolation and Intervention

To ITALY, Germany, and Japan the League of Nations was a conspiracy of nations, the possessive against the dispossessed. If the Japanese invasion of Manchuria was the turning point between war and peace in the 1930s, the central event was the rise of Germany under the National Socialist, or Nazi, dictatorship of Adolf Hitler. It was his alliance of October 25, 1936, with the National Socialist, or Fascist, dictatorship of Benito Mussolini in Italy, and subsequent pact with Japan of November 25, 1936, that brought the ambitions of the three countries together.

Hitler's foreign policy was expansionist and had two aims. The first was the unification of all German-speaking peoples in Europe in the Third Reich, whether they were minorities within other nations, such as the Sudeten Germans in Czechoslovakia and Germans in Poland, or other entire nations, such as Austria. The second aim was to grasp the hegemony of Europe. Both aims involved undermining the Treaty of Versailles. Yet Hitler's for-

Checkmate at Munich. All were not equal around the round table on September 29, 1938, among Mussolini, Hitler, Dr. P. Schmidt (translator), and Neville Chamberlain. Commenting later on Chamberlain's sacrifice of Czechoslovakia, and his proposed Anglo-German declaration of "peace for our time," little Adolf was supposed to have cheerfully remarked, "He seemed such a nice old gentleman and I thought he was only asking for my autograph." (Bundesarchiv, Koblenz, Germany).

eign policy was improvised and responded to situations as much as it created them. Whether opportunist in the manner of Bismarck's foreign policy—that is to say using situations for the furtherance of a central aim—or not, there was a long-term logic to its success for ten years. The prerequisite of the foreign policy was the rearmament of Germany in defiance of the Treaty of Versailles. Mussolini, who sought the creation of Italian blocs, began as Hitler's tutor in foreign affairs, continued as his accomplice, and declined into his lackey.

The ambitions of Hitler and Mussolini posed crucial strategic, diplomatic, and ethical problems for Britain and France. The Covenant of the League of Nations pledged members to respect one another's integrity and to unite against any agressor. However, states were unwilling to sink their national independence and aspirations in the creation of a multilateral force, or army, for the sake of collective security. Even less successful were attempts at disarmament that were floundering in fall 1933. On October 14, 1933, Germany withdrew from a London conference on disarmament and the following week it left the League. Hitler's policy of rearmament was completed on March 7, 1936, when he sent a token force to reoccupy the Rhineland. Public opinion in Britain would not brook resistance and the government could only renew assurances to France and Belgium guaranteeing their territorial integrity.

For its part in the tragic events that were about to unfold, Italy led a group of so-called "revisionist" powers—Hungary, Bulgaria, and, later, Austria—that also wanted to revise the settlement of 1919. Mussolini dreamed of a new Roman Empire. Italy had two colonies in East Africa, Eritrea and Somaliland, but they were barren, unlike fertile Ethiopia (or Abyssinia) that lay between them and had untapped mineral resources. Italy launched a full-scale invasion of Ethiopia on October 3, 1935, and was able to conclude the war with the decisive battle of Lake Ashangi of March 31 to April 3, 1936, after which the emperor of Ethiopia, Haile Selassie, fled the country. Despite the outrage to the Kellogg Pact and its own Covenant, the League of Nations demurred before briefly imposing economic sanctions against Italy in the form of an oil embargo. Indeed, Britain and France were willing to come to some sort of dishonest compromise with Italy, whereby Ethiopia would be partitioned between Mussolini and Haile Selassie. Neither Britain nor France would bite the bullet of collective security. Here was clear proof that the League lacked teeth.

More damaging to international security was the Spanish Civil War of 1936–1939, which began after a democratically elected but sometimes unstable and disorderly Popular Front government was challenged by a rebellion of right-wing generals led by Francisco Franco on July 17, 1936. The intervention of Italy and Germany on behalf of Franco and of Russia for the Republic transformed the Spanish Civil War into an international issue. Both Britain and France wanted to ignore the problem, principally to prevent its escalation into international war. Thus they undertook not to aid either side in Spain. This time the League was not consulted. It restricted its activities to keeping safe the paintings of the Prado Art Gallery in Madrid.

In the summer of 1937 Britain and France, in protest at the sinking of British, French, and Russian ships carrying food and civilian supplies to the Spanish Republic by "unknown" submarines, which were, in fact, Italian, organized a conference of Mediterranean countries at Nyon. Antisubmarine patrols were set up, a demonstration that a firm line would work. After the fall of Barcelona, the Spanish government's stronghold, in January 1939, many foreign governments extended recognition to Franco's regency and, besides Germany and Italy, these included, on February 27, Britain and France. But the United States delayed recognition until April 3, 1939, after the fall of Madrid in March.

What was true of Franklin Roosevelt's character and temperament in domestic politics was also true of him in foreign affairs. The facts that FDR was raised by a wealthy eastern family and had visited Europe several times, that he had served as assistant secretary of the navy under Woodrow Wilson, and that, as vice-presidential candidate in 1920, he had campaigned for American membership of the League of Nations—all these greatly influenced his foreign policy. At heart he was a committed internationalist and deeply interested in the well-being of Europe. However, the facts that his political education in New York had taught him the necessity of expedience and compromise, that he had had to struggle to overcome the crippling limitations of his poliomyelitis, and that he was temperamentally incapable of adhering to rigid formulas—all these affected the way he would lead America back into the concert of nations and into World War II.

Foreign Relations in the Mid-1930s

When Roosevelt first took office the New Deal subordinated all other issues and throughout his first term he concentrated on domestic policy, leaving his secretary of state, Cordell Hull (1933–

1944), almost in full charge of foreign policy after the abortive London Economic Conference of 1933. Hull had been largely responsible for that part of the Democratic platform of 1932 calling for reciprocal trade agreements and he was too tenacious and persistent a politician to give up the aim of increasing world trade after the setback in London. Hull had sometimes denounced the protective tariff as the "king of evils" and "the largest single underlying cause of the present panic." Thus his critics mimicked his lisp and southern drawl by declaring, "We must eliminate these trade baa-yuhs heah, theah, and ev'ywheah." Hull persuaded Roosevelt and Secretary of Agriculture Henry A. Wallace to seek bipartisan support for a bill to make tariffs the prerogative of the president rather than Congress. By the Reciprocal Trade Agreements Act of June 4, 1934 (renewed in 1937 and 1940), the president was given power to negotiate bilateral concessions with other countries and thence to raise or lower tariff rates by as much as 50 percent, provided other countries made reciprocal arrangements. Within eighteen months agreement had been reached with fourteen countries.

However, Hull went further than the specific terms of the act in order to lower tariff barriers. He turned to the "most favored nation" clause of the old Fordney-McCumber tariff of 1922. This clause enabled him to extend tariff reductions on specific items to all other countries whose duties did not discriminate against America. By 1940 there had been a 61 percent increase of trade with twenty-two countries, compared with only a 38 percent increase with countries not sharing the trade agreements. The acts of 1934, 1937, and 1940 thus reduced the average tariff rates from 40 or 50 percent to 13 percent. However, the value of exports from 1933 to 1939 rose only from $1.7 billion to $3.2 billion, while imports rose from $1.4 billion to $2.3 billion—below the levels of the twenties. Nevertheless, the government had abandoned the openly selfish economic policies of the previous decade. Yet Congress, in an act sponsored by Senator Hiram Johnson of California, and signed by FDR on April 13, 1934, forbade Americans to lend or buy from nations that defaulted on payment of their war debts.

However, some policies, while equally self-serving, were more enlightened and constructive. In 1934 the Roosevelt administration used funds from the RFC and created an Export-Import Bank as another government agency to stimulate foreign trade by offering credits and loans to finance the purchase of American goods. The Export-Import Bank loaned money to European countries so that they could buy American agricultural produce and to Latin-American countries both to stabilize their currencies and to enable them to buy equipment for such projects as road construction.

In the thirties arguments about trade were more propitious than earlier and influenced America's relationship with Russia. In 1930 the U.S.S.R. had bought 36 percent of all American exports of agricultural implements and 50 percent of all tractors; in 1931 it had purchased 65 percent of all machine tools exported. After the rise of the Nazis in Germany and military factions in Japan, both Roosevelt and Joseph Stalin recognized in the other a potential ally. On November 16, 1933, despite opposition from American conservatives, the two nations agreed to resume diplomatic relations. On September 18, 1934, the U.S.S.R. went further and joined the League of Nations. The economic advantages of the new relationship proved disappointing for the United States. Russia was unable to export much, defaulted on its debt agreements, and, in violation of its agreement, continued to foment communist activities in America.

Roosevelt became deeply interested in foreign affairs in 1935. Reforms had achieved modest economic recovery but international relations had begun to deteriorate so badly that they could no longer be ignored. The aggressive acts of Mussolini and Hitler made more urgent the fears first awakened by the Japanese invasion of Manchuria and the collapse of collective security. For fifteen years the issue of American membership of the World Court had hung in the balance of the prevalent isolationism. Now Roosevelt asked the Senate to approved the protocol governing membership that Elihu Root had drawn up in 1929. FDR knew that membership would have little practical effect but it would be an important symbolic gesture. It was not to be. Isolationist sentiment in the country suddenly revealed its latent strength when Father Charles E. Coughlin, the radio priest, and William

Randolph Hearst, owner of the most influential newspaper chain, joining vociferous isolationist Senators Long, Borah, Johnson, and Norris, were able to arouse public opinion against the proposal. American membership of the World Court was rejected by the Senate on January 29, 1935, by 52 votes against to 36 in favor, and with 7 abstentions. For FDR, who had staked his reputation on the issue, the defeat was deeply embarrassing. Defeat of American membership of the World Court marked a turning point in American foreign policy, signifying that a powerful isolationist lobby now threatened to wrest the initiative from the president.

Isolationism

In the 1930s the term "isolationist" had a particular application to those unilateralists or continentalists who wanted the United States to have complete independence of diplomatic action, to avoid what Washington called "entangling alliances," and, most of all, to remain neutral in any war. Isolationists and pacifists agreed that World War I had been a disaster, that a second war would be even worse, and that renewed American intervention would profit only bankers, arms makers, and other industrialists. The cost would be borne by the American people who would lose their lives, their money, and their democratic institutions.

Socially, isolationists were more likely to come from small towns and the countryside in the Midwest than from the great cities of the Northeast, or from the South, and to work as farmers, small businessmen, and manufacturers of light and service industries. Ethnically, they were drawn from the Irish-, German-, and Italian-American blocs.

In Congress their champions included: progressive Republican Senators William E. Borah of Idaho; Hiram Johnson of California, Arthur Capper of Kansas; Gerald P. Nye of North Dakota; Republican Senators Arthur H. Vandenberg of Michigan; Robert A. Taft of Ohio; Republican Congressman Hamilton Fish of New York; progressive Democratic Senator Burton K. Wheeler of Montana; progressive Senators Robert M. La Follette, Jr., of Wisconsin and George W. Norris of Nebraska; and Farm-Labor

Senator Henrik Shipstead of Minnesota. However, it should not be imagined these men all thought and voted consistently or as one. For example, Republican Arthur Capper of Kansas voted for the World Court protocols in 1926 and 1935 while Democratic Burton K. Wheeler of Montana voted for the protocols in 1926 but against them in 1935.

They were, however, crucial allies to FDR in domestic affairs, being committed to the New Deal, and their support was invaluable, especially on the more controversial legislation. It is a political axiom that a wise politician never alienates his support. In short, FDR dared not risk their antagonism in domestic affairs by provoking them on foreign policy, particularly in his second term when he was engaged in adversary politics and when the slide to war was more obvious in Europe and Asia.

Outside Congress, isolationist champions included Governor Philip M. La Follette of Wisconsin; revisionist historian Charles A. Beard; former New Dealers Hugh S. Johnson and George N. Peek; socialist leader Norman Thomas; and, most famous and controversial of all, star aviator Colonel Charles A. Lindbergh. In the mass media they had the voice of press magnate William Randolph Hearst. Their views were also expressed in a whole range of periodicals from the conservative *Scribner's* to the liberal *Christian Century* and *New Republic*.

In convincing the American public that their foreign policy of unilateralism was to be preferred to that of FDR and Hull, isolationists were most fortunate that the slide to war in Europe and Asia could be represented in the syndicated press as the inevitable outcome of a conflict of imperialist rivalries from which the United States would do best to remain aloof. Moreover, as the tragic sequence of events unfolded abroad, the ravages of the Great Depression and a series of domestic crises at home proved of consuming interest to the American people. As historian William Manchester has shown, the preoccupation of Americans with internal events partly explains the slowness of American response to the deterioration in international relations. The actual timing of international crises was partly responsible for confused American reaction to them. Such was the backdrop to the isolationists' campaign to insulate America from war.

The Senate investigation of the munitions industry, led by Republican Senator Gerald P. Nye of North Dakota, and the ensuing four Neutrality Acts of 1935, 1936, 1937, and 1939 represented the high tide of American isolationism in the 1930s.

American demands for the regulation of arms traffic had intensified after the collapse of the Geneva Disarmament Conference in 1933. Dorothy Detzer, executive secretary of the Women's International League for Peace and Freedom, believed that pacifist ideas on restricting the arms traffic would be accepted by the public if an official enquiry were conducted into the munitions industry. Detzer and her ally in the Senate, George W. Norris, persuaded Senator Gerald P. Nye of North Dakota, a humorless zealot of the isolationist cause, that it would be to his advantage to promote such an enquiry. His state had no heavy industry and thus his constituents could not be harmed by any revelation. Moreover, the chair of an important Senate committee could provide him with an ideal base from which to launch his presidential ambitions. On April 12, 1934, the Senate approved Nye's motion calling for a seven-man Senate investigation into the munitions industry of which Nye himself was subsequently chosen as chairman.

The time was ripe. A month earlier H. C. Engelbrecht and F. C. Hanighen had had their sensational article, "Arms and the Men," published in *Fortune* magazine. In asking exactly who had profited from the world war, the authors produced evidence to show that the only financial profits were made by the munitions manufacturers. It was said that the motto of the munitions makers was "When there are wars, prolong them; when there is peace, disturb it." Shortly afterward, Walter Millis added fuel to the fire of economic interpretation of the causes of World War I with his *The Road to War* (1935), a best-seller described as the isolationists' bible.

The Nye committee held its public hearings from September 4, 1934, until February 20, 1936, and during those eighteen months heard evidence from around 200 witnesses and produced a final report of 13,750 pages in thirty-nine volumes. Its star witnesses were the brothers Du Pont (Irénée, Pierre, and Lammot) and J. P. Morgan, Jr., and his senior partners. Newspapers across

America gave somewhat lurid accounts of the hearings, especially the most sensational revelations.

The hearings confirmed the worst suspicions of isolationists and pacifists of double-dealing in aid of arms sales. For instance, a series of letters between Lawrence Y. Spear, a vice-president of Electric Boat, a submarine manufacturer, and Charles Craven, head of the British arms firm Vickers, disclosed the apparently compulsive need of big companies to make profits at the expense of human life. In one letter Spear told Craven, "It is too bad that the pernicious activities of our State Department have put the brake on armaments orders from Peru by forcing the resumption of formal diplomatic relations with Chile." It seemed that countries existed to be cajoled and corrupted by munitions makers whose dupes they were. Nye could sardonically "wonder whether the army or the navy are just organizations of salesmen for private industry, paid for by the American government."

Indeed, some arms sales were supported by the American government. Bernard Baruch, one of Roosevelt's advisers, sent FDR a memorandum on the subject of governmental supervision of arms sales in February 1935 in which he emphasized that the United States had to find ways of maintaining capacity to make arms in peace. This could be done by selling to foreign belligerents:

Governments of industrial countries . . . almost universally . . . encourage the manufacture of lethal weapons for exportation to belligerent countries actively preparing for war, but which have an insufficient munitions industry. . . . This is a method of providing a laboratory to test killing implements and a nucleus for a wartime munitions industry by maintaining an export market for instruments of death. Of course, it is absolutely indefensible. . . .

Historian Charles A. Beard's interpretation of the Nye committee came in a series of articles for the *New Republic* that show a fascination with an economic interpretation of the origins of World War I. In the first article, on March 9, 1936, he said the revelations of the Senate committee made

The files of the newspapers that reported and commented on events look like the superficial scribblings of ten-year-old children. . . . People who imagine that they 'know what is going on' because they read the great metropolitan dailies will find in the Nye records the shallowness and irrelevance of their 'knowledge' gathered from the press in 1914–17.

In a further series of articles for the *New Republic,* Beard made his famous comparison between war and the explosion of a chemical compound, the so-called "devil theory of war." Was the explosion caused by the last ingredient added or did it merely precipitate the explosion in the end? In times of peace men prepared for, and encouraged, the coming of war by their insatiable greed for territory, capital, and profit.

Nye believed he knew the answer and overstated his findings, telling the Senate on January 15, 1935, how he had discovered the existence of a vicious partnership between the federal government and the munitions industry. What Nye considered perhaps "the most important part of the investigation" came in March 1935 when the committee examined the files of American banks relating to loans to European governments in World War I before American intervention. In particular, an announcement by committee member Senator Bennett Champ Clark of Missouri on January 15, 1936, that President Woodrow Wilson and Secretary of State Robert Lansing "had falsified" their knowledge of secret treaties between the Allies caused a minor explosion. Over the next two days Wilson was roundly defended by Tom Connally of Texas and Carter Glass of Virginia on the floor of the Senate. By his angry insistence on Wilson's duplicity, Nye succeeded in uniting somewhat diverse opposition in the Senate to the munitions investigation and thus nothing came immediately of the committee's final recommendations.

However, the damage had been done. The committee had provided the initiative for the Neutrality Acts of 1935, 1936, 1937, and 1939. Much to his subsequent regret, Secretary of State Cordell Hull had acquiesced in the establishment of the committee. In his *Memoirs* he explains how disastrous was the outcome.

The Nye Committee aroused an isolationist sentiment that was to tie the Administration just at the very time when our hands should have been free to place the weight of our influence in the scales where it would count. It tangled our relations with the very nations whom we should have been morally supporting. It stirred the resentment of other nations with whom we had no controls. It confused the minds of our own people as to the real reasons that led us into the First World War. It showed the prospective aggressors in Europe and Asia that our public opinion was pulling a cloak over its head and becoming nationally unconcerned with their designs and that, therefore, they could proceed with fuller confidence.

Naval Construction

In the meantime, FDR, who was distrusted by pacifists and isolationists alike as a big navy man, had begun a program of naval expansion, partly to compete with Japan and partly to satisfy domestic economic needs. In June 1933 he allocated $238 million from public works funds for the construction of thirty-two ships of a total of 120,000 tons. Congress had already provided for five new ships of a total of 17,000 tons. The two programs represented the biggest expansion of the navy since 1916 and, because he knew it would cause controversy at home and abroad, FDR, in his public statements, minimized what was being accomplished. He did the same in 1934 when the Vinson-Trammell naval bill authorized the construction of 102 new ships, taking the replacement of ships to limits set by the Washington and London naval treaties of 1922 and 1930.

The Washington and London naval agreements were, according to different conditions, due to end in December 1936 but FDR wanted to keep the treaty system intact. Japan now sought parity; Britain wanted certain qualitative alterations. If FDR rejected these proposed revisions, he would, in effect, help destroy the treaties; if he accepted them, he would save the treaties but oblige the United States to engage in an extensive program of naval construction in order to assure its security in the Pacific. Whichever he chose, the outcome would be the same—major naval construction in the United States.

Nevertheless, the three powers continued to negotiate naval limitation until January 1936 when the Japanese abandoned a London conference. Their withdrawal allowed FDR to request the largest peacetime naval appropriation ever for the construc-

tion of two new battleships and replacements for outmoded destroyers and submarines. On March 25, 1936, the United States,
Britain, and France agreed to naval parity.

Neutrality Acts

In America the outcome of fascist adventures abroad and the
isolationist sentiment they engendered at home was a series of
Neutrality Acts. The pivotal role in shaping the Neutrality Acts
was played by Democratic Senator Key Pittman of Nevada,
chairman of the Senate Foreign Relations Committee from 1933
to 1940, a most shrewd, if alcoholic, politician, who steered a
mid-course between isolationism and internationalism.

The First Neutrality Act was a direct outcome of the imminent
Italian war of conquest in Ethiopia and, in its final form, determined by compromises between FDR, Pittman, leading isolationists, and Congressman Sam D. McReynolds of Tennessee, chairman of the House Foreign Affairs Committee. FDR felt deeply
divided on the subject. While utterly opposed to the neutrality
legislation, he recognized that he dare not jeopardize the New
Deal by antagonizing his progressive Republican allies in Congress.
In fact, the First Neutrality Act was only passed after a group of
isolationist senators, led by Borah, Clark, Nye, Long, and Vandenberg, threatened to institute a filibuster to block ten pieces of
domestic legislation unless the administration would agree to accept the First Neutrality Act. FDR gave in to them, partly for the
sake of a compromise to limit the life of the act to six months,
and partly because he wanted to silence Republican criticism that
he was assuming excessive presidential powers. Thus, when he
signed the first act on August 31, 1935, he did so with a heavy
heart, announcing ruefully, "History is filled with unforseeable
situations that call for some flexibility of action. It is conceivable
that situations may arise in which the wholly inflexible provisions
of Section I of this Act might have exactly the opposite effect
from that which was intended. In other words, the inflexible
provisions might drag us into war instead of keeping us out."

The First Neutrality Act required the president formally to
recognize foreign conflicts and to deny shipments of arms to all

belligerents indiscriminately. Thus, when Italy finally invaded Ethiopia in October 1935 Roosevelt invoked the act and ensured federal control of arms sales by the new National Munitions Control Board it had established and from which arms makers had to apply for a license. He also warned businessmen that trade with belligerents would not be protected by the American government. Moreover, American ships were prohibited from carrying arms to a belligerent. The Second Neutrality Act of February 18, 1936, not only extended the terms of the first until May 1, 1937, but also forbade loans or credits to any belligerent and made the president's action obligatory.

But the neutrality acts made no provision for a civil war and the Spanish conflict involved such divisive loyalties within the United States, especially among committed socialists, that Roosevelt and Hull asked Congress for speedy legislation that would uphold the policy of containment established by the European Nonintervention Committee organized by Britain and France, and thus anticipate any pressure from religious, political, and ethnic groups within America on the federal government to choose between Loyalists and Falangists. Whereas American Catholics were torn between loyalty to the Spanish Catholic church, and, thus, to Franco, and dismay at the repression they represented, American Protestants and Jews were not so divided in their support for the Loyalists. At Madison Square Garden they formed a Spanish Ambulance Committee, with Ernest Hemingway as chairman, that sent four ambulances and a medical unit to the Loyalists. Despite the attempt by the State Department to prohibit enlistment in foreign forces, over a thousand Americans died in service to the Loyalists as members of such organizations as the Abraham Lincoln or George Washington battalions among the international brigades serving the Republic.

Hitherto, the State Department had asked American firms for a voluntary embargo to ensure impartiality. On December 24, 1936, Robert Cuse, president of a company dealing in used aircraft, applied for export licenses to sell planes and engines worth almost $3 million to the Spanish Republic. The request was perfectly legal but in conflict with the spirit of official government policy. However, the case prompted the administration to ask Congress to waive the arms embargo for countries fighting civil wars, and this was achieved by an enabling act passed on January 6, 1937, with only one dissenting vote.

The savage bombing of the Basque town of Guernica on April 26, 1937, by German planes, with the indiscriminate killing of 1,654 civilians and wounding of another 889, aroused deep outrage in the United States and renewed discussion about the neutrality acts. It was now impossible to ignore the involvement of Italy and Germany in the war and various pacifist and radical groups began to lobby FDR to apply neutrality provisions to them. Socialist leader Norman Thomas spoke for many when he told FDR on June 29, 1937, that it was both immoral and grossly unfair to deny arms to the Republic while giving them to the technically neutral but active participants, Germany and Italy. As usual, FDR was evasive, sensitive to Catholic opinion in America that supported Franco and knowing he could not count on firm lines from Britain and France. He would only impose an arms embargo on Italy and Germany in response to a general European war. The neutrality acts and FDR's use of them, far from containing aggression, had, if anything, encouraged it.

The Third Neutrality Act of May 1, 1937, was another compromise. The provisions of the 1936 act were extended and included a new measure that allowed belligerents to buy any goods but arms from American firms, provided they paid for them in cash and carried the goods away on foreign ships. The cash-and-carry provisions could be applied by the president with discretion. It was thought that cash-and-carry would help Britain in a war against Germany, by allowing it to take advantage of its navy.

The influence of the revisionist histories on the first three neutrality acts was clear enough. The acts were specifically designed to prevent the "mistakes" of Woodrow Wilson being repeated by FDR. On the assumption that the United States had been drawn in to World War I to protect its foreign loans, Congress forbade war loans. On the premise that the export of arms in 1915 and 1916 had been another cause of intervention, Congress prohibited the export of arms. Because a third cause of intervention had been, supposedly, trade with the Allies, the act of 1937 insisted that if belligerents bought American goods they paid for them with cash and carried them on their own ships. In the belief that the loss of American lives through submarine warfare had contributed to American involvement, Congress forbade Americans to travel on belligerents' ships.

War in China

The slide to world war worsened with the full-scale Japanese invasion of China in 1937. Moreover, the three Axis powers moved closer together. On October 25, 1936, the Berlin-Rome Axis was formed. On November 6, 1937, Italy and Germany signed an Anti-Comintern Pact and on December 12 Italy left the League. Japan had already abrogated the Washington and London disarmament treaties at the end of 1934 and in December 1936 signed an Anti-Comintern Pact with Germany. As we have observed, Japan was deficient in crucial raw materials, especially oil, and the place to obtain them was South East Asia. When fighting broke out between Japanese and Chinese troops near Beijing on July 7, 1937, the prime minister, Prince Fumimaro Konoye, acceded to the demands of his war minister, Hajime Sugiyama, to dispatch reinforcements and escalate an incident into undeclared war. After China had appealed to the League Assembly, a conference opened at Brussels on November 3, 1937, to discuss the Sino-Japanese War. Japan and Germany absented themselves and their part was taken by Italy. Although Russia participated with the United States, Britain, and France, none of the states was willing to take action under the terms of the Nine Power Treaty and the conference was a failure.

The immediate reaction in America was timid. The House rejected Roosevelt's request for funds to defend Guam on July 21, 1937, by 205 votes to 168, mainly on the grounds that Japan should not be provoked. One member, Bruce Barton, author of a best-seller about Jesus, *The Man Nobody Knows,* whether in praise or pique at Margaret Mitchell's even better seller, parodied her title, calling out, "Guam, Guam with the Wind." This, indeed, happened in the week after Pearl Harbor and the recapture of Guam in August 1944 cost almost 8,000 casualties. Yet on August 17, 1937, the United States sent 1,200 marines to Shanghai to safeguard American interests in China.

With the outbreak of war in Asia as well as Europe and Africa, Roosevelt decided to explore the possibility of public support for a discriminatory foreign policy, in place of the neutrality legislation that he criticized for the way it helped aggressor nations. On October 5, 1937, Roosevelt delivered his famous Quarantine Speech in Chicago in which he proposed that the peace-loving nations should contain warlike states, or else aggression could not be checked: "When an epidemic of physical disease starts to spread the community approves and joins in a quarantine of the patients in order to protect the health of the community against the spread of the disease." Judge Samuel I. Rosenman of New York observed "the reaction to the speech was quick and violent—and nearly unanimous. It was condemned as warmongering and sabrerattling."

Events now occurred in such a way as to allow isolationists an opportunity to try and seize the initiative of foreign policy. The bone of contention was the power to declare war. Congressman Louis Ludlow of Indiana had proposed an amendment to the Constitution whereby the president and Congress could not declare war (unless American territory were attacked), without first securing public support in a national referendum. His proposal remained locked in the judiciary committee until the *Panay* incident of December 12, 1937. The *Panay*, an American gunboat on the Yangtze River in China, was attacked and bombed by Japanese planes for reasons never fully explained, despite the suspicion that the unprovoked attack was meant as a test of American nerve. There were three casualties and another eleven sailors were seriously wounded.

Roosevelt and Hull handled a difficult situation with tact and dignity, eventually accepting a Japanese apology and payment of an indemnity of $2.21 million. Nevertheless, the incident stimulated renewed discussions about the danger of the United States getting caught up in foreign wars inadvertently. The controversy over the *Panay*, aggravated by pacifist societies, such as the National Council for the Prevention of War, brought the Ludlow resolution onto the floor of the House. The arguments against the Ludlow amendment were clear enough. If it were adopted, the roles of the president and Senate in foreign affairs would be circumscribed, giving the impression that America could not back up its foreign policy with force, that the American public did not really trust its administration, and leaving wide open the possibility of an enemy victory during the strategic delay whilst a war referendum was held. Moreover, advocates of the Ludlow amendment failed to appreciate that overseas wars could only be sustained by public consent to government policies and that, once public opinion was aroused by government propaganda, it was most unlikely to be deterred from war by some artificially imposed cooling-off period. Nevertheless, it was perhaps a personal letter from FDR to the speaker, William H. Bankhead, that persuaded enough congressmen to defeat the amendment (which would have required a majority of two-thirds) in a vote of 209 against to 188 in favor in the House debate on January 5, 1938.

Checkmate at Munich

Attention was now concentrated on Europe. In January 1938 Roosevelt, still deeply concerned by the turn of events in Europe, proposed to the British prime minister, Neville Chamberlain, that there should be an international conference to discuss territorial possessions and access to raw materials. Chamberlain rejected the proposal: it would undermine Britain's policy of coming to terms with the dictators.

Hitler invited the Austrian chancellor, Kurt von Schuschnigg, to Berchtesgaden to induce him to accept a union of Austria with Germany, or, rather, its incorporation. Schuschnigg refused but resigned on March 11, 1938. On March 12 Hitler and his army entered Austria at Braunar, his birthplace, and on March 13 he took Vienna. From the back benches Winston Churchill warned the House of Commons on March 14 that Europe was "confronted with a programme of aggression, nicely calculated and timed, unfolding stage by stage." After the Anschluss leading psychologist Sigmund Freud was admitted to England without the usual formalities and became a British citizen the next day although the usual practice was to require five years' residence. Like other refugees from Central Europe, his very presence was effective propaganda against the Nazis, especially for their oppression of the Jews. Nazi anti-Semitism, which became a central feature of German policy in 1938, quite undermined arguments in favor of Hitler's foreign policy based on the injury done to Germany at Versailles, Germany's economic rights, and the self-determination of nations.

In response to the growing threat of war, American isolationists now conceded that the United States required a larger navy for the defense of the western hemisphere and Congress voted for the Vinson Naval Act of 1938, which was to expand the navy at a cost of $1 billion. Moreover, FDR was able to rally public opinion behind statements about the territorial integrity of nations in the western hemisphere.

British Prime Minister Neville Chamberlain disliked the uncertainty of foreign policy. He could not rely for safety on treaties and pacts, as the French were determined to, and thus he asked himself what was the alternative but appeasement of Hitler's demands? Not the League, nor an alliance with France, presumed secure behind its defense fortifications, the Maginot Line. Rather, Hitler and Mussolini had to be treated like rational, if unpleasant, statesmen. As English historian A. J. P. Taylor suggests:

The opponents of appeasement . . . often failed to distinguish between "stopping" Hitler and defeating him in a great war. Hitler could be stopped only in areas directly accessible to Anglo–French forces. . . . Austria was the last occasion when direct opposition was possible. Great Britain and France could not have stopped a German invasion of Czechoslovakia. . . . Similarly, they could not stop the German invasion of Poland. They could only begin a general war which brought no aid to the Poles. There were thus two different questions. At first: shall we go to the aid of this country or that? Later: shall we start a general war for the overthrow of Germany as a Great Power? In practice . . . the two questions were always mixed up.

In other words, while Britain and France could defend areas close to them and restrict the conflict, they could not do so in Central Europe, which could only be defended by full-scale military invasion and a general war.

However, in the next crisis Neville Chamberlain took the initiative, believing that Hitler would strike at Czechoslovakia, unless his "grievances" were met in advance. He did not regard Czech independence as a British interest and both he and Hitler disliked Czech alliances with France and Russia.

The rights of 3 million Sudeten Germans, citizens of Czechoslovakia, were guaranteed in name by the League, to whom they could protest against injustice. Rarely had they done so. However, Germany now made claims on their behalf. On September 4, 1938, President Edvard Benes agreed to these demands. But on September 12, 1938, when Hitler spoke to the annual Nazi party rally in Nuremberg, it became clear that the concessions were insufficient. The speech was broadcast live to America by CBS and translated by Kurt Heiman. Historian William Manchester recalls, "Millions of Americans, hearing Hitler for the first time over shortwave, were shaken by the depth of his hatred; on his lips the Teutonic language sounded cruel, dripping with venom." The following day, September 13, there was a revolt in the Sudetenland that the Czech government quelled.

The French government dithered at the prospect of confrontation with Germany, having believed that Hitler would only attack Czechoslovakia if he were certain there would be no Anglo-French opposition. Chamberlain flew to Munich on September 15 and met Hitler at Berchtesgaden where he offered the separation of the Sudeten Germans from the rest of Czechoslovakia: "I didn't care two hoots whether the Sudetens were in the Reich or out of it according to their own wishes." Hitler agreed: "We want no Czechs." However, Edouard Daladier, French prime minister, and Georges Bonnet, his foreign secretary, now argued with Chamberlain on September 18 that Hitler's real aim was the domination of Europe itself. Thus, if Chamberlain believed that Hitler only wanted the unification of all German peoples and was now satisfied, would Britain guarantee the new truncated Czechoslovakia? Chamberlain and three of his Cabinet did so, although they had refused to guarantee the whole state. On September 21 the British and French told the Czech president, Benes, that Czechoslovakia could either capitulate to Hitler's demands or fight alone.

Chamberlain believed the affair was settled and on September 22 again flew to Germany to meet Hitler at Godesberg on the Rhine. However, Hitler now wanted immediate occupation rather than a negotiated transfer of power. Nevertheless, he promised to wait until October 1, 1938, before marching on Czechoslovakia. Chamberlain knew nothing could be done to assist Czechoslovakia but agreed to Mussolini's proposal for a Four Power Conference in Munich. On September 29 Chamberlain met Hitler there and, without much reference to Daladier, the two of them accepted a plan submitted by Mussolini that had actually been prepared by the German foreign office. The Czechs were obliged to agree.

Superficially, it was Mussolini who dominated the Munich conference: he was the only one among Daladier, Hitler, and Chamberlain, who could speak the others' languages. The idea of four incompetent linguists discussing world affairs in cod accents led to a bitter, apocryphal anecdote at Italy's expense. "Remember, if it comes to war," Hitler is supposed to have told Chamberlain in his most gutteral tones, "we shall have Italy on our side this time." More in sorrow than anger, Chamberlain is said to have replied in his most upper-crust accent, "That's only fair. We had to have her last time."

On September 30 Hitler met Chamberlain for the last time and welcomed a statement the prime minister had prepared: "We regard the agreement signed last night and the Anglo-German Naval Agreement as symbolic of the desire of our two peoples never to go to war with one another again." The same evening Chamberlain told cheering crowds in London, "I believe it is peace for our time." (Some later accounts have Chamberlain saying "in our time.") The overwhelming majority of press, public opinion, and Chamberlain's own Conservative party approved, as did the governments of the British Dominions. In fact, it was checkmate. As A. J. P. Taylor says, "The triumph of appeasement also marked its failure. . . . Appeasement had been designed by Chamberlain as the impartial redress of justified grievances. It became a capitulation, a surrender to fear."

From Hitler's point of view, there was also a crucial military consideration to the seizure of Czechoslovakia. The annexation of the Sudetenland by the Reich involved handing over to Hitler the

Nazi artist Josef Plank produced a series of scurrilous but stylish cartoons and posters reviling the United States, Britain, and Russia during the years of the Third Reich. In this cartoon of the Munich crisis and partition of Czechoslovakia, an overpainted nanny, taking mischievous children to the zoo, Benesch (as Czechoslovakia) has his skirt pulled up by such howling brats as Yugoslavia, Romania, and Hungary while the caged Russian bear and conniving Italian ice-cream vendor salivate at the prospect of uproar in Europe. At the end of World War II the Americans confiscated Plank's portfolio and a collection of 250 drawings is now held in the Library of Congress.

powerful fortifications that protected Bohemia and Slovakia, and hence eastern Europe, from invasion by Germany. It was this single achievement, more than any other, that ensured German dominance of Central Europe. A yet more sinister advantage was that Czechoslovakia was comparatively rich in U^{235}, the sort of uranium essential for nuclear fission.

In three stages members of the League had abandoned collective security and common action in the face of aggression. The invasion of Ethiopia was considered by the Council and its members had briefly imposed economic sanctions; the great powers made decisions about the Spanish Civil War through a special Non-Intervention Committee but laid their plans before Council and Assembly; the Czech crisis was never submitted to the League in any form. Winston Churchill's comment was: "Britain and France had to choose between war and dishonour. They chose dishonour. They will have war." Plans for rearmament in Britain were put into effect with great urgency.

Hitler's diplomatic success at Munich encouraged him to intensify his persecution of the Jews. Already the Nuremberg laws of 1935 had divested Jews of their political and civil rights. In November 1938 a new, and even more terrible, wave of persecution began as Nazi gangs attacked Jews and their businesses and synagogues. The streets of German cities were strewn with broken glass, giving the name of *Kristallnacht* to the outrage to humanity. The pretext was the assassination of a German diplomat in Paris by a Jew. In these months hundreds of victims were killed and thousands were transported to concentration camps. While the American press deplored the violence, only the *New Republic,* in its issue of November 23, 1938, urged a revision of the immigration laws to allow the entry of persecuted Jews into the United States. Subsequently, in 1939, Senator Robert Wagner of New York introduced a bill to allow the entry of 200,000 German refugee children above the official quota but, lacking the support of FDR, who was reluctant to press Congress after the failure of the court-packing scheme, the refugee bill expired in committee.

A survey in October 1938 by *Fortune* showed that only 11.6 percent of American public opinion approved of the Munich settlement and that 76.2 percent believed the United States would become involved in a European war. As the editors pointed out, in March, 1937, only 22 percent had thought then that America would get involved in a foreign war.

The Good Neighbor in Latin America

Roosevelt's attempts at a Good Neighbor policy toward Latin America ran into troubled waters when they encountered a mix of Latin-American nationalism, American commercial interests, and the gales of contrary diplomatic doctrine.

Despite their concentration on developments in Europe and the Far East, Roosevelt and Cordell Hull recognized just how significant were Latin-American affairs for the United States. They, and the Senate Foreign Relations Committee, were deeply committed to the Good Neighbor policy and understood exactly how important it was to convince Latins of America's benevolent disinterestedness. Moreover, when it came to Latin America, FDR was exercising his executive role to further his interests elsewhere. As the historian of American isolationism, Wayne S. Cole, explains, "In subtle but increasingly significant ways . . . Roosevelt's policies toward Latin America helped educate the American people in the wisdom and practical benefits of a more active leadership and multilateral peace-keeping role by the United States. It accomplished that from a direction the isolationists were not well prepared to defend." For one thing, FDR's policies toward Latin America were consistent with those advocated by isolationists such as Borah, Nye, and Norris, especially in regard to repudiating dollar diplomacy and the big stick. For another, the administration's policies to defend the western hemisphere from attack from the eastern almost always met with the uniform approval of the American people.

Roosevelt and Hull tried to persuade Latins of America's friendly intentions.

Since 1929 the people of Cuba had been in open revolt against the corrupt dictatorship of Gerardo Machado. The decisive factor in the overthrow of Machado in 1933 was the weight of the army and its pivotal leader, Colonel Fulgencio Batista, who were able to place in power, first, Carlos Manuel de Cespedes, a former diplomat, and, then, Dr. Ramon Grau San Martín, surgeon and professor at the University of Havana. Grau condemned the ascendancy of privileged foreign interests in Cuba and refused to continue the earlier favoritism shown to foreign investors. This policy aroused the indignation of Ambassador Sumner Welles, who advised FDR to intervene with military force under the terms of the Platt amendment of 1901. Instead, FDR simply denied recognition to the Grau regime and sent gunboats to patrol Cuban waters. Of course, the withholding of American recognition precluded Cuba's ability to export sugar to the United States and thus the new, subtle form of pressure threatened Cuba's very economic future. Accordingly, Batista transferred his support to Colonel Carlos Mendieta who was able to seize power in January 1934 and resume more conservative policies toward foreign investors.

Having successfully applied pressure tactics rather than outright force, FDR then abrogated the Platt amendment, retaining only rights to maintain an American naval base at Guantanamo Bay. In May 1934 Congress reduced the tariff on Cuban sugar by 25 percent, and, several months later, reduced the tariff by another 40 percent.

In July 1934 FDR embarked on a goodwill tour of the Caribbean and the Pacific. In Haiti he advanced the withdrawal of American troops from October 1 to August 15, 1934; in Colombia he praised the peaceful resolution in the settlement of the Leticia dispute with Peru; in Panama he promised pacific and just settlement of its differences with the United States. In short, FDR, by his open manner and conciliatory gestures, earned the reputation of being a good neighbor.

In 1935 the State Department reached reciprocal trade agreements with Brazil, Colombia, Haiti, and Honduras and initiated discussions with another nine Latin-American countries. Hull also negotiated a new treaty with Panama, signed on March 2, 1936, by which the United States abandoned its unlimited rights of intervention agreed in 1903, and in which both countries agreed to joint operation and defense of the Panama Canal.

Moreover, FDR and Hull resisted lobbying of Congress by American Catholics, led by the Knights of Columbus, to put pressure on the Mexican government of Làzaro Càrdenas to end its anticlerical policy, if necessary by recalling the U.S. ambassador to Mexico, Josephus Daniels. Neither FDR nor Hull was prepared to jeopardize his reputation of nonintervention in the internal affairs of any Latin-American country, especially over such an emotive and ephemeral issue as religious practices. However, on March 18, 1938, President Cárdenas of Mexico announced the appropriation of the $400 million Mexican oil industry, much of it in foreign hands, because the foreign oil companies had defied the Mexican Supreme Court's decision in a labor dispute. FDR, Josephus Daniels, and the Treasury adviser, Henry Morgenthau, were united in their determination to prevent Cordell Hull and the State Department from sensationalizing the issue and causing an open break with Mexico.

In December 1936 FDR attended the opening of the Inter-American Peace Conference in Buenos Aires, Argentina, where he received a tumultuous public reception. However, Cordell Hull's proposals for a common hemisphere policy on arms and neutrality were shot down by Saavedra Lamas of Argentina who wanted to assert Argentinian supremacy in Latin America. The only U.S. proposal accepted in its original form was that of nonintervention, first put forward at Montevideo, Uruguay, in 1933.

In 1938 and 1939 FDR took action to strengthen the defense of the western hemisphere. In April 1938 he created a Standing Liaison Committee to strengthen military missions to Latin America, establishing firm control over commercial airlines. In November the Joint Army and Navy Board discussed contingency arrangements in case of attack. In 1939 the five so-called Rainbow Plans defined strategy for defending the United States by safeguarding the hemisphere as a whole. Moreover, in December 1938 the American republics attending the Pan American Conference in Lima, Peru, had unanimously adopted a Declaration of Lima, condemning religious and racial prejudice and alien political activity in the western hemisphere. Fear of Nazi infiltration preceded World War II. On January 4, 1939, George C. Stoney advised readers of the *New Republic,* "How the Dictators Woo Argentina."

The Dark Valley of 1939

Roosevelt's annual message to Congress on January 4, 1939, was largely devoted to foreign affairs: "All about us rage undeclared wars—military and economic." Therefore, the United States, without getting involved, should revise its neutrality legislation: "We have learned that when we deliberately try to legislate neutrality, our neutrality laws may operate unevenly and unfairly— may actually give aid to the aggressor and deny it to the victim. The instinct of self-preservation should warn us that we ought not to let that happen any more." Congress continued to oppose any change that indicated the United States would distinguish between aggressor and victim and thereby incur hostility. Yet Gallup public opinion polls of spring and summer 1939 showed 65 percent of Americans favored an economic boycott of Germany and 56 percent wanted a revision of the neutrality laws. For, 51 percent expected a war in Europe and 58 percent expected that the United States would become involved. Thus when the danger of war was greater, fewer Americans feared its inevitably because there was, in early summer 1939, no dramatic crisis such as Munich to focus people's minds on the danger. Yet, although 90 percent said they would fight if America were invaded, only 10 percent said they would do so regardless of invasion.

Despite setbacks, FDR and Hull continued to put pressure on Congress to repeal the neutrality laws. On June 6, 1939, the House Foreign Affairs Committee voted to repeal the arms embargo by only 11 votes to 9. However, seven days later, the committee voted on party lines by 12 votes to 8 to report a new measure, giving the president discretion as to how, where, and when, the law should be applied. On June 29 the House voted by 159 to 157 in favor of an amendment proposed by Congressman John M. Vorys of Ohio, placing an embargo on arms and ammunition but not on other war materiel. This amendment was then incorporated into the main bill of Congressman Sol Bloom of New York that passed the House most narrowly on June 30 by 200 votes to 188.

In the Senate, it fared worse. On July 11 the Foreign Relations

Committee rejected FDR's proposed revision of the neutrality legislation by 12 votes to 11. Originally, the Committee had been divided, with 11 in favor, 10 against, and 2 undecided. The undecided were the Democrats Walter George of Georgia and Guy Gillette of Iowa and both favored repeal. However, because FDR had opposed them in his attempted purge of 1938, the isolationists were able to persuade them to take their revenge by voting against repeal of the neutrality laws.

On July 18, 1939, Roosevelt and Hull invited congressional leaders to discuss European affairs at the White House. Roosevelt predicted war and said he believed France and Britain had only an even chance of survival. He hoped Congress would agree even now to a revision of the neutrality laws in their favor to deter Hitler. However, the most prepossessing senator there, William E. Borah of Idaho, declared, "There's not going to be any war this year. All this hysteria is manufactured and artificial." Brushing aside Hull's references to State Department telegrams, he went on, "I have sources of information in Europe that I regard as more reliable than those of the State Department." He meant newspaper articles. The vice-president, John Nance Garner, is supposed to have advised Roosevelt, "You haven't got the votes and that's all there is to it." Thus, the policy of the United States would continue to be to forbid the sale of munitions to all belligerents, even if there were another European war. The prospect of that war moved closer.

The newly diminished state of Czechoslovakia was divided by ethnic dispute. The Czechs insisted the country was one state, the Slovaks said it was two and, from October 1938, it was spelled Czecho-Slovakia. On March 15, 1939, Slovakia became independent. Hungary claimed the Ukraine district of lower Carpathia. Thus the new president, Hacha, allowed "Czechia" (or Bohemia) to become a German protectorate. The Sudeten territories had not been Hitler's "last territorial demand in Europe," after all. Speaking in Birmingham on March 17, 1939, Neville Chamberlain declared that no one "could possibly have saved Czechoslovakia" but added, "any attempt to dominate the world by force was one which the Democracies must resist." On March 19 he drafted a declaration of resistance to a reported, but nonexistent, German invasion of Romania, which he then invited Russia, France, and Poland to sign. Poland had used the Munich crisis to take Tesin from Czechoslovakia and was negotiating in secret with Germany over Danzig (or Gdansk, the free city created in 1919), and thus refused any proposed alliance with Russia. Yet on March 31 Chamberlain promised Poland a British and French guarantee of its integrity. He had not consulted France. Britain had no way of keeping its bargain with Poland, nor did it advance money or military aid. Hitler called the bluff on April 28 by repudiating Germany's nonaggression pact with Poland of 1934 and an Anglo-German naval agreement of 1935.

Britain and France could not guarantee Poland without the support of Russia. Chamberlain did not trust a Russian alliance but, nevertheless, his government pursued protracted negotiations in Moscow in the spring and summer of 1939. However, on August 23 the foreign ministers of Russia and Germany, Viacheslav Molotov and Joachim von Ribbentrop, signed a Nazi–Soviet Pact in Moscow by which Russia was to stay neutral if Germany went to war. This seemed a prelude to a partition of Poland and on August 25 the Anglo–Polish alliance was signed. A clause by which Danzig was guaranteed as well as Poland was kept secret so that Hitler would not be provoked. The rights of Germans in the free city of Danzig had long been the pretext for German "grievances" against Poland. In reality, Hitler wanted Poland's industrial resources and to recover Germany's ascendancy over Poland lost in 1919. Joseph Kennedy, the American ambassador to Britain, told Cordell Hull that Chamberlain "says the futility of it all is the thing that is frightful; after all they cannot save the Poles." Despite Britain's public assurances, Viscount Halifax, the British foreign secretary, urged Poland to negotiate with Hitler. The Polish foreign minister, Beck, refused to do so and on September 1, 1939, German troops crossed the frontier into Poland.

Chamberlain, Halifax, and Georges Bonnet, the French foreign minister, supported a proposal from Mussolini for another conference. But when Chamberlain reported this to the House of Commons on September 2 the response made it clear that the only British policy could now be an ultimatum delivered to Germany on September 3 and war if it expired without satisfactory assurances. This was what happened. Thus, in the end, Britain and France went to war over a state that they could not defend. World War II had begun. France and the four British dominions of Australia, New Zealand, Canada, and South Africa followed the British declaration of war against Germany with their own. Within eleven days the Nazis had subdued Poland. This was the *blitzkrieg*—lightning war.

While there is no doubt that the prime cause of war was Hitler's aggressive foreign policy, Britain's reluctance to address German aggression earlier was a contributing factor to the terrible crisis. Christopher Andrew shows in *Her Majesty's Secret Service* (1986) how British intelligence officers in the 1930s were incapable of evaluating information about Germany. As a result, the British government was so overwhelmed with alarmist rumors about German intentions and capabilities that it found it impossible to arrive at quick, appropriate, and effective decisions. Thus Neville Chamberlain had made his decision to join staff talks with France in January 1939 on a false intelligence report that Germany was about to invade the Netherlands. He was rushed into guaranteeing the independence of Poland in March 1939 by rumors of German action against Romania. Even more surprisingly, British intelligence failed to realize that a Nazi-Soviet Pact would be signed, a fact that dissident Germans leaked to the United States. Most tragic of all, it concluded that the entire German economy was being overmobilized to such an extent that it must soon crack under the strain of war—an illusion that it took three years of fighting to dispel. It seemed as if British foreign policy was based on Lady Bracknell's dictum to her prospective son-in-law, "Ignorance is like a delicate exotic fruit; touch it, and the bloom is gone. Fortunately in England, at any rate, education produces no effect whatsoever."

Having fought Russia in skirmishes in 1938 and 1939, Japan regarded the Nazi-Soviet Pact as a betrayal by Germany and thus remained neutral at the outset of the European war.

In October 1939 Russian troops occupied eastern Poland. Russia, eager to make sure of the Baltic, also occupied Latvia, Estonia, and Lithuania. Russia demanded that Finland cede, or lease, parts of its territory considered essential to Russian security. Ready to accede to most of the demands, Finland refused a thirty-year lease on the port of Hanko as a Russian naval base and also refused to give up territory across the isthmus of Karelia by Leningrad. On the pretext that Finns had fired across the frontier, Russian armies invaded Finland on November 30 and established an exiled Communist, Kuusinen, as head of the Democratic Republic of Finland. He then acceded to the specific Russian demands. But, buoyed up by what it felt to be the tide of world opinion, Finland protested to the League against Russia on December 2. It was almost as if World War II were not taking place. Whereas Finland wanted the Assembly to persuade Russia to stop fighting, or to provide military and economic aid, the League simply expelled Russia on December 14, 1939, the only time it excluded a member that had broken the Covenant. On March 12, 1940, Finland sued for peace and accepted Russian terms. Once again, Britain and France had paraded their intention of aiding a small victim of aggression and had failed to do anything about it. In France, Daladier's government fell and was replaced by one led by Paul Reynaud.

"Battle of Washington"

Never again would American isolationists hold the dominant position in American politics that was theirs in 1939. But, although they were gradually forced to retreat, they consistently deployed considerable influence against every proposal to involve the United States more directly in world affairs. Responding to the Nazi invasion of Poland, FDR said in his radio "fireside chat" of September 3, "This nation will remain a neutral nation." But, going further than Woodrow Wilson in 1914, he added, "But I cannot ask that every American remain neutral in thought as well."

The cash-and-carry provisions of the 1937 act had expired; the munitions embargo was still in effect. Roosevelt called Congress into special session on September 21 so that the embargo could be replaced by a provision allowing belligerents to purchase munitions and raw materials on a cash-and-carry basis. The administration argued that such a measure would strengthen American neutrality rather than aid Britain and France. However, the real purpose was not in doubt. Germany had increased its own manufacturing capacity and, in seizing Czechoslovakia, had taken over its great munitions works, and thus already possessed military supplies on a scale that neither Britain nor France could match without American support. FDR's aides reported that public opinion was divided and that he could still not count on the votes of nominally loyal congressmen to get the neutrality law revised. FDR decided to compromise and thus, on October 27, 1939, the Senate by 63 votes to 30 and, on November 3, the House by 243 votes to 181, agreed to a revision, permitting the sale of goods to belligerents on the basis of cash-and-carry, provided Congress approved.

The inactive "phony war" of the winter of 1930–1940 lulled Britain and France into a false sense of security. They believed they now had time to make their own arms and thus reduced their orders from the United States. Moreover, since the Johnson act of 1934 had barred countries that defaulted on their loans from borrowing more American money, they decided to conserve their dollar and gold reserves by restricting their purchase of American goods to food, raw materials, aircraft, and machine tools. FDR insisted that Britain and France set up a special Purchasing Mission in the United States that had to operate through the Federal Reserve Board. By exercising such controls, FDR hoped to avoid the Allies' interests clashing with America's own military needs.

In fact, in early 1940 FDR had to fight a "battle of Washington" with his own administration over aid to Britain and France. Secretary of War Henry Woodring opposed Allied purchases of war material and aircraft that interfered with American needs and flatly refused Allied access to secret information necessary to fly the planes they had ordered. FDR became so exasperated that in March he told the War Department that its opposition must end, that leaks to the isolationist press must stop, and that he would transfer any truculent officers to Guam.

However, America was not even prepared for its own national defense, let alone to defend the democracies effectively. In May 1940 the War Department reported that the army could field only 80,000 men and had equipment for fewer than 500,000 combat troops. As to aircraft, America had but 160 pursuit planes, 52 heavy bombers, and only 260 fully trained pilots. This was partly why Air Corps Chief of Staff General Henry ("Hap") Arnold was reluctant to sell aircraft to Britain and France. At their current rate of loss, 100 planes would last only three days, while substantively reducing the number of American planes for self-defense and thus delaying the training of American pilots.

During the 1930s Congress had been miserly about defense appropriations. In May 1940 it could not provide enough. It voted $1.5 billion more for defense—$320 million above what Roosevelt had asked—and then voted another $1.7 billion to expand the regular army from 280,000 to 375,000 men and allowed the president to summon the National Guard for active service.

More ominously, FDR and his closest associates were also preparing the United States for the atomic age.

In a letter delivered to the White House on October 11, 1939, Albert Einstein, the world-famous Jewish physicist, warned FDR that the Germans were working on an atomic bomb and that with this weapon they could conquer the world. Einstein's letter was the outcome of the research and moral courage of distinguished physicists from different countries—Otto Hahn, Niels Bohr, Lise Meitner, James Chadwick, Victor R. Weisskopf, and Edward Teller (who translated the letter from German into English), many of whom had emigrated to the United States. When Niels Bohr arrived in New York from Denmark on January 16, 1939, a telegram awaited him from his Viennese colleagues Lise Meitner and O. R. Frisch, now working in Copenhagen. It explained how, in a recent experiment, they had used TNT and split an atom that had freed 200 million volts of electricity. If uranium could be used, the explosion would be twenty million times greater.

The Meitner-Frisch experiment was repeated at Columbia University by other physicists, including Nobel Prize winner Enrico Fermi of Italy, on January 25, 1939. Discussions at Columbia were open but only briefly reported in the New York press. Bohr told the American Physical Society meeting in Washington that a projectile armed with a fragment of U^{235} bombarded with slow neutrons could produce an explosion that would destroy the

News of the terrors of the German Blitz, or aerial bombardment, of London in fall 1940, which devastated the city and partly damaged St. Paul's Cathedral, helped unite English-speaking peoples across the world in a central purpose of World War II—the elimination of nazism. (British Press Services; Office of War Information; Library of Congress).

District of Columbia. Moreover, it was clear that the Third Reich was committed to the development of such an atomic bomb. Accordingly, Roosevelt was persuaded to enter the atomic race. With the support of pivotal leaders in Congress, FDR secured the necessary funds to start the Manhattan Project, to make an atomic bomb that could be dropped by air.

In the autumn of 1939 Kennedy and Bullitt, America's ambassadors to Britain and France, both consistently predicted that, unless the Allies were given more immediate material aid, they would fall victim to a German assault from the air. At this time FDR expected Germany and Russia to divide Europe between them and then extend their control to Asia Minor and thence the European colonies in Africa and Asia. The United States would be imperiled. Thus, in his State of the Union message on January 5, 1940, he expressed his anxiety in a significant distinction, explaining "there is a vast difference between keeping out of war and pretending that war is none of our business. We do not have to go to war with other nations, but at least we can strive with other nations to encourage the kind of peace that will lighten the troubles of the world, and by so doing help our own nation as well." FDR was anxious to assert, for both domestic and international consumption, that America must play a decisive part in shaping postwar peace. "For it becomes clearer and clearer that the future world will be a shabby and dangerous place to live in —yes, even for Americans to live in—if it is ruled by force in the hands of a few." Moreover, he warned, "I hope we shall have fewer ostriches in our midst. It is not good for the ultimate health of ostriches to bury their heads in the sand."

The degree of sympathy for Europe and support for American intervention varied throughout the United States and depended partly on ethnic origins. According to opinion polls, New York City was more interventionist than any other part; Texas was more anti-German; the South showed itself most ready to fight; the West Coast was more concerned with Japan than Germany. The upper classes were most interventionist: in 1940 more than 66 percent of America's business and intellectual elite wanted increased supplies to be sent to Britain; almost half the people in *Who's Who in America* wanted an immediate declaration of war.

Almost everybody favored increasing military and naval strength. Yet opinion polls indicated an unwillingness to accept the inevitable. In late 1939, after the outbreak of war in Europe, 40 percent thought the United States would become involved. In 1940, after the fall of western Europe, when the likelihood was greater, only 7.7 percent thought so. But one pattern was consistent in these months. To the Gallup question, "Do you think the United States should keep out of war or do everything possible to help England, even at the risk of getting into war outselves?" the public showed increasing acceptance of involvement during 1940. Those willing to take the risk by helping England were 36 percent in May, 50 percent in November, and 60 percent in December.

The *New Republic,* an openly isolationist magazine before the war, underwent a change of attitude that reflected the shift in public opinion. There was a period of transition when it advocated all aid short of war to England and France and supported cash-and-carry legislation before calling on the government to declare war on the Axis. Emphasizing the possibility of Nazi success and the ensuing dangers of Nazi encroachment on the United States, the editors decided on September 6, 1939, that the devil they knew, imperialist Britain and war, was better than the one they had no experience of, Nazi Germany and peace. The *New Republic* accurately assessed the undercurrent of public opinion on February 12, 1940: "You cannot go on day after day and month after month believing with all your heart that one party in a desperate struggle is both dangerous and despicable and must at all costs be defeated, without feeling a sort of moral delinquency in failing to contribute your own strength to the cause." This was the essential point of pundits such as prominent theologian Reinhold Niebuhr and popular columnist Walter Lippmann, who, in various articles and books, showed they, too, were moving from isolationism to interventionism.

Proponents of intervention did not simply keep their own counsel. They mobilized theor forces. The Committee to Defend America by Aiding the Allies was organized in May 1940 by William Allen White with the aim of rousing public opinion to support, first, all aid to Britain short of war, and later, outright intervention. Leading speakers included John McCloy, Robert

Sherwood, and Elizabeth Morrow Cutter, author and mother-in-law to Charles A. Lindbergh. The organization had chapters across the country but was strongest in the East.

In Congress the old guard of the isolationists was changing. Senator William E. Borah died in January 1940. Of the survivors, Senators Hiram Johnson and Arthur Capper were seventy-five years old and no longer had the stamina for a sustained war of words with FDR, while Senator George W. Norris was being drawn increasingly into the Roosevelt camp. The younger men, Nye (who had replaced Borah on the SFRC), Robert La Follette, Clark, and Vandenberg, now led the isolationists in the Senate. Moreover, with the death in November 1940 of Key Pittman, Democratic chairman of the SFRC, and his replacement by Senator Walter F. George, the congressional battle lines had changed once and for all.

Battle of Britain

In April 1940 Germany invaded Denmark and Norway and on May 10 Germany invaded western Europe. At last, Winston Churchill became prime minister of Britain. In a speech with phrases borrowed from Garibaldi and Clemenceau but with an urgency of his own, Churchill told the House of Commons on May 13, 1940, "I have nothing to offer but blood, toil, tears and sweat. You ask, What is your policy? I will say: It is to wage war. . . . You ask, What is our aim? I can answer in one word, victory —victory at all costs." No one foresaw even the immediate cost that entailed placing Britain in pawn to the United States.

Holland capitulated to Germany on May 14, Belgium on May 16. The British army in Europe evacuated the beaches of Dunkirk with such heroism that propaganda almost succeeded in transfiguring the unmitigated disaster into a symbolic victory. Italy then declared war on Britain and France on June 10, 1940. The French government of Paul Reynaud survived the German occupation of Paris on June 14 by two days. In the week when ministers, deputies, and civil servants left the capital, two American films were being shown in cinemas in the Champs Élysées, *Going Places* and *You Can't Take It With You*. This was the philosophy of Renaud's successor, Marshal Philippe Pétain, the eighty-four-year-old hero of Verdun in World War I, who was determined to use the defeat of France to rid his country of the ideologies of the Left. He reached an armistice with Germany on June 22 and established a fascist government, first at Bordeaux and then at the resort of Vichy in southern France that arranged terms of collaboration on October 24. To prevent it falling into German hands, the British government then ordered the scuttling of the French fleet at Mers-el-Kebir (Oran) on July 3, 1940, with considerable loss of life. The fall of France was devastating not only for Britain and the rest of Europe but also for the United States, where it was taken as a clear signal that, unless Britain were given substantive material aid, it could not stand alone against the Nazis, far less turn the tide of the German advance and shield America from the greatest military threat ever. Robert Sherwood in *Roosevelt and Hopkins* has said that during the early war Roosevelt was at a loss to know what to do—"a period of terrible, stultifying vacuum."

The Battle of Britain of the summer of 1940 began with German attacks on convoys of merchant ships. On August 13 the second part of the battle commenced, with a full-scale German attack on England with bomber aircraft protected by fighters. Provided with 500 new fighters, Air Marshall Hugh Dowding concentrated on the destruction of the bombers. Hence the Germans set out to destroy the fighter bases in the county of Kent and nearly succeeded. Then on September 7 the Germans began to bomb London, with massive loss of life and the dislocation of society but the Kent airfields were saved. The German Luftwaffe made its last effort on September 15, and then conceded air superiority to the British by withdrawing. Hitler postponed his immediate invasion of Britain on September 17. However, the Germans bombed London every night from September 7 to November 2 and then turned to other industrial cities and western ports. The last severe air raid of the so-called "Blitz" came on Birmingham on May 16, 1941. Thereafter, the Luftwaffe prepared to cooperate with the German army in the invasion of Russia that began on June 22, 1941. The conflict with Britain then turned to battle on the seas, essentially Germany's attempt to destroy the convoys carrying

American supplies that reached its first climax between March and July 1941 in the Battle of the Atlantic. That April, 700,000 tons of shipping were sunk.

The artistic metaphor for the physical hurricane and political holocaust of 1938 had been Orson Welles's radio version of *War of the Worlds*. *The Great Dictator,* Charles Chaplin's film parody of Hitler and Mussolini, which opened in New York on October 15, 1940, served for America as tragicomic comment on the condition of continental Europe. A simple plot has a little Jewish barber returning to his ghetto after World War I to find the whole country, Tomania, dominated by the despot Adenoid Hynkel, with his aids Herring and Garbitch, under the sign of the double cross. When the little fellow is mistaken for Hynkel complications ensue to provide a series of comic and sentimental divertissements. Chaplin could thus play his beloved tramp and caricature Hitler to whom he bore "a coincidental resemblance." The parody is at its peak when Hynkel and his associate, the dictator of Bacteria, Napoloni, allowing Jack Oakie to ridicule Mussolini expansively, debate their apportionment of the globe, a balloon that never quite manages to balance.

Increasing Involvement

American foreign policy from the summer of 1940 to the winter of 1941 developed in response to Germany's conquest of Europe and Japan's conquest of South East Asia in five stages. Three — the destroyers-bases deal, Lend-Lease, and the war at sea — led to the Atlantic Charter signed by Roosevelt and Churchill. The other two — economic restrictions on Japan and intransigent opposition to Japan's territorial claims — led to Pearl Harbor and the full intervention of the United States in the war.

After Italy's declaration of war and the conquest of Holland, Belgium, and France, it was possible for Roosevelt to arouse the American people to the needs of national defense. Roosevelt said at Charlottesville, Virginia, on June 10, 1940, "We will extend to the opponents of force the material resources of this nation and, at the same time, we will harness and speed up the use of those resources in order that we ourselves in the Americas may have equipment and training equal to the task of any emergency and every defense." The next month representatives of the American republics at the Havana Conference in Cuba agreed to take action to prevent any change in the status of the European colonies in the western hemisphere and to consider aggression against any one of them as aggression against them all. This solidarity lasted until Pearl Harbor when Chile refused, temporarily, and Argentina, permanently, to sever their relations with the Axis. Some countries offered the United States military bases, others replaced German military advisers with Americans. The United States increased its purchase of raw materials within the hemisphere and sold its products to the other countries, deprived of European goods, at restricted prices.

In an attempt to widen his base of support Roosevelt appointed two prominent Republicans who had opposed the New Deal, Henry L. Stimson and Frank Knox, as respectively, secretaries of war and navy, on June 19, 1940. They replaced the two most isolationist members of the Cabinet, Henry Woodring and Charles Edison. Knox, the Republican vice-presidential candidate in 1936, favored considerable military expansion, an army of a million men, the strongest air force in the world, and the immediate shipment of late model planes to Britain. Stimson wanted the repeal of all neutrality legislation and the introduction of military conscription. In fact, it was now Harry L. Hopkins who exercised more influence on Roosevelt than either Hull or Welles in this period. Called "Lord Root of the Matter" by Churchill, he had the same sort of position with Roosevelt that House had known with Wilson. Unlike House, he did not pretend to know his chief's mind when he did not and, since his sole aim was to serve, he did not quarrel with the president.

On July 21, 1940, Winston Churchill made a specific plea to Roosevelt for a transference of destroyers from America in exchange for leases of British naval bases. Although Roosevelt had announced all aid short of war in June, he delayed action until the transfer could be presented as an act of defense and accomplished without reference to Congress. The eventual agreement, incorporated in letters exchanged between Cordell Hull and Philip Kerr, Lord Lothian, the British ambassador, on September 2,

1940, gave British bases in Newfoundland and Bermuda to the United States as an outright gift and granted to the United States ninety-nine-year leases on other bases on the Bahamas, Jamaica, St. Lucia, Trinidad, British Guiana, and Antigua in exchange for fifty old American destroyers, built in World War I, now out of commission, and not needed while the British navy controlled the Atlantic. Only nine destroyers entered British service before 1941. The gesture was one of sympathy, rather than support, and afforded by Roosevelt in a calculated and careful maneuver.

However, after the destroyers-bases deal, the United States was not neutral in any real sense of the term. It seemed Roosevelt and Hull believed that total aid short of war would be the best way of avoiding attack or intervention. Joseph Kennedy, former ambassador to the Court of St. James, declared that talk about Britain fighting for democracy was "bunk." John Foster Dulles, a prominent lawyer and later secretary of state, said, "Only hysteria entertains the idea that Germany, Italy or Japan contemplates war upon us."

Election of 1940

The dispute over intervention was exacerbated by the presidential campaign of 1940. The dark horse of the Republicans' campaign was utility tycoon Wendell Willkie of Indiana, president of the Commonwealth and Southern Corporation, who had fought the Tennessee Valley Authority and could thus present himself as a hapless business victim of the encroaching power of the state. He was a liberal and an internationalist. On the radio he was so persuasive that lawyer Oren Root, Jr., was moved to establish the Associated Willkie Clubs of America among his Ivy League associates in order to advance Willkie's campaign. Thus at the Republican National Convention in Philadelphia Willkie took the nomination on the sixth ballot over favorites Thomas E. Dewey of New York and Robert A. Taft of Ohio. Willkie's nomination in preference to some midwestern party regular signaled the start of a new domination of the Republican party by its eastern establishment that would continue for twenty years. The Democrats charged

Willkie with "an electric background, an electric personality and an electric campaign chest."

FDR was as enigmatic over the issue of running for an unprecedented third term as he was about much else. His enemies accused him of being ravenous for unlimited power. His close associates recognized that he was deeply divided as to whether to break the two-term tradition. None of his preferred successors, Hopkins, William O. Douglas, and Robert Jackson, developed any sizable popular following nor did the plausible conservative alternatives, Hull, Garner, and Farley.

The international crisis was the most crucial factor in prompting FDR to decide on his candidacy in May 1940. Ironically, he was supported by a group of leading politicians that included both the proponents and opponents of intervention. Although he chose Chicago as the site of the Democratic National Convention, because he could rely on the local political boss, Ed Kelly, to "pack the galleries," he would not openly campaign for his nomination, seeking instead the fiction of a spontaneous draft. Kelly had his superintendent of sewers rouse delegates for FDR through loudspeakers around the hall. After a dutiful show of reluctance and deference, Roosevelt was nominated by 946 votes on the first ballot. Commented Thomas Gore, former senator from Oklahoma, "You know I have never doubted for one moment since he was nominated in 1932 that he would seek a third term. . . . Caesar thrice refused the kingly crown—but this Caesar, never."

In place of John Nance Garner, FDR chose Secretary of Agriculture Henry A. Wallace as his running mate because Wallace was a committed New Dealer who could carry the Corn Belt and his choice was accepted, reluctantly in some quarters, by the delegates.

FDR was most vulnerable to criticisms that the New Deal had failed to meet America's minimum defense needs, although the wartime economic boom had already begun. Expanded industrial production was providing about 3 million new jobs. Roosevelt retaliated by campaign visits to defense plants and to military and naval sites that served both to demonstrate Democratic preparedness and illustrate his domination of the situation.

In the election FDR took 27,307,819 votes (54.8 percent) to Willkie's 22,321,018 (44.8 percent), and 449 votes in the electoral college to Willkie's 82. Socialist candidate Norman Thomas polled 99,557 votes. Roosevelt had won all but ten states, eight in the Midwest, and Maine and Vermont in the Northeast. Roosevelt won his victory in the cities and it was his decisive pluralities in New York, Chicago, Cleveland, and Milwaukee that gave him the pivotal states of New York, Illinois, Ohio, and Wisconsin. He attracted ethnic groups who had most at stake on his policy of intervention in the war, such as Norwegians, Poles, and Jews.

Because Willkie had, until the eleventh hour, been a committed internationalist, his campaign convinced isolationists they had been deprived of a genuine choice in the election. Against the wishes of Willkie, the Republican National Committee had made anti-intervention broadcasts that declared to mothers, "Don't blame Franklin D. Roosevelt because he sent your son to war—blame yourself because you sent Franklin D. Roosevelt back to the White House." Therefore, taking notice of his advisers, FDR consented to promise, immediately before the election on October 30, 1940, "Your boys are not going to be sent into any foreign wars." Most significant, under pressure from his advisers, FDR had dropped the crucial qualifying phrase, "except in case of attack."

Selective Service and America First

The issue of intervention was debated everywhere and discussion concentrated on peacetime conscription, student dissent, America First, and Lend-Lease.

Most Americans opposed compulsory military service in peacetime—the very idea represented the tyrannies whence their fathers had fled. When FDR courageously raised the issue in a speech on June 10, 1940, he was, perhaps, introducing the most controversial subject ever in an election campaign to that time. However, Willkie supported him. Draft legislation for conscription was introduced in the Senate by Democrat Edward R. Burke of Nebraska and in the House by conservative Republican James

W. Wadsworth, Jr., of New York. It moved comfortably through both houses of Congress between August 27 and September 14 and was signed by the president on September 16, two weeks after the destroyers-bases deal.

The Selective Service Act required the registration of all male citizens and resident aliens between the ages of twenty-one and thirty-five. Those inducted were to serve in the armed forces for twelve months but only either in the United States or in its territories and possessions overseas. On October 16, 1940, 16 million men registered for the draft. Owing to the effective lobbying of the peace churches, led by the Church of the Brethren, the act also provided Civilian Public Service Camps for those who could convince the National Service Board of their deep religious or ethical objection to military or naval service. The Civilian Public Service Camps became an adjunct to the military establishment, and, besides, conscientious objection was a declining phenomenon. Moreover, army doctors rejected almost half the men called for inspection before draft boards and FDR learned why from a national nutrition conference in spring 1941: most suffered from ten years' malnutrition. The census of 1940 disclosed that half of the nation's children came from families with incomes of less than $1,500.

One group, college students, was especially concerned about conscription and how it would affect them. Students throughout America, but particularly those at eastern colleges, indicated that they did not want to fight in another war. The editors of the *New Republic* summed up the way the students were making their protest felt on July 1, 1940:

During the past few months it has become apparent that there is an intellectual gulf between the generations, the post-war and the pre-war. It can be seen almost everywhere but it is especially obvious in the eastern colleges, where the majority of each faculty is already fighting Hitler, while a considerable part of the student body is against military intervention and lukewarm about aiding the Allies. That is the case at Yale, Princeton and Dartmouth, to judge by recent petitions. At Harvard a speaker who advocated help to Britain was booed on Class Day, something that has rarely happened in Harvard history. It would have been inconceivable in 1916.

To Greet the Bomber. A British antiaircraft gunner with gas mask and tin hat is photographed ready to take on the German Luftwaffe and give a vivid impression of the alertness and efficiency of Britain's defenses. People grew accustomed to the ghoulish uniform, and a new generation of science fiction novelists were ready to draw on the strange experiences for alien encounters in fiction of the 1950s. (Office of War Information; Library of Congress).

The attitude of young people was summarized caustically by Arnold Whitridge in the *Atlantic Monthly* of August 1940. His attack on their apathy and "hysterical timidity" initiated a debate between older people who believed that World War II was inevitable and necessary and the young who felt that it was an avoidable fracas. The gist of the article by Whitridge, "Where Do You Stand?" was an indictment of unpatriotic slothful youth when confronted with the task of subduing military dictatorship menacing Europe. The phenomenon was not confined to Ivy League schools. In November 1939 the Jesuit weekly, *America,* published the results of a poll of more than 50,000 students in 182 Catholic colleges and universities. More than a third expected the United States to become involved in the war and nine-tenths of them believed that a second intervention would not lead to a lasting peace. Moreover, they voted fifty to one against intervention.

However, increasingly in the early 1940s, isolationism was synonymous with the America First Committee. Here, it seemed, was where students did stand. America First was founded on September 4, 1940, by two students at Yale, Kingman Brewster, Jr., and R. Douglas Stuart, Jr. Stuart was the son of the Quaker Oats magnate, who arranged for considerable financial backing from Chicago businessmen, led by Robert E. Wood, chairman of Sears Roebuck. The strength of America First lay in its exceptional organization of 450 chapters across the country with a total membership of between 800,000 and 850,000 that drew on support from the rank and file of the National Council for the Prevention of War (NCPW) and the Woman's International League for Peace and Freedom (WILPF). Members included conservative opponents of FDR, college students opposed to the draft, and a few Communists. The big guns were Herbert Hoover, Joseph P. Kennedy, Hugh S. Johnson, and Henry Ford.

It was America First's association with star aviator Charles A. Lindbergh, Jr., that ensured intense and thorough press coverage of its activities. As we have remarked earlier, Lindbergh was always good copy and his visits to Germany in 1930, 1937, and 1938 had been widely reported. During those visits he had inspected German air power and reported his findings back to the U.S. military attaché in Berlin, Major Truman Smith. Lindbergh did not accept the general contemporary pro-British and anti-German interpretation of European affairs. His sympathies for Britain and France had been blunted by what he regarded as their inability to accommodate themselves to the new phenomenon of German air power. He thought American intervention in the war would be a disaster for the United States' economy and that American democracy might not survive it.

America First, knowing Lindbergh's views, wanted to attract him as its principal speaker. He was, quite simply, one of the most popular men in America. However, Lindbergh's popularity was as effervescent as a film star's. He could attract huge audiences—at least 23,000 at Madison Square Garden on May 23, 1941, and at least 40,000 at the Hollywood Bowl on June 20, 1941 —but he could only hope to keep people's sympathy by tapping indefinite fears. Furthermore, Lindbergh was a political novice who failed to realize that his generalizations divided where they were meant to unite. Thus, at Des Moines, Iowa, on September 11, 1941, he told an audience of 8,000 that the interventionists' "ever-increasing efforts to force the United States into the conflict" had been "so successful that, today, our country stands on the verge of war." Further, he identified the "war agitators."

The three most important groups who have been pressing this country toward war are the British, the Jewish, and the Roosevelt Administration. Behind these groups, but of lesser importance, are a number of capitalists, anglophiles, and intellectuals, who believe that their future and the future of mankind, depend upon the domination of the British Empire. Add to these the communistic groups who were opposed to intervention until a few weeks ago, and I believe I have named the major war agitators in this country.

He concluded that these particular groups were trying to involve the United States by advocating increased military preparedness for defense and creating "a series of incidents which would force us into the actual conflict." His designation of the British, the Jews, and the Roosevelt administration as "war agitators" was wide open to the interpretation that he and America First suffered from Anglophobia, anti-Semitism, and selfish conservatism. Of course, Lindbergh meant that, from their own points of view, these "agitators" believed, misguidedly, in the need for American involvement but the Des Moines speech was bitterly attacked by the press, deeply resented by Lindbergh's nominal allies, and, worst of all, praised by the very elements from which America First wished to dissociate itself.

For his part, FDR, by selective use of surveillance and propaganda, managed to give the somewhat erroneous impression that isolationists were narrow-minded, self-serving, and anti-Semitic conservatives. Lindbergh's foolhardiness helped him do so. The reaction to Lindbergh's Des Moines speech was so hostile that widespread support for America First seemed to evaporate almost overnight. In any case, it had already lost the battle against intervention with the passing of lend-lease.

H.R. 1776: Lend-Lease

Roosevelt realised that because Britain had exhausted its cash reserves it could not continue to pay for heavy purchases of materials in the United States without which it could not continue the war. Whilst on a Caribbean cruise recovering from his campaign, Roosevelt received a letter from Winston Churchill explaining the British plight and pleading with him to find a way of providing the necessary additional aid. Britain had less than $2 billion with which to pay orders costing $5 billion. Stimulated by Churchill, Lord Lothian, and the White Committee, Roosevelt proposed Lend-Lease. Roosevelt explained Lend-Lease at a press conference in Washington on December 16, 1940. He introduced it with a parable suggested by Harold Ickes,

Suppose my neighbor's house catches fire, and I have a length of garden hose. If he can take my garden hose and connect it up with his hydrant, I may help him put out the fire. Now what do I do? I don't say to him before that operation, "Neighbor, my garden hose cost me fifteen dollars; you have to pay me fifteen dollars for it." What is the transaction that goes on? I don't want fifteen dollars—I want my garden hose back after the fire is over. All right if it goes through the fire all right, intact, without damage to it, he gives it back to me and thanks me very much for the use of it.

Roosevelt proposed loans of tanks, planes, and ships to Britain without detailed suggestions as to how Britain might repay "in kind" after the war. The argument was sophistical, the appeal unsophisticated. Furthermore, Roosevelt renewed it in his fireside chat of December 29, 1940, when he told the country it was necessary for America to expand its industrial production. For, "We must be the great arsenal of democracy." Mail to the White House was 100 to 1 in favor, while polls of public opinion showed 80 percent who heard the talk direct or read about it approved, while only 12 percent were opposed to FDR's arguments. FDR repeated the argument in his State of the Union address of January 6, 1941, and went further, claiming that victory over the Axis would mean "a world [based] upon four essential human freedoms: freedom of speech and religion and freedom from want and fear."

FDR was swift to counter accusations from America First that he would use the law simply to give away the U.S. navy and convoy supples and to enhance his own powers. He was especially stung by Senator Burton K. Wheeler of Montana's remark that Lend-Lease was "the New Deal's triple A foreign policy; it will plow under every fourth American boy." He described Wheeler's charge as "the most untruthful, [as] the most dastardly, unpatriotic thing that has ever been said. Quote me on that. That really is the rottenest thing that has been said in public life in my generation."

Fortuitously numbered House Resolution 1776, the Lend-Lease bill gave the president power to lend, lease, sell or barter arms, food, or any "defense article," to foreign nations "whose defense the president deems vital to the defense of the United States." Of course, one reason for freeing Lend-Lease entirely from the question of loans was to avoid the sort of controversy attached to Wall Street loans to the Allies in World War I. On March 11, 1941, the Senate approved the bill by 60 votes to 31 and the House did so by 317 votes to 71. Once the president had signed the act, Congress voted an appropriation of $7 billion to implement its terms.

The conception was bold, the accomplishment a bare minimum. Historian Stephen A. Ambrose describes Roosevelt's reluctance to provide strong central control and assesses the conflicting interests of the officials involved: "Some American officials tried to use the new system as a wedge to get American firms into the British Commonwealth market and to force the British to sell their holdings on the American continents, and the Army resisted sending arms needed in the United States to Britain, so that the total amount of goods shipped, in comparison with the need, was small." British imports from the United States increased by only 3 percent in 1941 and the increase was principally in foodstuffs and steel. Most of the American arms obtained were still bought with cash in 1941 and Britain lost most of its remaining dollars. Naturally, Britain could not turn Lend-Lease goods into exports, but exports not made from Lend-Lease materials were cut down so as to avoid an outcry from American manufacturers.

Senator Arthur Vandenberg of Michigan wrote in his diary after the passing of H.R. 1776 that he thought this was the suicide of the Republic: "We have torn up 150 years of traditional foreign policy. We have tossed Washington's Farewell Address into the discard. We have thrown ourselves squarely into the power politics and power wars of Europe, Asia and Africa. We have taken the first step upon a course from which we can never hereafter retreat."

War in the Atlantic

Lend-Lease was no use unless American supplies reached Britain. In February and March 1941 German submarines sank or seized twenty-two ships. Despite the opposition of about half the Senate to the idea of American convoys supporting British freighters across half the Atlantic, Roosevelt announced that the United States's security zone would be extended a thousand miles into the Atlantic from April 11, 1941. The air force was used to patrol the North Atlantic as far as Iceland in order to warn British ships of the presence of German submarines. A majority of the Cabinet favored a declaration of war on Germany. Henry Stimson was concerned that Roosevelt did not follow his victory with the Lend-Lease Act with more positive policy but continued to move with great caution. In this concern he was supported by Secretary of the Navy Frank Knox, Attorney General Robert H. Jackson, and Secretary of the Interior Harold L. Ickes. Stimson tells in his diary for April 25, 1941, how Roosevelt introduced a program for patrolling the western Atlantic and then added defensively, "Well, it's a step forward." Stimson answered, "Well, I hope you will keep on walking, Mr. President. Keep on walking." Clare Booth Luce said Roosevelt's symbolic gesture was not, like Churchill's defiant one, two fingers raised in a V shape, but, rather, a moistened finger held to test the wind.

Unlike Theodore Roosevelt or, for that matter, Winston Churchill, FDR did not believe in war as social therapy, a means of strengthening national fiber. As William Manchester observes, "Divided countries do not win great wars. [FDR] could be a step ahead of the people, perhaps even two steps. But if he ever lost them he would fail them and his oath of office."

Nevertheless, despite FDR's caution, British military staffs had already had secret conversations in Washington with the American combined chiefs from January 29 to March 27, 1941. Britain and the United States were not yet formal allies. However, they were already "associated powers" with a common goal.

Elsewhere, other weaker countries were seeking support from strong allies. By early 1941 Hungary, Bulgaria, and Romania had been conquered by Germany. After making war on them, Italy had failed to subdue Yugoslavia and Greece but, once Germany had launched an offensive on these countries on April 6, 1941, they, too, were made subject to the Axis within three weeks.

In May 1941 the American freighter *Robin Moor* was sunk by Germans in the south Atlantic. Roosevelt declared an "unlimited national emergency," froze all German and Italian assets in the United States and closed their consulates. In June popular support for convoys was 52 percent, according to public opinion polls, and 75 percent approved if it seemed that Britain would not win the war without the security of supplies they provided.

To make the Atlantic patrols more effective, Roosevelt and his advisers decided to secure territories on the edge of the zone. On April 9, 1941, the State Department concluded an agreement with the exiled Danish minister in Washington to occupy the Danish possession of Greenland. In June and July the administration negotiated with Iceland to replace British and Canadian troops stationed there with an American force that landed on July 7. The American patrol ships were given secret orders to extend their duties beyond patrolling rather than allow any hostile force to deflect them from their course.

On June 22, 1941, Hitler repudiated the Nazi-Soviet Pact and invaded Russia. On June 26, 1941, the United States announced that the neutrality laws would not be invoked against Russia because American security was not endangered. But on July 26 Roosevelt sent Hopkins to Moscow to ascertain Stalin's needs and on August 2 promised Russia aid against aggression. On November 7, 1941, Lend-Lease was applied to Russia as well as Britain.

In an attempt to discuss the objectives of Britain and the still technically neutral America in the war, Roosevelt met Churchill at sea in Placentia Bay off Argentia, Newfoundland, from August 9 to 12, 1941. Their meeting had been planned by Harry Hopkins. Intending a complement to Woodrow Wilson's Fourteen Points, the two leaders declared in the Atlantic Charter that their countries sought no new territory in the course of the war; that territorial changes would only be made with reference to the populations involved; that all peoples had the right to choose the form of their government; that all nations had equal right of access to raw materials and trade throughout the world; and that after the war aggressor nations would be forced to disarm until a permanent system of international security was established. In short, the future peace should, as FDR's earlier promise had suggested, give all peoples freedom from want and freedom from fear, and freedom of speech and religion. Roosevelt's recollection of how the United States had treated Woodrow Wilson's scheme for the League of Nations led him to have explicit references to systems of international security deleted. Roosevelt appreciated the tenacity and charm of Churchill and Churchill liked Roosevelt's subtlety and sense of timing.

In response to Churchill's desire that America should declare war, FDR explained that a request to Congress for a declaration of war would simply produce a political debate lasting three months. Instead, according to Churchill's report of August 19, 1941, to his own cabinet, FDR had "said that he would wage war, but not declare it, and that he would become more and more

provocative. . . . Everything was to be done to force an 'incident'
. . . which would justify him in opening hostilities."

American public opinion was overwhelmingly favorable to the
principles of the Atlantic Charter, provided it did not lead to
outright intervention in the war. Moreover, isolationist sentiment
in Congress was still strong. The occupation of Iceland by 4,000
marines on July 7, 1941, opened debate about the appropriate size
and disposition of American forces. The Selective Service Act had
allowed for 900,000 draftees for one-year's service in the western
hemisphere. Military strategists agreed this was inadequate.
However, Congress was reluctant to take the initiative in as unpopular a measure as would be increasing and extending the draft.
Therefore, FDR agreed with congressional leaders on July 14 that
he would take the responsibility in his strong recommendation to
Congress on July 21, warning against the "tragic error" of allowing the "disintegration" of the comparatively modest army. The
Senate voted for an extension of service to eighteen months—
rather than for the duration of the emergency as FDR had asked
—with 45 in favor and 21 senators not voting at all. On August
12 the House agreed by a majority of one, 203 votes in favor of
202 against. That narrow victory was essentially due to the work
of Chief of Staff General George C. Marshall from behind the
scenes.

On September 4 the United States and Germany began an
undeclared naval war after an incident in which the commander
of a German submarine U-652 off Iceland sent torpedoes at what
he thought was a British destroyer. It was an American, the
Greer. Describing the attacks on the *Greer* and other ships as "acts
of international lawlessness" intended by Germany to destroy
freedom of the seas, Roosevelt said in a radio address of September
11, 1941, that American vessels and planes "will no longer wait
until Axis submarines lurking under the water, or Axis raiders on
the surface of the sea, strike their deadly blow—first."

Had FDR said that the U-boat had fired in self-defense, which
was what had really happened, and admitted that Hitler did not
intend to attack American ships in the Atlantic, which was what
Churchill told his colleagues, he would have had to wait for the
imminent collapse of Britain and Russia before getting nation-

wide support for declared military intervention. Yet here was cause for future unease of a different sort, the manipulation of incident by a president, acting on the basis that the end justifies the means. Historian Robert Dallek observes, somewhat ruefully, "Yet for all the need to mislead the country in its own interest, the President's deviousness also injured the national well-being over the long run. His action in the *Greer* incident created a precedent for manipulation of public opinion which would be repeated by later Presidents in less justifiable circumstances."

In October another destroyer, the *Reuben James,* was sunk off Iceland with the loss of 100 American lives. However, when Roosevelt signed a revision of the neutrality laws on November 17, 1941, permitting the arming of American marine ships and allowing them to carry cargoes to belligerents' ports he was giving assent to an act that was passed by narrow margins in both houses — 50 to 37 in the Senate and 212 to 194 in the House — that reflected the still-prevalent division of opinion.

War in the Pacific

In the Pacific, the United States was on a collision course with Japan and it was this that led to its formal entry into World War II.

In December 1938 the Japanese prime minister, Prince Konoye, had announced Japan's ambitious foreign policy for a "Greater East Asia Coprosperity Sphere." From 1938 the State Department issued protests against Japanese interference with American rights in China and the bombing of Chinese civilians. Moreover, Cordell Hull had gone further than the letter of the neutrality laws and asked American bankers not to extend credits to Japan and requested American manufacturers not to sell airplanes and airplane parts to any nation that might attack civilians. American disapproval of Japan's foreign policy culminated in an announcement of July 1939 that the commercial treaty of 1911 would be terminated at the end of the year. The actual sale of goods did not come to an end immediately in January 1941, but within months such exports as gasoline, steel, and scrap iron were made subject to government license.

Japan took full advantage of the fall of France to extend its imperial ambitions to northern Indochina, a French colony comprising the three states of Laos, Cambodia, and Vietnam. Unable to resist Japanese demands for airfields, Vichy France consented to Japanese occupation of Indochina in September 1940. That month Japan concluded the Axis with Germany and Italy by which the three powers were obliged to come to one another's aid if any one of them were attacked. Japan thereby extracted from the others acceptance of its own sphere of influence in South East Asia and the Pacific. Germany hoped the tripartite pact would deter the United States from entering the European War as did Japan for the Sino-Japanese War.

Senator Robert A. Taft of Ohio, who succeeded Vandenberg as Republican spokesman on foreign policy, commenting on opposition within the White House to the Japanese invasion of Vietnam, said no American mother was prepared to let her son be killed in war "for some place with an unpronounceable name in Indochina." Ironically, those who advocated strict neutrality toward Europe did not advance the same arguments toward South East Asia. For example, Senator Burton K. Wheeler of Montana criticized Roosevelt's policy to Europe for its tendency to intervention but supported the stronger line on Japan.

In April 1941 Germany and Japan discussed plans for a projected war on two fronts against America when the Japanese foreign minister, Matsuoka Yosuka, visited Berlin. Joachim von Ribbentrop, the German foreign minister, urged him to commit Japan to an immediate assault on the British protectorate, Singapore. By July 1941 Japan had completed occupation of southern as well as northern Indochina. The United States looked askance at a situation in which the oil, tin, rubber, bauxite, and other resources of South East Asia were controlled by a hostile power and on July 24, 1941, Roosevelt froze all Japanese credits in the United States. When Britain and the Dutch colonial governor in Djakarta in the Netherlands East Indies took similar action, Japan's sources of petroleum dried up. The American ambassador in Tokyo, Joseph Drew, warned Cordell Hull that if America humbled Konoye by its action he would fall and be replaced by a more belligerent prime minister.

Konoye suggested a meeting at sea between himself and Roosevelt at the end of August 1941. Cordell Hull advised the president against discussions without prior agreement on the basic principles underlying any prospective negotiations. This proved impossible and in September an Imperial Conference of cabinet ministers and chiefs of staff met in Tokoyo to consider preparations for war, should talks between Japan and the United States fail.

It was obvious that the United States would not allow Japan to become a great power. Japan had to choose war while it was able to do so. Without war, economic collapse was inevitable and thus, even if Japan lost a war with the United States, there would still be nothing to regret. With the failure of the Japanese ambassador in Washington, Admiral Kichisaburo Nomura, to secure terms with the United States, Prince Konoye was, indeed, humbled as Joseph Drew had predicted. He was succeeded as prime minister, on October 16, by the former war minister, General Hideki Tojo.

Because the Washington ambassador was not a trained diplomat, Tojo sent Saburo Kuruso, a veteran diplomat and once ambassador to Berlin, to assist him in November 1941. He brought an offer of conciliation: Japan would withdraw from Indochina and halt its advance in South East Asia if the United States agreed to Japanese control of China. The American reply on November 26 was equally candid: if Japan withdrew its troops from both China and Indochina America would resume liberal trade with Japan. In this period Winston Churchill, perhaps out of consummate political strategy, appeared content to let the United States negotiate with Japan in a matter affecting not only Britain but also Australia, New Zealand, Malaya, and Hong Kong, as well as Guam, the Philippines, and Hawaii. The last Japanese offer, with a final deadline set at November 29, contained nothing new. Hull originally decided to propose a three-month truce during which limited withdrawal of troops from Indochina would be complemented by limited economic offers from the United States, but when he learned on November 26 of large Japanese convoys moving down the South China coast, he submitted stiff terms leaving no room for compromise.

The outcome of the negotiations was an undeclared attack on American naval bases in Pearl Harbor. The attack, led by the waves of carrier-based Japanese dive-bombers, torpedo planes, and fighters, lasted two hours and demolished the American fleet and air and military installations at Pearl Harbor, Honolulu, and Hawaii. Altogether, 2,403 Americans were killed and another 1,178 wounded. Not only did American intelligence officers, in possession of the Japanese secret code by the decoding system "magic," predict the attack by following telephone conversations between Saburo Kuruso in Washington and Isoroku Yamamoto in Tokyo, but they also made this known to General Walter Short, the army commander in Hawaii, and Admiral Husband E. Kimmel, the naval commander there. Short and Kimmel decided not to put the war plan into operation: their men would become exhausted by being put into a state of constant alert.

As Gordon Prange concludes in his *At Dawn We Slept* (1981) and his associates Donald Goldstein and Katherine V. Dillon conclude in a later edition, *Pearl Harbor: The Verdict of History* (1985), the fundamental causes of the American defeat were the skill, boldness, and luck of the Japanese in planning and carrying out the operation and the inability of American leaders to believe in, and act upon, the idea that the Japanese would dare to make a surprise attack on Pearl Harbor. Those who seek to defend Admiral Husband E. Kimmel, such as Edwin T. Layton in *"And I Was There"* (1985) contend that Kimmel was "shortchanged" by Washington, denied full intelligence information by incompetents in the Navy Department who then tried to cover up their errors. Whatever the failures in Washington, it is also true that Kimmel failed to conduct as much aerial reconnaissance as he might have, and that both army and navy commanders at Pearl failed to coordinate their efforts sufficiently. Thus Gordon W. Prange's emphasis on the states of mind and preconceptions of the principal officers in Washington and Pearl is a more important part of the explanation for the disaster that overtook the United States than any surprise revelation about code-breaking.

An old man in New Jersey asked about the attack answered a reporter, "You got me on that Martian stunt; I had a hunch you'd try again." Senator Gerald P. Nye reacted with the bad grace of a

"A day that will live in infamy." The Japanese air attack on the American naval base at Pearl Harbor, Hawaii, on December 7, 1941, left 2,403 American servicemen and civilians dead and 1,178 others wounded; 149 planes were destroyed; and the battleships *Oklahoma, Tennessee, West Virginia, California,* and *Nevada* were either sunk or damaged beyond repair. Meanwhile, a Japanese air raid on Manila devastated the army's air force in the Philippines. The following day Congress declared war against Japan. (Library of Congress).

small-minded man who saw the desert of political oblivion stretching out before him. "Sounds terribly fishy to me," he told a reporter. However, Senator Burton K. Wheeler was more positive. "The only thing to do now is to lick the hell out of them."

While noting how shocked was FDR, Frances Perkins also recognized that he was relieved to have the decision about war made for him, although he was reluctant to admit this. On December 8, 1941, Roosevelt sent his war message to Congress:

"Yesterday, December 7, 1941 — a day which will live in infamy — the United States of America was suddenly and deliberately attacked by naval and air forces of the Empire of Japan." Congress authorized a declaration of war against Japan on December 8. This time there was only one dissenting voice, that of the Quaker pacifist Jeanette Rankin, who had also voted against intervention in 1917.

For three days Hitler's advisers argued against declaration of war on the United States, whatever the terms of the pact with Japan. However, frustrated by setbacks on the Russian campaign and infuriated by American opposition in the Atlantic, Hitler made his declaration of war on December 11.

The most bitter lesson learnt in the wake of Pearl Harbor was that, if America was going to get drawn into others' wars, it would be better to do so on its own terms. Never again would the United States seek to isolate itself from world affairs. Churchill was especially jubilant after Pearl. "Now at this very moment I knew the United States was in the war, up to the neck and in to the death. So we had won after all! . . . Hitler's fate was sealed. Mussolini's fate was sealed. As for the Japanese, they would be ground to powder. . . . No doubt it would take a long time. . . . But there was no more doubt about the end." This was true. The United States was on the eve of an Atomic Age.

SOURCES

ANY HISTORIAN who attempts an interdisciplinary history of a country over a period of twenty or more years immediately puts himself in the debt of others. If he is to be alert in his scholarship, there must be something of Rossini's thieving magpie in his nature. Notwithstanding original research into such papers as those of the NAACP in the Library of Congress, Walter Lippmann at Yale, Jane Addams at Swarthmore College, Norman Thomas in the New York Public Library, and other primary sources, mainly in the Library of Congress—all of which were studied for this volume—the historian will undoubtedly seek interpretations and essential facts from numerous secondary works.

He or she is likely to be moved and captured by a select few. In my case, such writers as Alfred Dupont Chandler, Jr., on industrial corporations and their management, J. K. Galbraith and Milton Friedman on economics, William Leuchtenburg on political and social history, especially in the New Deal period, C. Vann Woodward on the South, Frank Freidel and James MacGregor Burns on Franklin D. Roosevelt, Richard Polenberg and Gaddis Smith on America and World War II, Richard Guy Wilson on the machine age and Gerald Mast on motion pictures, have all had a profound influence upon me. Their very different histories are judiciously written and persuasively argued, and their facts and ideas are represented, and acknowledged, in this work. Similarly, a series of social historians, beginning with Mark Sullivan, Frederick Lewis Allen, and Ray Ginger on the 1920s and 1930s, and continuing with William Manchester for the 1930s and 1940s, provides us with numerous anecdotes, much wit, and a sense of the thrust of popular and cultural history not readily available in more specific political or economic histories. Certain authors like Daniel Snowman on domestic history and Stephen Ambrose on foreign policy are able to sum up their points and present conventional enough material in a fresh way that also makes its mark.

The following bibliography is, like the book itself, intended as a basic guide for anyone new to the history of the United States in the period. It does not include every book or article mentioned in the text, but rather a representative selection of those that we might expect to find in a good university library, such as those of NYU, GWU, or the University of Manchester, England.

Statistics provided in this book on population, immigration, agricultural and industrial production, and election returns are usually taken from the United States Bureau of the Census, *Historical Statistics of the United States,* 2 vols. (Washington, D.C., 1975). A useful abridged version of the bicentennial edition is Ben J. Wattenberg (ed.), *The Statistical History of the United States from Colonial Times to the Present* (New York, 1976). I have taken supplementary factual or statistical information from Richard B. Morris and Jeffrey B. Morris (eds.), *Encyclopedia of American History* (sixth edition, New York, London, etc., 1982). The bibliography is arranged in subsections by chapter, with principal texts placed first in each subsection, and preceded by a list of general works.

BIBLIOGRAPHY

General

Daniel Snowman, *America Since 1920* (revised London, 1978; first published 1968).

William Manchester, *The Glory and the Dream: A Narrative History of America 1932–1972* (New York, 1974; London, 1975).

Ralph F. de Bedts, *Recent American History*, Volume 1 *1933 Through World War II* (Homewood, Ill., London, and Georgetown, Ontario, 1973).

Isabel Leighton, ed. *The Aspirin Age 1919–1941* (New York, 1949).

Jonathan Daniels, *The Time Between the Wars: Armistice to Pearl Harbor* (New York, 1966).

Edmund Wilson, *The American Earthquake: A Documentary of the Twenties and Thirties* (New York, 1979; first published 1971).

Jim Potter, *The American Economy Between the World Wars* (New York, 1974).

Warren I. Susman, *Culture as History: The Transformation of American Society in the Twentieth Century* (New York, 1985).

Chapter 1

A MACHINE AGE

Richard Guy Wilson, Dianne H. Pilgrim, Dickran Tashjian, with the Brooklyn Museum, *The Machine Age in America: 1918–1941* (New York, 1986).

U.S. National Resources Committee, *Technological Trends and National Policy* (Washington, D.C., 1937).

Roger Burlingame, *Engines of Democracy: Inventions and Society in Mature America* (Salem, N.H., 1976; first published 1940).

Stephen Fox, *The Mirror Makers: A History of American Advertising and Its Creators* (New York, 1984).

Chapter 2

THE 1920S

Frederick Lewis Allen, *Only Yesterday: An Informal History of the Nineteen Twenties* (New York, 1931).

Burl Noggle, *Into the Twenties: The United States from Armistice to Normalcy* (Urbana, Ill., 1974).

Paul A. Carter, *The Twenties in America* (New York, 1975; first published 1968).

——, *Another Part of the Twenties* (New York, 1977).

George Soule, *Prosperity Decade: From War to Depression 1917–1930* (New York, 1947).

Ellis W. Hawley, *The Great War and the Search for a Modern Order: A History of the American People and Their Institutions, 1917–1933* (New York, 1979).

J. W. Prothro, *Dollar Decade: Business Ideas in the 1920s* (Westport, Conn.; first published 1954).

Don S. Kirchner, *City and Country: Rural Responses to Urbanization in the 1920s* (Westport, Conn., 1970).

Robert S. Lynd and Helen Merrell, *Middletown* (New York, 1927).

Frank Stricker, "Affluence for Whom?" Another Look at Prosperity and the Working Classes in the 1920s," *Labor History* 24 (Winter 1983): 5–33.

F. May, "Shifting Perspectives on the 1920s," *Mississippi Valley Historical Review* 43 (December 1956): 405–27.

Winthrop Sargeant, "Fifty Years of Women," *Life* 28 (January 2, 1950): 64–67.

SACCO AND VANZETTI

Louis Joughin and Edmund M. Morgan, *The Legacy of Sacco and Vanzetti* (Princeton, N.J., 1976; first published 1948).

John Dos Passos, *Facing the Chair* (New York, 1970; first published 1927).

Francis Russell, *Sacco and Vanzetti: The Case Resolved* (New York, 1986).

William Young and David E. Kaiser, *Postmortem: New Evidence in the Case of Sacco and Vanzetti* (Boston, 1985).

Herbert B. Ehrmann, *The Case That Will Not Die: Commonwealth vs. Sacco and Vanzetti* (Boston, 1969).

NATIONAL PROHIBITION

Andrew Sinclair, *Prohibition: The Era of Excess* (London, 1962).

Charles Merz, *The Dry Decade* (Seattle and Washington, 1970; first published New York, 1930, 1931).

Thomas M. Coffey, *The Long Thirst—Prohibition in America 1920–1933* (New York and London, 1975, 1976).

E. Austin Kerr, *Organized for Prohibition: A New History of the Anti-Saloon League* (New Haven, Conn., 1985).

David E. Kyvig, *Repealing National Prohibition* (Chicago and London, 1979).

J. C. Burnham, "New Perspectives on the Prohibition 'Experiment' of the 1920s," *Journal of Social History* (Fall 1968): 51–67.

CRIME AND THE UNDERWORLD

Fred J. Cook, *The Secret Rulers: Criminal Syndicates and How They Control the U.S. Underworld* (New York, 1966).

Humbert S. Nelli, *The Business of Crime: Italians and Syndicate Crime in the United States* (New York, 1976).

Joseph L. Albini, *The American Mafia—Genesis of a Legend* (New York, 1971).

John Landesco, *Organized Crime in Chicago* (second edition, Chicago, 1968).

Francis A. J. Ianni with Elizabeth Reuss-Ianni, *A Family Business—Kinship and Social Control in Organized Crime* (New York, 1972).

John Kobler, *Capone* (New York, 1971).

Dennis Eisenberg, Uri Dan, and Eli Landau, *Meyer Lansky: Mogul of the Mob* (London and New York, 1979 and 1980).

Mark H. Haller, "Organized Crime in Urban Society: Chicago in the Twentieth Century," *Journal of Social History* (Winter 1971–72: 210–33.

H. L. MENCKEN

Edgar Kemler, *The Irreverent Mr. Mencken* (Boston, 1950).

William Manchester, *Disturber of the Peace: The Life of H. L. Mencken* (New York, 1951).

Charles Angoff, *H. L. Mencken, A Portrait from Memory* (New York, 1956).

THE NEW SOUTH

George Brown Tindall, *The Emergence of the New South 1913–1945* (Baton Rouge, La., 1967).

Ray Ginger, *Six Days or Forever? Tennessee v. John Thomas Scopes* (Chicago, 1969; first published 1958).

Jerry R. Tompkins, *D-Days at Dayton: Reflections on the Scopes Trial* (Baton Rouge, La., 1965).

David M. Chalmers, *Hooded Americanism—The First Century of the Ku Klux Klan 1865–1965* (Garden City, N.Y., 1965).

Kenneth T. Jackson, *The Ku Klux Klan in the City 1915–1930* (New York, 1967).

Charles C. Alexander, *The Ku Klux Klan in the Southwest* (Louisville, Ky., 1965).

Lawrence Levine, *Defender of the Faith: William Jennings Bryan: The Last Decade* (New York and Oxford, 1965).

Charles H. Martin, *The Angelo Herndon Case and Southern Justice* (Baton Rouge, La., 1976).

Wyn Craig Wade, *The Fiery Cross—The Ku Klux Klan in America* (New York, 1987).

Chapter 3

THE REPUBLICAN ASCENDANCY

John D. Hicks, *The Republican Ascendancy 1921–1933* (New York, Evanston, and London, 1960).

Arthur M. Schlesinger, Jr., *The Crisis of the Old Order* (Boston, 1958).

Wesley M. Bagby, *The Road to Normalcy: The Presidential Campaign and Election of 1920* (Baltimore, 1962).

Robert K. Murray, *Warren G. Harding and His Administration* (Minneapolis, 1969).

Burt Noggle, *Teapot Dome: Oil and Politics in the 1920s* (Westport, Conn., 1980; first published 1962).

Claude M. Fuess, *Calvin Coolidge: The Man from Vermont* (Westport, Conn., 1981; first published 1977).

Richard Gid Powers, *Secrecy and Power—The Life of J. Edgar Hoover* (New York, 1987).

David Burner, *The Politics of Provincialism: The Democratic Party in Transition, 1918–1932* (New York, 1968).

Robert K. Murray, *The 103rd Ballot: The Democrats and the Disaster in Madison Square Garden* (New York, 1976).

Paula Elder, *Governor Alfred E. Smith: The Politician as Reformer* (New York, 1982).

Matthew and Hanna Josephson, *Al Smith: Hero of the Cities* (Boston, 1969).

Richard O'Connor, *The First Hurrah: A Biography of Alfred E. Smith* (New York, 1970).

Allan J. Lichtman, *Prejudice and the Old Politics: The Presidential Election of 1928* (Chapel Hill, N.C., 1979).

Richard Lowitt, *George W. Norris: The Persistence of a Progressive 1913–1933* (Champaign, Ill., 1971).

Arthur Link, "Whatever Happened to the Progressive Movement in the 1920s?" *American Historical Review* (July 1959): 833–51.

David Noble, "The New Republic and the Idea of Progress, 1914–1920," *Mississippi Valley Historical Review* 38 (December 1951): 387–402.

Herbert Croly, "The Eclipse of Progressivism," *New Republic* 24 (October 27, 1920): 210–16.

——, "The Outlook for Progressivism in Politics," *New Republic* 41 (December 10, 1924): 60–64.

Charles Merz, "Progressivism, Old and New," *Atlantic Monthly* 132 (July 1923): 102–109.

Allan J. Lichtman, "Critical Election Theory and the Reality of American Presidential Politics, 1916–1940," *American Historical Review* 81 (1976): 317–51.

Chapter 4

THE WALL STREET CRASH

J. K. Galbraith, *The Great Crash–1929* (New York, 1979; first published 1954).

John Brooks, *Once in Golconda: A True Drama of Wall Street 1920–1938* (New York, 1969).

Gordon Thomas and Max Morgan-Witts, *The Day the Bubble Burst* (New York, 1979).

Peter Temin, *Did Monetary Forces Cause the Great Depression?* (New York, 1976).

THE GREAT DEPRESSION

Frederick Lewis Allen, *Since Yesterday: The Nineteen Thirties in America* (New York, 1940).

Broadus Mitchell, *Depression Decade: From New Era Through New Deal, 1929–1941* (New York, 1947).

Lester V. Chandler, *America's Greatest Depression, 1929–41* (New York, 1970).

Studs Terkel, *Hard Times: An Oral History of the Great Depression* (New York, 1970).

Robert S. McElvaine, *Down and Out in the Great Depression: Letters from the Forgotten Man* (Chapel Hill, N.C., 1983).

Leo Ribuffo, *The Old Christian Right: The Protestant Far Right from the Depression to the Cold War* (Philadelphia, 1983).

David Tyack et al., *Public Schools in Hard Times: The Great Depression and Recent Years* (Cambridge, Mass., 1984).

UNEMPLOYMENT

John A. Garraty, *Unemployment in History: Economic Thought and Public Policy* (New York, 1979).

Unemployment in the United States: Hearings before a Subcommittee of the Committee on Labor, House of Representatives, 72d Congress, 1st Session, on H.R. 206, H.R. 6011, H.R. 6066 (Washington, D.C., 1932).

Paul Webbink, "Unemployment in the United States, 1930–1940," *Papers and Proceedings of the American Economic Association* (February 1941).

Federal Aid for Unemployment Relief: Hearings Before a Subcommittee of the Committee on Manufacture, U.S. Senate, 72d Congress, 1st Session, on S. 174, S. 262, and S. 4592; U.S. Senate, 72d Congress, 2d Session, on S. 5125 (Washington, D.C., 1932).

Relief for Unemployed Transients: Hearings before a Subcommittee of the Committee on Manufactures, U.S. Senate, 72d Congress, 2d Session, on S. 5121 (Washington, D.C., 1933).

CONTEMPORARY ARTICLES ON UNEMPLOYMENT

John L. Leary, Jr., "If We Had the Dole," *American Magazine* (December 1931).

George R. Leighton, "And If the Revolution Comes. . . ?" *Harper's Magazine* (March 1932).

Joseph L. Heffernan, "The Hungry City: A Mayor's Experience with Unemployment," *Atlantic Monthly* (May 1932).

George R. Clark, "Beckerstown, 1932: An American Town Faces the Depression," *Harper's Magazine* (October 1932).

Frank A. Vandenlip, "What About the Banks?" *Saturday Evening Post* (November 5, 1932).

Mary Heaton Vorse, "Rebellion in the Cornbelt: American Farmers Beat Their Plowshares into Swords," *Harper's Magazine* (December 1932).

Remley J. Glass, "Gentlemen, the Corn Belt!," *Harper's Magazine* (July 1933).

"A Survey of Unemployed Alumni," *School and Society* (March 10, 1934).

"The Great American Roadside," *Fortune* (September 1934).

THE INCOMPLETE POLITICS OF HERBERT HOOVER

Herbert Hoover, *The Memoirs of Herbert Hoover,* vol. 2, *The Cabinet and the Presidency 1920–1933* (New York and London, 1952).

Martin L. Fansold, *The Presidency of Herbert C. Hoover* (New York, 1985).

Jordan A. Schwarz, *The Inter-Regnum of Despair: Hoover, Congress, and the Depression* (Urbana, Ill., 1970).

Gene Smith, *The Shattered Dream: Herbert Hoover and the Great Depression* (New York, 1970).

Joan H. Wilson, *Herbert Hoover: Forgotten Progressive* (Boston, 1975).

Gilbert Seldes, *The Years of the Locust—America, 1929–1932* (New York, 1973).

Roger Daniels, *The Bonus March: An Episode of the Great Depression* (Westport, Conn., 1971).

Donald Lisio, *The President and Protest: Hoover, Conspiracy and the Bonus Riot* (Columbia, Miss., 1974).

Malcolm Cowley, "The Flight of the Bonus Army," *New Republic* (August 17, 1932).

George Soule, "Are We Going to Have a Revolution?" *Harper's Magazine* (August 1932).

Frank Freidel, *Franklin D. Roosevelt: The Triumph* (New York, 1956).

Chapter 5

FRANKLIN D. ROOSEVELT AND THE NEW DEAL

William E. Leuchtenburg, *Franklin D. Roosevelt and the New Deal 1932–40* (New York, 1963).

Arthur M. Schlesinger, Jr., *The Coming of the New Deal* (Boston, 1958).

———, *The Politics of Upheaval* (Boston, 1960).

James MacGregor Burns, *Roosevelt: The Lion and the Fox* (New York, 1956).

Albert U. Romasco, *The Politics of Recovery: Roosevelt's New Deal* (New York and Oxford, 1983).

Paul Conkin, *The New Deal* (Arlington Heights, Ill., 1975).

Katie Louchlin, ed., *The Making of the New Deal* (Cambridge, Mass., 1983).

Harvard Sitkoff, ed., *Fifty Years Later: The New Deal Evaluated* (New York, 1985).

John Braeman, et al., ed., *The New Deal* (Columbus, Ohio, 1975).

THE NEW DEALERS

Joseph P. Lash, *Eleanor and Franklin: The Story of Their Relationship, Based on Eleanor Roosevelt's Private Papers* (New York, 1971).

William J. Youngs, *Eleanor Roosevelt* (Thorndike, Maine, 1984).

Joan Hoff-Wilson and Marjorie Lightman, ed., *Without Precedent: The Life and Career of Eleanor Roosevelt* (Bloomington, Ind., 1984).

Robert E. Sherwood, *Roosevelt and Hopkins: An Intimate History* (New York, 1948).

Graham White and John Maze, *Harold Ickes of the New Deal* (Cambridge, Mass., 1985).

George Martin, *Madam Secretary, Frances Perkins* (New York, 1977).

John M. Blum, *From the Morgenthau Diaries: Years of Urgency* (Boston, 1964).

Otis L. Graham, Jr., *An Encore for Reform: The Old Progressives and the New Deal* (New York, 1967).

Richard Lowitt, *George W. Norris: The Triumph of a Progressive 1933–34* (Champaign, Ill., 1978).

J. Joseph Huthmacher, *Senator Robert F. Wagner and the Rise of Urban Liberalism* (New York, 1968).

Peter H. Irons, *New Deal Lawyers* (Princeton, N.J., 1982).

Elliott Rosen, *Hoover, Roosevelt, and the Brains Trust* (New York, 1977).

NEW DEAL POLICIES AND PROGRAMS

Raymond Moley, *The First New Deal* (New York, 1966).

Susan Estabrook Kennedy, *The Banking Crisis of 1933* (Lexington, Ky., 1973).

Jordan Schwarz, *1933: Roosevelt's Decision: The United States Leaves the Gold Standard* (New York, 1969).

Jerold S. Auerbach, *Labor and Liberty: The La Follette Committee and the New Deal* (New York, 1966).
Theodore Saloutos, *The American Farmer and the New Deal* (Ames, Iowa, 1982).
Richard S. Kirkendall, *Social Scientists and Farm Policies in the Age of Roosevelt* (Ames, Iowa, 1982; first published 1966).
David E. Conrad, *The Forgotten Farmers: The Story of Sharecropping in the New Deal* (Westport, Conn., 1982; first published 1965).
Sidney Baldwin, *Poverty and Politics: The Rise and Decline of the Farm Security Administration* (Chapel Hill, N.C., 1967).
Betty Lindley and Ernest K. Lindley, *A New Deal for Youth: The Story of the National Youth Administration* (New York, 1938).
Timothy L. McConnell, *The Wagner Housing Act* (Chicago, 1957).
Gilbert Fite, *George N. Peek and the Fight for Farm Parity* (Norman, Okla., 1954).
Richard Polenberg, *Reorganizing Roosevelt's Government: The Controversy over Executive Reorganization* (Cambridge, Mass., 1966).
Bruce Bliven, "Boulder Dam," *New Republic* (December 11, 1935).
J. S. Auerbach, "New Deal, Old Deal, or Raw Deal: Some Thoughts on New Left Historiography," *Journal of Southern History* 25 (February 1969): 18–30.

THE DUST BOWL

R. Douglas Hurt, *The Dust Bowl: An Agricultural and Social History* (Chicago, 1981).
Walter J. Stein, *California and the Dust Bowl Migration* (Westport, Conn., 1973).
Donald Worster, *Dust Bowl: The Southern Plains in the 1930s* (New York, 1979).
F. Barrows Colton, "The Geography of a Hurricane," *National Geographic Magazine* (April 1939).

Chapter 6

ADVERSARY POLITICS

Alan Brinkley, *Voices of Protest: Huey Long, Father Coughlin, and the Great Depression* (New York, 1982).
T. Harry Williams, *Huey Long* (New York, 1969).
Sheldon Marcus, *Father Coughlin* (New York, 1973).
James Patterson, *Congressional Conservatism and the New Deal* (Lexington, Ky., 1967).
Geoffrey S. Smith, *To Save a Nation: American Countersubversives, the New Deal, and the Coming of World War II* (New York, 1973).
Marquis Childs, "They Hate Roosevelt," *Harper's Magazine* (May 1936).
——, "They Still Hate Roosevelt," *New Republic* (January 18, 1939).

NEW DEAL POLICIES

Ellis W. Hawley, *The New Deal and the Problem of Monopoly: A Study in Economic Ambivalence* (Princeton, N.J., 1966).

———, "The New Deal and Business" in John Braeman, Robert H. Bremner, and David Brody, eds., *The New Deal: The National Level* (Columbus, Ohio, 1975).

Chapter 7

WORKERS AND LABOR

James R. Green, *The World of the Worker* (New York, 1980).

David Brody, *Workers in Industrial America: Essays on the Twentieth Century Struggle* (New York, 1980).

Irving Bernstein, *The Lean Years: A History of the American Worker 1920–1933* (New York, 1983).

———, *The Turbulent Years: A History of the American Worker 1933–1941* (Boston, 1970).

———, *A Caring Society: The New Deal, the Worker, and the Great Depression* (New York, 1985).

Herbert R. Northrup, *Organized Labor and the Negro* (New York, 1944).

Matthew Josephson, *Sidney Hillman* (New York, 1952).

John Barnard, *Walter Reuther and the Rise of the Auto Workers* (Boston, 1982).

Sidney Fine, *Sit-Down: The General Motors Strike of 1936–37* (Ann Arbor, Mich., 1969).

———, *Frank Murphy: The Detroit Years* (Ann Arbor, Mich., 1975).

John W. Herever, *Which Side Are You On? The Harlan County Coal Miners 1931–39* (Champaign, Ill., 1978).

Melvyn Dubofsky and Warren Van Tine, *John L. Lewis: A Biography* (New York, 1977).

Melvyn Dubofsky, "Not So 'Turbulent Years': Another Look at the American 1930s," *Amerika Studies–America Studies* 71 (December 1984).

Bruce Bliven, "Sitting down in Flint," *New Republic* (January 27, 1937).

RADICAL MOVEMENTS

David A. Shannon, *The American Socialist Party* (New York, 1955).

Harvey Klehr, *The Heyday of American Communism* (New York, 1984).

Mark Navison, *Communists in Harlem During the Depression* (Champaign, Ill., 1983).

William Swanberg, *Norman Thomas—The Last Idealist* (New York, 1976).

James C. Duram, *Norman Thomas* (New York, 1974).

Harry Fleischman, *Norman Thomas* (New York, 1964).

Bernard K. Johnpoll, *Pacifist's Progress* (Chicago, 1970).

Philip S. Foner, *American Socialism and Black Americans* (Westport, Conn., 1977).

CLASSES AND ETHNIC GROUPS

Richard Polenberg, *One Nation Divisible—Class, Race, and Ethnicity in the United States Since 1938* (Harmondsworth, Middlesex, and New York, 1980), Chapters 1 and 2.

Maurice R. Stein, *The Eclipse of Community* (revised Princeton, N.J., 1972; first published 1960).

Ronald H. Bayor, *Neighbors in Conflict: The Irish, Germans, Jews, and Italians of New York City, 1929–1941* (Baltimore, 1978).

Federal Writers Project in the WPA, *The Italians of New York* (New York, 1938); *The Swedes and Finns in New Jersey* (Bayonne, 1938); *The Armenians in Massachusetts* (Boston, 1937).

Robert and Helen Lynd, *Middletown in Transition* (New York, 1937).

Mark Reisler, *By the Sweat of Their Brow: Mexican Immigrant Labor in the United States 1900–1940* (Westport, Conn., 1976).

Rodolfo Acuna, *Occupied America: A History of Chicanos* (New York, 1980).

Matt S. Meier and Feliciano Rivera, *The Chicanos* (New York, 1972).

WOMEN AND THE FAMILY

Carl Degler, *At Odds: Women and the Family in America from the Revolution to the Present* (New York and Oxford, 1980).

Sheila Rothman, *Woman's Proper Place: A History of Changing Ideals and Practices, 1870 to the Present* (New York, 1980; first published 1978).

Winifred D. Wandersee, *Women's Work and Family Values 1920–1940* (Cambridge, Mass., 1981).

William H. Chafe, *The American Woman: Her Changing Social, Economic, and Political Role* (New York, 1977; first published 1972).

Jacqueline Jones, *Labor of Love, Labor of Sorrow: Black Women, Work, and the Family from Slavery to the Present* (New York, 1985).

J. Stanley Lemons, *The Woman Citizen: Social Feminism in the 1920s* (Champaign, Ill., 1973).

Linda Gordon, *Woman's Body, Woman's Right: A Social History of Birth Control in America* (New York, 1976).

Susan Ware, *Beyond Suffrage: Woman in the New Deal* (Cambridge, Mass., 1982).

——, *Holding Their Own: American Women in the 1930s* (Boston, 1982).

Lois Scharf, *To Work and to Wed: Female Employment, Feminism, and the Great Depression* (Westport, Conn., 1980).

Glen H. Elder, Jr., *Children of the Great Depression: Social Change in Life Experience* (Chicago, 1984; first published 1974).

W. Andrew Achenbaum, *Shades of Gray: Old Age, American Values, and Federal Policies Since 1920* (Boston, 1982).

David H. Fischer, *Growing Old in America* (New York and Oxford, 1978).

INDIANS

David Murray, *Modern Indians: Native Americans in the Twentieth Century* (British Association for American Studies Pamphlets in American Studies 8, 1982).

Mary K. Grafmick, *Sociology of American Indians: A Critical Bibliography* (Bloomington, Ind., 1981).

Edward H. Spicer, *A Short History of the Indians of the United States* (New York, 1969).

Roger L. Nichols and George R. Adams, ed., *The American Indian: Past and Present* (Lexington, Mass., 1971).

Edgar S. Cahn, ed., *Our Brother's Keeper: The Indian in White America* (New York and Cleveland, 1969).

Alan L. Sorkin, *Indians and Federal Aid* (Washington, D.C., 1971).

Margaret Szasz, *Education and the American Indian: The Road to Self-Determination, 1928–1973* (Albuquerque, N.M., 1974).

Wilcomb E. Washburn, *Red Man's Land, White Man's Law: A Study of the Past and Present Status of the American Indian* (New York, 1971).

Kirke Kickingbird and Karen Ducheneaux, *100 Million Acres* (New York, 1973).

Russel L. Barsh and James Y. Henderson, *The Road: Indian Tribes and Political Liberty* (Berkeley and Los Angeles, 1980).

Stan Steiner, *The New Indians* (New York, 1968).

INDIANS AND THE NEW DEAL

John Collier, *From Every Zenith* (Denver, 1963).

Laurence C. Kelly, *The Assault on Assimilation: John Collier and the Origins of Indian Policy Reform* (Albuquerque, N.Mex., 1983).

Kenneth R. Philp, *John Collier's Crusade for Indian Reform* (Tucson, Ariz., 1977).

Donald L. Parman, *The Navajos and the New Deal* (New Haven, Conn., 1976).

Chapter 8

BLACK AMERICA

Lerone Bennett, Jr., *Before the Mayflower: A History of Black America* (Chicago, 1961).

Mary Frances Berry and John W. Blassingame, *Long Memory: The Black Experience in America* (New York, 1982).

L. Franklin Frazier, *The Negro in the United States* (Toronto, 1969; first published 1949, revised 1957).

Benjamin Quarles, *The Negro in the Making of America* (revised New York, 1969; first published 1964).

John White, *Black Leadership in America 1895–1968* (London and New York, 1985).

Joel Williamson, *The Crucible of Race: Black-White Relations in the American South Since Emancipation* (New York, 1984).

BOOKER T. WASHINGTON AND HIS CRITICS

Bernard A. Weisberger, *Booker T. Washington* (New York, 1972).

Louis R. Harlan, *Booker T. Washington: The Making of a Black Leader, 1865–1901* (New York and Oxford, 1972).

——, *Booker T. Washington: The Wizard of Tuskegee, 1901–1915* (New York and Oxford, 1983).

Hugh Hawkins, ed., *Booker T. Washington and His Critics* (Boston, 1974; first published 1962).

W.E.B. DUBOIS

Elliot Rudwick, *W.E.B. DuBois: Propagandist of the Negro Protest* (New York, 1969).

Francis L. Broderick, *W.E.B. DuBois: Negro Leader in a Time of Crisis* (Stanford, Ca., 1966; first published 1959).

Arnold Rampersad, *The Art and Imagination of W.E.B. DuBois* (London, 1976).

Rayford W. Logan, ed., *W.E.B. DuBois: A Profile* (New York, 1971).

E. M. Rudwick, "W.E.B. DuBois in the Role of *Crisis* Editor," *Journal of Negro History* 43 (1958), 214–40.

Mary Law Chafer, "W.E.B. DuBois' Concept of the Racial Problem in the United States," *Journal of Negro History* 41 (1956): 241–58.

MARCUS GARVEY AND THE UNIA

David Cronon, *Black Moses: The Story of Marcus Garvey and the Universal Negro Improvement Association* (Madison, Wis., 1955).

Theodore G. Vincent, *Black Power and the Garvey Movement* (San Francisco, 1972).

Tony Martin, *Race First: The Ideological and Organizational Struggles of Marcus Garvey and the UNIA* (Westport, Conn., 1976).

Robert G. Weisbord, *Ebony Kinship: Africa, Africans, and the Afro-American* (Westport, Conn., 1973).

Leonard E. Barrett, *Soul Force: African Heritage in Afro-American Religion* (New York, 1974).

Alphonso Pinkney, *Red, Black, and Green: Black Nationalism in the United States* (Cambridge, 1976).

Theodore Draper, *The Rediscovery of Black Nationalism* (New York, 1969).

Randall K. Burkett, *Garveyism as a Religious Movement: The Institutionalization of a Black Religion* (London, 1978).

Emory J. Tolbert, *The UNIA and Black Los Angeles: Ideology and Community in the Garvey Movement* (Los Angeles, 1980).

R. H. Brisbane, Jr., "Some New Light on the Garvey Movement," *Journal of Negro History* 36 (1951): 53–62.
C. S. Matthews, "Marcus Garvey Writes from Jamaica on the Mulatto Escape Hatch," *Journal of Negro History* 59 (1974): 170–76.

BLACK CULTURE IN THE NORTH

R. L. Kusmer, *A Ghetto Takes Shape: Black Cleveland, 1870–1930* (Evanston, Ill., 1978).
Gilbert Osofsky, *Harlem: The Making of a Ghetto, 1880–1930* (New York, 1963).
Nathan I. Huggins, *Harlem Renaissance* (New York, 1971).
Jervis Anderson, *Harlem: The Great Black Way, 1900–1950* (London, 1982).
Claude McKay, *Harlem: Negro Metropolis* (New York, 1968; first published 1940).
Roi Ottley, *"New World A-Coming"* (New York, 1968; first published 1943).
James Weldon Johnson, *Black Manhattan* (New York, 1968; first published 1930).
D. J. Hellwig, "Black Meets Black: Afro-American Reactions to West Indian Immigrants in the 1920s," *South Atlantic Quarterly* 77 (1978): 206–24.
Theodore Kornweibel, Jr., *No Crystal Stair: Black Life and the Messenger 1917–1928* (Westport, Conn., 1975).

WHITE OVER BLACK

Gunnar Myrdal, *An American Dilemma* (New York, 1944).
Morton Sosna, *In Search of the Silent South* (New York, 1977).
Charles S. Johnson, *Patterns of Negro Segregation* (New York, 1943).
Dan T. Carter, *Scottsboro: A Tragedy of the American South* (Baton Rouge, La., 1969).
Robert L. Zargrando, *The NAACP Crusade Against Lynching 1909–1950* (Philadelphia, 1980).
——, "The NAACP and a Federal Antilynching Bill, 1934–1940," *Journal of Negro History* 50 (April 1965).
Robert W. Dubay, "Mississippi and the Proposed Federal Anti-Lynching Bills of 1937–1938," *The Southern Quarterly* (October 1968): 73–87.

BLACKS AND THE NEW DEAL

Ralph Bunche, *The Political Status of the Negro in the Age of FDR* (Chicago, 1973).
John B. Kirby, *Black Americans in the Roosevelt Era: Liberalism and Race* (Knoxville, Tenn., 1980).
Nancy J. Weiss, *Farewell to the Party of Lincoln: Black Politics in the Age of FDR* (Princeton, 1983).
Harvard Sitkoff, *A New Deal for Blacks: The Emergence of Civil Rights as a National Issue,* vol. 1, *The Depression Decade* (New York, 1978).

Herbert Garfinkel, *When Negroes March: The March on Washington Movement in the Organizational Politics for FEPC* (Glencoe, Ill., 1959).

William H. Harris, "A. Philip Randolph as a Charismatic Leader, 1925–1941," *Journal of Negro History* 44 (1979): 301–15.

BLACK LITERATURE

Stephen J. Butterfield, *Black Autobiography in America* (Boston, 1975).

Addison Gayle, Jr., *The Way of the New World: The Black Novel in America* (New York, 1976).

Edward Margolies, *Native Sons: A Critical Study of Twentieth Century Black American Authors* (New York, 1968).

Chapter 9

RADIO

Erik Barnouw, *A Tower in Babel: A History of Broadcasting in the United States,* vol. 1, *to 1933* (New York, 1966).

——, *The Golden Web: A History of Broadcasting in the United States,* vol. II, *1933–1953* (New York, 1968).

Richard Levinson and William Link, *Stay Tuned* (New York, 1983).

Christopher Sterling and John M. Kitros, *Stay Tuned* (New York, 1978).

Philip T. Rosen, *The Modern Stentors: Radio Broadcasting and the Federal Government 1920–1933* (Westport, Conn., 1980).

Frank Buxton and Bill Owen, *The Big Broadcast 1920–1950* (a revised, expanded edition of *Radio's Golden Age*) (New York, 1972).

Hadley Cantril, *The Invasion from Mars: A Study in the Psychology of Panic, with the Complete Script of the Orson Welles Broadcast* (Princeton, N.J., 1940).

Alexander Kendrick, *Prime Time: The Life of Edward R. Murrow* (Boston, 1969).

Robert Lichello, *Edward R. Murrow: Broadcaster of Courage* (New York, 1972).

Robert Franklin Smith, *Edward R. Murrow — The War Years* (Kalamazoo, Mich., 1978).

Chapter 10

HOLLYWOOD AND THE MOVIES

Gerald Mast, *A Short History of the Movies* (revised New York, 1986; first published 1971).

Paul Michael, ed., *The American Movies Reference Book: The Sound Era* (Englewood Cliffs, N.J., 1970).

Lary May, *Screening Out the Past: The Birth of Mass Culture and the Motion Picture Industry* (revised Chicago, 1983; first published 1980).

Kevin Brownlow, *The Parade's Gone By* (New York, 1968).

Robert Sklar, *Movie-Made America: A Cultural History of American Movies* (New York, 1975).

Andrew Bergman, *We're in the Money: Depression America and Its Films* (New York, 1971).

Eugene Rosow, *Born to Lose: The Gangster Film in America* (New York, 1978).

Raymond Lee and B. C. Van Hecke, *Gangsters and Hoodlums: The Underworld in the Cinema* (New York, 1971).

James Agee, "Comedy's Greatest Era," *Agee on Film* (Boston, 1964), pp. 2–19.

DIRECTORS, MOGULS, AND STARS

Andrew Sarris, *The American Cinema: Directors and Directions, 1929–1968* (New York, 1968).

Iris Barry and Eileen Bowser, *D. W. Griffith: American Film Master* (New York, 1965).

Lillian Gish, *The Movies, Mr. Griffith, and Me* (Englewood Cliffs, N.J., 1969).

Charlie Chaplin, *My Autobiography* (New York, 1964).

David Robinson, *Chaplin: His Life and Art* (New York, 1985).

Isabel Quigley, *Charlie Chaplin: Early Comedies* (New York, 1968).

Mack Sennett, *King of Comedy* (New York, 1954).

Rudi Blesh, *Keaton* (New York, 1966).

Peter Cowie, *The Cinema of Orson Welles* (New York, 1965).

Robert Field, *The Art of Walt Disney* (New York, 1943).

Stephen Farber and Marc Green, *Hollywood Dynasties* (New York, 1984).

Philip French, *The Movie Moguls: An Informal History of the Hollywood Tycoons* (London, 1969; Harmondworth, Middlesex, 1971).

Bob Thomas, *King Cohn* (New York, 1967).

——, *Thalberg: Life and Legend* (New York, 1969).

——, *Astaire: The Man, the Dancer* (New York, 1984).

George Eells and Stanley Musgrove, *Mae West* (New York and London, 1984).

John Grierson, "Directors of the Thirties," *Film: An Anthology* (Berkeley and Los Angeles, 1966).

Chapter 11

THE LOST GENERATION

Alfred Kazin, *On Native Grounds* (New York, 1983; first published 1939).

——, *An American Procession* (New York, 1984).

——, *Starting Out in the Thirties* (New York, 1980).

Robert Crunden, *From Self to Society: Transitions in American Thought, 1919–1941* (Englewood Cliffs, N.J., 1972).

Malcolm Cowley, *Exile's Return: A Literary Odyssey of the 1920s* (Magnolia, Mass., 1983; first published 1934).

Frederick Hoffman, *The Twenties: American Writing in the Postwar Decade* (revised New York, 1965; first published 1962).
Edmund Wilson, *The Twenties* (New York, 1975).
——, *The Thirties* (New York, 1982).
Jerre Mangione, *The Dream and the Deal: The Federal Writers' Project 1935–1943* (New York, 1974).
Richard Wightman Fox, *Reinhold Niebuhr* (New York, 1986).

THE IMPACT OF FREUD

Ernest Jones, *The Life and Work of Sigmund Freud,* 3 vols. (New York, 1953–57; abbreviated edition in one volume edited by Lionel Trilling and Steven Marcus, New York, 1961).
Walter Lippmann, "Freud and the Layman," *New Republic* 2 (April 17, 1915); supp. 9–10.
A. A. Brill, "The Introduction and Development of Freud's Work in the United States," *American Journal of Sociology* 45 (November 1939): 318–25.

MUSIC, MUSICIANS, AND THE PERFORMING ARTS

Stanley Sadie, ed., *New Grove Dictionary of Music and Musicians,* 2 vols. (6th edition, New York and London, 1980).
Paul Oliver, *The Blues Tradition* (New York, 1970).
Marshall Stearns, *The Story of Jazz* (New York, 1956).
Aaron Copland and Vivian Perlis, *Copland: 1900 Through 1942* (New York, 1984).
Joseph Horowitz, *Understanding Toscanini: How He Became an American Culture-God and Helped Create a New Audience for Old Music* (New York, 1987).
Russell Lynes, *The Lively Audience: A History of the Visual and Performing Arts in America, 1890–1950* (New York, 1985).
Jay Gold, ed., *The Swing Era (1936–37: The Movies, Between Vitaphone and Video; 1940–41: How It Was to Be Young Then; 1941–42: Swing as a Way of Life)* (Time-Life Records, New York, 1970).
Charles W. Stein, ed., *American Vaudeville as Seen by Its Contemporaries* (New York, 1984).
Stanley Green, *The Great Clowns of Broadway* (New York, 1984).
Tony Thomas, *That's Dancing* (New York, 1984).
Otis Ferguson, "The Spirit of Jazz," *New Republic* (December 30, 1936).
Richard Hasbany, "Bromidic Parables: The American Musical Theatre during the Second World War," *The Journal of Popular Culture* 6 (Spring 1973).
Timothy B. Donovan, "Oh, What a Beautiful Mornin': The Musical *Oklahoma!* and the Popular Mind in 1943," *Journal of Popular Culture* 8 (Winter 1974).

Chapter 12

PAINTING AND SCULPTURE

Lloyd Goodrich and John Baur, *American Art of Our Century* (New York, 1961).

Sam Hunter, *American Art of the Twentieth Century* (New York, 1972).

Jean Lipman, *What is American in American Art* (New York, 1963).

Jack Burnham, *Beyond Modern Sculpture* (New York, 1963).

Clement Greenberg, *Art and Culture: Critical Essays* (Boston, 1961).

Richard D. McKinzie, *The New Deal for Artists* (Princeton, N.J., 1973).

Serge Guilbaut, translated by Arthur Goldhammer, *How New York Stole the Idea of Modern Art—Abstract Expressionism, Freedom, and the Cold War* (Chicago, 1985).

Susan C. Larsen, "The American Abstract Artists: A Documentary History, 1936–1941," *Archives of American Art Journal* 14 (1974): 2–7.

ARCHITECTURE

Wayne Andrews, *Architecture, Ambition, and Americans* (London, 1984).

John Burchard and Albert Bush-Brown, *The Architecture of America* (Boston, 1961).

William Coles and Henry George Reed, Jr., ed., *Architecture in America: A Battle of Styles* (New York, 1961).

James Fitch, *American Building: The Forces That Shape It* (Boston, 1948).

Talbot Hamlin, *The American Spirit in Architecture* (New Haven, Conn., 1926).

Huson Jackson, *A Guide to New York Architecture, 1650–1952* (New York, 1952).

Charles Jencks, *Modern Movements in Architecture* (second edition, Harmondsworth, Middlesex, and New York, 1985; first published 1973).

Lewis Mumford, *Sticks and Stones: A Study of American Architecture and Civilization* (New York, 1924).

Nikolaus Pevsner, *Pioneers of Modern Design* (New York, 1949).

Vincent Scully, *American Architecture and Urbanism* (New York, 1969).

RAYMOND HOOD AND FRANK LLOYD WRIGHT

Raymond Hood, *Raymond M. Hood* (New York, 1931).

Arthur Norton, *Raymond M. Hood* (New York, 1931).

Frank Lloyd Wright, *An Autobiography* (New York, 1932).

——, *Writings and Buildings* (New York, 1960).

Vincent Scully, *Frank Lloyd Wright* (New York, 1969).

Henry-Russell Hitchcock, *In the Nature of Materials, 1887–1941: The Buildings of Frank Lloyd Wright* (New York, 1942).

Brendon Grill, *Many Masks: A Life of Frank Lloyd Wright* (New York, 1987).

Chapter 13

AMERICA AND WORLD AFFAIRS

Foster Rhea Dulles, *America's Rise to World Power 1898–1954* (New York, 1963; first published 1954).

Richard W. Leopold, *The Growth of American Foreign Policy* (New York, 1962).

Robert H. Ferrell, *American Diplomacy in the Great Depression: Hoover-Stimson Foreign Policy, 1929–1933* (New Haven, Conn., 1957).

———. *Peace in Their Time: The Origins of the Kellogg-Briand Pact* (New York, 1969).

Warren I. Cohen, *The American Revisionists: The Lessons of Intervention in World War I* (Chicago, 1967).

Charles Chatfield, *For Peace and Justice: Pacifism in America 1914–1941* (Knoxville, Tenn., 1971).

Anthony Sampson, *The Seven Sisters* (New York and London, 1976).

———, *Empires of the Sky: The Politics, Contests, and Cartels of World Airlines* (London and New York, 1985).

Merlo Pusey, *Charles Evans Hughes,* 2 vols. (New York, 1951), vol. 2.

Herbert Feis, *The Diplomacy of the Dollar: First Era, 1919–1932* (Baltimore, 1950).

Charles Beard, "The American Invasion of Europe," *Harper's Magazine* 158 (March 1929): 470–79.

LATIN AMERICA AND THE GOOD NEIGHBOR

Bryce Wood, *The Making of the Good Neighbor Policy* (New York, 1961).

———, *The United States and Latin American Wars, 1932–1942* (New York, 1966).

E. David Cronon, *Josephus Daniels in Mexico* (Madison, Wis., 1960).

Chapter 14

ISOLATION AND INTERVENTION

Robert Dalek, *Franklin D. Roosevelt and American Foreign Policy, 1932–1945* (New York and Oxford, 1979).

Wayne S. Cole, *Roosevelt and the Isolationists 1932–1945* (Lincoln, Neb., 1983).

John E. Wiltz, *From Isolation to War, 1931–1941* (Arlington Heights, Ill., 1968).

Julius W. Pratt, *Cordell Hull* (Totowa, N.J., 1964).

Basil Rauch, *Roosevelt: From Munich to Pearl Harbor* (New York, 1975; first published 1950 and 1965).

Walter Johnson, *The Battle Against Isolationism* (New York, 1973; first published 1944).

Warren F. Kimball, *The Most Unsordid Act: Lend-Lease 1939–1941* (Baltimore, 1969).

——. *Franklin D. Roosevelt and the World Crisis 1937–45* (Lexington, Mass., 1974).

T. R. Fehrenbach, *F.D.R.'s Undeclared War* (New York, 1967).

Robert A. Divine, *The Illusion of Neutrality* (Chicago, 1962).

Robert A. Divine, *The Reluctant Belligerent: American Entry into World War II* (New York, 1976; first published 1965).

Gordon W. Prange, *At Dawn We Slept: The Untold Story of Pearl Harbor* (New York, 1981).

Wayne S. Cole, "American Entry in World War II: A Historiographical Appraisal," *Mississippi Valley Historical Review* 43 (March 1957): 575–617.

INDEX

INDIVIDUALISM RECONSIDERED

INDIVIDUALISM

David Riesman

RECONSIDERED

AND OTHER ESSAYS

The Free Press, Glencoe, Illinois

TO MY WIFE

TO MY WIFE

Contents

Preface

IN MAKING the selection of essays for this book, I decided to omit all articles published before 1946 when, having given up law teaching, I came to the University of Chicago. I have included most of my articles contributed to fifteen journals and half a dozen symposium volumes between 1947 and 1953. I am indebted to all these original sources for permission to reprint as well as for their original hospitality and in some cases, notably *Psychiatry* and *Commentary* and my article in *Years of the Modern,* helpful editorial criticism. I am also indebted to Reuel Denney, who took a major share in the research and writing on the football article, for his consent to its reprinting here; likewise to Nathan Glazer for allowing me to reprint, in a single revised piece, two articles we had jointly written on public opinion. My wife is co-author of the article on "Movies and Audiences," and her help at every step of the making and editing of these articles has been extensive.

The articles appear, for the most part, as they did originally, with a few cuts here and there and an occasional word changed or phrase clarified.

Mrs. Claudia Kren helped prepare the manuscript for the publisher and the latter, my friend Jeremiah Kaplan, did much to encourage this book and clarify its purposes.

D. R.

Chicago, Illinois
October, 1953

I.

INTRODUCTION

IN ONE of his speeches Justice Holmes remarks that he would like before he dies to comment on all the great questions of the law, while all he could encompass are some thousand cases, many of them petty. To be sure, he used some of those cases for obiter dicta on some burning philosophical and social issues, but he was still hedged in by the passivity of the role of the judge, who must await what litigants bring before him and decide, if he is conscientious (as Holmes wasn't always), at retail rather than wholesale. At the same time, the occasions provided by litigants may widen a judge's scope, may take him in the course of his occupation away from his preoccupations. As I looked over my own essays and reviews, including unpublished ones buried in files, in preparation for this volume, I was at first dismayed by the "scatter" of so many tentative themes begun and not returned to—some of them occasioned by specific requests which I should have had the strength to dismiss.

What I have written, for the most part, seems linked less by topic than by a certain attitude, best summed up in "Values in Context." That article concluded with the motto of William Blake I have adopted as my own: "When I tell any Truth, it is not for the sake of Convincing those who do not know it, but the sake of defending those that do." This implies a defense of people from themselves, as well as from outside pressures. To do this I must know something about the audiences reached by what I say. For instance, when I published in 1942 a monograph on "Civil Liberties in a Period of Transition," in which I criticized a number of traditional civil liberty assumptions (such as the "clear and present danger" test), I was writing for those already on the side of civil liberties, not for the unenlightened. And so I was very happy when I learned that the American Civil Liberties Union had distributed copies to its board; but when asked to debate with Roger Baldwin in a public meeting I declined because I felt that before a large lay audience I would prefer to support Baldwin on certain major issues rather than to attack him on minor ones. Indeed, I believe that when issues are complex, one must write for a special audience, because one can't say everything at once.

Not long ago *The Lonely Crowd* brought me a critical letter from a woman in North Dakota; she wrote:

"I am not a Dr. I never went to college, I have not even finished High

9

School, I am only a nurses aid, and I like things simple and clear. All really great things, characters and thoughts are simple and clear. . . ."

Lack of clarity may sometimes be the result of confused ideas. But it may also be the result of an attempt to speak to some audiences to the exclusion of others. A writer may pitch his discourse at a certain level, in a certain vocabulary or metaphoric language for that purpose. Indeed, for reasons just given, there have been times when I regretted that *The Lonely Crowd* was not more inaccessible. Thus, there is a section in it dealing with tendencies in a now traditional sort of progressive education: I criticize the frequent "groupiness" of teachers, their lack of concern for intellectual content, their preoccupation with watery, presumably tolerance-breeding "social studies." As it happened, publication of the book coincided with a renewed drive against "Deweyism" and progressive education generally; I was dismayed to find myself quoted (or misquoted) by angry people in their all too easy onslaught against "new-fangled" notions in the public schools. Dismayed because, of all occupational groups, school teachers are among the most vulnerable; under attack, often from virulent reactionaries, they were hardly in a mood for truly critical self-examination. Despite what seemed to me reasonable caution, I had furnished *outside* ammunition against them. In his book *Persecution and the Art of Writing*, Leo Strauss argues that political philosophers and other writers have engaged in a form of concealed exposition to avoid either punishment for their views or their spread in untoward quarters. Whether Strauss' interpretation is correct or not in any particular case, the problem he deals with is real enough for me, less because of the tyranny of the powerful, who probably do not read me, than because of what might be deemed "the tyranny of the powerless" over their group—the tyranny of beleaguered teachers, liberals, Negroes, women, Jews, intellectuals, and so on, over each other. These are my principal audiences and the power of these audiences to intimidate their own constituencies is a theme of many of the papers in the next two sections.

Naturally, I do not alter my critical appraisals of contemporary schools because reactionaries are also on the warpath; rather, I try to present my views in such a way as to carry challenge to the complacency of reactionaries if they should chance upon them. Unlike some of the men whom Strauss discusses, I do not a priori divide mankind into an elite which can understand, and a mass which needs to be fobbed off, and I am hostile even to the best excuses for censoring ideas.

"Individualism Reconsidered," the essay which has lent this book its title, may also serve to exemplify my contextual view of the intellectual's role. If one should compare it with the essay on civil liberties just mentioned, one would find in the latter (as well as in "Equality and Social Structure," also published in 1942) an effort to show some of the limitations of laissez-faire liberalism and individualism in the realm of ideas. Both of the earlier essays emphasize the cultural conditioning of thought; both aim to put civil liberties doctrines in the perspective of the sociology of knowledge. To some extent I have changed my views since then; to some extent, the world has changed, and "groupism" become ever more of a danger; but also, to some extent, my audiences have changed. The earlier essays were written when I was still a law professor, addressing colleagues who appeared slow to recognize the social-psychological roots of opinion—colleagues, often enough, still immured in the heavenly city of the eighteenth-century philosophers. In contrast, "Individualism Reconsidered," like most of the essays in this volume, was written with an audience of social scientists (including historians and philosophers) mainly in mind—groups which, as I see them, have sometimes been all too inclined to overemphasize the values of collective or folkish life and to damn the individualism they find rampant in bourgeois, industrial, urban society.

Towards my lacunae of training and erudition, my new-found colleagues, the social scientists, have been more generous and hospitable than I should have expected. Though I first dipped into the study of the social sciences as a law student (attending Carl J. Friedrich's courses as well as those of some Harvard economists), I have learned much of what I have put into these essays from my colleagues at Chicago. Moreover, my students at Chicago, free of immediate vocational aims, have been willing to join me in learning how to study society—though to be sure many of them, bent on immediate reform, have been impatient with my skepticism, which they considered a form of delaying tactics. The atmosphere is different from that even of the best law schools where both students and faculty are after the "straight dope" (though they define it differently) and are all too clear as to how to get it. While my legal colleagues had been eager to facilitate my research, the diversity of aims had made difficult the sort of colleagueship that I found on leaving the law. In coming to Chicago, I was in search of colleagues with whom it would not be necessary to spend time explaining and justifying one's indulgence in what Veblen termed "idle curiosity," colleagues who are heirs of a longer tradition of cosmopolitan disinterestedness. A number of my articles also reflect my training in psychoanalysis (primarily with Erich Fromm, and to a very minor extent with Ernest Schachtel and the late Harry Stack Sullivan of the Washington School of Psychiatry). Much of my work is in the "neo-Freudian" tradition of these analysts. Only briefly represented in the final section of this book, it has involved the effort to relate social structure to character structure, and to bring such psychoanalytic methods as the "depth interview" and interpretation of dreams and folk tales out of the consulting room and into the study of large-scale social systems. And, needless to say, this effort is part of a vast movement under way for several decades in social anthropology, social psychology, and sociology.

Implicit in what I have said is the belief that social science can no more be divorced from values than from other contexts. Much as I defend "idle curiosity" against other imperatives for research, I know this value too is contextual and that it takes effort if one is to become aware of one's biases and to make use of them in what one undertakes. No artist or scientist needs to seek "engagement" when he cannot help it: a measure of disinterestedness is, indeed, one of the great and fragile values which the Western world has achieved.

A generation ago, however, when social science was still struggling to free itself from theology and social work (from socialism, too), even the oversanguine efforts to establish a "value-free" social science made good pragmatic sense.[1] Social scientists, finding their professional passion to lie in casting a cold eye, could in this way disassociate themselves from American reformism and the optimism about the social process it usually implied. To get rid of the old fuddy-duddy moralists aroused the zest of the Young Turks who marched under such banners as "operationalism." Their work was essential in freeing American social science from much sentimentality and highly ethnocentric preaching.

For my part, I want to make my evaluative position clear, or at least to flag the reader with my prejudices. (Even so, scrupulousness in self-revelation can very well run into all the ambiguities of "sincerity" which I take up in "Values in Context.")

Some social scientists have sought escape from terms which common usage has loaded with values, escape into manufactured symbolism so lacking in overtones as to avoid connotations of praise or

---

1. When I read Max Weber's influential discussions of the place of values in the selection but not the treatment of problems, there comes to my mind the picture of an imposing German professor bewailing Versailles and urging his students to patriotic hysteria—it is against such that Weber contended. In this country, outside the ex cathedra context in which Weber wrote, his fine-spun distinctions are correspondingly less useful: in so pluralistic a country as ours, and in one so unlikely to be swayed by professors, there may perhaps be less danger than in Germany from their succumbing to a particular political program and smuggling it into their work.

blame. In the spirit of certain schools of logical positivism, they want to make only "meaningful" statements and only purely denotative ones. But, in my opinion, the relation of social science to its subjects, who are also its audience, forbids any such easy undialectical answer to the problem of the researcher's ethical judgments. Terminological opacity will itself be taken as a judgment upon the world, perhaps a manipulative, frightened, or unsympathetic one. Deadpan symbols may symbolize a deadly determinism in the researcher. Literate peoples are going to read what is said about them, no matter how many verbal formulae are set up as barriers, and what they cannot understand they may aggressively misunderstand. Communication involves "noise," redundancy—and overtones. And beyond these problems of misunderstanding lies the further point that all our understanding of society is in my opinion metaphorical or analogical in some sense. Among our most fruitful intellectual tools are those metaphors which remind us by their very nature—even their very outrageousness, as for instance Freud's metaphoric use of Greek mythology—that we are abstracting and selecting (not simply "inducting" and not simply model-building). Contrary to the situation of a generation ago, we live, I am inclined to think, in an era of a "safe and sane" Fourth of July and a "safe and sane" sociology, though the world itself has hardly got safer and saner in the interim. Even my own obscurities of thought, my unresolved judgments and uncontrolled overtones, reflect in part a necessary and inevitable tension between life and reportage.

II.

INDIVIDUALISM AND ITS CONTEXT

IN ESSAYS on the "nerve of failure," written in 1946-7 ("We Happy Few," "Community Plans and Utopia," and "'Minority' Living"), I am still persuaded that Americans are dominated by the success ethic; I am thinking of people who are jockeying for wealth and power. The self-abasement of avant-garde intellectuals that I criticize in "We Happy Few" struck me a few years ago as a minority reaction, not yet influential in American culture at large. That is, my picture of what was going on in the United States carried some hangover from the 20s and 30s. And of course it should, for the country has not changed overnight. Nevertheless, my later writings are less acrid and satiric; there is a somewhat more sanguine attitude toward American culture.

Throughout the articles in this and the following section I am defending individualism (of a certain sort) and being critical of conformity (of a certain sort). Yet I am perfectly sure that I would not be attacking "groupism" in America if I could not rely on its durable achievements—it is just these that make individualism possible. I attempt to deal with such shifting contexts of judgment in "Values in Context," the first article in this section. It was delivered as an address at a conference on Science and Human Values at Mt. Holyoke College.

"Individualism Reconsidered" and "The Saving Remnant" try to grapple in brief compass with intricate questions of salience and causation in the shaping of the modern temper. I feel that in this whole area we profit from many different interpretations. We know neither what produces autonomy in individual children nor independence in the social order; it is easier to locate blockages than to propose practicable remedies.

It is to this very issue that the paper on "Community Plans and Utopia" is directed, for there I ask why we have allowed ourselves to focus so exclusively on our social fears rather than our social hopes —a focus not entirely explained by the grim events reported in any day's press (more accurately, the reports themselves are a selection, and their availability reflects as well as shapes our times).

In this essay, I suggest that the utopian tradition has gone sour because of collectivist, especially Communist, abuse, and gone stale (especially in America) because so many of our earlier hopes for equality and abundance have been attained—leaving us either to try to put meaning back into outdated struggles or to find a political agenda not in planning for a better future, but in postponing a worse one. Many writers and statesmen have pointed out that America now has world responsibilities for the less fortunately situated countries, but it also needs pointing out that we have responsibilities to ourselves, to improve the quality of our own daily life, even while we concern ourselves with the miseries of the less fortunate parts of the globe. Otherwise, all we shall succeed in doing is to level down. Similar issues, of course, face the Socialists in Britain and in Scandinavia, for whom the old-time Fabian and social-democratic slogans have so patently worn thin.

1. Values in Context

LYMAN BRYSON, examining a few weeks ago the papers submitted for the annual [1952] Conference on Science, Philosophy and Religion, observed that only four out of forty-five dealt with values in any concrete and empirical way; the rest were hortatory, many of them assuming that the academicians there assembled understood each other and needed only some formula of belief to impose values on a world that had presumably lost them. Reading a number of these same papers, I also was struck by the frequent assumption that values in general, not merely some values or the speakers' values, had gotten lost or dissipated; moreover, that without consensus on values, our democratic society would not hold together. I see no convincing evidence for either of these assumptions. It seems plain to me that men cannot live without values, without preferences and choices, without the vocabulary of motives that we partly learn and partly teach ourselves. Those who bewail the loss of values seem disingenuously to bewail the loss—that is, the replacement—of their own values; and in many cases I believe this applies quite literally: for many of the men whom I find to be most hysterical about the loss of values appear to me to lack confidence in their own ongoing processes of valuation; they do not enjoy making choices, and their effort to escape from freedom is writ larger than life in their overly subjective appraisal of the society as a whole.

Something of this sort, I think, must lie behind the second assumption also, namely, that agreement on fundamental values is essential for democratic functioning. The attempt to enforce such agreement seems to me a good way to bring on civil war; and it is important to study those institutions in our society which allow society to function precisely in the face of profound disagreements on fundamentals. One of these institutions, I suggest, is the city bosses and their machines: these act as brokers among competing urban values, based as they are on religious, ethnic, regional, occupational and other identifications. These bosses can trade a park in a middle-class section for a symbolically important Italian judgeship, and otherwise keep a tolerable peace by appropriate pay-offs from the spoils of American productivity. The current attempt to unify the country against municipal patronage and bossism seems to me dangerous, because by enforcing an ideological unity on politics we threaten with extinction a few men, soaked in gravy we can well spare, who protect our ideological pluralism.

To be sure, there is a fundamental value underlying my own view, which is that men should not be forced by the needs of society to give more than conditional co-operation to specific, short-term goals. Thus, I think we can ask people to be vaccinated, but not to believe in its efficacy, or in science, or in long life. And on the whole I prefer that we win people's co-operation by offering concrete advantages—including such personal growth as they may gain from the co-operation itself—without asking them what their fundamental values are. (Incidentally, the Communists in our midst have made this program difficult, not only because their fellow-workers in the usual front organizations naively assume that since the Communists share the work they also share the liberal and humane values alleged to be involved in the joint enterprise, but even more because the country at large assumes that it is always the fellow-workers and never the Communists who are the dupes: the fact often is that the Communists are gulled into doing the work on the improvident speculation that they will win converts or make some other gain.) To put the matter another way, I believe it a fallacy to assume that people can co-operate only if they understand each other (this is the illusion of many semanticists), or if they like each other, or if they share certain preconceptions. The glory of modern large-scale democratically-tending society is that it has developed the social inventions—such as the market, the practices and skills of negotiation, and the many other devices which allow us to put forward in a given situation only part of ourselves—which allow us to get along and, usually, not to kill each other while retaining the privilege of private conscience and of veto over many requests made of us by our fellow men. No doubt, for this to occur there has to be some *procedural* consensus, some shared values of a very general sort like due process, and among sufficient people in strategic locations, some less-than-fanatical attitude toward compromise and even corruption. But this is far from saying that we would be better off if we could go forward by going back to some partly mythical state of value-agreement based on choicelessness.

§ II

THE PSYCHOANALYTIC psychologist can come at this same problem in another way. His clinical work makes him aware that in an individual values are contextual, with each value-element having a very different loading depending on the *Gestalt*, on the whole. It did not,

of course, take Freud to teach us that, for instance, the morally indignant person is often a sadist whose own impulses were his first
victims. But the analytic method does allow us to delineate such
observations in more detail and in more complexity. Let me take as
an illustration the virtue of sincerity, which is becoming a salient
and unquestioned value, so far as I can see, among a whole generation
of young people. One gifted boy of fifteen, whose interview I have
analyzed in detail elsewhere, stated that his best trait was sincerity,
and proved the point by a gallant effort to be totally frank with the
interviewer. It did not occur to him that such sincerity puts pressure on others in a social situation to be equally sincere: it is coercive, and tends to break down etiquettes which we use to protect
our emotional life from strangers, from over-inquisitive relatives and
friends, and at times from ourselves. Nor did it occur to him that his
very frankness concealed some of its driving motives, not only this
coercive one but also another equally coercive insistence that he be
regarded and valued for his truth-telling. He tells us everything about
himself without reserve—everything but what he doesn't know, namely,
that he wants the credit, or at least some response, for this very
frankness.

In this connection, it is interesting to note the study of values
made in Vienna some years ago by Else Frenkel-Brunswik. She
asked people what values they thought they possessed and then asked
their associates to rank them on the same values. And she discovered,
for example, that people who said they were sincere were not thought
to be so by their friends; rather, those who said "I try to be sincere
but I am often insincere," were regarded by others as sincere. Such
observations confirm my feeling of wanting to be particularly cautious when meeting someone who says, "I am going to be frank with
you."

But of course it would be going much too far to say that the
contemporary cult of sincerity is simply negative, a regression from
the superior age of manners. The *opportunity* to be sincere, particularly between men and women, is a tremendous achievement over the
past; the *opportunity* to convert a stranger into a friend in a Pullman car or academic convention is an American blessing; the growth,
through the practice of sincerity, of the One Big Union, the union
of sinners, has lifted intolerable burdens of moral underprivilege
from the isolated and the inarticulate. Moreover, in a big rich country, lifted above the needs of peasant guile and tenement-house suspiciousness, millions of us can afford sincerity, just as in many parts
of the country we can afford to leave our cars unlocked and would
in any case suffer—unlike the Italian victims of *The Bicycle Thief*

—only moderate discomfort from an instance of misplaced confidence.

My point rather is to show how a trait like sincerity must be studied in the life-plan of given individuals and of society as a whole before we conclude that it is a value we want to encourage or discourage. My own guess is that sincerity is today so much taken for granted as an unequivocal blessing that it becomes important, as it never was at an earlier historical point, to discover some of its ethical ambiguities and limitations. To do so may help curb the tyranny of the self-styled sincere over the rest of us.

§ III

I WANT to turn now from the problem of appraising the values of an individual or of an age to the analogous problem of evaluating the ethical positions of the great thinkers of the past and present. For here, too, I believe a contextual analysis is necessary if we as intellectuals are to live in some productive tension with our times and not merely to ride the waves of the past or of the future. Let me begin by taking as an illustration the great controversy opened up by the debate between Condorcet and Godwin on one side and Malthus on the other. The former, trusting to the increasing ability of science to make nature produce, believed that an age of abundance was dawning on mankind, and that the march of history was a march of progress toward human perfectibility. Malthus lacked trust. He was more impressed with the ability of fecund, improvident men and women to produce children than with the possibilities of technological advance. The only way he could see out of nature's trap was an ascetic "moral restraint," and sociological invention, and for this way he had scant hopes. Moreover, he was perhaps the first economist to foresee that depressions might be permanent. For him there was no question about perfectibility: man had his choice between late and frugal marriage, coupled with intensive work, and the various miseries from war to pestilence by which in the past the adult population was periodically aborted. His book on population was written as a reply to Godwin, Condorcet and the other utopians of his day.

Now it seems to me, though I may well be mistaken, that Godwin and Condorcet, though in their personal lives badly treated, were to a considerable extent in line with late eighteenth-century ideas: they might be vilified, but they did not stand alone. By contrast, Malthus, whose personal fortunes were much more secure, was heretical; and, indeed, his views on depressions remained so for many years. Trying to look at these thinkers in terms of their own day, I respect and admire both sides, and do not feel called upon to take a stand with one and against the other: each made a decisive and stimulating contribution to our understanding. However, when the argument shifts to our own day, my attitude shifts to some extent also. Moving in circles where Malthus is greatly esteemed, and Condorcet and Godwin, if regarded at all, sneered at as childish Enlightenment utopians possessed with *hubris*, my tendency in teaching and writing is, without derogating Malthus, to emphasize the courage which Condorcet and Godwin also had, and the importance today of faith that nature, including human nature, is not a trap, though we can make it one. On the other hand, where complacency still rules, there one would want to stress Malthus, and some of the neo-Malthusians are probably quite useful in this direction. But where, as in so many intellectual circles, there prevails an anti-Enlightenment temper which prides itself on its realism, its refusal to share any dreams of man's potentially fine future, there a reappraisal of Godwin and Condorcet is desirable—taking account, however, of all that Malthus and his followers have taught us.

§ IV

I MUST now confess—in an effort to communicate and to be relevant more than to be sincere—that what I have to say here has been guided in some part by a similar feeling for context. When I received this invitation, I assumed—perhaps unfairly—that the balance of opinion and assumption here would turn out not to be too radically different from the one that Lyman Bryson reported on for the Conference on Science, Philosophy and Religion; and I also assumed that I had myself been asked because the planners were themselves pluralists, at least to start with. So I felt it incumbent on me to stress that side of my thought which is skeptical about absolutes and, in a day when very few admit being relativists, to illustrate some of the possible advantages of a relative approach to values. By the same token, I would have done somewhat differently had I been asked to talk on scientific method before the American psychological or sociological societies; there, confronted with many who still believe in a value-free social science and a deceptively neutral operationalism, I might have stressed not only the importance of the study of values, but also the inescapable and creative role of values in the scientific process itself.

When I conduct myself in this way, a host of problems immediately arises, and in discussing them I may be able to clarify somewhat our elusive topic. In the first place, I may be mistaken about my audience: I may be hardening their prejudices when I am seeking to be liberating. I try to cope with this by insisting, when I discuss such matters, that there be an extended question period, or its sublimation in a panel like ours here; the question period may help correct my misapprehensions about the audience and simultaneously their misapprehensions about me. But it is not enough to know the audience; one must also know *their* context. They may be so buffeted by their adversaries that they need, at least temporarily, to have their prejudices confirmed rather than shaken. For instance, girl students at some of our liberal universities need occasionally to be told that they are not utterly damned if they discover within themselves anti-Negro or anti-Semitic reactions—else they may expiate their guilt by trying to solve the race question in marriage. But even that judgment has to be made in terms of the wider social context—in this case, a judgment that the lot of Negroes, let alone Jews, in America is not always so utterly desperate as to call for the ruthless sacrifice of protective prejudices. And, as I have indicated, each of these judgments of context, from the audience out in widening circles, may be mistaken.

In the second place, I may be mistaken about my own motives as a speaker. What may on the surface appear to me as my courageous choice of an unorthodox and unpopular position may turn out on closer examination to be a form of exhibitionism. Or I may be more conciliatory than is warranted because I want to be liked. More probably, I may be falling into the all-too-common academic pitfall of finding and clinging to a pet heresy, proud of my intransigence, while failing to realize that it has become, if not a popular orthodoxy, at least the vested heresy of an in-group. I must therefore try to keep up with myself, as I develop, as well as with my audience, and to watch for any symptoms showing that I prefer to shock or startle people rather than to enlighten them. At another level, I cannot help but be aware that a shifting position which takes a stand only against the need to take a stand on many exigently argued issues may have terrible moral pitfalls in convenient uncommitment—I say I cannot help this awareness because all my adult life I have been besieged by people who wanted to convert me to their loyalty and thought me cowardly for refusing to join. It has taken me a long time to recognize the possible values, including courage, behind such refusals. But still, this issue too has to be re-examined. To complicate matters further, I know that ambiguity is fashionable today in the literary world, so my plunging into it as a pedagogic device may not be entirely disinterested. Let me hasten to add, however, that I don't think I or anyone else need be faultless before opening his mouth, for the history of thought teaches us how many men were productive for the "wrong" or at least very neurotic motives, and vice versa.

Discussion may help somewhat, as I have said, to clarify an audi-

ence for me and me for an audience. Even so, someone is likely to
ask me: "Don't you think so-and-so is true, irrespective of time and
place? Isn't taking your audience into account a complicated form
of lying?" A somewhat more subtle questioner may ask: "Don't you
place yourself above your audience, and even above the ideas you
deal with, by making yourself into a governor or thermostat for the
society, trying to prevent its going to extremes? Can't 'extremes' be
right? And doesn't this conduct make you, after all, a servo-mechan-
ism, dependent for your own motion on that in the larger society?"
All I can do now is to begin an answer to some of these questions—
to deal with all of them would mean to discuss the function of intellectuals in our society; the possibilities of democratizing that function so that any number can play; and indeed a discussion of the play
itself, of the play of the mind, of what Veblen termed "idle curiosity."
But I can say right off what is perhaps already clear, that I do not
take a relativist position on *all* issues—that would be another abso-
lutism—but only on some. Santayana said of James that he didn't
think any questions were ever settled, whereas for me some questions
are settled, some positions are indefensible. I cannot, for instance,
agree that Plato, or anyone else, makes a tenable argument, in any
context I can conceive of, for banishing poets. And while I can see
that sadism when incorporated into certain personality types can be
socially useful, for example if sublimated into a surgeon's work, I
react negatively to the trait even in ameliorative contexts, and violently against it in destructive ones. In fact, destructiveness in its
grosser and its subtler forms—when, for example, I see students'
confidence that they can learn something being undermined by
teachers or classmates or parents—so arouses my combativeness that,
like Karl Popper in his book *The Open Society and Its Enemies*, I
tend to become a fanatic crusading against fanaticism. The very position I have described to you here is taken partly because I want no
possibly liberating voice in the thinkers of the past to be wholly lost
by destruction of the psychological roots in us enabling us to sympathize with it.

Thus, there are issues on which I am a relativist and issues on
which I am an absolutist and those in which I am in doubt as to what
I am, or should be. Such moral experimentalism, while it has the
perils I have already outlined and others I know not of, is essential
if we are to meet life flexibly, listening to the ancestor within and
the friend without, but not bound to obey either.

Let me add that I don't posit this as some sort of middle way:
what *is* the middle is a contextual problem in itself, and extremes
may be right. Nor would I quite define my role as that of a thermo-

stat or other simple feed-back mechanism. For I define the context as including not only what is "really" there, as your self-styled realist would see it, but as including what is potentially there, given what my intervention may evoke in others and theirs in me. To find out this potential, one has to take risks, and one may be disappointed; but the only alternative is to condemn society to an endless regress in which each thermostat is reacting to each other thermostat or to a Generalized Thermostat of some sort.

To put this another way: I believe that the processes of communication are inherently ambiguous, since we understand other people's symbols in terms of our own character and the experience it has let us have. Therefore even those people who are sure they know what the truth is may not succeed in communicating it, but something quite the opposite, as the history of every reform movement testifies. Perhaps in America communication is especially ambiguous, for reasons already partly indicated. I think, for instance, that the wild exaggeration and tall tales so characteristic of American humor may reflect, among other things, the speaker's fear that unless his stretching of the truth is highly visible, he may run the risk of being believed. On the whole, to our loss, we have had few gentle satirists, and the *New Yorker*'s development of some gentle cartoonists may signify the beginnings of a common culture among its readers.

Some will take this complexity of communication to American audiences as further evidence that we should seek lowered ambiguity through value-uniformity. But is it not better, while admitting that there are losses involved, to take heightened ambiguity as an indication of the great variety of experience available to Americans in the face of all standardizing tendencies? At any rate, I prefer to come to grips with this ambiguity directly, as the psychoanalyst uses his patient's resistance as a very central part of his cure, and to seek to develop values in the very process of discussing them. For I think we do well to take advantage of the fact that we live, as Albert Camus puts it, in *la civilisation du dialogue*, whence arises the problem of sincerity, and also the need upon occasion to interiorize and perhaps even to transcend the dialogue, in such recesses of privacy as we can make for ourselves, even at some cost in sincerity.

§ V

TO RETURN now to the beginning: I suggest that the anxiety manifested by so many intellectuals about values, especially other people's values, may be on the point of being overdone. Having watched what happened when the experimentalist progressive education of John

Dewey, via the patronage networks of various teachers' colleges, was installed in many ill-equipped schoolhouses throughout the country, I am not attracted by the picture of a crusade to implant self-consciousness about values in all the pious and platitudinous teachers of America: I would rather have them teach languages and algebra and biochemistry. Movements of thought, it seems to me, do not so much reflect the society in which they arise as take account of what that society appears to have left out of account—to emphasize individualism when mercantilism reigned, or groupism when laissez-faire did. But as society becomes more highly differentiated, and as the audiences among whom intellectuals talk become more stratified, it becomes more and more difficult to know whether, let us say, a preoccupation with values is at fruitful odds with the times or a cruel addition to its excesses. In this, as in other cases, it may begin as the one and end as the other. I think that ways of observing our society with some detachment, such as literature and social science, offer us the chance to understand these dialectical relationships better than we now do, and to safeguard our judgment as to what intellectual tasks need doing; some tasks, of course, are hardy perennials. And then when we communicate what we have observed back to these audiences, we will find that the same pluralism which exists in the society exists in many of its individuals, and that we are talking to one part of a person and against another. For such a situation, I like the motto of William Blake: "When I tell any Truth," he wrote, "it is not for the sake of Convincing those who do not know it, but for the sake of defending those that do."

2. Individualism Reconsidered

Since such terms as "society" and "individual" tend to pose a false as well as a shifting dichotomy, I must anticipate misunderstanding; if I succeed in being suggestive to at least a few, I shall be satisfied. We live in a social climate in which, in many parts of the world and of the United States, the older brands of ruthless individualism are still a social danger, while in other parts of the world and of the United States, the newer varieties of what we may term "groupism" become increasingly menacing. Actually, we can distinguish conceptually between the needs of society (as a system of social organization) and those of the environing groups (as a system of psychological ties and expectations). As so defined, society, the larger territorial organization, often provides the mechanisms by which the individual can be protected against the group, both by such formal legal procedures as bills of rights, and by the fact that large-scale organization may permit the social mobility by which individuals can escape from any particular group. Prior to the rise of passports and totalitarianism, the modern Western city provided such an asylum and opportunity for many, while the existence of this safety-valve helped alleviate the pressure of "groupism" everywhere.

§ I

Just as a self-proclaimed "realist" is a different fellow in the Middle Ages, in the Enlightenment, and in modern America, so also the meaning of "individualism" depends on the historical setting. And it is worth tracing here the paradoxical development which, in the course of the modern era, freed Western men progressively from many previous restraints while at the same time developing a seemingly individualistic character-type enclosed within new psychological restraints. Men of the emerging middle classes, after the Renaissance, were turned loose in an economic order freed from the supervision of mercantilism, in a political order freed from the supervision of an hereditary aristocracy, in a religious order freed from the supervision of ecclesiastical hierarchy. To many observers of this process, whether radical or reactionary, these men who were freed of external restraints under the slogans of laissez-faire economics, utilitarian philosophy, and so on, appeared fiercely and viciously individualistic and

26

competitive.[1] But if we look at these new men from the inside, so to speak, we can see that it was precisely their internalization of a great deal of restraint that allowed them to become free of the group sanctions that might have been arrayed against their "individualism." They could disregard the religious anti-money-making attitudes that had survived from the medieval and early Reformation period only because (as Max Weber pointed out) their Puritan religious ethics provided them with stern justification and with a shell of protection against the shocked attitudes of their contemporaries.

Today, with some old evils behind us, we can admit that the hardy men who pioneered on the frontiers of production, exploration, and colonization in the last three hundred years were usually men who acted according to a code and who, though of course there were many pirates like Daniel Drew and the slave traders among them, were more likely to subscribe to high moral principles (e.g. the elder Rockefeller). These men were bound by a character orientation I have termed "inner-direction": they were guided by internalized goals and ideals which made them appear to be more individualistic than they actually were. Often, they were men who walked in the imagined footsteps of idealized parents—and this gave them their seven-league boots, and their feeling of having a personal destiny. And since the ideals that were internalized included many vestiges of older traditions, they were frequently paternalistic men, who, despite nominal belief in free enterprise, helped ameliorate the worst abuses brought about by their innovations. They shared, then, more than appears of the ethics of their anti-individualistic critics, from Owen and Marx to Karl Mannheim and Tawney. Evidence of this may be found in comparing these Western enterprisers with their counterparts in other countries, such as South America or China or the Soviet Union, where when traditional restraints on ruthlessness broke down, fewer internalized restraints were available to take their place. In sum, it proved possible in the West in early modern times to carry individualism to its limits of usefulness—and, in some cases, far beyond these limits—because a fair amount of social cohesiveness was taken for granted. . . .

Moreover, the same sort of moral compulsions which many of these "freedmen" carried within themselves, as the result of their socialization in a patriarchal family, were also turned loose upon the society at large. Individualistic "promoters" turned up not only in business and colonization, but in the many zealous reform movements

---

1. To Werner Sombart, these men appeared free of "scruples"—that is, free from such traditional obligations as those of guild morality. The fighting slogans were, of course, often blatantly individualistic.

of the last several hundred years. These movements fastened new restraints on a society that was shaking loose from old ones—how effectively, we can see by contrasting the attitudes towards law and society in India today, as the legacy of British rule, with the attitudes in neighboring countries which were not compelled to internalize the "white man's burden." In the West, the nineteenth century witnessed the triumph of the Victorian way: a triumph of legal and orderly justice, of honesty in business and government, of greater concern for women and children, and so on. (Inclined as we are today to patronize the Victorians, we generally see the seamy side of their attainments and emphasize their hypocrisy, failing to observe that this hypocrisy was itself some evidence of their success in driving corruption, vice, and social sadism underground.) In the eighteenth century it was impossible to walk unarmed in many English cities, let alone in the country; public and private violence abounded; corruption was taken for granted; the slave trade was thriving. By the middle of the nineteenth century, the lower orders had been freed, the lower impulses (as well as some higher ones) subdued. The development in America ran parallel, but was never, of course, as complete or as spectacular; as we all know, lawlessness reigns in many areas of American life today.

Nevertheless, anti-individualist writers such as Tawney, while they may have neglected the dangers of collectivism out of their disgust with their acquisitive society (and their failure to appreciate that medieval society was in some ways more acquisitive still), do express a very common mood of dislike for the cash nexus—a mood which appears in more astringent form in Veblen. It is hard for people to find satisfaction in a society whose best defense is that it is a lesser evil than some other social form. People can become greatly attached only to a society which takes account of their longings for connection with each other, and they may even opt for totalitarianism because it pretends to satisfy these longings and to get rid of the felt indecency of the cash nexus. To the degree that capitalist individualism has fostered an ethic of callousness, the result has been to undermine all forms of individualism, good and bad.

§ II

IN THE PERSPECTIVE of hindsight, we can see how Darwin's *Origin of Species* came to be so completely misinterpreted when it first appeared, as a brief for struggle to death *among individuals*. We can see, as the pendulum has swung towards groupism, that Darwin's book might just as well be interpreted as demonstrating the need for social solidarity or symbiosis within and among given species in order to achieve survival; thus (as Kropotkin pointed out) the book has much to say about cooperation as a technique of competition.

But the hardy Victorians, who had freed themselves from external restraints on economic competition and who were at the same time still sensitive, as I have indicated, to anti-moneymaking ethics, welcomed their interpretation of Darwin as a support in their continuing polemic against restraints—a polemic carried out also within themselves. One can, for instance, almost watch William Graham Sumner trying to stamp out, with the aid of Darwin, any softness and tenderness towards those who were pushed aside in the competitive struggle; he would have been less violent towards "do-gooders" if he had not feared their echo inside himself.

Today the argument against Sumner, and against this nineteenth century variety of individualism, seems very dated. We have come to realize that men who compete primarily for wealth are relatively harmless as compared with men who compete primarily for power (though, to be sure, there are violent, even totalitarian, implications in the treatment of labor, at home and abroad, as a commodity). Nevertheless, we are still inclined to use the word "bourgeois" as an epithet; we are well aware of the vices of the money-grubber, and perhaps less sensitive to the meannesses of spirit that develop in a monastery or a university where wealth as a goal is minimized. Even so, the centuries-old campaign against the middle class should not have hidden from us the advantages of a social system in which some men seek wealth (including wealth through power), pretty much for its own sake, and others seek power (including power through wealth), pretty much for its own sake, thus establishing a dichotomy of drives in which protective separation of specifically political powers can take its stand.

I recall Walter Duranty talking some twenty years ago about the Soviet abandonment of the "New Economic Policy," the policy by which, in the early twenties, a moderate capitalism had been encouraged in Russia. He spoke of the horror with which the ascetic Communists had reacted to the champagne parties and lovely ladies of the burgeoning NEP-men who were speculating in commodities, and making fortunes overnight by methods hard to distinguish from black-marketing. I felt then, and still feel, that if these Communists had been more historically minded and less morally indignant they might have seen that the NEP policy offered the only chance of curbing the totalitarianism which sets in when only power, and not money, talks. (The Communists were like those farmers who, in their hatred of varmints, get rid of the very creatures on whom the whole ecological balance depends.) At the same time, we can see that if the

Russian capitalists had not allowed moral restraint to be monopolized by the Communists, they might have aroused less of this sort of antagonism. (Today, it is the top Party functionaries—and occupation troops—who have access to champagne and ladies!) And we also see that economic control through the "impersonal" market mechanism (Adam Smith's "invisible hand"), where this is at all possible, is decidedly preferable to the all too visible and personal hand of the state or private monopolist.

§ III

IN THE EPOCH when "money talked," the conception of human nature underwent a series of changes quite as ironical as the social developments themselves. The view of man as naturally cooperative runs through the writings of a number of otherwise quite diverse nineteenth century thinkers: St. Simon and Comte, Kingsley and Marx, Durkheim and Bellamy, Kropotkin and Ruskin. All these writers, more or less explicitly, reject competitive capitalism in favor of a medieval type of guild harmony and order, while differing in their attitudes towards the machine and in their remedies for the diseases of industrialization.

Likewise, the view of man as naturally antagonistic has given rise to a number of diverse solutions to the problem of the social order thus presented. Freud, for example, deeming men innately aggressive, thought that a strong elite, with a monopoly on the capacity for being reasonable, would have to compel the majority to cooperate in the tasks of civilization, at once demanding submission from the masses and providing them with consolation. In Elton Mayo and in other recent writers, one can find a similar elitism and a similar concern with the formation of group consensus through strong leadership.

All these writers thus arrive at positions in which they become advocates of what I have labelled "groupism," whether they start from reactionary or revolutionary political positions, or from Rousseauistic or Freudian and even Hobbesian views of human nature. That is, whether one begins with the assumption that cooperation is man's natural state, which he is prevented from attaining by a reactionary social order, or with the assumption that the "state of nature" is one of war of all against all, one can readily end by focussing on forcing or allowing men to define themselves entirely as social animals. (To be sure, in the early Marx, and even in Bellamy, one finds more anarchistic strains; and some thinkers of the last century and of this one, such as John Stuart Mill and Bertrand Russell, have worried less about order than about liberty.)

Obviously, the preoccupation with the desires and needs of men for group affiliation testifies, often enough, to the actual presence of disorder in the society. But it often testifies also to the obsessive feeling on the part of some intellectuals that disorder in itself is a terrible thing. Furthermore, one of the themes that unifies many of these writers is their attitude towards the disorderly trait of "selfishness"; in true medieval fashion, they denounce it and welcome, if not always altruism as such, then at least a class or national consciousness that submerges individual self-interest. The confidence in self-interest that ran from Mandeville through Smith to Sumner, seems to have been almost utterly defeated among influential thinkers by the end of World War I; it is still assumed that self-interest is natural —and sometimes, indeed, that an "enlightened" self-interest is called for—but on the whole, reliance is placed on concern for the needs of the group.

This altruism might have worked during the 1900-1950 shift toward emphasis on the group, if those group needs had themselves been clear. In that case, people might have developed a pattern of obedience to the group in certain limited spheres (regarding the group demands as a kind of tax collection), while retaining individuality in other spheres. If this had happened, the shift from the preceding attitudes of subtly socialized individualism would hardly have been noticeable. But in fact, the group needs have not been clear; moreover, they have been constantly changing. There has developed today a great preoccupation, less with specific needs, than with group mood —a feeling on the part of individuals that they wanted or felt they had to spend their energies, first in making a group, and second, in attending to and improving its morale.

This groupism, which rests not on obvious group emergencies but on the vague disquietude of lonely individuals, is probably strongest in America, where people appear to be most vocally concerned about the problems of group participation and belongingness. Americans have devoted less scientific attention to the measurement of group needs and potential wants through market research techniques (save in the most obvious commercial forms) than to what we might term "mood engineering" in work, play, and politics. Mood engineering leads not so much to specific "altruistic" behavior as to a general readiness to participate in the given group activities of the moment, even if their only purpose is to help other people pass the evening. As Margaret Mead has pointed out, Americans feel selfish if they stay at home when they might be amusing people who are "underprivileged" in the skills of self-amusement.

It would take us too far afield even to begin to try to explain the reasons for the psychological changes which have occurred at least as rapidly as those in social and political organization. For example, shifting patterns of child socialization are important: among other things, parents today face the responsibility of "making a group" with their children—are on the defensive vis-a-vis their children's moods—in a way quite different from the attitude of parents in an earlier day. Not all the developments towards groupism are to be deplored. Groupism rests in part on an increasing sensitivity to subtle states of feeling, and this is an advance. Only, as always, such advances bring with them a dialectical train of new perplexities and limitations. We must skeptically question the demands for greater social participation and belongingness among the group-minded while, on another front, opposing the claims of those who for outworn reasons cling to individualism as a (largely economic) shibboleth.

§ IV

IT IS NOT EASY, for obvious reasons, to discover the actual state of this conflict in Soviet Russia today. We do not know, for instance, to what extent people have become cynical and apathetic as a way of resisting an enforced group belongingness. However, occasional arguments appear in the press which, by claiming that the issue is settled, show that it is not settled. Thus, in 1940 there was a discussion of a psychology textbook which was attacked, not only for its "objectivity," but for its failure to realize that the whole science had undergone a profound change in the Soviet Union. "The tragedy of the loneliness of the individual," it was asserted, "which characterizes a society founded on classes, has been liquidated. The conflict between the individual and the community has disappeared. The interests of the Soviet people are harmoniously identified with the interests of Soviet society." Furthermore, theories about "unchanging human nature" are damned as bourgeois (an issue not absent from American social science polemics)—it would seem that Lysenko-ism operates in the field of psychology too.[2]

---

2. A poignant newspaper story from Warsaw indicates that the Poles may be maintaining some resistance to the Stalinist extremes of groupism. A young Polish girl loosed a flood of abuse and correction on herself by writing a letter to the newspaper *Standard of Youth* declaring that "my private life does not concern anyone." She continued that the ideal member of the Union of Polish Youth was a "creature with wings . . . wearing a long and clean cloak of sackcloth. When it meets a pal it discusses only Marxism. It does not push in tramways nor spit on the floor and walks only on the right side of the street. . . . According to you we should wear only a spotless uniform of our organization, straight hair and, of course, no trace of makeup . . .—all, in order to discuss the development of education in the New China! . . . I am young and lucky enough to have survived the war and have a right to live as I like. Z.M.P. meetings, discussions and some artistic shows are not enough for me."

To be sure, it is no adequate answer to Western advocates of groupism to show how the idea has fitted so well into the totalitarian pattern (which eventually serves to destroy all local groupings). In fact, the advocates of an anti-individualist position use the seeming success of the dictatorships to buttress their views (not seeing to what extent the dictatorships, beneath their ideology, are seeking to imitate *us*), pointing out that men welcome social solidarity even if they must pay, in the loss of freedom, a high and terrible price for it; and that actually they want demands made on them—a point to which war experience also testifies—rather than to be left alone and forced to direct their own efforts. Still other voices argue that, in order to defeat the USSR, we must evoke our own spirit of sacrifice and devotion to the group: our alleged anarchy will be our undoing in the war of the two worlds. And still other, though few, voices would like to see international anarchy put down by an all-powerful world state.

What strikes me in many of these proposals is an ascetic uninventiveness reminiscent of the discussions which bored the Polish letter-writer quoted in the footnote. We assume that all possible forms of human relatedness have already been experienced, so that if present forms are unsatisfying, then better ones must be looked for in our own past, in wartime comradeship, or in the grisly present of the Soviet Union. Ironically, the very people who extol groupism, whether as an inexorable necessity or as desirable in its own right, usually do not themselves lead parochial and "groupy" lives; they draw sustenance from all the continents and all of history; they have friends everywhere, just as their material needs, through the modern division of labor, are met from everywhere. But like Plato and many other unhappy intellectuals since, they believe that those others, the masses (obviously, the very term "masses" is heavily value-loaded), can be saved from a Durkheimian anomie only by an enforced groupism and its concomitant ideology.

We can see, moreover, other forces than a simple nostalgia, or even simple elitism, at work. Anti-urbanites, for example, argue among themselves, in the guise of instructing the "masses." Unable to stand alone, lacking the "nerve of failure," they tend to project onto others their own uneasiness and frequently their own contempt for intellectuality. I do not mean, of course, that there is no malaise in our great middle and working classes in urban life; but rather, on the one

---

For this display of "selfishness," the writer was termed demoralized by war and occupation, said to "almost sanction(s) debauchery," and informed that "exceeding the production target . . . is happiness. Work in the organization provides happiness certainly greater than that gotten out of dancing or making up."

hand, that the intellectuals greatly underestimate the terror, misery, and disorder of the "status society" of the past which they so much admire, while underestimating, on the other hand, the tremendous achievements of modern men in making themselves comfortable in the face of the novelty of a fluid industrial society.

Americans of the more mobile classes have not only adapted themselves to a fluid society, but have also begun to adapt the society to their own needs. They have achieved an extraordinary ability to make judgments about, and friends with, a great variety of humankind. Whereas more traditional societies have an etiquette to govern the relation between people of different age, class, and sex groups, these Americans have abandoned etiquette for a more individualized and personalized approach. And while we are familiar with the negative aspects of this development—its enforced joviality of the "greeter" and glad-hander, its enforced politeness of the Helen Hokinson type— we may in our self-contempt be less ready to see its great adventurous- ness: the liberation of people and their movements from the chain mail of etiquette.

In the arts of consumption as well as in the arts of production, Americans have moved so fast that, in architecture and design, in moving pictures and in poetry and criticism, we are living in what I believe to be one of the great cultures of history. It is not fashionable to say this. Yet we may ask, as Crane Brinton does in *Ideas and Men*: What is there in Pericles' famous praise of Athens that does not apply to us, in some or even in extended measure?

Sensitive Americans—and they are more in number than each individually is apt to think—have become exceedingly allergic to anything that smacks of chauvinism; this very symposium is in part a testimony to this development. Vis-a-vis Europe, we have lost the defensive aggression of Mark Twain, though his was a needed cor- rective; vis-a-vis Asia, we were until recently taken in by the image of the peaceable, unaggressive, technologically-unseduced Chinese. It now seems likely that we shall fall for the idea that the Russians have more to offer the Far East than we; and that they have unequivocally convinced the peasants that this is so. While this attitude stems in part from our disenchantment with machine civilization and our failure to use machinery as a means to greater, more creative leisure, it would appear ludicrous to that part of the world which needs machines before it can realize the possibility of becoming disenchanted with them!

One of the interesting semantic expressions of our own disen- chantment is that of bewailing our society as "impersonal." What would the member of the village group or small town not give at times for an impersonal setting where he was not constantly part of a web of gossip and surveillance? Furthermore, this use of the term "impersonal" is a way of deprecating our great human achievement of turning over productive routines to machinery and to formal organization. One result of this attitude is clear enough: the sphere of work tends to come increasingly under the supervision of the engineers whose concern is less to reduce the time and strain of the worker, than to render the workaday world "meaningful" in terms of shared emotions reminiscent of the guilds, or perhaps of our nostalgic image of the guilds.

A contrary attitude would assume that we should be grateful to find, in our work, areas of freedom from people, where the necessary minimum of productive activity could be accomplished without the strain and waste of time involved in continuous concern for the morale of the working group. If men were not compelled to be sociable at work, they could enjoy sociability in their leisure much more than they often do now. In fact, while men in the nineteenth century may have underestimated their satisfactions from solitary occupations, hobbies and other pursuits, we tend today to reverse these extremes and to forget that men can enjoy, let us say, the physical rhythms of work or the private fantasies of leisure even when they are for long periods deprived of social comradeship at work and play. What is necessary is some sort of balance which will find room for quite idiosyncratic individual desires to be, variously, alone and with others. The flexibility of modern industrial organization, no longer bound geographically to rail lines and power sites, the steady decrease of hours of compulsory work which our abundance allows, and our increasing sensitivity to the psychic as well as physical hazards of the different occupations—these developments permit us to move towards the reorganization of work so that it can offer a greater variety of physical and social challenges and stimulations. But work should never be allowed to become an end in itself simply out of a need to keep ourselves busy.

§ V

APART FROM the everpresent threat of war—not seldom used as a rationalization to sop up our "excessive" comforts, leisures, and painfully-attained easy-goingnesses—most of our social critics cannot imagine a society being held together without putting organized work in the forefront of its goals and agendas. Their efforts to restore the participative significance of work, allegedly enjoyed in earlier social stages, show the same poverty of imagination as their belief in the inevitable need for the parochial group as the only conceivable building block of society. When we turn to formal politics, we see that the same fundamentally reactionary ideology leads to a demand for national unity and a distrust of the chaos of democratic politics and of the war among the so-called "special interests."

The notion that there must be "agreement on fundamentals" in order that democratic politics may go on is an illusion. Carl J. Friedrich, in *The New Image of the Common Man*, provides a discriminatory critique. While it is true that people must be prepared to accept the fact of a vote or election going against them, and to accept certain legal and juridical minima of the same sort, this is not what is meant when agreement on fundamentals is asked as the price of national unity and survival. What is meant is actually a surrender of special interest claims, whether these grow out of ethnic loyalties, church affiliation, regional, occupational, or other ties. What is meant is agreement that democracy itself (defined to mean more, much more, than the legal minimum) is a good thing; agreement on equality of races; agreement to put American needs ahead of any foreign loyalty. Yet the fact is that our democracy, like that of Switzerland, has survived without securing such agreements. In our country, this has been attained by a party system that serves as broker among the special interest groups: the parties do not ask for agreement on fundamentals—certainly, not on ideological fundamentals—but for much more mundane and workable concessions. At the same time, our expanding economy (and concomitantly expanding state services) has made these concessions possible without bankruptcy and, on the whole, with a steady reduction in hardship and injustice.

Those who would like to see the parties "stand for something," and those who have framed their own image of the future in terms of some Armaggedon of proletarian revolution or overthrow of the "interests," feel unhappy and misgoverned under such a system. To them it seems simply a lack of system. Thus, we are in part the victims of ideals of polity which turn our virtues into vices and which have confused the Western world since Plato's *Republic*, if not before. What we need are new ideals, framed with the future rather than the past in mind—ideals closer to the potentialities actually realizable under the impetus of industrialization.

One of the elements in such a new ideal would seem to be a relaxation of the demand for political dutifulness now made by many citizens who are worried about apathy. Apathy has many meanings. Its expression today may be one of the ways the individual—in the Soviet zone or Franco's Spain, no less than here—hides from ideological pressures, hides from "groupism." Lacking an active counterfaith in individualism, or any way of meeting up with others who share his resentments, he falls back on apathy as a mask behind which he can protect the remnants of his privacy. If it were widely recognized that not all people in a democracy need concern themselves continuously with public affairs (or with the union, or with the PTA, or what not), but that all should have a "right of veto" of which to make sparing, residual exercise, they might more readily agree to comply with the minimal demands for information and participation that such a veto would need for its effectiveness. And with politics no longer regarded as a continuous duty, people might feel less resistance to participation.

§ VI

IF THE INTERNATIONAL (and hence domestic) outlook continues to be as grim as during recent months [written in early 1950], readers may wonder whether this advocacy of "irresponsible" individualism is not sheer escapism. It would be insufficient to answer that "escape," like "compromise" or "appeasement," has become a bad word to the crusaders for political and group commitment. It would perhaps be a better answer to observe that if America is to be saved from destruction or self-destruction, it will be by preserving, as part of our armory of significant escapes, our humor and creativity and sense of perspective.

I recognize, of course, that many Americans feel guilty about their "luxuries" if others are forced to fight and suffer, and so would welcome a kind of edited hardship as an alleviation of their guilt. But though this is understandable and, in many ways, desirable, it provides the privileged countries and groups with much too limited and hence too easy a morality. The present international dangers menacing America (real enough in the view I hold of Stalinism) can obviously be used by many people in America to rationalize their partiality for the shared hardships of war against the solitary hardships of developing their individuality in time of peace.

Again, it should be obvious to the reader that I speak in a social context in which anarchy and "unbridled" individuality are much less likely prospects (except on the international scene) than the all-too-evident danger of the "garrison state." This danger must make us particularly sensitive to the fact that we depend for advance, in morals no less than in physical science, on individuals who have developed their individuality to a notable degree. We must give every encouragement to people to develop their private selves—to escape from groupism—while realizing that, in many cases, they will use their freedom in unattractive or "idle" ways. Our very abundance makes it possible for us, even in the midst of war, to take the minor risks and losses involved in such encouragement as against the absolutely certain risks involved in a total mobilization of intellect and imagination.

Yet in these remarks I find myself, as a final irony, addressing the defense of individualism to some presumed director of unselective service: I am using, Adam Smith style, group-survival arguments to justify the "selfish" living of an individual life. (Much of the same irony overtakes many devout people who "sell" religion as a variety of group therapy—because it is good for morale rather than for morals.) Possibly I am thereby revealing my own arguments against my own guilts. But I think more is involved. I am trying to answer Dostoevsky's Grand Inquisitor in terms that he would understand, as well as in the transcendent terms that his interlocutor, Jesus, understands. I am insisting that no ideology, however noble, can justify the sacrifice of an individual to the needs of the group. Whenever this occurs, it is the starkest tragedy, hardly less so if the individual consents (because he accepts the ideology) to the instrumental use of himself. . . .

Social science has helped us become more aware of the extent to which individuals, great and little, are the creatures of their cultural conditioning; and so we neither blame the little nor exalt the great. But the same wisdom has sometimes led us to the fallacy that, since all men have their being in culture and as the result of the culture, they owe a debt to that culture which even a lifetime of altruism could not repay. (One might as well argue, and in fact many societies in effect do, that since we are born of parents, we must feel guilt whenever we transcend their limitations!) Sometimes the point is pushed to the virtual denial of individuality: since we arise in society, it is assumed with a ferocious determinism that we can never transcend it. All such concepts are useful correctives of an earlier solipsism. But if they are extended to hold that conformity with society is not only a necessity but also a duty, they destroy that margin of freedom which gives life its savor and its endless possibility for advance.

3. The Ethics of We Happy Few

WE HAPPY FEW[1] is the ironic title of Helen Howe's study of an academic community. The community happens to be Harvard, and the English Department. But both Miss Howe and her readers have insisted that this is merely coincidental, and that the same sort of self-centered behavior is to be found on other campuses and in other departments. It is a study of intellectuals, and my interest in it here is in the representative character of its ethical attitude towards them.

The central character of *We Happy Few* is Dorothea Natwick, accomplished daughter of a liberal New England family. In observing the Natwicks, Miss Howe has seen through the conventionalities of people who seek desperately to be unconventional. "To *épater* the bourgeois both of the faculty of St. Cuthbert's and the countryside around Constable was the crusade into which Mrs. Natwick was forever flinging herself, while from her tilted lance fluttered the pennant of the good, the true, the beautiful, and the 'interesting.' And the greatest of these was the 'interesting.' " When Mr. Natwick dies, Mrs. Natwick holds a service in her barn: "Isn't it too good to be true?" she announces gaily to Dorothea, "I've got the Gordon String Quartet to say they'll play. I thought the Mozart Clarinet Quintet would be just right. . . . Then there's a chapter from Fabre's *Life of the Fly* which your father was particularly fond of. . . ."

The picture of the Harvard faculty into which Dorothea marries is drawn in the same spirit. Everything is "interesting"; nothing is serious—nothing, that is, except the bitter rivalries for prestige and place. There is a terrible striving always to be *avant-garde*: to "discover" Henry James, T. S. Eliot, Melville or the more obscure modern English poets. There is a standing rule for admission to the happy few, who call themselves "The Little Group": *never to be taken in* by any person, idea or emotion.

So far, very good. Miss Howe has had the nerve to tackle not the easy targets of the Babbitts or the Hucksters, the Sammy Glicks, et al., but people who are far above the average, even among intellectuals and academes, in intelligence, sensitivity, and breadth of view. She has not been taken in by the self-deceptions of the élite of culture. She has their number with the wit of a Helen Hokinson, but with a mordancy of her own.

---

1. Helen Howe, *We Happy Few*, Simon & Schuster (1946).

The main sin of The Little Group is pride, meaning self-centered-
ness. Dorothea symbolizes arrogant unconcern for ordinary people,
ordinary emotions and ordinary events. The war news annoys her.
She finds Basic English more interesting than the RAF. Miss Howe's
criticism of these "selfish" attitudes and preoccupations becomes clearer
by contrast with the brave, unselfish males in Dorothea's life. The
males—Dorothea's suitor, husband, son, and father—are completely
uninterested in themselves. The suitor is a gauche Idaho crusader who
becomes a fighting liberal Senator. Uncultivated and inhospitable to
the play of ideas, he is out of sorts in the Natwick atmosphere. He
is a sterling democrat from the great open spaces. He gets things
done. He finally rejects Dorothea because she is too snobbish, frivolous, and unworthy. The husband, John, is immersed in the study of
seventeenth-century England as Dorothea's father had also been immersed in his teaching, his research, and his hobbies. John, despite
Dorothea's pushing, refuses to angle for the mastership of "Bromfield
House," one of the swank Harvard Houses. When war comes he
enlists in the British Navy, quietly, without fuss or feathers. When
Dorothea consoles herself with a lover, he is not jealous, but only
concerned lest Dorothea be wounded. He dies at sea. Their son,
Johnny, is exempt from service as a medical school student and is
fascinated by his work. But he, too, is unselfish. Again quietly, without fuss or feathers, he seeks to enlist and finally gets Dorothea's permission to do so. Even Dorothea's lover, a wonderfully sketched portrait of the slick success-boy who makes women and money for the
love of making, comes off at least no worse than The Little Group.
Since he is uncomplicated and unintellectual his selfishness is undis-
guised. He debunks the academic airs, and is billed as a more intrepid
and successful lover than any Harvard professor could possibly be.
Except for him, then, the men close to Dorothea and thus contrasted
with her and The Little Group, are models of unselfishness, devoted
to their work, their cause, or both. They are not always looking out
for number one.

§ THE ETHICS OF INDIVIDUALITY

IF WE LOOK at The Little Group and Dorothea, we must grant the
charge of selfishness. But we must grant it from a quite different
critical position, namely in terms of Erich Fromm's distinction between selfishness and self-love.[2] Fromm points out that a "selfish"
person has no real self, and no fondness for the self; therefore, he
must continuously seek security in terms of conquests and power to

2. See "Selfishness and Self-Love," *Psychiatry*, (1939) 2:507-523. I am also
indebted to his forthcoming book, *Man For Himself*.

compensate for his lack of "self-love." In other words, the selfish person is not interested in himself, but only in others' evaluation of himself. He shines in their reflected light—he is their satellite, even when he dominates them. On the other hand, the self-loving person is confident of his own self-evaluation. He does not need others for psychic security, but is capable of loving them as he loves himself. He has an erotic attitude towards the world, not a greedy one. Dorothea and all The Little Group were selfish and lacking in self-love as thus defined. Dorothea depended on the Group for admiration, and won it; the Group basked in its conviction of superiority over the less esoteric and advanced. Lacking any conviction of their individuality, they needed constantly to appear "original" and "interesting"; the war on banality was a major problem. Lacking ambition for personal quality and distinction, their aims were necessarily petty. Their fault was not an excess of pride but a deficiency of it.

"Moralists are constantly complaining," De Tocqueville observed in 1834, "that the ruling vice of the present time is pride. This is true in one sense, for indeed everybody thinks that he is better than his neighbor or refuses to obey his superior; but it is extremely false in another, for the same man who cannot endure subordination or equality has so contemptible an opinion of himself that he thinks he is born only to indulge in vulgar pleasures. He willingly takes up with low desires without daring to embark on lofty enterprises, of which he scarcely dreams.

"Thus, far from thinking that humility ought to be preached to our contemporaries, I would have endeavors made to give them a more enlarged idea of themselves and of their kind. Humility is unwholesome to them; what they want most is, in my opinion, pride."[3]

Pride in De Tocqueville's sense, like self-love as Fromm uses the term, is an essential ingredient of true individuality, which is based on an awareness of, and liking for, one's self in its particularity and uniqueness. The individuality of the members of The Little Group was factitious—a put-up job with differentness cultivated for its ability to create status. The Little Group is liberal-minded, but its method of achieving individuality resembles that of the reactionary Uncle Jules, in Sartre's "Portrait of the Anti-Semite," whose one claim to fame was that he could not stand the English. Thus true individuality goes together with pride, while a want of individuality frequently appears in our culture as selfishness.

§ THE ETHICS OF COLLECTIVISM

A SELFISH PERSON, then, if he is to change, needs to cultivate above

---

3. *Democracy in America,* (Phillips Bradley ed., 1945), Vol. II, p. 248.

all else a feeling of pride, and an understanding fondness for his own individuality. As is evident, Miss Howe's therapy for Dorthea's selfishness is just the opposite. Dorothea finds in suffering and humility the cure for her Little-Groupish pride, and in the collective activities made available by the war the cure for her Little-Groupish individualism. With the war, Dorothea suffers a series of losses and defeats: husband, lover, son, and maid abandon her in one way or another; Bromfield House and Basic English also fall away. Then she is put through a number of "experiences" which bring her close, physically at least, to the troubles and pains of ordinary folk. Becoming a nurse's aid, she meets other nurse's aids socially; they are fine and dull. Traveling to Coeur d'Alene to be near her son in training, she "sees" America: in the stench of the ladies' room, the sadness of platform partings, the good-heartedness of Middle-Westerners. The townsfolk of Coeur d'Alene are another "experience"; they, too, are fine and dull. At the end, Dorothea returns to Cambridge a sadder and wiser woman: her pride is gone, and she has learned humbly to admire the great open spaces and the open sentiments usually associated with them in song and story.

Suffering and physical discomfort, however, do not always succeed in submerging one's individuality, though they are among the most useful weapons. Nor are feelings of identification with others, whether in Coeur d'Alene or elsewhere, adequate; such feelings are quite consistent with a strong feeling of individuality and personal value. So Dorothea, following the penances set out for her by Miss Howe, must further submerge her own self by the device of self-belittlement: in order to build up the common man, she must learn to run herself down. This lesson of submersion begins, rather mildly, when Dorothea discusses with her mother, Mrs. Natwick, the "original" arrangement for burying Mr. Natwick at the cheery barn funeral already described.

"Even Dorothea," Miss Howe writes, "found herself wondering if it might not have been 'simpler' to accept the common lot, and to take death with all the other trappings and the suits of woe decreed by the organized morticians, along with millions of other anonymous human beings who had never hoped to assert an individuality in life and certainly would not have the temerity to storm the ramparts of eternity on their own momentum." Is there any greater virtue in bowing to the pressure of the organized morticians than in bowing to the private need to be "original"? At least the Natwick style of life was an attempt at individuality, even if it failed as too external a "creation."

Dorothea has absorbed this anti-Natwick lesson of acceptance by

the time her own husband dies. At the service "the beautiful words
of the Burial of the Dead engulfed her. It was comforting to lose
oneself in their blanketing anonymity. *The burden of being one's
own arbiter of taste and feeling had been removed.* John was not
narrowed into a gifted young man, with nice tastes and a knowledge
of the seventeenth century. He had become enlarged, enfolded. He
was simply one more 'man that is born of woman who hath but a
short time to live.' . . . One must go with it, accept it, believe that
some transubstantiation was wrought, beyond our power to understand."[4] Where have we heard before of loss of oneself in blanketing
anonymity? Of the burden of taste and choice? Of one's duty to
accept what one neither likes nor understands? Is not that the essence
of the denigration of the individual in the reactionary ideology—
none the less so because here put in the context of John's anti-fascism?

Dorothea continues learning the lesson of self-belittlement. After
John's death, her lover deserts her. Dorothea is overwhelmed with
shame for having slept with him, for having given way to her desires. "She had been dethroned by her own flesh." As a result, she
feels she has no right to condemn Japanese atrocities; she had finally
"made up (her) mind that (she) was not one bit better than the
meanest of earth." She says to herself caustically: "What insuffer-
able hypocrisy and arrogance that she should dare to hand out moral
judgments. . . ."

Having been dethroned by the flesh, Dorothea must mortify it;
hating illness and filth, she is taunted into becoming a nurse's aid by
a fellow-traveling and wholesome member of The Little Group who
has already joined. "Don't tell me the lady has an idea she's somebody!" is the friend's irrefutable comeback to Dorothea's protest
that the work would not make use of her special gifts. Dorothea's
education continues; she learns that: "What makes a good nurse is
simply the power to forget yourself—completely." Staggering through
the agonizing days at the hospital, she learns in her few off hours to
enjoy Schumann as well as her beloved Bach and Mozart: "Her
aesthetic as well as her human taste was stretching, too—cruder, possibly, but warmer and more inclusive." In other words, whatever
makes for individualization and idiosyncracy in taste requires "stretching"; in compensation for this, she makes herself believe that "quintes-
sential beauty is to be found at the very heart of human pain." How
convenient! *Ad astra per aspera.*

The pain, submission, and self-belittlement which put an end to
Dorothea's efforts to achieve individuality are symbolized by her
change of attitude towards Harvard. No longer is it a subject for

4. Italics mine—D. R.

jokes, or for Natwick insouciance. Listening to Churchill's speech at Harvard in September 1943, she glows with thoughts of sacrifice: "Here, in this dark, mellow, sanctified hall was the distilled essence of values worth dying for." The institution, too, is sanctified: Dorothea concludes that "Harvard College—like any community of men dedicated to a goal higher than themselves—was greater than the sum of its parts."

At the end, in a touching scene, Dorothea shows that she is "cured," she has learned her lesson well. She is taking leave of her son Johnny at Coeur d'Alene; he is about to be shipped out. He is a gifted, sensitive lad, just eighteen. He is also Dorothea's one remaining human tie with life, and she is genuinely devoted to him. But now she sees him, "for the first time, as only part of the general whole—no longer anything special or remarkable or favored—just one more American gob." Again, how convenient! These are precisely the sentiments of passivity and resignation which make it possible for the underlying population to take the miseries of war with a minimum of fuss and feathers. But why should people not weep, protest? Why should they so easily be reconciled?

Dorothea's soul is "saved" by the most humble and uncritical surrender. Her surrender must be humble, in Miss Howe's ethics, because her claims at the beginning of her career were regarded as so proud. It is the very American morality of the higher they come the harder they fall.

§ THE ETHICS OF AFFIRMATION

ARE "LITTLE GROUPS" of intellectuals, then, more proud than most people, or more selfish? As Miss Howe is aware, frantic concern about status is to be found in almost all groups, little and big. The notion that sensitive and educated people are more conceited or more vicious than the average is a romantic fiction; and, like romantic fictions generally, serves a social function. That function is to justify attack on a weak and powerless minority: the intellectuals. They are, Miss Howe says, detached from America. But what does this mean, except to say that they are weak; otherwise, one might claim that America is detached from them, and that is too bad for America.

I do not, of course, intend to deny that the intellectual, like everyone else, faces a staggering problem of relating himself genuinely to other people and other problems than his own. How can he give up selfishness for self-love, in a culture which practices selfishness and preaches self-abasement? How can he maintain a feeling of belonging in the world, of having just claims on life, if the world ignores or rejects him? Miss Howe lets us and herself down into the one easy answer which we know to be false. That is also the judgment of Diana Trilling, whose brief, brilliant review of *We Happy Few* stimulated my own attempt at a more extensive analysis. "Miss Howe is scarcely alone among current novelists," Mrs. Trilling writes, "in regarding democracy—or the proletariat, or the fight against fascism, or a sweeping view of the multitudinousness of American life—as if it were a medicine especially prepared to cure the sick soul of the modern individual. One recalls, as an extreme instance, the novel of a few years ago in which a young woman was cured of neurosis by giving visas to refugees; or the more recent example in which the heroine was saved from nervous collapse by joining the movement for cooperatives. As a matter of fact, asked to name, on the evidence of the novels I read, the one dominant trend of our progressive literary culture, I would probably specify this mechanical notion that the individual finds himself by losing himself in some larger social manifestation."[5]

In fact, we can observe the same trend in writers of such different backgrounds from Miss Howe, of such tremendous power, and of such exceptional awareness of the issues, as Koestler and Silone. In *Arrival and Departure,* Koestler is frightened by his own mocking of contemporary liberal and democratic values, mocking which he puts into the mouths of Bernard the fascist and the woman psychoanalyst. He is unwilling to face his fear, and to take the responsibility for his mockery, for if he dealt with them in their own terms he might be defeated. His answer? A symbolic plunge into "affirmation." Peter, the hero, is parachuted into enemy territory, a dangerous war exploit; by his act, he seems to reject the mockery, which nevertheless remains verbally persuasive and unanswered. He drowns the self-doubts with which the analyst has filled him in violent, unreflective anti-fascism.

Silone's recent play *And He Hid Himself* is a good deal more ambivalent in its conclusions; yet it contains a similar lesson. Murica, a revolutionary student who has been living beyond his psychological means, under pressure betrays his comrades to the Fascist police. No one knew; no one would know; he is safe. But he finds it intolerable to be alone in the sense of being detached from the revolutionary movement, and also in the sense of having no one to submit to. He is tormented by remorse and confesses, first to his girl, then to Don Benedetto, a sympathetic cleric, and finally to Pietro Spina, the socialist leader who has disguised himself as a priest. By these confessions he risks his life, for he knows the law of the underground:

_____
5. 163 *The Nation,* 50, 51, 1946.

traitors are assassinated. However, Spina forgives him, permitting him
to rejoin the movement; Murica remains unpunished until, at the
end of the play, he is captured and tortured to death by the authorities. He dies without betrayal but instead with psychological solvency.
Silone treats this final act of heroism as redeeming not only Murica
but also the peasants whose revolutionary ardor and hope it stimulates after they had become cynical and apathetic.

The play throughout is framed in Christian imagery. The priestly
robes in which Spina hides himself are more than make-up for a
getaway: they represent an effort to combine Socialist and Catholic
traditions. And though the allegory is not, for me, quite clear, it
seems that Murica's sacrificial return to the illegal movement symbolically resembles that of Christ, who also took upon himself the
guilt of the suffering poor. Thus, while Silone has wonderful things
to say about the virtue of pride, he nevertheless is also, with part of
himself, on the side of those who believe that man is redeemed from
weakness and neurosis by "taking punishment" and by joining,
through submission, the hierarchies of Church and Party.

§ THE NERVE OF FAILURE

NONE OF THESE AUTHORS means to be popular. They do not intend to
join the chorus, and they are certainly unaware of doing so. They
believe themselves to be daring and heretical. What, then, is going
on in them? Sidney Hook has referred to the contemporary "failure
of nerve" among intellectuals.[6] The concept is significant and correct,
but it is only part of the story. It assumes that, if there were no
failure of nerve, the intellectuals might win battles, might save themselves from defeat, from the rout of democratic and liberal values.
But such defeat, for the time being, seems inexorable. Hence, the
other part of the story is the courage to accept the possibility of
defeat, of failure, without being morally crushed. This courage I
would call "the nerve of failure." The "failure of nerve" concept
looks at the problem primarily from outside; it assumes there is no
failure but that of nerve. The "nerve of failure" concept looks at the
problem primarily from the inside; it assumes there is no nerve but
that of failure. Plainly, little nerve is required on the winning side:
nerve has no meaning except when we must face the possibility,
today the probability, of failure.

What is feared as failure in American society is, above all, aloneness. And aloneness is terrifying because it means that there is no
one, no group, no approved cause to submit to. Even success—the
seeming opposite of failure—often becomes impossible to bear when

6. 10 *Partisan Review*, No. 1 (1943).

it is not socially approved or even known. This is perhaps why successful criminals often feel the need to confess, that is, to submit to the community's judgment, represented in the person to whom the confession is made. They will confess, as Murica did, even under circumstances where this will probably, if not certainly, endanger their previous success: proof, I think, that aloneness is more intolerable than mere failure. For mere failure, provided it is found in company, can rather easily be borne; many ideologies have the function of making it possible for people to digest the worst miseries and even death. Under the sway of the ideology, they do not feel the impact of their failure; they are in the grip of an authority, even if it lets them down. On the other hand, one who is alone lacks this solace which can make even failure comfortable.

Of course, this problem of aloneness existed before democracy and before fascism. It is part of the problem of man's relation to the world and to other men which intellectuals today face with such specialized acuteness. The nerve of failure is needed to face the fact that the problem remains unsolved, and the possibility that it is insoluble. Thus we may experience defeat in our personal life-goals as well as in our social aims. Franz Kafka expressed these problems in his writing. He had the "nerve of failure"; he faced failure without illusion and without affirmation.

§ THE USES OF GUILT

KAFKA WAS VIRTUALLY ALONE. Most writers—writers of the sort we have been discussing—lose their nerve of failure by allowing themselves to succumb to feelings of guilt. Such feelings are accompanied by the need to submit to others and to affirm others' affirmations. An intellectual today, simply by virtue of being an intellectual, has perhaps a harder time than most people to escape such feelings of guilt. He is weak; he is despised; he has no assured social role and status; he is out of step. In a culture which values strength and power, the weak and powerless are easily made to feel that there is something wrong with them. What is taken to be wrong, of course, are all their individual defects which they share with other men. But beyond that material which is always available, the intellectual can focus on those very elements which differentiate him from the majority. Do I prefer Bach to Schumann? Do I prefer sensitive and cultivated people to squally brats on trains? Do I fail to thrill to mass ceremonials in Sanders Theatre? Then I must be guilty; I am impious. But this is only the beginning. What is really differentiating and most valuable in the intellectual is his gift of sharply and critically seeing through many conventional values, "democratic" as well as fascist, "wholesome" as well as treacherous. Since he cannot help, given his originality, having a critical attitude toward the dominant culture, he either represses those insights which detach him from that culture, or mixes them, as we have just now seen, with penances of "affirmation." What kind of authority has laid down the rule that it is wrong to be critical or negative if one cannot also be constructive? It is the same kind which favors the yes-man and yes-woman in business, politics, and domesticity. It is the same kind which, long ago, alleviated and manipulated guilt by inventing the confessional and coupling it with a system of penances.

In the conventional judgment, confession is regarded with approbation; it is good for the soul. We are invited so to regard it, although with qualifications, in Silone's play. Yet confession is often more immoral than the original act which is confessed, because it means that the person is unwilling to bear the responsibility for his actions; by confession they become no longer *his*, but are shared. Penance serves to destroy the last vestige of aloneness. Had Murica, for instance, been a moral person, able to stand alone, he would have felt neither remorse nor the need to confess; he would have recognized his betrayal as *his*, not to be shifted, not to be wiped out in the bookkeeping of the heavenly authorities. He would have decided what he was, and wanted to become, on the basis of his potentialities for the future, rather than on the basis of the judgment of his past made by outsiders.

Of course, the intellectuals and the novelists who represent them and speak for them are not Muricas; they are not dissembling traitors. Yet they, or the characters with whom they identify, go in heavily for self-accusation. Dorothea becomes expert at accusing herself. Koestler luxuriates in the guilty self-doubts which assail Peter, through the words of Bernard and the psychoanalyst. Silone's *mea culpa* is more complicated and more ambiguous; it deserves greater respect. Yet is has led him from the wonderful irreverence and humor of *The School for Dictators* (1938) and the early novels, to the sticky piety of some parts of *And He Hid Himself* (1945).

It is, I think, guilt which lies behind this sticky piety which is, in turn, the trade-mark of all these writers' "affirmations." Consequently, while talent and passion enliven their satire and criticism, their affirmations turn out to be "negative" and "unconstructive." *And He Hid Himself* ends lamely with the once-disillusioned and apathetic peasants uniting for new revolutionary action, although nothing in their character makes this turnabout convincing. Koestler concludes *Arrival and Departure* with a Hollywood trumped-up ending, also disguised as anti-fascist heroism. Such an ending shows a lack of respect for the previous seriousness of the book. In Miss Howe's book the ironic contradiction is even more striking, because so much of the book is devoted to Dorothea's discovery of American democracy, common or garden style. As Mrs. Trilling observes: "It is the lesson of democracy that finally cuts Dorothea down to size. The only flaw is that, with her, democracy itself also gets cut down to size—Miss Howe's firmest intentions to the contrary notwithstanding. *We Happy Few* ends with the wide American panorama presenting itself as little more than a series of small-spirited, harassed, and unhappy people who in their uneducated fashion are just as egotistical as the well-educated Dorothea. The commonalty of man, therapy for a poorly balanced emotional nature, shows itself to be largely a matter of helping make sandwiches with the other ladies or holding a neighbor's crying child. . . . It is as if the eye and ear that can catch the subtle nuances of the first section of *We Happy Few* cannot but go on to betray Miss Howe's formulation of conscience. While Miss Howe's program calls for Dorothea's regeneration through contemplation of some vast body of corporate virtue called the United States of Democracy, her literary senses feel out all the petty snobberies and prides that are bound to inform a nation of human beings. . . . Because draughts of solemnity taste so bad, we deceive ourselves that they are our eye-openers instead of our newest opiates."

To answer serious questions with trivial "solutions" is deceptive. For it puts the weight of the writer's earnestness, ethical conviction, and insight into the business of telling the reader that *his* doubts, too, are "negative" and bad. The reader is only too ready to believe this, and to indulge in his own orgy of identification with the pride of a Dorothea and the fall that follows. He, too, convinces himself that he is guilty, and thus rationalizes climbing on the bandwagon and stifling his critical uniqueness. There results a failure to develop his potentialities and, in Fromm's terms, an "escape from freedom." Readers, like writers, need support of their "nerve of failure" not anaesthesia. The ethical convictions that they lack are the belief in their own values, and the belief that only in their differences from others will they find their identity with them.

I trust no one will misunderstand me as saying that anti-fascist or pro-democratic activity is worthless or immoral. My point is that many people engage in such activity without ever deciding whether it has real meaning for them, and without the realistic judgment as to the practical possibilities which cannot be made in the absence of the nerve of failure. Instead, collective activity appears affirmative, sustains illusions, assuages doubt, and finds guilt useful; these are some of its attractions for powerless and isolated intellectuals.

§ THE ETHICS OF EXPERIENCE

THERE IS, however, another side to this powerlessness and isolation. The intellectual believes that he wishes to submerge his pride—i.e. his independence—in the fate of common humanity. In Silone's play where Murica offers himself up to almost certain death; in Koestler's novel where Peter returns to the wars despite conduct which should make him feel entitled, if any one ever did, to a passage to America and relative peace; in Miss Howe's book where Dorothea gives up her intellectual life and shares the hardships of a hospital, of war-time travel, of the camp-followers of servicemen, the motives appear noble. To a large extent they are. But there are other aspects of this type of behavior which are not noble at all. In many cases, the attempt to share wider human burdens and situations is a disguise for the greedy cult of experience, an anxious fear of missing those experiences which others have had or claim that they have had. Dorothea doesn't want to let any pitch of life go by. But the "experience" is not given raw by nature; we really experience only what we as individuals can inter- pret and assimilate as our own. In the phoniness of "sharing" com- mon experiences, there is masochism of two sorts, one obvious, one indirect. The obvious masochism is that the experience is usually painful and humiliating, as in Dorothea's case. (In an earlier genera- tion of novelists who were less religious and less ideological, the experience was generally supposed to be pleasureful, e.g., sleeping around or getting drunk.) The more concealed masochism lies in submission to the experiences everyone is supposed to have. It is really easier to do this than to experience one's course of life directly, let us say as an intellectual; for this latter requires an individuality of interpretation: the interpretation is not given by the culture. Dorothea does not ask herself what she, as a unique person, can uniquely experience in the very process of living; rather she welcomes being overwhelmed by what might be called the collective experience. "The burden of being one's own arbiter of taste and feeling had been removed." Her son loses his poignant closeness to her to become "just one more American gob." . . .

§ THE ETHICAL ELITE

THIS SUBMISSION to generally shared interpretations of experience is the most self-effacing form of the intellectual's response to his feel- ings of social weakness. Often, however, if not usually, his response disguises a strong desire for power and status. In joining the common man, the intellectual really wants to lead him; he feels called upon to save society. Apparent submission to the common lot and the common work—rather than the specialized work called for by his gifts—conceals delusions of grandeur. The intellectual is not willing to accept himself as he really is, with his unusual assets and their compensatory drawbacks, but he must be an "operator"; he must be "versatile"; he must be "practical." Coupled, therefore, with the masochism of pain and of rejection of the person's own talents and values, there is an even more concealed desire for domination, in which great claims are covertly staked out for leadership in the day-to-day social scene. Such a person privately feels that he has his finger in the dike against fascism, or whatever other evils threaten, and that if this finger were removed, but only then, the flood would overwhelm us. (Of course, situations can arise where this fantasy will be true; but where there is no "nerve of failure," judgments of social need and personal capacity cannot be realistic.) Thus the intellectual who professes to engage in the activities of ordinary folk only partially wants to lose his individuality in the collective whole; since he believes with Dorothea that the whole is greater than the sum of its parts, he wants the difference for himself. That is, he makes the secret stipulation that he is not really lost but will become one of the élite.

The form this stipulation takes in *We Happy Few* is subdued. Miss Howe demands of Dorothea, of her class, and perhaps of her sex, that they suffer more pain, become more unselfish, more humble, and in general lay claim to higher, more altruistic standards of behavior. Dorothea is harder on herself for sleeping with Gordon than she is on Gordon, or than she probably would be with one of the girls in Coeur d'Alene. This in itself may conceal pride—the arrogance of the member of the élite who must be a hero, or at the very least, an "example." Dorothea begins her mature life by rejecting marriage with the Idaho crusader. In this rejection there are some elements of snobbery: she laughs at his crudity and lack of sophistication. In her later encounter with him she feels herself inferior to him—this time he has rejected her. He is so much nobler and finer; his lack of aesthetic sensitivity, his simple moralistic sureness, become assets in her eyes. Dorothea, it is plain, has learned to value his differentness from her, but also to undervalue her differentness from him. If she does not belong among the happy few, he surely must. Our culture lives by these judgments of superiority and subordination, and differences among races, classes, and individual personalities are largely made use of to place oneself and others in the social hierarchy. In feeling unworthy, just as in feeling superior, Dorothea practices not the ethics of democratic equality but those of the collectivist discrimination between élite and mass.

This feeling of unworthiness, this need to rank herself, brings us back to the role of the romantic myth mentioned earlier: that intellectuals, that is, the self-conscious people, are more vicious than ordinary folk. Others are of course glad to hear this, for it means that demands are not to be made on them, but on the intellectuals who had the nerve to challenge them. And their envy is assuaged by learning that intellectuals are not only immoral but unhappy. More generally, this teaching means that people who are aware of the problem of choice are morally inferior to those whose choices are largely made for them by the culture. If this is so, a rational individualistic ethics becomes impossible. For where is new moral insight to come from, if not from the self-conscious few, from the morally perceptive Helen Howes and Koestlers and Silones? It is not likely to come from the "shared values" of some collective enterprise.

§ THE ETHICS OF SACRIFICE

CATHOLICISM is older than the answers of the Koestlers and the Howes, and it is illuminating to compare the attitude of Miss Howe towards Dorothea with the virtually identical attitude of the Catholic nuns towards the heroine, Nanda, of Antonia White's novel *Frost in May*. This is a very moving story, plainly autobiographical, of a young girl growing up in a convent school. At the school, one finds precisely the same feeling as in *We Happy Few* that pride, in the form of self-love, is the most intolerable sin. When one of the school girls really enjoys her excellent performance as Beatrice in *The Inferno*, she is removed from the role, lest she become vain. And Nanda is told by a nun: "It is a hundred times better to knit a pair of socks humbly for the glory of God than to write the finest poem or symphony for mere self-glorification."

Nanda is warned not to choose her friends "for such superficial attributes as cleverness and humour, and even for the still more unworthy and frivolous reasons of mere 'good looks' and a social position . . ." but instead for "solid piety" and a lower social status.

Beauty is, in fact, a great temptation: "A saint said it was dangerous to walk through a beautiful wood." For it means that things, and people, are looked at for their own sakes rather than as manifestations of collective purposes, in this case called God. When thirteen-year-old Nanda begins to write an adolescent novel, she is brutally expelled, and the head nun explains: "God asks very hard things from us, the sacrifice of what we love best and the sacrifice of our own wills. That is what it means to be a Christian. For years I have been watching you, Nanda. I have seen you growing up, intelligent, warm-hearted, apparently everything a child should be. But I have watched something else growing in you too—a hard little core of self-will and self-love. I told you once before that every will must be broken completely and re-set before it can be at one with God's will. And there is no other way. That is what true education, as we understand it here at Lippington, means." In return for this sacrifice of self, the convent offered collective security. If one did penance for one's own individuality, one was deprived of "the burden of being one's own arbiter," and permitted to feel at one with God.

The nuns were especially severe with Nanda for two reasons: she was remarkably sensitive and gifted, and she was not of an old wealthy Catholic family. It is always the individually gifted and socially weak who are the first to be asked to give themselves up. The same point might even be put more strongly. It is a truism that certain qualities or behavior traits are differently valued, depending on the social position of their possessor. What is offensive arrogance in an underling is charming insouciance in a lord. What is squirming subservience in the lower middle class is lovable modesty in the upper. At Miss Howe's hands, Dorothea's pride comes off more shabbily than that of Mrs. Calcott, the "true" aristocrat into whose family Dorothea climbs by matrimony. Likewise, the galling pride and independence of the intellectual is impressive in a "temperamental" movie star or ball player. Conversely, Nanda had, from the nuns' viewpoint, too many stubborn intellectual gifts for her sex and station.

Nanda escapes the nuns, very probably because she was ejected for rebellion, which was scarcely conscious and not at all planned. And it is generally not too difficult to escape the nuns, for their Puritanism—the especially virulent Puritanism of the Counter-Reformation—is other-worldly and is out of fashion. But, as Max Weber pointed out, the western world has closed the monasteries and turned earth itself into a nunnery. It is very much harder to resist the diluted but pervasive Puritanism of sacrifice and subservience which takes modern and "progressive" forms. It is harder for Dorothea to resist the "education" given her by what her society calls "life"—as in the phrases "that's life," "that's how things are"—than for Nanda to resist the "education" of antiquated Lippington.

Intellectuals today do have a hard time resisting their education, resisting attack. They need to be defended not attacked, if they are to succor their "nerve of failure." Miss Howe, a member of the class, attacks the "Happy Few" for their selfishness and pride. As we have seen, the intellectuals turn against themselves because they are few, and because they are not happy enough; that is, they have not enough love for themselves, or pride in what they are. "We ought to have our own class-consciousness," William James declared in his 1907 speech *The Social Value of the College Bred.*[7] " '*Les Intellectuels!*' What prouder clubname could there be than this one, used ironically by the party of 'redblood,' the party of every stupid prejudice and passion, during the anti-Dreyfus craze, to satirize the men in France who still retained some critical sense and judgment!"

7. *Memories and Studies* (1911) p. 323, quoted in 2 Ralph Barton Perry, *The Thought and Character of William James* (1936) p. 299.

4. A Philosophy for "Minority" Living

THE "NERVE OF FAILURE" is the courage to face aloneness and the possibility of defeat in one's personal life or one's work without being morally destroyed. It is, in a larger sense, simply the nerve to be oneself when that self is not approved of by the dominant ethic of a society.

In America, "success" is central; we are provided with a catalogue of what is success and what is failure, and nothing matters except achieving the first and avoiding the second. Whoever accepts the prevailing social standards of our times is not alone, not morally isolated; even if he is a "failure" he remains related, if only in fantasy, to the dominant theme. Such a person has no more need of the "nerve of failure" than a gambler who has had a bad day at roulette: for him life is centered on the wheel, and he remains related, though anxious and miserable, so long as he can go on watching the others who are still in the game. The "nerve of failure" is needed only for really heretical conduct: when one renounces even the company of misery and takes the greater risk of isolation—that is, the risk of never rejoining the company.

The "nerve of failure" is akin to the traditional virtue of "courage in defeat," praised in a number of ethical systems. But it differs in this sense: it comes into play before defeat is actual, when it is only a possibility. To be sure, one may have a good deal of the "nerve to fail" and still be cowardly in extreme situations. But, on the other hand, while many can find courage in defeat only when others are defeated too, those endowed with the "nerve of failure" have the capacity to go it alone.

A man may maintain a lonely course by other means. He may not realize that he is heretical—Rousseau, the "primitive" painter, seems to have thought he was painting just like everybody else. He may be more or less crazy, constructing an elaborate system to justify himself—as did Fourier and Comte. He may attach himself to nature and to imagined transcendental forces—as did William Blake. He may overestimate his personal influence and the extent to which others are listening to what seems to him self-evident and reasonable —as did Robert Owen, the English manufacturer and utopian socialist, whose later life was on the surface one long series of failures. He may convince himself that history, or science, is inevitably on his side—as did Karl Marx. He may protect himself from aloneness by remaining conventional in many spheres—as Darwin did. He may surround himself with a small body of ardent disciples and limit his contact with contemporaries—this also was Comte's way. Only very rarely will an individual with enough originality to disturb society be able, without such adventitious aids, to face his situation realistically and yet be unshaken by what the majority considers "failure."

These moral attitudes in the face of frustration and defeat become even more complicated, enormously more so, in the life of groups lacking material power, whether domestic "minorities" or small nations. Negroes, Jews, intellectuals, and women as domestic "minorities"; Poles, Irishmen, Italians as small nations coping with big powers —all feel the need of protecting themselves in one way or another from the moral impact of power. In different historical periods they develop different means and modes of coping with this problem. If I discuss the fate and problems of the Jews here, it is because, despite all differences, they still provide one of the most suggestive paradigms of the relatively powerless group.

§ I

FOR THE LAST two thousand years the Jews have been a minority; before that, it may be suggested, they were a "small power," a buffer state.[1] But until recent times, many Jews did not have what we might today regard as a typical minority outlook. Their ethical regime was quite defiantly Ptolemaic, revolving about the small group of Jews, not the larger Gentile group—and, accordingly, they learned to remain unimpressed by Gentile temporal power. Being unimpressed did not mean being unafraid—material power might beat or starve one to death; it did mean refusing to surrender moral hegemony to the majority merely because it had power. Instead, the Jews saw through power by observing its blindness in comparison with the vision possible to the weak. A saying of Nahman of Bratzlav exemplifies this outlook: "Victory cannot tolerate truth, and if that which is true is spread before your very eyes, you will reject it, because you are a victor. Whoever would have truth itself, must drive hence the spirit of victory; only then may he prepare to behold the truth."

In other words, since the Jews' ethical scheme placed no great premium on material power, on material success, the majority was not

---

1. I am indebted to Dr. Erich Fromm for calling my attention to the relations between Jewish power and ethics in their historical changes. The reader will recognize, of course, how difficult it is to generalize about Jewish ethics, as about anything else concerning "Jews"—or indeed any group.

looked up to with envy and admiration; hence its verdicts, both as to the ends of life and as to the value of the minority itself, did not echo in the Jews' self-consciousness.

A related attitude was expressed in the belief—which kept the Jews Jews and not Christians—that the Messiah was still to come. To be sure, many Jews during the dark periods between the 11th and 17th centuries were deceived at times into believing that the Messiah had indeed come. But these aberrations were limited in scope and time: Jews in general continued to have faith in the continuance into the future of the process of revelation and to be unimpressed by contemporary events and the would-be Messiahs who, consciously or unconsciously, exploited these events. If we do not take this belief, that the Messiah will yet come, too literally, we can see that one of its meanings is an attack on the powers that be, and an emphatic statement that justice and peace shall some day—as they do not today—prevail everywhere among men.[2]

Jewish ethics, though not devoid of authoritarian strains, is, like Greek ethics, based primarily on reason, although reason has sometimes descended to casuistry. It is an ethics of reason both in its ends, which are human and earthly, and in its means, which are argumentative rather than dogmatic. Even the casuistry seems often to have been turned to the humanizing of authoritative texts, as a lawyer might "interpret" a statute or decision in order to reach a more humane and reasonable result.

Such an ethical pattern as the one just described would seem admirably fitted to the psychic situation of a powerless minority which —unlike, let us say, the Republican party during recent years—has no chance of soon becoming a majority. But, as we know, ethical systems are not developed in the abstract; though they have a momentum of their own, Jewish ethical patterns arose in connection with given social and economic conditions; and they were embroidered by complex, demanding rituals and racial myths.

Occasionally, the group's "nerve of failure" was supported by the notion that its very powerlessness proved the Jews to be in fact the Chosen of God. In this way, defeat itself could strengthen the faith of the "saving remnant" of Jews. On the other hand, we should recognize that the spiritual forces that gave the Jews their immense moral resistance in the ghetto rested on a material base that, though often pre-

---

2. There are many Messianic, or as we should say, utopian elements in Christianity, of course; but the established institutionalized churches have always tended to play down these disturbing notions and to treat revelation as a completed or at least a centralized process. Dissenting sects have tended to restore the Messianic faith.

carious, had considerable solidity. The Jews were part of the medieval order, which gave them, like everyone else, a relatively fixed psychic place, even though theirs was that of pariah. (See Daniel Bell, "A Parable of Alienation," *Jewish Frontier*, November 1946.) Within the medieval order, moreover, the Jews developed a near monopoly of certain skills, in artisanship as well as in trade, which were handed down, as in the guilds, from father to son.

Thus, the ghetto walls buttressed the Jewish ethical walls.

§ II

THE RISE of modern capitalist society and the levelling of ghetto walls may be said to have started an uneven dialectic of change in the spiritual and material bases of Jewish life. Many Jews in the main Western countries surrendered their inherited ethical system in return for a chance to participate in the wider world, thus losing their special sources of spiritual strength. Sometimes this was done out of opportunism; more often than not this drive was mixed with more idealistic motives. For among the forces that broke down ghetto barriers from the outside was the Enlightenment. Liberty, Equality, and Fraternity were a set of values with great moral appeal—as well as with many parallels in Jewish ethics.

The Enlightenment was impious towards authority, utopian about the future, and hospitable to reason. What then could have been more attractive to many of the most ethically sensitive Jews, especially at a time when the ghetto tradition itself seems to have become somewhat impoverished in Western Europe? Such Jews could move from a religious to a political minority position with hardly any change in ethical attitude.

The great Jewish intellectual and political leaders of this period represented, in highly individual ways, mergers of Jewish and Enlightenment ethics, and the retention of the "nerve of failure." At the same time, certain skills and attitudes nurtured by ghetto life became useful and rewarding assets in the modern world. In the expanding era of international finance and international markets, the developed financial and commercial skills of a Rothschild, as later of a Rosenwald, were important: some Jews, that is, had a head-start. Jewish cultivation of a particular type of intelligence, moreover, could be turned to account in modern managerial, professional, and intellectual capacities; while the Jewish view of an open future (the Messiah still to come) was well adapted to leaders of progressive political or labor movements. In sum, many Jews gained personal power and self-confidence during the free capitalism that lasted until the close of the 19th century.

In those days, Jewish self-contempt did not exist in its characteristic contemporary forms. While rising Jews often shared the attitudes common to parvenus, they had confidence in their ultimate social acceptance, or that of their progeny; consciously or unconsciously, they felt they had something of particular value to offer. Likewise, those Jews who took a direct share in the struggles of the Enlightenment felt no insecurity or self-belittlement as Jews; they could be wholeheartedly indignant at discrimination since they had confidence in the ultimate triumph of the ideals of the Enlightenment. They, too, felt that they had something to offer—namely, a social program that the majority needed and would learn to want.

During this period, therefore, the consequences of Jewish acceptance of a largely Gentile ethics were positive: both because that ethics was rational and progressive and because the role and material power of Jews were on the increase.

§ III

HOWEVER, HISTORICAL DEVELOPMENTS soon began to undermine the material position of the Jews and give a different meaning to their new ethical position. As heavy industry grew in importance, it gradually freed itself from the free market. Jewish family and group "trade secrets" soon became common property. "Fair trade" acts and similar autarchic limitations on the free market came to restrict Jewish merchandising talents (while permitting, however, the marginal survival of many small Jewish shopkeepers). Though Jews shared in the growing managerial and professional openings of the "new" middle class, they began to be faced with increasing competition.

This lessening of the Jew's sense of economic value, and of his self-confidence in the possession of a special skill, helped lessen his feeling of ethical security, and made him increasingly a psychological victim of the dominant social and economic systems of the modern world.

But this is also a fate that, both in its economic and its psychological aspects, has overtaken vast numbers of the less "successful" classes in our new society, and condemned them to "alienation." For them, as for Jews, the relative security of a social role fixed by skill, family, age, and sex has vanished. One must now "show one's stuff" in a competitive market, and one's stuff is one's "personality," an externalized part of the self, and not primarily one's matter-of-fact skill. (See Erich Fromm, *Man for Himself* pp. 67-82.) In other words, it is not the genuine self that is put on the market in the race for success, or even economic survival, but the "cosmetic" self, which is free of any aroma of personal, non-marketable idiosyncracy as it is free of "B.O." or last year's waistline. If this artificial self succeeds, then doubts may be temporarily quieted. However, since self-evaluation has been surrendered to the market, failure in the market, or even fear of failure, is translated into self-contempt. (The market in this sense includes all spheres of life—business, politics, art, love, friendship.)

For the dominant groups—those that, by birth or temperament or luck, have been able to make the grade—the subjection of all values to the test of the market is convenient. It justifies their own existence in what amounts to moral rather than merely power-political terms. In a market situation pervaded by what Karl Polanyi has termed the "market mentality" (*Commentary*, February 1947), control of the economy will carry with it, to an unusual degree, control of the ethical regime. And the market, we must remember, has had perhaps a more complete sway in America than elsewhere.

Now, add to this the fact that America happens to have colonials —Negroes and other ethnic minorities—within its borders, and that we have developed a racialism not to be found in Europe. Upon the Jewish minority, this situation operates with special force, as can be seen in the encounter between Jewish traditions and the melting pot.

The melting pot had, especially in its early days, valuable elements: a kind of Whitmanesque equalitarian vigor and a seeming hospitality to cultural diversity—but it increasingly became a form of internal imperialism in the interest of the earlier arrivals. Its aim was narrowed to producing "Americans all" of a starched uniformity, freed of all cultural coloring, maladjustment, or deviation. The main burden was on the minorities, while few demands were made by the ethical system of the Protestant majority. (Protestantism and modern capitalism, having grown up together, have always been congenial.)

Even today, the typical Protestant businessman still makes money as a by-product of his devotion to his work and his organization; the money, as Max Weber pointed out, serves as a proof of fulfilment of ethical duty, of having found one's "calling," one's proper—and therefore prosperous—social niche. But there is no such compatibility between non-Protestant ethics and modern capitalism; hence the moral disorientation worked by the latter among Mexicans and South Americans generally, Eastern and Southern Europeans, and Treaty-Port Chinese. The same moral disorientation was produced among these people when they emigrated to America, affecting not only Jews from pre-capitalist Eastern Europe, but also Italians, Greeks, Mexicans. For these non-Protestants, business was not originally the expression of their religion, but a by-product of the need for money, status, or family security. For the dominant groups, the Protestant—or, more accurately, the Puritan—strain in our culture permitted a development of a kind of ethics intertwined with business. "Mere" money-making, for example, was open to criticism when not accompanied by an ethos of business as "calling" or as service. The non-Protestant, on the other hand, was often led, both by the special pressures of modern capitalism upon him and the strangeness of the Protestant market ethic to his own, to discard his own values without assimilating prevailing values. As a result he often became a caricature of the American careerist.

In this process, certain elements in Jewish ethics—the attitude towards power, towards the future, and towards reason—often tend to become distorted. The irreverent attitude towards power becomes contempt for what remains of the Puritan ethics of business and professional enterprise, which is interpreted as softness or hypocrisy. Irreverence towards authority degenerates into an indiscriminate disrespect for convention, whether that convention is an exploitative device or a crystallization of decent standards of personal intercourse. This Jewish irreverence may also appear as a cynicism that seeks money and power without the conviction that they represent the fruits of virtue or that they are genuinely important ends—or even the means to such ends.

Similarly, the Jewish attitude towards the future, with its Messianic devaluation of present reality, can be fitted, by distortion, all too nicely into the American success tradition, where—as the Lynds have remarked—people live "at" the future, eternally "on the make," either awaiting a lucky break for themselves, or planning for one for their offspring.

Finally, the Jewish attitude towards reason can also suffer a change. "Pure" reason for its own sake, what we might call Talmudic intelligence, is at a discount in America: it is not "practical." On the other hand, manipulative intelligence is exceedingly useful; in fact, the entire Jewish constellation of intelligence, humor, and charm is often humiliatingly exploited—for instance, by so many Jewish comedians—as entertainment and self-ingratiation.

Jews in America, like other Americans, go in for hero-worship; and it is possible to trace, in the types they frequently select for admiration, patterns of compromise between the American Protestant tradition and their own. Though they can afford to admire the "impractical" Einstein because he has been such a world-famous success, they tend more to bestow their medals on intelligent operators like Brandeis and Baruch. Though these men have the ear of presidents, they are not mere "court Jews": they are quite outspoken; moreover, they are old and white-haired, appropriate to the Jewish reverence for aged wisdom—yet they are also energetic and eupeptic, in keeping with the American worship of dynamic youth.

It goes without saying that—like Jewish ethics—American Protestant ethics contains many divergent themes, and that the Enlightenment still lives in its best representatives. However, the Jew emerging from the European ghetto was not met at Ellis Island by the representatives of enlightenment. At most, he was given a choice between accepting the melting pot and the ethics of success—as interpreted by earlier immigrants often bent on exploiting him economically or psychically—or trying to retain his traditions as a transient in a voluntary ghetto. If he took the latter course, he was seldom stimulated towards any effort to reinterpret the meaning of his ethical background in terms of the American context; rather he tended to freeze defensively in his memories and rituals. If he took the former —perhaps more typical—course, he altered his ethical and intellectual inheritance so that it could be turned to account in the struggle for success, just as a neurotic makes use of his illness, or a cripple his misery, for fragmentary advantages.

However, the same recent social and economic changes that have weakened the material position of Jews have also tended to alter the meaning of success as such. The mere matter-of-fact achievement of high economic or even political position no longer satisfies. Since we market our personalities, it is imperative that we be popular, accepted; and handicapped ethnic minorities are not popular. The Jew who plays the power and success game can hardly help viewing himself through the eyes of the more successful players.

Bernard Marx, a character in Aldous Huxley's *Brave New World*, despises himself because he is short. The majority, stunted lower-caste people, are also short, but he compares himself with the tall top-caste to which in other respects he "belongs," and to which, though with some ambivalence, he surrenders his ethical judgment. That is, he accepts from them the same cultural emphasis on height that sells Adler Elevator Shoes (the sexual reward being, as so often, a symbol for the reward of status). Since his society puts a high value on science, Bernard Marx's shortness is explained in seemingly rational terms by the rumor that some alcohol accidentally got into his feeding solution when he was a bottled embryo (alcohol being intentionally used only to stunt the lower castes). In any rational ethics, of course, there would be no correlation between height and human value. Yet Bernard does not quite dare look behind the "scientific" social judgment, and so must turn the blame upon himself. Among Jews, this relation between physical appearance and ethical valuation is seldom quite so obvious (there is more of this among Negroes, who tend to rate each other according to lightness of skin and other white characteristics); nevertheless, the Jewish devaluation of Jewish physiognomy is not confined to Hollywood, as the flourishing state of plastic surgery in Manhattan would testify.

§ IV

IF A MINORITY accepts the majority's definition of good looks, we would expect that the majority's definition of good conduct would be likewise accepted. And so it turns out. But is the Jew who sharply criticizes the behavior of his fellow-Jews accepting the majority's standards, or is he not simply exercising his human privilege—from which it would be anti-Semitic to exclude him—of disliking certain kinds of behavior? We cannot tell at first glance, though we may wonder why, amid all the evil in the world and all the examples of vicious and mean conduct, he fastens on the Jews. Moreover, even when the traits he selects for attention are not so obviously differentiated according to race—where, for instance, a Jew claims to despise Italian and Greek as well as Jewish manners—we may ask the same sort of question: why is he preoccupied with differences in manners and not, let us say, with differences in coldness and warmth, gloominess and wit? Has he not accepted the majority's judgments as to what is important and the majority's criteria of good and evil?[3]

However, the Jew whose focus of criticism is the poor behavior of his fellow-Jews may urge that, far from accepting the majority's standards, he feels merely threatened by them: he is worried by the menace of anti-Semitism if Jews do not conform, and is being "realistic." Here we may ask why, among the many "causes" of anti-Semitism, he selects primarily those over which Jews themselves seem to have some control. Perhaps better manners on the subway would mitigate anti-Jewish feeling; perhaps if Jews did not appear in public at all—no Frankfurter on the Supreme Court, no Dubinsky in the labor movement—they would not be noticed. But in advocating such things, has this timorous Jew done anything more than accept the majority's anti-Semitic stereotype, as well as their rationalizations for refusing to accept Jews as individuals on their own merits? Is this Jew really concerned about the daily quality of direct personal contacts between Jews and non-Jews, which might, in the long run, have some marginal effect on anti-Semitism?

---

3. I don't mean to enter here upon complicated questions of national character and to examine whether Jewish manners are characteristically undignified, or British behavior is really lacking in warmth; I am raising the problem rather of the way in which majority ethics gives rise to a process of stereotyping and selection in which certain traits are valued, others devalued, still others ignored.

But ordinarily I think it can be shown that the threat such a Jew feels is that of being himself caught, in his own deeper consciousness, in the majority stereotype of "the Jew." This involves not only contempt for "the other Jews," but his own self-belittlement. The real cause of his concern with the behavior of his fellow Jews is the moral retreat he has made in servilely accepting the majority's ethics, not the so-called undesirable Jewish traits that provoked his anxiety. And if he wanted to do something about anti-Semitism—and if he understood what in the face of fear is difficult to understand—he might begin with his own moral subservience, where he has at least a real chance to change things, instead of trying to reform the manners or career choices of his fellow-Jews.

If we confined our attention to such instances of the acceptance of majority judgments as these (and of course we are selecting a particular segment of majority opinion and not the entire spectrum), we might underestimate the extent of present-day Jewish ethical bondage. However, since many Jews, especially in recent years, have tried to repress their tendencies towards group-belittlement of themselves, evidence of this self-belittlement—where not covertly released in gibe or gesture—is less obvious since it issues in reactions that are seldom fully conscious.

Apologetics as a reaction to attack hardly needs discussion in these pages. It surrenders the ethical initiative, for it permits the anti-Semite to frame the issue of debate and the norms of criticism. Denials that Jews are rich, radical, or rude concede to the anti-Semites that it is a crime to be rich, radical, or rude.

Another reaction is self-denial, in which Jews deny as Jews that there are such things as Jews. Sometimes this self-denial is a "liberal" reaction, an insistence that there are no anthropological (racial) differences, out of a fear that such differences would be exploited. Sometimes this self-denial is rationalized as a "radical" reaction, by the insistence that there is no "Jewish question" whatsoever, but only some other question, such as the question of capitalism. Jews who take this latter course do at least identify themselves with a submerged group larger than their own, but they run the risk of carrying the position to extremes in believing that the Jewish problem, despite cultural and historical differences, is in all respects similar to—let us say—the Negro problem, or the problem of the working class as a whole. In this way, the specifically Jewish overtones are lost; but indeed this is precisely what the self-denier wants.

Still a third reaction occurs as a revulsion against all traits associated with the majority stereotype of "the Jew." Are Jews pushing? Very well, we will be retiring. Are Jews over-critical? Very well, we will swallow our protest.[4] The minority group actually expects more from itself than from the rest of the population; that is, it applies the majority ethics but with a double standard.

It is evident that this timid double standard is very different from the feeling of *noblesse oblige* of certain ruling classes. These classes have no doubts of their right to rule, even when they are far from perfect; in contrast, the "double-standard" Jews seem to say that Jewish claims for full equality are invalid if Jews are merely human.

In all these instances Jews try to cope with American anti-Semitism in terms of majority stereotypes, which by their very irrationality prevent both minority and majority from making any fresh approaches to reality.

§ V

RECENT EVENTS have brought still another aspect of Jewish self-doubt to light. I think that exaggeration of the uniqueness of the crime committed by the Nazis against the Jews may sometimes be read as betraying an unconscious doubt as to the ethical justification of the Jewish case. When some Jews claim that no injustice was ever so great, nor any dictator the peer of Hitler, they are not always simply venting an understandable grief. They are afraid that the very enormity, the irretrievable quality, of the killing of the Jews must prove something about them, something in fact against them. For there is no way that a success ethics can cope with unavenged material defeat. Some may try to still the doubt—whether, after all, Hitler was not right—by racist vindictiveness against the German people. What seems to be lingering in the minds of so many is the notion that Hitler somehow won a victory over the Jews.

On the other hand, a Jew who has found his way to an independent ethics would say with Rabbi Johanan: "All distress that Israel and the world bear in common is distress; the distress confined to Israel alone is not distress" (From *In Time and Eternity*). On the ethical side, he would find little to choose between the Nazi murder of Jews and of Poles, or between the concentration camps

---

4. Some Jews indulge in what looks on the surface like just the opposite reaction. They aggressively play up what they accept as Jewish traits; sometimes they select the very ones that are detested in the majority stereotype; sometimes they indiscriminately fasten their affection on those traits, good or bad. Are Jews pushing? Very well, pushing is nice, and we will push. Are Jews critical? Very well, let us exploit this fine cultural resource. Some young Negroes, too, play this pathetic game, accepting the whites' judgments in the very act of making an issue with them. Likewise, many middle-class intellectuals spend their lives reacting against middle-class standards and values, for instance in bohemianism, as if this were the only ethical contrast to what they conceive as the middle class.

of Hitler and Stalin; on the political side, he would be free to perceive that the slaughter of the European Jews was to some extent a historical accident in which they happened to become material game and spiritual symbol for a congeries of reactionary forces.

Victory and defeat, success and failure, are facts. But they are facts in the world of power, subject to an evaluative judgment in which defeat may become victory and victory defeat. Who "really" won in the war between Athens and Sparta? It is conventional today to decide in favor of Athens. What, for example, about Weimar Germany? Are many of its critics, who attack its experimentalism, its pacifism, its artistic and intellectual "irresponsibility" and lack of consensus only disapproving of these tendencies because they did not ward off political defeat? Many generations hence, may not people look back with admiration on the cultural and even some of the political and social achievements of that brief period between 1919 and 1933, and pay little attention to all our elaborate explanations for its "failure," explanations which, as in the case of the slaughtered Jews, consciously or unconsciously subordinate ourselves to an ethics of success pure and simple, and overemphasize what was wrong with the victim?

Even such devastating defeats as those of the last decade the truly moral man must find the courage and the capacity to face with the nerve of failure.

§ VI

OF COURSE, it would be applying a double standard to expect Jews to have the nerve of failure when other groups do not. Moreover, it would be as unfair to blame Jews for losing their traditional ethics in the melting pot, as to blame them for not emerging from it as Anglo-Saxon gentlemen. But the opposite error, which tolerantly understands all minority behavior as the inevitable consequence of persecution, is not helpful either. The real question is, what choices do the Jews now have?

There is no want of proposed solutions, many of which seem to me to repeat or exacerbate the circular problems in which a minority is so often caught. One is a plea for a return to the ritual and religious elements historically linked to the ethical resources of Jewish life. It is not surprising that this same plea for what amounts to a medieval revival is also being made at this time by many non-Jews as a general therapy for modern alienation.

The usual criticism of such efforts to restore psychic security and dignity is that they are impractical, since the change from medieval to modern times cannot be reversed. But another criticism can be made from the standpoint of the very Jewish ethics which one wants to recapture. That ethics contains a fervent claim for a more decent future, a claim that takes the form of Messianic hope. Though the glories of biblical Palestine are looked back upon with pride and sorrow, utopia lies in the future, not in the nostalgic past. To seek restoration of an earlier time is to confess intellectual and ethical impoverishment. The "nerve of failure" implies the ability to face the *possibility* of failure, but it is rooted in the assumption that past and present failures need not mark the limits of human powers. To be satisfied with something no better than that which medieval Jewry had—assuming, in defiance of all reason, that this could be attained—is a surrender of that demand typical for Jews (though of course not exclusively theirs) for a more decent future for Jews and non-Jews alike.

The surrender of utopian claims is one of the most revealing symptoms of the current state of minority ethics. Despite differences in shading, such claims are a part of Judaic, Christian, and Enlightenment ethical systems. But they are very much at a discount today. The powerful do not need visions; they either fear or scorn them. Their response to such claims is: "If you don't like it here, why don't you go back where you came from?" Some minority representatives aggressively propose to do just that, to go back—in time. Whereas the older success game permitted many minorities to be easily satisfied with petty gains in the American scene, the newer religious revival would satisfy them with petty dreams from the past.

Political Zionism is another suggestion proposed as a means of obtaining psychic as well as physical security for Jews. Jewish nationalists seem to be even more impressed by worldly power than Jews who urge a religious revival; they have given up the success game on the domestic scene only to transfer it to the international sphere; this entails a complete acceptance of majority attitudes towards force and *raison d'état*. Thus they abandon the critical attitude which subjects to principle and to reason all claims of power and all demands for loyalty—an attitude which I believe to be among the significant contributions of Jewish ethics to the general problem of the powerless minority and the small nation.

If Jews are to avoid self-defeating courses of action, it would seem necessary to clarify the themes in their ethical tradition that fit the problem of the powerless, and then to separate these from their cultist and ritualistic trappings. The way food is prepared or the style of beards are locally various and ethically quite indifferent matters—questions of taste and not of value. To attach one's love and admiration to them is to risk putting the superficial or parochial aspects of Jewish culture in the center of affection, rather than its ethically significant elements. And it is this sort of love that so easily runs over into fondness for, or defensiveness about, even the weaker sides of Jewish life in America. This sort of chauvinism is particularly easy to rationalize today, just because the Jews seem at the moment a defeated people on the world's stage. It would be well, however, to recall Nietzsche's advice not to love a defeated nation. (Nietzsche seems to have meant that an honorable person finds it harder in defeat than in victory to detach himself from his nation —witness German nationalism after the First World War.)

The concept of minority ethics suggested here is not meant as an invitation to minority fanaticism or as a condemnation of all majority ethics as such; the minority position in itself is no guarantee of ethical superiority. Rather, it points out that the Jewish minority in America must discover what are the ethically significant themes relevant to its present situation, which in turn requires reinterpretation of Jewish tradition.

Such a reinterpretation of tradition would in itself do something to overcome Jewish self-belittlement by giving the past meaning without mystery. But the more direct function of this reinterpretation would be to foster a Jewish self-image counterposed to the majority ethics. Adherence to majority ethics may be a help in social climbing, or in rationalizing one's acceptance of the values of the culture that happens to be dominant. But the experience of many Jews in America must be that this adherence is emotionally precarious, and that it easily becomes self-destructive once things do not go well for oneself or one's group. There are more ways of acquiring a feeling of "belonging" in the American scene than the alternatives of melting pot or parochial separation.

Yet is it not merely wishful to ask that Jews today, of all people, be reasonable men looking for guidance in their personal and political lives to a rational, and therefore experimental and tentative, ethics? No matter how ethically inadequate the ritualist, racialist, and nationalist therapies may be, does not their very existence prove that the vast bulk of Jews cannot be expected to defend themselves morally against power without the encompassing support of daily ritual observances, or without the *ersatz* program of Palestinian terrorism? Is not one of my own arguments—that Jewish ethics has been closely related to Jewish material circumstance—proof of the impracticality of any therapy that begins with ethics and not with environment? I would answer that movements of thought among a people are never entirely determined by the material setting. On the contrary, an ethical and intellectual feature—such, for instance, as an eloquent tradition of utopian thought—may itself become one of the institutional forces of the environment. In the case of the Diaspora history of the Jews, utopian thought was even a decisive force. Of course, such a program does not pretend to "save" the Jews; its goal is moral independence from the majority, not physical survival or a solution of "the Jewish problem." Its gains would largely be in the happier lives of Jews and other powerless folk. Nevertheless, a reduction of Jewish self-contempt and an increase in the Jewish "nerve of failure" is bound to make for more realistic, as well as attractive, behavior by individual Jews and Jewish agencies, and so reduce those minor, pointless tensions and self-defeating patterns that Jews themselves may create.

Specific groups of Jews in America are meeting widely different problems and experiences. There is room for research into the intricate relations between their ethics and their attitudes toward themselves, research that would test and refine such hypotheses as those suggested here. Such work has meaning for minority groups in general. At the same time American Jews have much to learn from other minority experiences and traditions—from Negroes in America and South Africa; from anti-fascists in Mussolini's Italy, Hitler's Germany, Franco's Spain, Peron's Argentina; from intellectual and cultural dissenters from modern capitalism and Stalinist Communism; and so on. Moreover, the utopian traditions of Christian sects, of the Enlightenment, of America itself—these have contributions to make to the development of a minority ethics. In fact, is not such development enjoined on almost all of us by our human situation? For who does not face at some time—at least as a child—a conflict between his own values and those of a stronger and oppressive power? Until a time when power is no longer used oppressively, minorities will have a compelling need of the nerve of failure to defend an independent view of the self and of what life holds.

5. Some Observations on Community Plans and Utopia

$\mathbf{A}$ REVIVAL of the tradition of utopian thinking seems to me one of the important intellectual tasks of today. Since we live in a time of disenchantment, such thinking, where it is rational in aim and method and not mere escapism, is not easy; it is easier to concentrate on programs for choosing among lesser evils, even to the point where these evils can scarcely be distinguished, one from the other. For there is always a market for lesser-evil thinking which poses immediate alternatives; the need for thinking which confronts us with great hopes and great plans is not so evident. Yet without great plans, it is hard, and often self-defeating, to make little ones. Such utopian thinking requires what I have termed "the nerve of failure," that is, the ability to face the possibility of defeat without feeling morally crushed. Without this sort of courage, any failure implies a personal defect, and brings feelings of intolerable isolation; to avoid this fate, people tend to repress their claims for a decent world to a "practical" point, and to avoid any goals, personal or social, that seem out of step with common sense.

Curiously enough, however, in a dynamic political context, it is the modest, common-sensical goals which are often unattainable—therefore utopian in the derogatory sense. I do not mean, of course, that "anything can happen"; I do mean that the self-styled realist tends to underestimate the strength of latent forces because he is too impressed by what he "sees." To take only one example, it often seems that the retention of a given status quo is a modest hope; many lawyers, political scientists and economists occupy themselves by suggesting the minimal changes which are necessary to stand still; yet today this hope is almost invariably disappointed; the status quo proves the most illusory of goals. To aim at this goal requires little nerve, for many people share the same hope; so long as things appear to go well, anxiety is stilled; and even when things go badly, many people will join in providing rationalizations for the failure: misery will have company.

The problem of how individuals can fortify themselves, without insanity, to the point at which they will believe their own, isolated imaginations, is of course a very old one. It is this problem that Spinoza deals with when he discusses how the Biblical prophets attempted to assure themselves of certainty:

"For instance, Jeremiah's prophecy of the destruction of Jerusalem was confirmed by the prophecies of other prophets, and by the threats in the law, and therefore it needed no sign; whereas Hananiah, who, contrary to all the prophets, foretold the speedy restoration of the state, stood in need of a sign, or he would have been in doubt as to the truth of his prophecy, until it was confirmed by facts. 'The prophet which prophesieth of peace, when the word of the prophet shall come to pass, then shall the prophet be known that the Lord hath truly sent him.' "[1]

Today in America, at least in intellectual circles, the Jeremiahs share a widespread, and in that sense comforting, defeatism; there are few Hananiahs who prophesy restoration and peace. The recent book *Communitas: Means of Livelihood and Ways of Life*,[2] by Percival and Paul Goodman, is therefore particularly welcome; it is avowedly utopian, both in its critique of earlier community plans and in its presentation of new ones. I propose in this article to indicate some of the Goodmans' contributions to utopian thinking; but first to place these in perspective by a review, necessarily sketchy, of the present state of such thinking in America.

§ I

A HUNDRED YEARS AGO, in the *Communist Manifesto*, Marx and Engels welcomed the criticisms which their so-called utopian predecessors, such as St. Simon, Fourier, and Owen, had made of capitalist society, but they rejected the peaceable methods of these men for achieving socialism. Their label "utopian" (expanded in Engels' *Socialism: Utopian and Scientific*) stuck as a derogatory term. Moreover, having taken their polemical position, they were themselves bound by it, and carefully avoided setting forth more than fragmentary views on what the classless society might look like: this refusal became a mark of realism and orthodoxy—and a great convenience to left-wing politicians and writers. While some Europeans, such as William Morris and Theodor Hertzka,[3] continued to work in the older utopian tradition as late as the '90's, the masses were soon recruited either for Marxist "scientific," *i.e.* hard-headed socialism, or for Fabian and Social-Democratic versions of practical, unmessianic politics.

In the rough and ready America of the last century, a serious interest in utopian thought found other obstacles than Marxism. However,

---

1. *The Philosophy of Spinoza* (Ratner ed.), p. 51.
2. University of Chicago Press. All quotations are from this source unless otherwise indicated.
3. For discussion and bibliography see Lewis Mumford, *The Story of Utopias*.

the country itself seemed to be a functioning utopia to peoples elsewhere, and it was the scene of most of the utopian experiments of the
period, as in Oneida and New Harmony. Immense enthusiasm greeted
Bellamy's *Looking Backward* (1888); during the same period, huge
audiences in the Midwest were inspired by the utopian prophecies of
Ignatius Donnelly.[4] All this ferment has vanished. The appeal of such
writers as Bellamy appears to have declined just about the time that
the socialism of Debs and DeLeon began to make some headway in
America. But since this type of socialism, too, has died out (of course,
economic determinism has always been influential in America, from
the Founding Fathers on down), we must look for deeper causes at
work.

The idea of a dialectical opposition between "ideology" and "utopia" is suggested by Karl Mannheim's book, though I use the words
here in a somewhat different sense from his.[5] A "utopia" I define as a
rational belief which is in the long-run interest of the holder; it is a
belief, not in existing reality, but in a potential reality; it must not
violate what we know of nature, including human nature, though it
may extrapolate our present technology and must transcend our present social organization.[6] An "ideology" I define as an irrational system
of belief, not in the interest of the holder. It is sold to him by a group
which has an interest in swindling him; he accepts it because of his
own irrational needs, including his desire to submit to the power of
the vendor group. An ideology may contain elements of truth; these
serve to lend plausibility, rather than to open the eyes and increase
the awareness of the recipient. Contrariwise, a utopia may contain elements of error, initially less significant than its truth, which assist its
later conversion into an ideology: in this way, the utopias of one age
tend to harden in a distorted form into the ideologies of the next,
taken on faith rather than rationally rediscovered.

The America of the last century, I suggest, made room for a limited amount of utopian thought and experiment because, among many
other factors, the capitalism of that period was singularly unconcerned

4. The early chapters of Dorfman, *Thorstein Veblen and His America* evoke
and document this atmosphere.

5. Mannheim, *Ideology and Utopia* (translated from the German by Wirth
and Shils). See also Mannheim, "Utopia," in 15 *Encyc. Soc. Sci.*, p. 200.

6. These features distinguish utopian thinking from, on the one hand, a mere
dream, and on the other hand, a mere description of existing facts. In other
words, "utopia" is a place—in contemporary terms, a plan—that now is nowhere,
save maybe for pilot models, but that may someday be somewhere, so far as
science can say; thus, heaven is not a utopia in my sense, while the Boston of
Looking Backward is one. An element of ambiguity remains in these, as in
Mannheim's definitions, perhaps reflecting the complexity of the topics themselves. For a thoughtful discussion, see Kenneth Burke, "Ideology and Myth,"
7 *Accent*, p. 195.

about propagandizing itself as an ideological system. Perhaps this is because it was so much taken for granted that it did not need verbal defense, though Southern writers continued to attack its Northern version. The system was written into the landscape, so to speak; it did not need to be written into books. After the Civil War, a dominant capitalism got brutal, but it did not get especially articulate; its critics, from Mark Twain to Veblen, treated it with an impiety and irreverence which we seldom find today. A few preachers continued to mumble grace over the economic system, but their combination of theology and economics was on the wane, while the new one of Social Darwinism coupled with laissez faire seems to have made little impression before William Graham Sumner started writing such essays as "The Absurd Effort to Make the World Over."[7] Throughout the period, to be sure, Eastern capitalists met resistance from the Populists, and perhaps the gold standard should be called an ideology; but on the whole dissent could be bought off without too much debate, e.g., by homestead rights, or by subventions to the appropriate political rings.

By the turn of the century, however, many developments, including tremors of socialism, put the capitalists on the defensive; they could no longer quite so freely use Pinkertons; they began to talk, to bargain collectively "through instruments of their own choosing." Then, a whole new class of university-trained demi-intellectuals began to find jobs and status in doing the talking: personnel men, trade-association men, organization-chart men, lawyers, economists, house-organ men, advertising men, etc. Meanwhile the school system had taught almost everyone to read. Thus both the quantity of and the receptivity for capitalist ideology grew enormously, most of it paid for—as Veblen pointed out in his article on "The Breadline and the Movies"[8]—by the underlying population, which subscribes to the mass media.

Business enterprise in America has, however, always tended to disguise its ideological pressures under a coating of apparently utopian aims, such as the promise of a chicken in every pot or a car in every garage. These promises, when made in U. S. A., can scarcely be called utopian. First, given our resources, it is not difficult to fulfill them; they are, in very fact, just around the corner. Second, attainment of these goals would not make the great mass of well-fed Americans noticeably happier. The fulfillment of utopian aims, on the other hand, is a revolutionary affair; it makes substantial demands on the community, and promises substantial gains in human happiness. While in the Age of Liberalism, capitalism was associated with just such great

7. 17 *Forum*, p. 92, reprinted in *Sumner Today*, p. 99.
8. An editorial in *The Dial*, reprinted in *Essays in Our Changing Order*, p. 450.

human aims, it has become distanced from them in its later phases of complacency, ideology, or reaction. But the utopian coating referred to has tended to satisfy masses of people with spurious social goals, while many thoughtful folk rebelled by doubting the whole Enlightenment concept of gradual progress towards a liberal utopia.

With minor exceptions, moreover, the large-scale anti-business movements in America have tended more and more to copy business methods in covering an essentially ideological approach with a few utopian trimmings. Populism, for example, was ambivalent: it included not only ancient rural hatred for city slicker "usury" but the scarcely veiled "me too" cry of the farmers, unions, small businessmen and small debtors to be cut in on the big money. The New Deal added to these Populist aims (expressed in the Holding Company Act and other anti-Wall Street measures) the goal of achieving the Social Democratic attainments of the Continent, such as social insurance, a minimum wage, and public assistance in housing; none of these measures promised a fundamental change in the quality of American life. The T.V.A., some F.S.A. projects, and a few housing ventures such as Arthurdale and Greenbelt—these pushed beyond relatively easy attainment towards utopian goals; the T.V.A. particularly serves as a pilot model for a new way of life, a new community plan. But the general poverty of aim of the New Deal is shown by the fact that, by 1937, it had reached its own limits, a point obscured by its continuing ideological competition with "The Interests." The war provided a welcome agenda for avoiding insight into this impasse; the government ideologists sold war bonds (or "unity") by the same sort of specious arguments as had sold N.R.A.'s blue eagle.

The more recent political developments which have tended to engender disillusion with all systematic thinking—ideological and utopian alike—hardly need review. The positive goals of both world wars were oversold; peace movements have seemed so futile, and have been in such bad company, as to be discredited among all but the most courageous and independent (or religiously-supported) thinkers. Marxian Socialism, once a branch of bourgeois Enlightenment utopianism despite its founders' assertions to the contrary, has tended, like capitalism, to degenerate into an ideology, notably, of course, in Communist hands. In fact, the Stalinist bureaucracy has brought Russia under the sway of the most leaden and impenetrable of ideologies; its propagandists continue to make utopian claims which conceal from the faithful the actual abandonment of those utopian advances, as in the treatment of women, which the Old Bolsheviks had fought for. As hypocrisy is the tribute vice pays to virtue, so ideology pays tribute to utopian thought. But as hypocrisy revealed discredits the very possibility of virtue, so people who are disillusioned find it hard not to reject the utopian aspirations as well as the ideological pretense.

While these disillusionments are general, the fear of being intellectually out of step, of belonging to a political party with no chance of immediate power, seems to be considerably greater here than in Europe; this was true even in the nineteenth century, as Tocqueville and Bryce observed. In the absence of a tradition of respect for independent thinking, many Americans have found only one workable defense against the pressure of their ideological environment, namely apathy, often touched with humor, or a self-protecting cynicism. This attitude resembles the way in which many adolescents cope with the ideological authority of their parents: they brush it off as the mouthings of the "old man" or the "old lady," and largely disregard it in practice, without ever taking the genuine risks of commitment to an untried and independent ethics. This is the way soldiers dealt with the ideological output of the Information and Education branch of the Army; and it is the way in which many civilians cope with the public-relations staffs of business, government, and labor.

However, these amiable defensive aspects are not the whole story: apathy and cynicism—and a kind of self-deprecating humor which is often attractive—also serve the function of gaining status through toughness or slickness, or through the smoother type of indifference to enthusiasm of the well-bred. These attitudes are so strong in America that decent, constructive people, too, come to fear being taken for suckers, or enthusiasts; from childhood on, boys especially have been made ashamed of their own impulses towards warmth, commitment, generosity. Among intellectual groups, one fears to be accused of the "bourgeois" virtues; or more fashionably today, fears lest some humane reaction escape one which might be translated in the Freudian dictionary, where, e.g., "justice" may be read simply as "envy." It is a characteristic of utopian thinking, however, that it springs from humane enthusiasm; those whose greatest fear is to be gullible, serious, or "soft" are immune. But, as we know, those who fear most to be taken in, while they will escape utopia, are in fact among the easiest prey for ideology. Astrologers, anti-Semites, editors of the *Daily News*, and other confidence men make their living from the very cynics who will fall for the craziest story or ideology, if only it appears sophisticated, brutal, illegal or mysterious.

These seem to me to be among the many factors which have contributed to destroying the market for utopian thinking in America. The increasing division of labor characteristic of an industrial society has meantime played a part in inhibiting the production of such thinking which by its very nature requires a broad approach to the problems of the society as a whole. Specialists shrink from this task; being "in the know" as to a particular set of details, they are suspicious of the injudicious who make large plans without such knowledge. Indeed, a whole theoretical analysis, typified by Von Hayek, holds that large-scale planning is a human impossibility without a compulsory limiting of choices, on the ground that no planner can know enough to do the job if choice remains free. Where scholars and men of superior intellectual training fear to tread, cranks and charlatans—e.g., Howard Scott of Technocracy—fill what market there is for big, bold, bad plans.[9] More sedate is the work of men like Ralph Borsodi, and the Southern Agrarians; while seemingly just the opposite of the Technocrats, these nostalgic writers are quite as insouciant in prescribing for the power-relations of modern industrial society.

These writers, moreover, can hardly be called utopian, in the sense in which I use the word. For utopia is time-located in the future: it is a social order which has not yet been tried, though it is a realistic possibility, not a mere idle dream. But the agrarians and anti-industrialists generally seek to restore something—their picture of the earlier age is usually distorted by convenient historical amnesias—without too much serious attention to limiting technological factors. Thus their writings have often an uneasy similarity to dream-work on a more popular level, like the cults of California.

If we turn to the universities, we shall not completely escape such literary restoration movements. However, American social science has in general sought escape from ideological pressures—where this is not guaranteed by specialization—by means of ethical relativism, a value-free attitude which might be thought of as the academic counterpart of popular cynicism. (Curiously enough, Sumner represents both tendencies: the hardening of capitalist ideology and the beginning of a relativism which would have revolutionary implications vis-à-vis capitalist as well as other mores and ethnocentric prejudices.) In recent years, under the influence of thinkers such as Dewey and the Lynds, this sort of relativism has been under attack, and properly so. However, the insistence on an immediate plan-for-action and a somewhat Puritan distrust of "idle" curiosity and "irresponsibly" speculative scholars have tended to bring utopian as well as relativist-descrip-

---

9. Of course, such writers often make slashing, though hardly original, criticisms of contemporary society, but what they would substitute for it is left vague. For instance, a recent issue of *Technocracy Briefs* has the running-head: "Technocracy Engineers Have Designed a Blue Print for A 'New America,'" which appears in the repeated injunction to "Think North American!" and in such statements as: "Not 'Dictatorship of the Proletariat,' but Dictums of Technology; Not 'Equality of Birth,' but Equality of Opportunity; Not 'Geopolitics,' but Geotechnics; Not 'Sovereign States' but Mechanics of Area Operations."

tive thinking under condemnation.[10] Both academic movements—
value-free and action-oriented schools—are reinforced by a stereotyped notion as to what constitutes research. Research is organized
either about the methodological framework of the existing disciplines
or about "problems." But the problems are those things which we
know bother us, such as poor administration, too much employment
or too little, race and international tensions, etc. Researchers do not
go looking for other problems which we ought to have, and indeed
do have; in any case, the problems we are aware of are so urgent that
they are felt to provide not only a necessary, but also a sufficient
agenda.

By and large, the people whose function it is to think, under the
division of labor, are over-impressed by what they think about. That
is, they are over-receptive to their data, which they take at face value;
even where they are not ethical relativists, they are terribly concerned with "what is." On the other hand a few intrepid heirs of an
older tradition try to impress themselves on their data, without too
much respect for "what is," e.g., Spengler, Sorokin. These latter,
therefore, come closer to the cranks and poets already mentioned for
whom "what is" is to be found inside their heads; the aggressiveness
of such thinkers towards the facts, the enormous empirical material
they deal with, may perhaps be related to the reactionary content of
their approaches to questions of social reorganization. Few scholars
achieve the kind of sensitive and friendly relation in reality which is
necessary for utopian creation—a relation in which one respects "what
is" but includes in it also "what might be" and "what ought to be."

One small group in our society, the architectural fraternity, has
continued to produce and to simulate thinking in the utopian tradition—thinking which at its best combines respect for material fact
with ability, even enthusiasm, for transcending the given. (Perhaps the
architects are in a good position to do this since they have had so little
building to do!) Veblen was mistaken in hoping for great things
from the engineers; the unideological matter-of-factness which he
thought their work-a-day tasks would encourage usually succumbs
to a pedestrian acceptance of the prevailing ideologies—a more uncritical acceptance, often enough, than that of their businessmen or
governmental bosses. Architects, however, are engineers with a difference: their profession would have no future if there were no dif-

---

10. In view of the reactionary onslaughts against Dewey today, I wish to
make plain that I speak here only of a tendency in his thought (something of
the same sort can be said of Lynd's *Knowledge for What?*), which is not actually central to it. In fact, Dewey is not nearly so narrowly "pragmatic" as his
enemies often assume; on the whole, he is certainly a "utopian thinker."

ference. Architects, that is, are paid to dream—paid even to waste, Veblen would say—but they must not ignore engineering requirements if they wish their structures to stand. Of course, most architects do not dream; they are simply businessmen, and their "waste" is of a most prudent kind, since their customers buy just the right amount of it to qualify for the social status they want. There remains a minority: *e.g.*, Wright and Le Corbusier; Behrendt and the Bauhaus group; the young editors of *Task* magazine; also there are community planners, such as Lewis Mumford, Charles Ascher and Catherine Bauer, who have worked with architects and have learned to relate their social thinking to this form of technological experience. This minority, despite the fundamentally reactionary character of Wright's and Le Corbusier's types of planning,[11] has helped to keep alive the utopian tradition both in the drawing of plans and in the experimental demonstration of new possibilities for living.

However, the architectural utopians have generally remained isolated from other forms of technological experience and analytical tools (classical economics and social psychology, for example); they have indulged, like most isolated men, in fanaticism and wars of sectarian annihilation, as in Wright's assault on Le Corbusier; we might even suggest that such eccentricities and blindnesses were necessary to preserve their "nerve of failure," their courage to be different and to stand alone.[12] The book *Communitas* is one attempt to break down this intellectual isolation. One author, Percival Goodman, is an architect and city planner; the other, Paul Goodman, a novelist and social critic. They have studied, not only the physical plans of some predecessor architects, but the intellectual constructions of some predecessor utopians. Their effort is ambitious to see what man is and may become, what society is and may become.

---

11. For Wright see, e.g., *The Disappearing City; When Democracy Builds;* and the remarkable interchanges between Wright and a group of English architects in *An Organic Architecture*. For Le Corbusier see, e.g., *When the Cathedrals Were White*.

12. Since writing the foregoing, I have read the brilliant review by Meyer Schapiro of *Architecture and Modern Life* by Baker Brownell and Frank Lloyd Wright. "Architect's Utopia," 4 *Partisan Review*. Mr. Schapiro argues that the utopias of such contemporary architects as Wright serve no constructive function but rather operate as reactionary middle-class ideologies, glossing over class relations by the use of words like "organic," "construction," "framework," which mix metaphors taken from architecture and from social thought. He sees the architects, especially of the depression period, as just another underemployed profession with delusions of its central role; these men, contemplating architecture as the mirror of society, fail to grasp those social realities which cannot be read directly from the physical forms. I am persuaded by Mr. Schapiro that there is less difference between architects of this stripe and engineers than I had supposed.

§ II

AS UTOPIANS, the authors' ethical and moral platform rests on a scientific psychology only hints of which are given in the text. It is a psychology which sees man as fundamentally good, capable under proper social and physical arrangements of enjoying work, family life, nature, privacy and cooperation—and alternating, temperamentally varied, rhythms between them. They see their fellow-Americans as, by and large, an unhappy folk, trapped in their competitive production and competitive consumption, strenuously passive, sourly emulative. They believe them, even now, to be capable of more spontaneous pleasures and more democratic cooperation. Thus, they have not fallen into the contemporary mood of a gloomy, Niebuhrian view of man, but have remained attached to more optimistic Enlightenment traditions, as represented in such various men as Godwin, Owen, Kropotkin and Dewey; like these thinkers, they see "what external conditions have grown inordinately large and are obstructing the harmony of society and the internal freedom of the people"; like them, they look for counterforces, for unmanipulative leverage, especially education. To hold this view today takes, I think, a certain amount of courage, more so, paradoxically, than to confess defeat at the outset. For the person who has the "nerve of failure" takes the risks of failure but also the risks of an improbable success; he dares to look at life in all its contingency. It is easier, and also more fashionable, to play the Cassandra role, and thus to reap from each new atrocity and impasse in world affairs new moral assurance and confirmation for one's position—like Prince Bagration in Tolstoy's *War and Peace* who gave the appearance of calm mastery by looking wise at each bit of catastrophic news from the battle as if he had not only foreseen but planned it just that way.

In one way or another, the Goodmans feel, most contemporary city planners avoid any responsibility for the ultimate values which their plans will freeze, destroy or serve. Believing that planning only makes sense on the assumption of peace, with its economic surplus and political choices, they are critical of those planners who are concerned simply with finding methods to minimize atomic destruction though this might become the easiest kind of planning to sell.[13] They

---

13. Lewis Mumford writes of an earlier city planner, who faced somewhat similar problems: "Leonardo da Vinci . . . dealt in his notebooks with the city proper, suggested the separation of pedestrian ways from heavy traffic arteries, and went so far as to urge upon the Duke of Milan the standardized mass production of workers' houses. But despite these pregnant suggestions, his contributions to the art of city building remain poor and meager compared with his extraordinary zeal in improving the art of fortification and assault." *The Culture of Cities*, p. 86.

are also critical of those more modest plans which aim at no positive good, but merely at the minimizing of lesser evils than atomic war: for instance, the relief of traffic congestion, or of unemployment (community development subordinated to make-work and pump-priming). For they feel that the planner, by virtue of his position and skill, has a responsibility to see, not only what people think they want, or have been persuaded to want, but what they might want, if they knew of its possibility. Unlike many utopian radicals, however, they sympathize with those planners who limit themselves to what can be realized at any given time, provided that the choice of evils, or of small gains, is informed by larger aims, and a full realization of the social consequences of amelioration.

It is also clear that the Goodmans do not think of utopian planning as a kind of exercise in legislation, in which the planners fit people to their theory; rather, it is an exploration of alternative possibilities. It is, therefore, a piecemeal approach: there is no one plan, no philosopher's stone. Technologies of scarcity, such as the Orient, pose entirely different alternatives than technologies of surplus, such as the U.S.A. Each geographic region, each cultural constellation, each stage of industrial development, presents material for exploiting quite different optima. This sounds like relativism or eclecticism, but it is not; among the utopias they sketch, the authors have reasoned preferences which are grounded in a systematic ethics; the same ethics leads them to dismiss as immoral still other alternatives—such as an improved Garrison State—which are conceivable, even probable.

The Goodman brothers evaluate those great city and community plans of the recent past which, on the basis of the attitudes just indicated, they feel to be of continuing importance. They ask of each plan: what does this tell us about the architect's underlying assumptions as to the ends of life? How, for instance, does he feel about modern industrial work—is it something to be belted off from the wives and children? In the design of the suburb, what are his implicit attitudes towards cultural variety—is he freezing in his plan the one-class, one-race, one-outlook ghettos which, as Catherine Bauer has observed,[14] are increasingly fostered by government and philanthropic planners and builders today? In the location and design of the factory, is his only value the goal of more commodities—and even within the limits of this goal, has he been taken in by current conventions, technologically outdated, as to the efficiency of mass production and the limits of machine-analysis of parts and subcontracted assemblies? In the design of the home, and landscaping, how does he feel towards

---

14. Bauer, "Good Neighborhoods," 242 *Annals,* p. 104.

children—is it, for instance, more important for them to have a workshop and climbable trees than, since choices must be made, for their parents to have standard plumbing and a white picket fence? In this fashion, by looking at the plans—the book is full of drawings and sketches—the Goodmans read off from them the implicit social values of the planners and those for whom they worked: in their hands the recent history of architecture becomes a record of evaluations and ideas. It is also a dialectical process in which the avoidance of some evils has brought others, usually unanticipated, and in which the commitment of social resources in physical form has its own logic, opening some possibilities and foreclosing others.

We may compare the Goodmans' method to that of a psychoanalyst who examines the unconscious choices, and values which have crystallized in the posture, the gestures and the character structure of a given individual. His task is to help the individual bring these values into conscious awareness and then to see what other structures can be built from the materials already given. This type of study owes much, in my opinion, to Mumford's writings; he has seen the interconnectedness of city shape, city movement, and city values;[15] the Goodmans, however, do not deal either with his analyses or with his own plans, such as those for Honolulu or post-war England.

The Goodmans feel that the central problems for the modern planner are posed by the Industrial Revolution. Is the planner revolting against its coal and iron slums, like the creators of Garden Cities and Greenbelts (*e.g.*, Ebenezer Howard,[16] Unwin, Stein)? Is he concerned with its economic insecurity, its Frankenstein qualities, like Frank Lloyd Wright? Or is he, on the contrary, fascinated with capitalist technology, anxious to speed the Industrial Revolution and plunge us all at once into a World's Fair kind of city, like Le Corbusier? Does he think primarily of consumption values, like Buckminster Fuller, or of production values, like the planners of the Soviet state farms, or is he concerned with restoring the relation between consumption and production which preceded the Revolution, like Borsodi? Or does he have his eye primarily on the possibilities of economic surplus given by the Revolution, and on the alternatives

---

15. See especially *The Culture of Cities* and *City Development*. I am indebted to Mr. Mumford for a number of helpful references and suggestions.

16. The Goodmans view the work of Howard too narrowly. Like them, he made plans not to divorce, but to reunite, work and residence. Far from espousing bigger and better suburbias, he insisted on the integration of industry, agriculture, and dormitory along regional lines which took account of local resources and cultural patterns. Significantly, he was inspired by Bellamy. See Giedion, *Space, Time and Architecture,* p. 509.

in production and consumption offered by these in turn, like the planners of the T.V.A.? To illustrate the Goodmans' analyses, I shall select their treatment of Buckminster Fuller and of the T.V.A.

Most readers will remember Fuller's Dymaxion House as a prefabricated mushroom—a mobile hexagonal house on a mast, one of the absurd technocratic dreams of the depression days. Fuller (who was trained not as an architect but as an engineer) called it a machine for realizing the "Eternal Now," without commitment to site, cities, or tradition. Fuller also roams all fields, untroubled by the division of labor. His "economics" rests on "automatic minimum existence credits selectively contractable . . . based on foot-pounds per hour of physical effort, with time study credits for labor-saving contributions of individual activity . . . plus sex-segregated maintenance of anti-social laggards," combined with a system of mass speculation in 10¢ industrial shares. His "politics" is abbreviated by securing, through patents and city services (though what role these would play in the self-contained Dymaxion House is not clear), world control for the Universal Architects, a self-effacing elite "after the manner of the Ford planning department." His "religion" is a new phase of Christianity where, through mass-production and divorce from material concerns, especially landed property, men will again become (rather curiously isolated) brothers. His "psychology," starting from the child's fear of noise and falling, analogizes the structure of the House to the structure of the human body (however, in the World War II version of the House, the functions of "fueling" and "refusing," *i.e.* elimination, are put on one side rather than in the central shaft).

One might dismiss all this as a mad pot-pourri, including Fourierist, money-crank, and possibly fascist bits. The Goodmans, however, take Fuller seriously both for what he says and what he symbolizes. They note the importance of the Dymaxion House's freedom from ground rent and public utilities (this is an as yet unimplemented aim: Fuller's proposed machine for using sun-power has not yet been invented; perhaps a little atomic pile will do instead). And the Goodmans see in the utter convenience of the House, its drive for complete consumer's effortlessness—no furnace to fix, no garden to putter in, no screens to hang—a symbol of the current craze for photoelectric doors, button-lowered car windows, and other magic-carpet fantasies. I find this search a very puzzling phenomenon, since the effort which is saved, for instance of cranking a car window, is not actually unpleasant; on the surface it appears to be a pathological laziness, but the people who go in for it probably play golf or go bowling. The Goodmans do not try to give a complete explanation, but they observe that the consumer, by the proliferation of these magic, fool-proof devices, becomes progressively enslaved and helpless in the hands of the "Universal Architects" who, in Fuller's scheme, monopolize all creative and decisive steps in the productive process.

In some respects, the T.V.A. may be thought of as a complete contrast to Fuller's work, though the Goodmans call attention to the Dymaxion-like section-trailers developed by the Authority for its mobile construction workers. For the T.V.A. does not divorce production from consumption; in its efforts at grass-roots democracy, as in its use of electric power, the two are brought into novel and multiple relations. The T.V.A.'s success rests on the adaptation of its plan to the logic of the man-nature pattern in the Valley: to keep the dams from silting up, it is necessary to prevent erosion, the land must be fertilized, and some restored to grass; to get these grass-roots, it is necessary to teach good land-use practice and to make possible a more intensive cultivation of the plowland; this requires encouragement of the cooperative movement, the sale of cheap fertilizer, and the easing of the farmer's tasks by cheap power and cheap appliances; and so on. People are freed from their primary, archaic relationship to the land; but are then enabled to relate themselves to the land and their neighbors on it in a more abundant, though more complicated, way. The authors, in their brief treatment, do no more than hint at the full meaning of the T.V.A. experience; they say little that is concrete; they move altogether too quickly from T.V.A.'s achievements to the issues it has not so far touched: "the problems of surplus and leisure, of the relation of culture and work, the role of great cities." For the solution of these, they turn to their own model plans.

§ III

THE AUTHORS PRESENT three such models. Each chooses to solve one problem to the exclusion of the others. The first model aims to increase leisure and the consumable surplus; the second, to reintegrate culture and work; the third, to reduce to a minimum both economic regulation and economic insecurity while maintaining large urban concentrations. The authors believe that the great plans of their predecessors expressed mixed aims; and they realize that any conceivable plan would likewise blend patterns from each of their three separated goals. In their logical abstractness, the plans are "ideal types" in Max Weber's sense; but they are also ideal types in the vernacular sense of something to be striven for, something utopian. Thus, the models, or, as the authors call them, paradigms, may be thought of as tools for analysing any existing plan; but in their statement, they are also efforts at analysing the conflict of aims in contemporary America.

The latter purpose comes out most clearly in the first plan, which rather sardonically assumes that there is to be no change in dominant American cultural values and socio-economic organization and raises the question: how can such values be unequivocally represented in the plan? Here the authors present a paradox in Veblen's thought: Veblen wanted to remove the archaic and pecuniary fetters on production by applying the matter-of-fact logic of the engineer; however, having stepped up production, he also wanted to step down consumption by getting rid of leisured waste and emulative luxury; would not the result be still greater mass insecurity through "overproduction?"[17] The Goodmans feel that this paradox is not solved by Keynesian methods, both because, short of building pyramids, there are not sufficient objects of public spending to sop up the excess production, and because such public works do not give sufficient incentive, including psychological incentive, to profit. Their "solution" in this case is therefore an advertising man's dream: *city planning for efficient consumption of luxury goods.*

This requires the following physical arrangements: (1) Metropolises, large enough to permit mass production of luxuries, and to encourage the sway of emulation and thereby the insatiability of desire. Buildings will be crowded together to lower distributive costs, so that even more resources may be devoted to production, shopping, and consumption. (2) The center of the city becomes a huge shell of a department store; the shell also provides room for offices, entertainment and other light industry, and hotels; the corridors of the department store are the streets, so that no one may walk without being tempted to buy; and of course people are forced to walk—they need not and cannot drive their cars in these corridors. By thus merging streets and corridors (Bellamy suggested enclosable streets in *Looking Backward*), and building a cylindrical 21-story skyscraper one mile in diameter, the authors calculate that they could include all the non-residential facilities for the population of Manhattan—and New York of course comes closest as it is to their model. A tremendous gain in servicing and construction efficiency would ensue. But the most important gain would be in the opportunities for display and advertising—a world's fair every day and everywhere. (3) In their irony, the planners naturally fear lest the poetry of the great writers compete with the poetry of advertising. Hence the universities, museums, and other great institutions of non-popular culture are zoned—like any nuisance—outside the central cylinder; how-

---

17. The authors realize that Veblen did not live to see the present potentialities for abundance in America.

ever, by visits there, people weary of the fashion-show at the City Center, weariness which would be economically disastrous, may renew themselves for further bursts of consumption. (4) A somewhat similar renewing function is served by planning a zone of open country, a real "escape," quite near, perhaps five miles from the concentrated Center, beyond which would lie a further zone of state parks and adult camps. (5) Since the authors believe that the true alternative to the city is country, not suburbs, the residence zone is not a satellite town of free-standing homes, but an encircling ring of apartment houses. The apartments, however, are merely service shells, permitting the individual occupants to partition and decorate their space to taste—and emulation.

At the time of spring inventory, by a revival of carnival practices, there would be a season of immense idleness, with bonfires of outmoded furniture, a crescendo of waste—in preparation for the next organized spurt of highly efficient consumption.

The reader of this abstract, as of the text, may not always be sure here what is sexy but serious satire (as in Huxley's *Brave New World*), what plain silliness, and at what point the authors are stating their own genuine goals. In general, however, the moral of the plan comes through without ambiguity: it is a criticism of popular culture, with its drive for less work, more pay and more play; it is also an effort to reveal certain hidden elements of moral worth in modern capitalism. The criticism—the air-conditioned nightmare theme—is familiar enough among radical writers, who sometimes tend to attack with equal fervor the worst abuses, such as lynching, and the most venial foibles, such as radio commercials. But the implicit ethical defense of capitalism on the ground of its provision of bounteous consumption is seldom found outside Chamber of Commerce circles. Sophisticated people who defend capitalism do so either on lesser-evil grounds, or as an interim system, or as a support for political and intellectual freedom; they tend to be apologetic about its encouragement of consumer self-indulgence, if not about consumer values generally.

This general attitude springs, it seems to me, from a growing intellectual hostility to the values of consumer free choice.[18] It is not simply a question of poverty, for many people do not even enjoy window shopping. The left-wingers feel the choice is immoral, because unequally distributed; many, Puritan at heart, would prefer to distribute scarcity. Social hygienists feel it is bad for people: they

---

18. For discussion of the percolation of consumer attitudes into all spheres of life and the overreaction against those attitudes, see my article, "The Cash Customer," 11 *Common Sense*, p. 183.

eat too much rich food (a feeling often rationalized by reference to starving people elsewhere in the world), go to too many movies, etc. Snobs, especially in the older Seaboard cities, react against popular emulative consumption—and the growing cult of effortlessness referred to above—by cultivating an indifference to material things; driving Fords, for instance, until they, too, became designed for comfort, rather than more plushy "petit bourgeois" cars such as Oldsmobiles. Those influenced by Veblen or theorists of functionalism in design are hostile to "waste," to conspicuous consumption, and to competition in sale and display. And many people seek to assert their individuality, not by enjoying choice among available consumption products, but by making an issue of resistance to all salesmanship and advertising. Indeed, it has become fashionable even for advertising men to attack advertising.

These attacks are indiscriminate: the joys of consumption, of free consumer choice, of "waste" and frivolity and excess, are thrown out along with the obvious evils of inequality and of anxious emulation. Yet while we are waiting for a better social order, or more meaningful job-opportunities, it would be a mistake to overlook this freedom and the available chances for making it still more free.

This, if I understand them, is one of the points the Goodmans have in mind in their "City of Efficient Consumption." The efficiency they seek is of two sorts. On the side of production, they follow Veblen in seeking to eliminate waste, for instance excessive distribution costs, in order to increase, while lowering hours, the total annual consumable product of goods and services. But on the side of consumption, the "efficiency" is of a different order: it is an effort to heighten waste and emulation in order to make sure that everything produced is consumed, lest the economy be choked by its own superlative productiveness; the pump to be psychologically primed is that of the individual spender. Perhaps, too, the Goodmans seriously feel that by enhancing the efficiency of consumption of the population as a whole, it might be possible to avoid the economic, maybe even political need for periodic creation of an enlarged class of professionally-efficient consumers, namely the armed services. If by consuming luxuries, we could avoid "consuming" armaments, most of us would settle for their City, any day. But it is intended rather as a caricature than as the best of their possible worlds.

In their second model or paradigm, the Goodmans present their own values explicitly. There they try to deal with the divorce of production from consumption in modern industrial society, and to recreate forms of work which will be meaningful without a futile

attempt at full retreat to handicraft production. But unlike most of
the writers from Marx on who discuss this problem, often in terms
of modern man's "alienation," they are fully aware that the impersonality of work today has certain advantages, even if these advantages are analogous to the "secondary gains" of a neurotic illness.
They see, for example, that punctuality on the job, which seems to
enslave man to the clock, "makes the work itself much more tolerable; for it establishes it in an impersonal, secondary environment
where—once one has gotten out of bed early in the morning—the self
has already resigned all claims." At work, one is "relieved" of one's
family; by the same token, after hours one is "free" of work. Nevertheless, it is, humanly speaking, a crazy divorce, which is simply made
smoother by those planners of suburbs who shield the residential area
from any contact with the productive economy. The Goodmans try
to see what utopian reunions are possible.

To reunite workshop and home, they advocate restoring some
work to the home, as domestic industry or subsistence farming, while
taking out of the home, and into the larger economy, some domestic
services. As to the former, they point to the decentralization made
possible by electricity and the new types of small machine tools; as
to the latter, they rearrange the home itself, and the role of children.

What the Goodmans are suggesting here is a program which, by
increasing the self-sufficiency of the home, the city, and the region,
will both lend variety and meaning to work and provide the economic
basis for freedom. In this, they follow Frank Lloyd Wright on the
physical side and Kropotkin on the social and political; they insist
that each producer must have a say in the distribution of "his" product. They believe that the solution of the problem of political power
in an industrial economy lies in planning for farm-factory units on
a regional basis, where each unit will have enough self-sufficiency
to defend itself in bargaining against other like units. This involves
"the close integration of factory and farm workers—the factory hands
taking over in the fields at peak seasons; farmers doing factory work
in winter; town people, especially children, living in the country;
farmers making small parts for the factories." But the self-sufficiency
must not go too far; each farm, each unit, each region will be
integrated into the national and international market as to some of
its dealings; there is to be none of the "wilful provincialism that is
so nauseating in movements of regional literature and art." Education
on and off the job, and frequent changes of job, are to give the producers the knowledge to support their control of distribution, and the
world-minded outlook which will guide trading of their regional
surpluses for surpluses from elsewhere.

The Goodmans say nothing as to how such a redistribution of resources is to be set up, nor how it will differ in operation from certain patterns of bargaining we have at present, when, let us say, Montana trades its copper for Pennsylvania's coal. In their effort to create a kind of internal balance of economic power, they are up against the same sort of problem which is faced in the Acheson-Lilienthal report on atomic energy: namely, how to find the leverage to distribute economic (or war) potential in such a fashion as to prevent either raids or autarchy. Those who now have the potential (in the atomic case, the United States) hesitate to surrender it, even for the hope of peace; those who lack it (in the atomic case, the U.S.S.R.) hesitate to surrender the chance of getting it, even for the fear of war.

The authors are more instructive in their psychological analysis of the problem of bringing productive work back into human scale. They see the problem as even more difficult, since they see man as even more complex, than many of the industrial psychologists who have been influenced by Elton Mayo. To illustrate: they do not insist, as the Mayo group does, that most workmen want always to work in teams, but rather that men want both group and individual work, both city and country work, both supervision and apprenticeship. Now, since it is undeniable that many factory workers today do not seem to want such diversity, but prefer their accustomed routines and their cluster of associates, we would have to say that this is not what they might want under a different social structure and a different educational system. While many industrial psychologists attempt to adjust workers as they find them to their malaise, as by seeing that they have "recognition" from management and agreeable team-mates, the Goodmans, being utopian, are more interested in adjusting the factory-system to their vision of what man is "really" like. For instance, adolescents would spend five months in general education, two in study-travel, and four in productive work, divided between farm and factory; older workers would shift around less, but would still work on a rhythmic basis with some time devoted either to supervision or to work at their highest technical skill. The jobs themselves would be reanalyzed, not with an eye to technical efficiency, either for production or consumption, but with an eye primarily to joy in work and the assurance of freedom: "Any end is prima facie suspicious if its means, too, do not give satisfaction."

"Supposing one of the masters, away on his two months of individual work, drafting designs for furniture, should decide—having studied the furniture of the Japanese—to dispense with chairs!

"It is problems like this that would create a bitter struggle in the national economy."

It is important to observe, in this otherwise idyllic passage, that the Goodmans do anticipate "bitter struggle" even in Utopia. This is an advance on the work of Bellamy as well as earlier utopians (including Marx) who, focussed on the sordid struggles which spring from capitalist relations, were not sufficiently attentive to clashes of temperament and interest which would spur the making of new utopias even when theirs had been achieved.

The Goodmans illustrate their plan—which they term "The New Commune: the Elimination of the Difference between Production and Consumption"—with drawings of the farmhouses in which families with children will be living. The farms are to be diversified, and zoned quite near to the smallish (200,000) urban nuclei. All children will do farm chores and thus enter "the economy" at a point where it is most comprehensible; the family-sized farms, aided by cooperative marketing and mechanization, will develop a cultural tone which can compete with, rather than submit to, the metropolitan culture.

The metropolitan milieu itself is to recapture something of the quality of leisureliness and sociability of the medieval city square. In their illustrative plan for "Printers' Square," for example, there would be a place for causerie among the gathering workmen, more typical of the French cafe than of the American tavern or coke-bar. Fronting on the Square is the printing factory, with its attached technical school of printing and engraving; a library with terrace-tables for drinks and snacks; some shops; an apartment for urban (childless) dwellers, whose meals are home-cooked after the dirty-work of vegetable washing and peeling, etc., has been communally done. The concept of the Square is, however, rather artificial. Printing happens to be a noisy industry, though not perhaps inevitably so; its relation to the rest of the activities that front on the Square seems tenuous: mere ecological proximity will not produce the kind of local color and culture which the Goodmans seek. Any utopian planning faces the problem of visualizing the intangibles that would give social meaning to physical form and layout. The problem is symbolized by the authors' puzzle as to what kind of public monument they should locate in the Square. A church? Hardly, though Frank Lloyd Wright, despite the idiosyncratic character of his own religion, plunks one down in his plan for Broadacre City. The Goodmans half ironically suggest a Sir Patrick Geddes Regional Museum as the focal point of their Square.

Bellamy's *Looking Backward,* published 60 years earlier, gives us, I think, a more imaginative glimpse of the social and domestic life of a utopian city which in spaciousness and cultivation resembles the more fragmentary picture of the "New Commune"; however, Bellamy's handling of the problems of work and economic life generally is about as different as can be from the Goodmans'. Unlike so many of his contemporary utopians, Bellamy did not turn his back on the Industrial Revolution; he welcomed the increasing pace of mass production and trustification; under his plan, industry was to be "efficiently" run on a national scale, under the direction of the generals of the Industrial Army. All youth were to serve a three-year term at common labor in the Army (rather like a compulsory C.C.C.); those who lacked the ability or desire to specialize would stay on in its lower ranks. The political leaders were to be chosen from among the top administrators who had risen in the Army; in fact, politics was to be largely the process of industrial administration. In some senses, then, Bellamy was a precursor of the theorists of the "managerial revolution."

Since consumption goods and services were to be equally distributed, without regard to rank in the Army (invalids, too, would receive an equal share), Bellamy was particularly concerned to meet the charge of capitalist critics that there would be no "incentive" either to work or to rise—this old, but ever renewed charge based on man's alleged innate laziness. He met this argument partly as the Goodmans do, by an effort to make work meaningful and pleasureful in itself and by encouraging feelings of benevolence and human fellowship in work, but also by reluctant though heavy reliance on the love of praise and the fear of censure. Men were to be educated to seek glory through their industrial ardor, and to avoid being held in contempt for ducking their social responsibilities; officers would rise on the basis of the zealous performance of their underlings.

It seems plain today that production can all too easily be organized on such an emulative and centralized system (compare the "socialist competition" of the Russians); in fact, the motives of hunger and gain which are supposed to operate our market economy have been very largely dispensed with even there.[19] Bellamy, it seems, was not quite utopian enough. One reason is that, though he foresaw the possibility of abundance, if the nationalized industries were properly organized and competitive and distributive wastes abolished, he did not foresee—who could have?—the possibilities of overabundance, the bountiful surplusage of means of production. Equality, and a comfortable, unostentatious standard of living had therefore to be his principal goal, not joy and freedom in work.

Moreover, as we have just observed, the earlier socialists and uto-

19. Karl Polanyi's *The Great Transformation* raises the question whether hunger and gain were actual motives as well as approved ones to any large extent, even in the heyday of the market.

pians, including Bellamy, believed that politics would disappear, once the community owned the means of production; and that universal peace would reign, once people were no longer educated to meanness and fear by the ruthlessness of the capitalism of their day. Today, an Industrial Army would give us nightmares; our awareness of totalitarian dangers leads the Goodmans to turn to regionalist and syndicalist writers as against the authoritarian-nationalist Bellamy for suggestions how to limit the power of the managerial bureaucracy. But as indicated above, their suggestions do not meet the issues.

On the side of the manner of living, however, life has not caught up with Bellamy to the same degree; if we judge by the Goodmans' work, he is still utopian here. The city pictured in *Looking Backward* has about as much sociability and amenity as the Goodmans' "New Commune."[20] There is ample leisure; there are goods enough to satisfy all "genuine" needs (Bellamy even foresaw the radio); domestic life is urbane, with the lot of women improved by communal services. A citizen who is willing to settle for a somewhat lower standard of living is permitted after a time to avoid industrial service, and to devote himself to study, the arts, or whatever he pleases—a suggestion which is also made in the Goodmans' book. Above all, human relations are to be friendly and unexploitative; women are the companions and equals of men (though organized for work in a separate hierarchy); and the individuality of children is respected; in fact from early years on, children are encouraged to develop their taste and their vocational bent. What is similar here to the quality of the Goodman's Commune is the emphasis on quiet happiness, as against excitement, as the aim of life. There is to be neither war nor economic competition; the excitement of the chase, of sadism, of exploitation will be disapproved; the city plan calls for contemplative, easy-going, and cultivated joys.

The Goodmans do not really hope that we could move directly to such a utopia, when our values are so very largely the excitement-values of the "City of Efficient Consumption." They offer, therefore, a third plan which they term an interim measure: its purpose is to minimize economic regulation, and thus to permit once more a choice of economic goals.

Over-regulation in our surplus economy arises, the Goodmans argue, because "overproduction" jeopardizes the jobs of the poor and the profits of the rich; the government is forced to interfere to assure full employment, thus making employment itself—in all its modern meaninglessness—the very end and aim of the community's political

20. In his sequel, *Equality*, Bellamy dealt more fully with decentralization; Manhattan was to have 250,000 people.

activity. Then the free market, one of the few remaining freedoms, becomes entangled in regulation (private, of course, as well as governmental) and taxes (private, of course, as well as governmental) to raise funds to subsidize, insure, and otherwise shore up the economy. The authors propose: that the problem of subsistence be divided off from the problem of luxury; the subsistence market, occupying a small fraction of the country's resources, would be government-controlled, with some scheme akin to rationing providing everyone with his basic needs; while the luxury market would be free of control and entitled, since no one would starve in any case, to its privilege of boom and bust.

"The retrenchment might go very far, relaxing kinds of governmental regulation that are now indispensable; for, where the prospective wage earner has a subsistence independently earned, the conditions under which he agrees to work can be allowed to depend on his own education rather than on the government's coercion of the employer."[21]

The industrialist would then lose the subsistence market and its labor force; the worker, unless in post-adolescence he could afford a paid substitute, would be coerced for the fraction of his time (recall again Bellamy's conscription) needed to produce the subsistence goods and services.

The authors believe that such a pattern (its economic details, obviously complex, are barely sketched) would commit the community to less irreversible change, in architecture and layout, than is demanded by the present type of Keynesian-New Deal methods for insuring full employment. They fully realize, however, that the basic question "what is subsistence?" is a cultural, not a medical problem, and that its solution requires a decision as to how much in consumers' emulative goods (the "standard of living") we are willing to give up in order to gain a greater measure of freedom from regulation. The Goodmans assume that much of our expenditure on clothing, cars, etc., is really forced on us by a competitive race, failure in which threatens even the minimum of self-support. The subsistence economy will, accordingly, provide food, clothing, and prefabricated shelter which is adequate but not varied or stylish. On the other hand, since people are to be freed for such work in the luxury economy as they want, they must be assured, as part of their subsistence, more physical and psy-

---

21. By giving those who want to pursue wealth an entire economy to themselves, insulated from the subsistence economy, the plan retains one of the chief advantages of nineteenth-century capitalism, where power was divided because some men sought it directly in the political sphere while others went primarily after money. Thus, unlike the modern managerial state, politics and economics were not entirely overlapping spheres; the result was some freedom in the interstices and a lessening of ideological pressures.

chological mobility than at present; hence, full transportation (and medical service) are handled as subsistence items also.

The most difficult political and economic questions arise in attempting to relate the two economies, the free one and the subsistence one. (It is here, as the authors point out, that similar attempts—Robert Owen's plan for New Lanark, Louis Blanc's Workshops, the FSA and the WPA—have failed.) To keep the subsistence economy non-competitive, its standards cannot be permitted to rise; to keep the private, free economy from oppressing it, for instance by control of facilities such as transport that both would use, the government might have to use its power over the labor supply. In times of prosperity, demand for subsistence products such as clothing and shelter will diminish, since almost everyone will be able to afford the greater variety of offerings on the private, free economy; in times of crisis, the subsistence demands will rise—but this very pattern will tend to mitigate the business cycle. By the (admittedly) very roughest of calculations based on national income and production figures, the authors guess that no more than one-seventh of the available resources (in labor-time or money) would be required to produce subsistence for all Americans; and that this figure is less than that to which the country, in pursuit of the same security goals, is already committed. Obviously, these calculations, financial and political, would need refinement before one could be pretty sure that the plan of the Goodmans would be any less fragile than the Keynesian approach which they attack.

Most interesting on the architectural side are the elevations and layouts for the residences of the subsistence workers. The Goodmans, unlike Mumford, have faith that prefabrication can produce really cheap mass housing. Many of their trailer-type houses would not need public utilities; others would operate with community kitchens and showers; families could combine their allotments to secure more commodious quarters. The subsistence houses are not meant to be especially inviting—though, as drawn, they look better than millions of rural and urban slum dwellings—for if one wants better housing, one must work in the free economy to pay for it: the subsistence economy's purpose is freedom, not luxury.

Once the obligations to the subsistence economy have been met, one would not have to work at all; whatever one needed, within the subsistence limits, would be free (again compare *Looking Backward*). But do we really want freedom?

"Suddenly, the Americans would find themselves rescued from the physical necessity and social pressure which alone, perhaps, had been driving them to their habitual satisfactions; they might suddenly find the commercial pleasures flat and unpalatable, but they would not therefore suddenly find any other resources within themselves.

"Like that little girl in the progressive school, longing for the security of the grownup's making her decisions for her, who asks: 'Teacher, today again do we have to do what we want to do?' "[22]

Escape from bored freedom into compulsive activity and excitement might become a powerful political movement, until education had been able to nourish the instinct of workmanship, of spontaneous creativity, the capacity for happiness as against excitement, which the Goodmans, along with their utopian teachers, believe to exist in everyone. Perhaps, they suggest, there would be a revival of small business ventures (in fact, we have actually seen this among the veterans, who today come closest to having a subsistence claim devoid of moral strictures); "for the risk of fundamental insecurity of life has been removed, and why should one not work to amass a little capital and then risk it in an enterprise that was always close to one's heart?" In any case, there would be renewed emphasis on the problem of one's "calling," one's true vocation, when all have behind them the security and experience of the subsistence economy and can take their time, as only the rich can now do, before choosing one's work in the free enterprise economy. (Again, a theme from Bellamy.) Or, one might choose not to choose, but to travel or study, a modern (and therefore quite different) Thoreau.

The Goodmans, however, share values with Thoreau (and Frank Lloyd Wright) but also with Marx, who spoke of the "idiocy of rural life"; they do not want to dismantle the metropolis. But trailers will not work in a large city; even a city slum will be too dear for the subsistence economy—as, indeed, the poor today cannot afford big city housing where there is no direct or indirect subsidy. So, then, a man must pay for his metropolitan advantages by work in the private economy, without thereby securing exemption from his subsistence duties. Thus many might desert the metropolis for the subsistence centers, and the Goodmans realize that this problem is not fully solved in their theoretical structure. But, since the purpose of their plan is security with minimum regulation, it cannot be said to leave most big city dwellers worse off than today. Especially if they want freedom.

§ IV

IT HAS NOT BEEN my purpose in these pages to criticize the Goodmans'

---

22. Bellamy had observed: "The fact that all the world goes after money saves a man the necessity of anxiously debating what his life is for." From the unpublished papers of Bellamy, quoted in Arthur E. Morgan, *Nowhere Was Somewhere.*

own models, nor their discussion of earlier community plans. The real value of their book lies not in this or that detail but in their explicit attachment to the now-languishing tradition of utopian thought. Their text, like a physical plan, does not render up all its meaning at first glance: an innocent-looking phrase may conceal a whole philosophy; I hope that they and others who are qualified will proceed with the necessary follow-up. The sort of imaginative courage, the sort of detail-work, which is required to plan today even for the development of a single city or region, is no news to the readers of this Law Journal, since the Yale Law School was one of the first institutions to recognize that community planning demands both a policy goal and a novel integration of the sciences.[23] But it may be news to the many community planners, at least of the older generation, who view their work as just another specialty. This problem of interdisciplinary cooperation may be illuminated by a brief comparison with a bold contemporary plan which is [1947] being put into effect, the Plan for the community of Warsaw. What follows is based on a conversation in the spring of 1946 with Szymon and Helen Syrkus, the former being one of the principal architects (now a director of the National Ministry of Reconstruction) and the latter an executive of the Plan.

Long before 1939, a small group of architects, city planners, social scientists and social workers had begun, in isolation from the dominant soddenness of the Polish government, to develop rather utopian conceptions of community planning. To a large extent, they seem to have been inspired by Robert Owen. They had an opportunity to build a "pilot model," a spacious though inexpensive cooperative in Racasiewicz, a Warsaw suburb; then the War came. After the bombing and capture of the city, members of the group continued to meet secretly to make plans for the rebuilding of the capital after the War. As they proceeded, they drew into their circle additional scientific collaborators. They discovered, for instance, that proper residential layout required an analysis of how far children could comfortably walk alone—for this they went to the child psychologists and social workers. From the economists, they secured data as to the cost to the community if private automobiles had to be provided for. From the data of the engineers, the group concluded what factories still had to be treated as nuisances under modern conditions, and what other fac-

23. See Lasswell and McDougal, "Legal Education and Public Policy: Professional Training in the Public Interest," 52 *Yale Law J.*, pp. 217-32; Directive Committee on Regional Planning, Yale University, *The Case for Regional Planning*. On the diversity of interests and skills required of the community planner, see Martin Meyerson, "What a Planner Has to Know" in *Proceedings, Annual Conference on Planning* (1946), p. 167. I am indebted to Mr. Meyerson for helpful suggestions.

tories due, for instance, to the type of skill employed, might add to the culture and amenity of the city; they proceeded with zoning on this basis. Architects and landscape architects worked on the problem: what sort of vistas, what sort of décor, create what sort of social and psychological attitudes in people; they wanted the walls and roofs and other shapes to say to people: "what's your hurry?" (The subtlety of this problem is such that it seems hardly to have been touched scientifically; the Rorschach test provides certain clues to its investigation, as Schachtel's work has shown.)[24]

On the basis of these and other studies, the cooperating architects then began to draw the detail plans for post-war Warsaw. Most of the group were eventually killed by the Nazis; the Syrkuses were among the few who managed to survive the wounds they suffered in concentration camps; many of the plans also survived. But after the isolation of the War, the survivors felt the need to see what had been learned elsewhere in their field; they journeyed to Sweden, to Russia, to the United States to find out.

It is my impression that they discovered little (save a few technical points such as new types of building materials) which their interdisciplinary group had not already explored. Reading *Communitas* fifteen months later, it was striking to see the resemblances between the Warsaw plans and those of the Goodmans' favorite utopia, the "New Commune," both with respect to some of the social values implicit in the plans and with respect to their physical features. The Warsaw residences are to be formed in super-blocks, but without the monotonous regularity of most of our own urban redevelopments; rather, with an eye to vistas, the paths will wind; the walk-up apartments will be variously grouped. At the calculated radii there will be: trees and play-yards for small fry; schools and libraries and meeting halls for the older folk; shopping centers will be on the through highways no further away than a mother can easily walk with a small child. Since the women are to be freed as much as possible from domestic drudgery, laundries, crèches, cooking will be communal; there are rooms where they can park their children at night to attend political meetings or go to the library with their husbands. But since women also enjoy cooking, when they are not compelled to it, and gain a feeling of status from the quality of a particular soup or casserole, the Polish planners insisted that each apartment have a private kitchen too, even though they were trying desperately to save on

---

24. Ernest Schachtel, "The Dynamic Perception and the Symbolism of Form: With Special Reference to the Rorschach Test," 4 *Psychiatry*, p. 79; "On Memory and Childhood Amnesia," 10 *id.*, p. 1.

plumbing and all dispensable expense. In this decision, they expressed their own values, and also, they felt, those of the people.

Interdisciplinary cooperation and scientific surveys, however, will not solve the problems which arise when the planners' values diverge from those of the general community. This point was raised by my question: suppose a family prefers the amenity of an automobile to the amenity of a kitchen, or would even sacrifice for it the minimum standards as to square feet of space per person that the planners had fixed upon; how could the family exercise consumer free choice and make its preference felt? The Syrkuses replied that, apart from obvious economic obstacles in present-day Poland, the example of America had convinced them that the automobile will spoil the best of urban residential plans; moreover, the factories and even open country will be within easy walking or bicycling distance from the homes; there will be a rapid transit system and a highway net along the River outside the City (I suppose, for common carrier and military traffic). They also added that the appropriate legislative bodies had enthusiastically approved the Plan. I was not entirely satisfied with this explanation.[25] Abstract as the question was in 1946, I had the impression that the planners might be freezing the shape of the City against private cars, perhaps without fully acquainting their constituents with the meaning of the choice being made in their behalf. Yet since health and the general welfare are clearly involved in minimum housing standards, I asked myself if the question really differed from the forcible vaccination of individual recalcitrants by public health authorities. Anyhow, the car question came to symbolize for me the whole issue of coercion in utopian community planning.

The very gap that separates the thinking of the advanced planner from that of his clients tends to lead him to dictatorial measures. For his work teaches him that he can do little to achieve his goals by verbal persuasion: if the walls and streets and vistas, the cars and subways, the kitchens and showers—if these say "hurry, hurry," how can his message of communal quiet and calm possibly be heard, or, if heard, emotionally understood? If people are drugged with excitement, will they not crave more of the same, like any addict, especially when the whole economy would flounder if they failed to respond? Must not the planner at least jazz up his plans and elevations? I suggest that

25. Before the reader becomes too skeptical of the Polish dictatorship—on *this* score—let him recall that rent subsidies, multiple dwelling laws, etc., compel the renter in American cities to buy space and fixtures where he might prefer to spend his share of the social income on something else. A group of American architects and city planners, visiting Warsaw, recently commented on the "extremely humanistic" and undoctrinaire quality of the Poles' physical planning. N. Y. Times, Sept. 13, 1947, p. 6, col. 3.

the true utopian errs if he allows himself to be seduced by such arguments. The moment he begins to manipulate (let alone use physical coercion)—even if the manipulation only consists in the use of reasoning which does not convince *him* but which he feels may "sell" his audience—he leaves the realm of utopia for that of ideology. Thereby he demonstrates, in many cases, his lack of the "nerve of failure." For it is not always his benevolence which leads him to force or manipulate people to do what is in their objective interest. It is his doubt as to his own correctness, which can be assuaged only by securing confirmation in plans and behavior he will live to see—these are his prophet's "sign."

The Goodmans quote Daniel Burnham who lived at a time (the turn of the century) when, or so it appears to us, faith was a less difficult virtue:

"Make no little plans; they have no magic to stir men's blood and probably themselves will not be realized. Make big plans: aim high in hope and work, remembering that a noble, logical diagram, once recorded, will never die, but long after we are gone will be a living thing, asserting itself with ever growing insistency."

So might the Warsaw underground planners have thought, who later perished in the concentration camps, or in the city's battles of liberation. Their diagrams did survive. But this strikes us as somewhat accidental, a rather insubstantial ground for faith. The real question is one about people, not plans: are they really hopeless addicts or can they, enough of them, appreciate what a good community plan would be like even when they have grown up under a bad plan? The utopian's faith is that the answer is affirmative, though its timing—here he can learn from Marx and Engels—depends on a congeries of social forces. That faith is supported by the very tradition of utopian thinking in which the planner works, and which is a record of just such human ability to transcend the ideologies provided by the culture and to add something new to the small precious stock of social ideas.

6. The Saving Remnant: An Examination of Character Structure

In 1794 the Marquis de Condorcet, in hiding from the French Revolutionary Terror, ill and near death, wrote his *Sketch of an Historical View of the Progress of the Human Spirit,* a great monument to faith in human power to shape human destiny. Condorcet refused to be dismayed either by his own experience of human meanness and savagery or by his wide historical reading in the annals of cruelty and error. For he rested his hopes, not only on "observation on what man has heretofore been, and what he is at present," but also on his understanding of the potentialities of human nature.

It has proven more difficult than he had perhaps supposed to develop those potentialities. Today we are aware that the raw material of human nature is shaped by what we call culture into the organized force of a particular character strucure; that this character structure tends to perpetuate itself from parent to child; that, largely determined by early experience, it determines in turn the adult modes of life and interpretations of new experience. The combination of character structure and social structure in a given culture is therefore relatively intractable to change. Though in America we are near Condorcet's dream of the conquest of poverty, his dream of the conquest of happiness seems ever more remote. It has become fashionable to sneer at him and other philosophers of the Enlightenment for lacking a sense of the human limitations on improvement. The sneer, however, is unimaginative. Condorcet's scientific, empirical method urges us to see precisely how recent changes in character structure, as well as in the conditions that gave rise to them, have helped to deny utopia. His philosophy then invites us to apply human reason and effort to the improvement of the human condition as thus understood.

My purpose here is to advance such understanding by tracing a shift I believe to have occurred in very recent times in this character structure of modern man: a shift from the predominance of a type I have called "inner-directed," whose source of guidance in life is an internalized authority, to a type I have called "other-directed," dependent on external authorities. We shall further explore the relationship between these two types of character and the changing feelings

99

in people as to their power to resist social pressures. For obviously, given the objectively identical social pressure, the individual's feeling and experience will depend upon his character, in which his previous life-experiences, especially those of mastery and submission, have been crystallized.

While our helplessness in the world is historically the condition of every advance in our mastery of it, the feeling of helplessness may today be so overpowering that regression, and not advance, ensues. But only when we have understood those forces that make for helplessness can we assay the probable outcome, and see what might be required for the new leap to security and freedom envisaged by Condorcet. One requirement is a type of character structure that can tolerate freedom, even thrive on it; I call persons of such type "autonomous," since they are capable of conscious self-direction. The very conditions that produce other-direction on the part of the majority today, who are heteronomous—that is, who are guided by voices other than their own—may also produce a "saving remnant" who are increasingly autonomous, and who find strength in the face of their minority position in the modern world of power.

§ I

THROUGHOUT MOST of history, people have lived in the bosom of nature, and at her mercy. They have sought a kind of defensive power and command of nature through magic and animism, by which they attempted to personalize and to propitiate the environment. The Pueblo Indians of the American Southwest, for instance, still cope with fear of drought by preoccupation with word-perfect rituals of rain making—and by very practical communal organization of the available water supply. These tribes quiet their anxiety over the weather by substituting for it anxiety over the ritual, which remains in their control. In such a society, as in the feudal past, people live on a relatively unawakened level, with limited life-expectations and limited potentialities for choice. An over-all balance is struck between helplessness and power; institutions mediate this balance, and character structure builds upon it.

This balance altered radically in the West during the age that opens with the Renaissance and closes, to set an equally arbitrary date, with the virtual cutting off of immigration from Europe following World War I. During this period, men were forced to face a world of changed dimensions, changed social relations, and changed meanings. As a result, some felt increasingly helpless and alone: the Calvinist doctrines appealed to them because those doctrines stressed man's helplessness to secure grace, the "chosen" being predestined by a terrifying and inscrutable God. The practical Calvinist, however, did not merely wait for the day of judgment; he tried to force God's hand by a ritual. This ritual, unlike the Pueblo Indian's rain making, was symbolized by hard work in the worldly processes of production—even though the ultimate aim was otherworldly. The result for many was success in mundane pursuits—which was regarded as a sign of election. Thus both hard work and its practical fruits assuaged the feeling of helplessness in the new conditions of life and led to the attainment of a new balance between power and weakness.

This period was the age of the early physical and industrial frontiers—the frontiers of expanding industry and trade, as well as expanding geographical frontiers. This age also enlarged the frontiers of intellectual and emotional discovery, excavating man's past and acquainting him with other cultures. To pioneer on a frontier, whether an external one—at the edge of a white settlement—or an internal one —at the edge of the known in science, art, or industry—requires a somewhat new type of character that is, to a degree, capable of self-piloting, a type that can act when the guidance of custom breaks down or when a choice must be made among several different sets of customs.

I call this type inner-directed, since the source of direction is internalized. By inner-direction, however, I do not mean genuine autonomy, but rather obedience to an internal psychic "gyroscope" which, installed in childhood, continues to pilot the person as he struggles to master the exigent demands of the frontier. This gyroscope is set going by the parents, or rather by their subconsciously internalized ideal image; or by heroes or great men of antiquity or revered elders taken as models. Driven by these internal voices, the inner-directed person is often ambitious—for fame, for goodness, for accomplishment in the world; and this is as true of the bold men of the Renaissance as of the hard, ascetic Puritans. By their own efforts at self-discipline and self-development, these men often helped to "produce" their own characters; the conquering of this internal frontier was accompanied and rewarded by mastery over others and over nature.

In all I have said, I speak primarily of the middle classes, for it was among them that inner-directed types arose; the lower classes moved more slowly out of feudalism. In time, as the doctrine of pre-destination became attenuated or forgotten, these middle classes developed an ideology of liberalism and individualism that proclaimed for all men the values of freedom and self-reliance compatible with char-acterological inner-direction. The inner-directed person came to *feel* free and to *feel* self-made: in his psychological innocence, he was not aware how many of "his" choices had been made for him already by his parents and his conditioning generally. He might have read the famous phrase of Heraclitus—"Character is fate"—to mean that he, as an individual, possessed his own fate, working in him through his own self-mastery; while we today would read the same sentence to mean that our own character is not truly ours, but is produced by our social environment, our "fate" of living in a particular place and time —a new, more sophisticated doctrine of predestination. Moreover, the inner-directed person, living in a time of expanding frontiers, could in fact achieve a small degree of the freedom that he felt. Many inner-directed persons achieved a measure of psychic autonomy and independence as theocratic controls declined in the eighteenth and nineteenth centuries.

§ II

THIS SECURITY of character was reinforced by the experience of a world which itself appeared to be inner-directed. Adam Smith and other late eighteenth-century thinkers saw society as operating "gyroscopically" in a beneficent direction. In general the men who established the industrial revolution in England and America were as unaware of their countries' good luck[1] as of the forces shaping their own characters. A world that seemed to be running on schedule was, of course, an illusion.

A number of great thinkers during this period did not, however, share the widespread optimism of the rising inner-directed middle class.[2] Of these, Malthus is one of the most interesting. He insisted on the entirely temporary quality of any victory over nature, and, contrary to Condorcet, Godwin, and other progressive thinkers, warned that the natural bounty of the earth—now, so it seemed, thoroughly explored—stood in danger of being turned into parsimony by the "natural" growth of population. Yet even Malthus was, by modern standards, optimistic; for he saw the world, not as a bad joke on man, but as a meaningful obstacle race designed to develop man's capacities for rational self-restraint. In our terminology, though not of course in his, he advised people to become inner-directed as the sole means of keeping population in line with subsistence: that is, he advised them to plan ahead, to work hard, and to postpone marriage —thus accumulating wealth without accumulating children. Thus, in

---

1. Karl Polanyi well describes in *The Great Transformation* the series of happy accidents that made liberal capitalism work in the period before 1914.

2. Most of these thinkers—Brooks Adams, for example, in America—were isolated men. Matters stand very differently today, when the prophets of despair are more popular.

effect, he proposed a way out of nature's trap by characterological change.[3]

We can see now, with the advantage of hindsight, that such a program never really had much chance of success. Inner-direction was never very widespread, but rather represented the ideal model toward which people strove. We have evidence that many people of that era tried desperately to conduct themselves in the approved inner-directed way, but were unable to conform. Thus, in Vermont of the eighteenth and nineteenth centuries many more people started diaries and account books—perfect symbols of inner-direction of which Malthus would have approved—than kept them up. Such people must have felt helpless in their efforts at self-mastery, particularly since they took as models those pre-eminent men, from George Washington to Andrew Carnegie, who then stood unshaken by disciples of Marx and Freud. Thus, in a very special sense, the feelings of potency were monopolized by those whose inner-direction was relatively stable and successful in the public mind, while a reservoir of hidden impotence existed. Yet for many of the unsuccessful, failure never seemed quite final, and so long as the future beckoned, or the belief in grace persisted, helplessness could be staved off.

§ III

INDIVIDUAL HELPLESSNESS and collective power play leapfrog with each other throughout history. Today, the helplessness foreseen by a few thinkers, and sensed even in the earlier age of frontiers by many who failed, has become the common attribute of the mass of men. We turn now to discuss some of the factors responsible for this development: in economic and political life, in methods of child-rearing, and in their consequences for character structure.

When immigration from Europe was cut off in 1924, a great symbol of hope in the Western world was destroyed. The "no help wanted" sign had been posted on the American frontier in 1890, but it was now hung out along our borders for all to see. Today, in the advanced industrial countries, there is only one frontier left—that of consumption—and this calls for very different types of talent and character.

The inner-directed type fitted the conditions of an essentially open capitalism, which rewarded ability to envisage new possibilities

---

3. Malthus' non-ecclesiastic successors substituted birth-control for chastity—which required less, but still something, in the way of character change. Actually, as far as food supply goes, Godwin, with his high hopes for technological change in agriculture, has turned out to be the better prophet. But, to complete the irony of the account, only for those industrialized countries where inner-direction—and Malthusian attitudes toward life—actually made great strides!

for production, and zeal to realize those possibilities. To a degree, this is still the case. Nevertheless, it would seem that, on the whole, contemporary society, especially in America, no longer requires and rewards the old enterprise and the old zeal. This does not mean that the economic system itself is slowing down: total production may continue to rise; but it can be achieved by institutionalizing technological and organizational advance, for instance in research departments, management counsel, and corporate planning staffs. The invention and adoption of new improvements can be routinized, built into the system, so to speak, rather than into the men who run the system. Therefore, the energies of management turn to industrial and public relations, to oiling the frictions not of machines but of men.

Likewise, with the growth of monopolistic competition, the way to get ahead is not so much to make a better mousetrap but rather to package an old mousetrap in a new way, and then to sell it by selling oneself first. People feel they must be able to adapt themselves to other people, both to manipulate them and to be manipulated by them. This requires the ability to manipulate oneself, to become "a good package," to use a phrase current among personnel men. These pressures are, of course, not confined to business, but operate also in the professions, in government, and in academic life.

As work becomes less meaningful and intense, however, leisure grows and men who are discarded as workers are cultivated in the one role that still matters, that of consumer. This is not an easy role, and people become almost as preoccupied with getting the "best buys" as they once were with finding their proper "calling" in the production economy. They turn, then, to the mass media of communication for advice in how to consume; at the same time, these media help make them anxious lest they fail in the role of consumer. I speak here not merely of "keeping up with the Joneses"— this is part of an older pattern—but rather of the much more unsettling fear of missing those leisure-time experiences, including sex, love, art, friendship, food, travel, which people have been induced to feel they should have.

These changes in the nature of work and leisure have made themselves felt most strongly among the middle classes of the American big cities in the last twenty-five years or so. It is here that the character type that I call other-directed appears to be concentrated, a type whose source of direction is externalized. The clear goals and generalized judgments of the inner-directed types are not implanted in the other-directed person in childhood. Rather, he is taught, vaguely, to do the "best possible" in any given situation. As soon as he can play with other children, he is made sensitive to the judgments of this play group, looking to it for approval and direction as to what is best. Parents and other adults come to value the child in terms of his ability to live up to the group's expectations and to wrest popularity from it.

The adult never loses this dependence, but continues to live psychologically oriented to his contemporaries—to what sociologists call his "peer group." Of course, it matters very much who these others are: whether they are his immediate circle of the moment, or a higher circle he aspires to, or the anonymous circles of whose doings he learns from the mass media of communication.[4] But the great psychological difference from inner-direction is that this modern type needs open approval and guidance from contemporaries. This new need for approval goes well beyond the human and opportunistic reasons that lead people in any age to care very much what others think of them. People in general want and need to be liked, but it is only the other-directed character type that makes others its chief source of direction and its chief area of sensitivity and concern.

These differences in the source looked to for direction lead to different modes of conformity in the two types. The inner-directed person will ordinarily have had an early choice made for him among the several available destinies of the middle-class child. What holds him on course is that he has internalized from his elders certain general aims and drives—the drive to work hard, or to save money, or to strive for rectitude or for fame. His conformity results from the fact that similar drives have been instilled into others of his social class. As against this, the other-directed person grows up in a much more amorphous social system, where alternative destinations cannot be clearly chosen at an early age. The "best possible" in a particular situation must always be learned from the others in that situation. His conformity to the others is thus not one of generalized drives, but of details—the minutiae of taste or speech or emotion which are momentarily "best." Hence, he internalizes neither detailed habits nor generalized drives, but instead an awareness of and preoccupation with the *process* of securing direction from others.

We can find exemplars of the other-directed character in leisured urban circles of the past, where the preoccupations were those of consumption, not production, and where status depended on the opinion of influential others. What is new is the spread of such an out-

---

4. These are some of the "anonymous authorities" of whom Erich Fromm has written in *Escape from Freedom* and *Man for Himself*.

look over large sectors of a middle class that was once inner-directed. Elements of this outlook, moreover, have now filtered down in America to many members of the lower-middle class.

It is my tentative conclusion that the feeling of helplessness of modern man results from both the vastly enhanced power of the social group and the incorporation of its authority into his very character. And the point at issue is not that the other-directed character is more opportunistic than the inner-directed—if anything, the contrary is true. Rather, the point is that the individual is psychologically dependent on others for clues to the meaning of life. He thus fails to resist authority or fears to exercise freedom of choice even where he might safely do so.

An illustration may clarify my meaning. I have sometimes asked university students why they come to class so regularly day after day, why they do not—as they are technically free to do—take two or three weeks off to do anything they like on their own. The students have answered that they must come to class or otherwise they will flunk, though the fact is that many students get ahead when they finally do break through the routines. It has become apparent that the students cling to such "rational" explanations because, in their feeling of helplessness, freedom is too much of a threat. They fail to see those loopholes of which they could take advantage for their own personal development; they feel safer if they are obeying an authoritative ritual in sympathetic company. Their attendance at class has much the same meaning as the Pueblo Indian's rain-making dance, only the student has less confidence that his "prayer" will be heard. For he has left "home" for good, and all of modern thought teaches him too much for comfort and too little for help.

We can, of course, find more drastic illustrations of the loss of individual self-reliance by looking to the field of political theory and practice. We may, for instance, compare the attitude which Hobbes held toward state power in the seventeenth century with the attitude of some nineteenth and twentieth century advocates of tyranny. Hobbes, in the *Leviathan,* held that the only intelligent recourse of the individual in a world of power was to surrender to it and to form with his fellows an all-powerful state that could repress internal violence and resist external foes. Above all an individualist, Hobbes saw the state as a necessary evil, useful only so long as it delivered physical security, but without any *ideological* claims. He wrote that a state was entitled to obedience only so far as its strong arm reached, but he did not think kings ruled by divine right nor would he have been deceived today by the equivalent superstition of nationalism. Hobbes believed people needed a strong state as a physical umbrella, not as a psychic altar. For example, he defended the individual's privilege against self-incrimination: the state, he wrote, had every right to kill a subject, with or without reason, if it had the power; but it could not expect cooperation from the victim, who had every right to resist. In his whole outlook, Hobbes spoke for the individual, whose interests, he felt, could be protected in a time of anarchy only by strong, tyrannical rule.

In the last hundred years, many thinkers have echoed Hobbes' desire for a strong, centralized state. But until very recent years their concern has been primarily with an attempt to satisfy psychological cravings—their own or those of the masses—for the sake of unity and emotional cohesion. Comte, for instance, desired a secular state that would match the medieval Church in evoking men's devotion. Freud, who resembles Hobbes in his view of man's aggressiveness, believed this aggressiveness could not be curbed by appeals to self-interest, but only by providing leaders with whom and through whom men might establish emotional ties. (See his *Group Psychology and the Analysis of the Ego.*)

In general—this is not true of Freud—modern reactionary thinkers begin with the society and not, like Hobbes, with the individual. Their fastidious distaste for disunity and "chaos"—their uneasiness in the open rough-and-tumble of democratic politics and capitalist economics—leads them to a blind worship of group solidarity and the "leader." Modern totalitarianism, however, exploits these psychological attitudes and fosters an internal as well as international anarchy far worse than that which plagued Hobbes. Only on the surface can a totalitarian movement provide solidarity and emotional cohesion even for its own following. The struggle for power goes on inside the movement, and the reactionary thinkers who abetted the seizure of power are among the first to become disillusioned—and dispensable.

During the last war, the British and Americans captured a number of Russians who had been taken prisoner by the Nazis. Most of these men were quite sure that they would be killed if they returned to Russia. This is not surprising, but what was striking to us was their apparent lack of indignation at the prospect. Some simply took it for granted; others even justified it. One man, a schoolteacher, said that Stalin would be entirely justified in killing him or anyone else who had been in the West, for such a person could never again be completely satisfied in Russia. The *Leviathan* of Hobbes stands outside the individual and tells him to join, or else suffer the consequences; but these Russians carried *Leviathan* inside them.

This modern nationalism has a very different psychological meaning from that of the businesslike nationalism of Hobbes. It also differs from the more progressive nationalisms of the pre-totalitarian era, which date from a time when the state did not exist, or was weak, and had to be created by individual effort. *Modern* nationalism, on the other hand, insists on emotional submission to a power that is already armed with unbeatable military force and with immense economic and propaganda powers. Shortly before his death, Largo Caballero, former Republican premier of Spain, said:

I would like to see every bricklayer go to work with his rifle slung on his shoulder. Then I know that nothing could exist in Spain except the will of the great mass of Spaniards.

For us, in "the years of the modern," the statement has an archaic ring. We happen to live at a moment when, as Hannah Arendt has pointed out, the state is so overwhelming that even martyrdom—the last despairing appeal of the individual human spirit against the group— is no longer possible.

Americans may feel that all this does not apply to them, but only to the totalitarian states. The latter, to be sure, are extreme instances, but Americans are perhaps not sufficiently aware of the current changes in the quality of their own nationalism. For many people, the program of their lives is determined by fear of a fifth column, and what the Russians or their allies do is an urgent and an all-embracing preoccupation. To such persons there is little identification with America in terms of positive aims, but rather a neurotic clinging to a shadow-war in which our national Superman is engaged.

We may conclude that while the state, through technological and organizational change, has become immensely powerful, the individual, through characterological change, has become less capable of psychological resistance to his contemporaries. Modern man feels helpless, and justifies this feeling by looking at the frightening world around him. Like a hypochondriac, he uses the undeniable threat of real danger to rationalize an even greater anxiety than a balanced view might warrant. During the long Victorian period, people assumed as the norm of life an existence in which a few external dangers, such as germs and foreigners, would soon be vanquished; possibly our present hypochondria comes in part from learning the falseness of that assumption. People of a different history have often lived comfortably in the face of impending misery.

§ IV

LET US EXAMINE several further factors that have robbed the middle-class individual of his defenses against the pressure of the group. We shall deal in somewhat more detail with changes in the nature of private property, of work, and of leisure, all of which at one time functioned as defenses.

In the feudal era, the individual was attached to property, largely land, by feudal and family ties. The breakdown of feudalism meant helplessness for many peasants, who were thrown off the land; but for the middle class the result was a gradual gain in consciousness of strength. A new type of relationship between persons and property developed: the person was no longer attached to property, but attached property to himself by his own energetic actions. Property, including land, became freely alienable; at the same time, it was felt to be an individual, not a family, possession. And property was satisfying, substantial—an extended part of the self. Inside the shell of his possessions, the inner-directed person could resist psychological invasion.

Today, however, property is not much of a defense. Taxes and other state activities, inflation and the panicky desire for liquid assets, have made it factually friable. Moreover, the fears of property-holders outrun the actual dangers. Thus, even powerful groups in America feel more frightened of Communism than its actual power warrants. Property no longer represents the old security for those who hold it, and the fear that it may vanish any day makes it as much a source of anxiety as of strength. The rich no longer dare flaunt wealth, but tread softly, guided by considerations of "public relations." Wealthy students often act as if ashamed of their wealth; I have sometimes been tempted to point out that the rich are a minority and have rights, too.

The change in the meaning of work is even plainer. For the inner-directed person, work seemed self-justifying: the only problem was to find the work to which one felt called. As we have seen, the age of expanding frontiers provided the individual with an inexhaustible list of tasks. Work, like property, moreover, was considered a mode of relating oneself to physical objects, and only indirectly to people. Indeed, the work-hungry inner-directed types of this period sometimes found that they were cut off from family and friends, and often from humanity in general, by their assiduity and diligence. And work, like property, was a defense against psychological invasion, a "do not disturb" sign guarding the industrious man of the middle class.

Today the meaning of work is a very different one, psychologically, though in many professions and industries the older modes still persist. To an increasing degree, the self is no longer defined by its productive accomplishments but by its role in a "friendship" system. As the isolate or rate-buster is punished and excluded from the work force in the shop, so the lone wolf is weeded out of management; up-to-date personnel men use deep-probing psychological tests to eliminate applicants, whatever their other gifts, who lack the other-directed personality needed for the job.

To be sure, out of anxiety, a lingering asceticism, and a need for an impressive agenda, the professional and business men and women of the big cities continue to work hard, or more accurately, to spend long hours in the company of their fellow "antagonistic cooperators": "work" is seen as a network of personal relationships that must be constantly watched and oiled. Increasingly, both work and leisure call on the same sort of skills—sociability, sensitivity to others' feelings and wants, and the exercise of taste-preferences freed from direct considerations of economic advantage. Work in this case has a certain unreality for people, since it has almost floated free from any connection with technical crafts. The latter have been built into machines, or can be easily taught; but people must still go to the office and find ways of keeping, or at least looking, busy. Thus in many circles work and leisure are no longer clearly distinguished—as we can see by observing a luncheon or a game of golf among competitors.

The feeling of powerlessness of the other-directed character is, then, the result in part of the lack of genuine commitment to work. His life is not engaged in a direct struggle for mastery over himself and nature; he has no long-term goals since the goals must constantly be changed. At the same time, he is in competition with others for the very values they tell him are worth pursuing; in a circular process, one of these values is the approval of the competing group itself. Hence, he is apt to repress overt competitiveness both out of anxiety to be liked and out of fear of retaliation. In this situation, he is likely to lose interest in the work itself. With loss of interest, he may even find himself little more than a dilettante, not quite sure that he is really able to accomplish anything.

From this it follows that this type of other-directed person is not able to judge the work of others—for one thing, he is no longer sufficiently interested in work as such. He must constantly depend on specialists and experts whom he cannot evaluate with any assurance. That dependence is an inevitable and indeed a valuable fruit of the division of labor in modern society; but the inability even to dare to pass personal judgment is a defect rooted in the character of the other-directed person.

When we turn from the sphere of work to the sphere of leisure,

we see again that roles in which the individual could once find refuge
from and defense against the group have become stylized roles,
played according to the mandates and under the very eyes of the
group. The individual in the age of inner-direction had little leisure;
often he was so work-driven he could not even use the leisure given
him. On occasion, however, he could escape from the pressures and
strains of the workaday world into a private hobby or into the resources of culture, either high-brow or popular. In either case, the
stream of entertainment and communication was intermittent; to
come into contact with it required effort. Leisure, therefore, by its
very scarcity, provided a change of pace and role. Moreover, beyond these actual leisure roles stood a group of fantasy roles—roles
of social ascent, of rebellion against work and inhibition, dreams of
world-shaking achievement; the individual was protected against
invasion at least of his right to these dreams.

Today, leisure is seldom enjoyed in solitude, nor is it often used
for unequivocal escape. Hobbies of the older craft type seem to have
declined, and a baseball game is perhaps the only performance where
the mass audience can still judge competence. The torrent of words
and images from radio, the movies, and the comics begins to pour on
the child even before he can toddle; he starts very early to learn his
lifelong role of consumer. The quantity of messages impinging on
the child becomes increasingly "realistic"; instead of "Just-So Stories"
and fairy tales, children are given "here and now" stories of real life,
and escape into imaginative fantasy is therefore held at a minimum.

Likewise, movies, fiction, and radio for adults increasingly deal
with "here and now" problems: how to handle one's relations with
children, with the opposite sex, with office colleagues away from the
office. Story writers for the better woman's magazines are instructed
to deal with the intimate problems faced by the readers, and soap
opera is one long game of Going to Jerusalem: when one problem
sits down, another is left standing. Indeed, to put it paradoxically,
there is no "escape" from leisure. Wherever one turns, in work or
in popular culture, one is faced by his peers and the problems they
present, including the pressure they put on one to "have fun." A
kind of ascetic selflessness rules much of the greatly expanded leisure
of the other-directed person: selflessness disguised by the craving for
comfort, fun, and effortlessness, but ascetic nonetheless in its tense
use of leisure for preparing oneself to meet the expectations of others.

Thus, the newly reached horizons of leisure and consumption
made possible by our economic abundance have not been as exhilarating for the individual as the realized horizons of work and production
proved to be for many in the age of expanding frontiers. On the

frontiers of consumption, limitless in quality and almost equally so in quantity, men stand anxiously, haunted by the fear of missing some consumption-experience which they are supposed to have enjoyed. Young men and women today, for instance, in some urban middle-class circles, often feel they must walk a tightrope in their sex lives: they must have "experiences," yet they must not become involved emotionally on any deep level of human tenderness and intimacy. And the while they are worried lest they are incapable of loving anyone. The word of the "wise" to the young—"don't get involved" —has changed its meaning in a generation. Once it meant: don't get, or get someone, pregnant; don't run afoul of the law; don't get in the newspapers. Today the injunction is more deeply psychological; it seeks to control, not the overt experience, but its emotional interpretation in terms of smooth, unruffled manipulation of the self. This transformation is characteristic of the change from inner-direction, with its clear and generalized mandates, to other-direction, with its emphasis on the process of receiving from others very detailed stage directions in the work-play of life.

To sum up, the inner-directed person had a sense of power as he faced the group because of his relationship to property, to work, and to leisure; and because both he and the group accepted certain specific rights that encouraged any individual to be himself. Such persons often became men of substance and men of the world—they made the world *theirs*. If we look at the portraits of the more eminent men in a centuries-long gallery stretching from Holbein to John Singer Sargent, we can see that they were indeed solid citizens. Today the solid citizen has given way to the "solid sender," the "good Joe," not solid enough to risk offending anyone and afraid of disobeying the subtle and impermeable injunctions of the contemporary peer group to whom he looks for approval. He is a sender and receiver of messages in a network of personal ties which, unlike the personal ties of a folk society, neither warm nor protect him.

On the surface, it might appear that the individual today feels powerless because he finds no protection from the hazards of war and depression. He feels weak because he has no control over these vast matters that are decisive for him; to avert war or internal catastrophe he cannot even turn to a ritual. Yet, granting these objective reasons for anxiety and weakness, we must nevertheless ask, why is war so likely, when few people want it? I suggest that one reason— certainly not the only one!—is simply that great numbers of people do not in fact enjoy life enough. They are not passionately attached to their lives, but rather cling to them. The very need for direction that is implied in our phrases of inner-direction and other-direction signifies that one has turned over one's life to others in exchange for an agenda, a program for getting through the day.

To be sure, the abdication is not complete. But the fact remains that the person who is not autonomous loses much of the joy that comes through strength—through the effort to live one's life, not necessarily heroically, but, come what may, in full commitment to it. Modern life, for many people, is full of tense and anxious relationships to people, to production and consumption; therefore, these people are prepared to resign themselves to war which does, after all, promise certain compensations in group companionship and shared meanings.

Thus, we have come full circle from Hobbes' view of man. For him, people risked war because they were selfish individualists, and he reasoned with them that they were better off in the *Leviathan*. Modern man does not want to risk war, but allows it to come with astonishingly little protest because, fundamentally, he is not an individualist. It is tractable men who operate the intractable institutions that now precipitate war, and when it comes, it is they who conduct it.

§ V

I DO NOT MEAN to imply that our society "produces" other-directed people because such people are in demand in an increasingly monopolistic, managerial economy. The relations between character and society are not that simple. Moreover, neither character nor society changes all at once. But it would take us too far afield to trace the many formative agencies in the still far-from-complete shift from inner-direction to other-direction in the middle classes.

Furthermore, I must guard against the implication that I think inner-direction is a way of life preferable to other-direction. Each type has its virtues and its vices: the inner-directed person tends to be rigid and intolerant of others; the other-directed person, in turn, is likely to be flexible and sensitive to others. Neither type is altogether comfortable in the world. But in different ways each finds the discomforts it psychologically needs in order, paradoxically, to feel comfortable. The inner-directed person finds the struggle to master himself and the environment quite appropriate; he feels comfortable climbing uphill. The other-directed person finds equally appropriate the malaise that he shares with many others. Engrossed in the activities that the culture provides, he can remain relatively unconscious of his anxiety and tonelessness. Moreover, the character type must always be judged in context. Many persons who are inner-directed and who, in an earlier age, would have gone through life in relative peace, today find themselves indignant at a big-city world in which they have not felt at home. Other-directed persons also may not feel at home, but home never had the same meaning for them. It would appear to the envious inner-directed observer, that the other-directed manage their lives better in a mass society. Conversely, the other-directed may envy the seeming firmness of the inner-directed, and look longingly back on the security of nineteenth-century society, while failing to see that firmness was often merely stubbornness and security merely ignorance.

§ VI

WHAT I HAVE SAID about the loss of the individual's defenses is recognized by many thinkers who, however, feel that through voluntary associations people can attain security analogous to that which family and clan provided in the era of primary ties, and for which work and property made additional provision in the days of expanding frontiers. They see labor unions as giving a feeling of solidarity to the working class, and even to increasing numbers of white-collar employees; they see racial minorities protected by their defense organizations, and farmers by their cooperatives; they see "group belongingness," in some sort of informal association, available to all but the most depressed. The advocacy of this as the chief remedy for the loneliness of the individual is an admission of his weakness. But it is more than that. It bolsters another set of power-combinations, only slightly democratized by individual participation. And it adds to the pressure on the individual to *join,* to submerge himself in the group—any group—and to lower still further not only his feeling that he can, but that he has a right, to stand on his own.

Conceivably, these associations in the future will succeed in strengthening the individual's feeling of his own powers by providing him with defenses, political, economic, and psychological, and by encouraging him to gain, outside his work, a variety of skills, encounters, and experiences. In the meantime, however, with the balance between helplessness and power tipped in favor of the former, the "voluntary" associations are not voluntary enough to do this job.

I turn now to examine another voluntary association, that between the sexes, whose nature, in our age as in any age, provides a profound clue to the state of subjective feelings of power and helplessness. In this context, the rapid change I discern in the denigration by American women of their own sex seems ominous. Eighty years ago, John Stuart Mill (turning to a theme touched on by Condorcet's *On the Admission of Women to the Rights of Citizenship*) wrote *The Subjection of Women* in order to show how attitudes toward this "minority" poisoned all social life; how both men and women suffered from the power-relations that prevailed between them; and how women's potentialities, even more than those of men, were crushed by social pressure. He observed that "the greater part of what women write about women is mere sycophancy to men." But he was gentle with women for he added, "no enslaved class ever asked for complete liberty at once. . . ."

In the intervening period, women did not attain "complete liberty," but they came a long way toward equality with men. In the years after 1890 and until recently, American young women of the middle class insisted on sharing with men the tasks and excitements of civilization. Today there is some evidence that many women of this class have retreated; they have again become enemies of emancipation of their sex; as the weaker power, they judge each other through the eyes of men.

Women today feel under almost as great a pressure to get married as did their pre-emancipation ancestors. In a certain way, they are under greater pressure, since all sorts of psychological aspersions are cast at them if they stay single too long.[5]

Perhaps all this means simply that women have won the battle of emancipation and can relax. I am inclined, however, to think that there is an increasing submissiveness of women to what men want of them, and to the world as men have largely made it. I interpret this, in part, as testimony to the fact that men today are far too anxious, too lacking in psychological defenses against each other, to tolerate critically-minded women. The women they want must be intelligent enough to flatter their vanity but not to challenge their prerogatives as men. Men once complained to their mistresses that their wives did not understand them; now they would complain if they did. For in their own competitive orientation to the world, men would interpret understanding from the side of women as still another, and underhanded, form of competition. This is partly because, since Mill's day, the economic and social power of women has grown; they can no longer be so obviously kept in their places. Hence their gifts, their critical powers, can no longer be patronized by powerful men, but must be subtly destroyed by anxious ones and their willing allies among the women themselves. Men and women, in their weakness, act like those minorities who throughout history have kept each other in subjection in the face of an oppressive power.[6]

---

5. Indeed, men, too, feel under pressure to get married early—among other reasons, lest they be thought homosexual.

6. Something of the same transformation has occurred in the relation between parents and children. Even as men are worried lest they might not pass the test with women, so parents are afraid that their children will not approve of them— a problem that would hardly have troubled the person of inner-directed char-

In sum, men and women eye each other not as allies, but, at best, as antagonistic cooperators. In their roles as parents, they are uncertain of their children and whether they will be liked by them; in turn, this anxiety is absorbed by the children. In earlier epochs of history, events outside the home were interpreted, often somewhat narrowly, through the perspective of family needs and family morality. Today, the situation is reversed, and the home must be adjusted to the values of the outside. As with the state, "domestic policy" and "foreign policy" are interdependent, and the conflicts and strains of each sphere add to weakness in the other.

We come, then, to a conclusion that would seem paradoxical: certain groups in society have grown weaker, but others have not gained in strength at their expense; rather, weakness has engendered weakness. And the state, the beneficiary of individual weakness, is ruled by men who are themselves no less weak than the rest. Even the dictators and their henchmen only seem strong under the imagery of modern propaganda. While the savage believes he will gain in potency by drinking the blood or shrinking the head of his enemy, in the modern world no individual gains in strength of character from the weakness of his fellows.

§ VII

NEVERTHELESS, even under modern conditions, and out of the very matrix of other-directed modes of conformity, some people strive toward an autonomous character. An autonomous person has no compulsive need to follow the other-direction of his culture and milieu—and no compulsive need to flout it, either. We know almost nothing about the factors that make for such positive results; it is easier to understand the sick than to understand why some stay well. It hardly helps to repeat that man's helplessness is the condition for his every advance, because this generalization tells us too little about individual cases. However, it seems that the helplessness of modern man in a world of power has been one element in the genesis of some of the extraordinary human achievements of our age. Some of these achievements are the physical and literary productions of men's hands and

---

acter. While parents appear to be terribly concerned to give their children approval—as they are told by all the textbooks to do—this disguises the parents' own dependence on being approved of by the children, who stand, as Margaret Mead has noted, for the New, for Youth, for the American Way—or, as I might say, for better other-direction. Moreover, parents assume the role of advisors and managers of their children's competitive struggles. This new family constellation is in fact one of the changes that may partly account for the formation of the other-directed character.

minds, but other achievements lie in the internal "productions" of men—their characters; it is of these that I speak here.

There were autonomous people of course, in the era of inner-direction, but they were made of sterner stuff; the barriers they encountered were the classic ones: family, religion, poverty. On the other hand, the person who seeks autonomy today in the upper socio-economic levels of the Western democracies is not faced with the barriers that normally restricted him in the past. The coercions against his independence are frequently invisible. An autonomous person of the middle class must work constantly to detach himself from shadowy entanglements with his culture—so difficult to break with because its demands appear so "reasonable," so trivial.

For my study of autonomy, I have drawn freely on Erich Fromm's concept of the "productive orientation" in *Man for Himself*. Fromm shows the orientation of a type of character that can relate itself to people through love, and to objects and the world generally through the creative gift. The struggle for a productive orientation becomes exigent at the very moment in history when solution of the problem of production itself, in the technical sense, is in sight.

All human beings, even the most productive, the most autonomous, are fated, in a sense, to die the death of Ivan Ilyitch, in Tolstoy's "The Death of Ivan Ilyitch," who becomes aware only on his death-bed of his underlived life and his unused potentialities for autonomy. All of us realize only a fraction of our potentialities. Always a matter of degree, always blended with residues of inner-direction or other-direction, autonomy is a process, not an achievement. Indeed, we may distinguish the autonomous by the fact that his character is never a finished product, but always a lifelong growth.

I speak of autonomy as an aspect of character structure, and not in terms of independence of overt behavior. The autonomous person may or may not conform in his behavior to the power-requirements and conventions of society; he can choose whether to conform or not. (The Bohemians and rebels are not usually autonomous; on the contrary, they are zealously tuned in to the signals of a defiant group that finds the meaning of life in a compulsive non-conformity to the majority group.) Yet the separation of "freedom in behavior" from "autonomy in character" cannot be complete. Autonomy requires self-awareness about the fact of choice, about possible ways of living. The autonomous person of today exists precisely because we have reached an awareness of the problem of choice that was not required among the Pueblos, or, for the most part, in the Middle Ages, or even in the period after the Reformation, when the concepts of God's will and of duty confined choice for many within fairly narrow bounds.

The very fluidity of modern democratic social systems, that, for the mass of people, results in anxiety and "escape from freedom," forces those who would become autonomous to find their own way. They must "choose themselves," in Sartre's phrase, out of their very alienation from traditional ties and inner-directed defenses which inhibited true choice in the past. However, I think Sartre mistaken in his Kantian notion that men can choose themselves under totalitarian conditions. If most of the choices that matter are made for us by the social system, even if it is in appearance a democratic system, then our sense of freedom also will atrophy: most people need the opportunity for some freedom of behavior if they are to develop and confirm their autonomy of character. Nevertheless, the rare autonomous character we have been describing, the man of high, almost precarious, quality, must arise from that aloneness, that helplessness of modern man, that would overwhelm a lesser person. It is in this quality, and in the mode of life he is groping to achieve, that he has made a contribution to living in a somewhat unstructured world. Often, in vanity, we judge our own era as the most advanced or the most retrograde, yet the type of perspective on the world and the self that thousands of people have today was probably matched in the past by only a few.

The people I speak of live under urbanized conditions in every land, but they are world citizens in thought and feeling. Sensitive to wide perspectives of time and space, they have largely transcended prejudices of race or time or class. Their guides are diverse, and they feel empathy and solidarity with their colleagues across all national boundaries. There have been cosmopolitans before, but their horizons were limited by want of knowledge, and their view of man was necessarily abstract. There have been internationalists before, but they have been restricted by class and region. The contemporary autonomous person has all the sensitivity to others of the other-directed type: he needs some interpersonal warmth, and close friends mean much to him; but he does not have an irrational craving for indiscriminate approval.

In one relationship, that between the sexes, the men and women who are striving for autonomy are seeking an equality that takes account of differences, an equality of which Mill would have approved. Here women are not the subtle slaves of men, nor do they flatter them as the feminists did by seeking to adopt men's particular privileges and problems. Though we have as yet to attain a new model of marriage, grounded neither in contract nor in sex alone but in mutual growth towards autonomy, we see new sets of roles developed by people who have achieved relationships to which both partners contribute from their productive gifts. It is unlikely, however, that beyond such families, and small groups of friends or colleagues, there exist any sizeable institutions or organizations predominantly composed of autonomous folk. It is hard to imagine an autonomous society coming into being now, even on a small scale, or perhaps especially on a small scale.[7]

The fact is, moreover, that the autonomous are hardly aware of others like themselves. Those who are to some degree autonomous may not always reveal themselves as such, preferring to conform overtly out of conscious choice. As a result, the potentially autonomous often do not discover each other, though they would in that very process strengthen and defend their own autonomy.

Indeed, the potentially autonomous person tends to bewail as a tragedy his isolation from the masses and from power. He neglects the opportunity of his lot—an opportunity to develop his individuality and its fruits in art and character. Hence he wishes he could undergo a metamorphosis and rid himself of the problem of choice, indeed of his very autonomous strivings; he wishes he were like the others—whose adjustment he often overemphasizes—thus revealing his own other-directed components. By these very tendencies to betray himself and his partially achieved autonomy, he becomes weaker and less autonomous.

The autonomous few can do little enough to reduce the strength of atom bombs and of the hands that now hold them, but some can at least defend their own and others' individuality, and pioneer in various ways of living autonomously. They will enjoy this pioneering to a degree, though it will be held against them by the envious and frightened ones who have abandoned the effort toward autonomy.

If these conjectures are accurate, then it follows that, by a process of unconscious polarization which is going on in society, a few people are becoming more self-consciously autonomous than before, while many others are losing their social and characterological defenses against the group. The latter, though politically strong, are psychically weak, and the autonomous minority, by its very existence, threatens the whole shaky mode of adaptation of the majority.

Nevertheless, joy in life has its own dynamic. I have said that people today are not sufficiently attached to life. We have traced this to their other-directed character structure, and this in turn to large-

---

7. Mary McCarthy describes with humor and insight the fate of an imaginary enclave of intellectuals seeking autonomy in her novel *The Oasis*.

scale social changes. Yet character structure is not completely fixed for the individual, so long as life lasts, or for the group. Men have some control over the fate by which their characters are made. By showing how life can be lived with vitality and happiness even in a time of troubles, the autonomous people can become a social force, indeed a "saving remnant." By converting present helplessness into a condition of advance, they lay the groundwork for a new society, though, like Condorcet, they may not live to see it.

III.

MARGINALITY, MINORITIES, AND FREEDOM

IN THIS SECTION the theme of individualism is viewed from a perspective slightly different from that of the preceding one. Yet the placing of individual essays in one or in the other section is somewhat arbitrary. Thus, in "The Ethics of We Happy Few" I examined some consequences for the intellectuals of their minority status, while in the first essay herein, "Some Observations on Intellectual Freedom," I probe some of the ways in which intellectuals, in fighting for freedom against McCarthyism, can endanger their individuality in a "united front" interpretation of the contemporary scene. Likewise, in "A Philosophy for 'Minority' Living" in the preceding section I used the situation of American Jews to illustrate my treatment of the alternatives open to the lone individual, while in "The 'Militant' Fight against Anti-Semitism" I discuss how the Jewish minority, in response both to Hitler and to the generic problems of ethnic newcomers to America, has tended (like the intellectuals) to embrace victim-psychology and to adopt its enemies' tactics in trying to censor hostile communications, or those believed to be such.

The political pressures of intellectuals upon each other with which my article on intellectual freedom deals are, however, relatively mild in comparison with the pressures American Jews have lately put upon each other to support Israel and the various other idols of the Jewish party line. "The 'Militant' Fight against Anti-Semitism" was delivered as an after-dinner speech to a meeting (in April, 1949) of the National Community Relations Advisory Council, a coordinating group of Jewish agencies concerned with defense, propaganda, and race relations at national and local levels.

I return to the Jews as a source of illustrative material in the first of the two articles on "Marginality"; the life of the Negro, Richard Wright, furnishes illustration for the second. Both were given as lectures, and here again something should be said about the audiences in order to indicate context. "Some Observations Concerning Marginality" was presented to graduate students in an introductory course at the University of Chicago on "Society, Culture, and the Individual"—at the time, they were reading excerpts from Robert Park's *Race and Culture*; more important, they were reading

anthropological writings critical of modern urban society in comparison with the "folk society"—of course, they would hardly need to
read anything so specialized to encounter a very widespread nostalgia
for preliterate times. This is one reason for my emphasis in the
lecture on certain positive aspects of marginality and for my all
too brief critique of current ideals of the "integrated" personality
and of the "integrated" culture which provides no discontinuities
in the life-cycle of its members.

The second article, "Marginality, Conformity, and Insight," carries both these matters a bit further, though it is far from constituting
a satisfactory critique of contemporary personality ideals. It was first
presented as the Billings Lecture at Smith College. Needless to say,
some remarks in a lecture (and both of these on marginality were
recorded, and retain much of their oral chattiness and meandering)
can only begin discussion of such exigently argued issues.

Whether in these papers I deal with women, Negroes, Jews, intellectuals, or such unorganized minorities as the physiologically over-
privileged or underprivileged, my concern is continuously with the
individual. It is his freedom, rather than the freedom of the group
as a whole, to which I address myself; and again I write in context,
for I know that many are preoccupied with Negro rights against
whites, or women's rights against men, and so on, whereas I speak
for the individual against, if need be, the very group that protects
him. And this brings us back to the discussion, in "The Saving Remnant," of whether the voluntary associations which have done so
much for a pluralistic freedom in America, so much to establish what
Galbraith terms "countervailing power," are as voluntary as they
appear to be, when looked at from within their constituencies. Negroes who want to "resign from the race" are violently criticized as
self-haters, but Negroes who can't admit having such a wish may
be as badly off as self-deceivers. Insight, it seems to me, and with it
a certain measure of freedom, comes when one can face and question
one's marginalities rather than simply accept them as given by the
order of nature or of the group to which one "belongs."

7. Some Observations on
Intellectual Freedom

> And if the ice was really to be broken, laughter and jest must be introduced into the consideration of the matter. In politics or business it would be obvious enough that one could not achieve a realistic view of what was happening if one was debarred from discussing principles or acts save in terms of respectful solemnity. Fun and ridicule must be allowed to play their part in the analysis of the motives or characters or doings of the principal actors; otherwise political discussion would remain at an unrealistic level, and those who discussed them would have a sense of servitude.
> —R. F. Harrod, *The Life of John Maynard Keynes*

VAGUE AND HORTATORY ARTICLES and speeches about the crisis of our age are a sign of the "respectful solemnity" we ethnocentrically reserve for *our* problems. I myself have sinned by entitling a monograph "Civil Liberties in a Period of Transition," falling too uncritically in with the comfortably disquieting supposition that the time in which I happen to be alive is by definition such a period! Such rhetorical grandiosity may illustrate Tocqueville's observation that, as a result of living in a democracy, the American's "ideas are all either extremely minute and clear, or extremely general and vague; what lies between is an open void."

This article is an effort to enter, in a somewhat dialectical fashion, into the open void, and to do so without the sense of servitude that characterizes much contemporary talk and writing about the fate of the intellectuals. I shall discuss some new-found conformities that seem to be emerging among many people who claim, often with good right, the mantle of liberalism; I am also curious about general tendencies influencing the position and self-confidence of intellectuals. Archibald MacLeish's article on "Loyalty and Freedom" is therefore the occasion compelling me to set down observations long accumulating. If, in what follows, I sometimes refer to his piece, I do so because it provides a ready illustration; many others could be found. I want to make it clear that I respect Mr. MacLeish's integrity and generosity; his motives recall Yeats' lines: "All things can tempt me from this craft of verse. . . . The seeming needs of my fool-driven land. . . ." If, to a person of my trade and training, certain poets and other artists appear at times politically naive when they make proclamations (while I must appear naive in another sense to them), this naivete doesn't bother me and doesn't require an "answer"; I will fight with any censor for the right of such people to go on being naive and "irresponsible." At best, my article is intended not to engender a debate, but to qualify a tone and thereby the better to represent the pluralism which is one of the glories of liberalism.

§ I

INTELLECTUALS TRY TO COPE with their anxiety by telling each other atrocity stories about America. When this is done in science fiction, as in *Galaxy's* serial "Gravy Planet" (recently republished in a pocket book as *The Space Merchants*), it can be be witty and even revealing. But when it is done with seriousness and portentousness, the consequences can only be anti-intellectual, can only stultify thought in the listener who, bemused at once by guilt and by self-righteousness, murmurs "Amen," "how true."

Other than as the expression of a current mood of a priori despair, the tales about America currently in circulation are often not entirely true. When, for instance, America's justly criticizable follies and excesses are compared with the systematic and calculated terror of the Soviet Union and the Nazis, the double standard applied misleads us in our estimation of events on both sides of the Iron Curtain. Totalitarianism, though it draws on attitudes and on techniques of organization available in the Western, and perhaps the whole world, becomes in its totality something new as soon as it seizes power; as Hannah Arendt has observed, we quite fail to understand totalitarianism when we simply extrapolate from (or back to) societies where the party system and its ideological competition still function, however badly. In my opinion totalitarian societies, once in power, dispense to a large extent with group or national loyalty (which involves danger of overadherence to principle), much as they dispense with ideological propaganda for internal consumption (replacing it with instructions in what the "line" now is, and who has hold of it). If many writers appear to overestimate the loyalty engendered under totalitarianism, they also fail to count their blessings when they attack the apathy, that is, the lack of loyalty to ideals, of many Americans. For this very apathy has its positive side as a safeguard against the overpoliticization of the country: the apathetic ones, often not so much fearful or faithless as bored, may be as immunized against political appeals, good or bad, as against much commercial advertising. Though, of course, there is much pressure for an undiscriminating chauvinistic loyalty and belongingness to a wide variety of groups, including the nation, I am impressed by the fact that among GIs there is far less nationalism than in the first World War—indeed, the pressure for loyalty may be, among other things, one, often unconscious, form of the battle between older and younger generations.

Moreover, the conflict between loyalty and freedom may be quite absent from the minds of many politically apathetic people who appear to be "followers" of Senator McCarthy: they see him in terms of the drama of his career: has he found a gimmick that will get him ahead? The meaning they see in him resembles what they find in figures of the entertainment world or the underworld who have risen to the top without gentility, without connections, and apparently without education. Some of those who have this dramatic view of what on the surface operates as an "anti-Communist crusade" are quite prepared to continue to befriend neighbors who have been called, as ex-Communists, before congressional committees; because for them the salient issue is not one of loyalty, or politics at all, they may even be a bit proud to know somebody who got into the papers. I don't know how widespread this apolitical reaction is, but I do know it is terribly difficult to interpret what Mr. MacLeish refers to as "our silence as a people"—European intellectuals can make very little of it either, perhaps because American cynicism and European cynicism exist in very different contexts. When we try to deal with so big and stratified a country as ours—so big it often cannot hear the talk of the articulate—we ought not begin by reading into others our own fears and idealisms.

Something of a double standard is also employed in many conventional comparisons of the American present with the American past. If, despite the Know-Nothings, a rough toleration has at times been maintained within our country, fears and hatreds have found outlets against Indians, Mexicans, Spaniards—and Japanese (wars often fought, or prolonged, for social-psychological reasons after the enemy had virtually capitulated). Moreover, to exalt the Founding Fathers as having faith in man, as Mr. MacLeish does, would certainly come as a surprise to crusty John Adams, and to Madison; Jefferson might be willing, periodically, to accept the accolade. The Constitution exists, and is the magnificent job it is, in large part because the Fathers had so very limited a faith in man that they sought to protect us from our own and each other's weaknesses wherever possible. The more we know about American 18th-century thought the more complex it appears: strands of religious pessimism persisted from the Great Awakening; the Enlightenment itself was no single-voiced adventure in optimism (recall Diderot's *Rameau's Nephew*); much talk of Reason took account not of all men but only of the educated; and so on. I am inclined to think we have, with a few exceptions, much more faith in man than the Fathers had, and I think this is in some respects a sign of our progress.

Very likely, however, we do not have as much faith as our parents did: we know a bit more, we have seen a lot more, and our aspirations are hardly less. The New Deal and World War II gave many intellectuals and academic people a pleasant feeling of being close to the seats of power, of being in on big doings. To some extent, this feeling was delusive—an aspect of the amiable come-on Franklin Roosevelt practiced with many different groups, from Groton graduates to Hollywood stars. Correspondingly, for all too many intellectuals it drew a connection between being influential and having self-confidence, a connection any even temporary fall in the "market" might sever; in the process, enjoyment of study and intellectual functioning for their own sakes became too much devalued. The post-War inflation which has raised the level of living for organized workers, many small businessmen, and other groups has relatively squeezed our financial security at the same time that, still prominent but no longer so politically protected, the intellectuals have faced a new (but I am hopeful to think presently receding) wave of loyalty oaths, investigations, and other marks of special suspicion and special attention.

Even so, I am inclined to think that many intellectuals today, so far as I can judge their views, overestimate the monolithic power of Reaction. Peter Viereck once remarked that anti-Catholicism is the anti-Semitism of the intellectuals. Certainly in many strata people like to exaggerate the Church's power as in less educated circles they enjoy exaggerating the power of the Jews; very seldom can one hear or read much discussion about the cleavages within American Catholicism or read analyses of the great reservoirs of decency there, analyses which show understanding of the role of the Orders, of missionary parishes, etc.

Likewise, gloomy talk about the "fascist menace" in America overlooks the fact that all efforts of fascist groups to join forces have in the past come to nought because the very suspiciousness and paranoia which are the fascist leader's stock in trade make it well-nigh impossible for him to cooperate with other salesmen on his side of the street—splinter movements seem endemic to "true believers." Moreover, our ethnic diversity, our regional and religious pluralism, our vested corruptions, all tend to confine a fanatical leader to "his" people and section. While only the smug would assert "it can't happen here," it does seem reasonable to assert that it is unlikely, and that the Nazi parallels that undoubtedly exist can be overdrawn. We are neither a small, nor a defeated country.

The naming of evils, intended as a magical warding-off, can have the opposite effect. It is easy to imagine a group of academic people or civil servants, sitting about in the hot summer of 1953, and swapping stories about who got fired from the Voice of America because he subscribed to *The Nation*, and how so-and-so was not rehired at Benton College because his wife had once joined the League of Women Shoppers—each capping the other's whopper of the reactionary menace. What is the consequence? A stiffening of spines? A clearing of the mind and will for action? I doubt it.

I often suspect [if I may quote an earlier article of mine[1]] that the people who tell such stories are, unconsciously, seeking to create a climate which will justify in their own minds the concessions they are making—or, sometimes, a climate which, being worse in those they have spoken to and convinced, is better "inside" than "out." That is, the person who tells such stories (and, as I've indicated, it doesn't matter that they are true stories, one must distinguish between the weight and purpose of different truths) can feel he is bowing to strong pressures when he himself for instance drops a friend who might be suspected of an undue interest in racial equality. . . .

In short, intellectuals who, for whatever reason, choose to regard themselves as being victimized contribute to the very pressures they deplore. These pressures are not so strong as alleged; thinking them strong helps make them so.

§ II

IN A WAY, the attention that intellectuals are getting these days, though much of it is venomous and indecent, testifies to the great improvement in our status over that of an earlier day. What might not Henry Adams have given for such signs of recognition! In his day the intellectual was no threat to anybody: whether clergyman or scholar, he had to defer to the "practical" men, the men of business and affairs. It is almost inconceivable today that a father should say "Where Vanderbilt sits, there is the head of the table. I teach my son to be rich." In the much more fluid and amorphous America of our time, the writer, the artist, the scientist, have become figures of glamour, if not of power. It is harder to say where the head of the table is. The practical, non-intellectual man feels uneasy with these changes; he resents the fact that his own importance, as well as his own understanding of the world, are threatened by the intellectual and the intellectual's ability to change ideas. There is a tendency for the older "class struggles," rooted in clear hierarchical antagonisms, to be replaced by a new status warfare: the groups which, by reason of

---

1. "Some Observations on the Limits of Totalitarian Power," *Antioch Review*, XII (1952), at p. 156. [Reprinted below, p. 414.]

rural or small-town location, ethnicity, or other parochialism, feel
threatened by the better educated upper-middle-class people (though
often less wealthy and politically powerful) who follow or create
the modern movements in science, art, literature, and opinion generally.[2] In other words, anti-intellectualism has increased in this
country in proportion to (though not only because of) the growth
of intellectualism. City slickers are no longer only bankers, lawyers,
and drummers—they are drummers of ideas, that is, professors, teachers, writers, and artists.[3]

The reaction of many intellectuals to Stevenson's defeat may be
taken as an illustration of my point about their real strength despite
their professed weakness. They acted throughout the campaign as
if *they* were up for election: they identified themselves with Stevenson's pathos as well as with his lovely wit. They saw the campaign
through his eyes as an Oxford Union debate in which the opposition mulishly refused to answer "points" or explain contradictions.
The same over-ideological outlook allowed them to be bemused by
the notion, so strenuously promulgated by F. D. R., that the Democrats were the party of virtue and progress, the Republicans of
reaction. Surprised, as I hardly think they should have been, that Ike
swept the country, they felt they had been rejected. In their despair,
they neglected the impressive fact that their man, their identity, had
garnered over 27,000,000 votes against one of the most appealing
candidates ever put up, and in spite of all the inherited handicaps of
the Democrats. Perhaps, like any rising class, we do not feel we are
rising quite fast enough, and momentary setbacks unduly dismay us.

§ III

AS ONE MOVE toward greater differentiation, we should review some
case-histories of people who have refused to make concessions urged
upon them, and consider whether and to what extent they have suffered for it. I think that such a study would show how, for instance,
a professor can call and be called names and survive unscathed. An
account of the detailed reasons why Harvard, Sarah Lawrence, Chicago, and many other places have not succumbed to the first trumpet
blasts of investigating committees would seem to me both more
illuminating and more important than to add to the well-rehearsed

2. Cf. Eric Larrabee's discussion of the Gathings Committee majority and
minority reports in "Obscenity and Morality," address to the American Library
Association, Los Angeles, June 1953.

3. Many of the humanists are in a paradoxical position, for they suffer the
vulnerabilities without attaining the glamour and glory of other academics—one
reason, possibly, for their frequent very great resentment of their colleagues who
lay claim, justified or not, to the mantle of Science.

choruses of academic degradation. Without doubt, liberals as well as fellow-travelers are under attack in many parts of this country. But are these places where they were formerly secure?

I do not overlook the fact that liberals teaching in small colleges in fundamentalist or reactionary communities are still less secure now.[4] And such people do need succor and defense. Articles in Mr. MacLeish's tone may give such people succor through recognition, if not clarification, of their plight: through giving labels to their mood. But by and large I would assume that the *American Scholar* circulates, not in these areas, but in the larger centers where, in sizeable groups, views such as Mr. MacLeish has expressed are not news. In these latter groups, there seems to exist a blind fright and frenzy about "witch-hunts," all committees and their membership being lumped together in a composite caricature.

From the Hiss[5] case we may perhaps date the beginning not only of the excessive power and renown of many Johnny-come-lately anti-Communists but also, on the other side, of what might be thought of as a new united front in some liberal colleges and universities, admission to which is gained by denouncing "witch-hunts" and refusing to cooperate with them. Much as the Communists were forgiven their earlier treacheries when they joined in the Resistance against the Nazis in occupied Europe, and indeed fought their way to leader-

---

4. A balanced estimate would have to take account of shifts in the issues, manifest and covert, to which the community is sensitive. In 1890, Veblen was refused a post at St. Olaf's College because he "does not see the difference between science and religion," and "would treat the historical content of the Bible as he would handle an old document that one might find in China." (See *Scandinavian-American Studies and Records*, XV, 1949, pp. 128-9.) Neither such views nor sexual irregularities would cause a professor similar trouble today. In our time, professors may have become conformists in many respects—there may be fewer "characters" among us—but I am struck with how many, provided they are anti-Communist, have held on to Marxist views without being vilified or pressured.

5. I believe Hiss, in his arrogant treatment of Chambers and the Congressional Committee, was doing the country a far more serious disservice than in his earlier, very likely inconsequential espionage and other efforts to influence foreign policy. If he had told the Committee, as less publicized witnesses have done since, how it happened that a more or less idealistic and successful young lawyer could get involved with the Communist Party, he would have contributed to clarification instead of mystification, and perhaps partially disentangled the knots of identification binding so many decent people to him and hence to the view that he was being victimized. It might have been revealed that his case had special elements (special guilts, special arrogances, special impatiences) and that therefore, despite appearances, it was not a generation on trial but a fringe. Perhaps Hiss thought he could brazen it out. As the square-jawed, clean-cut hero of the two he would have a comic-strip advantage. Perhaps he was ashamed to disillusion his non-Communist friends and preferred to drag them down with him.

ship, so in the new American front the menace of McCarthy helps bring about a similar factitious solidarity among those who are sympathetic to, or apologetic about, or opposed to Communism. In some colleges, professors who testify before the Velde or Jenner committees with dignity and restraint (often educating committee members in the process, as Hiss so notably failed to do) are slandered as appeasers. To the extent that Communists, by such tactics, can get non-Communists to claim the Fifth Amendment, they too can pass off their men as martyrs to principle. This is the general confusion that let Odysseus out of the giant's cave; and in the scramble, the chief ethical problem—to what extent one should tell the committee not about oneself but about others—is obscured. The very term "witch-hunt" is obscurantist.

It may be true that, as this new-found front gains momentum, in AAUP chapters and elsewhere, it will shift the context into which such articles as Mr. MacLeish's fall. While the view of America they bespeak is so dispiriting that in some circles a kind of internal neutralism may be encouraged—why defend freedom if it is already beaten?—in united front circles these writings may well stiffen resistance to loyalty investigations, and thus in some degree serve to strengthen academic freedom. But this might turn out to be an ambiguous dividend, won only because many professors will have become afraid of being thought scared, and because many who share Mr. MacLeish's premises will have concluded that any intra-academic dissension is treachery. However, in my opinion achievement of this airless conformism under the banner of non-conformity would be a confession of academic defeat and vulnerability.

Even critics of articles like Mr. MacLeish's may fall in with this kind of "don't wash dirty linen" clannishness: they may fear that his attitude would encourage European and Asian neutralism. Doubtless, many Europeans are already too inclined to accept some American intellectuals' estimate of their own situation. (In our tradition, what is critical often seems more plausible than what is approbatory.) And since the Soviet Union, Red China, their satellites and mass parties remain the chief threat to freedom, such writers as Mr. MacLeish may be criticized for giving indirect aid and comfort to the foreign foe. But at this point, I would come to their defense and say that we are not so weak as to need a unity chorus at home to persuade intellectuals abroad to love and admire us! Since I share Mr. MacLeish's enthusiasm for freedom of thought and expression, I gladly take the risks of Europeans or Indians overhearing our conversation, and drawing their own conclusions—not the ones, I feel sure, that Mr. MacLeish would expect them to draw.

IT IS CHARACTERISTIC of our times that we raise public relations considerations, if only to reject them. I agree with the implication of Mr. MacLeish's article that we are not the men our ancestors were—we tend to be less rigid, more agreeable, more cooperative and conciliatory. In an earlier, less "other-directed" age, polemics could be carried on, as they still are among Europeans, with fewer restraints based on one's resonance with the other, one's awareness and sympathy and misgiving. Such "weaknesses," when judged by an older standard of intransigent self-righteousness, are among those that Mr. MacLeish would perhaps like to see expunged in favor of the Spartan virtues he attributes to an earlier America. In Lionel Trilling's novel, *The Middle of the Journey*, we can see the power of such virtues, in Mrs. Croom or in Maxim, as against the hesitant and conciliatory Laskell in whom all voices echo.

Yet if we are to find our way out of the tricky personal and social perils peculiar to our day, as well as out of those that afflict any given day, it does not profit us to strive for the moral athleticism and heroism that not even a William James could drill into us. We must work with the psychological tools available to us, and not waste time bemoaning the loss of those blunter ones our forefathers possessed. We know today, for example, that all communication is problematic, a trap of serried ambiguities and obscure consequences. One must always bear in mind—can hardly help bearing in mind—for whom one is writing, even if one violently disagrees with Sartre's theory of "engagement." (I am aware that I am writing this for the *American Scholar*, not *Life*, the new *American Mercury*, or even *The New Leader*.)

However, a writer may make mistakes both about his audience and the pressures they are under: in aiming to challenge complacency wherever he finds it, he may instead strengthen it, or he may further harass people too wounded to listen.[6] I have often been in just this dilemma, as a result of the domestic repercussions of the cold war, in my relations with students and audiences. For instance, when I speak, usually on non-political topics, in the Midwest or in smaller communities in the East, someone is almost sure to ask out of the blue what about Owen Lattimore or don't I think America is going fascist or something of the sort. Often, he turns out to be a *Nation* reader, isolated and bereft, decent and dogmatic, frozen in middle life into what may earlier have been a less spiky carapace of liberalism. He has been waiting eagerly for the coming of light and learn-

6. For fuller discussion of this problem see my article, "Values in Context," *American Scholar*, XXII (1952), p. 29, at pp. 34 et seq. [Above pp. 21-25.]

ing from the University of Chicago to help lift the siege he has been laboring under among his townsfolk: he wants to be told that he isn't crazy, but that the others are. What am I to do when I share his associates' opinions of his opinions, if not of his character and motives? Am I to add one more blow to his self-esteem? To deny my own principles to support his? The mixture of therapy with education is characteristic of our time, and we have no easy answer for a problem that would not have bothered the Victorians.

With students, similar problems arise. Before World War II, I had moderate good luck in getting totalitarian-minded students to chuck some of their stereotypes about America, even if they did not accept mine. When very little penalty, and often even kudos, befell the members of the Party-dominated student groups, I could attack their criticisms without seeming to attack them as individuals; one can do this with the young—their ideas are not affixed to them but are part of a diffuse process of development and discovery; individually, I could encourage them not to be intimidated by the fear of being thought bourgeois. They would not suspect me of worrying about the reputation of my university. Now, as I need hardly say, all that is changed. Radical-minded students have learned in high school or even earlier to be wary of adults; afraid of being seduced by expediency, they have put a kind of intellectual chastity belt around their views. Since some of the nobler-spirited young still want risk and emancipation from parents, the educator who offers them a less clear and less violent set of ideas tends to be fanatically resisted.

Another curious kind of situation arises when the question of the books one uses in teaching comes under the scrutiny of an investigating committee. One of the general education courses in the College at Chicago was criticized by the Broyles Committee of the Illinois legislature because it assigned the *Communist Manifesto* and other writings of Marx and Engels. Before that, some of us had felt these works to be inappropriate for the particular course—for one thing, because the students had not yet had any historical background to understand the portrait of English industrial misery in the 1840's; for another, because we felt the course already too overweighted on the side of the "great books" as against more empirical or experimental materials. But ever since the investigation, the *Manifesto* has been frozen into the course: to replace it now would be regarded as a symbol of knuckling under to egregious, ill-meant criticism; and we and our students have become to that extent a captive audience.

While perhaps a majority of students in this course find Marx dull—in a way, they feel they know all that, and it's irrelevant—a minority feels called upon to speak up for or about Marx, lest they conclude they have betrayed themselves. I hesitate to put students into a position where they must make such a choice (our course is required), but would prefer to have them select their Armageddons at their own time and place. And this is one reason among many why I am opposed to most teaching of social studies in the high schools or earlier, for neither students nor teachers can be protected there against at least some kind of inquisition; the result will either be mushy piety or muddled bravado: in neither case will it be critical understanding. The schools, I think, would do better to teach subjects less vague and less inviting to censorship, leaving the social studies until later or for independent student exploration.[7] But again, the context makes it difficult to say this, or for the schools to do anything about their curricula, without being put in the position of seeming to bow to reaction, or to the intemperate attacks on John Dewey and progressive education. Thus, captive audiences spring up all around, precisely in the most advanced sections of the intellectual community.

I recall in this connection a conversation with the energetic editor of a liberal periodical who had suggested in one of his articles that there was something to be said for the investigating committees: they were not all vicious, and after all Communist conspiracies had existed. As a result, he was bombarded by letters charging that now he, too, was betraying the cause, was giving in to hysteria, was leaving his loyal readers in the lurch. He *did* give in to hysteria—to his readers'—and decided to publish no more such articles. Who can blame him, for where will he find another audience if he alienates his present one?[8]

In sum, the current atmosphere tends to inhibit thought in ways other than those generally recognized. United fronts for political action are one thing: intellectuals need lobbies and pressure groups just as other minorities do who in that way contribute to the pulling and hauling of American politics; but united fronts for intellectual understanding are as impotent as for artistic creation. In that area, each of us must go it alone, and, on occasion, even muster the courage not to take a stand.

---

7. It is an ironic symptom of the vulnerability of the school system that even Mr. MacLeish, in search of an explanation for our "escape from freedom," turns at the end to attacking education! "The underlying failure," he writes, "is a failure of education." Educators are fond of this kind of boasting, which so greatly over-estimates our role in the total culture.

8. In her otherwise admirable article, "The Menace to Free Journalism in America," in *The Listener*, May 14, 1953, p. 791, Mary McCarthy goes too far, in my judgment, in seeing such instances of editorial subservience as typical. It has even become the formula of many magazines to provoke or needle their readers; and certainly many seek to stay ahead of them.

§ V

BUT I WOULD also maintain at the same time and in the same connection, that the effort to rid ourselves utterly of cowardice is inhuman (it is analogous to the effort to rid the country utterly of corruption, Communism, or McCarthyism). We must learn to fight battles while admitting our fear of the enemy, as the American soldier has increasingly learned to do. Otherwise, we encourage a needless martyrdom in some, and an excessive self-contempt in those many valuable people who cannot live up to the courage and stern morality our ancestors represent for us. A friend who recently visited some members of the New Deal government-in-exile in Washington wrote me that his own high spirits were taken as a kind of physiological affront. To be gay or glad about anything in these days is considered by many who share Mr. MacLeish's views to be a sign of idiocy, ill-will, or both.

To be sure, the guilt for being well-off (or well-to-do) is a notable and not wholly negative feature of the American educated classes—we feel it vis-à-vis our own poor and vis-à-vis the ill-nourished of the rest of the world. Likewise, those of us who are reasonably safe from attack by school boards or investigating committees because, out of good luck, timidity, good judgment, or whatnot, we never flirted with Communism, and because the hatred with which we have regarded Communism is now widespread—we, too, do not feel quite happy in our security, even if we do not share the widespread convinction that liberals as well as Communists and their fellow-travelers in general are being victimized. As intellectuals, we the "Pollyannas" inevitably and properly ask ourselves if we can be right, when the country is in some rough measure with us—and so many respected intellectuals are against us. In any case, we cannot but be sympathetic with the many decent people who are anguished, even if their anguish appears to us frequently self-defeating and the source for a monotonous style of talking about America.

But I regret that they do not see that we in America now live in what in many ways is a great age. Terrible things are happening but wonderful things too, and the former do not cancel out the latter any more than they do in one's personal life. The sudden rise to relative affluence of millions of people has intensified the struggle—no new thing in America—between the "old," Eastern-oriented merchant and professional middle classes and the "new," half-educated small business and small-town-manufacturing middle classes. In this confrontation, an astonishing number of the latter seek culture or worldliness in a benevolently energetic way—the heroine of *South Pacific*, for an exotic instance. But another group, as I have indicated, feels put upon and dominated by the intellectuals who seem to control or at least understand the respectable and influential people, media, and opinions; the very ferocity with which these anti-intellectuals sometimes try to outlaw the worldly and the educated is a sign of their resentment of their inferior status in the traditional hierarchies of prestige and comprehension. We are witnessing, not only a tremendous increase in the number of intellectuals in the occupational structure, but an anxious resurgence of some aspects of Populism. This springs not merely from rural areas, so greatly diminished, but also from the half-urbanized and far from urbane city folk for whom nationalism provides an identity of sorts when all else shifts.

And not only nationalism but other narrower groupings. The Pole in Cicero who has helped build a family, a parish, a neighborhood which Negroes threaten to invade, evicting him (and where shall he begin over again?), may find in a crusade against intellectuals some surcease for his own guilt for his inability to sacrifice much of the status he has precariously erected to the values of tolerance and charity the respectable teachers, media, and pastors urge upon him. The violence of his response makes him at least momentary prey for politicians who refuse to abide by the orderly rules of their body, just as he wants to smash the orderly rules of property and mobility which permit anyone with the money to buy a house, and hence school his children, anywhere. Increasingly, Congress and our state legislatures have become more democratic, more representative and less corrupt; they often speak for these previously under-privileged millions, and less often for the "wise, the good, and the [very] rich." By continuing to think of our country as banker-ridden or boss-ridden, we have sought not to recognize these sometimes tenuous changes in the sources of social and personal control of violence and impulse, or to find scapegoats in "demagogues" who whip up "the people," otherwise innocuous. Doubtless, demagogues play a part in "legitimizing" frictions within and among Americans—and how should there not be frictions with vast new populations entering the market for goods and ideas in little more than a decade?

These large-scale and scarcely understood changes and resistances to change in the bases of American life and allegiance are likely to have far greater long-run effects on the climate of freedom in America than the tendencies to conformism within liberalism to which this article has mostly been devoted. We should not allow short-run rises or falls in temperature, even while we suffer from them or oppose them, to obscure these climatic changes. But by the same token, we cannot predict the outcome of the complex, sometimes silent, sometimes vocal struggle against the influence and prestige of intel-

lect and education, nor is there any course we can take which will
guarantee victory to the scholar. However, in personal or political
life I think there are limits to the usefulness of speculation on ultimate outcomes for oneself, one's group, one's nation, the white race,
the Western world, or even the planet. Defeat is not the worst fate.
The Athenians were "defeated." So were many other great civilizations. We must recognize the tragedy of every loss, every defeat,
without banking too much on the quantifiable measure of longevity
as proof of value. To become too fascinated by eventualities of destruction is not only not the way to ward them off but a way to distract
ourselves from equally important questions about America: Why,
for instance, are Americans often so anxious and unhappy, when
Europeans, who live much closer to military or economic disaster
are so sanguine in their personal lives, often expressing philosophies
of despair with exuberant arrogance? Why are American young
people so frequently aimless, lacking private passions and pursuits,
when a greater variety of skilled careers are open to them than ever
before? Why in intellectual circles is there so much malice, when
there are jobs and prestige and tasks enough for everybody and to
spare? The American culture, high, low, and middle, nearly always
lacks the gamut of qualities our best and most creative spirits have
evoked and represented, and the list of reasons for our not having become the promised land is endless—not to be dealt with by such
general terms as "loss of faith" or "growth of reaction." Since small
actions can have large consequences, the future of America is as
bewilderingly open as the present is opaque. Nevertheless, it seems
to me that individuals in America have still an undiminished potential
for good and great, rich and fortunate lives. In living up to this potential, we express our freedom.

§ POSTSCRIPT

AS THE FOREGOING ARTICLE implies, it represents one side of a debate
staged in the pages of *The American Scholar* (the official organ of
Phi Beta Kappa) between Archibald MacLeish and me. I had, as a
member of the *Scholar's* editorial board, opposed our running an
address by Mr. MacLeish entitled "Loyalty and Freedom," for I felt
that the views expressed in it were not news to our readers, did not
illuminate the issues, and—whatever value these views might have in
magazines not read by people like ourselves—would, in the context
of other articles previously published in the *Scholar*, only contribute
to an atmosphere of resignation, depression, and misunderstanding
of the intellectuals' plight. The article was, however, accepted, and
I was encouraged to write a reply (something I would have refused

to do in any more public forum not only because Mr. MacLeish has suffered greatly from patrioteers but also because our differences, as far as the great anti-intellectual world goes, are marginal and intra-academic). Mr. MacLeish in turn wrote a brief reply to me, chiding me for lack of passionate concern for intellectual freedom and for a social scientist's presumed preference for cold analysis over eloquence and rhetoric.

Very much the same argument arose between me and Professor Laurence Sears of Mills College when I drew on this article in giving a lecture there. This argument attracted the attention of local papers and was reported in a distorted fashion, especially by the Hearst press: the argument itself could scarcely be understood from the reports, but the pleasure outsiders always take in seeing insiders fighting each other was evident enough. I had been trying to talk to liberal intellectuals and thoughtful college students, but was overheard by reactionary editors to whom I was not talking, to whom I would have said something very different. But of course one irony inside this irony is that it is very difficult to get across to people outside the academic world any such complex intention: such people want to know whether something is so or isn't so, and can't see any harm in broadcasting a debate especially if it encourages them to feel superior about professors! At the same time, as my article declares, I have never been willing to accept the "don't wash dirty linen" position, which implies that a group under attack must stop talking unless all exits are sealed. If we are not to succumb to overwhelming "inside" pressures, we have to take a good many chances.

Even so, I must add that when I wrote this article (in the spring and early summer of 1953), I did so with a good deal of misgiving lest it comfort those intellectuals, rather rare in my own circles but no doubt plentiful, who might take it as an excuse not to worry. At times, even the most intrepid among us may secretly long for excuses for inaction, and I was aware that, in criticizing the panic doctrine that America is on the road to fascism (my opinion in part based on the none too hopeful ground that we have always had illegality and violence in this country), I might leave some readers even more smug than before. I now think that I did not pay sufficient heed to my own misgivings, for some reactions favorable to my article have had this smug quality; on rereading what I wrote, I feel I should have emphasized more some of the impalpable erosions of intellectual freedom that are related both to the general pressures hostile to individualism and to the specific tensions and irritabilities of the cold war.

Certainly, since my article was written, I have encountered painfully little evidence of the willingness of American intellectuals, let alone businessmen, lawyers, broadcasters, and government officials, to come out swinging in the old free-hand way, not only against McCarthy but against the careful, excessively fine-spun arguments of many of those whom McCarthy has attacked: the latter, if innocent of Communist ties, are often deferential and conciliatory, expressing neither firmness and conviction nor making use of the traditional American pattern of political villification for one's own protection. What is involved here is perhaps not so much the rational fear of people for their careers; rather, people fear public embroilment with a bully, which can become an unbelievably harrassing and time-consuming job. Many of us can recall, or prefer not to recall, our dismal encounters with bullies in high school or earlier; being Americans, unprotected by arrogance of class or family, we could not be sure we were in the right if we lost or ran away from such a fight. Thus, in dealing with a demagogue, we often lack assurance and are unprepared for virulence and bad faith; at times, we fall back on argumentative weapons deemed weak by a sports-loving public. And this weakness would seem especially grave when one is dealing with Senator McCarthy, whose sales appeal to the newly well-paid but socially uneasy strata in his constituency is as much his outspoken contempt for all symbols (such as Harvard, England, the State Department, or Army brass) of older and better educated strata, as is his opportunistic and picayune domestic anti-Communism.

Moreover, I sense among many members of the intellectual community an understandable tendency to establish our patriotism, our incontrovertible loyalty and anti-Communism, as a kind of public-relations gesture. And we are likely to argue that we are better fighters against Communism at home and abroad than McCarthy or *Counter-Attack*. These declarations are true, yet they have an air of enforced piety about them, like the declarations of some comic-book and pocket-book publishers who, instead of ridiculing the Gathings Committee's hypocrisy and denouncing its unfairness and mistrust of freedom, proclaim their own desire to avoid "obscenity" in cover and content. The fact that we feel such politic declarations must be made, that we cannot have our virtue (or the viciousness of our critics) taken for granted, is one of the many signs of the increasing pressure against freedom that I think now I did not take sufficiently into account in this article.

8. The "Militant" Fight Against Anti-Semitism

IT WAS NOT so long ago that Jews sought to defend themselves against anti-Semitism by discreet and persuasive apologetics and by the quiet intercession of their "best people" with the authorities. Though these methods survive, the past two decades have tended to replace them by pressure-group tactics in which Jewish organizations take the offensive—by means of picketing or boycott, or the threat of these weapons—against books (*The Merchant of Venice*), movies (*Oliver Twist*), teachers (City College's Knickerbocker), performers (Gieseking, Furtwängler), and exhibits (the German Industries Fair) that are thought to promote or condone anti-Semitism. It must be at once conceded that much has been accomplished by these methods in the last years in the field of civil rights and fair employment practices. Yet the new "militancy" has brought with it new problems, at once ethical and practical.

The classic American pattern encourages personal self-reliance, hitting back as an individual against attack, but Jews have scarcely felt themselves more free to do this than the Negroes in the South have. This situation promotes smoldering resentment and repressed aggression, which often seek release through the channels of Jewish organizational life. So, for example, a Jew who in private life puts up with mildly anti-Semitic friends, or has changed his name, may support an organization whose public "militancy" assuages his own private discomfort. At the same time, the "leader" of such an organization, afraid of losing his following to still more militant leaders, may be far more outspoken in his public "militancy" vis-à-vis non-Jews than he is in private life.

Whatever the effect of pressure-group tactics in reducing anti-Semitism in the larger American community, they do seem to have gone a long way toward enforcing unanimity among Jews themselves. Though only a small minority of Jews would seem to be what Alfred Kazin has called "mindless militants," this group has steadily gained a disproportionate power, often enabling them to intimidate the community, so that many Jewish "leaders" are actually the captives of the most violent and intemperate of their "followers." When a part of this article was presented in an address to a meeting of the National

Community Relations Advisory Council (April 30, 1949), a number of people told me they agreed with my views but were in no position to say so publicly. Apparently, they were afraid of being called "scared Jews."

Just as liberals in the days of the Popular Front could often be forced to take extremist positions in order to prove that they were not "petty bourgeois," not "enemies of the working class," so today the more comfortably situated Jews, who are very likely a numerical majority, can often be brought into line to support ill-advised policies which are justified by picturing the Jews (in America as well as elsewhere) as an oppressed group—a picture that plays much the same role in these tactics as the Stalinist picture of the workers as members of a "proletariat." Thus, many American Jews who feel guilty about having been untouched by the Nazi holocaust, guilty about their "assimilation," guilty perhaps about not being Palestinian soldiers or pioneers—in addition to all the other guilt-feelings they have as middle-class Americans—are easy ideological victims of Jews with more aggression and (frequently) lesser social standing, whom, in an earlier day and for equally bad reasons, they would have snubbed. In fact, in order to "prove themselves," the most assimilated occasionally become the most militant. Every threat or presumed threat to Jews anywhere in the world can be converted into a lever for the "militant" minority of Jewish organizational life, much as Russian threats to American interests anywhere reinforce the power of our self-proclaimed militant anti-Communists to put a blanket of "unity" over American life as a whole.

§ II

IT SHOULD, however, be noted that there are factors not peculiar to the Jews that motivate similar cycles of "appeasement" and "militancy" among many other ethnic groups in America.[1] The first generation of immigrants enjoyed an improved lot. They had come to this country, or migrated within it, in order to find greater economic and social opportunity, and they had found it. The standard of comparison was always with the old country—an old country assumed to have remained unchanged.

The second and third generations apply a different standard of comparison. For they are sufficiently Americanized, which means sufficiently middle class, to judge their experience in terms of a creed of complete equality of opportunity. While the older generations were glad to get into a college, the more recent ones are terribly hurt

---

1. I owe much to Professors Oscar Handlin and Everett C. Hughes for my understanding of this cycle.

if they do not get into a fraternity; while the older generations were happy to achieve economic security and civic equality, the younger generations find exclusion from the Racquet or Hunt Club a grievous burden. Sensitive to rebuffs to which their parents would have given scant heed, they turn in their disillusionment and resentment towards ethnic nationalism. National revivals—Irish, Polish, Czech, Italian— are thus mainly the prerogative of the native-born; in this sense, ethnic nationalism is paradoxically a sign of Americanization. Those American-born Jews who today seemingly reject America's promise in favor of Israel have been shaped by American schools, American economic institutions, and American culture in general: their very effort and style of protest against America proceeds mainly along American lines, even though colored by specifically Jewish factors, and testifies to their "assimilation."

In terms of most objective indexes of discrimination, it is undeniable that the position of Jews has substantially improved in the last generation. There are many more Jews in the universities, and on the whole there is considerably less prejudice. Though indeed it is still a long way towards complete equality, I would guess that there is today, both in the fields of law and academic life,[2] more discrimination against women than against Jews. Yet, the improving situation of Jews in America corresponds to a mounting sensitivity by Jews to all manifestations of prejudice.

§ III

FURTHER UNDERSTANDING of the psychological complex behind the need of many American Jews to assert themselves aggressively can be found if we look at some of the targets against which Jewish groups have recently directed their fire. Almost invariably, these targets have been weak ones. In some cases, those attacked (or "pressured") have been movie exhibitors or movie lords—"lords" who tremble so readily before an archbishop or a Hearst or a Congressional committee. Another target is the public school boards, so often submissive to whoever in the community can make a big noise. Jewish bigots cooperated with Catholic bigots years ago to deny Bertrand Russell a chair at City College in New York. In descending on Pro-

---

2. In the field I know best, that of academic life, the situation has changed very much, even in the last ten years. I recall that when in 1938 and 1939 I tried to find places for Jewish refugees in American law schools, as the executive secretary of a committee headed by John W. Davis, I found my efforts hampered not only by anti-Semitism but also by well-intentioned persons who felt that Jews had so little chance in academic or professional life that they had best go into business. Today the men our committee succeeded in helping find very few of the old obstacles: they teach in the top law schools and have jobs in the government and in Wall Street law offices.

fessor Knickerbocker at the same institution, Jewish organizations had of course a rather different case, since he was charged not only with anti-Semitic opinions but with actual discriminatory practices in running his department. But what about the assumption apparently made in this case that if he could be proved to have made anti-Semitic remarks he should be fired—as if private anti-Semitism in City College (of all places!) is the menace that it might be, say in Congress, or in the utility industries.

Still another target for American Jews is supplied by all things German. Although Germany is, of course, potentially strong, she has been weak since the war in the important sense that American educators, trust-busters, and others have found it easier to influence (or at least make a fuss about) American policy in Germany than about comparable problems on the domestic political scene. Just as anti-Semites portray Jews as powerful, in order to justify attacking them under the code of fair play, so the anti-German Jews have utilized allegations of "the German danger" to justify notions as cruel and crazy as the Morgenthau Plan. To be sure, the American Jews have probably not been strong enough to affect appreciably the course of events in Germany, either for good or ill. But they have been strong enough to keep Gieseking out of the country—and to harden in the Jewish community the picture of a solidly unregenerate German people, as openly and intensely anti-Semitic today as were the Nazis, thus inhibiting any serious discussion of German realities. This last is yet another example of the attempted *Gleichschaltung* of Jewish organizational life.

In the case of Germany, Jewish concern is often rationalized in terms of fighting alleged resurgences of anti-Semitism there. Actually, however, it would seem to be motivated by a natural desire to remind the world of the slaughter of fellow Jews. It is probably inevitable that those who have not suffered should feel a certain guilt about that very fact, especially if one feels that not all was done that might have been done to rescue the doomed—and if one also has to combat one's own desire to forget and gloss over what happened. But the sensitive person should need no reminders: he lives all too constantly with the memory of history's crimes and disasters. Conversely, the insensitive person may react negatively to reminders, especially if he feels that they are sometimes a form of moral blackmail. At the same meeting at which my own address was delivered, another speaker who had been concerned with Jewish affairs in Germany mentioned how, when he would lay his complaints before a certain American general, the latter would say, in a friendly tone, "Now, don't throw the six million at me again."

True, the American Jews who attack weak and easy targets in this country, or who applaud such tactics at home and abroad, certainly do not interpret their action as bullying or blackmail; and they would be horrified to be classified with those groups who use force or threats of force to censor art, or to suppress free discussion. And let us grant that there may be some warrant, emotionally at least, in viewing a Furtwängler or Knickerbocker as a symbol both of the European massacre and the worldwide threat of political anti-Semitism. Nevertheless, while any instance of anti-Semitism *may* testify to a fascist potential, there is a grave danger of distortion when a hotel's restriction, a chance remark, or a silly book come to be automatically identified with Nazi cruelties, and call forth a reflex action of violent indignation and an effort at aggressive suppression. A kind of fantasy is built up which, though it has much more justification behind it, curiously resembles that of the anti-Semite who sees in the acts of an individual Jew the systematic conspiratorial intentions of a whole race.

In coping with anti-Semitism, Jews have a problem similar to that with which all Americans are faced in coping with the Russians. As Americans we have to learn to live with relative comfort and self-control in a state of cold war that in all likelihood will go on for many years. If we get panicky, and unable to keep our heads in the face of even serious hostility, we can bring disaster on ourselves as well as on the world. Thus, for instance, if Americans were to concentrate on hating the Russians, we should already be reduced by them part-way to their own level. As Jews we have even less choice. We are going to be able at best only to contain anti-Semitism in America, to prevent its spread, to prevent violent incursions and active discrimination; we have no chance whatsoever of wiping out anti-Semitism by force, although maybe some Jews, underneath fantastic fears, nourish even more fantastic hopes. But since this is so, those Jews who are over-alert to anti-Semitism and go to all lengths to lash out at any and every sign of it are likely to waste too much of their time and resources. And they will tend to neglect the things that might be done to better the lot and widen the horizon of all Americans, including Jews.

Perhaps Jews, looking at the European experience, consciously or unconsciously feel that no dividing line separates an anti-Semitic remark from an extermination camp. This is to assume more or less that there are no social and psychological barriers between thought and action, and between moderate action and extreme action. And it also assumes that Americans are not bound by specific traditions and habits. We Americans, Gentile and Jew, like big talk, and much that passes for anti-Semitic expression is big talk, with no thought or dream behind it of real action. And, happily, it is a fact that Americans draw a line between anti-Semitic remarks and actual persecution, and it is by virtue of this distinction (and the political and social institutions built upon it) that Jews in America have little more occasion for anxiety as Jews than for anxiety as Americans.

§ IV

SO FAR I HAVE ASSUMED that the books and movies Jews are attacking are in fact anti-Semitic. But is this really so? Who will deny that there have been Jewish Fagins? And are these the worst men to be found in the gallery of literature and life? If these things are the worst that can be said in serious literature about Jews, they are surely no worse than what can be said about other people. Indeed, as I recall *Oliver Twist*—the book, I mean, since I haven't been permitted to see the film—Dickens never makes Fagin's Jewishness an excuse for general charges against the Jews.[3] And Shakespeare in *The Merchant of Venice* puts into the mouth of Shylock one of the most eloquent pleas for the humanity of Jews that has ever been written.

But even if I were wrong about these particular works, it still would not change my view. There are violently anti-Semitic writers, such as Ezra Pound or Louis-Ferdinand Céline, who have the right to say what they please, just as Montherlant, Farnham, and Lundberg have the right to say what they please about women. When Jews try to suppress such writers, they act as if they had something to hide. My own feeling is that Jews have nothing to hide, either in literature or in life. At one time I thought it might be practicable to draw a line between group-libel of the Jews which included false statements of fact—such things as are now peddled by Curt Asher and William Dudley Pelley—and works of art in which Jews are dealt with perhaps unsympathetically, but as part of a whole picture of life. But in time, my studies convinced me that there were virtually insuperable administrative difficulties in drawing such a line, and in entrusting it to public officials and juries, and that the dangers outweighed the possible benefits. Suits for libel by individual Jews and replies in the forum of public discussion are, of course, another matter entirely, though hardly one of great importance. My general feeling is that our tradition of civil liberty is the best defense we have for individuals

---

3. Since writing the above, my British-born friend, John Seeley, has informed me that Fagin does make a profound impression on British boys as to what happens when a Jew "reverts to type"—just as Bligh is what happens when an Englishman does. And Fagin, he adds, by virtue of the very humanity with which he is portrayed, is made to seem far more human, near, and threatening than Bligh.

and for minorities; and Jews have every interest, as Jews and as Americans, in seeing that this tradition remains strong and vital.

In view of what happened in Europe and of the existence of anti-Semitism in America, it is not surprising that Jews feel weak and therefore lack confidence that full and free discussion will be just to them. Nevertheless, I feel that we should encourage such discussion. Jews are, after all, much more interesting to talk about than anti-Semitism. And I think it best that we should be prepared to take our chances in such a discussion, only making efforts to see that it is stimulating and abundant.

At present we may distinguish four levels of talk about Jews in America, four levels that hardly mix or meet. At the top level are the intellectual and artistic circles, of Jews and non-Jews, where there is at the same time curiosity and matter-of-factness about things Jewish. The pages of *Commentary* are an excellent illustration of this kind of discussion. There one finds reporting of Jewish life without a fearful concern for public relations; philosophic and sociological debate about what, if anything, it means to be a Jew; and, in the department "From the American Scene," occasional pictures of the fabulously interesting, rich, and varied life of Jews in America. On this level, one can also find literature that is not a tract against anti-Semitism but an exploration of Jewish consciousness and unconsciousness; there comes to mind Saul Bellow's fine novel, *The Victim*.

Our second level of discussion is in the liberal middle class, both Jewish and non-Jewish, the class responsible for putting car cards about brotherhood in the New York subways. A friend of mine claims to have heard a radio jingle over a New York station, "He's no Jew, he's like you." I suspect him of satire. But if it didn't actually happen it might well have, given the notion of "defense" prevailing in many advertising minds. It is here that a mythical world is constructed in which Negroes and whites, Jews and non-Jews—and, for that matter, men and women—are "really" alike; such differences as there still are, being expected to wither away like the Marxist state. On this level Jews fail to see that it is their very difference which may be both worthwhile and appealing. This insistence on denying differences, or on seeking to eradicate them, identifies "American" with "Americanization"—and insists that for people to be treated as equals they must have more than their humanity in common.

The chief quality I sense in discussion about Jews on this second level is piety, a kind of dreary piety, filled with platitudes about unity, amity, democracy, and so on. This piety, it seems to me, as it spreads throughout "official" culture, through our churches, schools, and many voluntary associations, has two consequences. On the one hand, in the obedient circles it tends to stultify observation and thought. On the other hand, it enables those rebellious souls who refuse to subscribe to it to appear as terribly dashing and bold and "militant." The violent anti-Semites and those Jews who throw eggs at Bevin both achieve an easy victory for their image of the Jew over the official picture. Just this appearance of toughness is, I think, one of the great attractions of the Chicago *Tribune* and even more of the New York *Daily News*: such organs appear to monopolize daring and impiety. The only way to combat this is by open and honest discussion about Jews, to make people aware that Jews are *real*, and to make an effort to talk about them as they are.

The third level of discourse about Jews is on what we might call the Catskill-Broadway plane, in which there thrives a form of culture spread throughout America by the press, film, and radio. Perhaps we find its beginnings in *Abie's Irish Rose*. Danny Kaye, the Goldbergs, Eddie Cantor, Billy Rose—day by day and night after night they exploit aspects of Jewish life and Jewish character. Many non-Jewish comedians play the same circuit; perhaps they have Jewish gag-writers. I wish I knew what Billy Rose's readers in Dubuque and Dallas, Charleston and Seattle, have made of his accounts of life and love at Lindy's; and I wish I knew what America makes of Milton Berle. Does this add to that identification of Jews with big-city life which —as Arnold Rose has observed—is so powerful an element in modern anti-Semitism? Do the lower-middle-class non-Jewish audiences of this Catskill culture have personal contacts with Jews of their own and other social levels, or is their only "contact" through these images of stage and screen? What is the attitude of these audiences towards the Jewish comic or, for that matter, the Jewish Winchell—are these performers patronized as something exotic and foreign? Are they felt to be Jews at all? I expect we would find a good deal of ambival-aspect of Jewish culture that he symbolizes. The same listener, for ence, a mixture of emotions, both towards the performer and the instance, may both despise and be fascinated by Winchell. I would like to know a lot more about this whole area for the sake of the light it would shed on both the myths of the Americans and the myths of and about the Jews.

The fourth level of discussion about Jews I would locate primarily in the working class, but with ramifications in the lower-middle-class. These people have little opportunity to express their own attitudes except through conversation—on the workbench, in the bar, on the street corner. The only medium of publication available is the walls of toilets. Even apart from the question of interstate commerce, group-libel laws—such as those being pushed by the Commission on Law and Social Action of the American Jewish Congress —can hardly be effective here! These toilet walls, indeed, are the distorted reflection of—and rebellion against—middle-class piety in respect to the two things, race and sex, that so many Americans find both indecent and alluring. If this level is reached at all by the propaganda of the dreary pietists, the principal effect might perversely be only to make Jews seem even more mysterious than before—and official culture more mendacious and mealy-mouthed. Working-class anti-Semitism is very strong indeed, if I may judge from recent studies of prejudice conducted under the auspices of the Scientific Department of the American Jewish Committee. Whether much of it is anti-Semitism that yearns for action or just big talk and griping, I do not know. . . .

§ V

SO FAR, I HAVE MADE clear my conviction of the futility of much that passes for militancy and—the other side of the coin—much that passes for sweet, pious reasonableness. I want now to draw a few needed distinctions.

First, I think Jewish attacks on anti-Semitism should aim at its containment, not its extirpation. In general, human efforts to eliminate vice totally, rather than to contain it within tolerable bounds, run the risk of a total "politicization" of society. That is, there are totalitarian implications in permitting political measures to encompass all of private, academic, and literary life.

Second, I think Jews go beyond the legitimate containment of anti-Semitism when they seek, as a pressure group, to limit freedom of teaching and expression. Naturally, a Jew need not himself support anti-Semitic expression; why should he? If a Jew resigns from a welcoming committee for Gieseking, he stands on his personal dignity. So does a Jew who declines to read or to place advertising in an openly anti-Semitic newspaper. But just as soon as such Jews band together and try to prevent other people from reading a paper or hearing a pianist, then they are no longer exercising a personal privilege but interfering with the personal privileges of others. In the present context of American society, freedom of expression is one of the great safeguards for Jews and all other minorities subject to prejudice. As we know, this freedom needs to be protected not only against government, but even more against private censorship—whether by Legionnaires, businessmen, unions, the Legion of Decency, or the Commission on Law and Social Action. Above all, freedom needs active support and encouragement from its friends, as well as protection from its many powerful foes.

Third, I would suggest that Jews are on the whole wisely advised not to spend their lives as anti-anti-Semites. We suspect that the vice crusader probably enjoys pornography and perhaps the anti-anti-Semite is fascinated by what he fights.

In any case, paradoxical as it may seem, Jews could become more at ease if they accepted the fact (I believe it to be a fact) that their fate as Jews in America is largely beyond their control. As many realize, Jewish well-being depends on the health of society as a whole, and only anti-Semites will claim that Jews are powerful enough to save or sink America. And it is relatively futile for Jews to address themselves to hardened anti-Semites as an audience: why should the anti-Semite listen to the Jew, especially when the latter speaks, not as one human being to another, but through the mass media of communication? We are always better off in devoting ourselves to talking to people who, at least in part, want to hear us.

Since, therefore, Jews waste their time when they spend it all trying to impress or repress their enemies, their very lack of power becomes an invitation to devote their major energies to self-development. This, too, may involve combat, but of a different sort and with a different goal, for the focus would shift away from the question as to what menacing things are being said about Jews to more challenging questions: What kind of better, more creative Jewish communities and American society would we like to see in the future? What are the arts that give us pleasure and enrich our lives, and how do we go about encouraging them? What will make America a more interesting and lively place to live in?

There are, I will agree, times so desperate in the life of a society, that repression of a totalitarian movement on its way to power may be required. That is not, in my opinion, the situation now—and if it were, as I have said, the Jews would not be the ones most able to do much about it. But Jews, like other Americans, can always find the situation they are in to be grim and desperate if they look hard enough, and can thus rationalize their failure to concern themselves with the possibilities of a more abundant life.

The policy I propose, as should be evident, is motivated not by a fear that in a contest of strength and fanaticism the Jews are bound to suffer because they are fundamentally weak, but rather by a fear of the evil Jews inflict on themselves and on other Americans by interfering with freedom of expression. We seem to be building a society in which any reasonably well-organized minority group can get itself a limited veto over the mass communications industries and, with some exceptions, over public political debate. Let us return to the movies as a prime example. The focus on the problem of repression that the organized Jews share with other organized groups tends to give us movies in which disagreeable things cannot be shown about doctors, veterans, Jews, morticians, priests, labor leaders, Negroes, Marshall Plan countries, and so on; only lawyers, gangsters, night-club operators, and Russians lack effective Hollywood lobbies. Curbed on these scores, and also on the score of open sex, the movies cater to sadism—even movies which are "good for race relations" do this. Perhaps if Jewish energies were spent, not in adding to the list of taboos, but in trying to free the mass media and the public mind from taboos, they would not get very far. But the advantage of choosing freedom as an ally is that, while it may sometimes be defeated, it is always a more interesting and agreeable side to be on.

A dangerous disregard and contempt for artistic work is evident in the easy condemnations of allegedly anti-Semitic movies, books, and performers by the militants. But a more subtle contempt also appears in those who view every act from the standpoint of real or imaginary "others" and therefore would like to use the arts to promote "better race relations." Indeed, we find that while the militants profess scorn for tactical considerations, they are in agreement with these public-relations-minded Jews in their view of culture as a mere expendable. Recently, for instance, a producer's representative, typical of the latter group, wanted me to go on record in favor of *Home of the Brave* on the ground that it was "good for race relations." When I asked him (the somewhat ironic question) whether he thought *Symphonie Pastorale* was good for race relations, he did not understand me—what did this movie about a pastor's family tragedy have to do with race relations? In his attitude, he patronized both his own craft of movie-making and the movie audience: he assumed that people get out of a movie a message as simple as the fortune-teller's printed slip in a penny arcade. The notion that the art form itself, over a period of time, could affect the quality of American life, and hence of its race relations, is forgotten in anxious concern for the presumed immediate results. This producer's representative did not ask himself what kinds of movies he himself enjoyed seeing, but looked at his product from the stance of an outsider—this is the hallmark of the public-relations approach. But it is evident that a person who seems only to patronize others also patronizes his own human reactions and, while he thinks he manipulates the emotions of the audience, also manipulates, and eventually causes to evaporate, his own emotions.

In fact, it is on a platform of contempt and distrust for people that the militants and the public-relations-minded groups, whatever their internecine quarrels, can unite. While the militants assume that most Jews not of their faction and all non-Jews except their certified "friends" are anti-Semitic, and sally forth to fight them, the public-relations-minded people assume that Americans are governed only by expediency and sally forth to cozen them. Instead of defending in their own membership and among its allies the best traditions of American freedom, they devote themselves to specious arguments with which to manipulate the indifferent mass.

An instance of the latter practice is the argument against racial discrimination frequently advanced by Jewish organizations—and not only by them, of course—that restrictive covenants and other discriminatory practices are economically expensive. Or, in another form, the argument says that racialism makes trouble for our foreign policy. People are hardly going to like Jews and Negroes better because hating them costs money or looks bad in Indonesia! The people who put out such arguments do not "believe" them; that is, the arguments are true enough, but it is not because of them that the arguers were themselves won over to the cause of racial justice and equality. To offer arguments that do not have weight for oneself is, I think, patronizing and arrogant. Wishing, each in his way, to be "realistic" and hardboiled, the militants and the public-relations people both are apt to forget that people need ideals and that the human passion for freedom is one of the recurrent experiences of mankind.

§ VI

INDEED, to defend freedom by appeals to public-relations considerations is, in a fundamental sense, to weaken it. One reason why the American tradition of freedom is perhaps less vital now than a hundred years ago is precisely that it has become enmeshed in piety and propaganda. This, of course, is not something the Jewish defense organizations have done; it is part of a long historical development in which freedom and democracy have become schoolbook words, have been linked with reactionary economic programs, and have been made available for the export trade. To see what has happened we need only compare the kind of writing about American democracy current in Jefferson's day with that of our own. From Jefferson to Mark Twain and Veblen there was a bite and vigor in American letters that is seldom dared today. Our various official doctrines of unity—the phrase, "the" American way of life, is revealing—and our various pressures of censorship are both symptoms and causes of the shift.

The picture of America which gets through the censorship is a stereotype, and not a very interesting one. During the last war, we experimented with an effort to create a stereotype both of America and of the GI, and to sell this to the soldiers through advertising, radio, and the military indoctrination agencies. The soldiers resented it, but took their resentment out in swearwords and apathy, since they lacked the resources and encouragement to develop their own picture of themselves and what they were doing. Today, we seem to be marketing to the civilian population a picture as spurious, as lacking in complexity and savor, as the GI Joe myth. Jews in America, like the other minorities who make up the majority, will not thrive on such stereotypes, even though severally favorable to racial tolerance—if freedom is the price, tolerance comes too high. But, in fact, this is an unreal alternative, since minorities thrive, not on a colorless uniformity but on diversity, even conflict—including diversity and conflict among themselves.

Many Americans have lost faith in freedom and have lost hope in the future. Many Americans have imitated the methods of their totalitarian enemies and have swung away from complacency and over-timidity in the direction of paranoia and over-aggression; still others have swung away from tolerance as a fighting faith to tolerance as a public-relations maneuver. Many Americans are attracted by force and repression, many by the veiled (and hence in many ways preferable) force of manipulative public relations. The "mindless militants" among the American Jews, and the public-relations soothsayers, have therefore plenty of company, though not good company. But what is particularly sad and ironic in this development is that those very Jews who often violently attack the policy of "assimilation" and who make much of their Jewish consciousness seem to have been completely uprooted in America from the mainstream of Jewish values. For in the past Jews learned to depend for life, liberty, and the pursuit of happiness on very formidable weapons of another order: namely, good judgment, the free exercise of reason, and hospitality to intellect and hatred of force, traditions which go back almost three thousand years.

Since analogous developments have overtaken many Jews and many Americans, we may suppose that the explanation for the historical shift in Jewish attitude lies less in the miseries peculiar to Jews than in those that they share with their fellow Americans. Specifically, as I have already indicated, many Jews, like many other Americans, do not know how to be happy—do not even know how to become aware of whether they are happy or not. Despite, as things go, a fair degree of security, despite very considerable material abundance, we find it somehow easier to be miserable. In our private lives, we look for, or easily fall into, agendas—ways of getting through the day and the evening. In our public lives, we live under a sense of menace and doom, create a context of chronic emergency, and are drawn to crusades against enemies, real and imaginary, because our lives are not sufficiently rewarding in their own terms. We think we would be happy in a world free of anti-Semitism and such evils, but I doubt it.

Any programs of "action" that rob us of any part of our intellectual heritage, that inhibit our curiosity and wonder about the world and the people in it, or that substitute the miasma of "piety" for the élan of truth, cannot make for happiness. And a life filled up with activities, aggressions, and anxieties is not my conception of a full life.

9. Some Observations
Concerning Marginality

THE PREVAILING ATTITUDE toward marginality on the part of social scientists, it seems to me, is one of dislike for it (it is sometimes called "alienation"). They would like to see us go back to a social system in which every one was supposedly rooted, in which there were no marginal people; everyone had a place and knew it. Now it has occurred to me that this attitude, which is so prevalent here [at the University of Chicago], might have something to do with the fact that we live in the city of Chicago, and that current uneasiness about this city might have given its particular tinge to some of the more recent discussions of urbanization and migration.

What I have in mind is that it has become fashionable to dislike Chicago, to view it as the very model of the "impersonal," sprawling, and disorganized metropolitan blob. The older, Sandburgian attitude of admiration for the steel plants, the packing houses, the railroads, and the other majesties of the city seems almost to have disappeared, and with it the studies of an earlier day which explored the city with fascination, even awe, and a certain touch of romance.

I propose in these remarks to take up first two kinds of marginality, which I shall call "open" and "secret"; then to turn to a brief case study of the Jews; and, finally, to make some comments about the ethical aspects of marginality.

§ I

"OPEN MARGINALITY" is the kind that we read about in the writings of Robert E. Park, that we are familiar with: the situation created when we have the educated Negro, the self-made man, the woman engineer, all the various kinds of marginality which have become, so to speak, institutionalized, defined. And they become institutionalized and defined for many reasons, for one thing because people in our society can make a living by these definitions: that is, by giving roles to marginal people. This seems to me one of the important functions of such organizations as the National Association for the Advancement of Colored People, the American Jewish Congress, the Portia Society of women lawyers, even on occasion the Rotary Club —all these groups, and in a way social scientists too—include those who make a living by defining other people's marginalities for them.

Now in the case of all these open, defined, institutionalized marginalities, we find people who are marginal to their marginality: that is, people who exist in one of the groups as defined and yet do not feel the group protest quite fits them, or their feelings. They do not feel as they are supposed to feel as inhabitants of that margin. And if that is true, then they join the ranks of those whom I would like to speak of as the bearers of a "secret" marginality. These are the people who subjectively fail to feel the identities expected of them. Obviously this dichotomy that I am suggesting between open and secret marginality cannot be made too sharp.

Let us look at some instances of secret marginality. The most obvious is the case of the passer. And we must think of the passer not only in the color ranks, but also in the status ranks and in the "brow" hierarchy. We may define the passer, drawing from Professor Hughes' article on "Social Change and Status Protest" (*Phylon*, X, First Quarter, 1949, 59-65), as a person who can identify with his new group in every attitude it has except its attitude towards the group he has left. And it is this sore point, of course, which makes his passing a problem of psychological marginality, rather than simple espionage. While this is the most discussed, it is perhaps the least important or prevalent of the kinds of secret marginality. For instance, there is the girl in Samoa, as Samoan culture is described by Margaret Mead, who feels more passionately, who has more jealousy, than she is expected to have. She feels marginal in a way which the culture does not allow her to credit, to recognize, to label, to give a name to, and therefore, in a way, to feel comfortable with. Or, to take a recent example that came to my notice, a girl came to see me, a university co-ed, who felt that she was quite crazy. When I tried to find out why she felt crazy, it came out that it was because she felt guilt about sexual adventures. That is, she had the feelings that would have been perfectly normal in earlier decades, but she had been convinced that it was wrong for her to feel the least bit troubled or problematic about sexual experience—she should be "cool" —and therefore she felt somewhat alienated from her group as she interpreted it, and felt marginal in a way that the youth culture did not define.

We may ask what are the factors that lead to this kind of secret marginality? I think that these factors arise from the "shape" we are in, from all the variety of human character and temperament and physique which separates us from others, which makes us individual; likewise, our position in the family, and many other individualizing experiences. Think, for instance, of the problem of the beautiful girl. Some years ago a friend of mine met a celebrated beauty-contest winner. She spent all her time trying to tell him how much she admired Harvard; she wanted to be thought of as a great brain and not as a great body; and she felt furious with the brutal, as she thought, qualities of the publicity men who moved her around the country. Contracted to appear at an exposition as sponsor of a House Beautiful, she felt all this as vulgar and materialistic. This is a well-known problem, yet we are inclined to be so envious that we cannot be quite sympathetic enough with the plight of the beautiful girl whose role is defined in a way which does not fit her as she feels herself to be; she cannot avail herself of the strategy of hiding behind her mask, because her mask is too much of a cynosure. I have known girls in this position to try to appear less beautiful than they are, for instance by wearing glasses (before these, too, became sexy), or ill-fitting clothes, or by, so to speak, wearing their body in an ill-fitting way, as some tall, big, handsome men also do.

All these people who do not fit, who do not hang together in the way that they are supposed to, who do not feel the identities they are supposed to feel, are unorganized. They have nobody to define them. They lack both the advantages and the dangers of the cultural compartmentalizers, who make their living by defining others' marginalities for them.

We must compare with this the concept of the invisible church: the union of people who, without organization, that is, formal organization, but through piety and through print (the Bible) feel close to one another and feel they "belong" through some invisible set of bonds which are irontight. They are as sure of the existence of this church as a spy is sure of the writing he has just done with invisible ink; in both cases, the future will reveal the presence of the now-invisible. But the group of people who are secretly marginal seldom have this confidence that there are recognizable others who share their situation and feeling; rather, they feel isolated because the marginalities that are talked about are precisely those they cannot bring themselves to share.

§ II

THOSE OF YOU who are familiar with the concepts of inner-direction and other-direction that my collaborators and I have developed in *The Lonely Crowd* will perhaps be in a position to raise the question whether characterological marginality may not be spreading with the spread of other-direction. Perhaps I can put this in best and clearest form by a reference to the concept of marginal differentiation. Marginal differentiation is a term I have developed from the economists who sometimes speak of "marginal" and sometimes of "product" differentiation under conditions of monopoly. What they have in mind is that each product in a monopolistic economy differentiates itself from other products by slight deviations in brand name and packaging. Each sector of the economy in this way is isomorphic, that is, tries to be similar—yet at the same time to be different. (I recently heard that one of the leading textbook publishers has the slogan, "We will sell books that are new, but not too new," and I think that puts the slogan of marginal differentiation very well.) Now with the spread of psychological other-direction in the upper-middle class, people themselves go in for marginal differentiation of personality. In order to do this they must be sensitive enough to themselves and each other to know how they appear to others, and to be aware concerning the degree to which they are different from others without being too different. This is an anxious, precarious business, to look at it negatively; it can be sensitive and comradely, to look at it positively, because it keeps people in touch both with themselves and with others. It creates a kind of attitude towards oneself which was absent in the earlier era of inner-direction, when conformity was in some ways perhaps more rigid, and in which people were less aware of these nuances of personality difference.

This awareness, this radar-like sensitivity to how one is navigating in the social world, and this tendency to make that navigation into an end of life as well as a means—these seem to me to be characteristic of the psychological type I have termed other-directed. By the same token, the idea can be advanced that the spread of this type will carry with it the spread of awareness that one is different, in secret and subtle ways. That is, we become so greatly interested in interpersonal relations, in our own sociometric location on friendship charts, and so on, that we are enabled to realize discrepancies between our internal states and those we sense in others. Moreover, as our growing economic abundance allows us to rise above the problems of sheer subsistence, we have time and energy to speculate about our fitness in the interpersonal scheme of things.

There is, furthermore, a connection between these characterological developments of our day with respect to marginality and certain social changes. On the social side what we see is a group of new hierarchies springing into existence, under which the older, relatively clear hierarchies of class and caste become amorphous and diffuse. We find, for instance, problems arising as to who rates whom, as between intellectuals and businessmen; we find problems of protocol in all walks of life, which imply that we can no longer easily speak of someone as marginal to a defined class or a defined caste. Instead, we are witnessing the rise of all kinds of, so to speak, brown and mulatto societies, groups who, with various shadings of slight difference from each other, occupy a place in the social system, not clearly distinct from other places. This confusion as to location is one of the reasons for the development of other-direction as a psychological trait, and in addition, one of the reasons why marginality may be on the increase in the sense that secret marginality (undefined marginality) is dependent on situations which are not yet fully understood and recognized by the participants. There is no union of the people who have, let us say, not quite the *New Yorker* attitude toward life, whereas they have the economic and educational position which would permit or require them to have this attitude, this being a more subtle differentiation than the older ones of sheer economic and social class. As a matter of fact, we can think of Lloyd Warner's work, with its emphasis on consumption values, as, in a way, a symptom or indication of the change in hierarchies; and all the arguments which go on so tiresomely, as I think, between Warner and the Marxists, seem to me an argument as to which status system runs the country when, in fact, neither does.[1]

§ III

WE HAVE TO THINK of marginality in terms of the social function of the marginal man before we can make any adequate inquiry into his psychology and ethics. Pirenne describes the man who, in the late Middle Ages, began to move around in the burgeoning cities and ports where one's position, as Pirenne says, instead of being measured by social status depended only on intelligence and energy. Now the court Jew is one of the most famous examples of this type of person, and he begins to take a prominent place in the society sometime after the period with which Pirenne deals, when the rise of absolute monarchy begins. The court Jew, with his international connections, is the banker of the embryo king, trying to help the king to do what the king wants to do. But the court Jew is not a marginal man at all in Park's sense; that is, he does not have the psychological consequences Park describes, be-

---

1. Perhaps a word of explanation should be added here concerning the challenge in this paragraph to some prevailing theories of social stratification in America. I am inclined to believe that researchers, by their very techniques, tend to "prove" their assumption that everyone, and not only a large number of people, is aware of his class membership (as against simply sharing values and behavior with others who are aware of the class cues of those values and behavior). Moreover, the problem of class has been investigated largely in the smaller communities where the number of parallel hierarchies is at a minimum; matters may stand very differently in large metropolitan clusters where people cannot establish a single common basis for ratings. This is not to be read, of course, as one of the now conventional criticisms of the stimulating and important explorations of Lloyd Warner and his coworkers, without which we would not be able to move on to these further complications which research has not yet found a way to handle.

cause there is little questioning on his part as to what his mission is, and there is no break on his part with the traditional Jewish values. He lives amid those values, though he moves in court circles, quite as comfortably as the British civil servant often lived amid his traditional values in India or Egypt. The British civil servant is out among strange people, but they do not exist for him except as objects to be organized, to be manipulated—the detachment of a Lord Cromer in Egypt is a good example. In the same way, the court Jew is very much a Jew: still orthodox, still tribe-connected, still the leader of the other Jews by virtue of his role in the non-Jewish economy, and using whatever power he has in that other economy simply to better the position of the Jews (in much the same way that the Rothschilds are reported to have improved the position of the Jews in Frankfort through intercession with Count Metternich).

Since, then, this kind of court Jew has a definite function both in the Jewish and the non-Jewish worlds, he does not have the psychological outlook of the bearer of either open or secret marginality. Likewise, the Jewish rebel who found his way to a political and intellectual role in the nineteenth century lacked many of the psychological consequences of social marginality; lacked some of the misery of Heinrich Heine. One good clue to this, I think, is the fact that such Jewish rebels as Marx or Börne could be violently yet not uncomfortably anti-Semitic, both in polarization from the court Jew on the one hand and from the Jewish masses on the other. For these rebel Jews of the nineteenth century found their security, found the end of their seeming marginality, in their clear vision of a future when no irrational margins of class, or ethnic group, or caste, would be left; rather than finding security, as the court Jew did, in past values. They held only to the future, with such tenacity that they could be violently anti-Semitic without self-hatred; ironically, they had some assistance here from the Messianic trend in Jewish thought itself.

The position of the Jew as marginal man really develops when he no longer has either his economic function as the court Jew or his political function as the socialist rebel.[2] Then only his marginality is his function. To a very considerable degree this is what has happened to the Jewish intellectual in the period of the last fifty to seventy-five years. (It is this which is described brilliantly in Hannah Arendt's book, *The Origins of Totalitarianism*.) The society Jew, welcomed

---

2. As one would expect, there are marginal cases to any statement one can make about a group. Thus, Ferdinand Lassalle, Marx's great contemporary, sought not only to climb in the class system as a social, but also as an ethnic parvenu. Tied securely neither to the past nor to the future, he was vulnerable to aristocratic aspersions on his Jewishness.

into the salons of the Faubourg Saint-Germain, as Proust relates, has nothing to sell in the way of an economic function; once democracy gets established, there is no longer a court for the court Jew to attend, and the Jew is not needed to finance the republic since taxes are so much more effective. Instead of goods and services, the society Jew is selling his Jewishness. In a sense, he is selling his marginal differentiation in which he claims to be different from the other Jews; and at the same time, if he were not a Jew, there would be no peculiar mutual attraction between him and the anti-Semitic aristocracy. For it is precisely because the aristocracy is anti-Semitic that he is drawn to it, as this keeps out the other Jews, while the aristocracy in its turn enjoys playing with "vice": Proust observantly describes how Jewishness and homosexuality play the same role because both are vices of the aristocracy. In the extraordinary study called the "Portrait of the Anti-Semite," Sartre recognizes something of this, and sees that the Jew in modern France, at least the emancipated Jew, is in a way created by the expectations of the anti-Semite, toward which he reacts, and against which he may sometimes later polarize himself.

We all know that it is possible to enjoy skating on thin ice, and so we must not be too sorry for some of these Jews who may have enjoyed the very risks of their marginality—the point is important because we tend all too often in social science to look only at the punishing aspects of such phenomena as alienation, marginality, and social mobility. Think, for instance, of the enjoyment some theologians derive from skating on the thin ice of their orthodoxy, while at the same time embracing avant-garde movements of thought; such men seem almost to have consciously sought out the most precarious margins one could find in the society; they are challenged, as well as tortured, by the intellectual reconciliations they must constantly make. . . .

§ IV

I WANT NOW to turn to a theme touched on at the outset, namely the contemporary influential view that marginality is some sort of disgrace, which should be abolished in all well regulated social and psychic systems. One evidence for this, to continue with our example of the Jews, can be taken from contemporary efforts, from both sides of the ethnic line, to erase Jewish marginality wherever found, to "normalize" the Jewish situation. Whereas once such efforts were manifested by plastic surgery on "Jewish" noses, they are now manifested by psychic efforts on "Jewish" souls, taking such forms as Zionist nationalism, the religiosity of the self-Judaizing Jews, artificially sustained Jewish and Yiddish usages, and so on. The chauvinistic and normalizing Jews are in turn quite aggressive against the "homeless

cosmopolitan," that is, the margin-hugging Jew who owes his existence to the Enlightenment—some Zionists here employ a similar vocabulary to that of the Soviet Union today and show the prophetic
quality of Veblen's fear that the loss of marginality might also mean
the loss to Western culture of the distinctive Jewish achievements in
intellectual life. These Jewish efforts are abetted, in America, by those
non-Jews who are so afraid of being thought ethnocentric that they
overeagerly welcome all signs of Jewish folksiness from their Jewish
friends, much as jazz was welcomed as so beautifully Negro by some
white Bohemians.

A further example of the attempts to abolish marginality by psychic surgery can be found if we examine the compulsion put on many
rapidly self-emancipating people to erase any feelings of prejudice
they may have against those of different class and ethnic background.
On this campus, for instance, students sometimes fail to realize that
they are being asked to cross both class and ethnic lines at the same
time—the situation appears to them to involve only the ethnic line.
A middle-class boy from a small Midwestern town may be confronted
with a Jewish boy from Brooklyn who is of working-class parentage,
but the former may define the encounter as a test of his ability to
shed any latent anti-Semitism; he fails to see that class and rural-urban
differences may be much more important. Or again, an upper-class
white girl may meet a lower-middle-class Negro boy and be horrified
at what she thinks is her own race prejudice, since all the marginalities
in the meeting have been packaged under the single ethnic label.
People may even break down—I have seen such cases—out of a feeling
of inadequacy to rise to such demands put on their tolerance of differences, because they do not realize how great and many-sided those
demands are. Here, as I have stated, the psychic surgery operates on
the member of the group which, in the society at large, is the dominant one—of course, such situations are probably confined to fairly
small cultural enclaves.

Reflection on such examples has increasingly forced upon me the
feeling that children have the right to be prejudiced and to move at
their own pace across class and ethnic lines; that they should not be
compelled by psychic surgery to move at a pace not of their choosing. I realize this view creates many problems to which I have no
ready answer, because one might say that they do not choose their
prejudices either; if they are given their prejudices they may be
frozen in them and unable to move or to be liberated. Nevertheless I
think we can do things which set up the educational system in such
a way as to make young people aware of what is being asked of them,
so as to reduce the loss of identity by children who are being invited

to normalize in their own proper persons relations which are a product of history, often centuries of history.

I feel this most clearly in the case of the relationship between men
and women. What seems to me to be going on today is that the marginality which always exists between the sexes—because men are not
quite men and women are not quite women, and wish in each case
that they were surer which they were—leads under conditions of
coeducation to confusion in which men are not able to establish their
identity as men without being forced at once to polarize themselves
against women, and much more strongly is this so for women. Men
are deprived today of the latency period; they must take girls to
proms from the age of—well, the sixth grade or the seventh grade on.
When older, they are deprived of taverns, country clubs, and factories as sanctuaries against women. They tend to retaliate by trying
to lock all women up in the suburb so as to avoid the dilemmas of
confronting them outside; thus being able to meet them at their own
pace and timing, without the women being aware that there are other
paces and other timings.

In sum, the person who is on the other side, on the majority side,
on the dominant side, of the sexual, ethnic or class line, may be forced
to move rapidly, and with little awareness, across all these lines under
the imputation that if he is not prepared to do so gracefully and at
once he is bigoted or unemancipated.

This raises a question as to what the relation is in a given case
between the life-cycle of an individual and the race-relations or sex-
relations cycle in which he happens to live. It may be that the problem
I am discussing is a problem of a temporary sort because it happens
there is a concurrence between the particular phase of the race-
relations cycle in our liberal upper-middle-class culture with the life-
cycle of some of you. But I suggest that the life-cycle, even in the
best of cultures, involves some marginality. We are all of us going to
live too long for somebody else, though not long enough for ourselves, and I sense a tendency in contemporary social science to
ascribe to marginality and to all the things that have brought marginality about—mixing of peoples, urbanization, and the rest—the
problems which are the dilemmas of living in any culture. While the
discovery of marginality as a concept and a topic for investigation
is recent, the problem of marginality must be about as old as organized
social life.

§ V

LET ME IN THIS CONNECTION say a word about the attitude of many
social scientists and intellectuals today that a socially mobile person

is punished and hurt by his drives to climb in the class system, by the ambiguities and marginalities of his ever-changing position. The implication is, even among thinkers who feel in the abstract that an open society is a good thing, that such mobility is hard on those who strive for it; they would be happier if they stayed put. And of course this view operates much more strongly among those increasingly active voices who sing the charms of the static society. Here it is thought that marginality can be eliminated largely by operations on the social structure, to ensure its rigidity (an utterly futile ideal, I think, but that is not my point here), though there will also be operations on psychic structure to eliminate the "anal" motivations which impel to climbing.

What appears to be left out in such views is the possibility that people use the mobility the system gives them in part to minimize the discomforts of secret marginalities, of which often they may not be aware. A lower-class person may actually feel more at home with middle-class people, not just because they have higher status—in fact, this higher status is one source of his sufferings at their hands—but because they are actually "his kind" of people. Some Negroes may actually feel more comfortable in white society. In both cases, movement which is "up" is also movement into the larger pool, and of course into a pool whose members differ from the members of the lower pool in many ways other than "upness."

What looks like the climbing of the parvenu may also be simply movement as such, or the search for challenge, or the desire for a greater amount of "social space." Conversely, we should not frown on those who want to "climb down"—a motive which is perhaps sublimated in some anthropologists and sociologists who, in their romantic belief that the lower classes or the Negroes or the preliterates have more fun, manage to spend most of their time with them. In neither case should we make people feel guilty about their desire to find new associates, or stigmatize as "uprooted" or "mobile" a person who does not care to be sedentary or parochial. Save for the rarely fortunate person who happens to be born and to live among his true peers (and is this always so fortunate?), most of us need to move around to find peers as we mature. We should not be intimidated from seeking liberation by the fear of becoming marginal both to the groups we leave behind and the groups to which we aspire. Most of the punishments meted out to the mobile person come, not from either old or new associates, but from within—from his own interpretations of what he is doing.

§ VI

MY OWN VIEW, it should be clear, springs from the ethical postulate that for a rational system of conduct one needs insight and the possibility of choice. So our problem becomes one of seeing what positions in society are conducive, more or less, to insight and choice. Whether marginality fosters insight and choice depends, of course, on the given case. Marginality can freeze people with anxiety or nostalgia, while the absence of marginality can give people so much power that they need not choose, but can make all the other people choose. That is, if one is powerful, one may be marginal in a quantitative sense, but not in a social and psychological sense. The English ruler of India did not need to choose: the Indians were the ones who had problems in dealing with him, like Aziz in *A Passage to India.*

On the other hand we must not assume, contrariwise, that powerlessness is always conducive to ethical superiority. While the powerless need insight to avoid being impressed by power, precisely because they are powerless they may not have the opportunities for insight which they need. They may not have the position, the mobility, even the marginality which they need in order to be aware of other ways of living and therefore of the possibility of choice. We must not, incidentally, assume that the upper class in America is necessarily powerful in the sense I have spoken of. If we think of the marginality of Henry or Brooks Adams or of Santayana, we will realize that in this country the upper class since perhaps the Eighties of the last century, has been in many ways quite as marginal as any other sector. This, indeed, is an aspect of the lack of clear class structuring on which I commented earlier.

To put all this another way, I am saying that the intellect is a controller of the consequences, an interpreter, of marginality, and that the intellect is at its best, and its ethical insights are at their best, when one is in a marginal position that is not too overpowering—just as one may have one's best ideas when one is on the margin between sleep and waking.

Now, finally, we might end with some questions about the implicit ideals of human life and of human society in the minds of those intellectuals and social scientists who are hostile to marginality. Park used to tell a story of an old ex-slave whom he met in Alabama. The old man was poor, and undoubtedly worse off in all material respects than under slavery. In fact, he used to boast about what a good life he had had under his old master. Park asked him whether he was not sorry about having been emancipated, and the old man replied that, no, he liked freedom—for, he said, "There's a kind of looseness about this here freedom." I myself feel that a certain looseness and disorderliness and variety of attitude are a part of the good life. One might ask, why do I have to take my stand on every issue? Why need I be all of a piece? . . .

Much the same might be said about continuity. The integrated life is connected with the straight career line, with life in the integrated neighborhood, with lack of discontinuity between the stages of the life cycle, and so on. Yet it seems to me that in taking this attitude, we patronize the skills of people in handling discontinuities. We tend to patronize the primitive when we think of him as someone who cannot move into the industrial culture. We certainly patronize the child when we think he is hard up if he has to move sometimes to a new neighborhood. We patronize the rural person when we think that he is so rural he cannot move into an urban way of living. And in our patronization we prove ourselves right. In all this it seems to me that our very gifts, especially, perhaps, in America, our ability to move in different directions, to be unintegrated to a degree, to operate on discontinuities of life and career, come to be regarded as liabilities, at least if they exceed the tolerated margin of marginal differentiation.

Plainly, this problem of ideals for human life is immensely complex, and terms such as "integration" are traps of ambiguity—I would not quarrel with someone who defined my kind of unintegrated, loosely ordered life as a form of integration on a higher level! At any rate, we can be fairly sure that the intellectuals who, in their dislike for marginality, would erase the sources of their intellectuality, are not likely to be successful in reforming society as a whole: life will continue to create both secret and open marginalities and secret and open defenses for them.

Park, in his essay on "Personality and Culture Conflict," is aware of this; he writes:

Considering that man lives so largely in the minds of other men, and is so responsive to the attitudes and emotions of those about him, it is nevertheless true that he is rather less dependent upon his environment . . . than other animals. He maintains, as over against other individuals—their attitudes and their claims—a certain degree of reserve. It is only in states of exultation and of ecstasy that he lets himself go completely, and yields himself wholly to the occasion and to the influences of the persons about him.

Ordinarily he is able, by means of his rationalizations, his cynicism and his casuistry—

And you see Park treats these, as I would, as at least in part valuable traits,

to defend himself against the psychic assaults which the presence of other persons makes upon him. He can, when he chooses, make his manners a cloak and his face a mask, behind which he is able to preserve a certain amount of inner freedom even while mingling freely with other persons. He can withdraw from the world on occasion, and men have always consciously and unconsciously devised means for maintaining social distances and of preserving their independence of thought even when they were unable to maintain their independence of action.

And, incidentally, it is just this that is one terrifying thing in totalitarian society: that it may bring this possibility to an end.

And this fact is just as significant and as charactristic a trait of human behavior as is the opposite disposition to respond to every change in the social atmosphere of the world about him.

It is for this reason, as much as for any other, that man invariably builds himself somewhere and some time a home, a retreat, a refuge, where, surrounded by his family and his friends, he can relax, and, so far as it is possible for so gregarious a creature, be wholly at home and at ease, and in more or less complete possession of his own soul. This is no more than to say that most men and some women possess a sales resistance which not even the magic of the new salesmanship can always overcome.

10. Marginality, Conformity, and Insight

LET ME WARN YOU in advance that I am not going to talk about this massive topic by laying out for you a scheme or typology of analysis, or by presenting interview material or projective test protocols, and so on. Rather, I propose to get at my subject by indirection and by implication. I shall raise many questions to which I have no answers. I shall deal heavily and designedly in ambiguities. Else Frenkel-Brunswik, Donald Campbell, Rokeach, and various other psychologists have made experiments to demonstrate the relationships between nonconformity and tolerance for ambiguity—willingness to look at a picture without having to decide at once whether it is a this or a that. Just such tolerance will be required if you are to follow me without discomfort in a mutual effort at understanding. Among other things, I shall discuss the ways in which several well-known literary men—Edmund Gosse for one, and Richard Wright for another, both of whom were brought up in extremely doctrinaire homes in which there was no other extravagance than that of doctrine—found their way to a measure of nonconformity, fruitful both for them and for society. Members of minorities in the society, they also grew up as minorities of one within the home. One of my objectives will be to emphasize that a minority position can be a blessing as well as a curse, and particularly that a marginal position—not quite in the minority, not quite outside it—may be a superior vantage point for understanding and for self-development.

§ I

LET ME BEGIN, then, with the episode in Edmond Gosse's *Father and Son,* in which Gosse as a boy experimented with idolatry, a sin severely condemned by his zealously religious father, a leader in a Puritanical sect known as the Plymouth Brethren:

All these matters drew my thoughts to the subject of idolatry, which was severly censured at the missionary meeting. I cross-examined my Father very closely as to the nature of this sin, and pinned him down to the categorical statement that idolatry consisted in praying to any one or anything but God himself. Wood and stone, in the words of the hymn, were peculiarly liable to be bowed down to by the heathen in their blindness. I pressed my Father further on this subject, and he assured me that God would be very angry, and would signify His anger, if any one, in a Christian country, bowed down to wood and stone. I cannot recall why I was so pertinacious on this subject, but I remember that my Father became a little restive under my cross-examination. I determined, however, to test the matter for myself, and one morning, when both my parents were safely out of the house, I prepared for the great act of heresy. I was in the morning-room on the ground-floor, where, with much labour, I hoisted a small chair on to the table close to the window. My heart was now beating as if it would leap out of my side, but I pursued my experiment. I knelt down on the carpet in front of the table and looking up I said my daily prayer in a loud voice, only substituting the address "Oh, Chair!" for the habitual one.

Having carried this act of idolatry safely through, I waited to see what would happen. It was a fine day, and I gazed up at the slip of white sky above the houses opposite, and expected something to appear in it. God would certainly exhibit His anger in some terrible form, and would chastise my impious and wilful action. I was very much alarmed, but still more excited; I breathed the high, sharp air of defiance. But nothing happened; there was not a cloud in the sky, not an unusual sound in the street. Presently I was quite sure that nothing would happen. I had committed idolatry, flagrantly and deliberately, and God did not care.

The result of this ridiculous act was not to make me question the existence and power of God; those were forces which I did not dream of ignoring. But what it did was to lessen still further my confidence in my Father's knowledge of the Divine mind. My Father had said, positively, that if I worshipped a thing made of wood, God would manifest His anger. I had then worshipped a chair, made (or partly made) of wood, and God had made no sign whatever. My Father, therefore, was not really acquainted with the Divine practice in cases of idolatry.

It is clear that Edmond Gosse had trapped his father in the latter's own theology. But he is not entirely happy about it; indeed, the incident remains in his memory all his life long.

For us, the episode can serve to recall an age when parents and children dealt with each other, so to speak, at arm's length; an age when parents, either with conscious or unconscious hypocrisy, sought to exclude their children as much as possible from the social and sexual know-how of adult life. Yet this marginal and excluded position of children was not without advantages for those who were not completely crushed or swindled by parental authority. The slight furtiveness of the boy making the prayer seems not unconnected with the development of his understanding of adults—to get round his father became for him almost a matter of life and death. In many Victorian novels, one gets a similar sense that the child struggles for identity through a fog of parental moral obfuscation—in *The Way of All Flesh*, the father is again a very pious man, while in *David Copperfield* he is that dream of Victorian parental neglect, the step-parent, who forces David into what seems on the surface like servitude but what turns out in the long run to be independence.

In Freud we can find explicitly the lesson we have teased out of the Victorian novelists. He writes (in his *General Introduction to*

Psychoanalysis): "The feeling of having been deceived by grown-up people, and put off with lies, contributes greatly to a sense of isolation and to the development of independence." While in this passage and quite generally he had in mind sexual life and where babies come from, he elsewhere equates lies on this topic with religious illusions and sees both together as an effort by authority to keep mankind in subjection. But his genius lay in seeing that deception isolates people and so may strengthen them, or at least those who survive and do not succumb to neurosis.

The domineering parent or teacher, as in Gosse's case or Richard Wright's, may force the child into a rebellious or sly independence —but he is quite as likely to crush the child entirely. Conversely, in a general atmosphere of permissiveness, the friendly or relaxed parent or teacher may smother children in a mood of amiable camaraderie. This may be done in the name of encouraging criticism, and in my portrait of a hyper-progressive school in *Faces in the Crowd*, I have sketched some of the ways in which nonconformity itself can become a uniform, cramping the child into an uncritical tolerance (in certain areas) and a sort of Stalinoid pessimism. The nonconformity which I admire may be defined as a map of the world made from where the given individual sits, not from where somebody else sits—an individualized map but not a crazy one, since it has some basis in reality, including social reality. We know almost nothing about the conditions in home and school and street which encourage such map-making —a therapeutic milieu does not necessarily produce it, or adversity eliminate it.

Apart from these larger questions raised by Freud's statement, I think we may take it as a good thing that sexual mysteries are today no longer the great divide between teachers and pupils, parents and children. For with secrecy the premium on a merely sexual initiation was so great that many Victorians defined maturity in terms of getting married and starting a family. Their portraits give us a sense that after adolescence they grew old—or as old as they ever did grow— quite young; unlike many people today, they were not very concerned about continued development in middle life. In fact, Freud's concept of the "genital" character as the final stage on life's way, after one has passed successfully through what he termed the oral, anal, and phallic stages, symbolizes this sudden accretion of final maturity and insight. By, let us say, the age of twenty, Freud assumed that the individual contained no more inner worlds to conquer if he had sexually joined the ranks of the grown-ups and been initiated into the secrets of the tribe.

We should bear in mind these constricting features of regularized initiation rites, as well as the obvious emancipating ones, before we grow too nostalgic over the simplicities, virilities, and easy conformities of an era in which, at a certain age, a young man put on his first long pants and smoked a pipe to the accompaniment of his mother's sobs while, at another certain age, a young woman put on her first party dress. Lacking these compartmentalizations, our young people are in some ways much more knowing and precocious, if less independent, than their predecessors were in Freud's day; and their initiation into life, while less sharp, may last longer, not stopping with the acquisition of sexual or theological enlightenment. While there are undoubted losses in the fact that parents in our time want very much to be pals with their children, to keep no secrets from them, or barriers against them, the parents may themselves be kept more alive by this interaction with their growing children.

What seems to have happened, among many other things, is that parents in the educated classes today have become terribly, even terrifiedly, aware of their power to make or to mar their children's fates and fortunes. They can no longer oppress children with a good conscience, and then blame the child's bad impulses or the mother-in-law's poor heredity if things do not turn out well. The twentieth century is not likely to be the Century of the Common Man, but it may well be viewed as the Century of the Child, this being actually the title of an influential book by Ellen Key written at the turn of the century. Since children have remained small powers in a world of big powers—a point brilliantly underplayed by the New York *Herald-Tribune's* comic strip, "Small World"—it is parental concession and not child rebellion which is responsible. The child has been brought into the United Nations, given access to news and opinion, and permitted to make his voice heard long before he himself is ready to arm himself and take on adult occupational, preoccupational, and procreational roles. The paradoxical result is that one can go into many modern homes and get the feeling that it is the parents, and especially the fathers, who are marginal, who are in a precarious position, who are the frightened conformists, while the children hold the strategic initiative. Like the willing self-subordination of the British Tories in the last generation, this parental abnegation is one of those rare historic cases where power has not shut off insight into the situation of the weaker classes, but has actually facilitated it, even to the point of weakening the power.

§ II

ORDINARILY, of course, if one has power one does not feel the need of insight; it is up to others, the powerless ones, to obtain insight as a means of anticipating the wishes of the power-holder. That is one reason why the possession of power and being shackled by a rigid conformity—an undifferentiated map of the world—often go together. Thus, we can see in the South that the amiably prejudiced white who feels that he "knows" Negroes is continuously deceived by Negroes who know him much better than he knows himself. They are in a marginal position and their livelihood, even perhaps life, depends on the acuteness of their responses, their often highly graceful ability to know what the "boss-man" wants before he wants it, while at the same time appearing insouciant and stupid. Their surface conformity is a form of nonconformity. To be sure, the white has some awareness of being deceived, just as he knows that the Negro maid is taking "totings" from the ice-box to her friends and family. But the awareness of a little deception and sabotage comforts him by establishing complicity and by demonstrating his power, just as the falsely friendly greetings he receives demonstrate his power. He is, however, not aware of the full extent to which he is seen through, manipulated, and controlled in many ways by those he believes himself to dominate. He resembles in this the husband who likes to boast that the "little woman" makes all the decisions, because he really feels, contrary to the much more ambiguous fact, that he is truly boss, bearing, if not the *white* man's burden at least the white *man's* burden; we would expect in such a case that the wife would know her husband much more coolly and unsentimentally than vice versa. The fiction that Negroes and women are sentimental is, it seems to me, plainly wishful thinking by people who do not have to know any better.

Actually, however, there are limits to the sort of knowledge the powerless person can gain in this way, for this knowledge is too close to cynicism to fit all cases. The Negro is protected by his cynicalness from an over-ready response to the white liberal, whose generosity he mistrusts as an unsentimental woman will mistrust a Don Quixote, a noble-minded man. In many cases, the suspicion of nobility is well-founded; it prevents one from being disillusioned, saves one from involvement in reform movements which will get nowhere. But a rule of thumb, no matter how useful, is not insight, and it is my judgment that the person who is completely powerless is seldom able to rise above animal cunning. And such cunning cannot cope with wholly novel, unanticipated situations. It is again an undifferentiated map, not individualized, and hence no matter how rebellious the individual may feel himself to be, he is incapable of fruitful nonconformity.

While I was reflecting on this problem, I had occasion to leave my office building at an unaccustomed mid-afternoon hour—I am living now in Kansas City. The old Negro janitor was standing outside in the sun, unconcernedly whistling a tune, when I came up from behind him. He was at once aware of my presence and, without an instant of guilt or gear-shifting, he was in the middle of the old Darky act, mumbling "yassir," "yassir," his eyes vacant, his feet shuffling. Even in his sleep such a man is instantly ready for vacuous inaction, for an uninnocent innocence of regression to childhood. Kansas City appears to retain enough of a Southern exposure not to threaten this janitor with a great deal of resentment from fellow-Negroes who would tease him as an "Uncle Tom," although to be sure the editors of the alert Kansas City Negro weekly, *The Call*, have very different ideas as to how Negroes should behave. Even so, however, the janitor's instantaneous, near-automatic response deprives him of the perplexities many Negroes confront in Northern communities, where not only other Negroes but other whites would be displeased by the actions of a handkerchief-head. In that sense, such a Negro is not marginal enough to have to make choices among complex alternatives, and to gain in the process more insight than simple sight and smell of the color white.

§ III

OFTEN, SUCH INCIDENTS bring me back to Richard Wright's remarkable autobiography, *Black Boy*. For this book can be of great help to us in understanding the subtle relations between marginality and insight. As man and boy, Wright has found it, as it seemed to him, physically impossible to respond in an automatic conformist fashion. In job after job that he held as a youngster, when he desperately needed money, his eyes would not be vacant enough when a white man was looking at him; try as he might, he could not suppress the critical nonconforming look of an equal. Angry white men would say, "What you looking at, black boy?"; friendly whites would take him aside and urge him to conform, at least while he was still in the South. As a bellboy in a hotel, he had to enter a bedroom to bring whiskey on a white man's order, and on one occasion he found a man naked on the bed with a woman. Other bellhops in such a situation could always appear not to see anything. Or they could enter into the bawdy yet subservient camaraderie of poor whites and poor blacks of the sort movingly portrayed in James Agee's book, *Let Us Now Praise Famous Men*. But Wright could not veil his frank curiosity —curiosity of the sort that, in one of the most revealing of adages, is death on cats. During all his time as bellhop, Wright feared some slip would cost him his life.

One job he held was in an optical company, making lenses. The boss was a Northerner who appreciated Richard Wright and wanted

him to get on. But the two white lens-grinders for whom Wright ran
errands and carried water no more liked the way he watched them
work than the man in the hotel room did; they feared he would
steal their trade secrets, which in his area of the South were white
secrets. To amuse themselves, they set Wright to fighting against a
black boy in another shop, but finally, afraid of their own boss'
sympathy for Richard, they threatened to kill him if he did not quit
the job. In this situation, his white protector was as helpless as he,
and resignedly let him go.

I should add that, far from admiring him for his intransigence, the
Negro world in which he moved was much less sympathetic than this
white employer. Some tried very hard to help him cotton on to the
ways of the white world, ways which to them came easily as second
nature so as almost to seem like original nature: they could not grasp
what it was that Wright found difficult, much as a good dancer cannot understand why anybody, having once watched him do a step,
cannot do it in turn. The Negro school principal and other Negro
intellectuals sought to teach him how to gain what seemed to be his
ends without antagonizing the benevolently influential whites as well
as the menacing if uninfluential ones. But his own uncle and other
relatives, and many of his school-fellows and work-mates, hated him
for putting on airs—which is how they interpreted his inability to
"act right," as they termed it, in inter-racial situations. They did not
realize that he wanted nothing so desperately as to "act right," to
know the ropes; how little he thought of himself and how little he
sought any friction or provocation!—as little as a new waiter who,
out of trembling fear to hold his job, drips gravy down the back of
the hostess. Not until much, much later, when he was becoming
known as a writer and finding in the Communist Party certain re-
capitulations of his experiences in the South, did he encounter people
who respected the very qualities in himself which he had vainly sought
to destroy.

In *Black Boy*, as in other personal documents, our job is to try
to understand the author better than he understood himself—in this
case, to see if possible some of the sources of Wright's inability to
conform to his "own" family, to his bellhop peers, and eventually to
his Communist cellmates in Chicago. Again and again, in *Black Boy*
and in the chapter Wright contributed to the book by former Communists, *The God that Failed*, we find him missing a cue that all the
others got. His failure to understand something everybody around
him took for granted seemed endemic. Thus, in childhood, he took
the word "white" literally and could not understand why his light-

colored grandmother was socially defined as Negro. This is the first example, perhaps, of Wright's problem in "looking through" a person, a problem which was interpreted by him and all his associates simply as a form of blindness. He was confused by his grandmother's being physically white. And, though he does not himself observe this, we can assume that in her ways, too, she was white in the sense of following lower-middle-class Puritanical norms. She and all the Wright family were Seventh Day Adventists, a sect which celebrates the Sabbath rather than Sunday and is in other respects much more strict than most of the denominations to which Negroes belong. Separated in many ways from other Negroes, the colored Adventists come as close as one can without "passing" to resigning from the race.

I can illustrate this by a story a friend of mine tells about a Seventh Day Adventist maid they had in their Chicago apartment. The maid was indubitably dark. But she acted "white" in her way of maintaining distance from the other colored maids in the apartment house; in her religion there are no races, and this theology influenced her posture, her manners, her whole behavioral set. It is not irrelevant to this that she would be going to church on the day, Saturday, that is the festive day for others. Finally, one of the maids next door could not stand the confusion any more and one Saturday knocked on the door to ask our friends whether that maid of theirs was colored or not. For she, like most whites, had been trained to look at the social uniform a person wears and not at the underlying color. And we may suppose that Richard Wright, having a grandmother who was both an Adventist and physically white, had a double reason for confusion. One source of his later creativity would seem to lie in his inability as a boy to put an easy end to his confusion and bewilderment.

Yet we know that other members of his family were not confused; why was he? We have no way of fully understanding this. But it seems to me that Wright's great intelligence, his artistic power and a certain unconscious stubbornness made it difficult for him to acquire cultural understandings which, in the most literal sense, were superficial. Consciously, he experienced these qualities when he was a boy as "stupidity," which is how his behavior was interpreted by others; since he could not see what they saw, he became convicted in his own eyes of being a dope. And of course once such a process of interaction with one's social environment begins, it may be cumulative; since he *is* a dope, others do not give him even such cultural understandings as he might grasp, and what begins as a slight and marginal nonconformity to the group ends up as a more sharply differentiated one.

§ IV

I HAVE CHOSEN Richard Wright as an example because he has so brilliantly described his experiences; but it is no news that these processes are universal and not confined to poor Negroes in the American South. I could as well have chosen Stephen Spender's semi-autobiographical novel, *The Backward Son,* in which the hero is defined, at home and school, as "backward" in comparison with an older brother who is "forward"—a brother to whom everything comes easily. Spender was made to feel stupid, as we now can see, because he was more alive, more sensitive, more inquisitive than his school-fellows. He was marginal to his group in ways nobody—least of all himself—could recognize; there was no definition of schoolboy intellectual at his public school. It was only much later, when he could move around the globe, that he could find people like himself and feel, instead of backward, that he was avant-garde—so much so that, like Wright, he ended up as an ex-Communist and a contributor to *The God that Failed!*

Spender comes of an upper-middle-class British intellectual family; for him, travel came naturally, once he was out of school. But Wright desperately needed the railroad fare, which he finally partly stole, in order to escape from the South. Yet in each case it often seems like an accident whether or not the step is finally taken by which the subconscious observations such a person is making all the while he is berating himself for not understanding anything—whether these observations are recognized and validated by others—consensually validated, as Harry Stack Sullivan liked to say. No matter how deeply buried, an element of irrepressible personal confidence appears to be involved. But, as with some unrecognized geniuses, a too hopeless and hapless marginality gradually shuts out experimental behavior and nonconformity, replacing it with craziness or apathy. Only in the rarest and greatest instances, that is, can one individual's inner, generative power lift him by his own bootstraps, and give him enough energy to combat the overwhelming atmospheric pressure of the total culture. By the same token, however, such power, once it has been confirmed in use—once it has established some contact with the world—becomes strengthened still further. Richard Wright tells the story in *Black Boy* of his mother's sending him as a very small youngster to shop for groceries; on his way a gang of boys beat him up and stole his money. When he came back and told his mother this, she did not comfort or protect him, but locked the door on him and gave him a stick—he was not to come back without the groceries. Even more terrified of his mother than of the boys, when he had to face their attack again, his frenzy lent him strength, and laying about him wildly with his stick he chased them off and brought home the bacon; he was never again molested.

But frenzy, while it can be momentarily salutary, is not insight; it does not help us draw a working map of ourselves or the world, nor does it have cumulative life-giving adequacy. The way out that Wright seems to have found as a non-fighter was through print; newspapers and books gave him access to a wider universe; through his literary imagination he could make contacts that surmounted the gang. At first, *any* newsprint would do: hair-raising fantastic tales, love stories, any amount of "trash" he could get hold of. The unreality of such tales, their lack of direct bearing on his situation, on race relations, on the economy—all this was probably to the good. For Wright was surrounded by people who "knew" what reality was, who had definite views on race relations, and who, like the school principal, did not lack dialectical skill in argument. Even to argue against them on the "realistic" plane would have been a kind of submission to the overriding Puritanism of the whole Negro middle-class world which brought him up and schooled him. By what was defined as "self-indulgence" in such bootless reading, and later in trying to write such far-fetched stories himself, Wright actually came in contact with a self for which the Seventh Day Adventist code made no provision. (We must remember that the middle-class Negro, eager to appear sober in the eyes of the whites, and to distinguish himself from the lower-class Negroes with their permissive, promiscuous ways, is apt to be far more inhibited than the middle-class white of the same epoch, more like a throwback to the middle-class white Puritan of an earlier day.)

When, years later in Chicago, Wright came in contact with another Puritan code, that of Communism, he finally broke from it on what amounts to the same set of issues. For he insisted again on "self-indulgence" in imagination; he refused to allow himself to be swallowed up in "agit-prop" work. He wanted to write fictionalized biographies of the South Side Negro Communists, and he frightened his less wide-ranging cell-mates by probing into details of their lives they believed to be irrelevant to the Cause. And once again Wright was defined as "stupid"; he did not seem to understand the rules of the Party, its manipulative use of writers, its internal intrigues. He tried as hard to conform to the Party code as he had to the race etiquettes of the South; he tried to suppress his curiosity and his individuality.

Eventually, however, he learned from the response of a wider, indeed an international, audience to appreciate his own qualities; no longer only as a reader of print but as a writer he could find support outside the cells in which he had previously been imprisoned. And he could begin to accept as his own insights what he had previously experienced as mere backwardness and confusion. He could win his way to the courage that is surely no less important in human affairs than physical courage: the courage of his free associations with both ideas and people.

§ V

WHEN WRIGHT encountered the Communist Party, its "line" was, and I assume still is, to use such experiences as he had had as a source of organized "minority" animus against American capitalism. To do this, it had to interpret his sufferings as due to his being a Negro first of all, an unhappy proletarian besides. That is, it had retroactively to "re-educate" his memory so that all his confusions and misgivings appeared to fall into a schematized theory of oppression of ethnic minorities, and of the working class. In turn, much as an oil company expects us to buy gas at its stations because it has given us a road map, the Party demands of people that they do its bidding because it has given them a map describing (in color) the places they have been and where they are going. And since it is simpler to navigate with a map, even if it is a distorted one, a great many people have accepted such assistance as part of a tie-in sale of ideological commodities. It is a rare person who, like Richard Wright, rejects the map in order to grope his own way.

The Communist Party, with its now-defunct plans for a Black Republic, is only an extreme instance of an organization whose existence depends on interpreting for people the source and the internal and external meaning of the discomforts they have experienced. The NAACP, the Chicago *Defender,* and other Negro "defense" agencies and media exist by defining for their constituencies the meaning of what happens to them as individuals and to the colored group in the wide white world. If, unlike Richard Wright's white-complexioned grandmother, one is obviously Negro, one can fall back on what Myrdal termed "the advantages of the disadvantages," including an ability to organize one's life around a status protest which serves as an explanatory key. And status protest can become a way of life, furnishing one not only with an alibi for the past but an agenda for the future.[1] . . .

I recall the outburst of a Negro student in a college class last fall at the University of Chicago, who said he was sick and tired of having to hear about every incident in the worldwide struggle of color,

---

1. Everett C. Hughes, "Social Change and Status Protest: An Essay on the Marginal Man," *Phylon* (First Quarter, 1949), 58-65.

no matter how trivial or distant. He could not pick up a Negro paper, he said, without having to discover the story of a Negro who had failed to have his windshield wiped by a station attendant in West Virginia, or a Negro hockey player who had been fouled, or a new pronouncement by Premier Malan. The more vocal students in the class were shocked at this, and asked him if he was against the progress of his own race, which was being won by just such agitation. They acted as if he had betrayed the cause of the oppressed merely for the sake of a little peace and comfort—a cause in which many of them were also engaged. Thus, if I had not intervened, they would have forced him to admit his guilt, as he was ready to do, for objecting to a daily diet of atrocities, and would have deprived themselves of the insight into the individual who becomes marginal to the very marginality which has previously been organized on his behalf. In some ways, I think it is more oppressive to be a minority within a minority than to be a minority within a more loosely organized and defined majority group.

§ VI

ONE WAY of looking at what I have said is to realize that every institution or label brought into being to define human experience is out of date almost as soon as created. Every sect tends to become a church; every noncomformist idea, an orthodoxy. People, therefore, are constantly under pressure to accept social definitions which do not apply to them in their ever-renewed individuality, and the resistance to these definitions is apt to generate uneasiness and guilt. . . .

I believe that social organizations draw much of their energy from unavowed and hidden marginalities. Marginality and nonconformity can, so to speak, be sublimated, much as Freud reasoned that sexual energy could be. And this is an aspect of the broader observation that people tend to systematize and rationalize their feelings in terms of socially-provided vocabularies of emotion. To be sure, such social provision must operate with certain limits given by the human condition. There are physiological as well as cultural reasons for the fact that we can discriminate many more shadings of color than of taste, which makes things difficult for those who write labels on wine bottles as well as those who seek to experience what intimations of dryness or nuances of asperity the label talks about. (In this connection, the Chinese dishes which are called "sweet and sour," such as sweet-and-sour pork, have always appealed to me semantically, for there are sweet-and-sour things which taste at once sweet and sour, as there are sweet-and-sour people and sweet-and-sour swing music.) In the same way, there is apt to be some physiological or temperamental base to the differences among people that a given culture can exploit, a theme Margaret Mead has thoughtfully explored. And all other differentiating factors, either those arising from the "shape" we are in, or from our intellectual and imaginative endowments, or from individualizing experiences such as position in the family or unique encounters, can serve, depending on circumstance, to set us apart from people or to force us together with them for protective coloration, or can leave us on some margin between belonging and not belonging. Insight and a creative rather than sterile nonconformity, I would argue, depend on one's ability to accept one's differences from others and one's similarities to them, without an artificial forcing of identity, without, that is, accepting entirely the definitions as to "who am I" and "who are we" that every family, clan, ethnic group, class and nation seeks to furnish to, and fasten on, its members. . . .

We are afraid of a chaotic situation in which people do not know their own "names," their own brand names, that is. In fact, under the mantle of cultural pluralism we often intensify these tendencies, by telling the Polish girl in Cleveland, for instance, who does not really feel very Polish, that we want to see her country's folk-dances and to put a Christmas tree in the Public Library which she will decorate after the Polish customs she has had to look up in a book. And it is evident that we are able to face these more subtle problems of identity because we have moved away from the earlier quite ferocious practices of "Americanization," when newer arrivals in this country were subjected to a kind of hazing on the part of the older arrivals. It always happens in the dialectic of social advance that the solution or abandonment of older problems has given us the fortune of newer ones. . . .

IV.

CULTURE: POPULAR AND UNPOPULAR

"LISTENING TO POPULAR MUSIC" was written as an interim research memorandum in 1947: it was intended simply as a prologue to more systematic research in musical tastes and their meanings. This, however, was one of the projects interrupted by my taking leave from Chicago to do some research at Yale. Only in this last year have I been able to return to the sociology of music, this time as consultant to a study being undertaken of the patronage of the Philharmonic Orchestra (and the relation of the Philharmonic to the whole musical culture) in Kansas City, Missouri, and I have had once again to confront the challenging and nearly insuperable difficulties of interviewing people about their musical interests and relating what they say to other relevant data about them.

I should report, in fact, that, in a seminar on "popular culture" which Reuel Denney and I gave for the Committee on Communications at Chicago in 1950, musically literate students who sought to establish correlations between preferred musical form and personality type got nowhere; the same fate has met analogous efforts elsewhere. Perhaps music in its setting contains too many subtleties for our still crude methods, for of course we do know that listening to music is the outcome of a great variety of influences, social and idiosyncratic. "Listening to Popular Music" may be read as an essay on these methodological conundrums, and perhaps as a demonstration of the virtues as well as the limitations of the small-scale project—a theme to which I return in the concluding section devoted to research method. For I firmly believe that fifteen interviews—even one—if properly understood can teach us a great deal.

The second essay in this section, "Movies and Audiences," touches lightly on analogous questions and suggests explicitly (what is implicit in the music study) that humanistic criteria of taste and judgment may help focus scientific research aims in the field of mass communications. This of course is highly controversial: many social scientists will insist that all audience behavior must be viewed relativistically, without preferring more independent reactions to stereotyped ones—or passing such judgment only in terms of social "function." But the fact remains that the most stimulating audience researches

—Robert K. Merton's *Mass Persuasion,* for example—have come out of passionate if controlled preferences for critical as against passively manipulated response. Indeed, both articles included here—on music and on movies—as well as "Bookworms and the Social Soil" and "How Different May One Be?," could just as well have been put in the preceding sections on individualism and minorities, concerned as they are with the opportunities of the audience to individuate responses to canned, mass-distributed products.

If social scientists find these articles controversial because they make qualitative judgments of the contents and consequences of the media, and do not stop with describing them, some humanists (in the narrow sense of many who call themselves that) may find just these judgments unpalatable. Many of the humanists feel on the defensive vis-à-vis the social sciences (as symptoms of all that they fear and dislike in the modern world). And they are ready to excommunicate colleagues who refuse to share their contempt for TV, opinion polls, Hollywood movies, swing music, Kinsey, and other forms of what they regard as vulgarized mass taste. While the highbrow gamesmanship of finding savor in lowbrow tastes has become fairly common in recent years, English and art departments in some universities remain refuges for those who judge a culture entirely by its traditionally packaged products, such as poetry and easel painting, and dismiss all newer forms as base and "commercial." In one sense, I respect this attitude because of its refusal to give in to sheer numbers, though often it gives in to the localized pressure of "near numbers." Those who are imprisoned by it miss a lot. They also fail to evaluate a culture properly, because they fasten on one or two conventional indices, and these may not be adequate: thus, novels may decline in quality while films rise; music may wither while architecture improves; manners may dwindle while understanding rises; and so on.

A number of my essays, in making such general appraisals, are somewhat more hopeful than the article on popular music—the same shift in my perspective I have noted earlier in this volume. Yet my sanguinity is very tentative. It is based in part on the personal experience that the culture of an earlier, more aggressively highbrow generation of Americans—my parents' generation—was thin and donnish. The very lack of a strenuous dialectic vis-à-vis lowbrow and middlebrow culture made the possession of correct taste too easy and complacent a matter. Few of the refined Americans of this period, as I meet them in person and print, seem to me as interesting and various as a great many of my own contemporaries and still younger people, even if the earlier group had more assured taste. At the same time, I recognize that there is a lot to be said for the position held by the critic

Clement Greenberg and many others that the social mobility of the middlebrow—the rise of a great culture-hungry but undisciplined group—has damaged and deranged high culture.

This same rise of a new, enormous leisure class in need of tutelage has been one of the factors responsible for the development of new professions engaged in taste leadership and education for leisure. From the sponsors of book clubs and home decoration magazines to travel agents and cruise directors, occupations have altered and originated to cope with unoccupied time. My article on "Recreation and the Recreationist" is at once an analysis of the motives behind professionalization and a warning against the dangers of a narrowing of the means and ends of play through well-meant supervision. In suggesting, for example, that a new supermarket might do as much for a community's leisure as a new park—indeed, that "chores" can often be redefined as play—I was urging my audience of professionals to examine critically conventional judgments as to the worthiness of play.

What is work for the recreationist is presumably play for his clients. In "Football in America: A Study in Culture Diffusion," Reuel Denney and I sought tentatively to indicate some of the ways in which collegiate football had become not only a highly speculative big business for the schools involved but a route of career ascent and career training for one after another of America's ethnic groups, whose mobility is reflected in the increasing degrees of movement within the game itself. Since the game was imported from England, it is possible to trace the detailed steps by which the English rules were modified to reflect different folkways among audiences and players alike; that is why we wanted, for a non-anthropological audience, to emphasize the theme of diffusion of cultural patterns.

Naturally, no simple and heavy-handed conclusions are to be drawn, such as that football is a mere reflection of American assembly lines and industrial teamwork. All we can do is to suggest certain compatibilities between the changing game, the changing factory, and the changing class mores of the country. It is one of a series of studies of sports and audiences which Mr. Denney has stimulated. I am in Mr. Denney's debt in less palpable fashion for many of the ideas in the two articles which deal with changes in leisure attitudes and standards. The first of these was presented to a group of school superintendents at the Harvard Summer School in 1952, under the auspices of the Harvard School of Education; the second was one of a series of appraisals of changing standards in contemporary American life which Professor Basil Rauch arranged at Barnard College.

The two concluding pieces in this section, "Bookworms and the

Social Soil," and "How Different May One Be?," deal with more or
less high culture and defend it from middlebrow enemies. The former
grew out of the Conference on Reading Development called by the
American Book Publishers Council to examine the fate and future of
reading in America. I found myself among some people who seemed
more concerned with adjusting books to people than vice versa; my
own view is that a certain amount of social maladjustment might be
a small price to pay for the glories of literature. When, in "How Different May One Be?," I restated this point with reference to a hypothetical girl whose passion for music separated her somewhat from
her age-mates, I was surprised to get letters from angry mothers
insisting I must be an old-fashioned Simon Legree, prepared to sacrifice a child's happiness, at worst, to parental pride, and, at best, to
the advance of the musical arts. Indeed, it was very hard for some
readers of the article, bemused by mothers who wanted to push their
child prodigies, to realize that more "permissive" and less insistent
mothers might also harm a child's development, by anxious concern
for the child's day-to-day adjustment rather than her long-run happiness. To be sure, I am not prepared to imprison any given child beneath the weight of its talents—to turn it into a cultural asset at its
own developmental expense; nevertheless I am quite prepared to bore
a number of children with difficult or classical subjects for the sake
of the few who will profit from them. Again I am an individualist,
but one who believes that, for most people, competent exercise of
one's talents leads in the long run to a happy life.

11. Listening to Popular Music

§ I

THE STUDY OF POPULAR CULTURE—radio, movies, comics, popular music, and fiction—is a relatively new field in American social science. Much of the pioneering in this field has been done by or on behalf of the communications industry to prove to advertisers that it can influence buying habits, and to pre-test its more expensive productions, such as potential best sellers and movies. At a more theoretical level, a good deal of current interest in popular culture springs from the motives, seldom negligible in scientific investigation, of dismay and dislike. Gifted Europeans, horrified at the alleged vulgarization of taste brought about by industrialization, left-wing critics in the traditions of Marx or Veblen who see popular culture as an anti-revolutionary narcotic, high-brows who fear poaching on their preserves by middle-brow "culture diffusionists"—all these have contributed approaches, and sometimes methods as well, to the present state of research in this field.

In using Harold Lasswell's formula—"who says what to whom with what effect"—the question of effects has proved most intractable to study, being at the same time in my opinion the most important and rewarding area. By its very nature, popular culture impinges on people unceasingly; it is part of their environment, part of the background noise, color, and verbal imagery of their lives from the age at which they can first listen to the radio, watch television, or "read" comics. The researcher has two courses open to him. He can either question listeners and readers to see what uses they make of popular culture materials, or he can study the materials themselves and make guesses about the uses made of them. He is usually pushed by the difficulties of interviewing toward the latter procedure, that is, toward some form of content analysis. This is especially the case where he wants to discover the effects of nonverbal materials such as music and paintings. For he will find that, on the whole, people can talk more readily about their responses to words than about their responses, say to a tune. Yet this very readiness to talk, this availability of a critical vocabulary, may hinder as well as help the researcher; words about words may screen rather than reveal underlying meanings. The current preference for the Rorschach test or the Thematic Apperception test ("inkblot" or pictorial stimuli) as a way of getting at underlying character is evidence that verbal responses to verbal cues are likely to be stereotyped and conventionalized.

I do not mean to deprecate content analysis where this is used to suggest possible audience effects. T. W. Adorno's essays on radio music[1] and recently the Wolfenstein-Leites' book on the movies[2] indicate how suggestive such work can be, where it is informed by a grasp of the social structure into which and out of which the content comes. We must be on guard against a tendency to sniff at library or arm-chair research as against field work; certainly the quickest short cut to understanding what popular culture does for people— and hence to understanding a great deal about American culture as a whole—is to make oneself the relevant audience and to look imaginatively at one's own reactions. But the danger exists then of assuming that the *other* audience, the audience one does not converse with, is more passive, more manipulated, more vulgar in taste, than may be the case. One can easily forget that things that strike the sophisticated person as trash may open new vistas for the unsophisticated; moreover, the very judgment of what is trash may be biased by one's own unsuspected limitations, for instance, by one's class position or academic vested interest.

While field work may not cure this attitude, it may chasten and modify it, provided that we can find the vocabulary to talk to people about experiences which are not particularly self-conscious ones. My judgment is that the same or virtually the same popular culture materials are used by audiences in radically different ways and for radically different purposes; for example, a movie theater may be used to get warm, to sleep, to neck, to learn new styles, to expand one's imaginative understanding of people and places—these merely begin an indefinitely expansible list. What these various ways and purposes are, we can scarcely imagine all by ourselves; we must go out and talk to various sorts of people in various moods to get at them. It may then appear that it is the audience which manipulates the product (and hence the producer), no less than the other way around.

This is a particularly important consideration in the field of popular music, where the music industry, with its song pluggers, its jukebox outlets, its radio grip, seems to be able to mold popular taste and to eliminate free choice by consumers. The industry itself may like to think it can control matters, even at the price of feeling a good deal of guilt over trashy output or dubious monopolistic practices. Nevertheless, there seems to me no way of explaining by reference

1. T. W. Adorno, "On Radio Music," in *Studies in Philosophy and Social Science* (New York: Institute of Social Research, 1941), vol. 9, and "A Social Critique of Radio Music," *Kenyon Review*, vol. 7, p. 208 (1944).
2. Martha Wolfenstein and Nathan Leites, *Movies: A Psychological Study.*

to the industry controllers the great swings of musical taste, say, from jazz to sweet in the last decade; actually the industry ignores these swings in consumer taste only at its peril. Even in the field of popular music, there is always a minority channel over which less popular tastes get a hearing, eventually perhaps to become majority tastes.

These, then, are some of the very general assumptions which guided me in setting down the following hypotheses about a majority and a minority audience for popular music among teen-age groups. These hypotheses were directed to the Committee on Communication of the University of Chicago as a tentative basis for research, and in the period since their drafting several students have been working in this area. They have, as was to be anticipated, come up against the great methodological obstacles already indicated: how to isolate music from the influences of other media; how to understand the relations between musical conventions and the conventions of the peer-groups (the groups of age-mates); how, in the case of popular tunes, to separate the mélange of words and music, performer and piece, song and setting.

It has proved easy enough, through *Billboard*, *Variety*, and other trade sources, to establish popularity ratings for hits; through a study of juke-box preferences in particular neighborhoods to get an indication of class and ethnic, sex and age differences; through an analysis of chord progressions or arrangements to get clues to what musical patterns and conventions might be common to a group of hit tunes. But to move from there to the more basic problems of the use of music for purposes of social adjustment and social protest, or the role of music in socializing the young, teasing the adolescent, and quieting the old—such things as these loom on the far horizon as unsolved problems.

§ II

BEARING THE DIFFICULTY of these problems in mind, I venture to suggest, nevertheless, that one role of popular music in socializing the young may be to create, in combination with other mass media, a picture of childhood and adolescence in America as a happy-go-lucky time of haphazard clothes and haphazard behavior, jitterbug parlance, coke-bar sprees, and "blues" that are not really blue. Thus the very problems of being young are evaded—the mass media also furnish comparable stereotypes for other deprived groups, such as Negroes, women, GIs, and "the lower classes." I do not mean to suggest that in thus presenting the young with a picture of Youth

drawn by adults there is conspiratorial intent—rather there is a complex interplay of forces between the adults who are the producers
and the young who are the consumers.

Most teen-agers, though much more "knowing" than the picture
gives them credit for being, do not think about this situation at all.
Among those who do, some are aware that their group standards are
set by outside forces. But their loss of innocence has made them
cynical, not rebellious; and they are seldom even interested in the
techniques of their exploitation or its extent.

A small minority is, however, not only aware in some fashion of
the adult, manipulative pressure but is also resentful of it, in many
cases perhaps because its members are unable to fit themselves by any
stretch of the imagination into the required images. Such a "youth
movement" differs from the youth movements of other countries
in having no awareness of itself, as such, no direct political consciousness, and, on the whole, no specialized media of communication.[3] If we study, for instance, the hot rodders, we see a group of
young (and pseudo-young) people who, in refusing to accept the
Detroit image of the automobile consumer, create a new self-image
though one in turn liable to manipulation. Likewise, the lovers of
hot jazz, while not explicitly exploring the possibilities of how youth
might take a hand in formulating its own self-images, do in fact
resist certain conventional stereotypes. But they do so by making
a differential selection from what the adult media already provide.

Thus, we may distinguish two polar attitudes toward popular
music, a *majority* one which accepts the adult picture of youth somewhat uncritically, and a *minority* one in which certain socially rebellious themes are encapsulated. For the purposes of this analysis, I
shall disregard the many shadings in between, and also neglect the
audiences of hillbilly and "classical" music.[4]

---

3. This is of course not intended to deny that there are certain very small
groups in the United States who follow the patterns of European youth movements. Many teen-age followers of Henry Wallace and young left-wing Zionists
preparing for emigration to Palestine seem to have all the emotional paraphernalia
of European movements, whether nominally "right" or "left."

4. Actually, both these areas are very important ones. It would be interesting
to study urban fanciers of hillbilly music as possible exemplars of the many city
folk who, though they depend on the city for income, friends, and entertainment,
despise or pretend to despise it and long nostalgically for the very rural life
from which they or their parents may have fled; perhaps for such people to
define themselves as country folk in their musical and other leisure tastes is the
only way they can accept the city. As for "classical" music, it is worth observing
that people who tell the interviewer that they like, or "don't mind," classical (or
"symphonic") music almost invariably in my own experience mean Tchaikovsky,
sometimes Chopin, and occasionally Brahms. People of serious musical taste
almost never describe their interests by means of a rubric, but rather by reference

MOST OF THE TEEN-AGERS in the majority category have an undiscriminating taste in popular music; they seldom express articulate preferences. They form the audience for the larger radio stations, the "name" bands, the star singers, the Hit Parade, and so forth. The functions of music for this group are *social*—the music gives them something to talk or kid about with friends; an opportunity for competitiveness in judging which tunes will become hits, coupled with a lack of concern about how hits are actually made; an opportunity for identification with star singers or band leaders as "personalities," with little interest in or understanding of the technologies of performance or of the radio medium itself. Thus I assume that the psychological functions of this medium for most of its audience include those that Herta Herzog has found in the radio daytime serial or the quiz program and that Leo Lowenthal has found in popular biographies.[5]

It is not easy at this stage to state the precise way in which these indiscriminate listening habits serve to help the individual conform to the culturally provided image of himself. To discover this is one of the tasks of research. And to this end some further lines of inquiry suggest themselves.

First, it has often been remarked that modern urban industrial society atomizes experiences, isolating each experience from other experiences. Does this same pattern operate, as T. W. Adorno suggests, in the auditory experience of popular music? Such music is presented disconnectedly, especially over the radio—where it is framed by verbal ballyhoo and atomized into individual "hits"—like the disparate items on a quiz program. Can it be established that this mode of presentation reinforces the disconnectedness often associated with modern urban life?

Second, by giving millions of young people the opportunity to share in admiration for hits, hit performers, and the hit-making process, are identifications subtly built up which serve to lessen the effects

---

to specific composers or, perhaps, distinctive musical epochs. It is striking that some of the new, big, hundred-selection jukeboxes will have a "classical" section, which is apt to include some Tchaikovsky (in an André Kostelanetz version) along with music from *Oklahoma!* or other similar shows (in an André Kostelanetz version). Indeed, "classical," for this sizable audience, might be defined as whatever music Kostelanetz will arrange and play.

5. Herta Herzog, "Professor Quiz—A Gratification Study," *Radio and the Printed Page*, Paul F. Lazarsfeld, ed., and "On Borrowed Experience," *Studies in Philosophy and Social Science*, vol. 9 (1941). Leo Lowenthal, "Biographies in Popular Magazines," *Radio Research 1942-43*, Paul F. Lazarsfeld and Frank Stanton, eds.

of social conflicts and to sustain an ideology of social equality?[6]

Third, does the music tell these people, almost without their awareness, how to feel about their problems in much the same way that the daytime serials package their social lessons?

Fourth, since this music is often dance music, does it help to create and confirm postural and behavioral attitudes toward the other sex? Does the facial expression assume the "look" the music is interpreted as dictating? Is the music felt as inculcating the socially right combination of "smoothness" with stylized "spontaneity," of pseudosexuality with reserve? Do these psychic and gestural manifestations then carry over from the dancing situation to other spheres of life? We should not be surprised to find that such molding of the body-image and body responses affects girls more powerfully than boys; as the subordinate group, with fewer other outlets, girls can less afford even a conventionalized resistance.

It is not unlikely that we will discover that the majority role represents in many of its aspects a pattern of "restriction by partial incorporation."[7] That is, the majority is continuously engaged in the process of adapting elements of the minority's musical outlook, while overtly ignoring or denigrating minority patterns. Jazz itself,[8] many of the dance steps, and lyrical images are almost entirely minority products to begin with. But they undergo significant changes in being incorporated into the majority style, just as radical intellectual and ideological developments are modified by academic acceptance.

§ IV

THE MINORITY GROUP is small. It comprises the more active listeners, who are less interested in melody or tune than in arrangement or technical virtuosity. It has developed elaborate, even overelaborate, standards of music listening; hence its music listening is combined with much animated discussion of technical points and perhaps occasional reference to trade journals such as *Metronome* and *Downbeat*. The group tends to dislike name bands, most vocalists (except Negro blues singers), and radio commercials.

The rebelliousness of this minority group might be indicated in some of the following attitudes toward popular music: an insistence on rigorous standards of judgment and taste in a relativist culture; a preference for the uncommercialized, unadvertised small bands rather

---

6. Cf. my article "Equality and Social Structure," *Journal of Political and Legal Sociology*, vol. i, p. 72 (1942).

7. See Harold D. Lasswell, *World Politics and Personal Insecurity*.

8. Cf. Kurt List, "Jerome Kern and American Operetta," *Commentary*, vol. 3, p. 433 (1947).

than name bands; the development of a private language and then a
flight from it when the private language (the same is true of other
aspects of private style) is taken over by the majority group; a profound resentment of the commercialization of radio and musicians.
Dissident attitudes toward competition and cooperation in our culture might be represented in feelings about improvisation and small
"combos"; an appreciation for idiosyncrasy of performance goes together with a dislike of "star" performers and an insistence that the
improvisation be a group-generated phenomenon.[9]

There are still other ways in which the minority may use popular
music to polarize itself from the majority group, and thereby from
American popular culture generally: a sympathetic attitude or even
preference for Negro musicians; an equalitarian attitude toward the
roles, in love and work, of the two sexes; a more international outlook, with or without awareness, for example, of French interest in
American jazz; an identification with disadvantaged groups, not only
Negroes, from which jazz springs, with or without a romantic cult
of proletarianism; a dislike of romantic pseudosexuality in music,
even without any articulate awareness of being exploited; similarly
a reaction against the stylized body image and limitations of physical
self-expression which "sweet" music and its lyrics are felt as con-
veying; a feeling that music is too important to serve as a backdrop
for dancing, small talk, studying, and the like; a diffuse resentment
of the image of the teen-ager provided by the mass media.

To carry matters beyond this descriptive suggestion of majority
and minority patterns requires an analysis of the social structure in
which the teen-ager finds himself. When he listens to music, even if
no one else is around, he listens in a context of imaginary "others"—
his listening is indeed often an effort to establish connection with
them. In general what he perceives in the mass media is framed by
his perception of the peer-groups to which he belongs. These groups
not only rate the tunes but select for their members in more subtle
ways what is to be "heard" in each tune. It is the pressure of conformity with the group that invites and compels the individual to
have recourse to the media both in order to learn from them what
the group expects and to identify with the group by sharing a common focus for attention and talk.

Moreover, many factors, including the youth orientation of the
culture generally, lower the age at which children venture into the

---

9. This combination of respect for group cooperation along with individual
spontaneity can be found here in both unconscious preference and explicit formulas. Sometimes hot jazz constitutes a satire on sweet or corny music, hence
of the attitudes that go with them.

"personality markets" to be judged by their success in terms of popularity. As high schools adopt the social customs and listening habits previously postponed until college, so the grammar school tends to ape the high school in dating patterns, proms, and so on. At the same time, the personalities of the popular music industry have every reason to cultivate the child market and are quite willing to "rob the cradle." This convergence of forces means that children are compelled to learn how to respond to music, in a fashion their peer-group will find acceptable, at increasingly earlier ages. Under these pressures, music can hardly help becoming associated with both the excitements and the anxieties of interpersonal relationships.

§ V

SO FAR, I HAVE OBTAINED some fifteen long interviews with young people about popular music. Since these interviews were in the nature of a limited pre-test, simply part of the long process of developing a questionnaire which could then be used on a selected sample, I made no effort to obtain a sample but engaged in random house and street interviewing in white (and Nisei) South Side Chicago, seeking to vary only sex, age, and economic standing in a very rough way. The respondents ranged from fourteen to twenty-two and from probably upper-lower to middle-middle class. In addition, I sought data on the higher social strata from the always available "sample" of traditional social psychology—namely, my students—and data on the Negro community from a few discussions with Negro students and musicians.

One advantage in interviewing teen-agers about their music listening habits is that—as compared, for instance, with interviewing on politics—one meets little resistance (save for an occasional overprotective mother), since all do listen and like to talk about their tastes; if the interviewer had cards with hits listed on them, they would doubtless enjoy ranking the cards and then explaining their rankings. However, the group as a whole—as compared with housewives—tended to be inarticulate, even if not shy; a good deal of direction was needed in some portions of the interview, and this ran the obvious risk of tilting the responses.[10] After introductory questions concerning the respondent's age, schooling, family data (for example, siblings, father's occupation, residential mobility, and, where

---

10. I have also found that dual interviewing, in which my colleague Reuel Denney participated, can help to establish easier rapport and deeper probing and can allow much closer analysis of the interviewing process itself. Here one of the pair of interviewers can take notes—or fend off the baby—while the other chats with the respondent; of course, the two interviewers have to be sensitive to each other's cues if they are not to get in the way.

possible, socio-economic status and mobility strivings), I turned to general questions about radio listening habits: length of time, place (that is, where, and with whom, listening occurs), favorite types of programs, and the like. Then came the questions about music. (Depending on the rapport, the order was sometimes reversed.) The schedule was long and open-ended, pointing toward the problems indicated in the analysis above.[11]

One question which sometimes led to illuminating answers was this: "How do you and they (your friends) decide what is a good or bad piece?" One seventeen-year-old girl, the daughter of a railroad telegrapher, said, "If it's popular we go for it; if it's played on the Hit Parade." Her answer to whether her social life would be affected if she hated music was, "That's all there is to do for kids our age." Yet the time she craved music most was when she was alone; the somewhat sultry love ballads that were her favorites were perhaps vicarious company. Like virtually all the other respondents, she vigorously denied attending broadcasts or having any desire to meet her favorite performers. "I don't swoon over anybody," she said.

I also discovered that respondents generally felt much safer in stating their musical dislikes than their musical likes; the former were volunteered readily, while the latter came out only if approval for the preference seemed in the offing. That is, many would quickly reject a whole area: "I hate hillbilly," or "I can't stand fast music," or "Negroes are too jumpy." More rarely something specific was rejected: "I dislike Tommy Dorsey; he has no rhythm, just blasting of horns." Or, " 'Bubble Gum' is the craziest song." Many said they disliked commercials and several that they would not buy anything that was advertised. As in high-brow circles, so in middle-brow and

11. A few sample questions: favorite tunes (and how far back these, and the lyrics, can be recalled); favorite bands; perhaps a discussion about the shift from swing to sweet and the reasons for it; what the hit-making process is and what effect a disclosure of such information has on the respondent; questions about the function of popular music in the peer-group, e.g., for dancing, kidding around, appearing sophisticated, and what would be the effect on his popularity —or on his more general feelings of "belonging" to the community—if the respondent could no longer listen (where I went into this, and the respondent was willing to make the experiment of thought, he said, in effect, "I would be isolated," or "I would be lost," or sometimes, "It would make no difference"); attitudes toward Negro musicians; favorite movie stars and fan attitudes generally; feelings about people with different musical tastes (often revealing within a family constellation, either vis-à-vis adults or vis-à-vis siblings); attendance at radio broadcasts; possible relations between mood and amount and type of music listening. Of course it often turned out that a whole congeries of questions was irrelevant for the participating respondent, or he was incapable of answering them; further interviewing should sharpen the questions that can be asked and shed further light on those that provoke anxiety, sudden awareness, sudden rapport, and so forth.

low-brow ones, enthusiasm would seem to be a greater social danger than negativism: the fear is to be caught liking what the others have decided not to like.

Among these young people, music seemed to be one of the principal areas for peer-group training in the appropriate expression of consumer preferences; by learning to talk about music, one also learned to talk about other things. Yet the vocabulary used to discuss music, as it turned up in the interviews, was in the majority of cases not a very differentiated one, but rather the "swell," "lousy," "I go for that," and so on which signify preferences for other cultural commodities, tangible and intangible. Indeed, one differentiation, as already indicated, between my hypothetical majority and minority wings lies in the latter's development of strict and often highly articulate standards for judging jazz.

This leads us to a final paradox. The hot jazz lovers are protesters. They are individualists who reject contemporary majority conformities. In the very process, however, do they not in many, perhaps most, cases simply move into another peer-group which holds them fast, and adopt a new conformity under the banner of nonconformity? While my handful of interviews in white South Side Chicago brought to light only a single hot-jazz fan, there have been a number of such fans among the students at the University of Chicago. Sometimes these are young men—strikingly enough there are very few hot-jazz girls, save in an occasional "symbiotic" relation to a hot-jazz boy—who grew up as somewhat rebellious individuals in a small high school group where they stood almost alone in their musical orientation. Then, when they came to the university, they found many other such people and for the first time experienced the security and also the threat of peers who shared their outlook.

What happens then, when this discovery is made, is something we are far from understanding; obviously, the problem touches on the whole congeries of issues connected with social and intellectual mobility, the American *rites de passage,* the role of big cities and intellectual centers. We may perhaps assume that the hot-jazz fan can employ his *musical* deviations (from the standpoint of the great majority) to conceal from himself other surrenders he makes to his peer-group. Or, he may find within the field of jazz further possibilities of protest by taking a still more esoteric stance, for example in favor of "pure" Dixieland or of some similar now-frozen cult. But what if his peer-group, conceivably as the result of his own initiative, moves with him there also? Does popular music itself offer him enough variety to permit him to use it alternatingly to establish prestigeful social distance from others and needed ties to them? And how does it compare in this respect with other cultural products, such as books, movies, art, and modern furniture?

Difficult as these questions are, it seems to be easier to understand the uses of music in this sociological sense than it is to understand the variations in what people of different psychological types actually hear when they listen to music. Is it foreground noise for them or background noise? What is it, precisely, that they "perceive?" Ernest Schachtel has made a brilliant beginning on the question of what meaning physical forms have for people, through seeing what they make of Rorschach inkblots. Experts in auditory perception have not succeeded, so far as I know, in finding an auditory stimulus as useful as the Rorschach test in circumventing cultural stereotypes. Our problem is to reach the people for whom music or plastic art or the movies are appealing in part just because they are more comfortable with sounds and images than with print and words. We are brought back to our problem of how to communicate with them.

§ VI

WHILE THE INTERVIEW GUIDE I developed on the basis of these research suggestions covered movies, magazines, and favorite radio programs as well as music, it did not explore the whole range of popular culture activities (and inactivities such as just sitting), or pay sufficient attention—though it did pay some attention—to hobbies, pets, dating, and other leisure pursuits. I am convinced that we cannot understand the role of any communication medium in isolation from the other media and from other leisure activities, any more than we can understand individual manipulation of the materials in the media without understanding the group which the individual belongs to, wants to belong to, or wants to be set apart from.

This truism led me to the further conclusion that one cannot hope to understand the influence of any one medium, say music, without an understanding of the total character structure of a person. In turn, an understanding of his musical tastes, and his use of them for purposes of social conformity, advance, or rebellion, provides revealing clues to his character, to be confirmed and modified by a knowledge of his behavior and outlook in many other spheres of life. . . . Plainly, we cannot simply ask "who listens to what?" before we find out who "who" is and what "what" is by means of a psychological and content analysis which will give us a better appreciation of the manifold uses, the plasticity of music for its variegated audiences.

12.   Movies and Audiences*

IT IS SAID by film critics (Gilbert Seldes, for example) that older people stay away from movies because the latter are not sufficiently adult and mature. (We know that the "average" moviegoer is 19, and that comparatively few people over 30 are to be found in the film audience.) The facts, however, may be just the reverse: films are too mature, move too fast, for older people to catch on to and catch up with. The same may be true of other newly-developed media whose conventions and emotional vocabularies the American young have learned as a mother tongue. Possibly realization that the old have to learn the new language of films (or TV) would be a first step toward appreciating some of the ambiguities of communication in which the movies and other media are involved—ambiguities related to the tensions between the generations, between the social classes, and between character types.

§ I

AN EFFORT TO UNRAVEL some of the ambiguities hidden in the term "escape," often used in connection with films and other media, may be a good place to begin. It seems to us that association of movies with the concept of escape may be a way of playing down the revolutionary or insubordinate rôle of the media, for one's children, or the lower strata, or even the childlike or less responsible parts of oneself. Children and adults often toss off a movie as "just a show," as if it made no more impression on them than the popcorn did which they ate there. But parents are right to suspect, in moments when they do suspect, that there is more to movies than that, though the nature of that "more" seems to have been changing over the years.

In the studies of the movies made under the Payne Fund twenty years ago, much evidence was gathered concerning use of the movies by young people who wanted to learn how to look, dress, and make love. What has changed since then, perhaps, is the kind of enlightenment that is sought. The young people whose reactions were studied by the Payne Fund investigators were often of lower-class origin; in the films they were suddenly brought face to face with sex and splendor, with settings and etiquettes remote from their own experience and observation. Today, however, American audiences are, with

---

* With Evelyn T. Riesman.

the rising standard of living, less remote from splendor, and with the rising standard of education, less remote from etiquette and social know-how generally.

While the movies are still a place where social class-learning goes on, the mixture of messages has become a more complex one; many other, less palpable skills are taught in addition to the linguistic lessons which enabled Eliza Doolittle to be received among those whose passport was their control of R.P.—"received pronunciation." Though the evidence is tantalizingly little, we have the impression that young people of, let us say, sixth grade level and up resort to the movies today, not so much to have a look at an exotic and make-believe world (though of course, as in the films of DeMille, these older patterns survive), but increasingly in order to understand complex networks of interpersonal relations. . . . Children who meet each other in the shifting peer-groups of city high schools are driven, somewhat more even than children of an earlier time, to depend on a precarious popularity as their main security. Athletic prowess may be declining as an unequivocal assurance of status, and certainly no other prowess can substitute for interpersonal competence as a guarantor of social success.

There have been analogous developments in the occupational world, and middle-class adults, with the loss of older certainties, religious and secular, look to their contemporaries for cues as to what in life is worthwhile. The flood of "peace of mind" books is one illustration. To take another example, audiences at race-relations "problem" films may take the movie, not in terms of getting worked up themselves about racial injustice, but as a cue concerning proper race-relations attitudes in a group in which they may want to move. Or they may take it as a cue to "interesting" experiences they might want to have with Negroes or Jews. An advertisement for *No Way Out* in the New York papers (August 15, 1950) declared it to be "an ADULT picture . . . it challenges your own ability to experience the emotions of others."

§ II

TO PUT THIS another way, the "problem" film may be a far wider category in fact than it is in popular belief. Not only do the movies portray scenes that duplicate or foreshadow the audience's own leisure-time problems in dealing with people, but the movie-going itself increasingly becomes an experience-with-people, one which makes demands on the audience for having the proper reactions. This focus may be beyond the grasp and even the interest of those who grew up in a more "inner-directed" era. Although on one level—and, to be sure, for many people entirely—the movie fills in between people who go in company, so that they avoid any demand for conversational or sexual gambits, on another level the performance is not simply a way of killing time: it makes the demand that it be appraised. A doctoral thesis by Eliot Freidson on children's attitudes towards the media shows how early they place themselves on a critical "taste-gradient," with a peer-oriented vocabulary for describing the comics, TV shows, and movies; these children are often very critical critics indeed, in terms of documentary detail if not of ultimate values. In their feeling, they are seldom alone at the movies; rather, the films are a place to show sophistication. At another age and class level, movie audiences coming out of a "little" or "art" theatre are even more concerned with their reactions and criticisms, and how these affect the company they are with. On a more abstract level of research, the degree to which contemporary movie *content* may be seen as involving common interpersonal angles and triangles can be seen in the psychoanalytic interpretation of plot-themes in the Wolfenstein-Leites book *Movies: A Psychological Study.*

§ III

IT IS IN this context of shifting meanings—based both on shifts in movie form and content, and concomitant shifts in audience situation and mood—that cultivated upper-middle-class parents and teachers today carry on their battle against their children's and charges' addiction to the media. It sometimes seems that they object to all "passive" forms of recreation, and are angry that their children do not play out in the open air, or go folk-dancing, or learn handicrafts. That this cannot be the whole story becomes evident when these same adults accuse the media of destroying children's reading habits, at least for "good" books. The fact is, that parents feel about these newer media much of the way paternalistic employers have felt about union organizers—strangers who are coming in with strange gods to break up the one big happy family. For these parents can share the culture of books with their children, but often cannot share the culture of comics, movies, or TV; the personalities of the latter appeal to children over the heads of parents, much as the Pied Piper of Hamelin did.

Occasionally, the parents band together in PTA groups or otherwise to bring pressure on movie exhibitors and others. More often, they succeed in convincing their own children that their (the parents') tastes and values are superior. But the results of such a victory are not always happy. When Katherine Wolf and Marjorie Fiske of Columbia's Bureau of Applied Social Research made their pioneering study of child comic-book readers, they discovered that those children who did not read comics (or who strongly felt, though they did read, that they shouldn't) were often oppressively and neurotically under parental domination, pathetic imitators of adult attitudes. Unable to invent counter-stimulations for their children, these parents had had to resort to manipulative intimidation, as those did who convinced their children (shades of the crusade against masturbation!) that comic reading was bad for the eyes.

To be sure, social class is one of the main factors determining parental stances towards the media as Margarete Midas shows in her article, "Without TV," in a previous issue of *American Quarterly*. There, interviews done immediately in the wake of a controversial advertisement for television sets, in which Angelo Patri testified that children without TV were likely to be left out of the popularity game, showed that only in the better educated strata was there any parental concern about children's media habits; in the working classes, of whatever income level, TV was taken for granted as part of the furniture, as pleasant and as apt to be shared as a sofa.

It is perfectly possible that working-class insouciance toward children is superior to middle-class anxiety. But to draw this conclusion would be to accept too readily the prevalent versions of urban pastoral. The working class, both as price and asset of its position, avoids by greater or lesser degrees of passivity some of those ambiguities in the dialectic between children, peers, parents, and media that the middle-class person cannot avoid who aims, in Ortega y Gasset's phrase, to "live at the height of the times." Middle-class parents, however, have been too ready to conclude that the media are in the trough rather than the height of the times (a judgment Ortega himself would share). They have therefore taken a defeatist or a censor's attitude toward the products of Hollywood and Madison Avenue.

§ IV

CENSORSHIP ALMOST ALWAYS miscarries when it is merely negative—in the media it has ironically (as G. Legman has so carefully documented in *Love and Death*) helped substitute sadism for sex. Censorship either of the act of looking at movies, TV, etc., or of the quality of the media looked at can best be avoided by providing something even better. But this is difficult to accomplish at a time when parents feel they have lost influence over their children. Indeed, the media are blamed for all our ills because by chance they have developed at the historical moment when the philosophy about bringing up children has been to leave them to their own devices. "Their own devices" have been the media, and parents have begun to beat a retreat from laissez-faire, without as yet arriving at a well-administered domestic economy. If they had more conviction about making their children practice music, for example—less misgivings both about music and their own authority rôle—they might have less objection to other things that their children did in their "free" time. But nobody is going to find for parents the films and other media performances which are as sure cross-generational bets as *Huckleberry Finn* or *Treasure Island;* in order to guide children, parents must first make an effort to understand them and the media —as already indicated, the one presents no fewer problems of acculturation than the other.

Let us take as illustration the movies of W. C. Fields. We don't suppose that Sam Goldwyn would contend that they are problem films. Yet in a society where we are frequently urged to be tolerant of others and to understand them, and where the others are presented as amiable, if manipulative, the huge suspiciousness of Fields may be liberating. It may allow children to come to terms with their own paranoiac though unacknowledged fears, and parents to recollect their own, and thus move closer to their own childhood. We may also learn from Fields to acknowledge our inhumanities—and thus paradoxically to become more human. Yet our critical conventions may lead us to deny these virtues in Fields and to see him (unaware that clowns are never simple) simply as a clown.

§ V

SUCH CONSIDERATIONS lead us to raise questions about the various levels of movie criticism both by the audiences and by the reviewers. The children studied by Eliot Freidson knew that *Born Yesterday* had won an Academy Award—indeed, for many who were Catholics, this seemed to legitimate the film at least as sound entertainment despite the ban on it pronounced by the local priest. But in general the children's judgments were cramped by a narrow "realism"—"why is it that cowboy heroes never get killed?" or "how could he fire seven shots out of a Colt six-shooter?"—although they did move, as they grew older, away from the excitement of "exciting" films (cowboy, gangster, etc.) to the subtler pleasures of supposedly adult films (*Bird of Paradise*). Yet perhaps this gradient itself is a sign of "realism": they know what is becoming to their age-grade. They were, perhaps, preparing to make the same sort of judgment later on that many of our friends made about *King Solomon's Mines*, whose complaint that "Hollywood *would* have to put in the love interest" and "keep Deborah Kerr looking too well-groomed for a safari" nearly spoiled their pleasure in an excellent movie. For they, too, in their purism, were misled by a very rigid idea of "realism."

From the side of the reviewers and critics, we all know that it has become standard operating practice to urge Hollywood to cope with real-life "problems." These people, however, are frequently all too sure what the "problems" of American life are, in all our great variety of subcultures; in this sense, even the problems are comforting in their timelessness and stereotypy. It takes imagination to look for problems that are not recognized as such, and films can remain a resource for such imagination only if children and adults alike are taught—or not untaught—to reject the gloss finish of "realism" and to appreciate what the literal-minded might reject as fantastic. Possibly the vogue of science-fiction testifies to an effort to blend both tendencies; but there is all too little fiction in most of it, indeed only banal extrapolative predictions of things to come.

On a more general level, it seems to us that many of the older generation who find films vulgar and shallow simply miss what is there. If we look at movies even ten years old, we see how quickly naunces of expression and phrasing replace the (as it now seems) strident and stilted acting of the earlier sound films. Thus, the "good-bad girl" heroine, as Wolfenstein and Leites describe her, is a tissue of ambiguities compared with the clear outlines of vamp or good girl in less sophisticated films of the 20s and 30s. While the young are often also unable to appreciate these ambiguities—and certainly to verbalize them—they can take such movies in their stride without any feeling of alienation from contemporary usage and convention.

We have almost no movie criticism concerned with such questions. After seeing and greatly enjoying the film of *The Great Gatsby*, we examined some of the critical reactions to it. The fan magazines carried such comments as "a terrible vehicle for Alan Ladd"—made by those who wanted Ladd to stay typed as a private eye or something like that. In the daily press, the comments on the film were as conventional as these "program notes" usually are. In the occasional mentions of the film in the critical reviews, it was also panned as a poor vehicle for Ladd—this time in terms of sacrilege to Fitzgerald's memory. The actual directorial achievement with Ladd, the gifted casting of Betty Field and Shelley Winters, and the many subtle qualities in the film—these, as it seemed to us, were not recognized by any of the critical notices at any "brow level." And if we are even half-way right, the makers of the film must have felt that their intentions failed to communicate to any significant sector of their audience—certainly not to the motion picture exhibitors who wrote in to their trade journals about the "poor biz done by this stinkeroo."

It goes without saying that anyone who sought to discuss "Gatsby" in terms of stage and literary traditions—or, for that matter, to adapt the book to the film medium in overdeference to those traditions—would overlook many of the very themes which might illuminate the understanding of films and so create modes of criticism in which older and younger generations might eventually converse. (To be sure, in any such cross-generational effort there are timing problems involved: the young have time to see films they don't have time to understand, while adults have time to understand films they don't have time to see!) In all likelihood, any improvement of the grown-up audience of films would encourage those in Hollywood who must now feel that only "message" films get a message across. The failure of quality in the movies that is now so endemic might then become less frequent.

To be sure, the reactions to *Gatsby* may be a poor example; and in any case there are some fine media critics—James Agee, the late Otis Ferguson, Mark Benney, John Crosby come to mind—who are developing an independent tradition of media criticism.

In saying this, however, we realize that any substantial increase in critical awareness for films and other popular culture products may tend to reduce still further their limited function as avenues of escape. While there is much to be said for teaching young and old an understanding of film art, we are all too aware of the ambiguities of the educative process, the dangers of overseriousness and over-preciousness and overcompetitiveness. Any declaration that American films can be taken seriously means guilt for many that they had missed this, and strenuous efforts to climb this newly revealed gradient of taste. On the other hand, such a declaration may liberate some from a prejudice which virtually forbade them to enjoy American films—and made others feel secretly guilty for falling for "corn." Parents and children who seek to come together in terms of mutual appreciation of the newer media will doubtless often find themselves facing similar dilemmas.

§ VI

WE HAVE DONE little more than open up discussion of some of the complex relationships which exist between movies (and other media), parents, children, and critics. Actually, students know almost nothing about these various audiences. This is so in part because movie audience-research (having the "Hooper" of the box-office) has lagged behind radio audience-research (where it was needful to show advertisers that radio, and now TV, do have effects). It is also because we have looked too much for the overt "messages" the movies bear and too little for the ways in which different audiences shape their experiences of the movies in terms of their character structures and daily-life situations. Moreover, the influence of films may lie in seeming irrelevances—in the handling of shape and color, for instance—and not in what they "say." But this remains in the realm of the speculative. The painstaking studies of film-effects by the Research Branch of the Army (see Carl Hovland *et al., Experiments in Mass Communications,* 1949) indicate how terribly difficult it is to come up with valid quantifiable results even where, as under Army conditions, we can shift audiences and create control groups with some freedom and resourcefulness of method.

Yet we suspect that the difficulties in qualitative analysis of the effects of films are not unconnected with the present low state of criticism of the movies as an art form. While the translation of esthetic experience into verbal form presents in any case an almost insurmountable problem—how much music criticism is there, for example, which is more than gossip or pedantry?—the movies have hit us so suddenly that we have not had time to begin a tradition of appreciation on which a tradition of research might build. Here, then, is one of the places where humanists and social scientists, equally at a disadvantage, might come together to see what each set of skills might contribute to heighten the awareness of Americans of all ages for the imaginative qualities of their best films. As it took the Romantics to "invent" the beauty of mountains, so it may take an analogous effort to "invent" the beauty of "the Hollywood hallucination."

13. Some Observations on Changes in Leisure Attitudes

> . . . our sole delight was play; and for this we were punished by
> those who yet themselves were doing the like. But elder folks' idle-
> ness is called "business"; that of boys, being really the same, is
> punished by those elders; and none commiserates either boys or
> men. For will any of sound discretion approve of my being beaten
> as a boy, because, by playing at ball, I made less progress in studies
> which I was to learn, only that, as a man, I might play more unbe-
> seemingly? and what else did he who beat me? who, if worsted
> in some trifling discussion with his fellow-tutor, was more embit-
> tered and jealous than I when beaten at ball by a playfellow?
> —*The Confessions of St. Augustine*

TEN YEARS AGO, I sat as a member of an international committee engaged in drawing up a Bill of Rights to be presented to some presumptive postwar agency. Among the rights proposed was one stating that all men and women had a right to "reasonable leisure," and that it was the duty of governments to make this right effective. In the ensuing debate, this was dubbed (by a Harvard professor) "Riesman's freedom from work" amendment, and, though the amendment carried, many of the hard-working delegates regarded it as a concession to the modern cult of effortlessness. Others thought the issue irrelevant, on the ground that, until the right to work was secure, the right to leisure could wait. This was my first introduction to the discovery that many people are uncomfortable when discussing leisure: as with sex, they want to make a joke of it. And there is no doubt that most of us feel vulnerable in a milieu that increasingly asks us whether we are good players as well as good workers—a problem St. Augustine's serious-minded, self-deceiving elders do not appear to have faced. For us, at any rate, there is nothing easy about effortlessness. I want here to trace some of the sources of vulnerability.

§ I

IN HIS NOVEL, *The Bostonians*, written about seventy-five years ago, Henry James describes a week that his hero, Basil Ransom, passed at Provincetown on the Cape. He smoked cigars; he wandered footloose to the wharves; perhaps he read an occasional book; it does not appear that he swam. He was, *pro tem*, a "gentleman of leisure." It may be that a few fossils of the species are preserved in the Athenaeum, but I rather doubt if they can be found in Provincetown. At least my impression is that people who go to such places for the summer appear to lead strenuously artsy and craftsy lives: even if they lie on the beach, they are getting a competitively handsome tan, but most of the time they appear to be playing energetic tennis, taking exhausting walks, entertaining children and guests by that mixture of grit, insects, and tomatoes known as a picnic; and in the evening attending lectures, the experimental theatre, and colloquia in private houses. While they may be less systematically engaged than many students in laying by credits, they are gainfully improving themselves in body and mind; and, perhaps unlike many students, they are subject to the additional strain of having to feel and to claim that they are having a good time, being victims of that new form of Puritanism which Martha Wolfenstein and Nathan Leites in their book *Movies* have termed "fun-morality."

All this in a country in which the average industrial work-week has declined from 64 hours in Henry James' day to around 40 in ours, not including the mid-morning coffee break and the other sociabilities which have crept into the hours which the census registers as working ones. We are in the ambivalent position described by Lynn White, Jr., President of Mills College, commenting on a roundtable on "leisure and human values in industrial civilization" of which he was chairman at the Corning Conference a year ago:

> We said, "Ha, ha, I have no leisure; why am I involved in this?" It was a sense of guilt and, at the same time, a sense of pride. In other words, we feel leisure is a cultural value. Theoretically we would rather like to participate in it, but we are sort of proud that we are such responsible members of society that we really have no time for leisure.[1]

Our responsibility extends, in fact, to a concern for how other people —our children, our pupils, our union members, the community at large—are spending their leisure. In fact, those of us who are in the education industry and its allies, such as the library industry, have developed quite substantial interests—vested interests—in other people's leisure. We see their loose time, as others see their loose change, as our problem and our responsibility. This is, I suggest, one reason why the "gentleman of leisure," whose portrait Thorstein Veblen drew so sardonically in the '90's, is obsolete today. Instead, we are all of us—that is, almost all—members of the leisure class, and face its problems. As Eric Larrabee pointed out at Corning, the expansion of the leisure "market" has brought "friction" in its wake.

---

1. For this and later quotations, see *Creating an Industrial Civilization: A Report on the Corning Conference,* Eugene Staley, ed. I have drawn on the materials prepared for this conference by Reuel Denney and myself.

It is, of course, characteristic of American life that our bonanzas, our windfalls, whether treasures of the soil or treasures of the self, have been interpreted by the most sensitive and responsible among us as problems. I'm not sure but that the hue and cry against Puritanism isn't beginning to be overdone, and that we won't come to realize that our moral seriousness—in fact, our fun-morality—is not wholly negative. At the Corning Conference, the Wellesley-educated Hindu author, Miss Santha Rama Rau, scolded us; she commented:

> I am wondering why leisure is a problem at all. Surely, nowhere else in the world do people fuss about what to do with their spare time. I think it is rather sad that some kind of guilt has been built up in this particular society so that people feel that they should be productive in their spare time. . . . What is wrong with lying on the beach and relaxing?

I suppose one, perhaps unfair, answer to her is to be found in the six- and seven-year old Indian children standing guard over their families' fields all night long, lest a sacred bull trample the crops down and leave the family to starve. It is Puritanism that, in considerable part, has brought us to the point where leisure is or can become a problem for the vast majority. In fact, so great is the sheer quantity of our available leisure and leisure resources, that I do not think we can find very helpful models in other countries.

Recent reading and reflection, and discussion with Mark Benney of the London School of Economics (now visiting lecturer at the University of Chicago), has convinced me that this is true enough, at any rate, for England, from which we once derived our working model of the gentleman of leisure, and from which, too, I suspect the Hindu aristocrats such as Miss Rama Rau have learned more than many will admit. The English remain torn between the aristocratic leisure pattern, which is rural, sportsmanlike, casual, and on the edge of such quasi-criminal activities as cock-fighting, and the middle-class leisure pattern, dating from the sobersides of the Puritan revolution, which is urban, uplifting, strenuous. (The urban working-class pattern, as represented in the London music hall and a vivid "street culture," is pretty much dying out.) A recent extensive survey by Seebohm Rowntree and G. R. Lavers, entitled *English Life and Leisure*, was evidence to me that the English today on the whole know even less than we how to spend leisure—that there is a sameness and lack of imagination about their pastimes and pursuits. The English aristocrats with their natural allies, the lower class, have won the day in the sense that the Victorian middle-class morality appears to be almost dead in England, and sexual intimacy seems the chief leisure resort after puberty. But while the young people are uninhibited, they **are not joyful.** They have to watch every penny they spend on liquor, but again seem to take no great pleasure in it. They gamble, but often with desperation. The truth is that they can no longer afford the aristocratic vices which are now, with the decline of religious sanctions, psychologically available to them. And the middle-class values of self-improvement are still strong enough so that many are dissatisfied with the aimlessness of their lives; I recall one young middle-class girl, for instance, who told the interviewer that she slept with young men who asked her to, but wished she could find something better to do.

What, then, do Rowntree and Lavers, who are distinguished students of English social life, recommend? They plug the old middle-class model, only more of it. After touring the Scandinavian countries to study leisure practices there, they urge more folk-dancing, more hobbies, more adult education, better books—and, I need hardly add, fewer Hollywood movies.   ,

In fact, their attitude towards Hollywood may be regarded as symptomatic of the attitude of a great many students of leisure—"recreationists" perhaps we'd better call them—here and abroad. In their view, Hollywood is a source of disruptive leisure patterns, of vulgarity, spendthrift living, and false values generally. You know the indictment, I'm sure—an indictment which includes most of our popular culture, radio, TV, and bestsellers as well. Rowntree and Lavers put themselves up, as many school officials have, as angry competitors with this commercial popular culture, waging a losing fight. If they can offer nothing better, I am afraid that both the old aristocratic pattern, which is too expensive, and the old middle-class pattern, which is too didactic, will evaporate from England, leaving nothing of much quality to take their place.[2]

§ II

NOW IT IS MY OPINION that Hollywood movies not only are often shoddy but are often profoundly liberating and creative products of the human imagination. And I am not referring to so-called "message" films, pleas for better race relations or labor relations. I refer rather to such films as *The Asphalt Jungle*, or *All About Eve*, or *An American in Paris*, or *The Marrying Kind*, or *The Great Gatsby*, and many others without any patent social message; some successful, some not; movies which take us out of ourselves or force us back in; movies which open a window on life, and movies which exhibit a nightmarish

---

2. Mr. Benney believes that English leisure is not quite so dreary as this book indicates: the interviewers seem to concentrate on the activities that shock them and, indeed, to encounter a high proportion of rather sad and isolated people; moreover, nothing appears in the book about such gregarious leisure pursuits as political meetings and dart matches in the pubs.

fantasy. If English leisure is sterile and mean-spirited, I doubt if such movies have made it so. Rather, I think English, and American life also, would be enriched if people learned to understand and appreciate the movies, and could enjoy them in the spirit, at once critical and friendly, with which people at different times and places have enjoyed literature. The thought occurred to me some years ago that our schools and colleges, and particularly our altogether too pious adult education ventures, might begin experimenting with courses on movie appreciation, and popular culture appreciation generally—a movement which would require us to develop something we have not yet got in this country: a corps of gifted movie and radio and TV critics. The beginnings are evident in the work of John Crosby, for instance; what is lacking is any program for developing such critics, operating in the different media and at different levels of irony and sensibility. I argued that such a program might help close the gap which now separates the literary culture of the schools—the culture which such men as Rowntree and Lavers narrowly regard as the only true and genuine culture—from the popular culture of RKO and CBS.

I argued too that such a program might help us get rid once and for all of the current distinction between active and passive recreations—"active" being such things as sports, hobbies, and square dancing, and "passive" such things as movie-going, TV-watching, and other things parents and teachers wish their children wouldn't do. For I am convinced that this is not a real distinction: much leisure which appears to be active may be merely muscular: its lactic acid content is high, but there may be little other content, or contentment. And conversely, such supposedly passive pursuits as movie-going can obviously be the most intense experience, the most participative. Indeed, Hollywood movies could hardly corrupt England and Europe if they were as passive and as pacifying as is charged! And so I wanted to teach people to enjoy the movies as participants in a fine performance, and not merely as a place to pass the time out of the old folks' reach. In fact, I was particularly eager to develop courses just for the old folks in the understanding of popular culture, thinking in this way not only to open up to them a wide range of imaginative experience but also of helping to close the gap which separates the young, who have been raised with movies, comics, radio, and now TV, from the old who have come to them late if at all. . . .

But now I am not so sure that the problem I have in mind can be solved by courses, or possibly by any sort of conscious social program. I vividly recall my experience a few years ago when, asked to talk informally at a men's dormitory at the University of Chicago, I chose the movies as my topic, and started to say some things about the contemporary tendency among educated Americans to regard the movies as "just a show," to be "taken in" when one has nothing better at hand. I was talking to an audience most of whom devoutly believed that Hollywood movies other than Chaplin and the early Griffith are without exception junk, and that only England, France, and Italy make movies seriously worth seeing. I was trying to rebut this prejudice by saying something about the differing film conventions on the Continent and in this country: how, for example, we had had a convention of a happy ending which our more arty directors were now tending to exchange for an equally conventional, though Continental, unhappy ending, and that no necessary superiority lay in one convention rather than another, any more than in one sonnet form rather than another. Likewise, I sought to show how the undoubted inanities of the Production Code often resulted in a movie treatment—the so-called Lubitsch touch, for instance—which was a creative surmounting of the constricting forms. And then suddenly I stopped in the middle of my lecture, and for a while could not continue.

For I had realized, as I looked at the intent faces of the students, that I might well be engaged in closing off one of the few casual and free escape routes remaining to them; that I might be helping to inaugurate a new convention: namely, that one had not only to attend Hollywood movies but to understand and appreciate them. I might be imposing on a group of students already zealously engaged in self-improvement, in social and intellectual mobility, still another requirement—and this in the very act of seeking to liberate them from a common prejudice against American movies. I could continue my lecture only after I had made some of these misgivings explicit, and had indicated that I came to offer some of them an opportunity, not another extra-curricular curriculum.

I realized the problem here was not so much mine of becoming a possible taste-leader, as it was one for the students who were looking for such leadership, if not from me, then from somebody. Contrary to the situation in my own undergraduate days, when we were, at least for external consumption, stoutly individualistic, these students were more malleable, more ready to be told. One reason for this is that the general level of teaching has improved, despite all the attacks currently being made against our educational system. Not only has the teaching improved, but the teachers have changed their pace and style; we try to get close to our students, to be good group leaders rather than platform ham actors, and to concern ourselves with more aspects of student life than simply classroom performance. We are perhaps today less distant from the student than we once were, both in terms of social class position and in terms of intellectual attitude. . . . The students I was talking to, were ready to shift their leisure behavior at a moment's notice; I could envisage a group of them going to a Sam Goldwyn movie and, coming out, being very self-conscious as to how they ought to respond to it, whereas earlier they would have gone to it with the excuse that they needed to relax a bit before hitting the books again. Since so much of their leisure was already highly self-conscious, I hesitated to add to the burden. All planning for other people's leisure has to face this fundamental ambiguity, a form of the ever-present problem of the unintended consequence.

To be sure, leisure is a burden of the sort I am describing only among the educated, among the great many high school and college graduates who have some aspirations towards culture; men and women who, in the absence of any visible aristocratic model of leisure in American life, look to their fellows for clues, look to the magazines and the press, and the "how to" books. For the working class, there is leisure now too, and often money to spend, but it is not usually a burden, not perhaps a burden enough. Hunting and fishing and bowling; puttering about the house, garden, or car; watching television with and without discrimination; playing the numbers—these are recreations, not so very different from those turned up by Rowntree and Lavers in England, which my students have observed among steelworkers in Hammond and Gary. To be sure, there is considerable aspiration towards improved taste on the part of some of the younger wives, who read the women's service magazines. And the unions make sporadic efforts to give political education to the men; you will hardly be surprised to hear that some of the leaders blame the mass media for seducing the rank and file away from meetings— a charge which Mark Starr, educational director of the Ladies Garment Workers' Union, leveled at David Sarnoff of NBC at the Corning Roundtable. I think the charge is quite unjust, for I see no reason why people should spend their leisure in political activity unless that is their form of sport and they enjoy it, save in those cases where conditions are really so terrible that every good man has to come to the aid of the party—and, contrary to what is so widely urged, I believe such conditions are rare in this country.

One reason why the steel workers have so few problems with their leisure is that their work today is itself often quite leisurely and gregarious. It was not like that even thirty years ago when, as we know, there were ten- and twelve-hour shifts, and when the work was so hot and heavy that many men, on returning home, lay exhausted on the kitchen floor before they could get the energy to eat and tumble into bed. Now at the big sheet and tube mill in Gary the men often take naps on mattresses they have brought in, and cook meals on burners attached to the fiery furnaces; if a new foreman doesn't like the practice, production is slowed down until he does like it. Think here, too, of the extent to which the schools train young people in this kind of comradely slow-down against the teachers and against the system generally, so that I sometimes think of school teachers as foremen who conspire with their pupils, the workers, to conceal the true state of affairs from top management, the principals, and from the parents who are the absentee stockholders, who grouse now and again about their dividends. At any rate, since work has now become so relatively lacking in strain—though it is not nearly so routinized in feeling as it may seem to be to observers of factory life—the worker leaves the plant with a good deal of energy left, which carries him readily through his leisure hours.

By contrast, the professional and business person is apt to leave his work with a good many tensions created by his reactions to interpersonal situations, and as a result his leisure "needs" may have to be satisfied before he can rise above the level of needs—before he can rise from the level of re-creation to the level of creation. But it is just this very person on whom fall most of the demands for participative, active, constructive leisure which we have been examining earlier; and he may move from a job, where he is constantly faced with others and their expectations, to leisure pursuits, again in the company of others, where workmanlike performance is also expected of him. While he may nominally have a short work-week—though in many middle-class occupations such as medicine and teaching, hours are as long or longer than ever—he has not got much time which is not filled with stress. As my colleague, Nelson Foote, likes to put it, he has very little reverie as a balance to his sociability.

§ III

LET US LOOK at a concrete example. A friend and former colleague, Professor John R. Seeley, is now engaged in directing a large research project on the relations between school and community in a wealthy, upper-middle-class suburb. It is a suburb which has one of the finest public school systems on this continent, one which is often held up as a model to others; in fact, the magnificent new modern high school dominates the community, even physically, as the cathedrals did in the Middle Ages. The very fact that this elaborate research is

going on there—it is to take a period of at least five years before any
final conclusions are reached—is indicative of the alertness of the
school officials, the school board, and the other community leaders.
Yet, from my own very limited observation and from what has been
reported to me, it is plain that the community, despite all material
advantages, is not happy. The parents have neuroses; the children
have allergies; and the teachers—well, I don't know. What has gone
wrong?

If we follow the life of the children after school, we can perhaps
get some clues. They are being prepared now for their later careers
and their later rather hypothetical leisure. Their parents want to
know how they have fared at school: they are constantly comparing
them, judging them in school aptitude, popularity, what part they
have in the school play; are the boys sissies? the girls too fat? All
the school anxieties are transferred to the home and vice versa,
partly because the parents, college graduates mostly, are intelligent
and concerned with education. After school there are music lessons,
skating lessons, riding lessons, with mother as chauffeur and sched-
uler. In the evening, the children go to a dance at school for which
the parents have groomed them, while the parents go to a PTA
meeting for which the children, directly or indirectly, have groomed
them, where they are addressed by a psychiatrist who advises them
to be warm and relaxed in handling their children! They go home
and eagerly and warmly ask their returning children to tell them
everything that happened at the dance, making it clear by their
manner that they are sophisticated and cannot easily be shocked. As
Professor Seeley describes matters, the school in this community operates a "gigantic factory for the production of relationships."

Since, moreover, the same interpersonal concerns dominate life
within this "plant" and outside it, there is no sharp change of pace
between work and play, between school and home activities. The
children and their mothers—the fathers who work in the city at
least make a geographical shift and also something of an emotional
one—are characterized by a pervading anxiety. This is connected, I
think, with the fact that the older, clear goals of achievement have
been called into question, and these family units must decide not
only how to get what they want but also what it is they should want.
To answer this question, the community makes much use of professionals—the school principals and teachers themselves, who have
a very high standing; child guidance experts and mental hygienists;
and the packaged professionalism which can be bought in books or
over the radio. The result is a well-known paradox: here is a suburb
devoted to the arts of consumption and leisure, where these arts are

pursued with such dogged determination that leisureliness as a quality of life is very largely absent. While all the appurtenances of variety are present, life is monotonous in the sense that it is steadily gregarious, focussed on others, and on the self in relation to others. As I have observed among some students, at Harvard and elsewhere, even casualness can be an effortful artifact.

§ IV

YET IT IS all too easy to deride these parents and children and assorted experts, to urge them—as some people are now doing in the anti-progressive education movement—to drop all this new-fangled nonsense and get back to hard work and traditional curricula and nineteenth century or classical "values" generally. It is perhaps not surprising that both aristocratic and working-class stances towards leisure combine in this derision. When, for example, this suburban community was recently discussed in my seminar on leisure, many people, both faculty and students, took the position that what these suburbanites needed was more direct and uninhibited aggression, more toughness and less talkiness. They compared the community unfavorably to a working-class community where, for reasons I indicated a moment ago, leisure is undoubtedly more casually dealt with. What they admired was aristocratic or artisan insouciance, as against upper-middle-class anxiety and preoccupation. Yet I do not know by what standard of value one prefers a broken nose to asthma, or lumbago or gout to ulcers. There is no doubt that the suburb in question, and others like it, is anxious and vulnerable, individually and collectively; otherwise, it would not be quite so receptive to a team of researchers. But I think that overadmiration for toughness is part of a romance which the middle class, in Europe as well as in America, has been carrying on with the lower class for a good many years. . . .

Thus, I think we can look at the people of this suburb rather differently from the way I have been doing so far, or from the way my seminar reacted to them. We can see them, for one thing, as explorers. Whereas the explorers of the last century moved to the frontiers of production and opened fisheries, mines, and mills, the explorers of this century seem to me increasingly to be moving to the frontiers of consumption. They are opening up new forms of interpersonal understanding, new ways of using the home as a "plant" for leisure, new ways of using the school as a kind of community center, as the chapel of a secular religion perhaps. But frontier towns are not usually very attractive. And frontier behavior is awkward: people have not yet learned to behave comfortably in the new surroundings. There is formlessness, which takes the shape of lawlessness on the frontier of production and of aimlessness on the frontier of consumption. In both instances, the solid citizens who stayed home are likely to feel superior, both to the formlessness and to whatever may be emerging from it, just as most Europeans of the educated strata have felt superior to most aspects of America throughout most of our history. The move to the suburb, as it occurs in contemporary America, is emotionally, if not geographically, something almost unprecedented historically; and those who move to any new frontier are likely to pay a price, in loneliness and discomfort. When the physical hardships are great, as they were for earlier generations of pioneers, the psychological hardships may be repressed or submerged—though we cannot be too sure even of that, for (as Oscar Handlin makes clear in his book on immigration to America, *The Uprooted*) the most devastating strains on the newcomers were in fact the emotional ones, rough though the physical conditions were.

To carry my analogy further, I do believe that discoveries are being made on the frontiers of consumption. Take the American diet, for instance. Once upon a time, and still in many quarters, this was in charge of the nutritionists, the exponents of a balanced meal, adequate caloric intake and colonic outlet, and plenty of vitamins. These good people bore the same relation to food that recreationists do to leisure: they want it to be uplifting, salubrious, wasteless. But now, among the better income strata at any rate, their work is done: it is incorporated into the formulae of bakers, into the inventories of chainstores, the menus of restaurants and dining cars. We have, as I sometimes like to put it, moved from the wheat bowl to the salad bowl. In consequence, in the suburb I have been describing, and elsewhere throughout the country, there is an emphasis, which was once confined to small sophisticated or expatriate circles, on having the right responses to food, on being a gourmet. Save for a few cranks, the housewives are not concerned with having enough wheat-germ, but with having enough oregano, or the right wine—and more than that, with having the right enjoyment of the wine. In the middle of the shopping center in this suburb is a store which stocks a stupendous array of delicacies, spices, patisseries, delicatessens, and European gadgets for cooking; the casserole replacing the melting pot!

Now, as I have indicated, the residents of this suburb are anxious about food and their attitudes towards it. They want to be knowledgeable about it and also to enjoy it, but they are not yet easygoing in the matter. Among men particularly, the demand that one must enjoy food, and not simply stow it away, is relatively new, and again these pioneers are awkwardly self-conscious. (Let me make clear in passing that I am not talking about old-fashioned conspicuous consumption. I am not talking about the hostess' fear of making a gastronomic *faux pas*, or fear that her children's table manners will disgrace her; no doubt these fears may still exist, although greatly muted, in the group I am describing. No, these parents are afraid that they are missing some taste experience, which in turn reveals the lack of a basic personality attribute.) We are observing these families, it appears, in a time of transition, when they have left old food-conventions behind and are exploring, without settling on, new ones. They are, in effect, paying the society's cost of research and development.

And can there be any doubt but that the result will be—in fact, has already been—an addition to the stock of American leisure bounties and benefits? The self-service supermarket, with its abundance of foods capably displayed, where the shopper's caprice and imagination can roam without interference from officious clerks or sabotage from indifferent ones, seems to me as significant an invention on the side of consumption as the assembly-line on the side of production. But the invention would be meaningless without a group of experimentalist families prepared to develop new eating patterns, new combinations of color and taste. And here enters still another service industry: the cookbook and recipe industry, which has ransacked the world's cuisines and produced a host of books and newspaper columns, as well as those restaurants which serve as pilot plants. I think there can be no doubt that the children of the children now growing up in our demonstration suburb will be reasonably free of fears, guilts, and awkwardness about food prepared as a matter of course for the pursuit of happiness in this area of existence. In fact, I see only one caveat: the return of the nutritionist ghost in the craze for reducing, which makes not only women but men choose between food and figure, with one eye on mortality tables and the other on the way one appears in the hall of mirrors which is society! Even so, the reduced diets on which these figure-chasers bravely live are, item for item, unquestionably superior to anything known before in the American provender—which a generation ago made our food, like our bootlegging, an international joke. Moreover, the cult of one's figure, as of one's dress and one's coiffure, is certainly not an illegitimate one for one's happiness and aesthetic sense.

In other fields of consumption such as music, painting, and literature; in the whole subtle field of sociability and conversation; in sports; in the changing style of vacations I think the pioneers are also paying a high price in emotional outlay, particularly in anxiety. I have already raised the question of whether our intellectual and literary culture is not too severe and derisive about the middle-class vice of anxiousness, compared with its benign tolerance for the aristocratic and

lower-class vices of brutality and indifference. Such very general questions of value judgment are of great importance in determining contemporary attitudes towards leisure. I think, for example, that we make
life and leisure harder for the already anxious person—whose anxiety
is in fact thoroughly understandable in the light of our discussion so
far—by making him also anxious about his anxiety, so that we heap
on him a cumulative burden. . . .

Teachers also feel it compulsory not to be anxious, but to be
always easygoing, warm, and relaxed—what a burden this puts on
teachers in the better public and private schools!—whereas lack of
discipline and firmness would have worried teachers in an earlier day.
I am inclined to think we should form a union of the anxious ones,
to defend our right to be anxious, our right to be tense, our right
to aspirin and to our allergies. I was shocked when one of my colleagues remarked, after our seminar had had a description of life
in the suburb I have here used as a case, that children were worse off
there than they had been under the *ancien régime*. Historical amnesia
had blinded him, as it blinds many now-fashionable critics of progressive education, to the brutalities and savageries in the treatment
of children a hundred years or so ago. Then children were harnessed
to the engine of society with often little concern for their own
development. Many were too frightened or too cowed to be
anxious.[3] . . .

§ V

I HAVE STRESSED as much as I have the conflicts in our attitudes towards
the proper use of leisure, and the kind of training children should get
with their later lives of leisure in mind, because I feel that a recognition of ambiguity at the very heart of our problem is a first step
towards perspective and a certain necessary detachment. I can't
emphasize enough how rapidly our country is changing, and how
hard it is even for the wisest among us to grasp what is going on.

Let me give just two illustrations: Recently a friend of mine
who works for one of the pocket book companies visited an Ohio
Valley city of about 75,000. There is no bookstore in the town, but
a few books are kept, along with stationery and oddments, in the
main department store. My friend asked at the department store why

---

3. Stephen Spender's novel, *The Backward Son*, and George Orwell's account
of his schooldays, "Such, Such Were the Joys" (which appeared in *Partisan
Review* since the above was written), can remind us that even a generation ago
the English public school could still treat the sensitive young with ferocious
bullying. Likewise, the fictional hero of Salinger's *Catcher in the Rye* might have
profited from some of the humaneness and sensitivity introduced by the now
maligned progressive educators.

they didn't put in a real bookstore, and was told, "Well, this is a steel town. People here don't read; they just look at television or go to the taverns." Yet over three-quarters of a million pocket books were sold in this same town in 1951 at restaurants, at newsstands and in drugstores, many of them in the Mentor line of modern classics. This is well over a book a month for those old enough to read. I wish we had some knowledge and understanding of what these citizens made out of all they read: the Faulkner novels, the Conant *On Understanding Science*, the Ruth Benedict *Patterns of Culture*, along with the Mickey Spillane and other mixtures of sadism with sex. But studies of this kind in the field of leisure have not yet been made, as far as I know.

I draw my other illustration of the laggard state of our knowledge even of the basic data from an article by Gian-Carlo Menotti which appeared in a recent issue of the New York *Times Sunday Magazine*. As you know, Menotti is a gifted and widely hailed young composer who, after some twenty years residence here, considers himself an American. He was complaining about the precarious position of the creative artist in American life, particularly in the field of music. Here, he points out, we bestow all our adulation on the performer: the glamorous conductor or singer, the Menuhin or Serkin or Reginald Kell, who interprets music but does not create it, while the modern composer, unless he writes for the movies or gets some help from a foundation or a rich wife, will starve (as Bela Bartok did)—and is certainly not in any case featured in the billing along with the star performers. And he goes on to say that many parents in America are ashamed if their sons choose an artistic career; not only do they fear they will not make a living—even if they (the parents) could afford to support them—but fear, too, that they will be sissies; fathers try to force their sons to becomes businessmen or doctors or something else equally reassuring. Now I am sure that Menotti has a very good case about the plight of the composer, who seems so much worse off than the painter or writer, having more impresarios standing between him and his public. However, it seems to me that Menotti does not take account of the rapid and widespread change which has been going on in just the attitudes he is attacking. Through amateur chamber music groups and through the fabulous growth of the long-playing record industry, many thousands of Americans are today discovering modern music with a rush, just as they are discovering wine and other pleasures that were once confined to a small cultivated indigenous group and a somewhat larger group of immigrants who brought this culture with them from the old country. Likewise, it seems to me unlikely that millions of middle-class parents would not in 1952 be pleased if their sons exhibited artistic gifts and interests, even if not commercially promising. . . . When I said as much, however, at the Corning Conference, Miss Rama Rau and others said I was mistaken: parents would only accept art if it was advertised in *Life* magazine. . . . I would be greatly interested in comments on this topic, for I feel that here again we simply do not know.[4]

§ VI

SO FAR we have been looking at our culture from inside. We have asked ourselves some questions about what is going on, about what attitudes are prevalent towards it, what models of competent use of leisure exist, what differences there are among different social strata, and so on. But there is another way of going at our problem which is to ask, not what play and leisure are like, or were like, in our culture but what they are like in any culture. Is there, for instance, any natural or biological basis for leisure or is it entirely conventional? *Homo Ludens,* a book by the late Dutch scholar Huizinga, offers some interesting clues to this. Huizinga points out that every language he examined had a word for play which is different from the word for work, and that many cultures have a pattern of sport, of noneconomic serious and yet playful competition. Many if not all cultures, moreover, operate on a periodic or seasonal rhythm between heavy work and heavy play—and I might add that many societies also have feasts even if they do not suffer from famines. That there is a cross-cultural solidarity of play may be indicated by a well-known example. Our Army advised soldiers and aviators to always carry a piece of string with them and when downed in a Pacific jungle to start playing cat's cradle if a suspicious native approached; the native would sometimes start to play, too.

All this must rest on something basic in the biological substratum of man and many animals. We know of course that children play even without instruction, provided certain basic minima of security are met. Thus, while children's play has aspects of artifice which the ever-renewed child's culture elaborates, much of it is

4. In discussion [at the Harvard Summer School], it was argued that parents will now often accept art as a glamorous stairway to quick success, but that this makes it even harder than earlier for a youngster whose interest in art cannot be readily commercialized: his parents are impatient with him, not because he is an artist or composer—which would lead to a total break and a relatively good conscience on the artist's part—but because, being in a glamorous field, he has not made his way; since the youngster in part also wants success, he finds it harder to cut himself off from his parents' values and anxieties. For thoughtful discussion of this problem, and a critique of the art schools which cash in on this craving for success, see Lyman Bryson, *The Next America.*

simply given. In fact, work and play are not yet, for the child, independently organized; and what he makes of play as he develops depends to a very considerable extent on the society's interpretation of his play—is it regarded as "child's play," as useless, as preparation for life, or is it disregarded?

I think we can say, indeed, that the child's play serves as the principal model for all later efforts to free leisure time from its burdens and to cope with its puzzling ambiguities. We all of us know, if we think about it, that children's play is by no means always free and spontaneous; it is often filled with terror and morbidity; but at its best it is surely one of the unequivocally good things of this earth, and no wonder we try to recapture it as Paradise Lost. But if we look closely at children's play we can observe something else which may even give us a clue as to how that recapture can, in part, be achieved, namely that the child's greatest satisfaction appears to arise from experiences of mastery and control. As Erik H. Erikson has noted in imaginative detail, the developing body provides a graded set of experiences; anyone can observe this who watches children play with their new-found mastery of walking or running or talking or diving. Play seems to reside in a margin, often a narrow one, between tasks which are too demanding, and those which are not demanding enough to require the excited concentration of good play. A child or adult who is simply going through the motions is not engaged in play or leisure as we have been talking about it here, however the society may define it. But without some social forms for leisure and play, forms which have to be broken through, yet have to be there to be broken through, I do not think we will have much play either. For the demand that play be constantly spontaneous, unchanneled by social forms, is too overwhelming; spontaneity, as we have already seen, is lost if we strive too hard for it. Thus, play would seem to consist in part of giving ourselves tasks, useless in any immediate sense, which challenge us but do not overwhelm us —tasks which allow us to practice our skills on the universe when not too much is at stake. Some of us, who lose this ability in our waking lives, retain it (as Erich Fromm points out in *The Forgotten Language*) in our dreams, which can be astonishingly witty, brilliant, and artistic—an indication, perhaps, of the child still buried within us, not so much in Freud's sense of the vicious child but rather of the child natively gifted with the capacity for imaginative play.

I have spoken of mastery of tasks, but I do not want to be understood as implying that this necessarily means physical activity—that is only one example. The child in the front of a subway train who intently watches the motorman, the signals, and the tracks may be quiet, but is undoubtedly playing, and may be playing very well—a point Reuel Denney eloquently voiced at the Corning Conference. When we speak of "role-playing," we should have something of this sort of vicariousness in mind. And this leads me to the complicating point that many of our workaday tasks as adults can be handled with a certain quality of leisure if we are able to regard work as a series of challenging tasks to be mastered, where the net of expectations surrounding us is at the same time not too frightening. On the other hand, we can be playful at work as a way of *evading* demands, sometimes by being one of the boys, pretending to ourselves and others that, if we really worked, we would get to the top. Students often play such games with themselves. But this is not really carrying out in adult life the effort at competence which is our lesson learned from the play of the child. That requires that we work at the top of our bent, while at the same time enjoying the very processes of accomplishment—enjoying our awareness, for example, of all that is going on in a classroom; enjoying our understanding of a technical problem; enjoying ourselves, in other words, as functioning and effective human beings.

We get here, it is apparent, into very deep waters indeed, where the boundaries between work and play become shadowy—as I think, for other reasons, they are tending to become in our society anyway —waters where we are looking for a quality we can only vaguely describe: it is various and rhythmical; it breaks through social forms and as constantly recreates them; it manifests itself in tension, yet not too much of it; it is at once meaningful, in the sense of giving us intrinsic satisfaction, and meaningless, in the sense of having no pressing utilitarian purpose. It is some such model as this, I suggest, which haunts us when we consider leisure and judge its quality in ourselves and others. It is a model which has been elaborated in our culture, and yet which transcends most, and perhaps all, given cultures.

14. New Standards for Old: From Conspicuous Consumption to Conspicuous Production

§ I

In a recent column, John Crosby affectionately quoted a remark of Sylvester L. Weaver, vice-chairman of the board of NBC: "The kids," said Weaver, "are already getting the full picture. 'The kids running around in space suits are smarter than the adults who are laughing at them.'" The parents' imagination, Weaver implied, is localized, whereas that of their children floats free even of planetary boundaries. A recent story in the science-fiction magazine *Galaxy* preaches a similar moral. It is a tale of two children, aged ten, who take off on a Moebius ring for other times and places. These children, at home in an Einsteinian universe, patronize their parents, are sorry for them, and obey them, not out of fear or favor, but lest they cause them pain. The parents are bound to a specific time and place, a specific job, whereas the children, free of chores for the most part both at home and school, are not hindered, as they would have been in an earlier day, from rapidly overtaking and surpassing their parents' know-how on the frontiers of consumption. It would be my guess, for instance, that more children than parents today favor "modern design" not only in space suits but in cars, bars, houses, and furniture.

Margaret Mead and others have pointed out that immigrant parents in America have always been on the defensive, because their children were more "American" than they. But the tendencies I am discussing seem to extend beyond this country, for they are the consequences of industrialization and urbanization and the growing leisure that, in later stages, accompany these developments. Indeed, when countries without a long Christian and Puritan heritage adopt the techniques of modern industry, they may appear more "American" than America in their readiness to slough off older ideologies of thrift and workmanship; they may hanker for leisure and consumption before they have solved the problems of production. The Coca Cola bottlers, the Hollywood film distributors, and other consumption missionaries preach a gospel that may be premature in Thailand or Egypt. But whatever the gospel, it is doubtless the young—lacking

219

the trained incapacities of their elders—who catch on to it most quickly, but at times, as I myself think may be true with space suits, most shallowly.

§ II

I AM GOING to illustrate some of these matters by referring to a play many of you have doubtless seen: *Death of a Salesman*. Whereas in 19th-century literature, children often fear that their parents will catch them out in some frivolity, it is Willy Loman, the father in *Death of a Salesman*, who is caught out by his son in a hotel room. And the other son, Happy Loman, openly ridicules his father as a fool for working hard; Happy—how meaningful his nickname!—has latched on to American consumption know-how at its most garish: his eyes are on the pleasure frontier while his father's are still on the production-achievement frontier. Not that Biff or Happy escape defensiveness towards their father—today as in an earlier day sons are still trapped by the irrelevance of their parents' hopes and fears for them—but the initiative is certainly changed.

The changes that have taken place can scarcely be fitted into a simple chronology of parent-child relations. Too many other factors are involved. The east coast is different from the middle west—and the differences, despite our stereotypes, are not well understood. There are very great differences in social class. It has been said that the upper class is oriented to the past, the lower class to the present, the middle class to the future. The upper class therefore tends to be strongly family-centered—think of the social memories of the Apleys, cemented by estates, portraits, memoirs, family names, and other impedimenta, as these are portrayed in Marquand's novel. Willy Loman, by contrast, seems to live always in the future, even though he spends much time listening to voices out of the past which point him to a future he didn't take or that didn't take him. Willy, in fact, appears to have no past, which is part of his pathos. . . . And Willy faces the problem that he is not really identified with salesmen but—as happens among some particularly outstanding salesmen—with the customers. It is often taken for granted that the good salesman should identify with the customers on whom he is dependent. Actually, the motives of men in business are more complex, and ambivalence towards the customer is common. Recently, a friend of mine, a market researcher, told me how a shaving lotion manufacturer stubbornly refused to alter his product, even to meet complaints of customers: it was the best on the market, and that was that. Similarly, another client, a pie-mix maker, while steadily losing business, would not agree to change his advertising to suit what market research had uncovered as to its effects: if potential customers who read his copy were "biased," that was their hard luck. Here, strikingly enough, resentment of the customer survives in firms highly dependent on sensitivity to consumers, companies which go so far as to employ market researchers but not far enough to cater to what they regard as customer prejudice. . . .

Willy Loman, however, failed to establish such emotional distance from his clients, and lacking support from his own occupational group, he became something of an anomaly among salesmen, exceptionally vulnerable, without the occupation's long-built-up defenses against the demands of work. In his ignorance of the ropes, Willy again strikes me as unusually deracinated—something Arthur Miller mislocates, I suggest, in the intangible nature of the occupation.

§ III

SO MUCH may be regarded as an overture to a somewhat more systematic account of why some of these developments have come about, why our work and leisure have changed so considerably. Naturally, such an account must be speculative and abbreviated; I will have to confine myself to institutional changes and to such intellectual currents as *Babbitt* or *Death of a Salesman* represent.

Let me emphasize, first of all, that such changes are never wholesale. Thus, the attitude towards the middleman in *Death of a Salesman* is nothing new. The idea that the middleman doesn't produce anything can be found in medieval thought and in the Reformation; the idea was very strong in 19th-century American populism. Populism, though it appears to have vanished, has left its mark. For example, nostalgia for a rural past is still very strong in America. Even so urban a writer as Arthur Miller is obsessed in *Death of a Salesman* with the fencing in of a once-rural Brooklyn and with the virtuousness of working with one's hands close to the soil. What is interpreted as "close to the soil" is, to be sure, partly a matter of cultural definition; thus, in Kansas City the leading annual social event, at which debutantes are presented, is the American Royal, a stock show at which grain traders and cattle buyers parade around under huge Stetsons—perhaps believing for a moment that they can identify with ranch life although they make their living as down-town brokers, and although ranchers themselves would seldom wear such head-gear. These identifications, as they become ritualized, have much more influence on our conceptions of our work than anything "intrinsic" to that work (such as the soil itself) or to man's biological potentiality for work and for avoiding work.

An illustration of the slow way in which cultural definitions change lies in the fact that, as Americans have sloughed off to a considerable extent the Puritan's exalted valuations of work, we have nevertheless not on the whole sought jobs that would provide a maximum of income with a minimum of work. Rather, what has happened is that our aims have become more complex: we now seek "the right kind" of work, including the right blend of leisure with work and inside work. For instance, a recent series of articles in *Fortune* indicates that we are witnessing the death of our salesmen in general: companies are finding it more and more difficult to recruit salesmen, even or especially when they work on a commission basis. The old-fashioned salesman set his own pace; he had a great deal of leisure, and, if he was good and business was good, he could make money. But today such opportunities seem often to go begging, and corporations engage in all kinds of semantic niceties, such as redefining sales jobs as sales engineering to get around the problem; they try to replace direct selling by advertising, and by using the retail store as the point-of-sale as in the Supermarket. College graduates today want jobs in personnel work or other "service" occupations, rather than in the exposed and isolated position of the salesman. For one thing, their wives make more demands of them than Willy's wife did: they want them home, and free of ulcers—and these new-style wives are more help to their men than the neutral misery of Mrs. Loman was any comfort to Willy. In the old days, Biff might have become a salesman without afterthought, but his ambitions are confused by some of the newer currents.

One reason for this is that young people seem to be increasingly choosing the role of an employee in a large organization, with pensions and perquisites, rather than the chance to make a quick killing by commission selling or other risky and entrepreneurial job. One company reported to *Fortune* that they now look for salesmen among Greeks—an ethnic group not yet acculturated to the newer American values; another, that they do their recruiting for sales in Texas and Oklahoma—states where also old-fashioned crazy millionaires can still be found. Sometimes people refer to high income taxes as a determining factor, but I think taxes, though certainly an element, are frequently used as rationalizations by men who don't want to take risks. Taxes are simply part of the managerial climate in which enterprise is now carried on, in which innovation is entrusted to a research and development staff trained at the Columbia School of Industrial Management and the Harvard Business School—men who take courses which deal with human relations in order that they will be able to get along with their colleagues in the office, or at least to discuss problems of human relations at American Management Association meetings.

And this leads me to a further reflection on *Death of a Salesman*. You will remember the terrible scene in which Howard Wagner fires Willy, while listening to an idiotic recording. Some of my colleagues at Chicago have recently been studying retirement practices and find that one reason many companies have a firm rule compelling retirement at, let us say, 65 is that people today are too soft-hearted to fire other people. At one large steel company, a number of older men have jobs which are make-work because no one can bring himself to discharge them. A retirement rule locates the responsibility elsewhere, makes it impersonal. This is true of the retirement regulations in universities also. Indeed, wherever I have observed such matters—in business, in government, in academic life —I have noticed the lengths to which people will go before firing somebody. Howard Wagners are hard to come by. (Now again you will notice that I am criticizing the play on the basis of a sociological estimate, but I must say that the play invites such criticism by its own effort at documentary realism.)

§ IV

so FAR, I have spoken as if fear of risk was the chief factor in the actual dearth of entrepreneurs and of salesmen in the American economy at present. But there is also a growing desire to be serviceable to others—this is one reason for the current high prestige of the medical profession. The attraction of personnel work for many college graduates rests on their urge to work *with* people (the fact is, they more often work with files—but that is in a way beside the point) rather than, as they interpret selling, *against* people. People want to be part of a team, part of a group. Work is done in groups, research is done in groups. It is this security which is often more important than pension plans. (I am discussing at such length the problem of work and the salesman today, because in order to see clearly the changes in the standards for judging consumption, we have to see how work itself has changed. For work and play seem to be fundamental dualities in culture, like day and night, male and female, parent and child, self and not-self.)

It may be that the changes I have been discussing are partly kept from clearer view by the American belief that men must be tough, not soft and sentimental; thus, we tend to conceal from ourselves as well as from others our conciliatory attitudes, our moods of fearing success and display, our sensitivity to envy. And so we continue to talk about free enterprise, about getting ahead—about all the older values which the Loman family, in its several ways, has taken so literally. But often this talk is big talk, or whistling to keep up our courage.

Such interpretation of contemporary talk, in fact, requires us to go back historically and raise the question whether in the 19th century, underneath all the Horatio Alger talk and the Samuel Smiles talk, similar ambivalences towards an all-out individualism were not present. The Christian values which are so strong in Mr. Gosse's group of Plymouth Brethren not only helped to spur the rise of a competitive, individualistic capitalism, but also moderated that capitalism by feelings of social responsibility, of concern for the other—after all, they were called "Brethren." And Christianity always contains the latent dynamic of a potential return to the values of the early Christian era, before the Church became a great going concern; in other words, there is always the available material for a reformation—within Catholicism as well as within Protestantism. Christianity may have become something of a shell in the 19th century, for many pious frauds, but it was always more than that and was not for long successfully allied with the more ferocious forms of competitiveness. Bruce Barton's notion of a generation ago that Jesus was really a big advertising man would hardly go over today among people of Babbitt's station, let alone among the advertising men who relish Mead's satiric *How to Get Ahead in Business without Really Trying*.

By the same evidence, we may conclude that there *have* been changes, very profound ones, although their origins can be traced back to an earlier day. Values once confined to a small elite group, or to an elite place within the hearts of many people—a kind of Sunday rather than weekday place—have now become much more widespread. For example, we can see this in attitudes towards conspicuous consumption. Veblen noticed in his book on the leisure class, published in 1899, that some small groups among the very rich were learning to be offended by conspicuous display, they were going in for "natural-looking" estates, "natural-looking" contrivances, and presumably "natural-looking" dress, too. He realized that when a leisure class gets large enough, and sufficiently in touch with itself, it can depart from grossly vulgar display—it can whisper rather than shout. And he saw how renewed attitudes of "workmanship," as against the earlier "waste-manship" at the top of the social pyramid, could spread downwards, as more people gained leisure, and as more came in contact with leisure class values.

Yet even he, perhaps because of his farm origin and midwest experience, did not see fully the extent to which nonconspicuous non-consumption (or, as one of my friends more appropriately terms it, "conspicuous under-consumption") was already a powerful American pattern. He seems to have escaped contact with Boston Unitarians or Philadelphia Quakers whose display was much more veiled. Although in Henry Adams' novel, *Democracy*, we are treated to an inauguration ball more gaudy than the un-top-hatted one of a few weeks ago [January, 1953], when we read Henry James's *The Bostonians*, which appeared in 1876, we are confronted with wealthy young women who were plain of dress and disdainful of display. For them, good intangible causes took the place of good commodities.

I should add, in fairness to Veblen, that he saw some of this. But he largely overlooked the possibility that these attitudes were being shaped by intellectual as well as by merely technological currents. Thus it would not have occurred to him that his own books would influence people's attitudes towards consumption, that he would be the godfather of the consumers' movement—that, indeed, a whole series of books, including his own and coming right down to Marquand's novels or *Death of a Salesman*, have helped inter certain American values with irony and sarcasm. For him, as for Marx, men always conform eventually to economic necessity, not to cultural or ideological necessity.

Nevertheless, Veblen's *Theory of the Leisure Class* fitted not too badly the American scene from the gay 90s to the not quite so gay 20s. The hero in the novel *Jefferson Selleck* who suffers agonies on his wedding night because he is of lower social origin than his bride; the drama of *The Great Gatsby,* and the miseries of Charlie Gray in *Point of No Return* and of Mary Monahan and her intimidated Beacon Street lover in the *Late George Apley*, are so many testimonies to the Veblenian cruelties of the American status system, with its unmerry emulative chase. And yet the last novels I mentioned are testimony also to a newer note in American life and literature, that of the failure of success, rather than, as in *Death of a Salesman*, the failure of failure.

§ V

IT HAS, I BELIEVE, been the bounteousness of modern industry, especially in America, which has done more than almost anything else to make conspicuous consumption obsolete here. It would go much too far to say that consumption bores us, but it no longer has the old self-evident quality; it no longer furnishes our lives with a kind of simple structure or chronology of motives, as it did for William Randolph Hearst, for instance. To collect objects in Hearst's manner required a certain confidence, even arrogance, a certain imperviousness to ridicule and criticism. Hearst's "whim of iron" appears to be a thing of the past.

It is not only or primarily, however, that our interest in goods has been drowned by the boundless cornucopia of goods, by analogy with Engel's law that food consumption declines proportionately as income rises. The same expansion of the economy has created new fortunes much faster than their possessors could possibly be tutored by the old rich in the proper consumption values of the latter. No mere "400" located in a single city can any longer dictate appropriate leisure-class behavior in terms of what estates, houses, furniture, and so on to collect. The absence of titles in America, and of many old-family names equivalent to titles (judging by names, many Negroes and onetime Kabotskys belong to some of the best families), also makes such hegemony very difficult—indeed, from the point of view of an Italian count (unfamiliar with American distinctions even in the days of Daisy Miller), a Dallas oil heiress in seven figures and Neiman-Marcus clothes may be preferable to a Saltonstall in six fig-ures and Jordan Marsh clothes. In this situation, the more established wealth and its auxiliary leaders of high taste have sought to fight back, not by a futile outspending, but by a conspicuous underspending. A Hearst has been ridiculed, not only for poor taste in *what* he bought, but *that* he bought in such quantity.

No doubt, universal education—itself part of our bonanza of good fortune—has exposed many people who later have come into means to tasteful critiques of working-class extravagance. The mass media, too, carry along with the prodigality of their advertising the relative emaciation of their judgments on expenditure: the *Vogue* style of restrained elegance is made an accessible model for millions. However, the movement of style has not only been from the top down—and how could it be when people can't tell, for reasons already indicated, where the top is? A relaxation of standards has spread upwards: the new rich gentleman needs no longer to struggle into a dress suit to hear Mary Garden at the Opera House, nor need he learn to ride to hounds or to send his sons to Groton or St. Marks. All he has to learn to do—and this, as Robert L. Steiner and Joseph Weiss point out in "Veblen Revised in the Light of Counter-Snobbery," is not easy for him—is to mute the wish for wild and gaudy spending that he learned as a lower-class lad, the very wish that may have helped propel him into the millionaire ranks. Frictions on this score are indi-cated by the concern of the Cadillac people with the consequences for their older clients of the fact that the Cadillac (rather than, as some years ago, the Buick) has become "the" car for well-off Negroes.

Today, men of wealth, fearful of making a wrong move, harried not only by taxes but by public relations and their own misgivings, are apt to give over the now-dreaded responsibilities for spending to a foundation, which then on their behalf can collect research projects or artistic works—protected by bureaucratic organization and corporate responsibility from imputations of extravagance. (As I write this, however, the big foundations such as Ford and Rockefeller are under Congressional Committee scrutiny—there seems to be no escape from money save anonymity!)

Another form of putting spending at arm's length is to delegate it to one's children. Whether for toys or for schools, for space in the home or advice on child management, more money is being spent on children and by them than ever before. The trouble with children, of course, is that they grow up—unlimited amounts cannot be spent on them. Before too long, in the same strata that Veblen and Arthur Miller have influenced, the children now grown up are denouncing advertising and disdainful of waste and extravagance. The parents, of course, can have more children, and as you may know, this is what has happened to the country in the last decade, much to the bewilderment of the demographers, who thought that the American urban middle classes would continue to have fewer and fewer children and more and more commodities. Demographers do not know, and I do not know, why the shift has occurred; doubtless the causes are complex and ramified—the same thing has happened in France and elsewhere. But I do suspect that the changes in value-patterns we have been discussing have been among the factors. I started several years ago reading college class books for the light they might shed on subtle shifts in attitude. I was struck by the emphasis on the family that began to appear in my own and other college classes of a few years back. People in writing about themselves no longer started off by saying they were Vice-President of Ozark Air Lines and a director of the Tulsa National Bank, and so forth; they began by telling about the wife and five kids and how they had a home in the suburbs where they all enjoyed barbecues in the back yard. The occupational achievement was played down; the family scene, with its pastoral virtues, played up. Since then I have found similar tendencies in other groups. This would seem to hang together with the devaluation of individual success we have been discussing: children are a kind of unequivocal good in a world of changing values, and we can lavish on children the care and emotions we would now feel it egotistical to lavish on ourselves. The younger age at which people are marrying today is a further factor; having started to go steady at fourteen, they want to settle down at twenty. Whereas a generation ago a career man and a career girl would have considered marriage an obstacle to their work aims, today marriage and children are in a way part of the consumption and leisure sphere, the side of life currently emphasized.

§ VI

THUS, CHILDREN ABSORB some of the surplus and foundations some more of it. Especially the biggest foundation of all—the federal government. Conspicuous consumption has been socialized, and appears of necessity largely in the form of weapons, with something left over for national parks. When we speak of government spending for armaments, it is clear that the line between consumption and production is hard to draw, and the much more general point I want to make is that with the decline in conspicuous consumption—a relative rather than an absolute decline perhaps—has come a great rise in what we might call conspicuous production.

As I have implied earlier, the company for which Willy Loman worked did not engage in conspicuous production—else they would have kept him on, finding a place for him in overhead. The companies that do engage in it begin by locating and designing their plants and offices for show as well as for "efficiency" in the older sense of nearness to suppliers, distributors, and other facilities. It would be interesting to know to what extent the immense tax-facilitated rebuilding of American industry since World War II has been influenced by management's desire to have a plant that looked like the *Fortune* ads of the Austin Company and other designers of low-slung, "streamlined" factories. To be sure, if such factories are good for morale, they are by definition efficient, but the Hawthorne experiments are some evidence that workers respond more to interest taken in them than to lighting, cooling, or other circumambient factors—very likely, such factories are good for executives' and directors' morale. (These experiments were made nearly a generation ago.)

Conspicuous production takes a great variety of forms. If a company leads the procession in granting paid vacations or in providing some new service for employees—that may be partly conspicuous production. Many additions to overhead both constitute such production and spend time advertising it—even some incumbents of the president's chair may have that as their principal role. Officials, who would no longer be as eager as their predecessors were to buy their way into an exclusive country club, suburb, or resort, are most eager to have their companies' ads appear in the pages of *Business Week*, *Fortune*, or on television, whether or not their market research can wholly justify each instance of space- or time-buying. I understand that some large companies have issued manuals to their officials on how to live up to their expense accounts, and we may properly regard such manuals as successors to all the educative literature by which previous ruling groups have been taught to spend—something which, strange as it may seem to some of you, needs always to be learned.

Professor Richard Hofstadter has suggested that these practices should be called conspicuous corporate consumption rather than conspicuous production. Certainly, it is as difficult to distinguish one from the other as to distinguish work from play among many of the managerial work-force. It would take a very close scrutiny of factory lay-out, for instance, to be sure what changes were the result of desires for corporate prestige rationalized as cost-cutting methods, and to know whether to allocate the costs of prestige itself to the production or the consumption side of the ledger. The aesthetics of the machines of production, factories and plants express a slightly different kind of conspicuous production. It is only when we adopt an "economizing" point of view that we can distinguish, in the activities centered around the economy, between the end of maximizing the product and the other ends, ceremonial, religious, prestige-laden, that are contextually being pursued. The conspicuousness of these other ends is the result, as Professor Martin Meyerson has pointed out to me, of our taking for granted as the sole end of work that of maximizing product—from that distorted, if traditional, perspective other ends embedded in the context of social life appear out of order, even garish. Men who in the 19th century or today seem to be pursuing wealth or efficiency as a single uncomplicated goal were certainly self-deceived as to their total gamut of motives. Nevertheless we can say, I think, that corporate consumption, in which each company goes into business as a junior welfare state, does currently rearrange our motives in a new configuration.

One factor, as I have already indicated, is the increasing professionalization of management, a development which has had consequences rather different from those Brandeis or Taylor hoped for. The 18th- and 19th-century industrialist came out of a rural background or ideology: he regarded his firm as a farm, and his work-force as hired hands, often transient and easily replaced, or as a small-town business, paternalistically run. He did not think of himself as having to be an expert on human relations—that could be left to the clergy, the main professionals in his purview. Feeling, moreover, some doubt as to where he stood socially, vis-a-vis the clergy and vis-a-vis Eastern aristocrats, he built a big feudal castle of a house for himself to show everybody that he had arrived, as if to declaim that he was personally worthy by visible evidences of his net worth: if he could not outshout the clergyman and the statesman, he could at least outshine them. And his wife, lacking the cultural tutelage of aristocratic wives and excluded by patriarchal convention from any contact with the workaday world, had nothing more to occupy her than to act as his deputy in conspicuous spending, his ambassador to the dominions of culture he was too busy and too bored to bother with.

Such an industrialist, when he met his competitors, frankly regarded them as such, and whatever conviviality he might show, he kept his secrets of production to himself. He met with others, that is, in terms of money, not in terms of a specialized profession which freely exchanges its own secrets while keeping them from the lay public. Today, the communication of industrialists and businessmen with one another is frequently quite different. Meeting as professionals, the former individuality which distinguished the American businessman is rubbed off. He seeks status in his ability to run a smooth, attractive, and pleasant social and technological organization. Unions obviously have done something to encourage this, and so has government, in its tax and labor policy, but the desire of businessmen themselves to become professionals in human relations seems to be a major element.

And their wives, too, have changed. If they are college trained, it isn't enough for them to spend their husband's income. Often they have had jobs themselves; they may be professionals in their own right, or potential professionals. They want to become pals and companions of their business spouses—sleeping partners, so to speak—aware of what goes on at work, and vicarious consumers of corporate conspicuousness, flaunting not so much their own now-standardized fur coats but their husband's firms—a more indirect display. Both husband and wife are urban, not small-town and rural, in their orientation; and they tend to view the factory work-force as a human collectivity in which there are roles to be played and maneuvers to be made. The earlier 19th-century horrors of rapid urbanization, in which human relations tended to become depersonalized and older social groupings disintegrated, now appear to be giving way to new institutional forms adapted to the conditions of contemporary city life. The presence of women on this scene, in fact or in feeling, helps alter the atmosphere, introducing a consumption mood into work relations, with its refreshing congeniality of association as contrasted with a male society of tycoons.

The divorce of corporate ownership from control and the consequent disenfranchisement of the stockholders (plus federal tax policies) have put responsibility for spending the corporate surplus on the executive in his capacity as an official, for corporate savings are only to a limited extent distributed to stockholders but are increasingly retained in depreciation funds or other concealment or reserve accounts. Business management schools play a part in deciding what it is that the corporation should now spend money for—whether it is for training directors, or market research, or philanthropic activity (which now supports much "pure" research)—all the multifarious forms of conspicuous corporate consumption.

In general, I think it can be said that many of the motives which were in earlier decades built into the character structure of individuals are now built into the institutional structure of corporate life. On the whole, I would rather see our surplus used to allow individuals a still greater amount of leisure, so that each of us would work, let us say, a four-hour day, than keep us at work eight hours so that our large organizations can generously spend the difference. And yet, in making such a judgment, I know I must continuously keep in mind the complex and stratified nature of the changes going on in our American life. If I had to choose between having Lever Brothers spend the American surplus on its beautiful Park Avenue offices and having the Happy Lomans and Glenn McCarthys spend it, I could easily come down on the side of Lever Brothers. Corporate consumption may be, as it has often been in architecture, a pleasure in its own right and sometimes a model for individual consumption.

15. Recreation and the Recreationist

§ I

As I was reflecting on our coming meeting, there came into my hands an article by Aileen Ross on the development of philanthropy in a Canadian city, which showed how from small amateur beginnings, the running of campaigns had become a professional job handled with increasing skill and cynicism on the part of the insiders—the designers of letterheads; the spearheads of the Special Gifts Committee; the full-time planners of other people's short-time bursts of energy and masochism—and with increasing apathy by the rank-and-file. I was thinking, too, about the notion, put forward in a recent book by Kenneth Boulding, that the most significant invention of modern times is the invention of the full-time organizer. The organizer moves in with his trained energy and skill, reminds people of identities and of needs they had only barely felt before, and builds a job for himself or somebody else as executive secretary. The full-time organizer is the answer our society has given to the problems created by rapid social change; the formula might be put this way: where the organizer is, disorganization was.

The trouble with the full-time organizer, however, is that he is apt to want not only a full-time job for a short time, but a life-time career. This means that he has a stake in the dependency of those he organizes. In the recreation field, he may want to do more than make facilities available to people, through books, magazines, and other media as well as in person; he may want to establish a group of clients who can't get along without him. I have watched this happening in the "field" of old age where, instead of trying to help young and middle-aged people prepare for old age by widening their leisure horizons, many spend much energy painfully organizing Golden Age clubs which turn the existing group of elderly people into the first wave of a permanent clientele. And we have all seen what has happened to teaching when the teachers' colleges and professional bodies forced those who entered it to make a career commitment, which has meant expulsion from teaching of those gifted amateurs for whom it could be a way-station on the road to something else, and has also meant that those who were in it for good were highly vulnerable to colleague pressures for conformity and not stirring up anything. It would be tragic if the still embryonic field of recreation should similarly become so professionalized that, for instance, able sociology graduates couldn't take a hand in it for a time, and then go on to something else (as my colleague Everett Hughes worked for the Chicago Park District while a student and learned thereby some of the ways in which different ethnic and class groups in Chicago like to amuse themselves, get married, and fight). Since recreation at its best depends a great deal on adaptability, spontaneity and enthusiasm, the field needs particularly to remain open at both ends, so that people can leave it and do something else, without feeling that there must be a loss of all ties, and can enter it either early or late in life without encountering restrictive barriers. The full-time organizers in the field can perhaps question the wisdom of giving up all claim to amateur standing, and come to think of themselves as a semi-permanent cadre, constantly bringing in short-term people.

§ II

THE FULL-TIME ORGANIZER, however, not only solves the problems of others but is a problem for himself. In this he is simply human. He wants to have people around who share his professionalization and the detachment this gives him, and with whom he can discuss his most intimate career concerns, share his "trade secrets," and get the news and gossip of colleagues. Since his clients constitute his major source of headaches, he can obviously not talk over his concerns with them; with them, he must maintain a front of piety, or permissiveness, or omniscience, or whatever else is the going mode of impressing clients in that line of work. He may find an audience in his wife, but she is not likely to fully understand a new business such as the one he is in, and he may in any case want to bring her his problems of play rather than his problems of work. Thus, the drive for professionalization among full-time organizers is in part a drive to regularize a colleague grouping, a drive to create a setting in which one is "understood."

But there is another sense in which the professional wants to be understood, in which what he really wants is to be appreciated, to have recognition and status for what he does. It is not only that he wants to impress clients, but he wants to impress himself, to feel he belongs, has a place; that he really exists and is not a figment of his own fertile imagination. When we are very young, we are apt to be asked: "How old are you, little man," and when we get out of school, we are asked: "What do you do for a living?" We want in the second case as in the first to make a self-evident answer, so that if, for instance, we reply that we are "in group work," we won't be asked, "Well, what the hell is that?" Recognition is, in fact, something to which the full-time organizer has every reason to be preternaturally sensitive, since he has to make his way not within a traditional going concern but within the very area which is to employ him and give him scope. He needs recognition outside the community in which he works in order to strengthen his hand inside, and so he devotes part of his effort to organizing his colleagues horizontally as well as his clients vertically.

The question still remains, however, as to who is to be admitted to, and who excluded from, the colleague group. How is one to draw the line between recreation as the "recreationist" sees it and the many different "industries" which contribute to the recreational side of life? Let me take, as an illustration, a traveling organizer of Columbia Concerts, or some similar service, who goes out to communities and organizes their previously dormant musical interests so that they will support a winter series of six or eight concerts. This person is adding to the recreational facilities directly and indirectly; for instance, many women will be led to spend their leisure as local volunteer helpers to put the concerts over; and the concerts may themselves stimulate local musical enterprises. Such concerts typically involve as many family members as can be persuaded to go, and the music offered is geared to a set of compromises between the musical tastes and fancies of young and old. The concerts may stimulate record sales—and vice versa—and perhaps the owner of the record shop should be viewed as a recreationist.

To take another example, the local movie theatre owner is certainly a recreationist, and if he is intelligent and public-spirited, he can play a not inconsiderable role in providing films for the family as a unit. With the ban on block-booking, he has come to have not inconsiderable power over the choice of individual films. I once knew a theatre manager in Brattleboro, Vermont, who regularly showed "art" and moderately highbrow films which he knew would lose $500 a run, because as he said he got tired of the usual stuff and figured he owed this to himself. Many of the films he got in this way provide a tight conversational web between parents and children, whereas other types of films either stratify the audience age-wise (and also, of course, in other respects) or bring the parents simply as bored guardians of the children or bring the children because the parents couldn't find a sitter. (I might express here in passing my prejudice against the drive-in theatre. It seems to me to have contributed to recreation within the family at the expense of the communal quality of an audience, being in this much like television. In a hall, one is aware of others being there. The quality is different; it is more festive. In the same way, I prefer to eat at restaurants rather than have food brought out to my car—but perhaps in this I am being merely old-fashioned.)

The theatre manager has another kind of power, in the voice the exhibitor has over the studios and the large distributing chains. He is the grass root which Hollywood sucks, and his comments are taken very seriously. If he says that Katie Hepburn in a film on tennis is box-office poison, he is going to make it hard for directors to make Katie Hepburn films, or they will try to change Katie Hepburn's style. And he in turn is vulnerable to local pressures. One theatre manager in Chicago told me that he was going to show no more Italian films because a local American Legion post had protested that it was "un-American." The recreationist who has a vision of the total leisure culture of his area will want to try to make an ally of this exhibitor, and to support him against both his own worst impulses and those of the pressure groups around him.

I am sure that a careful inventory would discover that any number of recreationists exist who do not realize their membership in a larger fraternity. And I think there is a good deal to be gained by the non-commercial recreationists from bringing them in. I belong to one professional group, the American Association for Public Opinion Research, whose meetings are worth attending because they bring together in one organization academic and governmental and business people concerned with opinion. To have market researchers and professors in the same outfit is stimulating to both—provided mutual defensiveness is not too great. The professors get to be a little more worldly, the market research people a little more curious about long-run developments. It may be that the analogy does not hold, and that camp directors and playground supervisors would find too little in common with the bowling-alley proprietor, the movie operator, the concert business manager, the bookseller, the sports promoters and pros.

I recall in this connection the feeling many educational broadcasters seem to have towards commercial radio and TV. Instead of looking for allies there, and finding here and there a program which, though not piously billed as "educational," actually stimulates the imagination and liberates a round of good family talk, they see the commercial broadcaster as the enemy almost by definition. Not recognizing in many cases the forms taken by their own commercialism under the disguise of an anti-commercial crusade, they draw an artificial line between private and public. . . . These are at least some cautionary themes which I would bear in mind before getting the profession of recreationist organized in such a way as to cut itself off from people who are not on a governmental or philanthropic payroll, but whose potentialities for a creative view of their work should not be underestimated.

§ III

NOW I WANT to turn to another set of misgivings, which are based less on the problem of professional boundaries as such and more on the ambiguity of the relation between recreation and public supervision. The recreationist, when he looks at other people's play, finds it hard to escape some of the biases the social worker is apt to have when he looks at other people's budgets, or the housing official when he looks at other people's accommodations. The latter, for example, when designing new housing or setting up standards for old tenements, is likely to give more space to cleanliness and less to cooking than a lower-class Italian or Polish family might choose if left to its own devices. He may without knowing it cramp the family's recreation, traditionally stove-oriented, in favor of the bathroom. (I don't mean to overlook the value of the bathroom as a cubicle of privacy in our society, provided the planner knows his clients' needs in this respect.) The social worker may feel it is extravagant for a slum family to buy a TV set on time, and fail to appreciate that the set is exactly the compensation for sub-standard housing the family can best appreciate—and in the case of Negroes or poorly dressed people, or the sick, an escape from being embarrassed in public amusement places. Likewise, the recreationist—especially if he comes out of a sports and camping background—may insist too much on getting families out to play in the open, and stress too little the solidarity a family can gain simply by dining out. Any of you who have seen a whole family, in its Sunday best, fighting away at lobsters at a seafood place with a sawdust floor, will recognize what I mean; such feasts may be no less important as a family ritual—and the similar feasts held at home—than the more muscular activities organized by school and park people.

At the same time, I believe that recreation people need to be very careful lest they place too much of a premium on families being together as such. John Crosby remarked in a recent column (about the TV program "Private Secretary"): "This is what is known as family entertainment, which I guess means it's designed to bore the whole family rather than entertain one section of it." We should not assume that keeping the family together for recreation is a good to be gained at the sacrifice of sharpness and vitality. However, there are, of course, ways it can be done that do not have this watering down effect. I think, for instance, of the Decca album of some years ago called "Saturday Night at Tom Benton's," a pot-pourri of Tom, his wife, and son playing the harmonica, guitar, and flute respectively, to the accompaniment of a harpsichordist, folk singers, and other stray instrumentalists. It is all the more entertaining and dramatic as a family experience because others are present, allowing each member of the family to see the other in new and inventive roles. And this includes the little daughter, Jessie, who, in Tom Benton's cover for the album, stands looking on at all the doings—a recreationist might not define her as an active participant, but she is surely taking it all in.

In this connection, perhaps one main problem of the recreationist, as of the teacher, is to see that children and parents are neither brought together nor pulled apart in their leisure behavior by undue adult moralizing. If there is too much pious censorship of film-fare, some of the family are going to get their fancy fantasies somewhere else, perhaps surreptitiously. If the culture of the school and the culture of the street connect in no way with one another, the children are likely to find the street unduly exciting and the school a fraud. Certainly, some dichotomy there will always be. The family never can, and never should, become a "company town" controlling all aspects of its members' lives and budgets. It is a question of degree, the degree to which adult and child worlds can communicate—even communicate hostility— in the dramatized forms of recreational activity. I am pretty sure that the movies made by the Stephen Basutow group, such as "Gerald McBoing Boing" and "Mr. Magoo," have bridged parent-child hiatuses in a way that neither party alone could have done, just as I have found films and novels that could tell my children things which I am glad I don't have to.

Very likely, the best thing we can do for many families is to give its members vacations from each other, by introducing them to wider friendship constellations, or helping them form what Nelson Foote terms "quasi-families," those groupings of elected uncles and grand-parents and cousins who are so characteristic of a mobile, urban so-ciety. There is a lot to be said for putting children fairly young into boarding school, or sending them to camp or on visits and trips, if for no other reason than that when they come home the reunion is both gay and intense; moreover, teen-agers can sometimes reveal themselves by letter-writing as they cannot do orally. And by the same token, I am inclined to think there is much to be said for periodic separation of sexes, in school and camp and later life; for here, too, reunions can be glamorous and more highly ritualized. I suspect that this goes against the grain of such a group as this, which prides itself on its informality and an easy familiarity between all sexes and all ages. But I am not convinced that good family life depends more on familiarity than it does on novelty and rhythm in relationships.

On the whole, it is probably easier for the recreationist to deal with people in groups, whether family groups or peer-groups. They take up less room, and perhaps need fewer facilities. But these considerations of material may be strengthened by the recreationist's own bias in favor of groups as such—he is apt to think of himself as a group worker, a facilitator of group enterprises and skills: after all, he has chosen a profession that means "working with people." In dealing with the many underorganized sectors of American life—the many isolated adults and deprived children—this professional bias is useful, but it needs to be guarded against in those sectors of American life where play outside the group is already under extreme pressure. We can perhaps remind ourselves how great this pressure is by asking whether such a poem as the following could be written today (at least without leading to a therapist's door!), and whether something very important in the valuation and protection of privacy is not now in danger:

> The "last man"—so I've heard it said—
> Will find his situation frightful;
> With all the other people dead;
> But *I* should think twould be delightful;
> There's nothing I'd enjoy
> Like being the last boy.
>
> That candy-store just up the street—
> I wouldn't lose a single minute
> In choosing what I'd like to eat,
> And spending several hours in it;
> With nobody to say
> I mustn't do that way.
>
> I'd go and visit all the shops,
> And fill my pockets—fill them, mainly,
> With little guns, and kites, and tops,
> And other things I've teased for vainly,
> And nobody would care,
> If nobody was there!
>
> I'd never go to bed—for then
> There'd be no horrid nurse to take me;
> I'd never go to school again:
> There wouldn't be a soul to make me:
> There's nothing I'd enjoy
> Like being the last boy.
>
> From *Slate-and-Pencil People*
> Verses by Emma A. Opper
> Frederick A. Stokes and Brother
> New York, 1885

§ IV

ONE MORAL of all this for me is that the recreationist needs to think of himself, less as the vanguard of a movement for the more participative use of leisure—long-term developments in our economy and culture are taking care of that—and more as a facilitator and stimulator, encouraging tie-ins with already existing activities. Thus, he may be living in Kansas City and discover that a TV show in Chicago is creating interest in the art galleries, and he may want to persuade the TV station in Kansas City to use that show in cooperation with the Art Museum; a telephone and a letterhead may be all the equipment he needs. On the whole, I should think it a good rule of thumb that the smaller his personnel budget and capital budget the better, lest he get a vested interest in a passing phase of play and recreation—an area whose very virtue lies in its fluidity. It may turn out that the community needs a tavern with tables for husband and wife groups more than it needs an adult education center; or a good supermarket more than a swimming pool. In fact, one of the most striking developments in family life in recent years appears to be the practice of husband and wife shopping together for groceries and staples, as one can see them of a Saturday morning, or of an evening in those shopping centers that have sparked and followed the new trend by staying open until nine or ten or even until midnight. Involved in this change are many things: the husband's shortened hours, and lengthened pocketbook (which has also influenced the superior design of the store itself) which makes purchasing an exercise in prodigality rather than in consumer's research; the self-service supermarket which does not demand good connections with the clerk to get waited on or with the butcher to get steak; ease in parking, which permits the family to come for the price of one; above all, perhaps, the modern middle-class families' re-arrangement of pleasures and duties which encourage bringing the husband in on what used to be the wife's private preserves. It would, I am inclined to think, be a muscle-bound recreationist who would think these evening or week-end shoppers were not engaged in recreation because the facilities they patronized were not labeled as a resort or park or camping-ground.

§ V

I AM NOT SAYING THIS, it should be clear, to urge the recreationist to follow majority vote, and if more dollars vote for a supermarket than a park, not to build or staff a park. There are many situations, many communities, where the majority can take care of itself, and where facilities for the minority may be the significant area of influence for the recreationist. It is a form of unrewarded sellout for the public receationist—or librarian or broadcaster—to worry too much about how many people patronize his facility. I know that librarians, for instance, are often under pressure from their boards as well as from their own success-ethic, to turn the library into a kind of road-show, hauling customers in by public-relations stunts and catering to the large mystery-reading public (who could just as well buy pocket-books) at the expense of the few active library-users in town who depend on the library for their emotional lifeblood. I remember talking to the chief librarian of a small Western city about this. Her board judged her effectiveness by a traffic-count of the number of people she could entice into her premises, while it seemed to her that it was a more important function to sustain the intellectual life of the few ranchers and professional people who depended on books for communication with the great world beyond. Of course, if there is money enough to go round, such choices do not have to be made, but for the time being—I needn't tell you!—the budget will compel clarity in evaluating alternative facilities. And I suggest that we be not too frightened of the label of snobbery when we insist on providing leisure funds for those who want to do the rare and infrequent thing, whether that means taking out the book that is seldom used, or going to the camping spot accessible only to the young, spry, and moderately well-off. Indeed, so fast do American leisure habits change that what is rare today becomes a mass activity tomorrow, as we have seen happen in our generation with horseback riding, tennis, boating, record-collecting, painting, gourmandizing, ballet dancing, and a host of other pursuits.

The matter of budgets for leisure raises one final consideration. Such economists as Colin Clark have espoused the view that as an industrial society moves into a plateau of high mechanization and high labor productivity, more and more of the workforce comes to be employed in what he terms the "tertiary" industries—the service trades, including those catering to leisure. Those require, in comparison with manufacturing and transport, little capital plant but many workers. Think, for instance, of the beauty shop, both in terms of what it does for recreation—for the housewife who can escape from her children, telephone, bill-collectors, and sit under a dryer with her conscience appeased by the ads that make beauty a duty—and what it does for employment. Economists are now concerned with what may happen to the national income if and when military spending tapers off; they emphasize the vast increase in capital plant and the great rise in installment buying as indicating that private spending cannot easily take up the slack. Here is the point at which an Office of Recreation might come forward with plans for a great increase in recreational facilities and personnel, as a means at once of maintaining reasonably full employment and reasonably full family life. I am inclined to think, as I've already indicated, that these facilities and personnel should perhaps preferably not be public, but privately owned and publicly encouraged; although in a severe recession it may turn out that a "Play Progress Administration" rather than a WPA will be necessary to spend the money fast enough. Consequently, while some of us will remain as private tutors in effective spending, I am inclined to think it makes sense for others to make their voices heard when decisions are being made as to how to spend the national surplus no longer on the common defense of life and liberty but on the common pursuit of happiness.

16. Football in America:
A Study in Culture Diffusion*

* With Reuel Denney.

§ I

On OCTOBER 9, 1951, Assistant Attorney General Graham Morrison instituted an anti-trust action against a number of universities on account of their efforts to limit TV broadcasts of their games—efforts dictated by the terrible burdens of what we might speak of as "industrialized football." This action occurred only a few weeks after the scandal of the West Point student firings, which, along with the William and Mary palace revolution, indicated that football was indeed reaching another crisis in its adaptation to the ever-changing American environment. Small colleges such as Milligan—a church-supported school in the mountains of Eastern Tennessee—were discovering that football was now so mechanized that they could no longer afford the necessary entry fee for machinery and personnel. Last year, Milligan spent $17,000, or two-thirds of its whole athletic budget—and did not get it all back in the box-office net. Football had come to resemble other industries or mechanized farms, into which a new firm could not move by relying on an institutional lifetime of patient saving and plowing back of profits, but only by large corporate investment. The production of a team involves the heavy overhead and staff personnel characteristic of high-capital, functionally rationalized industries, as the result of successive changes in the game since its post-Civil-War diffusion from England.[1]

It would be wrong, however, to assert that football has become an impersonal market phenomenon. Rather, its rationalization as a sport and as a spectacle has served to bring out more openly the part it plays in the ethnic, class, and characterological struggles of our time—meaning, by "characterological struggle," the conflict between differ-

---

1. The growing scale of college football is indicated by its dollar place in the American leisure economy. In 1929, out of $4.3 billion recreation expenditures by Americans, the college football gate accounted for $22 million. In 1950, out of $11.2 billion in such expenditures, it accounted for $103 million. While something less than 1% of the total United States recreation account, college football had ten times the gross income of professional football. The 1950 gate of $103 million suggests that a total capital of perhaps $250 million is invested in the college football industry. The revenue figures, above, of course, do not include the invisible subsidization of football, nor do they hint at the place that football pools occupy in the American betting economy.

ent styles of life. The ethnic significance of football is immediately
suggested by the shift in the typical origins of player-names on the
All-American Football Teams since 1889. In 1889, all but one of the
names (Heffelfinger) suggested Anglo-Saxon origins. The first name
after that of Heffelfinger to suggest non-Anglo-Saxon recruitment
was that of Murphy, at Yale, in 1895. After 1895, it was a rare All-
American team that did not include at least one Irishman (Daly,
Hogan, Rafferty, Shevlin); and the years before the turn of the century saw entrance of the Jew. On the 1904 team appeared Pierkarski,
of Pennsylvania. By 1927, names like Casey, Kipke, Oosterbaan, Kop-
pisch, Garbisch, and Friedman were appearing on the All-American
lists with as much frequency as names like Channing, Adams, and Ames
in the 1890's.

While such a tally does little more than document a shift that most
observers have already recognized in American football, it raises questions that are probably not answerable merely in terms of ethnic origins of players. There is an element of class identification running
through American football since its earliest days, and the ethnic
origins of players contain ample invitations to the making of theory
about the class dimensions of football. Most observers would be inclined to agree that the arrival of names like Kelley and Kipke on
the annual All-American list was taken by the Flanagans and the
Webers as the achievement of a lower-class aspiration to be among
the best at an upper-class sport. The question remains: what did the
achievement mean? What did it mean at different stages in the development of the game? Hasn't the meaning worn off in the fifty-odd
years, the roughly two generations since Heffelfinger and Murphy
made the grade?

There are many ways to begin an answer to such questions, and
here we can open only a few lines of investigation. Our method is
to study the interrelations between changes in the rules of the game
(since the first intercollegiate contest: Rutgers, 6 goals—Princeton,
4 goals, in 1869) and to analyze the parallel changes in football strategy
and ethos. All these developments are to be seen as part of a configuration that includes changes in coaching, in the training of players,
and in the no less essential training of the mass audience.

Since football is a cultural inheritance from England, such an analysis may be made in the perspective of other studies in cultural
diffusion and variation. Just as the French have transformed American
telephone etiquette while retaining some of its recognizable physical
features, so Americans have transformed the games of Europe even
when, as in track or tennis, the formalities appear to be unaltered.
Even within the Western industrial culture, there are great varieties.

on a class and national basis, in the games, rules, strategy, etiquette, and audience structures of sport. In the case of college football—we shall leave aside the symbolically less important professional game—the documentation of sportswriters (themselves a potent factor in change) allows us to trace the stages of development.

§ II

A STUDY OF Anatolian peasants now under way at the Bureau of Applied Social Research indicates that these highly tradition-bound people cannot grasp the abstractness of modern sports. They lack the enterprise, in their fatalistic village cultures, to see why people want to knock themselves out for sportmanship's remote ideals; they cannot link such rituals, even by remote analogy, with their own. These peasants are similarly unable to be caught up in modern politics, or to find anything meaningful in the Voice of America. Nevertheless, football itself, like so many other games with balls and goals, originated in a peasant culture.

Football, in its earliest English form, was called the Dane's Head and it was played in the tenth and eleventh centuries as a contest in kicking a ball between towns. The legend is that the first ball was a skull, and only later a cow's bladder. In some cases, the goals were the towns themselves, so that a team entering a village might have pushed the ball several miles en route. King Henry II (1154-89) proscribed the game, on the ground that it interfered with archery practice. Played in Dublin even after the ban, football did not become respectable or legal until an edict of James I reinstated it. The reason was perhaps less ideological than practical: firearms had made the art of bowmanship obsolete.

During the following century, football as played by British schoolboys became formalized, but did not change its fundamental pattern of forceful kicking. In 1823, Ellis of Rugby made the mistake of picking up the ball and running with it towards the goal. All concerned thought it a mistake: Ellis was sheepish, his captain apologetic. The mistake turned into innovation when it was decided that a running rule might make for an interesting game. The localism, pluralism, and studied casualness of English sports made it possible to try it out without securing universal assent—three or four purely local variants of football, football-hazing and "wall games" are still played in various English schools. Rugby adopted "Rugby" in 1841, several years after Cambridge had helped to popularize it.[2]

---

2. A commemorative stone at Rugby reads as follows:
THIS STONE
COMMEMORATES THE EXPLOIT OF

This establishment of the running or Rugby game, as contrasted with the earlier, kicking game, had several important results. One was that the old-style players banded themselves together for the defense of their game, and formed the London Football Association (1863). This name, abbreviated to "Assoc," appears to have been the starting point for the neologism, "Soccer," the name that the kicking game now goes by in many parts of the English-speaking world. A second result was that the English, having found a new game, continued to play it without tight rules until the Rugby Union of 1871. As we shall see, this had its effects on the American game. The third and most important result of Ellis' "mistake," of course, was that he laid the foundations for everything fundamental about the American game between about 1869 and the introduction of the forward pass. (The forward pass is still illegal in Rugby and closely related football games.)

§ III

IN THE COLONIAL PERIOD and right down to the Civil War, Americans played variants on the kicking football game on their town greens and schoolyards. After the war, Yale and Harvard served as the culturally receptive importers of the English game. Harvard, meeting McGill in a game of Rugby football in 1874, brought the sport to the attention of collegiate circles and the press—two identifications important for the whole future development of the game. But if Harvard was an opinion leader, Yale was a technological one. A Yale student who had studied at Rugby was instrumental in persuading Yale men to play the Rugby game and was, therefore, responsible for some of Yale's early leadership in the sport.

It happened in the following way, according to Walter Camp and Lorin F. Deland.[3] The faculty in 1860, for reasons unknown, put a stop to interclass matches of the pre-Rugby variety. "During the following years, until 1870, football was practically dead at Yale. The class of '72, however, was very fond of athletic sports, and participated especially in long hare and hound runs. The revival of football was due in a large measure to Mr. D. S. Schaft, formerly of Rugby School, who entered the class of '73 and succeeded in making the

WILLIAM WEBB ELLIS
WHO WITH A FINE DISREGARD FOR THE RULES OF
FOOTBALL, AS PLAYED IN HIS TIME,
FIRST TOOK THE BALL IN HIS ARMS AND RAN WITH IT,
THUS ORIGINATING THE DISTINCTIVE FEATURE OF
THE RUGBY GAME
A. D. 1823

3. Walter Camp and Lorin F. Deland, *Football*.

sport popular among his classmates, and eventually formed an association which sent challenges to the other classes."

Soon after the period described by Camp, it became clear that American players, having tasted the "running" game, were willing to give up the soccer form. It became equally clear that they either did not want to, or could not, play Rugby according to the British rules. "The American players found in this code [English Rugby Rules] many uncertain and knotty points which caused much trouble in their game, especially as they had no traditions, or older and more experienced players, to whom they could turn for the necessary explanations," says Camp. An example of such a problem was English rule number nine:

"A touchdown is when a player, putting his hand on the ball in touch or in goal, stops it so that it remains dead, or fairly so."

The ambiguity of the phrase "fairly so" was increased by the statement in rule number eight that the ball is dead "when it rests absolutely motionless on the ground."

Camp's description of these early difficulties is intensely interesting to the student of cultural diffusion not only because of what Camp observed about the situation, but also because of what he neglected to observe. Consider the fact that the development of Rugby rules in England was accomplished by admitting into the rules something that we would call a legal fiction. While an offensive runner was permitted to carry the ball, the condition of his doing so was that he should *happen* to be standing behind the swaying "scrum" (the tangled players) at the moment the ball popped back out to him. An intentional "heel out" of the ball was not permitted; and the British rules of the mid-nineteenth century appear to take it for granted that the difference between an intentional and an unintentional heel-out would be clear to everyone. Ellis' mistake became institutionalized— but still as a mistake. This aspect of Rugby rule-making had important implications for the American game.

British players, according to tradition as well as according to rules, could be expected to tolerate such ambiguity as that of the heel-out rule just as they tolerated the ambiguity of the "dead" ball. They could be expected to tolerate it not only because of their personal part in developing new rules but also (a point we shall return to) because they had an audience with specific knowledge of the traditions to assist them. In America it was quite another matter to solve such problems. No Muzafer Sherif was present[4] to solidify the perceptions of "nearly so," and the emotional tone for resolving such question

---

4. Cf. his *An Outline of Social Psychology*, pp. 93-182.

without recurrent dispute could not be improvised. Rather, however, than dropping the Rugby game at that point, because of intolerance for the ambiguities involved, an effort was undertaken, at once systematic and gradual, to fill in by formal procedures the vacuum of etiquette and, in general, to adapt the game to its new cultural home.

The upshot of American procedure was to assign players to the legalized task of picking up and tossing the ball back out of scrimmage. This in turn created the rôle of the center, and the centering operation. This in turn led to a variety of problems in defining the situation as one of "scrimmage" or "non-scrimmage," and the whole question of the legality of passing the ball back to intended runners. American football never really solved these problems until it turned its attention, in 1880, to a definition of the scrimmage itself. The unpredictable English "scrum" or scramble for a free ball was abandoned, and a crude line of scrimmage was constructed across the field. Play was set in motion by snapping the ball. Meanwhile Americans became impatient with long retention of the ball by one side. It was possible for a team that was ahead in score to adopt tactics that would insure its retention of the ball until the end of the period. By the introduction of a minimum yardage-gain rule in 1882, the rulemakers assured the frequent interchange of the ball between sides.

The effect of this change was to dramatize the offensive-defensive symmetry of the scrimmage line, to locate it sharply in time ("downs"), and to focus attention not only on the snapping of the ball, but also on the problem of "offside" players. In the English game, with no spatially and temporally delimited "line of scrimmage," the offside player was penalized only by making him neutral in action until he could move to a position back of the position of the ball. In the American game, the new focus on centering, on a scrimmage line, and on yardage and downs, created the need for a better offside rule. From that need developed offside rules that even in the early years resembled the rules of today. American rulemakers were logically extending a native development when they decided to draw an imaginary line through the ball before it had been centered, to call this the "line of scrimmage," and to make this line, rather than the moving ball itself, the offside limit in the goalward motion of offensive players. At first, lined-up players of the two sides were allowed to stand and wrestle with each other while waiting for the ball to be centered; only later was a neutral zone introduced between the opposing lines.

Even with such a brief summary of the rule changes, we are in a position to see the operation of certain recurrent modes or patterns of adaptation. The adaptation begins with the acceptance of a single pivotal innovation (running with the ball). The problems of adaptation begin with the realization that this single innovation has been uprooted from a rich context of meaningful rules and traditions, and does not work well in their absence. Still more complex problems of adaptation develop when it is realized that the incompleteness of the adaptation will not be solved by a reference to the pristine rules. In the first place, the rules are not pristine (the English rules were in the process of development themselves). In the second place, the tradition of interpreting them is not present in experienced players. In the third place, even if it were, it might not be adaptable to the social character and mood of the adapters.

Let us put it this way. The Americans, in order to solve the heel-out problem, set in motion a redesign of the game that led ultimately to timed centering from a temporarily fixed line of scrimmage. Emphasis completely shifted from the kicking game; it also shifted away from the combined kicking and running possible under Rugby rules; it shifted almost entirely in the direction of an emphasis on ball-carrying. Meanwhile, to achieve this emphasis, the game made itself vulnerable to slowdowns caused by one team's retention of the ball. It not only lost the fluidity of the original game, but ran up against a pronounced American taste for action in sports, visible action. There is evidence that even if players had not objected to such slowdowns, the spectators would have raised a shout. The yardage rule was the way this crisis was met. This, in turn, led to an emphasis on mass play, and helped to create the early twentieth-century problems of football. But before we consider this step in the game's development we must turn to examine certain factors in the sport's audience reception.

§ IV

A PROBLEM posed for the student of cultural diffusion at this point can be stated as follows: What factor or factors appear to have been most influential in creating an American game possessing not only nationally distinct rules, but also rules having a specific flavor of intense legality about many a point of procedure left more or less up in the air by the British game?

We can now go beyond the rule-making aspect of the game and assert that the chief factor was the importance of the need to standardize rules to supply an ever-widening collegiate field of competition, along with the audience this implied. The English rule-makers, it appears, dealt with a situation in which amateur play was restricted to a fairly limited number of collegians and institutions. The power of localism was such that many an informality was tolerated, and intended to be tolerated, in the rules and their interpretation. Ameri-

can football appeared on the American campus at the beginning of a
long period in which intercollegiate and interclass sportsmanship was
a problem of ever-widening social participation and concern. Football etiquette itself was in the making. Thus, it appears that when
early American teams met, differences of opinion could not be resolved between captains in rapid-fire agreement or penny-tossing as
was the case in Britain. American teams did not delegate to their
captains the rôle of powerful comrade-in-antagonism with opposing
captains, or, if they did, they felt that such responsibilities were too
grave.[5]

Into just such situations football players thrust all of the force of
their democratic social ideologies, all their prejudice in favor of equalitarian and codified inter-player attitudes. Undoubtedly, similar considerations also influenced the audience. Mark Benney, a British sociologist who is familiar with the games played on both sides of the
Atlantic, points out that, whereas the American game was developed
in and for a student group, the English game was played before quite
large crowds who, from a class standpoint, were less homogeneous
than the players themselves, though they were as well informed as
the latter in the "law" of the game. Rugby football was seldom played
by the proletariat; it was simply enjoyed as a spectacle.

Held by the critical fascination the British upper strata had for
the lower strata, the audience was often hardly more interested in the
result of the game than in judging the players as "gentlemen in action." "The players," Mr. Benney writes, "had to demonstrate that
they were sportsmen, that they could 'take it'; and above all they had
to inculcate the (politically important) ideology that legality was
more important than power." The audience was, then, analogous to
the skilled English jury at law, ready to be impressed by obedience
to traditional legal ritual and form, and intolerant of "bad form" in
their "betters." The early Yale games, played before a tiny, nonpaying
audience, lacked any equivalent incentive to agree on a class-based
ritual of "good form," and when the audiences came later on, their
attitude towards upper-class sportsmanship was much more ambivalent
—they had played the game too, and they were unwilling to subordinate themselves to a collegiate aristocracy who would thereby have
been held to norms of correctness. The apparent legalism of many
American arguments over the rules would strike British observers as
simply a verbal power-play.

---

5. "Fifty years ago arguments followed almost every decision the referee
made. The whole team took part, so that half the time the officials scarcely knew
who was captain. The player who was a good linguist was always a priceless
asset." John W. Heisman, who played for both Brown and Penn in the 1890's,
quoted in Frank G. Menke, *Encyclopedia of Sports*, p. 293.

Such differences in the relation of the game to the audience, on this side of the Atlantic, undoubtedly speeded the development of the specifically American variant. Native, too, are the visual and temporal properties of the game as it developed even before 1900: its choreography could be enjoyed, if not always understood, by non-experts, and its atomistic pattern in time and space could seem natural to audiences accustomed to such patterns in other foci of the national life. The mid-field dramatization of line against line, the recurrent starting and stopping of field action around the timed snapping of a ball, the trend to a formalized division of labor between backfield and line, above all, perhaps, the increasingly precise synchronization of men in motion—these developments make it seem plausible to suggest that the whole procedural rationalization of the game which we have described was not unwelcome to Americans, and that it fitted in with other aspects of their industrial folkways.

Spurred by interest in the analysis of the athletic motions of men and animals, Eadweard Muybridge was setting out his movie-like action shorts of the body motion (more preoccupied even than Vesalius or da Vinci with the detailed anatomy of movement)[6] at about the same time that Coach Woodruff at Pennsylvania (1894) was exploring the possibilities for momentum play: linemen swinging into motion before the ball is snapped, with the offensive team, forming a wedge, charging toward an opposition held waiting by the offside rule. In Philadelphia, the painter Eakins, self-consciously following the tenets of Naturalism and his own literal American tradition, was painting the oarsmen of the Schuylkill. Nearby, at the Midvale plant of the American Steel Company, efficiency expert Frederick Winslow Taylor was experimenting with motion study and incentive pay geared to small measurable changes in output—pay that would spur but never soften the workman.[7]

Since we do not believe in historical inevitability, nor in the necessary homogeneity of a culture, we do not suggest that the American game of football developed as it did out of cultural compulsion and could not have gone off in quite different directions. Indeed, the very effectiveness of momentum play, as a mode of bulldozing the defense, led eventually to the rule that the line must refrain from motion before the ball is snapped. For the bulldozing led, or was thought to

6. Sigfried Giedion, *Mechanization Takes Command*, pp. 21-27.

7. In view of the prejudice against "Taylorism" today, shared by men and management as well as the intellectuals, let us record our admiration for Taylor's achievement, our belief that he was less insensitive to psychological factors than is often claimed, and more "humane" in many ways than his no less manipulative, self-consciously psychological successors.

lead, to a great increase in injuries. And while these were first coped with by Walter Camp's training table (his men had their choice of beefsteak or mutton for dinner, to be washed down with milk, ale, or sherry), the public outcry soon forced further rule changes, designed to soften the game. After a particularly bloody battle between Pennsylvania and Swarthmore in 1905, President Roosevelt himself took a hand and insisted on reform.[8]

Camp's colleague at Yale, William Graham Sumner, may well have smiled wryly at this. Summer was exhorting his students to "get capital," and cautioning them against the vices of sympathy and reformism—a theme which has given innumerable American academes a good living since—while Camp was exhorting his to harden themselves, to be stern and unafraid. In spite of them both, the reformers won out; but the end of momentum play was not the end of momentum. Rather, with an ingenuity that still dazzles, the game was gentled and at the same time speeded by a new rule favoring the forward pass. But before going on to see what changes this introduced, let us note the differences between the subjects of Sumner's and Camp's exhortations on the one hand, and Taylor's on the other.

Frederick Taylor, as his writings show, was already coming up against a work force increasingly drawn from non-Protestant lands, and seeking to engender in them a YMCA-morality, whereas Camp was inculcating the same morality into young men of undiluted Anglo-Saxon stock and middle- to upper-class origins. Not for another fifty years would the sons of Midvale prove harder, though fed on kale or spaghetti, and only intermittently, than the sons of Yale. Meanwhile, the sons of Yale had learned to spend summers as tracklayers or wheat harvesters in an effort to enlarge their stamina, moral toughness, and cross-class adventures.

---

8. "In a 1905 game between Pennsylvania and Swarthmore, the Pennsy slogan was 'Stop Bob Maxwell,' one of the greatest linesmen of all time. He was a mighty man, with amazing ability to roll back enemy plunges. The Penn players, realizing that Maxwell was a menace to their chances of victory, took 'dead aim' at him throughout the furious play.

"Maxwell stuck it out, but when he tottered off the field, his face was a bloody wreck. Some photographer snapped him, and the photo of the mangled Maxwell, appearing in a newspaper, caught the attention of the then President Roosevelt. It so angered him, that he issued an ultimatum that if rough play in football was not immediately ruled out, he would abolish it by executive edict." Frank G. Menke, *Encyclopedia of Sports*.

Notice here the influence of two historical factors on football development: one, the occupancy of the White House in 1905 by the first President of the United States who was a self-conscious patron of youth, sport, and the arts; two, the relative newness in 1905 of photographic sports coverage. Widespread increased photographic coverage of popular culture was the direct result of the newspaper policies of William Randolph Hearst, beginning about 1895.

Nevertheless, certain basic resemblances between the purposes of Taylor and those of Sumner and Camp are clearly present. In contrast with the British, the Americans demonstrated a high degree of interest in winning games and winning one's way to high production goals. The Americans, as in so many other matters, were clearly concerned with the competitive spirit that new rules might provoke and control. (British sports, like British industry, seemed to take it more for granted that competition will exist even if one does not set up an ideology for it.) Much of this seems to rest in the paradoxical belief of Americans that competition is natural—but only if it is constantly recreated by artificial systems of social rules that direct energies into it.

Back of the attitudes expressed in Taylor, Sumner, and Camp we can feel the pressure not only of a theory of competition, but also a theory of the emotional tones that ought to go along with competition. It is apparent from the brutality scandals of 1905 that President Roosevelt reacted against roughhouse not so much because it was physical violence, but for two related reasons. The first and openly implied reason was that it was connected with an unsportsmanlike attitude. The second, unacknowledged, reason was that Americans fear and enjoy their aggression at the same time, and thus have difficulty in pinning down the inner meanings of external violence. The game of Rugby as now played in England is probably as physically injurious as American football was at the turn of the century. By contrast, American attitudes toward football demonstrate a forceful need to define, limit, and conventionalize the symbolism of violence in sports.

If we look back now at England, we see a game in which shouted signals and silent counting of timed movements are unknown—a game that seems to Americans to wander in an amorphous and disorderly roughhouse. Rugby, in the very home of the industrial revolution, seems pre-industrial, seems like one of the many feudal survivals that urbanization and industrialization have altered but not destroyed. The English game, moreover, seems not to have developed anyone like Camp, the Judge Gary of football (as Rockne was to be its Henry Ford): Camp was a sparkplug in efforts to codify inter-collegiate rules; he was often the head of the important committees. His training table, furthermore, was one of the signs of the slow rise in "overhead" expense—a rise which, rather like the water in United States Steel Stock, assumed that abundance was forthcoming and bailing out probable, as against the British need for parsimony. But at the same time the rise in costs undoubtedly made American football more vulnerable than ever to public-relations considerations: the "gate" could not be damned.

§ V

THIS PUBLIC RELATIONS ISSUE in the game first appears in the actions of the rules committee of 1906—the introduction of the legalized forward pass in order to open up the game and reduce brutal power play. Between 1906 and 1913 the issue was generally treated as a problem centered about players and their coaches, and thus took the form of an appeal to principles rather than to audiences. However, the development of the high audience appeal that we shall show unfolding after 1913 was not autonomous and unheralded. If public relations became a dominant factor by 1915, when the University of Pittsburgh introduced numbers for players in order to spur the sale of programs, it had its roots in the 1905-13 period. The rules committee of 1906, by its defensive action on roughhouse rules, had already implicitly acknowledged a broad public vested interest in the ethos of the game. Let us turn to look at the speed with which football was soon permeated by broad social meanings unanticipated by the founders of the sport.

By 1913, the eve of the First World War, innovation in American industry had ceased to be the prerogative of Baptist, Calvinist, and North of Ireland tycoons. Giannini was starting his Bank of America; the Jews were entering the movies and the garment hegemonies. Yet these were exceptions, and the second generation of immigrants, taught in America to be dissatisfied with the manual work their fathers did, were seldom finding the easy paths of ascent promised in success literature. Where, for one thing, were they to go to college? If they sought to enter the older eastern institutions, would they face a social struggle? Such anxieties probably contributed to the fact that the game of boyish and spirited brawn played at the eastern centers of intellect and cultivation was to be overthrown by the new game of craft and field maneuver that got its first rehearsal at the hands of two second-generation poor boys attending little-known Notre Dame.

The more significant of the two boys, Knute Rockne, was, to be sure, of Danish Protestant descent and only later became a Catholic.[9] During their summer vacation jobs as lifeguards on Lake Michigan, Rockne and Gus Dorais decided to work as a passing team. Playing West Point early in the season of 1913, they put on the first demonstration of the spiral pass that makes scientific use of the difference in shape between the round ball used in the kicking game and the oval that gradually replaced it when ball-carrying began. As the first players to exploit the legal pass, they rolled up a surprise victory over Army. One of the effects of the national change in rules was to bring

---

9. "After the church, football is the best thing we have," Rockne.

the second-generation boys of the early twentieth century to the front, with a craft innovation that added new elements of surprise, "system" and skull-session to a game that had once revolved about an ethos of brawn plus character-building.

With the ethnic shift, appears to have come a shift in type of hero. The work-minded glamor of an all-'round craftsman like Jim Thorpe gave way to the people-minded glamor of backfield generals organizing deceptive forays into enemy territory—of course, the older martial virtues are not so much ruled out as partially incorporated in the new image. In saying this, it must not be forgotten, as sports columnist Red Smith has pointed out, that the fictional Yale hero, Dick Merriwell, is openly and shamelessly represented as a dirty player in the first chapters of his career. But the difference is that his deviation from standard sportsmanship consisted largely of slugging, not of premeditated wiliness. In fact, the Yale Era, even into Camp's reign, was characterized by a game played youthfully, with little attention to the players' prestige outside college circles. Again, the second-generationers mark a change. A variety of sources, including letters to the sports page, indicate that a Notre Dame victory became representational in a way a Yale or Harvard victory never was, and no Irish or Polish boy on the team could escape the symbolism. And by the self-confirming process, the Yale or Harvard showing became symbolic in turn, and the game could never be returned, short of intramuralization, to the players themselves and their earlier age of innocent dirtiness.[10] The heterogeneity of America which had made it impossible to play the Rugby game at Yale had finally had its effect in transforming the meaning of the game to a point where Arnold of Rugby might have difficulty in drawing the right moral or any moral from it. Its "ideal types" had undergone a deep and widespread characterological change.

For the second-generation boy, with his father's muscles but not his father's motives, football soon became a means to career ascent. So was racketeering, but football gave acceptance, too—acceptance

---

10. One of us, while a Harvard undergraduate, sought with several friends to heal the breach between Harvard and Princeton—a breach whose bitterness could hardly be credited today. The Harvards believed Princeton played dirty—it certainly won handily in those years of the 20's—while Princetonians believed themselves snubbed by Harvard as crude parvenus trying to make a trio out of the Harvard-Yale duo. The diplomatic problems involved in seeking to repair these status slights and scars were a microcosm of the Congress of Westphalia or Vienna—whether the Harvard or Princeton athletic directors should enter the room first was an issue. A leak to the Hearst press destroyed our efforts, as alumni pressure forced denials of any attempt to resume relations, but the compromise formulas worked out were eventually accepted, about the time that the University of Chicago "solved" the problem of the intellectual school by withdrawing from the game altogether.

into the democratic fraternity of the entertainment world where performance counts and ethnic origin is hardly a handicap. Moreover, Americans as onlookers welcomed the anti-traditional innovations of a Rockne, and admired the trick that worked, whatever the opposing team and alumni may have thought about the effort involved. One wonders whether Rockne and Dorais may not have gotten a particular pleasure from their craftiness by thinking of it as a counter-image to the stereotype of muscle-men applied to their fathers.

It was in 1915, at about the same time that the newcomers perfected their passing game, that the recruitment of players began in earnest. Without such recruitment, the game could not have served as a career route for many of the second generation who would not have had the cash or impetus to make the class jump that college involved.[11]

The development of the open and rationalized game has led step by step not only to the T formation, but also to the two-platoon system. These innovations call for a very different relationship among the players than was the case under the older star system. For the game is now a coöperative enterprise in which mistakes are too costly —to the head coach, the budget, even the college itself—to be left to individual initiative. At least at one institution, an anthropologist has been called in to study the morale problems of the home team, and to help in the scouting of opposing teams. To the learning of Taylor, there has been added that of Mayo, and coaches are conscious of the need to be group-dynamics leaders rather than old-line straw bosses.

Today, the semi-professionalized player, fully conscious of how many people's living depends on him, cannot be exhorted by Frank Merriwell appeals, but needs to be "handled." And the signals are no longer the barks of the first Camp-trained quarterback—hardly more differentiated than a folkdance caller's—but are cues of great subtlety and mathematical precision for situations planned in advance with camera shots and character fill-ins of the opposing team. James Worthy and other advocates of a span of control beyond the usual half-dozen of the older military and executive manuals might find support for their views in the way an eleven is managed. Industrial, military, and football teamwork have all a common cultural frame.

Yet it would be too simple to say that football has ceased to be a game for its players, and has become an industry, or a training for industry. In the American culture as a whole, no sharp line exists between work and play, and in some respects the more work-like an activity becomes, the more it can successfully conceal elements of

---

11. See George Saxon, "Immigrant Culture in a Stratified Society," *Modern Review*, II, No. 2, February 1948.

playfulness.[12] Just because the sophisticated "amateur" of today does *not* have his manhood at stake in the antique do-or-die fashion (though his manhood may be involved, in very ambivalent ways, in his more generalized rôle as athlete and teammate), there can be a relaxation of certain older demands and a more detached enjoyment of perfection of play irrespective of partisanship.

The rôle of football tutor to the audience has been pushed heavily onto radio and TV announcers (some of whom will doubtless be mobile into the higher-status rôle of commentators on politics or symphony broadcasts). The managerial coalescence of local betting pools into several big oceans has also contributed to the audience stake in the game. Yet all that has so far been said does not wholly explain alumnus and subway-alumnus loyalties. It may be that we have to read into this interest of the older age groups a much more general aspect of American behavior: the pious and near-compulsory devotion of the older folks to whatever the younger folks are alleged to find important. The tension between the generations doubtless contributes to the hysterical note of solemnity in the efforts of some older age groups to control the ethics of the game, partly perhaps as a displacement of their efforts to control youthful sexuality.

And this problem in turn leads to questions about the high percentage of women in the American football audience, compared with that of any other country, and the high salience of women in football as compared with baseball imagery (in recent American football films, girls have been singled out as the most influential section of the spectators). The presence of these women heightens the sexual impact of everything in and around the game, from shoulderpads to the star system, as the popular folklore of the game recognizes. Although women are not expected to attend baseball games, when they do attend they are expected to understand them and to acquire, if not a "male" attitude, at least something approaching companionship on a basis of equality with their male escorts.[13]

For all its involvement with such elemental themes in American life, it may be that football has reached the apex of its audience appeal. With bigness comes vulnerability: "inter-industry" competition is invited, and so are rising costs—the players, though not yet unionized, learn early in high school of their market value and, like Jim in Huckleberry Finn, take pride in it.[14] The educators' counter-reforma-

---

12. Compare the discussion of Freud's playful work, pp. 331-333, below.

13. Anthropologist Ray Birdwhistell convincingly argues that football players play with an eye to their prestige among teammates, other football players, and other men.

14. Their pride varies to some extent with their place on the team. Linemen, with the exception of ends, have lower status than backfield men. Many players

tion cannot be laughed off. With the lack of ethnic worlds to conquer, we may soon find the now-decorous Irish of the Midwest
embarrassed by Notre Dame's unbroken victories. Perhaps the period
of innovation which began in 1823 at Rugby has about come to an
end in the United States, with large changes likely to result only if
the game is used as a device for acculturation to America, not by the
vanishing stream of immigrants to that country, but by the rest of
the world that will seek the secret of American victories on the playing fields of South Bend.

---

believe that backfields are consciously and unconsciously recruited from higher
social strata than linemen.

17. Bookworms and The Social Soil

In the bringing up of children today there seems to have been a definite shift in the attitude toward what books should and do mean to a child. Ever since Lucy Sprague Mitchell started writing the "Here and Now" books, parents and teachers have been told that imaginative books and fairy tales are bad and disturbing; that they may impart false values; that in dealing with princesses and giants they are trivial and unreal. In place of such fare it is said that children should have books that will enlighten them about the world, about reality. Reality turns out to be how things work, how water gets into the bathtub, for instance, or milk onto the doorstep; the human meanness of ogres and stepmothers is definitely not reality.

More recently parents have been told that children should not read too much, that it is better for them to learn through experience and to spend their time with other children—as if life were long and varied enough to find out very much about people without the aid of the social storehouse of books and other artistic works. There has been engendered a real fear of books among the very social groups that once upheld standards of cultivation, on the grounds that books may interfere with a child's development. A psychologist recently wrote in his daily newspaper column that "a child's main interest should be in doing things not in reading about them," and he added, "Living too much in the realm of imagination retards the development of his ability to distinguish reality from daydreams." Parents are also advised not to allow children to become bookworms—they will grow up lacking personality.

In the earlier years of settlement of this country many parents had just the opposite fear. Moving from Europe or from the cultivated seaboard to the frontier, they feared that their children would become illiterates; they struggled desperately to see that their children were taught to read and that a few books, including of course the Bible, would be part of their sparse furnishings. Perhaps, indeed, it is a sign of American abundance that we can now take literacy virtually for granted and can discover some of its ambiguities for personal adjustment. But such tendencies easily become self-confirming, and if psychologists tell us that a bookworm will lack personality we will have fewer bookworms and those we have will feel on the defensive.

To be sure, not only books can disturb "adjustment." Once, doing

a study of teen-age attitudes towards music, I talked with the mother
of a fourteen-year-old boy. "John likes to practise [the piano]," she
told me, "but I don't let him play more than an hour a day. I want
to keep him a normal boy." Possibly a daughter would have been
allowed somewhat more freedom in this as in other areas of genteel
accomplishment, though on the whole girls even more than boys
would seem to be defenseless against the demand that they be adjusted. At any rate, when they grow up they do not take upon themselves the duty of reading books on behalf of the whole society;
after leaving school both boys and girls in nine cases out of ten drop
anything that could be called serious reading.

The bookworm, then, is the one person in ten who reads 70 per
cent of the books, including the pocket-size books, that are sold or
shelved in the United States. I am inclined to view these bookworms
as performing something of the same service in aerating our society
that earthworms perform for the soil. Yet worms and other invaluable contributors to the earth's ecology are sometimes considered
"varmint" by farmers, despite all the Soil Conservation Service can
do—very much as even adult bookworms are considered to be poor
personalities by some personnel managers. Fortunately, the Committee on Reading Development has set itself up as a kind of Soil Conservation Service for the field of ideas and has gone to bat on various
fronts to defend the bookworm's interests, including not only the
stimulation of research but also a lobby in Congress.

One thing seems pretty clear, namely, that books remain the least
censored of media. This is in part, I suggest, precisely because of the
smallness of their audience; as pocket books somewhat widen the
market the problem of censorship is bound to grow more acute. But
print has an old tradition to defend—older than that of movies and
radio—and it has had for many reasons less intimidated defenders.
True, minds may be closed to new ideas even if books are not. But
since people are seldom all of a piece books can usually get into
their crannies and use parts of them for leverage to open up the rest.
Books, that is, can be disturbing, disintegrating forces in people
and in society.

There is actually little evidence that the people who read the most
books have in general the fewest social contacts and hence suffer for
performing the bookworm function for the community at large.
Most studies of the audience for books and other media serve rather
to demonstrate the principle of "the more, the more." The more books
one reads, the more magazines one reads, too, the more movies one is
apt to see, and the more organizations belonged to, and so on. Books,

in spite of all I have said, still carry enough of a prestige tag so that many non-readers will tell the interviewer: "I would love to read but I have no time." Freudian implications to the contrary, if they do not have time to read they are also apt not to have time for much voluntary leisure activity of any sort.

On the whole I cannot feel that by allowing children to be book-worms one is providing for the aeration of the social soil at their emotional expense; reading is one of those functions where tragic contradictions between social and individual interest are at a minimum. But obviously this judgment depends in part on my view that "adjustment" is one of the sadder fates which can overtake a child in our society and that "integration" of personality is a somewhat doubtful ideal as usually defined—that contradiction and discontinuity of personality have to be part of any ideal which is not merely wan and flaccid.

Some people who have given thought to the problem contend that a short way to get rid both of the allegedly high price of books and of any ambiguities in being a bookworm is to go over completely to pocket books, which could be disposed of without a pang or trace as readily as a magazine, and beyond that to substitute transmission of information by facsimile for books altogether. Apparently, it is now technically feasible to scan entire libraries electronically, so that by pushing a button a "reader" could have flashed onto a television screen a series of moving images containing the capsulated information or amusement that he wanted. When these prospects struck horror into some of the more cultivated members of the publishing fraternity one of the Conference experts urged us to abandon any sentimental attachments we might have to the moss on the bucket which had previously dragged up ideas and to focus our emotional eye only on the bucket's content.

Yet it is precisely on the good-sized, hard-cover book that the bookworm is nourished. He cannot bury himself in a moving image or even, unless he is very small, in a pocket book. He is a creature who needs wide margins. For he tries to create amid all the pressures of contemporary culture a kind of "social space" around himself, an area of privacy. He does this by tying himself in his thinking and feeling to sources of some relative permanence—hence impersonal— while remaining somewhat impermeable to the fluctuating tastes, panics, and, most menacing of all, the appeals to be "adjusted" from his contemporaries. Hard-cover books are essential as protection for our all-too-small tribe of "hard-cover men."

There can be no doubt that many publishers do take very seriously their crucial mission in the defense of the hard-cover men. It is often this that leads them to be troubled by the rising break-even point of hard-cover books which makes it difficult to take chances with those first novels and non-fiction not entirely sure-fire. However, in view of the social and psychological pressures generally operative against becoming a bookworm it seems doubtful that the high price of books is one of the more serious deterrents to good reading (though, as just indicated, it may be a deterrent to new, creative writing). Rather, the fact that books are *believed* to be high-priced would seem to be a sign of public hostility to books and reading: the publishing industry is one of the few whose costs and prices create comment on the outside and guilt on the inside of the industry. The question seems worth raising as to why publishers as compared with other manufacturers should be deprived of the American right to a reasonable inefficiency and a reasonable Hotel-Algonquin-style expense account.

In fact it is my impression that the large, streamlined publishers of textbooks are somewhat more "efficient" and feel less guilt—but should feel more. Textbooks are hard-cover books which often lack—or even in the long run destroy—the hard-cover function. (In the short run a great many of the important ideas in society appear to be spread by textbooks rather than by more current writings: this is where ideas end up to pasture, after a few runs at Belmont Park.) Textbooks increasingly associate reading with "government issue," something which is handed out rather than bought. In some college towns bookstores carry only texts and students do not learn to browse among books or how to collect and cherish them. (I should add, of course, that this development is not so much the responsibility of the publishers as of my own teaching profession, whose occasional monopolistic practices in the promotion of texts make use of quite a few of the devices, such as tie-in sales and captive markets, that the FTC has condemned.)

This all too brief consideration of whether textbooks are really books leads into an even more difficult question: what is a good or a serious book anyway? What kinds of books should publishers feel responsibility to publish and readers to read? It is my own impression that much that is forced upon people as good reading may turn them against reading as a chore and help create a protective apathy against all ideological appeals. The "Here and Now" books have been followed by the waves of Little Golden Books such as "Let's Go Shopping," and "Scuffy the Tugboat"; similar developments have taken place in the adult world where books about international relations and race relations, whether fiction or non-fiction, are promoted because they are intended to awaken people to "reality," to the various critical issues of today such as foreign policy.

All this assumes that we know more than we do know about the consequences of reading one or another sort of book. There is always an element of indeterminacy in art; in the relation of a reader to a book many things—many unintended things—can and do happen. It seems possible to argue, for instance, that "Huckleberry Finn" is a more serious book on race relations than any of the recent crop, among other reasons because of the artistic ambiguities in the reflections of Huck on the problem of helping Nigger Jim escape. Likewise it seems possible to argue that people need to read less that deals with the present and more that deals with the past and future. The very expense and solidity of the hard-cover book—its quality as furniture—may bear some relation to the long-run timetable of its impact, as compared with those media that cannot as readily be preserved, annotated, reread, or inherited. And among such things it is perhaps precisely the more "escapist" ones which for many can nourish the longer perspectives and the detachments that this country with its abundant resources of people and goods can afford even—or especially —in wartime.

True, there is no necessary conflict in principle between the "escape" book which is a craftsmanlike treatment of literary themes and the topical book which is a tract for the times. It follows from what I have said that what is a liberating book for one person may not be for another—a point often overlooked by those who, nostalgically overestimating the uncorrupted tastes of an earlier day, assume that all those who read good books in the eighteenth century or saw Shakespeare's plays in Elizabethan days found the good things in them. (In her excellent historical study, "Fiction and the Reading Public," Q. D. Leavis does present some evidence, such as material from letters and diaries as well as analysis of best sellers, to indicate a decline of English taste in the last century and a half, but it is terribly difficult to be sure of any such judgment about a dead audience when we cannot even tell much about a live one.) In the "Road to Xanadu" John Livingston Lowes traced some of the kaleidoscopic influences which had seeped into the mind of Coleridge, but similar detective work has not been done to trace the impact of books in the lifespan of less notable figures. Beyond the well-thumbed indexes of reading by age, sex, and previous condition of social-class servitude, research, I must repeat, can so far tell us very little about the subtle interplays between books of different kinds and people of different kinds. Reading a sheaf of book reviews is evidence enough that any book of moment can be interpreted in a fantastic variety of ways.

I recall, for example, the hue and cry among many parents and teachers, already leery of comics, when the story appeared about the boy who had jumped from an apartment-house window wearing a Superman cloak and been killed. It was naturally assumed that children identify themselves with Superman and with other heroes of the newer media. But a careful study of comics readers—one of the very few sophisticated studies we have of any sort of reader—shows that perhaps the majority of children do *not* identify themselves with Superman or other potent wizards of the comics. . . . The reader's fear of being a sucker; the fear of seeming to make ambitious, envy-arousing claims; the here-and-now interest in aviation coupled with disinterest in imaginative "flying"—all these things may inhibit the child's power and willingness to identify with a fictional hero.

Much in the same way, I suggest, readers do not learn in school to identify themselves with writers, that is, to identify themselves actively with great literary achievement. Such identification is, obviously, not the same as that which is encouraged by gossip columns about authors as "personalities." Anyone can identify with a personality in this sense. He can wear the same Superman cloak, he can drink the same coffee, drive the same make of car. But the writing of books of the sort we are concerned about would seem to thrive only where readers can identify with the author as craftsman, as performer—where they are capable of an objective identification with performance as such. This doesn't mean, of course, that they have to be able to write themselves but I do suspect that schools might do more for reading if they worried a bit less about pupils' reading skills and tastes and a bit more about their writing.

Of course everyone damns the schools for the crushing of literary talents and enthusiasms; indeed, this may be one reason why the schools have tended to abandon the classical tradition in favor of social studies and other supposedly less spinsterly and more true-to-life topics—topics, however, which can seldom be taught "realistically" and honestly to school children. The schools in turn tend to shift the blame for the dissatisfaction of the book-reading minority—about the fact that they *are* a minority—onto the shoulders of the mass media.

However, just as we are in no position to declare what is a serious book for every type of reader so we cannot assume offhand that books are inevitably more liberating than the newer media. Furthermore, the school-teacher who feels TV as unfair competition with Jane Austen not only fails to realize that Jane Austen's audience may not have gotten out of her what the teacher herself would hope to get across; more important, the teacher may also be unaware of how much she could do for a gifted and sensitive child or two if she was not afraid of boring a hundred others. Or her attack on TV may be based on her own succumbing to the very values she deplores (often unfairly) in TV; she is apt to accept somehow the inverse snobbery and class romanticism of the prevailing assumption that the non-readers have more fun and are closer to the "natural" and to "life" than the rare gifted bookworms are. It is when she feels she must reach everybody that she compares the Hooper rating of books with that of the supposedly competing media.

The result of all this is neither to make TV more interesting and artistic nor to create social space for the minority of bookworms but rather to make the use of leisure from childhood on a matter for anxiety, inter-generational tension, and concern for social status. I notice among my own students, who are moving up to the top of the "brow" hierarchy, an all-too-ready tendency to adjust to this new set of tastes and to diminish to a safe point the total number of risky enthusiasms for books. They are not worried about being conspicuous for a Superman stunt but for liking a "middlebrow" best seller. (It is safer, of course, for intellectuals to have low tastes than middling ones.) They worry, let us say, that they like Dylan Thomas less than Stephen Spender.

For them the problem is not whether to read or not to read (as it is for the average textbook student mentioned earlier), but how to have read "everything" by the age of twenty-four. This kind of self-demand is historically new in American education and is due to the quiet revolution in standards of teaching which has occurred in the last decades in the more active colleges and universities. Around these students the social space is often small because they want in a few years to fill in an area that took earlier generations of students a lifetime. A small minority even within the small minority of bookworms, they indicate in their own way how haunted and unleisurely our leisure often is.

Yet Americans, despite their ability to make themselves unhappy by efforts to achieve the right amount of adjustment (or, depending on the group, of maladjustment), are an inventive people. I think it quite possible that there exist new and as yet unknown ways by which people may protect their privacy and social space for liberation through books and other mass media even against all the obstacles presented by their peers and by the society at large. When for such suggestions I am accused of fostering "escape" I usually ask: is the world so wonderful, then, that you can think of no better 'ole, even in a book? The world is what it is in considerable measure because of the books that have been written and read. Likewise, any hope of finding a better world—and therefore of making one—rests on books and on other imaginative productions of some permanence. But until moving day comes and we go to our new utopian quarters I think we have every right to insist on our prerogative of escape.

The question comes back to the quality of that escape, as the problem of the mass media comes back to their quality, for their variety of audiences, in all the concreteness of their impact. And it is here, partly because we are so much in the dark, that we tend to engage in polemics and in admonitions. We need neither to praise escape nor to blame it but to differentiate it. It is even conceivable that only the escapists will turn out to be living in a real world—while the ascetic promoters of serious and dutiful reading are inhabiting some other planet of their own fantasy!

18. How Different May One Be?

... IN AN EARLIER DAY, parents and other authorities held out to children certain objective goals: they should get rich, for one thing, or become great scholars, or maybe even become president. And parents drove their children toward these goals. The traits of character which mattered were such things as diligence, honesty, and thrift—the injunctions of Ben Franklin's Almanac. If the child delivered the goods according to these reasonably clear criteria, it mattered rather less what he was like as a person; parents neither knew enough to observe his psychological make-up nor were they very interested in it. As a member of society's work-force the child would be expected to produce, rather than to be a particularly well-adjusted or even happy person. Thus both his character, with its implanted goals, and his situation, as he turned to make his living or his mark, combined to intensify the demands made on him as a producer, while the demands made on him as a person were slight. This gave him a certain freedom to be different, provided he did his work adequately.

What matters about the individual in today's economy is less his capacity to produce than his capacity to be a member of a team. Business and professional success now depend much more than ever before on one's ability to work in a team in far-flung personnel networks; the man who works too hard or in too solitary a way is, by and large, almost as unwelcome in the executive offices, the universities, or the hospitals of urban America as he would be in a union shop. He cannot satisfy society's demands on him simply by being good at his job; he has to be good, but he has also to be cooperative. When translated into child-rearing practices, this means that parents who want their children to get along and to succeed will be quite as concerned with their adjustment in the school group as with their grades or with their industry on an after-school job.

I don't mean to suggest that parents consciously calculate their children's job-chances and train the youngsters accordingly. Rather, the same great and still not fully understood social changes that have altered the nature of attitudes toward work and the worker have also influenced the home (the parents, or at least the father, are also workers), the school, the movies and radio and other institutions which divide among themselves, in none too friendly a fashion, the tasks of defining the goals for modern children.

These goals are no longer clear-cut. The older goals—such as sheer money-making—were often shallow and have been to a considerable degree abandoned. New goals—such as a full and happy life —have not yet had a chance to become more than vague mandates that cannot guide a parent or a child from day to day. Consequently there is every opportunity for one goal, namely popularity, to outstrip all others in importance. This is a means of rating the child when there is no other means available. Parents can no longer prefer to have a child who is diligent to a child who is "one of the gang." So parents, too, though perhaps with some misgivings, share the concern with popularity. Unlike their predecessors of the Victorian Age, they know—from the teacher, the P.T.A., their own children—what the popularity score is.

Matters would be relatively simple for parent and child if the market demanded complete conformists. Then, at least, expectations would be clear—and rebellion against them equally clear. But matters are not simple. What is expected of children and adults, in the middle and upper educated strata at least, actually *is* difference—but not too much. That is, one must be different enough to attract attention, to *be* a personality, to be labeled and tagged. . . .

Progressive parents, taught for the last several decades to "accept" their children, have learned to welcome a certain amount of rebelliousness or difference. Likewise, business and the professions, especially perhaps in the growing number of fields catering to consumption and leisure, welcome a certain amount of eccentricity, if this goes together with a cooperative team spirit. Thus children often find themselves in the paradoxical position in which their "difference" is simply evidence that they are conventional and up-to-date. Perhaps more important, they are compelled to learn to find their way among exceedingly subtle expectations on the part of others. They are expected both to be spontaneous and not to disrupt the mood of a particular group; to a degree they must conform and yet maintain the personality they have already built up. . . .

And the parents themselves become concerned and anxious, and understandably so, if the child's age-mates reject him; they fear his differences are of the wrong sort, and perhaps, too, that their differences from their neighbors are of the wrong sort. Are they to defend their child's differences, then, at the cost of his undoubted present and possible future misery?

I think the answer to this crucial question depends at least in part on whether the parents are secure enough and capable enough to provide the child with an environment that will give him some protection against the expectations of his peers. They must offer him a way of life which will help him suffer less from his loneliness and his fear of it. They do this in part by altering the valuation put on loneliness and in part by encouraging interests that, while making his adjustment to his present group no easier, make his adjustment to a future group no more difficult.

Let me take a specific, wholly imaginary case. It is, perhaps, not a very frequent case. It may be less frequent than that of parents who push their children into academic or aesthetic pursuits beyond the children's potential gifts and interests, injuring the children's self-esteem (since they cannot live up to adult expectations) and sacrificing their present happiness to an impossible future goal. But it is a case of a sort that, I believe, occurs more often as parents are taught the gospel of "adjustment to the group" and apply it both in their own lives and in their concern for their children.

Isobel is very gifted musically. Her parents and teachers eagerly encourage her musical zealousness. Already in her early teens her passionate preoccupation with music begins to set her apart somewhat from the other girls, not to mention boys, in her group who have no such individual interests. Isobel takes music lessons while the other girls go to the movies; she practices while others gab in a friend's house.

But Isobel's problem arises not only, if at all, from the time taken out of play by her musical interests; it arises because a concern with music, regarded in the group as too highbrow, goes beyond the limits of marginal differentiation in her circle. Gradually, without her full awareness of what is happening, Isobel is labeled as "different" (that is, as *too* different); and in the ceaseless game of friendship-ratings that the other girls play, she is left near the bottom or put to one side.

Meanwhile Isobel has become devoted to her music teacher, who encourages her to go on with music as a career; but Isobel's parents and schoolteacher—and Isobel herself—become worried that she may diverge from the path of a "normal" girl. . . . Isobel's mother may even feel guilty that she has allowed Isobel's musical interests to develop to this point.

What are some of the alternatives that may be open to Isobel's mother in this situation? Certainly, I do not expect her to make decisions that will press Isobel toward martyrdom to some once-existent ideal. But I think that Isobel's mother and teacher might be making a mistake if they concluded that acceptance in the group was more important for Isobel than music. For one thing, it is easy for parents and children to believe that they want mere acceptance, whereas what they really crave is popularity going far beyond acceptance. (This confusion is all the easier to make because of the clique structure of many school classes where, indeed, there may be no midpoint between popularity and ostracism.)

But the real question is whether popularity or even acceptance is a goal worth the sacrifice of precious, genuine musical talent. What the group offers is attractive but precarious and evanescent; music is a delight and an endless resource. In due time Isobel will be old enough to journey to an environment where there will be other girls and boys who care more passionately about music than about anything else—perhaps even than about *anybody* else. While our society has done an extraordinary job in the cultivation of the social skills, these must never be allowed to become ultimates of existence; they are far from being the only skills from which people can derive pleasure and profit. Some social skills Isobel will have to learn as part of her musical training, but this can wait.

And, indeed, it really is the ability to wait that is involved here. Parents never ask themselves what will give their child (or themselves, for that matter) pleasure at the age of sixty or seventy. While our life-expectancy has lengthened, our life-timetables have shortened considerably; and our flattened perspective makes it hard for us to see our children suffer, even for a short time, let alone to be the cause of this suffering ourselves. Yet thousands of parents throw away their children's special gifts—which can best be cultivated during youth—in return for gifts of social adjustment to a particular group at a particular time and place. Though certainly an unhappy childhood is not desirable, it is true that many unhappy children do grow up to be happy, productive, befriended adults.

For Isobel's mother to make such a choice as to let her daughter suffer now in anticipation of her future satisfactions would require that she herself believe that music, no matter what its momentarily estranging qualities may be, is worth a child's devotion. She is likely to doubt this, despite the evidence of her own child's attachment, if her own reactions and values are largely influenced by the opinions and values of relatives, friends, and neighbors, for then she will look to the other children for cues as to what is "normal" adjustment.

How can she defend Isobel against the others, if they are taken as the norm? Indeed, she is likely to fail to defend Isobel if she cares too much whether Isobel likes her, for there will be times when Isobel will deeply resent her mother for permitting her to be "different," even if Isobel herself, pushed by her gifts and her music teacher, takes the first steps in this direction. Isobel's mother has some power to define the values in the home in such a way that a child's loneliness is not regarded as the worst possible fate, while a failure to develop potentialities is felt as a real tragedy. Thus, gradually Isobel may learn to defend herself against the expectations of any particular group, and can move toward genuine autonomy—toward the ideal, which we humans seek but never fully achieve, of cultivation of our genuine differences as these develop from our unique capacities and life experiences.

Furthermore, Isobel's parents are not only members of a particular family but members of a particular community. If they want to protect Isobel's future they are not entirely confined to giving her marginal guidance in the direction of marginal differentiation. As members of a P.T.A., for instance, they can insist that schools concern themselves not only with children's social adjustment, with forming them into tolerant, amiable members of a cooperating group, but with children's skills, musical, linguistic, mathematical, or whatnot. They can raise the question whether we may not have gone too far in de-emphasizing academic performance, thus concentrating the teachers' as well as the children's attention on the more intangible aspects of social development. And as members of the wider community, they can apply their efforts to increasing the appreciation of what people can do, even if this means decreasing the appreciation of "personality" as the chief focus of concern.

VEBLEN AND THE BUSINESS CULTURE

THE FIRST OF THESE ESSAYS, "The Social and Psychological Background of Veblen's Economic Theories," follows the same plan as the Freud studies in the next section, for it is an effort to relate Veblen's ideas to each other and to his milieu. While, however, with Freud I kept as clear of biographical detail as possible, with Veblen I combined close textual analysis of his writings with reading what I could find, and talking with whom I could buttonhole, about the man himself. I'm not sure how much I would have guessed about Veblen from his writings alone, regarded as interview material for projective analysis, especially as Veblen took enormous pains to cover his tracks and hide himself in what he wrote—as compared with Freud's brave but unshowy effort to reveal himself through his dream-analyses and autobiographical writings. (Veblen, indeed, ordered all his letters and possessions destroyed—hardly any have been made public—and his last wish was that there should be no biography or even tombstone to recall him, a wish that reminds us of another ailing son of a strong-willed father: Kafka.) In this article, as well as in the book from which it is partly drawn, I offer some very tentative suggestions about Veblen's character structure and the relation this bore to his choice of profession, choice of intellectual weapons such as irony, and choice of topic. I am more concerned here with the sources of Veblen's ideas, and some of their consequences for intellectual history, than with whether they were right or wrong. That is, I am not here arguing with Veblen nor opposing him so much as trying to explain him.

My talk on "Relations between Social Progress and Technical Progress" was, *inter alia*, an effort to raise questions about the changing patterns and changing nature of the American business culture before a group of young technical people brought from all over the globe to attend a conference sponsored by M.I.T. students. These conferees, chosen mostly by twos from the various applicant countries, had been spending the summer at M.I.T. and were preparing for a bus tour of American industrial centers. As the discussion following my talk made clear, most of them were eager to adapt

American techniques for their home countries, while avoiding what they considered the debasement and vulgarity of American life; they were reluctant to admit that this country might be changing, and that their stereotypes about it were insufficiently complex. As one Dutch chemist rather aggressively said: "I am only in this country for a few months; I have *got* to see it in black and white!" Fortunately for him, other American speakers presented a not un-Veblenian view of the American business tycoon, his ruthlessness, raw empiricism, and lack of cultivation, which permitted him and others to feel I was seeing things which weren't there.

And to be sure, the question is left open in all my work as to how far and how fast the newer-model business values have spread: I have described a business typology without marking the boundaries and quantitative distribution of the several types. Certainly in my research in Kansas City I have found thriving exemplars of un-chastened enterpreneurship—businessmen who leave culture to their wives and ministers and remain untroubled by professionalizing tendencies within management. But these are small businessmen mostly, sometimes traders, wealthy but not economically influential; they are not "the transients" within large corporate businesses that William H. Whyte, Jr., has so imaginatively described in *Fortune*. With a strong hold on Congress and the state legislatures, on chambers of commerce and American Legion posts, on the businessmen's Bible classes which struck me in Kansas City as more energetic, optimistic, and bouncy that even small business itself, men such as those Veblen mercilessly satirized in his section on the country town in *Absentee Ownership* remain a potent political and cultural force, uneasily hostile to wealth and cultivation older and more secure than theirs.

However, theirs is not the only force and if I do no more in this article than raise questions for further searching, I shall be quite content. As Eric Larrabee remarked during the conference, the delegates were having trouble because American culture had become, in some ways, more sophisticated than they realized. I myself constantly feel that it escapes my efforts at interpretation, that I have a sense of only a very small fragment of what goes on, and that neither social science nor other forms of reporting are quite keeping up with the growing differentiation of our national life.

19. The Social and Psychological Setting of Veblen's Economic Theory*

IN VEBLEN'S OWN CRITIQUE of other economists—and a major portion of his theory is just that—he relied securely on quasi-Marxist simplicities concerning causation. Other economists "got that way" because they were members of or sycophants of the kept classes, aristocratically disdainful of the actualities of production. Their theories, if they were classicists, were "superstructural" in the sense of being both above and behind the battle, for Veblen was one of the pioneers in the use of the cultural-lag concept which has done so much to confuse the understanding of the relations between technology and society. If they were *American* classicists, such as (in Veblen's view) J. B. Clark, they were likely to couple a pallid reformism with their "fine-spun technicalities," offering palliatives at the level of pecuniary theory for evils rooted in the very divorce of the pecuniary culture from its industrial base. And this reformism Veblen saw as a leisure-class product, along with female philanthropy, the arts and crafts movement, social work, and vegetarianism—the archaic by-products of the sheltered life of the better-off and the better-educated strata whose menial and hence life-giving work was done for them by others. Reformism was archaic because it was pre-evolutionary, pre-Darwinian; for Veblen, "A.D." meant "After Darwin." His emphasis on the datedness of economic theory—a charge to which Americans are especially sensitive since we like to be progressive and up-to-date—led Veblen to express recurrent hopes for the "younger generation" of economists, whom he wanted to make less literate and theoretical, less parasitic and less sanguine, less refined and more machine-minded. For Veblen as for Rousseau, what was young was not so likely to be corrupted and spoiled.

Veblen, however, never explained why some economists, himself included, were historically minded and literate in spite of being "younger." He admired Sombart and borrowed much from him; he had good words to say for Schmoller; and he attacked the German

* In the footnotes I have taken account of some of the points made in the discussion following the presentation of this paper to the Economic History Association, meeting at Bryn Mawr, September 1953. I gratefully acknowledge many helpful suggestions from Staughton Lynd.

Historical School only for not being completely free of chauvinism
and reformism; for Karl Marx, in his role as economic historian and
not in his role as prophet, Veblen had a good deal of sympathy. In
his efforts to make economics a historically relativistic science, in
his refusal to "take the current situation for granted as a permanent
state of things," Veblen contributed to economic history rather than
to economics proper (I happen not to share his bias that the classicists were all too proper), granted that his Morganatic anthropology
was a kind of history, a Just So story of stages in a universal unilinear
human destiny. And perhaps it can be said that Veblen's unremitting
warfare with what he called "the guild of theoretical economists"
opened up possibilities for a more historical or anthropological economics which later students, more cautious and less given to economistic explanations, have been exploiting.

§ I

BUT HOW, drawing from Veblen, are we to explain Veblen? In my
forthcoming book, I make a very tentative effort to show how his
theories reflect the conflict between his harsh, intrepid, and technologically adept father and his Bible-reading, softer, and whimsical
mother.[1] Take, for example, his view that in the matriarchal past life
was at its best, but that modern man is simply nostalgic if he dwells
on this, for modern man must adapt to the discipline of the machine,
its cold, impersonal calculus, or go under. Might we not say that
this outlook, like analogous lost paradises, reflects the co-existence in
his mind of periods of his own life: the earliest childhood, dominated
by his mother, and the succeeding harsher if more productive phases,
dominated by his father? Plainly, neither such a theory nor such a
family constellation is idiosyncratic to Veblen; such families, indeed,
peer out at us from Victorian portraits and memoirs—and, in fact,
justify themselves by reference to ideologies of masculine work-
mindedness and domination of nature, of masculine mathematics and
calculation. Yet such correspondence between family and ideology,
while fruitful for speculation, are not explanatory: they illustrate compatibilities but do not show why some children of ascetic fathers,
like Samuel Butler, rebelled to become antagonists of the machine
and admirers of luxury, while others, like Veblen, rhapsodized their
fathers and defended their coldness, asceticism, and solemnity. In fact,
a closer look at Veblen, while it shows the father portrayed as the
philosopher-king of the future, the engineer, also shows the father
attacked in the son's muted praise for "idle curiosity" and muted

---

1. *Thorstein Veblen: A Critical Interpretation.*

contempt for pragmatism—contempt expressed also in his unceasing and successful effort to make a failure of his own career.

Veblen's father, though notably progressive in his use of farm machinery and interest in science, never learned English; Rolvaag's statement is applicable to him: "We have become strangers—strangers to the people we forsook and strangers to the people we came to."[2] But Veblen's Norwegian heritage is important not only because it made him a marginal man, linguistically and intellectually cosmopolitan, socially awkward, and emotionally expatriate, but also because of certain specific values he seems to have acquired as a youngster. Blegen notes the fact that the Norwegian immigrants could not understand competitive sports and games. Recalling Schumpeter's observation that for the entrepreneur "economic action becomes akin to sport,"[3] it would seem plausible to connect Veblen's fear and distrust of the entrepreneur with his Norse peasant's sort of Puritanism which rejected sport.[4] Indeed, Rolvaag's novels show how the Norwegian immigrants viewed plays and dances as sinful; their ministers urged them to hold fast to their racial traits and not to emulate American ways. While Veblen emancipated himself from this piety in certain respects, sexually and theologically for instance, he remained in many ways a seventeenth-century sort of Puritan protesting against the more commercially minded and urbanized Yankee Puritans whose faith seemed to him as watered as their stock, whose expenditures appeared as wasteful as their wars and their agronomy, and whose Anglo-Saxon ideal of sport struck him as a form of juvenile delinquency.

Staughton Lynd, who has collaborated with me in the study of Veblen's background, has observed that Simon Patten was born on better, richer land than that of Veblen's parents—and Patten of course went on to emphasize American abundance and consumption whereas Veblen, ever fearful of scarcity, remained an ascetic and aesthetic enemy of consumption, above an efficient subsistence minimum. (Patten had studied in Germany and been impressed by *Gemütlichkeit*, by how well the Germans made use of their leisure.) Veblen did not feel, with Willa Cather, that "it took more intelligence to spend money than to make it,"[5] but rather that getting and spending were

---

2. Quoted in Theodore Blegen, *Grass Roots History*, p. 113.

3. *The Theory of Economic Development*, p. 93.

4. A genealogy of the Veblen family indicates that most of Thorstein's siblings married other Norwegian-Americans (judging from names, and the names given children) and apparently remained in rural areas: one brother, and his favorite nephew Oswald, entered academic life. Only in the next generation would there appear to have been widespread assimilation to American middle-class norms.

5. *One of Ours*, p. 102.

both frivolous pecuniary diversions from modern man's essential problem: habituation to the machine and its relentless logic. In turning in his own career from philology and Kantian philosophy to economics, he was not only converted, as his first wife later declared, by Bellamy's *Looking Backward*, but also seems to have wanted to immerse himself in the study of livelihood. But perhaps at the same time he was attracted as well as repelled by the almost philological intricacy the science of economics, in comparison with other social sciences, was beginning to attain.[6]

This last point is important, for it introduces us to the fact that Veblen did not remain a Populist or a Bellamy Nationalist: he outgrew both movements in part. Thus, while a good deal of his economics may be interpreted as a farm boy's stubborn empiricism—a show-me attitude toward theory and refinement, a dislike of classics and the classical, a fear of art and artfulness, a chronic suspicion of lawyers and financiers—Veblen is neither a Bryan nor a Dreiser. Soon after moving to Chicago in 1892, he ended his concern with agricultural economics and the price of wheat and began his lifelong preoccupation with the most subtle market and monopoly tactics of business enterprise. He was thoroughly aware that the future, not only of the United States but of the planet, lay with industry and not, by any fond hope, with the rural, the tribal, the fundamentalist. Though proud all his life long of his Scandinavian ancestry, and happier with farmers and Wobbly workers than with professors who could not chop a tree, make furniture, or saddle a horse, he nevertheless identified himself with the international world of scholarship and only on occasion with the more folksy and destructive vulgarities of Populism.[7] Indeed, as a self-proclaimed matter-of-fact scientist, he was able to conceal from himself (and from many of his readers) the extent of his animus against the rich and the scholastics who

6. To be sure, in Veblen's America economics was still often taught by divines and other amateurs, but Veblen, a gifted linguist, was familiar with the work being done on the Continent. On coming to Chicago, he translated Ferdinand Lassalle's polemical *Science and the Workingman*, and in the *Journal of Political Economy* he reviewed scholarly as well as socialist European economic literature. These reviews—some of them reprinted in *The Place of Science in Modern Civilization and Other Essays*—exhibit Veblen's skill in handling complex Marshallian types of argument in economic theory.

7. Neither Veblen's idealized engineer nor his footloose Wobbly hero has much in common with the masterful, muscular hero of Jack London's *The Iron Heel*. During the first World War, Veblen, though ferociously anti-German, was concerned about how international scholarship might be preserved through American aid. In this man of multiple and wavering identities, a concern for scholarship and especially economics—if not for particular scholars and economists—remained an abiding concern even when he became a "left-wing" journalist on *The Dial*.

neither toiled nor spun—save for spinning theories to justify their idleness and prestige. Through science he could sublimate his alienations and harness his hostility.

§ II

HE CAME LATE to economics, as he came late to the English language and the genteel tradition, to cities, and, in a way, to America. And this, too, is not idiosyncratic but reflects an era in which it was very difficult for the underprivileged young to get higher education, although it was also an era in which professors, secure in their own status, enjoyed polishing and bringing along those rare ethnics—a Veblen, a Bernard Berenson, a Morris Cohen, an Alvin Johnson—who did manage to get access to them. The zeal and enthusiasm of these newcomers for the classical culture was thus stimulated and preserved (as compared with the situation today in which professors and students, no longer so different from each other, are cool, sharing know-how rather than isolated excitement). The very backwardness of America then held certain advantages for the pioneers of scholarship who, even if like Veblen they turned hostile to classicism, came as individuals to a library with the same passion that whole nations have come to literacy when the printing press is first introduced. I should add, moreover, that but for this backwardness I doubt if we would be taking Veblen very seriously today; he stands out among turn-of-the-century thinkers in this country as he would hardly do in an international conspectus that took account of his great contemporaries on the European continent.

To return to Veblen as a late-comer: Trained initially in philosophy, the field in which he took his doctorate with a thesis on Kant, he turned his critical intelligence and linguistic acuity onto what he termed the "received homilies" of economic theory; his papers on Clark, Marx, Böhm-Bawerk, and others are magnificent forays in criticism. Often unaware of what he had learned from the men he attacked, he tested their theories for both internal consistency and relevance, not to "the economy" in the narrower sense in which that sphere is the province of a special breed of men called economists but to "the economy" in the broader sense which includes all human use of resources, political and cultural, tangible and intangible. By bringing the "state of the industrial arts" into the discussion of market relations, he forced attention to the cultural and technological prerequisites which many theorists of marginal utility had taken for granted. Likewise, he insisted on bringing into technical academic discussion the usages of the common man. Thus, in a review of Irving Fisher's *Capital and Income*, he argued that "capital" can only be

defined by empirical observation of how businessmen use the term
—there is no point in a more refined definition. Indeed, the study of
economics becomes the study of businessmen's habits of thought;
changes in businessmen's linguistic usage, therefore, reflect changes
in what they do. Here the outsider speaks—or, in terms of his own
theory (see *Imperial Germany and the Industrial Revolution*), the
late-comer who takes over modernity without the encrustations of
habit, sport, and dilettantism. In this and other papers, he stresses that
price, interest, value, and other categories are conventions, not given
in the nature of things or in human nature but through the institutional processes and social learnings we would today summarize as
culture.

§ III

MOREOVER, like many outsiders and late-comers—including some of
the most significant minds of the nineteenth century—Veblen employed the search for economic origins as a way of discrediting capitalism's claim to be sacrosanct and traditional, as well as the claim
of particular capitalists to be innovators and contributors to welfare.
In regard to the latter, when he did not charge them with usurpation
and sabotage, he observed that they lazily engrossed the community's
common stock of industrial understanding: they stole not so much
surplus labor (a metaphysical concept Veblen derided) as a racial
inheritance of instinctive workmanship (Veblen's racism was metaphysical, too, as he sometimes admitted). Concerning the former,
Veblen pointed to the historically late entrance of substantial capital
assets upon a population already somewhat crowded by growing
scarcity of land, giving rise to the exceptional and unstable phenomenon of modern capitalism—a parvenu likes to pretend he has always
been there. But the "assets," Veblen insisted (in line with single-tax
thinking), are such only because the institutions so define them; thus
when metals came into use, flint-beds were no longer assets, and in
general "the maker's productivity in the case was but a function of
the immaterial technological equipment at his command, and that in
its turn was the slow spiritual distillate of the community's time-long
experience and initiative."[8]

While Veblen was simply one of a number of nineteenth-century
thinkers who, by ennobling earlier ages or submerged classes, challenged the capitalists' own lately attained patents of nobility, he was
distinctly stimulating and original in his emphasis on the insubstan-
tiality of capital, not only in terms of its historical uniqueness in its

8. "On the Nature of Capital," in *The Place of Science in Modern Civilization*, p. 339.

contemporary form but also in terms of its resting on interpersonal expectations and understandings much more than on plants and tools. Under Veblen's analysis the impressive physical apparatus of industrialism is separated from the interpersonal racketeering, the "intangible assets," the absentee ownership, the salesmanship and propaganda—all the vendible imponderables that truly dominate the business culture and constitute specifically modern "capital." His awareness of the role of propaganda, of confidence and confidence men, of "good will," is sophisticated, and links him with such political scientists as Harold Lasswell or such sociological economists as Pareto or Schumpeter, rather than with the classical or, for the most part, the institutional economists either then or now. Just as he saw socialism as grounded in large part on emulation, he saw capitalism resting on Kwakiutl-like motives of waste and display and on the airy romance of unstable hopes rather than on the solid substance of land, labor, and equipment. Indeed, one can trace anticipations in Veblen of Keynes's and Schumpeter's theories of crisis. And Veblen also anticipated their sense of the precariousness of future prosperity and the historically limited nature of the capitalist world of the nineteenth century.

§ IV

HE GOT THERE, however, I suggest, in part by the skeptical farm boy's route of distrusting the words, the promises, of city slickers, while being fascinated by them. His father, who had lost his first farm to a shrewd claimant, had been a man of very few words—and those in Norwegian; Veblen's own style is a conscious parody of the prolixity, pedantry, and legalism of the half-educated country lawyer or deacon. His distrust, moreover, is not only that of the farm boy who can never quite accept the reality of things beyond the palpable necessities of life but also a quite far-reaching distrust rooted in his character structure—a fear of being caught, made a fool of, taken in. This is one reason he was never willing to commit himself to a cause, a movement, a colleague, or a woman. All obligations seemed unstable to him. He was so ready to see the role of expectations in society in part because he himself was so fearful lest anything be expected of him; his whole academic career may be viewed as a sidling out of commitments, and his unfactual attitude toward getting the facts and unscientific attitude toward himself as a mere scientist may be seen as efforts to escape from amorphousness and to relate himself to something solid, if not to somebody. His crusade to get theory "down to earth" was thus in part the argument with himself of a refugee from the farm.

This fear of constraint and commitment, coupled with a fear of the freedom that would result from their absence, is one of the most distinctive themes of Veblen's character structure, visible in his writings as well as in other behavior. His writings, for example, have as a formal matter no principle of flow, of organization; they are endlessly repetitive in the large and in detail; sentences have style but little structure. Moreover, as we have seen, Veblen insisted on man's subordination to the machine, to the slow evolutionary drift of things, while at the same time he identified with the Wobblies, the less bemused portions of the underlying population, the masterless men who bowed to no authority save logic and to no rule save the slide-rule. This ambivalence we can relate once more to his parents, who thought him bright, expected much of him, but gave him little warmth—and these parents in turn provide a link with the tight patriarchal family and the no less tight ethnic group—a group who supported the post-doctoral Veblen while he loafed and read, read and loafed, because as a traditional culture they accepted the responsibility even for such kin as were deviants. And on the other side, we can relate Veblen's character structure to his choice of field, for I suggest that economics then, with its undefined boundaries and unmathematical, more or less speculative, often historical methods, attracted those who feared constraint, much as sociology and anthropology have more recently done. That is, economics may have appeared to Veblen to mix agreeable proportions of intricacy and openness, methodology and topicality. Veblen broke down the boundaries of economics even further: his very fluid definition led him to subtitle *The Theory of the Leisure Class* "an Economic Study of Institutions." The state of the art allowed him not to be cabined by his chosen discipline; and his eloquent pleas for opening it up to new areas of investigation—business practice, anthropology, psychology, as well as politics—have helped create such cadres of no longer quite marginal but also not wholly free men and women as yourselves, the economic historians.

§ V

ALL THIS ONLY BRINGS US to another paradox in Veblen's relation to his *Zeitgeist,* if this term can still be used. The psychology he went to school with, so to speak, was that of Peirce, James, and Dewey—a psychology that stressed, as indeed Kant's did, man's selective perception and active organization of the world, his adaptation of it to him, rather than his mere passive response to hedonistic drives. Again and again, Veblen states that man is an agent, an actor, shaping the institutions which in turn shape him; moreover, his concept of idle curiosity is a sort of instinctual basis for autonomy. He had some sympathy for Lester Ward, who drew humane implications from Darwinism; he was friendly with W. I. Thomas, who stressed the subjective nature of social life;[9] he even saw in animism a projection of the human will. And yet, because as already indicated he was afraid of his own fear of constraint, afraid too of the freedom he regarded, as his father might have, as soft and sentimental, he resisted the implications of his psychological affiliations for his economics. For him, Darwinism came as a discovery of mankind's submergence in blind, cumulative drift over which it would be naïve and vain to seek control. In counseling adaptation to the machine, he urged on men a ferocious surrender to the existent, even at the cost of distorting instincts which Veblen thought had been shaped for all time in a savage past. And in his aggressive scientism, no less deterministic than that of Comte and St. Simon and more so in some ways than that of Engels, he urged his fellow economists to give up their personal wishes for amelioration and to bind themselves, in fraternal anonymity, to become consultants for industrial managers, statisticians for project engineers (shall I say "policy scientists"?). In a famous passage, he criticizes Marx and his followers:

> The neo-Hegelian romantic, Marxian standpoint was wholly personal, whereas the evolutionistic—it may be called Darwinian—standpoint is wholly impersonal. . . . The romantic (Marxian) sequence of theory is essentially an intellectual sequence, and it is therefore of a teleological character. . . . On the other hand, in the Darwinian scheme of thought . . . the sequence is controlled by nothing but the *vis a tergo* of brute causation, and is essentially mechanical. The neo-Hegelian (Marxian) scheme of development is drawn in the image of the struggling ambitious human spirit: that of Darwinian evolution is of the nature of a mechanical process.[10]

Indeed, I think William Graham Sumner, hard-boiled at least on the surface, had more influence on Veblen than his gentle colleague, John Dewey, with his, at least on the surface, more hopeful view of man. In making his choice among "influences"—and it will be seen

---

9. I have relied heavily, for information on Veblen's life and times, on Joseph Dorfman, *Thorstein Veblen and His America.* I am also indebted to a conversation with Professor Max Fisch concerning Veblen and Peirce. Since my address was written, an interesting essay has appeared comparing Veblen and William James: Lewis Feuer, "Thorstein Veblen: the Metaphysics of the Interned Immigrant," *American Quarterly,* V (1953), 99-112. Feuer, somewhat less sympathetic to James and more to Veblen than I am, stresses that Veblen was too close to a precarious personal existence to afford James's middle-class optimism about the human will.

10. "The Socialist Economics of Karl Marx and his Followers: II," in *The Place of Science in Modern Civilization,* pp. 436-37.

that I myself see men as having some leeway in choosing their influences rather than simply succumbing to tropisms—Veblen may have been picking his father over his mother, his enemies over his friends, his need to be restrained over his fear of restraint. Beyond that, a certain personal passivity and shyness may have been at work which made him dislike any theory or custom that gave renown to individuals or brought them into the limelight. Veblen, having early handed in his resignation to life and being in many ways a very dependent person, seems to have felt that the "struggling ambitious human spirit" could neither found a scientific system nor change the world, even though, as in many fatalist schemes, this discovery heartened him to espouse, with a very personal style, the claims of impersonality and, with a very unexpedient life, the mandates of expedient adaptation and determinism.

§ VI

SUCH PSYCHOLOGICAL EXPLANATIONS, however, leave me somewhat unsatisfied, not only because I know all too little about the details of Veblen's parentage and childhood but also because I know all too well that men of very different background espoused quite similar views of the economy—while of course other farm boys, such as Alvin Johnson, differed from Veblen. Nevertheless, we must ask how Veblen happened to select, among available careers and themes, the particular contradictions that he made his own. The question is in principle answerable even though others could achieve outcomes similar in general, though never in detail, from different motives and, of course, follow him for again different motives. And if we then ask why so intelligent a man as Veblen did not go farther, why he failed in so many ways appreciably to transcend his age, we are once more brought back sharply to his biography. We see, for instance, that his country-boy late-comer skepticism and bitterness had its opposite side in a certain gullibility. He was overimpressed by the very captains of industry he derided. He gave them more power to do damage, as saboteurs of production and Goliaths of consumption, than they actually possessed; their personalities and even their success impressed him, in his shy, resigned failure, despite his Darwinist defense. Their values impressed him even more. In making the canon of efficiency the standard for judging all social life, he was able to demolish much Victorian cant and pretense, but by the use of a Philistine weapon borrowed from businessmen. Veblen contended that businessmen were unbusinesslike, though only by insisting that they were single-mindedly in pursuit of profits rather than production; this very single-mindedness, though some of the robber barons came close to it, was for most of them an unachieved ideal. In his own attempt to be single-minded, Veblen would have very little quarrel with the businessman today who wants government to be run like General Motors: if technocracy was a caricature of his gospel, it was not without his co-operation. Even the businessman who despises art, culture, and philanthropy finds something of an ally in Veblen, whose hatred for all archaic, inefficient, untechnological pursuits has at times a very militant quality. Believing himself a critic of his culture, he fell into some of its most characteristic nineteenth-century crudities and self-deceptions.

Even more striking, perhaps, is Veblen's unconscious acceptance of nineteenth-century rationalistic individualism. Veblen never seriously concerned himself with the problem of social solidarity: he assumed that men, once freed of the imposed incubus of pecuniary rivalry, would work together in obedience to both their instincts and their self-evident subsistence needs. While he spoke occasionally of the "parental bent" as a kind of instinct of social solicitude, he more typically took it for granted that "masterless men" would find in engineering mandates a sufficient basis for co-operation. During the same era that Durkheim and Freud, Brooks Adams and Sorel, Max Weber and Pareto were in one or another way preoccupied with centrifugal tendencies in modern society, Veblen saw the role of leaders and elites as sheer unnecessary swindle and expense. His preconceptions concerning human relations were those of a market economy —impersonal, rationalistic, calculable. Here again, Veblen is the very "American" efficiency expert, and paradoxically one who is attacking orthodox economics for its reliance on premises of hedonism and rationality. All of us suffer from the illusion that we are outside what we are criticizing.

To be sure, all this needs to be qualified by recalling once again that Veblen kept a kind of ikon corner for the impractical and the "un-American," the inefficient, the unbusinesslike, and the irrelevant, in the form of his concept of "idle curiosity." He called it an instinct, to give it a biological base beyond criticism—and obviously biology is the true nobility, coming first before all learned parvenus. But under idle curiosity he smuggled the university and research, his own vested interest and the one he cared most about. While everywhere else his mentality is that of the engineer or accountant, the Puritan and debunker, the person who has no truck with frills, frivolity, and nonsense—a mentality that drew him at once to the Bolsheviks in 1919—his design for the universities, and hence by implication even for economics, is impractical and indeed remains an attractive dream for many of us who are harassed by demanding students, repetitive committees, administrative chores, and foundation benevolence; we may be grateful here, as with other thinkers, for a certain lack of consistency.

§ VII

ONE MORE PARADOX and we are done. For reasons partly indicated, Veblen failed to account for modern capitalism in its specifically American variant—he gave the captains too much power, saw credit only as collusive and collapsible, and otherwise overestimated the destructive elements in the system; his asceticism prevented him from seeing the constructive role of waste and luxury on both the production and consumption sides.[11] In my judgment, he is a poor, if often amusing and provocative, guide to America.[12] But he really comes into his own when taken as a guide to the economics of underdeveloped countries—"underdeveloped" being our not wholly satisfactory semantic substitute for "backward." By simplifying and empiricizing economics, by putting it back into its cultural context and rejecting partial equilibrium analyses, by teaching us that every society draws on motives which are left over from previous epochs, he introduces an essential curriculum for Point Four missionaries. The new theorists of economic development, working where there is only a rudimentary market and not even a semblance of entrepreneurial ideology, may find Veblen's anthropological economics, with its iteration of the interrelatedness of everything, good and even inspiring reading. Someday we may be able to trace a United States Technical Assistance project in aid of Javanese home industry (tied to matrilineal descent lines) to a set of ideas set off originally by Veblen's own encounter

---

11. After the meeting, Mrs. Edna Macmahon of Vassar College told me the following incident, which occurred when she was a student of Veblen's: After a New School lecture, a pretty girl (a species usually able to overcome Veblen's defenses) presented Veblen with a gold clasp to substitute for the safety pin with which he attached his pocket watch to his clothes. Veblen declared, pulling out his pin, that it had true beauty, which he would not exchange for anything: that it could be bought at any five and ten, six for five cents; that the pin did not damage his clothes; finally, that if the girl could not grasp the functional aesthetics of the pin, she had learned nothing from the course!

12. For this judgment, I was gently chided by Professor Willson Coates of the University of Rochester and others who felt that to criticize Veblen in terms of developments since his time was unjust. The problem, of course, would not arise had Veblen not sought to transcend his times, both critically and prophetically; indeed, were he not to some degree original, there would be no point in seeking to understand him as an individual rather than simply as a type. It may well be that I expect too much illumination from Veblen, of a sort he is not equipped to give, and in this paper insufficiently stress his accomplishments. However, since many still move in evaluating contemporary America within the ambit of Veblen's rhetoric, it is important to emphasize that Veblen's America, to the extent it ever existed, predeceased him—while, to name a profounder guide, Tocqueville's America is in some ways more ours than his.

with a magisterial father and with a society which, for much of his life, insisted on defining him as impractical, even at times subversive, but mostly not good for much. And that would be the final ironic verdict on a man whose great discovery, in his own eyes, was the vanity of any human effort to oppose "the *vis a tergo* of brute causation."

20. Some Relationships between Technical Progess and Social Progress

THE REPORTS of previous conferences of this sort make fascinating reading. They suggest some of the ways in which certain American values and ideals are spreading throughout the globe at the same time that they are becoming devalued in this country. Technical progress is such an ideal. The MIT students who invited you here are not simply or single-mindedly devoted to it: they and many of their professors are increasingly concerned with *relations*—human relations, international relations; and with culture as a set of relations, including both the anthropologists' culture and the humanists'. The American ideal of social mobility takes all sorts of forms, in addition to the well-documented pattern of individuals moving upwards in a corporate hierarchy or an income bracket. One somewhat abstract form of the ideal is to move "up" from preoccupation with "merely" technical problems to preoccupation with social and psychological problems, with human relations. This is perhaps less a form of mobility for the individual scientist or engineer (though it may help groom him for higher position) than a form of mobility for the engineering profession as a whole. My very presence here may be taken as an indication that the tycoon of culture, the professor of social science or humanities, is beginning to rank with the tycoons of metallurgy or finance.

I have had several recent reminders of the increasing defensiveness of engineers—a group which, as recently as the Age of Hoover, had ranked comfortably high among the professions as the bearers of progress, hard common sense, efficiency, and other indisputably good things. On one occasion, an engineering society invited my colleague, Reuel Denney, and me to advise them about what could be done to make engineers more cultivated and more aware of interpersonal relations: the group felt very defensive about being good with sliderules or transistors but not with people or Shakespeare. On another occasion, students at the Sheffield Scientific School at Yale indicated their bewilderment and resentment at the fact that, when they spoke to their girl-friends, or to literary Yalemen, about jet engines they were accused of shop-talk, while the latter, when they chatted about Proust, Elizabethan poetry, or the future of the United Nations were thought to be unequivocally cultivated and fit for social gatherings! In each instance, the engineers rather mournfully asked what they must do to be saved. Surely, their misgivings do not spring from want of employment—as a glance at the glowing want-ads for engineers in any paper can establish. Rather, full or even overfull employment for engineers is part of that great wave of American abundance (which some of you, no doubt correctly, think we are far too ready to boast about), abundance which encourages the development of tertiary industries (the service, entertainment, education, and "culture" industries) and, within the secondary industries, an increasing concern with the supposedly higher things in life which can now be afforded. Indeed, if we want full employment without war, we cannot afford not to continue this development of turning out fewer tool and die makers and more museum directors and novelists.

It seems to me an open question whether there are such things as "higher things," apart from human meanings and cultural definitions. Is "Guernica" a greater work of the imagination than a telephone relay or a theory of nuclear fission? In the curious and paradoxical reversals of emphasis I am discussing, however, many of the less industrially developed countries seek immediate self-respect and status, as well as more obvious goals such as autarchy, by going in for steel plants and automobile assembly lines, despite the fact that improvement of agricultural techniques or distributive mechanisms might promise more immediate gains—gains, moreover, not requiring suffering severe deprivations in order to import heavy capital equipment. When at the 1952 meeting of this group Professor Walt Rostow pointed this out, he was criticized by representatives of "underdeveloped" countries for his emphasis on "mere" material well-being; he was put in one typically American position in international exchanges of having to reply that, while he wanted to put a practical base under ideals, he was of course not against ideals—he understood the Quixotic appeal of assembly lines. What also irked his questioners was his relative pessimism, his belief that the world could not be changed overnight. By contrast, his critics appear to me to have been somewhat reckless in their eagerness to hasten impressive industrial advance at no matter what human cost. Indeed, it was the Africans and Asians at the Conference who tended to be the eager-beavers, the romantic strivers after "efficiency," the unquenchable optimists, whereas the Americans were worldly wise, full of sober second-thoughts, and quite free of missionary zeal or cant. It was almost as if the traditional trans-Atlantic and trans-Pacific conversations had somehow got their labels switched, with the United States the age-old country and Europe and Asia the unexplored utopia, the millenary land!

I realize, of course, the complex processes of selection at work which might give one such an impression from last year's Conference. You who come from other countries are, I assume, not typical of your countries, not even typical of your countries' upper strata, else you would not be here. I remember the committee which met in this country from 1942 to 1944 to draw up an international bill of rights for presentation to some presumptive post-war official body. Representation was sought from all the Allied powers. It turned out that the non-Anglo-Saxons (such as Hu Shih from China) were often more "English" in their ways than the English: this was as true of the Hindu, who hated the English, as of the Egyptian, likewise Anglo-phobic, who had been co-opted to "represent" Islam.[1] I had greatly hoped in the committee meetings to learn something about the cultures of a number of other countries, but instead I mostly got one or another Westernized version of culture, often at the hands of men so bedazzled by the West that they could not help but be impatient with their native cultures, no matter how much they might chide us Americans for our lack of spirituality, our haste and hurry, our standardization. Many were marginal men, like the Hindu doctor in Orwell's *Burmese Days;* they could never really go home again even if, unlike Dr. Veraswami, they hid their admiration for the West under a superficial contempt. As is generally recognized, the mixing of peoples that industrialization has brought with it everywhere (mixing of peoples from town and country, from East and West, from Catholic and Protestant and other denominational folds, etc.) involves a mixing also of values, and these 20th-century casualties among stranded, half-Westernized intellectuals are often as

---

1. No other remarks in my address provoked quite so much active and acrid rebuttal as my suggestion that the delegates were not "typical." None wanted to feel he was in any way different from "his" people to whom he would perforce return; the "Moslem bloc" was particularly vociferous in insisting that their cultures were as progress-minded as the American and that hence they themselves were in no way alienated from Islamic tradition; they denied that they were reinterpreting that tradition to find room in it for their own activities, their own ideologies. Most eager to rebut any inferences of his untypicality was an Egyptian who spoke perfect English, and who, it turned out, had been educated in England; not surprisingly, he saw England as the root of all his country's difficulties in overtaking and surpassing American prosperity. Surely, the strength of nationalism, and often Communism (i.e., the new National "Socialism"), among non-Western intellectuals springs in part from the effort to submerge any doubts that one is a 200% Egyptian or Thailander or Nigerian in the face of one's knowledge of and desire for Western-model forms of technology, education, and values generally.

tragic as the more evident casualties among half-urbanized peasants whom Engels described in 19th-century Britain or as those among the detribalized whom Boeke has written about in modern Indonesia.

Conversely, as Americans begin to rise above the industrial evangelism of our own past, we make things very uncomfortable for those of us who are too much in love with older definitions of efficiency. Even in his best days, the efficiency expert, Frederick Winslow Taylor, had a terrible time trying to persuade Americans to work efficiently; he would raise productivity and real wages only to be hated by workmen and fired by management—and today the zeal he expended in trying to help workmen do their tasks with a minimum of strain is forgotten in easy denunciations of "Taylorism." It is men trained in the thinking of Elton Mayo, not of Taylor, who are now in demand—men who don't drive too hard, men who can create a happy atmosphere among companionable work groups, men who aren't too infuriated with waste. Sometimes I think that we tend to export our remaining zealots of efficiency, on Point IV or Ford Foundation missions, where they can speak for "American methods" as they never could at home! Don't mistake me: these men we send abroad are far more humane than Carl Peters, or the hero of Conrad's *Heart of Darkness*, and they are genuinely concerned with welfare; however, in their single-minded drive and energy, their dedicated willingness to fling themselves into what appear to be lonely and hopeless situations, they are true descendants of Taylor and the Puritan entrepreneurs. And of course, such people are not likely to be around here to address this Conference along with your panelists who (like myself) take a four-months summer vacation in New England!

It follows that we would expect recent immigrants to America and their immediate descendants to be today a principal locus of traditional American values. For these people, in their complex effort to become "Americanized," engage in some of the same misinterpretations of what that process means that foreign visitors are apt to accept: that is, they conceive America in terms already out of date among the better educated and more assimilated groups. They oversimplify America whether they resort to crime and competitive sports in order to get rapidly ahead, as good Americans are supposed to get ahead, or whether they resort instead to more unremitting (as well as more disagreeable) work than would have been appropriate in the old country. Just the other day I had a letter from a former student, now a private in the army, concerning the army's dependence on this latter sort of immigrant behavior; he writes:

"A great center of inner-direction [i.e., behavior in pursuit of a clear internalized goal] still exists—and it has particular strength among the rising second-generation kids. Several of our cadre around the Fort here are Armenians, Greeks, Italians, Hungarians, and Yugoslavs, etc.—and almost without exception they are great believers in the meritoriousness of 'hard work,' and 'principled behavior.' The Army depends on these plus the few Anglo-Saxon Puritan ethic people to get its work done. The Army requires such work-minded people who try to do a good job of whatever they're told to do no matter how odious the task, simply because it is 'wrong' and 'disgraceful' to do anything but a good job."

To be sure, the perspective of this letter is somewhat one-sided: it necessarily leaves out of account what the East and South Europeans have done to make Americans fonder of good food, good song, and the leisurely life generally. But at the same time, it is part of the evidence for the generalization that industrial development usually requires new sorts of people, just as kings and popes learned that commercial development required Hollanders or Jews or Lombards or Jansenists—part of the omen of what may happen to America for having virtually cut off immigration, a traumatic blow to world development both within and without this country.

In this connection, I was struck by the study of Knapp and Goodrich on the origins of leading American natural scientists. A disproportionately high number, they point out, come from small-town or rural backgrounds and attended small liberal arts colleges in the Midwest and Far West. One might plausibly interpret their data as follows: as youngsters, these men had known little luxury and less occupational diversity; hence their college science teacher could strike them as a figure of moment and if he invited them to work, let us say, on a carbon ring or a physics text, they were wedded to science (in a perhaps somewhat narrow and pragmatic view of it) for life. They had formed a work-minded character while young, but had not hitched it to a particular interest; the life of research seemed to them the pinnacle of service and ambition. By comparison, students from the cities, from the upper strata, attending larger and more cosmopolitan universities, would more often find such a career too narrow, and a college chemistry teacher too unexhilirating a model.[2]

---

2. In the light of a more recent study, *The Younger American Scholar: His Collegiate Origins,* by Knapp and Greenbaum, these comments must be somewhat revised, for more recent data indicate that the high-status, high-cost Eastern universities are now also producing a proportionate number of scientists. The authors suggest that this shift may be due, in part, to the increasing vogue of intellectualism among well-to-do Americans, but also think that the scientists turned out from these strata will be less pragmatic than those from the "grass roots." To complicate the picture, boys from the grass roots are now increasingly financially able to attend the more expensive institutions—migration within the country here replacing immigration as a source of talent, of novelty and enterprise.

What I have been getting at, in a number of different illustrative ways, is that American society, on the basis both of technological and cultural development, appears to be undergoing profound transformations at the present moment which are carrying us increasingly further away from those concerns which are still a matter of life and death in the countries where population presses heavily on food supply—countries which, now aware of other ways of life than their own, want the "technical progress" which for many educated Americans has either become a game or something towards which to feel snobbish and superior.[3] Is it any wonder the productivity teams that have come here from Europe to discover the "secrets" of American know-how have been often baffled: they cannot always tell which elements in our managerial and factory cultures are "scientific" and which are "magical"—the latter needed for American morale but not necessarily transportable. And of course we Americans do not understand our own system—I am much less sure of the things I am telling you than I may seem to be if you miss the ironies in my voice and the ambiguities in my argument. But we feel under pressure, both for the sake of our sanity and of our foreign relations, to discover ex post facto rationalizations for why we act as we do.

It is interesting that it was an American, Peter Weiss, at last year's meeting who asked Professor Rostow how non-American countries could without prior mechanization acquire the industrial *esprit* that could spark general economic advance. Machines, he felt, gave an air to a society, a heady and impetuous air, which somehow went together with high productivity—in my own terms, I would say that machines help educate and inspire, symbolize and socialize, at least once a proper cultural context is there for mediating and defining them. Certainly the enthusiasm and aesthetic sense of the Italians for modern machine design may be connected with their rapid post-war recovery: it minimizes the snobbery or strangeness traditional cultures sometimes feel towards the very machines they also envy and desire. Skill and competence in making machines that excite international admiration engender confidence: they have a halo effect. Athens and Venice in their commercial heydey had this confidence; many American industrialists and organizers have it now. But how can one borrow confidence from another country, especially

---

3. In extensive discussion, the delegates insisted that the "rest of the world" wants more factories, better medical care, and so on—but not American "mass culture" or "juvenile delinquency." Some appeared to want industrialization without urbanization, and perhaps without democratization. On the degrees of choice involved here, as illustrated by Mexican experience, see *inter alia* the work of Robert Redfield and Wilbert E. Moore.

when that confidence rests in part on the very achievements one is oneself seeking?

Equally perplexing for the borrower is the realization of how much American productivity depends on a casual yet calculated disregard or sabotage of standard operating procedures. The industrial sociologist William F. Whyte of Cornell tells the story of the workmen in an oil-cracking plant in Oklahoma who got angry because, in a collective bargaining session, the management had referred to them as semi-skilled. They proceeded to carry out literally the instructions of the chemist, instructions which they had previously treated as a good chef will treat a recipe—soon bringing the plant to a halt. It turned out that they understood the idiosyncracies of the machines better than did the supervisory staff—and they won a pay increase. Warner Bloomberg, Jr., a colleague of mine who has spent some years as a factory worker, recounts many similar experiences, including the important role workmen play in modifying a customer's requirements for accuracy according to their own knowledge of what is actually needed, thereby minimizing the number of rejected pieces. Such "corruptions" and "indulgences" mediate between the formally prescribed and the empirically provided elements of production—they comprise an invisible overprint on a blueprint.[4] I might add that similar practices, which many oversimple moralists regard as reprehensible, keep us from getting completely bogged down in the separation of powers our Constitution prescribes—I suppose that in any society the people who save other people from the pitfalls of their rituals are likely to be either notorious or unknown. All this again suggests that countries which think it is easy to install "American methods" by copying blueprints or our own copybook maxims may be in for serious disillusionment.

Let me choose, as one illustration, an American business practice which has impressed a number of the productivity teams—the willingness of businessmen to share their production methods with each other. Instead of trade secrets, kept in the family or in the business,

---

4. Mr. Bloomberg also cautions me not to take at full face value the extensive talk among managers concerning personnel practices and what I have sometimes called "mood engineering": at least in the heavy industries in which he has worked, an enormous concern for cutting down waste and increasing man-hour productivity hangs on, underneath the newer forms of talk. Even the labor force, he feels, is still productivity-minded, in spite of itself; as he reports workers as saying: "Give us a new machine and we'll end up making it do even more than the engineers thought it could. That's our trouble. We can't hold back forever. We're like a kid with a new toy." This is perhaps not so much work-mindedness as a game-mindedness which does not exhaust itself in factory loafing or in obstruction of management

our managers often cannot wait to tell other managers, through the appropriate journals or meetings of the American Management Association and other trade associations, what short-cuts they have discovered. This sharing of information and devices has perplexed European observers who had perhaps learned from American novelists, if not from Balzac or Dickens, that business was a cut-throat affair. To "explain" what they find, there is a tendency to rationalize this sharing as a conscious policy of tit-for-tat, a kind of Miltonian free trade in secrets, even a conspiratorial pool; and the Americans themselves, if charged with disloyalty within their own organizations, would very likely fall back on similar justifications. (I should add that the sharing might be even more extensive in some industries if it were not for fear of the anti-trust laws, though the spirit behind these laws is only one of a number of reasons why companies often pretend to themselves and to others that they are more competitive than in fact they are.) It is my impression, though of course very difficult to support, that the sharing of business information has more to do with the growing professionalization of management than with any conscious decisions to trade one secret for another. Officials who regard themselves as professionals find their fraternity, not among rentiers, but among people doing the same work in other companies as well as in their own company. They are tied to the company for which they work by that work, its interest and its perquisites, and not by stockholdings or family connections or tradition. . . .

Sharing of information can actually be quite expensive to individual companies, not only in "giving away secrets" but in the actual costs of distribution. It costs money to compile and publish reports, to send people to conventions, to receive visitors from other companies or (as you will discover when you go on tour) from abroad; yet all this is done by American companies without afterthought, uncomplainingly; neither the accountant nor the internal revenue agent is likely to object, any more than to the charitable donations or the "pure" research which corporations are increasingly going in for.[5]

All this, I suggest, is a facet of what I have elsewhere described as the shift from "conspicuous consumption" to "conspicuous production" in American life, in which our surplus is spent at the source, so to speak, in the very processes of production, rather than distrib-

---

5. Several M.I.T. students at the Conference objected that not all companies shared information or admitted visitors—proprietary drug houses were notably guarded. But others felt that the general point I was making was valid, although there was considerable variation among industries.

uted to stockholders or bankers and spent or hoarded according to private whim. Professor Walt Rostow observed last year that even in the late 19th century the American business leader was ordinarily at least as much concerned with finding an outlet for his social energies as with making a fortune—one that, in European style, he could use as a counter in acquiring status. Indeed, in retrospect it is sad to contemplate the vain struggle of the millionaires of that day for good repute: many pious ones sought to obey all the rules, and won only ridicule or antagonism; for a Carnegie or a Rockefeller there were few long-established, socially-approved roads to take. While today of course there are many Americans who want to make a fast buck and succeed, mostly in small business, in doing so, many big businessmen don't even dare spend a fast buck, but have their companies do it for them. If you want to find big businessmen still mightily driven by the entrepreneurial ethic in getting and spending, you may do best in the South and Southwest—or in Toronto: Canada already surpasses us proportionately in some indices of productivity, it has for generations exported many of its more enterprising French Canadians to the United States, thus keeping Quebec quaint for habitants and tourists alike.[6]

Since up-to-date American corporations now have to learn the arts of conspicuous spending, they need tutors—just as European princes did or American tycoons. Business schools (including very probably M.I.T.'s own school of management) play a part as such tutors; so do management consultants; so do industrial architects and designers. There are corporate officials who are addicts of one or another of the many fads—committee management, incentive systems, operations analysis, and a hundred other plans—and go about the country stumping for these devices and their morale-building and profit-building virtues. For these "muscular Christians" of enterprise, trade does not necessarily follow the flag and the Bible; these men act in obedience to their self-image as proper businessmen, no matter how strenuously they insist (as, depending on mood, most Americans will insist) that they act only out of self-interest. In this modern atmosphere of sharing, of geniality, of muted competition and unmuted conspicuous production, who would be the Scrooge who would hoard trade secrets, or hoard capital (like Sewell Avery, to the fury of his associates), or hoard time (very few top businessmen are actually as inaccessible as their secretaries like to pretend)?

In some ways, the Soviet Union is more "capitalistic" than Amer-

6. Cf. Everett C. Hughes, *French Canada in Transition,* on significant changes now occurring in this pattern—and for illumination of the general problem of the ways in which technical "progress" mixes different ethnic groups together.

ica; having learned what it could from American engineers in the Age of Hoover, it still plainly lives in an epoch of tight-fisted capital accumulation and secrecy—though it will be interesting to see to what extent its managers, as they become more professional, will begin to imitate American patterns of conspicuous production. Conceivably, this tight-fistedness may be one among many reasons why, beneath competing ideologies, Soviet agents have an appeal to "underdeveloped" countries which are even further away than the Soviet Union itself from the American plateau of opulence. Likewise, the wealthier parts of Europe do not appear to be captivated by the American example, even if they could afford it: a psychology of scarcity has become embedded there; and the state rather than the corporation is looked to for the appropriate spending of whatever surplus there is—while industrialists know what to do with profits, namely, buy land and a title and escape from *"les mains sales."*

The growing bureaucratization of business in America is one reason why a career in business no longer captures the imagination of our most gifted young people; as in Europe, there is a tendency to look down on business as demeaning. The tragedies common enough even a generation ago, of young men forced to go into their father's businesses when they would like to have become artists or scholars, are much rarer today. For one thing, it isn't father's business any more, but the corporation's—the kinds of taken-for-granted nepotism Douglass North has recently described for life insurance companies at the turn of the century are now frowned upon. For another thing, father has lost his easy confidence that his way is the only way. So we find that the talents which in the 19th century found their entrepreneurial outlet in building a railway, a department store, a foundry, now find it in building a diocese (what industrialist is a match for Cardinal Spellman?), a labor union (what tycoon is as fiercely individualistic as John L. Lewis?), a new university or foundation (what promoter could not learn from Robert Hutchins?)—all the "tertiary" areas of the economy.

One way of looking at this development is to see that the most extensive and radical social changes seem to occur when there is a sudden breakdown of old traditions—so sudden the traditions cannot recover quickly and develop new institutional and ideological protections. Thus, in this country there was a period of ten to twenty years when the movies, an altogether new industry, could experiment quite freely without successful censorship from the outraged fundamentalists or successful bureaucratization from the side of outraged bankers and investors; only much later was the "cancerous" growth halted and the industry forcibly routinized in its financing and management, and partially subjected to the popular mores it had previously succeeded in flouting and indeed in altering. In the same way the auto industry went haywire, so to speak, in its initial stages, before the settling down of union resistance, standardized consumer taste, and corporate "responsibility"—even that old-time new-style tycoon, Henry Kaiser, could not shake loose from the traditions. In sum, much of the economy consists of more and less stabilized ways of doing business. The more stabilized ways, the traditions, provide a cushion against the shock of new developments, just as precapitalist motives and ideas protected capitalism from its own destructive tendencies; the traditions at the same time invite radical new developments by their very inelasticity in the face of moderate reform. In this country after the Civil War it was the economy that appeared more open to innovation than the churches or the law, whereas today the economy appears to many people as the official or vested part of society, where change is likely to be very slow. Who would have heard of Henry Luce if, like other of his Yale classmates, he had gone into banking or the railroads or the plate glass business?

All these changes indicate that the United States may at the present time be an ambiguous model for countries wanting to be rich, or to be less poor. As you go on tour you may discover how inefficient Americans frequently are, how lacking in precise technical or professional knowledge, how inexpert and fuzzy our "experts" often are—a theme to which my own lecture might be an introduction in itself. Our industrial system is geared to, or around, this inefficiency; our amiability makes us put up with it; our concept of know-how is often a way of generalizing our amateur spirit into a confident mood. There may well come a time when we will be sending productivity teams elsewhere, having exhausted our immigrant and rural resources of painstaking efficiency and workmindedness prematurely—before, that is, having made production wholly automatic. At a recent *Fortune*-magazine-sponsored conference on the automatic factory (an abbreviated write-up appears in the magazine for Oct. 1953, vol. 48, p. 168), I got the distinct impression that very few American engineers and industrialists were capable of easily conceptualizing a factory without operatives; this blockage of imagination appeared to be limiting experimentation with full automatization (as against experiment with ever more specialized transfer machines and machine tools). The American technicians seem not to have been able to overlook the needs, at least for employment, of those who presently do the manufacturing—at any rate sufficiently to put their organized ingenuity behind the up-to-date "requirements of manufacture" that might lead them to automatization. They fear unconsciously, and often vocally, to go too far in replacing men with machines.

Perhaps on your travels you will be shown the new Ford engine plant in Cleveland, and be told that this is automatic. But you will actually find it designed in terms of operatives who, to be sure, do little physical work, but are attached to the highly specialized machines which move and shape material, whereas in a truly automatic factory a tape or other source of coded information would "instruct" far less specialized machines in the specialized procedures for handling the particular product. The Ford engine plant is a huge, new, proud investment in the antithetical procedure—possibly, an example of the hardening of the American industrial imagination at its allegedly most advanced.

There is, however, one problem connected with automatization which is not likely to come up on your trip, though it is highly relevant to what I have been saying about the image of American industry as efficient. Let me remind you here of Warner Bloomberg, Jr.'s observation that the work-force in large modern plants covertly mediates between the rigid specifications insisted upon by the customer or the supervisor and their own informal knowledge that much looser specifications will still do the job. They know the idiosyncracies both of the customer and of the individual machines—in general, they know much more about the industrial process than they appear to know or get credit for knowing. Literal fulfillment of all plant regulations and obedience to blue-prints would either halt production or make it excessively costly. How, Bloomberg provocatively asks, can a tape be taught to deceive itself or disobey itself? How can the engineer who gives information to the machine know all the factory folklore which is in the workmen's heads and which he has previously, often unknowingly, depended upon? Will not the punched tape become a form of red tape, snarling the plant by virtue of its very orderliness and clarity, with which machines without men cannot cope?

Given the kinds of gaps that exist in America between what we do and what we say we do, I have no good answer to these questions.[7]

---

7. Professor Richard L. Meier, who has had extensive experience with automatic processes, believes that they have become increasingly necessary for quality control as a counter to labor inefficiency and sloppiness. He agrees that one cannot keep two sets of books with automatic factories—one for the tax collector or the customer and one for an inner circle—but feels that large corporations, worried about how to control deviations in the lower ranks, would welcome precisely this assured clarity. And he does not feel it is impossible for engineers, observing skilled workmen, to build the latter's know-how into the automatic process itself and thus stabilize it.

Furthermore, he points out that the rise of automatic processes will, like any

However, when I speculate about the prospects for the automatic factory in less industrially developed countries, I can see certain compensating advantages that might make experimentation with it worthwhile. Hitherto, whenever industry has gone into a folk culture, a tribal culture, it has been necessary forcibly to disrupt that culture to provide workmen. They have had to be taxed (as in South Africa or Dutch Indonesia) or tempted (as in the Tata Mills in India or the textile plants that have migrated from New Hampshire to North Carolina). Everywhere, people have had to be forced off the land, off the "reservation," and almost everywhere new values—punctuality, for instance—are instilled into them. It is only in the very late stages that the questions arise of the American song: "How are you goin' to keep 'em down on the farm . . . ?"; earlier, the problem is how to get them off. The fully automatic factory could conceivably be installed with very little shift in values: it needs a tiny workforce—even less than an oil refinery. Speaking now not in terms of questions of investment and trade which I am not equipped to answer, such a factory, with its electronic brains, could obviate in some measure the historic process of having natives work under non-native supervision, or the supervision of members of a different ethnic and religious group; for once the prefabricated plant was erected, nobody except a few maintenance men would work within it. Conflict would occur over what it should make and what should be done with the product by whom, but no conflict would arise—or human beings be "reformed"—within its walls.

Perhaps such talk of a magic carpet may seem very remote to you, struggling as many of you are with exigent questions of heavy machinery import or unfavorable terms of trade. Or you may share the worry of some American engineers, about what would happen to millions of workers if factories needed them no longer—whether they could be shifted rapidly enough to such service trades of high labor utilization as teaching, barbering, poetry, or social research. But if you do harbor such feelings, it would be some evidence for my hypothesis that the way the Western world happened to achieve industrialization exercises great fascination as the only way. As generals typically prepare for the last war, so many prepare to imitate an American industrial plant that may already be obsolete. When it was suggested to some people from Asia that vitamin factories, which are

technological revolution, alter the character of the managers: they will have to become more statistics-minded, more adept at handling complex chains of information, but may need less skill than before in the executive leadership of a workforce and in decision-making on the basis of hunches. His forthcoming book on world technological development will deal fully and imaginatively with these themes.

relatively inexpensive, might rather rapidly improve diet and well-being, it seemed to me that objections were too quickly found to a project which lacked "weight"—which approached industrial development, not the hard way but the easy way.

A certain asceticism operates here to limit the imagination. There were cracks at the Cadillacs in Kuwait in last year's sessions. There was competition in appearing unmaterialistic. There was recognition of the undeniable virtues of British austerity in the post-war period. Yet I sometimes wonder if this asceticism and austerity provide the best climate for the kind of thinking we need if we are to experiment with other as yet untried roads to economic development, and if we are to subvert our principal vested interest: that in prevailing models and patterns. A certain luxuriousness, a certain lack of dutifulness, may stimulate the imagination, as against the portentousness by which some of you pay for your privileges in being here when so many of your countrymen are in want. In the past, Puritanism has accompanied industrialization, but now that the going concern of industry is here, and diffusable, I wonder if that ethic is still as essential.

That crazy, gifted traveling salesman, Charles Fourier, makes the point quite well in his book, *Social Destinies*. After referring to poverty as "that most scandalous of all social disorders," he asks:

"In what parts of the world, has Civilization made the most progress? In Athens, in Paris, in London, where men have been in no sense the friends of mediocrity or of truth, but on the contrary have been the slaves of their passions, and devoted to intrigues, to wealth, and to luxury. And where has Civilization languished and remained stagnant? In Sparta, and in primitive Rome, where the voluptuous passions and the love of luxury had but a feeble development."

Fourier's point is especially significant for those countries which are seeking simultaneously to bring about industrialization and the welfare state. The spirit of luxury and playfulness exerts its force when it provides contrast with the workaday world and its grim tasks and not, of course, when it simply reinforces a traditional idleness among a privileged caste. Economic and other development may require an increase of asceticism among some strata and a moderate diminution of it among others. At least, if it is to take new forms rather than those already exhibited in the West.

We should, in sum, be wary of assuming that there is only one pattern, that which Pirenne, Sombart, Schumpeter, Robertson, Max Weber, and a host of other scholars have sought to delineate. We do know from the work of these men that technology is not separate from the rest of culture, but is part of a climate which in the modern

West includes Bach and Newton, Descartes and Calvin, and the monk who invented double-entry book-keeping. But we cannot know that there are no other combinations capable of producing similar end-results in industrial plant. (We do know that similar behavior can come in individuals as the result of radically different patterns of motivation.) There is no reason to assume that we have exhausted human inventiveness in recombining cultural forms.

Nineteenth-century systems of thought tend to obstruct us here. Thinkers of that epoch were preoccupied by the search for origins, the search for the stages through which historical development was bound to pass. Linear thinking prevailed. It was ethnocentric both in putting the West at the pinnacle of progress (or, in rare instances of inverse boastfulness, of decay) and in a kind of point-to-point evolutionism consonant with Western teleological modes of thinking and speaking. Various forms of belief in monolithic inevitability fell in with the misleading analogy between societal development and the stages through which an individual organism must pass. Today, we have become more skeptical, but not always more creative. It is easier for us to break down the schemes of Malthus and Marx, Comte and Spencer, Veblen and Pareto, than to imagine potential alternative sequences.

An illustration of what I have in mind can be drawn from contemporary studies by anthropologists of the character structure of both small Pacific tribes and larger national entities. The studies seem to me to indicate that some character types are more adaptable to industrial civilization than others who appear to share a similar culture pattern. For example, the inhabitants of the island of Truk in the Pacific (an island occupied by the Japanese between the wars and then by the Americans) seem to typify the biting variant of what the Freudians term the "anal" character: they deal with the environment by seizing it, by active mastery and aggression. Not only did they take readily to machines, they took readily to those who could instruct them in technical matters. The American Navy found them adaptable and teachable; the Trukese even beat a Navy baseball team. Their adaptability led the Americans to encourage them to become mechanics and speed-boat operators, but by the same token little pressure was put on their culture as a whole to succumb to Western values. Because of this closeness of fit, the impact of occupation and mechanization on Truk seems not to have been destructive or revolutionary: characterological compatibility was sufficient to minimize the problems of cultural dissimilarity. Such compatibility, to be sure, need not always have this consequence; we deal here with highly complex and also controversial matters; Truk is described very differently by the anthropologists George P. Murdock and Edward Hall, both of whom have been there (my own interpretation is based on Hall's work and on Erich Fromm's analysis of Trukese character in a seminar with Murdock and Ralph Linton at Yale).

By way of contrast, let us look at one or another of the Caribbean cultures, such as that of Cuba or Puerto Rico, which the Fromm-Linton seminar characterized as "male vanity" cultures: in some strata, mothers early encourage their boys in exhibitionism and older males likewise encourage younger ones. The individual of this character type has difficulty in learning to master new aspects of his environment because vanity dictates that he already know it. Any discrepancies tend to be "resolved" by words, by quick and facile verbalization. Thus, a number of my colleagues who have taught at the University of Puerto Rico report how difficult they find it to teach young men whose vanity is humiliatingly wounded if they don't already know everything—who therefore are blocked in doing homework, or serious studying, or patient apprenticeship to new methods. (To be sure, among students everywhere there is a good deal of this —male vanity is not a Latin monopoly!)

A "male vanity" culture can inhibit industrialization on at least three counts. First, all work, certainly sweaty or evidently pedantic work, tends to be regarded as dirty work. Men talk or fight; they do not grease machines or even draw blueprints. Secondly, they take to teamwork, to the building of industrial harmony, rather angularly: envy (symbolized in the ability of women to force their men to fight on behalf of their honor) is too uncontrolled; narcissism, as represented in Sebastiano in *The Fancy Dress Party* and other Moravia male characters, is too unsublimated. Thirdly, along with these difficulties on the side of production comes the equally important role of vanity in dictating consumption so that, as I have already indicated, conspicuous consumption may be very powerful in such cultures. Bert Hoselitz' study of San Salvador for the U.N., for instance, shows that the wealth accumulated by the leading families there is either invested in showy, if stony, ground or in flashy purchases in San Francisco or New York, whereas the Jews of San Salvador re-invest their money in industry and commerce; traditional Jewish culture, though it favors the male, does not encourage the prickly sensitivity to masculine honor of Spain or Latin America. (I need hardly add that a male vanity culture imposes a considerable barrier to the spread of contraception—other perhaps than oral contraception—among wives.) Yet it would be rash to say that the male vanity character type is incompatible with economic advance; rather, such advance might proceed by seeing how the energies mobilized by this type could be harnessed to new forms of work, perhaps through nationalistic ideology.[8] Conversely, any steps that would alter the fear men of this type have of what other men think of them, might have cumulative consequences far greater than direct and often wounding efforts to teach them new industrial techniques. A map of the world in terms of character type would be useful to the harbingers of economic development, if only in saving them heartbreak and in pointing to those groups whose character is such that industrialism is unlikely to be adopted without very considerable dislocation; the Arapesh, as Margaret Mead describes them, whose men are too passive, too unaggressive either for vanity or for current forms of industrial work, might be an example.

The difficulties inherent in this approach must be fairly evident to you. While speaking of male vanity cultures, I could not help thinking of Spaniards I have known who can hot-rod with the best of our American young people; indeed, hot-rodding is a very male pursuit precisely in its use of machines. I thought, too, of the extraordinary renaissance of Italian industrial design typified by Olivetti. The characterological descriptions of peoples which we now have are crude. Furthermore, not every society can be usefully described in psychoanalytic terms, even apart from the problems presented by the character differences within any large and complex population— and we scarcely have other terms than psychoanalytic ones which possess the necessary inclusiveness. All the same, I think the approach worth working with, both for its intrinsic interest and for the light it might shed on the variable consequences of the spread of industrialization, accompanied by very different ground-rules, in Asia and Africa.

To conclude: while much of the rest of the world seeks ways of accumulating the capital, characterological and financial, on which to base industrialization, a great many of us in America, I have suggested, can find no good reasons for such accumulation. We have lost not only many of the motives impelling industrialization but many

---

8. Richard Meier, who has studied the "case" of Puerto Rico with this perspective in mind, believes that progress in any traditional culture, including a "male vanity" one, depends on deviant types; he has found one source of "inner-directed" types in Puerto Rico in exceptionally energetic "poor but honest" families in rural areas, all of whose children, irrespective of sex, get education somehow and move up in the society. Such families cannot be separated from their neighbors on any easily evident demographic bases—the educated children say they "owe it all to their mothers." These children, Professor Meier believes, are the backbone of rural economic and technological innovation. But of course just what it is in their families that spurs them on remains a problem for further research.

of the motives which gave structure and meaning to life itself. We have approached the accomplishment of one mission and are searching for another.

Very possibly, it will prove as difficult to find a moral equivalent for capitalism as William James discovered it was to find a moral equivalent for war. But I don't believe new goals are beyond human powers to invent. We Americans are tempted to extrapolate from our present situation rather than to invent, much as I have here suggested that other peoples are tempted to imitate Western industrial development rather than invent alternative patterns. I differ from many pragmatists in believing that one must go on imagining new goals, new aspirations, even if at any given time one cannot imagine their implementation; I hope you will feel the same way about such tentative and illustrative suggestions as that of the automatic factory even if you cannot quite see how to get from here to there. We know one thing for sure: that the future is going to be different from what we think, and probably more various. Among many reasons for this, our creativity, stimulated by such conferences as this, is one element. The M.I.T. students who brought us together dreamed up the whole idea, then found the means to implement it. They exemplify the new generation of American entrepreneurs who engage in team-work, are not profit-minded, and seek outlets in the world beyond our borders. It will be hard for you to understand their motives, but if you succeed in doing so, you will grasp a good many of the difficulties I have thrown your way this afternoon.

FREUD AND PSYCHOANALYSIS

THE ESSAYS in this section (and one on Veblen in the previous section) represent, as the rest of the volume does not, my abiding interest in intellectual history, especially in the relation between great thinkers and their milieu. I suppose in one aspect this is part of my preoccupation with individualism—with how some unique figure in the history of thought is able to arrive at and to maintain an independent view; I have touched on this earlier in the essays on utopian thinking and the "nerve of failure." However, I find intellectual history one of the subtlest of fields: I am skeptical of most accounts of "influences," and think that the road to or from Xanadu can be traced only with the greatest caution coupled with intense disquiet. Even when I speak, let us say, of the influence of Freud on middle-class marital relations or vice versa, I can not get rid of a sociologist's query as to how many were influenced by how much, and the "obvious" relations do not quite assuage me. All of history seems to me beset by similar pitfalls of causality and coincidence, and intellectual history is the more dangerous because of the delusive confidence its documents and texts, letters and journals, may engender.

In these essays, I have bypassed most of these issues in the history of ideas by concentrating primarily on the writings of Freud in terms of certain familiar dualisms: work and play, authority and liberty, heroism and weakness—I had also planned to include love and hate, reason and unreason (day and night), and others. My work on Freud, in which I profited from discussion with Philip Rieff and Murray Wax, was intensively carried on in 1946 and 1947 but, like the music project, was interrupted by my leaves of absence at Yale. Since these articles were written, a great deal of new information has been assembled on Freud's beginnings and the precise intellectual meteorology of his education has been carefully delineated—in articles by Siegfried and Suzanne Cassirer Bernfeld, in the Harvard doctoral thesis of Richard L. Schoenwald (done under Crane Brinton), and in the first volume of Ernest Jones' biography. In addition, the discovery of Freud's letters to Fliess has thrown unexpected and revealing light on the period of his greatest isolation—and greatest achievement—

the period after the break from Breuer and prior to the publication of the book on dreams. In reprinting my essays, however, I have taken no account of this accumulated learning which, to take an instance, shows Freud to have been somewhat less isolated than he leads one to think, even when he was most under the ban of traditional Viennese psychiatry. Nor have I taken account of the remarkable article of Erik H. Erikson, "The Specimen Dream of Psychoanalysis," which shows what a really skillful dream interpreter, familiar with the background, can do with Freud's own dreams.

One qualification, however, should be noted. The original context of these articles was an audience almost wholly sympathetic to Freud —students and staff in the College at the University of Chicago to whom I presented three lectures on Freud in the fall of 1946. Freud's writings had already been admitted there to the elite list of "Great Books," and a number of my colleagues were then rather orthodox adherents of Freud. Nor was Freud news to the majority of students; on the contrary, they seemed to me to be too inclined to swallow him whole as part of their progressivism. The situation was very different from my own undergraduate days when no course I took had Freud on a reading list and when the only classroom reference I heard to him was a sneering reference to "Saints Sigmund and Karl" who were presumably up to no good—days when my mother, an early and ardent admirer of Freud, hesitated to call my attention to him lest my father, a physician, object. In this context I did not have to worry lest I give cause for new sneers at Freud, nor was this a problem in the catholic, if often "Neo-Freudian," pages of *Psychiatry*. Here, let me state explicitly for the critical reader that what I know or think I know of Freud, I owe to Freud; that no one else has contributed so much to the vitality of the social sciences today; that my admiration, indeed wonder, at Freud's achievement remains undimmed by my criticisms of many of his views. These essays were not intended to please the orthodox, but neither were they intended to encourage glib dismissals of Freud, among those who know his work only through snippets and hearsay (as someone said when asked if he'd read a certain book: "not personally").

Schoenwald in his doctoral dissertation makes one serious criticism of these essays, namely that they regard Freud's work as if it had all been done at one time, not allowing for chronological development. This is correct: I rely primarily on Freud's early works, and I develop my themes irrespective of dates. But I think this is less of a drawback than would be the case were it my aim to state Freud's position on one or another issue of theory or therapy; rather, my central concern is Freud's outlook on man in society, and this changed I believe very little over the years, save for an obvious growth in pessimism. What is interesting is to find in a dream-interpretation of the nineties the germ of an idea that was not to receive the full treatment from Freud until a generation later when he turned to explicit philosophizing. While some distortion doubtless results from treating his remarks, spread over a long and active life, as if they had all been uttered in one breath, and while this may sometimes discover contradiction where there was dialectical development, I am inclined to think that no essential injustice has been done to a man one of whose principal claims to eminence was, as he once remarked, the courage of his prejudices—or, as we might say of him, the stubbornness of Moses.

These essays also deal, all too briefly, with one of the most interesting social movements of our day: the psychoanalytic movement of the last half century. In this aspect, the essays are to be compared with the one on the law in the final section, or on recreationists in Section IV, as studies of an occupational group and its vicissitudes as professionalization sets in. To survivors of an earlier analytic era such as Theodor Reik, this professionalization is as unwelcome as a settled grievance procedure is to the union militant who recalls the glorious and unsettling days of sit-down strikes; and perhaps my essays reflect a shade too critical and unperspectivistic a view of the contemporary regularization and "secularization" of analysis. For this stage of the movement has of course its positive sides. I am especially impressed with these after a recent visit to Winter Veterans' Administration Hospital in Topeka where a huge institution, of the sort which before World War II would have been a retreat for doctors on a permanent lost weekend, is now fired with the Menningers' enthusiasm for analytic therapy and their Foundation's enthusiasm for research.

"Freud, Religion, and Science," the final essay in this section, also deals with the contemporary situation of psychoanalysis, especially vis-à-vis organized religion. It was originally a wire-recorded lecture in a series on "Attack and Counter-Attack in Religion," which dealt with such figures as Nietzsche, Marx, Malinowski, Schweitzer, Niebuhr, and Toynbee—a series organized by the Unitarian student group at the University of Chicago. Excerpts have been published in *The American Scholar* and (under the title, "Freud: Religion as Neurosis") in the *University of Chicago Roundtable*. The remarks on American Catholicism in this address might well have been included in the section on Marginality, Minorities, and Freedom; they spring out of the interest I share with Everett C. Hughes in the sociology of American religious groups, a field in which a few of our students have been active. As the paper indicates, I believe Freud has done more than any other psychologist to stimulate the scientific study of religion—something that William James was unable to accomplish. (Max Weber and the anthropologists, if we include Durkheim, have probably done more.) But of course what I say about Catholicism remains at the most general and tentative level—a beginning of discourse rather than a terminus.

Students at Chicago sometimes ask why they are given Freud to read and not Jung, Adler, Rank, and other dissidents. Indeed, why should Freud rather than Jung be chosen in a series on religion? The answer must be institutional as well as individual: for a variety of reasons, it is Freud and his followers who have had the principal impact on American social science; it is they who have helped give direction to the new field of "culture and personality" studies, who have sent anthropologists to the field to study totems and taboos— if only to disprove Freud. Freud's followers were here first with the most, and no one can understand American cultural anthropology or social and clinical psychology or psychiatry without understanding Freud's work. Conceivably, Jung's theories or Adler's might have had this role; they didn't. One reason, I suspect, has to do with social status. Jung's theories, with their mystical flavor and racial emphasis, their "archetypical" focus, tend to appeal to the aristocracy—and indeed, humanists, often the aristocrats of academia, have been in some cases disciples of Jung. Adler's theories, with their common-sense flavor, their socialist humanitarianism coupled with underdog understandings, tend to appeal to the rare scientist who has a working-class identification; such men, in fact, working in clinics with poor patients and with an unequivocal therapeutic focus, are apt to have little time and resource for research and writing. By comparison, Freud is definitely bourgeois or upper-middle class; his theories have enough complexity to intrigue the highly educated, without frightening them by Jungian vagueness or offending them by Adlerian vulgarity; there may even be a connection between a certain compulsiveness in Freud's rationalism (a theme discussed in all these essays) and the ferocious industry of the Freudian adherents for whom, like Freud himself, therapy is not enough, but must be legitimated by research and by publication, despite the arduousness of the resulting daily round. While what I term in these essays the "third generation" of analysts is less preoccupied than Freud was with philosophic, religious, and generally "metapsychological" questions, they are no less research-minded and no less hard working bourgeois; their questions tend to be more technical, less "theoretical," more cautious—after all, they have been taught where Freud went wrong, as he did in his anthropology.

Very soon, I expect, the psychoanalytic movement will be hardly distinguishable from the broad front of research in personality—even now, psychoanalysis and psychiatry are in many institutions virtually interchangeable. (However, I also expect that there will continue to be men—cranky ones—who rediscover Freud with the freshness of first seeing, and who seek to lead reformation movements based on his books.) But of course such a sociology of intellectual movements must always halt before it pushes trend-thinking too far, realizing the importance of the role of single, unpredictable individuals. No one could have predicted the theories or the human accomplishment of Freud, or his first gifted disciples, even if one might have foreseen that, given a few energetic adherents, he would take hold in the United States as he has in no other land.

21. The Themes of Work and Play in the Structure of Freud's Thought

THE PROCESS of incorporating Freud's thought into our living heritage of social and humanistic studies has moved bewilderingly fast, especially in America. But incorporation, as always with great thinkers, has been partial. There has been a tendency, among Freud's medical followers, to "empiricize" him, to forget about his philosophical interests and outlook in order to get on with the clinical job. Among non-specialists, however, it is this philosophical side of Freud's thought that has often been most influential. In generally accepting it at face without an effort to refer it back to its base in Freud's own experience, people have neglected the very kind of reference he taught us to make. In my opinion, it is not possible to separate his technique from his cultural outlook and setting. It is sometimes said that he was a therapist and medical man in his earlier writings and a gloomy and speculative philosopher in his later writings. But we must be wary of such dichotomies by which, for many, the "good" Freud is separated from the "bad" Freud as, by similar measures, the "good" early Comte is separated from the "bad" later Comte, or the "good" Marx of *The German Ideology* from the "bad" Marx of the *Manifesto* or *Capital*. Though of course there are important differences in emphases, these men are of a piece—this, too, Freud would teach us—and their earlier writings contain the germs of the later views.

I have sought to establish this wholeness of the man in the light of certain important themes in Freud's philosophic and social outlook, by examining some of the implications of his early writings, making particular use of his own reported dreams. The later explicit statements in such writings as *Civilization and Its Discontents* or *The Future of an Illusion*[1] often merely confirm and elaborate a position that can be inferred from the "Dora" history, for instance, or from the book on dreams. I have, so far as possible, avoided coming into contact with biographical material or gossip about Freud, in order to see what the works themselves, so bravely revealing, have to say.

For my purposes here, it is not of very great importance to decide

1. *Civilization and Its Discontents* develops, *inter alia*, certain themes set forth in "'Civilized' Sexual Morality and Modern Nervousness," *Collected Papers* 2:76, published in 1908, and the Clark University lectures of the following year.

at what point Freud's writings reveal him as a unique person—reveal, that is, his own deep affective involvement in an idea—and at what point he simply speaks, without much affect or individuation, in terms stereotypical of the general attitude of the era.[2] Certainly, his utilitarian and Philistine attitudes toward work and play were both central to his own view of life and a dominant note in his cultural environment. But what really matters for us is that by virtue of his greatness —by virtue, too, of the fact that he was on the whole a liberator of men—Freud has succeeded in imposing on a later generation a mortgage of reactionary and constricting ideas that were by no means universally held even in his own epoch. Like so many original thinkers, he was ambivalent; he provides the texts for the partialities of incorporation, and for contradictory life-paths and social policies.[3]

In this essay, I deal with Freud's basic attitudes to work and to play. They were formed in a society that was primarily job-minded; they circulate today in an American society that has much more chance to be leisure-minded and play-minded. While my preoccupation is with the social and cultural implications, it will I think be clear that the more technical contributions of Freud—for instance, his theory of dream interpretation, or his concept of the analytic transference—were to a very considerable degree shaped by his class and cultural outlook. This, of course, does not mean that the contributions are wrong; rather it helps us understand them, and puts us on the lookout for unsuspected pitfalls of ideological bias that may be hidden beneath questions of technique.

§ WORK: FREEDOM OR NECESSITY

FREUD VIEWED work as an inescapable and tragic necessity. Although he was no student of population problems, he implicitly agreed with Malthus' gloomy conclusion that men would be forever caught between the drives of hunger and sex—lucky to be one jump ahead of starvation. And sex, too, was for Freud a realm of necessity. He saw it, not as presenting men with a problem to be solved, nor with a

---

2. To decide this question, in each specific case, could be often highly speculative and difficult. Problems of the same sort arise when one seeks to interpret contemporary interview material, at least of a nonpsychoanalytic sort. There one must always ask: Does what the respondent reports say much about him as an individual, or is it mainly testimony—and, of course, that he gives this testimony says something about him—to the norm of his group, his social class, or the group or class to which he aspires? In Freud's case, we have the advantage of his reported dreams and associations, and many stray remarks, which it is sometimes possible to reinterpret by use of the method he discovered.

3. See Erich Fromm, "Individual and Social Origins of Neurosis," *Amer. Sociological Rev.* (1944) 9:380; reprinted in Clyde Kluckhohn and Henry A. Murray, eds., *Personality in Nature, Society, and Culture.*

game to be played, nor, coupled with love, as a road to human closeness and intimacy, but rather as a "teleological" prime mover, charged
with the task of socializing and civilizing men and thus preserving the
species. Sex could fulfill this task because of its ability to bribe with
an elemental pleasure and to appease with an elemental release. Work
was, then, the means by which the species maintains itself while performing its endless procreative mission.

This outlook, heavily influenced by Puritanism, took shape in the
early nineteenth century, in part as a reaction against the views of
utopian visionaries—men such as Condorcet, Godwin, and Owen—who
envisaged the possibility that, beyond this realm of necessity, might
lie a realm of freedom where work had social meaning and where the
economy would be our servant, not our master.

Needless to say, men are producing animals and must work in
order to live. Moreover, it is altogether likely, men being the creatures
they are and work being what it is, that some drudgery will continue to be associated with it. The question of the meaning of work, of
how it is experienced, is primarily a cultural problem; and cultures
differ enormously in the way work is interpreted in their value-
scheme. In some, work is not sharply differentiated from other aspects of life. It may be viewed as fulfilling religious duties; it may
have the pleasurable variety, creativeness, and interpersonal texture
which is associated with some kinds of farming, or artisanship, art,
or science. It may be viewed in other ways. Only, probably, in our
Western industrial culture, has work in fact the features Freud at-
taches to it; is it sharply set off against love, against pleasure, against
consumption, against almost every sort of freedom. Only here is it
a curse for most people, mitigated as such, often enough, not by its
own nature, but by the fear of boredom, which can be even greater
than the irksomeness of toil.

In the nineteenth century, dominated by scarcity economics and
Malthusian fears, work could nevertheless be given the rational meaning of the avoidance of hunger. And hunger and gain (ambition)
could be viewed as the self-evident motives of a market economy, the
former operating on the poor, the latter on the well-to-do.[4] In the
mid-twentieth century, in the countries of the Industrial Revolution
and especially in America, it is likely that with very little human
toil a full abundance can be assured to all inhabitants as the result
of the machine technology. But although the result has already been
a great lowering in the hours of work and vast improvement in physical conditions, work itself is still subjectively felt as a duty, without

---

4. Cf. Karl Polanyi, *The Great Transformation.*

meaning in its own terms. This is most striking evidence of the fact that the pattern of a culture can disguise, even distort, the inescapable problem of work. Neither the basic physiological drive of hunger, nor the basic equipment of production—man's brain and eyes and hands—instruct him in what meaning, what pattern, he shall give to work, any more than the basic drive of sex, and its genital equipment, tell him what meaning, what pattern, he shall give to love.

It is, as I shall try to show, the more pessimistic, middle-class, nineteenth-century attitudes that are reflected and elaborated in Freud's thought. I shall consider, first, his view of the "real," the workaday world, including his view of his own role in it, and, second, his attitude towards the subordinated world of play.

§ THE WORKADAY WORLD

FREUD, LIKE SO MANY scientists of a system-building cast of mind, was always in search of simplifying dichotomies, of polar opposites. As the "self" was the opposite of the "other," as the pleasure-principle and the reality-principle—or Eros and Thanatos—divided life between them, so the workaday world with its productive machinery, its markets, its other economic processes, was sharply marked off from the play-world, the world of fantasy and gratification. The former world, Freud took for granted as he found it; he reserved his insight and his unconventionality largely for the latter.

Freud regarded the world of business and professional life—of all areas where hunger and gain were alleged to hold sway—as unquestionably real. The views of critics, such as Veblen or Thurman Arnold, who see the mythical or fantastic elements of business enterprise,[5] are foreign to his mode of thought. It did not seem to occur to him that much work was obsessive busy-work, that businessmen often fled into work to avoid women, or that the seeming pursuit of business self-interest might be the sheerest rationalization for activities that were quite differently motivated. To be sure, the European businessman is more of an "economic man" than his American counterpart; his compartmentalization of work, separate from home and from play, is more complete; he *does* seek gain as his principal end, rather than friends, prestige, or an agenda. Nevertheless, Freud's attitude towards the work that men do in their occupations was almost that of a behaviorist who does not probe into motives.

Indeed, Freud concluded his book on dreams on the qualifiedly behaviorist note that "actions, above all, deserve to be placed in the front rank" in judging human character, since the dark and daemonic

---

5. See, for example, Thorstein Veblen, *The Theory of Business Enterprise;* Thurman Arnold, *The Folklore of Capitalism.*

psychic forces he had been describing had usually only the most limited consequences in the real, that is, the workaday, world.[6] In the same volume, Freud described the dream-experiments of his colleague, Dr. Schrötter, and concluded: "Unfortunately, the value of this important investigation was diminished by the fact that Dr. Schrötter shortly afterwards committed suicide."[7] There was no note of sympathy or grief for this human tragedy: what mattered to Freud was the work and not the man. Such behavioristic views seem to be a reflection of the psychology of a market-economy: it does not matter what men think or how they feel, but only that, overtly, they react "appropriately" to the stimuli of hunger and gain.

Middle-Class Conventions Concerning Work

Freud's friends and patients, mainly upper-middle-class folk, were not supposed to be motivated by the spur of hunger, but by the hope of gain. Freud knew penury as a youth—financial needs drove him out of the laboratory and into practice—but it was still the penury of the rising student, not of the destitute proletarian. He assumed that the individualistic motives of getting on in the world, the desires of fame and success, were perfectly "natural"; it did not occur to him that they might be culturally stimulated or produced, let alone that they might be in themselves, neurotic drives. While he was apt to minimize the extent of his own ambition, it did not trouble him to avow his wish to be a full professor, to be famous, to be "an authority." With the exception of the cases where he had personal experience of bigotry or incompetence, he rather easily assumed that his teachers such as Brücke or Meynert were "great masters," entitled to "veneration";[8] there was nothing unreal about their attainments and position. And, just as he assumed without question the conventions about greatness, he also assumed the other conventions of the workaday world—for instance, about the great importance of priority in scientific work. In one of his dreams he is anxious to "give Professor N. due credit for his diagnosis."[9]

The Playboy Classes

Three social groups seemed to Freud to be immune to the demands of the workaday world. These were the aristocrats, who needed only

---

6. Freud, "The Interpretation of Dreams," in *The Basic Writings of Sigmund Freud*, p. 548.

7. Reference footnote 6; p. 386.

8. Reference footnote 6; pp. 407, 409, 417. For a disavowal of ambition, see p. 219, and cf. pp. 257, 446.

9. Reference footnote 6; p. 333.

to be born in order to be fed;[10] the professional artists and writers, who were privileged not only to live in the play-world of illusion but to draw from it the realities of fame and fortune;[11] and the monks and priests.[12]

The artist, as Freud viewed him, had the gift of being able to sell his day-dreams, his fantasy productions, even his megalomania, on the market; he could appeal to the hidden dreams and desires of his audience who responded by bestowing on him the admiration he could not have won in direct economic or sexual competition. The artist, moreover, was free from the arduous conventions of the scientist; by his gift, he could obtain a release from what others have to do and gain as direct an access to truth as to the hearts of mankind. While for the scientist, too—such as Freud—dreams and fancies might be real data, he must work and not play with them in order to make a profit.[13] But he must on no account "waste" his talents; Freud found Leonardo da Vinci infantile when, instead of turning his powers to account, he employed them in ephemeral toys and antic jests.[14] In a different vein, he also found Leonardo's passion for investigation neurotic: where one investigates the universe (instead of acting on it, or moving one's fellowmen by great art), one obviously misses real values for which a normal person would strive.[15] Naturally Freud applied to his own work a similarly conventional judgment: what helped him to cure patients was "real"; all else was "speculation."[16]

While, however, the artist had a privileged position in the native ease with which he won success, he remained, in Freud's eyes, a mere decoration upon the economic and political processes which mattered in the workaday world. Freud, the middle-class patron of the theatre and collector of figurines, wrote of art as a monarch might speak of his court jester: "Art is almost always harmless and beneficent, it

---

10. See Freud's dream of Count Thun (reference footnote 6; p. 415).

11. "A kindly nature has bestowed upon the artist the capacity to express in artistic productions his most secret psychic feelings hidden even from himself, which powerfully grips outsiders, strangers to the artist, without their knowing whence this emotivity comes." Freud, *Leonardo da Vinci*, p. 84.

12. See, for example, Freud, "A Neurosis of Demoniacal Possession in the Seventeenth Century," in *Collected Papers* 4:436; see especially pp. 470-471.

13. However, even a scientist may sometimes be lucky; thus Freud writes: "From the reports of certain writers who have been highly productive, such as Goethe and Helmholtz, we learn, rather, that the most essential and original part of their creations came to them in the form of inspirations, and offered itself to their awareness in an almost completed state." Freud, reference footnote 6; p. 543.

14. Reference footnote 11; p. 108.

15. Reference footnote 11; pp. 42-43.

16. Freud, *A New Series of Introductory Lectures on Psycho-analysis*, pp. 207, 218.

does not seek to be anything else but an illusion. Save in the case of a few people who are, one might say, obsessed by Art, it never dares to make any attacks on the realm of reality."[17] Freud's attitude towards Count Thun, the aristocratic "do-nothing" Prime Minister of Austria, was not very different: he, too, was a privileged idler.[18]

Work as the Man's World

Only in one respect did Freud deal with success as anything but an obvious, self-evident goal which justifies the expenditure of immense efforts: he observed that in day-dreams men seek to throw their laurels at the feet of beautiful women. Does it follow from this that the real world, too, was in Freud's eyes subordinate to sex? The question raises all sorts of ambiguities. On one level, Freud saw men's libidinal drives, coupled in various harnesses with their aggressive ones, as the source of all their productions: work was a channelling and sublimation of these drives. But on another level, the nighttime sphere of sex was clearly subsidiary to the daytime sphere of work, of accomplishment in the real world. For one thing, in Freud's eyes the man of potency and means, unintimidated by cultural taboos, would have no difficulty in finding appropriate sexual outlets. Achievement —making a dent in the world—this was the problem. Indeed, women were only trophies, to be tied, metaphorically, at the conqueror's wheel: they were a by-product, pleasant enough, of his achievement, but only incidentally an aim.

The workaday world then was clearly a man's world. Speaking again of Leonardo, Freud referred to his "manly creative power" prior to his homosexual, reflective and investigative stage;[19] Freud's attitude towards Hamlet's indecision expressed a quite similar judgment. This "man's" world was threatened, not only by homosexual tendencies, but by an excessive, uncautious interest in women. In connection with one of his dreams, Freud tells us his fear that his sons' talents will be "ruined by women," just as the great Lassalle was killed in a duel over a lady.[20]

The place of women in this man's world was rather like that as-

---

17. Reference footnote 16; p. 219.
18. See Freud's dream of Count Thun (reference footnote 6; p. 415).
19. Reference footnote 11; p. 115.
20. Reference footnote 6; pp. 333-334. Freud does not see that Lassalle was lured to his death, not by feminine wiles, but by his highly ambivalent ambition for social status and fear of social humiliation. The plebian Jewish Lassalle, despite his leftist views, was moved by the unconscious wish to prove his patent of nobility; therefore, his real "folly" lay precisely in acceptance of the motives and outlook which Freud took as the highest, most realistic wisdom. Cf. George Brandes, *Ferdinand Lassalle*.

signed to them in Veblen's ironic *The Theory of the Leisure Class.*[21]
Their very narcissism makes them desirable objects of display; their
role is to be fed, tended, exhibited. But they must remain tractable in
their gilded cage, and neither lure men to failure by giving them
syphilis or otherwise draining their work-potential, nor, above all,
enter the world of men as competitors.[22] Indeed, any effort of a
woman to take part in the real world, in any capacity other than
consumer of goods and libido, was interpreted as a desire to make
up for her lack of a penis, the organ of power and creativeness. So
strong were Freud's psychoanalytic rationalizations of the conventional Victorian—or, as Veblen would hold, predatory—attitude towards women, that they still impress many psychoanalysts, even
women psychoanalysts.[23] Freud seems to have coped with the inconsistency, from his viewpoint, of his own daughter's entry upon
analytic work by assigning to women analysts the field of child-
analysis—very much as women in industrial management today are
assigned the job of handling the morale problems, not of men and
women, but of women only.

§ MAN'S NATURAL LAZINESS AND THE FUTILITY OF SOCIALISM

THE GRIMNESS of today's workaday world, as Freud saw and accepted
it, is so great that it is understandable that men should exhibit signs of
laziness, as if to justify the charge that they would not turn a hand,
without the spur of hunger and gain. It is not surprising therefore to
find Freud falling in with the hoary argument which seeks to derive
the futility of socialism from the observed laziness of the working
class.[24]

The Passive Paradise

This attitude Freud expressed in his interpretation of the myth of
the Garden of Eden, which he saw as meaning that man longed for
the idyllic idleness of the womb, or of childhood—the next-best in
dependent passivity. But man was driven by his "original sin"—

---

21. Veblen, *The Theory of the Leisure Class.*
22. "We say also of women that their social interests are weaker than those
of men, and that their capacity for the sublimation of their instincts is less."
Reference footnote 16; p. 183.
23. Cf., for example, Helene Deutsch, *The Psychology of Women*, vol. I,
chapters 7 and 8 .
24. Reference footnote 16; p. 246. Freud found socialism impossible on other
grounds as well, namely man's natural aggressiveness, which departs somewhat
from the conservative Malthusian pattern; but aggressiveness, too, comes down,
though only in part, to the scarcity of possessions and men's desire to seize them
from each other, rather than to work for them.

apparent in the sexual-aggressive Oedipus complex—to violate the conditions under which he might be taken care of in carefree bliss. Forced out of Paradise, he had ever after to work in the world, as sign and as penance; only in illusion could he momentarily return. Freud, who was accustomed to overturn many myths and see through them, accepted this myth as an historical truth, or rather as a primitive anticipation of the Victorian conviction that "life is real, life is earnest." A similar view is implicit in Freud's theory that man, as child and primitive, passed through a stage of belief in the omnipotence of thought. This magical thinking, in which wishes are automatically gratified, as they almost are for the infant, seemed to Freud to constitute one part of the charm of Paradise; men give it up for reality-thinking only under the pressure of frustration and pain. "If wishes were horses, beggars would ride"—or, more accurately, would fly. By a word, men would annihilate bothersome rivals, as Freud actually did in one of his most striking dreams.[25] The intensity of wishes and their violent ability to propel a dream thus arise from the fact that wish-fulfillment was once effortless, and that men never become reconciled to a workaday world in which this is no longer so. Freud assumed that men do not grow psychically, that nothing new happens to them in the course of development which might lead them to desire activity for its own sake.

Thus Freud had no doubt whatever that man needs to be driven into reality, by an angry God or his earthly deputies. Children, he felt, naturally did not want to grow up; they must be forcibly socialized, forcibly adapted to reality.[26] Parents who fail early to acquaint the child with pain, with what he must expect from the world, will create neurotics, recusants to their workaday tasks. Freud had no faith in his own children's talents as self-realizing, and he enjoined upon his wife the "training" by which these would be husbanded.[27]

In all this, I feel that Freud patronizes infancy and childhood. Even small infants seem to want to explore the universe—and not only in search of food and sex. Children—though, of course, like all of us, they have moments of regression—often are stifled in their wish to grow up, to accept responsibility and arduous tasks, by adult authorities who underestimate them. Conversely, adults, and children, too, forced to work at a pace that is not their own, react by rejecting work, in fantasy if not in featherbedded fact.

---

25. Reference footnote 6; p. 406. Freud says in the introduction to the second edition of the book on dreams that many of the dreams reported were connected with the poignant and emotionally significant period of his father's death.

26. Reference footnote 16; p. 201.

27. Reference footnote 6; p. 333.

§ FREUD'S ATTITUDE TOWARDS HIS OWN WORK

FREUD'S VERY DEFINITION of pleasure as release of physiological tension contains, in capsulated form, the essence of his attitude towards work. Even though he might, under certain conditions, regard work as a sublimatory release of tensions which are sexual in origin—which permits him on occasion to speak of "intellectual pleasures"—still he viewed these as only a poor second-best, purchased through a stunting of the primary, libidinal releases.[28] But if pleasure is release of tension, then toil—ordinarily the opposite of release—is by definition arduous. Nevertheless, despite the elaborateness of Freud's physiological and metapsychological explanations, despite all his talk about pleasure-principle and reality-principle, we must not forget the cultural setting: How could he as a self-respecting Victorian admit that his work was anything else but a chore? To speak of his job, as Americans today often do—usually with like conventionality—as "good fun," would hardly befit a practitioner of the Harley Streets of the world; we need merely remind ourselves of the unspeakable boredom from which even the most exciting case could hardly rescue the languorous Sherlock Holmes.

The Slave of Science

Freud's work, as I read his own account of it, seems to me of the very greatest intellectual interest; beside such detective work, even that of Sherlock Holmes is pallid and limited. But Freud seems to have found—or at least admitted to—almost no pleasure in it; on the contrary, his writings are full of references to his weariness, to the arduousness, rather than the ardor, of his unique intellectual adventure. "It is a habit of mine to run up two or three steps at a time"[29]— how blithely he speaks of "habit" rather than symptom when it is himself he is describing. His hurried days were almost incredible: ten or twelve hours of analysis—made especially anxious by the novelty of the task and the dangerously isolated position of the therapist— followed by writing up his notes on his cases;[30] then working far into the night on his writing, lectures, and correspondence; at night, writing and interpreting his frequent dreams, sometimes pages in length—only *once* did he not make "careful notes" on a dream;[31] finally, rousing himself in the morning with the greatest effort to begin another weary round.[32] Even when he suffered from the most

---

28. Reference footnote 11; p. 46.
29. Reference footnote 6; p. 290.
30. Reference footnote 6; p. 197.
31. Reference footnote 6; p. 349.
32. Reference footnote 6; p. 210.

painful boils, he refused to rest from "my peculiarly strenuous work."[33] until ordered to by the doctor. And of course in later life, his agonizing cancer of the throat gave him no excuse to slow the pace of his labor. Like other middle-class, self-made, self-driven men, he could only relax at the conventional times: on his vacation, or at the parties to which he infrequently went. He said of himself, characteristically, after a summer evening's lecture: "I was tired; I took not the least pleasure in my difficult work, and longed to get away from this rummaging in human filth. . . ."[34] But, even on vacation, Freud could not abandon his vocation. Just as he "amused" himself by examining starfish on his first visit to the Irish Sea at the age of 19[35]—how different his preoccupations from those of James Joyce by the Irish Sea—so he drove himself even in his beloved Italy, like any harried tourist.[36] Though he reproaches himself, or permits himself to be reproached, for his hobbies,[37] as for his other "vices" such as smoking which did not directly contribute to his work, he did in fact manage to turn most of his "play" to economic account, like a cook who saves her leftovers for a stew. He enjoyed jokes—and collected them for a book on wit; he loved Michaelangelo—and wrote a long analysis of his "Moses" statue; his wide reading of novels and poetry was automatically and unaffectedly ransacked for analytic clues. So in fact, nothing was "wasted"—nothing, that is, but Freud, who took for himself Claude Bernard's motto, "*Travailler comme une bête.*"

In return for his Spartan zeal, Freud allowed himself to take pride in his conscientiousness, especially in cases involving no admixture of interest, like the twice-a-day injections he gave a cranky old lady;[38] while he scolded those "spoilt" gentlemen, the devout, who "had an easier time of it with their revelation."[39] And, indeed, the Sisyphus task of science, endlessly pursuing truth, becomes for Freud the very core of his personal philosophy of life.[40] Nevertheless, while Freud would agree with Spinoza that "the joy by which the drunkard is enslaved is altogether different from the joy which is the portion of the philosopher,"[41] still he would have insisted that there is little joy, but much enslavement, in the philosopher's quest.

33. See Freud's dream of not working; reference footnote 6; pp. 284-285.
34. Reference footnote 6; p. 441.
35. Reference footnote 6; p. 475.
36. Reference footnote 6; p. 414. Freud speaks of wearing out his brother "by rushing him too quickly from place to place, and making him see too many beautiful things in a single day."
37. See the dream of the botanical monograph; reference footnote 6; p. 243.
38. Reference footnote 6; pp. 204, 206 *et seq.*
39. Reference footnote 16; p. 237.
40. Reference footnote 16; pp. 236-238.
41. *The Philosophy of Spinoza*, edited by Joseph Ratner, p. 245.

"Per Ardua ad Astra."

In one very important respect, Freud's Puritan attitude towards work in general, and to his own work in particular, had a profound influence on the whole psychoanalytic method. For he assumed, as a matter of course, that any answer to which one came without arduous toil must be wrong. It was this feeling, that truth must cost something if it is to be worth anything, which, among other factors, led Freud to feel that the more far-fetched and "difficult" the solution, the more probable its correctness. Thus, despite his reference, which we have earlier quoted, to the successful "intuitions" of his admired Goethe and Helmholtz, he distrusted intuition in psychoanalysis. Repeatedly, he attacked the "intuitive" method of dealing with dream-symbolism.[42] Moreover, not only in dream-interpretation, but in all his work, Freud played down the role of intuition, just as he distinguished between mere "speculation" and real scientific work. Again and again, he referred to himself as a sober-sided, meticulous investigator, who never jumps to conclusions, but constantly acknowledges his dependence in observation and theory, on "the real external world."[43] Understanding is the reward, not of the gifts of genius, but of the "expenditure of effort."[44] Undoubtedly, Freud expended tremendous effort, but of course it is not only this which led him to his genuine innovations. While he accused intuition of arbitrariness, the very logical, and often pedestrian, rigor of his own treatment of symbols led repeatedly to highly arbitrary, indeed quite fanatical, constructions. But, of course, these were "work"; they did not spring from an alerted, but at the same time unstrenuous, "listening" for what the symbol was attempting to convey, but rather from a forceful, categorical insistence that the symbol surrender its meaning to Freud's intransigence. Perhaps his relative disregard for his own imaginative gifts was not only a defense against the critical pettifogging researchers of his day, but also a rationalization of his envy for those whom he considered still greater geniuses such as Goethe, who appeared to him to have had an easier, sunnier path.

Every so often, however, Freud did refer to his pleasure in mastering difficulties.[45] But, like most political conservatives, he did not assume that men generally could share his own loftier motivations.[46] Among Puritans, such a hierarchy of toilsomeness is not uncommon. Compare the statement of Mrs. Gromyko: "Oh, Andrei does work

---

42. For example, reference footnote 6; pp. 369, 371, 374, 401.
43. Reference footnote 16; p. 239.
44. Reference footnote 16; p. 238.
45. For example, reference footnote 6; p. 275n.
46. *Civilization and Its Discontents;* reference footnote 1; pp. 24-25.

hard, yet not as hard as Mr. Vishinsky, and even that is not so hard as Mr. Molotov works."[47]

Freud's Own Dream-work

A single, magnificent example illustrates Freud's method, and at the same time these limitations. In his famous "Dream of the Botanical Monograph," Freud says:

> I have written a monograph on a certain plant. The book lies before me; I am just turning over a folded coloured plate. A dried specimen of the plant, as though from a herbarium, is bound up with every copy.[48]

His associations to the dream were manifold and revealing. Among other things, Freud noted an association to his own monograph on the coca plant. He has told us elsewhere of his frustration because he did not become known as the discoverer of the anaesthetic properties of cocaine, the reason being that he let a friend continue the research so that he (Freud) might take time out to become engaged to his future wife.[49] He also made reference to the fact that his wife often remembered to bring his "favourite flower"—the artichoke—from the market where she diligently shopped, while he was less "thoughtful" of her, seldom bringing her flowers.[50] The artichoke reminds him of a childhood scene where he tore up a book containing "coloured plates" and of his later fondness for collecting books; he reproaches himself, both for this expensive hobby, and for the "onesidedness" of his *Gymnasium* studies, which had led him close to failing his botany examination.[51] In sum, after pages and pages of examining separately each dream-detail, he permits himself in his analysis a slight awareness of his "thoughtlessness" towards his wife, of envy and grandiose ambition, and a memory of destructiveness, safely remote in childhood and in any case blamed upon his father. The worst thing he can say about himself is that he has expensive and distracting hobbies! In fact, he calls the childhood memory itself a " 'screen or concealing memory' for my subsequent bibliophilia."[52] A curious "screen" in which he concealed the amiable and redeeming veniality of a hobby for collecting books behind the less amiable vice of destroying them—perhaps the vice of destructiveness itself! But play—that is, preoccupations and hobbies, especially if expensive, not

47. *Time*, August 18, 1947; p. 25.
48. Reference footnote 6; p. 241.
49. Freud, *An Autobiographical Study*, pp. 23-25.
50. Reference footnote 6; p. 242.
51. Reference footnote 6; pp. 243, 323.
52. Reference footnote 6; p. 243.

directly advancing one in one's profession—did appear to Freud as sinful.[53]

In his associations to the dream, Freud pushed aside his unconscious recognition of what the dream was about and disregarded the significance of flowers as a symbol. Instead, he tore the dream word-from-word like the leaves of an artichoke; he viewed the dream, not as a *Gestalt,* but in a series of concentric verbal associations. I would like to suggest another possible interpretation of the dream, on a fairly obvious symbolic level. Freud seems to have been aware in the dream that flowers—a symbol which he elsewhere recognizes as plainly sexual[54]—do not speak to him; his love has become "a dried specimen of the plant, as though from a herbarium. . . ." Is it not also correct to assume that he is unconsciously aware that he has sacrificed his wife's love to his ambition—that *this* is screened by the mild, and yet symbolic charge he elsewhere makes against her that, but for his devotion to her, he would be famed as the discoverer of cocaine? Indeed, he scarcely permits himself to realize that he is readier to buy himself a monograph—he speaks of his "fondness for . . . possessing books"[55]—than to buy flowers for his wife; this, although the dream commentary refers to his seeing at a bookseller's on the previous day a monograph on the cyclamen, his wife's favorite flower.[56] (His wife has, in fact, become "puffy," like a stuffed animal, while Mrs. "Gardener," whom he met the night before, is still "blooming," presumably from Mr. "Gardener's" care.)[57] Flowers are, by their very nature, a symbol of emotional feeling, even waste; in the act of "possessing" them, they dry up; the artichoke, on the other hand, is not a real extravagance—it is edible. Yet there is more than "possessing" involved; Freud has imprisoned love within the covers of an illustrated monograph; he has crushed it; in penetrating to the heart

---

53. In speaking of the absence of affect in this dream, Freud writes that the dream "corresponds to a passionate plea for my freedom to act as I am acting, to arrange my life as seems right to me, and to me alone." Reference footnote 6; p. 439. But the "freedom" he refers to is that of his collecting mania, against the reproaches of his own conscience and those of his even more puritanical friends like the eye specialist, Dr. Koenigstein, who had told him the evening before that he was "too absorbed" in his hobbies. Reference footnote 6; p. 243. He reproaches himself: for not inventing cocaine, for "neglect" of botany; but he answers "I am entitled to freedom for, after all, I am conscientious and have made some good monographic studies." Thus, he assumes that he must justify not driving himself 100 per cent—"allowing himself," as he says, some small vices. By his standard, even his meagre vacations from the workaday world were sinful, especially where he "missed something," such as the cocaine discovery, as a result. Reference footnote 6; p. 268.

54. Reference footnote 6; pp. 382-383.

55. Reference footnote 6; p. 243.

56. Reference footnote 6; p. 241.

57. Reference footnote 6; p. 245.

of the artichoke, he has a lifeless specimen in his hand. I strongly suspect that the mild scene of childhood destructiveness, which Freud treats as screening his bibliophilia and, on a deeper level, his sexual curiosity, actually conceals the way in which his own life and that of those around him is torn by his almost total incapacity for love and spontaneity—this is his true "onesidedness." It is like the Irish Sea, which means little more to him than the examination of a starfish and the recollection of its Latin name.

Dream-work and Entropy

The concept of "dream-work" attributes to the process of dream-formation the same economics of affect which Freud employed in the process of dream interpretation. He writes, "we take pains to dream only in connection with such matters as have given us food for thought during the day";[58] that is, the dream-work is the processing plant which prepares the material with an eye to the driving wishes behind it, the inspection of the censor, and the economical and convenient packaging of the imagery. Behind this concept, there lies again the assumption of man's laziness. If we had our way, Freud is saying, we would not even dream; we would lie in the blissful fetal state. But our wishes, and external stimuli also, prevent this; these create tensions in our otherwise flaccid state of rest; the *purpose* of the dream-work is to release this tension and thus, by permitting us to go on sleeping, to restore us to the workless state. As Freud divided his year between his workaday months and his vacation period, so he divided the day between the waking tensions and the night's release. But this is not the only way to live! A vacation may be restful, though strenuous, if it lends variety and enjoyment to life; likewise, sleep is not merely the opposite of waking tension. In fact, recent studies have shown that restful slumber is accompanied by frequent changes of position; motionless sleep is not nearly so refreshing. Dreaming, too, is assumed to be an almost continuous process, of which the dreamer is only occasionally aware.

This feeling of Freud's, that he needed to explain the fact of having a dream, and to find the energy-source for the amount of "work" involved, misled him in at least two ways. It was one factor in his insistence that every dream represents a—probably libidinal—wish-fulfillment, the wish being the primal source of energy; this insistence led him to over-elaborate explanations of those dreams, such as anxiety dreams, judgment dreams, and so on, which did not appear to fit his formula. Secondly, it made him suspicious of dreams which, by their

---

58. Reference footnote 6; p. 245.

baroque imagery, their eloquent speeches, or other luxuriance, seemed to have required much "work"; since work is unnatural to man, this effort must hide something, must cover up a most forbidden thought. Thus, when Freud recalls in a dream the formula for trymethylamin, he takes this as "evidence of a great effort on the part of my memory,"[59] and goes off accordingly on a long, interpretative search.

This attitude towards effort pushed Freud towards over-interpretation in his analytic thinking generally. Being a strenuously effortful man, his thoughts and dreams, even without further elaboration on his part, would naturally tend to be complicated and far-flung. Moreover, Freud's work-drive compelled him to go beyond even his initial reaction, towards sometimes over-intricate structures of thought—the *Moses* book is a final and brilliant testament of this obsession which was at the same time part of the drive which made him great and courageous. And yet, concealed beneath all this work, is it possible that Freud is occasionally "playing" with us, and with himself? Is it not likely that, outwardly denying himself any playfulness or frivolity as doctor and scientist, he may have unwittingly sublimated his play-impulses, so that they can be glimpsed only in an "unnecessary" metaphor, a fine-spun interpretation of a dream, a tenuous reconstruction of history?

However that may be, it would seem an important task to track down, in Freud's more technical writings, some of the over-interpretations that may have resulted from his attitude towards effort. Here all I can do is to indicate some of the implications of this attitude. It seems clear that Freud, when he looked at love or work, understood man's physical and psychic behavior in the light of the physics of entropy and the economics of scarcity. For him, life was not self-renewing, or self-producing; he viewed the process of life as drawing on the given natal store, as on a bank account. Hence, for him, effort, expenditure, was problematical: it needed to be explained; something must lie behind it.

One views dreams quite differently if one holds a different view of the nature of life itself. If one thinks that growth is characteristic of life, that life can unfold unsuspected potentialities and resources, one feels that it is not *effort* that needs to be explained—that is life itself—but the *absence* of effort. Then it is the absence which appears pathological. So, if one comes upon a dream which is rich in invention and the use of symbolic expression, or which exhibits indignation, or judgment, or wit, or other human faculties which one appreciates in waking life, one will not feel that this is strange and that the dream

59. Reference footnote 6; p. 203.

must *necessarily* be about something altogether different. Any dream ordinarily requires interpretation, but its prima-facie opacity need not be due to a censorship over malign or outrageous wishes; the necessity for interpretation may result from the fact that symbolic expression is simply a different language, often a more abundant one than the dreamer allows himself in waking life.[60] Or it may be due to the fact that the memories called up in the dream have not been pigeonholed into the dreamer's organized, waking categories and thus appear with a freshness and intensity of experience which he may have had as a child.[61]

§ THE WORLD OF PLAY

ALREADY, in order to talk about the world of work, as Freud saw it, I have had to picture in contrast the opposing world of play. For, indeed, Freud saw these two worlds as sharply separated as was the *Aussee* where he spent vacations, from the urban Vienna where he did his analytic work. Freud's world of play, as we shall see, is a world of children, of artists, and, only surreptitiously, of adults—that is, those adults who are real men and not idlers or escapists.

The Nursery Years

Freud regarded childhood as an auto-erotic haven where all one's pleasures are within reach. Nor is there any conflict between the drives of hunger and sex: "Love and hunger meet at the mother's breast." Soon, moreover, the child discovers the pleasures of onanism; these, too, require no work, not even the labor of object-choice. But this cannot go on; Freud writes:

This age of childhood, in which the sense of shame is unknown, seems a paradise when we look back upon it later, and paradise itself is nothing but the mass-phantasy of the childhood of the individual. This is why in paradise men are naked and unashamed, until the moment arrives when shame and fear awaken; expulsion follows, and sexual life and cultural development begin. Into this paradise dreams can take us back every night. . . .[62]

But this view of childhood as not subject to the laws of the adult world of reality was only one side of Freud's position. He noticed that children liked to play at being grown up, and indeed wished to grow up;[63]

---

60. I have leaned heavily on Erich Fromm's lectures on dream interpretation. See his article, "The Nature of Dreams," *Scientific Amer.* (1949) 180:44.

61. See Ernest Schachtel, "On Memory and Childhood Amnesia," *Psychiatry* (1947) 10:1; also Evelyn T. Riesman, "Childhood Memory in the Painting of Joan Miró," *Etc.*, (1949) 6:160.

62. Reference footnote 6; p. 294.

63. Reference footnote 11; p. 107.

and he had a clear vision, unusual for his epoch, of the terrors, phobias, and conflicts which beset even the most protected child. Unlike most adults, he did not condescend to the battles and nightmares of the nursery; these he accepted as real. And with his usual pessimistic sense, he observed that "the excited play of children often enough culminates in quarrelling and tears."[64] Thus he saw the child as more adult, and the adult as more child, than was the conventional opinion.

This contradiction in Freud's thought can be reconciled if one observes that he saw through the current myths regarding "the innocents of the nursery" only insofar as sex and aggression or matters related to them were concerned—and, obviously, this was no small achievement but one of his most decisive contributions. He saw, clearly enough, the sexual elements in children's play, the onanist practices, the animistic fantasies.[65] But he was at one with his adult generation in looking down on play in general as childish; he did not entirely grasp its reality-testing and reality-expanding functions, its nature as a part of or an aspect of preparation for human adult existence, any more than he respected the creative functions of the playful moods which he criticized in Leonardo's life.

Indeed, even to talk about "functions" when discussing play runs the risk of catching us in an anthropological or psychoanalytic functionalism which means that human freedom is limited to being "unfunctional"—a privilege, paradoxically, most relevant to human existence when seemingly most irrelevant, as many great teachers of mankind have understood.

Play and Foreplay

This divorce between work and play which sharply separates the world of the adult from the world of the child is not reconciled by maturity. Rather, once the genital stage is reached, play becomes attached primarily to the sexual function and continues in an underground, often unconscious existence. In his utilitarian attitude towards sex, Freud was much interested in what he called "foreplay," the preliminary stages of lovemaking. Foreplay seemed to him a kind of come-on which tempted couples onto the path of biological fulfillment; by its tension-heightening nature, it seemed to violate the pleasure-principle and to demand ejaculative release. By this ambiguity, it impelled otherwise reluctant people to comply with the "laws of propagation."[66] (The term "foreplay," itself, seems to carry its

---

64. Reference footnote 6; p. 315.

65. See, however, his discussion of children's food wishes and disappointments; reference footnote 6; p. 214.

66. The phrase is from Freud's *Leonardo da Vinci;* reference footnote 11; p. 70.

own linguistic self-contradiction: if it is play for a purpose, it is robbed of most of its spontaneous, amiable, frivolous, or tender playfulness.) In other words, just as Freud "allowed himself" his book-collecting and other hobbies for their recreative functions, so he "allowed" mankind this apparent frivolity of foreplay for its procreative functions: in both cases, pleasure is not really free, it merely baits the trap. After intercourse, so Freud felt, there is sadness; after play, one pays by sorrow and work.

Dreams and Day-dreams as Play

Fantasy and art are among the secondary and derivative efforts of mankind to obtain sexual pleasure; they constitute a kind of bargain basement, in which a meed of pleasure is sublimated—no other pleasure could equal direct sexual pleasure in Freud's view—in return for a modification in the ensuing pain. The discovery of this *ersatz*, inexpensive pleasure is made by the child, Freud argued, in the form of a hallucinatory wish-fulfillment, a kind of mirage in which the hungry infant, for instance, can persuade himself that he is being fed.[67] In later life, the adult can restore this state in dreams and day-dreams.

Freud perhaps tended to exaggerate the extent to which one can actually escape reality, unless one is crazy, by means of these fantasies. For although he is correct in believing that in the passive state one can afford wishes which would endanger one in real life, by the same token one diminishes one's satisfaction: somehow one realizes that "it's only a dream"[68] or a day-dream—and that it will never come to pass. Moreover, our individual and cultural imagination sets limits to wishes; they are often as poverty-stricken as that of the woman in the famous tale, which Freud quotes, who used the first of her three fairy wishes to procure some sausages which she had smelled next door.[69] The "damned wantlessness of the poor," against which Lassalle protested, is not dissipated when they sleep.[70]

My conclusion here is that Freud was romantic about dreams, as he was about more overt sexual life. By his insistence that, underneath the manifest dream, there must lie a wish, and that this wish, in an adult, would have a dark, luxuriant, and forbidden quality, he avoided

---

67. Reference footnote 6; pp. 509-510.

68. This phrase is from Freud's "The Interpretation of Dreams"; reference footnote 6; p. 513.

69. Reference footnote 6; p. 520n.

70. In a recent *Fortune* poll, a cross-section of the American people was asked what income they would like to have, if there were no limits to their demands. The average person gave a figure less than 25 per cent above what he was at the moment making; the mean figure was less than $4,000. See "Portrait of the American People," *Fortune* (1947) 35:10.

seeing how flat and conventional, how sorrowful and anxious, many dreams actually are. There is, for example, little that is wish-fulfilling in his own "Dream of the Botanical Monograph." Actually the censorship, to which he himself called attention, is not so easily evaded as he supposed; the most daring, and therefore frightening, wishes do not even exist in our unconscious, let alone rebel in the night against the dictation of the censorship.

But though there is a romantic element in Freud's view of the dream, this did not prevent him from subjecting it, like every other psychic performance, to the laws of scarcity economics. One dreams, he says, in order to continue sleeping, for otherwise the ungratified wish or outside stimulus, would wake one—one continues sleeping, of course, to prepare for the labor of the following day.[71] Thus the dream represents an elaborate compromise, a deal between the psychic forces: with the censorship relaxed by sleep, the repressed wishes are able to go in search of pleasure, using the thought-residues of the day, but at the same time the dream-work "binds the unconscious excitation and renders it harmless as a disturber . . . of sleep," while satisfying through displacement and other devices of evasion the censorship's one open eye. This involves, Freud writes, a lesser "outlay of . . . work, than to hold the unconscious in check throughout the whole period of sleep."[72]

Art as Play and Display

So far, I have been discussing the play-world in its private aspects, to which one has access principally in sexual "play" and in dreams. There is also a public play-world; it has virtually the same economy as that of the dream. It is built on fairy-tales[73] and other folk-myths, on wit, and on art.

71. Reference footnote 6; pp. 518-519.

72. Anxiety dreams do not seem to fit in this economy, and their explanation caused Freud no end of trouble. He finally concluded that anxiety is the response of that part of the dreamer's psyche which is displeased by the forbidden wish; this part, at least, is pleased by the suffering the anxiety occasions, which is felt as punishment. Reference footnote 6; p. 520; Freud, *A General Introduction to Psychoanalysis*, p. 192.

73. Freud had the genius to see that fairy tales were *"nichts für Kinder,"* that they had an adult meaning though one which the adults did not permit themselves to see. He applied to them the same interpretative process he had used on dreams; he analyzed their symbolism; he tried to see what really happens in them beneath their decorative screen. He found it typical that the heroine, for example, Cinderella, marries the prince; he took the status-striving, as well as the sexual, even incest, elements, as "real"; naturally, every girl would want to marry a prince and lead the do-nothing life of an aristocrat. Reference footnote 6; p. 371. Moreover he held that in fairy-tales we commit the Oedipal offenses; we are the "great criminals"; we indulge in the totem feast, with its sacrilege. All this gives us pleasure whose true nature, like that of dream, is concealed from us by its apparently harmless, innocent garb.

The artist's job is that of giving public expression to his private fantasies, fantasies which others may share; his work is others' play. Moreover, art, as Freud viewed it, is not bound by the rules of the workaday world—it is free. Like religion, the other great operator in the play-world of illusion, it can dissolve the dichotomies of human existence; it can deny the fact of death, or, as in the Greek and Egyptian sculptures which fascinated Freud, it can unite man and woman.[74] The pleasure in art is, as one would expect, partly Oedipal and rebellious sexuality, partly narcissism, in which both artist and audience identify with the hero. Licit gratification of illicit wishes is secured by these projections.

The relative thinness of the role assigned by Freud to art is surprising, in view of the amount of attention which he gave the subject both in his own writings and in his "hobbies." Of art as critic of society, as transcending the given cultural divisions and definitions of work and play, as conscious creator of new values, Freud does not speak. His own tastes in art seem to have been conventional for his time, place, and class. Like so many nineteenth-century bourgeois, he admired the Renaissance, perhaps finding in it an age less cramped than his own. His great hero was Goethe, regarded as a late-Renaissance figure. He seems to have had little taste for music. Though he admired Ibsen, who was also a defier of sexual convention in his writings, he was not in general interested in "modern art." But it is modern art which has most strongly rebelled against being a plaything for rich patrons; sometimes it has done so by its very "ugliness" according to accepted patterns. Moreover, Freud paid little attention to the formal problems of art, being primarily concerned with its psychological causes and effects; when he thought about form at all, he said that the problem was insoluble.[75] Thus, his attitude towards art, as well as his taste, was conventional: by assigning it to the world of play, of regression, of sex, he patronized it, as a sober, cultivated bourgeois should. Perhaps one could say that he viewed it, as a modern city-planner views a zoo or park, as a territory zoned off from the workaday world, which is there to delight but not to be taken with full seriousness.[76]

The Play of Words

Somewhat the same attitude governs Freud's view of wit. He saw the role of language as a reality-instrument in a way that could hardly have been done before the development of his theory of dreams. For

---

74. Reference footnote 11; p. 96.
75. Reference footnote 11; p. 120.
76. See Freud's remarks on the uselessness of beauty, including parks, in *Civilization and Its Discontents;* reference footnote 1; pp. 54-55.

by means of words, one delays gratifications, and tests reality experimentally before, so to speak, setting foot in it. Though the infant, like the primitive, uses them as magic handles, in his phase of thought-omnipotence, they nevertheless become tools, not pleasures. By their nature, moreover, they are logical, un-autistic: they relate us to the world and to the other people in it; only children and lovers are permitted a private language. But even here, in this instrument of communication, there is a domain reserved for pleasure: this is word-play or wit. At one point in his dream-theory, he speaks of comical effects as a "surplus" which is discharged by laughter;[77] wit is, indeed, the theatre and poetry of the poor. But the pleasure which Freud found in wit is not only that of release of the tensions of obedience to the laws of language;[78] it is also that of direct rebellion. While he collected for study jokes and stories of Jewish humor, he enjoyed also the richness of its satiric and sardonic elements.[79] And even the sexual elements which Freud emphasized in his analysis of wit are not only pleasurable in their own right, but in their rejection of convention. Freud, so meticulously clean as a physician, was quite "rebelliously" fond of "dirty" stories, just as he enjoyed spitting on the stairs of an old lady patient whom he detested.[80]

§ CONCLUSION

I HAVE INDICATED that Freud's ascetic rationalistic dichotomy between work and play, and the very limited role he assigned the latter, belong to the work-morality of nineteenth-century Europe—to the years when the advancing industrial revolution had still not shown its potentialities for drastically shortening labor and expanding leisure horizons. The chances are, moreover, that Freud went much further in the direction of asceticism, of eliminating "waste," than did most of the members of his class and culture: he actually did what it was only their ideal to do. But when one looks at contemporary American attitudes towards work and play, one cannot be too critical of Freud —one can, indeed, see much in his view that is refreshing. Thus he never adopted the notion that work and play must alike be "fun"— and, more particularly, fun with people. This notion forces men in the American upper-middle class to merge the spheres of work and play, often without advantage to either. An anxious gregariousness and concern for the expression of appropriate consumer tastes can permeate a business or professional conference as easily as a cocktail

---

77. Reference footnote 6; p. 538.
78. Reference footnote 6; p. 332n.
79. Freud, *Wit and Its Relation to the Unconscious;* pp. 164 *et seq.*
80. Reference footnote 6; pp. 269, 272, 291.

party. To a degree, Americans have substituted fun-morality for work-morality. But this, among other things, makes it difficult to admit that one is tired: one has not done enough to "deserve" it. Conversely, one tends to exploit his vacations not, as Freud did—when he was not traveling or climbing mountains—by doing productive work, but by seeking to train oneself for advances in status or in the solution of vexing interpersonal problems.

I can put my point another way by saying that there are certain advantages to making fun and play surreptitious—even sinful. For then, play is less apt to be socially guided, less apt to be compulsively gregarious. Freud's view of play as a kind of underground in adult life protects it—gives it some of the same chaotic freedom that the carnival provides in Catholic countries. As against this, the contemporary social focus on recreation sometimes tends to leave no room either for whorehouses or for underground passages of any sort; everything must be out in the open. And while in a utopian society this would not be so bad, today it often means that play is exploited in fact—as it was for Freud in principle—for physical and psychic hygiene.

Indeed, Freud's own account, in a somewhat distorted version, is one of the factors which has shaped this modern view. Many women, for instance, indulge in sexual play not because they seek pleasure but because they have been told, and told themselves, that repression is bad. Men justify their vacations on the ground that they "owe it to themselves." Emancipated parents are anxious if their children do not masturbate, lest they become neurotic. Men who have stomach trouble feel that they must "relax," must have more fun, to avoid further psychosomatic disorder—the give-away clue of psychic imperfection. And those men who cannot play are robbed, both by cultural developments and by the loss of psychological innocence Freud helped bring about, of the older defenses provided for them in a work-oriented society. So it turns out that, under the guise of fun and play, we remain today almost as truly ascetic as Freud, often enough without the very real satisfactions which—in spite of himself and in spite of his views as to the supremacy of sexual pleasure—he derived from his intellectually demanding and adventurous work. The threat of work today is not that it is arduous, but—in the some ways far worse fact—that it boring and without meaning.

As against this, Freud, despite his skepticisms and reservations, had no doubt that work was worthwhile and that scientific work, whatever its uncanny "primal" sources in sexual or aggressive drives, had its own logic, its own convention, and its own tradition. Moreover, while he was a utilitarian in his attitude towards play, and, in a way, towards life in general, he was actually much less of a utilitarian about science than many of his successors. The pursuit of truth was for him self-justifying: man had every right to penetrate the secrets of nature without giving an account of himself to academic, priestly, democratic, or other moralizing authority. Although he thought the truth would set men free, he was, nevertheless, far from the mood of many "policy-oriented" researchers today, who hedge their curiosity about by all sorts of expediential considerations and concern for various good causes. One of the things that makes Freud such perennially exhilarating reading is the sense of the "play of the mind" that he communicates.

It may be a long time before middle-class people, in America, will feel themselves free to play when they are not free to really work—if their work has degenerated into sociability or featherbedding. Those who are excluded from meaningful work are, by and large, excluded from meaningful play—women and children, to a degree, excepted. The kind of passionate fondness and excitement about his work that Freud had, although he would seldom admit this to himself, is also a good base from which to learn to play. And people have to learn to play—or stop unlearning; in this enterprise they are faced with the whole long tradition of the driving and driven men who created Western industrial society, Western political organization, and Western scientific thought, including psychoanalysis.

Perhaps it is time now for the analysts, and for other social scientists, to pay more attention to play, to study blockages in play in the way that they have studied blockages in work and sexuality. Yet, in studying play, one must be aware of the ambiguities that haunt play, be aware of the elusiveness and privacy that are its main defenses. We have far to go before we move to a new integration of work and play unreservedly superior to the Freudian dichotomies—an integration allowing us more work in work and more play in play.

22. Authority and Liberty in the Structure of Freud's Thought

Sᴜꜰꜰɪᴄɪᴇɴᴛ ᴛɪᴍᴇ ʜᴀꜱ ᴇʟᴀᴘꜱᴇᴅ since Freud built his system—not perhaps in years but in the movement of thought—to permit and require critical re-examination of the sort undertaken here. Such re-examination depends for its very method on Freud's own work, and its aim is less to point to weaknesses in that work, which have already been sufficiently discussed, than to contribute to the sociology of knowledge and to the ongoing effort, both in psychiatry and in the other social sciences, to separate what is essential in Freud's thought from the garb, determined very largely by the time and the culture, in which that thought made its debut. The texts of Freud which I will primarily use are not those in which he himself spelled out his *Weltanschauung*, but rather those more technical writings in which his outlook on such problems as those of authority and liberty appears only inferentially, and often without his own full awareness.

§ THE MEANING OF HUMAN HISTORY

Kᴇɴɴᴇᴛʜ Bᴜʀᴋᴇ ᴏʙꜱᴇʀᴠᴇꜱ, in a remarkable essay on "Ideology and Myth," that when historical thinking succeeded philosophical thinking in the West, writers who wanted to establish some thing or some authority as essential declared that it was temporally prior:

Thus, whenever they wanted to say that man is "essentially competitive" or "esentially good," they said that the "first men" were constantly at war or that men were "originally" good but were later corrupted by society. They postulated such "firsts" in some hypothetical past time, their thinking in this regard often being much more mythical than they suspected, and no more based on actual scientific knowledge about the past than was the "mythical" doctrine of "original" sin (which, translated philosophically, would mean "essential" sin, that is, some ineradicable difference between individual and group which the individual, eager to socialize himself, might experience as a sense of guilt).

Freud was similarly concerned with establishing status-rankings between different orders of the given, either on the basis of temporal priority or on the basis of what essentially *belongs* and what is merely additive or artificial. For him the "essentially" human was the ur-human—one reason, perhaps, why the myth of the primal horde held such attraction for him. Likewise his view of original sin—namely, the primal crime of Oedipus which is both deposited in our racial memory and repeated by each of us in the modified form of childhood fantasy and feeling—fits Kenneth Burke's description.

A concept of original sin is typical of a view of life which makes the past an authority over the present, in which the individual is mortgaged to society, and both the individual and society are mortgaged to the preceding generations. All through recent history, one finds secular variations of this outlook, and secular castes who, replacing the priests, have the duty of collecting the interest on the mortgage. The most striking, because extreme, example of this is in the work of Auguste Comte who was so impressed with the legacy of past ages that he invented quantities of new holidays to celebrate a calendar of secular saints; immortality was, for him, the continuation of the hold of the past over the present. Though he did not believe in original sin, he did believe that the individual owed to his parents, and to all the past, so enormous a debt that it could never be repaid even by a lifetime of altruism. In Ruth Benedict's *The Chrysanthemum and the Sword*, there is a recent analysis of this principle in operation in Japanese society. In Japan too the individual feels that he must spend his life in repaying his debt to his parents, and to society—symbolized by the Emperor. Payment of the debt in all such cases is never a mere matter of contract; it is always a matter of morality, enforced by feelings of shame and self-abnegation.

Freud's metaphorical doctrine of original sin is, at first glance, emancipated from such rigors. He does not believe in altruism, nor, of course, does he give a literal meaning to original sin. Nevertheless, in his manifest thinking, he seems to stand on the side of the past's authority. The most striking illustration appears in *Moses and Monotheism*. He suggests there that anti-Semitism may be due at least in part to the "stubborn" refusal of the Jews to acknowledge their share in the primal crime, which in their case took the historical form of the killing of Moses, their "father." And he points out that the ascetic renunciation which he attributes both to Jewish ethics and theology —the bare bones of monotheism—are the consequence of unconscious guilt feelings for this consciously forgotten offense. But the reader may well ask: Does Freud not accept here the authority of those of the dominant majority who are hostile to Jews and rationalize their hostility by swinging the club of the past over the present? Freud took his own Jewishness very seriously, as shown in his well-known letter to the B'nai B'rith.[1] To some extent he seems to be renouncing the present claim of the Jews to equal and decent treatment, and justify-

---

1. "On Being of the B'nai B'rith," reprinted in *Commentary* (1946) 1:23.

ing this renunciation on the basis of the past as forcibly reconstructed by him.

In fact, Freud traced all authority back to this source of the original father; as he writes in his book on dreams:

> The sovereign is called the father of his country (*Landesvater*), and the father is the first and oldest, and for the child the only authority, from whose absolutism the other social authorities have evolved in the course of the history of human civilization (in so far as "mother-right" does not necessitate a qualification of this doctrine).[2]

It is significant to see what short shrift he gives, here and elsewhere, to matriarchy. The possibility of the ur-existence of matriarchy is obviously inconvenient, if one wants to justify contemporary authority by throwing over it the mantle of the primal father. Freud takes this latter step explicitly in his *Group Psychology and the Analysis of the Ego.*

Freud had, however, to face the fact that some children do not know their fathers, or know them only as lenient ones; and the fact that it was not easy to find convincing evidence for the existence of repressed Oedipal desires in every adult whom he analyzed. One way in which he dealt with this problem was by the concept of racial memory: from this, no one can escape. This memory included a realization of the primal crime, which, however, needed usually to be revived by some symbolic repetition; it also included a kind of ur-language and universal symbolism.

The concept of ur-language and ur-symbolism is of particular importance in Freud's thought. For its implication is that language and imagery are prisons, set up in the long-distant past, from whose categories and modes of thinking man cannot free himself; it is a kind of phylogenetic rather than epistemological Kantianism. Since mankind originally thought dichotomously, with ur-words meaning two polar opposites, the implication is that all real or basic thinking continues to be of this sort; neither cultural diversity nor individual style can do much but add trimmings to the racially inherited pattern.[3] Even in our word-play when, according to Freud, we put aside adult reality for a moment, we fall back upon puns and images which are part of the racial stock; so, too, with symbols, whether found in dreams or works of art. A small number of these have a given, usually

---

2. Freud, "The Interpretation of Dreams" (Brill, tr.), in *The Basic Writings of Sigmund Freud*, p. 275n.

3. Freud, "'The Antithetical Sense of Primal Words,'" *Collected Papers* 4:184; London, Hogarth Press, 1925. In his essay on "Ten Levels of Language," Albert Guérard has shown the differentiated richness of the lingual inheritance, which both groups and individuals are free to alter in many ways; no one level is superior. *Amer. Scholar* (1947) 16:148.

sexual, meaning: a tool or stick is always a penis; a lake or river signifies birth or the womb; a room or wood means a woman; a dream
of flying symbolizes sexual intercourse. No deviations are permitted;
the racial memory controls the individual or cultural experience.

Yet in Freud's position there is a concealed element which is not
at all authoritarian; this is the notion that, since all have the same
memory, there are no fundamental differences between classes of
men or between nations. The upper classes are subject to the same
crude unconscious memories as any peasant: "None is so big," he
writes, "as to be ashamed of being subject to the laws which control
the normal and morbid actions with the same strictness."[4] Underneath, he is arguing, men are, after all, the same. Thus the dialectic
of history is turned around so as to deny privilege as well as to defend it.[5]

The same mortgage which binds society to its past, and to the
reincarnation of its primal father, also of course extends to every
single individual. Freud's utilitarian teleology led him to see the individual as a piece of somatic tissue indebted to its own sperm or ovum
until released by death—"the common fate . . . which subdues us
all."[6] Everyone is bound to procreate;[7] that is his purpose on earth,
and all else is preparation. This task he inherits, just as he inherits his
unconscious memories and passions; the neurotic tries to subdue these
—to escape their domination—and falls ill as a result.[8] From this point
of view, Freud's attack on narcissism is quite understandable: narcissism is, so to speak, the last refuge of the individual from his creditors, social and personal. And yet—here again we see the ambivalence
of his view—he was the inventor of a therapy designed to lift from the
individual his oppressive mortgage, or at least to provide for a stay
of foreclosure and a remission of payments long since due.

It is now necessary to see somewhat more particularly the ways
in which mankind is bound to its destiny, at once phylogenetic and
teleological. Just as all are guilty of the primal crime, even if they
did not participate in or even consciously remember it; so all are sad-
dled with the prospect of a future which is not capable of much voluntary change. Immutable laws limit man's control over his physical environment and over his own desires for aggression and nirvana. The most
that could be hoped for is the slight amelioration of the inherited

4. Freud, *Leonardo da Vinci*, p. 38.
5. Cf. Freud, "Wit and Its Relation to the Unconscious" (Brill, tr.), in *The
Basic Writings of Sigmund Freud;* p. 778.
6. Reference footnote 2; p. 411.
7. Reference footnote 4; p. 70.
8. Reference footnote 2; p. 520.

framework; no radical transformation of society has any chance. This is a curious position for a thinker who discovered whole areas of untapped human resources, richer than the wealth of the Americas, and who in his clinical practice actually assisted men and women to make abundant use of their own latent energies which had been crippled by conflict and repression.

Since this *is* an ambivalent position, it is not surprising that Freud's whole attitude towards history combines elements from both the progressive and the cyclical theories which were current in his time. The progressive theorists, both before and after Darwin, saw mankind's development as linear—up from the ape, up from slavery, up from animism, as the case might be. Thinking of this sort goes back to the Enlightenment, to men like Turgot and Condorcet; it was refined by nineteenth-century writers who, like Hegel and Marx, introduced dialectical elements—or, like Comte or Maine, conservative ones—without changing the fundamental pattern. That pattern viewed history not as a series of alternatives which were rather accidentally chosen, but as entirely "necessary": what happened had to happen in accordance with the progressive laws. In such a late thinker as Bergson, even the laws evolve; nothing is static; everything moves forward according to a vital principle or spiritual gyroscope.

Cyclical theories of history, though old, did not find favor until late in the century. Antibourgeois writers such as Brooks Adams and Pareto reacted against the optimistic assumptions of the linear theorists. Whether they spoke of the circulation of elites or of the rise and fall of civilizations, their cynical platitude remained: *plus ça change, plus c'est la même chose.* Moreover, increasing historical and anthropological knowledge made the simple progressive theories difficult to maintain. Despite the efforts of the nineteenth-century ethnologists, for instance, no single sequence of tribal social development could be discerned. Those who were attracted to cyclical theories were not only rejecting modern capitalistic society as the best of worlds to date or even the prelude thereto. They were also rejecting the parochialism which viewed the fate of the planet from the perspective of Western Christianity or even, as in Comte's case, from the perspective of a single country thereof; that is, these thinkers chose their illustrations from a wider range of cultures—seeing less to respect in their own, and more to respect in the others. Thus, with the assistance of such men as Sumner, they laid the foundations of cultural and historical relativism.

Freud picked and chose among these contrasting attitudes. His notion of the gradual development of a phylogenetic inheritance, of the linear change from primitive to modern times, as recorded both

in language and in social organization and as deposited in the unconscious—this borrows from the progressive theorists. On the other hand,
his conception, most explicitly set forth in *Civilization and Its Discontents,* that epochs of repression and refinement are always succeeded by epochs of explosion and barbarity,[9] and his further, more
implicit belief that, from here out, nothing new can happen in history
—these are reminiscent of the cyclical theorists. This ambivalence follows not only from Freud's ambivalence towards authority but also
from his feelings towards his own civilization. Sometimes he was inclined to view this, ethnocentrically, as the height of human attainment, and to accept without question the values of science and cultivation and the middle-class world generally. But, except for the value
of science—which he never questioned so far as I can find—he could
also be quite sharp in his hostility towards the culture in which he
lived, and admire, without condescension, earlier ages and earlier
civilizations, such as the Egyptian. About the shape of the future,
however, no such conflict was necessary: this was virtually governed
by the past. Under these circumstances, Freud advised mankind to
"submit to the inevitable."[10]

To a degree, this attitude towards the future may be closely related to Freud's acceptance of scarcity economics. Where scarcity
prevails, there will authority also be found—the authority of the generalized past and the more direct authority of the ruling class which
must control the distribution of the limited resources. Freud was quite
skeptical that there could be alternative outcomes or abundant ways
of organizing man's relations to nature and to his fellows. For where
history appears as a series of determined events—and historical writing
almost always makes it so appear—the future can hardly be regarded
as open: at most it will present a dichotomy, an either-or.

Today, we are all short-run pessimists. But Freud's long-run pessimism has also become fashionable, perhaps prevalent, though it is
often linked to a religious base which Freud explicitly rejected. How
radical it was when he first expressed it may be gathered from an
essay by Bertrand Russell on "Current Tendencies,"[11] written in 1920.
This essay attacks the "cosmic impiety" of such thinkers as Bergson—
their delusions of omnipotence, of automatic progress, which he felt
ignored or trivialized man's existential problems. In such a climate of
late Victorian evolutionary optimism, Freud's pessimism was chal-

---

9. *Civilization and Its Discontents* (first published in 1930).
10. *New Introductory Lectures on Psycho-analysis,* p. 221. Compare, however,
his high hopes for the spread of psychoanalytic modes of thought in "The Future
Prospects of Psychoanalytic Therapy," in *Collected Papers* 2:285.
11. Bertrand Russell, *Selected Papers.*

lenging. Today, we stand in need of more impiety, cosmic and otherwise. It is pessimism which has become complacent.

Freud's pessimism, furthermore, was strictly limited. In his day-to-day clinical task, he acted without question on two progressive beliefs: the unfolding nature of science, and the linkage of knowledge to therapy. At least once, moreover, in his published writings, he permitted himself to face the possibility of economic abundance and its social consequences, saying that "a fundamental alteration of the social order will have little hope of success until new discoveries are made that will increase our control over the forces of nature, and so make easier the satisfaction of our needs."[12] History, then, is not hopeless after all. From this it follows that man, far from bowing to the inevitable, must imitate Prometheus; he must not only understand, but act: "He has the right to make an effort to change that destined course of the world. . . ."[13]

To sum up, it may be said that Freud's view of history is a compromise among ambiguous and contradictory elements. On the one hand, there is evolution and advance; there are great men who "make an effort to change that destined course," men such as Moses. On the other hand, there are definite limits, now in all probability reached, beyond which neither man as a biological product nor society as a bio-historical product can move; the future holds neither miracle nor messiah.

§ INDIVIDUAL DESTINY

ONLY LATE IN LIFE did Freud begin to write on these general social and historical problems, although as early as 1900, in his book on dreams, his attitudes were already fairly explicit. For most of his life he was concerned not with social but with individual destiny. Some of his case records constitute what today would be called a "life history," and what medical men in any case term a "history"; from analyzing these, one can see what Freud thought of as open in human history and what as closed.

The theory of the birth-trauma can be a starting point. If all of a person's life is viewed as determined by the one crucial event which commences his independent history, all later events have been reduced to mere repetitions or reminders, over which the person has no control. That is why the theory is so forcibly reminiscent of the strictest Calvinist predestinarianism; it has the same universal, uncontrollable quality.[14] In this strict form, Freud rejected the theory as

---

12. Reference footnote 10; p. 248.
13. Reference footnote 4; p. 43.
14. The theory of the birth-trauma appears to be scientific, but it was never

it was developed by his disciple, Otto Rank; but he continued to believe that this trauma was the prototype, though not the source, of all later anxiety, while the womb became the prototype of the Garden of Eden. To the constitutional inheritance, the phylogenetic memory, and the birth experience, Freud added a fourth source of the later life-pattern—namely, the early years of childhood. Though "the development of the individual is only an abridged repetition" of the phylogenetic experience, it can nevertheless be influenced "by the fortuitous circumstances of life," particularly of the first five years.[15] It is in these "circumstances" that liberty lies, as against the authority of the past.

The childhood experiences, however, are not fortuitous in any extensive sense. The child has no more control over who his parents are —except in dreams where, Freud delighted in pointing out, children always create different parents for themselves, or in the myths of birth such as that of Moses—than over the manner of his obstetrical delivery or his sex. And in his early years, the child is unavoidably helpless, dependent for life itself on the surrounding adult world. Freud's great contribution was to relate these "obvious" facts to a dynamic theory of character. Character is determined, once and for all, in the childhood situation. Writing of Leonardo's illegitimate birth, Freud states: "the love of the mother became his destiny; it determined his fate. . . ."[16]

In Freud's theory of character, the final (genital) stage is reached with the physical and psychic changes of puberty. This is the terminal; beyond puberty there are no further stages; before it, lie the various way-stations—oral, anal, phallic—at which the destined neurotic or pervert lingers too long or to which he returns. Just as the sex role, given at birth, is unalterable—short of castration—so these childhood phases determine the interpretation of the events of adult life: choice of mate, of livelihood, of *Weltanschauung*. Even the most dramatic and unexpected experiences, such as those of war, serve chiefly to revitalize and repeat a childhood pattern; that is, the traumas of war and death are perceived within the characterological limits which are already set. After puberty at the latest, and probably much earlier, nothing new can be added; the life pattern is already fixed— short of psychoanalytic therapy.

The decisive importance of this concept of character for contemporary work in the social sciences can scarcely be over-estimated. In

actually tested, though as Freud pointed out it offers itself easily to empirical scrutiny. *The Problem of Anxiety*, pp. 94-96.

15. Reference footnote 2; p. 497.
16. Reference footnote 4; pp. 94-95.

our attempts to understand social and political movements, historical changes within a culture, conflicts of class and caste, and many other similar problems, the theory permits us to advance in our methods and hypotheses.

If all men are prisoners of their childhood character-structures, over whose formation they have had no control, it easily follows that all their later motives, tastes, and judgments are not, in any real sense, theirs at all. Men are viewed less as individuals than as the representatives of their sex-and-character roles. In what is perhaps his most famous case history, that of "Dora," Freud dates the onset of the patient's hysterical neurosis from her rejection of a sexual advance from an older, married man, a long-time friend of the family. Freud assumes that not to be excited by a reasonably presentable and potent male is itself neurotic, and some of his analysis is based upon this assumption. He scarcely grants Dora, or any other woman, the privilege of taste and idiosyncrasy even—indeed especially—in the most intimate relations of life: a penis is a penis, and that is enough for a "normal" woman who has physically attained, as 14-year-old Dora had, the genital stage. That Freud believes this, may be inferred from a footnote to his report on Dora's case, in which he remarks, as if in answer to possible critics, that he has seen the man who attempted Dora's seduction, and that he is attractive![17] Hence Dora's refusal must be neurotic. Of course, it *may* have been neurotic, though the man as Freud describes him seems rather a dubious character. Our quarrel is only with Freud's implication—to be sure, qualified by other arguments—that Dora had no freedom of choice, so to speak, in the matter: she *must* be neurotic since she refuses to "bow to the inevitable," the fact of being a woman.

But men are subject, in Freud's analysis, to an authority identical to that which women face in their sex roles. So when he finds a patient who, instead of visiting a girl about whom he has heard, takes a train in the opposite direction, this, too, *must* be neurotic—of course, it *may* have been. Freud insists that the biological equipment of men and women, rather than the cultural definition of that equipment, is determinative of normalcy.

Given the crucial importance of sex and sex-roles in the Freudian theory, little new can happen; whatever does happen will be explained as essentially a repetition or recombination of the past. The figures

---

17. "Fragment of an Analysis of a Case of Hysteria," in *Collected Papers* 3:38. The case of Dora is, of course, exceedingly complex, and Freud could argue that Dora was in fact in love with Herr K. Note also Freud's reference (in "Further Recommendations in the Technique of Psycho-analysis," in *Collected Papers* 2:377, 385) to "all the individual details of [a patient's] way of being in love."

created in dreams Freud compares to dragons or centaurs.[18] These composite creatures, like the unicorn, seem to me to symbolize man's difficulty in imaginatively transcending nature. Just as deterministic theories of history, whatever their differences *inter se*, put the historian in the position of an authority who, in the name of History, sets limits to mankind's future development, so the Freudian analyst makes himself into an authority in the name of Character or Sex. In his view, motives are without opacity, and actions, though often ambivalent, are without ambiguity. If a person cares about justice, that must be because he is essentially envious; if he shows pity, that must be because he is reacting against a basic sadism; he gives himself away to the observing authority in the very act of concealment. One can see that the same deterministic principle is at work here as in the concept of universal symbolism or as in some of the historical constructions—for instance, Freud's insistence that Moses *must* have been killed by rebellious Jews.

Now it may be argued that Freud in these instances is simply expressing the scientific postulate that everything is, in principle, capable of being explained, and that science has no room for the concept of freedom of the will or for accident. One might question so flat a statement of the postulate, by reference, for instance, to recent theories of probability; but that is not my purpose: it is not the fact of explanation but the nature of the explanation that I question. Just as in his psychic economics Freud applies the second law of thermodynamics and assumes that libido is indestructible, so he assumes in his analysis of the individual that one's childhood-formed character and role are indestructible; these form the real self, all else is trimming. His men and women are allowed little future, other than a repetition of the past; whatever happens to them is *"déjà vu."* Freud takes on himself the role which so fascinated him intellectually, the role of the Parcae; before him, as the representative of destiny, all men are humbled. Freud held that even in dreams man does not escape. He closes his book on dreams on this characteristic note: "By representing a wish as fulfilled the dream certainly leads us into the future; but this future, which the dreamer accepts as his present, has been shaped in the likeness of the past by the indestructible wish."[19] But even the predestining wish is not the person's own; it goes back to the childhood situation which was anything but unique and which in turn is merely a repetition of the primordial pattern. Would it be going too far to say that—for Freud—life itself, ever renewed in the individual, is subjected to the repetition-compulsion of the race?

---

18. Reference footnote 2; p. 350.
19. Reference footnote 2; p. 549.

§ THE STRUCTURE OF AUTHORITY WITHIN THE INDIVIDUAL

I HAVE POSTPONED consideration of the mechanics by which the person is, so to speak, held to his destiny, while being permitted a limited illusion of freedom. This is the function of the ego and the superego—the internal delegates of external authority.

The Walking Delegate from Economics: the Ego

The ego has the task of curing the child's addiction to the pleasure-principle and of encouraging his operation according to the reality-principle. This means somatic self-preservation—fundamentally coping with hunger; when that is taken care of, the ego can turn to its teleological duty of finding appropriate hetero-sexual objects, outside of the incest taboos, and thereby giving pleasure to the id. What is the nature of the "reality" to which the ego relates itself? It appears to be the given state of economic development in Freud's milieu, as interpreted by capitalist scarcity economics. The ego is concerned with survival, and with whatever happiness is attainable within this context. Thus from the viewpoint of the individual his ego is that part of himself which is charged with mastering reality; from the viewpoint of society his ego is merely the administrative organ which sees to the carrying out of the workaday tasks. In other words, the ego not only *develops* out of man's helplessness "in the presence of the great forces of life,"[20] but it exercises over the id the authority of those forces and administers their demands. It is an "official" agency, though of course on the lowest rung. But according to Freud it never achieves full control of its assigned internal territory.

The Walking Delegate from Ideology: the Superego

The ego, as the agent of economic or technical "reality," divides authority with the superego, which is the agent of parental and public opinion. This opinion is, in a sense, just as real a force as the other, for it depends on the given state of social ideals and patterns for identification. Nevertheless, Freud views the superego—as a Marxist might—as a sort of ideal superstructure. He does not credit it with the full power he attributes to the material base. Hence enforcement here does not spring from the ego's role of adaptation to life itself but rather from emotional, indeed irrational, pressures in the child's upbringing. While at one point Freud remarks, "When our student days are over it is no longer our parents or teachers who see to our punishment; the inexorable chain of cause and effect of later life has taken over our further education,"[21] it does not follow that the superego loses its

---

20. Reference footnote 4; p. 103.
21. Reference footnote 2; pp. 316-317.

function with adulthood. As an unceasing source of guilt feelings, it cooperates with external authority in subduing the rebelliousness of the id. By holding the individual up to his internalized ideals—ideals he can never attain—the superego sees to it that he does not violate the cultural taboos appropriate to his social station.

If one assumes with Erich Fromm that the function of parents and teachers in any historical culture is to see to it that the individual will *want* to do what, under the given social and economic conditions, he *has* to do,[22] further light is shed on the relation between ego and superego in Freud's thought. Freud seems to realize, half consciously, that "reality" itself, namely what *has* to be done, is actually not a sufficient spur to human performance. By the reality-principle alone, mankind could not be governed. What is required is an actual reversal within the personality of its native attitudes towards work and play, as Freud regarded them: it must learn to enjoy what is inherently painful—its workaday tasks; and to fear what is inherently pleasureful —satisfaction of the desires of the id. This transformation of the affects of pleasure and pain is carried out under the aegis of the superego; it is never left to matter-of-fact "cause and effect."[23]

How does this come about? Freud's account is exceedingly involved; I will oversimplify for purposes of this paper. The motive power for this change of affect is the child's dependence on the parents, not only for physical survival but for love. By using love as a reward for renunciation of pleasure, the child is trained in the way he should go; he becomes tractable, the word Freud uses in reference to his own sons.[24]

At first, this is an ego-adaptation; the parents represent "reality," and the child does what is necessary to manipulate them. But under the pressure of the parental demands for renunciation of instinctual gratification, this mode of adaptation proves economically inadequate. Some release for the suppressed impulses must be found. In this situation where the child is economically so hard pressed, torn between his need for further gratification and the necessity of not jeopardizing the margin of gratification that he does secure from his parents, he has recourse to the mechanism of identification. He internalizes the parental figures, particularly the one of the same sex, as part of his ego, and endows this new entity with his surplus of instinctual energy. So an outlet for the thwarted aggressive impulses is found—but at what a cost! For the superego now directs against the child the same

22. Erich Fromm, "Individual and Social Origins of Neurosis," *Amer. Sociological Rev.* (1944) 9:380-384.
23. Reference footnote 2; pp. 521, 533-534.
24. Reference footnote 2; pp. 333, 335.

aggression for which he could previously find no target. Continually the idealized parental figure is held before him as a norm, and every deviation in conduct or thought from this norm is followed by inescapable punishment. And since the energy for this punishment comes from the frustrated id, no actual conduct, no pure thought is satisfactory: the nobler the behavior, the less the id gratification, the more energy at the disposal of the superego, and the more the flagellation of the self.

To the historically-oriented Freud, the internalized parents were more than the child's idealization of his own particular parents. As well and beyond, they were historical figures, carried in the germplasm and evoked by the particular socialization process. The superego is not merely the precipitate of the particular Oedipus complex, but of the original Oedipal slayings. Thus, just as the child carries his ancestral germ-cell as both legacy and mortgage, so he continues in his superego a morality which springs not from his own direct experience, or even from that of his parents, but one which goes back into the phylogenetic past. This inheritance, Freud wrote, is only slowly altered in response to economic factors,[25] thus perceiving that the superego drives a person, in actual fact, not to the tasks required in his generation but to those required in the past. If there is rapid change in the economic environment, therefore, the superego and the ego would point in different directions; this, of course, is what actually happens when society moves from a technological economy of scarcity to a technological economy of abundance.

Ordinarily, and apart from neurotic outcomes, the ego and the superego divide between themselves the bureaucratic job of id-supervision, the role of authority shifting from one to the other depending on the balance of internal and external forces. Under conditions of civilization, this dual monarchy appears to grow very strong, while the original wishes of the id become more and more repressed or, with the transformation of affect, turned into their opposite. Moreover, with the transition to adulthood, the ideals of the superego undergo a change, attaching themselves no longer to the parents, but to outside powers—to God, to Public Opinion, and so on. Political leadership makes use of this mechanism; social groups are formed among people who have within themselves the same superego image. In this way, the internal bureaucracy and the external bureacracy remain in touch with each other, with the former able to supervise the execution of not only the parents' commands but also those of the parent-surrogates of later life.

---

25. Reference footnote 10; p. 244.

Mechanisms of the Internal Revolution

I rather doubt if any one would be as sensitive to the way in which authority actually operates within the individual as the foregoing shows Freud to have been, if he himself were not at least ambivalent towards authority. If Freud had been wholeheartedly on authority's side, he would have tended to overlook the extent of its power and the subtle infiltration of its operations, especially in modern society, into the very citadel of the personality. But beyond that, he would scarcely have been so aware of the seething rebelliousness which underlies outward conformity—of the civil war continually in progress within. For while many frightened bourgeois at the turn of the century were overanxiously afraid of socialism, few recognized, as Freud did, that the "revolt of the masses" was an affair not confined to the proletariat, and that hatred of civilization burned like an underground fire in even the strongholds of the *bourgeoisie.*

The fire burns in the id which, despite all efforts at repression, remains the stronger force—"the *daemonic* power," Freud calls it.[26] Indeed, the repressory forces must draw their energies from the great energy reservoir of the id, just as in modern society the masses supply the police force by which they are kept in check; the battle of revolution and counter-revolution—"cathexis" and "counter-cathexis," in Freud's terminology—goes on unceasingly. The proud ego and superego might be able to persuade both the outside world and the individual himself that everything is under control, only to be disestablished by the despised and rejected id.[27]

Thus in Freud's view the id is the great liberator, constantly struggling to overcome authority. The struggle is carried on according to the patterns familiar to us in a lenient, bureaucratic autocracy such as the Austrian Monarchy was in the nineteenth century: by sly evasion, by constant pressure, by satire, but rarely by open revolt. Freedom, then, is found in these interstices where the hierarchy is deceived or held at bay. Finally, the future lies with the oppressed id which will not take "no" for an answer.[28] This is one meaning of the well-known doctrine of "the return of the repressed." Let us see somewhat more precisely the forms taken by the internal fight for freedom.

---

26. Reference footnote 2; p. 543.

27. Cf. Freud, "The Origin and Development of Psychoanalysis" (Chase, tr.), *Amer. J. Psychol.* (1910) 21:181-218. Freud writes, in "My Contact with Josef Popper-Lynkeus," in *Collected Papers* 5:295, 297: "Our mind . . . is rather to be compared with a modern State in which a mob, eager for enjoyment and destruction, has to be held down forcibly by a prudent superior class."

28. It is interesting to compare John Dewey's view of the liberating role of impulse. See *Human Nature and Conduct.*

Because the ego and superego draw their energies from the id, they are forced to relax their hold in sleep. They feel, moreover, that they can afford to relax since they have, as Freud puts it, closed the gates to motility;[29] nothing very serious can happen to the workaday authorities. Thus, every night is *Walpurgisnacht* for the id; in dreams these revels are recorded. But since the dreams are on the record, since they are recalled during the working day, they cannot express openly the desires and the revolts of the underground; in Freud's metaphor, they evade the censorship by the characteristic devices of obscurity and concealment known to all underground movements. These devices lull the censorship—viewed by Freud as just as stupid as the Austrian bureaucracy—by flattery, *double entendre*, and the invisible ink of symbolic language. Under these conditions, anything can be expressed, provided only that it is properly veiled.

In Freud's own dreams, for example, as interpreted by him, no authority is safe from attack. Count Thun, the Austrian Prime Minister; Meynert, the great psychiatrist to whom Freud in his waking life deferred; Brücke, Freud's inspiring teacher; the Emperor; Freud's own father—all are accused in his dreams of the vilest habits, the greatest absurdities; but all accusations are safely disguised by distortion, caricature, and obsequiousness.[30] Thus dreams, as Freud explained, play the role of the court jester, or of the Hamlet who is "mad north-northwest."[31] The authorities can rationalize their leniency with the remark, "After all, it's only a dream."[32] But it is the id which has the last word, for it maintains an unrelenting pressure; and since it forgets nothing and never misses an opportunity,[33] it will someday catch the censorship unawares and present the authorities with really frightening demands. The censorship will ring the alarm, and the sleeper will wake, frightened and anxious, finally aware that underneath the seemingly placid surface of his life there flow deep and dangerous currents—the "daemonic power." The play-world, to which Freud assigned dreams in one part of his theory, turns out to be not so innocent after all; in fact, Freud believed that there simply were, for adults at any rate, no guileless dreams.[34]

While dreams evade the bureaucratic censorship through their elaborate concealments of style, jokes and artistic productions escape by their wit and charm; it was indeed through these qualities that the

29. Reference footnote 2; p. 510.
30. Reference footnote 2; pp. 269 (Count Thun), 417 (Meynert).
31. Reference footnote 2; p. 423.
32. Reference footnote 2; pp. 455, 513, 548.
33. Cf. reference footnote 2; p. 268.
34. Reference footnote 2; pp. 250-251.

Viennese often coped with their rulers and with the problems presented by the Empire's ethnic mixture. The id expresses its criticism by what Freud called tendency-wit, but then turns to its masters with a smile, saying, "After all, I don't mean it; it's only a joke." The censor is as humorless as he is stupid; he either misses the point of the joke or is tempted by it to let the villain through. To prove his point, Freud made an elaborate analysis of Jewish humor which, like so much of the underground humor which circulates in totalitarian states, is often a bitter attack upon authority. In the many jokes, for instance, which on their surface poke fun at the lies and sales talk of the *schadchen,* the Jewish marriage brokers, Freud saw that the underlying theme was an attack on the whole system of arranged marriage which put the fate of the young in the hands of the ghetto elders.[35] Similarly, in jokes of which poor Jews were the apparent butts, he saw that the real attack was on the dominant majority. Jokes, then, like dreams, are never guileless; they are skirmishes in the unending civil war within the individual and within the group.

Another evasion, in Freud's view, lies in the belief of adults that children's play is innocent and therefore need not be severely and closely supervised by the bureaucratic hierarchy. The "authorities" however are mistaken, just as mistaken as when they leave the dreamer, the jokester, the artist to their own devices. For children, Freud insisted, are naturally rebellious against authority; they hate their parents; they hate the sibling who displaces them; they have an eye, for which they are not given credit, for what goes on in their world.[36] When the individual child grows up, when his ego and superego take over their respective duties, a convenient amnesia covers over these early perversities and revolts. As Freud pictures the process, it is rather like the way in which American Negroes so quickly forgot their stirring history of slave revolts after emancipation. But the forgetting is only in the conscious mind. The id, which never forgets and never denies itself, is therefore constantly able to refresh its powers by harking back to these childhood perceptions and experiences. But as an adult, one is not aware on the conscious level of what one's own children are up to. Thus the internal authorities, despite their power, are not really able to suppress all claims for liberty, simply because they cannot get access to the claims; they are in the position of a jailer who has lost the records of his prisoners. No matter how he strives, the "liberation cannot be inhibited."[37]

Still another evasion rests on the fact that sexual activities, by

---

35. Cf. reference footnote 5; pp. 700-701.
36. Reference footnote 2; pp. 298-299, 499-500.
37. Reference footnote 2; p. 537.

their very nature, are carried on in private; the bureaucracy would have to have a far-flung network indeed to catch all evaders. Of course, as Freud saw, sexual intercourse is not quite free of bureaucratic regulation. He realized that a patriarchal society necessarily is an authoritarian one, since fatherhood, unlike motherhood, is not a palpable fact but must be inferred from circumstances. The inference is stronger or weaker depending on the amount of supervision—which in the Middle Ages took the form of chastity belts and in the Victorian Age of an overwhelmingly strong female superego. Even so, the civil war goes on. While virtually totalitarian pressures may limit illicit intercourse to a minimum, since interpersonal relations can be fairly well controlled, no pressures whatsoever can control the intrapersonal relations to the point of suppressing all sexual protests from the id. Masturbation, though carried out in private, and almost universally present in childhood, is too obvious to the waking self to escape censorship. But it was Freud's genius to see that in hysterical neurotic symptoms the sexual wish was, in spite of everything, expressed. To all appearances, and even in her own mind, a woman might seem most refined, but her gestures, her compulsions, her eating habits might betray an unmistakably sexual note.

Reference to the "refined woman" leads to still another area where the bureaucracy is easily evaded—namely, the lower classes generally, the peasants, the simpletons. While in the Marxian view these are the oppressed classes, in Freud's eyes they were freer from internal and external censorship than their "betters." Because they are not supposed to know any better, because their superegos are relatively weak, they can get by with assaults on the prison of language or the prison of sex; their transgressions will simply amuse the "authorities." In his book on wit, Freud explains that misuses of the language—obscenities, for example—which would make us indignant if committed on purpose, make us laugh if committed by a naive person; he is not dangerous, and we can afford to laugh. Such people are like children, except that they happen to be adult.[38]

But people of the upper and middle classes do not get off so easily.[39] A very few—the elite, the leaders—are strong enough knowingly to defy the hierarchy within and the hierarchy without; Freud admired them. The rest, however, adapt themselves as best they can to the world and its opinions as they find them, content to evade only in dreams and daydreams, and in jokes and art. Another residue are unable to adapt at all; they are too weak, the pressures are too strong; moreover, they do not know how to achieve even the per-

38. Reference footnote 5; pp. 766-767.
39. Reference footnote 14; p. 90.

mitted evasions. These are the neurotics; Freud pitied them. Yet even they are not entirely devoid of liberty. They have, so to speak, a choice among neuroses. Perhaps they will become hysterical, expressing a sexual rebellion in a physical symptom such as vomiting. Or perhaps they will choose a phobia, refusing, for instance, to go out on the street lest they encounter temptation there. Or they may become obsessive as in the remarkable case of Dr. Schreber whose homosexuality took the form of constant preoccupation with thoughts of God's getting into him.[40] These "choices" hardly strike one as the essence of freedom. But one must remember that Freud did not believe there was much freedom to be had, even for the "normal" man. The point is rather that Freud did believe that the id was, in the last analysis, ungovernable; that the bureaucratic structure of civilization rested on a precarious foundation, since its agents were at the mercy of the oppressed; and therefore that the last word lay with the revolution.

§ AUTHORITY AND LIBERTY IN SOCIAL RELATIONS

AS ONE MIGHT EXPECT from his acceptance, in part, of cyclical theories of history, Freud was a believer in the theory of elites: that society was inevitably divided between a small class of leaders and a large class of led. Unlike the Marxists, he did not attribute this to any particular form of property relations; even under communism of goods, he felt that there would still be an elite, and the course of the Bolshevik revolution seemed to him to confirm his claims. His views rested not only on his belief in man's natural laziness, his need to be pushed into reality-work, but also on the theory of the death instinct, that man's aggressiveness would dissolve society into atoms if leadership ties did not hold it together. Thus authority has two independent psychological sources in the modern world: In the first place, it must ration those goods for which men will work; it does not matter so much whether these goods are directly economic commodities, as under capitalism, or are such things as fame and love, under communism. In this respect, the leader merely takes over the function of the parent who, as we have seen, brings children up by withholding love; conditional "love" is always the method of authority. Indeed, Freud attacked progressive education, which he felt would spoil children by giving them unrationed love. In the second place, the authority must keep order; without it, men's passions, envies, greeds, and superstitions would atomize society. With it, these same passions can form the basis of relatively enduring institutions.

These views are remarkably similar to those of the great theorist

---

40. Reference footnote 3; vol. 3, p. 390.

of autocracy, Thomas Hobbes; for he, too, tried to build a social order on a psychology—and one emphasizing men's fears and passions. Just as Freud imagined that society began from a compact of the brothers who had slain their tyrant father and realized that only in union and renunciation could they avoid the war of all against all, so Hobbes saw men in the state of nature as engaged in ceaseless combat, with peace attainable only by renunciation of virtually all individual rights. But there are significant differences, as well as striking comparisons, between Hobbes and Freud. The former, writing in a period of chaotic civil war, believed that men could be persuaded to make this surrender by an appeal to their reason—in Freud's terms, to their ego; that is, to their quite rational fear of being killed since no one man could be—like Freud's mythical primal father—strong enough to stand off all the rest. Hobbes said to men: Look here, is not death the worst thing? Is it not sensible to surrender everything else—freedom of speech, of religion, and so on—to assure plain physical survival? Moreover, if it should turn out that the leader on whose behalf you have surrendered these things does *not* bring peace, then you owe him no obligation; go find a better one.

In other words, Hobbes saw men endangered by their rational self-interest, which led them to aggressive striving to attain and secure the good things of this world. But he also thought men could unite through appeals to this same self-interest—self-preservation being, after all, a rational business for any living thing. And he thought all men equal, not only in the state of nature, but in the possession of this fundament of reason which could lead them to unification in a national state. He distrusted illusion—which he called superstition—because it clouded men's reason and led them to do fanatical things which were not in the interest of self-preservation.

While, like Hobbes, Freud saw aggression as native to man, he saw it as fundamentally an irrational striving rooted in the death instinct. He felt, moreover, that men could not be persuaded to renounce any desire by reason alone; the id is altogether too strong. Most men, that is; for only the elite could learn to live on a plane of sublimation. But the masses, in Freud's view, could be led to renounce aggression only through authority and what today would be called ideology—the cement of emotional ties. Thus the elite, producers of efficacious illusions, could live without these illusions, but not the masses.

While Freud did not publish his *Group Psychology and the Analysis of the Ego*[41] until after the first World War, his belief that the

---

41. Both this book and *Beyond the Pleasure Principle* reflect the impact of the war on Freud.

masses needed to be subjected to the authority of forceful leaders can be traced in his earliest psychological writings. Like Hobbes, he was afraid of anarchy; but he did not live in a period of anarchy, but rather, up until 1914, in one of the most stable and peaceful epochs in Western history. One of his dreams is especially interesting in this respect. It shows his admiration for Szell, the Hungarian parliamentary leader, who knew the arts of "leading men and organizing the masses" and was able to cope with the "anarchy" of the Hungarian delegates.[42] While Freud admired the rebel Garibaldi, who unified Italy, he seems from this dream to have had a typical Austro-German's contempt for the rebellious national minorities within the Hapsburg Monarchy. To one of these minorities, the Jews, Freud himself belonged; but he repeatedly insisted on the need for scapegoats in order to maintain the national solidarity—outgroups and ingroups, in present-day terms. Indeed, notions of racial solidarity run through his work.[43] While Hobbes took the value of the nation for granted, he did not see it as the focus of sentimental ties.

For Hobbes, moreover, the leader had no special emotional qualities—no aura of charisma; he was simply the man who happened to take up the vacuum of power, and he was the leader only so long as he was powerful. Freud, following LeBon, saw the leader as having a quasi-magical influence on the mass. He was attracted to orators—such as Szell and Garibaldi—men who could cast a spell. In his article on the Moses of Michelangelo Freud seems fascinated by charisma, by the physical and psychic strength which emanates from the great man—both the portrayer and the portrayed. So it is with his other historical heroes, such as Hannibal and Napoleon. These are the men who are above illusion, but who create it; above fear, but who inspire it; above loyalty, but who demand it.

All this sounds familiar enough today. But at the turn of the century, it was a far less conventional view. Nietzsche, for whom Freud had profound admiration, stood almost alone. Other elements in Nietzsche's theory are also found in Freud: the attack on reformers, the ridicule of humanitarians,[44] and the contempt for the bewitched masses,[45] who look always for the "happy ending" in their fantasies.[46] Nor, obviously, did Freud much care by what ideology the leader secured the necessary mass submission; late in life, he expresses con-

---

42. Reference footnote 5; pp. 271, 411.

43. See reference footnote 10; p. 242. Cf. reference footnote 2; p 272. ("In the dream I am surprised at my German Nationalistic feelings").

44. Note, however, that Freud states that he was a member of the Humanitarian Society. Reference footnote 2; p. 240.

45. Reference footnote 10; pp. 194-195.

46. Reference footnote 10; pp. 220-221.

siderable respect even for the Bolsheviks who, he feels, have known how to organize the masses.[47]

This, as will be apparent, is only one side of Freud's view; perhaps it is the more conscious and explicit side. But before turning to the more libertarian themes, it is necessary to see how Freud, in his day-to-day writing and work, treated the powerless groups in his society. This will, I think, afford more insight into his personal authoritarian tendencies than will his writings on leadership. For the latter might, or so one could claim, spring from a realistic judgment of social needs; the former, while less explicit, had a more deep-lying effect on psycho-analysis itself.

§ THE HIERARCHY OF DIFFERENCES

I MENTIONED at the outset that Freud tended to view differences as implying relations of super- and sub-ordination; this, in fact, was my definition of authoritarian thinking. In comparison with man, for example, Freud saw the other animals as a powerless group, a down-trodden class. It is interesting that they never appear in Freud's writings, so to speak, in their own right; they are always the objects of phobias or the stuff of symbols. Where a little 5-year-old boy is afraid of draft horses falling down in the street, Freud cannot believe this could be pity, or any form of human sympathy; it is simply a sexual symbolism.[48] Of course, it might have been that alone, or that plus a special feeling for struggling horses in harness—a frightening sight to a sensitive onlooker. The point is that it seems hardly to have occurred to Freud that one might identify with oppressed and struggling animals, and that what might have been so frightening to Hans was seeing in these huge horses the same struggle that he felt himself engaged in.

Freud's attitude towards the lower classes of human society was actually not very different. Wherever servants, nurses, porters, and so forth, appear in his writings, they are viewed as dubious rather undifferentiated beings, scarcely credited with personality. Freud repeatedly warns parents against the damage that nurses can do to children; they are viewed as seductresses, rather than as persons who might give a middle-class child the love and stimulation withheld by his parents.[49] As one gets glimpses of his own behavior towards the few lower-class people he came in contact with, such as maids and

---

47. Reference footnote 10; p. 247.

48. "Analysis of a Phobia in a Five-Year-Old-Boy"; reference footnote 3; p. 149; but cf. p. 254, and also "Totem and Taboo" (Brill, tr.), in *The Basic Writings of Sigmund Freud;* pp. 906-907.

49. For young men, actresses constitute a similar danger. Reference footnote 2; p. 325.

cabdrivers, one finds a tendency in him to be exploitative, even mean. He spits on the stairs to annoy a particularly neat housekeeper. He drives cabbies too hard. He seeks bargains from shopkeepers. He upbraids the conductor of an express.[50] In all this, he is the nineteenth-century bourgeois gentleman, for whom the lower classes are not really people, scarcely seen as individuals, and not respected.

Another social difference is that between adults and children; and here, too, Freud is partly on the side of the powers-that-be, the grown-ups. He frequently refers to children's questions as a "nuisance";[51] it seldom occurs to him that adults' questions of children—"And how old are you, my little boy?" and, "What are you going to be when you grow up?"—may also be a nuisance. More seriously, he makes the famous charge that children are "polymorphous-perverse"—that is, that their sexual life is not confined to the genital zone. Despite all his qualifications, this seems to me to be the application of adult standards to child behavior. He does not see that our language patterns, to which he was so sensitive in other connections, are adult-oriented; the child is forced into them both as object and subject. Likewise Freud speaks of children as immoderate,[52] lacking the ego and superego controls by which the adult has learned to govern his behavior. In this way, he justifies the authoritative controls which are applied to them. But it is at least an open question whether children are as wanting in moderation as Freud supposed. Just as recent experiments have shown that children, left to themselves, will choose the foods that their particular metabolisms need, there is evidence that they are far from immoderate in satisfying their other desires where they have not already been cramped by adult interference.

"The child's ambition," Freud writes, "is not so much to distinguish himself among his equals as to imitate the big fellows. The relation of the child to the grown-up determines also the comic of degradation, which corresponds to the lowering of the grown-up in the life of the child. Few things can afford the child greater pleasure than when the grown-up lowers himself to its level, disregards his superiority, and plays with the child as its equal. The alleviation which furnishes the child pure pleasure is a debasement. . . ."[53] Does this not sound a bit patronizing? So a white man would talk about Negroes, or a colonial about the "natives." In all these instances, a civilization that is

---

50. Reference footnote 2; p. 269.

51. See, for example, reference footnote 5; p. 796.

52. Reference footnote 5; p. 796. But of course he also regards the adult demands made of children as immoderate. See, for example, "The Sexual Enlightenment of Children," in *Collected Papers* 2:36.

53. Reference footnote 5; p. 796.

different is judged by a kind of unconscious ethnocentrism. And of course a vicious circle is created. For the powerless do tend to imitate the powerful, and to "enjoy" degrading them.

Freud, as I have already noted, wanted "tractable" sons. So, in his psychoanalytic theory, he accused children of not wanting to renounce illicit goals—and emphasized less adults' reluctance to renounce their privileges vis-à-vis this helpless minority; in the same way, Freud viewed the Oedipus complex from the side of the adult who is the focus of the child's rivalry and love—more often than from the side of the child of whom the adult wants greedily to take possession.

That Freud sides with the authorities in this warfare is most sharply shown by his relative lack of indignation against the crimes parents commit on their children, even when those crimes have landed the children in his office. He takes for granted that that is how things are, and while he succors the victims he feels little fury against their oppressors. He never notes that the threat of castration is a more severe punishment than warranted even for the Oedipal crimes which he believes children would like to commit. Even in the most extreme case, when a patient is taken from him by her parents who fear she will recover, he records the fact with only a marginal protest.[54] On the other hand, where he does have some control over an upbringing, as in the famous case of little Hans, he is critical of the mother for "spoiling" the boy, but much less of the prying father who pesters the child with psychoanalytic questions and interpretations from morning to night—a father who, as the report implicitly reveals, had no respect for the child's integrity, privacy, and idiosyncrasy.[55]

The Analyst as an Authority

A further example of Freud's attitude towards the powerless, lies in his treatment of neurotics, a minority, as against the "normal" majority. On one level, Freud consciously accepted the standards and outlook of the normal man and branded the neurotics as weaklings, constitutionally and psychically inadequate. These attitudes find their way into psychoanalytic therapy in Freud's primarily one-way concept of the transference. "Transference" means that the patient transfers to the analyst the constellations of love, hate, and other affects, which developed in his childhood; he treats the analyst, in feeling, as if the latter were his father or another significant figure. The theory, obviously, contains a great deal of truth. And, while Freud

54. See Freud, *A General Introduction to Psycho-analysis*, pp. 400-401; and cf. "The Psychogenesis of a Case of Homosexuality in a Woman," in *Collected Papers* 2:202, 206.

55. Reference footnote 48; p. 207.

does deal with the "countertransference," in which the analyst's own resistances get in the way of his work, he does seem to set up an ideal in which only the patient is affected by the patient-analyst relationship, and where the analyst is merely a neutral figure.

But suppose the patient rebels, and refuses to accept the analyst's authority? Freud called this the "resistance," and set himself the methodical task of breaking it down. If a patient expresses a doubt about the content of a dream, Freud is apt to interpret this as a resistance.[56] If a patient is unable to give associations to a dream, Freud will supply the answers from the symbolic dictionary;[57] in other words, Freud, in effect, tells the patient, If you do not come across and reveal the mechanisms which I know to be at work within you, I will find them anyway. Once, he succeeded in producing from a patient the desired sexual key, after saying he would have to discontinue the analysis.[58] Though, theoretically, Freud called "resistance" anything which impeded the analysis, in practice he seems at times to have regarded such resistance as a personal attack: he said, in effect, to his patients, If you oppose me, that is your "resistance," your preferring to remain ill, and, perhaps, you wish to have me fail. In part, Freud thus avoided debate upon the merits of the case. A most striking single example of this outlook appears in the book on dreams. A patient knows Freud's thesis that all dreams are wish-fulfillments. Then she dreams of something so disagreeable—spending the summer with her mother-in-law—that it cannot be a wish-fulfillment, even in the most far-fetched interpretation. Freud replies that the patient wished to prove *"that I should be wrong, and this wish the dream showed her as fulfilled."*[59]

Though Freud insisted that the analyst should counsel and direct the patient as little as possible, he seems to have been not entirely aware of the degree of authority he exercised. In one of his earlier cases, he reports that he "expected her [the patient] to accept a solution which did not seem acceptable to her";[60] in the dream-associations he accuses her of showing him up by not getting well and responds by telling her that her symptoms are her own fault,[61] that he would prefer to have a more "docile" patient.[62] And, like God, there are no secrets from him; few things so engaged his efforts as attempts

56. For example, reference footnote 2; p. 474.
57. For example, reference footnote 2; p. 381.
58. Reference footnote 2; p. 334.
59. Reference footnote 2; p. 229.
60. Reference footnote 2; p. 195.
61. Reference footnote 2; pp. 196-197.
62. Reference footnote 2; p. 199.

of patients to hide something—this was "resistance" with a vengeance.[63] He prided himself that they could seldom, if ever, succeed. In this he had the advantage of a "phonographic memory";[64] if a patient got fuzzy about a dream, Freud could always catch him up.[65] Moreover, since not even the slightest error escaped him,[66] he must have given patients the feeling that they could not get away with anything.

This same congeries of attitudes towards the powerless—towards children, women, neurotics—is manifested towards the intellectual problems with which Freud was concerned; one might view this as sadism towards the (powerless) material of theory. Freud himself gives us, as one of his favorite quotations, a similar comparison which was once made by Lassalle:

A man like myself who, as I explained to you, had devoted his whole life to the motto *Die Wissenschaft und die Arbeiter* (Science and the Workingman), would receive the same impression from a condemnation which in the course of events confronts him *as would the chemist, absorbed in his scientific experiments, from the cracking of a retort. With a slight knitting of his brow at the resistance of the material, he would, as soon as the disturbance was quieted, calmly continue his labor and investigations.*[67]

Freud's intellectual powers seem to have been excited by that very "resistance of the material," whether the "material" was the reception of his theories at the hands of the Vienna profession, the "resistance" of a patient in analysis, or the intractability of facts which he wished to order into a theoretical framework. "How many seemingly absurd dreams have we not forced to give up their sense!"[68] Freud says of himself with pride. And elsewhere he refers to a type of dream which "stubbornly refuses to surrender its meaning."[69] In such a case, he advises the analyst to turn the inexplicable symbol into its opposite— say exchange night for day, or wet for dry—a technique that sometimes led him to great discoveries and sometimes simply to victory over a stubborn fact. One might even suppose that Freud's great admiration for Moses, Hannibal, Michelangelo, and others, may have sprung in part from his identification with the effort to shape and hew the hardest materials, physical or human.

---

63. See, however, the benevolent attitude towards patients' denials Freud takes in "Constructions in Analysis" in *Collected Papers* 5:358.

64. Reference footnote 10; p. ix.

65. Reference footnote 2; pp. 472-473.

66. Cf. "Psychopathology of Everyday Life" (Brill, tr.), in *The Basic Writings of Sigmund Freud*.

67. Reference footnote 5; p. 682.

68. Reference footnote 4; p. 65.

69. Reference footnote 2; p. 352.

Many illustrations could be given of this effort of Freud's to fit everything into a comprehensive system, even at the cost of distorting. When he deals, for instance, with dreams, he establishes that they are all wish fulfillments—and if, later on, a dream turns up which does not seem to fit this system, Freud can become very ingenious in nevertheless finding a wish. When he deals with Biblical history, as in *Moses and Monotheism,* his arbitrariness in selecting as true those narratives which fit, and rejecting as "tendentious" those which do not, strikes me as a somewhat aggressive handling of the data.

Moreover Freud was particularly attracted by anything which savored of mystery or challenged his powers of unmasking.[70] He was fascinated by the uncanny, by the dark and secret springs of life. But he was not awed; on the contrary, he responded by attack, by an insistence on penetrating the secret, coming to the heart of the artichoke.[71] The sign "Keep Out" has attracted many great thinkers, some of them Jews and other "marginal men" for whom exclusion touched a sensitive spot. But here we see that the material on which a thinker works is only apparently powerless; though it cannot talk back, it "resists," and it is "protected" by all the categories of convention. Sometimes it seems as if a certain tendency to overpower is necessary for the creation of any radically new intellectual system; like Lassalle, the pioneer must be as deaf to the objections as the chemist to the cracking of his retort. Yet it is also this refusal to "listen" to the material which results in the distortions and overstatement of such a system.

§ FREUD AS PROMETHEUS

BUT ALL THIS is only one aspect of Freud's view. I have stressed this aspect because, for one thing, this hierarchical, reactionary side of Freud is just what attracts a number of contemporary intellectuals to him. Freud fits in with the current vogue of the "tough guy." And it is understandable that his tendency towards dogmatism should be admired by people who today force themselves to sound dogmatic even though they lack Freud's real self-confidence. However, in seizing upon the dogmatist in Freud, and upon the power-worshiper, they actually disregard his much more complicated view of things. In the remaining pages, I want to take up some of those themes in Freud that are liberating and equalitarian, and it will be seen, I think, that these themes are interwoven with their opposites. It is just such textures of ambivalence that Freud taught us to unravel.

---

70. Speaking of the occult, Freud writes that "prohibitions will not stifle men's interest in an alleged mysterious world." *The Question of Lay Analysis,* p. 104.

71. See the "Dream of the Botanical Monograph"; reference footnote 2; p. 243.

Liberating Underprivileged Reality

I have already indicated that another way of looking at the elements of sadism in Freud's handling of data is to see them as a source of the energy and drive needed to liberate those aspects of reality that convention had submerged or hidden. And it cannot fail to strike us that the same man who intransigently sought to organize the material of experience into the shapes of his theoretical constructions also "listened" to that material with a rare attentiveness and respect. And what he listened to particularly were the little things—the unnoticed words, gestures, silences, and so on—which previous thinkers had considered too trivial for notice. And not only little things but despised things too: "absurd" dreams, "debasing" perversions, "infantile" memories. Freud admitted them all into the structure of his thought and gave them all the credit of having meaning. Since, for Freud, these secret things are also the basic, the *Ursache,* they are even credited with an eminence over the more "powerful" and accepted data of experience. In other words, not only was no fact too humble to be lifted into the theoretical structure, but it might easily find itself outranking the more obvious and insistent facts which had been stressed by earlier thinkers.

Liberating Underprivileged Illness

It is the same with Freud's treatment of neurotics. Before his time, neurotics had generally been regarded as malingerers in whom no organic symptom could be found; or their ailment was credited to bad heredity. Instead, Freud insisted that psychic injuries ranked at least equally with the more obvious physical ones, were entitled to as much consideration, and were subject to the same causality. Everyone knows with what abuses the insane were treated before Freud's time, and how they are treated even today; the most innocent treatment for neurotics was to give them placebos, the harmless pills which swell the doctors' income. On the whole, medicine seemed to rank highest those specialists, such as surgeons, and eye, ear, nose, and throat men, who had the least close contact with the patient as a human being. And by and large when Freud started in psychiatric practice, only the hypnotists attempted to establish contact with the mentally ill; Freud soon rebelled against the authoritarianism of these men, with their inflexible "suggestions." He chose instead the far more respectful technique of "free" association. By this, he hoped to be able to listen to the voice of the id, freed from the supervision of the ego and superego, as well as from the surging noises of the external world.

Thanks to Freud, the powerless and despised neurotic finds himself, in the analytic situation, in a new relationship. Instead of being cursed out of the doctor's office with an accusation of malingering, or breezed out with a "why don't you just relax," or gentled out with a prescription for placebos, his every "thoughtless" word and act is taken with the utmost seriousness, and for a length of time—often years—unknown in any analogous professional relation. He can "make" the analyst listen to his stream of consciousness, his outcries, his silences, subject only to the injunction of sincerity, of keeping nothing back. But even this injunction bespeaks respect: not only the obvious respect for confidences, but the belief that what the patient seeks to hide is, after all, a human act or thought; and that, fundamentally, he has no thought or experience which cannot be matched among the dominant, the so-called normal.

Liberating Women and Children from Suffocating Piety

While in Freud's day the typical note in the treatment of the neurotic was brutality, the typical note in the treatment of women and children was sentimentality. In both cases, the powerless were treated with contempt; but in the second case the contempt, though it could be brutal enough, was veiled by hypocrisy and the assignment of angelic virtues to the group in question. Thus, Victorian middle-class womanhood—like the Southern white woman of today's romance—was put on a pedestal compounded of chastity, pity, and pretense. In showing up the falsity of this picture, Freud, despite acceptance of antifeminine bias, did much to put women in the same class with men. In the first place, his concept of bisexuality meant that women and men had come from the same original format—rather than from a male, as in the Adam and Eve myth; moreover, in the life of each sex, there existed elements from the other sex, one source of homosexual ties. In the second place, though Freud stressed the differences between the erotic and workaday roles of men and women, these after all are smaller than the similarities: both are subject on the whole to the same ontogenetic as well as phylogenetic destiny; both have the same internal structure of ego, superego, id; both may fall into the same characterological formations—both may fall ill of hysteria.

By similar leveling measures, Freud reduced the gap between the upper and lower classes of society. For him, the king was naked—with the ur-nakedness common to all mankind.[72] All women, of high and low degree, lost control of themselves in their destined labor of

---

72. See reference footnote 2; pp. 293-296.

childbirth. Freud liked to tell the story of the obstetrician who played cards with a baron while the baroness was in confinement. When the latter called out, "Ah, mon Dieu, que je souffre," the husband jumped up, but the doctor said, "That's nothing; let us play on." Later she called, "My God, my God, what pains," but still the doctor said it was not yet time to go in. "At last, there rang from the adjacent room the unmistakable cry, 'A-a-a-ai-e-e-e-e-e-E-E!' The physician quickly threw down the cards and said, 'Now it's time.' "[73]

Likewise, in rescuing children from sentimentality, Freud in one sense put them on the same footing with adults. As I have pointed out, he credited them with vices, with rebellion, with lust and hate and murderous intent. His ur-thinking made every adult at heart a child, by the very process of debasement he himself described as central to the process of wit. Even the first difference—the one between animals and men—was broken down in the pattern of Freud's thought; he viewed men as, at bottom, animals and found the source of their most human traits in the sexual instincts which they share with the mammalian phylum.[74]

Furthermore, whatever markedly ambivalent deference Freud paid to the temporal authorities of his day—the upper classes, the males, the distinguished—he retained more than most men the obedience of the true scientist to the truth and to the scientific tradition which the Renaissance revived and glorified. While he was forced against his will to quarrel with scientists, he never broke faith with Science. The things he rendered unto Caesar are trivial coin in comparison with the devotion he rendered to his fierce, yet fundamentally humane and passionately secular deity of Science.

Thus, we may compare his taking the side of the adult against the child in some of his views, such as the Oedipus complex, with his protest against adults who lied to their children. He realized quite clearly that children who can see through their parents' lies will become free of the parents, and he wrote that children who reject the stork fable begin their "psychic independence . . . from this act of disbelief. . . ."[75] Even more strongly, he denounced the "sadly antiquated" *patria potestas* which survives in modern society: "Even in our own middle-class families the father commonly fosters the growth

---

73. Reference footnote 5; p. 681.

74. Cf. Fenichel, *The Psychoanalytic Theory of Neurosis*, p. 213. "The child is not as arrogant as the adult person, who tries to believe in a fundamental difference between human beings and animals."

75. Reference footnote 4; p. 47.

of the germ of hatred which is naturally inherent in the paternal relation, by refusing to allow the son to be a free agent or by denying
him the means of becoming so."[76] And the mother, too, he added,
circumscribes her daughter when the latter's "budding beauty" reminds the envious parent "that for her the time has come to renounce
sexual claims."[77] More searching still is Freud's awareness that the
father's strictness evokes the child's criticism and the latter's close
awareness of every weakness in the authority, but that this criticism
is repressed and remains unconscious.[78] No truer statement as to the
operation of authority has ever been written than this: that criticism
is called into being by interest and need, and that the findings are then
repressed and remain operative in the unconscious mind. Ambivalence
towards the father, one may assume, is the inevitable outcome of this
process, with conscious love and admiration acting as a cover for
unconscious criticism and hate. Of this ambivalence, Freud's own attitude, which I have just reviewed, is an example; the phrases just
now quoted hardly spring from an unequivocal worshiper of authority.

As one would expect, Freud's reported dreams indicate his ambivalence towards his own parents. He reports, without apparent indignation, his mother's deceiving him, her strict middle-class restraints.[79] But certain dreams are polemics against his father; Freud
interprets these either to mean that the manifest father represents
some other authority—when it could more easily refer both to the
father and to the other authority—or by accusing himself, for example, of sexual curiosity, thus putting his father in the right.[80] Nevertheless, the dreams stand as proof that Freud rebelled against his
father, but, like so many sons, did not carry the rebellion through.[81]

Promethean and constricting elements seem to me similarly intertwined in the thought and heritage of many great thinkers throughout history, whether one thinks of Confucius or of Marx, of Plato
or of St. Simon. To be born is to be mortgaged; to live is to be
crippled; to be socialized is to be limited as well as freed. And, as
violent social revolutions have their Thermidors, so do violently original social thinkers look both forward and back. However, such an
attempt at generalization will be misleading if it obscures the profound differences among thinkers in the degree to which they blend

76. Reference footnote 2; pp. 303-304.
77. Reference footnote 2; p. 304.
78. Reference footnote 2; p. 416.
79. Reference footnote 2; pp. 266-267.
80. Reference footnote 2; pp. 416, 433. Cf. also the dream on p 411.
81. Cf. "A Disturbance of Memory on the Acropolis," in *Collected Papers*
5:302, 311-312.

the prejudices of their class and age with means of escaping from those prejudices. Moreover, elements in a thinker which may have been peripheral in his own time may turn out to be decisive in his reception by later ages.

One can already see in Freud's case the divergent streams of social philosophy that trace their origins, more or less justly, to his work. I have spoken of the fashion among certain intellectuals to use Freud—along with Dostoevsky, Kierkegaard, and others—as a spokesman of man's irrationality, his need for mystery and authority. Among some psychiatrists, Freud's stress on reality-orientation can be read as justifying therapies aiming to adjust the patient to society as given, whether reality happens to be deserving of such sacrifice or not. And among a large lay public, diluted Freudian interpretations are used by people to evaporate their own hostility; and to explain others' hostility to oppressive life-conditions as simple transfers of Oedipal rivalry to the social scene—or things of the same sort. There is a side of Freud that warrants these abuses of his contributions, just as there is a side of Marx that cannot completely disavow the atrocities committed in his name.

For Freud did share, in the ways which I have tried to trace, many attitudes which, in his epoch and in his class, were used to establish and support differences of value and rank. On one level, he sided with the authority and looked at the powerless through authority's eyes. But on another, and more characteristic level, he rebelled against authority. As in many such rebellions, his tactic was not to exalt the underdog but to degrade the top dog. "You are all the same," he seems to be saying, "princes and paupers, gentlemen and pimps, philosophers and babies." And, just as a lord has no secrets from his valet, so the illustrious could not dazzle Freud's eyes; in the very highest attainments of man—his art, his speculation, his juridical institutions—Freud found the cloven hoof of sex. As on the western plains the Colt revolver was called "Old Equalizer," so Freud saw the legacy each man carried on his person as the fundamental equalizer of the race.

23. The Themes of Heroism and Weakness in the Structure of Freud's Thought

Sᴛᴜᴅᴇɴᴛs ᴏғ ɪɴᴛᴇʟʟᴇᴄᴛᴜᴀʟ ʜɪsᴛᴏʀʏ tend to exaggerate, so it seems to me, the importance in contemporary life of the ideas whose derivations they trace. Since they are themselves intellectuals, for whom ideas are very important, they fall prey to the error of the specialist who sees the world from the angle of his own routines. Thus, one can find Nazism blamed on a congeries of alleged fathers from Machiavelli to Nietzsche, from Gobineau to Spengler or Carl Schmitt. Likewise, in much current discourse, William James and John Dewey are treated as the founts of all that is alleged to be shallow, manipulative, and complacent in American life. A whole school of critics, led by Van Wyck Brooks, blamed on the debunking writers of the twenties the cynicism and pacifism which they thought prevalent in the pre-World War II era. In this fashion, people whose trade is words cry their own wares even in the very act of claiming to be overwhelmed by the far more powerful words of their chosen enemies.

Obviously, it would be absurd to rush to the opposite extreme and to contend that words and ideas have only negligible influence on the stream of events. Indeed, a just appraisal in a concrete social context is always exceedingly difficult, as are efforts to isolate *any* single item in a cultural complex. We know well enough that institutions often come close to reversing their founders' intentions: that Christ was not a Christian, Marx not a Marxist (let alone a Stalinist), Dewey not a school principal in the Teachers College patronage network. And where a man's thought and action do not lead to creation of a new institution but mingle in a general climate of opinion, the tracing of the consequences of his work is even more a shadowy and impalpable task: no Mendelian law governs the unembodied transmission of ideas. Even when men acknowledge indebtedness, what does that prove? They often say they owe it all to their mothers. We are, I think, quite far from even knowing how to begin the job of evaluating the weight of any single person's ideas in the historical process. Conceivably, the sort of studies now undertaken by social psychologists concerning the impact of the mass media—radio, print, and film—on people will give us some clues as to the influence and social distribution of particular words and images.

Yet when all this is granted, it remains plausible to say that Freud has had tremendous impact on our popular culture. As radioactive tracers allow us to follow chemical substances in the physiologist's laboratory, so the verbal tags adopted by Freud and his followers give us some way of tracing the rapidity of the diffusion of his inventions. The number of psychoanalysts even today is a mere handful—in America, it would seem, less than 500—fewer than the number of "missionaries" who spread Marxist gospel as members of the International Workingmen's Association in the 1850's and 60's. And while the devotion, diligence, and productiveness of these analysts—who fill journals while treating patients and training the young—could scarcely be excelled by any band of missionaries, these qualities, without the aid of a powerful ideology, would not have given them their present place in popular discourse.[1]

It would be valuable to make a comparative study in detail, and to see how, in different countries and different social strata, Freud's thought has been received and modified, used and abused. Plainly, the process that Lasswell, with reference to political ideologies, termed "restriction by partial incorporation"[2] has also occurred with Freud. One would expect this process to occur when students in their courses read some watered-down or textbook version, but this process even occurs when students read Freud in his own words. For the revolu-

---

1. Freud, in one of his moments of sober self-judgment—at other times, as I shall try to show, he was overmodest—ranked his contribution alongside those of Copernicus and Darwin: he saw it as reducing man's stature and self-pride. So he found it easy enough to explain why he had enemies, and could defend himself by explaining the "resistance" he met with. But he made less, at least in his published work, of the fact that after 1902 or so he attracted friends and followers—at a time when it still cost something to be a friend of Freud—and that before the Second World War his thought had spread to all industrialized or even semi-industrialized lands. To be sure, in "The Future Prospects of Psychoanalytic Therapy," he allowed himself to speculate, as early as 1910, on the possibility that analytic thought would permeate education, would be made available to the poor, and would finally make therapy unnecessary by the progress of what would today be called preventive mental hygiene. (*Collected Papers* 2:285; London, Hogarth Press, 1925.) But he seems not to have realized that men were and would be attracted to his work, not only because it was socially useful, but because it was adventurous—that men would, in effect, trade their vanity for the pleasures of disinterested discovery and understanding. Indeed, it is striking that a number of the ideologies which are popular today, such as Marxism and Freudianism, cannot adequately explain the appeal they have for many of their devotees. A good many people embrace Marxism, for instance, in order to make sense of the world, or to contribute to it, and not only because of class consciousness; people embrace psychoanalytic thinking because it adds to the interest they find in observing human beings, and not only because of such motives as narcissism.

2. Harold D. Lasswell, *World Politics and Personal Insecurity*, p. 6.

tionary concepts of Freud can no longer have the same impact when they have their teeth drawn by the very nature of most classroom situations—when, moreover, students already come with some familiarity with major themes: the unconscious, childhood sexuality, the importance of dreams, slips and errors, and so on. But it follows from this that it makes little sense to blame Freud for the untoward consequences of some aspects of his thought as it is currently modified and received —if we find, for instance, "neurotic" used as a term of apology for the self and of vicious denigration against others. That certain elements in Freud's view of life were narrow, class-biased, and reactionary is one of the points made in the preceding two papers and in this one. But this must not blind us to the fact that Freud expressed his views at a time when, in many quarters, democratic sentiments were powerful and when the "common man" was, in America especially, given a great deal of lip service. His opposition to those dominant trends, even when the latter happened to be progressive, was stimulating and productive; and this is not altered by the fact that today some of his views on work, on authority, on heroism, may no longer liberate thought but, in the present context of Freud's reception, may confine it.

It is, then, up to each generation to read Freud as if it were for the first time, much as men in the sixteenth and seventeenth centuries sought—and even today such men as Schweitzer and Buber still seek —to approach the Bible anew. I would like to succeed in sending at least some of the readers of these articles back to Freud to see whether the themes I trace in his work actually exist and, if so, whether they can be stated in a more fundamental and searching way. By such ever-renewed readings, I hope that Freud can be saved from the fate of "partial incorporation," and that his power to challenge, inspire, and perplex can be retained. If so, we need worry less about tendencies to put his work to manipulative uses and his authority behind socially regressive ideologies.

In depicting Freud's view of human nature and social organization in the previous articles, I have already touched on Freud's ideal of human life—what he admired in people and, conversely, what he despised. Indeed, such ideals, explicit or implicit, are ordinarily part of that image of human nature from which everyone makes judgments as to the meaning of life and the value of, and possibilities for, social relations. Here I want to examine Freud's ideal and its counterimage of weakness in more detail.

Note that I have taken heroism and weakness—not heroism and villainy—to be polar opposites in Freud's view. Such a polarity ostensibly eliminates ethical considerations. It accompanies a view which sees men as divided into a strong elite and a numerous but vacillating mass. But here again one finds ambivalence in Freud's outlook. For while he shared with thinkers such as Nietzsche and Carlyle elements of an elitist position, he also emphasized, as I have indicated before, the fundamental similarity of all men, their obedience to the same instinctual laws and infantile survivals.

§ PORTRAIT OF A HERO

FREUD'S IDEAL MAN is harmonious within and successful without. He has conflicts and meets obstacles but they are all in the external world. Out of polymorphous infantile sexualities he has developed a definite gential supremacy; the hero neither lingers at the childhood way-stations of sex nor returns regressively to them. His potency is unproblematical and his choice among sexual objects is unrestricted by fetish or fixation. Freud, in commenting on a statement by Leonardo that "great love springs from great knowledge of the beloved object," declares that people in love "are guided by emotional motives which have nothing to do with cognition; and their consequences are rather weakened by thought and reflection."[3] In this light, "genital maturity" means for Freud lesser rather than greater complexity and differentiation of emotions. But one must qualify this by observing that such maturity involves a man's ability to make love to women of the same social class and refinement as his mother and sister; he remains immature so long as, hounded by the incest taboo, he can let himself go only with women whom he socially despises—that is, who do not forcibly remind him of the forbidden objects of his childhood. By implication, therefore, mature love involves more than mere ability to secure genital heterosexual release.[4]

Nevertheless, the course of the hero's sexual gratification, as one senses it from Freud's writings, takes the shortest line between the unconscious wish and the conscious gratification; there is no occasion for the procrastination of daydreaming nor, indeed, for the 'waste' of

3. Freud, *Leonardo da Vinci*, p. 40.

4. One must remember, moreover, that more was involved in such ability in the days before the advent of easy and reliable contraceptives and of easy and reliable women who were not courtesans. While at one point Freud pleads for the spread of contraceptive knowledge among married couples ("Sexuality in the Aetiology of the Neuroses," in *Collected Papers* 1:237-239), this is not inconsistent with his statement in which he speaks of nongenital forms of sexuality: "ethically they are reprehensible, for they degrade the love-relationship of two human beings from being a serious matter to an otiose diversion, attended neither by risk nor by spiritual participation." " 'Civilized' Sexual Morality and Modern Nervousness," in *Collected Papers* 2:95.

dream-stimulated emissions.[5] There is none of "the tendency to reflection and delay" that Freud noted in Leonardo's art.[6] Freud attributed a similarly uncomplicated quality to the dreams of the normal person. "Indeed," he writes, "the natural dreams of healthy persons often contain a much simpler, more transparent, and more characteristic symbolism than those of neurotics, which, owing to the greater strictness of the censorship and the more extensive dream-distortion resulting therefrom, are frequently troubled and obscured, and are therefore more difficult to translate."[7]

The hero, viewed economically, follows, without scruple, without hesitation, without doubt, the hedonistic calculus in his sexual life. Freud declares:

> The man who in consequence of his unyielding nature cannot comply with the required suppression of his instincts, becomes a criminal, an outlaw, unless his social position or striking abilities enable him to hold his own as a great man, a 'hero.'[8]

Moreover, the hero is a person of great energy potential: "psychic greatness like somatic greatness is exhibited by means of an increased expenditure."[9] Viewed topologically, this pattern means that the ego of the hero is in unquestioned command, and that conflict between the conscious and unconscious levels of the personality is at a minimum. As the wise statesman never veers too far from the demands of the mob he leads, but controls and channels them in the very process of carrying them out, so the hero's ego is in the closest touch with the wishes of the id, of which it is in one sense a most effective "public servant."[10]

Plainly, all this does not mean that the hero is as completely free of internal superego restraints as he is unintimidated by society's efforts at repression. While his ego does not cringe before an internalized father-imago, the superego functions to provide an ideal to which the narcissistic elements in the personality can aspire and to

---

5. The dreamer, Freud writes, "thinks in his sleep: 'I don't want to continue this dream and exhaust myself by an emission; I would rather save it for a real situation.'" "The Interpretation of Dreams" (Brill, tr.), in *The Basic Writings of Sigmund Freud*, p. 514.

6. Reference footnote 3; p. 116.

7. Reference footnote 5; pp. 381-382.

8. *Collected Papers* 2:82.

9. Freud, "Wit and Its Relation to the Unconscious" (Brill, tr.), *The Basic Writings of Sigmund Freud;* p. 777.

10. Even so, Freud pointed out that "the subjection of the *Ucs.* by the *Pcs.* is not thorough-going even in perfect psychic health; the extent of this suppression indicates the degree of our psychic normality." Reference footnote 5; p. 520. See also Freud, *The Ego and the Id*, pp. 81-83.

demand a high level of performance in line with that ideal. The restraints so imposed may perhaps be compared to the concept of
"noblesse oblige." For they are voluntarily accepted—even though
their original imposition may have been far from voluntary—as a
nobleman's code is supposed to be, rather than submitted to through
the operation of the bureaucratic internal machinery based on fear
of castration, of God, of public opinion. The hero has a certain
Spartan, uncomplaining attitude towards life, and a sportsmanlike adherence to the rules of good breeding. Freud's heroes are at farthest
remove from the spoiled Bohemian attitudes, seemingly free of
superego and of inhibition, which Freud detested.[11]

Nevertheless, there is, I feel, something romantic and parochial
in Freud's image of the ideal type of man as one who goes directly
at what he wants, including sexual objects, without getting lost in
the toils and discontents of thought.[12]

With a different outlook, one might describe neurotics as people
for whom life is insufficiently complicated; they over-simplify it by
seeing new events within the stereotype of old ones; they find nothing new under the sun. The ideal of a mentally healthy person would
then be someone able to differentiate his experience in every field; to
see other people, for example, in terms of subtle changes in them so
that they are never the *same* people. Such a person would make only
minimal use of the categories and conventions which culture provides
in order often to simplify life to the point of bareness.

We may make the comparison more concrete by another glance
at Freud's picture of genital love. For him, "two on an island" was
the ideal; he wrote in *Civilization and Its Discontents* that a pair of
lovers needed no one else to complete their happiness but wished to
withdraw their libido from the task of building civilization.[13] This is
an adolescent moviegoer's dream of love, but not something which
mature lovers actually seek: love rather leads them to widen and
complicate their dealings with other people, with art, and with other
civilized matters. In those cultures, whether 'civilized' or 'primitive,'
where human relations are marked by subtlety of feeling, sexual love
can become filled with overtones. Moreover, one may today observe,
among the groups where Victorian morality has waned, that love
can become even more complex and, if you please, more 'intellectual,'

---

11. Cf. his well-known remark that "revolutionary children are not desirable
from any point of view." *A New Series of Introductory Lectures on Psychoanalysis*, p. 206.

12. There is a similar note in Elton Mayo's critique, based on Janet, of "obsessive thinking" in modern industrial society. See, for example, Mayo, *The
Human Problems of an Industrial Civilization.*

13. Freud, *Civilization and Its Discontents*, p. 80.

precisely because it lacks the artificial spur of taboos and inhibitions.[14] Contrary to what many think, romantic love does not depend on delayed gratification but on gratification and mutuality which occur on many levels of the love relationship. Indeed, as Simone de Beauvoir has so well observed in *Le Deuxième Sexe*, such love can grow only when women are emancipated, when they no longer, as in Freud's day, have "only the choice between unappeased desire, infidelity, or neurosis."[15]

For other elements in Freud's picture of the hero, one may turn to his two loving studies of Moses. In his essay on "The Moses of Michelangelo,"[16] Freud describes the hero admiringly—his great frame and impressive beard, his noble brow and piercing, inscrutable glance, his fiery anger and his equally powerful restraint. In *Moses and Monotheism*,[17] Freud pays more attention to the hero's intellectual than to his physical qualities. The hero is shown to be a proud Egyptian nobleman, his monotheism the product of the kingly temper of Ikhnaton, which brooked no illusions and required no orgies of belief. This Egyptian Moses is undeterred by the resistance of the image-worshiping masses; he is unafraid of the fate of pioneers. This intransigence, so similar to his own, appeals to Freud. Likewise, as he indicates obliquely in his book on dreams, Freud admires "those powerful personalities who, by their sheer force of intellect and their fiery eloquence, ruled" the course of the French Revolution; and he also admired the eloquence and virility of Garibaldi.[18]

Views of this sort, largely implicit in Freud's pre-World War I writings, became of course much more explicit in his *Group Psychology and the Analysis of the Ego*, where he writes:

... from the first there were two kinds of psychologies, that of the individual members of the group and that of the father, chief, or leader. The members of the group were subject to ties just as we see them to-day, but the father of the primal horde was free. His intellectual acts were strong and independent even in isolation, and his will needed no reinforcement from others. . . .

---

14. Cf. Freud's remark that "the view may also be accepted that the differentiation of individual character, now so much in evidence, only becomes possible with sexual restraint." *Collected Papers* 2:91. It depends, of course, on what one means by "restraint."

15. *Collected Papers* 2:93. Since writing the foregoing, I have been glad to find the searching article by Edith Weigert, "Existentialism and Its Relations to Psychotherapy," in PSYCHIATRY (1949) 12:399-412, which takes much the same attitude as the text.

16. *Collected Papers* 4:257.

17. Freud, *Moses and Monotheism*.

18. See reference footnote 5; pp. 461, 410-411.

He, at the very beginning of the history of mankind, was the *Superman* whom Nietzsche only expected from the future. Even to-day the members of a group stand in need of the illusion that they are equally and justly loved by their leader; but the leader himself need love no one else, he may be of a masterly nature, narcissistic, but self-confident and independent.[19]

Evidently, there is a solipsistic tendency in this Freudian hero. In his contempt, in the style of his idealism, in his egocentric insistence on having his way, he reminds one of certain Hollywood types, or of the Hero Roark in Ayn Rand's best-selling novel, *The Fountainhead*, which was later made into a movie. This hero is tall, dark, handsome, and young.[20] But it would be manifestly unfair to push the comparison with Hollywood too far. Freud's hero is no rich playboy; his orientation is entirely toward reality, toward serious tasks in this world. He is in fact quite grown up; like Leonardo in his later years, he has attained "the resignation of the man who subjects himself to the 'Aνάyxn, to the laws of nature, and expects no alleviation from the kindness or grace of God."[21] He has faced the fact that "dark, unfeeling and unloving powers determine human destiny," or, again, that "the world is not a nursery."[22] In other words, the hero is one who is able to live without illusions—but this includes an end to illusions about the self, an end to vain regrets, wasteful mourning,[23] feminine pity, and sentimentality.[24]

---

19. Freud, *Group Psychology and the Analysis of the Ego*, pp. 92-93. It is interesting to note, in this connection, one of the charges that Freud brings against the United States; namely, that in this country "leading personalities fail to acquire the significance that should fall to them in the process of group-formation." Reference footnote 13; p. 93. In other words, America in Freud's eyes lacked dominating leaders, through identification with whom the masses could be bound to one another and to the system.

20. Several of Freud's dreams or dream-associations refer to his feeling of aging. Reference footnote 5; p. 220 (his black beard turning color); p. 447 (growing grey); p. 446 (youth as a time of many loves).

21. Reference footnote 3; p. 105.

22. Reference footnote 11; pp. 229, 230. Perhaps it should be added that, in Freud's view, the nursery becomes very like the world.

23. Freud again and again returned to the problem of mourning and sought to explain its "wastefulness" in terms of mental economics. See, for example, "Mourning and Melancholia," in *Collected Papers* 4:152. It is typical of his outlook that he was baffled whenever men seemed to extend themselves, whether in grief, in love, or in work, without the pressure of apparently overwhelming need. With a different outlook, one would find a problem in an inability to mourn, as in affectlessness generally.

24. Finding that Leonardo was "kind and considerate" to his young male disciples, Freud regards this as a correlate of his homosexuality. (Reference footnote 3; p. 77.) Freud also notes his "exaggerated sympathy for animals" (pp. 114, 36). He may, of course, be right with regard to Leonardo; my point is that he seems to accept, though not without qualification, conventional definitions of masculinity.

This stern reality-orientation of the hero includes the related element of steadiness and practicality in the pursuit of goals. Subject to "storming passions of the soul-stirring and consuming kind"[25] though he may be, he is nonetheless able to hold his fire, even to sublimate if need be. While he seeks, by the exercise of his "manly creative power,"[26] to change the course of the world, he faces the delays and frustrations of his self-appointed task with stoicism. Freud admired the insouciance in the face of death of aristocrats in the French Revolution,[27] or indeed of any criminal who could go to the gallows with a laugh.[28]

But to enter Freud's Valhalla it is not enough to be brave; one must also succeed. Sexual achievement is, in fact, the sign of success as of maturity. Freud writes:

A man who has shown determination in possessing himself of his love-object has our confidence in his success in regard to other aims as well. On the other hand, a man who abstains, for whatever reasons, from satisfying his strong sexual instinct, will also assume a conciliatory and resigned attitude in other paths of life, rather than a powerfully active one.[29]

Freud agrees with those critics of Leonardo, the homosexual, who object that the latter did not finish all the work he started; and he comments on Leonardo's "lack of ability to adjust himself to actual conditions."[30] And yet in writing about Leonardo, Freud states that he himself "succumbed to the attraction which emanated from this great and mysterious man, in whose being one seems to sense forceful and impelling passions, which nevertheless evince themselves in a remarkably subdued manner."[31] There are, moreover, other heroes of

To be sure, Freud criticizes German Army leadership in the First World War as too harsh, resulting in a failure to create sufficient libidinal ties between officers and men, hence among the men *inter se;* but this seems really to be a critique not of harshness as such, but of unskilful manipulation of men. Reference footnote 19; p. 44, n. 1.

25. A phrase Freud uses in explaining why the over-ratiocinative Leonardo missed those loves and hates that "others experience [as] the best part of their lives. . . ." Reference footnote 3; p. 43.

26. Freud, reference footnote 3; p. 115.

27. Cf. reference footnote 5; p. 461.

28. Cf. reference footnote 9; p. 798.

29. *Collected Papers* 2:93-94. Freud goes on in the same passage to point out that since women are intimidated from sexual curiosity, they are likewise rendered submissive in other spheres of life: "the undoubted fact of the intellectual inferiority of so many women can be traced to that inhibition of thought necessitated by sexual suppression." Such observations on Freud's part must be taken as a counterpoise to what has been said earlier about the exclusively masculine qualities of the hero.

30. Reference footnote 3; pp. 101, 116.

31. Reference footnote 3; pp. 117-118. Cf. his reference to "the magic of his [Charcot's] aspect and his voice," in "Charcot," *Collected Papers* 1:15.

Freud who were in the long run unsuccessful; he admired Hannibal and Ikhnaton. Thus, plainly enough, the men whom Freud looked up to are not cast in a single stereotype. They must leave a mark on the world, but there are different types of marks which count.

Perhaps the most important evidence of this is Freud's lifelong reverence for "the immortal Goethe."[32] He writes that his decision to become a medical student came about through reading, at 17, Goethe's essay on Nature;[33] and quotations from Goethe, meant to illustrate the latter's psychological wisdom, are scattered throughout his writings. Moreover, with his own desire "to fathom with coldest reflection the deepest secret,"[34] he was preoccupied with the "secret" of Goethe's genius, as with that of Leonardo and of other artists. In "A Childhood Recollection from 'Dichtung und Warheit'" Freud traced the early source of "that victorious feeling, that confidence in ultimate success, which not seldom brings actual success with it"[35] —that smiling destiny which Freud felt he himself perhaps lacked.

While Freud, not unlike Goethe, took for his subject matter all of human life and history, and many of the sciences, social and physical, while he wrote with the style of a novelist and ran the psychoanalytic movement with the style of a statesman, he continued to view himself as a restrained and plodding specialist. He speaks of "an inclination to concentrate my work exclusively upon a single subject or problem," and seems to accept, as I noted in a previous paper in commenting on his "Dream of the Botanical Monograph," the charge of being "one-sided."[36] In a way, this is quite fantastic: it is hard to think of anyone in the last seventy-five years who has roamed and rummaged so widely in so many different fields. Yet

---

32. See Freud's dream of Goethe, reference footnote 5; pp. 418-420, 352.

33. Freud, *An Autobiographical Study*, p. 14.

34. A phrase Freud quotes with reference to Leonardo. Reference footnote 3; p. 39.

35. *Collected Papers* 4:367. Freud, like many worshipers, failed to see the bitter tensions and surrenders in Goethe's life, which are dealt with in a fine, and to me convincing, essay by Ortega y Gasset, "In Search of Goethe from Within," reprinted in *Partisan Review* (1949) 16:1163-1188. Possibly, Freud was taken in by his envy of just those phases of Goethe's life that Ortega y Gasset finds suspect—his role as a courtier, his inability to commit himself to his art. Freud would not call this last an inability, but rather an ability to lead a well-rounded life. However, from this other point of view, Goethe's sunny freedom seems to be more apparent than real.

36. See reference footnote 33; p. 17. One may perhaps speculate as to what claims to grandiose versatility may lie concealed behind this self-image—or what truth in the sense of Freud's recognition of his unremittingly rational and intellectualized rhythm of life; that he did not care for music, an art whose meanings are difficult to seize by means of intellect, may be of some relevance here. Cf. *Collected Papers* 4:257.

this modesty, whatever its source, saved Freud from supposing that when he had analyzed the "family romance"—that is the Oedipal constellation—of a great artist, he had also fathomed the latter's gift for writing romances. Artistic gift and artistic technique Freud felt to be beyond the reach of psychoanalytic scrutiny. Since he had no similar hesitation in explaining other great human attainments psychoanalytically, one may suppose that his deference to the artist shows by implication that he retained to the end of his life what he felt at seventeen: unquestioning admiration for talent and achievement, such as Goethe exemplified for him. Whatever one may say of the limitations of the qualities Freud sometimes admired, the fact is that, in spite of his growing pessimism, he continued to be able to admire.

A further and quite remarkable example of this ability appears in Freud's *Festschrift* essay, "My Contact with Josef Popper-Lynkeus." There Freud quotes a story of Popper's, published in 1899, which described a man so pure and whole in heart that his dreams lacked opacity. He adds:[37]

And if Science informs us that such a man, wholly without evil and falseness and devoid of all repressions, does not exist and could not survive, yet we may guess that, so far as an approximation to this ideal is possible, it had found its realization in the person of Popper himself.

Here we find Freud admiring, though not without a characteristic touch of irony, a utopian reformer, a mere scribbler of impractical plans for social amelioration! At the close of the essay, Freud refers to the disappointments he had suffered when great men whom he had "honoured from a distance" turned out to be unsympathetic to psychoanalysis. With such experiences, it is surprising that Freud did not become more soured on those heroes, such as Popper, who were his contemporaries.[38]

§ FREUD'S ATTITUDE TOWARD HIS OWN QUALITIES

THIS BRINGS US to inquire directly how far Freud himself, in his own eyes, measured up to his portrait of a hero. It is hard to say, but there are a few stray remarks which we may take as clues. Unlike Leonardo,

---

37. *Collected Papers* 5:300-301. It is interesting to recall that Edward Bellamy once described in his story, "To Whom This May Come," a society in which people would know each other's inmost thoughts, hence have no need for guile. See Arthur E. Morgan's *Nowhere Was Somewhere;* Chapel Hill, Univ. of North Carolina Press, 1946; p. 142. Cf. the pungent observations of Harry Stack Sullivan concerning an anthropological report about an isolated Malay tribe whose members engage in mutual dream interpretation. "The Study of Psychiatry," *Pyschiatry* (1949) 12:326.

38. Cf., for example, Freud's warm tribute to Romain Rolland, in "A Disturbance of Memory on the Acropolis," in *Collected Papers* 5:302.

he is not the son of a "great gentleman,"[39] and while in his dreams he compares his father to Garibaldi, or to the statesman Szell who leads the unruly Magyars,[40] his father seems to have been a somewhat small-minded and unsuccessful man who could not imagine great things for his son.[41] Freud's boyhood and youth, moreover, were anything but glamorous. Instead of killing insolent Egyptians, he was a "good boy" at the *Gymnasium;* later, in Brücke's laboratory, he was afraid of arousing the master's ire by being unpunctual.[42] In contrast with those of his heroes who were courtiers or leaders of great armies, Freud spent what he terms "this unfruitful and actually somewhat humiliating period of my student days" at the Chemical Institute.[43] Compelled to wait five years before he could afford to marry,[44] he settled down with a prudent *Hausfrau*, remaining, he implies, sexually "above reproach."[45] In his daily life, he trained himself to wear a mask of politeness.[46] Nor was his routine varied by wild drinking bouts or Dionysian orgies. Freud was plagued, as I have already noted, by aging; and also by the Job-like but quite unheroic afflictions of boils, swellings in the nose, rheumatism,[47] and finally cancer. He bore these painful afflictions, as he bore the approach of death, with an extraordinary stoicism, but one feels that he was far from thinking himself a hero on this account.

Despite his family's poverty, Freud appears, moreover, to have been a sheltered lad, educated among the professional and business classes. And this diligent student, though he went through medical school, seems to have been astonished at his later realization of the prevalence of sex and sadism. For it is with a certain recollected innocence that he tells us of his surprise that other highly esteemed doctors —Breuer, Charcot, Chrobak—knew about the sexual etiology of neu-

---

39. Reference footnote 3; p. 100. In fact, Freud notes that his very name— *"Freude"* means "joy" in German—is the butt of jokes. Reference footnote 5; p. 268.

40. Reference footnote 5; pp. 410-411. In another dream (p. 418) he makes his father "a professor and a privy councillor."

41. Cf. Freud's discussion of his feeling of guilt for having outdistanced his father, in "A Disturbance of Memory on the Acropolis," reference footnote 38; pp. 311-312.

Even as a student at the University, Freud felt that, as a Jew, he could look no higher than for "some nook or cranny in the framework of humanity" from which to make a contribution. Freud, reference footnote 33; p. 14.

42. Freud, reference footnote 5; p. 407 (see also p. 450): "What overwhelmed me was the terrible gaze of his [Brücke's] blue eyes, before which I melted away. . . ."

43. Reference footnote 5; p. 445.

44. Reference footnote 5; p. 418.

45. Cf. reference footnote 5; p. 221.

46. Reference footnote 5; p. 223.

47. See reference footnote 5; pp. 199, 201, 220, 284.

rosis all along;[48] they took for granted what for Freud was a discovery—one that landed him, as it were by default, into greatness and controversy. In one respect, however, these discoveries did not disillusion Freud. For he seems never to have shed the illusion, perhaps typically middle class, that there *are* people who experience the wildest sensuality, or who abandon themselves in orgies of destruction. In *Civilization and Its Discontents* there are passages about intense pleasures of this sort which culture has forced us to surrender.[49] Such passages remind me of the newspaper advertisements several years ago for the movie "Anna and the King of Siam": "A strange, barbaric world of unendurable pleasures . . . infinitely prolonged." This is language to arouse excitement, to suggest experiences from which we, a humdrum people in a workaday world, are inevitably cut off and can only share by sublimation. If such pleasures are to be won by the adventuring hero, Freud was in his own eyes no hero.

Yet such romanticism about sexual conquest is of course only one aspect of Freud's complicated view of things. Though there was no pleasure to compare with sexual excitement, Freud convinced himself that even this delight was fundamentally unsatisfying in the long run: it had to contend not only with obstacles in the external world but with the fact that in the civilizing process, sexual energy itself seemed, in Freud's view, to be diminishing. And true lasting greatness, Freud believed, was generally paid for by libidinal sacrifice. Indeed, the tragedy implicit in this outlook runs through his last long philosophic essay, *Civilization and Its Discontents*, in which he argues that since men can only be happy in a state of idleness and sexual gratification, no conceivable culture can meet their requirements: both biology and culture forbid. The reader is led to conclude that the earth is a trap, for it tempts men to have wishes which it cannot satisfy, and the adult's only realistic course is that of Odysseus: to stop the ears of others and tie oneself firmly to the mast of sublimation, until in old age and finally in death the wishes lose their power to torment.

Work, then, and especially science and art are surer bets than sex. But how did Freud regard himself in his chosen field of scientific work? One of his dream associations is quite poignant evidence of his unsatisfied wishes to be uncontroversially great and famous. He imagines himself going anonymously to be treated for glaucoma by a doctor in Berlin; the doctor applies cocaine which makes the operation pos-

---

48. "The History of the Psychoanalytic Movement," in *The Basic Writings of Sigmund Freud;* pp. 937-938; also in *Collected Papers* 1:294-296.

49. Reference footnote 13.

sible; and Freud takes pleasure in the secret knowledge of his share in discovery of the drug.[50] Thus Freud in this fantasy plays the role of a prince of science in disguise. Since he came close to being in fact the discoverer of cocaine's anaesthetic uses and never forgave himself for missing the opportunity, the fantasy, with its image of eye illness, is obviously touched with self-pity. Today, many people learn of the discovery of cocaine only through Freud!

One may find similar notes of self-pity based on a quite understandable feeling of isolation in Freud's long essay "On the History of the Psychoanalytic Movement."[51] Freud speaks there of those "lonely years" when he alone *was* the Movement—when he thought "science would ignore me entirely during my lifetime," though he believed that at a much later time his discoveries would be found and honored. While on the one hand he regards those years as "a glorious 'heroic era,'" on the other hand he seems to have been unduly impressed by his invitation to accept an honorary degree and to deliver lectures at Clark University, in Worcester. In his *Autobiographical Study*, he writes:[52]

> As I stepped on to the platform at Worcester to deliver my *Five Lectures upon Psycho-Analysis* it seemed like the realization of some incredible day-dream: psycho-analysis was no longer a product of delusion, it had become a valuable part of reality.

Even as of 1909 this seems slightly excessive, as does Freud's overgratefulness for the Goethe prize bestowed on him by the City of Frankfort—"the climax of my life as a citizen."[53] When disciples came, he accepted them, by his own later avowals, somewhat uncritically, and he worked with them to give to the minuscule "psychoanalytic movement" those congresses, journals, reports from abroad which one might expect from a world-wide organization of many thousands.

How is one to explain this disparity between Freud's altogether

---

50. Reference footnote 5; p. 241. While Freud would himself tend to assume that, once we have found the wish that was motive to a dream we must take it at face value, I would prefer to argue that the dream- or day-wish may be of much less weight in the total personality than explicit conscious considerations. Dreams may represent the husks, rather than the vital centers, of one's contemporary life, and it is far from decisive proof of childish ambition that one has a dream or daydream, perhaps in a mood of depression, such as Freud here reports and interprets. Today, indeed, dream-interpretation often permits people to discount themselves unduly and to take a passing thought, whether libidinal or aggressive, as better evidence of their "true" selves than a lifelong commitment.

51. Reference footnote 48; *Basic Writings;* p. 943; *Collected Papers* 1:304-305.
52. Reference footnote 33; p. 95.
53. Reference footnote 33; p. 135.

extraordinary achievements, which in the main he evaluated justly, and these scarcely heroic concerns? I think that here again one is confronted with the problem of Freud's ambivalence toward authority. To the extent that Freud irrationally admired the powerful and illustrious of his day and had not completely freed himself from his "innocent faith in authority"[54] it was almost impossible for him to avoid viewing himself and his work through their eyes, even or perhaps especially where that judgment was a negative one. Thus, though Freud's own method gave him an exceptional weapon for understanding the hostility and irrationality with which he was surrounded, a weapon which, ironically, distracted him from seeing in equally full light the friends who flocked to him, he nevertheless seems to have felt to some slight extent: *After all, my enemies are right; I am, like so many other Jews, a disturber of the peace and it is only right if I am badly treated.* He was anything but the rebel who likes to *épater les bourgeois* and who consciously feels worried only if he has the admiration of conventional circles. In spite of himself, Freud could not help his preoccupation with questions of rank within the institutions of solid-seeming Vienna[55] and, beyond Vienna, solid-seeming 'official' German science and chauvinistically hostile but culturally reputed Parisian science.

Elsewhere, I have briefly discussed the problem of "the nerve of failure," by which I mean the ability of a lonely thinker, or other minority-figure, to remain unimpressed by the judgments passed on his views, his personality, his system of values by the dominant authorities of his day.[56] Some thinkers defend themselves by a kind of paranoia, as Fourier did; others minimize their deviations, as for a time Robert Owen did; still others, such as Marx or Rilke, take refuge in understandable but hardly amiable dependency on a few loyal patrons. Very few men seem to have been able to rest secure in the knowledge of their qualities and conviction of their achievement without some support from authoritative contemporaries. Freud possessed the nerve of failure in great measure. To sustain himself, he depended on his reason, on his ability to trust his own experience—even after this ability was temporarily shaken by the dramatic disproof of the stories of seduction his early patients had told him and he had

---

54. Reference footnote 33; p. 27.

55. Cf. his dream of the memorial at the University, reference footnote 5; pp. 407-408.

56. "The Ethics of We Happy Few," *University Observer* (1947) 1:23 *et seq.*; "A Philosophy for 'Minority' Living," *Commentary* (1948) 6:413-422; "Some Observations on Community Plans and Utopia," *Yale Law Journal* (1947) 57:173. [All reprinted above, in Section II.]

believed.[57] He thought, not that he was crazy nor that the authorities were, but that he was a laborious worker and discoverer, while they were bigoted, frivolous, and hypocritical. Freud wrote in 1921 that "he who knows how to wait need make no concessions";[58] such a man may also, with good friends and good luck, avoid the fate of a Semmelweiss.

Furthermore, Freud was able to discover in his own case how the oppression of the child by the authority of the father, or other parental figure, can be prolonged in the obeisance of the adult toward father-surrogates. He recognized, in connection with the memory on the Acropolis, his unconscious feeling that to become unequivocally great would amount to an act of impiety toward his own father.[59] Freud therefore had to laugh at himself when, in interpreting a dream, he found that he compared himself with Hercules, with a superman.[60] Even at the age of 40, with distinguished contributions to neurology and related sciences behind him, and well started on his unique psychoanalytic enterprise, he dared not think he had grown so big.

Nevertheless despite the great distances which Freud felt separated him from his heroes, it is clear that he never surrendered his quite justified hope that he would be as great as they. This may be one factor overdetermining the devotion of his last major work to the story of Moses. As Freud pictured him, Moses found his "clients" among the weak and alien tribe of Jews, as Freud found his among the neurotics who were treated as hereditary pariahs by the medical profession of his day. Moses, in Freud's view, sponsored an ego-deflating system—a tight, logical monotheism which made no concessions to human frailty by the route of superstition or animism; here again the parallel to Freud's own contribution seems clear. Moses, according to Freud's account, was reviled and eventually killed by those whose illusions and indulgences he attacked; Freud, as we have seen, was intensely and continuously conscious of an ever-widening area of hostility—from the infuriated psychiatrists of Vienna, to the wider reading and writing public,[61] and finally even including the

---

57. See Freud, reference footnote 33; pp. 60-62; also "My Views on the Part Played by Sexuality in the Aetiology of the Neuroses," Collected Papers 1:275-281.

58. Reference footnote 19; p. 40.

59. Freud, reference footnote 38.

60. Reference footnote 5; pp. 440-41.

61. For early references, see, for example, reference footnote 5; pp. 420, 429; for later ones, for example, reference footnotes 11; pp. 186-191. Note also the form of his book, The Question of Lay Analysis (Procter-Gregg, tr.; New York, Norton, 1950): the discussion proceeds, as so often in Freud's writing, by an

Austrian Church, the Nazis, and other bitter enemies of his science, his outlook, and his Jewishness. And while, in Freud's view, the killing of Moses by the Jews only fastened them eventually more fully to his teachings of grim renunciation, so Freud hoped for the eventual victory of the persecuted wisdom of science and truth, including psychoanalytic truth.[62] To the end, so far as his writings show, Freud was not for any length of time impressed by the seeming strength of his opponents; he did not come to think that his own soft voice would be *spurlos versenkt.*

At no point, indeed, was Freud's consciousness of his enemies that of a timorous man; perhaps it was rather that of an ambitious one. It was precisely the most exposed and criticized positions in his theory to which Freud ardently held. He refused, as he says again and again, to play down the role of sex, either in the life of children or of adults, whatever might be gained by the concession; and, after the "defections" of Jung and Adler, he felt even more committed to holding the fort. In his book on dreams, he wrote: "An intimate friend and a hated enemy have always been indispensable to my emotional life; I have always been able to create them anew. . . ."[63] In the same book he declared that it was decades since he had had any anxiety dreams,[64] and in all probability this did not change with the further passage of years.

Freud had the courage to pursue his way in the face of common opinion and of the in some ways more substantial obstacle of congealed scientific opinion paraded as common sense. He learned, despite his university training, to pay more attention to what was said by an hysterical woman patient than to what was said in books and lectures by professors of psychiatry. At the same time, he rejected neither the vested institutions nor the impalpable traditions of science; though he felt compelled in self-defense to found his own movement, he hoped eventually to rejoin the mainstream of scientific thought and communication. If one judges the heroes of mankind not in terms of the power they wielded over masses of men but in terms of their contribution to the control of nature, including human nature, and to the enrichment of the human spirit; if one adds consideration of the courage, the nerve of failure, needed to achieve that contribution in the face of obstacles, then surely Freud deserves to be regarded as

argument with an untutored critic and, with other evidence, makes me think that Freud constantly internalized the voices of his foes.

62. Cf. Freud, *The Future of An Illusion*, p. 93, quoted below, p. 400.

63. Reference footnote 5; p. 451.

64. Reference footnote 5; p. 522. He worried (see p. 420) about the future his own children would meet as Jews, but not about the hostility he himself encountered.

one of the great intellectual heroes of all time. It is not the least of his triumphs that he was willing and able to go on to the very end of his long life reopening questions and laying himself open to criticism by writing; perhaps his failure fully to see and foresee his laurels was in part a way to avoid any resting on them.

§ WEAKNESS AND NEUROSIS

IN SKETCHING Freud's portrait of a hero, I have already very largely indicated his portrait of the weakling; it remains only to review several cumulative themes. The weakling, as Freud depicts him, comes of "poor stock"; he possesses a quantitatively small libido and has other constitutional inadequacies.[65] This hereditary taint is magnified by a poor educational environment. The weakling is apt to be overgratified as a child: Freud traced one type of homosexuality in part to a boy's having "too much love" from the mother.[66] To at least some degree, he seems to have believed that only a rigorous training would produce a manly sexuality. And indeed one can agree that there is something to this view if the love of the mother is actually the smothering pseudo-love of overprotection, which neither gives the child a basic sunniness and security nor gives him the chance to free himself by fighting a patently oppressive parental authority.

At any rate, Freud felt that the combination of poor heredity with poor training or supervision in childhood expressed itself in adult sexual inadequacies which might take form either as neurosis (repression of libido from heterosexual object-choice) or perversion (wrong object for libido). In either case there is a failure to surmount the Oedipus complex, to break with the father and at the same time to identify with his masculine role, and this may show up in a Hamlet-like wavering as in a Leonardian overreflectiveness. This attitude of considering the unaggressive as weak appears with special clarity in Freud's famous letter to Einstein. There he writes:

Why do you and I and so many other people rebel so violently against war? Why do we not accept it as another of the many painful calamities

---

65. It is evident that, behind the argument over "constitutional" factors in neurosis, lurk many social struggles, just as most eugenic considerations hide class or ethnic bias; today a similar argument rages over William Sheldon's studies of delinquency but, thanks partly to Freud, the weight of scientific opinion has shifted and "hereditary factors" are viewed with great (perhaps excessive) skepticism.

66. Reference footnote 3; p. 73. Freud also believed, at least in his early practice, that strict watch should be kept over children to prevent "excessive" masturbation, as well of course as sexual assaults by relatives, nurses, and tutors. But cf. footnote 29.

of life? After all, it seems quite a natural thing, no doubt it has a good biological basis and in practice it is scarcely avoidable.[67]

He adds that the pacifists' attitude "is not merely an intellectual and emotional repudiation; we pacifists have a constitutional intolerance of war, an idiosyncrasy. . . ."[68] And while he ends on the note of hope that the rest of mankind, with the growth of culture, may become equally organically intolerant of war, the whole essay assumes that it is pacifists who need to be "understood," while warlike people can, on the basis of the death instinct, be taken for granted. We may compare with this Freud's essay on "The Taboo of Virginity,"[69] in which he seeks to explain on grounds of fear, and not at all on other possible grounds (such as culturally organized sympathy), those customs which in some tribes have a maiden deflowered before marriage by an instrument—again the point at issue is not the facts of preliterate psychology but the trend of Freud's mind.

Yet there is more to Freud's view of the matter than a mere criticism of "over-refinement" and a readier understanding for those who take easily to blood and thunder. As one can see by studying his essay on " 'Civilized' Sexual Morality and Modern Nervousness," written in 1908, he was preoccupied with the loss of individual enjoyment as well as racial vitality that he felt accompanied Victorian sexual repressions. In this same essay he suggested that neurotics are those who only partially succumb to such repression:[70]

Neurotics are that class of people, naturally rebellious, with whom the pressure of cultural demands succeeds only in an apparent suppression of their instincts, one which becomes ever less and less effective.

The neurotics, in this view, were those who had too much libido to permit them to surrender completely to the cultural ideals of sexual restriction, and too little fortitude to resist the hypocritical social norms imposed on them by the beguiling authority, first of the father and later on of society at large. It is, therefore, not only out of weakness of will but out of strength of libido that the neurotic falls ill. It seems that Freud does not maintain a wholly consistent position regarding the source of the neurotic's inability to attain heterosexual success.

Later experience led Freud to considerable skepticism as to the

---

67. "Why War?" in *Collected Papers* 5:285; see also "Thoughts for the Times on War and Death," in *Collected Papers* 4:288.

68. Reference footnote 67; p. 287.

69. *Collected Papers* 4:217.

70. *Collected Papers* 2:76, 86. Cf. the development of the point by Erich Fromm, *Man for Himself*, pp. 22-23, 36-37.

ability of such people to overcome their dependence; instead, he saw that in the analytic situation they often only renewed it in a new form.[71] However, despite his awareness of the contrast between the neurotic's irresolution and stubbornness in remaining ill, and the mastery of self and others which he admired in his heroes, Freud never for a moment doubted that neurotics suffer, that they are oppressed, that society bears on them much more harshly than it does either on the elite who succeeded discreetly in getting their way or on the mass of men who have very little to get. In other words, Freud, in his daily work, took the neurotic with complete seriousness, and one must set this consistent behavior over against the passages in his writings where he glorifies the strong and ruthless males.

Indeed, I think that one of Freud's greatest contributions, though it is one he took more or less for granted, lay in his willingness to spend years if necessary with patients who were neither fatally ill nor important people,[72] without, moreover, any great confidence on his part that they would inevitably get well. To be sure, he declared that "a certain measure of natural intelligence and ethical development may be required of him [that is, the person amenable to psychoanalytic therapy]; with worthless persons the physician soon loses the interest which makes it possible for him to enter profoundly into the mental life of the patient."[73] Nevertheless, without a great deal of willingness to "enter profoundly into the mental life" of people who were very far from his image of the hero, he could easily have gotten rid of his "interminable" patients, as other doctors did. Today, it is just this 'luxury' aspect of psychoanalysis—its prolonged concern with individuals as such, and for their own sake—that is sometimes under attack. Popularly, analysis is often regarded as occupational therapy for wealthy women; hostility to the neurotic is easily disguised by charging him with the crime of being middle-class, or the double crime of being middle-class and a woman.

Unquestionably, efforts to hasten analysis, and to broaden its scope beyond the middle class and beyond the well-to-do, are desir-

---

71. See "Analysis Terminable and Interminable," in *Collected Papers* 5:317 *et seq.*

72. Erich Fromm takes a very similar position in *Psychoanalysis and Religion*, p. 98.

73. "Freud's Psycho-Analytic Method," *Collected Papers* 1:270-271. Since Freud's day, a number of his followers have been trying to widen the bounds of what they find "interesting" and endurable in patients. See, for example, Frieda Fromm-Reichmann, "Notes on the Personal and Professional Requirements of a Psychotherapist," *Psychiatry* (1949) 12:361, and the insistence of O. Spurgeon English that manic-depressives are not as insensitive as they seem and can be reached by therapy, "Observation of Trends in Manic-Depressive Psychosis," *Psychiatry* (1949) 12:125.

able, but I cannot conquer the suspicion that some psychiatrists—not to speak, of course, of medical men who are not psychiatrists—share to a degree the popular impatience, sometimes dimly veiled by fascination, with the seemingly endless talkfest of individual analysis. Among the many motives which impel the physician to resort to shock therapies (and the community to consent to this), a lack of Freud's generous concern with the well-being of a single all-too-human person may perhaps be one. Indeed, one cannot read Freud's article, "Sexuality in the Aetiology of the Neuroses,"[74] written in 1898, as well as other writings of this early period, without seeing how passionately Freud protested against injustice in the treatment of neurotics, and the medical hypocrisy which veiled that injustice; he adds that "the layman is deeply convinced inwardly of the unnecessariness, so to speak, of all these psychoneuroses, and therefore regards the course of the disease with little patience. . . ."[75] Nearly forty years later, in one of his last papers, he recurs to a similar theme; he begins "Analysis Terminable and Interminable," published in 1937, with these remarks:

> Experience has taught us that psycho-analytic therapy—the liberation of a human being from his neurotic symptoms, inhibitions and abnormalities of character—is a lengthy business. Hence, from the very beginning, attempts have been made to shorten the course of analysis. Such endeavours required no justification: they could claim to be prompted by the strongest considerations alike of reason and expediency. But there probably lurked in them some trace of the impatient contempt with which the medical profession of an earlier day regarded the neuroses, seeing in them the unnecessary results of invisible lesions. If it had now become necessary to deal with them, they should at least be got rid of with the utmost dispatch.[76]

This outlook made Freud a "rate-buster" among his medical colleagues—a person, that is, who violated "production norms" as to how much sympathy and time were to be given to patients; and it seems not unlikely that hostility based on this ground may sometimes have been rationalized as based on the *content*, especially the sexual content, of Freud's discoveries.

Conversely, one should expect that Freud himself, with his ambivalence toward authority, would be to some degree affected by such medical attitudes. Just possibly, his tough, 'masculine' talk might therefore be considered, among other things, as a defense mechanism against so 'unmanly' a drain on his sympathy for the weak and oppressed as, on one level, he may have felt his therapeutic work to be —a drain he could not, however, avoid as his experience with free

74. *Collected Papers* 1:220.
75. Reference footnote 74; p. 247.
76. Reference footnote 71; p. 316.

association and transference problems developed. In this interpretation, I suggest that he may have been frightened by the dangers for him of what he regarded as sentimentality, of identifying too closely with his patients. He justified his conduct to himself and others by stressing his preoccupation with research—research which, by his bad luck, had to be done with patients.[77] But that he was haunted by the problem appears in his discussions of the analyst's role, in which he concluded that complete neutrality and impassivity of behavior in the transference situation were not always tolerable.[78]

A number of those analysts who belong to what one might term the third generation from Freud are, perhaps especially in America, not much interested in his ethical concerns and 'metaphysical' explorations. For example, they dismiss the death instinct as a late aberration and do not inquire into the latent tragic import behind its manifestly dubious biology. They strenuously avoid 'jargon' or any other eccentricity and try to become indistinguishable from the other hard-boiled medicos from whose ranks they have sprung. By insisting on medical training, they tend to eliminate at the outset some of the more sensitive spirits who might seek careers in analysis. The *American Imago* struggles on largely supported by some of the old-timers; many of this new generation prefer to report clinical findings. This tendency among some analysts is part of the process of 'normalizing' Freud which I have referred to earlier. Such a development is perhaps inevitable when what has begun as a sect becomes an institution with a more approved and lucrative cultural niche.

But such analysts make a mistake if they suppose that they can avoid the metaphysical issues Freud raised by a matter-of-fact focus on therapy and clinical research. The words they use, to describe to their patients or to each other what is going on in the patients, are inevitably loaded with cultural meanings and ethical judgments. No matter how they may duck the issue of the goals of therapy, their own ideals of heroism, their own views of what is weakness, will affect whom they accept or seek out as patients, what they say to them,

---

77. Cf. also the following remarks from *The Question of Lay Analysis*: "Not every neurotic whom we treat may be worth the trouble of analysis, but there are many valuable personalities amongst them. The goal of our achievement must be to secure that as few human beings as possible are left to confront civilized life with such defective psychical equipment; and to that end we must collect much material, and learn to understand much. Every analysis is instructive and can be made to yield fresh elucidation, quite apart from the personal worth of the individual patient." Reference footnote 61; p. 78.

78. See, for example, "Observations on Transference-Love," in *Collected Papers* 2:377; and cf. "Recommendations for Physicians on the Psycho-analytic Method of Treatment," in *Collected Papers* 2:327, 331.

and the tacit models they themselves are for their patients. Since they want to be just like other doctors, they try to push all problems of ethical responsibility under the tent of 'professional [that is, medical] ethics,' an ethics which less friendly critics of the profession might see as principally a code of trade secret and trade association tactics.[79] In his writings on lay—that is, nonmedical—analysis, Freud showed himself fully aware of the dangers of medical incorporation and regularization of his work. As I have tried to show in this paper, he very much wanted official recognition—but not at the price of emasculation.

---

79. However, the therapeutic duty of the doctor was a strong support to Freud in his early days when he was attacked in medical circles for prying into sexual matters. See, for example, reference footnote 74; pp. 220, 221-224.

24. Freud, Religion, and Science

I WANT TO BEGIN by saying a few words about the social setting in which such a series topic as ours—Attack and Counter-attack in Religion —occurs. Then I want to say something about the use made of Freud in the religious counter-attack before turning more explicitly to Freud's own views. Finally, I shall touch on possible rapproachements between certain tendencies in religion and certain tendencies in psychoanalysis.

§ I

WE MAY TAKE IT as a principle of social observation that, when we find the words "attack" (or "counter-attack"), we must always ask, who is really hitting whom? If we listen to the rhetoric of Southern whites, they talk as if the Negroes, and Northern "do-gooders," were hitting *them*. The Nazis gave it out that the Jews were the attackers. Any child learns to say, "He hit me," to justify an attack. Obviously, we cannot accept at face value the clamor of many religious organizations that they are under attack from psychoanalysis, Marxism, secularism, and so on: we must examine the power relations actually involved. It may be that the very rhetoric of being attacked used by these groups is a sign of their crescence and of the weakening of the allegedly attacking groups.

In *Patterns of Culture,* written in 1934, Ruth Benedict discussed the problem of criticism of contemporary American institutions and how such criticism might be advanced and enlightened by anthropological and comparative studies. We have accustomed ourselves, she observed, to shedding our ethnocentrism when it comes to religion; nobody gets into trouble because he attacks religion; we have not done that, however, with respect to our economic institutions, with respect to capitalism. Here we have remained ethnocentric, and an attack may be dangerous.

Now I wonder if you will agree with me that, fifteen years after this book appeared, the situation is very nearly reversed. The massed social pieties which ranked themselves behind the economic order in the pre-Roosevelt era now seem to rank themselves behind religion and nation. The economic order is today nothing one has to be particularly pious about—unless one is a Communist and then, indeed, religion and nationalism are both involved. But one has to be (and, more important, feels one ought to be) considerably more careful about the religious order. To give an interesting example which comes to mind, the magazine *Commentary*, published by a secular and on the whole conservative group, the American Jewish Committee, has contained many profound critiques of capitalism, articles for instance by John Dewey and Karl Polanyi. These caused no trouble for anybody. But when the gifted novelist Isaac Rosenfeld wrote an article suggesting a psychoanalytic interpretation of Jewish dietary laws, noting a possibly sexual undertone in separating meat from milk, a violent storm broke out upon him and the magazine and it became necessary for the editors to print a disclaimer and apologia.

The movies, with their extraordinary sensitivity to pressure, provide another illustration. In the twenties or thirties there was a Lillian Gish picture in which a minister seduced a young girl who was his ward. I doubt if such a movie would be made, or could be made, today. Religion, much more than free enterprise, is sacred in the movies—many films are devoted to sentimental glorification of churchly figures—and in popular culture generally. Even capitalists enjoy going to plays and reading books which either make fun of business or, as in *Death of a Salesman*, make tragedy of it; and, so far as I know, no one has criticized the play, *The Madwoman of Chaillot*, for the silliness, let alone the offensiveness, of its handling of the bourgeois class.

If we wanted to give a psychoanalytic interpretation, we might think of the image of the rebellious son who carries out a partial, not wholly successful, rebellion against his father. Because of his ambivalence and partial failure, the son feels guilty; because of his partial success, the father gives in; and there is a reconciliation on a new level. Similarly, the revolt against the Hoover economic order (or, more accurately, the radical change in economic conditions) carried out since 1934 has been partly successful—too successful to allow the "father" to hope more than nostalgically for the restoration of "free enterprise." But father and son have come to terms on religion and nation, and the continuing and perhaps even increasing social anxieties and rigidities, displaced from economics, have found a new, "spiritual" fold. This shift permits religious organizations today, which in some ways are much stronger than in the thirties, to feel themselves aggrieved by any scientific and intellectual tendency which is at all outspokenly irreligious. Such a tendency can then be attacked as an "attack on religion," without violating the code of fair play.[1]

1. When I expressed this tentative view of the shift in power positions between "science" on the one side and "religion" on the other, in the course of my lecture, many in the audience questioned my interpretation. Some pointed to Blanshard's *American Freedom and Catholic Power* as evidence that the older Mencken atti-

We can recall that when the psychiatrist Brock Chisholm stated in a lecture to the Washington School of Psychiatry that the myth of Santa Claus was a swindle on children, the Canadian cabinet was forced to meet, and he very nearly lost his job as health minister.

I may be mistaken—and certainly there are counter-tendencies which indicate the weakening of organized religion. But assuming that I am right, how are we to explain this alteration in the climate of discussion concerning religion? Obviously, in this article I can touch on only a few of the many factors involved. One factor is the increasingly sympathetic attitude toward religion taken among avant-garde groups. Intellectual anti-clericalism, like anti-clericalism in the labor movement, is out of fashion; and it is not surprising that psycho-analysts—even those "orthodox" in other respects—seem to have fallen in with the general trend, and either stick to their clinical work or claim religion as an ally.

To be sure, the avant-garde has little social power and less political influence. Nevertheless, its loss of the barbed and merrily agnostic elan of a Mencken, a Veblen, a Haldeman-Julius is not without effect, especially among those who are or want to be young. The avant-garde had power enough during the twenties to put religion on the defensive among those upper-class and upper-middle-class Catholics and other communicants who wanted to feel socially and intellectu-ally accepted and up-to-date. Such people did not want to appear backwoodsy and bigoted. Today, however, it is "backwoodsy" to be anti-religious, and in fact I find among my students that only, on the whole, small-town, especially Southern, boys will go whole hog with Freud's view of religion. The revival of interest in religion (if not in church-going) among intellectuals means that many in the upper social strata who are affiliated with organized religion need no longer flinch in pressing the claims of religion and in attacking its few remaining outspoken foes. They can now accept without embar-

---

tude toward organized religion is still strong. A more important argument, in my opinion, was raised by those who contended that the *lack* of strong scientific attacks on religion today was caused, not by the strength of religion and the weakness of the scientific temper, but by its opposite: religion is no longer an issue which the young, emancipated by science, find worth arguing about. And to be sure, scientists now go their way with less worry than ever before about those theological issues which developed in the great battles between science and organized religion from the sixteenth to the beginning of the twentieth century; the turmoil in which such a man as the biologist Gosse was caught by Darwinism is today hardly conceivable. But one reason for this "peace of West-phalia" is that religionists are at last resigned to leaving natural science alone— it is only philosophers, humanists, and psychologists who, dealing with man, face even the possibility of jurisdictional dispute with organized religion.

rassment the anti-scientific position of the devout of lesser social standing.

This alliance of the classes in defense of religion is facilitated by a development much more important in its bearing on our topic than the altered mood of the avant-garde—namely, the rise in the social position of American Catholics in the last several decades. Everett C. Hughes, a very thoughtful and sympathetic student of church institutions and especially of Catholicism, has pointed out that one of the greatest sources of anxieties among middle-class Catholics is the problem of the relation between their church affiliation and their social mobility. Because they are mobile, these Catholics have looked for the definition of "good American" in the past largely to non-Catholics: to high-status Protestants, to Jewish intellectuals and mass-media opinion leaders, and (to a degree) even to the "leakage," as those are called who seep away from the Church. But as Catholics have increasingly moved into the managerial and professional classes, they have been able greatly to influence the definition of "good American," and have taken the lead, since they were among the "earliest arrivals" in the crusade against Communism, in defining the "bad un-American" as well. At the same time, non-Catholic opinion leaders, for the reasons given earlier, do not define the middle- and upper-class style of life in such a way as to exclude good Catholics—save, perhaps, for the still differentiating and hence exceedingly anxiety-provoking issue of birth control.

Yet, while the Catholics have risen substantially, they have not yet gained full social security on the American scene—and the same, of course, is true of the Jews, whose "religious" revival deserves a chapter to itself. Consequently, they are not yet able to laugh off such criticisms of religion as, despite religious censorship of the mass media, continue to crop up. It is unlikely that, fifteen years ago, a high Catholic churchman would have dared to attack an Eleanor Roosevelt after the recent fashion of Cardinal Spellman; it is unlikely that, fifteen years hence, a high churchman will find such a polemic fitting and needful.

So far, I have stressed the tendencies to censor science and intellectual discourse that are implicit in the new "united front" of religionists and intellectuals. But in this same development there are liberating aspects. The seriousness with which religion is now taken has made an interest in it respectable among many scientists who would earlier have considered an irreligious attitude—a village atheist's outlook—an essential mark of emancipation. While William James was considered by many of his professional colleagues to be a kind of nut for concerning himself with religious experience, especially of a mystical and sectarian sort, no such scorn would greet a similar student, for instance Gordon Allport, today. Nor do I think we should bemoan the passing of the village atheist, with his easy monotone of a debunking approach to questions of faith and morals.

§ II

IT IS IMPORTANT to realize, in the light of this changing political and social context, that Freud, when he wrote on religion, seems generally to have thought of himself as the attacked, not the attacker. In *The Future of an Illusion*, written in 1928, he showed his sensitivity to the charge that he was robbing people of their faith. He pointed out that *he* had no such faith in his own arguments: people, he said, were capable of great "resistance" to unacceptable thoughts; their emotional bonds had shown enormous tenacity which even the great Voltaire, let alone Freud, could not shake. Hence, Freud argued, he and his movement were the only ones likely to suffer from an attack on religion. Likewise, when he wrote *Moses and Monotheism* ten years later, he for a while did not dare publish the last chapters—though these raised no new points against or about religion—because he thought it would give the Austrian Church an excuse for closing down the psychoanalytic movement in Nazi-threatened Vienna. Beyond that, Freud felt that whenever it was attempted to put bounds on the inquiries of science—to confine it, for example, to the "material" universe—this actually constituted an attack on science's right to deal with everything. No matter how small the enclave which, like some Vatican City, was preserved against the inquiries of science, Freud felt a real challenge to the total claim and method of empirical investigation.

Now it is ironical that, in the continuing campaign of organized religious thought against organized scientific thought, Freud is today frequently thrown into the fray on the side of the campaigners. It is worth devoting some attention to this paradox, because it will help both to illuminate Freud and the kind of orthodoxy which currently makes use of him. We may consider four themes: the allegation that Freud has dethroned reason and crowned irrationality and mystique; the emphasis on anxiety in Freud's writings; his pessimism about man's fate; and his concept of original sin.

In thinking about these uses of Freud, I was reminded of the figure of Squire Gaylord in William Dean Howells' novel *A Modern Instance*, written in 1881. Gaylord is the crusty village atheist, and also the lawyer, of a small Maine town which Howells calls Equity. A cantankerous man, with a low opinion of mankind. "For Liberal

Christianity," Howells writes, "he has nothing but contempt, and refuted it with a scorn which spared none of the wordly tendencies of the church in Equity. The idea that souls were to be saved by church sociables filled him with inappeasable rancor; and he maintained the superiority of the old Puritanic discipline against them with a fervor which nothing but its re-establishment could have abated." There is something of the Squire in Freud. As he says in *Civilization and Its Discontents* (pp. 23-24), he is happier with, or at least more respectful of, the old-time religion than with its liberal variants which have pretensions to accommodate science. And yet, as we shall see, the "hard" religion which often appeals to Freud for support would be considered by him quite as comfortable and lacking in real strength as a church social.

The first such appeal to Freud is made on the basis that he dethroned the claims of rationalism and positivism and upheld those of the dark, irrational forces in man. The neo-orthodox today like to talk about such forces as a way of slapping down the liberals who are alleged to believe that man is good and his life a feast of reason. They cite Freud's findings as evidence for man's daemonic powers and also for his need for unquestioning faith. This view, I think, comes from a misunderstanding of Freud—and it is probably also a misunderstanding of the "liberals" such as John Dewey who are set up as straw men on the other side. Freud is fundamentally a rationalist—in fact, it would be difficult to find anyone in the Enlightenment who was more so. His whole effort as a scientist was to make the irrational understandable—to capture it for rationality—while as a therapist he had the same goal for the patient—that he should gain control over his irrational strivings by an understanding of them. To a degree (and perhaps we tend to overestimate the degree) the Enlightenment had overlooked and Victorian hypocrisy had buried the *materials* which Freud drew attention to; but the *method* of Freud was invariably the method of science, of positivism if you like, and the morality he demanded of himself and shepherded in his patients was a modified, but far from rebellious and Bohemian, Victorianism.

If we look at the whole body of Freud's work, we can see that he was attracted, like many great scientists, by puzzles, by mystery, by what was veiled and hidden whether by prevailing medical doctrine, by religious dogma, or by the uncanny and perplexing nature of the material itself. Yet always his effort was to order this material, sometimes with pedantic rigor, and he sharply criticized those who used "intuitive" methods in dealing with symbolic data. As other nineteenth-century entrepreneurs took upon themselves the white man's burden of subduing foreign customs and procedures which seemed irrational from the standpoint of Ricardian economics, so Freud sought to subject to laws—for which he often used the term "economic"—all the seemingly irrational phenomena he uncovered. In *Beyond the Pleasure Principle,* there is a typical passage where he expresses these scientific goals. He is arguing that the purpose of an instinct is the restoration of an earlier state in the history of the human race, and that since living matter was once inorganic, there must be an instinctive drive to restore that earlier condition; the goal of life must therefore be death. Yet in the middle of this highly speculative flight, Freud writes as follows:

"If what results gives an appearance of 'profundity' or bears a resemblance to mysticism, still we know ourselves to be clear of the reproach of having striven after anything of the sort. We are in search of sober conclusions of investigation or of reflections based upon it, and the only character we wish for in these conclusions is that of certainty."

Moreover, it is interesting to see that, when he dealt with religion —and he recurred to it again and again in his work—he analyzed only its more rational forms. Despite his discussion of the "oceanic feeling" in *Civilization and Its Discontents,* a discussion which ends in dismissal, he seems nowhere to have dealt with Western mysticism in its wide variety of expressions. Unlike William James, he was less interested in the religious *experience* than in the meaning of the rules and rituals laid down under religious auspices. (There are some partial exceptions to this, as we shall see.) In general, he looked for this meaning in terms of a disguised statement of an historical truth. Like an archaeologist, he asked, "what does this religion say about these people's past?" And he found the answer in, for example, a father-murder at an earlier point, followed by guilt and remorse, and the deification of the slain. Here, typically, we find Freud asking rational questions of, and giving rational answers about, data whose source lay in the unconscious of men and in their irrational feelings. The source of religion lay in the repressed, irrational childhood of the race. He was able to interpret it as he did myths and dreams in a rational way.

True, Freud was not very sanguine about reason. He thought that to trust it might sometimes be to trust in an illusion. But at least it was capable of disproof as an illusion, according to the canons of reason itself; and therefore it was superior to the illusion of religion which did not offer itself to proof or disproof. In other words, while Freud was skeptical about how much science could explain, he was far more skeptical about the claims to explanation of any other system, including occult practices and religion.

Another theme in Freud which makes him appealing to some of the more sophisticated among the neo-orthodox is his repeated emphasis on anxiety. But here again, there is I believe a misapprehension of Freud, some of it perhaps of a semantic sort. Freud's "anxiety" has only a peripheral connection with the "anxiety" of the fear-and-trembling school. Far from being a sign of potential grace or of any religious significance, it is a sign of weakness and sexual inadequacy. Freud did not admire those who trembled in contemplation of the problems of living and dying. He himself did not tremble, but steeled himself in Stoic fashion against isolation, illness, and impending death. To be sure, he counselled resignation. But this was the resignation of the strong and not the resignation of the weak—moreover quite different in quality from the haughty self-abasement whose long religious tradition can be traced in St. Paul, St. Augustine, and their successors.

There is even perhaps a certain Philistinism in Freud's view, like that of the self-made man impatient with anyone unwilling to come up the hard way. What Freud admired in the Jews—and it seems to me he gives them just a bit too much credit—was their stiff-necked pride in the face of the universe, in the face of persecution. Skeptical as he was of religion, traces of his admiration for the tough, uncompromising monotheism of the Jews appear again and again in his work. The Jews in repressing the memory of having killed Moses, their "Father," could never enjoy the expiation of their guilt, as the Christians could in the Son's atonement for their sins.

I think it follows from this that Freud would interpret the seeming toughness of Christian neo-orthodoxy as not tough at all, but a new form of comfortableness: a refusal to defy the father, as all must do who wish to grow up; a refusal to face uncertainty; a wallowing in anxiety, rather than a resolution of it through action. Thus he would find a secondary gain of surrender hidden under the only apparent harshness of contemporary revivals of old-time religion.

Still another theme where some religious thinkers trace affinity with Freud is that of pessimism. Freud was undoubtedly a pessimist, but of a different brand from most religious writers. Not only did he have little faith in social reform or in man's innate goodness, he also had no faith at all in eschatological visions, let alone in any doctrine of election. In this sense his pessimism is more thoroughgoing than that of his new religious allies. Moreover, as we have already seen, Freud did have a qualified confidence in reason; through strengthening of man's ego—the wise arbitrator seeking to balance and control the passions—he hoped for a better future. More important, perhaps, than these statements of *Weltanschauung* or ideology is the fact that one cannot read Freud's work without realizing the passionate and sanguine admiration he had for human achievement, for human curiosity, for human mastery. What delighted him in monotheistic religion was its intellectual achievement, even if he saw elements of illusion in it.

The final theme in Freud to which some religious people point is his emphasis on original sin. Somewhere Freud writes, "Psychoanalysis confirms what the pious are wont to say, that we are all sinners." Certainly, there is something here from which the orthodox may take comfort, but it is less than they think. Freud's thought is filled with paradoxes and ironies and we must use his own method to make sure that we do not take him at face value: his text, like that of a dream, challenges us to interpret it. When we do this, Freud's concept of original sin appears at best as an analogy to the religious concept. For Freud saw its origin in biology, rather than in a religious framework. Its biological base was the death instinct, followed by the primal crime, the killing of the father, but this chronologically original sin was for him the source of god-making rather than the result of God's prior existence. More meaningful, perhaps, than these differences in the nature of the concept are the differences in the metaphorical use made of it by Freud and by some of the neo-orthodox. The latter, as Arthur Murphy and Gardner Williams have pointed out with reference to Reinhold Niebuhr, in saying that all men are sinners are creating a preferential position for those who recognize this fact. For Niebuhr, those men are in some ways the worst who think themselves good; those the most arrogant, who think they understand society.[2] This position elevates those who abase themselves, who acknowledge man's intellectual and moral limitations. Freud, on the contrary, used original sin as a democratizer of men. He liked to

---

2. In correspondence, Dr. Niebuhr has pointed out that I have been unjust to him here, and I accept his criticism. Quoting Pascal's remark that "Discourses on humility are a source of pride to those who are proud," he declares: "I have again and again insisted that such are the powers of human self-deception that those who have what I believe to be a correct analysis of human nature may use it as a source of pride. . . . There is a sense of course in which everybody who strives for the truth gives implicitly a 'preferential' position to those who perceive the truth, as you do for instance, in your article. I cannot help but feel, though this may be quite unjust, that you had to make some critical remark like that in order to establish the preferential position of irreligion as against religion in the matter of truth, for it would be embarrassing to grant that any truth could come out of a religious position. . . ." Dr. Niebuhr referred me to statements in *Faith and History* and *The Children of Light and the Children of Darkness* to show how thoroughgoing a foe of pretence and arrogance, in and out of theology, he has been; I needed no references for his zeal on democracy's behalf.

see the symptoms of sex and aggression in the work of the high and mighty, and in the very good of the "good" men who scorned his theory. And not only men, but men and animals and men and gods were equalized by Freud's view: his interpretation of the totem animal as both a sign of the original crime and as destined to become a god may be thought of as the symbol for this. So we must conclude that for Freud the phrase "original sin" is tinged with irony—and beyond irony, compassion.

§ III

THE FUNDAMENTAL PREMISE of Freud's view of religion is that we can understand it, not in its own terms, but only by understanding men and their human situation. For him, then, religion is a shared neurosis, having its origin, like any neurosis, in the Oedipus complex, that is, in hostile and rivalrous attitudes towards the father which have been replaced by identification and submission. Equally interesting and significant, however, is Freud's idea that neurosis is a private religion. One of his most interesting case studies is that of Schreber, a German jurist who, at the end of the nineteenth century, developed highly elaborate and quite original religious views while he was confined in a mental hospital. Through his conversion into a woman, Schreber felt God would "get into him," and he would found thereby a new race of Schrebers. Schreber's religion was socially defined as paranoia because, unlike the great religious leaders of history, he could not make others renounce claims in favor of his God as he had offered to renounce his masculinity. (In the nineteenth century and since, as we know, many cults hardly less fantastic have flourished in America.)

Furthermore, both private religion and shared neurosis resemble each other for Freud in that both seek to escape from reality, and as we have seen he criticizes those who, by whatever route, try to avoid facing life and pressing their claims. Once he allowed himself to say of the priests: ". . . they are spoilt, they have an easier time of it with their revelation." What he meant was that he himself was a scientist, arduously digging in the murky, the disapproved, the controversial, while at the same time obedient to the traditions and procedures of science. As against this, the priests took the easy way out of "*ipse dixit.*"

Freud's analysis of the monastic reports of the troubles of a seventeenth-century painter, Christopher Heitzmann, is revealing. It appears that, when Christopher was around thirty or forty his father died, and the son had tough going economically and psychologically. He could not work, could not paint, and was depressed. In a vision, the Devil appeared to him, and Christopher made a deal with him that, if the Devil would take him as his son for nine years, then he, Christopher, would belong to the Devil thereafter. When the nine years were up, Christopher wanted to welch (as Freud viewed it) on the bargain, and so hied himself to a monastery where he underwent conversion and was saved by the intercession of Mary. Much else is involved in Freud's essay, but important here is his position that Christopher-become-monk took the easy way out.

Freud had something of the same tough approach to the person who escapes through suicide and through mental illness—and even to the artist who, in Freud's eyes, deals with fantasy, not with the "real." Conversely, those whom he admired were those who were able to make others renounce, those who "civilized" others while remaining strong and unbowed themselves. Thus he admired Ikhnaton, the Egyptian monarch whom he credited with founding monotheism, the worship of an abstract sun god, and with forcing the Egyptians, at least for a time, to give up their comfortable beliefs in immortality and in a plenitude of gods. He admired Moses, whom he regarded as an Egyptian follower of Ikhnaton, who succeeded in imposing on the Jews the monotheism of his King. These were men who left an impress on the world, but for their followers—those who gave in to fear, to guilt, to remorse—Freud had scant respect.

Both the religious man and the neurotic in Freud's eyes are cowards who compromise the search for the meaning of life and the truth of social relations. The religious man is inhibited by the power of his racial memory, by collective authority. This blocks his inquiries in certain areas and this blockage spreads over other areas. Likewise, the neurotic is blocked in his search by his inability to rebel against parental authority. This inhibits his sexual curiosity; and this blockage, too, spreads over other areas. Similarly, Freud found analogies in obsessional ritual between religion and neurosis: the same compulsiveness, the same driven need to carry out acts the meaning of which had been repressed—meaning related in the case of the individual to his own childhood, and in the case of the religious man to the childhood of the race.

There is, however, in Freud's estimation an important difference between religion and neurosis, resulting from the fact that the former is *shared*. He speaks, for instance, of a compulsion neurosis as a caricature of a religion. It is this because it lacks the companionship, the close touch with others, secured by the religious devotee. The latter finds his way to others—and hence to a part of reality—through religion, while the neurotic is isolated by his very rituals, often practiced in secret, which he cannot and dare not share with others. This ability to share, even if it is only the sharing of a collective illusion, puts the religious man on the same psychological footing as the successful artist. The latter is one who, in Freud's eyes, is originally alienated from reality but who, through success in selling his private fantasies to the public, wins his way to fame, money, and beautiful women—and so at least to the realities of social existence. Thus, the privacy of neurosis endangers the individual escape, while the publicity of religion brings the devout into contact with others, even though reality be mutually distorted.

Now we must stop for a moment to ask again, what kinds of religion is Freud talking about here, what aspects of religion? In the first place, he is preoccupied with the search for origins that was so characteristic of nineteenth-century scientific thought. In company with the early evolutionary anthropologists, he was concerned with tracing religion back to a presumptive starting point. This led him to examine the beginnings of totemism and of monotheism—the latter interested him mainly in its Jewish and Christian forms. When he talks about modern religion, he seems to be referring to its more puritanical Victorian versions. I have already pointed out that he left out of account anything which might be called genuine religious mysticism. In this latter tradition, in some of its Christian, Jewish, and also Oriental forms, the religious man is placed on a footing of a certain equality with God. He is made in God's image, and God in his. They communicate with one another; the mystic may even talk back to God—recall Joseph wrestling with the angel. This kind of mysticism is, to be sure, rather individualistic, but its attitudes are not unknown to some of the Protestant sects of the seventeenth century and later that emphasize love, such as the Dutch cult of the Family of Love. Freud seems to have been unaware of these minority phenomena and, indeed, in view of his system it is somewhat hard to see what he would have made of them.

In fact, I am afraid that these kinds of religious experience are but infrequently considered. Perhaps we have a kind of bias in the sorts of religion we talk about, when we discuss the relations of religion to science and philosophy. We are influenced by what is powerful, rather than by what might teach us something.

However, that may be, Freud did not grant a great future to religion, in his own limited definition. This collective neurosis would not last. For, if the individual can grow up, can overcome his Oedipal ties, so can the race. He arrives at this conclusion after a magnificent dialogue with himself in *The Future of an Illusion*. We may call his

alter ego in this dialogue the Grand Inquisitor, though Freud does not
call him that.[3] When Freud suggests that perhaps the human race can
grow up, then comes the Inquisitor and denies it. Religion is useful,
the latter says, useful to force the mob to renounce and to console it
for having renounced, and to reconcile them to the culture from which
they reap so little gain. Moreover, the Inquisitor adds, religion has
this great advantage over science, that high and low strata of society
can come together in its folds, as in the Catholic Church, with the
high strata making their own sublimatory refinements yet remaining
in the same house with the low. Freud answers that we can hope that
all men (not merely some) will become rational and face reality. The
Grand Inquisitor returns and says, what is this reality? If you know
it, you know that most men cannot face it, and that religion, though
untrue, is useful and will if it passes be replaced by doctrine not calling itself religion but equally untrue, equally constricting for the
masses, and equally consoling to them. Freud replies:

"You shall not find me impervious to your criticism. I know how
difficult it is to avoid illusions; perhaps even the hopes I have confessed
to are of an illusory nature. But I hold fast to one distinction. My illusions—apart from the fact that no penalty is imposed for not sharing them
—are not, like the religious ones, incapable of correction, they have no
delusional character. If experience should show—not to me, but to others
after me who think as I do—that we are mistaken, then we shall give up
our expectations."

And then he adds:

"We may insist as much as we like that the human intellect is weak in
comparison with human instincts, and be right in doing so. But nevertheless there is something peculiar about this weakness. The voice of the
intellect is a soft one, but it does not rest until it has gained a hearing.
Ultimately, after endlessly repeated rebuffs, it succeeds."

So Freud ends the story.

We must take full account of Freud's tentativeness here. He is
often criticized as a dogmatist, and I am one of those who have made
this criticism of him. But concerning religion and its future, Freud
says that he may be mistaken, and that the last word will be said by
others besides himself. With this let us turn to look at some of the
elements in Freud's view of religion that may be overstated or mistaken

§ IV

IN WHAT HAS JUST BEEN SAID, I have adverted to the analogy Freud
draws between ontogenesis and phylogenesis, between the life-cycle

---

3. In his essay on "Dostoevsky and Parricide," Freud pays his respects to the
great scene in *The Brothers Karamazov*, and points out that Dostoevsky, out of
his neurosis, allowed his great intelligence to be humbled by the Little Father
of the Russians and the Great Father of the Russian Orthodox Church. Nowhere
does Freud make sharper remarks about the intellectual's "turn to religion."

of the neurotic individual who succumbs to the Oedipus complex and the history of humanity which has succumbed, in the form of religion, to the guilt of the prehistoric Oedipal crime. Obviously, all such "organicistic" analogies are as dangerous as they are alluring. Freud, though well aware of this, repeatedly resorted to such analogies and metaphors and, like many scientists, put more weight on them than was warranted. To be sure, when he came to study in *Moses and Monotheism* the history of the Jews, he abandoned the historical universalism which would have given all human beings the same phylogenetic experience and racial memory; instead, he traced those particular events of Jewish religious experience which, to his mind, gave the Jews a distinct national character and a distinct racial memory—one which the Christian world only repeated in considerably chastened and modified form. Those Jews who could not endure this guilt of the murder of the father, Moses, accepted Christ as the Messiah, the Son who came to atone for their racial crime, to expiate their guilt. It is plain, however, that Freud did not similarly differentiate between the historical experience of different social classes within a society, though in his day-to-day work he recognized of course that the lower classes suffered less from sexual inhibitions—and therefore should presumably have "inherited" a different set of Oedipal memories. Any attempt at racial, or "human-racial" interpretation of history, such as Freud builds on his analogy between individual and group, inevitably "de-classifies" societies and runs into trouble in dealing with the stratification and divisions of any complex social order such as that of the Western world, or even of the Jews of Biblical times. It follows, therefore, that Freud's approach to religion will prove unsatisfactory to the more sociologically-minded investigator.

To illustrate this, and to show the limitations in Freud's method, I should like to review briefly a discussion in the psychoanalytic periodical *Imago* concerning the development of Christian dogma. An orthodox Freudian position was taken by Theodor Reik; a more sociological view was taken by Erich Fromm, and it is from the latter's article on "The Origin of the Dogma of Christ" that I primarily draw.[4] Both Reik and Fromm were struck by the fact that there is a change in the image and symbolism of Christ in the early Christian era. He appears in early representations as a young man, sometimes a young man suffering on the Cross; in later representations He appears as a babe in the arms of His mother, the Virgin Mary, who had been very much in the background in the early period.

The orthodox psychoanalyst looks at this development and says,

---

4. On this problem I am indebted to Murray Wax for many helpful suggestions.

in effect: oh yes, we know all about such alterations; that is simply ambivalence; people cannot make up their minds whether they wish Jesus to be a man or a baby. Moreover, we often see such ambivalence in our patients; they, too, cannot make up their minds whether to be a man or a child. So again mythology confirms what we find in the study of the neuroses.

Erich Fromm's critique of this kind of psychoanalytic analogizing is, I think, sound. He points out that such a view does not take religion seriously enough, does not take society seriously enough, does not even take the individual seriously enough. For the development of Christian dogma can tell us much, not about the psychological complexes of individual men who may have been ambivalent in one respect or another, but about the social struggles which shook the Roman Empire at this period—struggles in which, despite their individual ambivalences, men took sides and developed important religious and social institutions. We cannot dismiss such struggles without examining them historically, any more than we can dismiss the tragedies of individual decision and indecision in a social setting by speaking only of ambivalence.

Thus, Fromm observes that the young Christ of the early decades represents the Messianic hopes of the peasants, of the oppressed classes. They identify with Him as a man, as a focus of social protest—and as a man who becomes God. True, He does not replace God—the movement is a Messianic one, not an actual and successful social revolution—but He joins God on high. Much later, when Christianity has become a state religion and when the Messianic hopes have evaporated, we find an entirely different image of Christ. He is the Son who is consoled and protected by His mother; moreover, He was God all the time, rather than attaining to Godhood by His own manly efforts. This shift is a sign, at one and the same time, of psychological regression among large social strata and of the defeat of these same strata. The peasants no longer challenge the Empire even in fantasy, and their religion mirrors their situation as earlier it mirrored their hopes for social change. Fromm notes that it is only with the coming of the Reformation that God re-emerges as a father-figure, while during the medieval epoch the challenge to the father, to authority, is muted and the mother-figure predominates. Thus the Reformation's change of Christian imagery presages new social stirrings and new possibilities of rebellion. In this analysis, the emphasis is on *social* authority, which is reflected both in the structure of the family and the structure of religious doctrine; whereas in Freud's or Reik's analysis, the emphasis is on the family—on the individual domestic constellation—from which the racial and religious imageries are developed.

I want, however, to warn you that Fromm's argument is a very complicated one—so, for that matter, is Reik's discussion of religious rituals—and I have only presented it in oversimplified form. I would not want to leave the impression that Fromm takes an entirely Marxist position, of saying that religion is a mere superstructure—a narcotic in the class struggle. Fromm criticizes Kautsky's view as to the origin of Christianity quite as sharply as he criticizes Reik's. For Fromm sees religion as playing an important part in social struggles, and not merely as a reflection or distortion of those struggles.

Taking religion seriously as a factor in man's long effort to free himself, Fromm also differs from Freud in the role he assigns religion within the individual's psychic economy. Freud, as we have seen, considers religion to be crippling for the individual, crippling to his intellectual curiosity and his emotional claims alike—and this holds for all religion which deserves the name. In contrast with this, Fromm sharply differentiates among religions in terms of their specific social functions. Some doctrines which are not *called* religion may be far more crippling than some which are called religion. That is, while all of us, by virtue of the socialization we have undergone, are crippled to some degree, we cannot differentiate the more crippled from the less crippled by the tags of church identification. If we look at the whole person and the interpretations he puts on his religion—the specific quality of his religion—we may very well find that a devout person is far more "free"—far less deluded—than a man who claims he has outgrown belief in God.

Religion, in other words, can tell us a good deal about the individual believer and the social system in which he exists. We can, in socio-psychological terms, interpret the part religion plays in the life of men and groups. But this part is seldom simple and monolithic. Paradoxically, Freud seems to have taken too much at face the religious opposition to science, and failed to see, at least in this particular, that we have not said the last word about a man's rationality when we have stamped him as a believer—his religion may be the very sign of his rationality, though a disguised one.

This leads me to a further criticism I would like to make of Freud's view of religion, namely concerning the problem of motivation. When Freud found a religious man, he was likely to assume that his altruism, for instance, covered something up—perhaps it was a reaction-formation to anal-erotic sadism. Surely, that often happens, and the time when Freud lived was particularly noted for its pious frauds, its hypocrites who concealed their meanness consciously or unconsciously under a cloak of fervent religious devotion or obsessive attention to ritual. But it seems to me that today we face an altered situation, in which the limitations of Freud's view have become more apparent. Partly as the very result of Freud's work, we have invented a new kind of hypocrisy in which we have to cover over anything decent in ourselves, and call it tough. If we do an altruistic or decent act, we don't dare admit it, even or perhaps especially to ourselves. We rationalize away what is good and genuine in us. The businessman, for instance, chalks it up to public relations if he does something generous. The student, if let us say he does not cheat or is not aggressive, will chalk it up to timidity, to his fear of what people might think—he will certainly not give himself credit for any nobility of impulse. This new hypocrisy strikes me as in some ways quite as displeasing, and socially perhaps considerably more dangerous, than the old.

It would seem to follow from this that we cannot regard religion as simply a method for controlling libidinal and aggressive drives in the interests of society or of some other ultra-individual power. Religion is not, as Freud thought it to be, a kind of tax collector that collects from everybody the energy necessary to power civilization, and to keep it going. Nor will we necessarily find in religious practices what Freud called "the return of the repressed," that is, the reappearance in distorted or symbolic form of the very tendencies that religion had served to inhibit. Freud's whole position here, while it contains much that is true for certain epochs and for certain social groups, rests on his "scarcity economics," his view of man as having only so much libido, so much benevolence, to go around. And if this structure of motivations, with its tendency to biological reductionism falls, with it does Freud's view that religion on its ethical side represents, in the individual no more than a reaction-formation, and, in the society, no more than a method of social control. As Freud saw an obsessional neurosis as a caricature of a religion, so we may regard Freud's picture of religion itself as a caricature of certain reactionary Augustinian tendencies within the Christian denominations—where the establishment comes close to being a method of social control and a reaction-formation against hatred and lust in whose very practices and doctrines hatred and lust reappear.

Furthermore, as I have already implied, there is in Freud's analysis of religion a somewhat pedantic treatment of religious symbolism. Freud does not, like Durkheim, study a religious ritual with the feeling that the ritual is trying to say something to him in another language —something which may be quite as rational as any scientific text. For example, he fails to see how a whole group, like the American Negroes, could guard their aspirations for liberation under a religious guise.

Though far less heavy-handed than some of his followers, he nevertheless handles symbolism, whether in religion, in dreams, or in works
of art, a bit too literally—not rationally so much as rationalistically.
He wants to force it into a certain framework, and to pierce through
the manifest symbol to its genetic origin. But the search for origins,
which we have already seen to be characteristic of his approach to
religion as to so much else, may tend to lead one to miss both artistry
and overtones of contemporary meaning. In a way, the origins of a
religious doctrine are relevant to contemporary men only insofar as
they have incorporated those origins in their reinterpretations of what
they do. Hence even if it were true that religion invariably arose
out of men's fear and guilt, it would not necessarily follow that it
is today propelled by fear and guilt.

§ V

HAVING MADE these criticisms of Freud's view of religion, I think we
must grant his tremendous contribution to our understanding of it.
As in so many other fields of his boundless curiosity and passionate
moral courage, he succeeded in his effort to win a new territory for
science, or at least a new angle of approach to the new territory. It
is an approach which, when combined with other approaches, can
be very fruitful, as I think Fromm's work indicates. Indeed, to make
the study of religion (apart, of course, from Biblical criticism and
other ongoing nineteenth-century efforts) respectable among scientists
was perhaps as hard when Freud wrote as it was to make science respectable among religious fundamentalists.

Another contribution Freud has made to the study of religion
leads me to introduce a kind of dialectic argument with the views of
Malinowski. Malinowski takes a functional view of religion. This
"functionalism" means that, if the investigator finds religion as an
element in the life of a man or a group, he will assume it has a function,
will seek to discover what it is, and will not consider it part of his
task to criticize the function. Whatever is, functions; whatever functions, is part of the ethnographic picture. Many cultural anthropologists—partly because of the almost inevitable contemporaneity of
field work, the lack of historical data—will not assess the historical
weight of anything that functions in the present, and will perhaps
overinterpret functions which may, in fact, no longer matter very
much. They may be simply relics.

Freud erred in the other direction by putting his emphasis almost
exclusively on origins and relics. This, however, provides him with
the perspective from which he says—whether he is right or wrong in

his prediction is not the question here—that the religion which seems to have such a strong hold on mankind will very likely disappear with the adulthood of the race. For he can look back historically and conclude that the hold of religion was not always what it now is; that there have been decisive historical events, such as the reign of Ikhnaton, or the Jews' killing of Moses, or the Crucifixion of Christ, which altered the social and individual function of religion. Malinowski finds it hard to do this with the Trobriand Islanders.

But Freud's look forward is not only based on his look backward into history. He also looks into himself, and asks: do I need religion, can I get along without it; and if I can, why not all men? By assuming the unity of men's psychic constitution, he was enabled by self-analysis to subject social institutions to criticism, whereas an anthropology that follows functionalism literally cannot criticize what it finds, if it "functions." In other words, Freud found within himself a scientific *Weltanschauung* which transcended religion in its historical givenness, and from this base he could criticize religion and look forward to its demise while granting its functional role in the development and cementing of Western civilization.

§ VI

LET ME TURN FINALLY, in the light of what has just been said, to the question of possible meeting grounds between psychoanalysis and religion. . . .

Within both fields, within psychoanalysis and within religion, there is an increasing preoccupation with meaning, with values. We must be as careful not to confuse psychoanalysis with one brand of it as we must be not to confuse religion with one brand of it. Indeed, I think it fair to say that the differences in attitude towards fundamental questions *within* religion and *within* psychoanalysis are greater than the differences between like-minded schools of religion and analysis.

As I have said, religion is today for many no longer the formal, often hypocritical shell that it frequently was in the nineteenth century. Great numbers of people can no longer coast on nineteenth-century religious observances, and they have been driven by modern life out of the religious communities that once held them fast. In the name of religion, they therefore meet together to consider where they are. It should not disturb or confuse us that these people put their quest for meaning in religious terms; he would be a bold person indeed who would allege that these terms cannot hold and develop new meanings.

A number of analysts have come to the same conclusion by a different route. In his therapy, Freud rejected the notion that he was a moral or ethical guide; he thought this would be a concealed dictatorship and that his job was done when he had helped the patient to find his own ego-ideals, free from compulsive obedience to, or flight from, a parental imago. Actually, he could largely coast on the implicit ends of the nineteenth century, and assume that his patients were on the whole sensible people whose neurosis did not itself originate in a moral conflict. Moreover, he was able to solve most moral problems which came up in his research and therapy by one ethical principle we have already seen at work in him: passionate devotion to the truth. Psychoanalysis in fact constitutes a great ethical achievement in its invention of a human relationship whose cardinal principle is scrupulous, or if you please ruthless, honesty *on both sides*. Freud's early patients, at any rate, were hysterics or obsessional people who had obvious symptoms and who wanted to be free of them, in order simply to lead good Victorian lives.

Perhaps is was Jung who first saw, in the immediate generation of analysts after Freud, that this (or training) was not the only reason people came to analysis. His patients seemed to be mainly men of middle age who were "in search of a soul"—who asked the analyst, "What is the purpose of my life? What should I do with it?" Their neuroses seemed to be bound up with moral problems, problems of choice. Increasingly today, this new type of analytic work with people who are not obviously ill—whose "symptom" is their malaise, their whole way of life—people who are troubled about moral issues, or who ought to be troubled about them, forces analysts to become concerned with problems of casuistry, of values, as part of the very task of therapy. Neurosis then appears, not so much as a conflict between "natural" libidinal demands and society's restraints, but as a conflict among moral strivings within the individual himself—though these, of course, reflect the conflicts within society. And, in terms of technique, the analyst's task may no longer lie in coaching sexual frankness. The analyst may have to help patients confront repressed moral issues about which they ought to be, but are not consciously, troubled.

In two books, *Man for Himself* and *Psychoanalysis and Religion*, Erich Fromm has made an effort to grapple with these moral problems as they present themselves in analysis, within an evaluative framework that finds much in common with what he terms "humanistic" religion. He takes religion much more seriously as a source of illumination for psychotherapy than most psychoanalysts (including Jung) have hitherto done. At the same time, he employs the Freudian methods to understand the hold over men of both humanistic and "authoritarian" religion, and its value for them. Thus he regards himself, not incorrectly, as working in the tradition of Freud, but (like John Dewey) he regards certain elevated ethical attitudes and cosmologies as truly religious, which Freud, when he adverted to them at all, regarded as too highbrow to be given the name of religion. Fromm represents a number of contemporary analysts who are preoccupied with theological questions, not simply as Freud was—i.e., as "evidence" of human weakness and as sources of historical data—but on their merits and in their own terms. At the same time, theologians, turning the tables, can look to psychoanalytic developments for evidence concerning basic human "needs" and the psychic mechanisms which give rise to problems of an ethical and religious sort.

Such reconciliations, however, are not likely to get very far in the prevailing atmosphere where people are afraid of criticizing religion. For if the onslaughts of organized religious groups succeed in putting psychoanalysis, along with other inquisitive sciences, on the defensive, psychoanalysis—far from joining in the possible creation of new, syncretistic religious patterns—will either leave religion alone, as too hot to handle, or will form expedient alliances and make expedient obeisances and denials of any claim to ethical and religious relevance. If, in other and more "emancipated" circles, psychoanalysis, in the form of a diluted popular Freudianism, can still put people on the defensive who would like to know how to live decent lives, they will look to analysis only for debunking cliches and for symptom-therapy, not for its moral illumination.

Indeed, if we are to get beyond such sterility and defensiveness on both sides, we must abandon the misleading notion that there is such a thing as pure science or pure religion. All thought—that of religion and psychoanalysis alike—is impure, or, as Freud would say, ambivalent; all thought must be constantly removed from its wrappings of this time or that place. This is true of Freud's views concerning religion, as their paradoxical uses traced here would seem to indicate. It is also true, I venture to say, not only of our religious inheritance as a whole, but specifically of our traditional religious way of dealing with the temerities of science.

No doubt, future developments in the relation between psychoanalysis and religion (including Fromm's attempt to break down this distinction and to develop new ones) will depend rather more on such larger issues of social structure as the fate of the Catholic middle class than on the success of the intellectual adventure of a handful of theologians and analysts. But religious and scientific advance must usually occur as relatively powerless movements within a precarious setting. Freud, like other innovators, started as a minority of one.

VII.

TOTALITARIANISM

THERE WAS A TIME when intelligent people tried to interpret totalitarianism either in terms of the ideological smoke-screens of the totalitarians or in terms of some theory of class conspiracy. Thus, many intelligent people before and even during World War II saw Nazism as a combination of Rhineland industrialists and Junker landlords and officers, making use of anti-Semitism and German chauvinism to "fool the masses," smash unions, and maintain the *Osthilfe*, the much-attacked Prussian farm subsidies. Popular support was summed up in a reference to the *Lumpenproletariat*, or possibly by an allusion to lower-middle-class malaise. I had been briefly in Germany in 1931, and my colloquial German, learned from a nurse "just off the boat" who knew no English, was enough to allow me to talk with students and other young men who were Nazis. Many of them were very idealistic—indeed, it was their ideals, as well as their unconscious aggressions, which were betraying them. I thought it likely that Germany would fall to Hitler, and wondered at the complacency of the older people I saw, who felt, with the wisdom of experience, that, if Hitler did reach power, the responsibility would sober him—as it had sobered the Social Democrats.

When it turned out that power did not sober or stabilize either Hitler or the Bolsheviks, many people jumped to the other extreme —represented in such a book as George Orwell's *1984*—and saw the totalitarian ruler in the image of the mad scientist: vicious but rational, his dreams of omnipotence come true. The earlier simplistic and economistic explanations (I don't intend to suggest I was myself immune from them) were exchanged for literary, philosophical, and theological ones, notably in Hannah Arendt's brilliant and evocative *The Origins of Totalitarianism*. Looking back at the record, however, it is all too easy to say that the observers who interpreted Nazism and Stalinism by extrapolation from their own experience underestimated the wilfulness, the lust for power and destruction, of the totalitarian movements and hence the inevitability of "permanent revolution." Without the aid of France and England, and then of the Soviet Union, Hitler would not have managed to bring on a war, and without war he could probably not have achieved his aim of full totalitarian domination—indeed, on taking over in 1933 he was in many ways quite inhibited and cautious. He himself was less confident of the outcome in the early years than many who now retroactively see a malign logic in all that occurred. Likewise, many Russian experts seem to believe that no move is made in the Soviet sphere without Politburo planning and approval—no move based on jurisdictional dispute, personal caprice and connection, or luck. Doubtless, the leaders wish it was like that! The real world puts limits—not enough, to be sure—on the wishes of even the most powerful and cruel men.

Today, however, those who think, for example, that McCarthy is bound to triumph in America, or that Malan and his party will succeed in their extremist program, appear to have "history" with them. In this new context, I feel we are witnessing an over-reaction against the earlier tendency to assimilate Nazi and Soviet phenomena to familiar despotic patterns: we have become extravagant in denying that these regimes had any imaginable connection with social structures of an ordinarily inefficient sort. My paper on "The Limits of Totalitarian Power," delivered at a meeting arranged by the American Committee on Cultural Freedom, gave me the opportunity tentatively to question this view before a group where there could be no danger of complacency towards the Communist countries—especially as I was on the program with such tried and true anti-totalitarians as Hannah Arendt, Bruno Bettelheim, and Nathan Leites. Even so, there was a tendency among some of my listeners to resent the suggestion that the Soviet regime could not completely cut the bonds of human solidarity and restructure human personality—not yet; there was a feeling that I, an unhurt outsider, was necessarily innocent, unable in my rationalistic liberalism to grasp the terrible monolithic quality of "the system."

Underneath some of these criticisms there lurked the belief which I have often encountered that social science, in its effort to probe and understand our times, must necessarily miss the basic evils and the deep irrationalities of totalitarianism and, besides, evaporate away our indignation and our will to fight. (The articles on intellectual freedom and on race relations in section III have of course come in for similar attack.) I think I recognize these dangers. We have all met people who diminish their sympathy with themselves by giving out parlor-Freudian analyses of their moods and conduct. When I have made myself read some of the literature on concentration and labor camps, I have been aware of my wish for mechanisms to put this terrible material at a distance, so as to diminish both my anxiety and my empathic suffering. Science can serve many concurrent aims—not only to disclose the truth but to give a safe-conduct pass to the scientist, an asbestos coating in hell. Yet at the same time I feel that an almost hysterical heavy-handedness can all too often cloak itself in righteousness and plead rank on the basis of more intense suffering; a refusal to use all available techniques for examination can also appear as a noble disdain for evil. I would hate to see the day dawn when intellectuals had to wear their piety (or their loyalty!) on their sleeves. We need both satire and sermon, both psychology and theology.

"The Nylon War" is a serious attempt, couched as satire, to suggest how the Soviet Union might be brought down short of war. Even if human beings have a good deal of unsuspected resistance to the totalitarian reformation of man, the regimes themselves are not likely to be destroyed from inside until one can make atom bombs in a bathroom; "The Nylon War" seeks to organize both American energies and Soviet limitations—it is a foray in Keynesian economics in reverse. I conceived the idea originally as something of a heuristic device to sharpen discussion among a group of social scientists meeting in 1947 under the auspices of the Harris Foundation for International Affairs to discuss "the world community." Two points of view had been vocal at the meeting. There were the self-proclaimed "realists," men like my colleague Hans Morgenthau, some of them geopolitically oriented, who thought in terms of the bipolar "big powers" and exchanged strategic details about Iranian oil or Skoda's output or de Gasperi's majority. Opposed to them was a smaller group, of whom the late Ruth Benedict was one of the more eloquent, who occasionally also sought the prestige of "realism" but did so in terms of psychology and culture rather than of steel plants or armored divisions. This latter group's theme-song was: "The Russians have a culture, too, and on this basis we can and must understand them." Although less patently nationalistic, this second group was no less devoted to the cause of the Western powers in the cold war, but it conceived of cross-cultural communication as a realistic possibility, once American ethnocentrism could be overcome. Some of them, to my mind, appeared to scant the fact that "the" Rusisans were not in charge, but had been conquered by a dictatorship, whereas some of the geopolitically minded were preparing to fight World War I over again with better military weapons—they assumed an enemy as rationalistic as they thought they themselves were; they missed the wild irrationality of a "people's imperialism" and underestimated the rational appeal of ideals to the West.

I recur to these events because the attitudes expressed at this conference are still so dominant, and especially the mood and method of realism. One limitation of this mood is that it robs academic life of one of its principal pleasures and functions, that of serving as a counterpoise to the life of statesmen and executives. My fellow-conferees tended to gravitate towards immediate policy questions—and to bind themselves to the alternatives the State Department might be willing or able to accept at the moment. Since we were a bunch of professors, and not the State Department, since we lacked its channels of information and misinformation, but also had less of an emergency mandate, I felt we should liberate ourselves from the conventions of thought which pass as realism. The notion of the Nylon War was intended to confront us with the very excess of realism in American domestic policy as well as with the fact the anthropologists sometimes understressed, namely that we Americans also have a culture, and one not capable of perennial patience or inaction. Thus, my satire sought to highlight some of the amiable qualities of the United States—industrial energy and romanticism, imagination, activism, generosity—as well as some of the salient qualities of the Soviets—inflexibility, cupidity, "projective" interpretation of the enemy, want, and fear.

I was encouraged by the Berlin airlift to revive the idea and write it up, and I was greatly stimulated by discussion of technical details with Kenneth Mansfield, then a graduate student in international relations at Yale and now a member of the staff of the Joint Congressional Committee on Atomic Energy. Many magazines rejected it—one on the ground that they'd "had enough articles on Russia"; for one thing, it was too long. After the Korean War began, I got it out again, cut it to a quarter its original elaboration, and published it in *Common Cause*, a tiny journal, since defunct. When after that it was picked up by *Etc.*, *The Christian Century*, and a Dutch monthly, I began to get letters and calls asking me if the "war" (whose fictitious date had by then been passed) had actually gotten under way! It was like a page out of *The Invasion from Mars* that people could feel so remote from the current of probabilities as to take my tale for literal fact. The still unresolved disquiet about flying saucers, coupled with the merely extrapolative and unfictional character of much "science fiction," are other indications that people often believe that anything can, and perhaps has, happened; the disorientation from reality that this misreading indicates is frightening.[1]

---

1. Since the above was written, I have had a letter from a man in Sydney, New South Wales, asking me for further references on the "war" on the assumption it has occurred and also whether *Common Cause* is not (as charged by a local representative of the U. S. Information Service) a "Commie magazine." In which case the war would not have occurred but would be "Commie propaganda." One hardly knows whether to laugh or weep at such a letter—and at so humorless and fearful an American representative abroad. "The Nylon War" has also

In a fine essay on "Democracy and Anti-Intellectualism in America,"[2] Richard Hofstadter has argued that intellectuals are characterized by both piety and playfulness—they care very much about what happens to truth, to ideas, and to their human carriers, and they also enjoy the play of the mind, the intellectual function, for its own sake. A dialectic must operate between these two contrasting attitudes, else one succumbs to fanaticism or stuffiness on the one side or dilettantism and debunking on the other. My own recent tendency has possibly been to err on the playful side and concentrate my fire against piety, perhaps as a counter to the relative asceticism and portentousness which seems occasionally characteristic of the University of Chicago. And certainly I agree with Hofstadter's insistence on maintaining the value of both attitudes, just as I feel that a tennis game should neither degenerate into "social tennis" and chit-chat nor lose its game-like quality in competitive ferocity.

When I was working on this manuscript, the June riots broke out in East Berlin, and filled millions of us with hopeful excitement. Even if, as seemed likely, the insurgency should be rapidly overcome, the reminder that totalitarianism could kill men and silence them, but not permanently crush them, cannot come too often—not only to us who stand by but to those Germans whose "Deutscher blick" (the furtive look out of the corner of the eye to see who is listening) has become a kind of totalitarian tic through twenty years of brown and red shirts. Thus, we are all of us fatefully indebted to the nameless ones who took the risks of the June days. And we are also indebted to the Americans whose energy overcome others' hesitations and provided food parcels for Eastern Germans who dared to "come and get it." If only we Americans had more faith in our own weapons, and the imagination to extend this operation into a full-scale "nylon war!" Perhaps we fear to be called materialists: no country was ever called this for its war materiel, but only for its consumer goods.

been reprinted in several anthologies edited by professors of English, where it has appeared as an example of satire; there at least, properly labeled, readers have not written to say that they've missed the papers lately and was the war over!

2. In *Michigan Alumnus Quarterly Review*, vol. 59 (1953), pp. 281-295.

25. Some Observations on the Limits of Totalitarian Power

Twenty and even ten years ago, it was an important intellectual task (and one in which, in a small way, I participated) to point out to Americans of good will that the Soviet and Nazi systems were not simply transitory stages, nor a kind of throwback to the South American way—that they were, in fact, new forms of social organization, more omnivorous than even the most brutal of earlier dictatorships. At that time, there were many influential people who were willing to see the Nazis as a menace but insisted that the Bolsheviks were a hope. And even today one can find individuals who have no inkling of the terror state—people who, for instance, blame "the" Germans for not throwing Hitler out, or for compromising themselves by joining Nazi party or other organizations, or who attribute Soviet behavior to the alleged submissiveness of the Russian character or trace it back to Czarist despotism and expansionism and whatnot. Yet it seems to me that now the task of intellectual and moral awakening has been pretty well performed, and stands even in danger of being overperformed; in pursuit of the few remaining "liberals who haven't learned," groups such as this [the American Committee on Cultural Freedom] may mistake the temper of the country at large, misdeploy their energies, and, paradoxically, serve complacency in the very act of trying to destroy complacency.

Intellectual communication, in this as in other cases, cannot avoid the ambiguities arising from the differing attitudes in the American audience at large. I know that I will be misunderstood. For one thing, those who have suffered directly at the hands of the totalitarians, and who can undoubtedly find many audiences where complacency still rules—where, for example, the Soviet Union is still sneakingly regarded as somehow on the right track as against "capitalist exploitation"—such people may feel that I take too lightly the domestic well-wishers of the Soviet Union, or the lethargic. No one likes being robbed of a well-earned agenda.

Yet I cannot help but feel that the telling of atrocity stories—undoubtedly true stories—may have ambivalent consequences and, after a time, may harm the very cause in hand. Let me give as an illustration the way in which many liberals today, in government service or in academic life, repeat tales of loyalty-probe incompetence or

414

injustice, of school board and trustee confusion between liberals and "Reds," of stupid F.B.I. questions, and so on. Such tales are meant to arouse us against the dangers of domestic reaction, but they have frequently the consequence of leading a government employee to burn back issues of *The New Masses,* of a faculty to drop the *Communist Manifesto* from its reading list, of a student to fear getting involved with even Americans for Democratic Action lest it prejudice his employment possibilities. Then such tales are in turn spread, to justify still further concessions to an alleged need to conform to the prevailing climate of opinion. . . .

Now I want to suggest that something of the same sort may occur if we begin, after greatly underestimating, to greatly overestimate the capacity of totalitarianism to restructure human personality. During the last war, I talked with many people who were concerned with the plans for occupying Germany at war's end. Most assumed that there would be not only physical but organizational chaos and that it was necessary to have skilled civil affairs officers to take over tasks that the Germans, broken by Hitler and the war, could not assume for themselves. I felt that this was unduly patronizing of a great and gifted people, capable of spontaneous organization and of settling affairs with the Nazis if the occupying powers merely held the ring and supplied some necessities of life. I think we can make the same mistake—for I believe it was a mistake—about the Soviet Union and its satellites, and fail to see that even the terror is not omnipotent to destroy all bonds of organization among its victims.

Similarly, I think we can become so fascinated with the malevolence of Stalinism that we may tend to overestimate its efficiency in achieving its horrible ends; and we may mistake blundering compulsions or even accidents of "the system" for conspiratorial genius. Overinterpretation is the besetting sin of intellectuals anyway and even when, with Hannah Arendt, we rightly point to the need to cast traditional rationalities aside in comprehending totalitarianism, we may subtly succumb to the appeal of an evil mystery; there is a long tradition of making Satan attractive in spite of ourselves. And the more practical danger of this is that we may, again reacting from underestimation,[1] misjudge not so much the aims as the power of the enemy and be unduly cowed or unduly aggressive as a result.

---

1. I have had some fairly extended experience of this. I remember in 1931 talking with American engineers in the Soviet Union who thought the Russians too incompetent in the mechanical arts ever to build tractors, let alone planes; they failed, as it seemed to me, to realize how the huge friction of Soviet incompetence could be partly overcome by the even huger burning up of human resources if one cared not at all about them. Likewise, when some seemed complacent about the Chinese Communists on the ground that "you could never

Consequently, I want to open up a discussion of some of the defenses people have against totalitarianism. Not that these defenses— I shall discuss apathy, corruption, free enterprise, crime, and so on— threaten the security system of the Soviets; that system is a new social invention and there are as few defenses against annihilation by it as against annihilation by atom bombs. Indeed, in some ways totalitarianism is actually strengthened by these partial defenses people are able to throw up against it, which make it possible for many people to compromise with the system as a whole. But at least a few European thinkers may be perplexed by the readiness of Americans, lacking firsthand experience of people's capacity to resist, to assume that totalitarianism possesses the kind of psychological pressure system pictured by Orwell in that sadistic but symptomatic book *1984*: here is a fantasy of omnipotent totalitarian impressiveness which I think may itself, among those who admire efficiency and have little faith in man, be an appeal of totalitarianism for those outside its present reach.

For we must distinguish, first of all, between the appeals of totalitarianism when it is out of power and its appeals when in power; my concern here is mainly with the latter. Out of power, totalitarianism competes like any other party, only more so: it can be all things to all men, attracting the idealist by its promise to reform society, to clean out the swindlers; attracting the disoriented and bewildered by its simplistic "explanations" of their misery and of their world, and by promising to get rid of seeming anarchy by enforcing social co-operation; and attracting the sadist in the way the Berkeley study of the "Authoritarian Personality" has documented. (In the Moslem countries and the Far East, the Communists do not need even this much of an armory: a promise to drive out the foreign devils while promising Western-style commodities to everyone may be almost enough.) Most large-scale societies will offer a spectrum of people available for the high-minded, middle-minded, and low-minded aspects of totalitarian politics, though probably a crisis is necessary to convert their organization into a fighting revolutionary party with a real hope of capturing power. That is, the fact that totalitarianism has captured a country doesn't tell us as much as some observers have supposed about the character of its total population; the mass base necessary can be far less than a majority and it can include people of

---

organize the unbelligerent Chinese for aggressive war," I felt that this left out of account the awful weapon of systematic terror and utter ruthlessness about killing one's "own" people that is Moscow's first export to its satellites and "national" Communist parties.

profoundly non-totalitarian personalities who have been fooled—to whom the appeal has not been a very deep-going one.[2]

When the latter wake up to the fact that the God they followed has failed them, it is of course too late to change deities. For many years it seemed to me that the Soviet Union was more dangerous in this respect than the Nazis, let alone the Fascists in Spain and Italy, because the latter were so clearly corrupt that they could not help but disillusion their idealists rapidly. Thus, during the Nazi regime, while the concentration camps were more or less hidden, the power and pelf struggles within the Nazi echelons were not: Hitler might remain for some unsullied. but hardly the party bums and barons of lesser magnitude, struggling to build up private empires of business and espionage. The ideological trappings fell away speedily enough. To be sure, there remained some fanatics, especially perhaps in the SS, savagely incorruptible. But many Germans who were drawn to the Nazis precisely by their claim to eliminate corruption were quickly enlightened when they saw the even greater corruption introduced. As against this, the Communists have seemed more incorruptible—a kind of Cromwellian type, hard-bitten and ascetic—thus perhaps retaining ideological impressiveness as well as gaining physical oppressiveness even after being installed in power. And certainly that impressiveness remains even today for many of those outside the system. Inside, however, there is some evidence—and of course only tantalizingly little—that corruption, blackmarketing, crime, and juggling of figures are widespread; presumably this makes it hard for the idealistic young to be overimpressed with the system's ethical rightness. To be sure, we have had such "training" in contempt for bourgeois comfort-seeking and the dangers of the desire for wealth, that if a Communist is desirous not of wealth but of power he can more readily appear idealistic; perhaps we should learn that the *auri sacra fames*, the cursed hunger for gold, is not half so dangerous to the human race as the ascetic drive for power—a point recently remade by Eric Hoffer in *The True Believer*. Indeed, anyone who claims he wishes to eliminate vice utterly is declaring a very dangerous and antihuman heresy—one all too prevalent, I might add, in today's municipal and national politics in this country. We must teach ourselves,

---

2. What I have said here needs to be qualified by an understanding of the less conscious motives which attract people to a totalitarian party. The Nazis, for example, were not really all things to all men; they gave the wink to some men that, for instance, their legality was merely window-dressing, and the latter could use the window-dressing to satisfy their conscious inhibitions against what at bottom drew them to the party. See, for example, Erik H. Erikson's discussion of "Hitler's Imagery and German Youth," in *Childhood and Society*, pp. 284-315.

and the young, to distinguish between genuine idealism and arrogant, curdled indignation against behavior which falls short of some monastic image of virtue.

More generally, I have long thought that we need to re-evaluate the role of corruption in a society, with less emphasis on its obviously malign features and more on its power as an antidote to fanaticism. Barrington Moore in *Soviet Politics,* and Margaret Mead in *Soviet Attitudes Toward Authority* present materials documenting the Soviet campaign against the corrupting tendencies introduced into the system by friendship and family feeling—some of Mead's quotations could have come from Bishop Baxter or other Puritan divines, and others from American civil service reformers. While Kravchenko shows how one must at once betray friends in the Soviet regime when they fall under state suspicion—and here, too, the Soviets are more tyrannous than the Nazis who expected friends to intercede with the Gestapo—it would appear that such human ties have never been completely fragmented, whether by Puritanism,[3] industrialism, or their savagely sudden combination in Bolshevism. Actually, people have had to defend themselves against the Soviet system's high demands for performance by building personal cliques, by favoritism, by cultivating cronies; thus, an informal network has continued to operate alongside the formal one, whose extraordinary expectations can in fact only be met in this way. (Similarly, Petrov points out that no amount of indoctrination has persuaded the Russian people to like and admire spies and informers, or to extirpate from their own reactions the profoundly human emotion of pity.)

To be sure, corruption does not always and inevitably work as a solvent for ideological claims. Hannah Arendt, returning from Germany last year, described the way in which many middle-class, educated Germans, in order to justify to themselves within their rigid code the compromises they made with the Nazi system, had to exalt that system ideologically; they were trapped by complicity as they would not have been had they been more cynical. Incidentally, their wives, who had to hunt for subsistence on the blackmarket, were probably better off in this respect—they did the needful things to keep going, while allowing their husbands to remain deceived in their older morality. And it could at least be argued that women—as the Bachofen-Fromm interpretation of the Oedipus trilogy would indicate

---

3. While I think that there are many revealing analogies between theocratic Calvinism in its heyday and Stalinism, I do not think the similarities should be pressed too far; among many other differences, the Puritans—in any case, far less powerful—believed in law.

—are more immune than men to impersonal and abstract ideals; they are more conservative in the good and in the bad sense—more "realistic."

I am not, it should be clear, discussing what are called resistance movements, but rather what might be called resistance quiescences. I am talking about the quieter modes of resistance to totalitarianism, not so much in practical life as in mental obeisance, in refusal to internalize the system's ethical norms. I am, moreover, quite unable to say what *proportion* of people, either under the Nazi regime or the Soviet, succumbed or managed to defend themselves in this way; I cannot assign quantitative weights to one mode or the other. It is one of our difficulties as intellectuals that we cannot easily assign such weights. We are likely to overestimate symbolic behavior that appears to give deference to totalitarian power. And the testimony of intellectuals who once believed in totalitarianism and have now fled it is further indication as to the dangers of a totalitarian regime for the emotional life of people like ourselves: ours is in many ways the most exposed position since overt obedience to mere power is least habitual, and since we need—whatever our rational beliefs about men's irrationality—to justify and integrate our behavior in some fashion, perhaps especially so when we ourselves are wholesalers or retailers of ideology.

Myrdal, when he visited this country, commented on the "protective community" of the Negroes and of lower-class people generally who, vis-a-vis the whites and the authorities, "ain't seen nothing or nobody"; long training has made them adept in duplicity, evasion, and sly sabotage. (A similar phenomenon exists in Italian peasant communities, under the name of "*la omertà*.") True, this kind of protective community breaks down on occasion, even under the relatively mild pressures and promises of white or official society; the Soviets have much more violent and fearsome methods. Moreover, the Soviet secret police are facing a population most of which is new to urban life, ways and byways: industrialization always stirs the melting pot and throws strange peoples together who have little understanding of or sympathy for each other, or whose suspicion of each other can be easily aroused. Whereas the workers of Hamburg were already accustomed to the industrial revolution and its problems and prospects of social interaction, the Soviet Union is in a sense one vast labor camp where social organization has to start pretty much from scratch.[4] Even so, I think it likely that there are protective

4. There is no space here to go into the analogous problem of the concentration camps themselves. Kogon's and David Rousset's accounts would seem to indicate that in these camps some prisoner rule developed, and much corruption

communities in Russian farms and factories, which punish Stakhano-
vites and cope with spies.

In a brilliant article in *The Reporter*, Lionel Trilling has delineated the anti-social, anti-societal bent of a great deal of American
literature: Huck Finn escaping the well-meant civilizing clutches of
the Widow Douglas is a good illustration of his theme. But we may
raise the question whether such escapes—if not to the open spaces then
to a protective community or an underground institution like a blind
pig or a whorehouse—are not to be found in all the major cultures
which have any complex institutions at all, and possibly even in the
simplest cultures if we only knew where to look for them. We must
never underestimate the ability of human beings to dramatize, to play
roles, to behave in ways that seem contradictory only if we do not
appreciate the changes in scene and audience. A friend of mine, Mark
Benney, riding a train with peasants in Nazi Germany, was struck
by their impassivity of feature. When he and another stranger, a
Nazi, got off the train, he could feel behind him a sudden relaxation
of facial and postural tensions, and looking back he saw people who
were, in a sense, not at all the same people.[5]

By the block system and the other machinery of a police terror,
the Soviets can cut off many of the traditional underground institutions, and make others too hazardous for all but a few heroes. But
even in such a case, human ingenuity is not completely helpless.
Overfulfillment—literal obedience to extravagant Soviet demands—
can be another form of sabotage; I have heard tell of one group of
Moscow cynics who would go to meetings and joyfully accuse all
and sundry of deviationism as a sure way to break up the party. All
fanatical movements, I would suggest, are as threatened by the real
or pretended deviations in the direction of perfect obedience as by
the underground. Beyond all this, there remains the escape into the
self, the escape of withdrawal, of what Kris and Leites have termed

---

(reminiscent of the kangaroo courts in the worst American jails), with various
groups of prisoners fighting among themselves, and with guard allies, for hegemony. When I raised this problem at the Committee's meeting, Hannah Arendt
insisted that the camps described by Kogon and Rousset were exceptions, and
that in most no such prisoner ingenuities and defenses developed. Reliable evidence is hard to come by; see, however, Theodore Abel, "The Sociology of Concentration Camps" in December, 1951, *Social Forces*, vol. 30, pp. 150-155, which
offers some support for my own position; and see, also, David P. Boder, *I Did
Not Interview the Dead.*

5. In a letter, Norman Birnbaum has suggested that the peasants' uneasiness
was pre-political—due to their natural reserve with urban people (city slickers)
not of their kind. But he also points out that if this were the case it would
not change the fundamental fact: the ability of people to be "two-faced" and to
practice social concealment on the basis of minimal cues.

"privatization." The Soviet press, by its attacks on the practice, gives evidence that depoliticization tendencies are strong, and one would expect people to develop ritualized ways of handling their political exhortations without inner conviction.

In my 1931 visit to the Soviet Union, I talked with students who had decided to go into medicine or engineering, rather than journalism or writing, as more protected, less polemical and sensitive areas; doubtless, many of them were sadly fooled when, in the purges, they found themselves accused of sabotage and wrecking, or even theoretical deviations based on their seemingly unideological decisions. Ever since then, I have sought to find out whether young people were able to choose army careers, or skilled labor, as ways of avoiding such dangers; I have found some evidence that such escapes are extremely unlikely since bright boys are already spotted in high school and compelled as well as bribed to develop their talents and deploy them; they cannot hide their light under a bushel.

One of the reasons why young people are willing to assume dangerous responsibilities is of course that the rewards of success in managerial posts are very great. It has become obvious that Soviet managers are no longer held, as in the earlier years of the regime, to ascetic standards of living. It is possible that, among the abler cadres, an entrepreneurial risk-taking attitude towards life is encouraged, which makes the prospect of becoming a factory manager with access to women, dachas, power, and glory worth taking the risk that it won't last, and may even be succeeded by exile and still grimmer fates —a psychology which bears some resemblance to that occasionally found among professional soldiers for whom battles mean promotions as well as deadly dangers.

But monetary rewards have their own logic. The loose change in people's pockets tends to encourage free enterprise or, as it is known in the Soviet Union, the black market. The black market also enters when managers scrounge for goods in order to fulfill production quotas and so remain managers. And business as usual, like other forms of corruption, is a wonderful "charm" against ideologies, useful particularly because of its own ordinarily unideological character. Under the Nazis, both in Germany and in the occupied countries, business was often almost an unconscious sabotage of the regime: people in pursuit of their private ends violated the public rules without, so to speak, intending any resistance. They did not have to be heroes, any more than the scofflaws were who drank under American prohibition, or the fellow who wants to make a fast buck in the Western war economies. Guenter Reimann in his book *The Vampire Economy*, tells as a characteristic story the answer to a question as to what a permit from a Party member for a certain commodity would cost: "Well, it all depends on what kind of a Party member you have to deal with. If he no longer believes in National Socialism, it will cost you a hundred marks. If he still does, five hundred marks. But if he is a fanatic, you will have to pay a thousand marks."[6]

In the past, we have tended to interpret such signs of passive resistance in terms of our hope for an eventual overthrow of the system from within; we have been like the Marxists who thought contradictions would bring capitalism down. Now we know that it takes more to destroy a system than its own contradictions, and we have been apt to go to the other extreme and assume that the system was, therefore, since it didn't collapse, all-seeing and all-powerful over the minds of men. Two errors common to the social sciences have worked together to this end. The first error, as just indicated, is to imagine social systems as monolithic, and as needing to be relatively efficient to remain in power. Actually, systems roll on, as people do, despite glaring defects and "impossible" behavior. We have created an imaginary image of what it takes for an institution to keep going; in fact, it can go on with little support and less efficiency. One reason for this mirage we have is that when a revolution does occur, we explain it as a matter of course by pointing to the defects of the previous system—and we fall here into the error of supposing that what happened *had* to happen. Barring relatively accidental factors, the system might well have gone on for a long while. (Incidentally, this same historicist error is an element in the overestimation of the power of totalitarian appeals; we assume, for example, that these appeals were responsible for Hitler's victory in Germany as if that victory were a foregone conclusion and not a series of reversible choice-points.) Social scientists, having logical minds and being efficient themselves— even when they sing the praises of irrationality—seldom take a sufficiently perspectivistic view of a society to see it as rolling along in spite of all the things which should bring it to a stop. In this error, of course, they do not stand alone; most of us tend to overinterpret the behavior of others, especially perhaps when we are menaced by them.

The second error, which is perhaps historically older, is more

6. Dr. Arendt in her rebuttal criticized the relevance of this and similar incidents on the ground that they occurred prior to Germany's entry into World War II—prior, that is, to the descent of the iron curtain which protected and facilitated complete totalitarianism. Without the slightest doubt, the Nazis grew ever more ferocious as the war progressed—thus, mass genocide did not really get under way until then; nevertheless, just because of the iron curtain, it is all the more necessary to examine whether the system did ever become efficiently monolithic even when all possible restraints of a humanitarian or public-relations sort disappeared. Cf. Trevor-Roper's *The Last Days of Hitler*.

formidable. It assumes that men can be readily manipulated and controlled, either as the earlier utopians thought in pursuit of some greatly uplifted state, or as the more recent anti-utopians such as Huxley and Orwell have thought, in pursuit of vulgarity and beastliness. (Orwell, to be sure, exempts his proles from the ravages of ideology.) Social science is concerned with prediction, with categorizing human beings and social systems. So it has perhaps a professional bias toward cutting men down to the size of the categories, and not allowing them to play the multiplicity of roles, with the multiplicity of emotional responses, that we constantly show ourselves capable of. Thus we run into a paradox. On the one hand, we think men can be adjusted into some Brave New World because of fundamental human plasticity and flexibility, while on the other hand we do not see that men's ability precisely to fit, part-time, into such a world is what saves them from having to fit into it as total personalities. We have assumed—and in this of course we reflect our own cultural attitudes —that people must be co-operative in order to co-operate, whereas throughout history people have co-operated because to do so made realistic sense, because certain conditions were met, and not because of the psychological appeal of co-operation per se. We have, under the pressure of recent events, reacted against the older view of writers like Sumner that people and cultures can hardly be changed at all towards the view that they can not only be changed but can be easily destroyed.

Ever since the rise of the bourgeoisie and of public opinion and mass politics, people have been afraid of the seeming chaos created by the open fight of special interest groups. The fight is open because there is a press and because each group tries both to solidify its own members and to recruit others by universalizing its appeals. In the contemporary world, there are many influential men who believe that this war of vested interests, occurring within the framework of a democratic society, will endanger consensus and disrupt the entire social fabric. Totalitarianism, in fact, makes an appeal, less to people's special interests as, let us say, workers, than to their fear of all competing interests, including even their own as these are organized by lobbies and pressure groups. Having an image of society as it ought to be, as orderly and co-operative, they tend to welcome, especially of course when the going gets rough, a system which promises to eliminate all social classes and other vested interests which impede co-operation. Thus, on the one hand they are frightened by the ideal of a pluralistic, somewhat disorderly, and highly competitive society— still the best ideal in the business, in my opinion—while on the other hand, their view of men as plastic allows them to suppose that the totalitarians will change all that and transform men into automatically socialized creatures like the ants. When we put matters this way, we can see that there may be grandiose fantasies at the bottom of the fears of people like Orwell, deeply repressed fantasies of human omnipotence such as Hannah Arendt has traced in the totalitarians themselves.

For me, the most striking conclusion to be drawn from the state of Germany today, from the stories of the refugees from behind the Iron Curtain, even from the present behavior of former concentration camp inmates, is precisely how hard it is permanently to destroy most people psychologically. Once the terror is removed, they appear to snap back, ravaged as in any illness, but capable of extraordinary recuperative efforts. In extreme situations such as Dr. Bettelheim has described, people sink to almost incredible abysses or more rarely rise to incredible heights; but if they survive at all, they exhibit an astonishing capacity to wipe away those nightmares.

As the concept of social harmony and integration has misled us as to the amount of disorganization a going society can stand, so I believe that the concept of psychological integration has misled us as to the amount of disintegration and inconsistency of response that an individual can stand. Even in our society, we tell lies to ourselves and others all day long; we are split personalities; yet, with a minimum amount of support from the system, we manage to keep going. All our days we give hostages to history and fortune, and yet are able to call on self-renewing aspects of the ever-filled cup of life.

A certain immunity to ideologies seems to me to be spreading in the world, if not as fast as totalitarianism, at least in its wake. This immunity is far from perfect, even in its own terms. Totalitarianism can appeal to cynics in their cynicism just as much as to idealists in their idealism. An ideology can be fashioned out of anti-ideology, as totalitarian parties have been fashioned out of an anti-party program. And a world is certainly ill-omened in which we must fear the enthusiasm of the young, and prefer their apathy, because we have learned (a hundred and fifty years after Burke) to fear ideas in politics.

We simply do not know whether, over a series of generations, it is possible to rob people even of the freedom of their apathy. Very likely people need at least some ability to communicate disaffection if they are not to conclude that only they alone are out of step. And privatization implies accepting the given regime as part of the order of nature, not to be fought by the likes of oneself—only in that way can terrible guilt feelings be avoided.[7] There comes to mind the story of

---

7. We must be careful in evaluating evidence here. A group of people near

a German anti-Nazi who, shortly after Hitler's coming, had taken a job as stenographer to an SS committee. Everything went well for a while; his convictions remained unshaken, and he continued old Socialist associations. But then one day he had a paralysis of his right arm; he could not move it at all. He went to a psychiatrist, who came quickly to the source of the paralysis, namely that the stenographer could not resign himself to the constant Heil Hitler salutes.

And, indeed, many of the defenses I have discussed are little better than forms of paralysis which, by their presence, evidence the resistance men put up against seemingly implacable destinies. I would prefer to see men fighting back through paralysis than succumbing through active incorporation of the enemy. But this is hardly an optimum way to live one's life, and we cannot be—even apart from the danger to ourselves—unmoved by the plight of those now living and dying under Communist regimes. All we can do while we seek ways to bring those regimes down without war is to find our way to a more robust view of man's potentialities, not only for evil, about which we have heard and learned so much, not only for heroism, about which we have also learned, but also for sheer unheroic cussed resistance to totalitarian efforts to make a new man of him.

Frankfurt remarked to my colleague Everett Hughes, when he had won their confidence, "Unter Hitler war Es doch besser." This did not mean they had been or were still Nazis, but just the opposite, namely that they were making an unideological judgment, immune as well to Occupation, to democracy, as to Nazism.

26. The Nylon War

T<small>ODAY</small>—A<small>UGUST</small> 1, 1951—the Nylon War enters upon the third month since the United States began all-out bombing of the Soviet Union with consumer's goods, and it seems time to take a retrospective look. Behind the initial raid of June 1 were years of secret and complex preparations, and an idea of disarming simplicity: that if allowed to sample the riches of America, the Russian people would not long tolerate masters who gave them tanks and spies instead of vacuum cleaners and beauty parlors. The Russian rulers would thereupon be forced to turn out consumers' goods, or face mass discontent on an increasing scale.

The Nylon War was conceived by an army colonel—we shall call him 'Y'—whose name cannot yet be revealed. Working with secret funds which the Central Intelligence Agency had found itself unable to spend, Y organized shortly after World War II the so-called 'Bar Harbor Project,' the nucleus of what, some five years later, became 'Operation Abundance,' or, as the press soon dubbed it, the 'Nylon War.' After experiments with rockets and balloons, it was concluded that only cargo planes—navigating, it was hoped, above the range of Russian radar—could successfuly deliver the many billion dollars worth of consumer goods it was planned to send. Nevertheless, when Y and his group first broached their plans to a few selected Congressional leaders in the winter of 1948 they were dismissed as hopelessly academic. America had neither the goods nor the planes nor the politics to begin such an undertaking. But in the fall of 1950, with the country bogged down in a seemingly endless small-scale war in Korea, Y's hopes revived. For one thing, the cargo planes needed for the job were beginning to become available. Moreover, a certain amount of overordering by the Armed Services, panicky over Korea, had created a stockpile of consumer goods. More important, the Administration, having locked up all known and many suspected Communists in one of the old Japanese relocation camps, had still not convinced the country that it was sufficiently anti-Soviet, though at the same time many Americans wanted peace but did not dare admit it. A plan which, in fact and in presentation, took attention away from alleged Far-Eastern bungling, and which was both violently anti-Soviet and pro-peace, appeared to offer the possibility of restoring the Administration's tottering position in the counry.

This is not the place to recount the political maneuverings that preceded Truman's success in securing a two billion dollar initial appropriation from Congress, nor the Potomac maneuverings that led to the recruitment of top-flight production and merchandising talent from civilian life. Our story begins with Truman going before Congress to secure authority to 'bring the benefits of American technology to less fortunate nations' by round-the-clock bombing, the day after the news of the first raids hit the American public.

The planners of the Bar Harbor Project had staked American prestige, their professional futures, and the lives of six thousand airmen on the belief that the Soviets would not know of these first flights nor meet them with armed resistance. When the opening missions were accomplished without incident, permitting Truman to make his appeal, Washington was immensely relieved; but when the second wave of planes met with no resistance either, Washington was baffled. It was at first assumed that the Soviet radar network had again simply failed to spot the high-flying planes—cruising at 48,000 feet and self-protected from radar by some still presumably secret device. We now know that what actually happened was a division of opinion in the Kremlin —we can piece the story together from intelligence reports and from clues in *Pravda*. A faction, led by foreign trade chief Mikoyan, maintained that the scheme was a huge hoax, designed to stampede Russia into a crusade against a fairy-tale—and so to make her the laughing stock of the world. He counselled, wait and see. And, indeed, it *was* a fairy-tale for secret police boss Beria, who argued that the raids had never taken place, but that reports of them had been faked by some Social Democratic East Germans who had somehow gotten access to the communications networks. When this idea was exploded, Beria counselled shooting the planes down, on the ground that they were simply a screen spying out plants for an atomic attack. Stalin himself believed with repentant economist Varga that American capitalism had reached so critical a point that only through forcible gifts overseas could the Wall Street ruling clique hope to maintain its profits and dominance. Coupled with these divisions of opinion, which stalemated action, was the fear in some quarters that America might welcome attacks on its errand-of-mercy planes as a pretext for the war of extermination openly preached by some only mildly rebuked American leaders.

At any rate, the confusion in the Politburo was more than mirrored by the confusion in the target cities caused by the baptismal raids. Over 600 C-54s streamed high over Rostov, and another 200 over Vladivostok, dropped their cargoes, and headed back to their bases in the Middle East and Japan. By today's standard these initial

forays were small-scale—200,000 pairs of nylon hose, 4,000,000 packs
of cigarettes, 35,000 Toni-wave kits, 20,000 yo-yos, 10,000 wrist
watches, and a number of odds and ends from P-X overstock. Yet
this was more than enough to provoke frenzied rioting as the inhabitants scrambled for a share. Within a few hours after the first parcels
had fallen, the roads into the target cities were jammed. Road blocks
had to be thrown up around the cities, and communications with the
outside were severed. The fast-spreading rumors of largess from above
were branded 'criminally insane,' and their source traced to machinations of the recently purged 'homeless cosmopolitan Simeon Osna-
vitch (Rosenblum).'

    But the propaganda of the deed proved stronger than the propa-
ganda of the word. As Odessa, Yakutsk, Smolensk, and other cities became targets of aggressive generosity, as Soviet housewives saw with
their own eyes American stoves, refrigerators, clothing, and toys, the
Kremlin was forced to change its line and, ignoring earlier denials,
to give the raids full but negative publicity. David Zaslavsky's article
in the June 10 *Izvestia* heralded the new approach. Entitled 'The Mad
Dogs of Imperialism Foam at the Mouth,' he saw the airlift as har-
binger of America's economic collapse. 'Unable because of the valiant
resistance of the peace-loving democracies to conquer foreign markets,
America's Fascist plutocracy is now reduced to giving away goods. . . .'
Taking another line, *Red Star* argued that to accept American consumer goods would make stalwart Russians as decadent as rich New
Yorkers.

    However, the Russian people who could get access, either directly
or through the black market that soon arose, to American goods
seemed not to fear decadence. Again, there was a change of line. Falling back on a trick learned during Lend-Lease, it was claimed that
the goods were Russian-made, and *Pravda* on June 14 stated that the
Toni-wave kit had been invented by Pavlov before World War I.
However, Colonel Y's staff had anticipated this altogether routine
reaction. On June 17, the target cities of that day—Kiev, Stalingrad,
Magnitogorsk—received their wares wrapped in large cartoons of
Stalin bending over, in a somewhat undignified pose, to pick up a
dropped Ansco camera. This forced still another switch of line. On
June 20 Beria went on the air to announce that the Americans were
sending over goods poisoned by atomic radiation, and all papers and
broadcasts carried scare stories about people who had died from using
Revlon or Schick shavers. And indeed booby traps (planted by MVD)
succeeded in killing a number of overeager citizens. For a while, this
permitted specially-recruited Party members to gather up the goods
and take them to headquarters for alleged de-radiation.

But here something unexpected occurred. We know from a few people who managed to escape to the West that a number of Party elements themselves became disaffected. Asked to turn in all American goods, they held on to some possessions secretly—there was a brisk underground trade in fake Russian labels. Sometimes wives, having gotten used to the comforts of Tampax and other disappearing items, would hide them from their more ascetic husbands; children of Party members cached pogo sticks and even tricycles. Thus it came about that when Party members were ordered to join 'decontamination' squads the depots were re-entered at night and portable items taken. By the beginning of July, all attempts to deceive the people had only made matters worse; things were getting out of hand.

Faring badly in the 'War,' the Kremlin turned to diplomacy. On July 5 at Lake Success Malik described the airlift as 'an outrage remindful of Hitlerite aggression' and, invoking Art. 39 of the U.N. Charter, he called on the Security Council to halt the 'shameful depredations of the American warmongers.' Austin replied that 'these gifts are no more or less than a new-fashioned application of ancient principles,' and the Russian resolution was defeated, 9-2. The next step occurred in Washington, when Ambassador Panyushkin handed Secretary Acheson a sharply worded note warning that 'should these present outrages continue, the U.S.S.R. will have no recourse but to reply in kind.'

Seattle was the first American city to learn the meaning of the Soviet warning as on July 15 a hundred Russian heavy bombers (presumably from bases in the Kuriles) left behind them 15,000 tins of caviar, 500 fur coats, and 80,000 copies of Stalin's speeches on the minorities question. When the Russian planes came, followed in by American jets, many were apprehensive, but as the counter-attack had been anticipated it proved possible to prevent incidents in the air and panic on the ground. Since then, Butte, Minneapolis, Buffalo, and Moscow, Idaho, have been added to the list of America's frontline cities. But in quantity and quality the counter-offensive has been unimpressive. Searing vodka, badly styled mink coats (the only really selling item), undependable cigarette lighters—these betray a sad lack of know-how in production and merchandising. In an editorial, 'Worse than Lend-Lease,' the N.Y. *Daily News* has charged that the Nylon War gives the Soviets free lessons in the secrets of America's success, but truly conservative papers like the *Herald-Tribune* see the comparative showing of Americans and Russians as a world demonstration of the superiority of free enterprise.

It is clear, at any rate, that free enterprise has not suffered much of a jolt—nor, indeed, has the mounting inflation been much reduced—

by the Russian campaign. To be sure, the massive air-borne shipments of caviar have made luxury grocers fear inventory losses and Portugal, heavily dependent on the American anchovy market, has been worried. But these pin-pricks are nothing to what is now becoming evident on the Russian side—namely the imminent collapse of the economy. For the homeland of centralized economic planning is experiencing its own form of want in the midst of plenty. Soviet consumers, given a free choice between shoddy domestic merchandise and airlift items, want nothing to do with the former and in a score of fields Russian goods go unwanted as the potential buyer dreams of soon owning an American version. Soviet housewives, eager to keep up with American-supplied 'Joneses,' pester their local stores, often to the point of creating local shortages—indeed, the American refrigerators have created demands, not only for electricity, but also for many foods which can now be stored (and hoarded).

Much of this disruption is the result of careful planning by the Bar Harbor Project's Division of Economic Dislocation. The Division, for example, early began studies of Russian power distribution, and saw to the landing of 60-cycle radios, shavers, toasters, milking machines, in 60-cycle areas; 25-cycle appliances in 25-cycle areas, and so on, especially with an eye to areas of power-shortage or competition with critical industries. In cooperation with G.E., methods were worked out by which the Russian donees could plug their appliances, with appropriate transformers, directly into high-voltage or street power lines; thus simply shutting off house current could not save the Russian utilities from overload. Similarly, drawing on the American monopolistic practice of tie-in sales, goods were dropped whose use demanded other items in short supply—oil ranges, for instance, were dropped throughout the Baku fields. Of course, mistakes were made and in one or two cases bottlenecks in the Russian economy were relieved, as when some containers were salvaged to repair a tin shortage of which the planners had not been advised.

But it is not only on the production end that the raids have been disruptive. Last Friday's raid on Moscow—when 22,000 tons of goods were dropped—may be taken as an illustration. For the first time General Vandenburg's airmen tackled—and successfully solved—the knotty engineering problem of dropping jeeps (complete with 150 gallons of gasoline and directions in simple Russian). So skillfully was the job done that half the three hundred vehicles parachuted down landed directly on the Kremlin's doorstep—in the center of Red Square. The raid was given wide advance publicity through the Voice and leaflets and when the great day came Moscow's factories were deserted as people fought for roof-top perches; in addition, an estimated

250,000 collective farmers swarmed into the city. In fact, as people drift from place to place hoping that their ship may fly in, the phrase 'rootless cosmopolite' at last assumes real meaning. Economists, talking learnedly of 'multipliers,' calculate that Russian output is dropping 3 per cent a month.

The Kremlin has reacted in the only way it knows, by a series of purges. Sergei Churnik, erstwhile head of the cigarette trust, is on trial for 'deliberate wrecking and economic treason.' Bureaucrats live in terror lest their region or their industry be next disrupted by the American bombardment, and they waver between inactivity and frantic Stakhanovite shows of activity. These human tragedies testify to the growing fear in the Politburo concerning the long-run consequences of the American offensive. The tangible proofs of American prosperity, ingenuity, and generosity can no longer be gainsaid; and the new official line that Wall Street is bleeding America white in order to create scarcity and raise prices at home, while 'believed,' has little impact against the ever-mounting volume, and fascinating variety, of goods and rumors of goods. Can the capitalistic gluttons of privilege be such bad fellows if we, the Russians, are aided by them to enjoy luxuries previously reserved for the dachas of novelists and plant managers? In an article in the *New Statesman and Nation,* Geoffrey Gorer has recently contended that the airlift serves to revive primitive Russian 'orality,' and that the image of America can no longer be that of a leering Uncle Sam or top-hatted banker but must soon become amiably matronly. It is thoughts along this line that most worry the Politburo although, of course, the MVD sees to it that only a tiny fraction of the mounting skepticism expresses itself openly or even in whispered jokes. But what is the MVD to do about a resolution of the All-Workers Congress of Tiflis that 'Marxist-Leninist-Stalinist democracy demands that party cadres install officials who can cope with the mounting crisis'?

Translated into plain talk, this means that the Russian people, without saying so in as many words, are now putting a price on their collaboration with the regime. The price—'goods instead of guns.' For Russia's industrial plant, harassed by the rapidly growing impact of Operation Abundance, cannot supply both, let alone carry on the counter-offensive against America. Intelligence reports speak of scheduled production cutbacks varying from 25 per cent on tanks to 75 per cent on artillery; it is symptomatic that washing machines, designed to compete with the American Bendixes which are being dropped in ever-increasing numbers, will soon start rolling off the assembly lines of the great Red October Tank Works—after its former manager had been shot for asserting that conversion to peacetime production could not be achieved in less than two years.

Meanwhile, diplomatic moves are under way—so, at least, the Alsop brothers report—to liquidate the Nylon War. It is obvious why the Russian leaders are prepared to make very considerable concessions in the satellite countries, in China, and in Indo-China in order to regain the strategic initiative in their domestic affairs. But on the American side the willingness of many to listen to Russian overtures is based on the success, rather than the failure, of the campaign. One sees a repetition of 1940 as the Washington *Times-Herald* and the *Daily Compass* join hands in attacking Operation Abundance, the former calling it 'an international WPA,' the latter arguing 'you can't fight ideas with goods.' Addressing the Stanford Alumni Club of Los Angeles, Herbert Hoover spoke for millions in observing that the monthly cost of the airlift has already exceeded the entire Federal budget for the year 1839. Still another tack has been taken by Senators who want the airlift to continue, but with different targets; some, insisting that charity begins at home, have wanted free goods landed on their districts; others have supported the claims of Japan, the Philippines, or Franco. Still others fear that many of the air lift items could be reconverted in some way for use by the Russian war machine; they are especially opposed to the jeep delivery program, despite reports it is wreaking havoc with the Russian road system as well as with the gasoline supply. And the House Un-American Affairs Committee has charged that trade secrets are being delivered to Russian spies by Red homosexual officials and professors disguised as plane pilots.

These are the obvious enemies, and against them stand some obvious friends of the Nylon War. Both AFL and CIO, now in their eighth round of wage increases, vigorously support the program, though it is rumored that the Railroad Brotherhoods have done so only in return for a fact-finding board's support of a 14-hour week. Farmers have become reconciled by the promise that bulk agricultural products will soon move over the aerial transmission belt—in part to encourage the wanderings of Russian farmers. The business community is divided, with the CED, Juan Trippe, and Baruch leading the supporters of the airlift.[1] But it would be a mistake to assume

---

1. It goes without saying that there are many fights within pressure groups as to *what* the airlift shall carry—and ideological considerations are not confined to the Soviet side. Thus, the Committee Against Juvenile Delinquency has registered strong protests against sending comic books. More serious issues revolve around the Planned Parenthood League's campaign to get contraceptives included in the airlift items. In addition to humanitarian arguments, the claim is made

that support of Operation Abundance springs only from hopes of material gain. The renewed fight against oppression and want, the excitement of following the raids in maps and betting pools, the ridiculousness of the Russian response—all these things have made many millions of Americans less anxious than they have been since the days in October 1950 when it seemed as if the Korean War would be quickly concluded.

Indeed, it is just this loss of tension which has given rise to much of the covert opposition to the Nylon War, as distinguished from the overt opposition already discussed. On the one hand, certain leaders are frightened that the Russian dictatorship may indeed be overthrown —as Colonel Y in his more optimistic moments had ventured to hope. This is thought to raise the possibility of all sorts of chaotic movements developing in Central and Eastern Europe, and even further west—Franco, for instance, feels threatened at the loss of his 'enemy,' and has offered to act as mediator in the Nylon War. On the other hand, it has become increasingly difficult for American politicians to frighten the American public about Russia: the once-feared monolith now appears as almost a joke, with its crude poster-and-caviar reprisals, its riots over stockings, soap, Ronsons, and other gadgets which Americans regard in matter-of-fact fashion. The sharp drop in war sentiment in the United States has resulted in psychological and even actual unemployment for a number of people.

What do the coming months hold? It is significant that this depends almost entirely on the outcome of the American domestic struggle: the Nylon War has altered the whole power-complex which, as the Korean War dragged on, still heavily favored Russia. It is now Russia, not America, whose resources are overcommitted, whose alliances are overstrained. In fact, Mao's visit to Moscow at the end of July seems to have been attended with apprehension lest he ask America to cut Red China in on Operation Abundance—at a price, of course. The possibility that this may redound to the credit of the Truman Administration in the 1952 campaign is not the least of the nightmares haunting many Americans, and at this writing it is impossible to predict whether the opponents of the program will win out.

Meanwhile, Operation Abundance marches on, solving technical problems of incredible complexity. The latest move is the perfection of an ordering system whereby Russians can 'vote' for the commodities they most want, according to a point system, by the use of radio-

that this will reverse the demographic trend now so favorable to Russia; the League's slogan is 'Give them the tools and they will do the job.' Walter Lippmann predicts a Rome-Moscow axis if the League should win out.

sending equipment, battery-run, with which we have provided them. The commodities available will be described over the Voice of America—now for the first time having something to 'sell'—by Sears Roebuck-type catalogues, and by dropped samples in the case of soft goods. The method making it impossible for the Russian government effectively to jam this two-way communication of distributor and consumer is still the great secret of the Nylon War.

VIII.

PROBLEMS OF METHOD IN THE SOCIAL SCIENCES

HOW OFTEN have I not sat with a group of lawyers and heard one of them say, "Of course, I know nothing about it, but . . ." The lawyer's feeling that he could master anything in a pre-trial two weeks, that there is no expertise but his own, is often arrogant and Philistine, and I used frequently to have to argue with my brethren of the bar that neither economics nor anthropology could be so easily encompassed. However, I suppose I did gain from my professional experience some of this confidence—for Justice Brandeis I became an "expert" in the making and shipping of berry boxes in one short spell, and in freight-rate making in another; for Lyne, Woodworth & Evarts, I learned how to cross-examine heart specialists in insurance cases, and learned something of paper-making for the reorganization of International Paper & Power. But it was not only the occupational mystiques of other people that I was encouraged to deflate, but of my own profession: the essay herein on "Law and the Legal Profession" represents my long-held belief that social scientists and other laymen stand too much in awe of the law, that its method of casuistry, its bibliographic techniques, and so on, don't take three years to learn. (I still have to find a profession, including medicine, that doesn't inflate its claims to the neophyte to some degree.)

At the same time, I know that in my writings on social science, I have often suffered from not studying under the guardian angels who would have kept me from treading where they rightly fear to; reading over my first forays into social science, made while I was still teaching law, I am in places abashed at my unwitting temerity. If the temerity survives in pieces written much later, at least it is witting; thus when I write now about the study of national character I know from long stewing that the term "character" in this context is filled with ambiguities, and that I have no satisfactory answer to problems with which writers I respect have struggled long before my time.

The article on the legal profession exhibits such temerity in the freedom with which it draws on my own exceedingly limited opportunities to observe lawyers; it is rather a program for field studies of the practicing bar than a formal statement of research results—my own or others'. It was first presented, at the invitation of Robert Redfield, a lawyer turned anthropologist, to the introductory graduate course on "Culture, Society, and the Individual" at the University of Chicago, in 1947. In the following two years, while I was at Yale, I sought to introduce a group of law students to the study of their own profession, encouraging them to use summer vacations to interview members of the bar in their home towns. Many of these students lacked confidence that they, untrained in social science techniques, could actually do interviews—perhaps they had not yet gained the confidence of the lawyer I dwelt on a moment ago. They found, however, that they could use a questionnaire on the basis of very inadequate briefing sessions I gave them; their project broke down less, I suspect, because of technical difficulties than because many of the faculty and students at the Yale Law School were more eager to use social science to prove something about the virtues or vices of juries, bar associations, or other polemicized themes than out of curiosity about the daily work and mythology of the practicing bar— curiosity not aiming to pin anything on anybody.

These experiences were in my mind when I revised my 1947 lecture for the 1950 annual meeting of the Association of American Law Schools. One of the commentators on the latter occasion was Professor Everett C. Hughes, from whose recurrent Chicago seminars on occupations and professions I have learned much of what value there may be in this article. In introducing the version of my talk which appeared in the *Chicago Law Review* (also drawn upon for the composite article here presented), he stated:

"Sponsorship in medicine is certainly strong, and there are those who say it is important in the academic career. American culture has stressed individual effort and ability, but never to the exclusion of family, class, religious and ethnic affiliations. We have had a kind of mixture of nepotism with insistence on delivering the goods. It may be that the law, or certain branches of it, demands abilities less amenable to social inheritance than those which make people company presidents. . . ."

Such considerations led me to draw on my own recollection of *Harvard Law Review* days, and on intermittent observation of other law reviews since, for rather hypothetical suggestions as to the role of the reviews—a unique student institution—in breaking down ethnic and class barriers in much the same way the Army has done: by putting people of different breeds on the same firing line, subject to Authority (the brass in the one case, the Law in the other), and forcing them to spend most waking hours in each other's company. But of course this would only apply to law reviews which, like the major ones, use some impersonal method of selection; and all this rests on the fact that law schools themselves, being cheap to run and even highly profitable, do not ordinarily if ever discriminate in their admissions policy. There are some 60 law reviews in the country, and very likely the pattern which I here suggest is not omnipresent—what are the patterns would be one of the topics for an anthropological or sociological study of the profession, as well as a basis for comparison and contrast with other professions.

This article, like the one on the recreationist in a previous section, might perhaps have been placed in a section on professions. However, it is apposite to a section on method because it is so largely concerned with the ways in which social scientists are drawn to certain fields of study and are repelled by others, such as the law. I suggest why there have been so few studies of lawyers and law, and what some of the theoretical rewards of such studies might be—but I would hate to see this suggestion taken as one more agenda for my fellow scientists. I believe strongly with Michael Polanyi that scientists are their own best planners, once they are in communication through print and congress and know what others are in general doing. Not very much of benefit to a field can be done by laying out programs; more can be achieved by providing a model which stimulates one's colleagues in a variety of ways and even produces new colleagues by making the field seem worthwhile and challenging to undergraduates. At best, my article is meant to suggest that the law is not so forbidding an area for social scientists to enter as it may appear; my remarks are intended as liberation rather than exhortation.

And the same is true of "Some Observations on Social Science Research," which treats some of these general themes as part of an effort to appraise the current state of affairs in sociology and social psychology. I decided to write this piece after I had heard a graduate student report in a seminar on a revolutionary plot he had had the good fortune to witness during World War II; he was miserable because he could not fit what he had seen into Max Weber's theory of charisma. It had not occurred to him that the theory, a very ambitious one, might not be the best way of approaching his particular problem; it had only occurred to him that he must be a very poor sociologist. And his doubts actually served to interfere with his report of incidents where precise observation would have been invaluable to a later Max Weber. This student was a casualty of current sociological polemics, and my article was aimed to clarify his and like situations.

In general, factors of spirit and stance have a great deal to do with what a social scientist feels prepared to study. When the Carnegie Corporation gave the Committee on Human Development a grant for the study of old age in a community, the question whether the community should be Chicago, a small town, or what, immediately involved such considerations of attitude. Chicago itself, despite apparent accessibility, was ruled out because it appeared too big, too unencompassable, too amorphous; we did not feel ready for it. Bravely we ruled out smaller cities—Peoria, Racine, South Bend, Decatur, and others for which we did feel more or less ready. Hearing of our search, an alert group in Kansas City invited us there, and, despite the distance, we accepted the challenge of a city far larger than the Muncies and Newburyports that have been studied, if smaller than such a megalopolis as Chicago.

In the study of aging, our difficulties are hardly less. Aging is almost as large a topic as life itself. There has been some good medical and physiological work but, despite the current vogue of geriatrics, little effective conceptualization in terms of social-psychological factors. In our Kansas City research, we decided to interview only those people who were over 40—though of course we realize that aging, like dying, begins much earlier. But this gives us a spread from 40 to 80 and up: a variety of contexts of obviously enormous range.

"Some Clinical and Cultural Aspects of the Aging Process" is drawn from a memorandum in which I sought to grapple with this issue. Since it was written, our Kansas City staff has been doing many interviews seeking to sharpen the criteria for aging as these can be applied to an interview, but we still feel we are a long way from delineating ideas that can be quantified, or that are especially applicable to our community rather than to aging in America as such.

I have included sections of two articles, "The Meaning of Opinion" and "Social Structure, Character Structure, and Opinion," jointly written with Nathan Glazer. The first of these articles was written before the 1948 election and published soon thereafter, with some afterthoughts on the Truman upset. It was an outgrowth of our curiosity concerning the ways in which public opinion pollers handled the "don't know" vote—the person who claims to have no opinion in areas where most respondents in America do have opinions. We saw this "vote" as one possible avenue for exploring the cross-cultural forms of opinion-formation and opinion delivery both among social classes in the United States and among different countries with different traditions of rapport and privacy—countries, for instance, in which conscientious women, aggressive enough to get in a door and polite and pleasant enough to stay safely there, may not be readily available. The second article (which I have telescoped into the first) was a somewhat more technical report of our own program for analyzing interviews, included as part of a post-election post-mortem on the polls in the now-defunct *International Journal of Opinion and Attitude Research.*

These articles indicate my view that social science is not soon likely to have available to it the great talents necessary to fulfill its present ambitions. Even if a society which had time and money and personnel enough for all the demands of social science might be attainable, I am not sure it would be wise to draw too many away from physics or business or psychiatry into sociology or social psychology! What does make sense is to make use of amateur and part-time observers; indeed, national surveys and many other projects could not get along without them. In several of the essays in this volume—in the one on movies and the one on social science research —I deal with the potentialities of "mass observation" as a resource for research, when for instance one wants to monitor TV throughout the country or observe movie audiences or parades or other non-recurring phenomena. But such observation is also important for the individuals who do it, for whom it can be a way both of contributing to science and to their own adeptness as observers. Thus, undergraduate students whom I have encouraged to do interviews, even though they did not intend to become professional sociologists, have not infrequently learned new confidence in approaching people, new awareness of the nuances of conversation, as well as enhanced appreciation of the complexities and even treacheries of the data out of which generalizations about human behavior are developed.

27. Toward an Anthropological Science of Law and the Legal Profession

Examination of the barriers to the study of law and lawyers in the United States helps at least make a beginning, depressing as it may seem, in the direction of an anthropological science. Among other things, by seeing what we are up against, we may prevent the disillusionment which is bound to set in (perhaps has set in) because so little has actually been accomplished by the realist movement in American jurisprudence.[1] Many times, programs and exhortations have driven law professors and their social science allies into the breach between them, but no junction has been provided for the American culture comparable to the brilliant pioneering work on preliterate culture by Llewellyn and Hoebel in *The Cheyenne Way*.[2]

§ I

Let us look first at the obstacles from the side of the lawyer who wants to take an anthropological look at himself and his role. He has been trained to move within a terminological system of abstractions which are (as Roscoe Pound has pointed out in his comments on the "ideal" or "normative" element) necessarily self-contained.[3] True, many lawers of recent years have moved away from abstraction toward a greater semantic hygiene. But law, however they define it, remains ethnocentric in the fundamental sense that it is the "law" of a particular jurisdiction, or bench, or board of officials. This ethnocentrism appears in many ways, among them the tendency to exaggerate the differences and underplay the similarities in the legal systems of Western society. Thus lawyers are brought up on dichoto-

---

1. Little, that is, in the domain of research; the realist movement has had a considerable influence on teaching and on actual practice and case law.

2. Karl N. Llewellyn and E. Adamson Hoebel, *The Cheyenne Way*.

3. A. R. Radcliffe-Brown (*Encyclopaedia of the Social Sciences*, pp. 531-34) points out: "If you examine the literature on jurisprudence you will find that legal institutions are studied for the most part in more or less complete abstraction from the rest of the social system of which they are a part." And he adds: "The system of laws of a particular society can only be fully understood if it is studied in relation to the social structure, and inversely the understanding of the social structure requires, amongst other things, a systematic study of the legal institutions."

mies between common and civil law: one is supposedly judge-made, the other statute-made—or one is supposed to rely on precedent, the other to disregard it. Such teaching may lead the lawyer to overlook the possibility that the use of precedent is not merely a legal game played in America and not in France, but is actually a human characteristic to be looked for everywhere.[4] (Pound's distinction between "Cadi justice" and "Western justice" also deprecates this possibility.)

If there is a touch of snobbery in the lawyer's trained ethnocentrism, there appears to be more than a touch in his focus on appellate litigation as the classical road to legal education. The rituals of the upper-court "opinion industry" are overt and impressive, and law students sometimes fail to observe that upper courts edit the "script" provided them by lower courts, much as a Hollywood producer edits his scriptwriters, in order to feel important and because institutional pressures compel him to assume this function and to give it weight in action. (Tammany has always known this and, one suspects, has made a tacit deal with the leaders of the bar to toss them the New York Court of Appeals, where the prestige lies, while holding on to the lower courts, where the money lies.)

To be sure, most lawyers today recognize that their most important work is done in the office, not in the courtroom; the elaborate masked ritual of the courtroom holds attraction only for the neophyte and the layman. Yet it is astonishing how strongly the image of the judge stands as the image of the lawyer-hero. While at the better law schools at least one and often nearly three years are spent in debunking upper-court opinions, in showing their largely derivative quality, their endless fallacies, their interminable self-confusion as to what they are "actually" deciding (as against what they *say* they are deciding), the better products of the better law schools want nothing more exciting when they get out than a chance to serve as clerk [as I did] to an appellate judge—the "upperer" the better. And as members of the bar they will move heaven and earth to get on the bench themselves (which is the source of much dirt in our political system, since many congressmen have partners who itch to be judges), although they know from practical experience how little power the judge has under the American system and how skilled lawyers are in emasculating that little.

---

4. Interesting light might be shed on this question by studying the adaptation to the United States of the refugee lawyers whom Hitler drove here. One surmises that they could draw on their European experience and therefore adapt most readily if they possessed an anthropological turn of mind and were inclined to look for institutional similarities under obvious—and often emotionally disturbing and distracting—differences; whereas they could not adapt if they capitulated too readily to the proposition that adaptation had to be a total, all-or-none process.

Why this is so would be a study in itself. We would have to find out why Holmes and Brandeis have been inflated to mythical proportions and have captured the imagination of the young law student, who is unlikely even to know the names of the brilliantly daring and inventive corporate and governmental lawyers who helped build our modern industrial society and its governmental stimuli and curbs. We would have to find out what there is in law practice, even in the most refined offices, which is felt as dirty work, from which the bench is an escape. We would have to find out whether the judge becomes an ideal before law school or in law school (certainly the federal circuit courts have a great attraction for law deans and professors!)—an ideal which later experience does little to influence.[5] And so on.

Moreover, we would have to draw class, ethnic, and regional distinctions in the image and appeal of the various levels of the judiciary. As Kentucky has its "colonels," so it, and the South generally, has its "judges": men of good family who represent the law as a scholarly, humanistic occupation and who, as R. L. Birdwhistell puts it, regard judgeships as their "natural right" by inheritance and early jurisprudential bent. In the big cities, on the other hand, judgeships become part of the system of ethnic brokerage by which the party machines keep the urban peace—the rise of the Italian judge is a recent illustration. Plainly, considerations of class and ethnic status influence the symbolic appeals of the robe to the profession and its lay audiences. Furthermore, is it not likely that, with the growth of concern for security as against risk, and for "plateau" positions as against achievement peaks, the judgeship, with its long tenure (even under elective systems) and fixed salary—and, save in rare cases, short hours—is preferred even to the most creative tasks in private practice?

The fact that law schools today spend their time in impious treatment of cases—this is what the "case method" means—is of course a tribute to the generations of lawyers who, especially since the time of Bentham, have reacted against the mystique of the law and have

---

5. It is not surprising that the public at large shares the lawyer's reverence for the judge: United States Supreme Court judges rated highest (doctors next) on a poll of occupation prestige, and the Supreme Court decision on racial covenants served to overawe a bunch of white Chicago hoodlums who had not been impressed by any other form of pro-tolerance propaganda. The hoodlums, indeed, are not so wrong. For, whether in general the judicial power is shadow rather than substance, there can be no doubt that in the field of Negro-white relations the Supreme Court has exerted enormous leverage, from *Dred Scott* to the *Civil Rights* cases to the latest decisions on segregation in education and transport.

sought to ridicule its fictions and ceremonies. Bentham did so under the banner of rationality: he wanted the law to make sense. The new-style debunkers, of whom Thurman Arnold is one of the most gifted,[6] are less sanguine about reason: indeed, they often come close to glory-ing in the claimed irrationality of legal myths, symbols, and rituals. This aspect of their work may be thought of as part of the general tendency of intellectuals to decry intellectuality wherever it appears to be overrationalistic while regarding more or less romantically those uneducated folk who are supposed to have not only more fun but also more common sense. This anti-snobbery is very clear in the writings of Judge Jerome Frank, who not only wants to elevate the study of lower courts to a position of academic respectability but attacks as snobbish and overintellectual antiquarians those who con-tinue to study upper-court verbalisms.[7]

Yet these contemporary legal critics of the law are not only amused by legal rigmarole and nonsense; under their wit they have hidden their anger at legal injustice, stupidity, and waste. While they may talk, as Veblen also did,[8] as detached observers, they are moti-vated by a profound concern for social policy, for the beneficent use of law in the public interest, and in this they remain the heirs of Bentham.

Yet this countermovement (which has captured the law school avant-garde) has had little concrete consequence in studies of legal process in America. A too immediate concern for public policy is perhaps one reason for this, for it tends to take away the curiosity and the patience of the observer: he is likely to assume that he has done his job if he has proved that a legal device is a myth or a fiction or a rationalization—though this does not even prove that it is irrational. The guilt of the more sensitive lawyers over the abuses and wastes of their profession—as these are seen in the Benthamite and the Veblenite view—may be one element in this preoccupation with "getting the goods on" the upper courts, the corporate bar, the bar associations (other than the Lawyers' Guild), as the case may be. Such guilt may even conceal a grandiose notion that the lawyers have a vocation, a "calling," to change the face of America.[9] In that case,

6. *The Folklore of Capitalism.* See also Fred Rodell, *Woe unto Ye Lawyers.*
7. E.g., in *Courts on Trial.*
8. Thorstein Veblen's chapter on the law in *Absentee Ownership,* pp. 40-68, is still a very stimulating classic.
9. Lasswell and McDougal's justly famed article on legal education, "Legal Education and Public Policy," *Yale Law Journal,* LII (1943), 203-95, suffers from such grandiose aims, which is perhaps one reason why it still stands as a huge land grant for research which has not yet found its occupants of quarter-sections, at least so far as I know. My own article, "Law and Social Science" (*Yale Law Journal,* L [1941], 636-53), suffers from the same high hopes.

guilt can become a vested interest which is hostile to research, even while it appears to invite it.

§ II

IF, WITH THIS ALL TOO BRIEF COMMENT, we turn now away from the legal profession and ask why the other social sciences have not, on their side, done more with the law, we find that some of the same explanations hold. Sociologists, for instance, have until quite recently been as much concerned with immediate social reform as their brethren of the bar; thus, they have looked at the law only where it impinged on the disadvantaged groups in society—on the criminal, the juvenile delinquent, the poverty-stricken seeker of divorce, etc. Like the criminologists still railing at the M'Naghten rule,[10] they view the law as unjust as well as irrational; their aim is to show up, perhaps to change, the law and the legal mentality rather than to understand it sympathetically. Furthermore, the sociologists who are theoretically inclined have concerned themselves with formal definitions of law (e.g., M. Georges Gurvitch) and with the problem of the origins of law—both perfectly valid enterprises but not good ways to bring the sociologist into actual contact with the legal profession as a going concern.

Meanwhile, anthropologists have been merrily analyzing some of the functions of law in preliterate societies—Sir Henry Maine's classic work may indeed be thought of as some sort of bridge between the study of legal origins and of functions. Malinowski, Hogben, Redfield,[11] and Llewellyn and Hoebel have tried, in Radcliffe-Brown's sense, to view primitive law in the setting of primitive social structure. They have not denounced legal myth and symbolism; rather, they have tried to see its function, sometimes with the admiration of one craftsman for the craft of another. Since they could approach primitive law with some knowledge of law in Western society, they needed no Rosetta stone to translate the symbolism which they found.

As soon as the search for origins lost its high priority, moreover, this anthropological enterprise could readily shed the ethnocentrism and snobbery which we have seen to be barriers on the side of the lawyer's study of law in our own culture; cross-cultural uniformities

10. Neither George Dession's paper, "Psychiatry and the Conditioning of Criminal Justice," *Yale Law Journal*, XLVII (1938), 319-40, nor the casebook of Jerome Michael and Herbert Wechsler, *Criminal Law and Its Administration: Cases, Statutes and Commentaries*, each with a very sophisticated approach, seems to have put an end to this sterile attack and counterattack between lawyers on one side and criminologists and psychologists on the other.

11. See, e.g., Robert Redfield, "Maine's *Ancient Law* in the Light of Primitive Societies," *Western Political Quarterly*, III (1950), 574-89.

as well as curious diversities could be looked for readily enough. By the same token, the anthropologist could be quite as interested in the law of a small group, lacking in political power, as in the law of a national state or "big power," and this very interest in what was intrinsically significant saved him from the frequent sterility of the "public policy" approach, which begins with what some other people (the officialdom, the liberals, the elite, etc.) think to be important in our own society, which is usually something pretty sizable in scope. Furthermore, the anthropologist's bias vis-à-vis institutions has in the past tended to be very different from the sociologist's: whereas the latter sees institutions as "vested," as restrictive, the former sees them (as united in the concept of culture) as fundamentally channeling and hence permissive. This leads the anthropologist to look for the channeling aspects of the law as well as the litigious and punitive ones —a point of view which, in Llewellyn's case, has governed his approach to American law as much as to Cheyenne law.[12] (Of course, this distinction between sociological and anthropological slants is rapidly breaking down; and elsewhere in this paper "anthropological," "sociological," and "social-psychological" are used as virtually interchangeable terms.)

Perhaps most important of all, the anthropologist is not likely to harbor the naïve assumption that the law, or any other institution, serves only a single function—say, that of social control—and that any other functions which in fact it serves are excrescences or "contradictions." The concept of ambivalence is part of his equipment; he tends to search for latent functions, transcending the ostensible.[13]

Yet despite this equipment and experience with primitive law, the anthropologist has still not turned back to American law with the *élan* he has shown in studying such other American institutions as the movies, child-rearing, and social class. My impression is that social scientists somehow believe that, since it takes three years to get through law school, law itself must be impermeable to them without long and arduous preparation. Many are willing enough to grant verbally with Thurman Arnold that the law is a set of irrational mystifications; but they feel nevertheless that the trained lawyer must "have something" that they could not possibly acquire in short compass. Men who are prepared, before going into the field, to learn a primitive language seem unready to tackle the hardly more difficult

12. See, e.g., Karl N. Llewellyn, "The American Common Law Tradition and American Democracy," *Journal of Legal and Political Sociology,* I (1942), 14-46.
13. Cf. Camilla Wedgewood, "The Nature and Functions of Secret Societies," *Oceania,* I (1930-31), 129-45, and the work of Robert K. Merton on manifest and latent functions in *Social Theory and Social Structure.*

semantics of American law. One of the few social scientists who has not been impressed, the psychologist Robinson, tried to explain matters as follows:

> The lawyers are a priesthood with a prestige to maintain. They must have a set of doctrines that do not threaten to melt away with the advances of psychological and social science. . . . They must, in order to feel socially secure, believe and convince the outside world that they have peculiar techniques requiring long study to master. In a way they have overplayed this card. Even laymen are coming to see that if The Law were as difficult to understand as the profession implies, nobody would ever be able to become a lawyer.[14]

What is the blockage which prevents other social scientists from doing what Robinson did? It seems to me that there *is* an irrational blockage, much like that among people who feel that they cannot handle simple mathematics or statistics—and so "prove" to themselves that they cannot. It is easy enough to see Robinson's point that the legal profession has an obscurantist interest at stake, but it is less easy to see why the social scientist falls for this. Has he at stake some self-image which his legal competence would threaten, in the same way that the girl who cannot read timetables believes her femininity at stake? I do not know the answer, but the blockage itself is a matter one can observe often enough—and not among social scientists only. Consider the manufacturer of soft drinks, a small businessman, who feels no awe of his chemist at all—there is no magic there for him—but who stands in terrible awe of his lawyer. Or the social scientists who, aware enough of specialization in their own fields, try to get free legal advice from a colleague with legal training about landlord and tenant law, divorces, wills, copyrights—even assault and battery! They assume, though they know he may not have practiced law for ten years, that he has some magic formula for them at his fingertips; moreover that there *is* a formula. They are astonished to find that he, as a lawyer, is much more casual about legal matters than they; that he goes on the principle (so often pointed out by Judge Frank) that the law in any given case is uncertain. In spite of their skepticism, they are surprised, for at bottom they believe in the certainty and majesty

---

14. E. S. Robinson, *Law and the Lawyers* (New York: Macmillan Co., 1935), p. 28. It would require a great deal of discussion to try to explain the one apparent exception to this, namely the group of political scientists who study and teach "public law." Many of these men treat Supreme Court cases with a reverence (even when they criticize them) that few lawyers would maintain; they are likely to be more literal than lawyers, for they have missed the three years of case-law debunking—training whose result is that the lawyer takes law less seriously than the typical educated layman. These teachers of public law do, however, share with law teachers the belief that cases on "public policy" are prima facie important.

of the law. But, again, this describes their attitude; it does not explain it.

Nor does it explain it to point to the over-reaction of many social scientists who, convinced that they cannot penetrate the opacity of the law, declare that there is nothing really there to be understood. The doctrine of Sumner and his followers that man-made law and legislation have minimal power to alter folkways and mores has influenced not only those who aver that law is fundamentally irrational but also those who aver that it is, if not wholly irrelevant, at best a cultural lag—or, in Marxist terms, an ideological superstructure. (An attitude basically not very different is to be found among those law teachers who see "the balancing of interests" as the formula of legal intervention and do not allow the law at any point a crucially innovating role—that is, they do not see law as an "interest" in its own right.) Despite the work of Max Weber, and, even more, his hints concerning the role of law in the development of Western "rationalization"; despite such a book as Commons' *The Legal Foundations of Capitalism*;[15] despite many other things which could be cited, the social scientists of this stamp believe that law is fundamentally a "secondary" or derivative institution—and thus feel they do not need to take a look to see whether and to what degree it is such.[16]

The American corporate bar played a decisive role in the development of our society, as Berle and Means have recognized.[17] Only lawyers had in the post-Civil War period the particular gift for the framing of corporate charters, security issues, and all the rest; the particular courage to work ahead of the cases and statutes in order to give powers to corporations which had never been tested (and often have never yet been tested) in court; the particular tradition to give body

---

15. John R. Commons, *The Legal Foundations of Capitalism*.

16. An interesting study of W. P. Webb's *The Great Plains* might be made from this perspective. Webb sees water law, manufactured in England and New England, as bowing to the rainfall pattern of the plains, and he attacks the doctrine of equal riparian rights as a bigoted and misguided "lag." Yet no one seems to have asked why, when it came to underground waters, and later underground oil, the developments in technique since *Acton* v. *Blundell* did not lead to compulsory pooling and a departure from *this* precedent. Was it simply the competitive ethos of Texas? Or the vested interests of the makers of oil derricks? I doubt it very much; I think that the law often cuts its own channel—in this case so deep that a court held a compulsory pooling law unconstitutional, although it would in 1846 have been quite conceivable to decide *Acton* v. *Blundell* the other way. This "watershed" role of developments within legal doctrine itself has been little studied, though obviously it has to be studied before we can dismiss law as mere ideology, superstructure, or lag. For a pilot effort of my own (which helps make me fully aware of the difficulties) see my examination of the development of libel law in "Democracy and Defamation: Fair Game and Fair Comment," *Columbia Law Review*, XLII (1942), 1085-1123, 1282-1318.

17. Adolph Berle and Gardner Means, *The Modern Corporation and Private Property*.

to such decisive inventions as the fiction of the corporation as a "person." This extraordinary achievement has neither created topics for the social scientist to study in close detail nor, as observed above, made heroes for the bar—perhaps because the social consequences have been so generally deplored among intellectuals;[18] perhaps, too, because the anonymity of office work—"paper work"—leads to its relative disregard.

Only relative disregard, however. Since the corporation is obviously important and glamorous for its friends and foes alike, students of the law from within and without the profession have paid some attention to its development. Such studies have been a junction point between law and economics,[19] or between law and political science, though hardly yet between law and anthropology. The place to begin the latter kind of junction is at a point which is neither glamorous nor obviously policy-oriented, but where the functions served by the legal process do not strike one at the first, and perhaps stereotyped, glance and need to be discovered anew.[20]

§ III

LET WHAT I HAVE TO SAY from here on be regarded simply as notes or prolegomena to some field studies of the functions of law and the lawyers in our culture, with an emphasis on those functions which perhaps have received less recognition than is warranted in view of what we might learn if we understood them. Here, as elsewhere in social research, curiosity does well to focus on what is changing rather than on what is more or less stable.

Take, for example, the apparent decline in the function of law as popular amusement or festivity. This decline may be viewed as a fairly good index of urbanization and the rise of modern leisure industries. But law still serves this function in the smaller country places. Here court sittings are seasonal affairs, not like a bank or a store which

---

18. Until the twentieth century it would seem that the truly inventive American lawyers and judges had been conservatives: Marshall, Field, Choate, for example. Since we like to think that inventiveness is a liberal monopoly, we do not find these men to be models for young lawyers today; Brandeis is a model, or Holmes—the latter thought to be both liberal and legally inventive, though he is neither.

19. Cf., e.g., the pioneering work of C. Reinhold Noyes, *The Institution of Property*. Noyes tries (in chap. vi) to treat the question as to the relation between property and social stratification in terms of politically enforced legal rules for the distribution of men and things upon land. And he sees that property may serve the function of stabilizing one's geographical location. See also the general framework of theory presented in *ibid.*, pp. 16-21.

20. Similarly, law and psychology will not really mesh while attention remains concentrated on the obvious junctions of insanity law, trial psychology, evidentiary rules, etc.

is open for business every day. James West, in *Plainville, U.S.A.*, is fully aware of it.[21] He describes the legal "party" thrown for Hobart Proudy, who shot his cousin, Mort Proudy, in the seat of the breeches with both barrels; a witness testified in Hobart's favor that he should be let off because "if he had intended to kill Mort, he would have, since Hobart won't shoot a squirrel down out of a tree, anywhere except in the eye." The legal "party" served thus to entertain the community and to throw a scare into Hobart—West is fully aware of compounding practices but sees them not as an excrescence but as an essential part of the legal order. He also describes the way in which an adultery suit between an undertaker and a garagekeeper over the affections of the latter's wife provided the town with an agenda for gossip: "The atmosphere was electric with spiteful talk for many months, though most people said 'Nobody will make any money out of that trial and it may break both men up.'" This remark leads West to comment on the ambivalent attitude toward law on the part of Plainvillers: they fear it, yet enjoy it; one suspects that they enjoy it, as one enjoys a roller-coaster ride, partly because they fear it. Even so, one of West's informants noted the decline of scandals as compared with her experience farther south: "The people here," she observed, "are either a lot better or a lot smarter." Perhaps it is only that they have increasing access to other amusements, such as the movies and radio.

But the word "amusements" does not convey the full significance of this function. "Amusements" are always more than individualistic escapes from monotony; they are, like the weather, an endless unifier of conversation and of attitude. The Plainvillers share a common focus for discussion, and politics and law may be seen in part as providing topics in this way, just as a high-school basketball team might do. By the same token, a trial may serve as a divisive point, not in terms of a factional split as between the friends of the garagekeeper and of the undertaker, but in terms of a moral turning point, such as is described in James Gould Cozzens' fine novel, *The Just and the Unjust*, or as the Western world experienced—perhaps for the last time?—in the trial of Sacco and Vanzetti.

It would be interesting to pursue these leads further and to inquire, as could be readily done by means of interviews, into the question as to what sorts of laymen talk on what occasions about what sorts of legal process today. One hypothesis is that in middle-class intellectual circles court cases play much less part in conversation than they did even twenty years ago; but that in labor and Negro circles they may

---

21. James West, *Plainville, U.S.A.*

play more part—certainly, many labor-union officials, in their upward intellectual and social mobility, seem to be quite law-oriented. Over all, there may be a general fading-out of law, not only of courts, from public view. But this remains to be seen.

§ IV

COULD THE AMBIVALENCE toward law observed by West be related to the possibility that the lawyer must do things the community regards as necessary—but still disapproves of? Hence, is the lawyer something of a scapegoat? Now, to be sure, this does not in itself distinguish lawyers from prostitutes, politicians, prison wardens, some doctors, and many other occupational groups.[22] What does distinguish lawyers in this role is that they are feared and disliked—but needed—because of their matter-of-factness, their sense of relevance, their refusal to be impressed by magical "solutions" to people's problems. Conceivably, if this hypothesis is right, the ceremonial and mystification of the legal profession are, to a considerable degree, veils or protections underneath which this rational, all too rational, work of the lawyer gets done.

Of course, this view of the matter is in plain contradiction to that of Thorstein Veblen, who, it will be recalled, saw the engineers and the skilled workmen as the bearers of the modern, skeptical, matter-of-fact temper, while the lawyers were typical for the archaic, predatory, pecuniary, and otherwise nonrational employments. Very likely, there has been a notable change in legal education since Veblen wrote, with the major law schools going ever more heavily into the systematic practice of skepticism concerning judicial authority. *Lawyers learn not to take law seriously*. They learn to make distinctions; they are trained in relevance—or at least in worrying about relevance—and they will discover when they get into practice that relevance is a concept which, to their chronic frustration, seems nearly absent from the mental equipment of most of the people they deal with.[23] While

---

22. I am greatly indebted to Professor Everett Hughes for my understanding of this occupational pattern.

23. Compare the following recollections from Lenin: "When I was in exile in Siberia . . . I was an undergraduate lawyer because, being summarily exiled, I was not allowed to practice, but as there were no other lawyers in the region, people came to me and told me about some of their affairs. But I had the greatest difficulty in understanding what it was all about. A woman would come to me and of course start telling me all about her relatives and it would be incredibly difficult to get from her what she really wanted. Then she would tell me a story about a white cow. I would say to her: 'Bring me a copy.' She would then go off complaining: 'He won't hear what I have to say about the white cow unless I bring a copy.' We in our colony used to have a good laugh over this copy. But I was able to make some progress. People came to me, brought copies of the necessary documents, and I was able to gather what their trouble was, what

teachers of evidence for several generations have punctured the absurdities of the rules of evidence, they may have paid less attention to the fact that their students were, in the process of learning to apply and criticize the rules, also obliquely learning what relevance means. . . .

In the wartime Army and Navy bureaucracies, it was often the lawyer-in-uniform who in my limited experience appeared prepared to cut red tape and to walk indelicately over red carpets; he might be, and generally was, out of his "field," but he was engaged in what may be his occupational role of being unimpressed by authoritative rituals.[24] He seemed less impressed than the accountants, bankers, businessmen, and engineers in similar slots. But, of course, such casual observations, while "relevant," are hardly "evidence."

More to the point, perhaps, are the observations of Ferdinand Lundberg in his article on "The Profession of the Law":

> The lawyer comes to know society not as a tenant or owner knows a house but as the architect, building contractor, and repair men know it. And his knowledge of society extends beyond the knowledge these technicians have of any building, for he is intimately acquainted as well with the servants that staff the structure. He either knows all there is to know about judges, public officials, business leaders, bankers, professional politicians, labor leaders, newspaper publishers, leading clergymen, and the like, or through that informal clearing house of esoteric information, the bar association, can find out from colleagues. The lawyer is a vast reservoir of actual or potential information about the social and political topography. . . .[25]

The layman is, however, not quite sure how he feels about such a person, whose usefulness he may need and whose knowledgeability may fascinate him: the more he needs him, the more he may be likely to project upon him his own tendencies to cynicism about authority and about procedure. Journalists also have this sort of knowledge about the culture, but, despite the best efforts of schools of journalism, they have not been able to turn their profession into a secret society. Indeed, it is the lawyer's LL.B. which allows his client to delegate this outlook, and the work it entails, to him: he can seek counsel from lawyers without loss of face, although the matter in hand may not,

they complained of, what ailed them" (*Selected Works*, IX, 355). I am indebted for this reference to Nathan Leites, *Operational Code of the Politburo*, pp. 13-14.

24. From this perspective, not the least shocking thing about the Korematsu cases is to see the Supreme Court bowing to the claim of "military necessity." A court which is unimpressed by patent cases, or by the accounting concepts used in rate litigation, or by most other factual grist, here falls for the flimsiest and most outrageous propaganda handouts General DeWitt's lawyers could dream up! Lawyers actually in uniform were less easily swindled by "military necessity" than these men of the robe. For details see Morton Grodzins, *Americans Betrayed*.

25. *Harper's* CLXXVIII (December, 1938), 10.

in any technical sense, be "legal" at all. It is, then, the lawyer who loses face on his client's behalf.

What is there, then, in the selection and training of lawyers that readies them for accepting such a role? Doubtless, many elements are involved, but an important one is the fact that the law schools throughout the country are still fairly wide open to "talent," irrespective of class, ethnic, and kin lines. Thus, they attract the more ambitious, the more mobile young people—the bright Grinnell graduate whose political science teacher tells him to "take a crack at Harvard Law," or the intellectual hope of a Bronx family which feels he is cut out to be a lawyer and sends him to Fordham. Law schools maintain a highly competitive atmosphere, and the law reviews are almost uniquely work-oriented institutions: they pay no attention to "personality" and concentrate on performance with a zeal as rare and admirable as it is savage.[26]

So far as I know, there is nothing in any other professional group which remotely resembles the law review, this guild of students who, working even harder than their fellows, manage to cooperate sufficiently to meet the chronic emergency of a periodical. Indeed, this cooperation often develops an island of teamwork in a sea of ruthless rivalry. Law review students frequently have a note-taking agreement, so not all have to attend class; and in other ways they are likely to cover for each other in dealing with the obstacles to their review work, and often enough to their education, that the curriculum offers.

To be sure, the major law reviews have a rather amiable rivalry inter se, as the boards of editors on the older reviews have a rather amiable rivalry with the records set up by earlier and deceased boards of editors. But there is little that is factitious about this school spirit; it is not whipped up by coaches (though here and there faculty advisors, public-relations conscious, may play this role) or by cheer leaders, but is self-perpetuating. The resulting standards often become so high that the contributed articles by law teachers and practitioners are markedly inferior to the student work both in learning and in style and, in fact, often have to be rewritten by the brashly serious-minded student editors. As democracy based on ability to *do* something (rather than that spurious democracy which is based on ability to *be* a right kind of guy) is strongest in the high schools and colleges in the field of sports, so in the professional world it appears strongest in the competitive-cooperative teamwork of the law reviews.

26. On the historical connection between social mobility and the law see my article, "Equality and Social Structure," *Journal of Legal and Political Sociology,* I (October, 1942), 72-95.

For it is a notable feature of this teamwork that it is based on impersonal and objective criteria in the sense that it ignores social class and ethnic lines and, beyond these, "personality" above a bare minimum. In many law schools, election is not really election, for it is based on grades alone; in others, it is based on performance, judged almost as impersonally as the grades themselves are judged by the scrupulous fairness of the faculty. (It is perhaps no accident that one or two law schools, as at Yale and Chicago, contain some of the most fervent devotees of Henry Simons' utopian vision of a free, impersonal, unmonopolistic economy; law reviews are the very model of such an economy, a model which it would be hard to duplicate elsewhere in the society.) I think that studies might reveal that, not only cooptation to the law review, but the election of officers thereupon, is heavily influenced by an ideology of impersonal, objective performance in which "merely" social and ethnic considerations are not only frowned upon but actually eliminated, so far as may be. Jews, for example, appear heavily represented in the upper mastheads of all the major law reviews. (They do on college papers, too, but that involves other issues of motivation and selection.) A great camaraderie, sometimes of a kidding and sometimes of a tacit sort, appears to develop on the reviews between the Jewish and the non-Jewish members. In what is left of their time away from school and books, sociability is often a duplication of the law review cliques themselves, these being based more on interest and congeniality than on fraternity-type considerations.

I do not doubt that members of law review staffs are pretty fully aware of how widely their mores diverge from those of the wider world, whether collegiate or business and professional, nor do I doubt that these "outside" considerations are sometimes brought inside, but when this happens they are felt as scandalous. The divergence from medical schools in this respect is obvious and striking. Medical school students do not edit journals in which, as not infrequently happens in the law reviews, students rewrite or even reject the work of their teachers. Already in the first year of medical school, the student has entered into a network of personal ties which will be decisive for his professional fate; he is judged, and judges himself, by his "personality" and connections quite as much as by his more intellectual qualities. "Personality" and connections, of course, have helped get him in to medical school in the first place, whereas law school admission, like law school life, is almost devoid of these tariffs. (The mathematical formula by which Harvard Law School selects its entrants is only an extreme illustration of this pattern.) The medical school student attends a "clinical" school in the very real sense that the values which dominate the school also dominate later medical practice, though perhaps in a somewhat muted form. Medical school students, no matter how service-oriented on entrance, soon learn that they live in a patronage network whose unspoken rules will govern internships and the whole complex ladder of medical practice today. A Catholic Italian boy will have to decide, for example, whether he dare play in the big-Protestant league, because one of his teachers has taken a shine to him, or whether he should take the safer course of playing in the Catholic minor league; if he misses his bet, he may easily fall between two stools.[27] In sum, the medical schools are "true to life" or clinical in a sense which the law schools are not; their pattern of social relations puts very little pressure on the medical community at large precisely because the students are in effect socialized as interns from the very beginning. To be sure, with respect to such issues as "socialized medicine," the medical schools controlled by full-time men may put some pressure on their students for progressive attitudes which are anathema to the medical associations, and at these same schools there is probably somewhat more impersonality than in most forms of medical practice. But on the whole, medical students do not need to face much re-orientation of values when they leave medical school; their problem is rather whether they can face treating patients without the full package of big-hospital facilities.

In contrast with this, the member of a law review staff who goes into practice suddenly confronts many of the class and ethnic barriers that his own team experience had lowered. He may enter a big non-Jewish or a big Jewish office, all of whose partners are themselves law review trained men, but all of whom are willy-nilly engaged in segregated practice. In the government, offices are unsegregated, which, however, often means largely ethnic in composition. And what is true of race is also true of sex; many large offices do not accept women as associates, though the men who run them may have worked closely with women in their law review days.

Nevertheless, the capitulation of the law review graduate to "life" is seldom complete. If he takes sex and race into account, he takes social class and religion into account much less than is the case in many other professions (e.g., architecture). It is partly this that permits the law to remain one of the careers open to talent, so that a railroad conductor's son from Altoona, who has done well at a name law school, may end up as head of a big manufacturing or utility com-

---

27. Hall, "Informal Organization of Medical Practice," 12 *Can. J. Econ. & Pol. Sci.* (1946); also, by the same author, "The Stages of a Medical Career," 53 *Am. J. Soc.* (1948).

pany, or a government agency, when he would never, without connections, have made the grade within the particular company or agency hierarchy. The career of the West Virginian, John W. Davis, is an excellent instance.

Furthermore, it may well be that a comparison of legal with medical practice would show that the former has been influenced, in its recent limited inroads on the barriers of race and sex, by the law school and particularly its law review ethos, as well as by the more generalized FEPC type of pressure. Certainly when, in the Christmas holidays before graduation, law students looking for jobs are confronted with the ethnic "facts of life," they return to their law review jobs with some uneasiness, and they may welcome bar association and other activities in which the old law review camaraderies are to some extent restored. This may be one source of the fact that Italians, Jews, and women seem of late years to have been finding jobs in the big offices, though these are understandably reluctant to duplicate in their own makeup the ethnic composition, often so heavily Jewish, of the law reviews from which they draw recruits.

If I am right in these suggestions, the law attracts people who can stand a certain amount of impersonality and who are trained to be objective, in the sense of being relevant and orderly. The very "ivory-towerism" for which the law schools are often attacked allows them to emphasize techniques which are relatively unclinical. The law student, and especially the law review student, does not encounter clients and is therefore not likely to be judged for what we might call his "briefcase manner."[28] The whole drift of the law is, in this sense, democratic, competitive, and impersonal. The law reviews put pres-

---

28. In considering the social and psychological consequences of professional education, it is at least as important to examine what has *not* been learned as to see what has been taught in the three years at school. The removal of apprentice lawyers from law offices during those years may be more significant than the items of instruction which have been substituted. This may sound strange, but we can see the problem clearly in an analogous case. As we know, industry turns increasingly to college-trained foremen, rather than promoting from the ranks, while at the same time proclaiming that the college-bred trainee might as well get a general education in college since he'll have to learn his technology and know-how in the factory anyhow. It would seem that college serves primarily to keep him for four years from learning the (often outmoded) ways of doing things he would learn if he were in the factory; when he starts fresh he can learn newer techniques developed in the meantime, and will be less disposed to sabotage them since all are equally strange. And perhaps the need to learn fast, to justify his college training and status, will lead him to short-cuts—certainly true of the greenhorn LL.B. who must acquire savvy fast. But the savvy acquired fast will be different—more rational—than the savvy acquired "the hard (clinical or 'real-life') way." Since coming to these conclusions, I regret the fact that law students do not have a better time during the three years when they are spared the mislearnings of practice.

sure on the profession, and the profession in turn puts pressure on the society.

Let it not be assumed that I am convinced this pressure is a good thing. Its concomitant is the rather scarifying emphasis on grades which is characteristic of law schools, for if the law review is a stepping stone to a high position, the stakes are more than a penny a point of average. Nor can we sensibly be too self-righteous about the more nepotistic atmosphere of the medical school, unless we would just as soon be attended when sick by Mr. Economic Man; indeed, the medical schools may conceivably be criticized as not snobbish enough but as simply typifying petty-bourgeois petty prejudice. A whole society run on the principles of the law review, in which everyone read Consumer's Reports in choosing services as well as commodities, while it would appeal to Myrdal and other radical democrats, might be a somewhat uncomfortable place, with none of the hominess provided by mild degrees of segregation and corruption. But a whole society run on the principles of the medical profession would, if anything, be even more intolerable, with guild controls dictating all choices. The tensions between these two systems of value and their two historic roots is characteristic of our modern industrial society.

The law review, then, would seem to present a kind of paradigm of impersonality combined with teamwork, to be studied in its own terms and also as a yardstick for the legal profession and, by contrast, other professions as well. Investigators would have to go on to see what the pace-setter is among the law reviews in these respects, and the degree to which different reviews represent, exaggerate, or modify the attitudes of their own law school communities. Is it only at the "national" law schools, for instance, where there is little parochialism in the *topics* treated by student editors, that there is little parochialism in the *choice* of editors? We should expect some subtle interplays between the interpretations of what is "law" at a given institution and the pattern of social relations for which the law review stands. But only careful observation can discover what the interplays are in each case, and what generalizations may be safely made about "the" law review and "the" school.

To repeat: law schools attract the more hard-working, ambitious young men; they drill them to respect top performance; they furnish them with models of, and perhaps contact with, previous graduates who moved rapidly into positions of influence. Under this combined nurturing, lawyers tend, I suggest, to become hard-working isolates. They are less inclined than the average client to be or appear to be "big-hearted," "good guys," etc.—the vocabulary by which they would be seduced into accepting the normal archaisms of the business world. The teamwork of a law review is very different from the teamwork of other, more clubby, professionals; this same atmosphere continues in the larger offices. An interesting illustration is gleaned from comparing the corporate bar's admiration for the SEC registration statement filed for the Kaiser-Frazer Company some years ago—a statement which whizzed through in record time—with the distrust of Henry Kaiser felt by his business competitors who view him as too streamlined for their comfort.

In sum, lawyers tend frequently to become paid rate-busters, mobile men in every respect, who find in devotion to their work and in the esteem of their professional colleagues rewards for serving clients in ways of which the clients do not entirely approve—and, what is more, do not want to have to approve. The "mystery" of the law is here a protection for the client: under an inevitable ignorance of *part* of a technical field, he can throw virtually the *whole* moral burden on his counsel and excuse himself on the ground that he could not possibly know enough to have an independent judgment. The lawyer, usually unaware of the psychological roots of this division of labor, may sometimes vainly try to "educate" his client into the whys and wherefores of his actions.

§ V

THE SO-CALLED PARTISANSHIP of the lawyer provides an interesting illustration of some of these problems. It is frequently said that lawyers are particularly partisan people; this is part of the stereotype. And it may be that the ambition of lawyers to go on the bench may spring to some extent from a wish to air opinions. Yet it is a question if lawyers are more opinionated than most people; they are ordinarily less partisan than nonlawyers and could hardly do their work if this were not so.

Every client realizes this when he sees the fraternizing of opposing counsel. He may suspect that his lawyer cares more for the opinion of other lawyers (including the judge) with whom he has to do business every day than he cares for the momentary problem of the client. The "rules of the game" of the law are so set up that lawyers can appear to fight hard without irretrievably hurting each other; yet, as with other games when *anomie* sets in and rules become purely instrumental, this restraint can break down. For many reasons, lawyers are more willing to bear each other's hostility for the sake of a client than other professionals (e.g., doctors); this would again seem connected—as Durkheim might predict—with the openness of the law-school world to talent, without ethnic and class barriers; and one of the important areas for sociological investigation would seem to be to study differences in type of professional camaraderie (at the client's expense) in different types of law practice. It seems likely that the lawyers' training in objectifying social relations permits them to tolerate not only the hostility of the public brought upon them for the disrespect of the public's image of the law they must show in order to get the public's work done but also this considerable amount of hostility to colleagues, or the risk of it.

But if there are times when the lawyer is less partisan than he should be in the client's interest (and it is hard for him not to confuse his own interest with the interest of his other present and potential clients who will exploit him as a bearer of a certain amount of good will from bench and bar), there are other times when the client cannot tolerate a non-partisanship which is clearly in his own interest.[29] There have been cases of quite conservative, but unfanatical lawyers, accustomed as few engineers are to taking account of human stresses and strains, who have lost their jobs as labor negotiators because management wanted, not success in the labor bargain, but a ritual of expletives against those damned union bastards. Sometimes businessmen and others dealing with the government have been similarly unwilling to accept, even in scapegoat fashion, their lawyer's matter-of-factness; they have wanted to pay, not for success, but for resounding speeches. And since they could find other members of the bar who would do this for them, they were deprived both of their success and of their comfortable assurance that they were morally superior to lawyers. Sometimes, as Everett Hughes has observed, this problem is handled by symbiotic teams of lawyers, one matter-of-fact, the other a ham actor. Similar demands are made today on our diplomats—men, of course, often trained in the law.

The demand for partisanship comes, moreover, not only from the client, but from the lawyer's own desire to believe in the client as a cause. John Brooks, in his novel *The Big Wheel*, describes the revolt of the writers for a newsweekly against a pious editor who wanted them to believe their own stuff: they felt their intellectual integrity depended on their being able to divorce their private beliefs from their daily writing stint. The law has a long tradition of rationalizing that divorce by an ethic of "invisible harmony" which assures each

---

29. This conflict between lawyer and client over the proper degree of affect which the former is to bring to the affairs of the latter is one of those conflicts between client emergency and occupational routine which has attracted the interest of Everett Hughes. As he observes, the client wants his problem given priority—yet he would be uneasy with a professional for whom his case actually was "the first" and who had neither been trained on other people's emergencies nor could control his own emotions in the face of the client's loss of control.

practitioner that if he fights hard for his client within the rules the general interest will be somehow advanced. Though obviously the matter is very hard to document, it appears that this ethic is breaking down and that lawyers consequently feel either the need to be partisan or to be iron-clad cynics.

When this outer and inner demand for partisanship is coupled with the perhaps increasing psychological need of lawyers to be liked by their clients, the lawyer's usefulness may be impaired. We must ask, in this connection, whether it is really a good idea to train lawyers in psychology, if the effect of this is to make them more sensitive to their clients' moods and judgments? If it is to make them more "other-directed"?[30] If it is to break down the psychological defenses of the "secret society"? Perhaps the lawyer, or certain kinds of lawyer, has to be a person with a thick skin, not very interested in how other people feel or in how he himself feels?

To put this another way, if the lawyer should become very concerned with others' feelings, might he not become merely a competitor with another kind of client-caretaker, namely, the public relations man? While to be sure many public relations men are LL.B.'s, can the law schools eventually do as good a job in training this crew as, let us say, schools of journalism or of applied psychology?[31] May not the eagerness of some law-school leaders to "modernize" their schools, by incorporating much social science, have the consequence, if what they introduce takes at all with their students, of cramping those mobility drives which have pulled and pushed lawyers along the particular career lines they have followed in this country to date? Obviously, we can say very little about such questions without knowing much more than we do about who goes to law school, what happens to him there, and how this is related to what happens to him later on.

Equally obviously, law schools differ very much *inter se* with respect to the kind of rate-busting ethos discussed above. It is not every law school whose graduates will carry to the courts (at their clients' expense) a real crusading effort to prove Williston right as against Corbin or vice versa, as some Harvard and Yale graduates in big law firms are said to have done in the pre-social-science era.

---

30. *The Lonely Crowd*, chap. vi.

31. It is interesting to watch how this new type of business and government counselor seeks to develop a ritual of his own in his competitive effort to displace lawyers as those who profit, in Lundberg's terms, from keeping their clients "in a condition of permanent convalescence, always dependent upon the expensive advice of specialists in obscure, often nameless disorders, never thoroughly ill, never wholly cured" (*op. cit.*, p. 2). This new ritual is usually based on public opinion research techniques and on psychological jargon—which perhaps has still some way to go before it becomes as impressive as law-talk.

CONNECTED IN SUBTLE and still opaque ways with some of these psychological shifts is the shift of awareness in the legal profession itself concerning the nature of legal rights. Whereas law has been very greatly preoccupied with property, with the relation of men to things, it is only in the most unsophisticated circles today that it is thought there are true rights *in rem;* elsewhere, it is recognized that all rights come at bottom down to relations among men, including relations among men concerning things, and that all rights are therefore creations of social organization. In the past lawyers have tended to be people who, so to speak, reified social organization; they moved among their complicated networks of personal relations (corporations, domestic relations, administrative rules, etc.) as physicists might move among their models of atomic nuclei. Their eye was on the structure, not on the personalities who happened at any moment to occupy various niches in it. This cultivated blindness to people, this ability to insist on the reality of legal fictions, helped to make it possible for lawyers to erect in confidence and good conscience the elaborate organizational machinery of our society. True, they lacked or repressed current sociological learning about the importance of the informal organization, whether in the bank wiring room at the Hawthorne plant of Western Electric or the higher reaches of the telephone company as described by Chester Barnard. But Danielian's book on the A.T. and T.—incidentally, one of the few corporate biographies which pays any attention to the role of lawyers—indicates that the development of the over-all telephone organization owes much to legal invention—and not alone in the patent suppression field.[32]

But anthropological and psychological learning offers not only the truism that legal rights are creations of culture, of human relations; it penetrates somewhat further into the question of what these rights are actually made of, what their effective sanction is. This may be illustrated by reference to an experimental psychodrama developed by the Veterans Administration in order to test candidates for jobs in the VA in terms of aggressiveness. A psychodrama is a playlet in which people play roles whose barest outlines are assigned to them; in this case, one of the testers plays the role of a Chinese laundryman who cannot speak English. The candidate is not told this but is told simply that his tuxedo has been left at a laundryman's, that he needs it for a big date at 7:00 P.M., and that he will see his tux hanging,

---

32. See Noobar Danielian, *A. T. & T.*, p. 97.

fully pressed, behind the counter. The following is a typical conversation.

CANDIDATE: Here is my claim check; there is the suit hanging there.
LAUNDRYMAN: Don't speak English. Boss back at 7.
C.: But I need this before 7. There it is.
L.: Don't speak English. (*Sits down behind counter and picks up paper.*)
C.: (*Hesitates, moves toward the counter.*)
L.: (*Lowers paper, looks up.*)
C.: (*Halts.*)
L.: (*Raises newspaper.*)
C.: (*Starts to cross counter.*)
L.: (*Rises, says nothing.*)
C.: (*Gives up and leaves, but in two cases only:*) God damn it, give me my suit! (*Goes and grabs it and leaves.*)

Our own problem here is not so much the question of aggression—though this has been of great interest, as it bears on law, in the work of Malcolm Sharp and others—as in the question: What is the counter made of?

There is no reason to assume that the counter is simply a culture barrier between Chinese and Americans, nor has the counter been charmed by a disease incantation. Rather, the counter seems to be made of some kind of interpersonal field situation connected with property rights and the nuances of trespass. Among these "generalized others" a line is drawn between the suit and its owner by some of the same considerations which created the relation between owner and tuxedo in the first place. (There being, apparently, some connection between the origin of property and of patriarchal society—a society, that is, which rests on inference and reasoning about paternity—one wonders if the VA would have gotten the same results in the psychodrama had the actors both been women!)

There are many unresolved complexities in this experiment. It may, however, serve to illustrate a further point, namely, that social psychology has much to gain from a study of the operation of law. In handling such incidents, psychologists sometimes show a tendency to overestimate the importance of individual personality, or of the "field" created by a number of personalities, while overlooking the bearing of a long historical development of a structural and institutional sort, to which these personalities, unless quite crazy, will defer, at least up to a point. The strength of the VA's imaginary counter depends not only on the weakness of the VA's candidates but also on the long and luxuriant growth of legal forms and practices. These have proceeded historically without becoming entirely the product, at any given time, of the private personalities of those who then fill the institution's statuses and perform its duties.

§ VII

ANOTHER ILLUSTRATION may be drawn from my observations when I
served a term in the Appeals Bureau of the New York District Attorney's Office. What struck me there was the fantastically unutili-
tarian character of many of the briefs we wrote. The head of the
office, a law-review-trained man, felt that no case was too humble not
to be loaded with all the erudition and art of brief-writing the
whole staff could muster. There were open-and-shut gambling cases,
for example, where our brief would draw, not only on Hawaii and
the law reviews, but even on New Zealand reports and perhaps something from the French Court of Cassation! Now, who was the audience for this display of professional activity? It was not a make-work
ritual such as James Caesar Petrillo might devise, for not only were
we all high-minded men but we were in fact shorthanded and were
actually more likely to lose men and even funds than to gain them
by our tactics. For they were certainly not appreciated by the trial
lawyers in the office who ridiculed us as some kind of fanatical brain
trust, pointing out, as we well knew, that we won 98 per cent of our
appeals anyway and that most of the judges did not, or perhaps could
not, read briefs. Nor did we endear ourselves to defense counsel,
often barely literate and often much too impecunious for such
displays of irrelevant learning. Nor did our briefs come to the attention of members of prominent downtown firms, who might appreciate our standards and hire our people—for such members enter the
criminal courts only, so to speak, by proxy.

    Thus, after eliminating rational explanations for our activity—
activity in which I found myself joining in spite of myself—I concluded that we were engaging in some sort of secularized religious
activity by which the members of the Appeals Bureau exploited a
long tradition of legal learning in order to lend meaning to their
daily lives. (Recalling how legalistic many of the Puritans seemed to
their more easygoing and worldly foes, we may think of the law
as one of the secular equivalents of seventeenth-century theology.)
On the face of it, these lawyers were worldly men, or at least worldly-
wise; behind their backs, in their unconscious, operated motives of
an unworldly sort they would have done their best to deny. Perhaps
something of what Veblen called "the instinct of workmanship" was
also at work here, some desire to do a good job apart from any
immediate audience. These nonutilitarian elaborations go on in the
law—our office was not unique, though it may have been extreme—
not in search of justice but in search of something which transcends
even justice, some kind of quest of the Absolute, some kind of art
for art's sake. Indeed, I am fairly sure that something of the same

sort happens in all occupations, but the lawyer is perhaps less able than others to conceal his intellectual orgies. They are often a matter of record, or they exist in filing cabinets. At the same time this very openness of the lawyer's play with reasoning may be a factor in the way the profession operates (of course, in conjunction with other professions, such as teaching and the more intellectual branches of the ministry) to drain off some of the culture's more adept and avid reasoners, who might find themselves deviants if these careers were not open to them as external defenses and internal sublimations.

It follows that the lawyer's sense of relevance—often greater than that of other people—must constantly struggle in this way with his desire to use his very rationality for ends he cannot admit to himself. And this in turn may link up with the ambivalent roles of the lawyer in our society, who stands at once for reason and for an excess of it.

It may follow, if what I am arguing here is supportable, that the lawyer, the person to whom society assigns the function of being peculiarly rational and relevant, protects himself from his clients by his mobility and professional *élan* and from himself by such ritualistic overwork. That is, he encysts his reason both within layers of professional mystique (much as the Delphic oracles may have done, or shamans of many tribes and climes) and within irrational work patterns of his own.

But, of course, lawyers are not the only examples of such irrational use of rationality. Any true effort to see the functions for the lawyer of his own functions in society must proceed in terms of a more general view of occupations and professions—such a view as my colleague Everett Hughes is engaged in developing.[33] Many lawyers, like many other professionals, have to work hard to down the suspicion that their work lacks meaning, lacks "reality." Lawyers sometimes feel that all they live by is words, that they perform operations which have been taught them but which have no non-solipsistic consequences. Watching lawyers at work, puzzled about the relation of that work to some larger and more embracing whole, one is reminded of the hero, Laskell's, attitude towards his fishing expedition, as Lionel Trilling describes it in *The Middle of the Journey*:

Lack of practice made him awkward with his casting. He dutifully reminded himself of all the things he must think about—arm close to the body, wrist loose, the fly to touch the water before the leader. He did

33. See, e.g., his articles, "Work and the Self," in John H. Rohrer and Muzafer Sherif (eds.), *Social Psychology at the Crossroads*, pp. 313-23, and "Institutional Office and the Person," *American Journal of Sociology*, XLIII (November, 1937), 404-13.

not believe that it made any difference. He did not really believe there were fish in the stream, or that he could catch them, or that fish had ever been caught by this method. You equipped yourself expensively, you learned the technique, you did everything the way you had been taught, and even, for the deceptive pleasure of it, you debated the theory of flies with other fishermen, arguing about just what it was that the fish saw when the fly floated over its head. But nothing really happened, or whatever happened happened for quite other reasons and not because you did what you did.[34]

Here, too, the more we find out about law, the more we will know about the meaning of work as a mode of relating people to some sort of physical and social reality, as culturally or existentially defined—and as a mode also of alienating them from reality and from each other.

§ VIII

ON ITS FACE, it seems not a difficulty but an advantage that the student of the legal profession can have ready access to records, files, and other materials accumulated by a diligently record-keeping lot of men. To be sure, no profession likes to be studied (apart from the public relations value of being professional and prominent enough to have studies made), and Judge Frank in *Courts on Trial* reports a striking example of judges' refusing to co-operate with would-be investigators,[35] but on the whole the lawyers are used to being visible. Perhaps, indeed, it is the very mass of material which is depressing to a prospective student. For the social scientist who wants to get beyond, on the one hand, generalizations about the unreasonableness of the law and, on the other hand, these peripheral touchings at the most obvious points of criminal justice and trial psychology, needs

---

34. Compare with Trilling's remarks the following observation by Llewellyn and Hoebel in *The Cheyenne Way*, p. 292: "Thus each law-job, and all of them together, presents first of all an aspect of pure survival, a bare-bones. The job must get done *enough* to keep the group going. This is brute struggle for continued existence. It is the problem of attaining order in the pinch at whatever cost to justice. But beyond this, each job has a wholly distinct double aspect which we may call the *questing-aspect*. This is a betterment aspect, a question so to speak of surplus and its employment. On the one side, this questing aspect looks to more adequate doing of the job, just as a doing: economy, efficiency, smoothness, leading at the peak to aesthetically satisfying grace in the doing of it. On the other side, the questing aspect looks to the ideal values; justice, finer justice, such organization and such ideals of justice as tend toward fuller, richer life. It no more does to forget the bare-bones in favor of these things than it does to forget these things in favor of the bare-bones." Cf. also Simmel's significant juxtaposition of art and play with law as activities which are purposeless in the sense that they are self-determining and independent of the original impulse that led to them (*The Sociology of Georg Simmel*, trans. Kurt H. Wolff, p. 42.).

35. *Op. cit.*, p. 116.

to wade into the lawbooks themselves and into office files, as well as to observe, as James West did, the ceremonial and festive functions of Ozark court sessions. He has to sit in on sessions between lawyer and client, especially lawyer and corporate or governmental client, to see if he can observe ways of thinking that are peculiarly legal. Maybe he will have to make distinctions not only among various kinds of law practice but among various groups of law-school graduates. At the same time he may discover that the first and easiest place to observe these tendencies of the American legal mind in the making is in the classroom, on the law review, and in the social life and the myths of the law students. For surely one mode of beginning any serious investigation of the kinds of problems being discussed is to look at the ways in which, on the day of entry, first-year law students already possess a kind of legal culture and personality and by seeing what happens to this as they go through their rites of passage to the LL.B.

Does this mean, to be concrete, that the sociological investigator has to go to law school himself? The law has been made out as much too esoteric—the investigator can pick up what legal lore he needs with relative ease and speed if he has any kind of flair for technical vocabularies. But knowledge of the law and knowledge of the culture of lawyers are obviously two different things; to gain the latter probably requires participant observation. And it may turn out that the investigator who has the best chance of picking up this culture in all its nuances will be one who is sufficiently familiar with the counters of legal discourse to share some of the culture of the lawyers among whom he will move. If he knows some, by the usual journalistic rule, he can pretend he knows more (or, sometimes, less), and find out still more. He will know where to look, where to probe. He will not be so taken up with imbibing legal phrases and mechanics that he will assign to the lawyers he is observing as much affect in the use of these phrases as is necessary for him in the original learning process.

An illustration may be drawn from anthropological field work. Sometimes ethnographic reports give the reader the impression that the preliterate tribe spent most of its emotional energies preparing breadfruit, or casting spells, or hollowing out canoes. All these activities had the same fascination for the anthropologist who had never engaged in them himself as the visiting of factories, nurseries, or prisons, which had been left out of their education in their own countries, had for Western tourists to the Soviet Union. In much the same way, the student of an occupation may be misled by the beat of his own rhythms of attention. His own interest may, without his full awareness, evoke a greater interest among his informants, who can perhaps recapture an earlier enthusiasm for their own shop thereby.

But to put it this way puts the task of participant observation too mechanically—too much as a problem in "rapport" and nondirective interviewing. I am enough of a fly fisherman to believe the legal problems have intrinsic interest; that they are one way of structuring the world—not so bad a way as lawyers in the present mood of defensiveness are often likely to think. The student who wants to see what the function of law is for the lawyer—and hence at least one of its important functions in the society of which lawyers are a substantial part—has to fall for it, just a little bit. Doubtless, he could also learn something if he hated it bitterly. But since there are many things to be studied, anyone omnivorous enough to choose the law and the legal profession might as well have some dessert in a diet that will at best contain a good deal of roughage.

28. Some Observations on Social Science Research*

Every work of social science today establishes itself on a scale whose two ends are "theory" and "data": that is, the great theoretical structures by which we attempt to understand our age at one end, and the relatively minuscule experiments and data which we collect as practicing social scientists at the other. In between are smaller schemes of generalization as well as larger and less precise observations. The relationship of the two ends of the scale to each other has never been completely clear, and all efforts simply to resolve the problem by comparisons with the natural sciences, or by drastic rejections of one or the other end of the scale, have failed to achieve general acceptance. Social scientists in pursuit of professionalization of their craft and of status as "scientists" are disturbed by this state of affairs, and are hopeful that, if not now, then soon the theory-data tension can be reconciled by some "operational" formula, and that there will then be no doubt as to what is social science. In this paper, I propose to indicate some reasons for skepticism as to these hopes, and some reasons for thinking that the tension is a productive one in the present state of the art, one we might as well enjoy.

To be sure, some deny there is any problem of reconciliation by arguing that only experiments and data are science while all the rest, though it may be produced by people who call themselves social scientists, is art or polemics, journalism or whatnot. Still others escape the problem of reconciliation by the opposite denial: they reject as pettyfogging make-work the meticulous technical operations of social science, and they use the club of late great essayistic thinkers to beat live field-workers into humiliation. Their trade-mark: did it take all this foundation money and all these IBM machines to tell us this, which Tocqueville already knew a hundred years ago!

What is today the most influential group of social scientists espouses neither of these extreme polarities. Rather, it hopes that the large visions of the "fathers"—of such thinkers as Marx, Simmel, Durkheim, Weber, Freud—can be broken down into smaller-scale parcels that could be subjected to empirical verification by contemporary researchers. In this way, it is thought, we should eventually be

---

* In collaboration with Nathan Glazer.

able to work our way from research projects testing rather small bits of generalization to large theoretical structures, no less illuminating than those of the past, but in their relation to data more closely parallel to the theories of natural science.[1] As yet, the hope that one can thus ascend from the twigs of research projects to the main trunk of social science theory remains only a hope—though one pursued with ingenuity and devotion by some of the most competent and gifted workers.

§ II

THE SHARPNESS of the polarity between theory and data varies with the age: we live in a third period, succeeding one in which theory reigned supreme, and another, data. Since the gospel of data is connected by personal, if not by inevitable intellectual ties to the concept of a value-free social science, its supremacy has fallen with the present self-consciousness of social scientists concerning values, and their desire to be useful in the formation of public policy; if we had to set a date for this development, we could set it in 1939, when World War II began and when Robert Lynd published his influential *Knowledge for What?* In this third period, each side in the theory-data conflict has strong defenders and the issue is joined with an exigent sense of mission. Moreover, it is part of the conflict that ambitious philosophies of history, past and present, should be sent tumbling down before some inconvenient facts energetically marshalled by the "data"-wing. But it is no less a mark of the intellectual history of our age that new philosophers of history, reacting against the slavery to fact of most contemporary historians and many contemporary social scientists, should be constantly exasperated by the paucity of data and tempted to stretch their theories over larger ground than those data allow. And in its turn this recrudescent temerity, especially when as with Toynbee it attracts a large lay audience, distresses many of the workers who prefer the data end of the scale, and then seek to arm themselves with still more data, first, to demolish the new philosophy of history, and, second, to build the pile of data high enough to compete with it.

In this climate of opinion, the theorist—and I speak here of the scholar who theorizes, who tries to pull together many facts in a large scheme of understanding, not of the person who is concerned with the problem of theory as a methodological specialty—can hope, at best, to be considered "stimulating," but irrelevant to the main

---

1. It goes without saying that the "natural science" that thus serves as a model is itself often a mirage: not natural science as it is actually practiced by its best contemporaries, but an ideology often based on Newtonian models.

course of social science. His "intuitions," as they are half-enviously, half-patronizingly, called, if they are not exploded out of hand by facts, may be considered worthy of processing by other social scientists—we have thus arrived at the strange position where the most seminal works in the social sciences, if they were published today, would probably be denounced in many professional quarters as sheer talk, though talk which might, under a particularly broad-minded thesis committee, be considered as a quarry for graduate students seeking a topic. That is, works of the type that in the past were most significant for the development of social science would today be considered, charitably, as plausible and interesting, but not as starting points for serious intellectual discussion among social scientists trying to evaluate their meaning and value and even validity.

It is argued, of course, that with the rise of empirical techniques social science has outgrown the need to rely on the type of "impressionistic" work of its early formative years. And we cannot dismiss this view as sheer error, for contrary to what many of the "theory"-wing suppose, these techniques have an unexampled richness and promise. Any kind of formal use of interviews, for instance, was not known in the social sciences even thirty years ago; the projective psychological tests are for the most part still younger; the formal, systematic effort at controlled observation that we find in the community survey or the professional ethnographic monograph is less than sixty years old, and in this period works in this genre have become increasingly more precise and many-skilled in method. In their general form and in their possibilities for technical validation and for mathematical treatment, these methods suggest a new vision of social science: superseding social science as an only moderately specialized development out of history and common observation, the goal now looms of a systematically organized body of observation and strict generalization as taut and impressive as the structure of natural science. In my judgment, attainment of the goal is still a long way off, for reasons that I shall come to in a moment; but the impatience of those to whom the goal seems close at hand, with any social science enterprise which does not appear to move directly towards it, is understandable.

Indeed, there is one problem which no amount of improvement in research methods will ever permit us to overcome, namely the limitation of our knowledge of the past imposed by the unfortunate fact that we cannot interview or test the dead. Historiography and archeology can do remarkable jobs of reconstruction, but they can seldom satisfy the ambitious social scientist in search of quantitative comparisons—a point well made in Paul Lazarsfeld's presidential address to the American Association for Public Opinion Research on "The Obligation of the 1950 Pollster to the 1984 Historian." Thus, if we are comparing, let us say, religious affects today with those of a generation ago, there is no need to be markedly more precise at the near than at the far end. Frequently the consequence is, however, that social scientists bemused by the richness of contemporary method confine their studies to the contemporary scene. And they do so not only when they deal with preliterate cultures where historical materials are scanty (though, if one is not perfectionist, less scanty than sometimes supposed), but also when they deal with civilizations where historical materials are abundant but frustrating. Yet it hardly needs argument in these pages that we cannot assay the weight of any prevailing pattern of attitudes and institutions without appreciating their historical development, and that if we do not study permanence and change in a time dimension we might as well surrender altogether the effort to understand society.

This, then, is the dilemma created by the development of our new tools: that they suggest to us a strict form of social science, in which every generalization refers directly or by a process of unassailable deduction to objectively available bodies of data—these generalizations being as meaningful, useful, and interesting as those of natural science; but for the present—possibly, indeed, for the foreseeable future—such generalizations are impoverished and hobbled by these self-same scientific forms, and consequently social science becomes less interesting, meaningful, and useful—as far as permitting us to understand a sequence of development goes—and less attractive altogether as an intellectual enterprise.

§ III

IN THE PRESENT STATE of controversy, there is tremendous pressure on students of social science (including especially sociology, social anthropology, psychology, and political science) to take sides either in the "theory" or in the "data" camp; this is easy to observe at such an institution as my own, the University of Chicago, or at Columbia, where both camps are well-armed but hungry for more arms, and where both can call on the support of a great tradition. When these students in their own research discover the really extraordinary difficulties of linking any important generalization to measurable data, and thereby closing the gap between the camps, they are apt to conclude, not that there is something wrong with the warfare, but that they are themselves lacking in what it takes to be warriors. The students would be much better off if they could take a stand against taking a stand: if they could realize that the dilemma is at present irresolvable, and nobody's "fault," and accept it as such; that it makes no sense, on the one hand, to reject the new techniques as grubby and inartistic, or, on the other hand, to discard the humanly valuable essence of social science: its power, as seen in the impact of certain great works in the past, to illuminate and describe in some larger framework the experienced details of social life.

Yet I know how difficult it is to convince anyone that one has not, even surreptitiously, taken a stand for "data" or for "theory." Margaret Mead can publish Samoan house-descriptions and genealogies, or co-operate in a wartime study of food habits using the most advanced techniques, and still be dismissed by many professional colleagues as "intuitive," or belabored by the even more fearsome term "insightful." The late W. I. Thomas would today perhaps be startled to see his work viewed as a storehouse of social-psychological theory, when his own much greater preoccupation was with the facts and forms of social reportage. On a much smaller scale, I find similar misunderstanding of my own teaching and writing. *The Lonely Crowd*, which lies towards the theory end of the scale, aroused misplaced enthusiasm from some historians and humanists because of its lack of graphs and tables, and perhaps misplaced animadversions from some social scientists who viewed it as more biased towards the "theory" end than was intended. For the book is full of data, mainly but not entirely in the traditional form of observation from everyday life: I speak there of movies, comic books, magazines; of progressive schools and traditional schools; of the way parents think of children, and vice versa; of the way executives think of workers, and vice versa. Many humanists fail to realize that such data require supporting data, and a more formal and systematic effort to demonstrate that what they and the author refer to as matters of common knowledge are really so. Conversely, many social scientists, prematurely dazzled by the new techniques, fail to realize how far we still are from being able to prove what we "know" by them.

To put matters another way, I do not believe that one is surrendering the strict demands of science to a human but unscientific desire for understanding if one accepts the theory-data dilemma and works within its limitations, while recognizing that at some future date those limitations will greatly change. For science itself arises out of the desire to explain, to understand: the technical operations are subsidiary to this. If the natural sciences did not satisfy this desire by real accomplishments, it is unlikely that they would enlist creative minds to serve the hard discipline of the techniques—though as a paying and going concern they can enlist many unadventurous minds drawn by motivations other than those of the pioneers. So, too, social scientists who insist that we must serve the machines and the techniques regardless of the quality of understanding that emerges from that service—for that service alone is real science—fail to appreciate not only the history of science in general but also that social science is still too untried to enlist and retain large-scale support without large-scale accomplishment.

Undoubtedly, science requires sacrifices of its acolytes, but the nature of those sacrifices differs with the age. By and large, American social science no longer requires of its personnel the humiliation, poverty, lack of recognition that were the fate of Marx, Comte, Freud, and, to a degree, of Sumner, Sorel, Veblen. But field-work is still arduous and heart-breaking, research still filled with disappointments, blind alleys, and want of adequate resources.[2] It is a sacrifice of vanity to realize that one will never even approximate the glorious achievements of the fathers, not perhaps live to see the edifice constructed by the technical adeptness of the great-grandsons. It is a sacrifice of impatience to be charitable both to one's work and that of others when this work has the status of "pilot projects," as social scientists overoptimistically dub most of their present enterprises—overoptimistically, because they assume that there will soon be a whole plant engaged in the production of results. In this situation, the claim that we should make the sacrifices of scientific work without the hope of gaining a better understanding of society—indeed while ridiculing whatever understanding is achieved, for instance by novelists, without training and technique—is to make vain demands on our willingness to wait for "production miracles."

I am quite aware that this formulation does not solve the question of how we know that an understanding not established directly or by strict reasoning on a sufficient volume of empirical data is a true understanding. I don't propose to unravel this epistemological mystery here: it is enough to observe that the acceptance of the position that only the generalizations founded on irrefutable data are true leaves us to conclude that all understanding of society (other than in economics, the social science with the greatest achievements to its credit) established up till now is pure illusion; and that all sociology is simply hypothesis awaiting proof, for I believe it can be shown that with rare exceptions even the most up-to-date data support the most up-to-date generalization only as example, not as proof in any (even probability-theory) scientific sense. Yet at the same time, only a data-extremist would insist that the study of Weber, Durkheim, Sim-

---

2. The scientific workers in the field of "culture and personality" must endure a particular kind of sacrifice, namely to have to live with heightened self-consciousness of all personal relations and cultural phenomena, making it hard for them to separate their professional work from the rest of their lives.

mel and other great turn-of-the-century founders is irrelevant to our understanding of social processes: some light emerges.

And the reason for this is that we are ourselves men living in society; and, as the saying goes, we were not born yesterday. Many social scientists, worried about bias and struck by what natural scientists have achieved in studying stars and atoms, being neither one nor the other, feel that when they approach work in their field they should cultivate a complete skepticism, at least until the not far distant day when theories will be buttressed at every point by data; ironically, this wanton innocence is itself the cultural product of some of the very thinkers whose writings they would reject as unscientific. Natural science deserves tremendous credit for having achieved so much when so inevitably distant from its objects; social scientists, rather than trying to impose on themselves similar handicaps, should take full advantage of the fact that they are themselves part of their universe of study, and heirs to a long and not utterly noncumulative tradition of thinking about man.[3]

§ IV

DOUBTLESS, more social scientists will agree that the problem is to proceed from one end of the theory-data scale to the other, so as to encompass a suitable combination of thought and fact, than will agree on which end should be taken as the starting-point. My own belief, already indicated, is that there is no "right" end, no royal road, but that one can fruitfully begin at either end, or anywhere between. One must be willing to take seriously theories which are not established, and even theories which are, in some formal sense, "refuted," when they offer a real illumination and insight, which will undoubtedly turn out to be a partial illumination. Thus, it makes not very fruitful use of Weber's book on the Protestant ethic to ask whether it is true or false. To be sure, the book evoked a whole historiography of disproof, but the book still helps us understand our world and our place in it. Certainly, no theory can have this success if it is in plain opposition to many facts, for the theory itself is an effort to explain and order facts; yet agreement with some large and crucial facts may be more important than contradiction by them in details.

At the same time, social scientists should be more willing than

---

3. Crane Brinton, in *Ideas and Men,* sees social science as largely noncumulative—having to be learned over again for each worker and each generation—while natural science is largely cumulative. And there can be no doubt that the truths of social interaction—of psychoanalysis, let us say—have to be experienced by each individual before he can make important use of them in research; yet there is a cumulative tradition which makes it possible to learn noncumulative truths, helping new field workers, for example, to face the ineluctable hardships of their initiation.

many of the ablest are, to begin at the "data" end of the scale, though without the illusion that they can move immediately therefrom to the grist of theory. Our obsession with our image of the natural sciences tends to make us think of data as only verification, as supporting a theory or destroying it. Yet the value of data as simple reporting on the quality and details of social life has been a most significant part of social science: Booth's *Life and Labour of the People in London*, Thomas and Znaniecki's *The Polish Peasant in Europe and America*, the Lynds' *Middletown* volumes, the Allison Davis and John Dollard studies of the Deep South, and many other works that present full pictures of some social phenomenon, partake of many of the qualities of good reporting. The theoretical schemes which the reporting supports usually seem less and less important with the passage of time: the data remain valuable and stimulating, and as useful in support of the theoretical schemes of the future as of those of the original authors.[4] Important branches of social science are even more clearly reporting rather than theory: this has been true, at least until recently, of most public opinion research: the poll data gathered in the public opinion journals, in the recent Cantril-Strunk volume, and in the *American Soldier,* form a rich body of materials, which we would never have had if we had had to wait for a structure of the theory-hypothesis-data-new-theory sort to justify gathering it.

Likewise, the scorn so frequently heaped on "gadgeteers," from without as well as within the ranks of social science, fails to grasp how much we owe, in all the sciences, to sheer fooling around with methods and techniques, more or less for their own sakes. In many ways, Freud was a gadgeteer, first in his work on the staining of cells for histological purposes, later in his experiments with hypnosis and other therapies; we forget this, since he also used his techniques to make brilliant discoveries. True, "gadgeteer" is often applied to those who see in a device or machine a panacea for all ills, or at the very least a solvent for hitherto intractable problems, and here certainly

---

4. In the middle '30's a type of reporting developed which had much in common with social science: in those days, reporters took to crossing the country and asking questions of various people they ran into (James Rorty, Benjamin Appel, John Dos Passos, Samuel Grafton, and others), presenting pictures which can support a number of different interpretations. At the same time, *Fortune* began to give large scope to reporters—some of whom have become very interested in social science and its problems—who developed a new kind of "story" which often surpasses the work of professional social scientists in information and even, though perhaps without intending it, in "theory."

My understanding of the origins and present importance of the reportorial tradition in social science has profited greatly from discussions with Everett Hughes.

scorn is justifiable. But scorn is also levelled at gadgeteers who make no such grandiose claims, and here it seems to reflect attitudes of a very widespread sort: our hierarchy of skill and learning snobberies, our gnawing uneasiness about "materialism" and mechanical know-how, our ambivalence towards those aspects of American life that John A. Kouwenhoven, in his book *Made in America,* sums up as the "vernacular." Science suffers, however, when the gadgeteer must justify himself by association with some immediate and high-flown purpose, whether drawn from the realm of theory or of social action.

In sum, whatever end of the scale one begins at, one is likely to be under pressure to move rapidly towards the other end—"to link theory and data" as the phrase goes—by people who have insufficient respect for either end in its own terms, and who fail to appreciate all the intermediate and frequently indirect and unplannable steps in between. This leads to the most paradoxical results: on the one hand, scholars think they have "proved" their case scientifically when they are very far from it—for if their case were not, to their own satisfaction, demonstrated, they could have no respect for themselves; and, on the other hand, other scholars are reduced to despair when they discover that the petty data they have accumulated in a stretch of painstaking and mayhap costly work bears little relation to the grand hypothesis with which they began. In this situation, work which is very far from technical validation, let alone from proving anything important about society, is often desperately seized upon by the promoters and defenders of social science in order to convince themselves and others that they are in a good line of work, and, beyond that, that they could produce far more if they got the funds and the go-ahead orders. As the design engineers in an industry feel harried by the demands and expectations of the product engineers who want to produce, and the sales engineers who want to sell, so the design engineers of social science are under the pressures just indicated from the production and sales staff who insist on putting on the social science assembly line what is still necessarily in the handicraft and mock-up stage.[5] In many quarters, the promoters of social science have aroused such unfulfillable expectations as to risk a disillusioning bust of the whole enterprise. Thus, while at an earlier time social scientists may have been overtimid, "ivory-towerish," and afraid of responsibility,

---

5. It should be added that this is often done in the friendliest spirit. At times, the production engineer will show an overgreat deference to the design engineer —as the result of snobberies already touched upon—leading the former to premature attempts to use and sell the work of the latter to raise his own status. Obviously enough, novelists and other artists are subjected to analogous briberies and temptations, and in the relation between highbrow and middlebrow art one can find similar tensions.

they seem today more endangered by check-kiting (in terms of reports leading to "pilot studies," to more reports, and so on endlessly) than by reticence.

§ V

ONE CAN IMAGINE the relief with which some promoters of social science have greeted a few recent very successful efforts to link theory and data. I shall discuss briefly two such major efforts—*The Authoritarian Personality*, by T. W. Adorno, Else Frenkel-Brunswik, Daniel J. Levinson, and R. Nevitt Sanford; and the *Yankee City* series by W. Lloyd Warner and his coworkers—in order to show that the difficulties we have been discussing arise even on the highest and most sophisticated level of research, and to show some of the risks one runs in taking such studies as models for slavish imitation.

The Authoritarian Personality is perhaps the most impressive attempt in recent American social psychology and sociology to link a large-scale and important theory to data which would support and demonstrate it. This thousand-page volume is the outgrowth of many years of study, first by members of the (Frankfort) Institute for Social Research, later by an able and energetic group at Berkeley that worked for another period of years: it was not a project set up to pay quick dividends out of capital to attract further capital, but rather one which took its time about the study of the authoritarian personality and its role in modern industrial society—a large order, indeed. The thinking at the "theory" end began in the late '20's and early '30's in Germany; a large volume dealing with many facets of the problem—*Autorität und Familie*—appeared in the mid-'30's, at which time empirical research projects had already begun; the research work that *The Authoritarian Personality* itself reports was carried out over a span of five years or more in Berkeley, and incorporates the use of the most subtle and advanced of psychological techniques. Time to work and think and experiment is essential for serious investigation, and this long period of maturation makes *The Authoritarian Personality* as good and significant as it is.

But there is just the rub. Society does not stand still—American society perhaps least of all—and the problem of twenty years ago is not the problem of today, and the problem of Germany then is not the problem of America now. Events continually outdistance our attempts to understand them; social scientists, no less than other people, must structure the world while at the same time keeping up with it. Economists kept talking about our economy as if its problems were those of underemployment for years after this problem had disappeared, and under circumstances that made its recrudescence unlikely for years to come, if ever.[6] *The Authoritarian Personality* rests on the equally irrelevant fundamental premise—as it appears to me—that European-style fascism is the great danger hanging over America, as well as on the minor premise—to me not important for America, and dubious even for Germany—that authoritarianism in character structure breeds and is bred by authoritarianism in social structure. As to fascism: there is no room here to set out all my reasons for believing that this is not the principal American menace—among them, is the position, developed in *The Lonely Crowd*, that virtually all sectors of American life (including would-be fascists) have an "in" on the political and social scene which would be disturbed by a *coup d'état;* moreover, that American big business is not as unified, ruthless, or conspiratorial as the authors of the book suppose; finally, if there exists a danger of internal repression in America today, it ensues more from the threat of totalitarian Soviet expansion than from sources in American "authoritarian personality."[7] As to the minor premise linking character and society, I suggest that, in America and England, the Puritan character, which qualifies in many ways as "authoritarian," actually helped foster a democratic social structure under given conditions of seventeenth-century life; conversely, the pliable "democratic" personality can be molded and made use of, under other social conditions and institutions, in developing a rigid and authoritarian society.

These may seem like drastic criticisms, and they certainly go to the heart of the authors' aims and conclusions. Yet the by-products of the study are invaluable: never, for instance, have we had, on such a large scale, such brilliant and brilliantly-validated use of "diagnostic" questions arranged in scales to test underlying attitudes, nor such grasp of nuances of verbal expression as clues to character, nor such an interesting discussion of the political attitudes of criminals, nor so capable an appraisal of the possibilities of typological treatment in social research. Nor is the study of fascism itself all waste effort by any means: there are undoubtedly some millions of fascist-minded people in the United States, and we now have an unexampled look at

---

6. We run here, among other things, into the matter of the "self-confirming prophecy" discussed by Robert K. Merton in *Social Theory and Social Structure*. Since people on all levels of our society believe that depressions are controllable (some, as the result of the Keynesians; others, as a result of their interpretation of our war experience), while they do not believe wars are controllable, the government will be under great if not irresistible pressure to live up to these expectations—by a war economy if necessary. This seemed evident to a number of observers before economists became concerned with the problems of full employment.

7. For a similar view, see Paul Kecskemeti, "Prejudice in the Catastrophic Perspective," *Commentary* (March, 1951).

many sides of their outlooks and personalities. Nevertheless, the study itself, as an effort to understand America, does not carry us far; the very gift and social concern of the planners of the work, which led them to the problem of fascism, led them off on what turned out, two decades later, to be a false scent; and if the study contributes, as I think likely, to the understanding of society, it will be indirectly, through its by-products.

Other examples of the complexites introduced by the necessarily long process of data-gathering and publishing are the studies of social class directed and inspired by Lloyd Warner. His first work in this field was done in a New England town at the beginning of the depression; the same techniques and concerns that were used in "Yankee City" in the early '30's have been carried over, with minor systematizations and modifications, to "Deep South" and to "Elmtown" ("Jonesville"), with way stations in between. But in these later studies the question is not raised whether class remains the most fruitful concept for understanding American culture and personality in 1951; or whether people today are as concerned with social mobility as they were twenty years ago, and as the technique then devised nearly inevitably makes it appear that they still are—for the technique tends to confuse membership in a social class, as symbolized by a brilliant variety of indices, with consciousness of that membership and of its implications, honorific and otherwise. The technique is not neutral—no technique is; it was devised at a time when certain problems relating to class were pre-eminent, and when Warner's insistence on their importance was stimulating and heretical; the technique took years to perfect, but now that it is perfected (a much debated point among experts), and relatively easy for students to apply, it must be asked whether other problems—divisions within social classes, for instance, or cutting across classes—may not have become more significant, even though class is still of great and obvious significance. Professor Warner himself, in fact, not being committed to a large and expensive apparatus, seems in his most recent work to be as interested in comparing the fantasy life of people on what he calls the "common man" level with that of the "uncommon man" as he is with new applications of the Yankee City scheme.

We must conclude, then, that the effort to link theory and data, at the present pace of work, runs into a most important set of logistical problems. It is hard enough to modify one's own conceptions to take account of a changing world, and perhaps to help change it; it is harder, much harder, to overhaul a huge research project, planned over the many years required for work, evaluation, and publication, so as to fit these changing conceptions. In answer to such dejections, it is often argued that money is the only bottleneck to the spectacular advance of social science—and that, if only a quarter as much were made available as was put at the disposal of atomic scientists, there would be no important areas of ignorance left about the world, let alone the United States! Conceivably, if there were *enough* money, and *enough* personnel, monopolistic competition among even large-scale research enterprises would tend to keep them flexible and fast on their feet to a degree—yet even here the logistical problem would remain, for a country that could be brought to devote such enormous resources to its own self-scrutiny would obviously be a very different land from the present U.S.A., so different perhaps that social science would no longer appear as inviting or necessary! One is almost awe-struck with the lack of humor, if not of humility, on the part of those social scientists who feel their trade so all-important that they can make such requests of the national income and the national man-power, and one could greatly admire the implicit utopian faith so displayed, if one did not feel an underlying insecurity prompting the frequent use of the nuclear physicists as a reference group.

It is evident, moreover, that the large-scale theory-testing operation runs the risks of encouraging mere discipleship which are always present in intellectual and artistic enterprise. The easiest way to do research is to apply the beautifully-engineered models supplied by such work as that of the Berkeley group and Warner—though actually, partly because this work has many complexities and is highly controversial, much inferior models are usually chosen. But while a proved sire may be the best bet in cattle-breeding, proved paternities in the social sciences are not so satisfactory. The discipline has much less chance, generally, of adapting his conceptions to the rapidly changing course of social development than the originator—but even the latter may be trapped by fear of disappointing, or "disemploying," his disciples.

Since I am myself a practitioner of social science, as well as a critic thereof, I must guard against the possible implication that I consider my own writing and teaching to have escaped these pitfalls —on the contrary, it is from falling in that I have learned to locate some of them. But I do suggest that certain aspects of my work which appear to some contemporary social scientists to be simply defects— a somewhat casual and unsystematic approach, and a refusal to set up the grand money- and time- and man-consuming research projects that would demonstrate my hypotheses—are not only defects, and certainly not unintended ones: if what I have said hitherto is sound, there are also virtues in the handicraft approach which, not entirely committed to a major course of action, is able to shift and turn with the development of the thought of the researcher, as well as with the course of social development. Without any question, however, this unmethodical method is subject to its own hazards, most of which have been examined at length in the social science literature of the recent, method-conscious decades.

§ VI

IT IS INTERESTING to speculate about what American social science would look like today if journalism had had as much prestige in the late nineteenth and early twentieth centuries as natural science, though perhaps the drive towards professionalization has been more important in shaping social science than the fact that the professional model chosen has generally been physics or biology. In England an organization has grown up in the last fifteen years—Mass Observation, or MO for short—which deserves to be better known in this country, for in conception it is a frontal attack both on the natural science model and on professionalization. It consists of a group of animated and amateur social observers who are encouraged to send in reports on assigned topics—and to suggest topics—to a central office run by social scientists: they have studied such British institutions as the pub, church-going, the last Coronation Day, and what happens at "all-in" wrestling. MO attempts to reduce the distance between observers and observed by allowing the latter to participate in the processes of social study—to bring to it what they have in the way of gifts of observation and to receive in return instruction and information based on others' observation. In intention, though not in its rather sloppy execution, it is an adult education venture in the social sciences.[8]

American (and British) public opinion specialists have heaped scorn on the MO sampling methods or lack of them; and one could also criticize the raw empiricism of such a book as *May the Twelfth*, which reports, without interpretation or selection or preliminary training of the reporters, what observers noticed on Coronation Day in 1938; there MO forgot that the first duty of a reporter is to be interesting, a duty which demands both selection and interpretation.[9]

In the United States there have been a few developments similar to MO but, significantly enough, all of them appear to have been

---

8. There is, of course, a tradition of local history studies, and also of local linguistics and folk culture studies, which goes back a long way in Europe, and to a lesser degree in this country.

9. Fortunately, Robert E. Park never got over his training as a Sunday Supplement feature writer for the Detroit press; he never managed, in his late career as a sociologist, to stay away from interest or "human interest" for very long at a time. See his "Autobiographical Note" in *Race and Culture*.

motivated by immediate problems of social policy rather than, as in the case of the British organization, by this coupled with "idle curiosity" about the society. During World War II the OWI ran what were called Correspondence Panels: men and women throughout the country who sent in reports on such assigned topics as how the draft was going, the effect of price control, and morale, receiving in return instructions and commentary; under the direction of Elizabeth Herzog, many small businessmen, housewives, and others learned for the first time to look at their communities with the detached and inquiring air which is the hallmark of the good reporter and the good social science observer. (With the end of the war, the program, like so much else that had been painfully built up, was hastily demolished.) More widely known is the "action-research" approach of the late Kurt Lewin and a group of his followers; their idea was that it might be possible to enlist ordinary citizens to study their own community problems; more than that, this self-study, they believed, would help in the solution of these problems, while the very effort at solution would in turn invigorate research. Under the influence of this approach there have been, for example, a number of "community self-audits," in which citizens, under the direction of social scientists, have examined their community from the point of view of its failings and fulfillments, particularly as to race relations. The method has much to be said for it, both as adult education and as social action, but I have some misgivings about its usefulness for research and deeper understanding: usually the social scientists in charge already know, in a rough way, that they will find anti-Negro bias in housing in Montclair or discrimination in employment in Northfield (two cities where successful audits were made), and "self-audit" can become, despite the democratic sympathies of the leaders, little more than a new gimmick to spur community activity.

At any rate, America much more than England seems to me to need both the reporting technique and the enlistment of the amateur observer that characterize MO—to need them for the basic job of finding out what goes on, apart from any question as to what can be done about it. This country is so big, so varied, so almost if not quite unencompassable, that social research cannot have enough observers who will break down its momentary generalizations and open up new views. Something like MO would permit what might be called "research by exception," where a researcher would count on his "far-flung correspondents" to tell him where something he had taken for granted was not so. Indeed, there are many fields of social research which simply cannot be handled by existing techniques. If we want to know, for example, the reactions of movie audiences to a nationally-exhibited film, as this varies from showing to showing, we cannot learn this at present, nor can sampling methods tell us how an audience, a group en masse, responds; the whole wide field of American popular culture needs mass explorers and mass observers: for sports events, dance-halls, bookie joints, fairs, and countless other pastimes. By bringing these observers into our research organizations, moreover, we are likely greatly to amplify our conception both of the complexity of our country and of its newly emerging problems, for there will be no want of stimulating queries and reports.[10]

Certainly, a social science militia of this type would go far to complement, and perhaps to check, the social science army of professionals envisaged by the logistics discussed earlier. We would be overwhelmed with data: our poor schemes would have to be sturdy indeed to stand up to it—perhaps, afraid of drowning in data, we would become fonder of theory! We would also have to focus on questions that interested our militia—and work on the problem of easy communication with them—for they would be bound to us, not by professional ties, but by mutual needs for understanding. We may perhaps not be prepared for the new functions that would be forced upon us. But at the same time, accepting our function as reporters as well as systematizers, we might continue to be happy even where we were unsuccessful.

§ VII

IN A THOUGHT-PROVOKING essay on "The Art of Social Science," Robert Redfield has called attention to some of the ambiguities of current emphasis on method in social research, pointing out that Tocqueville and other great and gifted observers had added much to our knowledge while ignorant of or violating the rules laid down by men who have added much less. If what I have said in this paper makes sense, we may draw a further analogy with contemporary problems of art, especially literary art. For it would seem that social scientists, too, have their "New Critics" who have been laying down a canon which, in the minds of some, operates to intimidate creative work. The canon is actually more perfectionist than its literary analogue, since it is based, not on actual work, but on often brilliant

---

10. Thanks to the cooperation of the National Opinion Research Center, I once had the opportunity to go over many reports sent in by interviewers to accompany their formal schedules—letters, really, rather than reports, which touched on how hard the interviewing had gone or how easy, on what types of questions made for trouble or interest, and on many of the day-to-day events and encounters in the interviewers' rounds. Often, these reports were more stimulating than the content of the schedules, which dealt with ephemeral opinions: what do you think of the UN, of Truman, of Palestine partition, or whatever else were the "issues" of 1948.

extrapolation from our old friends, the "pilot studies." And whereas the new critics in literature frequently have a verve and elegance in writing, and a depth in understanding, which compensates for much that may be lacking in creative writing, the new critics in social science—while they would hardly agree with William F. Ogburn's paper on "The Folklore of Social Science" that the social scientists of the future will not be gifted with wit or originality but will publish merely statistical reports—seem to feel that their ascetic laboriousness and lugubriousness in the content of criticism should also be reflected in its style.

Both developments, moreover, in literature and in social science, are in part the outcome of the tremendous advance in university teaching in the humanities and in the social sciences in the last several decades. At many institutions, large and small, there has been a heightening of critical standards, and students are confronted, not with easy-going teachers using casual texts, but with able and energetic new critics, who can discover the flaws in the finest poetry and fiction, or in the most heralded works of social science. And in both areas, as a price for this advance, there is a temptation for students to become easily discouraged about what they could contribute to creative work; they have to bear in mind so many injunctions, each of them "correct," that they can no more start their own enterprises than could a businessman in a completely regimented state—for their vanity and ambition are already low, as the result of other social developments than the rise of the new critics.

In the art world at least, the battle of artists and critics is an old one. But it is a battle of a noncumulative sort, which must be fought over in every era, because of changes in the division of labor, and in the strength and self-confidence of the several sides. In American writing, those seem to fare best who pay no attention to critics—symbolized by William Faulkner calling himself aggressively a farmer, and not a literary man. In American social science, many of the best contributions have been made by journalists and others who were out of the circle of academic life and criticism. But surely this is not an optimum solution, for it lowers the intellectual level of creative writing, and leaves critics as the audience for other critics. And while in art there is an inexhaustible storehouse for the critics to draw upon, in social science there is not enough good work to occupy many critics for a full-time day. Marx was right when he wrote in *The German Ideology* that it should be "possible for one to do one thing today and another tomorrow—to hunt in the morning, to fish in the evening, to criticize after dinner just as I have in mind, without ever becoming hunter, fisherman, shepherd, or critic."

29. Some Clinical and Cultural Aspects of the Aging Process

IF WE OBSERVE the aging of individuals, in the period after middle life, it seems to me that we can distinguish three ideal-typical outcomes. Some individuals bear within themselves some psychological sources of self-renewal; aging brings for them accretions of wisdom, with no loss of spontaneity and ability to enjoy life, and they are relatively independent of the culture's strictures and penalties imposed on the aged. Other individuals, possibly the majority, bear within them no such resources but are the beneficiaries of a cultural preservative (derived from work, power, position, etc.) which sustains them although only so long as the cultural conditions remain stable and protective. A third group, protected neither from within nor from without, simply decay. In terms more fully delineated elsewhere,[1] we may have autonomous, adjusted, and anomic reactions to aging.

§ THE AUTONOMOUS

IN THE CASE of someone like Bertrand Russell or Toscanini, one feels an essential aliveness of spirit that reflexively keeps the body alive, too, in the face of the inevitable physiological catabolisms. Such men create something new every day through their own reactions; in their work as in their general style of life they exhibit what Erich Fromm calls the "productive orientation."[2] It is most important to realize that such men are not necessarily "balanced" or "well-adjusted" people: they may have terrible tempers, neurotic moods; they may be shut out from whole areas of existence; they may get along well with very few people, or prefer the "company" of dead people as historians or musicians; they may relate themselves to the cosmos more through an emphasis on objects and ideas than on social relations. One can see in such cases that a passionate interest or preoccupation which has remained alive since childhood—though perhaps newly justified or rediscovered in middle life—may matter much more than the roundedness of interests we are today inclined to encourage among our two vulnerable groups of "clients": children and older people. It might be valuable to study, for instance, professional chess players of dis-

1. See chapter 14 of *The Lonely Crowd*.
2. *Man for Himself*.

tinction; my guess would be that they suffer very little deterioration as a social-psychological process, however constricted their lives may appear to the therapist whose norm is a superficial integration of a bundle of diverse activities.

Such individuals, I repeat, are fairly immune to cultural changes, or to cultural definitions of their own physical changes: they carry their preservative, their "spirits," within. Freud could continue to live with vigor in the face of cancer of the mouth which made eating embarrassing and difficult; as his life went on, it seems to me that he grew steadily more alive and imperturbable—*Civilization and Its Discontents*, written when he was over 70, belies its pessimistic theme by the very vitality of its presentation. Likewise Franz Boas, though he suffered from disfigurement and though he was in many ways a cramped person, does not appear to have experienced any decline of powers. The misfortunes brought by Nazism could no more shake either man than the misfortunes brought by their own bodies. Men of this sort exhibit in a dramatic way the specifically human power to grow and develop on a super-physiological level (with, of course, physiological consequences); as long as the body does not actively prevent, these men are immortal because of their ability to renew themselves.

In lesser degree, anyone who can experience anything for himself —whether he is a "man of distinction" or not—staves off by so much psychological death. Paradoxically, the premonition of death may for many be a stimulus to such novelty of experience: the imminence of death serves to sweep away the inessential preoccupations for those who do not flee from the thought of death into triviality. It is apparent that we enter here a cultural dimension and raise the questions how death is regarded or disregarded in America, compared to how it is viewed, for example, in existentialist philosophy.

I can think of several reasons why we have not paid very much attention to these autonomous reactions to aging. Such reactions are rare, and a spurious democracy has influenced both our research methods (I am sometimes tempted to define "validity" as part of the context of an experiment demanding so little in the way of esoteric gift that any number can play at it, provided they have taken a certain number of courses) and our research subjects (it would be deemed snobbish to investigate only the best people). Moreover, the period of life I am describing and its attendant qualities do not last long: men react productively to waning physical and often social power, only to die shortly thereafter. And we tend to view individuals as we do entire cultures: while we can admire the Hellenistic period although it was weak and vulnerable and soon perished, we do not on the whole admire declining empires nearer to us in time. We read their future fate—death—into our present judgment of them.

§ THE ADJUSTED

I SHOULD, I SUPPOSE, always put quotation marks around my use of the term "adjusted," for I define this, not in terms of my own value judgments but in terms of given cultural definitions. For instance, we all know the type of American executive or professional man who does not allow himself to age, but by what appears almost sheer will keeps himself "well-preserved," as if in creosote. For the most part, he lacks inner aliveness of the sort just discussed; the will which burns in him, while often admirable, cannot be said to be truly "his": it is compulsive; he has no control over it, but it controls him. He appears to exist in a psychological deep-freeze; new experience cannot get at him, but rather he fulfills himself by carrying out ever-renewed tasks which are given by his environment: he is borne along on the tide of cultural agendas. So long as these agendas remain, he is safe; he does not acquire wisdom, as the old of some other cultures are said to do, but he does not lose skill—or if he does, is protected by his power from the consequences, perhaps the awareness, of loss of skill. In such a man, reponsibility may substitute for maturity.

Indeed, it could be argued that the protection furnished such people in the United States is particularly strong since their "youthfulness" remains a social and economic prestige-point and wisdom might actually, if it brought awareness of death and what the culture regarded as pessimism, be a count against them. In a way, nothing happens to these people, which leads them (save possibly in rare moments of self-doubt and self-questioning) to regard themselves as well-off. They prefigure in complex and often imperceptible ways the cultural cosmetic that makes Americans appear youthful to other peoples. And, since they are well-fed, well-groomed, and vitamin-dosed, there may be an actual delay-in-transit of the usual physiological declines to partly compensate for lack of psychological growth. Their outward appearance of aliveness may mask inner sterility.

Like the women of an earlier day who were held up by stays, such "adjusted" people of the middle and later years are held up by endoskeletal (mesmorphic?) tensions. As I have said, they are literally held up: nothing advances, save their careers, their responsibilities. This sort of energy must surely be ranked among the world-conquering assets of Western man: it is impressive to Indians to find Englishmen, as well as mad dogs, out in the noonday sun—they are gods of a sort, who tell the sun to stand still. Only at night, perhaps, coming home from a party, does the mask drop or crack, to be ritualistically reorganized the following day. We who are the beneficiaries of such accumulated energies in the past cannot lightly scoff at their possessors.

Nevertheless, I am inclined to think that many of the geriatric suggestions currently made for improving the adjustment of the elderly are aimed simply at finding ersatz preservatives, not at any inner transformations that would allow self-renewal to occur. Thus, we may seek to persuade a retired doctor or executive to take up golf or fishing with the same undiscerning ferocity he once threw into his work and its social context; we may shift someone from the faculty club or the Kiwanis into the Golden Age Club; and so on. It would be unjust to criticize too severely these ameliorative measures in the absence of understood and institutionalized ways of assisting more basic transformation—ways it is often, one fears, too late to start with by the time of retirement. (We know, in principle, it is never too late; but, as with other therapeutic questions, it is a matter of available help, of the allocation of scarce resources.) Yet we may occasionally discover dilemmas in which too quick an effort to assure a smooth adjustment results in this merely substitutive activity, whereas allowing a person to be confronted for a time with nothingness might save him—or destroy him—depending on what inner resources he could muster in reaction to the challenge.[3]

And in this connection let me bring up reservations about our usual social-psychological discussions of roles and role theory—discussions which too easily assume that people *are* the roles they play, the willing or unwilling puppeteers of the social drama. In my own view, the ability to play roles not only involves, in a great many instances, some rewriting of the socially-provided script, but some saving grace of potentiality not bound up in the role; the role itself is what allows people to give to it less than their full selves; it clarifies one's economy of affects. Hence there are reservoirs of inner life in a great many individuals whose roles, almost by definition, do not wholly absorb them. (The same is true, as Toynbee observes in terms of world history, of many cultures and what had been thought to be their "roles.") We see in wartime or other socially-structured emergency the great efflorescence of unsuspected potentialities in people —unsuspected often enough by the very individuals concerned. Where do these potentialities come from? It is hard to say, though we are tempted to refer them, as we refer so many mysteries, to childhood,

3. I have just come upon the excellent article of Dr. Martin Gumpert, "Old Age and Productive Loss," *Bulletin of the Menninger Clinic,* vol. 17, pp. 103-109 (May 1953). Dr. Gumpert stresses that the very bodily defeats and impairments of the aging person may be and often are more than compensated for by inner growth.

and to say that the cultural preservative is a deep-freeze in the sense, too, that childhood potentialities, though long neglected, are seldom wholly crushed. (Very few projective test experts, in my limited observation, focus sufficiently on the discovery of such potentialities; the "deeper levels" they look for are ordinarily those that foreshadow trouble rather than liberation: they are understandably more worried that they will miss a hidden flaw than a buried asset.)

Professor Martin Loeb, the field director of our Kansas City research, in discussing these notions with me, has been inclined to question the making of such explicit value judgments, the positing of an ideal of aging as the basis for setting up a typology. He suggested that I might be in danger of projecting into a typology my own dream that the autonomous person does not "really" age, at least in any deleterious way. And he asked what was wrong with a grandmother's way of aging who had had a hard life and now preferred to sit passively on the porch and watch her grandchildren and the passing traffic? Who was to tell her she should be spontaneous?

I doubt if this was meant as a warning against value judgments as such, for we cannot avoid them, but rather against shallow and ethnocentric ones. Still, I sometimes feel that middle-class social scientists are today almost too ready to throw over their own values, as class-biased, while accepting values from groups whose life-conditions have permitted them fewer alternatives. Our circle of sympathy should not be too narrow—should even perhaps include the lower-middle-class grandmother who wears too much grease paint in a pathetic effort to look like a cover girl. And certainly a grandmother who decides out of her life-experience to observe her progeny and the passing show and who is capable of observing people as individuals and not entirely as stereotypes would strike me as making a productive reaction to aging—spontaneity and aliveness are of course not to be equated with activity and hep-ness. In general, I feel that we can sharpen our scientific awareness of what aging does to people, and vice versa, by bringing into play our preference for more creative as against more stultified ways of meeting the challenge of aging in individuals and in cultural groups.

As the Eisenhower Administration takes office, I think we shall have an unusual opportunity to observe the working out of some of these ways. Some of the military and business leaders newly drafted into government will be unable to grow and develop when robbed of the protective surroundings their social systems gave them; they may even appear to age rapidly, to decay. (Others, sufficiently high up, can try to recreate analogous protective systems, down to the secretary, the staffs, the shape of the desks and perhaps of the subordinates too—so as to avoid the need to leave "home.") Still others, however, will prove to have, or to gain, the quality of inner aliveness that enables one to adapt to radically new surroundings; fear does not prevent their seeing that these are new, or force them simply to curse the newness as "bureaucracy," "politics," or whatnot; rather, they will be stimulated.

One would want to watch, also, for the consequences of different occupational experiences before entering the government. Are the department store executives whom William E. Henry has described as having a tropism towards decision-making better off than bankers who are in the main accustomed to constrict decision-making? Is it a question of the nature of different preservatives in different occupational groups, as these mix or refuse to mix with the occupational experience of government officials? Can we develop tests that will help answer such questions, not for young people early in their careers, but for middle-aged people suddenly given a new lease on a new office, if not on a new life?

An illustration of how difficult it is to predict which of these several "careers of aging" an individual will pursue is presented by the notorious misjudgments teachers are apt to make about the prospects of their students. Some who appear to have spark and originality lose it very shortly. Then, retroactively, one can see that while young they were kept alive partly by physiological changes and that aging started for them at 25 if not before; nothing new has happened after that. In such cases, it depends hardly at all on the individual whether the culture keeps him going until death or does not prevent his obvious and grievous deterioration. In contrast, other individuals who in their 20s appeared to be quite set in their ways, without much ability to have new experiences, turn out to have been harboring reserves which slowly come to reshape their whole orientation. Whereas for some and perhaps most men the possession of power protects them from having to develop (others are compelled to adapt to *them*), there remain a number of men for whom power serves as a stimulant to late flowering.

Thus, it is plain that for the "adjusted" group it matters decisively what institutions they hitch or are hitched onto, and whether such institutions encapsulate them or awaken them or destroy them. Their one-and-only life-cycle gets fatally mixed up with the larger institutional cycles. And, to recur to our image of the aging business or professional person, it sometimes seems as if his tenacious efforts to keep himself from sagging into a flabby or relaxed age provide much of the motive power for our entrepreneurial expansion combined with institutional conservatism.

§ THE ANOMIC

REAL DECAY sets in when the physiological vitality is lost, and when the culture does not carry the individual onward but drops him. Here we get the sudden decompositions, as they appear, of some men who are forced to retire, where it becomes evident that the job and its emotional ambience kept the job-holder together: he held a job less than the job held him. Or we get the spouse who—though he or she did not greatly love the other spouse—cannot survive him or her, but dies shortly thereafter in a metaphorical Suttee. (We find the same pattern among the "quasi-families" of people who are not married, but are tied to each other in a similar symbiotic way.) Such people live like cards, propped up by other cards.

At first blush, they may look very much like the people who have a better cultural preservative, but the paths soon diverge, and their decay sets in earlier. They are not the lawyers and engineers and businessmen of springy step, but the prematurely weary and resigned. As against the person who, in a way, never grows up, never faces death, they sometimes appear never to have been young. But in both cases—the adjusted and the anomic outcomes—there is a truncation of the "seven ages of man," the variety and contretemps of the life cycle; there is an insufficient dialectic between physiological decline and psychological increment.

Moreover, both the autonomous and the anomic reactions to aging are alike in that the individuals concerned make little use of the standard cultural preservatives—the former because they transcend and reshape them, the latter because they cannot attain them or maintain them. If responsibility accompanies maturity for the autonomous, and takes the place of maturity for the adjusted, the anomic find their way to neither. Like a person who is afraid to overshoot the green when he drives from the tee (or, more probably, gives up acting as if he wanted to make the green at all), they start out in life with aims that will not carry them through a career. And they do not succeed in getting onto an institutional escalator that will define for them what it is to have a career.

Our research in Kansas City, having moved out of the clinic and into the community, will probably have to develop typologies less "universal" than this one I have proposed here. For the three types I have sketched have nothing to do with Kansas City as such—with its conflict of rural and urban ideologies, its history as an entrepot, its prospective future as an industrial base. Differences of sex (I have said almost nothing about women in this paper) and of social station have decisive consequences for the forms of aging felt to be appropriate—

but these differences, too, while illustrated in Kansas City as elsewhere, are not peculiar to it. Nevertheless, as we examine different occupational groups in the metropolitan area, we may find this typology useful as a critique of each group's way of aging. Thus the well-to-do and ceaselessly energetic medical men of Kansas City may buy a cultural preservative at the expense of being run ragged from the days when they did autopsies to the day when they are the subject of one—perhaps a bit raggeder because busier, more successful, and slightly more traditional, than medical men elsewhere. As against this, we may find the pattern Warren Peterson suspects to exist among Kansas City high school teachers, that they are "old maids" at 30 and for 40 years thereafter (they must retire at 70) do not appreciably age, being kept alive by their young charges, their community obligations, their summer school courses, and the rest of the diurnal round to which this helplessly exposed target of community hopes, fears, and envies is committed.

Even here, I doubt if we shall find patterns exclusively Kansas City's, or exclusively metropolitan. But it is in any case fortunate that our research objectives, and our setting in Kansas City, both force and encourage us to move back and forth between clinical and cultural considerations, in search of a typology, or a set of them, that encompasses both.

30. The Meaning of Opinion*

THE RELATION OF MANY SOCIAL SCIENTISTS—and of course of the public at large—to the failure of the polls to predict the American presidential election was itself an interesting social-psychological phenomenon. Some of the opinion researchers hope to find the cause of the failure in some simple "bug" in the polling machinery, such as a sampling error; possibly a good deal of their security has rested in their belief that social science is as "scientific" as they believe natural science to be. Others are worried about the reactions of potential clients, governmental and commercial, for applied social research; they are troubled that the pollers may have done a bad job of public relations; they feel let down in their task of selling social research; they, too, would like to see some quick and simple explanation emerge. Perhaps these responses indicate some doubts as to the value of social science as a human enterprise of curiosity and self-understanding, doubts which need to be assuaged by "success," both in terms of accurate prediction and of public usefulness and approval.

Many other social scientists had a positive reaction to the failure of the polls. Something interesting and new had happened. Here was a chance to justify re-examining old routines, and to test others which had not had much of a hearing—and perhaps to learn something. We take it that this is the spirit in which this Symposium has been called together. A reaction of ours was that the judgment of the polls in terms of success and failure of prediction—that is, not in terms of percentage of error, but in terms of picking the winner—was a striking indication of the success-ethos of America. (Gallup was just as far off in 1936, but having picked the winner, it hardly mattered.) In social research, if not in life, however, it is better to be right than to guess who will be president; that is, better to understand what goes on in society than to predict, empirically, what will happen if one doesn't know *why* one is right. And good public relations can be a menace to social research, in terms of forcing or encouraging scientists to work on trivial tasks or even on serious ones which the culture, rather than they, think are important. Likewise, success, and the craving for it, can be constricting for social research, as indeed for any scholarly or creative work, forcing it to go through routines with ever greater technical proficiency and ever greater boredom; while failure can be liberating in its challenge.

---

* With Nathan Glazer.

We make one or two technical suggestions as to why the polls may have "failed." But our principal concern in this article is with the further expansion of the use of polls in public opinion research, to garner not only opinions but also the less accessible situations and feelings which underlie opinions. Public opinion pollers have, of course, been moving in this direction, aware that their delicate apparatus, though designed and originally used to measure surface reactions, needs to be perfected not only for this purpose, but also to be adapted to new and even more demanding uses, if it is to help us understand social change. The election is another reminder, if any were required, that these two tasks—measurement of opinion, and discovery of its roots in social structure and character structure—are fundamentally interrelated. This interrelationship exists, we suggest, not only on the level of predicting political behavior but also in the day-to-day practice of political polling, which cannot help, in the process of gathering opinions, gathering also a good deal of information which might locate the opinions in a more meaningful context. At present, much of this information is thrown away, as a residue or by-product—or indeed, as an obstacle getting in the way of the true opinion. Partly, the problem is a practical one: keeping the residues, and analyzing them, is in the present state of the art a most expensive and time-consuming operation. In the first instance, however, the problem is one of intellectual clarification: it is one of tracing the relationship between the opinion which is reported as such and its residues, and of suggesting ways of viewing the complex totality as a *Gestalt*.

To avoid misunderstanding, we should make clear at the outset that we are not making a plea for polling conducted by "depth" interviews. We do not believe that the longer and more "freely" someone talks, the more truth he necessarily tells, nor that psychological probing is as useful as, say, study of group affiliation and activity in predicting an election. We agree with most of the penetrating remarks of Paul F. Lazarsfeld[1] on the problem of open-ended versus structured interviews: namely, that virtually all the functions for which intensive interviews are used today can be met by different types of conventional poll questions, if intelligently constructed. Our point is rather that new functions, at the moment perhaps best met by intensive interviews, must be taken on by polling, if it is to serve as an effective tool in "mirroring" the public mind.

---

1. "The Controversy over Detailed Interviews—an Offer for Negotiation," *Public Opinion Quarterly*, 8, No. 1 (1944), pp. 38-60.

§ SOME ASSUMPTIONS WHICH UNDERLIE POLLING

TO DIVIDE THE TOTAL POPULATION on any given question among those who are for, those against, and those undecided, gives an inadequate report of the state of public opinion on most types of issues; and this remains so even when the report is complicated by the use of such devices as George Gallup's quintamensional plan,[2] Roper's multiple-choice, or the various types of intensity thermometers. All these reports assume, in the first place, a qualitative equality among all those who select the same alternative, an equality reflected in the expectation that people in all social classes, and of all character types, will be equally habituated to the style of thinking which "makes up its mind" in terms of such stateable alternatives. These methods generally assume, in the second place, that the most significant division of opinion on any issue is between those who are for and those who are against, and between both of these and the "don't knows." But this simply reflects the structure of opinion as our political-legal tradition supposes it to be, with each view having its partisans and its "independent voters." This tradition is in turn supported by the way the mass media handle opinion, which is again in terms of a dichotomy or trichotomy, or in terms of categories and degrees of partisanship. Public opinion research comes along and confirms the existing ideology about opinion, both in its interviewing methods and in its manner of presenting its findings.

The scientific study of public opinion is thus today in the hands of neither the poll-takers nor the respondents: both are caught in an historical process which has not only set the questions to be investigated but also the form of the answer. We should at least assume that another structure of opinion may exist, in which every question has many sides, and many perspectives in which it may be viewed, each tinged with varying degrees of meaning and affect; we should try to work with models of opinion other than the conventional two- or three-sided one now in use. One such model, for example, might divide the population into those who had grounds for an opinion and those who did not. Among others, the National Opinion Research Center (NORC) has done much work along this line. Another model might divide those in whom the answer was deeply rooted from those to whom the answer was, so to speak, lightly attached. One might experiment with this by having the interviewer challenge or argue with the answer—contrary to the convention, which advocates of both structured and open-ended methods share, of "non-directive" interviewing.

---

2. ,"The Quintamensional Plan of Question Design," *Public Opinion Quarterly*, 11, No. 3 (1947), pp. 385-393.

Present-day polling, in its main assumptions, exemplifies the 19th-century liberal's approach to the individual as a social atom. By a convenient fiction, polling tends to treat its subject, in every social stratum, as a "responsible citizen"—one who considers the world in terms of "issues" and considers these issue in the terms in which they are discussed in the press and on the radio, holds a position in a political spectrum which runs in such single dimensions as left-right, or Republican-Democrat-Progressive, and feels it his duty to take sides on public issues both when polled and when called upon to vote.

To be sure, one can still find people like this—often people in the upper and upper middle classes, and many older persons of varying class position for whom opinion grows out of a feeling of responsibility, and out of a feeling of potency to affect political events which responsibility implies. Such people think that their opinion, and their vote, matter very much, and the mass media and the polling process encourage them in this belief. Maybe this is a good thing for society. But it unquestionably handicaps public opinion research to operate with assumptions which are no longer, if they ever were, a useful abstraction from the social reality of a mass society. The type of 19th-century citizen, whom we have characterized—a type we call "inner-directed"—becomes increasingly rare under the pressures of our era.

For most people in modern society, there is no such direct relation between responsibility for having an opinion and responsibility for action. They can see no relation between their political opinions and the actual course of political life—particularly those developments, such as war, which are most crucial to them. On the contrary, the obscurity and remoteness of the more decisive national and international political happenings, the general feeling that instead of "we" (the common people), it is some alien "they" (the distant powers) who manage events (among those social groups who assume events to be manageable at all)—these developments have made politics an anxious and frustrating topic. And this leads either to an obviously apathetic reaction to politics or to attempts (functionally no less apathetic) to view politics in some more tolerable framework, such as sports (the election as a race), chit-chat (the election as gossip), or the more amiable aspects of the American past (clichés about democracy). People today seem to us to be increasingly concerned with the opinions of others rather than with what they themselves think, and use their own opinions not so much to orient themselves in responsible action as to please, entertain, or simply get along with others. This psychic state increases their subjective feelings of powerlessness to affect the course of political events.

Yet the great majority of people, while they are actually power-less and while they feel as alienated from politics as from the other major foci of modern life, are called upon, in our democratic tradition, to act as if they had power. They are called upon to vote, and to expose themselves to information and exhortation from the mass media and to discussion in their clique groups about political affairs. The public opinion polls play a part in this call, though perhaps a minor one, not only in the way their results are presented, but also in the specific contacts between poller and pollee. The public opinion interviewer is a pervasive symbol of the demand to be opinionated. Most polls assume that people will have—and subtly therefore, that they should have—opinions on the "issues of the day" or "news of the week," though occasionally Gallup asks people "Do you have a cold?" or "Are you happy?" or some similar question which does not come straight out of 19th-century politics.

The fact is that people do respond, in overwhelming numbers, to this social demand that they have an opinion. Perhaps 10 per cent of the population refuses to be polled at all; another 10 per cent or so gets into the no-answer or undecided box; all the rest "have an opinion." If we took this evidence of the polls at face, we might conclude that politics had in fact not changed since the last century, that the masses who had entered the historical process had not with-drawn from it. Maybe so. But we think that the polls conceal as much as they reveal on this subject, and that if we look at the polls in unorthodox ways, we can even now see that the meaning of opinion is in flux.

§ HOLDING AN OPINION

THOUGH HARDLY MORE THAN HALF the electorate votes, a much larger fraction of those approached by pollers have opinions on whom they will vote for.[3] Asked to have an opinion, many people for whom the opinion has no significance—other than to proffer on demand like a password—produce one in accord with their station in life. And who has not at some time delivered himself of an opinion stronger and more pronounced than one he "really" held—as part of the conversation he holds with himself and with other people?

The poll interviewers (on the more cursory survey, where some form of area-sampling or other careful counter-measures are not

---

3. Of course the polling agencies eliminate from their sample Southern Negroes, and use relatively smaller percentages of certain social groups than their proportion in the general population in order to get a first approximation to the voting population. But even taking this into account, we think it is undeniable that many more people say they will vote than do vote; and this disparity is only partly accounted for by those who plan to vote and are prevented from doing so by technical accidents.

insisted on) can hardly help getting in on this conversation, subtly selecting as respondents the articulate and over-opinionated as against the recusant and under-opinionated. The interviewers can sense, even if they stick to their socio-economic quotas, who will be susceptible to the opinion-holding frame of the interview (and the interviewer) and who will not; in our culture, the opinionated are visible, while the under-opinionated, like our cripples and deformed people, are not visible. (The under-opinionated in the last election would probably have been, in the main, for the underdog candidate, Truman. But the over-opinionated would not necessarily have been conservative; they might also have been the more extreme and aggressive Jews and Negroes who were for Wallace. If this is so, then a quite unconscious bias—a bias, indeed, of the middle class, and of our culture generally —in favor of the opinionated might be one factor in the overestimation both of the Dewey and the Wallace vote; the interviewers simply "happened" to bump into more people who *held* opinions— this being the commodity they were looking for.)[4] . . .

These and many other sorts of variation in the style of response are important because a superficially identical answer coming from persons with different styles of response may well have very different meanings. We cite one instance, conceivably relevant for election polling, which was suggested to us by our study of files at NORC. It seems possible to differentiate between two, among many, styles of response: a *non-committal*, in which good rapport is not established; the respondent gives only as much as he has to, is not "friendly." And an *embarrassed*, in which, whether or not the respondent has answers for questions, he feels in a warm human environment permitting him to show and even enjoy his embarrassment (by gestures, giggles, coyness and laughter), and, often, his incompetence. We think that one might discover, if one were to rate respondents as embarrassed or non-committal, significant differences between them as to the sticking power of opinions. The embarrassed person is, we suggest, using his opinions more as a social device than the non-committal: he is trying to shift the encounter from one involving the transmission of information into one in which both parties get personal satisfaction;

---

4. Those who had "no opinion" were then handled by the home office with, perhaps, a similar psychological bias; they were treated as if they had had opinions, being divided up pro rata among those who had opinions, like wallflowers in a school tug of war. Since this had "worked" in earlier election polls, inadequate attention was paid to the latent meanings of the "no opinion" style of response. Similarly, the Elmira 1948 Election Study, mentioned hereafter, discovered after the election that those who had dropped out of the Panel, or refused—and probably also those who weren't at home despite several callbacks—formed a different group, in terms of vote, than those who were easily enticed onto the Panel and stayed with it throughout.

the personal satisfactions tend to become paramount, and the opinions to lose their factual importance. On the other hand, the non-committal person is "close" with, and to, his opinions: even when they can be pried from him, they remain his: they are not cooked to conversational short-order.

We would, moreover, expect the non-committals to decrease, and the embarrasseds to increase as the more socialized styles of response become more widely spread. Some indirect evidence on this may perhaps be gleaned from the study of refusals—the 10 per cent or so "hard core" who don't want to give the pollers any answers at all. NORC was able to get a few "foot-in-door" questions asked of those who refused on one survey, and a tabulation was made by Dr. Herbert Hyman (of NORC) as to who they were. A sizable proportion of the refusals gave explanations or said things that indicated they would chronically refuse to give answers, largely because of feelings of inadequacy. Significantly those who refused—in this survey—were generally older people and women, people whose style of response had, we suspect, been little affected by the currents of opinion and opinion-giving that circulate in contemporary culture.

§ THE FUNCTIONS OF OPINION IN THE UPPER CLASS

INDEED, THE UNRECORDED EXPERIENCE of observant poll interviewers seems to us one of the most important sources for discovering the meaning of opinion in the several social strata. This belief is confirmed by the opportunity given us by Herbert Hyman to read over some of his extraordinarily searching interviews with interviewers, and to interview several of these people ourselves. There is some evidence here, of course quite unsystematic, that the upper-class person—the pollers' "class A"—does not find emotional satisfaction in *voicing* an opinion to an interviewer, who is generally of lower social status, as distinguished from having and voicing an opinion at the dinner table, on the commuter train, and in clique groups generally. Perhaps the interviewer, according to the view of this social level, falls into the category of the cab-driver and the elevator man, with whom one exchanges seasonal pleasantries about the weather and the election, but with whom one is also reserved and close-mouthed.

We may interpret this reaction to the interviewer psychologically by saying that many of these upper-class respondents do not feel alienated from their opinions; they do not need to make either conversation or capital with them. Though in recent years they have often talked as if they felt politically frustrated, as if they could make no headway against "that man in the White House," or, indeed, against politicians in general, the premise of this apparent frustration is that they are not really powerless, but that they feel temporarily out of the seats of power. Actually, politics is a malleable domain for them, whether or not they feel responsibility for it. Yet even they tend to overestimate their power, and therefore the social importance of their having an opinion, and it is often this feeling which allows the interviewer to get by the doormen and secretaries at all.

§ ILLUSIONS OF OMNIPOTENCE IN THE UPPER MIDDLE CLASS

IN BOTH THE UPPER and upper middle class there is a high proportion of response on polls, particularly from men. People in these groups have been brought up to make choices and to consider their opinions significant. . . . In the working class, politics does not generally become a focus of interest, if ever, until after formal education is complete and the individual has entered on his work career, but in the upper middle class young people often begin to attend to political discourse earlier, in high school and college. Public opinion polling, and the election itself, meets such people on their own ground; they think about men and issues in the way that the polls, the mass media, and their clique groups all require of them. . . .

Such people are also tempted by their social situation to over-estimate their actual power. They are in contact with political "insiders" both in print and in person; this helps them to identify with the political world. In our interviews we often find such people to be possessed of a relatively high level of information about politics and a stock of opinions like a well-furnished wine-cellar, but lacking in any genuine affect about opinions which would lead them to discriminate between those opinions which have meaning in today's world from those which are mere opinionatedness.

The upper middle class tends to have an "inner-directed" ideology about politics, so that there is much talk and action in terms of responsibility. But the trend seems to us to lie with those whose opinions are lightly attached—hence easily secured by a poller—and yet who need opinions, for clothing, conformity, and comfort.

§ MAKING CONVERSATION BETWEEN THE SOCIAL CLASSES

AS ONE GOES DOWN the status ladder, one still finds an astonishingly high proportion of response on polls, both in permitting oneself to be interviewed and in having an opinion which can be fitted, without too much gerrymandering, into the dimensions of current polling work. In a sense, this is only another way of saying that America is a middle-class country and that middle-class values and styles of perception reach into all levels except perhaps the fringes at the very top and the very bottom. The study of polling, however, suggests two perspectives on this well-accepted statement: one is that people who are actually powerless and voiceless grasp at straws of participation, and the other is that the upper and lower levels of our culture converse with each other across status lines by means of the polls and, of course, also by means of the mass media and many other forms of exchange.

In the lower middle class, there often seems to be considerable satisfaction in voicing an opinion to the interviewer, even if it has to be manufactured on the spot for the purpose. Respondents in this group are not so often consulted as they might wish—"I told that fellow from the Gallup Poll . . ."—and at the same time, they do not want to be taken for ignoramuses who do not know, and consequently are quite happy to have a chance to show that they do know. And, of course, they *do* know. For, like the upper social levels, they have been trained to exercise consumption preferences, and they are willing, if not avid, cash customers for opinions on political issues. Through national and international affairs are for them mysterious realms, though they have no way of grasping what a political figure actually does, they can listen to Walter Winchell. . . .

Since such people have, however, no actual experience of potency in meaningful life situations—but only the imitation of potency in the consumption of goods and opinions—they will tend to be over-impressed by "public opinion." Frightened as they are of being taken for suckers, they assume public opinion to be much more given and set than it actually is, and, if anything, underestimate what *they* might do to change opinion by taking a strong stand against a current trend. Truman, no inside-dopester, was not impressed by the massive public opinion structure which the mass media talked about. Rather, like the self-made, inner-directed man of earlier generations, he thought it was up to him whether he got to the top, and his naïveté encouraged him where other-directed types would have despaired.

Added to the desire to participate on the part of the lower middle class is the cultural pressure, felt by both interviewer and interviewee, in favor of giving someone an answer rather than no answer. The situation is said to be different in France and some other countries, but the American attitude is summed up in the expression criticizing those who "wouldn't give anyone the right time." An opinion is considered a free gift in a culture where privacy is at a minimum, and people will feel that the interviewer is entitled to an opinion irrespective of whether they also try to guess which of several possible opinions he may want of them. Even the people who seem to enjoy slamming the door in the interviewer's face may be taking advantage of a rarely-given opportunity not to live up to expectations and to lord it over the (usually female) interviewer. It is not that they so value their privacy. And indeed, why should people not give their opinion freely when the opinions were often only created for this purpose in the first place? Opinions are not felt as part of one's underlying self; on the contrary, people have been so invaded, the threshold of personality has become such a highway, that they have very little private self left anyway. . . .

In this perspective, the polls may be thought of as a kind of political market research. Like most commercial market research, the effort is not really to find out what people might want under quite different social conditions, but rather to offer them a monopolistically-limited range of alternatives: just as they can choose between the four big weeklies. They can be for or against Truman, for or against Taft-Hartley, even for or against the United Nations, but they cannot be, in the given spectrum, in favor of trying to start a revolution within Russia, as against fighting or appeasing her. And probably they have been so conditioned that they would not know what to do with any radically new alternatives, but would try to fit them into the style of viewing "reality" which the existing polls reflect.

§ RAPPORT AND OPINION IN THE LOWER CLASS

EVEN THE LOWER CLASS participates in this "conversation between the classes." Some are left out, as indicated by the fact that the proportion of "don't knows" rises sharply in the lower class, particularly among women. Many of the "don't knows" and refusals in the lower social strata are actually frightened; frightened of authorities in general, of the FBI in some places, and of the Communists in others (as we found last summer in rural Vermont). Yet even among this group it is surprising how many respond.

There are few illusions of omnipotence here, as one finds them among the upper middle class; nor is there, we suspect, as much need as in the lower middle class for verbal aggression against interviewers —telling "them" (the powers) off, through the interviewer. Why, then, do people respond? Partly, of course, it is a matter of simple courtesy and needs no complicated explanations. But we think that the emphasis on rapport which dominates so much discussion of interviewing shows that there are other elements involved. The concern for good rapport as a requirement of good interviewing seems to us partly a reflection of the need of modern middle-class people to be liked by everybody. At any rate, rapport serves to insure the success of the "conversation of the classes" when it is conducted between the middle-class interviewer and the lower-class respondent. Thus great care is taken that the lower-class individual is approached sympathetically, and the polls try to use an interviewer of his own ethnic group, though they are rarely able to use one of his own class. This is not wholly pointless if one's goal is to maximize the number of responses, since rapport, by providing some interpersonal though usually spurious warmth, helps to repress unconscious feelings of powerlessness and distrust. But this is artificial; life-situations for the interviewee in the lower class are not typically suffused with rapport, and he is rarely treated with the consideration the interviewer shows him. Thus a false picture of the actual extent of political involvement is created, though it might be argued that it is a picture which would disappear under depth-interviewing and still greater doses of rapport. This needs testing, but it seems clear that the same culture which insists on "service with a smile" can also get answers with a smile—up to a point.

§ DOES THE ELECTION CHANGE THINGS?

THE FOREGOING OBSERVATIONS were sketched out by the writers in a memorandum written a year ago; naturally, we have had to ask ourselves whether Truman's victory does not show the power of the allegedly powerless. This may be. No doubt the union locals who put Truman over in the cities have a feeling of potency and elation, though coupled with misgivings they will be "sold out." Winning an election against odds, it may be argued, is different from merely having an opinion: affect is aroused and competence learned in the very process of getting out the vote. But even in the case of the union vote, many of the rank and file were simply pressured into going to the polls by a leadership which felt threatened by the Taft-Hartley Act; and while undoubtedly for many millions of Americans—somewhat more perhaps than we believed—opinion is formed by a realistic evaluation of alternatives, for these same persons, and for many others, the social and psychological meanings of opinion we have discussed become increasingly prominent. Whether we are interested in predicting elections or in understanding what is happening in America—and while the former may be hit by dint of sheer luck, ultimately it involves the latter—we must go past the level on which opinion research is now concentrating. Individuality and idiosyncrasy of response, up to now "processed out" of the polling process, is, we feel, the key to this next stage.

§ NEW APPROACHES IN INTERVIEWING AND ANALYSIS

A POWERFUL TENDENCY in current public opinion work is the attempt to stabilize and standardize the interview; idiosyncratic interviewing is another residue which is extruded as "bias." This effort is, in part, the necessary consequence of the methods of handling interview material in the home office, where the effort at standardization begins, ramifying out from there into pre-coded field techniques. For assembly-line work on a national cross-section, with an army of interviewers and coders to supervise, these methods are inevitable: their aim is to make interviewers, and the responses they obtain, virtually interchangeable on the verbal plane; as the skill grows of those who plan the survey, the interview and the interviewer are, in Karl Mannheim's terms, subjected to "functional rationalization." Opening up the interview to a wider ambit of human interaction cannot be done, therefore, without going back to handicraft methods in the analysis of the results. . . .

In our work we have tried to study first, the different types of interviews produced by different types of interviewers; second, the different types of responses to a challenging interview, using many difficult "why" questions, some "absurd" questions and unanswerable dilemmas, and, where possible, argumentative questions. Our effort was directed at confronting the respondent with a very large range of interpersonal meanings and styles in a single interview, as against the method now generally favored, which seeks to confront the smooth, middle-class side of the respondent with the smooth, middle-class side of the interviewer. The monotone of amiability called rapport, in which the interviewer must assume that all opinions received are equally valuable, equally inoffensive, undoubtedly finds out things which could be learned in no other way. But also one runs the risk of creating an unreal situation and of tapping a level of rationalization which may appear deep and intimate but which may actually be phony.

The Harvard Opinion Study has been making use of the "stress interview," in which a group of professors badger the respondent, to see how his political opinions stand up under pressure, and how he deals with contradictions in his views brought out in a series of interviews.[5] Arnold Rose has suggested other, somewhat less arduous techniques.[6] And as Hyman and Sheatsley have pointed out,[7] public opinion research can learn a good deal from Kinsey who, for example, excoriates liars and fixes interviewees with a steely eye, not a polite one. A fascinating range of possible interview techniques is suggested by Allen Funt, who conducts the "Candid Mike" radio program. Mr. Funt talks to people in all sorts of situations, and records the

5. We are indebted to M. Brewster Smith and Jerome Bruner for helpful information on this work-in-progress.
6. "A Research Note on Experimentation in Interviewing," *Am. J. Sociology*, 1945, 51, 143-144.
7. Herbert H. Hyman and Paul B. Sheatsley, "The Kinsey Report and Survey Methodology," *Int. J. of Opinion & Attitude Research*, 1948, 2, 183-195.

conversations with a concealed microphone for later rebroadcast: he has, for example, imitated a market researcher, but one using a meaningless double-talk in his interview instead of typical questions. His own style of talking to people is extremely interesting, in contrast to the current stereotype of rapport: he is in no ways charming, and has a dry, rather ordinary tone of voice, combined with a skeptical and even semi-hostile approach. Yet he has managed to get people to reveal themselves in ways—some of them outrageous—that no interviewer schooled in ordinary poll techniques could.

Obviously, there are ethical problems involved in more drastic interview procedures—as, indeed, in all social research which makes contact with human beings; and there are practical limits to what one can ask of interviewers and interviewees. But such problems are not avoided in conventional interviewing. A rapport-filled interview in which, while it lasts, the respondent is encouraged and assured that he is "doing all right," may leave him with a feeling of inadequacy, even perhaps trickery, if he should become aware of its lack of content. And conversely a challenging interview might actually give the respondent a vital experience, from which he learns something, as well as providing us with data.

We would like to cite an incident which indicates both how new techniques might plunge through the surface layer of opinion, and the practical difficulties in using these techniques. A panel study of the 1948 election campaign was made in Elmira, New York, a kind of follow-up to *The People's Choice* by Lazarsfeld, Berelson, and Gaudet. At one point questions were used which pointed out contradictions in the respondent's attitudes—for instance, asking him, if he were a worker and thought Truman was for the workers, why he was planning to vote for Dewey. Such questions would involve a loss of smooth rapport, but might reveal, in the very embarrassment of the respondent, something of his real feelings; and the authors urged that the interviewers be instructed to take note of the way the interviewee reacted to such questions, as well as of the words he uttered: to note, for example, whether he was embarrassed or at ease. The interviewers themselves balked on the pre-test, finding that they could not bring themselves easily to ask such questions, or to make much sense of the mode of reaction by the respondent. They were, naturally enough, too insecure psychologically, too drilled in obtaining rapport (especially in this study, interviewers were concerned over losing members of the panel, who would then be unavailable for subsequent waves of interviewing), and too eager to seize on easily-recorded and easily-classified replies to be able to experiment with more impolite and perhaps more fruitful types of interviewing. Despite the discomfort of the interviewers, the questions were asked. It is only with such approaches that one had a chance of discovering that, for example, those who were for Dewey, against their consciously understood class interests, might in the end turn to Truman.

Perhaps all we are doing here is suggesting that there may be other kinds of rapport than the conventional type. For to keep in human contact with an interviewee, while also making the interview a faceted and, at moments, barbed encounter, seems to us to require getting across to him that one is genuinely interested in the content of the interview, and in his reactions to it as an individual: we gather that this is Kinsey's conclusion, too. If one likes, one can call this less artificial footing rapport also—at least until it becomes too hard to take and the interviewer runs for it. . . .

§ DO WORDS HAVE A MEANING?

MUCH CURRENT SOCIAL RESEARCH proceeds on the assumption that if one wants to tap idiosyncratic meaning one must dispense with interviews altogether, except perhaps the psychoanalytic interview, and substitute projective tests such as the Rorschach, or the TAT, where the stimulus is non-verbal. A number of psychoanalysts, for instance, have said that Kinsey could not possibly have discovered anything veracious by his rapid-fire poll-type questionnaire. Indeed, some of the more orthodox Freudians, occasionally joined by some extreme semanticists, tend to take the position that people *never* mean what they say, and that the manifest replies to a question are inevitably a facade to be pierced rather than anything to be taken seriously.

We think that this outlook in social science is, among other things, an over-reaction against an earlier, naive reliance on the manifest content of answers to questions in personality inventories and other types of questionnaires. But today the best pollers no longer fall into such simplistic pitfalls; by pretesting with intensive interviews and converting these results into interlocking sets of questions, they try to follow the lead of Professor Lazarsfeld in the article already cited. We think it most unlikely that the failure to predict the election could have been repaired by depth interviewing in its present stage of development. On the contrary, we think it most likely that a better job of prediction might have been done by a conventional interview, had it dealt with such matters as group affiliation. . . . Let us move away from this sterile dichotomy between over-rational belief in words per se and over-skeptical nihilism about them, and see precisely in what direction public opinion research can advance if we

believe that words do, sometimes, possess their rational manifest
meaning, while being also projective of underlying character structure. . . .

Our own quite tentative hypothesis is that it is possible to work
with answers to a relatively structured interview as if the interview
itself as a whole, rather than as a set of separate questions, were a
projective test. Our interviews are not long, nor do they probe for
intimate data; skill in administering them helps, but is not essential.
The problem is in interpretation, not in administration. For we handle
the entire interview as a unit—a record of an experience—which we
try to translate into a set of latent meanings which may in any given
case include some of the literal, manifest meanings, too. This is done
before any single answer is coded for purposes of correlation and
comparison. That is, each single answer gives clues as to the latent
meaning, the plot, of the interview, and as the latter develops, so
it colors the meaning of the single answer, which must frequently be
reinterpreted in the light of other answers and of the whole. Eventually, in a dialectic process, we come to a point where the latent,
character-based meanings of answers are consistent and are seen to
spring from a total personality, no matter how seemingly contradictory
the surface answers are. The method we use thus resembles that used
by the more "intuitive" and less quantitative workers with Rorschach
and TAT. Moreover, to get beneath ideology, chit-chat, and rationalization that are always part of the manifest responses, we must look
at and rely on the way things are said, and when they are said in the
sequence of answers, and on what the interviewer can tell us as to
non-verbal modes of reaction to a question. (Of course, we must
know something of the interviewer, too, in order to evaluate the
report.) . . .[8]

§ THE FEAR OF THE LATENT

LATENT MEANING—either of an answer or of no answer—may be understood if we grasp the socially structured interpersonal situation between poller and pollee, and search it for the residues, verbal and
non-verbal, which now in our haste we throw away. But it is not
only haste which often steers the academic, as well as the commercial
poller, away from reliance on latent meaning. In our daily life we all

---

8. How much can be done by less elaborate analyses of less elaborate interviews is indicated by Babette Samelson's article, "Mrs. Jones' Ethnic Attitudes:
A Ballot Analysis," *J. of Abn. & Soc. Psych.*, 1945, 40, 205-214. Taking a single
NORC poll ballot—an ingenious ballot, with a number of open-ended questions
—she has analyzed the full responses somewhat in the manner of a case history,
to bring out a pattern of prejudice which purely extensive analysis of the whole
set of returns would hardly have disclosed.

know that a gesture, an inflection, a nuance of phrase, may show a latent meaning which is the opposite of the patent one. In our working life, however, we fear to rely on such human knowledge because of the difficulties of proof, of standardization, and of validation. We fear to be called unscientific by our colleagues. The failure of the polls to predict the election should give us a kind of back-handed courage, by demonstrating that the alternative, highly-quantified methods may at times be equally fallible.

Depth interviewing, it is apparent, does not avoid the problem of interpretation of latent meaning. One cannot assume that the interviewee's self-revelations may be taken at face, especially if they are intimate and of the sort usually hidden. For these, too, may be as spurious as any surface rationalizations; the excellent rapport which produced them may merely have served to encourage boasting or aggression by the respondent. What we want is the whole personality, and neither what is on the surface nor what is covered up will alone suffice. There is, we conclude, no escape from the social scientist's own judgment. He must train himself to hear, and to understand, latent response, even though the whole culture, as well as the demands of his training and his colleagues, make this difficult.

At the same time the rewards of even a fragmentary approach to latent meaning are great. The election shows—as did the British Labor Party victory of 1945—how little we know, polls or no polls, about what is going on in our society. We do not know what the election meant to people in different social classes. We know almost nothing about the underlying forces in American life which are not visible—forces which cannot fit themselves into the pollers' opinion-grid. . . . Now, by virtue of our proven ignorance, we can justify staving off demands for quick results, and can occupy ourselves with discovering what is fundamental and how to get at it.

Place of Original Publication

1. "Values in Context" was first published in *The American Scholar*, Vol. 22, No. 1, 1952.
2. "Individualism Reconsidered" was first published in *Religious Faith and World Culture*, ed. by A. William Loos, Prentice-Hall, 1951. It was later reprinted in *City Lights*, Vol. 1, No. 3, 1953.
3. "The Ethics of We Happy Few" was first published in the *University Observer*, Vol. 1, 1947.
4. "A Philosophy for 'Minority' Living" was first published in *Commentary*, Vol. 6, No. 5, 1948.
5. "Some Observations on Community Plans and Utopia" was first published in *The Yale Law Journal*, Vol. 57, December 1947.
6. "The Saving Remnant" was first published in *The Years of the Modern*, Longmans, Green and Co., Inc., 1949.
7. "Some Observations on Intellectual Freedom" was first published in *The American Scholar*, Vol. 23, No. 1, 1953.
8. "The 'Militant' Fight Against Anti-Semitism" was first published in *Commentary*, Vol. 11, No. 1, 1951.
9. "Some Observations Concerning Marginality" was first published in *Phylon*, Vol. 12, No. 2, 1951.
10. "Marginality, Conformity, and Insight" was first delivered as a lecture at Smith College, March 12, 1953, and later revised as an address to the Mental Hygiene Society of Greater Baltimore, May 26, 1953. It was published in *Phylon*, Vol. 14, No. 3, 1953.
11. "Listening to Popular Music" was first published in *The American Quarterly*, Vol. 2, No. 4, 1950.
12. "Movies and Audiences" was first published in *The American Quarterly*, Vol. 4, No. 3, 1952.
13. "Some Observations on Changes in Leisure Attitudes" was first published in *The Antioch Review*, Vol. 12, No. 4, 1952. It was later reprinted in *The Antioch Review Anthology*, ed. Paul Bixler, World Publishers, 1953, and in *Perspectives, USA*, No. 5, Fall 1953.
14. "New Standards for Old: From Conspicuous Consumption to Conspicuous Production" was given as a lecture in the Barnard College series on "The Search for New Standards in Modern America," March 10, 1953, and is here reprinted with the permission of Barnard College.
15. "Recreation and the Recreationist" was first delivered as a lecture at the Chicago Conference on a Federal Department of Welfare, February 27, 1953. It was published in *Marriage and Family Living*, Vol. 16, No. 1, 1954.
16. "Football in America: A Study in Culture Diffusion" was first published in *The American Quarterly*, Vol. 3, No. 4, 1951. It was later reprinted in *The University of Chicago Magazine*, Vol. 45, No. 2, 1952.
17. "Bookworms and the Social Soil" was first published in *The Saturday Review of Literature*, May 5, 1951.
18. "How Different May One Be?" was first published in *Child Study*, Vol. 28, Spring 1951.

19. "The Social and Psychological Setting of Veblen's Economic Theory" was first delivered as a lecture to the Economic History Association, Bryn Mawr, September, 1953. It was later reprinted in *The Journal of Economic History*, Vol. 13, No. 4, 1953.

20. "Some Relationships Between Technical Progress and Social Progress" was first delivered as a lecture at the Foreign Student Summer Project of MIT, August 28, 1953. It was later reprinted in *Explorations in Entrepreneurial History*, Vol. 6, No. 3, 1954.

21. "The Themes of Work and Play in the Structure of Freud's Thought" was first published in *Psychiatry*, Vol. 13, No. 1, 1950.

22. "Authority and Liberty in the Structure of Freud's Thought" was first published in *Psychiatry*, Vol. 13, No. 2, 1950.

23. "The Themes of Heroism and Weakness in the Structure of Freud's Thought" was first published in *Psychiatry*, Vol. 13, No. 2, 1950.

24. "Freud, Religion, and Science" was first delivered as a lecture to the Channing Club of the University of Chicago, January 9, 1950. It was later (as "Freud: Religion as Neurosis") reprinted in part in the University of Chicago Roundtable on *Psychoanalysis and Ethics*, No. 638, June 18, 1950, and in *The American Scholar*, Vol. 20, No. 3, 1951. It was later reprinted in full in *The Chicago Review*, Vol. 8, No. 1, 1954.

25. "Some Observations on the Limits of Totalitarian Power," was first published in *The Antioch Review*, Vol. 12, No. 2, 1952.

26. "The Nylon War" was first published in *Common Cause*, Vol. 4, No. 6. It was later reprinted in *The Christian Century*, Vol. 48, No. 18; in *Etc.*, Vol. 8, No. 3; and in *New Problems in Reading and Writing*, ed. H. W. Sams and W. F. McNeir, Prentice-Hall, 1953.

27. "Toward an Anthropological Science of Law and the Legal Profession" was first given as a lecture to the introductory graduate course in sociology and anthropology at the University of Chicago, December 1947, and a revised version was delivered at the meeting of the Association of American Law Schools, December 1950, and was later reprinted in *The University of Chicago Law Review*, Vol. 19, No. 1, 1951, and in *The American Journal of Sociology*, Vol. 57, No. 2.

28. "Some Observations on Social Science Research" was first published in *The Antioch Review*, Vol. 11, No. 3, 1951.

29. "Some Clinical and Cultural Aspects of the Aging Process" was first published in *The American Journal of Sociology*, Vol. 59, No. 4, 1954.

30. "The Meaning of Opinion" was first published in part in *The International Journal of Opinion and Attitude Research*, Vol. 2, No. 4 and in part in the *Public Opinion Quarterly*, Vol. 12, No. 4.

Bibliography

1 9 3 9

"Possession and the Law of Finders"—*Harvard Law Rev.*, 52:1105-1134.

1 9 4 0

"Government Service and the American Constitution"—*Univ. Chicago Law Rev.*, 7:655-675.

"Legislative Restrictions on Foreign Enlistment and Travel"—*Columbia Law Rev.*, 40:793-835.

1 9 4 1

"The American Constitution and International Labor Legislation"—*Internat. Labor Review*, 44:123-193.

"Law and Social Science: A Report on Michael and Wechsler's Classbook on Criminal Law and Administration"—*Yale Law J.*, 50:636-653.

"Government Education for Democracy"—*Public Opinion Quart.*, 5:195-209.

"What's Wrong with the Interventionists?"—*Common Sense*, 10:327-330.

1 9 4 2

"Civil Liberties in a Period of Transition"—*Public Policy* (Harvard Graduate School of Public Administration, Carl J. Friedrich and Edward S. Mason, eds.), 3:33-96.

"Democracy and Defamation: Control of Group Libel"—*Columbia Law Rev.*, 42:727-780.

"Democracy and Defamation: Fair Game and Fair Comment I"—*Columbia Law Rev.*, 42:1085-1123.

"Democracy and Defamation: Fair Game and Fair Comment II"—*Columbia Law Rev.*, 42:1282-1318.

"The Cash Customer"—*Common Sense*, 11:183-185.

"Equality and Social Structure"—*J. Legal and Pol. Sociol.*, 1:72-95.

"The Politics of Persecution"—*Public Opinion Quart.*, 6:41-56.

1 9 4 3

"An International Bill of Rights"—*Proc. Amer. Law Inst.* 20:198-204.

1 9 4 4

"The Present State of Civil Liberty Theory"—*J. Politics*, 6:323-337.

1 9 4 7

"Some Observations on Community Plans and Utopia"—*Yale Law J.*, 57:173-200.

"The Ethics of We Happy Few"—*Univ. Observer*, 1:19-28.

1 9 4 8

"A Philosophy for 'Minority' Living"—*Commentary*, 6:413-422.

1 9 4 9

"Social Structure, Character Structure, and Opinion" (with Nathan Glazer)—*Internat. J. Opinion and Attitude Resch.*, 2:512-527.

"The Meaning of Opinion" (with Nathan Glazer)—*Public Opinion Quart.*, 12:633-648.

"The Saving Remnant: An Examination of Character Structure"; pp. 115-147. In: *Years of the Modern;* ed. by John W. Chase, New York, Longmans, Green & Company.

1 9 5 0

"Do the Mass Media 'Escape' from Politics?" (with Reuel Denney). In: *Reader in Public Opinion and Mass Communications;* ed. by Bernard Berelson & Morris Janowitz, Glencoe, Ill., Free Press.

"Criteria for Political Apathy" (with Nathan Glazer). In: *Studies in Leadership;* ed. by Alvin Gouldner, New York, Harper & Bros.

"The Themes of Work and Play in the Structure of Freud's Thought"— *Psychiatry,* 13:1-16.

The Lonely Crowd: A Study of the Changing American Character (with the collaboration of Reuel Denney and Nathan Glazer), New Haven, Yale Univ. Press.

"Langdon Narbeth"; pp. 121-135. In: *Social Sciences 2, Syllabus and Selected Readings,* Vol. II, Chicago, Univ. of Chicago Press.

"One from the Gallery: An Experiment in the Interpretation of an Interview" (with Nathan Glazer) (Part 1)—*Internat. J. Opinion & Attitude Resch.,* 4:515-540.

"Listening to Popular Music"—*Amer. Quart.,* 2:359-371.

"Authority and Liberty in the Structure of Freud's Thought"—*Psychiatry,* 13:167-187.

"The Themes of Heroism and Weakness in the Structure of Freud's Thought"—*Psychiatry,* 13:301-315.

1 9 5 1

"The Nylon War"—*Common Cause,* 4:379-385. (Reprinted in *Christian Century,* 48:554, & *Etc.,* 8:163-170, & in *New Problems in Reading & Writing,* ed. by H. W. Sams & W. F. McNeir, New York, Prentice-Hall, pp. 480-488.)

"Some Problems of a Course in 'Culture and Personality' "—*J. General Educ.,* 5:122-136.

"How Different May One Be?"—*Child Study,* 28:6-8, 29-30.

"The 'Militant' Fight Against Anti-Semitism"—*Commentary,* 11:11-19.

"One from the Gallery" (with Nathan Glazer) (Part 2), *Internat. J. Opinion & Attitude Resch.,* 5:53-78.

"Bookworms and the Social Soil"—*Sat. Rev. Lit.,* 34:7-8, 31-32.

"From Morality to Morale"; pp. 81-120. In: *Personality and Political Crisis;* ed. by Alfred H. Stanton & Stewart E. Perry, Glencoe, Ill., Free Press.

"Individualism Reconsidered." In: *Religious Faith and World Culture;* ed. by William Loos, New York, Prentice Hall.

"Two Adolescents"—*Psychiatry,* 14:161-211.

"Comments on the Jewish Student"—*Commentary,* 12:524-525.

"Football in America: A Study in Culture Diffusion" (with Reuel Denney) —*Amer. Quart.,* 4:309-25.

"Freud, Religion and Science"—*The Amer. Scholar,* 20:267-276.

"Some Observations Concerning Marginality"—*Phylon,* 12:113-127.

"Some Observations on Law and Psychology"—*Univ. of Chicago Law Rev.,* 19:30-44.

"Some Observations on Social Science Research"—*Antioch Review*, 11:259-278.

"Toward an Anthropological Science of Law and the Legal Profession"—*Am. J. Soc.*, 57:121-135.

"Leisure in Urbanized America" (with Reuel Denney), pp. 469-480 in *Reader in Urban Sociology*, ed. by Paul K. Hatt & Albert J. Reiss, Jr., Glencoe, Ill., Free Press.

1 9 5 2

Faces in the Crowd: Individual Studies in Character and Politics (with the collaboration of Nathan Glazer), New Haven, Yale Univ. Press.

"Some Observations on the Limits of Totalitarian Power"—*Antioch Review*, 12:155-168.

"Ambassadors to the Machine"—*Griffin*, 1:6-11.

"Some Observations on the Study of American Character"—*Psychiatry*, 15:333-338.

"A Lecture on Veblen"—*J. General Education*, 6:214-223.

"Values in Context"—*Amer. Scholar*, 22:29-39.

"Our Country and Our Culture"—*Partisan Review*, 19:310-315. (Reprinted in *America and the Intellectuals, Partisan Review*, 95-100).

"Leisure in an Industrial Civilization" (with Reuel Denney). In: *Creating an Industrial Civilization: A Report on the Corning Conference*, ed. by Eugene Staley, New York, Harper & Bros.

Introduction to *Commentary on the American Scene*, Elliott Cohen, ed., New York, Alfred A. Knopf.

"Some Observations on Changes in Leisure Attitudes"—*Antioch Review*, 12:417-436.

"Movies and Audiences" (with Evelyn T. Riesman)—*Amer. Quart.*, 4:195-202.

1 9 5 3

Thorstein Veblen: A Critical Interpretation—New York, Scribner's & Sons.

"Some Observations on Intellectual Freedom"—*Am. Scholar*, 22:3.

"The Social and Psychological Setting of Veblen's Economic Theory"—*J. of Econ. Hist.*, 13:449-461.

"Marginality, Conformity, and Insight"—*Phylon*, 14:241-257.

"The Study of Kansas City: An Informal Overture"—*Univ. of Kansas City Review*, 20:15-22. (Reprinted as "The Study of the City"—*City Lights*, No. 4, Fall: 3-9.)

"Conspicuous Production"—*The Listener*, 49:1009.

The Lonely Crowd—abridged edition, New York, Doubleday.

"Psychological Types and National Character: An Informal Commentary"—*Amer. Quart.*, 5:325-343.

1 9 5 4 *(forthcoming)*

"Some Relationships Between Technical Progress and Social Progress"—to appear in *Explorations in Entrepreneurial History*, Vol. 6, No. 3.

"Some Clinical and Cultural Aspects of the Aging Process"—to appear in *Am. J. of Soc.*, 59:379-383.

"Veblen's System of Social Science"—to appear in *Explorations* I.

"Recreation and the Recreationist"—to appear in *Marriage & Family Living*, Vol. 16, No. 1.

"A Career Drama in a Middle-Aged Farmer"—to appear in *Bulletin of the Menninger Clinic*, Vol. 17.

Index

Abel, Theodore, "The Sociology of Concentration Camps," 420n.
Abundance in America, 37, 38
Action-research, approach in social science research, 481
Adams, Brooks, 102n., 163, 283, 338
Adams, Henry, 127, 163
Adler, Alfred, 381
   Psychoanalytical approach of, 308
Adorno, T. W., 187, 476
   "On Radio Music," 184n.
Affirmation, ethics of (in Koestler and Silone), 45
Agee, James, 200
   Let Us Now Praise Famous Men, 171
Aging, study of, in Kansas City:
   Cultural preservatives in, 486, 490
   Three reactions to, 484-489
   Superficial nature of, 486-487
Aggression, in Freud, 352
"Alienation," 153
Allport, Gordon, 392
Amateurs, in social science observation, 480, 481
Ambiguity:
   in America, 296
   as fashionable, 22
   in social science research, 482
   Value of, 166
America:
   Aloneness in, 46, 47
   Abundance in, 37-38, 287
   as an ambiguous model, 296
   the artist in, 215
   Asian attitudes toward, 130
   Censorship in, 150, 151
   Efficiency in, 289
   Fluid society in, 34
   "High" culture in, 180
   Humor in, 24
   Ideals at home and abroad, 286
   Pessimism about, 136
   Stereotypes of, 151
   Youthfulness in, 486
American Association for Public Opinion Research, 235, 469
American Committee for Cultural Freedom, 410, 414
American leaders, absence of, and Freud, 372n.
American Management Association, 293
American Scholar, 129, 136

Americanization, 178
   of recent immigrants, 289-290
Amusement, attitudes toward, 31
   and see Leisure, Play
Anthropologists:
   and functionalism, 405-406
   Attitudes toward law, 444-445
   Aware of ambivalent purposes in the law, 445
Anti-intellectualism, 128
Anti-Semitism, 75, 139, 145, 148
   Containment policy toward, 143, 147
   Decline in, 141
   European vs. American, 143
   and Freud, 335
   and Jews, 63
   in literature and movies, 144
   and marginality of Jews, 159
   Over-reactions to, 143
   in post-war Germany, 142
   Working class, 146, 147
Anxiety:
   in Freud, 395
   Jewish, 144
   Middle-class, 210, 211, 213
   of middle-class Catholics, 391
Apathy:
   Defense against ideological environment, 75, 424
   Political, 36, 37
   Positive side of, 124
   Role of in defense against totalitarianism, 416
Appel, Benjamin, 474n.
Architects, and utopian thinking, 77, 78
Arendt, Hannah, 108, 124, 410, 415, 418, 420n., 422n., 424
   The Origins of Totalitarianism, 158, 409
Arnold, Thurman, 443, 445
   The Folklore of Capitalism, 313n., 363, 443n.
Art:
   as affecting the quality of life, 149
   in America, 215
   as a career, 216, 216n.
   Disregard for by Jewish militants, 149
   Freud's view of, 315-316, 328, 330, 374n., 375, 398
   Indeterminancy in, 262

BOOKS PUBLISHED BY
The Free Press

LORD ACTON: *Essays on Freedom and Power* $6.00

ARISTIDES: *To Rome*   1.00

ARISTOTLE: *The Constitution of the Athenians*   temporarily out of print

MIKHAIL BAKUNIN: *The Political Philosophy of Bakunin*   6.00

EDWARD C. BANFIELD: *Government Project*   3.50

BERNARD BARBER: *Science and the Social Order*   4.50

SALO W. BARON: *Freedom and Reason*   5.00

REINHARD BENDIX AND SEYMOUR MARTIN LIPSET:
    Class, Status and Power: A Reader in Social Stratification   7.50

BERNARD BERELSON: *Content Analysis
in Communications Research*   4.00

BERNARD BERELSON AND MORRIS JANOWITZ:
    Reader in Public Opinion and Communication   5.50

BRUNO BETTELHEIM: *Love Is Not Enough*   4.50

BRUNO BETTELHEIM: *Symbolic Wounds*   4.75

BRUNO BETTELHEIM: *Truants from Life: The Rehabilitation of
Emotionally Disturbed Children*   5.00

HERBERT BUTTERFIELD: *The History of Science*   2.50

RICHARD CHRISTIE AND MARIE JAHODA: *Studies in the Scope
and Method of "The Authoritarian Personality"*   4.50

ALBERT K. COHEN: *Delinquent Boys: The Culture of the Gang*   3.50

MORRIS R. COHEN: *American Thought*   5.00

MORRIS R. COHEN: *A Dreamer's Journey*   4.50

MORRIS R. COHEN: *King Saul's Daughter*   3.00

MORRIS R. COHEN: *Reason and Law*   4.00

MORRIS R. COHEN: *Reason and Nature*   6.00

MORRIS R. COHEN: *Reflections of a Wondering Jew*   2.75

DONALD R. CRESSEY: *Other People's Money*   3.00

HERBERT DINERSTEIN AND LEON GOURE: *Two Studies in
Soviet Controls*   4.50

EMILE DURKHEIM: *The Division of Labor in Society*   5.00

EMILE DURKHEIM: *Elementary Forms of the Religious Life*   5.00

3,55